The California Legislature and Its Legislative Process

The California Legislature and Its Legislative Process

Cases and Materials

Chris Micheli

CAROLINA ACADEMIC PRESS

Durham, North Carolina

ISBN   978-1-5310-2039-2
LCCN   2021934083
eISBN   978-1-5310-2040-8

Carolina Academic Press
700 Kent Street
Durham, North Carolina 27701
Telephone (919) 489-7486
Fax (919) 493-5668
www.cap-press.com

Printed in the United States of America

Contents

Table of Cases

Foreword

I worked with my colleague, Jessica Gosney, California Deputy Legislative Counsel, to develop the first online course on legislatures and lawmaking for MSL students at McGeorge School of Law, including the federal and state legislative branches of government and their respective processes. As a result of this work, I wanted to more thoroughly explore the scholarly field and found through research that there are numerous books on statutes and regulations and the legislative process, almost all of which are focused on the federal government.

So, I decided to undertake an effort that was focused exclusively on California — its Legislature and its legislative process. The compilation of any casebook requires lots of helping hands, and this effort is not any different. I have received important guidance from Jessica Gosney, as well as my co-instructor for the Lawmaking in California course at McGeorge, who is Katie Londenberg, Deputy Legislative Counsel. Both Jessica and Katie have provided helpful suggestions regarding content of the casebook, both in topics covered and cases utilized.

I could not have completed this arduous task without the assistance of my family, colleagues, and friends who are always supportive of my academic and writing pursuits. In this regard, I am indebted to Liza, Morgan, Francesca, and Vincenzo.

Chris Micheli
May 2021

Preface

The purpose of this casebook is to provide students with an examination of the California Legislature and its lawmaking process — the state legislative process — that are set forth in the state Constitution, particularly Article IV, and relevant statutes, primarily found in the Government Code. The casebook provides extensive explanatory material on the different topics contained in this casebook and, of course, some of the key appellate court decisions.

How were the topics decided? Like other casebook authors, I spent considerable time trying to decide what topics were appropriate (and necessary) to cover. I poured over Article IV of the California Constitution and then began formulating the main topics. Always at the forefront was "How would I teach a course on the California Legislature and its legislative process, and what would I want students to learn?" That was quite a chore, because a casebook of several thousand pages would not be used by professors or students!

After I figured out the topics to cover and their relative order of presentation, I turned to reviewing cases. As one might imagine, some topics do not have any caselaw. In other subject areas, there are far too many cases to use in a single casebook. I also wanted cases that were well written, with analysis and explanation of both the law and the court's decision-making so that students can learn about the subject area, and they can see how courts analyze and decide issues.

Hopefully, professors and students using this casebook will find the right balance of informational material, cases, and notes and questions, that will educate and prompt thought and analysis of the extensive law regarding the California Legislature and its legislative process.

Chris Micheli
May 2021

Preface

About the Author

Chris Micheli is an attorney and lobbyist in Sacramento, California where he regularly testifies before policy and fiscal committees of the California Legislature, as well as a number of administrative agencies, departments, boards, and commissions. He often drafts legislative and regulatory language and is considered a leading authority on state tax law developments and the California legislative process.

Over the last twenty years, he has published hundreds of articles and editorials in professional journals, newspapers and trade magazines, whose diverse subjects range from tax incentives to transportation funding. He wrote a bi-monthly column on civil justice reform for five years for *The Daily Recorder*, Sacramento's daily legal newspaper, authoring over 100 columns. He has served on the editorial advisory boards for both state and national tax publications.

Micheli has been an attorney of record in several key cases, having argued before the Supreme Court of California (just two years out of law school), as well as the Court of Appeal several times. He has filed more than fifteen *amicus curiae* briefs in California courts. Additionally, Micheli has been qualified as an expert witness on California's knife laws in superior court, and has appeared as an expert witness before the State Board of Equalization in several tax cases.

He has published half a dozen peer-reviewed law review articles and is the co-editor and co-author of the book *A Practitioner's Guide to Lobbying and Advocacy in California*, as well as the author of the book *Understanding the California Legislative Process*, both released in 2020 by Kendall-Hunt Publishing Company. He is the author of two additional books published in early 2021: *Introduction to California State Government"* and *An Introduction to Drafting Legislation in California*.

He is a graduate of the University of California, Davis with a B.A. in Political Science — Public Service and the University of the Pacific, McGeorge School of Law with a J.D. degree. He currently serves as an Adjunct Professor of Law at McGeorge, where he teaches the course Lawmaking in California. He resides in Sacramento with his wife, Liza, two daughters, Morgan and Francesca, and son, Vincenzo.

The California Legislature and Its Legislative Process

Chapter One

The California Legislature

We begin with an overview of the California Legislature and its place within the state's Constitution. To properly frame Article IV and the legislative branch of state government, the following is an overview of the state Constitution.

A. California's Constitution — Its Structure and Functions

The California Constitution was first adopted in 1849, just prior to California becoming a state in 1850. The current Constitution was ratified on May 7, 1879. It is the governing document for the state, like the U.S. Constitution is the governing document for the country.

By most accounts, our state's Constitution is one of the longest in the world. In fact, the California Constitution has been amended or revised over 500 times.

While there are many provisions of the original Constitution, the main reason that the state's Constitution is so lengthy is that there are numerous provisions adopted by the people by ballot measures at statewide elections. California's signature requirement for placing measures on the ballot is one of the lowest thresholds of all states.

California's Constitution authorizes several state agencies, such as the University of California (and Stanford University, for certain property), the State Compensation Insurance Fund, and the State Bar of California. These provisions are intended to protect these institutions from governmental interference.

The state's Constitution also provides for counties and cities, as well as charter cities, whose local ordinances can be insulated from state laws. In addition, it specifies that cities are permitted to pay counties to perform governmental functions.

The California Constitution's Preamble provides, "We, the People of the State of California, grateful to Almighty God for our freedom, in order to secure and perpetuate its blessings, do establish this Constitution." In order to appreciate the length and complexity of the state's Constitution, the following are the Articles of the California Constitution:

Article I — Declaration of Rights [Sections 1–32]

Article II — Voting, Initiative and Referendum, and Recall [Sections 1–20]

Article III — State of California [Sections 1–9]

3

Article IV — Legislative [Sections 1–28]

Article V — Executive [Sections 1–14]

Article VI — Judicial [Sections 1–22]

Article VII — Public Officers and Employees [Sections 1–11]

Article IX — Education [Sections 1–16]

Article X — Water [Sections 1–7]

Article X A — Water Resources Development [Sections 1–8]

Article X B — Marine Resources Protection Act of 1990 [Sections 1–16]

Article XI — Local Government [Sections 1–15]

Article XII — Public Utilities [Sections 1–9]

Article XIII — Taxation [Sections 1–36]

Article XIII A — Tax Limitation [Sections 1–7]

Article XIII B — Government Spending Limitation [Sections 1–15]

Article XIII C — Voter Approval for Local Tax Levies [Sections 1–3]

Article XIII D — Assessment and Property-Related Fee Reform [Sections 1–6]

Article XIV — Labor Relations [Sections 1–5]

Article XV — Usury [Section 1]

Article XVI — Public Finance [Sections 1–23]

Article XVIII — Amending and Revising the Constitution [Sections 1–4]

Article XIX — Motor Vehicle Revenues [Sections 1–10]

Article XIX A — Loans from the Public Transportation Account or Local Transportation Funds [Sections 1–2]

Article XIX B — Motor Vehicle Fuel Sales Tax Revenues and Transportation Improvement Funding [Sections 1–2]

Article XIX C — Enforcement of Certain Provisions [Sections 1–4]

Article XIX D — Vehicle License Fee Revenues for Transportation Purposes [Section 1]

Article XX — Miscellaneous Subjects [Sections 1–23]

Article XXI — Redistricting of Senate, Assembly, Congressional, and Board of Equalization Districts [Sections 1–3]

Article XXII — Architectural and Engineering Services [Sections 1–2]

Article XXXIV — Public Housing Project Law [Sections 1–4]

Article XXXV — Medical Research [Sections 1–7]

Like its federal counterpart, California's Constitution is the "supreme law of the land" in this state, followed by state statutes, and then regulations promulgated by state entities. As with the federal level, the statutes and regulations cannot conflict with the Constitution.

California's Constitution is much more detailed than the federal Constitution, which is focused on the three branches of government. The U.S. Constitution sets forth the three branches of government in its first three articles (i.e., Article I provides for the Congress; Article II provides for the President; and, Article III provides for the Judiciary).

On the other hand, the California Constitution sets forth the three branches of state government in its Articles IV (Legislature), V (Governor) and VI (Judiciary). California's Constitution sets forth important personal rights in Article I of its Constitution, such as the right to privacy (Article I, Section I) and, my personal favorite, the right to fish in public streams (Article I, Section 25).

The provisions of direct democracy (initiative, referendum, and recall) are found in Article II. The state's Constitution goes on to cover the establishment of the state's governance system, as well as other important parts of state government, such as the University of California, in Article III.

Our state's Constitution also covers several other subject matters. For example, in keeping with our concerns for the environment and our educational system, there are provisions related to water and marine resources, as well as education.

The California Constitution also has numerous provisions related to taxation and transportation revenues, and it even establishes labor relations laws as well as the state's workers' compensation system. While there are many statutes and numerous regulations affecting California's workers' compensation system, it is enshrined in the state's Constitution.

Notes and Questions

1. Does California's Constitution have the right number of provisions or too many provisions? Are some of the Constitution's Articles more appropriate to be statutes in the Codes? What are some possible reasons for the length of California's Constitution?

B. The Legislature and California's Constitution Article IV

Now we turn to an examination of the constitutional provisions related to California's Legislature and some of the appellate court decisions that provide insights into how these provisions are interpreted by the courts.

Article IV provides powers to the Legislature and specifies aspects of the legislative process, including the consideration of legislation and the state budget. Some provisions are general in nature, while others are specific. Any student or practitioner of the legislative process needs to be familiar with these constitutional provisions and the appellate court decisions that provide guidance in interpreting them.

Article IV of the California Constitution deals with the legislative branch of government. Here are some interesting provisions about the legislative branch found in the state's Constitution (along with the relevant section):

The Legislature must convene its regular session at noon on the first Monday in December of every even-numbered year. and they must undertake their organization that day (e.g., election of leaders). And the Legislature must adjourn by midnight on November 30 of the following odd-numbered year. (Section 3)

Only the Governor can call extraordinary sessions (aka "Special Sessions") of the Legislature and does so by proclamation. The Legislature does not have to conduct any business in a special session but, if it does, then they only have power to legislate on the subject(s) specified in the Governor's proclamation. (Section 4)

A legislator cannot receive travel and living expenses (aka "per diem") during the times that the Legislature is in recess for more than three calendar days, except in specified instances. (Section 4) This explains why the Legislature will hold its normal Thursday floor session on a Friday preceding a Monday state holiday.

The Legislature has the sole power to judge the qualifications and elections of the Members of the Assembly and Senate. They also have the power, by a 2/3 majority vote, to expel a Member. The same vote is required if either house wants to suspend a legislator. Such a suspension requires findings and declarations setting forth the basis for the legislator's suspension. No such requirement exists for the expulsion of a legislator. (Section 5)

Legislators are prohibited from accepting any honorarium (e.g., a legislator cannot be paid for giving a speech to an interest group). The Legislature is also charged with enacting laws to ban or strictly limit gifts that might create a conflict of interest. (Section 5)

Legislators cannot accept compensation for taking any action on behalf of another person regarding any state government board or agency. This prohibition does not extend to actions before any local government board or agency, but in such cases, a legislator is banned for one year from using his or her official position to influence any action that would have a direct and significant financial impact on that person and not affect the public generally. (Section 5)

This prohibition does not extend to activities for the legislator himself or herself, or where the legislator is acting as an attorney before any court or in workers' compensation appeals. Legislators are prohibited from lobbying the Legislature for compensation for 12 months after leaving office. (Section 5)

Both the Senate and Assembly must choose its officers and adopt rules for their proceedings. Each house must keep and publish a journal of its proceedings. The proceedings of the Senate and Assembly, as well as their committees, must be open and public. And the public can record these proceedings by audio or video means. The Legislature must make audiovisual recordings of all of its proceedings and post them on the Internet within 24 hours after their conclusion and must maintain an archive of the recordings for 20 years. (Section 7)

Closed sessions are allowed in specified circumstances such as employment matters, litigation, safety and security, and party caucuses. Neither house may recess for more than 10 days without the consent of the other house. (Section 7)

No bill, other than the budget bill, may be heard or acted upon by a committee or either house until it has been in print for 30 days after introduction. Either house can dispense with this rule by a 3/4 majority vote of that house. The Legislature can only make a law by statute, and statutes can only be enacted by bills. A bill cannot be passed unless it has been read by its title on 3 separate days in each house. This rule can be dispensed with by a 2/3 majority vote of the house's members. (Section 8)

A bill cannot be passed or become a statute unless that bill and any amendments have been in print and published on the Internet for at least 72 hours before the vote, unless the Governor has submitted a statement that it is needed to address a state of emergency. No bill may be passed unless a majority of members of each house votes in favor of the bill. (Section 8)

A statute goes into effect on January 1 in a regular session, and on the 91st day after adjournment of a special session. Statutes calling elections, statutes providing for tax levies or appropriations for the usual current expenses of the state, and urgency statutes go into effect immediately upon their enactment (i.e., the day the bill is chaptered by the Secretary of State). (Section 8)

Urgency statutes are defined as those necessary for the immediate preservation of the public peace, health or safety, and a statement of facts constituting the necessity must be set forth in a section of the bill. An urgency bill and the urgency clause require a separate vote, and both require a 2/3 majority vote for passage in each house. An urgency statute may not create or abolish any office or change the salary, term, or duties of any office, or grant any franchise or special privilege, or create any vested right or interest. (Section 8)

There is a single subject rule for legislation (like the constitutional provision for ballot measures). That subject must be expressed in the title of the bill. (Section 9) There is a re-enactment rule that provides that a section of an existing statute may not be amended unless that section is re-enacted as amended by a bill. (Section 9)

Each bill passed by the Legislature must be presented to the Governor. The bill becomes a statute if it is signed by the Governor, or the Governor may veto a bill if he or she returns it to the house of origin along with any objections. If the Legislature votes again to pass the bill by a 2/3 majority vote, then the bill becomes a statute (i.e., when the Legislature overrides the Governor's veto). (Section 10)

Any bill in the possession of the Governor after adjournment of the Legislature that is not returned within 30 days becomes a statute. Any other bill presented to the Governor (i.e., prior to the end of session) becomes a statute if it is not returned within 12 days. Any bill that was introduced in the first year of the 2-year session that has not been passed by its house of origin by January 31 of the second year may no longer be acted upon by either house. (Section 10)

No bill may be passed by either house after September 1 in an even-numbered year, except those measures calling elections, statutes providing for tax levies or appropriations for the usual current expenses of the state, urgency statutes, and bills passed after being vetoed by the Governor. The Legislature is prohibited from presenting any bill to the Governor after November 15 in the second year of the session. (Section 10)

The Governor may reduce or eliminate one or more items of appropriation while approving other portions of a bill. In such a case, the Governor must include a statement of the items reduced or eliminated with the reasons for his or her action. Any appropriation item reduced or eliminated must be considered separately and can be passed over the Governor's objections by a 2/3 majority vote. (Section 10)

The Senate or Assembly or both houses may adopt a resolution that provides for the selection of committees to conduct the business of the Legislature. (Section 11)

Within the first 10 days of each year, the Governor must submit to the Legislature a budget for the forthcoming fiscal year (which begins July 1). Therefore, the Governor's first budget proposal is called the Governor's "January 10 Budget." The budget must include an explanatory message, as well as itemized statements for expenditures and estimated revenues. (Section 12)

The Governor may require a state agency or employee to furnish whatever information he or she deems necessary to prepare the budget. The budget bill must be introduced immediately in each house by the budget committee chairs of the Senate and Assembly. The Legislature must pass the budget by midnight on June 15. (Section 12)

Until the budget bill is enacted, the Legislature cannot send any bills to the Governor that propose to appropriate funds during the upcoming fiscal year unless it is an emergency bill recommended by the Governor. No bill, except the budget bill, may contain more than one item of appropriation. (Section 12)

All appropriations bills require a 2/3 majority vote, except the budget bill, budget trailer bills with appropriations, and those for public school appropriations (all of which require a simple majority vote). The Legislature can control the submission, approval and enforcement of budgets and the filing of claims for all state agencies. Legislators cannot be paid any salary or expenses in any year in which the budget bill is not passed by the Legislature by midnight on June 15. (Section 12)

A legislator cannot hold any office or employment with the state other than the elected office for the Assembly or Senate. This limitation applies during his or her elected term. (Section 13)

A legislator cannot be served a civil summons during a Legislative Session or for 5 days before Session and 5 days after Session. (Section 14)

A person who attempts to influence a legislator's vote or action by bribery, intimidation or other "dishonest means" is guilty of a felony. This also applies to a legislator who has been influenced by such means. (Section 15)

General laws have uniform operation, while a local or special statute is limited in its operation. A local or special statute is invalid when a general statute applies. (Section 16) This is why bills that are deemed special statutes must contain an explanation of why a general statute will not apply in the bill's particular circumstances.

The Legislature does not have power to grant extra compensation to a public officer, employee or contractor after service has been rendered or to authorize payment of a claim against the state or a local jurisdiction. (Section 17) This is why each year the Appropriations Committee Chair will carry a "claims bill" to require the state to pay claims properly owed by the state.

Only the Assembly has the power to impeach, but any impeachment must be tried by the Senate, and an individual can only be convicted of impeachment if the Senate votes to do so by a 2/3 majority. The power of impeachment applies to statewide elected officers, members of the Board of Equalization, and state court judges. These individuals are subject to impeachment only for misconduct in office. When a conviction occurs, that individual is removed from office and disqualified to hold any state office thereafter. (Section 18)

The Legislature has authority to divide the state into fish and game districts and may protect fish and game in those districts. (Section 20)

When each regular session convenes, the President pro tempore of the Senate, the Speaker of the Assembly and the two minority leaders must report to their houses the goals and objectives of that house during that session. At the close of each regular session, these four legislative leaders must report on the progress made toward meetings those goals and objectives. (Section 22)

No bill can take effect as an urgency statute if it authorizes or contains an appropriation for any alteration or modification of the State Capitol or the purchase of furniture for the Capitol. (Section 28)

Notes and Questions

1. What are some differences and some similarities between Article IV of the California Constitution and Article I of the U.S. Constitution? Is the California Legislature and its legislative process similar or different than its federal counterpart?

2. Are any of the sections of Article IV more appropriate for the Government Code? If so, which one(s)? Regarding the constitutional provisions related to the legislative process, should any of these instead be placed in the Assembly, Senate, or Joint Rules?

C. Other Constitutional Provisions Affecting the Legislature

Most of the provisions of the California Constitution concerning the Legislature are found in Article IV, Sections 1 thru 28. Nonetheless, there are a number of provisions found in other articles of the state Constitution affecting the duties and powers of the Legislature. The following highlights the other major constitutional provisions concerning the Legislature.

Article II — Voting, Initiative and Referendum, and Recall

The Legislature defines residence and provides registration and elections laws and must prohibit improper practices that affect elections. The Legislature also provides for recall of local officers.

Article IX — Education

The Legislature prescribes the qualifications required for county school superintendents, as well as appointment or election of the county boards of education. The Legislature has the power to provide for organizing school districts, high school districts, and community college districts, and may authorize all school districts to carry on programs and activities.

Article XI — Local Government

The state is divided into counties, which are legal subdivisions of the state. The Legislature prescribes uniform procedures for county formation, consolidation, and boundary changes. The Legislature provides for county powers, elected county sheriffs, district attorneys and assessors, as well as an elected governing body in each county.

In addition, the Legislature prescribes uniform procedures for city formation and provides for city powers. The Legislature provides that counties perform municipal functions at the request of cities within those counties.

The Legislature is prohibited from delegating to a private person or body any power to make, control, appropriate, supervise, or interfere with county or municipal corporation improvements, money, or property, or to levy taxes or assessments, or perform municipal functions.

The Legislature may prescribe procedures for presentation, consideration and enforcement of claims against counties, cities, their officers, agents, or employees.

Article XIII — Taxation

The Legislature may provide for property taxation of all forms of tangible personal property, shares of capital stock, evidence of indebtedness, and any legal or equitable interest therein not exempt. This must be done by a 2/3 majority vote of each house (i.e., to classify personal property for differential taxation or for exemption).

The Legislature may exempt from property taxation in whole or in part a number of types of property, such as personal residences for those injured in military service, and property used for religious, hospital or charitable purposes.

In addition, the Legislature by a 2/3 majority vote may authorize county boards of supervisors to exempt real property having a full value so low that, if not exempt, the total taxes and applicable subventions on the property would amount to less than the cost of assessing and collecting them.

The Legislature may define open space land and must provide that when this land is enforceably restricted to recreation, enjoyment of scenic beauty, use or conservation of natural resources, or production of food or fiber, it will be valued for tax purposes consistently those the restrictions on uses.

The Legislature may provide by law for the manner in which a person of low or moderate income who is 62 years of age or older may postpone ad valorem property taxes on the dwelling owned and occupied by him or her as his or her principal place of residence.

The Legislature may provide for the assessment for taxation only on the basis of use of a single-family dwelling and so much of the land as is required for its convenient use and occupation, when the dwelling is occupied by an owner and located on land zoned exclusively for single-family dwellings or for agricultural purposes.

The Legislature may authorize local governments to provide for the assessment or reassessment of taxable property physically damaged or destroyed after the lien date to which the assessment or reassessment relates.

The Legislature may provide maximum property tax rates and bonding limits for local governments. The Legislature may not impose taxes for local purposes but may authorize local governments to impose them.

The Legislature may not reallocate, transfer, borrow, appropriate, restrict the use of, or otherwise use the proceeds of any tax imposed or levied by a local government solely for the local government's purposes.

The Legislature may tax corporations, including state and national banks, and their franchises by any method not prohibited by the Constitution or the Constitution or laws of the United States.

The Legislature may authorize counties, cities and counties, and cities to enter into contracts to apportion between them the revenue derived from any sales or use tax imposed by them that is collected for them by the state.

Article XIV — Labor Relations

The Legislature may provide for minimum wages and for the general welfare of employees and for those purposes may confer on a commission legislative, executive, and judicial powers.

The Legislature is expressly vested with plenary power, unlimited by any provision of this Constitution, to create and enforce a complete system of workers' compensation by appropriate legislation.

Article XVIII — Amending and Revising the Constitution

The Legislature by a 2/3 majority vote may propose an amendment or revision of the Constitution and, in the same manner, may amend or withdraw its proposal. Each amendment shall be so prepared and submitted that it can be voted on separately by the electorate.

The Legislature by a 2/3 majority vote may submit at a general election the question whether to call a convention to revise the Constitution.

Article XX — Miscellaneous Subjects

The Legislature shall protect by law from forced sale a certain portion of the homestead and other property of all heads of families.

Members of the Legislature, and all public officers and employees, executive, legislative, and judicial, except such inferior officers and employees as may be by law exempted, shall, before they enter upon the duties of their respective offices, take and subscribe an oath of office.

The Legislature shall not pass any laws permitting the leasing or alienation of any franchise, so as to relieve the franchise or property held thereunder from the liabilities of the lessor or grantor, lessee, or grantee, contracted or incurred in the operation, use, or enjoyment of such franchise, or any of its privileges.

Legislative term limits are provided for Assembly Members and Senators for a total time of service of twelve years, which can be served in either or both houses.

The Legislature may authorize, subject to reasonable restrictions, the sale in retail stores of alcoholic beverages contained in the original packages, where such alcoholic beverages are not to be consumed on the premises where sold; and may provide for the issuance of all types of licenses necessary to carry on the activities.

The Speaker of the Assembly shall be an ex officio member, having equal rights and duties with the non-legislative members, of any state agency created by the Legislature in the field of public higher education which is charged with the management, administration, and control of the State College System of California.

All these provisions are of interest, because they are granted by the state Constitution and provide authority or limit power of the Legislature in specified areas. Some are narrow in their application, but others are quite broad.

Notes and Questions

1. Should all the provisions of the state Constitution related to powers and duties of the Legislature be placed in Article IV? Or is it appropriate to have the Legislature and some of its powers and duties be scattered around multiple Articles in the state Constitution? In theory, could the Legislature play a role in the remaining Articles? Does the Legislature need to be specified in those other sections to have a formal role?

D. Conflict of Laws with the Constitution

When it comes to the hierarchy of laws in this state, California follows the federal version, which places the Constitution at the top of the chart, followed by statutes (enacted by the Legislature), followed by regulations (adopted by the executive's branch's rulemaking agencies and departments). Based upon the Constitution being the supreme law of the state, statutes may not conflict with the state Constitution.

Where there is a conflict of laws, the Constitution prevails. Fundamentally, where statutes conflict with constitutional provisions, the latter must prevail.

Hart v. Jordan

(1939) 14 Cal.2d 288 (in bank)

OPINION

THE COURT.

By this proceeding in mandamus the petitioner seeks to compel the respondents, as Secretary of State and State Printer, respectively, to desist from taking any further steps in the matter of preparing for the ballot and submitting to the voters at the special election to be held on November 7, 1939, a proposed referendum on "The California Oil and Gas Control Act" enacted at the last session of the legislature (Stats. 1939, ch. 811). The question presented for determination is whether a referendum which has qualified for submission to the voters must be presented at a special election called for the purpose of presenting a particular initiative measure.

On July 1st the Governor of California by proclamation fixed November 7th as the date of a special election at which there shall be submitted to the voters for adoption or rejection an initiative constitutional amendment entitled "Retirement Warrants". It appears that on July 27th the attorney-general prepared a title and summary of the chief purpose and points of a referendum petition against "The California Oil and Gas Control Act", supra, and since that time this petition has been signed by approximately twice the number of persons required by the Constitution to submit the measure to the electors. If on or before September 18th this petition, certified as having been signed by "qualified electors equal in number to five per cent of all the votes cast for all candidates for Governor at the last preceding general election", is presented to the Secretary of State, the challenged enactment of the legislature shall be submitted to the electors "at the next succeeding general election occurring at any time subsequent to thirty days after the filing of said petition or at any special election which may be called by the Governor, in his discretion, prior to such regular election …". (Const., art. IV, sec. 1.) As the petitioner asserts that there are now on file the names of sufficient electors to qualify the referendum petition, the question for decision primarily concerns the construction of the constitutional provision in connection with certain statutes relating to elections.

Article IV, section 1, of the Constitution relates not only to referendums but also to initiative petitions. It specifies with particularity the requirements of each of such classes of petitions, and also the elections at which proposed or challenged laws are to be submitted to the voters. An act proposed by an initiative petition for submission directly to the electors must be presented "at the next succeeding general election occurring subsequent to 130 days after the presentation aforesaid of said petition, or at any special election called by the Governor in his discretion prior to such general election". This differs from the provision concerning initiative measures to be first submitted to the legislature, in that the general election must occur ninety days after the presentation of the petition and the special election need not be one "called for such purpose."

Issues raised by a referendum petition must be submitted to the People at the next succeeding general election occurring at any time subsequent to thirty days, after the filing of the petition or at any special election called by the Governor in his discretion.

In considering these different provisions, the petitioner contends that because the Constitution provides that "no law or amendment to the Constitution, proposed by the Legislature, shall be submitted at any election unless at the same election there shall be submitted all measures proposed by petition of the electors, if any be so proposed", in all other cases it is discretionary with the Governor which qualified initiative or referendum measures shall be submitted at a special election called for a particular purpose. There are two answers to this contention. In the first place, the Constitution, for obvious reasons, provides that in the particular situation specified, all qualified measures must be submitted to the People at one time. This requirement does not apply when initiatives to be submitted directly to the People and referendums are the only measures which have qualified for submission to the People. In the second place, the legislature in providing that a special election may be called by the Governor, left it within his power, as a matter of discretion, whether to call such an election. But when he has acted in the exercise of discretion, all measures which are qualified to go before the People by the constitutional provisions must be placed upon the ballot. This is the plain mandate of the Constitution and a court has no authority to change the requirements which the People have imposed.

The petitioner places considerable reliance upon the provision of the Constitution that the failure to submit any referendum measure "at the election specified in this section" shall not prevent its submission at a succeeding general election. This can only mean that if for any reason a referendum measure is not submitted to the voters as required by the Constitution, it shall not thereby fail but must be placed before them at a succeeding general election. This provision safeguards the power reserved by the People.

As against this construction, however, are certain statutory provisions fixing times for the doing of acts in connection with an election on a referendum measure greater than the constitutional period of thirty days. For example, the Constitution provides that "all measures submitted to a vote of the electors, under the provisions of this section, shall be printed, and together with arguments for and against each such measure by those in favor of, and those opposed to, it shall be mailed to each elector in the same manner as now provided by law as to amendments to the Constitution, proposed by the Legislature; and the persons to prepare and present such arguments shall, until otherwise provided by law, be selected by the presiding officer of the Senate". (Art. IV, sec. 1.) Under section 1195 of the Political Code, arguments for or against a proposed constitutional amendment or other proposition to be submitted to the People "shall be submitted to the secretary of state within ninety days after the adjournment of the legislature". A succeeding section authorizes the Secretary of State, in the event the argument for or against a referendum measure is not filed as required by the Constitution, to make a general press release eighty-five days prior to the date of the election, inviting electors to submit such arguments within sixty-five days prior to the election. (Sec. 1195c, Pol. Code.)

Another requirement laid upon the Secretary of State is that not less than forty-five days before the election he shall furnish each county clerk and registrar of voters a stated number of pamphlets containing the text of the measures to be submitted at such election, with the ballot titles and arguments thereon. The pamphlets are to be mailed to the voters not more than forty days nor less than fifteen days prior to the election. (Sec. 1195b, Pol. Code.)

The essential purpose of these provisions is to give the voters information concerning the measures on the ballot. It does not appear that the statutory requirements cannot be either fully or substantially complied with by the respondents in preparing material for the coming election, but wherever they conflict with constitutional provisions, the latter must prevail.

The alternative writ of mandate heretofore issued herein is discharged and a peremptory writ is denied.

Notes and Questions

1. Like at the federal level, California has a hierarchy of law. The hierarchy is the state Constitution, statutes (found in codes), and regulations (found in titles).

2. The Constitutions at the federal and state levels were created by the people. With direct democracy, California's electorate can amend the state Constitution and adopt statutes. The Legislature can propose amendments to the state Constitution (which must be approved by the voters) and adopt statutes. Executive branch administrative agencies promulgate regulations (sometimes called rules).

3. Neither a statute nor a regulation can contradict the Constitution, which sits atop the hierarchy of laws at the federal and state levels. The U.S. Constitution and U.S. Codes (statutes adopted by Congress) are above their state equivalents. Charters and ordinances adopted by local governments are below federal and state laws.

4. On this basis, it is common sense that a statute cannot conflict with the Constitution, and that a regulation cannot conflict with either the Constitution or a statute.

5. Why does the state Constitution provide that all qualified measures must be submitted to the people at one time? What is the purpose of such a requirement?

6. What rationale does the court use in determining that measures can be placed on the next succeeding election ballot?

Chapter Two

Power and Authority

The California Supreme Court opined in 2016 (*Howard Jarvis Taxpayers Assn. v. Padilla* (2016) 62 Cal.4th 486) that "Our Constitution vests '[t]he legislative power of this State ... in the California Legislature which consists of the Senate and Assembly ...' (Cal. Const. art. IV, Sec. 1.)" State constitutions, unlike the federal Constitution, generally do not grant only limited powers. (*Marine Forests Society v. California Coastal Com.* (2005) 36 Cal.4th 1, 29.)

Consequently, "unlike the United States Congress, which possesses only those specific powers delegated to it by the federal Constitution, it is well established that the California Legislature possesses plenary legislative authority as specifically limited by the California Constitution." (*Marine Forests Society*, 36 Cal.4th at 14–15.)

It has generally been recognized that the Legislature has inherently the implied authority to engage in activities that are incidental and ancillary to its lawmaking functions. As the Supreme Court explained, "A legislative assembly, when established, becomes vested with all the powers and privileges which are necessary and incidental to a free and unobstructed exercise of its appropriate functions. These powers and privileges are derived not from the Constitution; on the contrary, they arise from the very creation of a legislative body, and are founded upon the principle of self-preservation.

"The Constitution is not a grant, but a restriction upon the power of the Legislature, and hence an express enumeration of legislative powers and privileges in the Constitution cannot be considered as the exclusion of others not named unless accompanied by negative terms. A legislative assembly has, therefore, all the powers and privileges which are necessary to enable it to exercise in all respects, in a free, intelligent and impartial manner, its appropriate functions, except so far as it may be restrained by the express provisions of the Constitution, or by some express law made unto itself, regulating and limiting the same." (*Ex parte McCarthy* (1866) 29 Cal. 395, 403.)

Among the Legislature's necessary and incidental powers and privileges, which generally derive from parliamentary common law, is the authority to "establish its own rules of proceeding." (*Ex parte McCarthy.*)

In addition, the appellate court in *People's Advocate, Inc. v. Superior Court* (1986) 181 Cal.App.3d 316, 322, stated: "Since the inception of our state, the power of a legislative body to govern its own internal workings has been viewed as essential to its functioning except as it may have been expressly constrained by the California Constitution."

In California, the power of each house of the Legislature to establish its own rules of proceedings is not merely implicit in the state Constitution, but it has been explicitly set forth in Article IV, Section 7, which provides "[e]ach house shall choose its officers and adopt rules for its proceedings." As the Court noted in its *People's Advocate* decision, "[t]he provisions of the California Constitution (art. IV, Sec. 7) which empower the houses of the Legislature to govern their own proceedings were first enacted almost 150 years ago and have twice been reenacted by the electorate." (181 Cal.App.3d at p. 322.)

The fundamental question from one perspective is whether any provision of the state Constitution expressly constrains or prohibits the Legislature from doing something. As a general rule, doubts are to be resolved in favor of the Legislature's authority to act. "[A]ll intendments favor the exercise of the Legislature's plenary authority: 'If there is any doubt as to the Legislature's power to act in any given case, the doubt should be resolved in favor of the Legislature's action'." (*Methodist Hospital of Sacramento v. Saylor* (1971) 5 Cal.3d 685, 691, quoting *Collins v. Riley* (1944) 24 Cal.2d 912, 916.)

As a general rule, any constitutional restrictions on the Legislature's authority to act should be narrowly construed. For example, "such restriction and limitation (imposed by the Constitution) are to be construed strictly, and are not to be extended to include matters not covered by the language used." (*Collins*, 24 Cal.2d at 916.)

In addition, "Legislative power, except where the constitution has imposed limits upon it, is practically absolute; and where limitations upon it are imposed, they are to be strictly construed, and are not to be given effect as against the general power of the legislature, unless such limitations clearly inhibit the act in question." (*Amwest Surety Ins. Co. v. Wilson* (1995) 11 Cal.4th 1243, 1255, quoting *Martin v. Riley* (1942) 20 Cal.2d 28, 39.)

State courts have generally been concerned about violating the separation of powers doctrine, particularly between the legislative and judicial branches of state government. For example, only upon finding "a clear constitutional mandate" may a court overturn a legislative action as *ultra vires*. (*County of Riverside v. Superior Court* (2003) 30 Cal.4th 278, 285.)

Similarly, "[L]egislative restraint imposed through judicial interpretation of less than unequivocal language would inevitably lead to inappropriate judicial interference with the prerogatives of a coordinate branch of government. Accordingly, the only judicial standard commensurate with the separation of powers doctrine is one of strict construction to ensure that restrictions on the Legislature are in fact imposed by the people rather than by the courts in the guise of interpretation." (*Schabarum v. California Legislature* (1998) 60 Cal.App.4th 1205, 1218.)

Notes and Questions

1. Is the power of the Legislature absolute? Is it too simplistic a view to determine that, if Article IV does not provide a specific prohibition, then the Legislature can exercise a power? Should the state Constitution be construed more narrowly than that?

A. Legislative Powers and Duties by Statute

In California's Government Code, there are several code sections that set forth legislative powers and duties. These statutes were added by Proposition 24 in 1984 and are found in Title 2, Division 2, Part 1, Chapter 8, Article 2. The provisions of law are summarized below:

Speaker of the Assembly — Gov't Code Sec. 9910

The Speaker is responsible for the efficient conduct of the legislative and administrative affairs of the Assembly. The Speaker is elected upon organization of the Assembly at the beginning of each regular or special session and serves until adjournment sine die of that session, unless removed and a successor is chosen.

Assembly Committee on Rules — Gov't Code Sec. 9911

There is an Assembly Committee on Rules, which consists of the Speaker, who is the chairman of the committee, and six other Members of the Assembly, three to be elected by the party having the largest number of Members in the Assembly and three to be elected by the party having the second largest number of Members.

The Assembly Committee on Rules has a continuing existence and may meet and act during sessions of the Legislature or any recess and in the interim periods between sessions. The committee has all the powers and authority provided in Article IV, Section 11 of the Constitution.

Powers of the Assembly Committee on Rules — Gov't Code Sec. 9912

The Assembly Committee on Rules has the power to assign all bills to Assembly committees; appoint the Chairmen and Vice-Chairmen of all other Assembly Committees (who must be members of different parties); have general direction over the Assembly Chamber and rooms set aside for the use of the Assembly, including private offices; allocate all funds, staffing, and other resources necessary for the effective operation of the Assembly; and exercise such other powers and perform such duties as may be provided by statute.

Neither the Chairman nor any member or agent of the Assembly Committee on Rules has the power to perform any action on behalf of the committee including, but not limited to, the making of contracts, the payment of claims, the allocation of office space, or the hiring or dismissal of staff, without the express authorization of two thirds of the total membership of the committee.

Appointments by the Assembly — Gov't Code Sec. 9913

All statutory appointments delegated to the Speaker of the Assembly are subject to confirmation by the Assembly Committee on Rules, two thirds of the membership concurring.

President pro Tempore of the Senate — Gov't Code Sec. 9914

The President pro Tempore is elected upon organization of the Senate at the beginning of each regular or special session and serves until adjournment sine die of that session, unless removed and a successor chosen.

Senate Committee on Rules — Gov't Code Sec. 9915

There is a Senate Committee on Rules, which consists of the President pro Tempore of the Senate, who is the chairman of the committee, and four other Members of the Senate, two to be elected by the party having the largest number of Members in the Senate and two to be elected by the party having the second largest number of Members.

The Senate Committee on Rules has a continuing existence and may meet and act during sessions of the Legislature or any recess and in the interim periods between sessions. The committee has all the powers and authority provided in Article IV, Section 11 of the Constitution.

Powers of the Senate Committee on Rules — Gov't Code Sec. 9916

The Senate Committee on Rules has the power to assign all bills to Senate committees; appoint the Chairmen and Vice-Chairmen of all other Senate Committees (who must be members of different parties); have general direction over the Senate Chamber and rooms set aside for the use of the Senate, including private offices; allocate all funds, staffing, and other resources necessary for the effective operation of the Senate; and exercise such other powers and perform such duties as may be provided by statute.

Neither the Chairman nor any member or agent of the Senate Committee on Rules has the power to perform any action on behalf of the committee including, but not limited to, the making of contracts, the payment of claims, the allocation of office space, or the hiring or dismissal of staff, without the express authorization of two thirds of the total membership of the committee.

Joint Rules Committee — Gov't Code Sec. 9917

There is a Joint Rules Committee, which is comprised of the combined membership of the Assembly Committee on Rules and the Senate Committee on Rules and two other Members of the Senate, one to be elected by the party having the largest number of Members in the Senate and one to be elected by the party having the second largest number of Members.

The committee created has a continuing existence and may meet and act during sessions of the Legislature or any recess and in the interim periods between sessions. The committee has all the powers and authority provided in Article IV, Section 11 of the Constitution of California.

Any action of the committee requires an affirmative vote of not less than a majority of the Senate members and a majority of the Assembly members of the committee, except that any action which involves or anticipates the expenditure or allocation of funds requires an affirmative vote of at least two thirds of the Senate members and two thirds of the Assembly members.

Notes and Questions

1. These provisions of the Government Code deal with legislative leaders, including some of their powers and duties. Are these appropriate to be in statute? Or should

these provisions be contained in the Assembly Rules, Senate Rules, or even the Joint Rules instead?

2. The state Constitution provides that the Legislature may adopt rules for its internal proceedings. Based upon this provision, should rules be placed into statute? Or should they be specified in the internal rules of the Legislature?

B. Power of the Legislature

The power of California's Legislature is set forth in Article IV of the state Constitution and represents a grant of authority, rather than a limitation. That grant is broad when it comes to lawmaking. Although the people reserve their rights of lawmaking through the initiative process as set forth in Article II, the Legislature has significant authority to enact statutes and to place constitutional amendments on the statewide ballot for a vote of the people. The Legislature has obvious powers that have been vested in it by the state Constitution.

The California Legislature has plenary legislative power except as specifically limited by the California Constitution. (*Marine Forests Soc. v. Cal. Coastal Com.*, 36 Cal.4th at 43–44, 47–48; *Fitts v. Superior Court* (1936) 6 Cal.2d 230, 234 ["[T]he Legislature is vested with the whole of the legislative power of the state."].) Essentially, the limitation is based upon the electorate's direct democracy powers. (*Methodist Hosp. of Sacramento v. Saylor* 5 Cal.3d at 691.) And the people's power of initiative is not limited by subject matter.

Howard Jarvis Taxpayers Association v. Padilla
(2016) 62 Cal.4th 486

Opinion

WERDEGAR, J.

In 2014, the California Legislature sought to place on the general election ballot a nonbinding advisory question, Proposition 49. The measure would have asked the electorate whether Congress should propose, and the Legislature ratify, a federal constitutional amendment overturning the United States Supreme Court decision *Citizens United v. Federal Election Comm'n* (2010) 558 U.S. 310, 130 S.Ct. 876, 175 L.Ed.2d 753.

In response to a petition for writ of mandate urging the unconstitutionality of the Legislature's action, we issued an order to show cause and directed the Secretary of State to refrain from taking further action in connection with placement of Proposition 49 on the ballot. Our action did not rest on a final determination of Proposition 49's lawfulness. Instead, we concluded "the proposition's validity is uncertain" and the balance of hardships from permitting an invalid measure to remain on the ballot, as against delaying a proposition to a future election, weighed in favor of immediate relief. (See *American Federation of Labor v. Eu* (1984) 36 Cal.3d 687, 697, 206 Cal.Rptr. 89, 686 P.2d 609.)

We now resolve the merits of Proposition 49's constitutionality. We conclude: (1) as a matter of state law, the Legislature has authority to conduct investigations by reasonable means to inform the exercise of its other powers; (2) among those other powers are the power to petition for national constitutional conventions, ratify federal constitutional amendments, and call on Congress and other states to exercise their own federal article V powers; (3) although neither constitutional text nor judicial precedent provide definitive answers to the question, long-standing historical practice among the states demonstrates a common understanding that legislatures may formally consult with and seek nonbinding input from their constituents on matters relevant to the federal constitutional amendment process; (4) nothing in the state Constitution prohibits the use of advisory questions to inform the Legislature's exercise of its article V-related powers; and (5) applying deferential review, Proposition 49 is reasonably related to the exercise of those powers and thus constitutional. We deny the instant petition for a writ of mandate.

Factual and Procedural Background

In *Citizens United v. Federal Election Comm'n, supra,* 558 U.S. 310, 130 S.Ct. 876, a divided United States Supreme Court invalidated federal election law restrictions on the political speech of corporations, holding that a speaker's identity as a corporation, as opposed to natural person, could not justify greater regulation of speech than the First Amendment would have otherwise permitted. (*Id.* at pp. 319, 365, 130 S.Ct. 876.) In the few years since its issuance, *Citizens United*'s holding concerning the speech rights of corporations has generated considerable democratic debate, receiving criticism in the presidential State of the Union address, giving rise to resolutions in Congress to amend the Constitution, and sparking calls for reconsideration within the United States Supreme Court itself. Many have agreed with the Supreme Court majority, while others have concluded the Constitution must be amended to permit renewed restraints on corporate involvement in popular elections.

The Legislature first joined issue with *Citizens United* in Assembly Joint Resolution No. 1, introduced in 2012 and adopted by both houses of the Legislature in 2014. (Assem. Joint Res. No. 1, Stats. 2014 (2013–2014 Reg. Sess.) res. ch. 77.) The resolution declared: "Corporations are legal entities that governments create and the rights that they enjoy under the United States Constitution should be more narrowly defined than the rights afforded to natural persons." (*Ibid.*) Acknowledging *Citizens United*'s holding to the contrary, the resolution exercised the Legislature's federal constitutional power to "apply to the United States Congress to call a constitutional convention for the sole purpose of proposing an amendment to the United States Constitution that would limit corporate personhood for purposes of campaign finance and political speech and would further declare that money does not constitute speech and may be legislatively limited." (Assem. Joint Res. No. 1, Stats. 2014 (2013–2014 Reg. Sess.) res. ch. 77; see U.S. Const. art. V ["The Congress ... on the application of the legislatures of two-thirds of the several states, shall call a convention for proposing amendments. ..."].)

Separately, the Legislature enacted Senate Bill No. 1272 (2013–2014 Reg. Sess.) (Senate Bill No. 1272), "[a]n act to submit an advisory question to the voters relating to campaign finance...." (Stats.2014, ch. 175.) A lengthy preamble decried *Citizens United*, noted the article V process for amending the United States Constitution, and asserted "[t]he people of California and of the United States have previously used ballot measures as a way of instructing their elected representatives about the express actions they want to see them take on their behalf, including provisions to amend the United States Constitution." (Stats.2014, ch. 175, § 2, subd. (m); see generally *id.*, § 2.) The measure "call[ed] a special election to be consolidated with the November 4, 2014, statewide general election" (Legis. Counsel's Dig., Sen. Bill No. 1272 (2013–2014 Reg. Sess.); see Stats.2014, ch. 175, § 3) and directed the Secretary of State to submit to voters at that election an advisory question asking whether Congress should propose, and the Legislature ratify, a constitutional amendment overturning *Citizens United*, and thereafter to submit the results to Congress (Stats.2014, ch. 175, § 4). The measure became law in July 2014, after both houses passed it and the Governor declined to sign or veto it. (See Cal. Const, art. IV, § 10, subd. (b)(3) [authorizing bills to become statutes after gubernatorial inaction].)

Subsequently, then Secretary of State Debra Bowen designated the advisory question Proposition 49 and began preparing ballot materials. The proposition was to read: "Shall the Congress of the United States propose, and the California Legislature ratify, an amendment or amendments to the United States Constitution to overturn *Citizens United v. Federal Election Commission* (2010) 558 U.S. 310 130 S.Ct. 876, 175 L.Ed.2d 753, and other applicable judicial precedents, to allow the full regulation or limitation of campaign contributions and spending, to ensure that all citizens, regardless of wealth, may express their views to one another, and to make clear that the rights protected by the United States Constitution are the rights of natural persons only?" (Stats.2014, ch. 175, § 4, subd. (a).)

Petitioners Howard Jarvis Taxpayers Association and Jon Coupal (collectively, Howard Jarvis) promptly filed a petition for writ of mandate in the Third District Court of Appeal, seeking to prevent Secretary Bowen from proceeding with placement of Proposition 49 on the November 2014 ballot. A divided Court of Appeal denied relief.

Howard Jarvis next filed an original emergency petition for writ of mandate in this court. After expedited briefing, we issued an order to show cause and stayed Secretary Bowen from taking further actions in connection with Proposition 49 until after a final decision, effectively removing the advisory question from the November 2014 ballot. The order explained, "[t]ime constraints require the court to decide immediately whether to permit Proposition 49 to be placed on the November 4, 2014, ballot pending final resolution of this matter." A five-justice majority concluded Proposition 49's validity was uncertain and the cost of postponing a potentially lawful proposition to a later ballot, a course the Legislature itself had contemplated in an earlier version of the bill, was outweighed by the cost of permitting a potentially invalid proposition to reach the ballot. "'The presence of an invalid measure on the ballot steals attention, time and money from the numerous valid propositions on the same ballot. It will confuse some voters and frustrate others, and an ultimate decision that the measure is invalid, coming after the voters have voted in favor of the measure, tends to denigrate the legitimate use of the initiative procedure.' (*American Federation of Labor v. Eu* (1984) 36 Cal.3d 687, 697 206 Cal.Rptr. 89, 686 P.2d 609.)"

Our actions in August 2014 resolved whether Proposition 49 could be placed on the November 2014 ballot. Senate Bill No. 1272 directs only placement on that ballot (Stats.2014, ch. 175, §§ 3–4), and this case is thus technically moot. But whether the Legislature ever has power to place advisory questions on a statewide ballot is important and undecided, and in the event we were to conclude Senate Bill No. 1272 was indeed constitutional, the Legislature could pass an identical measure directing placement of the same advisory question on a future ballot. In response to our order to show cause, Howard Jarvis and real party in interest the State Legislature of California have briefed the larger questions the petition raises: whether legislative advisory questions are ever permissible, and whether in particular Proposition 49 is permissible or should be enjoined from placement on any future statewide ballot. Notwithstanding that the passage of an election cycle has interposed mootness as a potential obstacle to resolving a significant election law issue, we conclude retaining jurisdiction and addressing the merits is the better course here. (See *Independent Energy Producers Assn. v. McPherson* (2006) 38 Cal.4th 1020, 1024, 44 Cal.Rptr.3d 644, 136 P.3d 178; *Costa v. Superior Court* (2006) 37 Cal.4th 986, 994, 1005, 39 Cal.Rptr.3d 470, 128 P.3d 675.)

Discussion

I.

Proposition 49 and the State Legislature's Power to Investigate

Our Constitution vests "[t]he legislative power of this State ... in the California Legislature which consists of the Senate and Assembly...." (Cal. Const. art. IV, § 1.) It is in the nature of state constitutions that they, unlike the federal Constitution, generally do not grant only limited powers. (*Marine Forests Society v. California Coastal Com.* (2005) 36 Cal.4th 1, 29, 30 Cal.Rptr.3d 30, 113 P.3d 1062.) Consequently, "unlike the United States Congress, which possesses only those specific powers delegated to it by the federal Constitution, it is well established that the California Legislature possesses *plenary* legislative authority except as specifically limited by the California Constitution." (*Id.* at p. 31, 30 Cal.Rptr.3d 30, 113 P.3d 1062.) Lying at the core of that plenary authority is the power to enact laws. (*California Redevelopment Assn. v. Matosantos* (2011) 53 Cal.4th 231, 254, 135 Cal.Rptr.3d 683, 267 P.3d 580.) It has been said that pursuant to that authority, "[t]he Legislature has the *actual* power to pass any act it pleases," subject only to those limits that may arise elsewhere in the state or federal Constitutions. (*Nougues v. Douglass* (1857) 7 Cal. 65, 70.)

Although the Legislature notes in passing that Proposition 49 resulted from a statute, it does not rest its argument for constitutionality on the syllogism that the legislative power includes the power to enact statutes, Senate Bill No. 1272 takes the form of an enacted statute, and thus for that reason alone the bill and Proposition 49 are within a constitutional source of power. Instead, the Legislature argues it has the inherent power to conduct an investigation in order to select the wisest policy course. Pursuant to that implied investigative power, the Legislature contends, it may enact a statute placing an advisory question before the voters.

We have since the early days of statehood recognized the act of creating a legislature imbues that body with certain implied authority characteristic of parliaments: "A legislative assembly, when established, becomes vested with all the powers and privileges which are necessary and incidental to a free and unobstructed exercise of its appropriate functions. These powers and privileges are derived not from the Constitution; on the contrary, they arise from the very creation of a legislative body, and are founded upon the principle of self-preservation." (*Ex parte D.O. McCarthy* (1866) 29 Cal. 395, 403.) The scope and nature of these powers is "to be ascertained by a reference to the common parliamentary law." (*Ibid.*) Many or most of a parliament's common law powers relate to matters of self-regulation, such as determining membership and establishing internal rules of procedure (see *id.* at pp. 403–404), and are not relevant here. One, however, is: the inherent power "[t]o investigate, by the testimony of witnesses or otherwise, any subject or matter, in reference to which [a legislature] has power to act." (*Id.* at p. 404, italics omitted.)

The principal function of a legislature is "to enact wise and well-formed and needful laws" (*In re Battelle* (1929) 207 Cal. 227, 240, 277 P. 725), but a legislature cannot exercise sound judgment without information. Accordingly, "the necessity of investigation of some sort must exist as an indispensable incident and auxiliary to the proper exercise of legislative power." (*Id.* at p. 241, 277 P. 725; see *Special Assembly Int. Com. v. Southard* (1939) 13 Cal.2d 497, 503, 90 P.2d 304 [the power to enact legislation "'necessarily presupposes that the members of each house of the legislature must investigate the necessity for legislation'"].) The details of how this implied power is to be exercised are consigned to the Legislature's discretion in the first instance: "'The ascertainment of pertinent facts for legislation is within the power of the law-making department of government. When a legislative body has a right to do an act it must be allowed to select the means within reasonable bounds.'" (*Parker v. Riley* (1941) 18 Cal.2d 83, 91, 113 P.2d 873; see also *id.* at p. 90, 113 P.2d 873 ["Intelligent legislation upon the complicated problems of modern society is impossible in the absence of accurate information on the part of the legislators, and any reasonable procedure for securing such information is proper."].)

The investigative power is not unlimited. While the Legislature's powers and functions are extensive (see *Carmel Valley Fire Protection Dist. v. State of California* (2001) 25 Cal.4th 287, 299, 105 Cal.Rptr.2d 636, 20 P.3d 533), they must share space with powers reserved to the executive and judicial branches. Although the Legislature's activities can overlap with the functions of other branches to an extent, the Legislature may not use its powers to "defeat or materially impair" the exercise of its fellow branches' constitutional functions, nor "intrude upon a core zone" of another branch's authority. (*Marine Forests Society v. California Coastal Com., supra,* 36 Cal.4th at p. 45, 30 Cal.Rptr.3d 30, 113 P.3d 1062.) The investigative power, no less than any other, may not be used to trench upon matters falling outside the legislative purview.

Even aside from separation of powers concerns, the investigative power permits inquiry only into those subjects "in reference to which [the Legislature] has power to act." (*Ex parte D.O. McCarthy, supra,* 29 Cal. at p. 404, italics omitted.) Investigation is permitted as a necessary aid to the execution of other legislative powers, not as an expansion of matters with respect to which the Legislature may act. Where those other powers are subject to limit, so too an investigation in support of them may be constrained. (See *Special Assembly Int. Com. v. Southard, supra,* 13 Cal.2d at p. 504, 90 P.2d 304 [" 'when the power to legislate ceases, then the power to investigate for the purpose of aiding the legislature in exercising this power ceases, or stated another way, when the main power of legislating dies the incidental or implied power dies with it' "].) The investigative power, constitutionally implied as necessary for the execution of the Legislature's other powers, does not stand as an unbounded, freestanding power in its own right.

Finally, while the method of investigation is for the Legislature to choose in its broad discretion, within reason (*Parker v. Riley, supra,* 18 Cal.2d at pp. 90–91, 113 P.2d 873), we do not foreclose the possibility limits may arise from other constitutional provisions and the values they embrace.

Given these constraints, to determine whether a particular legislative action is authorized as an exercise of investigative power, we must in the first instance ascertain whether a nexus exists between the matter investigated and some potential action the Legislature has authority to undertake. Senate Bill No. 1272 seeks to conduct a statewide plebiscite on a proposed federal amendment and deliver its results to Congress. (*Id.,* § 4, subds. (a), (b).) The Legislature contends the plebiscite should be understood as part of an investigation into how and whether to exercise the Legislature's powers in connection with a potential future federal constitutional amendment. Accordingly, we examine next the extent of the role the federal Constitution contemplates for state legislatures in the amendment process.

 ....

III.

*The Use of Advisory Questions to Facilitate the
Exercise of Article V-Related Powers*

Text and tradition thus firmly establish a state legislature's power to petition for and participate in federal constitutional change, by proposing a national convention for the consideration of an amendment, by issuing a resolution calling on Congress to itself propose an amendment, by deciding whether to ratify amendments that emerge from either of these paths, and by establishing ground rules in the event ratification is to be by state convention. If a state legislature can exercise these powers, that a legislature can also avail itself of implied investigative powers to explore the wisdom or desirability of choosing one or another course of action necessarily follows.

(See *Parker v. Riley, supra,* 18 Cal.2d at pp. 90–91, 113 P.2d 873; *In re Battelle, supra,* 207 Cal. at pp. 240–241, 277 P. 725.)

As noted, however, the state law investigative power is not unbounded. Any investigation must be tethered to the exercise of other established legislative powers, and the method chosen in a particular instance must be reasonable. The issue we face is whether the Legislature may pose to the electorate a single advisory question concerning the People's support for a federal constitutional amendment. Its resolution depends on the answer to two sub-questions. First, in the abstract, does anything in the text or structure of the state or federal Constitutions preclude the Legislature from posing an advisory question when exercising its own article V authority or entreating other bodies with article V authority (Congress and fellow state legislatures) to act? Second, if there is no bar, is the specific question before us today, Proposition 49, a reasonable exercise of that implied state investigative power?

For example, federal environmental issues have been the subject of advisory questions in at least four states. The North Carolina Legislature asked voters if they were "for" or "against" location of a radioactive waste facility in the state, and directed that the results of the ballot be shared with the President, Congress, and other federal officials. Likewise, the Oregon Legislature asked: Should state officials continue challenges to federal selection of the state to house high-level nuclear waste repositories? The Wisconsin Legislature asked: Do voters support construction of a national or regional high-level radioactive waste disposal site in the state? The Massachusetts Legislature asked: "Shall the Commonwealth urge the President ... and ... Congress to enact a national acid rain program" requiring specific reductions in total national sulfur dioxide and allocate the costs of reductions equitably among the states?

A. *The Role in a Republic of Representative Consultation with the People*

The texts of the state and federal Constitutions are silent on the issue we face. The state investigative power is, as we have discussed, an inherent but implicit power of a legislature. The state Constitution does not otherwise clearly address the matter. The federal Constitution is even more terse: "As a rule the Constitution speaks in general terms, leaving Congress to deal with subsidiary matters of detail as the public interests and changing conditions may require; and Article V is no exception to the rule." (*Dillon v. Gloss, supra,* 256 U.S. at p. 376, 41 S.Ct. 510, fn. omitted.) Regarding what state legislatures may do when carrying out their article V roles, the federal Constitution leaves the scope of the powers and their limits unarticulated.

As for precedent, in our past decisions elucidating the constitutional principles that govern legislative investigations we have not been called upon to determine whether the investigative power may include the enactment of a statute placing an advisory measure on the statewide ballot. (Cf. *Parker v. Riley, supra,* 18 Cal.2d at p. 91, 113 P.2d 873 [approving formation of an independent commission]; *In re Battelle, supra,* 207 Cal. at p. 241, 277 P. 725 [approving formation of investigative committees]; *Ex parte D.O. McCarthy, supra,* 29 Cal. at p. 404 [approving summoning of witnesses].)

Where neither text nor precedent affords guidance, sometimes a "page of history is worth a volume of logic." (*New York Trust Co. v. Eisner* (1921) 256 U.S. 345, 349, 41 S.Ct. 506, 65 L.Ed. 963 (maj. opn. of Holmes, J.); see *Dyer v. Blair* (N.D.Ill.1975) 390 F.Supp. 1291, 1303–1307 [looking to historical practice to understand the proper scope of state legislative power in connection with federal constitutional amendments].) The history of legislative consultation with the people, and in particular the historical use of advisory questions to inform judgments concerning federal constitutional matters, is illuminating here.

. . . .

B. *Advisory Questions and State Constitutional Limits*

Legislatures in California and elsewhere thus have established a tradition of using advisory ballot measures to determine the will of the people on questions pertaining to amendments to the federal Constitution. While "'usage and custom, no matter how long continued, cannot create a right in the legislature that otherwise it does not possess'" (*Special Assembly Int. Com. v. Southard, supra,* 13 Cal.2d at pp. 508–509, 90 P.2d 304), we see no evidence the drafters of the California Constitution intended to deprive the Legislature of a tool other state legislatures have long used to ensure they are truly speaking on behalf of their states in the federal constitutional amendment process.

Nevertheless, Howard Jarvis offers a series of arguments for why the structure and implications of various provisions of our state Constitution necessarily bar the Legislature from using an advisory question as a means of investigating the will of the people with respect to federal constitutional amendments. We consider four separate contentions: (1) the Constitution confines the means of investigation to investigation by committee; (2) the Constitution confines the Legislature's access to the ballot to specifically enumerated circumstances that do not include advisory questions; (3) the Constitution prohibits anyone from placing on the ballot a measure that does not enact law; and (4) the Constitution allocates legislative power to the people and the Legislature in a way that preserves clear lines of accountability and implicitly prohibits devices such as advisory questions that would blur those lines. None has merit; no constitutional provision or set of provisions prohibits the use of advisory ballot measures concerning federal constitutional amendments.

1. The Committees Clause

Howard Jarvis argues that the power to investigate is limited by California Constitution, article IV, section 11, which authorizes investigations by committee. Under that provision, "[t]he Legislature or either house may by resolution provide for the selection of committees necessary for the conduct of its business, including committees to ascertain facts and make recommendations to the Legislature on a subject within the scope of legislative control." (*Ibid.*) From this language, Howard Jarvis reasons that the Legislature may ascertain facts *only* through committee investigations, and not by any other means. This argument misapprehends the import of the committees clause.

Prior to the clause's adoption in 1940 (see Cal. Const. art. IV, former § 37, added by initiative, Gen. Elec. (Nov. 5, 1940)), the extent of the Legislature's ability to act through less than all of the members of one house was the subject of dispute. (See *Swing v. Riley* (1939) 13 Cal.2d 513, 90 P.2d 313; *Special Assembly Int. Com. v. Southard, supra,* 13 Cal.2d 497, 90 P.2d 304; *In re Battelle, supra,* 207 Cal. 227, 277 P. 725.) In *Battelle,* this court considered but rejected the argument that the Legislature could not investigate by committee, explaining that the Constitution implied a power to investigate and committee investigations were a permissible exertion of that power. (*Id.* at pp. 240–244, 277 P. 725.) In *Special Assembly,* we again construed the state Constitution as implying a power to investigate, including a power to investigate by committee. (*Special Assembly,* at pp. 502–504, 90 P.2d 304.) We held, however, that the Legislature was not a continuing body, that it ceased to exist between sessions, that its express powers ceased to exist at the same time, and accordingly that the implied power to investigate died too. (*Id.* at pp. 504–507, 90 P.2d 304.) Consequently, an interim committee established by the Assembly to conduct investigations after legislative adjournment and report to the next session of the Legislature was unconstitutional. (*Id.* at p. 509, 90 P.2d 304; see *Swing v. Riley,* at pp. 517–520, 90 P.2d 313 [extending the same conclusion to a committee created by a joint resolution of both houses].)

At the next general election after *Special Assembly,* the Legislature placed on the ballot a constitutional amendment making explicit the power to investigate and act by committee and overturning the holdings that that power did not extend between legislative sessions. A ballot argument in support of amendment quoted directly from *In re Battelle, supra,* 207 Cal. at page 241, 277 P. 725: In "'the preparation of wise and timely laws the necessity of investigation of some sort must exist as an indispensable incident and auxiliary to the proper exercise of legislative power.'" (Voter Information Guide, Gen. Elec. (Nov. 5, 1940) argument by Assemblymember Voigt in favor of Assem. Const. Amend. No. 2, p. 24.) Another argument explained that, although the inherent power to investigate by committee had always been recognized, "[a] recent court decision has held, however, that this practice in our State is without constitutional authority." (*Id.,* argument by Assemblymember Cronin, at p. 24 [implicitly referencing *Special Assembly*].) The amendment's purpose was to supply, explicitly, the constitutional authority *Special Assembly* had found lacking. (*Id.,* at p. 24.)

Regarding the federal government's role in legislating concerning health care, the Massachusetts and New Jersey Legislatures each asked voters: Should the state urge Congress to enact a national health care program?

C. Nationwide and in California: Advisory measures submitted to voters by local legislatures (county boards and city councils)

Nationwide, the use of legislative advisory ballot measures to ask voters similar policy questions is even more frequent at the level of local legislatures — county boards of supervisors and city councils. (See <http://ballotpedia.org/Advisory_question> [as of January 4, 2016] ["Advisory questions are most commonly used at the local level, often to voice the opinions of [the] region to higher levels of government"].) Cities have made use of such advisory measures since the late 19th and early 20th centuries.

(See, e.g., Zimmerman, The Referendum, *supra,* at p. 140 [describing such measures in New York City, Buffalo, Chicago, and Wilmington]; Crouch, *Municipal Affairs: The Initiative and Referendum in Cities* (1943) 37 Amer. Poli. Sci. Rev. 491, 492, 501 [observing that "[m]any city councils have made use of ... the advisory referendum, or 'straw vote'" advisory ballot, and noting that between 1910 and 1938, 32 such measures were submitted to the voters in Detroit] [hereafter *Referendum in Cities*].)

Local legislatively initiated advisory ballot measures in California reflect a similar pattern. Prior to 1940, and even though there was at that time no explicit constitutional or statutory authority for doing so, advisory policy measures often appeared on the ballot in Los Angeles and San Francisco. (See *Referendum in Cities, supra,* 37 Amer. Poli. Sci. Rev. at pp. 492, 501 [noting 46 "[p]ublic [p]olicy [r]eferenda" on the L.A. ballot, and 21 on the S.F. ballot].) Eventually, in 1976, the Legislature specifically codified and acknowledged the propriety of advisory measures placed on the ballot by local legislative entities, including county boards of supervisors and city councils. Elections Code section 9603, subdivision (a), expressly contemplates advisory measures to allow "voters within the jurisdiction, or a portion thereof, to voice their opinions on substantive issues, or to indicate to the local legislative body approval or disapproval of the ballot proposal." Counted from 1995, the most recent year for which data is readily available, there have been, in California alone, 184 such measures — mostly by cities, with others by counties — averaging more than nine statewide each year.

Accordingly, we read the text of the committees clause as language of expansion, not restriction. The ballot argument in support endorses extant precedent establishing an implied power of investigation. The amendment simply removes doubt over whether the Legislature may investigate and carry out other necessary functions also by way of committee; it does not require the Legislature henceforth to inform itself of facts bearing on the need for action only by way of committee. Nothing in California Constitution, article IV, section 11 constrains the Legislature from placing advisory questions on the ballot.

2. Legislative Access to the Ballot

Various provisions of the state Constitution expressly authorize the Legislature to place measures on the ballot for voter approval. The Legislature may amend or repeal a statute adopted by voter initiative, but generally only if the amendment or repeal is first submitted to and approved by the electorate. (Cal. Const. art. II, § 10, subd. (c).) The Legislature may authorize the issuance of bonds, but above a certain amount they must be submitted to the voters for approval. (*Id.,* art. XVI, § 1.) Finally, the Legislature may propose state constitutional amendments, but such amendments must be submitted to the voters for approval. (*Id.,* art. XVIII, §§ 1, 4.)

Invoking the interpretive canon *expressio unius est exclusio alterius,* Howard Jarvis argues these three specific instances in which legislative action must be ratified by the voters demonstrate no others are permitted. (See also dis. opn., *post,* 196 Cal.Rptr.3d at 809–810, 363 P.3d at 692–693 [arguing that the constitutional scheme precludes legislative access to the ballot in other circumstances].) Under the canon, the explicit mention of some things in a text may imply other matters not similarly addressed are excluded. (*In re J.W.* (2002) 29 Cal.4th 200, 209, 126 Cal.Rptr.2d 897, 57 P.3d 363; *Lake v. Reed* (1997) 16 Cal.4th 448, 466, 65 Cal.Rptr.2d 860, 940 P.2d 311.) Applied to specific grants of power, the canon may support ""an implied negative; an implication that no other than the expressly granted power passes by the grant; that it is to be exercised only in the prescribed mode."" (*Wildlife Alive v. Chickering* (1976) 18 Cal.3d 190, 196, 132 Cal.Rptr. 377, 553 P.2d 537; see *Wheeler v. Herbert* (1907) 152 Cal. 224, 237, 92 P. 353 [applying the canon to interpret the scope of the Legislature's powers under the state Constitution].)

Here, however, the canon has no application. The *expressio unius* inference arises only when there is some reason to conclude an omission is the product of intentional design. (*Marx v. Gen. Revenue Corp.* (2013) 568 U.S. ___, ___, 133 S.Ct. 1166, 1175, 185 L.Ed.2d 242, 253; *Silverbrand v. County of Los Angeles* (2009) 46 Cal.4th 106, 126, 92 Cal.Rptr.3d 595, 205 P.3d 1047.) The text must contain a specific list or facially comprehensive treatment. (See *Barnhart v. Peabody Coal Co.* (2003) 537 U.S. 149, 168, 123 S.Ct. 748, 154 L.Ed.2d 653 [the canon "has force only when the items expressed are members of an 'associated group or series,' justifying the inference that items not mentioned were excluded by deliberate choice, not inadvertence"]; *Chevron U.S.A., Inc. v. Echazabal* (2002) 536 U.S. 73, 81, 122 S.Ct. 2045, 153 L.Ed.2d 82 [the canon requires a "series of terms from which an omission bespeaks a negative implication"]; *In re Sabrina H.* (2007) 149 Cal.App.4th 1403, 1411, 57 Cal.Rptr.3d 863 the canon "is generally applied to a specific statute, which contains a listing of items to which the statute applies" and may not have any application to "an entire code".) The provisions Howard Jarvis relies on are widely separated, both in where they are codified and as to how and when they were adopted. The provision allowing the Legislature to propose to the electorate amendments to initiative measures was adopted by the voters at the 1946 general election. (See Cal. Const. art. IV, former § 1b, enacted by Prop. 12 (Nov. 5, 1946 Gen. Elec.); *People v. Kelly* (2010) 47 Cal.4th 1008, 1038, 103 Cal.Rptr.3d 733, 222 P.3d 186.) The provision providing for bond measures to be placed on the ballot was adopted at the 1878–1879 Constitutional Convention. (Cal. Const. art. XVI, § 1.) the provision providing for the legislature to place constitutional amendments on the ballot traces all the way back to California's first Constitution. (Cal. Const. of 1849, art. X, § 1.) Nothing suggests these provisions were intended as a conscious and comprehensive treatment, such that one might infer powers not explicitly conveyed were intentionally omitted.

More fundamentally, Howard Jarvis's argument rests on a misconception as to the nature of the constitutional provisions it cites. Each involves not a grant of authority but a limitation on legislative power — an occasion when the Legislature must turn to the voters, where otherwise it would have been at liberty to act without voter input. Whatever might be said for the logic of inferring from a few specific grants of authority the *absence* of some more general authority, that logic cannot be turned on its head to infer from a few specific limits on legislative authority the *presence* of a broader, unstated limit on legislative authority. The *expressio unius* canon, were we to apply it here, would at most support the inference that the three cited instances are an exhaustive list of the circumstances in which submission of a matter to a plebiscite is mandatory. The canon and the scattered provisions Howard Jarvis cites offer no guidance at all on the actual question before us, whether the Legislature in its discretion *may* turn to the voters to ascertain their will concerning a possible amendment to the federal Constitution.

3. The Use of the Ballot for Nonlawmaking Purposes

In a closely related argument, Howard Jarvis notes this court's holding that the people by initiative may place on the ballot only measures that enact law. (*American Federation of Labor v. Eu, supra,* 36 Cal.3d at pp. 694, 708–714, 206 Cal.Rptr. 89, 686 P.2d 609; see Cal. Const. art. II, § 8, subd. (a) "The initiative is the power of the electors to propose statutes and amendments to the Constitution and to adopt or reject them.".) From this, Howard Jarvis reasons that the people's initiative and referendum power and the constitutional provisions mandating electoral review of particular actions by the Legislature (Cal. Const. art. II, §§ 8–10; *id.,* art. XVI, § 1; *id.,* art. XVIII, §§ 1, 4) define an exhaustive list of matters that may be placed on the ballot, that they all involve the adoption of law, and accordingly that the Constitution forbids ballot measures that do not enact laws.

This contention is a variation on the *expressio unius* argument just considered and rejected. It depends on the assumption that these scattered provisions of the Constitution—i.e., adding the people's right to place initiatives and referenda on the ballot to the Legislature's duty to place certain matters on the ballot—define the exclusive list of matters the electorate may vote on. But there is no reason to infer provisions governing what the people may put on the ballot, and what the Legislature must put on the ballot, limit the wholly separate category, what the Legislature may put on the ballot. *Expressio unius est exclusio alterius* has no interpretive force here.

Howard Jarvis and the dissent contend that if, under *American Federation of Labor v. Eu, supra,* 36 Cal.3d at 697, 206 Cal.Rptr. 89, 686 P.2d 609, the people are limited to placing on the ballot only proposed laws, then the Legislature must be too. We reject that argument as well. Our decision in *Eu* defined limits on the initiative power, not limits on what the Legislature might do or limits on the proper use of the ballot. Indeed, we explicitly recognized that the Legislature's powers were broader than those conveyed by the initiative power: "Even under the most liberal interpretation, however, the reserved powers of initiative and referendum do not encompass all possible actions of a legislative body." (*Id.* at p. 708, 206 Cal.Rptr. 89, 686 P.2d 609.) When the people established the Legislature, they conveyed to it the full breadth of their sovereign legislative powers. (*Nougues v. Douglass, supra,* 7 Cal. at p. 69.) When they adopted the initiative power in 1911, they restored to themselves only a shared piece of that power. (See *Eu,* at p. 708, 206 Cal.Rptr. 89, 686 P.2d 609.) There is nothing incongruous in reading the state Constitution as allocating broader powers to the deliberative body representing the people than to the people directly. Such is the nature of a republic. (See generally U.S. Const. art. IV, § 4 [guaranteeing a republican form of government]; Browne, Rep. of Debates in Convention of Cal. on Formation of State Const. (1850) pp. 393–394 [noting the fundamentally republican nature of the state Constitution]; 1 Willis & Stockton, Debates & Proceedings, Cal.

Const. Convention 1878–1879, p. 242 [the state Constitution implicitly establishes a republican form of government].)

Of course, *Eu* of itself does not establish that the Legislature has the specific authority to ask an advisory question about a federal constitutional amendment where the people might lack the power to opine unilaterally on the same matter; that issue, central to this case, was far afield from the question in *Eu*. The point, rather, is that nothing in *Eu* forbids this understanding, while the substantially broader powers assured the Legislature by the federal Constitution's article V and the state Constitution's article IV, section 1, in contrast to the narrower powers restored to the people by the latter section and the state Constitution's article II, section 8, support it.

Nor, contrary to the concern of our concurring colleague Justice Liu, does recognizing that the Legislature may pose an advisory question about constitutional matters impermissibly restore to the people a power constitutionally forbidden them. The state Constitution does not prohibit the people from speaking on such questions at the ballot box; it simply fails, in article II, section 8, as construed in *Eu*, to authorize their doing so unilaterally. That they may not speak when, pursuant to sources of constitutional power outside article II, section 8, they are asked, does not follow.

4. Accountability

Finally, Howard Jarvis argues the state Constitution contains an implicit structural barrier to the use of advisory questions by the Legislature. It asserts new laws may come into being by legislative enactment, with no participation by the people, or they may come into being by initiative, with no involvement from the Legislature (Cal. Const. art. II, § 8; *id.,* art. IV, § 1), and in each instance, accountability for a given law is clear. Advisory questions on legislative matters, in contrast, would supposedly blur lines of accountability and hamper the ability of voters appropriately to evaluate their representatives at the ballot box: should they be held responsible for a particular legislative action pre-approved by the electorate, or not?

As an initial matter, we note our system of government is one in which the lines of accountability are inevitably blurred to some extent. In a representative democracy, legislators are generally expected to be responsive to their constituents. If a representative votes in favor of a legislative measure that tracks the results of an advisory ballot measure, a voter may not be able to know if the representative is voting his or her own conscience or instead is following the views of a majority of the representative's constituents. But even in the absence of an advisory measure, questions will sometimes arise as to whether a representative's vote on a particular matter is based on the representative's individual views or instead reflects those of his or her constituents, as embodied in polls or other gauges of public sentiment.

Moreover, our state Constitution guarantees to the people "the right to instruct their representatives." (Cal. Const. art. I, § 3, subd. (a).) Although this court has not had occasion to delineate the bounds of that right, its very existence is telling.

....

C. Conclusion

The federal Constitution is our nation's fundamental charter and the source of its supreme law. Only supermajorities of the people's representatives and the several states can alter the course it sets for our country. (See U.S. Const. art. V.) Over the last century and more, state legislatures have seen fit to resort to the ballot box for guidance on whether to propose or ratify potential federal constitutional amendments. This past use of advisory questions to inform the federal constitutional process evidences a larger truth — a recognition of the particular appropriateness of consulting the polity in the course of exercising independent judgment with respect to such foundational matters.

That truth draws its strength from "the animating principle of our Constitution that the people themselves are the originating source of all the powers of government." (*Arizona State Legislature v. Arizona Indep. Redistricting Comm'n* (2015) 576 U.S. ___, ___, 135 S.Ct. 2652, 2671, 192 L.Ed.2d 704, 729–730.) If that be so, there can be little complaint with a legislature, before pursuing constitutional change, seeking to obtain from the people of the state "the deliberate sense of the community." (The Federalist No. 71, *supra,* at p. 482 (Hamilton).) Moreover, the solemnity of the matter to be considered justifies obtaining popular input through an equally solemn formal vote, rather than a mere opinion poll or other unofficial solicitation of views. While Hamilton (and many others) objected to binding instructions from the people, no similar constitutional objections attach to purely advisory votes. Legislators may solicit and consider the views of the people on fundamental matters pertaining to federal constitutional amendments, while at the same time remaining free ultimately to act differently after due deliberation with fellow members of their representative body. The Legislature possesses broad discretion, when conducting an investigation under its implied state constitutional authority, "to select the means within reasonable bounds." (*Parker v. Riley, supra,* 18 Cal.2d at p. 91, 113 P.2d 873.) We conclude the enactment of a statute placing an advisory question on the ballot in order to investigate popular sentiment on a matter of federal constitutional dimension falls within that discretion.

Our concurring colleague, Justice Liu, expresses concern that we, like the Legislature, have rested authority for the advisory question here on the investigative power rather than on the plenary lawmaking power alone. (Conc. opn. of Liu., J., *post,* 196 Cal.Rptr.3d at 803–804, 363 P.3d at 687–688.) He argues that the lawmaking power and power to enact statutes are coextensive, and resort to any other power to justify a statute would raise doubts about the plenary nature of the lawmaking power. This line of argument confuses the form of legislative action — statute, resolution, something else — with the nature of the underlying power justifying the exercise of that action — lawmaking power, investigative power, ratifying power, something else. Though the lawmaking power may be exercised only by statute (Cal. Const. art. IV, § 8, subd. (b)), we have never held the converse, that every statute may be justified only as an exercise of the lawmaking power. When California joined the wave of states enacting statutes governing the ratifying conventions for the Twenty-First

Amendment (*ante,* at 741, 363 P.3d at 635–636), its actions were not authorized by its general lawmaking powers alone, but pursuant to an implied article V power to regulate the procedures for that one-time only event. Justice Liu likewise would justify enactment of the statute here based not on the naked power to make laws, but on an implied article V power, albeit while adopting an unduly restrictive understanding of state legislative powers. Neither that explanation nor ours places in any doubt the plenary nature of the Legislature's lawmaking power.

Justice Liu also expresses concern that the means of investigation selected here is unlike the methods expressly addressed in previous cases. But novelty alone is no basis for imposing a categorical constitutional barrier where none otherwise exists. Here, as we have discussed, none does.

IV.

The Nexus Between Proposition 49 and the Exercise of Powers Related to Federal Constitutional Amendment

Having concluded the Legislature may use advisory ballot questions to facilitate the exercise of its article V functions, we next consider whether the specific measure before us, Proposition 49, is a reasonable exercise, not barred by any law, of the Legislature's power to investigate and determine the best course of action in connection with a potential federal constitutional amendment. Howard Jarvis contends that because the Legislature has already submitted to Congress a call for a national convention, no further purpose can be served by a ballot measure. We disagree.

In evaluating the connection between Proposition 49 and the Legislature's powers, we are mindful of our limited role. "'It is no small matter for one branch of the government to annul the formal exercise by another and coordinate branch of power committed to the latter, and the courts should not and must not annul, as contrary to the constitution, a statute passed by the Legislature, unless it can be said of the statute that it positively and certainly is opposed to the constitution.'" (*Methodist Hosp. of Sacramento v. Saylor* (1971) 5 Cal.3d 685, 692, 97 Cal.Rptr. 1, 488 P.2d 161.) "[A]ll intendments favor the exercise of the Legislature's plenary authority: 'If there is any doubt as to the Legislature's power to act in any given case, the doubt should be resolved in favor of the Legislature's action.'" (*Id.* at p. 691, 97 Cal.Rptr. 1, 488 P.2d 161.) Nor, in holding up the Legislature's actions to the light of the Constitution, will we inquire into underlying motives; our review is confined to determining whether an action itself is at odds with constitutional imperatives. (*City and County of San Francisco v. Cooper* (1975) 13 Cal.3d 898, 913, 120 Cal.Rptr. 707, 534 P.2d 403; *County of Los Angeles v. Superior Court* (1975) 13 Cal.3d 721, 727, 119 Cal.Rptr. 631, 532 P.2d 495.) If any reasonable connection between the proposed ballot measure and the Legislature's article V-related powers is discernable, it will suffice.

Other measures have probed the voters' policy preferences concerning a variety of miscellaneous local matters. The City of Milpitas has asked: Should the city council submit to the voters a proposal to revise the city charter in various ways, including enlarging the city council? The City of National City has asked: Should the city

council establish a Citizens' Police Oversight Commission? The City of South Gate
has asked: Should the city council enact a permit system regulating the number of
vehicles that may be parked overnight? The City of Half Moon Bay has asked: Should
the city adopt a policy of employing its powers of eminent domain only when the
stated "public use" is not "primarily ... based on the City's desire for 'increased City
revenue'"?

We conclude there is a sufficient nexus between Proposition 49 and, at a minimum, the potential exercise of every one of the Legislature's amendment powers.
For the legislators of a state collectively to call on Congress for a federal amendment,
or to call for a national convention, is one matter. For the people of a state, by the
millions, to vote in favor of pursuing an amendment is another. The 1892 plebiscite
concerning direct election of senators yielded a resounding 93 percent to seven percent majority in favor of constitutional change. (Rossum, *California and the Seven-
teenth Amendment* in The California Republic, *supra,* at p. 84.) The Legislature
rationally could believe that a decisive result in the present day might carry more
weight with members of Congress, when deciding whether to propose or vote in
favor of an amendment, and with other state legislatures, in their deliberations over
whether to join California's call for a constitutional convention, than the Legislature's
call alone. Election results might also inform the Legislature's decision whether to
formally supplement its convention call with a joint resolution asking Congress to
propose an amendment, just as both methods of soliciting amendment were employed in the late 19th and early 20th century in connection with senatorial selection
and in 1935 in connection with tax reform. (*Ante,* 196 Cal.Rptr.3d at 742–743, 363
P.3d at 636–638.) Finally, if either Congress or a national convention were to propose
an amendment, a plebiscite would inform the Legislature's decision on ratification.
(See Idaho Sen. J. Res. No. 101 (50th Leg., 1st Reg.Sess.1989), reprinted in 101 Cong.
Rec. S7911 (daily ed. July 13, 1989) [ratifying the 27th Amend. following solicitation
of a popular vote].)

Many other advisory measures have addressed housing, development, and related
public service issues. For example, the City of San Diego has asked: Do the voters
endorse development of up to 5,000 low-rent apartments and townhomes scattered
throughout the city? The City of Modesto has asked: Should the city council expand
sewer service to certain areas? Los Angeles County has asked: Should a new flood
control district be formed, or should an existing area be annexed to a current county
flood control district?

Numerous local advisory measures have inquired about specific land-related developments. For example, Siskiyou County has asked: Should certain river dams and
associated hydroelectric facilities be removed? Imperial County has asked: Should
the county create a new regional international airport to replace or augment the services provided by the county's existing international airport? The City of Hawthorn
has asked: Should certain public lands be sold to generate general or earmarked revenue? Still others have asked about gaming and related issues. For example, the City
of Calexico has asked: Should a local ordinance give a city authority to negotiate

agreements with Native American tribes concerning development and operation of gaming and entertainment resorts?

Moreover, even a result at the ballot box rejecting the proposal could afford material assistance to the Legislature in determining how to exercise its article V-related powers. Although the Legislature has already called for a constitutional convention, "[w]hat the Legislature has enacted, it may repeal." (*California Redevelopment Assn. v. Matosantos, supra,* 53 Cal.4th at p. 255, 135 Cal.Rptr.3d 683, 267 P.3d 580; see *Fletcher v. Peck* (1810) 10 U.S. (6 Cranch) 87, 135, 3 L.Ed. 162 ["one legislature is competent to repeal any act which a former legislature was competent to pass"].) Nothing in the text of article V establishes an intent to depart from this fundamental understanding about the nature of legislative bodies and to afford Congress and state legislatures only the power to make, but never to withdraw, proposals. Indeed, the logic of the amendment process the Article establishes urges strongly to the contrary. Convention calls take effect only when a supermajority, two-thirds of the legislatures, have joined in. A national consensus is a foundational necessity. To allow the making of calls, but not their subsequent negation, might place Congress under orders to call a convention when far fewer states, perhaps not even a majority, presently favored amendment. It follows that convention calls are not static; they can be, and as a matter of historical practice frequently have been, rescinded. (See, e.g., Nev. Assem. Res. No. 157 (1989 Reg. Sess.), reprinted in 101 Cong. Rec. S7911 (daily ed. July 13, 1989) [rescinding convention call]; Kyvig, Explicit & Authentic Acts, at p. 378 [noting N.C. and Okla. rescissions of convention calls]; Paulsen, *A General Theory of Article V: The Constitutional Lessons of the Twenty-Seventh Amendment* (1993) 103 Yale L.J. 677, 765–789 [cataloguing both state-by-state convention calls and their repeals].) The Legislature has called for a national convention; it might, upon sober and mature reflection informed by popular disapproval at the ballot box, reconsider and rescind as unwise that resolution.

Illustrative of the relevance an advisory vote can have even after a legislature has acted is the case of the Massachusetts legislature's 1924–1925 change of heart on the question of a child labor amendment. In 1924, Massachusetts was among those states petitioning Congress for submission of a constitutional amendment to the states to overturn United States Supreme Court decisions limiting Congress's regulatory power over child labor. However, when Congress complied and proposed an amendment, the state's legislature did not immediately act but instead submitted the question of ratification to a November 1924 advisory vote of the people. The plebiscite demonstrated widespread popular opposition, with the amendment losing by more than three-to-one. Taking those views into account, the legislature reversed its support from the year before and declined to ratify the amendment. (Kyvig, Explicit & Authentic Acts, *supra,* at pp. 259–260.) So too, an advisory vote may guide a legislature in deciding whether to persist with efforts to obtain, or rescind a call for, a national convention or congressionally proposed federal amendment.

Accordingly, we conclude Proposition 49 is a reasonable and lawful means of assisting the Legislature in the discharge of its article V-related functions. Howard

Jarvis has identified no constitutional obstacle. Proposition 49's placement on a statewide ballot may be upheld as an exercise of the Legislature's implied power under the California Constitution to investigate and determine the best course of action in connection with a potential federal constitutional amendment.

Disposition

We discharge the order to show cause, deny Howard Jarvis's petition for a peremptory writ of mandate, and vacate our previously ordered stay.

WE CONCUR: Cantil-Sakauye, C.J. Corrigan, Cuéllar, and Kruger, JJ.

Notes and Questions

1. Unlike the U.S. Congress, which possesses only those specific powers delegated to it by the U.S. Constitution, the California Legislature possesses plenary legislative authority except as specifically limited by the California Constitution, and lying at the core of that plenary authority is the power to enact laws.

2. A state statute passed by the Legislature to place an advisory question on the statewide ballot was a valid exercise of the Legislature's implied power to investigate the necessity to exercise its power to petition for a federal constitutional change, even though the Legislature had already submitted to Congress a call for a national convention to pass an amendment.

3. The state constitutional provision stating that the Legislature may provide for the selection of committees necessary for the conduct of its business does not implicitly prohibit the Legislature from using advisory ballot measures to determine the electorate's position on whether the Legislature should exercise its power to petition for federal change.

4. It is often explained that the California Constitution grants plenary power to the California Legislature so that the legislative branch of state government can exercise any legislative powers, except where that power is limited in the state Constitution. Note that this is opposite its federal counterpart, where the U.S. Congress can only exercise those powers that are specified in the U.S. Constitution.

5. The California Supreme Court said, "The Constitution is not a grant, but a restriction upon the power of the Legislature, and hence an express enumeration of legislative powers and privileges in the Constitution cannot be considered as the exclusion of others not named unless accompanied by negative terms." (*Ex parte McCarthy* (1866) 29 Cal. 395.)

6. More recently, the California Supreme Court ruled, "At the core of the legislative power is the authority to make laws.... Of significance, the legislative power the state Constitution vests is plenary. Under it, 'the entire law-making authority of the state, except the people's right of initiative and referendum, is vested in the Legislature, and that body may exercise any and all legislative powers which are not expressly or by necessary implication denied to it by the Constitution'." (*California Redevelopment Association v. Matosantos* (2011) 53 Cal.4th 231.)

7. The Legislature usually petitions Congress regarding a particular view on federal issues through its use of either an Assembly Joint Resolution or a Senate Joint Resolution. Is a question on the statewide ballot necessary for the Legislature to express its will to the federal government? As the court noted, the Legislature first entered this debate through adoption of Assem. Joint Res. 1.

8. The Court ruled that "nothing in the state Constitution prohibits the use of advisory questions to inform the Legislature's exercise of its article IV-related powers." Should this be the end of the inquiry for the judicial branch regarding the legislative branch's official actions?

9. The Court also notes an earlier precedent that "[t]he Legislature has the *actual* power to pass any act it pleases," subject only to those limits that may arise elsewhere in the state or federal Constitutions. (*Nougues v. Douglass* (1857) 7 Cal. 65, 70.) Should this broad of a reading of the state Constitution still control?

10. Why does the Legislature argue that its implied investigative power allows it to enact a statute placing an advisory question before the voters? Is seeking a vote of the statewide electorate a logical extension of the legislative branch's investigative authority? Do these investigational powers apply to investigating activities of the other branches of government? Or do they apply to investigating possible legislation? In other words, is this basis the wrong one, instead of relying on the Legislature's plenary lawmaking authority?

11. Does the Legislature need to seek guidance from the voters to determine "how and whether to exercise the Legislature's powers in connection with a potential future federal constitutional amendment"?

12. Is the Court's lengthy examination of state legislatures and the federal constitutional amendment applicable to its ruling in favor of the constitutionality of Prop. 49?

13. Is the Court's finding that "Legislatures in California and elsewhere thus have established a tradition of using advisory ballot measures to determine the will of the people on questions pertaining to amendments to the federal Constitution" sufficient to rule in favor of the Legislature's authority in this case? Were the other aspects of its analysis necessary to make this ruling?

14. What were the four contentions made by the plaintiffs in this case that the Legislature lacked the power to place advisory measures on the statewide ballot? Did the Court accept any of these arguments? If not, why?

15. Because the Legislature had already called for a constitutional convention, why is an advisory ballot measure necessary? By publicly calling for the convention, did the Legislature not already determine its position so that Prop. 49 was unnecessary?

C. Lawmaking Authority Is Plenary

The authority of the Legislature to make laws is absolute, as set forth in the Constitution and judicial branch decisions. Neither the executive branch of state government nor the judicial branch has such authority. Generally, the executive branch executes the laws while the judicial branch interprets the laws. The executive branch does play a small, but vital role, in lawmaking because the state's chief executive, i.e., the Governor, can sign or veto legislation that is sent to the Governor's desk for final action.

State legislative power is limited by Section 10 of Article I of the U.S. Constitution that prohibits states from enacting bills of attainder and *ex post facto* laws, as well as impairing the obligation of contracts.

Steinberg v. Chiang

(2014) 223 Cal.App.4th 338, rehearing denied

OPINION

BUTZ, J. —

Defendant John Chiang, in his official capacity as State Controller (Controller), appeals from a declaratory judgment in favor of plaintiffs Darrell Steinberg and John Pérez in their respective official capacities as President pro Tempore of the Senate and Speaker of the Assembly (collectively, the Legislature). The trial court concluded that the Legislature complies with the constitutional provision for a balanced budget when it enacts a budget bill in which its revenue estimates for the coming fiscal year exceed the total of existing appropriations for the fiscal year, new appropriations proposed in the budget bill for the fiscal year, and any transfer to the reserve fund. At that point, the Controller does not have the authority to make an independent assessment that the budget bill is not in fact balanced because it relies on revenues not yet authorized in existing law (or in enrolled legislation), and on that basis withhold the salaries of legislators as a penalty for failing to enact a timely budget.

The Controller appeals, contending declaratory relief should have been denied because this action does not represent an actual controversy, or because his undisputed power to audit the lawfulness of any request for a warrant entitles him to determine whether a budget is *in fact* balanced regardless of any legislative declaration to that effect. Because the parties are in an ongoing relationship in which this existing dispute over the Controller's asserted authority can arise again in the future, which presents a question of law regarding the interpretation of provisions of the state Constitution in the context of facts inherent in any future such dispute, we do not find a declaration of rights to be purely advisory. On the merits, we agree with the trial court that the Controller has failed to identify any basis for the exercise of a power to audit the accuracy of legislative estimates of revenues. We therefore shall affirm the judgment.

FACTUAL AND PROCEDURAL BACKGROUND

The pertinent facts are few. In 2011, the Legislature passed a budget bill on June 15 and sent it to the Governor for signature. The Legislature estimated revenues for the coming fiscal year of $87.8 billion dollars (rounded), and the appropriations in the budget bill (in combination with existing appropriations for the fiscal year) totaled $86.6 billion dollars (rounded). The Governor vetoed it on the next day, declaring that it did not present a "balanced solution" of spending cuts and revenue increases to address the "big deficits for years to come."

The Controller then undertook a determination of whether the budget bill complied with the constitutional provision for a balanced budget. (Cal. Const., art. IV, § 12, subd. (g) [the "balanced budget" provision].) Finding inter alia that some of the identified revenues were based on four bills that the Legislature had yet to pass, the Controller declared on June 21 that the Legislature failed to enact a *balanced* budget by midnight on June 15, which therefore subjected its members to the penalty contained in a 2010 constitutional amendment for failing to enact a budget bill before June 16: forfeiture of their salaries until the presentation of a balanced budget bill to the Governor. (Cal. Const., art. IV, § 12, subds. (c)(3) & (h) [the timely budget and forfeiture provisions].) The Legislature passed a balanced budget on June 28, which the Governor signed into law on June 30.

The Legislature never sought direct judicial review of the Controller's action. Instead, the Legislature filed the instant action in January 2012, seeking a declaration that it complies with the balanced budget provision of the state Constitution when it passes a budget bill in which appropriations (and monies transferred to the reserve account) do not exceed the legislative estimate of revenues, and that the Controller cannot thereafter make a determination that the budget bill was not *in fact* a balanced budget enacted on or before June 15, or enforce that decision by declaring legislative salaries forfeited until the enactment of a balanced budget. The parties made cross-motions for judgment on the pleadings. The trial court issued a lengthy minute order explaining the basis for issuing the requested declaratory judgment. This timely appeal followed.

DISCUSSION

I. An Actual Controversy Is Present in Which Relief Is Proper

Whether a probable future dispute over legal rights between parties is sufficiently ripe to represent an "actual controversy" within the meaning of the statute authorizing declaratory relief (Code Civ. Proc., § 1060), as opposed to purely hypothetical concerns, is a question of law that we review de novo on appeal. (*Environmental Defense Project of Sierra County v. County of Sierra* (2008) 158 Cal.App.4th 877, 885 [70 Cal.Rptr.3d 474] (*Environmental Defense*).) Whether such actual controversy *merits* declaratory relief as necessary and proper (Code Civ. Proc., § 1061) is a decision within the discretion of the trial court (*Environmental Defense,* at p. 885) except in the extreme circumstances where relief is "entirely appropriate" such that a trial court would abuse its discretion in denying relief (e.g., where there is an ongoing dispute over rights between parties that have an ongoing relationship, even if the dispute arises from past events, and where a declaration provides guidance for future behavior) or where relief would *never* be necessary or proper (e.g., a past dispute between parties lacking an ongoing relationship) (*Osseous Technologies of America, Inc. v. DiscoveryOrtho Partners LLC* (2010) 191 Cal.App.4th 357, 365, 367, 370 [119 Cal.Rptr.3d 346]).

In the present case, the parties have an ongoing relationship in the distribution of legislative salaries, and a continuing dispute over whether the facts of the events of

2011 (for which there is a reasonable expectation of recurrence) provide a basis for the legal authority that the Controller claimed and continues to claim. (*Environmental Defense, supra,* 158 Cal.App.4th at p. 887.) We reached a similar conclusion in *Gilb v. Chiang* (2010) 186 Cal.App.4th 444, 459–460 [111 Cal.Rptr.3d 822] (*Gilb*), where even though the dispute arose out of the Controller's past refusal to abide with an executive directive to withhold warrants in excess of federal minimum wage until a budget for the current fiscal year was signed, this was a dispute reasonably likely to recur, given the Legislature's then repeated failures to enact timely budget bills and the clear indication that the Controller would refuse to abide by a similar executive directive in the future, and thus presented an actual controversy. Unlike *Pacific Legal Foundation v. California Coastal Com.* (1982) 33 Cal.3d 158, 172, 174 [188 Cal.Rptr. 104, 655 P.2d 306] (speculative nature of possible projects and possible conditions on project permits pursuant to challenged guidelines made declaratory relief inappropriate), *Wilson & Wilson v. City Council of Redwood City* (2011) 191 Cal.App.4th 1559, 1583 [120 Cal.Rptr.3d 665] (statement of general intent to acquire property through eminent domain presents too many uncertainties to support declaration in favor of owner), or *Sanctity of Human Life Network v. California Highway Patrol* (2003) 105 Cal.App.4th 858, 871–872 [129 Cal.Rptr.2d 708] (too many variables to issue declaration regarding right to display signs on overpasses in circumstances other than case at bar), we do not need to guess at any additional facts that are *necessary* to our resolution of the issue. Unlike [*Teachers' Retirement Bd. v.*] *Genest, supra,* 154 Cal.App.4th at pages 1043–1044 (prospect that the Legislature would again attempt to borrow retirement funds in a manner ruled unauthorized is hypothetical), the Controller is continuing to litigate his authority to withhold salaries if, as often is the case, the revenues' estimate appearing in a budget bill relies on sources not presently authorized.

In addition, the refusal to grant declaratory relief would work a serious hardship on the Legislature. (*Farm Sanctuary, Inc. v. Department of Food & Agriculture* (1998) 63 Cal.App.4th 495, 502 [74 Cal.Rptr.2d 75].) The Legislature should not be put in the position of risking the forfeiture of future salary if its position is not sustained in a future confrontation with the Controller, grounded on the Controller's interpretation of the constitutional provisions at issue here. Declaratory relief is cumulative of any other remedy. (Code Civ. Proc., § 1062.) Availability of an alternative remedy, such as mandate in a future impasse (*Lungren v. Davis* (1991) 234 Cal.App.3d 806, 809–810 [285 Cal.Rptr. 777] [action in mandate to challenge refusal to pay salary]), is not generally a basis for denial of declaratory relief (*Filarsky v. Superior Court* (2002) 28 Cal.4th 419, 433 [121 Cal.Rptr.2d 844, 49 P.3d 194] [noting exception where statutory remedy indicates it is to be *exclusive*]; *Ermolieff v. R.K.O. Radio Pictures* (1942) 19 Cal.2d 543, 548 [122 P.2d 3]; *Holden v. Arnebergh* (1968) 265 Cal.App.2d 87, 91–92 [71 Cal.Rptr. 401] [court may decline to grant declaratory relief where *expeditious* alternative remedy exists]). A mandate proceeding is not necessarily expeditious. Each day consumed in the course of a mandate proceeding against the Controller would represent the risk of another day of forfeited wages if the Legislature ultimately did not prevail. We thus find that this action presents an actual controversy, and the trial court reasonably found declaratory relief is necessary and proper.

II. The Controller Cannot Second-guess Revenue Estimates

At the outset, we address the Legislature's suggestion that the constitutional forfeiture provision applies only to the timeliness of a budget bill and not any *other* substantive constitutional requirement for the budget bill such as the balanced budget provision or the single subject rule (Cal. Const., art. IV, § 9), a point the trial court declined to address. We will assume, as a matter of in pari materia (*Lexin v. Superior Court* (2010) 47 Cal.4th 1050, 1091 [103 Cal.Rptr.3d 767, 222 P.3d 214] [where different provisions address same purpose or object, courts should construe them to give effect to all]), that in seeking to enforce the timely presentation of a budget bill the electorate intended that the bill be *otherwise* valid, rather than allow the Legislature to evade the timely budget provision with a sham bill that does not satisfy other constitutional prerequisites.

We begin with a fundamental principle of our state Constitution: its grant of lawmaking authority to the Legislature is plenary (except for the reserved rights of initiative and referendum), which empowers that body to exercise this authority in any manner that is not expressly or through necessary implication prohibited elsewhere in the Constitution. As a result, we must resolve any ambiguity about legislative authority in favor of the Legislature. (*California Redevelopment Assn. v. Matosantos* (2011) 53 Cal.4th 231, 253–254 [135 Cal.Rptr.3d 683, 267 P.3d 580].)

All that the balanced budget provision prescribes for the budget bill is inclusion of a legislative *estimate* of revenues "made as of the date of the budget bill's passage" that exceeds the combination of the total amount of appropriations in the bill, the existing appropriations for the upcoming fiscal year, and transfers to the reserve fund. (Cal. Const., art. IV, § 12, subd. (g).) The balanced budget provision does not prescribe the manner in which the Legislature must calculate this estimate, the nature of the revenue sources the Legislature may or may not take into account, or any role for the Controller in overseeing the estimate. The constitutional text does not in any way expressly support the Controller's assertion that any revenue bills (which cannot be part of the budget bill itself) must be enrolled and sent to the Governor for signature before the constitutional deadline of June 15. Indeed, the Controller overlooks the extent to which California balances its budget with federal funds, the authorization for which is entirely *outside* the control of the Legislature (and the predicted total of which bespeaks more legislative artistry than accounting skills).

Given this absence of any express language to support the Controller's asserted concern with vouchsafing the absence of any phantom revenues included in a budget bill's estimate, it would amount to "inappropriate judicial interference with the prerogatives of a coordinate branch of government" to endorse his intrusion into the budget process under "the guise of interpretation." (*Schabarum v. California Legislature* (1998) 60 Cal.App.4th 1205, 1218 [70 Cal.Rptr.2d 745] (*Schabarum*).)

This does not mean the balanced budget provision is a dead letter. The Governor can enforce it either through vetoing the budget as a whole or exercising his power to veto line items to bring appropriations in balance with accurate revenues. (Cal. Const., art. IV, § 10, subds. (a) & (e); see *Schabarum, supra,* 60 Cal.App.4th at pp. 1240–1241 (dis. opn. of Morrison, J.) [noting Governor's oath to uphold Constitution in review of whether limits on legislative spending in budget honored].) Moreover, as with any legislation, the judicial branch is the ultimate arbiter of its constitutionality (although we eschew any attempt at pondering the form of action or the standard of review involved).

Given that constitutionally no role exists for the Controller to play because the revenue estimate in the budget bill is *not* limited to existing law (or enrolled revenue bills), his assertion — that the electorate necessarily implicated his existing audit function before issuing warrants for legislative salaries in the enforcement of the balanced budget and timely budget constitutional provisions — is beside the point. Additionally, its underlying premise is incorrect.

It is true that the Legislature (to which the Constitution has delegated the task of defining the duties and functions of constitutional officers) has vested the Controller with the responsibility for determining the lawfulness of any disbursement of state money. (*Tirapelle v. Davis* (1993) 20 Cal.App.4th 1317, 1327–1328 [26 Cal.Rptr.2d 666] (*Tirapelle*); Gov. Code, §§ 12410, 12440.) But this is primarily a ministerial function in which the Controller is not authorized to review and approve or reject an agency's approval of a disbursement if it is within the scope of the legislative grant of discretion to the agency (which we likened to jurisdiction in the "fundamental" sense); the Controller's limited discretionary function involves the determination of whether the factual circumstances of the claim come within the scope of the agency's approval. (*Tirapelle,* at pp. 1329–1330, 1335.) Thus, *Madden v. Riley* (1942) 53 Cal.App.2d 814 [128 P.2d 602] noted that the Controller was authorized to exercise discretion to determine whether a claim for approved travel expenses was in fact incurred for the approved purpose, but his legal conclusion that the travel did not constitute "state business" was not within his discretion to determine; we instead upheld the legal basis of the approval and issued a writ against the Controller. (*Madden,* at pp. 819–820, 823–824.) As a result, "Where a department or agency acts within the authority delegated to it by the Legislature, the Controller must defer to the agency or department and leave review of the [lawfulness of the] decision to the courts and/ or the Legislature" (*Tirapelle, supra,* 20 Cal.App.4th at p. 1335), the latter of which has reserved the authority to review the Controller's rejection of a claim (*id.* at p. 1329, fn. 18). (Accord, *Gilb, supra,* 186 Cal.App.4th at p. 463 [if Controller believes agency's action is unlawful, he or she cannot simply disregard it but must seek judicial review].)

Consequently, where the *Legislature* is the entity acting indisputably within its fundamental constitutional jurisdiction to enact what it designates as a balanced budget, the Controller does not have audit authority to determine whether the budget bill is in fact balanced. In addition, it would not make any sense as a matter of statutory interpretation to believe the Legislature granted such statutory review authority in defining the Controller's powers where the Legislature in turn can ultimately override the Controller's decision. As a result, the Controller is not a party to the enactment of the budget bill.

DISPOSITION

The judgment is affirmed.

BLEASE, ACTING P.J., and MURRAY, J., concurred.

Notes and Questions

1. The state Constitution's grant of lawmaking authority to the Legislature is plenary, except for the reserved rights of initiative and referendum which empowers that body to exercise this authority in any manner that is not expressly or through necessary implication prohibited elsewhere in the Constitution. The budget bill is limited to the one subject of appropriations to support the annual budget.

2. The Legislature's estimate of revenues used to determine whether the state budget complies with the balanced budget provision of the state Constitution may include revenue sources not yet authorized in existing law or in enrolled legislation. The Controller may not withhold legislators' salaries on the basis that a budget bill that the Legislature has designated as "balanced" is not in fact balanced under the constitutional provisions stating that legislators forfeit their salaries during the period that a balanced budget bill is past due, since such an audit is not within the Controller's statutory power to determine the lawfulness of a disbursement of state money.

3. An action brought by the President pro Tempore of the Senate and the Speaker of the Assembly for declaratory judgment that the Legislature had complied with the requirement to pass a balanced budget bill to preclude withholding of legislators' salaries presented an actual controversy as required for declaratory relief.

4. The Legislature's estimate of revenues used to determine whether the state budget complies with the balanced budget provision of the state Constitution may include revenue sources not yet authorized in existing law or in enrolled legislation. (*Steinberg v. Chiang* (2014) 223 Cal.App.4th 338.)

5. What was the basis for the court to find that the Controller did not have authority? The court cited the state Constitution's grant of lawmaking authority to the Legislature. Should the "absence of any express language to support the Controller's asserted concern" be a sufficient basis for the court to rule against another constitutional officer?

6. Could the court's ruling in this case also be based upon the separation of powers doctrine? Does the state Constitution's grant of authority to the Legislature to adopt the state's budget mean that the other branches of government (other than the Governor's presentation of a budget and consideration of it like any other bill) do not play a role in the state budget?

D. Roles of the Legislative and Judicial Branches

There are separate and distinct roles of the legislative and judicial branches of state government when it comes to lawmaking. Article IV sets forth the legislative branch, while Article VI sets forth the judicial branch. While the legislative branch is primarily involved with lawmaking, the main role of the judicial branch is to interpret the laws, ensure there are no conflicts between statutes and the Constitution, and ensure the executive branch does not infringe on the duties of the legislative branch. Keep in mind that, subject to constitutional constraints, the Legislature may enact legislation, but the judicial branch interprets that legislation.

1. Role of the Judiciary in the Lawmaking Process

Members of the state and federal judiciary branches play a role in the California lawmaking process as a part of our government's system of "checks and balances." When California statutes or regulations are legally challenged, for example, then the state or federal court that decides the challenge establishes a policy for the state. Of course, California statutes and regulations may be challenged on either federal or state constitutional grounds. As a result, both state and federal courts may play a role in the state lawmaking process.

In addition to a legal challenge, both federal and state courts may be called upon to interpret California statutes or regulations. The judicial branches of the state and federal governments are granted their authority by the California and U.S. Constitutions. In addition, the powers and duties of the judicial branch are enumerated in federal and state statutes. Statutory interpretation is the primary role of the judicial branch of government in the state lawmaking process. In fact, the courts are regularly called upon to interpret state statutes and regulations.

Sometimes to the dismay of elected officials in the executive and legislative branches of government, the third branch of government does play a crucial role in the state lawmaking process when the courts determine what the legislative intent was of a statute, whether a regulation comports with the Administrative Procedures Act, or whether a statute or regulation is constitutional. This is the critical role of the judicial branch in the state lawmaking process.

Occasionally, the California Legislature passes a law that does not comport with the state or federal Constitution. Despite claims by judges that they leave lawmaking to the elected branches of government, when judges modify statutes or provide a determination of how a statute or regulation is to be interpreted and applied, then judges do in fact become a critical part of state policymaking. Hence, all three branches of government play a role in developing state policy.

When a statute, regulation or government action is found to violate a provision of the Constitution (either the federal or state Constitution), the courts will not only invalidate the law, regulation or executive order, but may also impose injunctive or other relief that is tantamount to a new public policy being adopted.

When provisions of law (primarily statutes or regulations) are unclear in certain respects, the courts will engage in statutory interpretation to clarify the law and do their best to determine what the legislative intent was in adopting the statute. Sometimes the court's interpretation is tantamount to a new public policy being issued.

The California courts are not really vested with the power to legislate, as this authority would conflict with the constitutional separation of powers, and those are the roles of the legislative and executive branches of state government. However, the courts can and do become involved in developing public policy. And when they do, that policy has the same effect as a statute adopted by a legislative body.

For instance, the landmark case of *Serrano v. Priest* (1971) 5 Cal.3d 584, originated as a class action brought by public-interest attorneys on behalf of a class of all California public-school pupils. The case involved pressing issues of the day: public education as a fundamental right and discrimination against poor and minority students. The California Supreme Court struck down California's public-school, general-fund financing structure as a violation of the state Constitution's equal protection guarantee.

Under this system, per-pupil expenditures varied greatly and depended on a school district's tax base. These kinds of tax-base disparities resulted in significant inequalities in actual educational expenditures on a per pupil basis from school district to school district around the state. The Court's decision (including a follow up 1976 decision) in *Serrano* essentially gave instructions to the California Legislature on what would be required to fix the state funding statutes, and the Legislature subsequently did so.

The other major way in which the courts make state public policy is through statutory interpretation. In this instance, there is a statute or group of statutes which is unclear or silent on some aspect of policy. The court is asked to fill in the gap (i.e., to discern the intent of the legislature). Thus, to invoke this approach, the plaintiff challenging the statute will need: (a) a statute or statutory scheme which is unclear or silent on some public policy matter, and (b) a cause of action and standing to sue.

Finally, while the federal courts may be limited in terms of their ability to adopt or create policy, they often have a profound role in terms of public policy. In particular, newly adopted statutes, regulations, and executive orders are often challenged in the state and federal courts. For parties or interests that lost in the legislative process, the courts have long been used as a means of preventing adopted policy from going into effect.

McClung v. Employment Development Department

(2004) 34 Cal.4th 467

OPINION

CHIN, J.

"It is, emphatically, the province and duty of the judicial department, to say what the law is. Those who apply the rule to particular cases, must of necessity expound and interpret that rule." (*Marbury v. Madison* (1803) 5 U.S. 137, 177 [2 L.Ed. 60].)

This basic principle is at issue in this case. In *Carrisales v. Department of Corrections* (1999) 21 Cal.4th 1132 [90 Cal.Rptr.2d 804, 988 P.2d 1083] (*Carrisales*), we interpreted Government Code section 12940 (hereafter section 12940), part of the California Fair Employment and Housing Act (FEHA). Later, the Legislature amended that section by adding language to impose personal liability on persons *Carrisales* had concluded had no personal liability. (§ 12940, subd. (j)(3).) Subdivision (j) also contains a statement that its provisions "are declaratory of existing law...." (§ 12940, subd. (j)(2).) Based on this statement, plaintiff argues that the amendment did not *change*, but merely *clarified*, existing law. Accordingly, she argues, the amendment applies to this case to impose personal liability for earlier actions despite our holding in *Carrisales* that no personal liability attached to those actions.

We disagree. Under fundamental principles of separation of powers, the legislative branch of government enacts laws. Subject to constitutional constraints, it may *change* the law. But *interpreting* the law is a judicial function. After the judiciary definitively and finally interprets a statute, as we did in *Carrisales, supra*, 21 Cal.4th 1132, the Legislature may amend the statute to say something different. But if it does so, it *changes* the law; it does not merely state what the law always was. Any statement to the contrary is beyond the Legislature's power. We also conclude this change in the law does not apply retroactively to impose liability for actions not subject to liability when performed.

I. FACTS AND PROCEDURAL BACKGROUND

In January 1998, plaintiff Lesli Ann McClung filed a complaint against the Employment Development Department and Manuel Lopez, alleging claims of hostile work environment and failure to remedy a hostile work environment under the FEHA, as well as another cause of action not relevant here. The superior court granted summary judgment for defendants, and plaintiff appealed.

The Court of Appeal affirmed the judgment in favor of the Employment Development Department, but reversed it as to Lopez. In so doing, it held that Lopez was plaintiff's coworker, not supervisor. It also recognized that we had held in *Carrisales, supra*, 21 Cal.4th at page 1140, that the FEHA does not "impose personal liability for harassment on nonsupervisory coworkers." Nevertheless, it found Lopez personally liable for harassment under the FEHA. It applied an amendment to the FEHA that imposes personal liability on coworkers (§ 12940, subd. (j)(3)), even though the amendment postdated the actions underlying this lawsuit. It found that the preexisting statement in section 12940, subdivision (j)(2), that subdivision (j)'s provisions "are declaratory of existing law," "supports the conclusion that [the amendment] merely clarifies the meaning of the prior statute." Ultimately, it concluded that whether "the amendment merely states the true meaning of the statute or reflects the Legislature's purpose to achieve a retrospective change, the result is the same: we must give effect to the legislative intent that the personal liability amendment apply to all existing cases, including this one." "For Lopez," said the Court of Appeal, "the Supreme Court's interpretation of individual liability under FEHA can be said to have come and gone."

We granted Lopez's petition for review to decide whether section 12940, subdivision (j)(3), applies to this case.

II. DISCUSSION

A. *Background*

The FEHA "declares certain kinds of discrimination and harassment in the workplace to be 'unlawful employment practice[s].' (§ 12940.)" (*Carrisales, supra,* 21 Cal.4th at p. 1134.) In *Carrisales,* we interpreted the FEHA as imposing "on the *employer* the duty to take all reasonable steps to prevent this harassment from occurring in the first place and to take immediate and appropriate action when it is or should be aware of the conduct," but as not imposing "personal liability for harassment on nonsupervisory coworkers." (Carrisales, *supra,* at p. 1140, citing § 12940, former subd. (h)(1).) Later, effective January 1, 2001, the Legislature amended the subdivision of section 12940 that we interpreted in *Carrisales* (now subdivision (j)). (Stats. 2000, ch. 1049, §§ 7.5, 11.) As amended, section 12940, subdivision (j)(3), provides in relevant part: "An employee of an entity subject to this subdivision is personally liable for any harassment prohibited by this section that is perpetrated by the employee...." It seems clear, and no one disputes, that this provision imposes on nonsupervisory coworkers the personal liability that *Carrisales* said the FEHA had not imposed. Subdivision (j) also states that its provisions "are declaratory of existing law...." (§ 12940, subd. (j)(2).)

We must decide whether the amendment to section 12940 applies to actions that occurred before its enactment. If the amendment merely clarified existing law, no question of retroactivity is presented. "[A] statute that merely *clarifies,* rather than changes, existing law does not operate retrospectively even if applied to transactions predating its enactment" "because the true meaning of the statute remains the same." (*Western Security Bank v. Superior Court* (1997) 15 Cal.4th 232, 243 [62 Cal.Rptr.2d 243, 933 P.2d 507] (*Western Security Bank*).) In that event, personal liability would have existed at the time of the actions, and the amendment would not have changed anything. But if the amendment changed the law and imposed personal liability for earlier actions, the question of retroactivity arises. "A statute has retrospective effect when it substantially changes the legal consequences of past events." (*Ibid.*) In this case, applying the amendment to impose liability that did not otherwise exist would be a retroactive application because it would "attach new legal consequences to events completed before its enactment." (*Landgraf v. USI Film Products* (1994) 511 U.S.

244, 270 [128 L.Ed.2d 229, 114 S.Ct. 1483] (*Landgraf*).) Specifically, it would "increase a party's liability for past conduct...." (*Id.* at p. 280; accord, *Myers v. Philip Morris Companies, Inc.* (2002) 28 Cal.4th 828, 839 [123 Cal.Rptr.2d 40, 50 P.3d 751] (*Myers*).)

Accordingly, two separate questions are presented here: (1) Did the amendment extending liability in subdivision (j)(3) change or merely clarify the law? (2) If the amendment did change the law, does the change apply retroactively? We consider the former question first. Because we conclude the amendment did, indeed, change the law, we also consider the latter question.

B. *Whether the Amendment Changed the Law*

"The powers of state government are legislative, executive, and judicial. Persons charged with the exercise of one power may not exercise either of the others except as permitted by this Constitution." (Cal. Const., art. III, § 3.) "The judicial power of this State is vested in the Supreme Court, courts of appeal, and superior courts, all of which are courts of record." (Cal. Const., art. VI, § 1.) Thus, "The judicial power is conferred upon the courts by the Constitution and, in the absence of a constitutional provision, cannot be exercised by any other body." (*Bodinson Mfg. Co. v. California E. Com.* (1941) 17 Cal.2d 321, 326 [109 P.2d 935].)

The legislative power rests with the Legislature. (Cal. Const., art. IV, § 1.) Subject to constitutional constraints, the Legislature may enact legislation. (*Methodist Hosp. of Sacramento v. Saylor* (1971) 5 Cal.3d 685, 691 [97 Cal.Rptr. 1, 488 P.2d 161].) But the judicial branch *interprets* that legislation. "Ultimately, the interpretation of a statute is an exercise of the judicial power the Constitution assigns to the courts." (*Western Security Bank, supra,* 15 Cal.4th at p. 244; see also *People v. Cruz* (1996) 13 Cal.4th 764, 781 [55 Cal.Rptr.2d 117, 919 P.2d 731].) Accordingly, "it is the duty of this court, when ... a question of law is properly presented, to state the true meaning of the statute finally and conclusively...." (*Bodinson Mfg. Co. v. California E. Com., supra,* 17 Cal.2d at p. 326.)   In *Carrisales, supra,* 21 Cal.4th 1132, we interpreted the FEHA finally and conclusively as not imposing personal liability on a nonsupervisory coworker. This interpretation was binding on lower state courts, including the Court of Appeal. (*Auto Equity Sales, Inc. v. Superior Court* (1962) 57 Cal.2d 450, 455 [20 Cal.Rptr. 321, 369 P.2d 937].) "The decisions of this court are binding upon and must be followed by all the state courts of California.... Courts exercising inferior jurisdiction must accept the law declared by courts of superior jurisdiction. It is not their function to attempt to overrule decisions of a higher court." (*Ibid.*)

It is true that if the courts have not yet finally and conclusively interpreted a statute and are in the process of doing so, a declaration of a later Legislature as to what an earlier Legislature intended is entitled to consideration. (*Western Security Bank, supra,* 15 Cal.4th at p. 244.) But even then, "a legislative declaration of an existing statute's meaning" is but a factor for a court to consider and "is neither binding nor conclusive in construing the statute." (*Ibid.*; see also *Peralta Community College Dist. v. Fair Employment Housing Com.* (1990) 52 Cal.3d 40, 52 [276 Cal.Rptr. 114, 801 P.2d 357]; *Del Costello v. State of California* (1982) 135 Cal.App.3d 887, 893, fn. 8

[185 Cal.Rptr. 582].) This is because the "Legislature has no authority to interpret a statute. That is a judicial task. The Legislature may define the meaning of statutory language by a present legislative enactment which, subject to constitutional restraints, it may deem retroactive. But it has no legislative authority simply to say what it *did* mean." (*Del Costello v. State of California, supra*, at p. 893, fn. 8, cited with approval in *People v. Cruz, supra*, 13 Cal.4th at p. 781.)

A declaration that a statutory amendment merely clarified the law "cannot be given an obviously absurd effect, and the court cannot accept the Legislative statement that an unmistakable change in the statute is nothing more than a clarification and restatement of its original terms." (*California Emp. etc. Com. v. Payne* (1947) 31 Cal.2d 210, 214 [187 P.2d 702].) Because this court had already finally and definitively interpreted section 12940, the Legislature had no power to decide that the later amendment merely declared existing law.

On another occasion, the Legislature similarly enacted legislation overruling a decision of this court — which was within its power — but also purported to state that the new legislation merely declared what the law always was — which was beyond its power. In *People v. Harvey* (1979) 25 Cal.3d 754 [159 Cal.Rptr. 696, 602 P.2d 396], we interpreted Penal Code section 1170.1 as not permitting a certain consecutive sentence enhancement. The Legislature promptly amended the statute to permit the enhancement. (Stats. 1980, ch. 132, § 2, p. 306.) It also declared that its intent was "to clarify and reemphasize what has been the legislative intent since July 1, 1977." (Stats. 1980, ch. 132, § 1, subd. (c), p. 305.) The judicial response was swift and emphatic. The courts concluded that, although the Legislature may amend a statute to overrule a judicial decision, doing so *changes* the law; accordingly, they refused to apply the amendment retroactively. (*People v. Savala* (1981) 116 Cal.App.3d 41, 55–61 [171 Cal.Rptr. 882]; *People v. Harvey* (1980) 112 Cal.App.3d 132, 138–139 [169 Cal.Rptr. 153]; *People v. Cuevas* (1980) 111 Cal.App.3d 189, 198–200 [168 Cal.Rptr. 519]; *People v. Vizcarra* (1980) 110 Cal.App.3d 858, 866 [168 Cal.Rptr. 257]; *People v. Fulton* (1980) 109 Cal.App.3d 777, 783 [167 Cal.Rptr. 436]; *People v. Matthews* (1980) 108 Cal.App.3d 793, 796 [167 Cal.Rptr. 8]; see *People v. Wolcott* (1983) 34 Cal.3d 92, 104, fn. 4 [192 Cal.Rptr. 748, 665 P.2d 520].) As one of these decisions explained, this court had "finally and conclusively" interpreted the statute, and a "legislative clarification in the amended statute may not be used to overrule this exercise of the judicial function of statutory construction and interpretation. The amended statute defines the law for the future, but it cannot define the law for the past." (*People v. Cuevas, supra*, at p. 200.)

Plaintiff points out that *Carrisales, supra*, 21 Cal.4th 1132, itself postdated the acts alleged in this case and argues that before that decision, nonsupervisory coworkers had been personally liable under the statute. However, "[a] judicial construction of a statute is an authoritative statement of what the statute meant before as well as after the decision of the case giving rise to that construction." (*Rivers v. Roadway Express, Inc.* (1994) 511 U.S. 298, 312–313 [128 L.Ed.2d 274, 114 S.Ct. 1510]; accord, *Plaut v. Spendthrift Farm, Inc.* (1995) 514 U.S. 211, 216 [131 L.Ed.2d 328, 115 S.Ct.

1447].) This is why a judicial decision generally applies retroactively. (*Rivers v. Roadway Express, Inc., supra*, at pp. 311–312; *People v. Guerra* (1984) 37 Cal.3d 385, 399 [208 Cal.Rptr. 162, 690 P.2d 635].) It is true that two administrative decisions had previously interpreted the statute differently than we did. (See *Carrisales, supra*, at pp. 1138–1139.) But we merely concluded that those decisions had misconstrued the statute (*ibid.*); we did not, and could not, amend the statute ourselves. (See *People v. Guerra, supra*, at p. 399, fn. 13.) It is the courts' duty to construe statutes, "even though this requires the overthrow of an earlier erroneous administrative construction." (*Bodinson Mfg. Co. v. California E. Com., supra*, 17 Cal.2d at p. 326; see also *Rivers v. Roadway Express, Inc., supra*, at pp. 312–313 fn. 12 [explaining that a United States Supreme Court decision interpreting a statute stated what the statute had always meant, even if the decision overruled earlier federal appellate court decisions that had interpreted the statute differently].)

Our conclusion that the amendment to section 12940, subdivision (j)(3), changed rather than clarified the law does not itself decide the question whether it applies to this case. It just means that applying the amended section to this case would be a retroactive application. "The fact that application of [the statute] to the instant case would constitute a retroactive rather than a prospective application of the statute is, of course, just the beginning, rather than the conclusion, of our analysis." (*Evangelatos v. Superior Court* (1988) 44 Cal.3d 1188, 1206 [246 Cal.Rptr. 629, 753 P.2d 585].) We turn now to the question whether the amendment applies retroactively.

C. *Whether the Amendment Applies Retroactively*

"Generally, statutes operate prospectively only." (*Myers, supra*, 28 Cal.4th at p. 840; see also *Evangelatos v. Superior Court, supra*, 44 Cal.3d at pp. 1206–1208.) "[T]he presumption against retroactive legislation is deeply rooted in our jurisprudence, and embodies a legal doctrine centuries older than our Republic. Elementary considerations of fairness dictate that individuals should have an opportunity to know what the law is and to conform their conduct accordingly.... For that reason, the 'principle that the legal effect of conduct should ordinarily be assessed under the law that existed when the conduct took place has timeless and universal appeal.'" (*Landgraf, supra*, 511 U.S. at p. 265, fns. omitted; see also *Myers, supra*, at pp. 840–841.) "The presumption against statutory retroactivity has consistently been explained by reference to the unfairness of imposing new burdens on persons after the fact." (*Landgraf, supra*, at p. 270.)

This is not to say that a statute may never apply retroactively. "[A] statute's retroactivity is, in the first instance, a policy determination for the Legislature and one to which courts defer absent 'some constitutional objection' to retroactivity." (*Myers, supra*, 28 Cal.4th at p. 841.) But it has long been established that a statute that interferes with antecedent rights will not operate retroactively unless such retroactivity be "the unequivocal and inflexible import of the terms, and the manifest intention of the legislature." (*United States v. Heth* (1806) 7 U.S. 399, 413 [2 L.Ed. 479]; accord, *Myers, supra*, at p. 840.) "[A] statute may be applied retroactively only if it contains express language of retroactivity *or* if other sources provide a clear and unavoidable implication that the Legislature intended retroactive application." (*Myers, supra*, at p. 844.)

We see nothing here to overcome the strong presumption against retroactivity. Plaintiff and Justice Moreno argue that the statement in section 12940, subdivision (j)(2), that the subdivision's provisions merely declared existing law, shows an intent to apply the amendment retroactively. They cite our statement that "where a statute provides that it clarifies or declares existing law, '[i]t is obvious that such a provision is indicative of a legislative intent that the amendment applies to all existing causes of action from the date of its enactment. In accordance with the general rules of statutory construction, we must give effect to this intention unless there is some constitutional objection thereto.'" (*Western Security Bank, supra*, 15 Cal.4th at p. 244, quoting *California Emp. etc. Com. v. Payne, supra*, 31 Cal.2d at p. 214.)

Neither *Western Security Bank, supra*, 15 Cal.4th 232, nor *California Emp. etc. Com. v. Payne, supra*, 31 Cal.2d 210, holds that an erroneous statement that an amendment merely declares existing law is sufficient to overcome the strong presumption against retroactively applying a statute that responds to a judicial interpretation. In *California Emp. etc. Com. v. Payne*, the amendment at issue does not appear to have been adopted in response to a judicial decision. In *Western Security Bank, supra*, 15 Cal.4th 232, the only judicial action that had interpreted the statute before the Legislature amended it was a Court of Appeal decision that never became final. After considering all of the circumstances, we specifically held that the amendment at issue "did not effect any change in the law, but simply clarified and confirmed the state of the law prior to the Court of Appeal's first opinion. Because the legislative action did not change the legal effect of past actions, [the amendment] does not act retrospectively; it governs this case." (*Id.* at p. 252.) Here, by contrast, as we have explained, *Carrisales, supra*, 21 Cal.4th 1132, was a final and definitive judicial interpretation of the FEHA. The amendment at issue here *did* change the law.

Moreover, the language of section 12940, subdivision (j)(2), namely, that "The provisions of this subdivision are declaratory of existing law," long predates the Legislature's overruling of *Carrisales, supra*, 21 Cal.4th 1132. That language was added to the section in reference to a different, earlier, change to the statute. (Stats. 1987, ch. 605, § 1, p. 1945.) Any inference the Legislature intended the 2000 amendment to apply retroactively is thus far weaker than if the Legislature had asserted, *in the 2000 amending act itself*, that the amendment's provisions declared existing law.

Plaintiff and the Court of Appeal also cite statements in the legislative history to the effect that the proposed amendment would only "clarify" the law's original meaning. But these references may have been intended only to demonstrate that clarification was necessary, not as positive assertions that the law always provided for coworker liability. We see no indication the Legislature even thought about giving, much less expressly intended to give, the amendment retroactive effect to the extent the amendment did change the law. Specifically, we see no clear and unavoidable intent to have the statute retroactively impose liability for actions not subject to liability when taken. "Requiring clear intent assures that [the legislative body] itself has affirmatively considered the potential unfairness of retroactive application and determined that it is an acceptable price to pay for the countervailing benefits." (*Landgraf, supra*, 511 U.S. at pp. 272–273.)

Retroactive application would also raise constitutional implications. Both this court and the United States Supreme Court have expressed concerns that retroactively creating liability for past conduct might violate the Constitution, although it appears neither court has so held. (*Landgraf, supra*, 511 U.S. at p. 281 ["Retroactive imposition of punitive damages would raise a serious constitutional question"]; *Myers, supra*, 28 Cal.4th at pp. 845–847; but see also *Landgraf*, at p. 272 [describing "the *constitutional* impediments to retroactive civil legislation" as "now modest"].) "An established rule of statutory construction requires us to construe statutes to avoid 'constitutional infirmit[ies].' [Citations.] That rule reinforces our construction of the [statute] as prospective only." (*Myers, supra*, at pp. 846–847.) "Before we entertained that [constitutional] question, we would have to be confronted with a statute that explicitly authorized" the imposition of liability "for preenactment conduct." (*Landgraf, supra*, at p. 281.) The amendment here contains no such explicit authorization.

For all of these reasons, we conclude that section 12940, subdivision (j)(3), does not apply retroactively to conduct predating its enactment.

III. CONCLUSION

We reverse the judgment of the Court of Appeal and remand the matter for further proceedings consistent with this opinion.

GEORGE, C.J., KENNARD, J., BAXTER, J., WERDEGAR, J., and BROWN, J., concurred.

Notes and Questions

1. This case is one of the most cited appellate court decisions in California on the issue of retroactive application of a statute. Does the test enumerated by the Court make sense? Should there be exceptions to their general rule?

2. If the Legislature enacts laws, can it tell the judiciary what the law means? If the Legislature changes the law, should the judiciary interpret the law in accordance with how the Legislature changed it?

3. Is this case one of separation of powers? Or is the case one of retroactive application of an amended law based upon statutory interpretation guidelines?

4. The Court made a distinction between the legislature changing the law and clarifying the law. Whether there was a law change or a clarification impacts the determination whether the courts will apply the change or clarification retroactively. As a general rule, a statute that clarifies an earlier enactment does not apply retroactively.

5. The appellate court noted the general rule that, if the courts have not yet finally and conclusively interpreted a statute and are in the process of doing so, a declaration of a later Legislature as to what an earlier Legislature intended is entitled to consideration by the courts. However, if the Legislature "has no legislative authority simply to say what it *did* mean" regarding how a statute is intended to be interpreted, how

can the Legislature ensure that the courts will interpret statutes in the manner the legislative branch intended?

6. Why have the courts concluded that, "although the Legislature may amend a statute to overrule a judicial decision, doing so *changes* the law [and] accordingly, they refused to apply the amendment retroactively"?

7. If "a statute's retroactivity is, in the first instance, a policy determination for the Legislature," what is the role of the courts in reviewing whether a statute is to be applied retroactively?

E. Constitution Prohibits Certain Legislative Actions

The state Constitution, while it grants authority, also prohibits certain types of legislative actions from occurring. It is important to review the provisions of the state Constitution in order to ensure a particular action is not prohibited. Courts do not look to the Constitution to determine whether the Legislature is authorized to do an act, but only to see if it is prohibited.

Unlike the federal Constitution, which is a grant of power to Congress, the California Constitution is a limitation or restriction on the powers of the Legislature. The judicial branch, not the legislative, is the final arbiter of the constitutionality of a statute.

Mendoza v. State of California

(2007) 149 Cal.App.4th 1034

OPINION

CROSKEY, J.

Mayors in certain large cities around the country have been granted control of the school districts in those cities. Antonio Villaraigosa, the Mayor of the City of Los Angeles (the Mayor), sought similar control over the Los Angeles Unified School District (LAUSD) through state legislation. The California Constitution grants to the voters within the LAUSD the right to determine whether their board of education is to be elected or appointed. Therefore, the Legislature could not simply enact a statute granting the Mayor authority to appoint the members of the LAUSD Board of Education (the Board). Moreover, the California Constitution also prohibits the transfer of authority over any part of the school system to entities outside of the public-school system. Therefore, the Legislature could not simply enact a statute transferring control over the LAUSD to the Mayor. The Legislature attempted to avoid these prohibitions with the enactment of Assembly Bill No. 1381 (2005–2006 Reg. Sess.), known as the "Romero Act."

At issue in this appeal is the constitutionality of the Romero Act. At the heart of that statute are two main provisions: (1) the transfer of substantial power from the

Board to the LAUSD District Superintendent (the District Superintendent), and the grant to the Mayor of authority to ratify the appointment of the District Superintendent; and (2) the transfer of complete control of three low-performing high schools (and their feeder schools) from the Board to a partnership led by the Mayor.

We conclude that the Romero Act is an unconstitutional attempt to do indirectly what the Legislature is prohibited from doing directly. The Legislature cannot overrule the LAUSD's voters' determination that their Board is to be elected rather than appointed, nor may it transfer authority over part of the school system to entities outside of the public-school system. We will therefore affirm the trial court's issuance of a writ of mandate preventing the enforcement of the Romero Act.

....

c. *Provisions Relating to the Romero Act's Constitutionality*

The Legislature was clearly aware of the Legislative Counsel's opinions when enacting the Romero Act, and therefore took steps with the goal of ensuring the Romero Act's constitutionality. Thus, the general provisions of the Romero Act include a statement that "[i]t is ... the intent of the Legislature that, in performing the school-related duties set forth in this chapter, the [C]ouncil of [M]ayors ... and the [Mayor's Partnership] function as agencies authorized to maintain public schools, similar to a school district or county office of education. The [C]ouncil of [M]ayors and the [Mayor's Partnership are, therefore, a part of the public-school system of the state in performing the duties established in this chapter within the meaning of Section 6 of Article IX of the California Constitution." (Ed. Code, § 35900, subd. (e).) The clusters of schools that are under the control of the Mayor's Partnership shall, by statute, "continue to exist as district schools, and employees at the schools shall be deemed to be district employees with all the rights of district employees." (Ed. Code, § 35932, subd. (b).) Those schools "shall continue to be funded with district resources," although the funding may be supplemented by private funding accounted for by the Mayor's Partnership. (Ed. Code, § 35932, subd. (c).) The Romero Act also specifies that "any liability incurred by any member of the [C]ouncil of [M]ayors or [Mayor's Partnership] in undertaking any of the functions described in this chapter shall be borne by the school district and not by the County of Los Angeles, or any of the cities within its boundaries." (Ed. Code, § 35900, subd. (f).)

d. *Remaining Provisions of the Romero Act*

There are several other provisions of the Romero Act, which are not material to our main analysis. The Romero Act provides that the Southeast Cities Schools Coalition, comprised of several cities, shall have the power to ratify the selection of the local district superintendent serving those cities. (Ed. Code, § 35911, subd. (c).) The Romero Act contains provisions relating to the inspector general of the LAUSD (Ed. Code, § 35400). The Romero Act also contains provisions relating to the selection of instructional materials by the LAUSD, including that "[p]arents, teachers, and other certificated staff [shall] have an authentic and central role." (Ed. Code, § 35914, subd. (a)(1)(A).)

The entire Romero Act is repealed by its own terms on January 1, 2013, unless subsequent legislation deletes or extends that date. (Ed. Code, § 35950.) There is no severability clause in the Romero Act.

The Los Angeles City Charter provides that the mayor may serve no more than two four-year terms in office. (L.A. Charter, §§ 205, 206.) If Mayor Villaraigosa is elected to a second term, the Romero Act would expire shortly before he leaves office.

4. *The Instant Action*

On October 10, 2006, a verified petition for writ of mandate challenging the constitutionality of the Romero Act was filed. The plaintiffs include the LAUSD and certain individuals and organizational entities opposed to the law. The named defendants are the State of California, the Governor, the State Controller, the State Board of Education, the county superintendent of schools, and the Mayor. Plaintiffs took the position that the Romero Act violated sections 5, 6, 8, 14 and 16 of article IX of the California Constitution. On November 7, 2006, a group of individuals and organizational entities that support the Romero Act was permitted to intervene. Additionally, plaintiffs alleged the Romero Act violated the home rule provisions of article XI, sections 3 and 5, and the equal protection guarantee of article I, section 7 of the California Constitution.

After substantial briefing and argument, the trial court issued its opinion granting the petition for writ of mandate. The lengthy and comprehensive statement of decision issued by the trial court held the Romero Act unconstitutional on every basis on which it had been challenged. Concluding the Romero Act was not severable, the court issued a writ of mandate prohibiting defendants from enforcing or implementing the Romero Act in any way. The Governor, Controller, State Board of Education, Mayor, and interveners filed timely notices of appeal. At the parties' joint request, we have heard this case on an expedited basis.

Judgment was, however, entered in favor of the State of California.

Appellants are divided into two groups. Mayor Villaraigosa and the interveners filed a joint brief; the Governor, State Controller and State Board of Education filed another. When discussing their positions on appeal, we will refer to the groups respectively as "the Mayor" and "the State defendants."

ISSUES ON APPEAL

We are concerned solely with the constitutionality of the Romero Act. We first consider whether the Romero Act violates article IX, section 16 of the California Constitution, which grants charter cities the right to determine whether their boards of education are to be elected or appointed. We conclude that it does. We next consider whether the Romero Act violates article IX, section 6 of the California Constitution, which prohibits the transfer of control of any part of the public-school system to any authority not included within the public-school system. We conclude that it does. As we conclude that the Romero Act is unconstitutional on two separate bases, we see no need to consider the further challenges to its constitutionality. We next consider whether the unconstitutional provisions of the Romero Act can be severed and the remainder of the Romero Act allowed to stand. We conclude the Romero Act is not severable. We will therefore affirm the trial court's judgment issuing a writ of mandate prohibiting the implementation or enforcement of the Romero Act in its entirety.

DISCUSSION

....

2. *The Romero Act Violates Article IX, Section 16 of the Constitution*

"[T]he Legislature's power over the public-school system [is] 'exclusive, plenary, absolute, entire, and comprehensive, subject only to constitutional constraints.'" (*State Bd. of Education v. Honig, supra*, 13 Cal.App.4th at p. 754.) "Public education is an obligation which the State assumed by the adoption of the Constitution. [Citations.] The system of public schools, although administered through local districts created by the Legislature, is 'one system ... applicable to all the common schools....'" (*Butt v. State of California* (1992) 4 Cal.4th 668, 680 [15 Cal.Rptr.2d 480, 842 P.2d 1240].) Management and control of the public schools is a matter of state care and supervision; local districts are the state's agents for local operation of the common school system. (*Id.* at p. 681.)

However, certain powers of local districts *are* enshrined in the California Constitution. Thus, California Constitution, article IX, section 16 *guarantees* to charter cities the right to provide "for the manner in which, the time at which, and the terms for which members of boards of education shall be elected or appointed, for their qualifications, compensation and removal, and for the number which shall constitute any one of such boards." Moreover, article IX, section 14 provides that "[t]he Legislature may authorize *the governing boards of all school districts* to initiate and carry on any program, activities, or to otherwise act in any manner which is not in conflict with the laws and purposes for which school districts are established." (Italics added.) In other words, while the Constitution does not *require* that the Legislature delegate any powers to the governing boards of local school districts, the *only entities* to which the Constitution *expressly* permits the Legislature to delegate powers regarding education are the very same governing boards that the Constitution *mandates* charter cities have the right to elect.

The Mayor cites to *Grigsby v. King* (1927) 202 Cal. 299, 304 [260 P. 789], for the proposition that local school boards are "administrative agenc[ies] created by statute and invested only with the powers expressly conferred, subject to the limitations thereto attached by the legislature." Yet article IX, section 16 of the California Constitution clearly provides that local school boards, far from being created by statute, are every charter city's constitutional right to design by charter.

It cannot seriously be disputed that the Romero Act substantially interferes with the Board's control of the district. The provisions relating to the Mayor's Partnership *completely divest* the Board of its powers of control over the three school clusters in the demonstration project. The provisions relating to the Council of Mayors work a somewhat more subtle, but no less substantial, interference. A great many of the powers otherwise accorded the Board are, by the Romero Act, transferred to the District Superintendent. The Board is then stripped of its otherwise statutory right to "employ" a district superintendent, in that the approval and removal of that individual is now subject to the ratification of the Council of Mayors. Thus, it is clear that both major provisions of the Romero Act substantially interfere with the Board's powers of control over the district. One of the issues presented by this appeal is whether this interference violates the right of the citizens of Los Angeles to elect their board of education, as guaranteed by article IX, section 16 of the California Constitution.

We conclude that it does. It would be a clear violation of the plain language of article IX, section 16, if the Legislature passed a law giving the Mayor the right to appoint the members of the Board. But the constitutional provision would be annulled if the Legislature could simply bypass it by taking the powers of the Board away from that entity and giving them to the Mayor, or the Mayor's appointee. This is nothing more than an end run around the Constitution. If article IX, section 16 is to mean anything, it must mean that charter cities can not only choose the composition of their boards of education, but that charter cities are guaranteed freedom from legislative interference even when the Legislature is of the opinion that they have made the wrong choice.

While we need not determine whether the Romero Act's delegation of decision-making power over the cluster schools to the Mayor's Partnership is a violation of California Constitution, article IX, section 14's provision granting the Legislature the authority to delegate decision-making power to "the governing boards of all school districts," we find article IX, section 14 instructive. Proposition 5 (see fn. 4, *ante*), which adopted this language, was placed on the ballot because of a Legislative Counsel determination that the Legislature *lacked* the power to delegate decision-making authority to local governing boards in the absence of an express grant in the Constitution. When the voters considered whether to approve Proposition 5's language permitting the Legislature to delegate increased decision-making authority to the governing boards of local school districts, *article IX, section 16 provided voters in charter cities the right to elect their local governing boards*. It therefore appears that the voters understood that their approval of Proposition 5 would enable the Legislature to delegate increased authority only to the local governing boards that they could elect. There was never any suggestion that the Legislature somehow also possessed the authority to delegate increased decision-making power over local schools to a city's mayor and various appointees. (Cf. *Dean v. Kuchel* (1951) 37 Cal.2d 97, 99–100, 104 [230 P.2d 811] [holding that an express grant of permission to delegate legislative powers to one entity does not prohibit a delegation of such powers to another entity unless such powers are denied expressly or by necessary implication].)

On appeal, the Mayor and State defendants argue that the Constitution's grant of the power to choose whether to elect a board of education is limited *only* to that power, and does not imply that any such elected board of education would have any particular powers or duties. The Mayor relies on *State Bd. of Education v. Honig, supra*, 13 Cal.App.4th 720, for this proposition, while the State defendants rely on *Cobb v. O'Connell* (2005) 134 Cal.App.4th 91 [36 Cal.Rptr.3d 170]. Both cases are distinguishable. *State Bd. of Education v. Honig, supra*, 13 Cal.4th at p. 729, was concerned with a "turf battle" between the State Board of Education and the Superintendent of Public Instruction (State Superintendent). By statute, the State Board of Education is the legislative, policymaking branch of the State Department of Education, while the State Superintendent is vested with executive functions. The State Board of Education adopted certain policies and sought a writ of mandate directing the State Superintendent to implement those policies. The State Superintendent took the position that he was under no clear ministerial obligation to do so. (*Ibid.*) At one point, the State Superintendent argued that the Legislature had exceeded its authority by designating the State Board of Education as the policymaking branch of the department of education. The State Superintendent argued that the framers of the California Constitution had "intended to place the Superintendent 'in charge and control of the public-school system and the state education department.'" (*Id.* at p. 754.) He relied on article IX, section 2 of the California Constitution, which provides as follows: "A Superintendent of Public Instruction shall be elected by the qualified electors of the State at each gubernatorial election. The Superintendent of Public Instruction shall enter upon the duties of the office on the first Monday after the first day of January next succeeding each gubernatorial election." "Focusing on the language 'shall enter upon the duties of the office' and on portions of the debates of the 1878–1879 Constitutional Convention, the [State] Superintendent assert[ed] article IX, section 2 limits the Legislature's plenary authority to define the Superintendent's duties." (*State Bd. of Education v. Honig, supra*, 13 Cal.App.4th at pp. 754–755.) In short, the State Superintendent argued that the "duties of the office" the Constitution required him to perform could not be narrowed from the duties of the office which were *then* in existence when that language was adopted as part of the Constitution — those duties apparently including being in charge of the Department of Education. (*Id.* at p. 755.)

The *Honig* court disagreed, concluding that nothing in the plain language of article IX, section 2 limited the Legislature's authority to define the State Superintendent's duties, noting that, when the "duties of the office" language in question was adopted, the State Superintendent's duties were *then* defined by statute, and there was no reason to believe the constitutional language was intended to deprive the Legislature of the authority to ever amend the statute. (*State Bd. of Education v. Honig, supra*, 13 Cal.App.4th at p. 756.) The court added, "Nor does a commonsense reading of the language the Superintendent 'shall enter upon the duties of the office' create a right to take charge of and be in control of the public-school system and the Department by virtue of that office alone. Our reading of article IX, section 2 is consistent with article IX considered as a whole. [Citation.] Although the Superintendent is a constitutional officer whose office cannot be extinguished by the Legislature, the powers and duties of that office may, and have been, increased and diminished by the Legislature under its plenary authority." (*Id.* at p. 756.)

The above quoted language from *State Bd. of Education v. Honig, supra*, 13 Cal.App.4th at page 756, does not control our interpretation of article IX, section 16 of the California Constitution. The LAUSD does not question the power of the Legislature to increase or diminish the powers and duties of local boards of education; indeed, much of the Education Code can be seen as limits on the power of local boards of education. We are instead concerned with a *special law* which provides that, although every other charter city in California may elect a board of education that can exercise all powers statutorily delegated to such local boards of education, Los Angeles may not. This case does not present a challenge to the Legislature's plenary power to limit the authority of local boards of education; it is a challenge to a legislative attempt to act where the voters of Los Angeles are given the exclusive power to act — to determine the composition of the local board of education. The Legislature cannot transfer a local board of education's powers to *a different entity* and then say the charter city has no right to determine the composition of *that* entity since it is not a board of education.

Article IX, section 14 of the California Constitution provides that "[t]he Legislature shall have the power, *by general law*, to provide for the incorporation and organization of school districts, high school districts, and community college districts, of every kind and class, and may classify such districts." (Italics added.) The trial court concluded the Romero Act violated this provision as well, as it is a special law altering the organization of the LAUSD.

The State defendants fare no better with *Cobb v. O'Connell, supra*, 134 Cal.App.4th 91. To appreciate that conclusion, however, a brief discussion of *Butt v. State of California, supra*, 4 Cal.4th 668, is necessary. In April 1991, the Richmond Unified School District found itself in such dire financial straits that it intended to close the doors to its schools on May 1, thus cutting off the last six weeks of school. (*Butt v. State of California, supra*, 4 Cal.4th at p. 673.) Local parents brought suit against the state, seeking injunctive relief to keep the schools open. The trial court granted an injunction and the Supreme Court affirmed. The Supreme Court concluded that allowing the Richmond Unified School District to close its doors would constitute a violation of its students' *equal protection* rights. Concluding that "[t]he State itself bears the ultimate authority and responsibility to ensure that its district-based system of common schools provides basic equality of educational opportunity" (*id.* at p. 685), the court upheld, as a proper exercise of the trial court's authority to enforce its constitutional judgments, a preliminary injunction requiring the State Superintendent to take over governance of the Richmond Unified School District (in conjunction with a substantial emergency loan) until a recovery and payment plan could be established. (*Id.* at pp. 675, 694–697.) In the course of its opinion, the Supreme Court noted that, in extreme cases, the state has a duty to intervene to prevent unconstitutional discrimination at a local level. (*Id.* at p. 688.)

The Supreme Court was clear that its analysis was limited to an appeal from a grant of a preliminary injunction, not an appeal from a final judgment. (*Butt v. State of California, supra*, 4 Cal.4th at p. 678 fn. 8.)

There was no challenge raised in *Butt* that the State Superintendent's takeover of the Richmond schools was unconstitutional. Instead, the *state* had appealed, arguing that its delegation of educational authority to local school boards prevented it from having any additional duties to come to the aid of troubled districts.

It was just such an extreme case that led to *Cobb v. O'Connell, supra,* 134 Cal.App.4th 91. In 2002, the Oakland Unified School District discovered that it had a deficit of $31 million, with another $50 million deficit projected for the following year. (*Id.* at pp. 93–94.) The Legislature stepped in with emergency legislation "to ensure that this fiscal crisis in the Oakland schools did not deprive students of their educational opportunities." (*Id.* at p. 94.) The state provided a $100 million loan, and temporarily transferred control of the schools to the state. The State Superintendent was to appoint an administrator to run the schools, with the local governing board remaining in an advisory capacity, for two years or until the projected completion of a specified plan to resolve the fiscal crisis. (*Ibid.*) Some Oakland residents brought suit, contending the temporary removal of authority from the elected school board violated the "home rule" provisions of the California Constitution and the Oakland City Charter. The *Cobb* court disagreed. Specifically, it concluded that there was no conflict with the Oakland City Charter because, "[t]he Oakland school board continues to be elected as it always was before the emergency legislation, and the hiatus in the exercise of its ultimate responsibility is only temporary, during which period the board continues to serve an advisory role." (*Id.* at p. 97.)

They did not raise a challenge under article IX, section 16 of the California Constitution, although the court briefly mentioned that section's language in its opinion. (*Cobb v. O'Connell, supra,* 134 Cal.App.4th at p. 97.)

Butt v. State of California and *Cobb v. O'Connell* are clearly distinguishable from this case. Those cases stand for the proposition that the state may, and in some circumstances must, interfere with a local school board's management of its schools when an emergency situation threatens the students' constitutional right to basic equality of educational opportunity. The Romero Act is not such legislation. The Romero Act makes no findings of crisis in the LAUSD schools. Indeed, it could not, as LAUSD schools are not the worst in the state by any measure. Instead, the Romero Act purports to justify its interference with the Board's authority on the basis that the LAUSD "has unique challenges and resources that require and deserve special attention to ensure that all pupils are given the opportunity to reach their full potential." (Ed. Code, § 35900, subd. (a)(1).) In the absence of any looming constitutional crisis, the "unique" circumstances of the LAUSD do not, alone, constitute a basis for depriving the citizens of Los Angeles of their right to an elected board running their school district. The Romero Act is therefore violative of article IX, section 16 of the California Constitution.

3. The Romero Act Violates Article IX, Section 6 of the Constitution

We next consider article IX, section 6 of the Constitution, which provides, in pertinent part, "The Public-School System shall include all kindergarten schools, elementary schools, secondary schools, technical schools, and State colleges, established in accordance with law and, in addition, the school districts and the other agencies authorized to maintain them. *No school or college or any other part of the Public-School System shall be, directly or indirectly, transferred from the Public-School System or placed under the jurisdiction of any authority other than one included within the Public-School System."* (Italics added.)

"It is clear from early cases that the general purpose of article IX, section 6 was to adopt one uniform system of public-school education; the term 'system' itself imparting unity of purpose as well as entirety of operation." (*California Sch. Employees Assn. v. Sunnyvale Elementary Sch. Dist.* (1973) 36 Cal.App.3d 46, 57 [111 Cal.Rptr. 433], fn. omitted.) Providing a single system of public schools "means that the educational system must 'be uniform in terms of the prescribed course of study and educational progression from grade to grade.'" (*Wilson v. State Bd. of Education, supra,* 75 Cal.App.4th at p. 1137.) The purpose of article IX, section 6 of the California Constitution is to guarantee that "the ability of that *system* to discharge its duty fully is not impaired by the dissipation of authority and loss of control that would result if parts of the system were transferred from the system or placed under the jurisdiction of some other authority." (*California Teachers Assn. v. Board of Trustees* (1978) 82 Cal.App.3d 249, 254 [146 Cal.Rptr. 850].) It is "a fluid provision, one that must be interpreted by the facts of each case." (*California Sch. Employees Assn. v. Sunnyvale Elementary Sch. Dist., supra,* 36 Cal.App.3d at p. 57.)

To determine whether the Romero Act violates this provision, we first decide whether the Council of Mayors and Mayor's Partnership are entities within the public-school system. As we conclude that they are not, we then address the question as to whether the Romero Act *transfers* part of the school system to these entities.

a. *The Council of Mayors and Mayor's Partnership Are Not Public-School System Entities*

Article IX, section 6 of the California Constitution provides that, in addition to the public schools themselves, the school system includes "the school districts and the other agencies authorized to maintain them." We therefore must determine whether the Council of Mayors and Mayor's Partnership are agencies authorized to maintain the schools.

An examination of the voter materials for the proposition that added this language provides no insight into the voters' intent. (Ballot Pamp., Gen. Elec. (Nov. 5, 1946) summary and arguments related to Prop. 3, pp. 4–5.)

Our analysis begins with an acknowledgement that the Romero Act specifically declares that the Council of Mayors and the Mayor's Partnership *are* part of the public-school system. "[I]t is ... the intent of the Legislature that, in performing the school-related duties set forth in this chapter, the [C]ouncil of [M]ayors ... and the [Mayor's Partnership] function as agencies authorized to maintain public schools, similar to a school district or county office of education. The [C]ouncil of [M]ayors and the [Mayor's P]artnership are, therefore, a part of the public-school system of the state in performing the duties established in this chapter within the meaning of section 6 of Article IX of the California Constitution." (Ed. Code, § 35900, subd. (e).) While this determination is entitled to great weight, it is not controlling. We repeat, "A court may not simply abdicate to the Legislature, especially when the issue involves the division of power between local government and that same Legislature." (*County of Riverside v. Superior Court, supra*, 30 Cal.4th at p. 286.) To put it another way, the Legislature may not, by means of legislative declaration, foreclose or limit the scope of judicial examination and review of the constitutionality of a legislative enactment. As a result, the *substance* of the Romero Act must be evaluated on its merits, quite apart from any legislative declaration designed to address expressed constitutional concerns. Preliminarily, we reject the Mayor's contention that the article IX, section 6 prohibition against the transfer of part of the public-school system does not apply to acts of the Legislature. The Mayor takes the position that, since the Legislature can authorize entities to maintain the public schools, any entity authorized by the Legislature to do so is, by necessity, part of the public-school system. We disagree. As the Supreme Court stated in a slightly different context, "The act of delegation does not change a private body into a public body and thereby validate the very delegation the [Constitution] prohibits." (*County of Riverside v. Superior Court, supra*, 30 Cal.4th at p. 294.) Similarly, we conclude the act of delegation of authority over a part of the public-school system does not change the entity to whom the authority was delegated *into* a part of the public-school system. Moreover, if the Legislature could delegate authority over the public schools *at will*, there was little purpose in the voters' adoption of article IX, section 14, a provision then deemed necessary in order to give to the Legislature the authority to delegate increased authority over the public schools to "the governing boards of all school districts." (See fns. 4 15, *ante.*)

The critical question, therefore, is whether the Council of Mayors and the Mayor's Partnership can be deemed to be a part of the public-school system for any reason *other* than the Legislature's bald declaration that they are. The Council of Mayors is effectively directed by the Mayor, as it can take no action without his agreement. Likewise, by its terms, the Mayor's Partnership is "directed" by the Mayor. Yet the Mayor is not part of the public-school system. The Mayor is an elected official who, according to the city charter, is "the Chief Executive Officer of the City." (L.A. Charter, § 230.)

Article IX of the California Constitution governs education in California. It provides for a State Superintendent and Board of Education; county superintendents and boards of education; and local school districts with governing boards. *These* are the entities *constitutionally authorized* to maintain public schools, and we conclude they are, therefore, the only entities referred to in article IX, section 6. (See *Wilson v. State Bd. of Education, supra*, 75 Cal.App.4th at p. 1142 [each entity provided for in art. IX is an entity authorized to maintain schools in our public school system and is therefore part of the public school system].) As the Council of Mayors and the Mayor's Partnership are not article IX entities, they are not part of the public-school system.

We are unpersuaded by the suggestion that the presence of a single representative of the LAUSD in the Mayor's Partnership with respect to each cluster transforms the Mayor's Partnership into a part of the public-school system. This is particularly the case where, as here, the duties of the LAUSD employee are not supervisory, but simply defined as running the Office of Parent Communication.

. . . .

4. *The Unconstitutional Provisions of the Romero Act Are Not Severable*

The Mayor argues by analogy. The Mayor contends that the Council of Mayors' ratification of the selection of the District Superintendent is akin to the United States Senate's power to confirm nominees to the executive and judicial branches. (U.S. Const., art. II, § 2.) The Mayor argues that since the United States Senate is not thereby granted "management and control" over the executive and judicial branches, the Romero Act does not grant the Council of Mayors management and control over the functions performed by the District Superintendent. The analogy effectively serves to clarify the issue. The United States Constitution is set up as a system of checks and balances, in which powers are spread among the three branches so that no one branch has unrestrained authority. In contrast, article IX of the California Constitution addresses no such separation of power concerns, but rather is the means by which the people of California have constitutionally vested *complete* authority over the public-school system in the school districts and other agencies authorized to maintain it. The Mayor's argument simply begs the question as to whether the Legislature may grant to a nonmember of the public-school system veto power over the appointment of an important official in that system without running afoul of that constitutional mandate.

For similar reasons, the provision of the Romero Act granting the Southeast Cities Schools Coalition the power to ratify the selection of the local district superintendent serving those cities also violates article IX, section 6 of the California Constitution.

Having concluded that the great bulk of the Romero Act is unconstitutional, the issue becomes whether those provisions can be severed, allowing the remainder of the Romero Act to go into effect. For the unconstitutional portions of a law to be severable, they must be "grammatically, functionally, and volitionally separable" from the remainder of the law. (*Calfarm Ins. Co. v. Deukmejian* (1989) 48 Cal.3d 805, 821 [258 Cal.Rptr. 161, 771 P.2d 1247].) The dispute in this case is over the third factor. This determination focuses on whether the remainder of the statute would have been adopted by the Legislature had it foreseen the partial invalidity of the statute. (*Ibid.*)

In this case, we are guided by the legislative history. As the Romero Act proceeded through the Legislature, a severability clause was added by amendment on August 8, 2006. (Assem. Bill No. 1381 (2005–2006 Reg. Sess.) § 4, as amended Aug. 8, 2006.) On August 28, 2006, the Senate deleted the severability clause. (Assem. Bill No. 1381 (2005–2006 Reg. Sess.), as amended Aug. 28, 2006.) The Assembly Republican Bill Analysis regarding this version of the bill sets forth, at length, the political maneuvering that resulted in the deletion of the severability clause. It appears that the possible future invalidation of the Council of Mayors and Mayor's Partnership aspects of the Romero Act had been considered, given the Legislative Counsel's opinions. Certain proponents of the Romero Act were concerned that if those provisions were, in fact, invalidated, "'what was left would be a step backward.'" (Assem. Republican analysis of Assem. Bill No. 1381 (2005–2006 Reg. Sess.) as amended Aug. 28, 2006, p. 9.) They were concerned that provisions strengthening the District Superintendent and weakening the Board would not be desirable if the Council of Mayors did not have control over the appointment of the District Superintendent. They were also concerned that the concessions giving teachers added input in curriculum decisions "'would strengthen employee unions at the expense of actual school reform.'" (*Id.* at p. 10.) Therefore, they successfully lobbied for the removal of the severability clause.

The legislative history also indicates the Legislature was aware that there was already a severability clause in the Education Code (Ed. Code, § 6). Some took the position that the deletion of the severability clause from the Romero Act would have no effect as the Education Code's severability clause still existed. In his reply brief on appeal, the Mayor suggests that the Legislature did not delete the severability clause until "after being assured by Legislative Counsel that such a clause was unnecessary in light of the general severability provision in Education Code section 6." This is untrue. The referenced Legislative Counsel's opinion is dated November 6, 2006 — well after the severability clause had been deleted, the Romero Act had been enacted, and plaintiffs had already filed their petition for writ of mandate challenging the law. (Ops. Cal. Legis. Counsel, No. 0621957 (Nov. 6, 2006) Severability Clause: Education Code.)

Since the severability clause was removed in light of concerns that some proponents of the bill did not, in fact, want the provisions of the Romero Act to be severable, we conclude that the Legislature *had* considered the possibility of partial invalidity of the Romero Act, and had concluded that it would not, in fact, want the remainder of the law to be effective. We therefore conclude the provisions of the Romero Act are not severable.

On appeal, the State defendants argue only that the Council of Mayors provision or the Mayor's Partnership provision should be considered severable if only one of the two is invalidated. They do not argue that the remainder of the Romero Act should go forward in the event, as we have concluded, that *both* provisions are unconstitutional.

CONCLUSION

The citizens of Los Angeles have the constitutional right to decide whether their school board is to be appointed or elected. If the citizens of Los Angeles *choose* to amend their charter to allow the Mayor to appoint the members of the Board, such amendment would indisputably be proper. What is not permissible is for the Legislature to ignore that constitutional right and to bypass the will of the citizens of Los Angeles and effectively transfer many of the powers of the Board to the Mayor, based on its belief, hope, or assumption that he could do a better job. The trial court's order granting the writ prohibiting the enforcement of the Romero Act in its entirety must be affirmed.

DISPOSITION

The judgment is affirmed. Plaintiffs shall recover their costs on appeal.

KLEIN, P.J., and KITCHING, J., concurred

Notes and Questions

1. The judicial branch, not the legislative, is the final arbiter of the constitutionality of a statute. The presumption of constitutionality of a legislative act is particularly appropriate where the Legislature has enacted a statute with the pertinent constitutional prescriptions in mind. In such a case, the statute represents a considered legislative judgment as to the appropriate reach of the constitutional provision. Is this the appropriate approach for the judicial branch to take? If the Legislature states what it wants enacted, should that be controlling?

2. The Los Angeles Unified School District challenged the constitutionality of state legislation that would have removed the authority of the elected Board of Education and handed over control of a significant portion of the school district to a private entity headed by Los Angeles Mayor Antonio Villaraigosa.

3. What was the reasoning for the court's conclusion that the Romero Act is unconstitutional on two separate bases? Were there other challenges to its constitutionality? The court also addressed the issue of severability. What was the court's ruling in that regard?

4. Did the appellate court afford appropriate weight to the fact that the "Legislature was clearly aware of the Legislative Counsel's opinions when enacting the Romero Act, and therefore took steps with the goal of ensuring the Romero Act's constitutionality"? Does it matter to the court that the Legislative Counsel opined that each variation of the Romero Act was unconstitutional?

5. Despite the state Constitution granting the entire lawmaking authority to the Legislature, that does not ensure that the Legislature can enact any law it chooses. The court pointed out that certain powers of local districts are enshrined in the California Constitution. Is that the sole basis for the court's ruling against the legislative enactment?

6. The appellate court appears to have easily concluded that the Romero Act violates the plain language of Article IX, Section 16 because it would have given the Mayor the right to appoint the members of the Board. This was the same conclusion reached by the Legislative Counsel, which serves as the Legislature's lawyer and its bill drafter. Why did the Legislature enact the Romero Act if its own attorneys opined that the proposed statute would violate the constitution?

7. In addressing the issue of severability of the unconstitutional provisions, why did the court determine the entire Romero Act was invalid?

F. Doubt Construed in Favor of the Legislature

If there are doubts raised as to whether the Legislature can act, the courts generally defer to the power of the Legislature, and they will construe the activity toward being authorized by the Constitution. With this approach, there is a presumption of correctness of official actions by the Legislature. From the judiciary's point of view, if there is any doubt as to the Legislature's power to act in any given case, that doubt should be resolved in favor of the legislature's action.

City of San Jose v. State of California

(1996) 45 Cal.App.4th 1802, review denied

OPINION

BAMATTRE-MANOUKIAN, J.

In 1979 the voters of the State of California (State) adopted an initiative which added article XIII B to the state Constitution. This followed in the wake of Proposition 13, which had added article XIII A the previous year. Section 6 of article XIII B imposed limits on the State's authority to mandate new programs or increased services on local governmental entities, whose taxing powers had been severely restricted by Proposition 13. Under section 6, whenever the state mandated such a program, the State would be required to reimburse the local entity for the costs of the program.

We will refer herein to section 6 of article XIII B of the California Constitution simply as section 6.

The present proceeding arose after the Legislature enacted Government Code section 29550 in 1990 (hereafter, section 29550). Section 29550 authorized counties to charge cities, and other local entities such as school districts, for the costs of booking into county jails persons who had been arrested by employees of the cities and other entities. The City of San Jose (City) claims that at the time of trial it had incurred expenses of over $10 million as a result of costs imposed pursuant to section 29550.

City contends section 29550 is a state mandated program under article XIII B, section 6, and that the State must reimburse these costs. The State claims that section 29550 simply authorizes allocation of booking costs, which formerly were borne solely by the counties, among all the local entities responsible for the arrests; since there is no mandated shifting of costs from state to local government, section 29550 does not come within section 6 and no reimbursement is necessary.

We agree with the state and we therefore reverse the judgment of the superior court which had granted City's petition for a writ of mandate. We direct that the court issue an order denying the petition and enter judgment for the State.

. . . .

Discussion

We must determine whether section 29550 constitutes a "new program or higher level of service" which is "mandated" by the State on local government within the meaning intended by section 6 of the Constitution.

(3) As to the first part of the question, whether section 29550 establishes a new program or higher level of service, the leading case of *Lucia Mar Unified School Dist.*

v. Honig (1988) 44 Cal.3d 830 [244 Cal.Rptr. 677, 750 P.2d 318] (*Lucia Mar*) provides a useful focus for discussion.

Lucia Mar involved Education Code section 59300, passed in 1981, which required local school districts to contribute part of the cost of educating district students at state schools for the severely handicapped. Prior to 1979 the school districts had been required by statute to contribute to the education of students in their districts who attended state schools. (Former Ed. Code, §§ 59021, 59121, 59221.) However, those statutes were repealed following the passage of Proposition 13 in 1978, and in 1979 the state assumed full responsibility for funding the schools. When article XIII B was added to the Constitution, effective July 1, 1980, the State had full financial responsibility for operating the state schools, and this was the status when section 59300 was enacted in 1981.

In 1984 the Lucia Mar Unified School District and other school districts filed a test claim asserting that Education Code section 59300 required them to make payments for a "'new program or increased level of service,'" thus entitling them to reimbursement under section 6. The Commission denied the claim, finding that, although increased costs had been imposed on the district, section 59300 did not establish any "'new program or increased level of service.'" This decision was affirmed by the superior court, which found that section 59300 did not mandate a new program or higher level of service but simply called for an "'adjustment of costs.'" (*Lucia Mar, supra,* 44 Cal.3d at p. 834.) The Court of Appeal also affirmed, reasoning that a shift in the funding of an existing program is not a "new program."

The Supreme Court reversed the judgment in favor of the State. The court recognized that " ... local entities are not entitled to reimbursement for all increased costs mandated by state law, but only those costs resulting from a new program or an increased level of service imposed upon them by the state." (*Lucia Mar, supra,* 44 Cal.3d at p. 835.) "'Program,'" as used in article XIII B of the California Constitution, is "one that carries out the 'governmental function of providing services to the public, or laws which, to implement a state policy, impose unique requirements on local governments and do not apply generally to all residents and entities in the state.'" (*Lucia Mar, supra,* at p. 835, quoting *County of Los Angeles v. State of California, supra,* 43 Cal.3d at p. 56.) Under this definition the high court found that the contributions called for in Education Code section 59300 were used to fund a "program." This was so even though the school district was required only to contribute funds to the state-operated schools rather than to administer the program itself.

The court found further that the program established by Education Code section 59300 was a "new program" insofar as the school district was concerned since, at the time it was enacted in 1981, school districts were not required to contribute to the education of their students at the state-operated schools. The court concluded that a shift in funding of an existing program from the state to a local entity constitutes a new program within the meaning of section 6. "The intent of the section [section 6] would plainly be violated if the state could, while retaining administrative control of programs it has supported with state tax money, simply shift the cost of the programs to local government on the theory that the shift does not violate section 6 ... because the programs are not 'new.' Whether the shifting of costs is accomplished by compelling local governments to pay the cost of entirely new programs created by the state, or by compelling them to accept financial responsibility in whole or in part for a program which was funded entirely by the state before the advent of article XIIIB, the result seems equally violative of the fundamental purpose underlying section 6 of that article." (*Lucia Mar, supra,* 44 Cal.3d at p. 836, fn. omitted.)

In *Lucia Mar* the case was remanded to the Commission for a determination of the remaining issue, whether Education Code section 59300 in fact "mandated" the school districts to make the called for contributions. (*Lucia Mar, supra,* 44 Cal.3d at p. 836.)

City and the amici curiae cities contend that the principles expressed in *Lucia Mar* compel the same result here. Section 29550, they argue, is a classic example of the state attempting to shift to local entities the financial responsibility for providing public services. As in *Lucia Mar,* the program is "new" as to City because City has not formerly been required to contribute financially to services provided via the booking process. And, as the *Lucia Mar* court explained, it does not matter that City itself is not required to provide the services; a shift in funding of an existing program from the State to the local level qualifies as a "new program" under section 6.

The flaw in City's reliance on *Lucia Mar* is that in our case the shift in funding is not from the State to the local entity but from county to city. In *Lucia Mar,* prior to the enactment of the statute in question, the program was funded and operated entirely by the state. Here, however, at the time section 29550 was enacted, and indeed long before that statute, the financial and administrative responsibility associated with the operation of county jails and detention of prisoners was borne entirely by the county. In the recent case of *County of Los Angeles v. Commission on State Mandates, supra,* 32 Cal.App.4th 805, this distinction is the focus of the court's section 6 analysis.

In *County of Los Angeles,* the court of appeal addressed the question whether Penal Code section 987.9 was a state-mandated program for which counties were entitled to be reimbursed. That statute, enacted in 1977, provided that indigent defendants in capital cases could request funds for investigators and experts to assist in the preparation or presentation of the defense. Prior to 1990, costs of this program were reimbursed to the counties by the state by annual appropriations. In the Budget Act of 1990–1991, however, no appropriation was made and counties were obliged to absorb the costs. The County of Los Angeles filed a test claim with the Commission, arguing that the state's withdrawal of funding for section 987.9 costs constituted an unlawful shifting of financial responsibility for the program from the state to the counties, within the meaning of section 6 and in violation of the Supreme Court's holding in *Lucia Mar.*

The Court of Appeal in *County of Los Angeles* decided first that the requirements of Penal Code section 987.9 were not state mandated, but were mandated by the United States Constitution. As a separate basis for its opinion, however, the court found that the State's withdrawal of funds to reimburse section 987.9 costs was not a "new program" under section 6. The court distinguished *Lucia Mar* as follows: "In *Lucia Mar,* the handicapped school program in issue had been operated and administered by the State of California for many years. The court found primary responsibility rested with the state and that the transfer of financial responsibility from the state through state tax revenues to school districts through school district tax and assessment revenues in the school district treasuries imposed a new program on school districts. … [¶] In contrast, the program here has never been operated or administered by the State of California. The counties have always borne legal and financial responsibility for implementing the procedures under section 987.9. The state merely reimbursed counties for specific expenses incurred by the counties in their operation of a program for which they had a primary legal and financial responsibility. There has been no shift of costs from the state to the counties and *Lucia Mar* is, thus, inapposite." (*County of Los Angeles v. Commission on State Mandates, supra,* 32 Cal.App.4th at p. 817.)

This analysis applies equally to our case. It has long been the law in California that """"the expense of capture, detention and prosecution of persons charged with crime is to be borne by the county...."""" (*County of San Luis Obispo v. Abalone Alliance* (1986) 178 Cal.App.3d 848, 859 [223 Cal.Rptr. 846].) Government Code section 29602, which was enacted in 1947, provides that "[t]he expenses necessarily incurred in the support of persons charged with or convicted of a crime and committed to the county jail … and for other services in relation to criminal proceedings for which no specific compensation is prescribed by law are county charges." (See also *Washington Township Hosp. Dist.* v. *County of Alameda* (1968) 263 Cal.App.2d 272, 275 [69 Cal.Rptr. 442].) The Penal Code similarly provides that county jails are kept by the sheriffs of the counties in which they are located and that the expenses in providing for prisoners in those jails are to be paid out of the county treasury. (Pen. Code, §§ 4000, 4015.)

City acknowledges that counties have traditionally borne these expenses, but argues that they do so only in their role as agents of the State. Counties, it is argued, are political subdivisions of the State, organized for the purpose of carrying out functions of state government and advancing state policies, particularly in the area of administration of justice. (See, e.g., *Wilkinson v. Lund* (1929) 102 Cal.App. 767, 772 [283 P. 385]; Gov. Code, § 23002; *Marin County v. Superior Court* (1960) 53 Cal.2d 633, 638–639 [2 Cal.Rptr. 758, 349 P.2d 526].) For example, prosecutions take place in county courts but are brought on behalf of the people of the State of California; the state Attorney General has direct supervision over county sheriffs and district attorneys (Cal. Const., art. V, § 13, subd. (b); Gov. Code, §§ 12550, 12560.); and the state asserts substantial control over the operation of county jails. (Pen. Code, §§ 4000 et seq.; 6030 et seq.) Enforcement of the state's criminal laws is a governmental function, the expense of which the state imposes on the county as the administrative arm of the state. (See *Los Angeles Warehouse Co. v. Los Angeles County* (1934) 139 Cal.App.

368, 371 [33 P.2d 1058].) Thus, even though the costs of operating county jails and detaining prisoners are paid from the county treasury, City argues those functions are essentially part of a state program. The imposition of those costs on cities therefore constitutes a shift from the state to local government.

This characterization of the county as an agent of the State is not supported by recent case authority, nor does it square with definitions particular to subvention analysis. In *County of Lassen v. State of California* (1992) 4 Cal.App.4th 1151 [6 Cal.Rptr.2d 359], a county sought indemnity from the state for costs of defending against an action by inmates of the county jail alleging inadequate conditions in the jail facility. The county alleged that the State has the ultimate responsibility for setting forth rules and standards governing the operation of jail facilities, and that county jails are used principally to incarcerate persons convicted of or charged with violations of state law. Further, the county reasoned that "it [was] the agent of the State in enforcing the State's laws against third persons" and that as State's agent in this regard it was entitled to indemnity from its principal for expenditures or losses incurred in discharge of its authorized duties. (*Id.* at p. 1155.)

The Court of Appeal rejected this theory, squarely holding that the costs of operating county jails, including the capture, detention and prosecution of persons charged with crime are to be borne by the counties. (*County of Lassen v. State of California, supra,* 4 Cal.App.4th at p. 1156, citing Pen. Code, §§ 4000, 4015; Gov. Code, § 29602; see also *County of San Luis Obispo v. Abalone Alliance, supra,* 178 Cal.App.3d at p. 859.) Further, the court observed that the Legislature was entitled to make policy decisions in order to assist counties in bearing the financial burden of certain aspects of running jails, such as providing funding assistance for construction of new facilities; however, the Legislature had not decided to subsidize the operation of existing facilities or costs associated with their operation. Unless the Legislature otherwise provides, counties are required to bear costs associated with operating county jails. (Gov. Code, § 29602.)

City points out that *Lassen* is not directly relevant for our purposes because the court in that case specifically declined to comment on the question whether costs would be reimbursable under section 6. Apparently, that theory of recovery had not been pursued below. (*County of Lassen v. State of California, supra,* 4 Cal.App.4th at p. 1157.) *Lassen* nonetheless supports State's position that fiscal responsibility for the program in question here rests with the county and not with the State.

More importantly, in analyzing a question involving reimbursement under section 6, the definitions contained in California Constitution, article XIII B and in the legislation enacted to implement it must be deemed controlling. Article XIII B treats cities and counties alike as "local government." Under section 8, subdivision (d), this term means "any city, county, city and county, school district, special district, authority or other political subdivision of or within the state." Furthermore, Government Code section 17514 defines "costs mandated by the state" to mean any increased costs that a "local agency" or school district is required to incur. "Local agency" means "any city, county, special district, authority, or other political subdivision of the state." (Gov. Code, § 17518.) Thus, for purposes of subvention analysis, it is clear that counties and cities were intended to be treated alike as part of "local government"; both are considered local agencies or political subdivisions of the State. Nothing in article XIII B prohibits the shifting of costs between local governmental entities.

Furthermore, we do not believe that the shifting of costs here was a state "mandate," within the meaning of section 6. As the Commission observed, "[t]he pertinent words of the statute state that '... a county *may* impose a fee on a city....'" Thus section 29550 does not require that counties impose fees on other local entities, but only authorizes them to do so. City claims this is too literal an interpretation of the statutory language. If we take a closer look at the circumstances surrounding the enacting of section 29550, City argues, it becomes clear that it was designed to accomplish indirectly the exact result section 6 was intended to prevent.

Section 29550 was added by section 1 of Senate Bill No. 2557. Section 2 of Senate Bill No. 2557 amended Government Code section 77200 to reduce county revenues by reducing the block grants for trial court funding by approximately 10 percent. (Stats. 1990, ch. 466, pp. 2041–2042.) Moreover, Senate Bill No. No. 2557 was part of the overall state "budget package" of 1990–1991, which contained other shortfalls in county funding. In light of these budget cuts in other areas, City argues, the counties basically had no choice but to pass along booking costs as authorized by section 29550. Moreover, as to City the costs incurred are mandated because Ordinance No. NS-300.470, which is authorized by section 29550, is mandatory.

In support of its position, City submitted excerpts from the county board of supervisors meeting where Ordinance No. NS-300.470 was adopted. These excerpts reflect the generally held belief on the part of the Board members that section 29550 was passed to enable counties to make up for state revenue cuts in other programs.

We appreciate that as a practical result of the authorization under section 29550, City is required to bear costs it did not formerly bear. We cannot, however, read a mandate into language which is plainly discretionary. Nor are we persuaded by the argument that budget cuts in other programs trigger the subvention requirement in section 6. Funding decisions are policy choices. (*County of Lassen v. State of California, supra,* 4 Cal.App.4th at p. 1157.) Section 6 was not intended to entitle local entities to reimbursement for *all* increased costs resulting from legislative enactments, but only those costs mandated by a new program or an increased level of service imposed upon them by the State. (*Lucia Mar, supra,* 44 Cal.3d at p. 835.) Section 6 cannot be interpreted to apply to general legislation which has an incidental impact on local agency costs. (*County of Los Angeles v. State of California, supra,* 43 Cal. 3d at p. 57.)

A strict construction of section 6 is in keeping with rules of constitutional interpretation, which require that constitutional limitations and restrictions on legislative power "'"are to be construed strictly, and are not to be extended to include matters not covered by the language used."'" (*Pacific Legal Foundation v. Brown, supra,* 29 Cal.3d at p. 180; see also *California Teacher's Association v. Hayes* (1992) 5 Cal.App.4th 1513, 1529 [7 Cal.Rptr.2d 699] ["Under our form of government, policymaking authority is vested in the Legislature and neither arguments as to the wisdom of an enactment nor questions as to the motivation of the Legislature can serve to invalidate particular legislation."].) Under these principles, there is no basis for applying section 6 as an equitable remedy to cure the perceived unfairness resulting from political decisions on funding priorities.

One final point merits brief comment. City contends that the Legislative Counsel's determination that section 29550 imposed a state-mandated local program is deserving of some deference. Government Code section 17575 requires the Legislature's Counsel to determine whether a proposed bill mandates a new program or higher level of service pursuant to section 6. Here Legislative Counsel found "[t]his bill would impose a state-mandated local program by authorizing a county to impose a fee upon other local agencies ... for county costs incurred in processing or booking persons arrested by employees of other local agencies ... and brought to county facilities for booking or detention." (Legis. Counsel's Dig., Sen. Bill No. 2557, 5 Stats. 1990 (Reg. Sess.) Summary Dig., pp. 170–171.) Under Government Code section 17579, when Legislative Counsel makes such a determination, the enacted statute must contain explicit language providing that "if the Commission on State Mandates determines that this act contains costs mandated by the state, reimbursement to local agencies and school districts for those costs shall be made pursuant to Part 7 (commencing with section 17500) of Division 4 of Title 2 of the Government Code...." (Stats. 1990, ch. 466, §7, p. 2046.)

These findings and required statements are not determinative, however, of the ultimate issue, whether the enactment constitutes a state mandate under section 6. The legislative scheme contained in Government Code section 17500 et seq. makes clear that this issue is to be decided by the Commission. "'It is apparent from the comprehensive nature of this legislative scheme, and from the Legislature's expressed intent, that the exclusive remedy for a claimed violation of section 6 lies in these procedures. The statutes create an administrative forum for resolution of state mandate claims, and establish procedures which exist for the express purpose of avoiding multiple proceedings, judicial and administrative, addressing the same claim that a reimbursable state mandate has been created.... In short, the Legislature has created what is clearly intended to be a comprehensive and exclusive procedure by which to implement and enforce section 6.' [Citation.] [¶] Thus the statutory scheme contemplates that the Commission, as a quasi-judicial body, has the sole and exclusive authority to adjudicate whether a state mandate exists. Thus, any legislative findings are irrelevant to the issue of whether a state mandate exists...." (*County of Los Angeles v. Commission on State Mandates, supra,* 32 Cal.App.4th at p. 819, quoting from *Kinlaw v. State of California, supra,* 54 Cal.3d at p. 333, italics omitted.)

Disposition

We reverse the judgment and direct that the superior court issue an order denying City's petition for a writ of mandate and enter judgment for the State. Costs on appeal are awarded to appellants.

COTTLE, P.J., and MIHARA, J., concurred.

A petition for a rehearing was denied July 2, 1996, and respondent's petition for review by the Supreme Court was denied September 18, 1996. MOSK, J., was of the opinion that the petition should be granted.

Notes and Questions

1. What was the basis for the court's ruling that the "shifting of costs" did not constitute a "mandate"? If the court agreed that the practical result of the authorization under the state statute required the city to "bear costs it did not formerly bear," how is that not a mandate?

2. While the court states the general rule that limitations on the Legislature's power "are to be construed strictly," has the court too narrowly construed the statutory language?

3. The city relied upon the determination of the Legislative Counsel, who is charged under statute to specify in a bill whether the measure would impose a state-mandated local program. Should greater deference be provided to this determination? If the Commission is the sole determiner of the mandate question, should the role of the Legislative Counsel be removed?

G. Legislature and Subpoena Power

The Legislature has subpoena power, although it rarely uses it. In most instances, in the rare need for someone to appear before a legislative investigating committee, these individuals will appear voluntarily. There have been occasions where it has been required to issue a subpoena to ensure witness appearance and cooperation before a legislative committee. The Rules Committee of either house will need to be consulted and will ultimately authorize issuance of a subpoena.

A branch of the Legislature has power to require and compel attendance of witnesses and the production of documents before it or its duly accredited committees. The State Senate has the power to punish a person for contempt, but such power can only be exercised in strict conformity with the rules of procedure which the laws provide. (*In re Battelle* (1929) 207 Cal. 227.)

Notes and Questions

1. The California Senate has the power to punish a person for contempt, but such power can only be exercised in strict conformity with the rules of procedure which the laws provide. Should the judicial branch play a role in holding an individual in contempt of the Legislature? Or should this enforcement be limited to the legislative branch?

H. Authority to Repeal Laws

The Legislature has the authority to repeal laws that it has previously enacted because, once the Legislature enacts a law, it has comparable power to repeal that same law. In other words, "what the Legislature giveth, the Legislature can taketh away."

California Redevelopment Association v. Matosantos

(2011) 53 Cal.4th 231

OPINION

WERDEGAR, J. —

Responding to a declared state fiscal emergency, in the summer of 2011 the Legislature enacted two measures intended to stabilize school funding by reducing or eliminating the diversion of property tax revenues from school districts to the state's community redevelopment agencies. (Assem. Bill Nos. 26 & 27 (2011–2012 1st Ex. Sess.) enacted as Stats. 2011, 1st Ex. Sess. 2011–2012, chs. 5–6 (hereafter Assembly Bill 1X 26 and Assembly Bill 1X 27); see also Assem. Bill 1X 26, § 1, subds. (d)–(i); Assem. Bill 1X 27, § 1, subds. (b), (c).) Assembly Bill 1X 26 bars redevelopment agencies from engaging in new business and provides for their windup and dissolution. Assembly Bill 1X 27 offers an alternative: redevelopment agencies can continue to operate if the cities and counties that created them agree to make payments into funds benefiting the state's schools and special districts.

The California Redevelopment Association, the League of California Cities, and other affected parties (collectively the Association) promptly sought extraordinary writ relief from this court, arguing that each measure was unconstitutional. They contended the measures violate, inter alia, Proposition 22, which amended the state Constitution to place limits on the state's ability to require payments from redevelopment agencies for the state's benefit. (See Cal. Const., art. XIII, § 25.5, subd. (a)(7), added by Prop. 22, as approved by voters, Gen. Elec. (Nov. 2, 2010).) The state's Director of Finance, respondent Ana Matosantos, opposed on the merits but agreed we should put to rest the significant constitutional questions concerning the validity of both measures. We issued an order to show cause, partially stayed the two measures, and established an expedited briefing schedule. We also granted leave to the County of Santa Clara and its auditor-controller, Vinod K. Sharma (collectively Santa Clara), to intervene as respondents.

We consider whether under the state Constitution (1) redevelopment agencies, once created and engaged in redevelopment plans, have a protected right to exist that immunizes them from statutory dissolution by the Legislature; and (2) redevelopment agencies and their sponsoring communities have a protected right not to make payments to various funds benefiting schools and special districts as a condition of continued operation. Answering the first question — no and the second yes, we largely uphold Assembly Bill 1X 26 and invalidate Assembly Bill 1X 27.

Assembly Bill 1X 26, the dissolution measure, is a proper exercise of the legislative power vested in the Legislature by the state Constitution. That power includes the authority to create entities, such as redevelopment agencies, to carry out the state's ends and the corollary power to dissolve those same entities when the Legislature deems it necessary and proper. Proposition 22, while it amended the state Constitution to impose new limits on the Legislature's fiscal powers, neither explicitly nor implicitly rescinded the Legislature's power to dissolve redevelopment agencies. Nor does article XVI, section 16 of the state Constitution, which authorizes the allocation of property tax revenues to redevelopment agencies, impair that power.

A different conclusion is required with respect to Assembly Bill 1X 27, the measure conditioning further redevelopment agency operations on additional payments by an agency's community sponsors to state funds benefiting schools and special districts. Proposition 22 (specifically Cal. Const., art. XIII, § 25.5, subd. (a)(7)) expressly forbids the Legislature from requiring such payments. Matosantos' argument that the payments are valid because technically voluntary cannot be reconciled with the fact that the payments are a requirement of continued operation. Because the flawed provisions of Assembly Bill 1X 27 are not severable from other parts of that measure, the measure is invalid in its entirety.

. . . .

D. Assembly Bills 1X 26 and IX 27

In December 2010, then Governor Schwarzenegger declared a state fiscal emergency. (See Cal. Const., art. IV, § 10, subd. (f)(1).) On January 20, 2011, incoming Governor Brown renewed the declaration and convened a special session of the Legislature to address the state's budget crisis. (Legis. Counsel's Digest, Assem. Bill 1X 26; see also *Professional Engineers in California Government v. Schwarzenegger* (2010) 50 Cal.4th 989, 1001–1002 [detailing the ongoing crisis].)

As a partial means of closing the state's projected $25 billion operating deficit, Governor Brown originally proposed eliminating redevelopment agencies entirely. (See Legis. Analyst 's Off., Governor's Redevelopment Proposal (Jan. 18, 2011) p. 4.) Parallel bills were introduced in the Senate and Assembly to eliminate redevelopment agencies (RDAs) and specif[y] a process for the orderly wind-down of RDA activities.... (Sen. Rules Com., Off. of Sen. Floor Analyses, analysis of Sen. Bill No. 77 (2011–2012 Reg. Sess.) as amended Mar. 15, 2011, p. 1; Sen. Rules Com., Off. of Sen. Floor Analyses, 3d reading analysis of Assem. Bill No. 101 (2011–2012 Reg. Sess.) as amended Mar. 15, 2011, p. 1.) Ultimately, however, the Legislature took a slightly different approach; in June 2011 it passed, and the Governor signed, the two measures we consider here.

Assembly Bills 1X 26 and IX 27 consist of three principal components, codified as new parts 1.8, 1.85 (both Assem. Bill 1X 26) and 1.9 (Assem. Bill 1X 27) of division 24 of the Health and Safety Code. Part 1.8 (§§ 34161 to 34169.5) is the freeze component: it subjects redevelopment agencies to restrictions on new bonds or other indebtedness; new plans or changes to existing plans; and new partnerships, including joint powers authorities (§§ 34162 to 34165). Cities and counties are barred from creating any new redevelopment agencies. (§ 34166.) Existing obligations are unaffected; redevelopment agencies may continue to make payments and perform existing obligations until other agencies take over. (§ 34169.) Part 1.8's purpose is to preserve redevelopment agency assets and revenues for use by local governments to fund core governmental services such as fire protection, police, and schools. (§ 34167, subd. (a).)

Part 1.85 (§§ 34170 to 34191) is the dissolution component. It dissolves all redevelopment agencies (§ 34172) and transfers control of redevelopment agency assets to successor agencies, which are contemplated to be the city or county that created the redevelopment agency (§§ 34171, subd. (j), 34173, 34175, subd. (b)). Part 1.85 requires successor agencies to continue to make payments and perform existing obligations. (§ 34177.) However, unencumbered balances of redevelopment agency funds must be remitted to the county auditor-controller for distribution to cities, the county, special districts, and school districts in proportion to what each agency would have received absent the redevelopment agencies. (See §§ 34177, subd. (d), 34183, subd. (a)(4), 34188.) Proceeds from redevelopment agency asset sales likewise must go to the county auditor-controller for similar distribution. (§ 34177, subd. (e).) Finally, tax increment revenues that would have gone to redevelopment agencies must be deposited in a local trust fund each county is required to create and administer. (§§ 34170.5, subd. (b), 34182, subd. (c)(1).) All amounts necessary to satisfy administrative costs, pass-through payments, and enforceable obligations will be allocated for those purposes, while any excess will be deemed property tax revenue and distributed in the same fashion as balances and assets. (§§ 34172, subd. (d), 34183, subd. (a).)

Part 1.9 (§§ 34192 to 34196), however, offers an exemption from dissolution for cities and counties that agree to make specified payments to both the county ERAF and a new county special district augmentation fund on behalf of their redevelopment agencies. Each city or county choosing this option must notify the state it will do so and pass an ordinance to that effect. (§§ 34193, subd. (b), 34193.1.) If it does, its redevelopment agency will be permitted to continue in operation without interruption, as is, under the Community Redevelopment Law. (§ 34193, subd. (a).) The amounts owed are to be calculated annually by the state's Director of Finance based on the fractional share of net and gross statewide tax increment each redevelopment agency has received in prior years, multiplied by $1.7 billion for this fiscal year and $400 million for all subsequent fiscal years. (§ 34194, subds. (b)(2), (c)(1)(A).)

Payments are due on January 15 and May 15 each year. (§ 34194, subd. (d)(1).) While remittances are nominally owed by cities and counties, the measure authorizes each community sponsor to contract with its redevelopment agency to receive tax increment in the amount owed, so that payments may effectively come from tax increment. (§ 34194.2.) Finally, any lapse in payments will result in a redevelopment agency's dissolution. (§ 34195.)

On August 17, 2011, we stayed parts 1.85 and 1.9, with minor exceptions, to prevent redevelopment agencies from being dissolved during the pendency of this matter. (Health & Saf. Code, div. 24, pts. 1.85, 1.9.)

II. DISCUSSION

....

B. *The Constitutionality of Assembly Bill 1X 26*

We turn now to the merits. In assessing the validity of Assembly Bills 1X 26 and 1X 27, we are mindful that "all intendments favor the exercise of the Legislature's plenary authority: 'If there is any doubt as to the Legislature's power to act in any given case, the doubt should be resolved in favor of the Legislature's action. Such restrictions and limitations [imposed by the Constitution] are to be construed strictly, and are not to be extended to include matters not covered by the language used.'" [Citations.] (*Methodist Hosp. of Sacramento v. Saylor* (1971) 5 Cal.3d 685, 691.)

1. *The Dissolution of Redevelopment Agencies Under Part 1.85 of Division 24 of the Health and Safety Code*

In enacting Assembly Bill 1X 26, the Legislature asserted that [r]edevelopment agencies were created by statute and can therefore be dissolved by statute. (Assem. Bill 1X 26, § 1, subd. (h).) We conclude the Legislature was correct.

At the core of the legislative power is the authority to make laws. (*Nougues v. Douglass* (1857) 7 Cal. 65, 70 [The legislative power is the creative element in the government.... [It] makes the laws....].) The state Constitution vests that power, except as exercised by or reserved to the people themselves, in the Legislature. (Cal. Const., art. IV, § 1; *McClung v. Employment Development Dept.* (2004) 34 Cal.4th 467, 472; *Nougues*, at p. 69 [[I]n all cases where not exercised and not reserved, all the legislative power of the people of the State is vested in the Legislature ... (italics omitted)].)

Of significance, the legislative power the state Constitution vests is plenary. Under it, the entire law-making authority of the state, except the people's right of initiative and referendum, is vested in the Legislature, and that body may exercise any and all legislative powers which are not expressly or by necessary implication denied to it by the Constitution. (*Methodist Hosp. of Sacramento v. Saylor, supra,* 5 Cal.3d at p. 691; see also *Marine Forests Society v. California Coastal Com.* (2005) 36 Cal.4th 1, 31; *People v. Tilton* (1869) 37 Cal. 614, 626 [under the state Const., [f]ull power exists when there is no limitation.].)

We thus start from the premise that the Legislature possesses the full extent of the legislative power and its enactments are authorized exercises of that power. Only where the state Constitution withdraws legislative power will we conclude an enactment is invalid for want of authority. "In other words, 'we do not look to the Constitution to determine whether the legislature is authorized to do an act, but only to see if it is prohibited.'" (*Methodist Hosp. of Sacramento v. Saylor, supra,* 5 Cal.3d at p. 691, quoting *Fitts v. Superior Court* (1936) 6 Cal.2d 230, 234; accord, *State Personnel Bd. v. Department of Personnel Admin.* (2005) 37 Cal.4th 512, 523; *County of Riverside v. Superior Court* (2003) 30 Cal.4th 278, 284.)

A corollary of the legislative power to make new laws is the power to abrogate existing ones. What the Legislature has enacted, it may repeal. (See *People v. Superior*

Court (*Romero*) (1996) 13 Cal.4th 497, 518 ["if a power is statutory, the Legislature may eliminate it"]; *Estate of Potter* (1922) 188 Cal. 55, 63 [rights that "are creatures of legislative will" may be withdrawn by the Legislature]; *County of Sacramento v. Lackner* (1979) 97 Cal.App.3d 576, 589 ["Every legislative body may modify or abolish the acts passed by itself or its predecessors."].)

In particular, if a political entity has been created by the Legislature, it can be dissolved by the Legislature, barring some specific constitutional obstacle to a particular exercise of the legislative power. In our federal system the states are sovereign but cities and counties are not; in California as elsewhere they are mere creatures of the state and exist only at the state's sufferance. (*Board of Supervisors v. Local Agency Formation Com.* (1992) 3 Cal.4th 903, 914; see also *City of El Monte v. Commission on State Mandates, supra*, 83 Cal.App.4th at p. 279 [Only the state is sovereign and, in a broad sense, all local governments, districts, and the like are subdivisions of the state.].) It follows from the fundamental nature of this relationship between a state and its political subdivisions that "states have extraordinarily wide latitude ... in creating various types of political subdivisions and conferring authority upon them. [Citation.]" (*Board of Supervisors*, at pp. 915–916.) As the United States Supreme Court has recognized in the context of municipal corporations: "The number, nature and duration of the powers conferred upon these corporations and the territory over which they shall be exercised rests in the absolute discretion of the State.... The State, therefore, at its pleasure may modify or withdraw all such powers, ... expand or contract the territorial area, unite the whole or a part of it with another municipality, [or] repeal the charter and destroy the corporation." (*Hunter v. Pittsburgh* (1907) 207 U.S. 161, 178–179, quoted with approval in *Board of Supervisors*, at p. 915.) The state (and, in particular, the Legislature) has plenary power to set the conditions under which its political subdivisions are created (*Board of Supervisors*, at p. 917); equally so, it has plenary power to set the conditions under which its political subdivisions are abolished (*Curtis v. Board of Supervisors* (1972) 7 Cal.3d 942, 951; *Petition East Fruitvale Sanitary Dist.* (1910) 158 Cal. 453, 457).

As Redevelopment agencies are political subdivisions of the state and creatures of the Legislature's exercise of its statutory power, the progeny of the Community Redevelopment Law. (See § 33000 et seq.; 11 Miller & Starr, Cal. Real Estate (3d ed. 2001) § 30B:2, p. 6 ["The redevelopment agency is solely a creature of state statute, exercising powers delegated to it by the state legislature in matters of state concern, and the scope of its authority is, therefore, defined and limited by the Community Redevelopment Law...."].) Consistent with that nature, the Legislature has in the past routinely narrowed and expanded redevelopment agencies' various rights. (E.g., Stats. 1976, ch. 1337, p. 6061 et seq. [imposing low income housing requirements]; Stats. 1993, ch. 942, p. 5334 et seq. [Community Redevelopment Law Reform Act of 1993, enacting wide-ranging reforms]; Stats. 2001, ch. 741 [amending redevelopment sunset provisions].) Most significantly, the Legislature has mandated that redevelopment plans receiving tax increment have finite durations. (§ 33333.2; *Community Redevelopment Agency v. County of Los Angeles* (2001) 89 Cal.App.4th 719, 722.)

The Association offers a twofold argument for why, notwithstanding the legislative authority over redevelopment agencies historically inherent in the state Constitution, the dissolution provisions of Assembly Bill 1X 26 are invalid. First, the Association posits that Assembly Bill 1X 26 is inconsistent with article XVI, section 16 of the state Constitution, governing tax increment revenue. Second, the well, we have recognized the power to dissolve with respect to school districts: [T]he local-district system of school administration, though recognized by the Association argues that Proposition 22 (as approved by voters, Gen. Elec. (Nov. 2, 2010)) amended the state Constitution to effectively withdraw from the Legislature the power to dissolve community redevelopment agencies for the financial benefit of the state.

What is now article XVI, section 16 was added by initiative in 1952, shortly after the Legislature enacted the Community Redevelopment Law. It made express the Legislature's authority to authorize property tax increment financing of redevelopment agencies and projects. However, nothing in its text creates an absolute right to an allocation of property taxes. (See Cal. Const., art. XVI, § 16 ["The Legislature *may* provide that any redevelopment plan *may* contain a provision" diverting tax increment to redevelopment agencies (italics added)].) Nor does anything in the text of the section mandate that redevelopment agencies, once created, must exist in perpetuity. On its face, the provision is not self-executing and conveys no rights; rather, it authorizes the Legislature to enact statutes, and local governments to adopt redevelopment plans, that are consistent with its scope.

What is apparent from the constitutional provision's text is confirmed by its history. The ballot materials provided to the voters gave no hint that the proposed amendment was intended to make redevelopment agencies or tax increment financing a permanent part of the government landscape. Rather, consistent with the text's use of the permissive may, the Legislative Counsel explained that the proposed amendment was intended simply to authorize but not require the Legislature to provide for tax increment financing for redevelopment. (Proposed Amendments to Constitution: Propositions and Proposed Laws, Gen. Elec. (Nov. 4, 1952) Legis. Counsel's analysis of Assem. Const. Amend. No. 55, p. 19.) The arguments in favor of the proposed amendment similarly emphasized its nonmandatory character: "This constitutional amendment . . . is in effect an enabling act to give the Legislature authority to enact legislation which will provide for the handling of the proceeds of taxes levied upon property in a redevelopment project. It is permissive in character and can become effective in practice only by acts of the Legislature and the local governing body, the City Council or Board of Supervisors. It will make possible the passage of laws providing that tax revenues derived from any increase in the assessed value of property within a redevelopment area because of new improvements, shall be placed in a fund to defray all or part of the cost of the redevelopment project that would otherwise have to be advanced from public funds." (*Id.*, argument in favor of Assem. Const. Amend. No. 55, p. 20.)

Against these indicia of intent, the Association emphasizes the final sentence of article XVI, section 16: "The Legislature *shall* enact those laws as may be necessary to enforce the provisions of this section." (Italics added.) The word shall, however, depending on the context in which it is used, is not necessarily mandatory. (*People v. Lara* (2010) 48 Cal.4th 216, 227; *Nunn v. State of California* (1984) 35 Cal.3d 616, 625; see Garner's Dict. of Legal Usage (3d ed. 2011) pp. 952–953.) Moreover, consistent with its character as an enabling act (Proposed Amendments to Constitution: Propositions and Proposed Laws, Gen. Elec. (Nov. 4, 1952) argument in favor of Assem. Const. Amend. No. 55, p. 20), the final sentence directs only passage of those laws as may be necessary. This portion of the text confirms the Legislature's authority to pass legislation it deems necessary to carry out the ends of redevelopment, but imposes no obligation to enact any particular law. It does not mandate that redevelopment agencies, or the allocation of tax increment to them, be made permanent.

The Association also looks to our decision in *Marek v. Napa Community Redevelopment Agency, supra,* 46 Cal.3d 1070. There, we determined that indebtedness, the term used to measure how much property tax increment should be allocated to a redevelopment agency (see Cal. Const., art. XVI, § 16, subd. (b); §§ 33670, 33675), should be interpreted broadly (*Marek,* at pp. 1081–1086). We cautioned that neither article XVI, section 16 nor the Community Redevelopment Law, as then written, contemplated that other tax entities [would] share in tax increment revenues at any time before the agency's total indebtedness has been paid or the amount in its special fund' is sufficient to pay its total indebtedness. (*Marek,* at p. 1087.) The Association contends Assembly Bill 1X 26 is invalid because it fails to continue allocating tax increment for existing indebtedness as broadly as in the past, most notably by allocating tax increment for only some, but not all, obligations owed by redevelopment agencies to their community sponsors. (See §§ 34171, subd. (d)(2), 34178, subd. (b).)

This argument misperceives both the role of article XVI, section 16 of the state Constitution and the nature of the issue we resolved in *Marek v. Napa Community Redevelopment Agency, supra,* 46 Cal.3d 1070. Article XVI, section 16 does not protect the receipt of tax increment funds up to the amount of a redevelopment agency's total indebtedness, nor does it grant a constitutional right to continue to receive tax increment for as long as redevelopment agencies have debt; rather, it authorizes the Legislature to statutorily grant redevelopment agencies rights to tax increment up to the amount of their total indebtedness. As the Legislature may extend that authorization (and did, in the Community Redevelopment Law), so it may limit or withdraw that authorization (as it has, in Assem. Bill 1X 26) without violating article XVI, section 16. In *Marek,* we addressed only the scope of the statutory term indebtedness and the corresponding scope of the constitutional authorization for redevelopment agencies to be granted statutory rights to tax increment; that issue has no bearing on the question we face here — whether article XVI, section 16 limits the Legislature's power to dissolve existing redevelopment agencies in the midst of ongoing projects. *Marek* thus is inapposite.

Finally, the Association draws our attention to the first two sentences of an uncodified section (§ 9) of Proposition 22, which, it contends, confirms that article XVI, section 16 is a guarantee of tax increment funding and a protection against dissolution. That section begins: "Section 16 of Article XVI of the Constitution requires that a specified portion of the taxes levied upon the taxable property in a redevelopment project each year be allocated to the redevelopment agency to repay indebtedness incurred for the purpose of eliminating blight within the redevelopment project area. Section 16 of Article XVI prohibits the Legislature from reallocating some or that entire specified portion of the taxes to the State, an agency of the State, or any other taxing jurisdiction, instead of to the redevelopment agency." (Prop. 22, Gen. Elec. (Nov. 2, 2010) § 9.) Whether or not article XVI, section 16 originally required tax increment allocations to be made to redevelopment agencies, rather than simply authorizing the Legislature to pass legislation approving such allocations, the Association contends that after this voter-approved statement, article XVI, section 16 must now be read to so provide.

We reject this contention. The assertion in Proposition 22, section 9 that tax increment allocations to redevelopment agencies are constitutionally mandated, rather than constitutionally authorized and statutorily mandated, is a clear misstatement of the law as it stood prior to the passage of Proposition 22. Moreover, section 9 of Proposition 22 does not purport to amend article XVI, section 16 or to change existing law concerning the *source* of redevelopment agencies' entitlement, if any, to tax increment. Accordingly, we decline to treat its immaterial misstatement of law as a basis for silently amending the state Constitution.

The purpose of section 9, instead, is simply to explain that the Legislature had been requiring the transfer of redevelopment agency tax increment, and that Proposition 22 was intended to eliminate future transfers: The Legislature has been illegally circumventing Section 16 of Article XVI in recent years by requiring redevelopment agencies to transfer a portion of those taxes for purposes other than the financing of redevelopment projects. A purpose of the amendments made by this measure is to prohibit the Legislature from requiring, after the taxes have been allocated to a redevelopment agency, the redevelopment agency to transfer some or all of those taxes to the State, an agency of the State, or a jurisdiction; or to use some or all of those taxes for the benefit of the State, an agency of the State, or a jurisdiction. (Prop. 22, Gen. Elec. (Nov. 2, 2010) § 9.)

The various ways in which the Association contends Assembly Bill 1X 26 is inconsistent with article XVI, section 16 of the state Constitution all flow from the assumption that section 16 establishes for redevelopment agencies an absolute right to continued existence. Because we can find no such right in the constitutional provision, article XVI, section 16 does not invalidate Assembly Bill 1X 26.

The Association 's alternate constitutional argument rests on article XIII, section 25.5, subdivision (a)(7) of the state Constitution, added in 2010 by Proposition 22. Examining both the text and the various ballot arguments in support of and against that initiative, we find nothing in them that would limit the Legislature's plenary authority over the existence *vel non* of redevelopment agencies.

Article XIII, section 25.5, subdivision (a)(7)(A) of the state Constitution generally prohibits the Legislature from requiring a redevelopment agency to pay property taxes allocated to the agency pursuant to Section 16 of Article XVI to or for the benefit of the State or its agencies and jurisdictions,14 or otherwise restricting or assigning such taxes for the state's benefit. The provision, the Association reasons, both presumes and protects the existence of redevelopment agencies. Dissolving redevelopment agencies would entail an impermissible diversion of their tax increment to third parties, in contravention of section 25.5, subdivision (a)(7)(A). Moreover, if the state cannot assign tax increment to third parties, that increment must go to redevelopment agencies; hence, redevelopment agencies must be entitled to exist to receive it.

This argument suffers from a surface implausibility. The constitutionalization of a political subdivision the alteration of a local government entity from a statutory creation existing only at the pleasure of the sovereign state to a constitutional creation with life and powers of independent origin and standing would represent a profound change in the structure of state government. Municipal corporations, though of far more ancient standing than redevelopment agencies, have never achieved such status. (See Cal. Const., art. XI, § 2, subd. (a) [specifying the Legislature's authority over city formation and powers].) Proposition 22 contains no express language constitutionalizing redevelopment agencies. (Cf. Cal. Const., art. XXXV, § 1, added by initiative, Gen. Elec. (Nov. 2, 2004) [creating the Cal. Institute for Regenerative Medicine as a constitutional entity]; *id.*, art. XXI, § 2, added by initiative, Gen. Elec. (Nov. 4, 2008) [creating the Citizens Redistricting Com. as a constitutional entity].) It would be unusual in the extreme for the people, exercising legislative power by way of initiative, to adopt such a fundamental change only by way of implication, in an initiative facially dealing with purely fiscal matters, in a corner of the state Constitution addressing taxation. As the United States Supreme Court has put it, the drafters of legislation do not, one might say, hide elephants in mouseholes. (*Whitman v. American Trucking Assns., Inc.* (2001) 531 U.S. 457, 468.)

The principle of *inclusio unius est exclusio alterius* applies here. Proposition 22 expressly adds numerous limits to the Legislature's statutory powers (Prop. 22, Gen. Elec. (Nov. 2, 2010) §§ 3–5, 5.3, 6–6.1, 7), and in one instance withdraws from the Legislature a preexisting constitutional power (*id.*, § 5.6 [repealing Cal. Const., art. XIX, former § 6]), but makes no mention of any intent to divest the Legislature of the power to dissolve redevelopment agencies. If the initiative proponents and voters had intended to strip the Legislature of that power or to alter the Legislature's article XVI, section 16 permissive authority, it stands to reason they would have said so expressly.

Had the voters in fact intended to amend the Constitution to fundamentally alter the relationship between the state and this class of political subdivision, we would, moreover, expect to find at least a single mention of such an intention in the various supporting and opposing ballot arguments. Instead, we find silence. The Legislative Analyst's review of the initiative identifies no such anticipated effect. (Voter Information Guide, Gen. Elec. (Nov. 2, 2010) pp. 30–35.) Indeed, the ballot argument in favor of Proposition 22 and the rebuttal to the argument against it do not even mention redevelopment. (Voter Information Guide, at pp. 36–37.) Only the opposing arguments highlight redevelopment and then only to criticize the initiative for how it secretly channels tax dollars to redevelopment agencies. (*Ibid.*)

The Association suggests it is not asserting an absolute right to perpetual existence, only a right for some form of agency to exist to receive redevelopment funds for as long as there is an active redevelopment plan and indebtedness. This framing does not change the analysis or conclusions. It would mean the Legislature's power to dissolve vanished as soon as a redevelopment agency was created; thereafter, an agency or its similarly tasked successor effectively could expire only of natural causes, after every project it might undertake in its jurisdiction had been completed and paid off. No hint of such a right is disclosed in the text or history of either article XVI, section 16 or article XIII, section 25.5, subdivision (a)(7) of the state Constitution.

Contrary to the Association's contention, declining to imply into article XIII, section 25.5, subdivision (a)(7) a constitutional guarantee of continued existence for redevelopment agencies does not render the subdivision a nullity. Though the Legislature retains the broad power to dissolve redevelopment agencies, Proposition 22 strips it of the narrower power to insist on transfers to third parties of property tax revenue already allocated to redevelopment agencies, as it had done on numerous previous occasions. (See §§ 33680, 33681.7 to 33681.15, 33685 to 33692; former § 33681 (Stats. 1992, ch. 700, § 1.5, pp. 3115–3116); former § 33681.5 (Stats. 1993, ch. 68, § 4, pp. 942–944).) It is precisely such raids the text of Proposition 22 and the arguments in support of it denounce. (Voter Information Guide, Gen. Elec. (Nov. 2, 2010) p. 36; see Prop. 22, Gen. Elec. (Nov. 2, 2010) §§ 2, subds. (e), (g), 2.5, 9.) The protection so granted is not insignificant simply because it is conditioned on redevelopment agencies' existing and having property tax increment allocated to them.

Accordingly, we discern no constitutional impediment to the Legislature's electing to dissolve the state's redevelopment agencies under part 1.85 of division 24 of the Health and Safety Code.

....

C. The Constitutionality of Assembly Bill 1X 27

We turn to Assembly Bill 1X 27. The measure conditions the future operation of redevelopment agencies on continuation payments. (§§ 34193, subd. (a), 34193.2, subd. (a).) Analyzing its operation in light of the constitutional limitations adopted by Proposition 22, we conclude the condition the measure imposes is unconstitutional and Assembly Bill 1X 27 is, accordingly, facially invalid.

The Legislature may not "[r]equire a community redevelopment agency (A) to pay, remit, loan, or otherwise transfer, directly or indirectly, taxes on ad valorem real property and tangible personal property allocated to the agency pursuant to Section 16 of Article XVI to or for the benefit of the State, any agency of the State, or any jurisdiction...." (Cal. Const., art. XIII, § 25.5, subd. (a)(7), added by Prop. 22, Gen.

Elec. (Nov. 2, 2010).) That the continuation payments called for by Assembly Bill 1X 27 will benefit the state and its jurisdictions, i.e., special districts and school districts, is uncontested; for fiscal year 2011–2012, they replace funding the state otherwise would have to supply under Proposition 98 (see § 34194.1, subd. (b)), and in this and future years they go to funds supporting school districts and special districts (§§ 34194, subd. (a), 34194.1, subd. (e), 34194.4).

. . . .

Assembly Bill 1X 27 … [l]ike all prior ERAF legislation, it operates as a levy on the receipt of tax increment funds. That is, for each dollar a redevelopment agency receives, a set percentage must be paid back into ERAF's [sic]. (See § 34194 [calculating continuation payment as a fraction of the net and gross tax increment each redevelopment agency receives].) In 2011–2012, the levy rate is roughly 34 percent ($1.7 billion out of $5 billion in tax increment); in future years, it is substantially lower ($400 million out of $5 billion equates to 8 percent).

That Assembly Bill 1X 27 allows payment to come either from community sponsors (§ 34194.1, subd. (a)), or from redevelopment agencies pursuant to reimbursement agreements (§ 34194.2), does not distinguish it from past ERAF legislation. Nor does the leeway Assembly Bill 1X 27 grants redevelopment agencies and community sponsors to decide the source from which to make payments diminish the payments' character as a levy on tax increment funds. Reasoning by analogy, income tax is income tax, even if a taxpayer may pay the government out of nonincome assets rather than directly return a portion of his or her income; so too, section 34194 is a levy on the receipt of tax increment for the benefit of the state's subdivisions, whether the levy is paid directly out of the tax increment the redevelopment agency receives, or indirectly out of other assets it or its community sponsor may possess. The source of payment is a distinction without a difference in light of the Legislature's historic indifference to ERAF payment sources and Proposition 22's broad prohibition on even direct or indirect transfers.

As construed by the dissent, however, Proposition 22 would prohibit only funding schemes the Legislature has not employed for nearly a decade, while permitting the very schemes its adoption history plainly demonstrates the initiative was intended to prohibit. The dissent identifies as the saving grace of Assembly Bill 1X 27 the provision allowing community sponsors to make continuation payments. (Conc. & dis. opn., *post*, at p. 15; see § 34194.1.) But every ERAF scheme since 2003 has included that feature. (*Ante*, at p. 37). Consequently, every such ERAF scheme would, under the dissent's construction, remain valid in its entirety even after Proposition 22, and the Legislature could simply have reenacted without change 2009's scheme. Such an interpretation cannot be squared with the available evidence of the drafters' and voters' intent, which was to prohibit these modern raids. (See Voter Information Guide, Gen. Elec. (Nov. 2, 2010) Legis. Analyst's analysis of Prop. 22 by Legis. Analyst, pp. 33–34 [singling out recent ERAF shifts as the sort of raid on tax increment Prop. 22 was intended to foreclose]; Prop. 22, §§ 2, subd. (d)(3), 2.5, 9 [same].)

The dissent justifies this rejection of expressed intent by relying on the grammar and syntax of Proposition 22. (Conc. & dis. opn., *post,* at pp. 15–16.) However, "[t]he rules of grammar and canons of construction are but tools, 'guides to help courts determine likely legislative intent. [Citations.] And that intent is critical. Those who write statutes seek to solve human problems. Fidelity to their aims requires us to approach an interpretive problem not as if it were a purely logical game, like a Rubik's Cube, but as an effort to divine the human intent that underlies the statute.'" (*Burris v. Superior Court* (2005) 34 Cal.4th 1012, 1017–1018.) Grammar and syntax thus are a means of gleaning intent, not a basis for preventing its effectuation. Where, as here, ballot materials clearly demonstrate the drafters' and voters' intent, syntax is not dispositive.

Moreover, nothing in the grammar of article XIII, section 25.5, subdivision (a)(7) of the state Constitution precludes giving the provision its intended effect. A required indirect transfer of tax increment by a redevelopment agency may include circumstances where the redevelopment agency, governed by the same people as its community sponsor (see *ante,* p. 9 & fn. 5), must persuade that sponsor to pay, with or with out reimbursement, a specified percentage of the tax increment the agency receives as the price for that receipt.

In her briefing, Matosantos does not focus on whether Assembly Bill 1X 27 involves direct or indirect payments of tax increment funds, but instead on the argument that Assembly Bill 1X 27 does not [r]equire payment within the meaning of article XIII, section 25.5, subdivision (a)(7). She acknowledges that Proposition 22 forbids the Legislature from directly requiring payment to special districts and school districts on the state's behalf. She contends, however, that the payments provided for under Assembly Bill 1X 27 are not required but are voluntary and constitutional, because the measure affords local governments an option between payment and dissolution.

This is indeed the way in which Assembly Bill 1X 27 is most distinct from the past ERAF legislation Proposition 22 specifically targeted. Effectively, however, the difference is only a change in the sanction for nonpayment. Before, nonpayment resulted in a range of limitations on a redevelopment agency's operations (see, e.g., §§ 33686, subd. (e), 33691, subd. (e)); now, it will result in dissolution (§ 34195).

This is another distinction without a difference. Assembly Bill 1X 27 on its face imposes not an optional condition but an absolute requirement: going forward, *every* redevelopment agency must have its community sponsor annually pay the portion of its tax increment assessed by the state under Assembly Bill 1X 27. Cities and counties operating redevelopment agencies, whether agencies that existed before Assembly Bill 1X 27 or agencies they establish for the first time to address new blight, must pay without exception in this and every future year. (See §§ 34194, 34195.) A condition that must be satisfied in order for any redevelopment agency to operate is not an option but a requirement. Such absolute requirements Proposition 22 forbids. (See Cal. Const., art. XIII, § 25.5, subd. (a)(7)(A).)

The Association argues that this conclusion is sufficient to invalidate not only Assembly Bill 1X 27, but also the dissolution provisions of Assembly Bill 1X 26. Not necessarily. How broadly the taint of the invalid exercise of legislative power extends is a question of severability. (See, e.g., *Sonoma County Organization of Public Employees v. County of Sonoma* (1979) 23 Cal.3d 296, 319–320 [preserving the state's bailout of local governments notwithstanding an unconstitutional condition placed on that bailout because the one could be severed from the other].) Accordingly, we turn to an analysis of severability and the impact of the invalid continuation payment program (Assem. Bill 1X 27, § 2; Health & Saf. Code, div. 24, pt. 1.9) on the remaining provisions of Assembly Bill 1X 27 and on Assembly Bill 1X 26.

D. *Severability*

We conclude Assembly Bill 1X 27 is invalid in its entirety, while Assembly Bill 1X 26 may be severed and enforced independently.

In determining whether the invalid portions of a statute can be severed, we look first to any severability clause. The presence of such a clause establishes a presumption in favor of severance. (*Santa Barbara Sch. Dist. v. Superior Court* (1975) 13 Cal.3d 315, 331 ["Although not conclusive, a severability clause normally calls for sustaining the valid part of the enactment...."].) We will, however, consider three additional criteria: "[T]he invalid provision must be grammatically, functionally, and volitionally separable." (*Calfarm Ins. Co. v. Deukmejian* (1989) 48 Cal.3d 805, 821.) Grammatical separability, also known as mechanical separability, depends on whether the invalid parts "can be removed as a whole without affecting the wording" or coherence of what remains. (*Id.* at p. 822; see also *Santa Barbara*, at pp. 330–331.) Functional separability depends on whether "the remainder of the statute 'is complete in itself....'" (*Sonoma County Organization of Public Employees v. County of Sonoma, supra*, 23 Cal.3d at p. 320.) Volitional separability depends on whether the remainder "'would have been adopted by the legislative body had the latter foreseen the partial invalidation of the statute.'" (*Santa Barbara*, at p. 331; accord, *Gerken v. Fair Political Practices Com.* (1993) 6 Cal.4th 707, 714.)

With respect to the portions of Assembly Bill 1X 27 apart from the section 2 continuation payment program, the Legislature in section 5 included a nonseverability clause: "If Section 2 of this act, or the application thereof, is held invalid in a court of competent jurisdiction, the remaining provisions of this act are not severable and shall not be given, or otherwise have, any force or effect." (Assem. Bill 1X 27, § 5.) Such a clause conclusively negates the possibility of volitional separability: The Legislature would not have enacted the rest of Assembly Bill 1X 27 without the invalid section 2. Accordingly, the remaining provisions of Assembly Bill 1X 27 cannot be severed and are unenforceable as well.

In direct contrast, the Legislature in section 4 of Assembly Bill 1X 27 expressed in a severability clause its intent to preserve Assembly Bill 1X 26: "The provisions of Section 2 of this act [Assem. Bill 1X 27] are distinct and severable from the provisions of Part 1.8 (commencing with [Section] 34161) and Part 1.85 (commencing with Section 34170) of Division 24 of the Health and Safety Code [enacted by Assem. Bill 1X 26] and those provisions shall continue in effect if any of the provisions of this act are held invalid." (Assem. Bill 1X 27, § 4.) Grammatically and mechanically, Assembly Bill 1X 26 can be separated from Assembly Bill 1X 27: it was passed as a distinct measure and is codified in a different portion of the Health and Safety Code. Functionally as well, it is separate: the freeze (pt. 1.8) and dissolution (pt. 1.85) procedures can be implemented whether or not the continuation payment program (pt. 1.9) is valid. (Indeed, invalidating pt. 1.9 alone would produce a result no different than if each redevelopment agency and sponsoring local government entity had elected not to make payments and had instead chosen to dissolve.)

The Association concedes grammatical separability but contends Assembly Bills 1X 26 and 1X 27 are neither functionally nor volitionally separable. As to functional separability, the Association posits that the Legislature likely expected Assembly Bill 1X 27 to be upheld and Assembly Bill 1X 26 thus to come into play only for those redevelopment agencies that elected to dissolve. Speculation as to what the Legislature may have expected is immaterial here; the issue under this prong is simply whether Assembly Bill 1X 26 is complete in itself such that it can be enforced notwithstanding Assembly Bill 1X 27's invalidity. Assembly Bill 1X 26 outlines an independent mechanism for redevelopment agency dissolution that does not depend in any way on Assembly Bill 1X 27.

Alternatively, the Association identifies a small handful of provisions in Assembly Bill 1X 26 that are meaningful only if Assembly Bill 1X 27 is valid. (See §§ 34172, subd. (a)(2) [permitting communities to create new redevelopment agencies provided they make Assem. Bill 1X 27 continuation payments], 34178.7, 34188.8, 34191, subd. (a) [governing redevelopment agencies that fail to keep up with continuation payments].) The provision allowing communities to establish new redevelopment agencies subject to continuation payments under Assembly Bill 1X 27 is invalid for precisely the same reasons applicable generally to Assembly Bill 1X 27. Its invalidity does not, however, affect the rest of Assembly Bill 1X 26, as the provision is grammatically, functionally, and volitionally separable from the rest of Assembly Bill 1X 26. (See Assem. Bill 1X 26, § 12 [providing for internal severability for Assem. Bill 1X 26].) Those provisions applicable only to redevelopment agencies that start but then cease continuation payments are not invalid, but are simply irrelevant; in light of Assembly Bill 1X 27's invalidity, no redevelopment agency will ever become subject to them. Neither set of provisions impairs Assembly Bill 1X 26's functional separability.

As for volitional separability, the Association points to evidence that the Legislature rejected Governor Brown's proposal simply to end redevelopment agencies in favor of the two-bill package it ultimately passed. The Association further quotes statements from various individual legislators during the June 15, 2011, floor debates suggesting they (1) viewed Assembly Bills 1X 26 and 1X 27 as a package deal (remarks of Sen. Steinberg; remarks of Assemblyman Blumenfield) and (2) preferred to mend redevelopment rather than end it (remarks of Sen. Hancock).

We may accept that the Legislature treated Assembly Bills 1X 26 and 1X 27 as a package, and accept as self-evident that the Legislature preferred dissolution with an option to buy a reprieve over dissolution without any such option; after all, it passed

Assembly Bill 1X 27 in addition to Assembly Bill 1X 26, when it could have opted for some variation of Governor Brown's outright dissolution proposal. We need not further consider what weight, if any, to accord the statements of individual legislators because this evidence goes to answering the wrong question. The issue, when assessing volitional separability, is not whether a legislative body would have preferred the whole to the part; surely it would have, and the legislative history the Association points to tells us no more than that. Instead, the issue is whether a legislative body, knowing that only part of its enactment would be valid, would have preferred that part to nothing, or would instead have declined to enact the valid without the invalid. (See, e.g., *Gerken v. Fair Political Practices Com.*, *supra*, 6 Cal.4th at p. 719; *Calfarm Ins. Co. v. Deukmejian*, *supra*, 48 Cal.3d at p. 822; *Sonoma County Organization of Public Employees v. County of Sonoma*, *supra*, 23 Cal.3d at p. 320.)

As to that question, the interstatutory severability clause the Legislature enacted is conclusive. (See Assem. Bill 1X 27, § 4.) It is no generic severability clause, providing nonspecifically that if any provision of a measure is invalidated the remaining portions of an act should remain in force. (Cf. § 34168, subd. (b).) Rather, it deals with the precise severability question we face: whether, if section 2 of Assembly Bill 1X 27 were to be invalidated, the Legislature would have wanted the provisions of Assembly Bill 1X 26 to remain in force. The interstatutory severability clause answers that question unequivocally in the affirmative: Assembly Bill 1X 27, section 2 is severable from Assembly Bill 1X 26, and the Legislature intended the freeze and dissolution provisions to continue in effect notwithstanding the invalidation of the continuation payment program. (Assem. Bill 1X 27, § 4; see also Assem. Budget Com., Conc. in Sen. Amend., analysis of Assem. Bill 1X 27 (2011–2012 1st Ex. Sess.) as amended June 14, 2011, p. 4 [highlighting that while most provisions of Assem. Bill 1X 27 were not severable, the bill *was* severable from [Assem. Bill 1X 26], which eliminates redevelopment. Thus, if provisions of this bill are found invalid, the provisions of the first bill could remain in effect.]; Sen. Rules Com., Off. of Sen. Floor Analyses, 3d reading analysis of Assem. Bill 1X 27 (2011–2012 1st Ex. Sess.) as amended June 15, 2011, p. 6 [same].) Accordingly, whatever individual legislators may have said at one point or another, what the Legislature actually *did* establishes it would have passed Assembly Bill 1X 26 irrespective of the passage of Assembly Bill 1X 27, and that Assembly Bill 1X 26 is volitionally separable. Consequently, it is severable.

We summarize our conclusions concerning the constitutional landscape. The Legislature, pursuant to its plenary power to establish or dissolve local agencies and subdivisions as it sees fit, may, but need not, authorize redevelopment agencies. (Cal. Const., art. IV, § 1.) If it does choose to authorize such agencies, it may, but need not, authorize their receipt of property tax increment. (*Id.*, art. XVI, § 16.) However, if it authorizes such agencies and, moreover, authorizes their receipt of tax increment, it may not thereafter require that such allocated tax increment be remitted for the benefit of schools or other local agencies. (*Id.*, art. XIII, § 25.5, subd. (a)(7)(A).) Assembly Bill 1X 26 respects these narrow limits on the Legislature's power; Assembly Bill 1X 27 does not.

. . . .

III. DISPOSITION

For the foregoing reasons, we discharge the order to show cause, deny the Association's petition for a peremptory writ of mandate with respect to Assembly Bill 1X 26, except for Health and Safety Code section 34172, subdivision (a)(2), and grant its petition with respect to Assembly Bill 1X 27. We direct issuance of a peremptory writ compelling the state Director of Finance and state Controller not to implement Health and Safety Code sections 34172, subdivision (a)(2) and 34192–34196. We extend all statutory deadlines contained in Health and Safety Code, division 24, part 1.85 (§§ 34170–34191) and arising before May 1, 2012, by four months. Given the urgency of the matters addressed by the Association's petition, our judgment is final forthwith. (See, e.g., *Senate of the State of Cal. v. Jones* (1999) 21 Cal.4th 1142, 1169.)

KENNARD, J., BAXTER, J., CHIN, J., CORRIGAN, J., and LIU, J., concurred.

Notes and Questions

1. A corollary of the legislative power to make new laws is the power to abrogate existing ones. In other words, what the Legislature has enacted, it may repeal. At the core of the legislative power is the authority to make laws. The legislative power that the state Constitution vests is plenary.

2. Under the legislative power of the state Constitution, the entire lawmaking authority of the state, except the people's right of initiative and referendum, is vested in the Legislature, and that body may exercise any and all legislative powers which are not expressly or by necessary implication denied to it by the Constitution. Only where the state Constitution withdraws legislative power will the state Supreme Court conclude an enactment is invalid for want of authority.

3. The Court here ruled that Assembly Bill 1X 26, the dissolution measure, was a proper exercise of the legislative power vested in the Legislature by the state Constitution. That power includes the authority to create entities, such as redevelopment agencies, to carry out the state's ends and the corollary power to eliminate these agencies. The Court agreed with the Legislature's position that, because the agencies were created by statute, they can therefore be dissolved by statute.

4. Does this mean that a specific constitutional obstacle to a particular exercise of the legislative power is the only limitation on the Legislature's authority?

5. What was the Court's finding that provisions of the bill were grammatically separable? How did the Court interpret the statute as functionally separable? What was the Court's basis for ruling that the bill's provisions were volitionally separable?

6. Regarding the Court's reformation of the statute, in particular its effective dates and deadlines in state law, was this a proper exercise of a court's power of reformation? Was the Court's four-month extension appropriate?

I. Seat of Government

The seat of a government is generally defined as the building or buildings where a government exercises its duties and responsibilities as set forth in a constitution or charter. In most jurisdictions, the capital of the city, state or country is its seat of government.

California's Government Code, in Title 1 (General), Division 3 (Seat of Government, Political Divisions, and Legal Distances), Chapter 1 (Seat of Government), which was enacted in 1943, sets forth the seat of state government. Chapter 1 contains Section 450 of the Government Code, which specifies that the "permanent seat of government of the state is at the City of Sacramento."

Section 450 does authorize the Governor to designate, by a written proclamation, an alternative, temporary seat of state government. This alternative seat is only in the event of war or an enemy-caused disaster, or the imminent threat of such an event or disaster. The Governor's written proclamation must be filed with the Secretary of State.

A different, temporary seat of state government may be designated "at any time as circumstances indicate the desirability of such a change." In such an instance, the Director of General Services, and any other state agency as directed, would be required to provide facilities of any kind at the temporary seat of government as appear desirable for the functioning of state government.

Notes and Questions

1. Does the seat of government provision require the Legislature to always meet in Sacramento at the State Capitol? Does that perspective change during the time of a pandemic?

J. Legislative Operations during Emergencies

As a result of the COVID-19 outbreak, numerous state legislatures around the country have acted upon or are considering measures to deal with legislative operations, such as recesses and bill deadlines. And, as in other states, California's Legislature is examining whether it can conduct its official business remotely. California, like many other states, provides for legislative operations during emergencies, and the state Constitution speaks to such circumstances.

Recess

At least half of the state legislatures have temporarily adjourned or recessed their legislative sessions so far. California is one of the states that has a constitutional provision that requires the consent of both houses of the state Legislature to recess. Article IV, Section 7(d) of the state Constitution provides, "neither house without the consent of the other may recess for more than 10 days or to any other place." This is done by a resolution, which occurred on March 16, and so the Legislature was in recess until April 13.

Special Sessions

In 36 states, the governor and the legislature have the ability to convene a special session. In the remaining 14 states, however, only the governor has that authority. In California, a "special" session is one convened pursuant to a proclamation issued by the Governor. Pursuant to Article IV, Section 3(b) of the state Constitution, "on extraordinary occasions the Governor by proclamation may cause the Legislature to assemble in special session. When so assembled it has power to legislate only on subjects specified in the proclamation but may provide for expenses and other matters incidental to the session."

While the Legislature must convene the special session once it has been called by the Governor, there is no legal requirement that any legislation be enacted, nor even be voted upon. Aside from the fact that a special session is limited to the subject matter for which it was called, there are no significant differences in legislative process between a regular and special session.

However, the effective dates for bills enacted during a special session are somewhat different than those for a regular session. Regular session bills, except urgency clause bills that take effect when the Governor signs them, generally take effect on the following January 1. On the other hand, special session bills take effect on the 91st day after adjournment of the special session.

Both regular sessions of the Legislature and any special sessions not previously adjourned are adjourned *sine die* at midnight on November 30 of each even-numbered year. As such, neither a regular nor a special session will continue indefinitely.

Remote Voting

At least eight states are reviewing electronic or remote meetings and voting during this pandemic. However, many state constitutions require legislatures to meet in person. As a result, the legislatures in many of these states may be precluded from passing a resolution or adopting a statute to allow remote meetings or voting by state legislators.

As the National Conference of State Legislatures explains,

> In normal circumstances, legislatures typically operate under a "you must be present" rule — that is, legislators must be physically present in committee or on the chamber floor to participate in debate or voting. The rationale for this rule centers on the integrity of the legislative process. Requiring members' physical presence creates a comfort level that procedures can more easily be controlled and the public can witness debate and voting. State legislatures, however, more often allow the use of technology to facilitate public input into committee meetings.

Continuity of Legislature During Emergency, National Conference of State Legislatures, Nov. 27, 2020, https://www.ncsl.org/research/about-state-legislatures/continuity-of-legislature-during-emergency.aspx.

In two states — Oregon and Wisconsin — specific provisions allow remote or virtual meetings of the legislature if emergencies exist. In 2012, Oregon voters approved a constitutional amendment relating to catastrophic disaster. Wisconsin's constitutional provision on continuity of civil government allows the legislature to "adopt such other measures that may be necessary and proper for attaining the objectives of this section." In both instances, the state legislatures are relying upon grants of authority under their respective constitutions.

In California, we have to look at our state Constitution, Article IV, Section 7. Prior to the adoption by the voters in 2016 of Prop. 54, Section 7(c) already provided: "The proceedings of each house and the committees thereof shall be open and public." As a result of the passage of Prop. 54, this constitutional provision was strengthened by language that begins, "The right to attend open and public proceedings...." There are exceptions in the state Constitution, but those are for the traditional closed sessions to consider employment or security matters or to confer with legal counsel.

There are also provisions of the California Government Code that provide that the "seat of state government" is in the City of Sacramento. While the Governor by proclamation can designate a different seat of government, that is only allowed during war or an enemy-created disaster pursuant to Government Code Section 450.

In a similar vein, the Joint Rules (see JR 60(a)) prohibit bill actions from occurring outside the State Capitol. This is why only "informational hearings" can be conducted around the state by legislative committees, but no bills can be considered or voted upon. This begs the question whether the Legislature can conduct any remote voting or any other official business outside the State Capitol.

Nonetheless, California's State Senate adopted SR 86 on March 16, 2020, which added Rule 56 to the Senate Rules, and is entitled, "remote participation in meetings during emergencies." It would allow committees to conduct remote meetings by electronic means and allow senators to participate remotely in those proceedings. The State Assembly has not adopted any such rule, and the Joint Rules have not been amended.

Notes and Questions

1. If the Legislature decides to proceed with remote hearings and voting, how will members of the public participate? Ultimately, the practical question would be whether someone or some group would sue to overturn a statute that was passed utilizing remote voting. And, if so, would a state court overturn such a statute under these circumstances?

K. California Senate Allows Remoting Voting

The California State Senate, pursuant to a rule that it adopted on March 16, 2020 (SR 86), allows remote voting in its house. Senate President pro Tempore Toni Atkins announced the use of remote voting under certain circumstances. She explained that the Senate was authorizing the use of remote voting to protect the health of those involved in the legislative process and to be "consistent with our Constitution." Senator Atkins stated that the Senate had consulted with legal experts and open government groups before implementing this new procedure.

The Senate is limiting the use of remote voting to their policy and fiscal committees, but it is not authorized for use on the Senate Floor. Senators who request to vote remotely will have to obtain approval for their accommodation request "due to COVID-19" and will have to participate in the committee hearing from their district office. In addition, the committee chair and a majority of Members will have to be physically present in the Capitol for the committee hearing to take place.

The basis for this new procedure is SR 86 (Atkins) that was introduced and adopted by the Senate on March 16, the day that the Legislature began an extended recess in the spring. SR 86 added Rule 56 to the Standing Rules of the Senate, which is titled "Remote Participation in Meetings During Emergencies."

Rule 56 only applies during "emergencies," which is a state of emergency proclaimed pursuant to the Government Code, or even an imminent threat of a state emergency or local emergency. It allows the Senate Leader to assign, remove or replace any Member on a standing committee of the Senate as well as establish a special committee that is deemed necessary.

During such an emergency, the Senate Leader may authorize meetings to be held and for Members of the committee to participate remotely by telephone, teleconference, or other electronic means. In addition, the public may also participate remotely in the committee hearing by any means that the Senate committee would make available.

Pursuant to Rule 56, a Senator who participates remotely is to be considered present and in attendance at the committee meeting, including for purposes of determining if a quorum is present. With a quorum present, either in person or remotely as verified by the chair of the committee, a vote of a majority of the members of a committee will still be required to report a bill, constitutional amendment, or resolution out of the committee.

Rule 56 also authorizes the entire Senate to conduct meetings at which one or more Members will participate in the meeting remotely. Under the current procedure, that would not occur, but may be considered in the remainder of the 2020 Legislative Session.

Finally, Senator Atkins released the following requirements for permitting a Senator who needs a COVID-19 related accommodation to participate and vote during Senate committee hearings from his or her District Office, effective July 29, 2020:

- The Senator must submit a request for accommodation to the Secretary of the Senate and obtain approval from the Secretary prior to participating or voting outside the Capitol.

- The request for accommodation must be specific as to the day or days for which the accommodation is requested, and must be resubmitted at least weekly.

- Senators who are approved to participate and vote remotely must be present in their District Office for any committee hearings for which they are approved to participate and vote remotely. The District Office background must be visible without video alteration.

- While participating and voting remotely, the Senator may have only one person present with him or her, and that person must be a Senate staff person, who is to be identified by the Senator.

- While participating and voting remotely, a Senator may not chair committee hearings. A temporary chair will be appointed for this purpose.

- A Senator who votes remotely shall certify each vote in writing using the form or format provided by the Secretary.

- This accommodation for remote voting is adopted pursuant to Senate Rule 56 (adopted by Senate Resolution 86 of 2020) and will be in effect for the remainder of the 2019–20 Legislative Session.

Senate committee hearings conducted during the period for which remote voting is permitted shall be presided over by a chair who is present in the Capitol and shall have a quorum of the committee members in the Capitol. Senator Atkins did note as part of her announcement that remote voting on the Senate Floor "does remain an option for the Senate depending on how conditions develop." She also noted that the "Senate and Assembly are taking different approaches."

Notes and Questions

1. Is there a legal difference between remote voting in committee versus remote voting on the Floor? If there is, what would that legal distinction be?

2. Is there a distinction between remote voting and proxy voting? If so, what is the legal distinction(s)?

Chapter Three

Separation of Powers Doctrine in California

Separation of powers — what is it and what does it mean? Essentially, the powers of government are provided to separate branches of government to operate. These powers are set forth in the California Constitution and are granted to the legislative, executive and judicial branches of government.

The separation of powers doctrine essentially provides that those who exercise power in one branch of government cannot exercise the powers of the other two branches of government. The United States Constitution does not contain any express language dealing with the separation of powers of the federal government.

On the other hand, California's separation of powers doctrine is set forth in Article III, Section 3 of the state Constitution. Section 3 provides: "The powers of state government are legislative, executive, and judicial. Persons charged with the exercise of one power may not exercise either of the others except as permitted by this Constitution."

In addition, the three articles of the state Constitution dealing with the three branches of state government establish the roles of the three branches. For example, Article IV, Section 1 of the California Constitution provides: "The legislative power of this State is vested in the California Legislature which consists of the Senate and Assembly, but the people reserve to themselves the powers of initiative and referendum."

Thereafter, in Article V, Section 1, it provides: "The supreme executive power of this State is vested in the Governor. The Governor shall see that the law is faithfully executed." And, Article VI, Section 1 provides: "The judicial power of this State is vested in the Supreme Court, courts of appeal, and superior courts, all of which are courts of record."

Hence, in the California Constitution, the three branches of state government are clearly established and their roles are specified. As a result, the separation of powers can be readily ascertained. But the three branches sometimes operate in a manner that may overlap another branch's role in government.

Essentially, separation of powers as a legal doctrine refers to the division of governmental responsibility set forth in the Constitution for the distinct role of each branch of government that also limits each branch from exercising the main functions of the other two branches of government. This doctrine also provides for the system of "checks and balances" so that no branch has total control over the government.

Despite this separation of core powers of government, in reality, there is some overlap, because each branch does provide that check and balance. For example, in the legislative process, while the Legislature writes and passes bills, the Governor can sign or veto those bills. And, once enacted, the courts can validate or overturn those laws.

In addition, while the courts generally interpret the laws, the executive branch through its administrative agencies will also interpret the laws in how they enforce them and by means of adopting regulations (exercising a "quasi-legislative" role) to implement the statutes enacted by the Legislature. When a state agency enforces a statute or gives meaning to a law (exercising a "quasi-judicial" role), it partially overlaps with the judicial branch's jurisdiction.

Notes and Questions

1. The state Constitution's separation-of-powers doctrine compels the courts to respect the legislature's powers. There is a "strong presumption of the constitutionality of an act of the Legislature." (*Delaney v. Lowery* (1944) 25 Cal.2d 561, 569.) "In considering the constitutionality of a legislative act we presume its validity, resolving all doubts in favor of the Act. Unless conflict with a provision of the state or federal Constitution is clear and unquestionable, we must uphold the Act." (*Amwest Surety Ins. Co. v. Wilson* (1995) 11 Cal.4th 1243, 1252 (citations and quotation omitted).)

2. "[J]udicial decisions abound with declarations to the effect that all presumptions and intendments favor the validity of statutes; that mere doubt by the judicial branch of the government as to the validity of a statute will not afford a sufficient reason for a judicial declaration of its invalidity, but that statutes must be upheld as constitutional unless their invalidity clearly, positively, and unmistakably appears." *People v. Superior Court* (1937) at 298.

Carmel Valley Fire Protection District v. State of California

(2001) 25 Cal.4th 287

OPINION

GEORGE, C.J.

In this case we consider whether Government Code section 17581 and certain budget measures that suspend the operation of administrative regulations adopted by the Department of Industrial Relations violate the separation of powers clause of the California Constitution by encroaching on the power of the executive branch of government. (Cal. Const., art. III, §3.) We conclude that no separation of powers violation has been demonstrated.

I

Executive orders promulgated in 1978 by the Department of Industrial Relations require employers to provide certain items of protective clothing and equipment to employees assigned to firefighting duties. (Cal. Code Regs., tit. 8, §§ 3401–3409, formerly 8 Cal. Admin. Code, §§ 3401–3409.)

Carmel Valley Fire Protection District and other local fire protection agencies incurred expenses complying with this order and, in earlier proceedings, submitted a claim for reimbursement of state-mandated expenditures pursuant to California Constitution, article XIII B, section 6. In 1987, the districts prevailed in securing reimbursement for these state-mandated expenditures. (*Carmel Valley Fire Protection Dist. v. State of California* (1987) 190 Cal. App. 3d 521 [234 Cal. Rptr. 795] (*Carmel I*).)

In ensuing years, the state experienced severe fiscal difficulties and undertook various measures to reduce its expenditures. (See Governor's Budget Summary 1992–1993 (Jan. 9, 1992), State and Local Fiscal Relationship, p. 132.) In 1990, the Legislature enacted Government Code section 17581. That provision permits the Legislature to suspend the operation of statutes and executive orders that constitute state-mandated local programs from year to year and to withdraw funding therefor. The Legislature provided in the Budget Act of 1992 that 45 mandates, including the above regulatory requirements regarding protective gear for firefighters, would be suspended pursuant to section 17581 and that no funds would be forthcoming for reimbursement. Of these suspensions, the great majority were of statutory mandates, and only three (including the one presently before us) were regulatory suspensions. (Stats. 1992, ch. 587, item 8885-101-001, provision 4, including items (l), (m), (vv), pp. 2604–2609.) Ensuing budget acts contained the same suspension of the regulatory mandate at issue in the present case, as well as suspension of numerous predominantly statutory mandates. (See Stats. 1993, ch. 55, item 8885-101-001, provision 4, item (uu), pp. 763–768 [43 mandates suspended]; Stats. 1994, ch. 139, item 885-101-001, provision 4, item (w), pp. 1213–1217 [26 mandates suspended].)

On September 5, 1995, the Carmel Valley Fire Protection District, joined by the Alpine Fire Protection District, the Bonita-Sunnyside Fire Protection District, the City of Glendale, the City of Anaheim, the Ventura County Fire Protection District, the San Ramon Valley Fire Protection District, the American Canyon Fire Protection District (a subsidiary district of the City of American Canyon), the Salida Fire Protection District, the West Stanislaus Fire Protection District, the Sacramento County Fire Protection District, the Humboldt No. 1 Fire Protection District, the Samoa-Peninsula Fire Protection District, and the Mammoth Lakes Fire Protection District (collectively referred to as the districts) filed with the Commission on State Mandates (the Commission) a consolidated claim for reimbursement of the expenses they had incurred in supplying their employees with the protective gear noted in the regulations. On June 27, 1996, the Commission rejected the consolidated claim, relying upon Government Code section 17581 and the budget language that deleted funding for this expense.

On October 8, 1996, the districts filed a petition for writ of mandate and complaint for declaratory relief against the State of California, the Commission, the State Department of Finance, the State Department of Industrial Relations, the State Controller, and the State Treasurer, seeking an order that their claims for expenditures from 1992, 1993, and 1994 be paid from specified existing appropriations. Among other contentions, the districts claimed that Government Code section 17581 and the budget language suspending the mandate for firefighters' equipment violated the separation of powers clause of the California Constitution (Cal. Const., art. III, § 3) by purporting to permit the Legislature to veto executive action.

On April 30, 1997, the trial court denied the petition for writ of mandate and dismissed the declaratory relief action. It declared: "Government Code section 17581 having been satisfied, the mandate of California Code of Regulations Title 8, sections 3401–3409, requiring that petitioners provide their employees with specified equipment and clothing, was suspended by operation of the Budget Acts of 1992, 1993 and 1994, thereby making the provision of such equipment and clothing optional on the part of petitioners."

The trial court also concluded that the Legislature had not "usurp[ed] ... executive functions" in violation of the separation of powers clause of the California Constitution.

The districts appealed. As in the trial court, they challenged the suspension of the administrative mandate on several grounds, including the claim that the suspension violated the separation of powers clause of the California Constitution. The Court of Appeal reversed the judgment of the trial court, determining that Government Code section 17581, as applied to the districts, constituted a violation of the constitutional separation of powers provision. Because the appellate court reached this conclusion, it did not address the districts' other claims, including a claimed violation of the single-subject rule of the California Constitution. (Cal. Const, art. IV, § 9.)

We granted respondents' petition for review challenging the conclusion of the Court of Appeal with respect to the claimed violation of the separation of powers clause of the state Constitution.

II

A

To begin our analysis, we describe the statutory background of the administrative orders at issue in the present case, and note the conflict that has occurred over the provision of funding to carry out these orders.

In 1973, the Legislature enacted the California Occupational Safety and Health Act (Cal/OSHA). (Lab. Code, § 6300 et seq.) The purpose of the act is to ensure "safe and healthful working conditions for all California working men and women by authorizing the enforcement of effective standards, [and] assisting and encouraging employers to maintain safe and healthful working conditions...." (Lab. Code, § 6300.) The Occupational Safety and Health Standards Board within the Department of Industrial Relations is responsible for adopting occupational safety and health standards and orders. (Lab. Code, §§ 140, 142.3, 6305.) It is pursuant to this authority that the executive orders here at issue, relating to protective equipment, were adopted in 1978.

Article XIII B, section 6 of the California Constitution provides, with exceptions not applicable here, that "[w]henever the Legislature or any state agency mandates a new program or higher level of service on any local government, the State shall provide a subvention of funds to reimburse such local government for the costs of such program or increased level of service...."

Despite existing statutory provisions requiring reimbursement of expenditures for state-mandated local programs, however, the Legislature when it adopted Cal/OSHA also enacted uncodified measures stating that the costs of compliance with regulations imposed pursuant to Cal/OSHA were not subject to reimbursement, on the theory that the costs were minimal and that Cal/OSHA merely restated a federal mandate. (Stats. 1973, ch. 993, § 106, p. 1954; Stats. 1974, ch. 1284, § 36, p. 2787.) In later years, the Legislature appended control language to budget items appropriating funds for reimbursement of state mandates, stating with particularity that no application for reimbursement of the cost of compliance with the Cal/OSHA regulations (Cal. Code Regs., tit. 8, §§ 3401–3409) regarding protective gear for firefighters would be processed. (See, e.g., Stats. 1981, ch. 1090, § 3, p. 4193.)

In 1987, in *Carmel I, supra*, 190 Cal. App. 3d 521, the Court of Appeal examined this uncodified language in light of the districts' claim for reimbursement for expenses of firefighters' safety equipment. The appellate court rejected as unfounded the Legislature's declaration that it need not provide reimbursement for expenditures required by Cal/OSHA because Cal/OSHA simply restated a federal mandate. That court concluded that pursuant to article XIII B, section 6 of the California Constitution, expenses incurred to comply with the 1978 regulations at issue in the present case were state-mandated local expenses and that the districts were entitled to reimbursement.

The Court of Appeal also declared that the budget control language was invalid because it violated the state constitutional requirement that a bill have only a single subject. (Cal. Const., art. IV, § 9.) The appellate court explained that the statement that no application would be processed for reimbursement of expenses incurred to comply with Cal/OSHA orders was unrelated to the ostensible subject of the bill appropriations for reimbursement of state-mandated local programs. (*Carmel I, supra*, 190 Cal.App.3d at pp. 541–545.) That court declared that nothing in the bill "alert[s] the reader to the fact that the bill prohibits the Board [of Control] from entertaining claims pursuant to the Cal/OSHA executive orders. The control language does not modify or repeal these orders, nor does it abrogate the necessity for County's continuing compliance therewith. It simply places County's claims reimbursement process in limbo." (*Id.* at p. 545.)

Apparently at least in part in response to this decision, in 1990 the Legislature enacted Government Code section 17581, which provides in pertinent part: "(a) No local agency shall be required to implement or give effect to any statute or executive order, or portion thereof, during any fiscal year … if all of the following apply: [¶] (1) The statute or executive order, or portion thereof, has been determined by the Legislature, the commission [on state mandates], or any court to mandate a new program or higher level of service requiring reimbursement of local agencies pursuant to Section 6 of Article XIII B of the California Constitution. [¶] (2) The statute or executive order, or portion thereof, has been specifically identified by the Legislature in the Budget Act for the fiscal year as being one for which reimbursement is not provided for that fiscal year." Section 17581 also provides that if an agency nonetheless elects to implement such a statute or order, it may assess special fees upon persons or entities benefiting from the implementation. (Gov. Code, § 17581, subd. (b).)

As noted, in the Budget Acts of 1992, 1993, and 1994, the administrative regulations requiring protective gear for firefighters were identified in the manner noted by Government Code section 17581, and the districts' request for reimbursement for the expenses of compliance was refused.

B

Next, we review the parties' contentions and the reasoning of the Court of Appeal. The districts contend that Government Code section 17581 and the provisions of the Budget Acts of 1992, 1993, and 1994 suspending the administrative regulations here at issue represent an effort by the Legislature to invade the power of the executive branch to carry out its duties under Cal/OSHA, thereby violating the constitutional principle of separation of powers. The districts claim that the Legislature delegated broad authority to the Department of Industrial Relations to enact and enforce regulations to carry out the department's mandate to ensure worker safety, and that the Legislature violated the principle of separation of powers when it purported to retain supervisorial control over the manner in which the department executes its duties. The districts conclude that the Legislature usurped the executive power of the department by exempting local agencies from the administrative regulations rather than altering or revoking the department's statutory power over rulemaking and enforcement.

Agreeing with the position of the districts, the Court of Appeal declared that Government Code section 17581 represents an unwarranted intrusion into the operation of the executive branch: "By reason of the separation of powers doctrine, the Legislature's power to declare public policy does not include the power to carry out its declared policies." In the view of the Court of Appeal, the Legislature could not retain supervisorial power or veto power over the execution of Cal/OSHA, in the absence of a statute amending or revoking the delegation of executive power over Cal/OSHA, or at least a statute effecting an implied repeal of the Department of Industrial Relations' executive orders. The Legislature, the Court of Appeal said, lacks "the power to cherry-pick the programs to be suspended which is precisely what the Legislature has done by suspending the operations of only those [identified in the budget]." According to the appellate court, the enactment of Government Code section 17581, far from constituting a revocation of executive power or an implied repeal, constituted an "attempt to exercise an unconstitutional veto power over the [department's] administration of Cal/OSHA."

The Court of Appeal concluded that although the Legislature may choose to retain complete control over a function by itself enacting detailed rules, the Legislature cannot retain administrative control when it enacts a statute that provides "broad policy guidance and leave[s] the details to be filled in by administrative officers exercising substantial discretion." The appellate court declared Government Code section 17581 "constitutionally infirm as applied."

The Attorney General, representing the state, the Department of Industrial Relations, the Department of Finance, the State Controller, and the State Treasurer (collectively referred to for convenience as the State) responds that the Legislature has not attempted to control the exercise of executive power, but rather has exercised its own power over appropriations and expenditures. It is within the Legislature's power, the State contends, to suspend an executive mandate in the interest of an appropriate allocation of limited state funds. Once the Legislature has enacted a statute suspending a mandate, it is clear that the executive lacks power to enforce regulations inconsistent with that statute. Executive power is not thereby threatened or frustrated, the State concludes, because the executive branch always is dependent upon the Legislature for funds.

III

We now consider Government Code section 17581 in light of the constitutional provision for separation of powers, and, as we shall explain, conclude that the statutory and budgetary provisions involved in the present case do not violate the separation of powers clause of the California Constitution.

Article III, section 3 of the California Constitution states: "The powers of state government are legislative, executive, and judicial. Persons charged with the exercise of one power may not exercise either of the others except as permitted by this Constitution."

The separation of powers doctrine limits the authority of one of the three branches of government to arrogate to itself the core functions of another branch. (*In re Attorney Discipline System* (1998) 19 Cal. 4th 582, 596 [79 Cal. Rptr. 2d 836, 967 P.2d 49]; *Superior Court v. County of Mendocino* (1996) 13 Cal. 4th 45, 53 [51 Cal. Rptr. 2d 837, 913 P.2d 1046] (Mendocino); see also *Loving v. United States* (1996) 517 U.S. 748, 757 [116 S. Ct. 1737, 1738–1739, 135 L. Ed. 2d 36].) "'The courts have long recognized that [the] primary purpose [of the separation-of-powers doctrine] is to prevent the combination in the hands of a single person or group of the basic or fundamental powers of government.'" (*Davis v. Municipal Court* (1988) 46 Cal. 3d 64, 76 [249 Cal. Rptr. 300, 757 P.2d 11], quoting *Parker v. Riley* (1941) 18 Cal. 2d 83, 89–90 [113 P.2d 873, 134 A.L.R. 1405]; see also *People v. Superior Court (Romero)* (1996) 13 Cal. 4th 497, 509 [53 Cal. Rptr. 2d 789, 917 P.2d 628].) To serve this purpose, courts "'have not hesitated to strike down provisions of law that either accrete to a single Branch powers more appropriately diffused among separate Branches or that undermine the authority and independence of one or another coordinate Branch.'" (*Kasler v. Lockyer* (2000) 23 Cal. 4th 472, 493 [97 Cal. Rptr. 2d 334, 2 P.3d 581], quoting *Mistretta v. United States* (1989) 488 U.S. 361, 382 [109 S. Ct. 647, 660, 102 L. Ed. 2d 714].)

The doctrine, however, recognizes that the three branches of government are interdependent, and it permits actions of one branch that may "significantly affect those of another branch." (*Mendocino, supra*, 13 Cal.4th at p. 52.) In the context of asserted legislative encroachment on the judicial power, for example, although we have invalidated legislative measures that would defeat or materially impair this court's inherent power (see, e.g., *Hustedt v. Workers' Comp. Appeals Bd.* (1981) 30 Cal. 3d 329, 339–341 [178 Cal. Rptr. 801, 636 P.2d 1139] [judicial power to discipline attorneys could not be vested in Workers' Compensation Appeals Board]; see also *People v. Superior Court (Romero), supra*, 13 Cal. 4th 497 [construing a statute so as to preserve the essential judicial function of dismissal, free from interference by the executive]), we have rejected separation of powers claims when no material impairment appeared. (See *Mendocino, supra*, 13 Cal. 4th 45, 58–60.) With respect to encroachment on the power of the executive, we observed, in rejecting a claim that a statute providing for the expungement of certain criminal records duplicated the Governor's clemency power in some cases and therefore infringed upon the executive power, in violation of the doctrine of separation of powers: "The purpose of the doctrine is to prevent one branch of government from exercising the complete power constitutionally vested in another [citation]; it is not intended to prohibit one branch from taking action properly within its sphere that has the incidental effect of duplicating a function or procedure delegated to another branch." (*Younger v. Superior Court* (1978) 21 Cal. 3d 102, 117 [145 Cal. Rptr. 674, 577 P.2d 1014].)

The founders of our republic viewed the legislature as the branch most likely to encroach upon the power of the other branches. (See *Bowsher v. Synar* (1986) 478 U.S. 714, 727 [106 S. Ct. 3181, 3188, 92 L. Ed. 2d 583]; *Buckley v. Valeo* (1976) 424 U.S. 1, 129 [96 S. Ct. 612, 687–688, 46 L. Ed. 2d 659]; see also Madison, The Federalist No. 48 (Cooke ed. 1961) pp. 332–334.) The principle of separation of powers limits any such tendency. First, it prohibits the legislative branch from arrogating to itself core functions of the executive or judicial branch. (See *Younger v. Superior Court, supra*, 21 Cal.3d at pp. 115–117; see also *Wash. Airports v. Noise Abatement Citizens* (1991) 501 U.S. 252, 274–275 [111 S. Ct. 2298, 2310–2312, 115 L. Ed. 2d 236] (*MWAA v. CAAN*).) Second, legislative power also is circumscribed by the requirement that legislative acts be bicamerally enacted and presented to the head of the executive branch for approval or veto. (Cal. Const., art. IV, §§ 1, 8, subd. (b), 10, subd. (a); see *California Radioactive Materials Management Forum v. Department of Health Services* (1993) 15 Cal. App. 4th 841, 872 [19 Cal. Rptr. 2d 357] (*California Radioactive Materials*); *INS v. Chadha* (1983) 462 U.S. 919, 945–951, 958 [103 S. Ct. 2764, 2781–2784, 2787–2788, 77 L. Ed. 2d 317] (Chadha); see also *MWAA v. CAAN, supra*, 501 U.S. at p. 275 [111 S.Ct. at pp. 2311–2312].)

The core functions of the legislative branch include passing laws, levying taxes, and making appropriations. (Cal. Const., art. IV, §§ 1, 8, subd. (b), 10, 12; *In re Attorney Discipline System, supra*, 19 Cal. 4th 582, 595; see also *Butt v. State of California* (1992) 4 Cal. 4th 668, 698 [15 Cal. Rptr. 2d 480, 842 P.2d 1240].) "Essentials of the legislative function include the determination and formulation of legislative policy." (*State Bd. of Education v. Honig* (1993) 13 Cal. App. 4th 720, 750 [16 Cal. Rptr. 2d 727].) Further, it is settled that "'the power to collect and appropriate the revenue of the State is one peculiarly within the discretion of the Legislature.'" (*In re Attorney Discipline System, supra*, 19 Cal. 4th 582, 595.) Executive power over appropriations is limited and is set out in the state Constitution, which provides that each year the Governor shall submit a proposed budget to the Legislature (Cal. Const., art. IV, § 12; see *Butt v. State of California, supra*, 4 Cal.4th at p. 698) and that each bill, including the budget bill, shall be presented to the Governor for his or her signature or veto. (Cal. Const., art. IV, § 10.) Legislative determinations relating to expenditures in other respects are binding upon the executive: "The executive branch, in expending public funds, may not disregard legislatively prescribed directives and limits pertaining to the use of such funds." (*Mendocino, supra*, 13 Cal.4th at p. 53.)

The legislative branch of government, although it is charged with the formulation of policy, properly may delegate some quasi-legislative or rulemaking authority to administrative agencies. (*Bixby v. Pierno* (1971) 4 Cal. 3d 130, 142 [93 Cal. Rptr. 234, 481 P.2d 242].) For the most part, delegation of quasi-legislative authority to an administrative agency is not considered an unconstitutional abdication of legislative power. (*Davis v. Municipal Court, supra*, 46 Cal.3d at p. 76; *Bixby v. Pierno, supra*, 4 Cal.3d at p. 142.) ""'The true distinction ... is between the delegation of power to make the law, which necessarily involves a discretion as to what it shall be, and conferring authority or discretion as to its execution, to be exercised under and in pursuance of the law. The first cannot be done; to the latter no valid objection can be made.'"" (*Loving v. United States, supra*, 517 U.S. at pp. 758–759 [116 S.Ct. at p. 1744]; see also 7 Witkin, Summary of Cal. Law (9th ed. 1988) Constitutional Law, § 130, p. 186.)

The Department of Industrial Relations, however, as an executive agency created by statute, has only as much rulemaking power as is invested in it by statute. (See *Association for Retarded Citizens v. Department of Developmental Services* (1985) 38 Cal. 3d 384, 390–392 [211 Cal. Rptr. 758, 696 P.2d 150]; *State Bd. of Education v. Honig, supra*, 13 Cal.App.4th at pp. 750–752 [""'there is no agency discretion to promulgate a regulation which is inconsistent with the governing statute'"" (italics omitted)]; *Imperial Irrigation Dist. v. State Water Resources Control Bd.* (1990) 225 Cal. App. 3d 548, 567 [275 Cal. Rptr. 250] ["'[t]he powers of public [agencies] are derived from the statutes which create them and define their functions'"].) As we have explained, "[a]dministrative action that is not authorized by, or is inconsistent with, acts of the Legislature is void." (*Association for Retarded Citizens v. Department of Developmental Services, supra*, 38 Cal.3d at p. 391.) And, as another court has announced, "the rulemaking authority of an agency is circumscribed by the substantive provisions of the law governing the agency.... [R]egulations that alter or amend the statute or enlarge or impair its scope are void." (*Physicians & Surgeons Laboratories, Inc. v. Department of Health Services* (1992) 6 Cal. App. 4th 968, 982 [8 Cal. Rptr. 2d 565].) An executive agency lacks power, for example, to order the disbursement of funds for a purpose contrary to that stated in a legislative enactment. (*Assembly v. Public Utilities Com.* (1995) 12 Cal. 4th 87, 100–104 [48 Cal. Rptr. 2d 54, 906 P.2d 1209].)

Further, an administrative agency is subject to the legislative power of the purse and "may spend no more money to provide services than the Legislature has appropriated." (*Association for Retarded Citizens v. Department of Developmental Services, supra*, 38 Cal.3d at p. 393.) The power of appropriation includes the power to withhold appropriations. Neither an executive administrative agency nor a court has the power to require the Legislature to appropriate money. (*California State Employees' Assn v. Flournoy* (1973) 32 Cal. App. 3d 219, 234–235 [108 Cal. Rptr. 251].) For example, in *California State Employees' Assn. v. Flournoy*, the Court of Appeal rejected a separation of powers claim that, because the Regents of the University of California was the executive agency vested with the power to govern the university, the Legislature lacked authority to refuse to grant the salary increases recommended by the Regents. The court observed that although the Regents possessed broad discretion over governance of the university, a constitutional power that was beyond the control of the Legislature, the "'finances of the University are subject to legislative scrutiny'.... Hence, although ... the Regents may be granted salary-fixing authority by the state Constitution, there is nothing to suggest that they additionally are granted authority to compel the California Legislature to appropriate money to pay any faculty salary increases which the Regents may have authorized or 'fixed.'" (*Id.* at p. 233.)

The decision to relieve districts of the duty to comply with specified executive orders is a policy decision an act within the authority of the Legislature, although it incidentally affects the legislatively enacted authority of the Department of Industrial Relations to promulgate regulations. (See *Steiner v. Superior Court* (1996) 50 Cal. App. 4th 1771, 1785 [58 Cal. Rptr. 2d 668] ["revocation of legislative action is itself legislative"].) The circumstance that the department may have had concurrent authority to alter or rescind the regulations in the present case within the bounds of its statutory authority does not suggest that the Legislature lacked authority over the matter. (See *In re Attorney Discipline System, supra*, 19 Cal.4th at pp. 596, 602–603, 611 [the circumstance that the Legislature has authority to impose attorney discipline and fees does not mean that the court cannot]; *Mendocino, supra*, 13 Cal.4th at p. 58 [the Legislature may exert "the authority to establish a schedule providing when the court generally will be open to the public," although a court has "'inherent power' to control the hours and days of its operations"].)

Considering the appropriate function of the Legislature to define policy and allocate funds and considering the inability of an administrative agency to which quasi-legislative power has been delegated to adopt rules inconsistent with the agency's governing statutes, we believe that a legislative enactment that limits the mandate of an administrative agency or withdraws certain of its powers is not necessarily suspect under the doctrine of separation of powers. When the Legislature has not taken over core functions of the executive branch and the Legislature has exercised its authority in accordance with formal procedures set forth in the Constitution, such an enactment normally is consistent with the checks and balances prescribed by our Constitution.

Government Code section 17581 was enacted, of course, by both houses of the Legislature and presented to the Governor for approval, as were the budget items at issue in the present case. The adoption of the statutory provision and the budgetary limitations in the present case measures that suspend operation of executive orders and withhold state reimbursement for certain protective gear no longer mandated by the orders does not signify that the Legislature has taken over core functions of the executive branch. Although section 17581 and the noted budget items have some impact on the functions of the Department of Industrial Relations, they do not defeat or materially impair the ability of the department to carry out its mandate to protect worker safety: even in the realm of the protection of firefighters, the department retains authority to enforce other, generally applicable regulations and to issue orders intended to ensure firefighter safety. Rather, the effect on the department is incidental, while the statutory and budget measures under review constitute an expression of the Legislature's essential duty to devise a reasonable budget.

It is most significant to the present case that the Legislature is the branch of government that must, on a yearly basis, fit the needs of the state into the funds available. "Enactment of a state budget is a legislative function, involving 'interdependent political, social and economic judgments which cannot be left to individual officers acting in isolation; rather, it is, and indeed must be, the responsibility of the legislative body to weigh those needs and set priorities for the utilization of the limited revenues available.'" (*Anderson v. Superior Court* (1998) 68 Cal. App. 4th 1240, 1249 [80 Cal. Rptr. 2d 891].) In determining what funds to expend in a given year, the Legislature must consider many legitimate and pressing calls on the state's resources in addition to the safety of firefighters. (See *California Teachers Assn. v. Ingwerson* (1996) 46 Cal. App. 4th 860 [53 Cal. Rptr. 2d 917].)

This is not a case in which the legislative action deprives the administrative agency of the resources necessary to carry out its function. The present case is distinguishable, therefore, from *Scott v. Common Council* (1996) 44 Cal. App. 4th 684 [52 Cal. Rptr. 2d 161], a case cited by the districts. In that case, the Court of Appeal determined that a local legislative body's action in eliminating all funding for the city attorney's investigative staff was beyond the normal appropriation power of that body, because "the budget cuts materially impaired the city attorney in the performance of his prosecutorial duties." (*Id.* at p. 694.) Such is not the case here.

We are unaware of any authority, and the Court of Appeal did not cite any, establishing that the Legislature may not circumscribe the authority of an administrative agency in certain particulars without withdrawing the general delegation of rulemaking authority it has made to the administrative agency. Such a rule would be cumbersome in the extreme, requiring a major overhaul of administrative function when a minor change might suffice, and impairing the ability of the Legislature to allocate funds on a yearly basis.

Despite the contrary assertion of the Court of Appeal and the districts, the decision in *California Radioactive Materials, supra*, 15 Cal. App. 4th 841, does not compel a contrary conclusion. In that case, a committee of the state Senate exacted a promise from persons being considered for confirmation as officers of the Department of Health Services that an application to construct a low-level radioactive waste disposal site would be reconsidered at a hearing conducted pursuant to a formal procedure prescribed by the Administrative Procedure Act (APA), although such a procedure was not required by statute. The Court of Appeal issued a writ of mandate directing the department to set aside its order for further formal administrative hearings, because the legislative action requiring such a hearing had not been undertaken by vote of both houses of the Legislature and presented to the Governor.

. . . .

IV

The judgment of the Court of Appeal is reversed, and the matter is remanded for further proceedings consistent with this opinion.

Mosk, J., Kennard, J., Baxter, J., Werdegar, J., Chin, J., and Brown, J., concurred.

[Appellants' petition for a rehearing was denied May 23, 2001.]

Notes and Questions

1. Legislative enactment that limits the mandate of an administrative agency or withdraws certain of its powers is not necessarily suspect under the doctrine of separation of powers. When the Legislature has not taken over core functions of the executive branch and has exercised its authority in accordance with formal procedures set forth in the state Constitution, such an enactment normally is consistent with the checks and balances prescribed by the Constitution.

2. The statutes enacted did not signify that the Legislature had taken over core functions of the executive branch, but constituted an expression of the Legislature's essential duty to devise a reasonable budget. The Legislature's power of appropriation includes the power to withhold appropriations, and neither an executive administrative agency nor a court has the power to require the Legislature to appropriate money. Is there sufficient guidance from the Court for the Legislature to determine when legislation would meet the definition of "supervisorial control"?

3. In analyzing the separation of powers in this case, did the Court draw a distinction between the statutory and budgetary provisions?

4. In the view of the Court of Appeal, the Legislature could not retain supervisorial power or veto power over the execution of Cal/OSHA, in the absence of a statute amending or revoking the delegation of executive power over Cal/OSHA, or at least a statute effecting an implied repeal of the Department of Industrial Relations' executive orders. The Legislature, the Court of Appeal said, lacks "the power to cherry-pick the programs to be suspended which is precisely what the Legislature has done by suspending the operations of only those [identified in the budget]." Why did the Supreme Court disagree with this assessment?

5. "The purpose of the doctrine [of separation of powers] is to prevent one branch of government from exercising the complete power constitutionally vested in another [citation]; it is not intended to prohibit one branch from taking action properly within its sphere that has the incidental effect of duplicating a function or procedure delegated to another branch." (*Younger v. Superior Court* (1978) 21 Cal.3d 102, 117 [145 Cal.Rptr. 674, 577 P.2d 1014].)

6. The Supreme Court found that it is "the appropriate function of the Legislature to define policy and allocate funds." On this basis, to what degree could the Legislature limit the quasi-legislative actions of an executive branch rulemaking agency? How much can the Legislature limit an administrative agency's rulemaking mandate? To what extent can the Legislature limit the rulemaking mandate of an agency without precluding it from exercising its ability to implement and enforce the law?

7. Does the Supreme Court provide sufficient guidance for "when the Legislature has not taken over core functions of the executive branch"?

8. When does the system of "checks and balances" violate the separation of powers doctrine?

9. Supreme Court Justice Stephen Breyer, when he was on the federal court of appeals, opined that the Congress can enact a statute to set aside a regulatory action. Is the separation of powers doctrine not violated because, in this case, the Legislature adopted and the Governor signed the budget and the suspension of a regulation?

Marine Forests Society v. California Coastal Commission

(2002) 104 Cal.App.4th 1232

OPINION

The California Coastal Commission (the Commission) is the "state coastal zone planning and management agency" with the primary responsibility for implementing the provisions of the California Coastal Act of 1976. (Pub. Resources Code, §§ 30300, 30330; further section references are to the Public Resources Code unless otherwise specified.) It consists of 12 voting members, 4 appointed by the Governor and 8 appointed by the Legislature, who serve two-year terms at the pleasure of their appointing authorities. (§§ 30301, 30301.5, 30312.) The Commission acts by vote of a majority of its appointed members. (e.g., §§ 30333, 30512.)

When the Commission notified Marine Forests Society (Marine Forests) that it intended to commence cease and desist proceedings regarding Marine Forests' experimental man-made reef on the ocean floor off of Newport Harbor in southern California, Marine Forests filed an action seeking to enjoin the Commission from doing so. Marine Forests claimed, among other things, that the Commission did not have the authority to issue cease and desist orders or to grant or deny permits for coastal development because the scheme for appointment of its voting members gives the legislative branch control over the Commission, thus impermissibly interfering with the Commission's executive branch responsibility to execute the laws.

The trial court held that the ability of the Senate Committee on Rules and the Speaker of the Assembly to remove a majority of the Commission's voting members at the pleasure of those appointing authorities effectively makes the Commission a "legislative agency." Therefore, the court enjoined the Commission "as a legislative body from exceeding its jurisdiction and violating the Separation of Powers Clause of the California Constitution [Cal. Const., art. III, § 3] which precludes it from granting, denying or conditioning permits or [from] issuing and hearing cease and desist orders." The Commission appeals. (Code Civ. Proc., § 904.1, subd. (a)(6).)

For reasons that follow, we conclude that the Commission's interpretation and implementation of the California Coastal Act of 1976 is an executive function, and that the appointment structure giving the Senate Committee on Rules and the Speaker of the Assembly the power not only to appoint a majority of the Commission's voting members but also to remove them at will contravenes the separation of powers clause of California's Constitution. The flaw is that the unfettered power to remove the majority of the Commission's voting members, and to replace them with others, if they act in a manner disfavored by the Senate Committee on Rules and the Speaker of the Assembly makes those Commission members subservient to the Legislature. In a practical sense, this unrestrained power to replace a majority of the Commission's voting members, and the presumed desire of those members to avoid being removed from their positions, allows the legislative branch not only to declare the law but also to control the Commission's execution of the law and exercise of its quasi-judicial powers. Accordingly, we shall affirm the judgment. We emphasize, however, that Marine Forests made a timely separation of powers objection and pursued its remedies in a timely manner. We do not address the rights and interests of other parties to prior actions of the Commission.

   ....

DISCUSSION

I

Article III, section 3 of the California Constitution states: "The powers of state government are legislative, executive, and judicial. Persons charged with the exercise of one power may not exercise either of the others except as permitted by this Constitution."

"The separation of powers doctrine limits the authority of one of the three branches of government to arrogate to itself the core functions of another branch. [Citations.] "'The courts have long recognized that [the] primary purpose [of the doctrine] is to prevent the combination in the hands of a single person or group of the basic or fundamental powers of government.'" [Citations.] To serve this purpose, courts "'have not hesitated to strike down provisions of law that either accrete to a single Branch powers more appropriately diffused among separate Branches or that undermine the authority and independence of one or another coordinate Branch.'" [Citations.]" (*Carmel Valley Fire Protection Dist. v. State of California* (2001) 25 Cal.4th 287, 297, 105 Cal.Rptr.2d 636, 20 P.3d 533 (hereafter *Carmel Valley*).)

However, the separation of powers doctrine recognizes that the three branches of government are interdependent. Accordingly, "it permits actions of one branch that may 'significantly affect those of another branch' [citation]" as long as there is no material impairment of the other branch's core functions. (*Carmel Valley, supra*, 25 Cal.4th at p. 298, 105 Cal.Rptr.2d 636, 20 P.3d 533.) "'The purpose of the doctrine is to prevent one branch of government from exercising the *complete* power constitutionally vested in another [citation]; it is not intended to prohibit one branch from taking action properly within its sphere that has the *incidental* effect of duplicating a function or procedure delegated to another branch.' [Citation.]" (*Id.* at p. 298, 105 Cal.Rptr.2d 636, 20 P.3d 533, orig. italics.)

II

"In general, it may be said that it is for the Legislature to make public policy and for the executive to carry out the policy established by the Legislature. In practice the complexity of public business necessitates that many of the functions of government be accomplished by administrative agencies. [Citation.]" (*California Radioactive Materials Management Forum v. Department of Health Services* (1993) 15 Cal.App.4th 841, 870, 19 Cal.Rptr.2d 357 (hereafter *Radioactive Materials*); disapproved on another point in *Carmel Valley, supra,* 25 Cal.4th at p. 305, fn. 5, 105 Cal.Rptr.2d 636, 20 P.3d 533.)

There can be no doubt that "[a]dministrative agencies are part of the executive branch of government. [Citation.]" (*Radioactive Materials, supra,* 15 Cal.App.4th at p. 870, 19 Cal.Rptr.2d 357.)

And there can be no doubt that the Commission exercises executive powers.

For one thing, it has been given the authority to "adopt or amend, by vote of a majority of the appointed membership thereof, rules and regulations to carry out the purposes and provisions of [the Coastal Act]" (§ 30333.) Such authority constitutes "substantive lawmaking." (*Yamaha Corp. of America v. State Bd. of Equalization* (1998) 19 Cal.4th 1, 10, 78 Cal.Rptr.2d 1, 960 P.2d 1031.) Because the Legislature "may make no law except by statute and may enact no statute except by bill" (Cal. Const., art. IV, § 8), it has no power to make law by regulation. Hence, the authority to adopt and amend rules and regulations to carry out the purposes and provisions of the Coastal Act represents the delegation of the Legislature's lawmaking power to an executive agency. (*Yamaha Corp. of America v. State Bd. of Equalization, supra,* 19 Cal.4th at pp. 10–11, 78 Cal.Rptr.2d 1, 960 P.2d 1031.)

The Commission has other duties and powers that are executive in nature. As we have noted, it has the authority to contract with private or governmental agencies for the performance of any work or services that cannot be performed satisfactorily by the Commission's employees. (§ 30334.) It also has authority to investigate and to determine what, if any, action should be taken against any person or governmental agency that has undertaken, or is threatening to undertake, any action within the jurisdiction of the Commission. (§ 30809.) Other duties of the Commission include reviewing the coastal programs of local governments for compliance with the Coastal Act; the Commission has the authority to refuse to certify those plans if they do not conform with policies specified in the Coastal Act. (§§ 30510–30514.) These duties in the interpretation and implementation of the Coastal Act are the very essence of the power to execute the law. (*Bowsher v. Synar* (1986) 478 U.S. 714, 733, 106 S.Ct. 3181, 3191, 92 L.Ed.2d 583, 600.)

In executing the Coastal Act, the Commission also grants and denies permits, issues cease and desist orders, and performs other review functions (§§ 30600, 30601–30627, 30809–30811), all of which are exercises of quasi-judicial power. (*Yost v. Thomas* (1984) 36 Cal.3d 561, 572, 205 Cal.Rptr. 801, 685 P.2d 1152; *City of Coronado v. California Coastal Zone Conservation Com.* (1977) 69 Cal.App.3d 570, 574, 138 Cal.Rptr. 241.) An administrative agency may exercise quasi-judicial powers if (1) the exercise of such power is incidental to, and reasonably necessary to accomplish, a function or power properly exercised by that agency, and (2) the essential judicial power remains ultimately in the courts through review of the quasi-judicial determinations. (*Bradshaw v. Park* (1994) 29 Cal.App.4th 1267, 1275, 34 Cal.Rptr.2d 872; *In re Danielle W.* (1989) 207 Cal.App.3d 1227, 1236, 255 Cal.Rptr. 344.) Therefore, assuming the requisite judicial review exists, it generally is appropriate for an administrative agency to exercise quasi-judicial powers because this is incidental to, and reasonably necessary to effectuate, the agency's executive power to implement and execute the law. But this is an executive power to be exercised in aid of the agency's executive functions; it is not a legislative power.

III

The Commission contends that the California Constitution does not prohibit the Legislature from appointing members of an executive branch agency; therefore, in the Commission's view, the fact that the Speaker of the Assembly and the Senate Committee on Rules appoint the majority of the Commission's voting members does not violate the separation of powers doctrine stated in article III, section 3 of the California Constitution.

The Commission relies in part upon the California Constitution of 1849, which stated in pertinent part: "All officers whose election or appointment is not provided for by this Constitution, and all officers whose offices may hereafter be created by law, shall be elected by the people, or appointed as the Legislature may direct." (Former art. XI, § 6.) When the Constitution was redrafted in 1879, this provision was retained in former article XX, section 4. It was interpreted as giving the Legislature both the power to establish new offices in addition to those provided for in the Constitution and the power to declare the manner in which non-constitutional officers shall be chosen. This latter power included not only the ability to delegate the duty of appointment to some other person or body, but also the Legislature's ability to make the appointment in question itself. (*Ex Parte Gerino* (1904) 143 Cal. 412, 414, 77 P. 166; *People v. Freeman* (1889) 80 Cal. 233, 235–236, 22 P. 173; People v. Langdon (1857) 8 Cal. 1, 16.)

Article XX, section 4 of the California Constitution was repealed by Proposition 15 in the general election of November 3, 1970. Noting that the repealed provision "apparently was intended during the early days of statehood to confirm the power of the Legislature to establish departments and agencies other than those specifically created by the Constitution," the California Constitution Revision Commission concluded: "Since there is nothing elsewhere in the Constitution restricting the now accepted inherent power of the Legislature to establish new offices, agencies, and departments, this provision is constitutionally unnecessary." The ballot pamphlet stated that the repeal of this provision would place the subject matter of the deleted matter under legislative control through the enactment of statutes.

The enactment of a statute replacing former section 4 of article XX was unnecessary in light of Government Code section 1300, which was passed in 1943. (Stats.1943, ch. 134, § 1300, p. 960.) It provides: "Every officer, the mode of whose appointment is not prescribed by law, shall be appointed by the Governor."

Accordingly, despite the repeal of former section 4 of article XX, the Legislature retains the power to enact legislation creating new agencies, and the power of appointment that is not regulated by the California Constitution may be regulated by statute. If the law so prescribes, the appointment power may be exercised by the Legislature. Only when the appointing authority is not otherwise prescribed by law does this power reside in the Governor.

The Commission points out that, where there is no set term of office, the power to appoint an officer includes the power by the appointing authority to remove the officer at will. (Citing Gov.Code, § 1301 ["Every office, the term of which is not fixed by law, is held at the pleasure of the appointing power"]; *Brown v. Superior Court* (1975) 15 Cal.3d 52, 55, 123 Cal.Rptr. 377, 538 P.2d 1137; *People v. Hill* (1857) 7 Cal. 97, 102.) It follows, the Commission argues, that because the Legislature has the authority to enact statutes permitting it to appoint administrative agency officers and to provide for their removal at the pleasure of the appointing party, the Legislature's exercise of such power with respect to the Commission does not violate the separation of powers doctrine. We disagree.

The fact the legislative branch has the power to appoint executive branch officers and to provide for their removal at will does not mean that this authority is without limits. Nor does it mean that the Legislature's exercise of its power in structuring the appointment of the Commission's members does not violate the separation of powers doctrine.

For example, although Congress had the authority to create a Board of Review when relinquishing to an executive agency the operating authority over federal property, it violated the separation of powers doctrine by specifying that the Board of Review would consist of nine Members of Congress who would have veto authority over decisions of the executive agency. (*Wash. Airports v. Noise Abatement Citizens* (1991) 501 U.S. 252, 255, 263, 270–271, 277, 111 S.Ct. 2298, 2301, 2305, 2308–2309, 2312, 115 L.Ed.2d 236, 245–246, 251, 255–256, 259.)

A different example may be found in *Obrien v. Jones* (2000) 23 Cal.4th 40, 96 Cal.Rptr.2d 205, 999 P.2d 95, a case in which the California Supreme Court was asked to determine whether a statute permitting the Governor, the Senate Committee on Rules, and the Speaker of the Assembly to appoint three of the five judges of the State Bar Court Hearing Department violated the separation of powers clause of our state Constitution because "the power to discipline licensed attorneys in this state is an expressly reserved, primary, and inherent power of [the Supreme Court]." (*Id.* at p. 48, 96 Cal.Rptr.2d 205, 999 P.2d 95.)

The Supreme Court did not simply say that the Legislature had the power to make appointments or to dictate the appointing authority and, consequently, there was no constitutional violation. Rather, the relevant question was whether the appointment mechanism materially impaired the court's primary and ultimate authority over the attorney admission and discipline process. (*Obrien v. Jones, supra*, 23 Cal.4th at pp. 43–44, 50, 96 Cal.Rptr.2d 205, 999 P.2d 95.)

The Supreme Court noted that all applicants for appointment as a State Bar Court judge must be screened and evaluated in light of criteria specified by statute and rules of the Supreme Court (*Obrien v. Jones, supra*, 23 Cal.4th at p. 51, 96 Cal.Rptr.2d 205, 999 P.2d 95), and must be found qualified by the Applicant Evaluation and Nominating Committee, whose members are appointed by the Supreme Court. (*Id.* at pp. 52, 53, 96 Cal.Rptr.2d 205, 999 P.2d 95.) And once appointed, the State Bar Court judges "are subject to discipline by [the Supreme Court] on the same grounds as a judge of a court of record in this state." (*Id.* at p. 46, 96 Cal.Rptr.2d 205, 999 P.2d 95.) In addition, findings and recommendations of State Bar Court judges are subject to independent review by the Review Department, whose members are appointed by the Supreme Court (*id.* at pp. 54, 55, 96 Cal.Rptr.2d 205, 999 P.2d 95), and the Review Department has the broad authority to accept or reject the findings and recommendations of the hearing judges. (*Ibid.*) Furthermore, those findings and recommendations must then be presented for the Supreme Court's consideration. (*Id.* at p. 55, 96 Cal.Rptr.2d 205, 999 P.2d 95.)

Hence, there is no separation of powers violation because the appointment mechanism is subject to sufficient judicially controlled protective measures to ensure that the appointments do not impair the Supreme Court's authority. (*Obrien v. Jones, supra*, 23 Cal.4th at pp. 44, 55, 57, 96 Cal.Rptr.2d 205, 999 P.2d 95.) "As in the past, all hearing judges [are] subject to the primary authority and supervision of [the Supreme Court]. (*Id.* at p. 55, 96 Cal.Rptr.2d 205, 999 P.2d 95.)

Likewise, the relevant question with respect to the Commission is whether the appointment mechanism in sections 30301 and 30312 materially infringes upon the inherent authority of that executive branch agency, i.e., undermines the authority and independence of the agency, as Marine Forests alleges, or whether there are sufficient safeguards preventing such an infringement.

IV

In contrast to the appointments to the State Bar Court, the statutory scheme regarding the Commission gives the Legislature virtually unfettered discretion in appointing 8 of the 12 voting members of the Commission. (§§ 30301, 30301.2.) Other than the requirement that 4 of the 8 members appointed by the Legislature must be local elected officials, the scheme provides no standards or procedures for evaluating the qualifications of prospective appointees. Although those appointments are made from a list of nominees provided by the county and city governments within the regions, the appointing authorities have the power to reject all of the nominees on the list and to require the local governments to provide additional nominees. (§ 30301.2.) The only qualification concerning the appointment of public members is that the appointing authorities "shall make good faith efforts to assure that their appointments, as a whole, reflect, to the greatest extent feasible, the economic, social, and geographic diversity of the state." (§ 30310, subd. (b).) And there is no requirement that appointees be found qualified by a review committee controlled by the executive branch.

Even more significant is the fact that, unlike State Bar Court judges who serve set terms and are subject to removal on the same grounds applicable to a judge of a court of record, pursuant to proceedings under the exclusive control of the judiciary (*Obrien v. Jones, supra*, 23 Cal.4th at p. 46, 96 Cal.Rptr.2d 205, 999 P.2d 95), the Commission members who are appointed by the Legislature serve at the pleasure of the appointing authority and, thus, can be removed and replaced at any time and for any reason, or for no reason at all. (§ 30312, subd. (a).)

There are no safeguards and checks which would serve to ensure that the Commission is under the primary authority and supervision of the executive branch. Rather, the retention by the Legislature of the virtually unfettered power of appointment, and wholly unfettered power of removal, over two-thirds of the voting members of the Commission serves to ensure that the Commission is under the control of the Legislature.

This is not merely a paper conclusion. It is a political reality. On motion for summary judgment, the Commission stipulated that "[the Commission] is not appointed by the Governor and is not subject to the Governor. [It] has been placed by the Legislature in the Resources Agency but is not governed by that agency." Thus, the Commission regards itself as being free of executive branch authority and supervision. Of course, whether the Commission is free of executive branch supervision and control is a legal, not a factual, question. But the Commission's view of its own position in government serves to confirm our legal conclusion that the Commission is subject to the control of the Legislature rather than executive branch of government. And this control enables the legislative branch concomitantly to control the Commission's function of implementing the Coastal Act (§ 30330), which function is the very essence of the executive power.

It is true "[t]he Legislature may, by statute, exercise broad control over the policies to be implemented and the ways and means of their accomplishment. However, acts which are done to carry out the policies and purposes already declared by the Legislature are not a legislative function." (*Radioactive Materials, supra*, 15 Cal.App.4th at p. 871, 19 Cal.Rptr.2d 357.) The Legislature cannot exercise direct supervisorial control over the performance of the duties of an executive officer in his or her execution of the laws; rather, it can exercise control only indirectly by dictating the manner of execution of the laws via the enactment of legislation. (See *Carmel Valley, supra*, 25 Cal.4th at p. 304, 105 Cal.Rptr.2d 636, 20 P.3d 533; *Connerly v. State Personnel Bd.* (2001) 92 Cal.App.4th 16, 63, 112 Cal.Rptr.2d 5; *Radioactive Materials, supra*, 15 Cal.App.4th at p. 873, 19 Cal.Rptr.2d 357; cf. *Bowsher v. Synar, supra*, 478 U.S. at pp. 733–734, 106 S.Ct. at pp. 3191–3192, 92 L.Ed.2d at p. 601.)

Accordingly, by retaining the unilateral power to remove at will the majority of the voting members of the Commission, the legislative branch impermissibly controls the Commission's executive function of implementing the Coastal Act in violation of the separation of powers clause of California's Constitution.

. . . .

V

The Commission contends that the holding in *Bowsher, supra,* 478 U.S. 714, 106 S.Ct. 3181, 92 L.Ed.2d 583 is distinguishable and inapplicable in the present case because, under the United States Constitution, Congress has no power to appoint executive officers and no power to remove them other than by the impeachment process (U.S. Const., art. II, § 2, cl.2, § 4), whereas the California Constitution does not preclude the Legislature from making appointments to executive agencies or exercising the concomitant power of removal from office.

This is not a critical distinction. Bowsher did not hold that the separation of powers doctrine was violated simply because Congress lacked the constitutional authority to remove an executive officer except by impeachment. The doctrine was violated because Congress's ability to remove the Comptroller General virtually at will interfered with the execution of the laws, a matter plainly outside the Congressional sphere. The high court noted that, because the structure of the Constitution does not permit Congress to execute the laws, Congress could not grant to an officer under its control what it did not possess. (*Bowsher, supra,* 478 U.S. at p. 726, 106 S.Ct. at p. 3188, 92 L.Ed.2d at p. 596.) What is of particular importance to the resolution of the appeal before us is the high court's conclusion that "[t]o permit the execution of the laws to be vested in an officer answerable only to [the legislative branch] would, in practical terms, reserve in [that branch] control over the execution of the laws." (*Ibid.*) This commonsense principle applies with equal force to our state separation of powers determination that the appointment mechanism for the Commission, an executive branch agency, materially impairs one of its core functions, namely execution of the law.

The Commission also argues that Marine Forests's constitutional challenge is infirm because it has not presented an "as applied" challenge or made any factual allegations that the Legislature has directed or dictated the actions of its appointees; rather, it has made a facial challenge and thus must demonstrate that the statute's provisions "'inevitably pose a present total and fatal conflict with applicable constitutional prohibitions.'" (Quoting *Pacific Legal Foundation v. Brown, supra,* 29 Cal.3d at p. 181, 172 Cal.Rptr. 487, 624 P.2d 1215.)

However, Marine Forests does not need to demonstrate that the legislative appointing authorities have attempted to interfere with the Commission members' execution of the Coastal Act. It is the Commission members' presumed desire to avoid removal — by pleasing their legislative appointing authorities — which creates the subservience to another branch that raises separation of powers problems. (*Bowsher, supra,* 478 U.S. at p. 727, fn. 5, 106 S.Ct. at p. 3188, fn. 5, 92 L.Ed.2d at p. 597; *MWAA v. CAAN, supra,* 501 U.S. at p. 269, fn. 15, 111 S.Ct. at p. 2308, fn. 15, 115 L.Ed.2d at p. 254.) As noted previously, "[t]o permit the execution of the laws to be vested in an officer answerable only to [the legislative branch] would, in practical terms, reserve in [that branch] control over the execution of the laws." (*Bowsher, supra,* 478 U.S. at p. 726, 106 S.Ct. at p. 3188, 92 L.Ed.2d at p. 596.) Thus, this is not simply a hypothetical problem as the Commission suggests.

The Commission intimates that there is no problem with the Coastal Act's appointment mechanism because the Governor signed, and therefore approved of, the legislation giving the legislative branch the ability to appoint and remove at will the majority of the voting members of the Commission. But "the Governor can no more concede executive power to a legislative committee than a committee can be permitted to usurp it. [Citations.] And the Governor's consent to an unlawful legislative act does not validate the act. [Citations.]" (*Radioactive Materials, supra*, 15 Cal.App.4th at pp. 873–874, 19 Cal.Rptr.2d 357.) Hence, the Governor's approval of an appointment structure that interferes with the executive power does not rectify its constitutional infirmity.

Pointing out administrative agencies in which fewer than a majority of the members are appointed by the Governor or in which members are removable at will, the Commission argues that this demonstrates there is nothing unique about the setup of the Commission and, thus, there is no separation of powers violation. However, the Commission does not point to any administrative agency that (1) performs executive functions as opposed to merely gathering information and making policy recommendations, which are incidental to legislative functions, and (2) for which the Legislature appoints a majority of the members and may remove them at will. In any event, even if other administrative agencies exist with an appointment structure similar to that of the Commission, this does not establish there is no separation of powers violation in the present case.

We note that in *Parker v. Riley* (1941) 18 Cal.2d 83, 113 P.2d 873, the California Supreme Court concluded the fact that the Commission on Interstate Cooperation was comprised of five members of the Senate Committee on Interstate Cooperation, five members of the Assembly Committee on Interstate Cooperation, and five members appointed by the Governor did not violate the separation of powers provisions of the California Constitution, or violate the constitutional prohibition against legislators holding other offices or positions of trust. (*Id.* at pp. 85, 87–90, 113 P.2d 873.) This was so because the duties imposed on said commission were incidental and ancillary to the lawmaking functions of the Legislature. (*Id.* at pp. 88–89, 113 P.2d 873.) However, the Supreme Court warned "[i]t must not be assumed ... that legislative activities may be expanded indefinitely through the creation of separate agencies responsible primarily to the legislature. This sort of expansion would soon lead to a legislative usurpation of power incompatible with the proper exercise of its lawmaking function." (*Parker v. Riley, supra*, 18 Cal.2d at p. 88, 113 P.2d 873.)

The appointment mechanism specified in the Coastal Act is just such an impermissible expansion. It materially impairs the executive power's ultimate authority over the execution of the laws because it allows the legislative branch to retain majority control over the Commission's implementation of the Coastal Act, and the Commission's duties are not limited to those that are incidental and ancillary to the lawmaking functions of the legislature.

Because the majority of the Commission's voting members are controlled by the legislative branch, the separation of powers doctrine precludes the Commission from being entrusted with the exercise of executive powers or of quasi-judicial powers that are incidental to the executive function of implementing the law. (Cf. *Bowsher, supra*, 478 U.S. at pp. 726, 732, 106 S.Ct. at pp. 3188, 3191, 92 L.Ed.2d at p. 596–597, 600.) Accordingly, the trial court acted properly in enjoining the Commission from granting, denying, or conditioning permits, and from issuing and hearing cease and desist orders.

VI

It is appropriate here to emphasize that our legal conclusion that the process for appointing voting members of the Commission violates the separation of powers doctrine is limited to the specific facts of this case, where a majority of the Commission's voting members are appointed by the legislative branch and may be removed at the pleasure of the legislative branch and there are no safeguards protecting against the Legislature's ability to use this authority to interfere with the Commission members' executive power to execute the laws. We express no opinion regarding the propriety of legislative appointments to administrative agencies under circumstances different than presented here.

We also note that Marine Forests made a timely separation of powers objection and pursued its remedies in a timely manner. (See *Moffat v. Moffat* (1980) 27 Cal.3d 645, 656, 165 Cal.Rptr. 877, 612 P.2d 967 [the waiver rule may preclude a party from making a collateral attack on proceeding in which the party participated without objection]; *Armstrong v. Armstrong* (1976) 15 Cal.3d 942, 950–951, 126 Cal.Rptr. 805, 544 P.2d 941 [same]; see also *Ryder v. United States* (1995) 515 U.S. 177, 182–183, 115 S.Ct. 2031, 2035–2036, 132 L.Ed.2d 136, 143 ["one who makes a timely challenge to the constitutional validity of the appointment of an officer who adjudicates his case is entitled to a decision on the merits of the question and whatever relief may be appropriate if a violation indeed occurred"].)

We need not, and do not, consider the rights and interests of other parties to prior actions of the Commission.

DISPOSITION

The judgment is affirmed. The trial court is directed to vacate the stay that it issued.

SCOTLAND, P.J.

We concur: DAVIS and ROBIE, JJ.

Notes and Questions

1. The court wrote that "it is appropriate here to emphasize that our legal conclusion — that the process for appointing voting members of the Commission violates the separation of powers doctrine — is limited to the specific facts of this case." If that is the case, does this decision provide sufficient guidance for the legislative branch to follow concerning the separation of powers doctrine?

2. First the court found the role of the Commission and its implementation of the California Coastal Act of 1976 is an executive function. The appointment structure

forms the basis for its separation of powers analysis. The court made clear its view by saying, "In a practical sense, this unrestrained power to replace a majority of the Commission's voting members, and the presumed desire of those members to avoid being removed from their positions, allows the legislative branch not only to declare the law but also to control the Commission's execution of the law and exercise of its quasi-judicial powers."

3. How could the Legislature adjust the appointment structure to allow the Legislature to influence the Commission without running afoul of the separation of powers doctrine?

4. Is control by the executive branch determined just by an agency's leadership? What are other means of "control" that the Legislature could exercise that would effectively make an entity a "legislative agency" which would violate the doctrine? The court's opinion includes a possible test for determining a violation of the separation of powers doctrine: "as long as there is no material impairment of the other branch's core functions." Does this test provide sufficient guidance to the Legislature when crafting legislation?

5. The Commission unsuccessfully argued that the state Constitution does not prohibit the Legislature from appointing members of an executive branch agency. With the Legislature's plenary lawmaking authority under Article IV, why is the Commission's argument not correct?

6. The court cited a rather obvious violation of the doctrine when it stated: "For example, although Congress had the authority to create a Board of Review when relinquishing to an executive agency the operating authority over federal property, it violated the separation of powers doctrine by specifying that the Board of Review would consist of nine Members of Congress who would have veto authority over decisions of the executive agency." Does the fact that the Legislature made appointments to the Commission, rather than having legislators themselves as Commissioners, impact your legal analysis?

7. Did the court find it important that there were limited qualifications for appointment to the Commission? Was the court's finding that "the Commission regards itself as being free of executive branch authority and supervision" the ultimate reason for the court's ruling?

Fuller v. Bowen

(2012) 203 Cal.App.4th 1476, rehearing denied, review denied

OPINION

Mauro, J. —

In the 2010 primary election, Heidi Fuller and Tom Berryhill were both candidates for state senator in the 14th Senate district. Prior to the primary election, however, Fuller asked the superior court to issue orders that would prevent Berryhill's name from being placed on the primary election ballot. Fuller alleged that Berryhill had not resided in the 14th Senate district for at least one year as required by the California Constitution.

The superior court declined to prevent Berryhill's name from being placed on the ballot, concluding that the one-year residency requirement violated the equal protection clause of the Fourteenth Amendment to the United States Constitution. Fuller now contends on appeal that the superior court erred in ruling that the one-year residency requirement is unconstitutional.

We do not address whether the one-year residency requirement is unconstitutional, because a threshold jurisdictional issue resolves this case. The California Constitution vests in each house of the Legislature the sole authority to judge the qualifications and elections of a candidate for membership in that house, even when the challenge to the candidate's qualifications is brought prior to a primary election. Under the facts presented in this case, California courts lack jurisdiction to judge Tom Berryhill's qualifications to serve as a senator for the 14th Senate district.

We will affirm the judgment.

BACKGROUND

Heidi Fuller and Tom Berryhill both sought to be the Republican nominee for state senator in the 14th Senate district. But before the June 8, 2010 Primary Election took place, Fuller filed a petition for writ of mandate in the Sacramento Superior Court. To understand the basis for Fuller's court challenge, we begin with an overview of the relevant legal framework.

Article IV, section 2, subdivision (c) of the California Constitution provides that "[a] person is ineligible to be a member of the Legislature unless the person is an elector and has been a resident of the legislative district for one year ... immediately preceding the election." Elections Code section 8020 states that no candidate's name may be printed on the primary ballot unless a declaration of candidacy (§ 8040) and signed nomination papers (§ 8041) are delivered to the county elections official. The declaration of candidacy must substantially comply with the example set forth in the statute, which includes a declaration that the candidate meets the constitutional residency requirements. (§ 8040.)

After the signatures are verified, the nomination documents are forwarded to the Secretary of State, "who shall receive and file them." (§ 8082.) "At least 68 days before the direct primary, the Secretary of State shall transmit to each county elections official a certified list of candidates who are eligible to be voted for in his or her county at the direct primary." (§ 8120.) "Unless otherwise specifically provided, no person is eligible to be elected or appointed to an elective office unless that person is a registered voter and otherwise qualified to vote for that office at the time that nomination papers are issued to the person or at the time of the person's appointment." (§ 201.)

A candidate for state senate must also file a statement of intention and a recipient committee statement of organization. (Gov. Code, §§ 85200, 84101.) The Secretary of State is the designated filing officer for these documents. (Gov. Code, § 85200.) The filing officer has a duty to determine whether the original documents conform on their face with the Political Reform Act of 1974 (Gov. Code, § 81000 et seq.) (Cal. Code Regs., tit. 2, §§ 18110, 18410), but the filing officer is not required to seek or obtain other information to verify the entries. The filing officer must accept for filing any campaign statement which the Political Reform Act of 1974 requires to be filed with the filing officer. (Cal. Code Regs., tit. 2, § 18110.)

Section 13314 permits an elector to obtain a writ of mandate concerning impending election error under specified circumstances. Section 13314 provides in pertinent part: "(a)(1) An elector may seek a writ of mandate alleging that an error or omission has occurred, or is about to occur, in the placing of a name on, or in the printing of, a ballot, sample ballot, voter pamphlet, or other official matter, or that any neglect of duty has occurred, or is about to occur. ¶ (2) A peremptory writ of mandate shall issue only upon proof of both of the following: ¶ (A) That the error, omission, or neglect is in violation of this code or the Constitution. ¶ (B) That issuance of the writ will not substantially interfere with the conduct of the election.... ¶ (4) The Secretary of State shall be named as a respondent or a real party in interest in any proceeding under this section concerning a measure or a candidate described in Section 15375 ...," which includes a candidate for a member of the Senate.

Fuller filed a petition for writ of mandate pursuant to section 13314, subdivision (a), alleging that Berryhill had not met the one-year residency requirement set forth in article IV, section 2, subdivision (c). Fuller acknowledged in her petition that prior opinions by the Attorney General concluded that the Secretary of State could not refuse to file a declaration of candidacy based on an alleged failure to meet the residency requirement (56 Ops.Cal.Atty.Gen. 365, 367 (1973)), and that the Secretary of State was not authorized to enforce the constitutional residency requirement (62 Ops.Cal.Atty.Gen. 365 (1979)). Nonetheless, Fuller argued that those prior Attorney General opinions were wrong.

. . . .

DISCUSSION

Fuller contends the superior court erred in determining that the one-year residency requirement in the California Constitution is unconstitutional under the Fourteenth Amendment to the United States Constitution. According to Fuller, the superior court applied the wrong standard of review.

We do not reach Fuller's equal protection contentions, however, because the Secretary of State and Berryhill assert threshold contentions regarding mootness and jurisdiction. The jurisdictional contention is dispositive.

I

The Secretary of State and Berryhill contend that Fuller's challenge is moot. They point out that the relief Fuller sought in the superior court was limited to withdrawing Berryhill's nomination documents, but that Fuller's petition was denied, the election was held with Berryhill's name on the ballot, he was elected, and he has been seated by the California State Senate.5 They argue that Fuller can no longer obtain the relief she requested.

Fuller counters that this case falls within the public interest exception to the doctrine of mootness. Berryhill concedes that the exception may apply. They are both correct.

The public interest exception may apply where the issues presented "are of general public interest and likely to recur" (*Clark v. Burleigh* (1992) 4 Cal.4th 474, 481 [14 Cal.Rptr.2d 455, 841 P.2d 975]), and the exception is often applied in election cases (*Kunde v. Seiler* (2011) 197 Cal.App.4th 518, 527 [128 Cal.Rptr.3d 869]). "'Under certain conditions, disputes concerning election procedures are properly reviewable by an appellate court even though the particular election in question has already taken place.' [Citation.] Even though the relief requested is no longer available, review may be appropriate if the contentions raised are of general public interest 'and are likely to occur in future elections in a manner evasive of timely appellate review.' [Citations.]" (*Huening v. Eu* (1991) 231 Cal.App.3d 766, 770 [282 Cal.Rptr. 664]; see also *Unger v. Superior Court* (1984) 37 Cal.3d 612, 614 [209 Cal.Rptr. 474, 692 P.2d 238].)

Here, the Secretary of State and Berryhill assert that the Legislature is the sole judge of the qualifications and elections of a candidate for membership in the Legislature even when the qualification challenge is asserted prior to a primary election. This issue is likely to recur in a manner not subject to timely appellate review. The public interest exception to the doctrine of mootness applies in this case.

II

Accordingly, we turn to the assertion by the Secretary of State and Berryhill that the courts lack jurisdiction to address Fuller's challenge to Berryhill's qualifications, because the Legislature is the sole judge of the qualifications and elections of its members. (Art. IV, § 5, subd. (a).) The Legislature of the State of California filed an amicus curiae brief in support of this contention.

Responding to this jurisdictional argument, Fuller asserts that the trial court had jurisdiction to decide this case because the role of construing constitutional provisions rests with the courts. She cites *Powell v. McCormack* (1969) 395 U.S. 486 [23 L.Ed.2d 491, 89 S.Ct. 1944] (*Powell*) to support her argument, but *Powell* is not on point.

In the *Powell* case, Adam Clayton Powell, Jr., was elected to the United States House of Representatives, but a House resolution prevented him from taking his seat. Powell sued, alleging he could only be excluded if the House found he failed to meet the standing requirements of age, citizenship and residence contained in article I, section 2 of the United States Constitution. He maintained that the House excluded him unconstitutionally because it specifically found he met those requirements. (*Powell, supra,* 395 U.S. at p. 489 [23 L.Ed.2d at p. 498].)

The United States Supreme Court asserted jurisdiction over the claim even though article I, section 5 of the United States Constitution assigns each House of Congress the power to judge the elections and qualifications of its own members. (*Powell, supra,* 395 U.S. at pp. 513–514 [23 L.Ed.2d at p. 512].) The relevant determination was whether the issue was "a 'political question' — that is, a question which is not justiciable in federal court because of the separation of powers provided by the Constitution." (*Id.* at p. 517 [23 L.Ed.2d at p. 514].)

....

We agree with Fuller that it is the judiciary's role to interpret the law, including the Constitution. But as we will explain, our interpretation leads us to the narrow conclusion that it is not the judiciary's role to judge the qualifications and elections of candidates for membership in the Legislature. This interpretation does not invalidate section 13314, however, because the application of that section is not limited to challenging the qualifications and elections of candidates for membership in the Legislature. Moreover, because our interpretation resolves this case, it is unnecessary to reach any other constitutional questions, even if we might have jurisdiction to do so.

To support their argument that the courts lack jurisdiction in this context, the Secretary of State, Berryhill and the Legislature rely on *Allen v. Lelande* (1912) 164 Cal. 56 [127 P. 643] (*Allen*) and *In re McGee* (1951) 36 Cal.2d 592 [226 P.2d 1] (*McGee*). In *Allen, supra,* 164 Cal. 56, a candidate was nominated for the office of member of the Assembly by direct primary election. But mandamus was sought to compel the county clerk to strike the candidate's name from the general election ballot on the ground that he failed to meet the constitutional residency requirement. (*Id.* at p. 57.) The California Supreme Court denied relief, stating: "The constitution of the state (art. IV, sec. 7) reads as follows: 'Each house shall choose its officers, and judge of the qualifications, elections, and returns of its members.' By that article the assembly is made the exclusive judge of the qualifications of its members. The law providing for an official ballot cannot be held to have changed the intent of the people in adopting that constitutional provision that the assembly should be the sole and exclusive judge of the eligibility of those whose election is properly certified. For this court to undertake to try the question of eligibility and to deprive the candidate of any chance to be elected, would simply be to usurp the jurisdiction of the assembly." (*Ibid.*)

Later, in *McGee, supra,* 36 Cal.2d 592, the California Supreme Court addressed a challenge to a candidate for the Assembly under former section 8600, which set forth the procedure for a challenge to a candidate's nomination. (36 Cal.2d at pp. 593, 598.) Former section 8600 provided in relevant part: "Any candidate at a primary election may contest the right of another candidate to nomination to the same office by filing an affidavit alleging any of the following grounds, that: (a) The defendant is not eligible to the office in dispute...." (Stats. 1939, ch. 26, p. 267; now see § 16101.)

The plaintiff in *McGee* argued that the constitutional power conferred on the Assembly to judge the qualifications and elections of its members did not extend to primary elections. (*McGee, supra,* 36 Cal.2d at p. 595.) But the California Supreme Court disagreed, citing with approval its decision in *Allen*. It reiterated that the California Constitution confers exclusive jurisdiction on the Legislature to judge the qualifications and elections of its members, and observed that the separation of powers doctrine precluded one branch of government from exercising the powers of the other. (36 Cal.2d at pp. 594–595.) "[T]he jurisdiction to judge qualifications and elections of assemblymen lies exclusively with the Assembly and it cannot delegate that duty and it cannot achieve that result indirectly by authorizing the courts to decide contests after primary elections.... [P]rimary elections in this state are an integral part of the election process. [Citations.]" (*Id.* at p. 597.)

The California Supreme Court added, "The anomalous results that would follow if a court could make a binding determination under section 8600 of the Elections Code are apparent. If the trial court gave its judgment, either favorable or unfavorable, to the candidate after the primary election but nevertheless the candidate at the ensuing election received the majority of the votes cast, there can be little doubt that he could present his credentials to the legislative house to which he was elected and that body would be required to pass upon any claimed defect in his selection, regardless of the conclusion reached by the court. Such could easily happen as it has in the instant case.... For this court to rule upon the question would be futile, for the binding and conclusive decision rests with the Assembly. If the Legislature may, by authorizing court review of primary election contests, prevent a candidate from being on the ballot at the ensuing election for various defects as to the elections or qualifications, it would, in many situations, achieve indirectly what it could not do directly, that is, delegate to the courts its prerogatives under section 7 of article IV of the California Constitution." (*McGee, supra,* 36 Cal.2d at pp. 597–598.)

Under the circumstances, the California Supreme Court held in *McGee, supra,* 36 Cal.2d 592, that former section 8600 could not validly apply to the office of a member of the Assembly (36 Cal.2d at p. 598) and that the Legislature's sole authority to judge the qualifications and elections of its members applied prior to a candidate winning the general election and becoming a member. The Legislature could not statutorily delegate its authority to adjudicate this issue at earlier stages of the election process.

Fuller acknowledges the holdings in *Allen* and *McGee,* but contends their reasoning should not be extended to a qualification challenge occurring before a primary election. We disagree. As the California Supreme Court stated, a primary election is an integral part of the election process. (*McGee, supra,* 36 Cal.2d at p. 597.) A candidate's participation in the primary is no less important than his or her participation in the general election. For the judicial branch "to try the question of eligibility and to deprive the candidate of any chance to be elected, would simply be to usurp the jurisdiction of the [Legislature]." (*Allen, supra,* 164 Cal. at p. 57.) The Legislature cannot "delegate to the courts its prerogatives" under the Constitution to judge the qualifications and elections of its members. (*McGee, supra,* 36 Cal.2d at pp. 597–598.) Using section 13314 to adjudicate the qualifications of a candidate for the Assembly or Senate prior to the primary would be just as invasive as a postprimary, pregeneral election challenge.

Moreover, if section 13314 could be used to judge the qualifications of a candidate for the Legislature prior to a primary election, it could lead to the type of anomalous results anticipated in *McGee.* (*McGee, supra,* 36 Cal.2d at pp. 597–598.) A court could remove a candidate from the ballot before the primary election, possibly depriving the Legislature of the opportunity to judge the qualifications of that person. But a candidate who survives a court challenge and is elected could be judged again by the

Legislature, perhaps with a different result. As the California Supreme Court noted in *McGee,* the prior court proceeding could be futile because the binding and conclusive decision rests with the Legislature. (*Id.* at p. 598.) The prospect that separate branches of government could judge the qualifications and elections of candidates for membership in the Legislature at different times with different results is something to be avoided, no matter when the challenge first arises.

Nonetheless, Fuller focuses on the word "Members" in article IV, section 5, subdivision (a), arguing that "[e]xtending ... *McGee* to preelection controversies would necessarily broaden the definition of 'Members' to the whole of the general public before a single form had been filed...." Not so. A challenge under section 13314 cannot occur until the person's name has been placed or is about to be placed on the ballot. (§ 13314, subd. (a)(1).) The person's name cannot be placed on the ballot until he or she has filed a declaration of candidacy and nomination papers. (§§ 13, 8020, 8040, 8041.) Accordingly, extending *McGee* to preprimary controversies under section 13314 does not encompass "the whole of the general public," only candidates for the state Assembly or Senate.

Fuller asserts that if section 13314 is considered "an impermissible encroachment" on the Legislature's authority over the election of its Members, Californians will be denied judicial recourse in "all things related to the election of an Assemblyman or Senator." But our decision does not encompass "all things" related to the election of a member of the Legislature. In any event, our holding is compelled by the separation of powers doctrine. As the California Supreme Court stated in *French v. Senate* (1905) 146 Cal. 604 [80 P. 1031]: "Under our form of government the judicial department has no power to revise even the most arbitrary and unfair action of the legislative department, or of either house thereof, taken in pursuance of the power committed exclusively to that department by the constitution.... The legislature is a coordinate department of the state government. By article III of the constitution it is provided that one department of the state shall not exercise the functions of either of the other departments except as in that instrument, expressly directed and permitted. There is no provision authorizing courts to control, direct, supervise, or forbid, the exercise by either house of the power to expel a member [or to adjudicate the qualifications for membership]. These powers are functions of the legislative department, and therefore in the exercise of the power thus committed to it the senate [and assembly] is supreme. An attempt by this court to direct or control the legislature, or either house thereof, in the exercise of the power, would be an attempt to exercise legislative functions, which it is expressly forbidden to do." (*Id.* at pp. 606–607.)

We hold that the California Constitution vests in the Senate the sole authority to judge Tom Berryhill's qualifications to serve as a senator for the 14th Senate district.

DISPOSITION

The judgment is affirmed.

RAYE, P.J., and HULL, J., concurred.

Notes and Questions

1. Under the separation of powers doctrine and the provision of the state Constitution vesting in each house of the Legislature the sole authority to judge the qualifications and elections of a candidate for membership in that house, California courts lack jurisdiction to judge the qualifications of a candidate for a primary election for a state Senate seat who allegedly had not resided in his district for at least one year as required by the state Constitution.

2. It is the judiciary's role to interpret the law, including the Constitution, but it is not the judiciary's role to judge the qualifications and elections of candidates for membership in the Legislature. The Legislature cannot delegate to the courts its prerogatives under the state Constitution to judge the qualifications and elections of its members.

3. The superior court used strict scrutiny to find the one-year residency requirement unconstitutional. On appeal, however, the Third District Court of Appeal ruled that the court did not have jurisdiction, as the state Constitution provides the Legislature the authority to determine qualifications of its members. In June 2012, the California Supreme Court denied Fuller's appeal of the Third DCA's ruling. As long as the Legislature continues to allow members to be sworn in, the one-year durational residency requirement does not apply.

4. How do you think the court would have ruled on the key question it did not address — whether the one-year residency requirement is unconstitutional?

5. If the courts are unwilling to address whether a candidate for elected office in this state meet the requirements specified in the state Constitution, does a citizen in this state have a recourse for challenging whether those requirements have been met?

6. Would any of the other requirements for elective office (e.g., age) survive a strict scrutiny standard of review and serve a compelling governmental interest?

7. Does the court's ruling that it is the judiciary's role to interpret the law, including the Constitution, require it to examine and decide the claims that a candidate has not met the constitutional requirements for holding office? Did the court undermine that general rule by finding that "our interpretation leads us to the narrow conclusion that it is not the judiciary's role to judge the qualifications and elections of candidates for membership in the Legislature"?

8. The appellate court in this case declined to adopt Fuller's argument that a pre-primary challenge should be treated differently. What is the basis for the court's determination in this regard?

A. Judiciary Branch Does Not Play a Role in Lawmaking

While the legislative and executive branches play critical roles in the lawmaking process, the judicial branch does not have an enumerated role in the lawmaking process. Instead, the judiciary is charged under the state Constitution with interpreting the laws that have been enacted by the Legislature and signed into law by the Governor. The Constitution clearly defines the roles of the Legislature and the Governor in the lawmaking process. However, it does not provide a role for the third branch of government.

Serrano v. Priest

(1976) 18 Cal.3d 728*

(Opinion by Sullivan, J., with Wright, C.J., Tobriner and Mosk, JJ., concurring. Separate dissenting opinion by Richardson, J. Separate dissenting opinion by Clark, J., with McComb, J., concurring.)

OPINION

Sullivan, J.

The instant proceeding, which involves a constitutional challenge to the California public school financing system, is before us for the second time. In 1971, we reversed a judgment of dismissal entered upon orders sustaining general demurrers and remanded the cause with directions that it proceed to trial. (*Serrano v. Priest* (1971) 5 Cal. 3d 584 [96 Cal. Rptr. 601, 487 P.2d 1241], hereafter cited as *Serrano I.*) In so doing we held that the facts alleged in plaintiffs' complaint were sufficient to constitute the three causes of action there set forth, and that if such allegations were sustained at trial, the state public school financing system must be declared invalid as in violation of state and federal constitutional provisions guaranteeing the equal protection of the laws.

Upon remand answers to the complaint were filed by all existing defendants and certain school districts of the County of Los Angeles were allowed to intervene as defendants, adopting as their own the answers previously filed by the other county defendants. The California Federation of Teachers, AFL-CIO, was permitted to intervene as a plaintiff on condition that its complaint adopt the essential allegations of the original complaint. The trial court declined to accept defendants' suggestion that the Legislature and the Governor be joined as indispensable parties.

Trial commenced on December 26, 1972. After more than 60 days of trial proceedings the court issued its "Memorandum Opinion Re Intended Decision" on April 10, 1974, and on August 30 of the same year filed its findings of fact and conclusions of law, there being 299 of the former and 128 of the latter. Judgment was entered on September 3, 1974, and defendants' motion for a new trial was denied on October 28, 1974. This appeal followed.

---

* Although neither the former state Treasurer (now deceased) nor the present holder of that office is a party to this appeal, we continue to use the title *Serrano v. Priest* for purposes of consistency and convenience.

I

Our decision in *Serrano I*, which due to the then legal posture of the proceeding directed itself only to the sufficiency of allegations of the complaint to state a cause of action and contemplated full trial proceedings for the proof of such allegations, nevertheless attracted the immediate attention of the California Legislature. As a result, the lawmakers passed two bills — Senate Bill No. 90 (S.B. 90) and Assembly Bill No. 1267 (A.B. 1267) — which, upon becoming law during the pendency of trial proceedings, brought about certain significant changes in the public-school financing system then under judicial scrutiny. Recognizing this, all parties to the action thereupon entered into a stipulation that for purposes of trial the California system for the financing of public schools should be deemed to include all law applicable at the time of trial. This agreement was later incorporated as follows among the trial court's conclusions of law: "For purposes of this litigation, the California system of financing public schools, includes not only all pertinent provisions of the California Constitution, statutes, and administrative codes, and all pertinent provisions of federal statutes and regulations, but includes all modifications, amendments, and additions to the California statutes and administrative codes resulting from the California Legislature's enactment of those bills known as S.B. 90 and A.B. 1267." (See Stats. 1972, ch. 1406; Stats. 1973, ch. 208.)

In view of these developments we think it appropriate at this point, before undertaking a description of the particulars of the trial court's judgment, to review in some detail the specific nature of the changes in the financing system which were wrought by the Legislature following our decision. Because our understanding of these changes depends in large part on an understanding of the system as it existed at the time of Serrano I, we begin by reiterating the description of that system, based on the allegations of the complaint and certain matters judicially noticed, which we set forth in our earlier opinion. Clarity of exposition dictates that the following excerpt be extensive.

. . . .

B. Conclusions of Law and Judgment

Although we consider it unnecessary to set out a comprehensive review of the trial court's 128 conclusions of law, the most fundamental of those conclusions were incorporated into the judgment, which we now describe.

The trial court held that the California public school financing system for elementary and secondary schools as it stood following the adoption of S.B. 90 and A.B. 1267, while not in violation of the equal protection clause of the Fourteenth Amendment to the federal Constitution, fn. 19 was invalid as in violation of former article I, sections 11 and 21, of the California Constitution (now art. IV, § 16 and art. I, § 7 respectively; see and compare *Serrano I, supra*, at p. 596, fn. 11), our state equal protection provisions. Indicating the respects in which the system before it was violative of our state constitutional standard, the court set a period of six years from the date of entry of judgment as a reasonable time for bringing the system into constitutional compliance; it further held and ordered that the existing system should continue to operate until such compliance had been achieved. The judgment specifically provided that it was not to be construed to require the adoption of any particular system of school finance, but only to require that the plan adopted comport with the requirements of state equal protection provisions. Finally, the trial court retained jurisdiction of the action and over the parties "so that any of such parties may apply for appropriate relief in the event that relevant circumstances develop, such as a failure by the legislative and executive branches of the state government to take the necessary steps to design, enact into law, and place into operation, within a reasonable time from the date of entry of this Judgment, a California Public School Financing System for public elementary and secondary schools that will fully comply with the said equal-protection-of-the-law provisions of the California Constitution."

III

Defendants advance three substantive contentions on appeal.

First, it is urged that the trial court employed inappropriate criteria insofar as it focused on the notion of so-called "fiscal neutrality" to the exclusion of other factors relevant to its determination. If the trial court had employed appropriate criteria, it is suggested, the system as improved by S.B. 90 and A.B. 1267 would have been seen to be free from constitutional objection on equal protection grounds.

Second, defendants urge that an improper legal standard of equal protection review was utilized. The proper standard, it is contended, even under our state constitutional provisions, is that requiring no more than a rational relationship, critically analyzed, between the financing method chosen and some legitimate state purpose.

Third, and assuming that the financing system before the court is to some extent inconsistent with state constitutional provisions guaranteeing the equal protection of the laws, it is urged that those provisions are to that extent in conflict with other provisions of the state Constitution and, in accordance with the principle of consistency in constitutional interpretation, should be made to yield pro tanto in order to avoid such conflict.

IV

Before taking up the foregoing contentions, we first dispose of a preliminary procedural matter. Defendants urge that the trial court was without jurisdiction to proceed in this matter because two allegedly indispensable parties — the Legislature and the Governor — were not joined. (See Code Civ. Proc., § 389.) It is pointed out that "the operative and directory provisions" of the judgment "are addressed solely to the Legislative and Governor," and that the parties defendant in the action lack all power to bring about the relief sought by plaintiffs and awarded by the trial court — i.e., the restructuring of the state public school financing system in a manner which will comply with provisions of our state Constitution guaranteeing equal protection of the laws. Reference is made to certain legislative reapportionment cases, notably *Silver v. Brown* (1965) 63 Cal. 2d 270 [46 Cal. Rptr. 308, 405 P.2d 132], and to the fact that the Governor and the members of the Legislature were there made parties. To do otherwise in this case, it is urged, "would deny [the] people who created this financing system through their elective representatives of their day in Court...."

This contention is based on several misconceptions and inaccurate statements of the record.

First, it is clear that the trial court — wholly cognizant of the well-established principle, rooted in the doctrine of separation of powers (Cal. Const., art. III, § 3), that the courts may not order the Legislature or its members to enact or not to enact, or the Governor to sign or not to sign, specific legislation — by no means addressed the "operative and directory provisions" of its judgment to the Legislature and Governor.

On the contrary it simply declared that the public-school financing system before it, which was administered by the parties [sic] defendant, was in violation of state constitutional provisions guaranteeing equal protection of the laws. The trial court also indicated that it would retain jurisdiction over the matter so that any party might apply for "appropriate relief" in the event that the lawmakers and the Governor had failed within a reasonable time, set by the judgment at six years, "to take the necessary steps to design, enact into law, and place into operation" a system which would comply with those provisions. However, it explicitly and properly refrained from issuing directives to the lawmakers and the chief executive, stating in its judgment: "... [T]his judgment is not intended to require, and is not to be construed as requiring, the adoption of any particular plan or system for financing the public elementary and secondary schools of the state...."

Secondly, as the reapportionment cases themselves indicate, it is the general and long-established rule that in actions for declaratory and injunctive relief challenging the constitutionality of state statutes, state officers with statewide administrative functions under the challenged statute are the proper parties defendant. (See *Yorty v. Anderson* (1963) 60 Cal. 2d 312, 317–318 [33 Cal. Rptr. 97, 384 P.2d 417], and cases there cited; cf. *D'Amico v. Board of Medical Examiners* (1974) 11 Cal. 3d 1 [112 Cal. Rptr. 786, 520 P.2d 10]; *City of Carmel-by-the-Sea v. Young* (1970) 2 Cal. 3d 259 [85 Cal. Rptr. 1, 466 P.2d 225, 37 A.L.R.3d 1313].) The fact that in the reapportionment context the Legislature and its members may also be considered proper parties stems from the direct institutional interest of those parties in the determination. (See and cf. *Silver v. Jordan* (S.D. Cal. 1964) 241 F. Supp. 576, 579, affirmed (1965) 381 U.S. 415 [14 L. Ed. 2d 689, 85 S. Ct. 1572]; *Minnesota State Senate v. Beens* (1972) 406 U.S. 187, 194 [32 L. Ed. 2d 1, 8, 92 S. Ct. 1477].)

In the instant case, on the other hand, as in the great majority of cases brought against state administrative officers to challenge the constitutionality of a statute or statutes administered by them, the Legislature and the Governor lack any similar interest. The interest they do have — that of lawmakers concerned with the validity of statutes enacted by them — is not of the immediacy and directness requisite to party status; it may thus be fully and adequately represented by the appropriate administrative officers of the state.

Moreover, even should the Legislature and the Governor be considered proper parties to this litigation (i.e., parties subject to permissive joinder or capable of intervention), it is clear that they could in no case be considered indispensable parties, or parties without whom the action could not fairly proceed.

Indispensable parties, as we said in *Bank of California v. Superior Court* (1940) 16 Cal. 2d 516, at page 521 [106 P.2d 879], are parties "whose interests, rights, or duties will inevitably be affected by any decree which can be rendered in the action. Typical are the situations where a number of persons have undetermined interests in the same property, or in a particular trust fund, and one of them seeks, in an action, to recover the whole, to fix his share, or to recover a portion claimed by him. The other persons with similar interests are indispensable parties. The reason is that a judgment in favor of one claimant for part of the property or fund would necessarily determine the amount or extent which remains available to the others. Hence, any judgment in the action would inevitably affect their rights."

Manifestly, the Legislature and the Governor have no interest in this proceeding which is remotely comparable to that contemplated by this language.

Moreover, as we also said in the *Bank of California* case, in dealing with the doctrine of indispensable and necessary parties "we should ... be careful to avoid converting a discretionary power or a rule of fairness in procedure into an arbitrary and burdensome requirement which may thwart rather than accomplish justice." (16 Cal.2d at p. 521; see also *Muggill v. Reuben H. Donnelley Corp.* (1965) 62 Cal. 2d 239, 241 [42 Cal. Rptr. 107, 398 P.2d 147].) In the instant case it is quite clear that no governmental interest has lacked for able and willing advocates in the absence of the Legislature and Governor as parties. This case has been well-known to those entities since its inception, yet they have at no point sought intervention or indicated any interest in doing so. Even more significantly, this is a matter whose resolution has been anxiously awaited by the parties and the public at large for more than seven years. In light of these considerations we are convinced that to invoke the doctrine of indispensability, and thus require the renewal of trial proceedings on this ground, would indeed be to "thwart rather than accomplish justice."

....

VII

For the reasons above stated, we have concluded that the state public school financing system here under review, because it establishes and perpetuates a classification based upon district wealth which affects the fundamental interest of education, must be subjected to strict judicial scrutiny in determining whether it complies with our state equal protection provisions.

Under this standard the presumption of constitutionality normally attaching to state legislative classifications falls away, and the state must shoulder the burden of establishing that the classification in question is necessary to achieve a compelling state interest. (*Serrano I* at p. 597; see also *Weber v. City Council* (1973) 9 Cal. 3d 950, 958–959 [109 Cal. Rptr. 553, 513 P.2d 601].)

Basing our determination upon the amply supported factual findings of the trial court, which we have summarized in part II above, we conclude without hesitation that the trial court properly determined that the state failed to bear this burden.

Our reasons for this conclusion are essentially those stated by us on this point in *Serrano I*. The system in question has been found by the trial court, on the basis of substantial and convincing evidence, to suffer from the same basic shortcomings as that system which was alleged to exist in the original complaint — to wit, it allows the availability of educational opportunity to vary as a function of the assessed valuation per ADA of taxable property within a given district. The state interest advanced in justification of this discrimination continues to be that of local control of fiscal and educational matters. However, the trial court has found that asserted interest to be chimerical from the standpoint of those districts which are less favored in terms of taxable wealth per pupil, and we ourselves, after a thorough examination of the record, are in wholehearted agreement with this assessment.

The admitted improvements to the system which were wrought by the Legislature following *Serrano I* have not been and will not in the foreseeable future be sufficient to negate those features of the system which operate to perpetuate this inequity. Foremost among these — especially in a period of rising inflation and restrictive revenue limits — is the continued availability of voted tax overrides which, while providing more affluent districts with a ready means for meeting what they conceive as legitimate and proper educational objectives, will be recognized by the poorer districts, unable to support the passage of such overrides in order to meet equally desired objectives, as but a new and more invidious aspect of that "cruel illusion" which we found to be inherent in the former system. (*Serrano I* at p. 611.) In short, what we said in our former opinion in this respect is equally true here. "[S]o long as the assessed valuation within a district's boundaries is a major determinant of how much it can spend for its schools, only a district with a large tax base [per ADA] will be truly able to decide how much it really cares about education. The poor district cannot freely choose to tax itself into an excellence which its tax rolls cannot provide. Far from being necessary to promote local fiscal choice, the present financing system actually deprives the less wealthy districts of that option." (*Id.*)

It is accordingly clear that the California public school financing system here under review, because it renders the educational opportunity available to the students of this state a function of the taxable wealth per ADA of the districts in which they live, has not been shown by the state to be necessary to achieve a compelling state interest.

[3b] Defendants, however, have one more string to their bow: they, joined by one of the amici curiae, contend that even in the event of such a holding by this court the financing system before us cannot be held to be in violation of state equal protection provisions, because other provisions of our state Constitution specifically authorize just such a system. It is to this contention that we now turn.

VIII

Defendants' claim of specific state constitutional authorization for the public school financing system before us is primarily based upon the terms of article XIII, section

21, which provides: "Within such limits as may be provided under Section 20 of this Article [allowing the Legislature to provide maximum local property tax rates and bonding limits], the Legislature shall provide for an annual levy by county governing bodies of school district taxes sufficient to produce annual revenues for each district that the district's board determines are required for its schools and district functions." The argument, generally stated, is that a harmonious interpretation of this section along with other provisions requiring equal protection of the laws must operate to insulate distinctions based on district wealth disparities from state equal protection requirements. The argument proceeds on two distinct levels. First, it is urged, we held in *Serrano I* that the system there before us was "authorized" and "mandated" by the predecessor to article XIII, section 21 (former art. IX, § 6, par. 6); that holding, defendants and their supporting amicus assert, is now the law of the case, and to the extent that the system here in question shares in the shortcomings of the former system related to district wealth disparities, it too is so "authorized" and "mandated." Second, it is pointed out, even if we are not compelled to this conclusion by the doctrine of the law of the case, the terms of the section compel the indicated result. We take up these contentions in order.

At pages 595 and 596 of our opinion in *Serrano I*, in rejecting plaintiffs' contention that the system there alleged to exist was violative of the provisions of article IX, section 5 (requiring "a system of common schools"), we observed that former article IX, section 6, paragraph 6 (now art. XIII, § 21), the provision here at issue, "specifically authorizes the very element of the fiscal system of which plaintiffs complain." (*Id.*, at p. 596.) At a later point in the opinion, rejecting a contention of defendants that only de facto discrimination was here involved, we had occasion to observe that "[t]he school funding scheme is mandated in every detail by the California Constitution and statutes." (*Id.*, at p. 603.) It is urged that these two references, taken together, represent a holding that the system there before us was required by the terms of present article XIII, section 21. Insofar as the system now under examination shares in the features of the former system which we found objectionable in *Serrano I*, defendants argue, it is equally required by that section under the doctrine of the law of the case.

We reject such contentions as being utterly devoid of merit. Indeed, as we shall make clear, defendants' seizure upon such fragments of our opinion in *Serrano I* as a basis of argument not only results in an unreasoned distortion of such language but more unfortunately displays an attempt to circumvent the rationale of *Serrano I* (now the law of the case) by emphasizing isolated words out of context. It is beyond question — and beyond cavil — that in stating that former article IX, section 6 "specifically authorizes the very element of the fiscal system of which plaintiffs complain," we had reference to that "element" of the system permitting variations in expenditures per ADA among the several districts. This is made clear by the context of the statement and the language following it. Former section 5 of article IX (the "common schools" provision) should not, we held, be interpreted to apply to school financing and require "uniform educational expenditures" because such an interpretation would render it inconsistent with former section 6 (the provision here at issue) which allows variation in school district expenditures. This was not to say, however, that former section 6 "authorized" or "approved" a system in which such variation was the product of disparities in district wealth. Any such conclusion would clearly have been at odds with our ultimate conclusion in *Serrano I* that the system there alleged to exist was violative of state as well as federal equal protection provisions. (5 Cal. 3d at 596, fn. 11.) ...

Similarly, by saying later on in our opinion, in disposing of an entirely different contention, that the school funding scheme was "mandated in every detail by the California Constitution and statutes" (*id.*, at p. 603; italics added), we in no way implied that the constitutional provision in question "mandated" the system there alleged to exist. The constitutional provision, as we shall point out more fully below, "mandated" only that there be a system allowing for local decision as to the level of school expenditures and that the mechanism to be utilized in providing revenues to permit such expenditures be a county levy of school district taxes. It was the statutes enacted under the aegis of that provision which tied the efficacy of local decision to district wealth.

We conclude for the foregoing reasons fn. 50 that the doctrine of the law of the case is not helpful to defendants on this point. It remains for us to undertake an interpretation of article XIII, section 21 (former art. IX, §6, par. 6) in order to determine whether that provision requires a public-school financing system which, like that before us, makes local decisions affecting educational opportunity depend for their effectiveness upon the taxable wealth per ADA in the district. We conclude without hesitation that it does not.

As we have noted above, article XIII, section 21 of the state Constitution provides that the Legislature, within certain limits set by established maximum tax rates and bonding limits, "shall provide for an annual levy by county governing bodies of school district taxes sufficient to produce annual revenues for each district that the district's board determines are required for its schools and district functions." In so doing the provision both authorizes the Legislature to establish a mechanism by which the revenues "required" for each district are to be produced, and describes the character of that mechanism — i.e., "an annual levy by county governing bodies of school district taxes." The provision does not, however, address itself to the question of the tax base to which the levy is to be applied, nor does it speak in terms of assessed valuation in any respect. Manifestly it does not authorize disparities in school district expenditures based upon the relative wealth per ADA of a particular school district. Such disparities, insofar as they have been here shown to exist, are the result of legislative action, not constitutional mandate.

Article IX, section 14 of the state Constitution clearly establishes that it is the Legislature which bears the ultimate responsibility for establishing school districts and their boundaries. [10b] By its exercise of this power, and by the concurrent exercise of its powers under article XIII, section 21 to provide for a school financing mechanism based upon county levies of school district taxes, it has created a system whereby disparities in assessed valuation per ADA among the various school districts result in disparities in the educational opportunity available to the students within such districts. Thus, as we said in *Serrano I*, "[g]overnmental action drew the school district boundary lines, thus determining how much local wealth each district would contain [citations]." (5 Cal.3d at p. 603.) It is that action, which we reiterate is the product of legislative determinations, fn. 52 that we today hold to be in violation of our state provisions guaranteeing equal protection of the laws.

It seems to be argued, however, that because article XIII, section 21 authorizes the financing of schools by a county levy of school district taxes, the Legislature is free to structure a system based upon this mechanism in any way that it chooses. Such a notion, we hasten to point out, is manifestly absurd.

A constitutional provision creating the duty and power to legislate in a particular area always remains subject to general constitutional requirements governing all legislation unless the intent of the Constitution to exempt it from such requirements plainly appears.

In *In re Jacobson* (1936) 16 Cal. App. 2d 497 [60 P.2d 1001], for example, the Legislature, acting pursuant to its power to create a system of inferior courts (former art. VI, § 11a), did so in a manner which granted greater jurisdiction to city courts in populous townships than to the same class of courts of less populous townships — regardless of the population of the particular city. This, it was held, was in violation of the fundamental constitutional requirement that laws of a general nature have a uniform application. "The legislature derives its power to create courts from the Constitution," the court stated, *"but it may do so only in conformity with the provisions of the Constitution.* It doubtless has the right to classify cities according to population, and having made such classification to prescribe different powers and regulations for each of the classes. The powers and regulations must, however, be uniform for each of the classes." (16 Cal.App.2d at p. 500; italics added.)

Similarly, in *Mordecai v. Board of Supervisors* (1920) 183 Cal. 434 [192 P. 40] the Legislature, acting pursuant to its constitutional power to create and regulate the affairs of irrigation districts (former art. XI, § 13), enacted a comprehensive irrigation plan which exempted from its provisions those districts located in counties which had adopted a charter prior to a specific date. This, we concluded, it could not do. "It is argued, in effect, that this provision [former art. XI, § 13] empowers the legislature to pass what laws it sees fit in regard to irrigation districts untrammeled by the general requirement that laws of a general nature shall have a uniform operation. We cannot agree with this. There is nothing to indicate that the power granted the legislature by this provision was not to be exercised by it subject to the general requirements of the constitution governing the manner in which the power of legislation when conferred or possessed shall be exercised. *The legislature has the power as conferred by the provision of the constitution just quoted to legislate concerning the affairs of irrigation districts, but that power, like the power of the legislature to legislate on other subjects, must be exercised in the manner in which the constitution provides that the power of legislation when it exists must be exercised. Before any grant of power to legislate on a particular subject can be held to be free of a general requirement governing all legislation, the intent of the constitution to that effect must be plain. No such intent appears in the present instance."* (183 Cal. at pp. 441–442; italics added.)

By the same token, we are here confronted with a situation in which the Legislature has been granted the power to provide for the financing of schools through the mechanism of county levies of school district taxes. Nothing in the constitutional provision establishing that power, however, indicates that its exercise is to be freed from general constitutional limitations applicable to all legislation. Accordingly, the Legislature, in its exercise of the subject power in conjunction with other powers possessed by it, was obliged to act in a manner consistent with such limitations. This it has not done. Instead it has undertaken to create a school financing system which, by making the quality of educational opportunity available to a student dependent upon the wealth of the district in which he lives, is manifestly inconsistent with fundamental constitutional provisions guaranteeing the equal protection of the laws to all citizens of this state. That system, we hold today, can no longer endure.

We also reject as wholly without merit the contention that the school financing system before us is somehow made necessary or permitted by the provisions of article IX, section 1, of the state Constitution. That section provides: "A general diffusion of knowledge and intelligence being essential to the preservation of the rights and liberties of the people, the Legislature shall encourage by all suitable means the promotion of intellectual, scientific, moral, and agricultural improvement." We declare ourselves at a loss to understand how this provision can be said to mandate or authorize the creation of a system which conditions educational opportunity on the taxable wealth of the district in which the student attends school.

For the foregoing reasons we cannot accept defendants' argument that there exists some irreconcilable conflict between the requirements of our state equal protection provisions and other state constitutional provisions of equal stature — namely article XIII, section 21, and article IX, section 1. The latter provisions, as we interpret them, neither mandate nor approve a system such as that before us, and therefore the only conflict which here appears is that between the requirements of our state equal protection provisions and the proven realities of the present, legislatively created California public school financing system — a conflict which the trial court, by holding that system to be invalid, properly resolved.

IX

To recapitulate, we conclude that the trial court properly ordered and decreed that the California public school financing system for public elementary and secondary schools, including those provisions of the S.B. 90 and A.B. 1267 legislation pertaining to this system, while not in violation of the equal protection clause of the Fourteenth Amendment to the United States Constitution, is invalid as being in violation of former article I, sections 11 and 21 (now art. IV, § 16 and art. I, § 7, respectively) of the California Constitution, commonly known as the equal protection of the laws provisions of our state Constitution. This determination and the other related provisions of the judgment we find to be fully supported by the findings and the evidence; indeed, no attack has been made on the findings as lacking evidentiary support. For the reasons we have detailed, we discern no jurisdictional defect in the proceedings below based on the claim — rejected by us as devoid of merit — that the Governor and the

Legislature should have been joined as indispensable parties. We conclude that the holding of the trial court is grounded solidly and soundly on our earlier decision in *Serrano I* wherein we determined among other things that the California public school financing system, failing to withstand "strict scrutiny," denied plaintiffs the equal protection of the laws under the relevant provisions of our state Constitution. We therefore confirm that our decision in *Serrano I* was based not only on the equal protection provisions of the federal Constitution but also on such provisions of our state Constitution, and we emphasize that insofar as the latter provisions are applicable here, *Serrano I* constitutes the law of the case.

We observe that the trial court so deemed it and properly adhered to the law set forth in our earlier opinion in assessing for state constitutional purposes the same financing system as revised by S.B. 90 and A.B. 1267.

Since such system before the court was shown on substantial evidence to involve a suspect classification (based on district wealth) and to touch upon the fundamental interest of education, the trial court properly followed Serrano I in subjecting it to the "strict scrutiny" test under which the state has the burden of establishing that the classification in question is necessary to achieve a compelling state interest.

Applying this test, the court properly determined on findings supported by substantial evidence that the state had failed to bear its burden and that the financing system before it was invalid as denying equal protection of the laws as guaranteed by the California Constitution.

Finally we hold that, contrary to defendants' claim, there is no conflict between the requirements of our state equal protection provisions and other provisions of the California Constitution so as to compel the former to yield as the determinative law of this case.

The judgment is affirmed. We reserve jurisdiction for the purpose of considering and passing upon respondent's motion for an award of attorneys' fees on appeal, filed January 28, 1977.

WRIGHT, C.J., TOBRINER, J., and MOSK, J., concurred.

Notes and Questions

1. The courts may not order the Legislature or its members to enact or not to enact legislation, nor may it order the Governor to sign or not to sign legislation. This is based upon the separation of powers doctrine. Those lawmaking functions are left to the other two branches of state government as the Court ruled in *Serrano v. Priest* (1976) 18 Cal.3d 728, certiorari denied 432 U.S. 907.

2. The trial court ruled the state financing system violated state equal protection provisions. Was the period of six years to bring the financing system into compliance with the constitution a reasonable time period? Too long? Or too short?

3. Despite all of the efforts by the Legislature to make "admitted improvements to the system" due to the Court's earlier *Serrano I* decision, were you surprised

that the Court readily dismissed those efforts as insufficient to negate the objectionable features of the system that the Court called "operat[ing] to perpetuate this inequity"?

4. Is the main take-away from this case that, although the Legislature has plenary lawmaking authority under the state Constitution, the legislative branch cannot enact laws that violate fundamental constitutional provisions (e.g., those guaranteeing the equal protection of the laws to all citizens of this state)?

5. In a case where a law firm challenged the validity of a contract entered into by the Legislature to improve security measures at the state capitol, documents that the firm sought regarding the contract were exempt from public disclosure. If this is the rule to be followed by the judicial branch, will the public be able to challenge legislative contracting to ensure that it is in compliance with applicable laws? If not, what type of oversight is there of the legislative branch's actions?

Zumbrun Law Firm v. California Legislature

(2008) 165 Cal.App. 4th 1603

OPINION

BLEASE, Acting P.J.

Plaintiff, The Zumbrun Law Firm, brought this action as a taxpayer against defendants California Legislature, its Committees on Rules and others, seeking declaratory and injunctive relief, claiming that a contract for the Capitol Park Safety and Security Improvements Project (Capitol Project), entered into by the Committees on Rules of the Legislature to improve security measures at the Capitol by controlling access to the State Capitol building and grounds, violated the separation of powers doctrine of the state Constitution and unlawfully restricted competitive bidding under the State Contract Act (Pub. Contract Code, § 10100 et seq.) by requiring an all-union workforce. Plaintiff also sought, but was denied in part, records relating to the contract under the Legislative Open Records Act (LORA; Gov. Code, § 9070 et seq.).

The trial court concluded the contract did not violate the separation of powers or the State Contract Act. It also concluded that the denial of discovery of certain records did not violate LORA. We agree.

The contract did not violate the separation of powers doctrine of article III, section 3 of the Constitution because under article IV, section 7, the Legislature retains powers necessary to its lawmaking functions, including the power to protect the safety and security of the Legislature, its members and any buildings and grounds used by the Legislature. (See also *Ex parte McCarthy* (1866) 29 Cal. 395.) The Legislature did not delegate this function to the Department of General Services (Department or General Services) when it created the Department to provide management and technical services for the state. (§ 14600.) Lastly, the Legislature is not bound by the competitive bidding requirements of the State Contract Act, and the documents sought are exempt from discovery under LORA and the Constitution.

We shall affirm the judgment.

....

DISCUSSION

I

The Capitol Project Contract Did Not Violate the Separation of Powers

Plaintiff first argues that the Legislature's act of contracting for the Capitol Project violated the separation of powers doctrine set forth in the Constitution at article III, section 3. Plaintiff further argues, that even if the Legislature had passed a statute allowing it to enter into the contract, such an activity is not within the core functions of the legislative branch.

The separation of powers doctrine limits the authority of one branch of government to appropriate the core powers of another branch. (*Carmel Valley Fire Protection Dist. v. State of California* (2001) 25 Cal. 4th 287, 297 [105 Cal. Rptr. 2d 636, 20 P.3d 533] (*Carmel Valley*).) "The purpose of the doctrine is to prevent one branch of government from exercising the *complete* power constitutionally vested in another [citation]; it is not intended to prohibit one branch from taking action properly within its sphere that has the *incidental* effect of duplicating a function or procedure delegated to another branch." (*Younger v. Superior Court* (1978) 21 Cal. 3d 102, 117 [145 Cal. Rptr. 674, 577 P.2d 1014].) However, "[t]he doctrine has not been interpreted as requiring the rigid classification of all the incidental activities of government, with the result that once a technique or method of procedure is associated with a particular branch of the government, it can never be used thereafter by another." (*Parker v. Riley* (1941) 18 Cal. 2d 83, 90 [113 P.2d 873].)

"A legislative assembly, when established, becomes vested with all the powers and privileges which are necessary and incidental to a free and unobstructed exercise of its appropriate functions. These powers and privileges are derived not from the Constitution; on the contrary, they arise from the very creation of a legislative body, and are founded upon the principle of self-preservation. The Constitution is not a grant, but a restriction upon the power of the Legislature, and hence an express enumeration of legislative powers and privileges in the Constitution cannot be considered as the exclusion of others not named unless accompanied by negative terms. A legislative assembly has, therefore, all the powers and privileges which are necessary to enable it to exercise in all respects, in a free, intelligent, and impartial manner, its appropriate functions, except so far as it may be restrained by the express provisions of the Constitution, or by some express law made unto itself, regulating and limiting the same." (*Ex parte McCarthy, supra,* 29 Cal. at p. 403.) The core functions of the Legislature include passing laws, levying taxes, and making appropriations. (*Carmel Valley, supra,* 25 Cal.4th at p. 299.)

However, the Legislature has the power to engage in activity that is incidental or ancillary to its lawmaking functions. (*Parker v. Riley, supra,* 18 Cal.2d at p. 89.) In determining whether an activity is incidental to the Legislature's appropriate function, we look to the history of the parliamentary common law against which the fundamental charter of our state government was enacted, and which is implicit in the Constitution's separation of powers. (*People's Advocate, Inc. v. Superior Court* (1986) 181 Cal. App. 3d 316, 322 [226 Cal. Rptr. 640].) Among the powers and privileges a legislative assembly takes by virtue of its creation is the power "[t]o protect itself and its members from personal violence." (*Ex parte McCarthy, supra,* 29 Cal. at p. 404.)

This legislative power, which is intrinsic to article III, section 3 of the Constitution, is expressly recognized in article IV, section 7, subdivision (c)(1)(B). It provides that closed sessions of the Legislature may be held "[t]o consider matters affecting the safety and security of Members of the Legislature or its employees or the safety and security of any buildings and grounds used by the Legislature." The right of the Legislature to consider such matters clearly implies the right to act substantively to protect the safety and security of its members, and that includes the power to contract for the construction of facilities to provide for such safety.

II

The Department of General Services Has Not Been Delegated
Contractual Authority over Safety Matters Involving the Legislature

Plaintiff next argues that if the Legislature had the power to contract for the safety of its members, it delegated the authority to bid, award, manage, and oversee construction projects on state property to General Services by enacting section 14600, and that once delegated, the Legislature may not usurp the authority without enacting new statutory authority. We disagree.

The Legislature may delegate its incidental powers. (*Parker v. Riley, supra,* 18 Cal.2d at pp. 90–91.) It may select the means, within reasonable bounds, of accomplishing ancillary and subordinate tasks, and is not precluded from delegating them to committees, boards, commissions, or individuals. (*Ibid.*) However, the Legislature has not delegated its authority to contract for the Capitol Project, except as it has done so to its committees.

The Constitution provides that the Legislature may "provide for the selection of committees necessary for the conduct of its business...." (Const., art IV, § 11.) (6) The Legislature has created the Joint Rules Committee by statute and has promulgated joint rule 40, which gives the committee the power "[t]o contract with other agencies, public or private, for the rendition and affording of services, facilities, studies, and reports to the committee as the committee deems necessary to assist it to carry out the purposes for which it is created" and "[t]o do any and all other things necessary or convenient to enable it fully and adequately to exercise its powers, perform its duties, and accomplish the objects and purposes of this rule." (§ 9107; Joint Rules of the Sen. & Assem., rule 40(d), (*l*).)

While the Legislature's power to contract is not unlimited, the contract at issue falls within the ancillary power of the Legislature to carry out its lawmaking functions because, as noted, it is an action taken to protect the safety of the Legislature and its members, and the Legislature could properly delegate such incidental power to its Joint Rules Committee.

Plaintiff argues that the Legislature delegated this ancillary authority to General Services when it created the Department for the express purpose of the "centralization of business management functions and services of [the] state government" including "planning, acquisition, construction, and maintenance of state buildings and property...." (§ 14600.) However, the authority to engage in "business management functions and services" does not necessarily entail the authority to contract for them. Rather, the extent of the authority of General Services over state property and to enter into contracts on behalf of state agencies is to be found in other provisions of the codes.

Section 9110, subdivision (a) provides that: "The *maintenance and operation* of all of the State Capitol Building Annex, an annex to the historical State Capitol building (Gov. Code, § 9105),] is under the control of the Department of General Services, subject to this article." (Italics added.) Section 9108 provides that the "first floor of the State Capitol Building Annex is excepted from the provisions of this article. Such excepted space shall continue under the control of the Department of General Services. All other space in the State Capitol Building Annex shall be allocated ... by the Joint Rules Committee...."

Section 9124, subdivision (b) provides that the "Department of General Services shall provide maintenance and operation services in connection with the legislative office facilities as requested by the Legislature."

However, none of these provisions apply to this case. The Capitol Project is not in the State Capitol Annex, nor does it purport to allocate space in the annex or involve its maintenance and operation. Rather the project involves the construction of vehicle barriers on the perimeter of the grounds surrounding the State Capitol building and visitor pavilions to control access to the State Capitol building.

III

The Public Contract Code Does Not Apply to Contracts by the Legislature

Plaintiff further argues that when the Legislature enters into a contract it is subject to the State Contract Act and to the provisions which require that the contract be let by competitive bid. Again, we disagree.

"The Public Contract Code contains detailed provisions and requirements with regard to the acquisition of goods and services by state agencies." (58 Cal.Jur.3d (2004) State of California, § 65, p. 235, citing Pub. Contract Code, § 10290 et seq.) "The procedure prescribed by law calls for competitive bidding ..." (58 Cal.Jur.3d, *supra*, § 65, p. 236, citing Pub. Contract Code, § 10300 et seq.) In particular, Public Contract Code section 10295, subdivision (a), requires the approval by General Services of "contracts entered into by any state agency for ... (3) the construction, alteration, improvement, repair, or maintenance of property, real or personal...." However, subdivision (c)(5) of that same section provides that the provision does not apply to "[a]ny contract let by the Legislature."

This court has determined that projects in the legislative domain are outside the State Contract Act because the act, "embraces projects within the jurisdiction of the

Department of General Services and certain other departments in the *executive* branch of state government." (*Department of General Services v. Superior Court, supra,* 85 Cal.App.3d at p. 280.)

Plaintiff points to the fact that the money for the Capitol Project was transferred to the Architecture Revolving Fund, which contains funds "for expenditure on work within the powers and duties of the Department of General Services with respect to the construction, alteration, repair, and improvement of state buildings, including, but not limited to, services, new construction, major construction and equipment, minor construction, maintenance, improvements, and equipment, and other building and improvement projects...." (§ 14957, subd. (a).)

Plaintiff argues that this implies that the funds for the Capitol Project were subject to competitive bidding under the State Contract Act because they may be used only "for expenditure on work within the powers and duties of the Department...." We disagree.

The powers accorded the Department by the interagency agreement with the Joint Rules Committee were to provide services to manage the construction of the Capitol Project. Management involved the payment of monies for the construction to the contractor and in that sense was within the powers of the Department.

Thus, because the Legislature retained its constitutional authority over the "safety and security of any buildings and grounds used by the Legislature" (Const., art. IV, § 7, subd. (c)(1)(B)) and delegated its authority to contract for the Capitol Project to the Joint Rules Committee, it did not delegate such power to General Services. Rather, in entering into the interagency agreement with General Services, the Joint Rules Committee employed General Services' management skills, consistent with section 14600, to superintend the construction of the vehicle barriers around the Capitol and the visitor pavilions at the north and south annex entrances to the Capitol building.

IV.

The Legislature Did Not Wrongfully Withhold Documents

A. *Proposition 59 Did Not Nullify LORA Exemptions*

LORA was enacted in 1975. (Stats. 1975, ch. 1246, § 1, p. 3206.) It generally provides for the open access of "information concerning the conduct of the people's business by the Legislature...." (§ 9070.) LORA also specifies several categories of records that are exempt from disclosure, in particular, "[c]orrespondence of and to individual Members of the Legislature and their staff," and "[r]ecords the disclosure of which is exempted or prohibited pursuant to provisions of federal or state law, including, but not limited to, provisions of the Evidence Code relating to privilege." (§ 9075, subds. (h), (i).) As is relevant here, the language of section 9075, subdivisions (h) and (i) has remained unchanged since LORA was enacted in 1975.

In 2004, the voters approved Proposition 59, which added subdivision (b) to section 3 of article I of the Constitution. Like LORA, it provided generally for the open access to "information concerning the conduct of the people's business ..." (Const., art. I, § 3, subd. (b)(1).) Unlike LORA, it also provided for access to "the meetings of public bodies" as well as the writings of public officials and agencies. (Const., art. I, § 3, subd. (b)(1).)

Subdivision (b)(5) and (6) of article I, section 3 of the Constitution states:

> "(5) This subdivision does not repeal or nullify, expressly or by implication, any constitutional or statutory exception to the right of access to public records or meetings of public bodies that is in effect on the effective date of this subdivision, including, but not limited to, any statute protecting the confidentiality of law enforcement and prosecution records.

> "(6) Nothing in this subdivision repeals, nullifies, supersedes, or modifies protections for the confidentiality of proceedings and records of the Legislature, the Members of the Legislature, and its employees, committees, and caucuses provided by Section 7 of Article IV,[9] state law, or legislative rules adopted in furtherance of those provisions; nor does it affect the scope of permitted discovery in judicial or administrative proceedings regarding deliberations of the Legislature, the Members of the Legislature, and its employees, committees, and caucuses."

Plaintiff claims section 3, subdivision (b)(6) of article I of the Constitution must be read to embrace only those exemptions of article IV, section 7 and to ignore the exemptions provided by "state law, or legislative rules adopted in furtherance of those provisions...." In support of this claim, plaintiff offers the maxims *ejusdem generis* and *noscitur a sociis*. Neither of these aids to construction has any application here because the constitutional language is not ambiguous, and because the language is not amenable to their application.

The first principle of statutory or constitutional interpretation is to ascertain the intent of the enactors. We determine intent by first looking to the language of the text. "'If the language is clear, there is no need for construction.'" (*Professional Engineers in California Government v. Kempton* (2007) 40 Cal. 4th 1016, 1037 [56 Cal. Rptr. 3d 814, 155 P.3d 226].) Only if the language is ambiguous is it necessary to resort to evidence of the intent of the Legislature in the case of a statute, or the voters in the case of an initiative. (*Delaney v. Superior Court* (1990) 50 Cal. 3d 785, 798 [268 Cal. Rptr. 753, 789 P.2d 934].)

Ejusdem generis is an aid to be used if the language is ambiguous. (*Moore v. Conliffe* (1994) 7 Cal. 4th 634, 671 [29 Cal. Rptr. 2d 152, 871 P.2d 204].) In this case, the constitutional language presents no ambiguity. Proposition 59 expressly does not change or repeal any exemption to disclosure provided by article IV, section 7 of the Constitution, by state law, or by legislative rules adopted in furtherance of state law or article IV, section 7. (Const., art. I, § 3, subd. (b)(6).) The exemptions specified in LORA are state law exemptions. (See § 9075, subds. (h), (i).) The mere coupling of these exemptions with those in a particular constitutional provision does not create an ambiguity.

Judicial construction should not render part of the statute meaningless or inoperative. (*Hassan v. Mercy American River Hospital* (2003) 31 Cal. 4th 709, 715–716 [3 Cal. Rptr. 3d 623, 74 P.3d 726].) Plaintiff's construction, which would limit exemptions to those set forth in Constitution, article IV, section 7, would render two of the three enumerated exemptions meaningless or inoperative. "'[A] statute will be given its full effect, as far as possible, and will be so construed that the whole may stand, and that each part thereof may have the meaning and effect which, from the act as a whole, appears to have been intended.' [Citation.]" (*People v. Silver* (1940) 16 Cal. 2d 714, 721 [108 P.2d 4].) Plaintiff's construction is contrary to the principles of interpretation we are bound to follow.

Moreover, these maxims of construction are simply inapplicable here. *Ejusdem generis* is a subset of *noscitur a sociis,* which means the meaning of a word may be known from the accompanying words. (*Martin v. Holiday Inns, Inc.* (1988) 199 Cal. App. 3d 1434, 1437 [245 Cal. Rptr. 717].) *Ejusdem generis* is typically applied to phrases that list several specific items, then refer to a general reference, using the term "other." (*Texas Commerce Bank v. Garamendi* (1992) 11 Cal. App. 4th 460, 473 [14 Cal. Rptr. 2d 854].) "Other" being an inherently ambiguous term, the specific items enumerated are used to qualify the more general item.

However, *ejusdem generis* "'is by no means a rule of universal application, and its use is to carry out, not to defeat, the legislative intent. When it can be seen that the particular word by which the general word is followed was inserted, not to give a coloring to the general word, but for a distinct object, and when, to carry out the purpose of the statute, the general word ought to govern, it is a mistake to allow the *ejusdem generis* rule to pervert the construction.'" (*Hunt v. Manning* (1914) 24 Cal. App. 44, 48 [140 P. 39].)

In this case the exception to the rule of disclosure set forth in article IV, section 7 of the Constitution is a distinct object from legislative statutes and rules. Proposition 59 pertains to the right of access to both government documents and "meetings of public bodies...." (Const., art. I, §3, subd. (b)(1).) The exception contained in article IV, section 7 refers specifically to the "proceedings" of the Legislature, and allows "closed sessions" for specified purposes. (Const., art. IV, §7, subd. (c)(1).) LORA, on the other hand, applies not to the proceedings of the Legislature, but to the disclosure of its records. (See §9070 et seq.) Thus, the specifically enumerated exceptions in Proposition 59 are qualitatively different, one applying to proceedings (art. IV, §7), one applying to documents (state law), and one applying to both (legislative rules). Because they are different, it cannot be said that the electorate intended one example (art. IV, §7) to restrict the other examples (state law and legislative rules). For this reason, we also reject plaintiff's claim that the provisions of Proposition 59 conflict with the terms of LORA.

Plaintiff also argues that the exemptions set forth in LORA and claimed by defendants conflict with the "sunshine" policies of LORA and Proposition 59, and therefore violate the public's right of access. However, neither the language of Proposition 59, nor the exemption provisions under LORA are ambiguous provisions in need of interpretation through the vehicle of the statute's public policy. Proposition

59 expressly did not repeal, nullify, supersede, or modify the exemptions set forth in LORA. (Const., art. I, § 3, subd. (b)(6).) LORA, in turn, expressly exempts from disclosure "[c]orrespondence of and to individual Members of the Legislature and their staff...." (§ 9075, subd. (h).) A public policy argument serves to resolve the ambiguities of a statute, but it does not alone stand superior to the express terms of the statute. (*Garcia v. County of Sacramento* (2002) 103 Cal. App. 4th 67, 75 [126 Cal. Rptr. 2d 465].)

Accordingly, the exemptions to the disclosure requirements found in LORA are applicable here, and are not restricted to the subject of the safety and security of the Legislature found in Constitution, article IV, section 7, nor is there any reason on this record to narrowly interpret the LORA exemptions.

B. *Defendants Complied with LORA*

Plaintiff argues defendants' response to the records request did not comply with LORA's requirements that if any records were exempt from inspection the defendant "justify in writing the withholding of such record by demonstrating that the record in question is exempt under the express provisions of this article...." (§ 9074.) Plaintiff claims defendants' response was "conclusory and unsupported...."

Relevant to the claims of exemption, defendants' response stated as follows: "The [LORA] provides for a number of categories of documents that are exempt from the act's mandatory disclosure provisions. For example, the act exempts from mandatory production '[p]reliminary drafts, notes, or legislative memoranda;' '[c]orrespondence of and to individual Members of the Legislature and their staff;' and '[r]ecords the disclosure of which is exempted or prohibited pursuant to provisions of federal or state law,' which would include various evidentiary privileges (subds. (a), (h), and (i), Sec. 9075, Gov. C.; see also Sec. 1040, Evid. C.)." The response then lists the documents being produced, and concludes: "Upon reviewing our records, we find we are not in possession of any additional documents that are responsive to Categories 3 or 4 or to any of the other four categories of documents in your request, or the documents we do have fall within statutory exemptions."

Plaintiff concedes that pursuant to the authority of *Haynie v. Superior Court* (2001) 26 Cal. 4th 1061, 1074–1075 [112 Cal. Rptr. 2d 80, 31 P.3d 760], defendants were not required to produce the equivalent of a privilege log, but argue defendants were required to specify the exemptions upon which they relied.

Haynie v. Superior Court, supra, 26 Cal. 4th 1061, did not involve LORA, but it interpreted a section of the California Public Records Act (§ 6250 et seq.) containing near identical language to the section at issue here. In that case the plaintiff argued that a duty to create a log of documents exempt from disclosure could be inferred from the language of section 6255, which, like section 9074, required the public agency to "justify withholding any record by demonstrating that the record in question is exempt under express provisions of this chapter or that on the facts of the particular case the public interest served by not disclosing the record clearly outweighs the public interest served by disclosure of the record." (26 Cal.4th at p. 1074.)

The Supreme Court held that the California Public Records Act required the public agency to articulate the exemption being claimed, and that in so doing it would "necessarily reveal the general nature of the documents withheld." (*Haynie v. Superior Court, supra,* 26 Cal.4th at p. 1074.) However, the court held it was not necessary for the public agency to describe each document falling within a claimed exemption. (*Ibid.*)

In the present case, the response to the document request could have been worded more directly by assertively stating that the records were being withheld pursuant to the exemption for correspondence of and to members of the Legislature and their staff, and the exemption from disclosure pursuant to the law of privilege, rather than describing these as examples of documents that are exempt from disclosure. However, these were the exemptions pursuant to which records were being withheld, and both these exemptions were specifically set forth in the response. This response was sufficient to comply with LORA.

Plaintiff also points to documents that were disclosed during the course of the litigation, but not disclosed in response to the initial LORA request, and claims these documents prove defendants did not comply with LORA. However, the later produced documents were not responsive to plaintiff's initial request.

Broadly speaking, the initial request was for all records authorizing the Legislature to (1) administer public contracts for construction at the Capitol, (2) require the projects to be limited to union bidders, (3) include union-only provisions, (4) avoid compliance with the State Contract Act, (5) allow union-only contracts where federal money was received, and (6) oversee the construction. Also requested were records involving federal funds and union-only bidding.

The hearing minutes that were produced during litigation pertained to a Joint Rules Committee meeting on March 14, 2002, to consider the security perimeter options presented by the California Highway Patrol (CHP), and to vote on the various options. The meeting minutes do not reflect any effort to administer or authorize the public contract for construction. Nor do they mention federal funds, union-only requirements, or the State Contract Act. The only purposes of the meeting were to choose one of the presented options for the security perimeter and to request the CHP Commissioner to provide the most expeditious completion of the project by emergency declaration, if appropriate. Therefore, the minutes did not respond to plaintiff's original LORA request, and defendants did not violate LORA by failing to produce the documents earlier.

C. *The Legislature Did Not Waive the Right to Withhold Documents.*

Plaintiff argues that defendants have waived the right to withhold documents on two grounds: (1) by failing to comply with LORA by not describing the nature of the records withheld, and (2) by General Services' disclosure of some documents. With respect to the first ground, we have determined that defendants' response to the document request did not violate LORA; therefore, there has been no violation that would constitute a waiver.

With regard to plaintiff's second argument, we conclude that the statutory exemptions from disclosure are not the equivalent of evidentiary privileges, which may be waived by disclosure. Privilege, as defined by the Evidence Code, relates to proceedings in which testimony may be compelled by law to be given. (Evid. Code, § 901.) Plaintiff cites no authority to support its claim that an exemption to LORA's open records policy is to be treated as if it were an evidentiary privilege subject to waiver if disclosed, and we are aware of no such authority.

LORA contains its own enforcement mechanism. A person may institute proceedings to enforce the right to inspect legislative records, and may obtain a contempt order if such records are not disclosed pursuant to court order. (§§ 9076, 9077.) LORA does not provide for waiver of exemptions. We will not engraft penalties onto the legislative scheme that the statutes cannot fairly be read to contain.

Plaintiff argues the inconsistency in allowing the Legislature to withhold correspondence between its members and staff on the one hand and General Services on the other, while not similarly allowing General Services to withhold the correspondence, leads to absurd results. This situation is the result of LORA containing an exemption for "[c]orrespondence of and to individual Members of the Legislature" (§ 9075, subd. (h)), while the California Public Records Act contains no similar exemption for state agencies (see § 6254 et seq.). However, regardless of any seeming inconsistency, the language of these statutes is clear, and "[w]here the words of the statute are clear, we may not add to or alter them to accomplish a purpose that does not appear on the face of the statute or from its legislative history." (*Burden v. Snowden* (1992) 2 Cal. 4th 556, 562 [7 Cal. Rptr. 2d 531, 828 P.2d 672].) Accordingly, we will not simply ignore the express exemption for correspondence of and to legislative members and their staff merely because the correspondence of other state agencies is not similarly exempt.

V.

The Capitol Project Was Not a Misuse of Public Funds

Plaintiff contends the Capitol Project was a misuse of public funds because it unlawfully confined bidding to union only contractors in violation of the doctrine of separation of powers and the competitive bidding requirements of the State Contract Act, and because the Legislature did not use federal funds for the Capitol Project. The argument is flawed because there was no violation of separation of powers, the Legislature was not bound by the State Contract Act, and it was not required to use federal funds for the project.

The construction contract was entered into by the Senate and Assembly Rules Committees. General Services was not a party to the contract, although the Rules Committees hired General Services to manage the construction contract through an interagency agreement. Thus, assuming the contract did not comply with the competitive bidding requirements of the State Contract Act, such non-compliance was not unlawful because the Legislature was not bound by the act.

Plaintiff argues federal funds should have been used to fund the project, but cites no law mandating such federal funding. Plaintiff points to a news release from the

Governor of Missouri, and asserts that because Missouri used "federal homeland security funds designed to protect the state against terrorist threats" to fund, among other things, "an emergency response team for the State Capitol complex" the Legislature was required to spend California's homeland security funds on the Capitol Project.

No evidence was presented below to indicate how federal homeland security funds are allocated by the state, who has the authority to allocate such funds, what types of projects are eligible, how projects are prioritized, or whether any funding was available for the Capitol Project in question. On this record we cannot hold that the Capitol Project was a misuse of funds because no federal funds were used.

DISPOSITION

The judgment is affirmed. Each party shall bear their own costs on appeal. (Cal. Rules of Court, rule 8.278(a)(5).)

DAVIS, J., and CANTIL-SAKAUYE, J., concurred.

Notes and Questions

1. The Court of Appeal would not take judicial notice of the Legislature's internet site showing laws currently in effect, including a statute that the plaintiff alleged was in effect, in determining that the statute had been repealed. The website was not brought to the attention of the trial court, the website was not the official, printed Government Code, and the website made no promises regarding its accuracy.

2. A constitutional enactment providing for access to meetings of public bodies and to the writings of public officials and agencies did not nullify the exemptions from disclosure under the Legislative Open Records Act (LORA) for privileged material and legislator and staff correspondence. The express exemption from LORA's open records policy for correspondence of and to legislative members and their staff is not invalidated by the fact that the correspondence of other state agencies is not similarly exempt.

3. The Legislature's response to a LORA record request satisfied the statutory requirement that it justify in writing the withholding of exempt records where the Legislature's response stated that any additional responsive documents in its possession fell within the statutory exemptions and stated that examples of such exemptions were "preliminary draft, notes or legislative memoranda," "correspondence of and to individual members of the Legislature and their staff," and "records the disclosure of which is exempted or prohibited."

4. What were the three claims addressed in this decision? What was the factual background for each of the claims addressed by the court?

5. What was the basis for the court finding that the contract with the Department of General Services did not violate the separation of powers doctrine? How broad is the Legislature's power related to its lawmaking functions?

6. Would you add to the court's listing of the "core functions of the Legislature [that] include passing laws, levying taxes, and making appropriations" (*Carmel Valley, supra,* 25 Cal.4th at p. 299)?

7. Does the court's decision provide sufficient guidance to determine how far to extend the Legislature's power to engage in activity that is incidental or ancillary to its lawmaking functions?

B. Compel the Appropriation of State Funds

The authority to appropriate state dollars is held by the legislative branch of government. The legislature can choose or not choose to appropriate dollars and whether the appropriation will continue indefinitely. In other words, the legislature cannot be compelled to appropriate state funds. The authority to do so remains with the legislative branch of government. Just because the Legislature one year decides to appropriate monies for a specified purpose does not mean that the Legislature is required to do so the following year.

City of Sacramento v. California State Legislature

(1986) 187 Cal.App.3d 393

OPINION

BLEASE, J.

The City of Sacramento (City) appeals from a judgment dismissing the Legislature from an action in which it seeks to compel the Legislature to appropriate money. Its purpose is to secure a reimbursement, pursuant to article XIII B, section 6 of the California Constitution, of costs it expended in compliance with a state-mandated unemployment insurance program. We will affirm the judgment (order of dismissal) on the ground that the judiciary has no power, under the doctrine of separation of powers, to grant such relief.

Facts and Procedural Background

The circumstances giving rise to this action are set out in a prior opinion, *City of Sacramento v. State of California* (1984) 156 Cal. App. 3d 182 [203 Cal. Rptr. 258] (hereafter *Sacramento v. State*). We briefly recapitulate. The Legislature in 1978, by statute, required all local government employers to participate in the unemployment insurance system. In 1979 the electorate enacted an amendment to the California Constitution which says, in pertinent part: "Whenever the Legislature or any state agency mandates a new program or higher level of service on any local government, the state shall provide a subvention of funds to reimburse such local government for the costs of such program or increased level of service,...." (Cal. Const., art. XIII B, § 6.) In *Sacramento v. State, supra,* we upheld a peremptory writ of mandate compelling the State Board of Control to grant the City a hearing concerning its claim for reimbursement of costs of participation in the unemployment insurance system. (*Id.,* at p. 199.) We held that this statutory mandate was subject to the reimbursement requirement of the constitution. (*Ibid.*)

Following this decision, the City pursued its claim before the State Board of Control. The board concluded that eligibility for reimbursement of costs commenced when the statutory mandate to participate in the unemployment insurance program took effect, January 1, 1978. The City participates in the unemployment insurance program under a system in which the California Employment Development Department makes payments to unemployed city workers and is reimbursed by the City. The City seeks repayment of all of the amounts it has in this manner paid the state.

Subsequent to the commencement of this action the Legislature enacted Statutes 1985, chapter 1217. Chapter 1217 appropriates moneys to reimburse the costs of the unemployment insurance program for the fiscal years 1984–1985 and 1985–1986, i.e., July 1, 1984 through June 30, 1986. (Stats. 1985, ch. 1217, §§ 12, 17, subd. (b).)

The City named the Legislature as a defendant in this action, alleging: "Legislature has no discretion as to whether to appropriate funds to reimburse for all of City's costs associated with Chapter 2/78. Appropriation for such costs is a non-discretionary, ministerial act which Legislature, despite repeated demand and despite its specific awareness of Article XIIIB, § 6 and of *City of Sacramento v. State, supra,* has deliberately and stubbornly refused to perform." It sought a writ of mandate commanding the Legislature to appropriate funds for the reimbursement of all costs associated with the City's compliance with the mandate from the inception of its participation in the unemployment insurance program.

The Legislature demurred to the complaint on the ground that it is not a proper party to the action. The demurrer was sustained without leave to amend. The City appeals from the ensuing judgment of dismissal.

Discussion

The City acknowledges the fundamental rule that the separation of judicial from legislative powers precludes the judiciary from ordering the enactment of an appropriation, but argues that the rule should allow an exception when the Legislature's duty to do so is ministerial. We disagree.

"The powers of state government are legislative, executive, and judicial. Persons charged with the exercise of one power may not exercise either of the others except as permitted by this Constitution." (Cal. Const., art. III, § 3.) "The legislative power of this State is vested in the California Legislature which consists of the Senate and Assembly, but the people reserve to themselves the powers of initiative and referendum." (Cal. Const., art. IV, § 1.) "Money may be drawn from the Treasury only through an appropriation made by law and upon a Controller's duly drawn warrant." (Cal. Const., art. XVI, § 7.) The appropriation of moneys is a legislative function. (Cal. Const., art. IV, §§ 1 and 12.)

The cases construing these provisions uniformly hold that courts are prohibited "from directly ordering the Legislature to enact a specific appropriation...." (*Mandel v. Myers* (1981) 29 Cal. 3d 531, 540 [174 Cal. Rptr. 841, 629 P.2d 935].) [2] Indeed, the broader rule is that mandamus will not lie to compel the Legislature to enact any legislation. (See Cannot., Mandamus to Members or Officer of Legislature (1942) 136 A.L.R. 677, 679–680; 52 Am. Jur.2d, Mandamus, § 131, p. 267.)

An emphatic and eloquent statement of the rule is given in *Myers v. English* (1858) 9 Cal. 341, 349: "We think the power to collect and appropriate the revenue of the State is one peculiarly within the discretion of the Legislature. It is a very delicate and responsible trust, and if not used properly by the Legislature at one session, the people will be certain to send to the next more discreet and faithful servants.

"It is within the legitimate power of the judiciary, to declare the action of the Legislature unconstitutional, where that action exceeds the limits of the supreme law; but the Courts have no means, and no power, to avoid the effects of non-action. The Legislature being the creative element in the system, its action cannot be quickened by the other departments. Therefore, when the Legislature fails to make an appropriation, we cannot remedy that evil. It is a discretion specially confided by the Constitution to the body possessing the power of taxation. There may arise exigencies, in the progress of human affairs, when the first moneys in the treasury would be required for more pressing emergencies, and when it would be absolutely necessary to delay the ordinary appropriations for salaries. We must trust to the good faith and integrity of all the departments. Power must be placed somewhere, and confidence reposed in someone."

The City cites to no case in which a court has issued an order to a Legislature to appropriate funds. We are invited to create an unprecedented exception to the contrary rule on the ground that the duty to appropriate funds to reimburse the City under article XIII B, section 6, is patent and the amount "owed" is capable of certain calculation. [3] The City does not claim, nor could it, that article XIII B, section 6, by its terms, requires that the judiciary provide such a remedy. In fact, the section contains no remedy.

The City suggests that the need for departing from precedent is great because otherwise the will of the electorate embodied in article XIII B, section 6, will be frustrated. The difficulty with the City's argument is that it applies in every instance in which a claim of this nature is tendered. Such a claim always rests on some mandatory constitutional provision; how else could we be called upon to check the Legislature? But this has never sufficed to breach the rule. If the electorate is willing it may directly enact an appropriation. In the absence of such an explicit expression of the People's will we will not indulge the presumption that we can discern it more faithfully and accurately than the political branches.

The City argues that an exception is justified because the duty of the Legislature is mandatory and so well defined that the Legislature has no discretion upon which we might encroach. It must be admitted that the presence of a mandatory duty that is clearly specified is a significant consideration. (See *Jenkins v. Knight* (1956) 46 Cal. 2d 220 [293 P.2d 6].) "Where political power is vested in a public officer, he is responsible only in his political character to the country. Where discretion is vested in him, he but conforms to the law in exercising that discretion. But where a question of political power is not involved, where no discretion exists, but a specific legal duty is imposed, ministerial in its character, such as the issuance of a patent, the delivery of a commission, the payment of a specific sum, or the drawing of a particular warrant, and in the performance of that duty individuals have a direct pecuniary interest, the officer, like any other citizen, is subject to the process of the regularly constituted tribunals of the country." (*McCauley v. Brooks* (1860) 16 Cal. 11, 54–55, overruled on other grounds in *Stratton v. Green* (1872) 45 Cal. 149.)

If article XIII B, section 6, is read to require an appropriation of moneys for the reimbursement of mandated costs, the matter is nonetheless one in which political power to accomplish that end is vested in the Legislature. "Under our form of government, the judicial department has no power to revise even the most arbitrary and unfair action of the legislative department, or of either house thereof, taken in pursuance of the power committed exclusively to that department by the constitution." (*French v. Senate* (1905) 146 Cal. 604, 606 [80 P. 1031].) The legislative power to enact laws, including appropriations, is committed exclusively to the legislative department by the Constitution. (See Cal. Const., art. IV, §§ 1 and 12.)

The focus in questions of separation of powers is "the degree to which [the] governmental arrangements comport with, or threaten to undermine, either the independence and integrity of one of the branches or levels of government, or the ability of each to fulfill its mission in checking the others so as to preserve the interdependence without which independence can become domination." (Tribe, American Constitutional Law (1978) p. 15; fn. omitted.) A ruling that orders the Legislature to enact an appropriation necessarily implicates the independence and integrity of the Legislature and its ability to fulfill its mission in checking its coequal branches. The judgment of the judiciary concerning the construction of the language of the Constitution and the laws "can only be controlled by its intelligence and conscience." (*McCauley v. Brooks, supra*, 16 Cal. at p. 39.) It functions as the constitutional auditor. The danger of concentrating the power to audit and the power to spend in the same branch is manifest.

A separation of powers does allow for some incidental overlap of function. (E.g., *Younger v. Superior Court* (1978) 21 Cal. 3d 102, 115 [145 Cal. Rptr. 674, 577 P.2d 1014].) But a judicially compelled enactment of legislation is not an incidental overlap; it is the very exercise of legislative power itself. "One branch of the Government cannot encroach on the domain of another without danger. The safety of our institutions depends in no small degree on a strict observance of this salutary rule." (*Union Pacific R.R. Co. v. United States* (1879) 99 U.S. 700, 718 [25 L. Ed. 496, 501].)

The judgment (order of dismissal) is affirmed.

PUGLIA, P.J., and SIMS, J., concurred.

Notes and Questions

1. Is the separation of powers doctrine absolute? In other words, are there no instances where it is appropriate for one branch of state government to exercise the powers or duties of another branch of state government? Is doctrine clear to ensure that no branch infringes on the other branches' powers?

2. The City acknowledges the fundamental rule that the separation of judicial from legislative powers precludes the judiciary from ordering the enactment of an appropriation, but argues that the rule should allow an exception when the Legislature's duty to do so is ministerial. Why did the court disagree with the city?

3. "Therefore, when the Legislature fails to make an appropriation, we cannot remedy that evil. It is a discretion specially confided by the Constitution to the body possessing the power of taxation." Why does the court equate appropriation of state funds (through an appropriations bill or the budget bill) with the power of taxation?

4. "A ruling that orders the Legislature to enact an appropriation necessarily implicates the independence and integrity of the Legislature and its ability to fulfill its mission in checking its coequal branches." On this basis, is there no scenario where a court would order the legislative branch to appropriate funds for a deemed necessary purpose?

C. Delegation of Authority by the Legislature

Under constitutional separation-of-powers provisions, generally the laws are enacted by the legislative branch of government, the laws are administered by the executive branch, and the laws are interpreted by the judicial branch. With the executive branch charged with administering the law, as well as enforcing it, the state agencies and departments that administer the law need to engage in rulemaking activities, which are quasi-legislative in nature.

In delegating authority to the executive branch of government, a question that is often raised is whether legislatures can be expected to adopt statutes that address every detail of public policy? In some instances, they can, but in others they cannot. As a result, there is expected to be some delegation of legislative power to the executive branch of either the federal or state levels of government.

Issues are raised, however, regarding which powers can be delegated to the executive branch and to which agencies or departments, as well as to what extent that delegation can take without running afoul of constitutional limits. The question occasionally arises: how broadly can the Legislature delegate authority to state agencies and departments?

Generally, when this authority is delegated to state agencies, the Legislature will articulate guidance in the use of that authority by the state agency. To do otherwise is tantamount to an improper delegation of legislative power. There are many state appellate court decisions in this area of constitutional law.

In general, an unconstitutional delegation of authority occurs when the legislature (1) leaves the resolution of fundamental policy issues to others or (2) fails to provide adequate direction for the implementation of that policy. Interested persons can review appellate court decisions on the topic of delegation of legislative authority, such as *Carson Mobilehome Park Owners' Assn. v. City of Carson* (1983) 35 Cal.3d 184, 190. In that case, the appellate court stated:

> An unconstitutional delegation of power occurs when the Legislature confers upon an administrative agency the unrestricted authority to make fundamental policy determinations. To avoid such delegation, the Legislature must provide an adequate yardstick for the guidance of the administrative body empowered to execute the law.
>
> Underlying these rules is the belief that the Legislature as the most representative organ of government should settle insofar as possible controverted issues of policy and that it must determine crucial issues whenever it has the time, information and competence to deal with them.

Other cases have made similar determinations, such as *Clean Air Constituency v. State Air Resources Bd.* (1974) 11 Cal.3d 801, 816–817.

An interesting example occurred in *California Radioactive Materials v. DHS* (1993) 15 Cal.App.4th 841, 19 Cal.Rptr.2d 357, in which the parties litigated over an order for formal adjudicatory proceedings to determine whether that order was the result of unlawful coercion by members of the Senate Rules Committee during the confirmation hearings of senior officials to head the Health and Welfare Agency.

The Senate Rules Committee admitted that it obtained an agreement for further administrative proceedings from those appointees during the confirmation process, but the legislators characterized the agreement as a legally proper compromise between two branches of government.

The appellate court, on the other hand, concluded that the Senate Rules Committee's interference in the administration of the law was unconstitutional and the purported agreement with the administrative officers was void. The appellate court explained that formal adjudicatory hearings are not otherwise required by law, and the void agreement was the only basis upon which the Agency intended to conduct further proceedings.

In the end, the fundamental issue the courts look at is how much authority can be delegated to the agencies in the executive branch. It appears that the more that authority is delegated, the more likely it will be deemed unlawful. As such, the Legislature must remain vigilant in its delegation efforts.

An unconstitutional delegation of legislative authority occurs if a statute authorizes a person or group other than the Legislature to make a fundamental policy decision or fails to provide adequate direction for the implementation of a fundamental policy determined by the Legislature. (*Plastic Pipe and Fittings Association v. California Building Standards Commission* (2004) 124 Cal.App.4th 1390.)

Notes and Questions

1. Is the test for delegation of authority clear to provide adequate guidance to interested parties? What are some examples of fundamental policy decisions that should not be delegated by the Legislature?

2. What is required to provide adequate direction to an agency by the Legislature?

Plastic Pipe & Fittings Association v. California Building Standards Commission

(2004) 124 Cal.App.4th 1390

OPINION

CROSKEY, J.—

The California Building Standards Commission (Commission) and five other state agencies appeal a judgment granting a peremptory writ of mandate in favor of Plastic Pipe and Fittings Association (PPFA). The writ of mandate compels the Commission and the Agencies to adopt as part of the California Plumbing Code provisions of the Uniform Plumbing Code allowing the use of cross-linked polyethylene (PEX) pipes, vacate their exceptions to the adoption of those provisions, and vacate the Commission's finding that review is warranted under the California Environmental Quality Act (CEQA) (Pub. Resources Code Secs. 21000 et seq.) with respect to allowing the use of PEX.

The Commission and the Agencies contend (1) the superior court's conclusion that they acted arbitrarily and without evidentiary support by refusing to adopt the Uniform Plumbing Code provisions allowing the use of PEX was error; (2) the decision not to allow the use of PEX was not procedurally unfair; (3) the Commission's decision to defer approval of PEX pending CEQA review was proper; and (4) the writ of mandate impermissibly directs the Commission and the Agencies to exercise their discretion in a particular manner. We agree with the first three contentions and do not reach the fourth.

. . . .

DISCUSSION

1. *Building Standards Law.*

The California Building Standards Law (Health & Saf. Code, 18901 et seq.) provides for the promulgation of building standards by state agencies. State agencies adopt or propose building standards that are then approved or adopted by the Commission. (*Id.*, 18930, subd. (a).) ...

The Commission must either approve the building standards adopted by a state agency, return the standards for amendment with recommended changes, or reject the standards. (Health & Saf. Code, Sec. 18931, subd. (a).) If the Commission fails to act within 120 days after receiving an agency's adopted standards, the standards are deemed approved without further review. (*Ibid.*) Approved standards are codified in the Code. (*Id.* Secs. 18931, subd. (b), 18938.) The California Plumbing Code is part of the Code. (Cal. Code Regs., tit. 24, part 5, ch. 1, Sec. 101.0 et seq.)

The Commission receives proposed building standards from state agencies for consideration in an annual code adoption cycle, publishes the Code in its entirety every three years, and publishes annual supplements as necessary. (Health & Saf. Code, Secs. 18929.1, subd. (a), 18942, subd. (a).)

2. *The Commission's Decision Not to Allow the Use of PEX Was Proper.*

....

c. *The Model Code Provisions Were Not Automatically Adopted and Approved as a Matter of Law as to the Department of Housing and Community Development.*

Health and Safety Code section 17922, subdivision (a), states that the building standards adopted by the Department of Housing and Community Development and submitted to the Commission for approval "shall impose substantially the same requirements as are contained in the most recent editions of the following uniform industry codes as adopted by the organizations specified. The Uniform Plumbing Code of the International Association of Plumbing and Mechanical Officials." Subdivision (b) states, in pertinent part, "Except as provided in Part 2.5 (commencing with section 18901), in the absence of adoption by regulation, the most recent editions of the uniform codes referred to in this section shall be considered to be adopted one year after the date of publication of the uniform codes."

Health and Safety Code section 18931, subdivision (a), states that the Commission must, "In accordance with Section 18930 and within 120 days from the date of receipt of adopted standards, review the standards of adopting agencies and approve, return for amendment with recommended changes, or reject building standards submitted to the commission for its approval. When building standards are returned for amendment or rejected, the commission shall inform the adopting agency or state agency that proposes the building standards of the specific reasons for the recommended changes or rejection, citing the criteria required under Section 18930. When standards are not acted upon by the commission within 120 days, the standards shall be approved, including codification and publication in the California Building Standards Code, without further review and without return or rejection by the commission."

PPFA maintains that the Department of Housing and Community Development adopted the model code as a matter of law, including the provisions allowing the use of PEX, by failing to adopt building standards within one year after the publication of the model code in October 1999, and that the Commission approved the model code, including the PEX provisions, by failing to act on the adopted standards within 120 days after they were deemed adopted. Under PPFA's construction of the Building Standards Law, the most recent edition of a model code can become California law without any review by either the adopting agency or the Commission. The superior court rejected this argument, and so do we.

The legislative power of the state is vested in the Legislature. (Cal. Const., art. IV, Sec. 1.) An unconstitutional delegation of legislative authority occurs if a statute authorizes another person or group to make a fundamental policy decision or fails to provide adequate direction for the implementation of a fundamental policy determined by the Legislature. (*Carson Mobilehome Park Owners' Assn. v. City of Carson* (1983) 35 Cal.3d 184, 190 [197 Cal. Rptr. 284, 672 P.2d 1297]; *Kugler v. Yocum* (1968) 69 Cal.2d 371, 376–377 [71 Cal. Rptr. 687, 445 P.2d 303].) For the Legislature to grant a private association such as the International Association of Plumbing and

Mechanical Officials the power to make law with no direction from the Legislature and no review by a state agency would be unconstitutional. (*International Association of Plumbing etc. Officials v. California Building Stds Com., supra,* 55 Cal.App.4th at p. 253.)

We must construe a statute to avoid a constitutional invalidity if a constitutionally sound construction is reasonable. (*City of Los Angeles v. Superior Court* (2002) 29 Cal.4th 1, 10–11 [124 Cal. Rptr. 2d 202, 52 P.3d 129].)

Assuming arguendo that the model code was deemed adopted without amendment by the Department of Housing and Community Development under Health and Safety Code section 17922, subdivision (a), we construe section 18931, subdivision (a), to mean that the Commission is deemed to approve adopted building standards through inaction only if the Commission receives the adopted standards from the adopting agency. Section 18931, subdivision (a), states that the Commission must review and act on adopted standards "within 120 days from the date of receipt of adopted standards." We conclude that the Legislature contemplated that automatic approval by the Commission could occur only if the adopting agency affirmatively adopted the building standards and forwarded them to the Commission. If the Commission did not receive adopted standards from the adopting agency, as here, the Commission cannot be deemed to approve the standards through inaction. This ensures that building standards cannot be both deemed adopted by the adopting agency and deemed approved by the Commission with no determination by either the adopting agency or the Commission that the standards are appropriate.

d. *The Decision Was Not Procedurally Unfair.*

PPFA contends the decision was procedurally unfair because (1) the Agencies failed to adopt the model code within one year after its publication as required by Health and Safety Code section 18928, subdivision (b); (2) the Commission and the Agencies improperly delayed the decision to apply CEQA; (3) the Department of Housing and Community Development characterized its decision not to adopt the model code provisions allowing the use of PEX as "secret" and allowed counsel for the California State Pipe Trades Council to participate in drafting a public notice; (4) the Governor appointed two new members to the Commission shortly before its hearing in May 2002, one of whom formerly represented a trade group promoting copper pipes, and the Governor received a substantial amount of campaign contributions from the California State Pipe Trades Council; (5) the Commission's hearing in May 2002 was a sham because the Commission "seemed predetermined to exclude PEX" and presented a "pre-printed motion" a copy of which had been given to the California State Pipe Trades Council; (6) the Agencies failed to make independent factual findings and acted under the direction of the Commission; (7) the Commission secretly authorized advance publication of the Code before the May 2002 hearing, so the hearing was a sham and the Commission's decision was predetermined; and (8) the Commission "threaten[ed]" to impose the costs of environmental review on PEX manufacturers without justification.

We reject the contention that the Agencies' failure to adopt the model code within one year after its publication as required by statute rendered the decision procedurally unfair so as to invalidate the Agencies' and the Commission's decision. Statutory time limits ordinarily are considered directory rather than mandatory and jurisdictional unless the Legislature clearly expressed a contrary intent. (*California Correctional Peace Officers Assn. v. State Personnel Bd.* (1995) 10 Cal.4th 1133, 1145 [43 Cal. Rptr. 2d 693, 899 P.2d 79].)

The California Building Standards Law does not provide that an agency's adoption of a model code is invalid if it occurs more than one year after the model code was published or that the Commission has no authority to approve building standards that were not timely adopted. Moreover, [15] statutory language that appears mandatory may be considered mandatory only in the sense that an administrative agency can be compelled to act if it fails to render a timely decision, but this does not mean that the agency has no jurisdiction to act after the deadline has passed. (*Id.* at pp. 1146–1147.) If depriving an agency of the power to act after a deadline has passed would defeat the purpose of the statute, a court should reject such a construction. (*Ibid.*) We conclude that to deprive an agency of the power to adopt a model code more than one year after its publication would deprive the Commission of the agency's considered opinion and application of the agency's expertise, and would defeat the purpose of the statute.

We reject PPFA's second contention concerning procedural unfairness in section 4 *post.* The other contentions concerning alleged undue influence, a sham hearing, and the like are only unsubstantiated allegations and cannot justify the invalidation of the Commission's or the Agencies' decisions.

     . . . .

DISPOSITION

The judgment is reversed with directions to the superior court to vacate the peremptory writ of mandate issued on February 13, 2003, and enter a judgment denying the petition for writ of mandate. Appellants are entitled to recover their costs on appeal.

KLEIN, P.J., and ALDRICH, J., concurred.

Notes and Questions

1. What was the basis of the court's determination that the agencies' failure to adopt the model code within one year after its publication as required by statute did not render the decision procedurally unfair so as to invalidate the agencies' and the Commission's decision? The court ruled that "statutory time limits ordinarily are considered directory rather than mandatory and jurisdictional unless the Legislature clearly expressed a contrary intent." Is this what the Legislature would expect from a court looking at a statutory mandate?

2. What was the basis for the court's ruling that the Commission's approval of building standards under the Building Standards Law is a quasi-legislative act of administrative rulemaking?

3. Does the standard of review play a critical role in this court decision?

4. Is it appropriate that an administrative agency making a quasi-legislative decision is not required to make detailed factual findings supporting its decision?

5. According to the court, "An unconstitutional delegation of legislative authority occurs if a statute authorizes another person or group to make a fundamental policy decision or fails to provide adequate direction for the implementation of a fundamental policy determined by the Legislature." How does the court determine what a fundamental policy is?

D. Limited Mandate to an Administration Agency

While the legislature may delegate authority, it cannot delegate a significant amount of that authority to an executive branch agency or department. Because of this limitation on the delegation authority, the more expansive the authority being delegated, the more problematic it is likely to be. A legislative enactment that limits the mandate of an administrative agency or withdraws certain of its powers is not necessarily suspect under the doctrine of separation of powers.

In addition, when the Legislature has not taken over core functions of the executive branch and has exercised its authority in accordance with formal procedures set forth in the state Constitution, such an enactment normally is consistent with the checks and balances prescribed by the Constitution.

The Legislature's power of appropriation includes the power to withhold appropriations, and neither an executive administrative agency nor a court has the power to require the Legislature to appropriate money. (*Carmel Valley Fire Protection District v. State* (2001) 25 Cal.4th 287, rehearing denied.) Statutes enacted do not signify that the Legislature has taken over core functions of the executive branch, but constitute an expression of the Legislature's essential duty to devise a reasonable budget.

Gerawan Farming, Inc. v. Agricultural Labor Relations Board

(2015) 236 Cal.App.4th 1024

OPINION

KANE, J. —

Agricultural employer Gerawan Farming, Inc. (Gerawan), and United Farm Workers of America (UFW) have never reached mutually acceptable terms to enter a collective bargaining agreement (CBA) regarding Gerawan's agricultural employees. UFW was certified as the employees' bargaining representative in 1992, but after engaging in initial discussions with Gerawan, disappeared from the scene for nearly two decades. In late 2012, UFW returned and the parties renewed negotiations. A few months later, at UFW's request, the Agricultural Labor Relations Board (the

Board) ordered the parties to a statutory "Mandatory Mediation and Conciliation" (MMC) process pursuant to Labor Code section 1164 et seq. Under the MMC process, if a 30-day mediation period does not succeed in producing a CBA by voluntary agreement, the mediator decides what the terms of the CBA should be and reports that determination to the Board. Once the mediator's report becomes the final order of the Board, the report establishes the terms of an imposed CBA to which the parties are bound. (See §§ 1164, 1164.3.) Here, following the Board's final order adopting the mediator's report, Gerawan petitioned this court for review under section 1164.5, challenging the validity of the order and the MMC process on both statutory and constitutional grounds. Among Gerawan's claims is the contention that UFW's lengthy absence resulted in an abandonment of its status as the employee's bargaining representative.

We agree with Gerawan's statutory argument that it should have been given an opportunity to prove abandonment to the Board once UFW requested the MMC process. More fundamentally, we agree with Gerawan's constitutional arguments that the MMC statute violates equal protection principles and constitutes an improper delegation of legislative authority. Accordingly, the Board's order, *Gerawan Farming, Inc.* (2013) 39 ALRB No. 17, is set aside.

. . . .

DISCUSSION

In addressing the contentions raised in Gerawan's petition for review (case No. F068526), our approach will be to discuss the statutory issues first and the constitutional questions second. Lastly, we will briefly address the separate appeal filed by Gerawan (case No. F068676), which has been consolidated herewith.

THE STATUTORY ISSUES

Inasmuch as we will conclude that the MMC statute unconstitutionally deprives Gerawan of equal protection and unconstitutionally delegates legislative authority, we could confine our opinion to a discussion of those issues alone. However, the parties have extensively briefed other issues relating to statutory interpretation and application of the MMC statute. We are not the highest court of review and hence do not presume to have the last word on this subject. We deem it appropriate to address the following statutory issues should they become relevant following a higher court ruling or a future attempt by the Legislature to enact another version of the MMC statute. Additionally, we reach the statutory issues as an alternative basis for our ruling; that is, even if the MMC statute were constitutionally sound, we would still conclude under the *statutory* arguments that the Board abused its discretion. For the sake of efficiency, we place our discussion of the statutory issues first because doing so will provide a thorough overview of the MMC statute (i.e., how it works and its purpose), which will give helpful background to our consideration of the constitutional issues.

I. Overview of the Statutory Framework

The Labor Code provisions creating the MMC process (§§ 1164–1164.13; the MMC statute) were added in 2002 as a new chapter (ch. 6.5) to the part of the code dealing with agricultural labor relations (div. 2, pt. 3.5), known as the Alatorre-Zenovich-Dunlap-Berman Agricultural Labor Relations Act of 1975 (§ 1140 et seq.; the ALRA). (See Stats. 2002, ch. 1145, § 2, p. 7401.) Therefore, to understand how the MMC statute fits within its larger statutory framework, we begin with a brief description of the ALRA.

    ....

II. Standard of Review and Rules of Statutory Construction

Having introduced the MMC statute, we next consider the nature of the statutory claims raised in Gerawan's petition. In a nutshell, Gerawan argues the Board did not follow the law when it ordered the parties to the MMC process because several of the statutory requirements for such an order (set forth in §§ 1164, 1164.11) allegedly were not met. According to Gerawan, the Board adopted erroneous interpretations of the statutory provisions at issue, causing it to incorrectly conclude that the statutory requirements were satisfied. Additionally, Gerawan asserts the Board improperly rejected its argument that UFW abandoned its status as the employees' bargaining representative and, therefore, lacked standing to invoke the MMC process under section 1164.

It is clear that Gerawan's claims involve questions of law relating to statutory construction. The rules governing statutory construction are well settled. "We begin with the fundamental premise that the objective of statutory interpretation is to ascertain and effectuate legislative intent. [Citations.] To determine legislative intent, we turn first to the words of the statute, giving them their usual and ordinary meaning. [Citations.] When the language of a statute is clear, we need go no further." (*Nolan v. City of Anaheim* (2004) 33 Cal.4th 335, 340 [14 Cal.Rptr.3d 857, 92 P.3d 350] (*Nolan*).) In that case, "no court need, or should, go beyond that pure expression of legislative intent. [Citation.]" (*Green v. State of California* (2007) 42 Cal.4th 254, 260 [64 Cal.Rptr.3d 390, 165 P.3d 118].) "If the words themselves are not ambiguous, we presume the Legislature meant what it said, and the statute's plain meaning governs." (*Wells v. One2One Learning Foundation* (2006) 39 Cal.4th 1164, 1190 [48 Cal.Rptr.3d 108, 141 P.3d 225].)

However, when the language of the statute "is susceptible of more than one reasonable interpretation, we look to a variety of extrinsic aids, including the ostensible objects to be achieved, the evils to be remedied, the legislative history, public policy, contemporaneous administrative construction, and the statutory scheme of which the statute is a part. [Citations.]" (*Nolan, supra,* 33 Cal.4th at p. 340.) Using these extrinsic aids, we "'select the construction that comports most closely with the apparent intent of the Legislature, with a view to promoting rather than defeating the general purpose of the statute, and avoid an interpretation that would lead to absurd consequences.' [Citation.]" (*People v. Sinohui* (2002) 28 Cal.4th 205, 212 [120 Cal.Rptr.2d 783, 47 P.3d 629].)

Where judicial interpretation is required, courts give deference to an agency's reasonable interpretation of the statutory enactment that the agency has been entrusted by law to enforce. (*Montebello Rose* [*v. Agricultural Labor Relations Bd.*], *supra,* 119 Cal.App.3d at p. 24.) Nevertheless, it is fundamental in statutory construction that courts should ascertain the intent of the Legislature so as to effectuate the purpose of the law. (*J.R. Norton Co.* [*v. Agricultural Labor Relations Bd.*], *supra*, 26 Cal.3d at p. 29.) Thus, while an administrative agency is entitled to deference when interpreting policy in its field of expertise, it cannot alter or amend the statute that it is interpreting, or enlarge or impair its scope. (*Ibid.*; *Adamek & Dessert, Inc.* [*v. Agricultural Labor Relations Bd.*], *supra*, 178 Cal.App.3d at p. 978.)

To the above, we add the following basic precepts regarding a court's role in the interpretation of statutes. As expressed in *Cadiz v. Agricultural Labor Relations Bd.* (1979) 92 Cal.App.3d 365, 372 [155 Cal.Rptr. 213]: "The guiding principle of interpretation was laid down by the Legislature in Code of Civil Procedure section 1858: 'In the construction of a statute or instrument, the office of the Judge is simply to ascertain and declare what is in terms or in substance contained therein, not to insert what has been omitted, or to omit what has been inserted; and where there are several provisions or particulars, such a construction is, if possible, to be adopted as will give effect to all.' That prime rule of construction has been adopted and restated by the cases." Furthermore, it is not a court's function to second-guess the policy choices or wisdom of particular legislation: "'Courts do not sit as super-legislatures to determine the wisdom, desirability or propriety of statutes enacted by the Legislature.' [Citations.]" (*Ibid.*)

III. Requirements of Section 1164.11

Gerawan contends that two of the conditions for relief stated in section 1164.11 were not shown by UFW and, therefore, the Board should not have ordered the parties to the MMC process. Under that section, where the union's certification occurred prior to January 1, 2003, no demand to the Board may be made for referral to the MMC process unless the following criteria are met: "(a) the parties have failed to reach agreement for at least one year after the date on which the labor organization made its initial request to bargain, (b) the employer has committed an unfair labor practice, and (c) the parties have not previously had a binding contract between them." (§ 1164.11; cf. § 1164, subd. (a)(1).) Specifically, Gerawan argues that the requirements of criteria (a) and (b) of section 1164.11 (hereafter sections 1164.11(a) and 1164.11(b)) were not established based on Gerawan's proposed interpretations of those provisions. As explained below, we reject Gerawan's arguments regarding the construction of the statutory language and conclude that the Board followed the clear and unequivocal terms of section 1164.11 when it held that the requirements thereof were met.

A. The Parties Failed to Reach Agreement for at Least One Year

Section 1164.11(a) states a requirement for seeking the MMC process in cases involving pre-2003 certifications that "*the parties have failed to reach agreement for at least one year after the date on which the labor organization made its initial request to bargain....*" (Italics added.) In the proceedings before the Board, Gerawan insisted this language meant there had to be "'a good faith and sustained effort'" at negotiation for at least a one-year period. It further argued that since UFW did not make such a showing, the Board was constrained to deny UFW's request. The Board disagreed. It explained that section 1164.11(a) does not contain any language requiring proof of one year of sustained and active bargaining, but only that "the parties failed to reach an agreement for at least one year" after the initial request to bargain, which the Board found to be the case.

In its opening brief herein, Gerawan argues the Board erred because the provision should be construed to specifically require a showing that the parties "actively attempt[ed] to bargain for at last one year," since "one cannot 'fail' to reach an agreement if one does not try." We reject Gerawan's proposed interpretation. The plain language of section 1164.11(a) simply requires that (1) the parties have not reached agreement and (2) at least one year has passed since the initial request to bargain. The provision makes no mention of the particular circumstances surrounding the parties' failure to agree. Contrary to Gerawan's suggestion, nothing in section 1164.11(a) mandates an affirmative showing of active and/or sustained bargaining over a one-year period. "When the language of a statute is clear, we need go no further." (*Nolan, supra,* 33 Cal.4th at p. 340.) Whether or not it would have been wise to include a threshold requirement that before a party may invoke the MMC process, the party must demonstrate there was one year of sustained bargaining, the Legislature did not do so in the particular provision under consideration here. One may argue it *should have,* but we are constrained by the fact that it did not. That ends the matter, since it is not our function to insert what the Legislature has omitted, nor may we, "'under the guise of construction, rewrite the law or give the words an effect different from the plain and direct import of the terms used.' [Citation.]" (*People v. Leal* (2004) 33 Cal.4th 999, 1008 [16 Cal.Rptr.3d 869, 94 P.3d 1071].)

Although, as Gerawan points out, other provisions of the ALRA obligate the parties to bargain in good faith (e.g., §§ 1153, subd. (e), 1154, subd. (c), 1155.2, subd. (a)), those provisions do not alter the plain meaning of what must be shown under section 1164.11(a).18 Even if, based on the general bargaining obligation, the parties should have engaged (or attempted to engage) in active and/or sustained bargaining during the one-year period specified in section 1164.11(a), the latter provision does not require that such conduct be affirmatively demonstrated as part of the necessary prima facie showing to request the MMC process.

In this case, it is not disputed that UFW's initial request to bargain was made in 1992. Additionally, UFW followed up its request by making a contract proposal to Gerawan in 1994, and one bargaining session occurred between the parties in early 1995. Insofar as the parties have still not reached agreement, the discrete statutory requirement set forth in section 1164.11(a) was clearly satisfied.

Gerawan's Further Arguments Do Not Persuade Us to Depart from the Plain Meaning of Section 1164.11(a)

Having upheld the plain meaning of section 1164.11(a), we briefly explain why we have not accepted Gerawan's arguments that we should depart from the statute's clear and literal terms.

In essence, Gerawan asserts that if the statute were treated as simply a passage-of-time requirement, it would lead to absurd results and contravene the overall legislative purposes of the ALRA and MMC statutes. To avoid that outcome, Gerawan argues that we should construe the provision to include an active or sustained bargaining requirement, even if that is not its plain meaning. (See, e.g., *California School Employees Assn. v. Governing Board* (1994) 8 Cal.4th 333, 340 [33 Cal.Rptr.2d 109, 878 P.2d 1321] [stating rule that a court need not follow the plain meaning of a statute when to do so would frustrate the manifest purpose of the legislation as a whole or lead to absurd results]; *DaFonte v. Up-Right, Inc.* (1992) 2 Cal.4th 593, 601 [7 Cal.Rptr.2d 238, 828 P.2d 140] [stating rule that plain meaning may be disregarded only when that meaning is repugnant to the general purview of the act or for some other compelling reason].) In this regard, it is pointed out that the ALRA (of which the MMC statute is a part) has a purpose to promote good faith bargaining between the employer and the employees' chosen representative so they may potentially reach a mutually acceptable agreement, which purpose is supported by the duty to bargain collectively in good faith (see §§ 1140.2, 1155.2, subd. (a)). According to Gerawan, if the Board's interpretation were correct, a union could make an initial request to bargain and then simply wait out the clock or engage in surface bargaining until enough time had passed to demand the MMC process (i.e., precisely what Gerawan contends happened here). Allegedly, a union in that situation would have no incentive to make voluntary concessions or otherwise engage in serious or genuine efforts to reach an agreement. In short, Gerawan maintains that the Board's interpretation would lead to absurd results at odds with the legislative purposes by (1) undermining a union's incentive to bargain in good faith and (2) potentially forcing employers to undergo the MMC process without a sustained period of good faith bargaining for an entire year.

While Gerawan's arguments identify significant concerns as to the potential impacts of section 1164.11(a), we believe they fall short of showing that we should effectively rewrite the statute by construing it to include a sustained or active bargaining requirement that the Legislature did not put there. (See *Unzueta v. Ocean View School Dist.* (1992) 6 Cal.App.4th 1689, 1698 [8 Cal.Rptr.2d 614] [absurdity exception to plain meaning rule "should be used most sparingly by the judiciary and only in extreme cases else we violate the separation of powers principle of government"].) Among other things, Gerawan's analysis of the statutory purposes fails to adequately account for the fact that the ALRA was amended by the MMC statute. The Legislature determined that the ALRA, in its original form, was not adequately fulfilling its purposes. (Stats. 2002, ch. 1145, § 1, p. 7401; *Hess* [*Collection Winery v. Agricultural Labor Relations*], *supra,* 140 Cal.App.4th at p. 1600.) New measures were deemed necessary because it was perceived that many employers were unwilling to enter into an initial CBA. (*Hess, supra,* at p. 1593.) Therefore, the MMC statute was enacted as an amendment to the ALRA to create a "one-time" compulsory process to bring about an initial CBA between parties who have never entered into such an agreement, where certain statutory conditions were met. (*Hess, supra,* at pp. 1600–1601 [noting the purpose "to change attitudes toward collective bargaining by compelling the parties to operate for at least one term" with an imposed CBA].) Among those statutory conditions is the one now before us — the passage of the one-year time period described in section 1164.11(a). In that provision, the Legislature specified that expiration of the one-year time period without a CBA (i.e., "the parties have failed to reach agreement for at least one year after" the union's initial request to bargain) was one of the threshold requirements for seeking a referral to the MMC process in cases involving pre-2003 certifications. Evidently, the Legislature believed that if more than one year elapsed without a CBA being reached, that fact reasonably indicated the MMC process was appropriate, assuming that the other requirements were also met. Viewed in light of the entire statutory context, we are unable to conclude that the one-year provision of section 1164.11(a), when accorded its plain and literal meaning, would substantially frustrate the main purpose of the ALRA *as amended by the MMC statute,* or otherwise lead to absurd results.

In a further effort to support its position on this issue, Gerawan notes that the Board's own past decisions had, on at least two occasions, expressed an understanding of the relevant statutory provisions that sounded remarkably similar to Gerawan's position. (See *Pictsweet Mushroom Farms, supra,* 29 ALRB No. 3, p. 9 [to be sent to MMC process, employer "must have been through a period of bargaining for a year without having reached a contract"]; *D'Arrigo Bros. Co.* (2007) 33 ALRB No. 1, p. 5 [MMC process may not be invoked unless parties have attempted to negotiate on their own for the statutory period].) However, it appears that such comments were made by the Board in connection with tangential issues, and that once the Board directly considered the present issue of statutory construction, it followed the plain meaning (see, e.g., *Gerawan Farming, Inc.* (2013) 39 ALRB No. 5, p. 3). In any event, we are bound to do so here.

Still, the Board's earlier comments about the import of the relevant statutory provisions provide some evidence that Gerawan's proposed construction is not mere wishful thinking on its part. There is cogency and common sense in Gerawan's argument that active bargaining should precede the MMC process, and it is not unreasonable to suggest that the former should be a prerequisite to commencing the latter. But such argument is more properly presented to the Legislature, whose exclusive function is to enact statutes such as those at issue here. Moreover, if we were to adopt Gerawan's interpretation, what additional specific language would we incorporate into the statute: sustained bargaining, active bargaining, actual bargaining, attempted bargaining? Would we likewise be expected to delineate how much or what quality of bargaining effort would constitute sustained, active, actual, or attempted bargaining? And if there was no bargaining during the one-year period under any definition, would it matter why there was no bargaining, or whose fault, if any, it was for the parties' failure to reach an agreement? These are some of the prickly questions that would be raised if this court, or any court, felt inclined to impose additional substantive requirements beyond those specified in the statute before the Board could refer a case to the MMC process. The nature of these quandaries reinforces our concern that, if we went down that path, we would be intruding into the legislative arena. We decline to do so. As was aptly stated by another Court of Appeal: "[E]xcept in the most extreme cases where legislative intent and the underlying purpose are at odds with the plain language of the statute, an appellate court should exercise judicial restraint, stay its hand, and refrain from rewriting a statute to find an intent not expressed by the Legislature." (*Unzueta v. Ocean View School Dist., supra,* 6 Cal.App.4th at p. 1700.)

....

THE CONSTITUTIONAL ISSUES

Gerawan raises several constitutional challenges to the MMC statute, including that the law is invalid under the protections afforded to the liberty of contract by substantive due process, fails to comply with equal protection principles, unlawfully delegates legislative powers, violates procedural due process, and constitutes a taking of private property without just compensation. As explained below, we conclude the MMC statute violates equal protection of the law and improperly delegates legislative authority. Since we hold the MMC statute is constitutionally deficient on these two grounds, we find it unnecessary to address the several additional arguments made by Gerawan that the MMC statute is unconstitutional. (See *Santa Clara County Local Transportation Authority v. Guardino* (1995) 11 Cal.4th 220, 230 [45 Cal.Rptr.2d 207, 902 P.2d 225] [courts refrain from rendering unnecessary constitutional law decisions].)

V. Equal Protection of the Laws

Gerawan attacks the validity of the MMC statute on the ground that it violates the constitutional requirement of equal protection of the laws.

The equal protection clause of the Fourteenth Amendment to the United States Constitution provides: "No State shall ... deny to any person within its jurisdiction the equal protection of the laws." (U.S. Const., 14th Amend., § 1.) The California Constitution expressly provides the same guarantee. (Cal. Const., art. I, § 7, subd. (a).) In essence, equal protection of the law means that all persons who are similarly situated with respect to a law should be treated alike under the law. (*Cleburne v. Cleburne Living Center, Inc.* (1985) 473 U.S. 432, 439 [87 L.Ed.2d 313, 105 S.Ct. 3249]; *Arcadia Development Co. v. City of Morgan Hill* (2011) 197 Cal.App.4th 1526, 1534 [129 Cal.Rptr.3d 369].) "Of course, most laws differentiate in some fashion between classes of persons. The Equal Protection Clause does not forbid classifications. It simply keeps governmental decisionmakers from treating differently persons who are in all relevant respects alike. [Citation.]" (*Nordlinger v. Hahn* (1992) 505 U.S. 1, 10 [120 L.Ed.2d 1, 112 S.Ct. 2326].)

"The general rule is that legislation is presumed to be valid and will be sustained if the classification drawn by the statute is rationally related to a legitimate state interest. [Citations.] When social or economic legislation is at issue, the Equal Protection Clause allows the States wide latitude, [citations], and the Constitution presumes that even improvident decisions will eventually be rectified by the democratic processes." (*Cleburne v. Cleburne Living Center, Inc., supra,* 473 U.S. at p. 440; accord, *FCC v. Beach Communications, Inc.* (1993) 508 U.S. 307, 313–314 [124 L.Ed.2d 211, 113 S.Ct. 2096].)

As Justice Robert Jackson explained many years ago: "[C]ities, states and the Federal Government must exercise their powers so as not to discriminate between their inhabitants *except upon some reasonable differentiation fairly related to the object of regulation.* This equality is not merely abstract justice. The framers of the Constitution knew, and we should not forget today, that there is no more effective practical guaranty against arbitrary and unreasonable government than to require that the principles of law which officials would impose upon a minority must be imposed generally. Conversely, nothing opens the door to arbitrary action so effectively as to allow those officials to pick and choose only a few to whom they will apply legislation and thus to escape the political retribution that might be visited upon them if larger numbers were affected. Courts can take no better measure to assure that laws will be just than to require that laws be equal in operation." (*Railway Express v. New York* (1949) 336 U.S. 106, 112–113 [93 L.Ed. 533, 69 S.Ct. 463], italics added (conc. opn. of Jackson, J.), cited with approval in *Hays v. Wood* (1979) 25 Cal.3d 772, 786–787 [160 Cal.Rptr. 102, 603 P.2d 19].)

The same rational basis standard is applied for purposes of the equal protection provision of the California Constitution. (*Kasler v. Lockyer* (2000) 23 Cal.4th 472, 481–482 [97 Cal.Rptr.2d 334, 2 P.3d 581]; *County of L.A. v. Southern Cal. Tel. Co., supra,* 32 Cal.2d at pp. 389–390.) This deferential standard "'invests legislation involving such differentiated treatment with a presumption of constitutionality and "requir[es] merely that distinctions drawn by a challenged statute bear some rational relationship to a conceivable legitimate state purpose." [Citation.]'" (*Warden v. State Bar* (1999) 21 Cal.4th 628, 641 [88 Cal.Rptr.2d 283, 982 P.2d 154].) "Past decisions also establish that, under the rational relationship test, the state may recognize that different categories or classes of persons within a larger classification may pose varying degrees of risk of harm, and properly may limit a regulation to those classes of persons as to whom the need for regulation is thought to be more crucial or imperative." (*Id.* at p. 644, citing *Williamson v. Lee Optical Co.* (1955) 348 U.S. 483, 489 [99 L.Ed. 563, 75 S.Ct. 461] ["Evils in the same field may be of different dimensions and proportions, requiring different remedies. Or so the legislature may think. [Citation.] Or the reform may take one step at a time, addressing itself to the phase of the problem which seems most acute to the legislative mind."].)

A key principle that must be applied in the present analysis is that "[a]n administrative order, legislative in character, is subject to the same tests as to validity as an act of the Legislature. [Citations.]" (*Knudsen Creamery Co. v. Brock* (1951) 37 Cal.2d 485, 494 [234 P.2d 26] (*Knudsen Creamery Co.*).) As the majority opinion in *Hess* correctly observed, the action of the Board in approving a final CBA submitted by the mediator is essentially *legislative* in character: "There can be no doubt that the compulsory interest arbitration scheme provides for quasi-legislative action. Although the statutes refer to the end result as a 'collective bargaining agreement,' there is no agreement. In this case Hess not only did not agree to be bound by the terms of employment imposed by the mediator, it did not agree to submit to interest arbitration at all. The terms of the 'agreement' determined by the arbitrator were imposed upon Hess by force of law. [¶] The statutory scheme is not quasi-judicial. An administrative action is quasi-judicial, or quasi-adjudicative, when it consists of applying existing rules to existing facts. [Citation.] The creation of new rules for future application, such as is done here, is quasi-legislative in character. [Citation.] This is so even though the action is, as here, taken in an individual case. [Citation.]" (*Hess, supra,* 140 Cal.App.4th at pp. 1597–1598.) (23) Accordingly, when under the MMC statute the Board approves or adopts a mediator's report (such as the one in this case regarding Gerawan) and thereby establishes an enforceable CBA as to a particular employer and union, the resulting CBA is legislative or regulatory in character and is "subject to the same tests as to validity as an act of the Legislature" (*Knudsen Creamery Co., supra,* at p. 494), including the test of constitutionality under the equal protection clause.

 . . . .

Additionally, the results would not only be unequal, but also arbitrary. Because of the differences of each employer and the subjectivity of a process whereby the only objective standard or goal to be met in the MMC statute is *to resolve issues* so that a first contract may be imposed (see § 1164, subd. (d)), it would appear to be unavoidable that even similar employers will be subject to significantly different outcomes. Since the factors in subdivision (e) of section 1164 are broad and varied enough to permit a mediator to select from among a wide range of potential CBA terms that he or she may think best (as long as minimal support for the decision is provided), the risk is simply too great that results will be based largely on the subjective leanings of each mediator or that arbitrary differences will otherwise be imposed on similar employers in the same classification — particularly as there is no objective standard toward which the mediator is required to aim.

In so holding, we disagree with the Board and UFW that the MMC statute is analogous to a rent control ordinance where one apartment building in a municipality may be granted a right to charge a higher rent than another (i.e., different results would be acceptable as long as they were rationally based). In the case of a rent control ordinance, a local board or commission attempts to determine a rent ceiling or a rent adjustment based upon an administrative standard (such as a "'fair and reasonable return on investment'") by using a specified formula or a list of factors. (*Fisher v. City of Berkeley* (1984) 37 Cal.3d 644, 679–681 [209 Cal.Rptr. 682, 693 P.2d 261]; see *Kavanau v. Santa Monica Rent Control Bd.* (1997) 16 Cal.4th 761, 768–769 [66 Cal.Rptr.2d 672, 941 P.2d 851].) Here, in contrast, there is a broad range of factors but no standard. Moreover, we believe the inequality and arbitrariness of the MMC process are on a far grander scale than might occur under an inadequately worded rent control law because, unlike the case of rent control (which only decides on a single term of a broader contractual relationship), here the Board, through the mediator, establishes the *entire* CBA.

For all of the above reasons, we agree with Justice Nicholson's dissent in *Hess* that the MMC statute on its face violates equal protection principles.

VI. Improper Delegation of Legislative Authority

Gerawan argues that the MMC statute invalidly delegates legislative authority in violation of the California Constitution.

An unconstitutional delegation of authority occurs when a legislative body "(1) leaves the resolution of fundamental policy issues to others or (2) fails to provide adequate direction for the implementation of that policy." (*Carson Mobilehome Park Owners' Assn. v. City of Carson* (1983) 35 Cal.3d 184, 190 [197 Cal.Rptr. 284, 672 P.2d 1297].) "'This doctrine rests upon the premise that the legislative body must itself effectively resolve the truly fundamental issues. It cannot escape responsibility by explicitly delegating that function to others or by failing to establish an effective mechanism to assure the proper implementation of its policy decisions.' [Citation.] [¶] The doctrine prohibiting delegations of legislative power does not invalidate reasonable grants of power to an administrative agency, when suitable safeguards are established to guide the power's use and to protect against misuse. [Citations.] The Legislature must make the fundamental policy determinations, but after declaring the legislative goals and establishing a yardstick guiding the administrator, it may authorize the administrator to adopt rules and regulations to promote the purposes of the legislation and to carry it into effect. [Citations.] Moreover, standards for administrative application of a statute need not be expressly set forth; they may be implied by the statutory purpose. [Citations.]" (*People v. Wright* (1982) 30 Cal.3d 705, 712–713 [180 Cal.Rptr. 196, 639 P.2d 267].)

In *Birkenfeld v. City of Berkeley* (1976) 17 Cal.3d 129 [130 Cal.Rptr. 465, 550 P.2d 1001], the California Supreme Court held that the rent control scheme at issue in that case gave adequate guidance in its delegation of authority to the rent control board because, in addition to providing a nonexclusive list of relevant factors to be considered by the board in determining adjustment of maximum rents, the stated purpose of the charter amendment furnished an implied standard for the board to apply. (*Id.* at p. 168.) "[T]he charter amendment's purpose of counteracting the ill effects of 'rapidly rising and exorbitant rents exploiting [the housing] shortage' [citation] implies a standard of fixing maximum rent levels at a point that permits the landlord to charge a just and reasonable rent and no more." (*Ibid.*)

Applying the above principles, we agree with Gerawan that the MMC statute improperly delegated legislative authority. Although the MMC statute enumerates several factors for the mediator to consider when making his or her various decisions about the terms of what will become a compelled CBA (§ 1164, subd. (e)), it does not provide the mediator with any policy objective to be carried out or standard to be attained once those factors have been considered. Since there is no goal to aim for, no one would ever know if the mediator hit the correct target or even came close. As was observed by Justice Nicholson in his dissent in *Hess:* "Even though under the statute at issue the mediator must make factual findings and those findings must be supported by the record, there is no way to determine whether the facts found by the mediator support the decision unless one knows what basic public policy the mediator must vindicate." (*Hess, supra,* 140 Cal.App.4th at p. 1612 (dis. opn. of Nicholson, J.).)

Additionally, unlike the *Birkenfeld* case, the legislative purpose of the MMC statute fails to supply the necessary guidance to either the mediator or the Board. The stated purpose of the MMC statute is to "ensure a more effective collective bargaining process between agricultural employers and agricultural employees, and thereby more fully attain the purposes of the [ALRA], ameliorate the working conditions and economic standing of agricultural employees, create stability in the agricultural labor force, and promote California's economic well-being by ensuring stability in its most vital industry." (Stats. 2002, ch. 1145, § 1, p. 7401.) Justice Nicholson is correct that "[t]his pronouncement [is] so general it fail[s] to provide actual guidance." (*Hess, supra,* at p. 1612 (dis. opn. of Nicholson, J.).) In short, no implied standard is discernable in the MMC statute.

For this reason, the difference between the present case and *Birkenfeld* is substantial. In *Birkenfeld,* because there was an implied standard that the rent control board was to implement — a just and reasonable rental amount based on several factors — the rent control board had sufficient direction and guidance regarding the responsibility delegated to it. (*Birkenfeld, supra,* 17 Cal.3d at pp. 168–169.) In other words, there was a particular destination the rent control board was supposed to reach, and a reasonable roadmap for getting there. In theory, at least, all of the information gathered in the rent control proceeding could be weighed and considered in making the ultimate determination of a just and reasonable rental amount and, once so determined, the amount of rent that could permissibly be charged was thereby established. In contrast, under the MMC statute, there is no particular destination that is supposed to be reached by the mediator, no particular determination that is to be made, nor is any direction given as to the mediator's task or purpose other than to impose a CBA on the parties after considering the listed factors.

We may further illustrate the lack of adequate standards under the MMC statute by posing a few questions with no discernable answers. Other than to create and impose an agreement, what is the mediator's precise purpose, goal or aim under the MMC statute? Is it to raise workers' wages? Is it to improve working conditions? Is it to impose on the grower any and all union demands the mediator deems *reasonable* and which the mediator believes the grower can *afford* and, if so, how are *reasonable* and *afford* defined? Is it to ensure that wages paid are at least industry average for comparable work? Is the mediator's starting point to determine a *minimum,* fair profit margin for the grower and then to determine in what amount the workers are to be compensated without compromising that margin; or is it to first determine a *minimum* amount the workers are to be compensated without regard to grower profit margins? By posing these questions, we are not saying that any of our questions embody wise or legitimate statutory objectives. We are simply pointing out that we cannot tell what the mediator's task is supposed to be under the MMC statute, and these questions serve to highlight a number of hypothetical possibilities without in any way approving of them. The bottom line is this: In the MMC statute, the Legislature has delegated broad legislative authority to the mediator and the Board under the MMC process, but has not provided adequate standards to guide and direct the use of that delegated authority or prevent its misuse.

Finally, the delegation of powers under the MMC statute also lacks the necessary procedural safeguards or mechanisms to assure a fair and evenhanded implementation of the legislative mandate to impose a CBA. *Birkenfeld* held that even if there is "legislative guidance by way of policy and primary standards," it is not enough if the Legislature fails to establish safeguards or mechanisms to protect against unfairness or favoritism. (*Birkenfeld, supra,* 17 Cal.3d at p. 169.) Here, in addition to the lack of standards, we do not see how the highly deferential and limited review the Board undertakes of a mediator's report under the MMC statute could be deemed a realistic safeguard against unfairness or favoritism. For the most part, the Board *must* approve the mediator's report as the final order of the Board unless a challenged CBA provision is either (i) "unrelated to wages, hours, or other conditions of employment," (ii) "based on clearly erroneous findings of material fact," or (iii) "arbitrary or capricious" in light of the mediator's findings of fact. (§ 1164.3, subd. (a).) In practical effect, this means the Board must give virtually a rubberstamp approval to the mediator's reported CBA as long as the terms thereof have at least a small kernel of plausible support, are not wholly arbitrary, and the mediator has considered the factors listed in section 1164, subdivision (e). Except in perhaps the most egregious instances of overreaching, the Board's hands would be tied and the report would have to be approved. In light of the mediator's considerable range of power to determine all aspects of a compelled CBA, which would include a broad array of important economic terms and relationships, such a highly deferential and narrow review mechanism would not be able to meaningfully protect the parties against favoritism or unfairness in regard to the determination of the CBA's terms.

....

DISPOSITION

The Board's order in *Gerawan Farming, Inc., supra,* 39 ALRB No. 17 (case No. F068526) is reversed and set aside. In light of the above ruling, the trial court's denial of the writ in case No. F068676 is affirmed. Costs are awarded to Gerawan.

HILL, P.J., and LEVY, J., concurred.

Notes and Questions

1. Under the constitutional doctrine prohibiting the delegation of legislative power, standards for administrative application of a statute need not be expressly set forth; they may be implied by the statutory purpose. Under the constitutional doctrine prohibiting delegation of legislative power, after declaring the legislative goals and establishing a yardstick guiding the administrator, the Legislature may authorize the administrator to adopt rules and regulations to promote the purposes of the legislation and to carry it into effect. The constitutional doctrine does not invalidate reasonable grants of power to an administrative agency when suitable safeguards are established to guide the power's use and to protect against misuse.

2. If the court ruled that the MMC statute was unconstitutional, why did it thoroughly review the statute's provisions? What were the two bases for the court's ruling that the MMC statute was unconstitutional?

3. What was the basis for the court's holding that the Board had abused its discretion?

4. Was this case simply one of statutory construction? Was the intent of the Legislature properly ascertained in this case? When is it appropriate for a court to ignore the "plain meaning" of a statute?

5. Why did the court reject Gerawan's argument that the statutory language should be read to require "'a good faith and sustained effort'" at negotiation for at least a one-year period? Would we not expect such a requirement in all types of contract negotiations whether the requirement was explicitly set forth or not?

6. Was Gerawan correct in relying upon the ALRB's prior decisions concerning the regulatory agency's statutory views? Should the court have deferred to the expertise and interpretation of the regulatory agency in this particular instance? What was the court's view of Gerawan's reliance on the Board's prior comments?

7. On what basis can a court effectively rewrite a statute?

8. What was the impact in this case of the judicial doctrine that, when the Legislature enacts a statute, it is presumed to have knowledge of the existing judicial decisions construing the statute or related statutes and to have enacted new statutes or amendments in light of those decisions?

9. What reasons did the court rely upon to recognize the abandonment claim?

10. What were the constitutional challenges lodged by Gerawan? Which of these constitutional challenges were persuasive to the court?

11. An unconstitutional delegation of authority is generally defined to occur when a legislative body "(1) leaves the resolution of fundamental policy issues to others or (2) fails to provide adequate direction for the implementation of that policy." Which option is generally the basis for a court determination that a statute constitutes an improper delegation of authority? What are examples of "suitable safeguards [that] are established to guide the power's use and to protect against misuse"?

12. Why did the court hold that the legislative purpose of the MMC statute failed to supply the necessary guidance to either the mediator or the Board? Did the statute really leave the resolution of fundamental policy issues to others? Did the statute actually fail to provide adequate direction and safeguards for the implementation of that policy?

Chapter Four

Organization

A. California Legislature's Organizing Session

The California Legislature operates during two-year legislative sessions. At the commencement of the two-year session, the Legislature must organize itself. In that regard, there are several provisions related to organizing the Legislature that are found in the California Constitution and the Government Code.

<u>Constitutional Provision</u>

According to Article 4, Section 3(a) of the state Constitution, "The Legislature shall convene in regular session at noon on the first Monday in December of each even-numbered year and each house shall immediately organize." This date falls every two years about three weeks after the statewide general elections has taken place. The two houses convene that first session at noon and it usually lasts about two hours.

<u>Government Code Provisions</u>

Pursuant to Section 9020 of the Government Code, "The Legislature shall convene in regular session at the City of Sacramento at noon on the first Monday in December of each even-numbered year, and each house shall immediately organize." This provision is essentially a restatement of the constitutional provision.

According to Section 9021, "The certificate of election is prima facie evidence of the right to membership." The California Secretary of State prepares this document certifying that the individual has been elected to either the Assembly or the Senate.

Per Section 9022, "At the day and hour appointed for the assembling of any regular session of the Legislature, the President of the Senate, or in case of his absence or inability, the senior member present, shall take the chair, call the members and members elect to order, and have the secretary call over the senatorial districts, in their order, from which members have been elected at the preceding election. As the districts are called the members elect shall present their certificates, take the constitutional oath of office, and assume their seats. If a quorum is present, the Senate may then elect its officers."

This provision has several key components. Either the Lt. Governor or the most senior member of the Senate opens the session, and the senators (both the 20 who were just elected, as well as the 20 carryover senators) respond to the calling of the Senate District in numeric order, from SD 1 through SD 40. Once the new senators take their seats, then they elect the officers of the Senate.

Under Section 9023, "At the day and hour appointed for the assembling of any regular session of the Legislature, the Chief Clerk of the Assembly, or in case of his absence or inability, the senior member elect present, shall take the chair, call the members elect to order, and call over the role of counties in alphabetical order. As the counties are called the members elect shall present their certificates, take the constitutional oath of office, and assume their seats. If there is more than one senior member elect present and the senior members are unable to agree as to who shall call the session to order, the Attorney General or one of his deputies shall call the session to order. If a quorum is present, the Assembly shall then elect its officers, and there shall be no other business, motion or resolution considered before the election of the Speaker, save and except a motion to adjourn or a motion for a call of the house."

This provision has several key components as well. Either the Assembly Chief Clerk or the most senior member of the Assembly opens the session, and the Assembly Members (all 80 of them) respond to the calling of the 58 counties. Once the new Assembly Members take their seats, then they elect the officers of the Assembly. The first order of business is to elect the Speaker of the Assembly.

Section 9024 provides "Members of the Legislature who did not take the oath of office at the assembling of the Legislature may take the oath at any time during the term for which they were elected." This provision allows individuals elected to either house to take their oath of office at any time during their term, such as those elected during a special election to fill a vacancy.

Per Section 9025, "An entry of the oath taken by members of the Legislature shall be made on the journals of the proper house." This provision requires the *Assembly Daily Journal* and the *Senate Daily Journal* to publish all the oaths of office by their respective members.

At the organizing sessions, both the elected officials and their families and supporters are in attendance. They rarely engage in regular business, other than introducing their first bills, which not all legislators do on that first day. They visit with colleagues, former legislators attend, and they enjoy the "pomp and circumstance" of the organizing session. Thereafter, in the first week of January, legislators commence the serious work ahead that will last the following two years.

Notes and Questions

1. The organizing session occurs at the start of each two-year session of the Legislature. Legislators are permitted to introduce bills that first day of the new Session, and many often do so at that time, although most bills are introduced in February, mostly just days prior to the deadline for doing so.

2. What are the similarities between the processes used on the opening day of Session by the Senate and Assembly? What are the major differences between the processes used on the opening day of Session by the Assembly and Senate?

B. Adjournment in the California Legislature

When the California Legislature adjourned its 2020 Session in the early morning hours of September 1, many observers mistakenly called it "adjournment *sine die.*" There is a distinction between adjournment and adjournment *sine die.*

According to the Legislative Counsel's Glossary of Terms, adjournment means the termination of a meeting, occurring at the close of each legislative day upon the completion of business, which is accomplished by a successful motion to end the session, with the hour and day of the next meeting being set prior to adjournment.

In order for the Assembly and Senate to adjourn, a motion to adjourn must be made. The motion to adjourn is not debatable and may not be amended. It is always in order, except when another Member has the floor, when voting is taking place, or during a call of the Assembly. Pursuant to Assembly Rule 84, the details of the adjournment motion are entered in the *Assembly Daily Journal.* A motion to adjourn requires a majority vote.

In addition, under Assembly Rule 85, a motion to recess to a time certain is treated the same as a motion to adjourn, except that the motion is debatable and can be amended as to the time and duration.

This is distinguished from adjournment *sine die* which, in Latin, means literally to adjourn without days. According to the Legislative Counsel's Glossary of Terms, the phrase means that there are no more days left. It is used to describe the final termination of the two-year legislative session.

Pursuant to Article IV, Section 3(a) of the California Constitution, "each session of the Legislature shall adjourn sine die by operation of the Constitution at midnight on November 30 of the following even-numbered year." Both regular and special sessions of the Legislature adjourn *sine die* at midnight on November 30 of each even-numbered year.

So, when the Legislature terminated its Session on September 1, both the Assembly and Senate adjourned until they reconvened on Monday, December 7 at 12 noon. On the other hand, the 2019–20 Legislative Session adjourned *sine die* on November 30.

C. Legislative Calendar

The calendar for the California Legislative Session is important for those working in and around the State Capitol. The California Constitution provides the dates of convening and adjourning the legislative session. Other than that, the Legislature has freedom to set its own calendar of meetings and recesses.

The legislative calendar establishes a schedule for the two-year legislative session and provides important deadlines for the legislative process. While there is a general outline for the legislative Session, the Senate and Assembly Daily Files contain the scheduled events for each day the Legislature is in session, including such things as committee meetings and floor sessions, along with holidays and important dates.

Article IV of the state Constitution establishes when the Legislature is to be in session. Section 3 of Article IV states that the Legislature is to convene in regular session on the first Monday of December in each even-numbered year to organize. The Legislature must adjourn by November 30 of the following even-numbered year.

Generally, the Legislature begins meeting the first week in January each year and concludes its work for the year either in mid-September (odd-numbered year) or August 31 (even-numbered year). During the calendar year, the Legislature traditionally schedules two recesses: a one-week spring recess (which is generally the week before Easter) and a summer recess that typically lasts four weeks.

In addition, several one-day holidays are recognized by the Legislature. The Legislature eliminated the Columbus Day holiday and one of the President's Day holidays several years ago. Legislators are permitted to provide one floating holiday for their personal staff members.

In addition to the regular session, the Governor may, by proclamation, require the Legislature to meet in special session. Section 3 of the California Constitution provides the Governor with the power to call special sessions of the Legislature. A special session may run concurrently with the Legislature's normally scheduled meeting time and/or during its recesses. During the special session, the Legislature may act only on subjects specified in the proclamation.

Aside from the fact that a special session is limited to the subject matter for which it was called, there are no significant differences in process between a regular and special session. However, the effective dates for bills enacted during a special session are somewhat different than those for a regular session.

The legislative calendar for the California Legislature contains rules and guidelines that shape the day-to-day business of the Assembly and Senate. Some of the rules found in the calendar are from the California Constitution, such as the January 1 date for the day that new laws usually take effect. Others come from laws passed by the Assembly and the State Senate.

D. Legislative Deadlines

The California Legislature works on the basis of deadlines for moving measures (bills, resolutions and constitutional amendments) through the legislative process. The Assembly Chief Clerk and the Senate Secretary each maintain information related to these legislative deadlines.

Based upon the legislative calendar and the Joint Rules of the Assembly and Senate, the following are the key dates during the calendar year for individuals monitoring the legislative process to be aware of:

Statutes take effect on January 1 (Art. IV, Sec. 8(c)).

Legislature reconvenes (J.R. 51(a)(1)).

Budget Bill must be submitted by Governor by January 10 (Art. IV, Sec. 12(a)).

Last day to submit bill requests to the Office of Legislative Counsel.

Last day for bills to be introduced (J.R. 61(a)(1), J.R. 54(a)).

Spring Recess begins upon adjournment (J.R. 51(a)(2)).

Legislature reconvenes from Spring Recess (J.R. 51(a)(2)).

Last day for policy committees to hear and report fiscal bills for referral to fiscal committees (J.R. 61(a)(2)).

Last day for policy committees to hear and report to the floor non-fiscal bills (J.R. 61(a)(3)).

Last day for policy committees to meet prior to June 5 (J.R. 61(a)(4)).

Last day for fiscal committees to hear and report bills to the floor (J.R. 61(a)(5)).

Last day for fiscal committees to meet prior to June 5(J.R. 61(a)(6)).

No committee may meet for any purpose except for Rules Committee and Conference Committees (J.R. 61(a)(7)).

Last day to pass bills out of house of origin (J.R. 61(a)(8)).

Committee meetings may resume (J.R. 61(a)(9)).

Budget Bill must be passed by midnight (Art. IV, Sec. 12(c)(3)).

Last day for policy committees to hear and report fiscal bills for referral to fiscal committees (J.R. 61(a)(10).

Last day for policy committees to hear and report bills (J.R. 61(a)(11)).

Summer Recess begins upon adjournment, provided Budget Bill has been passed (J.R. 51(a)(3)).

Legislature reconvenes from Summer Recess (J.R. 51(a)(3)).

Last day for fiscal committees to meet and report bills to the Floor (J.R. 61(a)(12)).

Floor session only. No committee may meet for any purpose (J.R. 61(a)(13)).

Last day to amend on the Floor (J.R. 61(a)(14)).

Last day for any bill to be passed (J.R. 61(a)(15)). Interim Recess begins on adjournment (J.R. 51(a)(4)).

Last day for Governor to sign or veto bills passed by the Legislature on or before Sept. 15 and in the Governor's possession after Sept. 15 (Art. IV, Sec.10(b)(1)).

One of the critical aspects of the legislative calendar relates to Joint Rule 61 deadlines. As it relates to JR 61, the following are the key provisions:

1. Bills acted upon by a committee deadline for which amendments are recommended have two legislative days after that deadline during which they may be reported (J.R. 61(c)).

2. Rules Committees are exempt from these deadlines (J.R. 61(f)).

3. Bills which are referred to an Assembly or Senate committee (pursuant to J.R. 26.5 or A.R. 77.2) are exempt from these deadlines (see also J.R. 61(g), J.R. 61(h)).

4. Bills related to the budget under subdivision (e) of Section 12, of Article IV of the California Constitution are exempt from these deadlines (J.R. 61(i)).

5. A policy committee or fiscal committee may meet for the purpose of hearing and reporting a constitutional amendment, or a bill which would go into immediate effect pursuant to Section 8 of Article IV of the California Constitution at any time other than those periods when no committee may meet for any purpose (J.R. 61(i)).

6. Joint and Concurrent Resolutions are exempt from these deadlines (J.R. 6).

Another important calendar item is the listing of dates on which Assembly or Senate measures may be considered. Article IV, Section 8(a), of the California Constitution provides that at regular sessions, no bill other than the Budget Bill may be heard or acted on by committee or either house until the 31st day after the bill is introduced unless the house dispenses with this requirement by roll call vote entered in the Journal, three-fourths of the membership concurring.

In addition, Joint Rule 55 provides that no bill other than the Budget Bill may be heard or acted upon by committee or either house until the bill has been in print for 30 days.

These are the most critical deadlines for legislation being considered in the California Legislature. It is important to consult the most current versions of the Assembly Rules, Senate Rules, and Joint Rules in order to double-check any important deadlines that may impact legislation of interest to you. Individuals can also consult with the Office of the Chief Clerk of the Assembly or the Office of the Secretary of the Senate.

Notes and Questions

1. The calendar and deadlines are important for those involved in the legislative process. As opposed to the Congress, the California legislative process is primarily driven by deadlines, whether it is when bills can be introduced, acted upon, etc. These deadlines force legislative action by specified dates and for decisions to be made by elected officials.

E. What Happens in the First Part of the Legislative Session?

This is the first of three sections about the major happenings in a legislative session pursuant to the California Constitution and relevant statutes. This section is focused on the first part of the legislative session. Section F focuses on the middle part of the session, and Section G looks at the last two months of the session.

There are essentially three major parts to the legislative session: house of origin; second house; and final month and gubernatorial action. Obviously, there are key subparts in these three major parts, but the session can be viewed in this way. In the first part, there is also the significant subpart of bill introductions. This first piece is on the house of origin part.

Overview

During the first part of the first year of a two-year session, legislators await their committee assignments, consider proposals for authoring bills and, for the new Members, they have dozens of "meet-and-greet" appointments in which they meet their colleagues, constituents and lobbyists. This usually occurs in January and most of February.

By March, the budget subcommittees and policy committees begin hearing bills and budget proposals. After policy committees hear and vote on bills, the vast majority of measures are considered by the fiscal committee (which we call the Appropriations Committee). Once bills pass the fiscal committee, they head to the respective floor for final consideration in their house of origin.

Legislative Calendar

The Assembly Chief Clerk and the Senate Secretary prepared the following calendar for the 2019 Session with the corresponding authority (found in the Joint Rules — JR) for these dates:

Jan. 7: Legislature reconvenes (J.R. 51(a)(1)).

Jan. 10: Budget must be submitted by the Governor (Art. IV, Sec. 12(a)).

Jan. 25: Last day to submit bill requests to the Office of Legislative Counsel.

Feb. 22: Last day for bills to be introduced (J.R. 61(a)(1), (J.R. 54(a)).

Apr. 26: Last day for policy committees to hear and report to the fiscal committees all fiscal bills introduced in their house (J.R. 61(a)(2)).

May 3: Last day for policy committees to hear and report to the Floor non-fiscal bills introduced in their house (J.R. 61(a)(3)).

May 10: Last day for policy committees to meet prior to June 3 (J.R. 61(a)(4)).

May 17: Last day for fiscal committees to hear and report to the Floor bills introduced in their house (J.R. 61(a)(5)). Last day for fiscal committees to meet prior to June 3 (J.R. 61(a)(6)).

May 28–31: Floor session only. No committees, other than conference or Rules committees, may meet for any purpose (J.R. 61(a)(7)).

May 31: Last day for bills to be passed out of the house of origin (J.R. 61(a)(8)).

Constitutional and Statutory Requirements

The Legislature must convene its regular session at noon on the first Monday in December of every even-numbered year, and they must undertake their organization that day (e.g., election of officers) (Article IV, Section 3).

The constitutional officers take office on the Monday after January 1 following their election, which is Monday, January 7, 2019, for those elected in the November 2018 general election (Article V, Section 2).

The Governor must report to the Legislature each year on the condition of the state. This is called the "State of the State" address. The Governor may, but is not required to, make recommendations to the Legislature at that time (Article V, Section 3).

Within the first 10 days of each year, the Governor must submit to the Legislature a budget for the forthcoming fiscal year (which begins July 1). This is why the Governor's first budget proposal is called the Governor's "January 10 Budget." The budget must include an explanatory message, as well as itemized statements for expenditures and estimated revenues.

The Governor may require a state agency or employee to furnish whatever information he or she deems necessary to prepare the budget. The budget bill must be introduced immediately in each house by the budget committee chairs of the Senate and Assembly. The Legislature must pass the budget by midnight on June 15 (Article V, Section 12).

The budget submitted by the Governor to the Legislature within the first 10 days of each session must contain a statement of accounts payable for the prior fiscal year and for the current fiscal year, as well as the succeeding fiscal year (Government Code Section 12020).

The budget submitted by the Governor to the Legislature within the first 10 days of each session must contain a statement of cash flow for the prior fiscal year and for the current fiscal year, as well as the succeeding fiscal year (Government Code Section 12021).

When each regular session convenes, the President pro Tempore of the Senate, the Speaker of the Assembly and the two minority leaders must report to their houses the goals and objectives of that house during that session (Article V, Section 22).

No bill, other than the budget bill, may be heard or acted upon by a committee or either house until it has been in print for 30 days after introduction. Either house can dispense with this rule by a 3/4 majority vote of that house. A bill cannot be passed unless it has been read by its title on 3 days in each house. But this rule can also be dispensed with by a 2/3 majority vote of the house's members (Article IV, Section 8).

F. What Happens in the Middle Part of the Legislative Session?

This is the second section about the major happenings in the legislative process pursuant to the California Constitution and relevant statutes. This section is focused on the middle part of the legislative session, which is essentially the adoption of the state budget and consideration of bills in their second house. Section E is focused on the first part of the legislative session. Section G looks at the last two months of the session.

There are essentially three major parts to the legislative session: house of origin; second house; and final month and gubernatorial action. Obviously, there are key subparts in these three major parts, but the session can be viewed in this way. This section is on the second house and budget part.

Overview

Immediately after the house of origin deadline, the budget deliberations are in full swing and bills must quickly be considered in the second house. The first half of June is spent mainly on the adoption of the budget bill as well as about two dozen trailer bills, which often implement significant statutory changes as part of the adoption of the state budget.

For the month that follows, the policy committees in both houses work diligently to consider and vote on the hundreds of bills that have made their way over from the other house. This is followed by a month-long summer recess before the final two months of the Session.

Legislative Calendar

The Assembly Chief Clerk and the Senate Secretary prepared the following calendar for the 2019 Session with the corresponding authority for these dates:

June 15: Budget Bill must be passed by midnight (Art. IV, Sec. 12(c)(3)).

July 10: Last day for policy committees to hear and report fiscal bills to fiscal committees (J.R. 61(a)(10)).

July 12: Last day for policy committees to meet and report bills (J.R. 61(a)(11)). Summer Recess begins upon adjournment of this day's session, provided Budget Bill has been passed (J.R. 51(a)(3)).

Constitutional and Statutory Requirements

All meetings of a house of the Legislature or a committee must be open and public, and all persons must be permitted to attend the meetings (Government Code § 9027). Any meeting that is required to be open and public must be held only after full and timely notice to the public as provided by the Joint Rules of the Assembly and Senate (Government Code § 9028).

The Governor may reduce or eliminate one or more items of appropriation while approving other portions of a bill. In such a case, the Governor must include a statement of the items reduced or eliminated with the reasons for his or her action. Any appropriation item reduced or eliminated must be considered separately and can be passed over the Governor's objections by a 2/3 majority vote (Article IV, Section 10).

Until the budget bill is enacted, the Legislature cannot send any bills to the Governor that propose to appropriate funds during the upcoming fiscal year unless it is an emergency bill recommended by the Governor. No bill, except the budget bill, may contain more than one item of appropriation (Article IV, Section 12).

All appropriations bills require a 2/3 majority vote, except the budget bill, budget trailer bills with appropriations, and those for public school appropriations (all of which require a simple majority vote). The Legislature can control the submission, approval and enforcement of budgets and the filing of claims for all state agencies. Legislators shall not be paid any salary of expenses in any year in which the budget bill is not passed by the Legislature by midnight on June 5 (Article IV, Section 12).

G. What Happens in the Last Part of the Legislative Session?

This is the third section about the major happenings in the legislative process pursuant to the California Constitution and relevant statutes. This section is focused on the last part of the legislative session, which is the last month that the Legislature is in session, followed by the month in which the Governor considers all of the bills sent to his desk. Section E is focused on the first part of the legislative session. Section F focuses on the middle part of the session.

There are essentially three major parts to the legislative session: house of origin; second house; and final month and gubernatorial action. Obviously, there are key subparts in these three major parts, but the session can be viewed in this way. This section is on the final month and gubernatorial actions part.

Overview

The final weeks of the legislative session are a proverbial sprint to the finish line. Policy committees have finished the bulk of their work, but many bills get significant amendments that require the policy committees to hear additional bills as the session winds down. The main focus is now on the fiscal committees and their votes on measures that are pending on the Suspense Files in the respective Appropriations Committees of the Senate and Assembly.

The last two weeks of the Session are a whirlwind, as hundreds of bills are considered on the Floor of the second house, with most bills having to return for a final vote on the Floor of the bill's house of origin. Once the session adjourns, the work is not done. Instead, the focus turns to the Governor's office and his consideration of on average 1,000 bills over the course of 30 days.

Legislative Calendar

The Assembly Chief Clerk and the Senate Secretary prepared the following calendar for the 2019 Session with the corresponding authority for these dates:

Aug. 12: Legislature reconvenes from summer recess (J.R. 51(a)(3)).

Aug. 30: Last day for fiscal committees to meet and report bills to the Floor (J.R. 61(a)(12)).

Sep. 3–13: Floor Session only. No committees, other than conference and rules committees, may meet for any purpose (J.R. 61(a)(13)).

Sep. 6: Last day to amend bills on the floor (J.R. 61(a)(14)).

Sep. 13: Last day for each house to pass bills (J.R. 61(a)(15)). Interim Study Recess begins upon adjournment of this day's session (J.R. 51(a)(4)).

Oct. 13: Last day for Governor to sign or veto bills passed by the Legislature on or before Sep. 13 and in the Governor's possession after Sep. 13 (Art. IV, Sec. 10(b)(1)).

<u>Constitutional and Statutory Requirements</u>

A bill cannot be passed or become a statute unless that bill and any amendments have been in print and published on the Internet for at least 72 hours before the vote, unless the Governor has submitted a statement that the bill is needed to address a state of emergency. No bill may be passed unless a majority of members of each house votes in favor of the bill (Article IV, Section 8).

Each bill passed by the Legislature must be presented to the Governor. The bill becomes a statute if it is signed by the Governor, or the Governor may veto a bill if he or she returns it to the house of origin along with any objections. If the Legislature votes again to pass the bill by a 2/3 majority vote, then the bill becomes a statute (Article IV, Section 10).

Any bill in the possession of the Governor after adjournment of the Legislature that is not returned within 30 days becomes a statute. Any other bill presented to the Governor (i.e., prior to the end of session) becomes a statute if it is not returned within 12 days. Any bill that was introduced in the first year of the two-year session that has not been passed by its house of origin by January 31 of the second year may no longer be acted upon by either house (Article IV, Section 10).

At the close of each regular session, the President pro Tempore of the Senate, the Speaker of the Assembly and the two minority leaders must report on the progress made toward meeting the goals and objectives outlined at the beginning of the legislative session (Article IV, Section 22).

At each session, the Governor must report to the Legislature any reprieves, pardons or commutations granted, including the reasons for doing so (Government Code § 12017).

H. Challenging the Provisions of the Internal Rules of the Legislature

Pursuant to Article IV, Section 7 of the California Constitution, "each house shall choose its officers and adopt rules for its proceedings." The judiciary will generally defer to the legislature regarding its internal rules and procedures. For example, the Assembly Rules, Senate Rules and Joint Rules are given deference, because they involve the internal operating rules of the legislative branch of government. The Legislature is granted this authority pursuant to the state Constitution, and so it is unlikely that a challenge to any provisions of the internal rules of the Legislature will survive in court.

People's Advocate, Inc. v. Superior Court of Sacramento County

(1986) 181 Cal.App.3d 316

OPINION

THE COURT

At the June 5, 1984, election the people adopted a statutory initiative measure entitled the "Legislative Reform Act of 1983" (the Act). The "First" part of the Act repeals various Government Code sections; the "Second" part adds chapter 8, part 1, division 2 (§§ 9900–9937) to the Government Code. This latter part makes sweeping changes in the organization and operation of the Assembly and Senate and limits the content of future legislation which appropriates money for their operations. Petitioners, People's Advocate, Inc. and five California taxpayers, filed suit in the Sacramento Superior Court against the real parties in interest, the California Legislature, the Senate and Assembly of the State of California and their individual and joint rules committees. The suit sought a declaration that the Act was valid and an order compelling compliance with its terms.

The real parties moved for judgment on the pleadings, challenging the provisions of the Act which regulate the internal rules, the selection of officers and employees, the selection and powers of committees of the houses of the Legislature and which limit prospectively the content of budget legislation as violative of the California Constitution; real parties challenged the remaining provisions as inseverable from the invalid provisions. The superior court granted the motion and entered judgment declaring the entire Act unconstitutional and of no force or effect. Petitioners then filed an original petition for a writ of mandate in this court seeking to vacate the judgment of the superior court. We issued an alternative writ.

We shall deny relief as to those provisions of the Act found by the trial court to be violative of the Constitution. However, the remaining provisions of the Act relating to secrecy in legislative proceedings are severable and as to those we shall issue a writ directing the trial court to vacate its judgment declaring their invalidity.

Discussion

It is well to be clear at the outset what this case is and is not about. First, the issue before this court is one of law, not policy; it is whether the Act is constitutional, not whether it is necessary or wise. We address that issue and that issue alone. Second, this case is not about whether the will of the people shall be heeded. The Act is not the only relevant expression of popular sentiment in this case. (See *Fair Political Practices Com. v. State Personnel Bd.* (1978) 77 Cal. App. 3d 52, 56 [143 Cal. Rptr. 393].) The provisions of the California Constitution (art. IV, § 7) which empower the houses of the Legislature to govern their own proceedings were first enacted almost 150 years ago and have twice been reenacted by the electorate. They are part of a constitutional structure of government by which the people have made statutes . . . even initiative statutes … subordinate to the Constitution, and have empowered the courts of this state in the exercise of the judicial power to interpret the state's fundamental charter. We are not presented with a conflict between the voice of the people expressed directly and through their elected representatives, but between two conflicting directives from the electorate: The Act and the California Constitution.

The powers challenged by the Act are deeply rooted in constitutional soil. Since the inception of our state the power of a legislative body to govern its own internal workings has been viewed as essential to its functioning except as it may have been expressly constrained by the California Constitution. The fundamental charter of our state government was enacted by the people against a history of parliamentary common law. That law is implicit in the Constitution's structure and its separation of powers. As was said by the California Supreme Court over 100 years ago: "A legislative assembly, when established, becomes vested with all the powers and privileges which are necessary and incidental to a free and unobstructed exercise of its appropriate functions. These powers and privileges are derived not from the Constitution; on the contrary, they arise from the very creation of a legislative body, and are founded upon the principle of self-preservation. The Constitution is not a grant, but a restriction upon the power of the Legislature, and hence an express enumeration of legislative powers and privileges in the Constitution cannot be considered as the exclusion of others not named unless accompanied by negative terms. A legislative assembly has, therefore, all the powers and privileges which are necessary to enable it to exercise in all respects, in a free, intelligent, and impartial manner, its appropriate functions, except so far as it may be restrained by the express provisions of the Constitution, or by some express law made unto itself, regulating and limiting the same." (*Ex parte D.O. McCarthy* (1866) 29 Cal. 395, 403; see also *Macmillan Co. v. Clarke* (1920) 184 Cal. 491, 498 [194 P. 1030, 17 A.L.R. 288]; *Hilborn v. Nye* (1911) 15 Cal. App. 298, 303 [114 P. 801].)

McCarthy recognized as an integral part of this parliamentary common law the power of a house of the Legislature to "choose its own officers, and remove them at pleasure," to "establish its own rules of proceeding," and "[t]o be secret in its proceedings and debates." (*McCarthy, supra,* 29 Cal. at pp. 403–404.) However, it is unnecessary for us to found our decision on that law for these powers have been made an express part of the California Constitution. They are to be found in article IV, sections 7 and 11 of the Constitution. The real parties claim that, with the exception of sections 9926 through 9929.5 and 9936 through 9937 of the Second part and (impliedly) the unqualified repealer of the related provisions in the First part (existing §§ 9027, 9028, 9030, 9031 and 9131) each section of the Act facially violates these constitutional provisions. We agree with the claim.

I.

Article IV, section 7, subdivision (a), directs that "[e]ach house shall choose its officers and adopt rules for its proceedings." Article IV, section 11, provides that the "Legislature or either house may by resolution provide for the selection of committees necessary for the conduct of its business.…"

The Second part of the Act regulates the appointments of the Speaker of the Assembly and the President pro tempore of the Senate. (§§ 9910 and 9914.) It also seeks to regulate the appointment and powers of the standing, select, joint and interim committees of the houses. (§§ 9911, 9912, 9913, 9915, 9916, 9917, 9922, 9923 and 9924.) The Act would also regulate the method of adoption of rules for the conduct of the houses both generally and as applied to specific subject matters. (§§ 9920, 9921, 9925, 9930, 9931, 9932, and 9933.) It further provides that these statutory provisions may not be amended or modified except as permitted by the Act. (See §§ 9904 and 9905.) The First part of the Act repeals the existing provisions of the Government Code which relate to these subjects (§§ 9026, 9029, 9107, 9107.5, 9126, 9127, 9128, 9129, 9132, 9220, 9221, 9222, and 9223). These provisions of the Act manifestly invade one or more of the powers of the houses over their committees, staff and internal proceedings as expressly delegated to them by article IV, sections 7 and 11 of the Constitution.

A.

Petitioners respond that the Act is within a coordinate power of the people granted them by the Constitution, i.e., the initiative "power of the electors to propose statutes . . . and to adopt or reject them." (Art. II, § 8.) This power is shared with the Legislature and the Governor. (See art. IV, §§ 8, 10; *Carlson v. Cory* (1983) 139 Cal. App. 3d 724 [189 Cal. Rptr. 185].) A rule of resolution is solely the product of the house or houses which adopted it. The petitioners claim that a statute is superior to a rule or resolution and hence may supersede and control the subject matters of the rule making powers vested in the two houses by article IV, sections 7 and 11. Thus, so the petitioners' argument goes, there is no conflict between the Act and the Constitution. The claim presupposes that these subject matters are among those which may be regulated by statute. Therein lies the fallacy.

The subjects of statutes are categorically different from the subjects of the rule-making powers of article IV, sections 7 and 11. The subjects of statutes are laws. (Art. IV, § 8: "The Legislature may make no law except by statute. . . ."; see *American Federation of Labor v. Eu* (1984) 36 Cal. 3d 687, 708, 709 and [206 Cal. Rptr. 89, 686 P.2d 609].) The kinds of rules and principles which are subsumed under the statutory "law" are addressed to the world outside the Legislature. (See *INS v. Chadha* (1983) 462 U.S. 919, 955, [77 L. Ed. 2d 317, 103 S. Ct. 2764]; cf. *American Federation of Labor v. Eu, supra*, at p. 712.) Conversely, the internal rules of the Legislature do not have the force of law except as they may bind the house which adopted them. (*Mullan v. State* (1896) 114 Cal. 578, 584 [46 P. 670]. . . .) Since the subjects of statutory laws and rules of internal proceedings categorically differ, a statute may not control a rule of internal proceeding.

These subject matters are the prerogatives of different governmental entities. Laws, as expressed in statutes, are the prerogatives of the Legislature, together with the Governor, and of the electorate. Rules or resolutions which affect the selection of the officers of the houses or their rules of proceeding or rules for their committees or their employees are the exclusive prerogative of "[e]ach house" of the Legislature or the combined houses. (Art. IV, §7, subd. (a).) The people's initiative statutory power, being limited to the subject matter of statutes, does not extend to these matters.

There is one exception to this separation of powers, and it underscores this reading. Article IV, section 7, subdivision (c) (a part of the rule-making section at issue), provides that "[t]he proceedings of each house and the committees thereof shall be public except as provided by *statute* or by *concurrent resolution* ... adopted by a two-thirds vote ... of each house, provided, that if there is a conflict between such a statute and concurrent resolution, the last adopted shall prevail." (Italics added.) This is the only constitutional provision which authorizes the statutory control of a rule or resolution of internal proceeding and that authority is subject to revocation by resolution. The unmistakable implication is that none other was intended.

In sum, the people through the electorate have been given the power to make statutes, i.e., the power to make laws for all the people, but not the power to make rules for the selection of officers or rules of proceeding or rules which regulate the committees or employees of either or both houses of the Legislature. These powers (with the exception noted) are exclusively the province of the houses affected by them.

B.

Petitioners also defend the constitutionality of the Act by pointing to the apparent anomaly that the Legislature has in fact adopted statutes which purport to regulate the internal proceedings of its houses.

Petitioners offer no reasons why this practice is legally significant. There are none. The form (statute or rule or resolution) chosen by a house to exercise its rulemaking power cannot preempt or estop a house from employing its substantive powers under article IV, sections 7 and 11. A rule of internal proceeding made in the guise of a statute is nonetheless a rule "adopted" by the house and may be changed by an internal rule. "The enactment of statutes relating to internal proceedings was obviously accomplished by the voluntary participation of each of the two Houses. Thus, each House was essentially engaged in its rule-making function." (*Paisner v. Attorney General* (1983) 390 Mass. 593 [458 N.E.2d 734, 739–740].) A rule of proceeding adopted by the Legislature by statute is, notwithstanding its means of adoption or label, a rule or resolution within the provisions of article IV, sections 7 and 11. It is not the form by which the rule is adopted but its substance which measures its place in the constitutional scheme. The people wholly lack this power whatever the form of its application.

Nor could a house estop itself or a future house by use of the statutory form from adopting any rule the substance of which is within the powers exclusively delegated to it by the Constitution. "'The long indulgence in [a] custom cannot create a right in the legislature, or either house thereof, to do that which it has no power or authority to do.'" (*Special Assembly Int. Com. v. Southard* (1939) 13 Cal. 2d 497, 509 [90 P.2d 304].) A house "has power to adopt any procedure and to change it at any time and without notice. It cannot tie its own hands by establishing rules which, as a matter of power purely, it cannot at any time change and disregard. Its action in any given case is the only criterion by which to determine the rule of proceeding adopted for that case." (*French v. Senate* (1905) 146 Cal. 604, 608 [80 P. 1031]; see *In re Collie* (1952) 38 Cal. 2d 396, 398 [240 P.2d 275].) A power conferred exclusively upon a house of the Legislature cannot be delegated. (*In re McGee* (1951) 36 Cal. 2d 592 [226 P.2d 1] [jurisdiction to judge qualifications of members cannot be delegated]; cf. the limited exception now contained in art. IV, § 5.)

Lastly, the petitioners seek to trade upon an assumption about the extent of the legislative power of the people. They assume that the initiative power includes the whole of the legislative power within which they locate the rule-making power. The assumption is incorrect. "The legislative power of this State is vested in the California Legislature which consists of the Senate and Assembly, but the people reserve to themselves the powers of initiative and referendum." (Art. IV, § 1.) Such reserved powers are exclusively specified in article II, section 8, and are limited to that which has been specifically delegated. They do not include the power to regulate the internal workings of the houses. Accordingly, the provisions of the Second part of the Act which do (§ 9904, §§ 9910 through 9925 and §§ 9930 through 9935) and the repeal of the related existing law in the First part of the Act (§§ 9026, 9029, 9107, 9107.5, 9126, 9127, 9128, 9129, 9132, 9220, 9221, 9222, and 9223) are invalid as in conflict with the Constitution.

To accomplish the purposes attempted by the Act, a constitutional amendment is required. Only by means of an initiative constitutional amendment may the people modify or impinge upon the freedom of the Legislature to exercise its constitutionally granted powers.

II.

Section 9934 is invalid for different reasons. It seeks to govern the content of future legislation by limiting the amount of monies appropriated for the support of the Legislature. It provides that "within 30 days following the enactment ... the total amount of monies appropriated for the support of the Legislature, ... shall be reduced by an amount equal to thirty percent of the total amount of monies appropriated for support of the Legislature for the 1983–84 fiscal year, and the amount so reduced shall revert to the General Fund. For each fiscal year thereafter, the total amount of monies appropriated ... shall not exceed an amount equal to that expended for support in the preceding fiscal year" adjusted up or down by the percentage increase or decrease in the general fund spending for the same year.

Real parties argue that section 9934 runs afoul of the "familiar principle of law that no legislative board, by normal legislative enactment, may divest itself or future boards of the power to enact legislation within its competence." (*City and County of San Francisco v. Cooper* (1975) 13 Cal. 3d 898, 929 [120 Cal. Rptr. 707, 534 P.2d 403]; see also *In re Collie, supra,* 38 Cal.2d at p. 398; *French v. Senate, supra,* 146 Cal. at p. 608.) We agree.

Neither house of the Legislature may bind its own hands or those of future Legislatures by adopting rules not capable of change. (*In re Collie, supra,* 38 Cal.2d at p.

398.) "[T]he power of the electorate to enact legislation by use of the initiative process is circumscribed by the same limitations as the legislative powers resting in the legislative body concerned." (*Mueller v. Brown* (1963) 221 Cal. App. 2d 319, 324 [34 Cal. Rptr. 474], citations omitted; see also 1 Singer, Sutherland Statutory Construction (4th ed. 1985) § 4.09, p. 135.)

This principle has special application here. What is at issue is not the authority to amend a statute, however adopted, but the power to say what content a future statute may have. The authority to enact statutes which appropriate money for the support of the state government, including the Legislature, is set forth in article IV, section 12 of the California Constitution. It provides for the appropriation of such monies through the adoption of the budget bill. It also provides for special appropriations measures which may be adopted outside of the budget bill process. (Art. IV, § 12, subd. (c).) Although either vehicle may be used to provide for the support of the Legislature, the budget bill is the vehicle historically used for the adoption of the Legislative budget. (See, e.g., Stats. 1984, ch. 258, § 2.00, p. 39.)

The budget process takes special form. The Governor submits a budget bill accompanied by a budget document which supplies the budgetary detail for the budget bill. (Art. IV, § 12, subds. (a) and (c); see Doubleday, Legislative Review of the Budget in Cal. (1967) pp. 26–28, 175–202 (hereafter cited as Leg. Rev. of the Budget).) The Legislature is given the power inter alia to "control the ... enforcement of budgets...." (Art. IV, § 12, subd. (e).)

Section 9934 limits the amount of monies that may be "appropriated" by statute for the support of the Legislature in each fiscal year beginning with the fiscal year 1984–1985. The limitation is based upon a formula tied to the budget bill enacted for the fiscal year 1982–1983. Section 9934 thus seeks to operate upon and condition the content of future statutes, appropriations statutes. In so doing it invades not only the content of the Governor's budget bill but displaces the process (budget and budget bill) by which article IV, section 12, commands the adoption and enforcement of the budget. It also affects any alternative means of appropriation by placing limits upon the content of any Legislative appropriations bill. By these means, section 9934 "divest[s] [the Legislature] of the power to enact legislation within its competence" and violates the specific injunctions of article IV, section 12 of the Constitution. (See *City and County of San Francisco v. Cooper, supra*, 13 Cal.3d at p. 929.) Since the Legislature is denied such a statutory power, so are the people. For these reasons section 9934 is invalid.

III.

....

DISPOSITION

A peremptory writ shall issue directing the superior court to set aside its judgment declaring invalid the repeal of existing Government Code sections 9027, 9028, 9030, 9031 and 9131 on the First part and invalidating the sections 9926 through 9929.5 and 9936 through 9937 of the Government Code as added by the Second part of the

Act and the policy provisions, severability clause and effective date necessarily linked to them. In all other respects the judgment declaring the invalidity of the "First" and "Second" parts of the Act is affirmed. The alternative writ is discharged.

Notes and Questions

1. Basically, the courts have ruled that either house of the California Legislature "has power to adopt any procedure and to change it at any time and without notice." In other words, the Legislature is in charge of its own rules and how it wants to conduct its operations. Those internal rules of procedure are for the Legislature to determine and not to be second-guessed by another, co-equal branch of government.

2. The power conferred upon the Senate by the Constitution to determine the rules of its proceedings and to expel a member are exclusive; and the judicial department has no power to revise even the most arbitrary and unfair action of the legislative department. There is no constitutional provision giving persons who have been expelled the right to have a trial and opportunity to be heard in the Senate other than that which they have received.

3. What were the four challenges by the Legislature as real parties in interest to the initiative adopted by the People?

4. Is this case simply requiring the judicial branch to decide between two existing provisions of the state Constitution: The initiative power held by the people pursuant to Article II and the Legislature's power to adopt its internal rules pursuant to Article IV? Would the outcome of the case have been different if the initiative had amended the California Constitution rather than sections of the California Government Code?

5. The court in this case ruled that, "since the subjects of statutory laws and rules of internal proceedings categorically differ, a statute may not control a rule of internal proceeding." Does that mean anything that is the subject of an Assembly, Senate or Joint rule cannot be the subject of a statute and vice versa? Or did the court find an exception to this rule? And how did the court advise proponents if they wanted to be successful with their ballot measure?

6. Does your opinion change when the court finds "the apparent anomaly that the Legislature has in fact adopted statutes which purport to regulate the internal proceedings of its houses"? How does this court address this "anomaly"?

7. Much is said about the Legislature's inability to "bind a future legislature." Is limiting the amount of monies available to the Legislature to appropriate each year "binding a future legislature"? Why would this doctrine apply to the People who have the power of initiative pursuant to Article II?

8. How does the court describe grammatical severability? How does the court explain the "capable of independent application" rule? How does the court address whether the electorate's attention was sufficiently focused upon the parts to be severed so that it would have separately considered and adopted them in the absence of the invalid portions? Which is these three tests of severability appear most persuasive to the court?

French v. Senate of California

(1905) 146 Cal. 604

OPINION

SHAW, J.

This is an original proceeding in *mandamus* to compel the senate of the state of California to admit the petitioners as members thereof. The case was submitted to this court upon a general demurrer to the petition and the writ denied.

The petitioners were duly elected senators of the state from the respective districts which they represent, and each duly qualified and acted as a member of the senate at the thirty-sixth regular session until the twenty-seventh day of February, 1905, when they were by the senate expelled therefrom for malfeasance in office, consisting of taking a bribe to influence their conduct as senators. Since then they have not been allowed to sit as members of the senate nor to participate in its proceedings. It is alleged in the petition that in the proceedings expelling the petitioners the senate did not give them a hearing, nor afford them a trial upon the charges made, nor permit them to make any defense thereto; that the charges of bribery upon which they were expelled are false, and that neither of them has been convicted of such crime.

Even if we should give these allegations their fullest force in favor of the pleader, they do not make a case justifying the interposition of this court. Under our form of government, the judicial department has no power to revise even the most arbitrary and unfair action of the legislative department, or of either house thereof, taken in pursuance of the power committed exclusively to that department by the constitution. It has been held by high authority that, even in the absence of an express provision conferring the power, every legislative body in which is vested the general legislative power of the state, has the implied power to expel a member for any cause which it may deem sufficient. In *Hiss v. Bartlett*, 69 Mass. 473, the supreme court of Massachusetts says in substance that this power is inherent in every legislative body; that it is necessary to enable the body "to perform its high functions, and is necessary to the safety of the state"; that it is a power of self-protection, and that the legislative body "must necessarily be the sole judge of the exigency which may justify and require its exercise." In this state the power does not depend on implication. It is expressly given. Or, as the power would exist without the express grant, perhaps it is more accurate to say that it is expressly recognized and limited. The constitution provides that the senate "shall determine the rule of its proceeding, and may, with the concurrence of two thirds of all the members elected, expel a member." (Const., art. IV, sec. 9.) If this provision were omitted, and there were no other constitutional limitations on the power, the power would nevertheless exist and could be exercised by a majority. The only effect of the provision is to make the concurrence of two thirds of the members elected necessary to its exercise. In all other respects it is absolute. The legislature is a coordinate department of the state government. By article III of the constitution it is provided that one department of the state shall not exercise the functions of either of the other departments except as in that instrument, expressly directed and permitted.

There is no provision authorizing courts to control, direct, supervise, or forbid, the exercise by either house of the power to expel a member. These powers are functions of the legislative department, and therefore in the exercise of the power thus committed to it the senate is supreme. An attempt by this court to direct or control the legislature, or either house thereof, in the exercise of the power, would be an attempt to exercise legislative functions, which it is expressly forbidden to do. 63 Am. Dec. 768, and note.

Even if the court should attempt to usurp this legislative function, there is no means whereby it could carry its judgment into effect and give the relief demanded. The thirty-sixth session of the legislature has adjourned *sine die;* it is a thing past, and cannot be reconvened upon the mandate of the judicial power. (Const., art. III.) The senate could not reinstate the petitioners as members of that session except when lawfully in session. Nor can the body which composed the thirty-sixth session be again called together except in special session and at the behest of the governor. (Const., art. IV, sec. 2; art. V, sec. 9.) The next regular session of the senate will be composed of different persons and will be a different body from that now supposed to be before the court. The court is without power to issue its final process against a body not lawfully served with its original process and which has not submitted itself to its jurisdiction. Moreover, before the next session convenes, the terms of all the petitioners except Wright will have expired. The court cannot issue any effective mandate to reinstate the petitioners as members of the senate.

We think it is proper to say further, out of respect to a co-ordinate department of the government, that, notwithstanding the arbitrary action apparently charged against the senate by the language of the petition, we cannot give the statements therein contained their full force. Ordinarily when a case is submitted on a demurrer all the facts stated in the pleadings demurred to are taken as true. To this rule there are some exceptions, one of which is important here. Only those facts are admitted by a demurrer which it is necessary to allege in the pleading. It is not necessary to allege facts of which the court will take judicial notice. Such facts will be considered by the court, although not pleaded. (12 Ency. of Plead. Prac., 1; 1 Chitty on Pleading, 215, 217, 218; *People v. Mehany,* 13 Mich. 481; *Mullan v. State,* 114 Cal. 581; Bliss on Code Pleading, 177, 194.) Those allegations of a pleading which are not necessary, and which are contrary to the facts of which judicial notice is taken, are not admitted by a demurrer, but are to be treated as a nullity. (12 Ency. of Plead. Prac., 1; 1 Chitty on Pleading, 215; *Mullan v. State,* 114 Cal. 581; *Ohm v. San Francisco,* 92 Cal. 449.) The courts take judicial notice of the public and private official acts of the legislative department of the state. (Code Civ. Proc., sec. 1875, subd. 2; *Mullan v. State,* 114 Cal. 581; *Davis v. Whidden,* 117 Cal. 623.) Among these official acts are included the proceedings by which the petitioners were expelled and which are entered upon the journal of the senate. We are therefore bound to take notice that charges were preferred against the petitioners in the senate and were referred by it to a committee for investigation; that the committee reported that it had made the investigation and that the charges were true, and recommended that the petitioners be expelled; that this report was taken up and considered by the senate; that the petitioners, being then members, had upon such consideration an opportunity to present, or have presented, arguments in their behalf, and that the resolution expelling them was regularly offered and adopted by the senate. There being no direct allegation to the contrary, we must presume that the petitioners had notice of these proceedings, and that they were allowed as members to participate therein. In view of these facts we cannot consider the allegations of the petition as imputing to the senate the arbitrary and unfair treatment of the petitioners which might be inferred from the language used, but will rather consider them as a statement of the conclusion of the pleaders that the proceedings taken, of which we take judicial notice, did not constitute a trial or hearing, and did not give them the opportunity to be heard in their own behalf which they believe they were entitled to have.

There is no averment that the manner of the proceeding was contrary to the rules established. And even if it were as abrupt as the interpretation of the pleading most favorable to the petitioners would imply, the matter would be immaterial. The senate has power to adopt any procedure and to change it at any time and without notice. It cannot tie its own hands by establishing rules which, as a matter of power purely, it cannot at any time change and disregard. Its action in any given case is the only criterion by which to determine the rule of proceeding adopted for that case.

There is no constitutional provision given to the petitioners the right to have a trial and opportunity to be heard upon the charges made against them in the senate other than that which they have received.

The fourteenth amendment to the constitution of the United States does not affect the case, nor have its provisions been violated by the action of the senate. While it is true that, so far as private persons are concerned, the right to hold a public office duly conferred upon an individual has many of the attributes of private property, and is protected by the law of the land, yet, as between the office-holder and the sovereign power, such right is not violated when the proper governmental authority, acting in pursuance of a power expressly given to it by the fundamental law, has removed such person from the office. (*Matter of Carter,* 141 Cal. 319.) The sovereign power which created the office can also fix the terms upon which it is held and can delegate the power of removal. The title is held subject to the conditions thus imposed. The relations between the body politic and its officers are not in this particular essentially different from those existing between a private person and his servants. Although there may be a difference as to the liability for damages for a dismissal without cause, the right or power to dismiss always exists. The senate having expelled the petitioners in the manner prescribed by the constitution, in the exercise of the power therein given, it is not true that they have been deprived of the right to the office without due process of law.

With respect to the possible abuse of such power the case is analogous to that of the President of the United States with respect to officers of the United States subject to arbitrary removal by him. In regard to this the supreme court of the United States says that the only restraint upon the abuse of the power "must consist in the responsibility of the president, under his oath of office, to act as shall be for the general benefit and welfare." *(Shurtleff v. United States,* 189 U.S. 317.) The same is true of the power of the senate here under consideration. The oath of each individual member of the senate, and his duty under it to act conscientiously for the general good, is the only safeguard to the fellow-members against an unjust and causeless expulsion. This is the only practical rule that can be adopted as to those unrestricted governmental powers which are necessary to the exercise of governmental functions, and which must be lodged somewhere. Each department of the state is necessarily vested with some power which is beyond the supervision of any other department, and in such cases the only protection against abuse is the conscience of the individual in whom the power is vested.

The decisions holding that where a power is given to remove an officer "for cause" without requiring any previous notice or any hearing, such notice must nevertheless be given, and a hearing had, have been disapproved in this state. *(Matter of Carter,* 141 Cal. 319.) But, in any event, they clearly have no application to the present case, where the power to remove is, as we have seen, inherent and necessary to the exercise of the functions of the body possessing it, and are given without limitation or restriction.

It is claimed that the power to expel for bribery is, by section 35 of article IV, limited to those cases in which the member has been convicted of the crime defined in that section. The section provides that any member of the legislature who is influenced in his official action by any reward or promise thereof is guilty of a felony, and that upon conviction he shall be forever disqualified from holding any office or public trust. It is obvious that this section was not intended to have any effect whatever upon the power to expel members of the legislature given by section 9 of the same article. The two provisions are entirely independent and are made for different objects and purposes. The power to expel is given to enable the legislative body to protect itself against participation in its proceedings by persons whom it judges unworthy to be members thereof, and affects only the rights of such persons to continue to act as members. The provision of section 35 defines a certain crime and prescribes the effect of a judgment of conviction thereof upon the subsequent *status* as a citizen of the person found guilty. A resolution of the senate expelling a member, whether for bribery or for some other offense, or improper conduct, is not the equivalent of the conviction of the person of the crime set forth in the charges against him.

The proposition that a resolution or other action of the senate resulting in the expulsion of a member is in substance a bill of attainder and, therefore, a violation of section 16 of article I of the state constitution, and of section 10 of article I of the constitution of the United States, is scarcely worthy of notice. The charges upon which a member is expelled may or may not constitute a charge of crime, but the resolution expelling him has not the force of law, and it cannot, by any stretch of construction, be denominated a bill of attainder. At common law "a bill of attainder was a legislative conviction for an alleged crime, followed by a prescribed punishment therefor, with judgment of death." And even where a milder punishment was inflicted its effect was an extinction of civil and political rights and capacities. (Cooley on Constitutional Limitations, 7th ed., 368.) The resolution of expulsion has no effect upon the rights of the member expelled further than to terminate his right to sit as a member of the legislative body, and it bears no just resemblance to a bill of attainder.

We find no ground upon which the application of the petitioners can be supported, and we are of the opinion that the writ was properly denied.

ANGELLOTTI, J., VAN DYKE, J., HENSHAW, J., BEATTY, C.J., and LORIGAN, J., concurred.

Notes and Questions

1. Should the Court have determined this claim was moot because the legislative session had adjourned and the Court had no authority to reconvene the Legislature even if it had desired to do so? In other words, because the Court could not order the Senate to reinstate the petitioners as members, why did it need to entertain the case?

I. Legislature Adopts Internal Procedures

Mission Hospital Regional Medical Center v. Shewry

(2008) 168 Cal.App.4th 460

OPINION

NICHOLSON, J.

We enter here into the arcane world of Medicaid law to answer a fundamental question: does a federal statute imposing notice and comment requirements apply to actions taken or mandated by a state legislature? In 2004, the California Legislature, as part of adopting a state budget after the constitutional budget deadline had expired, proposed and enacted over only a three-day period a freeze on the rates the state would use to reimburse certain hospitals that provided services to Medicaid beneficiaries during the state's 2004–2005 fiscal year. A large number of those hospitals sued for writ relief, claiming the state's action violated federal Medicaid statutes that require a public notice and comment period as part of the process used when revising rates and rate methodologies and that impose substantive findings necessary to support those rates.

The trial court disagreed with the hospitals except to the extent the freeze affected services rendered prior to the freeze's enactment. Both the hospitals and the state department responsible for administering the Medicaid program appealed. We conclude the federal statute requiring notice and comment procedures applied to the state's action, and that the state's process did not satisfy the federal statute. We reverse the trial court's judgment on that basis.

. . . .

FACTS

In 2004, the Legislature adopted a freeze on the reimbursement rates paid to non-contract hospitals for inpatient services during the state's 2004–2005 fiscal year. The bill, Senate Bill No. 1103 (2003–2004 Reg. Sess.), imposed the freeze by modifying the PIRL calculation used for determining a noncontract hospital's final reimbursement.

The freeze provision is found at section 32 of Senate Bill No. 1103 (2003–2004 Reg. Sess.). Section 32 declares "the state faces a fiscal crisis that requires unprecedented measures to be taken to reduce General Fund expenditures." (Stats. 2004, ch. 228, § 32, subd. (a) (Stats, section 32).) The rate freeze at issue here was one such measure.

. . . .

DISCUSSION

. . . .

II Section (13)(A)

Plaintiffs claim the Department violated a mandatory duty imposed by section (13)(A) to provide a notice and comment process on the rate methodology change contained in Stats, section 32 prior to the statute's adoption. The Department argues, and the trial court held, that administrative law principles contained in section (13)(A) do not apply when the Legislature is the body changing the rates and methodology. We conclude section (13)(A) applied here, and that the adoption and implementation of section 32 did not comply with Stats, section (13)(A)'s notice requirements.

. . . .

B. *Analysis*

Plaintiffs claim the Department violated a mandatory duty imposed by section (13)(A) to provide notice and an opportunity for review and comment on Stats, section 32's rate freeze before the freeze became effective. They claim section (13)(A) applies to the Legislature's actions by the statute's plain language. The federal statute requires the state plan to provide for a public process for determining rates before the rates and their methodologies become effective. Plaintiffs argue the states are subject to federal Medicaid law, and section (13)(A) contains no exception for rates and methodologies adopted by the Legislature.

The Department disagrees with this argument, asserting that section (13)(A) does not apply to legislatively mandated rate changes. It claims section (13)(A) applies only to rates established by an administrative body. The Department concurs with the trial court's reasoning: "Notice and comment procedures such as that set forth in Section 13(A) are a central feature of administrative law and procedure, applicable when a state administrative agency takes action to set rates. Such procedures *do not appear to be applicable*, on the other hand, when the state administrative agency takes no discretionary action to set the rates itself, but is mandated to apply rates that have been set by the legislature." (Italics added.)

We conclude the principle vaguely espoused by the trial court does not apply in this instance.

We acknowledge that the Assembly and the Senate have power to adopt their own rules of proceeding, including rules for hearings and notice, and that these rules of proceeding "are the exclusive prerogative" of each house. (*People's Advocate, Inc. v. Superior Court* (1986) 181 Cal.App.3d 316, 325 [226 Cal.Rptr. 640] (*People's*

Advocate); see Cal. Const., art. IV, § 7, subd. (a).) Each house "has power to adopt any procedure and to change it at any time and without notice." (*French v. Senate* (1905) 146 Cal. 604, 608 [80 P. 1031], as quoted in *People's Advocate, supra,* 181 Cal.App.3d at p. 327.)

"A legislative assembly, when established, becomes vested with all the powers and privileges which are necessary and incidental to a free and unobstructed exercise of its appropriate functions. These powers and privileges are derived not from the Constitution; on the contrary, they arise from the very creation of a legislative body, and are founded upon the principle of self-preservation. The Constitution is not a grant, but a restriction upon the power of the Legislature, and hence an express enumeration of legislative powers and privileges in the Constitution cannot be considered as the exclusion of others not named unless accompanied by negative terms. A legislative assembly has, therefore, all the powers and privileges which are necessary to enable it to exercise in all respects, in a free, intelligent, and impartial manner, its appropriate functions, except so far as it may be restrained by the express provisions of the Constitution [such as the supremacy clause], or by some express law made unto itself, regulating and limiting the same." (*Ex parte D.O. McCarthy* (1866) 29 Cal. 395, 403.) These powers include the power of a house of the Legislature to "establish its own rules of proceeding," and "[t]o be secret in its proceedings and debates." (*Id.* at pp. 403–404.) These powers have also been made an express part of the California Constitution. (*People's Advocate, supra,* 181 Cal.App.3d at p. 323.)

Moreover, the due process principles of notice and opportunity for hearing do not apply to legislative action. "[O]nly those governmental decisions which are *adjudicative* in nature are subject to procedural due process principles." (*Horn v. County of Ventura* (1979) 24 Cal.3d 605, 612 [156 Cal.Rptr. 718, 596 P.2d 1134], original italics.)

The case before us, however, does not concern the Legislature's power to adopt or waive its own rules when it considers new state law, nor does it involve the application of due process principles as a matter of state constitutional law to legislative action. Rather, this case concerns the extent to which a federal statute constrains state legislative action—more particularly, a federal statute's imposition of notice and comment procedures to acts by a state legislature when the state voluntarily agrees to participate in the federal program. This is a matter of federalism, not administrative law.

Congress enacted the Medicaid Act pursuant to its powers under the federal Constitution's spending clause. (U.S. Const., art. I, § 8, cl. 1; *Independent Living Center v. Shewry, supra,* 543 F.3d at p. 1052.) The law is emboldened under the Constitution's supremacy clause (U.S. Const., art. VI, cl. 2), and preempts any state law that stands as an obstacle to its enforcement. (See *Independent Living Center v. Shewry* (S.D.Cal. Aug. 18, 2008, No. CV 08-3315) 2008 U.S.Dist. Lexis 77525 [pursuant to the supremacy clause, court enjoined enforcement of legislative reduction in Medi-Cal reimbursement rates due to Legislature's and Department's failure to comply with § (30)(A) prior to enactment of reductions].)

"'The Medicaid program ... is a cooperative endeavor in which the Federal Government provides financial assistance to participating States to aid them in furnishing health care to needy persons. Under this system of "cooperative federalism," [citation] if a State agrees to establish a Medicaid plan ... the Federal Government agrees to pay a specified percentage of "the total amount expended ... as medical assistance under the State plan....'" (*Harris v. McRae, supra,* 448 U.S. at p. 308.) Participation is voluntary, but 'once a State elects to participate, it must comply with the requirements of Title XIX.' (*Id.* at p. 301.)" (*Olszewski* [*v. Scripps Health*], *supra,* 30 Cal.4th at p. 809.)

Because of the extraordinary complexity of the Medicaid statutes, Congress has also conferred on the Secretary "'exceptionally broad authority to prescribe standards for applying certain sections of the Act.' (*Schweiker v. Gray Panthers* (1981) 453 U.S. 34,] 43 [69 L.Ed.2d 460, 469–470, 101 S.Ct. 2633]; see, e.g., 42 U.S.C. § 1396a(a)(4)(A) ['[a] State plan for medical assistance must ... [¶] ... [¶] ... provide ... such methods of administration ... as are found by the Secretary to be necessary for the proper and efficient operation of the plan'].) Regulations promulgated by the Secretary are therefore 'entitled to "legislative effect"' unless they exceed his or her statutory authority or are arbitrary or capricious. (*Schweiker,* at p. 44.) 'State Medicaid plans must [therefore] comply with requirements imposed both by the [Medicaid] Act itself and by the Secretary' (*id.* at p. 37), and must 'be approved by the Secretary' (*Elizabeth Blackwell Health Center v. Knoll* (3d Cir. 1995) 61 F.3d 170, 172 (*Elizabeth Blackwell Center*)).

"Despite these requirements, '[t]he [Medicaid] program was designed to provide the states with a degree of flexibility in designing plans that meet their individual needs. [Citation.] As such, states are given considerable latitude in formulating the terms of their own medical assistance plans.' (*Addis v. Whitburn* (7th Cir. 1998) 153 F.3d 836, 840.) 'Congress intended that states be allowed flexibility in developing procedures for administering their statutory obligations under the Medicaid statute and their state plans.' (*Elizabeth Blackwell Center, supra,* 61 F.3d at p. 178.)" (*Olszewski, supra,* 30 Cal.4th at p. 810, fn. omitted.)

In short, by agreeing to participate in the Medicaid program, the state subjected itself under the supremacy clause to comply with all federal Medicaid laws. Under those laws, the state would retain flexibility and discretion as allowed by those laws to develop methods and procedures, but those methods and procedures would have to satisfy the requirements of the federal law.

Plaintiffs and the Department acknowledge there are as yet no published judicial opinions addressing the application of post-Boren-Amendment section (13)(A) to legislative actions or administrative actions mandated by a state legislature. We thus review the federal Boren Amendment cases interpreting part 447.205, as they are instructive on the issue we face. These courts adhered to the concept of "cooperative federalism" when interpreting notice requirements imposed on a state under the Boren Amendment and its implementing procedural regulation, part 447.205.

     ....

Turning to our case, we have no doubt that the principle of cooperative federalism contained in part 447.205 as just discussed continues in current section (13)(A). Nothing in the language of section (13)(A) indicates Congress intended to abrogate the holdings of the cases just discussed and excuse a state from providing any notice of legislatively revised reimbursement rates. A state can develop whatever type of public process it chooses, including a legislative process for establishing and revising reimbursement rates. However, Congress clearly imposed a duty on a state participating in Medicaid to ensure that whatever process it develops and uses at a minimum satisfies the publication and comment requirements of section (13)(A). The supremacy clause superimposes that duty over any conflicting procedure the state may utilize.

The trial court and plaintiffs rely on one other Boren Amendment case, *Minnesota Homecare Ass'n, Inc. v. Gomez* (8th Cir. 1997) 108 F.3d 917 (*Minnesota Homecare*), and *Rank* [*California Ass'n of Bioanalysts v. Rank* (C.D.Cal. 1983) 577 F.Supp. 1342] to claim the notice requirements of section (13)(A) do not apply to legislative action. They misread the holdings of those cases. In *Minnesota Homecare*, the plaintiffs claimed the Minnesota legislature violated the substantive "equal access" requirements of section (30)(A) by adopting reimbursement rates without conducting any formal analysis of the factors listed in section (30)(A). The court disagreed. Although the Medicaid Act requires states to consider certain factors when setting rates, "it does not require the State to utilize any prescribed method of analyzing and considering said factors." (*Minnesota Homecare, supra*, at p. 918.) In that instance, the record demonstrated that the plaintiffs and others had in fact raised the required factors to the legislature as part of its consideration of the proposed rates. This was sufficient to find the state's methodology satisfied the requirements of section (30)(A).

One of the judges concurred separately, concluding the plaintiffs had not stated a claim because the legislature had set the rates in question. "Federal courts do not undertake administrative law review of legislative action, certainly not the action of a state legislature. Review of statutory rates must be limited to whether their result in the marketplace is consistent with the substantive requirements of federal law." (*Minnesota Homecare, supra*, 108 F.3d at p. 919 (cone. opn. of Loken, J.).) The trial court here relied upon this statement as the basis of its decision under section (13)(A).

The concurring judge's statement is not persuasive. First, as already stated, we are not asked in this case to conduct administrative law review of legislative action. Rather, we are asked to interpret federal statutes and regulations to determine whether they impose notice requirements on actions taken or mandated by a state legislature participating in the Medicaid program. If they do, the fact that notice requirements are usually associated with administrative action is irrelevant.

Second, the concurring judge's assertion goes far beyond the court's *per curiam* opinion that the state had in fact complied with the procedural requirements section (30)(A) imposed on it. Significantly, Minnesota had complied with those requirements at the legislative level. Nothing in the court's opinion suggests the legislature was free to ignore the requirements of the Medicaid Act and its regulations. *Minnesota Homecare* offers the Department no assistance.

We also disagree with the Department's and trial court's reliance on *Rank.* Contrary to the Department's arguments, the federal district court in *Rank* did not hold that no notice was required for legislatively mandated rate reductions. It stated that even when the legislative mandate vests only ministerial authority in the Department, the Department still must give notice under part 447.205(d) before the action goes into effect. At best, the *Rank* court simply held that where a state provides inadequate formal notice, an aggrieved provider with actual notice lacks standing to complain of notice defects. (*State v. Shalala* (10th Cir. 1994) 42 F.3d 595, 603, fn. 13; *State of Ill. v. Shalala, supra,* 4 F.3d at p. 517.)

Having concluded section (13)(A) applies to legislatively mandated or adopted rate revisions, we now turn to review the record and determine whether the public process utilized for Stats, section 32 satisfied section (13)(A)'s publication and comment requirements. To review, section (13)(A) requires the state to publish the proposed reimbursement rates for inpatient services, the methodologies underlying the establishment of the proposed rates, and the justifications for the proposed rates. (§ (13)(A)(i).) The state must then provide providers such as plaintiffs "a reasonable opportunity for review and comment on the proposed rates, methodologies, and justifications." (§ (13)(A)(ii).) The state must also publish the final rates, their underlying methodologies, and their justifications. (§ (13)(A)(iii).)

The Department asks us to remand the matter to the trial court to determine the adequacy of its compliance with section (13)(A). The Department and plaintiffs, however, submitted evidence concerning the adequacy of the notice and fully argued the matter to the trial court. Those facts are not in dispute and we may treat the matter as an issue of law. A new trial thus would be a waste of effort. We may proceed to judgment under these circumstances. (See *Mid-Century Ins. Co. v. Gardner* (1992) 9 Cal.App.4th 1205, 1220 [11 Cal.Rptr.2d 918].)

As the *Rank* court noted, the legislative process is a public process that usually satisfies the objectives of the notice requirements: securing public comment and promoting accountability among decision makers. (*Rank, supra,* 577 F.Supp. at p. 1348.) Under the usual process in California, for example, after a nonbudget bill is introduced, it cannot be heard or acted upon by a committee or either house for a period of 30 days, thereby giving the interested public time to review the proposal. (Cal. Const., art. IV, § 8, subd. (a).)

Indeed, the Assembly has a rule regarding budget spot bills that fulfills the same purpose. The Assembly's standing rules for the 2003–2004 session prohibited the Assembly from voting on the spot bill, as amended to include the budget provisions, until the bill had been in print for at least 15 days. (Assem. Res. No. 1 (2003–2004 Reg. Sess.) § 51.5.) Under these usual circumstances, a legislative process could provide notice and an opportunity for review and comment, but that did not happen here.

Unfortunately for the Department, the truncated process utilized with Senate Bill No. 1103 (2003–2004 Reg. Sess.) did not satisfy the object and purpose of section (13)(A), even when we assume a limited exemption for legislative action exists.

Stats, section 32 of Senate Bill No. 1103 (2003–2004 Reg. Sess.) appeared on July 27, was adopted by the full Assembly on July 28, and was adopted by the full Senate on July 29. Even the Department did not know of Stats, section 32 until it was enacted. The record does not support an inference, much less establish, that the proposed Stats, section 32 was made public in such a way that providers such as plaintiffs were given a reasonable opportunity to review and comment on the proposal. There is no evidence in the record that plaintiffs had actual notice of the proposed Stats, section 32. The only notice plaintiffs received concerning Stats, section 32's rate freeze arrived several months later, after the state's fiscal year to which Stats, section 32 applied had already ended and they had provided the services to which Stats, section 32 applied. This legislative process did not fulfill the purposes of section (13)(A).

Because we conclude the trial court erred in its ruling under section (13)(A), we need not reach the parties' remaining arguments, the Department's appeal, or the parties' requests for judicial notice. We note, however, that our reasoning on the application of section (13)(A) would also require the application of section (30)(A) to the adoption of Stats, section 32. (*Independent Living Center, supra*, 2008 U.S.Dist. Lexis 77525.)

DISPOSITION

The judgment is reversed and the matter is remanded to the trial court. The trial court shall issue a writ of mandate enjoining the Department from utilizing Stats, section 32 in its calculations of plaintiffs' reimbursement rates for the state fiscal year 2004–2005.

Costs on appeal are awarded to plaintiffs. (Cal. Rules of Court, rule 8.278(a).)

SIMS, Acting P.J., and CANTIL-SAKAUYE, J., concurred.

[The petition of appellant Sandra Shewry for review by the Supreme Court was denied February 11, 2009, S169393. WERDEGAR, J., did not participate therein.]

Notes and Questions

1. Each house of the Legislature has the power to adopt any procedure and to change it at any time and without notice. Both the California Assembly and Senate have the power to adopt their own rules of proceeding, including rules for hearings and notice, and these rules of proceeding are the exclusive prerogative of each house. Was this authority to adopt internal rules relevant to the final determination in this case?

2. Was the court's ruling that the federal statute required notice and comment procedures applied to the state's action an obvious outcome? Why did the court rule that the state's process did not satisfy the federal statute?

3. What were the five allegations put forth by the plaintiffs in this case? How did the court rule on each one of these claims?

4. What was the basis for the court's ruling that the plaintiffs had standing to bring this lawsuit? What does it mean to be a "beneficially interested party"?

5. Do you agree with the statement that the due process principles of notice and opportunity for hearing do not apply to legislative action because "only those governmental decisions which are *adjudicative* in nature are subject to procedural due process principles"? (*Horn v. County of Ventura* (1979) 24 Cal.3d 605, 612.)

6. What was the basis for the court to rule that this case concerns the extent to which a federal statute constrains state legislative action?

7. Is it an obvious statement by the court that, based upon the Supremacy Clause, agreeing to participate in the Medicaid program made the state subject itself to complying with all federal Medicaid laws?

8. If state legislative measures undergo a public process, why does that legislative action not satisfy the federally-require notice requirements? As the *Rank* court noted, the legislative process is a public process that usually satisfies the objectives of the notice requirements: securing public comment and promoting accountability among decision makers. (*Rank,* 577 F.Supp. at 1348.)

9. What was the significance of this statement by the court? "Review of statutory rates must be limited to whether their result in the marketplace is consistent with the substantive requirements of federal law."

10. What was the impact of the truncated legislative process on the court's decision? How did the court view the notice, or lack thereof, of the rate freeze? Was the late receipt of the notice more or less problematic than the fact that the fiscal year had expired?

J. Proceedings Refer to Entire Legislature

Watson v. Fair Political Practices Commission

(1990) 217 Cal.App.3d 1059

OPINION

COMPTON, Acting P.J.

In two separate actions, plaintiffs, consisting of several state legislators, their constituents, and other elected officials, initiated suit against the Rules Committee of the California State Senate and the Fair Political Practices Commission (FPPC), challenging the constitutionality of one portion of an initiative measure dealing with political reform, Proposition 73, adopted at the June 1988 primary election.

Article IV, section 3 of that measure amended Government Code section 89001 to read as follows: "No newsletter or other mass mailing shall be sent at public expense."

Although the trial court initially found the newly amended statute to be unconstitutional, it reversed its position in a subsequent action brought to enforce the original judgment. Since the appeals from these conflicting rulings involve similar issues and parties, we have consolidated the cases for purposes of our review.

We have concluded that the statute neither interferes with the Legislature's authority to govern its internal affairs nor burdens the exercise of any fundamental right. We therefore reverse the judgment of the trial court which declared section 89001 to be unconstitutional, and affirm the court's subsequent ruling upholding the validity of the statute.

The facts giving rise to this litigation are undisputed by the parties and may be summarized as follows.

Prior to its amendment by Proposition 73, former section 89001 prohibited the mailing of newsletters and other mass mailings by or on behalf of any elected officer to a constituent or potential constituent but only after the elected officer had filed either "[t]he nomination documents ... for any local, state, or federal office to be voted upon at an election governed by Chapter 5 ... of Division 6 of the Elections Code" or "[t]he last document necessary to be listed on the ballot as a candidate for any local, state or federal office to be voted upon at an election not governed by Chapter 5...."

Following the enactment of that statute, the state Legislature developed extensive "newsletter programs" which involved expenditures from the contingent funds of both the Senate and Assembly for the publication and distribution of mass mailings from legislators to their constituents and other members of the public.

The "Revised Senate Newsletter Rules" (Rules), effective December 1984, set forth the purpose of the program as follows: "The Senate Newsletter Program is conducted by the Senate Rules Committee. The purpose of the program is to inform and educate, through direct mail communication the citizens of the state by discussion of the legislative issues, problems, and suggested solutions that are being dealt with in Sacramento.... [¶] The Newsletter Program is designed to inform citizens about past, present and future legislative events, as well as provide constituent assistance.... [¶] No mailing may be designed or used for 'political purposes.'"

In keeping with this statement of intent, the Rules contained various restrictions on the format of the newsletters, their substantive content, and the frequency of the mailings. The Rules further required that all proposed mailings be submitted to the rules committee for approval of both form and content before being distributed. The Rules Committee of the Assembly promulgated similar rules for its members.

Both before and after the adoption of former section 89001, legislators and other elected officials, at both the state and local level, used publicly funded mass mailings to send a wide variety of written materials to their constituents. According to plaintiffs these mailings have been used by legislators to "address issues and legislation of special concern to their individual districts and of general concern to the state as a whole, to inform constituents of the activities of their elected representatives and of state government as a whole, to solicit views and comments from their constituents, to mobilize support for, or opposition to, proposed legislation, and to provide information concerning laws, regulations, and various governmental programs."

Based upon the total cost of the state newsletter program, the legislative analyst estimated in 1988 that the adoption of Proposition 73's prohibition against mass mailings by state elected officials would result in savings of approximately $1.8 million annually. Similar savings were also expected at the local level.

Against this backdrop, a majority of the electorate approved Proposition 73's limitation on publicly funded newsletter programs at the June 1988 primary election. Unlike the bulk of statutes enacted by the measure, however, the amended version of section 89001 became effective the day following its passage. (See Cal. Const., art. II, § 10, subd. (a).)

Immediately thereafter, the Senate Rules Committee began rejecting requests from senators to send, at public expense, newsletters, questionnaires, and miscellaneous material to their constituents, and other members of the public.

In July 1988, several state senators, including plaintiffs Diane Watson, Bill Greene, and Art Torres, and six of their constituents, initiated an action in Los Angeles Superior Court (case No. C691676) against the Rules Committee seeking a declaration that section 89001 was unconstitutional. Various other state and local elected officials, including members of the Los Angeles City Council, later intervened in that action as plaintiffs. Assembly Member Ross Johnson, one of the authors of Proposition 73, and Mark Pickens, a nonincumbent seeking election to the Legislature, intervened as defendants.

Plaintiffs subsequently filed a motion for summary judgment, arguing in part that the statute infringed on the state Legislature's authority to govern its internal affairs and control the budget and appropriations process. Plaintiffs further maintained that the newly amended law burdened the exercise of several fundamental rights guaranteed by the First and Fourteenth Amendments to the federal Constitution, and that Proposition 73 itself violated the California Constitution's "single-subject" rule.

In February 1989, after hearing extensive argument by the parties, the trial court granted summary judgment in favor of plaintiffs declaring section 89001 "unconstitutional and of no force or effect." Defendants subsequently filed their appeal from that judgment.

Following entry of judgment, the FPPC informed the Legislature that, under the authority of section 3.5, article III of the California Constitution, it would continue to enforce section 89001 until it had been declared unconstitutional by an appellate court. As a result, the Senate Rules Committee rejected all requests for publication and distribution of newsletters and other mass mailings pending the outcome of the appeal.

Plaintiffs thereafter sought relief by the filing of a petition for mandate and/or prohibition. Although Division Three of this court summarily denied the request for relief, its order suggested that plaintiffs initiate an action in superior court for injunctive relief against the FPPC.

Plaintiffs subsequently filed a new and separate complaint (case No. C722189) seeking to enjoin the FPPC from enforcing section 89001 and any interpretative regulations based thereon.

Several months earlier, in December 1988, the FPPC adopted regulation 18901 as a means of implementing section 89001. That rule, effective April 12, 1989, essentially provided that newsletters and other mass mailings were not prohibited under the statute so long as they did not "feature" (i.e., "single out for attention of the reader") any particular elective officer and were not "sent at the request of any elected officer or his or her agent." The regulation further permitted the mailing of press releases to the media, intra-agency communications, legal notices, announcements of official agency events and other public meetings, telephone directories, and documents "sent in connection with the payment or collection of funds" by a governmental agency, including tax bills and checks.

Plaintiffs took the position that the FPPC in promulgating regulation 18901, had impermissibly rewritten section 89001 by creating numerous exceptions and exclusions not authorized by the clear wording of the statute. At the hearing on plaintiffs' motion for a preliminary injunction, the trial court disagreed and ruled that when read in context of its placement in the Government Code and construed according to the FPPC interpretive regulation, the statute was constitutional. The request for injunctive relief was denied. Plaintiffs now appeal from that order.

In reviewing plaintiffs' challenge to the constitutionality of the statute, we do not consider or weigh the economic or social wisdom or general propriety of the initiative measure before us. Our sole function is to evaluate section 89001, and the FPPC's interpretive regulation, in light of established constitutional standards. (See *Amador Valley Joint Union High Sch. Dist. v. State Bd. of Equalization* (1978) 22 Cal. 3d 208, 219 [149 Cal. Rptr. 239, 583 P.2d 1281].)

As emphasized by our Supreme Court when confronted with a similar task, "'all presumptions and intendments favor the validity of a statute and mere doubt does not afford sufficient reason for a judicial declaration of invalidity. Statutes must be upheld unless their unconstitutionality clearly, positively, and unmistakably appears.' (*In re Ricky H.* (1970) 2 Cal. 3d 513, 519 [86 Cal. Rptr. 76, 468 P.2d 204]; *In re Dennis M.* (1969) 70 Cal. 2d 444, 453 [75 Cal. Rptr. 1, 450 P.2d 296]; *Lockheed Aircraft Corp. v. Superior Court* (1946) 28 Cal. 2d 481, 484 [171 P.2d 21, 166 A.L.R. 701].)" (*Calfarm Ins. Co. v. Deukmejian* (1989) 48 Cal. 3d 805, 814–815 [258 Cal. Rptr. 161, 771 P.2d 1247].)

These principles have particular application to enactments that are the product of the initiative process.

The courts of this state have often described the initiative and referendum as articulating one of the most precious rights of our democratic process. "'[I]t has long been our judicial policy to apply a liberal construction to this power wherever it is challenged in order that the right be not improperly annulled. If doubts can reasonably be resolved in favor of the use of this reserve power, courts will preserve it.' [Citations.]" (*Associated Home Builders etc., Inc. v. City of Livermore* (1976) 18 Cal. 3d 582, 591 [135 Cal. Rptr. 41, 557 P.2d 473, 92 A.L.R.3d 1038]; see also *Fair Political Practices Com. v. Superior Court* (1979) 25 Cal. 3d 33, 41 [157 Cal. Rptr. 855, 599 P.2d 46]; *Farley v. Healey* (1967) 67 Cal. 2d 325, 328 [62 Cal. Rptr. 26, 431 P.2d 650]; *Blotter v. Farrell* (1954) 42 Cal. 2d 804, 812 [270 P.2d 481].)

""""The words [of an initiative] must be read in a sense which harmonizes [them] with the subject-matter and the general purpose and object of the amendment, consistent of course with the language itself. The words must be understood, not as the words of the civil service commission, or the city council, or the mayor, or the city attorney, but as the words of the voters who adopted the amendment. They are to be understood in the common popular way, and, in the absence of some strong and convincing reason to the contrary, not found here, they are not entitled to be considered in a technical sense inconsistent with their popular meaning.'" [Citation.] To ascertain the intent of the electorate it is, of course, proper to consider the official statements made to the voters in connection with propositions of law they are requested to approve or reject. [Citations.]" (*Creighton v. City of Santa Monica* (1984) 160 Cal. App. 3d 1011, 1018 [207 Cal. Rptr. 78].)

Bearing in mind the foregoing interpretive aids, we turn first to plaintiffs' argument that the amended version of section 89001 usurps the state Legislature's constitutional and statutory authority to govern its internal affairs.

Article IV, section 7, subdivision (a) of the California Constitution directs that "[e]ach house shall choose its officers and adopt rules for its proceedings." Plaintiffs maintain that section 89001 violates this exclusive mandate by interfering with various statutory enactments and house rules which allow a contingency fund for legislative expenses (see § 9126), provide for the rules committee to determine how expenditures from that fund are allocated, and establish a newsletter program for legislators to communicate with their constituents.

As we see it, however, section 89001 does not attempt to regulate the manner in which the Legislature drafts its rules, appropriates its funds, or chooses its officers. The statute merely limits the Legislature's ability to utilize public funds for mass mailings to constituents and other members of the public. The mere labeling of the "newsletter program" as an internal procedure of the Legislature does not make it so.

While there can be no question that both the Senate and the Assembly possess the power to create and administer their own internal affairs, it does not strike us that the newsletter program in either house falls within the exclusive sway of the rulemaking process. These programs extend far beyond the halls of the Legislature and impact virtually every citizen of this state.

The rulemaking authority is limited to the internal workings of the Senate and Assembly and does not encompass matters which are addressed to the world outside the Legislature. We cannot agree with plaintiffs that section 89001 constitutes an impermissible attempt at rulemaking by the electorate. It is, instead, a valid effort by which the electorate seeks to control the allotment of limited state revenues and reform the electoral process. Said another way, the use of taxpayers' funds to pay for mass mailings by state legislators is not insulated from external control by article IV, section 7.

The limitations provided for in section 89001 are substantially different from the initiative measure struck down in *People's Advocate, Inc. v. Superior Court* (1986)

181 Cal. App. 3d 316 [226 Cal. Rptr. 640], a case upon which plaintiffs principally rely. There, the court held that the Legislative Reform Act of 1983, a statutory initiative measure, was violative of article IV, section 7 because it attempted to regulate the Legislature's adoption of rules, its selection of officers and employees, and the appointment of committee members. That measure also established, among other things, a formula for the Legislature's budget and sought to repeal section 9126, the statute granting the Senate Rules Committee the authority to disburse monies from the contingent fund. In declaring the majority of the act unconstitutional, the court observed that "the people through the electorate have been given the power to make statutes, i.e., the power to make *laws* for all the people, but not the power to make rules for the selection of officers or rules of proceeding or rules which regulate the committees or employees of either or both houses of the Legislature. These powers . . . are exclusively the province of the houses affected by them." (*People's Advocate, Inc. v. Superior Court, supra*, at p. 326, italics in original.)

Unlike the initiative measure at issue in *People's Advocate*, section 89001 does not attempt to regulate any of the proceedings of either the Senate or Assembly, but merely restricts individual members from using public funds to send self-aggrandizing newsletters.

We agree with the FPPC that the term "proceedings" as used in article IV, section 7, subdivision (a) does not refer to activities engaged in by individual legislators, but rather to activities by which the Legislature as a whole conducts its business. *People's Advocate* does not hold otherwise.

It is hyperbole to say that an initiative which merely prohibits legislators from spending public funds on mass mailings somehow strangles the legislative process as a whole. We take judicial notice of the fact that the state Legislature has not ceased functioning because of the passage of Proposition 73 in June 1988 or its enforcement by the FPPC. The Legislature has continued to fulfill its constitutional obligations.

Plaintiffs nevertheless insist that the statute interferes with the Legislature's power to budget and appropriate money under article IV, section 12 of the California Constitution. That argument, however, misses the point. Section 89001 as written places no limitation whatsoever on the Legislature's authority to appropriate funds for its internal operations. It merely curbs individual legislators from using public funds to finance mass mailings to their constituents. Again, *People's Advocate, Inc. v. Superior Court, supra*, 181 Cal. App. 3d 316 is inapposite. Under section 89001, the Legislature, as pertains to its internal operations, retains full control over the budget process and may continue to appropriate monies for such purposes as it sees fit. As to the other types of appropriations, article IV, section 12 does not operate to restrict the initiative process set forth in article II, section 8 and which vests the electorate with a power equal to that of the Legislature to enact laws. (Cf. art. II, § 9, subd. (a); see also *Bd. of Osteopathic Examiners v. Riley* (1923) 192 Cal. 158 [218 P. 1018]; *Carlson v. Cory* (1983) 139 Cal. App. 3d 724 [189 Cal. Rptr. 185].) Moreover, since the prohibition contained in section 89001 may be amended by statutory initiative or by referendum (see §§ 81012, 85103), the Legislature is not divested of its authority to enact future legislation within its competence. (See Castello, The Limits of Popular Sovereignty: Using the Initiative Power to Control Legislative Procedure (1986) 74 Cal.L.Rev. 491 499, fn. 44.) We decline to follow any suggestion to the contrary in *People's Advocate, Inc. v. Superior Court, supra,* 181 Cal.App.3d at pages 328–329.

Citing a vast array of state and federal cases, plaintiffs next assert that section 89001 violates numerous fundamental constitutional rights held by them as both elected representatives and as members of the electorate. Despite their broad assertion of such rights, plaintiffs have failed to identify any constitutional right to send newsletters and other mass mailings at public expense.

Although some of the federal "franking" privilege cases cited by plaintiffs refer to a legislator's "constitutional duty to communicate with and inform their constituents on public matters" (*Common Cause v. Bolger* (D.D.C. 1982) 574 F. Supp. 672, 677; see also *Bowie v. Williams* (E.D.Pa. 1972) 351 F. Supp. 628, 631; *Hoellen v. Annunzio* (7th Cir. 1972) 468 F.2d 522), none hold that the public must finance such communications.

For the most part, these cases dealt with whether Congress's statutorily granted franking privilege (see 39 U.S.C. § 3210) was unconstitutional, or whether it had been abused by the mailing of various types of literature to members of the public. That is not the issue before us.

Assuming arguendo that there exists a constitutional duty for legislators to communicate with the electorate on matters of public concern and a corollary right of the electorate to receive such communication, the United States Supreme Court has made it clear that so long as a legislative act is not aimed primarily at suppression of speech the failure "to subsidize the exercise of [such] right does not infringe [that] right." (*Regan v. Taxation with Representation of Wash.* (1983) 461 U.S. 540, 549 [76 L. Ed. 2d 129, 139, 103 S. Ct. 1997].)

We are not here concerned with an enactment that seeks to control the content nor suppress any particular communication between individual legislators and their constituents. The statute does not contain a wholesale prohibition against legislators communicating with their constituents nor does it prevent public officials from receiving information from the electorate on matters of general concern. The principle articulated in *Regan* squarely applies to section 89001's limitation against the use of public funds to finance mass mailings by state legislators.

Were the "duty" of a legislator to communicate and the corresponding "right" of members of the electorate to receive such communication equated with the freedom of speech as protected by the First Amendment, the question would immediately arise as to how that right would be enforced and by whom. What form of communication and with what frequency would discharge the duty or satisfy the right. In our opinion there is no such duty or right which can truly be said to enjoy constitutional protection in the manner urged by plaintiffs.

Plaintiffs further contend that limitation of section 89001 impermissibly burdens the rights to freedom of association, to vote, to petition the government for redress of grievances, and to instruct or recall elected representatives.

This overly broad assertion is merely makeweight in an endeavor to establish that somehow an elected official's constituents possess an absolute right to receive newsletters and other such communications at public expense.

We are further told that the statute's prohibition against publicly financed mass mailings "improperly dilutes and interferes with the meaningful exercise of constitutional rights because it prevents those rights from being exercised in a fully informed and effective manner." None of the cases cited by plaintiffs, however, support the proposition that they advance here.

The "Bill of Rights," as established in the first 10 amendments to the Constitution, simply bars governmental interference with those rights. It contains no guaranty that the government will monetarily subsidize the exercise of that right.

The statute in question neither seeks to "muzzle" elected officials nor impede the free flow of ideas between the electorate and the Legislature. It in no way diminishes the ability of any class of voters from exercising their right to vote, from petitioning the government, or from otherwise making their beliefs known to their elected representatives.

Having found that the statute has no real or appreciable impact on any right guaranteed by the state and federal Constitutions, we must also reject plaintiffs' contention that section 89001 be declared invalid unless its proponents demonstrate that it serves a compelling state interest and that it is narrowly drawn to achieve that end.

That form of analysis is generally reserved for those instances where the contested regulation impacts directly on the content of some restricted communication or directly interferes with the fairness and integrity of the electoral process. (See *Canaan v. Abdelnour* (1985) 40 Cal. 3d 703, 710–713 [221 Cal. Rptr. 468, 710 P.2d 268, 69 A.L.R.4th 915]; *Gould v. Grubb* (1975) 14 Cal. 3d 661, 670 [122 Cal. Rptr. 377, 536 P.2d 1337]; *Curtis v. Board of Supervisors* (1972) 7 Cal. 3d 942, 952 [104 Cal. Rptr. 297, 501 P.2d 537]; see also *Common Cause v. Bolger, supra*, 574 F. Supp. 672, 680–681.) Here, there is no such impact.

The ballot arguments in favor of and in opposition to the enactment of Proposition 73, in addition to the impartial appraisal of the measure by the legislative analyst, makes it clear that the initiative as a whole sought to reform the electoral process, at least in part, by prohibiting the public subsidy of political campaigns by incumbent officeholders and their challengers alike. As a means of implementing that goal, the measure-imposed restrictions on campaign contributions (see §§ 85200–85202 and 85301–85305), limited honoraria (see § 85310), prohibited candidates for public office from using state revenues in their election campaigns (see § 85300), and circumscribed the use of mass mailings by elected officials (§ 89001).

Even a cursory review of these provisions makes it manifest that the majority of the electorate who voted for Proposition 73 intended to control the conduct of both incumbents and those seeking public office by restricting the use of public funds. Section 89001 in particular appears to be directed at removing at least some of the substantial advantages enjoyed by incumbent office holders over their challengers.

This objective is, of course, in keeping with that portion of the Political Reform Act of 1974 which declares: "Laws and practices unfairly favoring incumbents should be abolished in order that elections may be conducted more fairly." (§ 81002, subd. (e).)

The statute at issue here helps in accomplishing that goal by prohibiting elected officials from using public moneys to perpetuate themselves in public office. The legitimacy of such an objective is made clear by the Supreme Court's observation in *Stanson v. Mott* (1976) 17 Cal. 3d 206, 217 [130 Cal. Rptr. 697, 551 P.2d 1]: "A fundamental precept of this nation's democratic electoral process is that the government may not 'take sides' in election contests or bestow an unfair advantage on one of several competing factions. A principal danger feared by our country's founders lay in the possibility that the holders of governmental authority would use official power improperly to perpetuate themselves, or their allies, in office [citations]; *the selective use of public funds in election campaigns, of course, raises the specter of just such an improper distortion of the democratic electoral process.*" (Italics added.)

We are convinced that section 89001, by denying elected officials of all political persuasions the advantage of using public funds to put or keep their name before the voters, advances the legitimate state interest in avoiding "arbitrary preferment of one candidate over another by reason of incumbency." (*Gould v. Grubb, supra,* 14 Cal. 3d 661, 677.) We also think it clear that the initiative serves the very legitimate aim of conserving limited state revenues by prohibiting the use of public funds for essentially political purposes. These twin goals of the statute constitute a permissible, if not significant, governmental interest.

Plaintiffs maintain, however, that even if section 89001 advances a compelling interest its scope is too broad to withstand constitutional scrutiny. In support of that argument, plaintiffs insist that the general wording of the statute not only prohibits the distribution of legislative newsletters, but all other forms of mass mailings by the government as well. We disagree.

Such an interpretation conflicts with the clear intent of the initiative measure as a whole. Nothing in Proposition 73 could have led the electorate to believe that the adoption of the measure would result in a total ban on all mass mailings, including legal notices, tax bills, sample ballots, and college catalogs. As previously discussed, supra, the initiative sought specifically to reform the political process by prohibiting the public subsidy of political campaigns and by attempting to limit some of the advantages enjoyed by incumbent office holders.

Any contrary interpretation would result in the repeal of countless statutes and regulations that require the mailing of various notices and other documents by governmental agencies. We seriously doubt that the electorate intended such a result by passing Proposition 73. In reaching this conclusion we are, of course, guided by the well-settled rule that "[t]he literal language of enactments may be disregarded to avoid absurd results and to fulfill the apparent intent of the framers." (*Amador Valley Joint Union High Sch. Dist. v. State Bd. of Equalization, supra,* 22 Cal. 3d 208, 245.)

In any event, regulation 18901, promulgated by the FPPC in exercise of the duties imposed upon it by the Political Reform Act of 1974 (see § 83112), clarifies any ambiguity that may exist in the practical application of the statute. Such regulations are deemed valid so long as they are "'consistent and not in conflict with the statute and reasonably necessary to effectuate the purpose of the statute.' ([§ 11342.2].)" (*Consumer Union of U.S., Inc. v. California Milk Producers Advisory Bd.* (1978) 82 Cal. App. 3d 433, 447 [147 Cal. Rptr. 265].)

Contrary to the argument advanced by plaintiffs, the FPPC has not rewritten section 89001, but has merely interpreted it in a manner consistent with the intent of the electorate in adopting Proposition 73.

In keeping with the spirit of the initiative, the regulation merely precludes the public funding of newsletters which feature any particular legislator or other elected official by name. It does not prohibit legislative committees and the like from using state revenues to disseminate information to the public as deemed necessary. We agree with the FPPC that the effect of regulation 18901 is to permit the free flow of necessary government information while reducing the political benefit realized by incumbent elected officials from the sending of newsletters and other such mass mailings. This is totally consistent with the FPPC's duty to implement the intent and not the literal language of the statute.

. . . .

The judgment in case No. C691676 declaring section 89001 unconstitutional is reversed, and the order in case No. C722189 denying injunctive relief is affirmed. All parties to bear their own costs on appeal.

GATES, J., and FUKUTO, J., concurred.

Notes and Questions

1. The proceedings of the Legislature concern the houses individually, as well as collectively, as California has a bicameral legislature. The term "proceeding" that authorizes the Legislature's self-government of its internal affairs does not refer to activities engaged in by individual legislators, but rather to activities by which the Legislature as a whole conducts its business.

2. The court ruled that the statute neither interferes with the Legislature's authority to govern its internal affairs nor burdens the exercise of any fundamental right. This is the basis of the court's ruling that upheld the validity of the statute. As the court noted, "statutes must be upheld unless their unconstitutionality clearly, positively, and unmistakably appears."

3. Did the court too narrowly construe Article IV, Section 7(a) when it said, "As we see it, however, section 89001 does not attempt to regulate the manner in which the Legislature drafts its rules, appropriates its funds, or chooses its officers"? Is the funding issue an important enough distinction that it takes the newsletter program out of the "internal procedures" of the Legislature?

4. Did the court decision achieve a fair balance between the electorate attempting control of a legislative program with the public's ability to control how limited state resources are expended?

5. What distinguishes this court decision from that in *People's Advocate*? Did the court find any First Amendment concerns in this case?

6. Was the court fair in its ruling that Prop. 73 was proper simply because the plaintiffs could not identify any constitutional right to send newsletters and other mass mailings at public expense? How did the court distinguish state legislative mailers to constituents and the federal "franking" privilege cases?

7. Was the court correct that a legislator does not have a "constitutional duty to communicate with and inform their constituents on public matters"?

8. If such a right did exist, would it be less important than the competing interest of preventing the use of public funds for what some see as political campaigning through the use of constituent mail programs? In other words, did Prop. 73 survive a constitutional challenge because it helped limit one of the perceived advantages enjoyed by incumbent office holders over their challengers by being able to communicate with constituents (i.e., voters) with publicly-funded mailers?

9. The court pointed to the provision of the Political Reform Act of 1974, which declares: "Laws and practices unfairly favoring incumbents should be abolished in order that elections may be conducted more fairly." (§ 81002, subd. (e).) The court ruled that "the statute at issue here helps in accomplishing that goal."

10. Should the court have provided a legal analysis regarding how it concluded that there was not a violation of the single subject rule when the electorate adopted Prop. 73? Or was finding that "[t]here is a reasonable connection between the prohibition of publicly financed mass mailings by elected officials and the reformation of the political process" sufficient?

K. Committees

1. Types of Legislative Committees

In both the California State Assembly and the State Senate, there are several types of committees that operate to conduct the business of the two houses of the Legislature. These committees are the Standing Committees (with a number of subcommittees), Select Committees, Special Committees (just in the Assembly), and Joint Committees.

Standing Committee hearings are the forums for public input on pending legislation. Measures are heard in **Standing Committees**, which meet on a regular basis throughout the legislative year. All of the Standing Committees are policy committees, except the two fiscal committees, which are the Appropriations and Budget Committees. **Joint Committees** have membership from both houses and consider issues of joint concern.

Committee information available online includes committee membership, staff, addresses, phone numbers, meeting schedules, and policy jurisdictions. In terms of the Standing Committees, there are 32 of them in the Assembly and 21 of them in the Senate. Created pursuant to Assembly and Senate Rules, the Standing Committees consider legislation, the state budget, and internal legislative matters, as determined by their jurisdictions. Jurisdictions are set by the Assembly and Senate Rules Committee. Standing Committees must meet specific standards for notice, analyses, quorums, and voting.

Both the Assembly and the Senate have Select Committees, which are technically subcommittees of each house's General Research Committee.

The Assembly also has Special Committees. In 2017, those Special Committees were the Assembly Legislative Ethics Committee as well as the Special Committee on the Office of the Attorney General.

Pursuant to Joint Rules 36.5 and 36.7, there are a number of Joint Committees of the Legislature. Many of them were established pursuant to statutes or resolutions adopted by the two houses. During the 2017 Session, the Joint Committees are:

Joint Committee on Arts (Resolution Chapter 101, Statutes of 1984. Continuous existence.)

Joint Committee on Fairs Allocation and Classification (Food and Agriculture Code §§ 4531, 4532, 4533, 4534, 4535. Continuous existence.)

Joint Committee on Fisheries and Aquaculture (Resolution Chapter 88, Statutes of 1981. Continuous existence.)

Joint Committee on Rules (Joint Rule 40. Continuous existence.)

Joint Legislative Audit (Government Code §§ 10501, 10502; Joint Rule 37.3. Continuous existence.)

Joint Legislative Budget (Government Code §§ 9140, 9141; Joint Rule 37. Continuous existence.)

Joint Legislative Committee on Climate Change Policies (Government Code § 9147.10.)

Joint Legislative Committee on Emergency Management (Resolution Chapter 31, Statutes of 2011. Continuous existence.)

2. Legislative Committees and Their Jurisdictions

Both houses of the California Legislature provide committees of legislators, based upon subject matter jurisdiction, to handle the business of the respective houses. With fewer legislators, the Senate has a fewer number of committees than the Assembly.

Nonetheless, they both consider legislation from their house of origin, as well as the other house. This chapter provides an overview of the Senate and Assembly standing committees and their basic jurisdictions.

Senate

There are 21 standing committees in the Senate pursuant to Rule 12 of the Standing Rules of the Senate. Those committees and their subject matter jurisdictions are as follows:

Agriculture — Bills relating to agriculture.

Appropriations — Bills that are subject to Joint Rule 10.5 and are not referred to the Committee on Budget and Fiscal Review. Bills that constitute a state-mandated local program.

Budget and Fiscal Review — The Budget Bill and bills implementing the Budget. Bills that directly affect the State Budget, including deficiencies and reappropriations.

Business, Professions and Economic Development — Bills relating to business and professional practices, licensing, and regulations. Bills relating to economic development, commerce, and international trade.

Education — Bills relating to education, higher education, and related programs. Bills relating to education employee issues and collective bargaining.

Elections and Constitutional Amendments — Bills relating to elections and constitutional amendments, ballot measures, the Political Reform Act of 1974, and elected officials.

Energy, Utilities and Communications — Bills relating to public utilities and carriers, energy companies, alternative energy development and conservation, and communications development and technology.

Environmental Quality — Bills relating to environmental quality, environmental health, air quality, water quality, waste management, recycling, toxics, and hazardous materials and waste.

Governance and Finance — Bills relating to local government procedure, administration, and organization. Bills relating to land use. Bills relating to state and local revenues, bonds, and taxation.

Governmental Organization — Bills relating to horse racing, public gaming, and alcoholic beverages. Bills relating to the management of public safety emergencies and disaster response. Bills relating to state government organization. Bills regarding the use of state-controlled lands and buildings, state contracting, and interstate compacts.

Health — Bills relating to public health, alcohol and drug use, mental health, health insurance, managed care, long-term care, and related institutions.

Human Services — Bills relating to welfare, social services and support, and related institutions.

Insurance, Banking and Financial Institutions — Bills relating to insurance, indemnity, surety, warranty agreements, financial institutions, lending, and corporations.

Judiciary — Bills amending the Civil Code, Code of Civil Procedure, Evidence Code, Family Code, and Probate Code. Bills relating to courts, judges, and court personnel. Bills relating to liens, claims, and unclaimed property. Bills relating to privacy and consumer protection.

Labor and Industrial Relations — Bills relating to labor, industrial safety, unemployment, workers' compensation and insurance, and noncertificated public school employees.

Natural Resources and Water — Bills relating to conservation and the management of public resources, fish and wildlife, regulation of oil, mining, geothermal development, wetlands and lakes, global atmospheric effects, ocean and bay pollution, coastal resources, forestry practices, recreation, parks, and historical resources. Bills relating to water supply management.

Public Employment and Retirement — Bills relating to state and local public agency collective bargaining; state and local non-school public employees; classified public school employees; public retirement systems; public employees' compensation and employment benefits, including retirement and health care; and state social security administration.

Public Safety — Bills amending the Evidence Code, relating to criminal procedure; the Penal Code; and statutes of a penal nature. Bills relating to the Department of Corrections and Rehabilitation and the Board of State and Community Corrections.

Rules — Proposed amendments to the rules and other matters relating to the business of the Legislature.

Transportation and Housing — Bills relating to the operation, safety, equipment, transfer of ownership, licensing, and registration of vehicles, aircraft, and vessels. Bills relating to the Department of Transportation and the Department of Motor Vehicles. Bills relating to highways, public transportation systems, and airports. Bills relating to housing and community redevelopment.

Veterans Affairs — Bills relating to veterans, military affairs, and armories. Bills amending the Military and Veterans Code.

Assembly

There are 32 standing committees in the Assembly pursuant to Rule 11 of the Standing Rules of the Assembly. Those committees and their subject matter jurisdictions are as follows:

Accountability and Administrative Review — Primary jurisdictions are identifying efficiencies in the management of state government, reviewing and studying the implementation, operation, and effectiveness of state programs and agencies.

Aging and Long-Term Care — Primary jurisdiction includes area agencies on aging, California Department of Aging, long-term supports and services, Older Americans Act, Older Californians Act, senior citizen advocacy activities, the California Senior Legislature, services for seniors in residential and day settings and the California Commission on Aging.

Agriculture — Primary jurisdiction includes agriculture, agricultural chemicals, agricultural commodities and commissions, Department of Food and Agriculture, expositions and fairs, food labeling, labeling of agricultural commodities, livestock and poultry, marketing law, milk and milk products, pest management, and veterinary issues relative to agriculture.

Appropriations — Primary jurisdiction is fiscal bills, including bonds and alternative public financing.

Arts, Entertainment, Sports, Tourism, and Internet Media — Primary jurisdictions are programs and policies affecting the recording, motion picture and other entertainment industries, tourism and arts programs and museums, professional and amateur sports including the State Athletic Commission and the regulation of athlete agents, and Internet media.

Banking and Finance — Primary jurisdictions are financial institutions, real property finance, consumer finance, and corporate securities law.

Budget — The Budget Committee's jurisdiction is the Budget.

Business and Professions — Bills involving "sunrise," the creation of new regulatory entities within the Department of Consumer Affairs (DCA); "sunset," the oversight and elimination of regulatory entities within the DCA; health care professional licensing; veterinarian licensing; occupational licensing; vocational education; the Department of General Services (building standards); product labeling (except agricultural and medical product labeling).

Communications and Conveyance — Primary jurisdiction over cable, common carriers, moving companies, broadband, telecommunications, and transportation network companies.

Education — Primary jurisdictions are education generally, certificated employees of schools, school finance, and school facilities.

Elections and Redistricting — Primary jurisdictions are elections and redistricting.

Environmental Safety and Toxic Materials — Primary jurisdictions are toxic substances and hazardous materials, hazardous waste regulation, drinking water regulation, and pesticides.

Governmental Organization — Primary jurisdictions include alcohol, Indian gaming, horseracing, gambling, tobacco, public records, open meetings laws, state holidays, outdoor advertising and emergency services/natural disasters (this can be shared with the Housing and Community Development Committee and Local Government Committee).

Health — Primary jurisdictions are health care, health insurance, Medi-Cal and other public health care programs, mental health licensing of health and health-related professionals, and long-term health care facilities.

Higher Education — Primary jurisdictions are university, state university, and community college systems, postsecondary education, and student financial aid.

Housing and Community Development — Primary jurisdictions are building standards, common interest developments, eminent domain, farm worker housing, homeless programs, housing discrimination, housing finance (including redevelopment), housing, natural disaster assistance and preparedness, land use planning, mobile homes/manufactured housing, redevelopment, and rent control.

Human Services — Includes child welfare services, foster care, child care, adoption assistance, CalWORKs, CalFresh, developmental disability services, In-Home Supportive Services (IHSS), community care licensing, adult protective services, and SSI/SSP.

Insurance — Primary jurisdictions are insurance (excluding health insurance), workers compensation, and unemployment compensation.

Jobs, Economic Development, and the Economy — Primary jurisdictions are business advocacy within California and the United States; business advocacy of import/export trade; California-Mexico relations; California overseas trade offices; Governor's Office of Business and Economic Development; development and expansion of new technologies, except energy; development of international high tech markets; economic disaster relief; economic impact reports; effect of balance of trade issues on California; expansion of overseas markets; foreign investments by California; foreign investments in California; impacts of federal budget on high tech projects; impacts of federal budget on international trade; industrial innovation and research; international capital, including capital formation; international trade, research and import/export finance; interstate commerce; seaports and physical infrastructure; sister state agreements and friendship agreements with other nations; small business development and operations; state and local economic development; women and minority business enterprises (WBME).

Judiciary — Primary jurisdictions are family law, product liability, tort liability, Civil Code, and Evidence Code (excluding criminal procedure).

Labor and Employment — Primary jurisdictions are wages, hours, employment discrimination, Cal-OSHA, employment development, and public job programs.

Local Government — Primary jurisdictions are General Plan, land use, housing element, local agency formation commissions (LAFCO), city and county organization and powers, special district governance and finance, special taxes, Subdivision Map Act, Brown Act, Public Records Act, redevelopment (as it relates to governance and financing), infrastructure financing districts, local government finance, charter cities and counties, eminent domain, joint powers authorities, Williamson Act, design-build (for local governments), military base reuse, public private partnerships (for local governments), state mandates, county clerks/recorders, and civil grand juries.

Natural Resources — Primary jurisdiction includes air quality, climate change, energy efficiency, renewable energy, California Environmental Quality Act (CEQA), coastal protection, forestry, land conservation, oil spills, solid waste and recycling.

Privacy and Consumer Protection — Jurisdiction spans a wide range of technology-related issues, and includes matters affecting consumer protection in both the digital and analog worlds. Specifically, the Committee has jurisdiction over matters related to privacy, the protection of personal information (including digital information), the security of data, and information technology, as well as false advertising, charitable solicitations, weights and measures, and consumer protection generally. The Committee is also responsible for oversight of the Department of Technology within the state's Government Operations Agency.

Public Employees, Retirement, and Social Security — Primary jurisdiction is oversight of classified school employees, Judges Retirement Law, public employee collective bargaining, and public retirement administration and investment strategy.

Public Safety — Primary jurisdiction is the California Penal Code.

Revenue and Taxation — Primary jurisdiction is the Revenue and Taxation Code.

Rules — Primary jurisdictions are proposed amendments to the rules and other matters relating to the business of the Legislature.

Transportation — Jurisdiction includes California High-Speed Rail Authority, California Highway Patrol, California Transportation Commission, Department of Motor Vehicles, Department of Transportation (Caltrans), driver's licenses, freight, regional transportation agencies, transit authorities, intercity rail, mobile sources of air pollution, fuels, rules of the road, state highways, local streets and roads, vehicles, aircraft, bicycle and pedestrian facilities, and vessels.

Utilities and Energy — Primary jurisdictions are California Energy Commission; California Independent System Operator; California Public Utilities Commission (CPUC); CPUC oversight and reform; electric generation: biogas, biomass, coal, geothermal, hydroelectric, natural gas, nuclear, renewables, solar, and wind; electric grid; energy efficiency, energy conservation, and demand response; energy service providers; natural gas; power plant siting; railroads; supplier diversity related to CPUC regulated energy, water, and railroad; utility rates: electric, gas, water, and vessels; water utilities.

Veterans Affairs — Primary jurisdictions are Cal-Vet loan program, Department of Veterans Affairs, National Guard, state military, and veterans.

Water, Parks, and Wildlife — Primary jurisdictions are water resources, flood management, fish and game, parks and recreation, and wildlife.

L. Contempt Powers

As part of their authority to conduct hearings and investigations, legislative committees have the power to hold individuals in contempt for failure to abide by a subpoena issued by a legislative committee. It is a rare occasion for a California legislative committee to issue a subpoena in order to compel a witness to appear before the committee. And it would be an even more rare instance where an individual called to testify before a legislative committee would refuse to do so. As such, the power of contempt is basically an unused power in the California Legislature.

M. Interim Committees

Legislative committees can be utilized during the recess or interim period when the Legislature is not in session. They can conduct hearings, take testimony and issue reports, but they cannot vote on legislation. Legislation can only be voted upon when the Legislature is in session. The Legislature and each house thereof have the power to appoint committees for obtaining information concerning proposed legislation and reporting back their findings to the body appointing them during the session or during the constitutional recess, but there is no power by a house resolution to appoint an interim committee to serve after adjournment of the Legislature *sine die.* (*Special Assembly Interim Committee on Public Morals v. Southard* (1939) 13 Cal.2d 497.)

Notes and Questions

1. What is the main purpose of interim committee hearings? Are they a necessary part of the lawmaking process?

N. Officers and Employees

1. Officers and Leadership of the Legislature

In both the California State Assembly and the State Senate, there are designated officers and elected leaders of these two bodies. The following is a listing of the officers and leadership positions in the Assembly and the Senate:

Assembly Officers and Leaders

Speaker — He or she is the highest-ranking officer of the Assembly; usually elected by the Members at the beginning of each two-year legislative session. The Speaker or his or her designee presides over Floor Sessions, and the Speaker's powers and duties are established by the Assembly Rules.

Speaker pro Tempore — This individual is an officer appointed by the Speaker that presides over Floor Sessions in the absence of the Speaker.

Assistant Speaker pro Tempore — This person is also appointed by the Speaker and presides over the Floor Sessions in the absence of the Speaker and the Speaker pro Tempore.

Majority Floor Leader — He or she is elected by the members of the majority party's caucus. He or she represents the Speaker on the Floor and oversees the Assembly Floor proceedings through parliamentary procedures such as motions and points of order.

Minority Floor Leader — He or she is elected by the caucus having the second largest membership in the Assembly and is generally responsible for making motions, points of order and representing the minority caucus on the Assembly Floor.

Majority Whip — Whips are essentially assistants to the political leadership of each party in the Assembly. They are elected by their respective caucuses and help count potential votes on matters which present particular party concerns. There usually are Assistant Majority Whips.

Minority Whip — Whips are essentially assistants to the political leadership of each party in the Assembly. They are elected by their respective caucuses, and help count potential votes on matters which present particular party concerns. There usually are Assistant Minority Whips.

Democratic Caucus Chair — Caucus chairs are elected by their respective parties. They convene caucus meetings, provide political advice to their leadership, and manage staff assisting Members in providing constituent services and communications with the public.

Republican Caucus Chair — Caucus chairs are elected by their respective parties. They convene caucus meetings, provide political advice to their leadership, and manage staff assisting Members in providing constituent services and communications with the public.

Chief Clerk — He or she is a nonpartisan, nonmember officer of the Assembly elected by the majority of the membership at the start of each two-year session as its legislative officer and parliamentarian.

Chief Sergeant-at-Arms — He or she is responsible for maintaining order and providing security for legislators. The Chief Sergeant-at-Arms in each House is elected by a majority of the Members of that House at the beginning of every legislative session.

Senate Officers and Leaders

President of the Senate — The Lieutenant Governor serves as the President of the Senate. However, by law and custom, the role of the Senate President is extremely limited, and he or she may be invited periodically to preside on ceremonial occasions, such as the opening of the Session. However, the only time the Lieutenant Governor is actually entitled to participate in the business of the Senate is in the case of a tie vote, when he or she casts the vote breaking the tie.

President pro Tempore — He or she is the leader of the State Senate and serves as the Chair of the Rules Committee. This individual is elected by the Members at the beginning of each Session. The "Pro Tem" is the presiding officer on the Floor, overseeing the appointment of committee members, assignment of bills, progress of legislation through the house, confirmation of gubernatorial appointees, and overall direction of policy. He or she is also the political leader of the majority party.

Majority Floor Leader — He is she is chosen by the Majority Caucus and serves as the main Floor manager for the President pro Tempore and majority party. He or she also is the chief assistant in political matters and strategy.

Minority Floor Leader — He or she is the second-most powerful position in the Senate. Elected by members of the minority caucus, he or she speaks for the minority party, maintains its inner discipline, and works with the President pro Tempore to set the Senate's order of business.

Majority Whip — Whips are essentially assistants to the political leadership of each party in the Senate. They are elected by their respective caucuses and help count potential votes on matters which present particular party concerns. There usually are Assistant Majority Whips.

Minority Whip — Whips are essentially assistants to the political leadership of each party in the Senate. They are elected by their respective caucuses, and help count potential votes on matters which present particular party concerns. There usually are Assistant Minority Whips.

Democratic Caucus Chair — Caucus chairs are elected by their respective parties. They convene caucus meetings, provide political advice to their leadership, and manage staff assisting Members in providing constituent services and communications with the public.

Republican Caucus Chair — Caucus chairs are elected by their respective parties. They convene caucus meetings, provide political advice to their leadership, and manage staff assisting Members in providing constituent services and communications with the public.

Secretary of the Senate — The Secretary of the Senate is one of the three officers of the Senate who are elected by the total Membership, the other two officers being the President pro Tempore and the Chief Sergeant-at-Arms. He or she is the chief parliamentarian and keeper of the legislative records. The Secretary of the Senate is responsible for the accurate drafting of bills and the presentation of bills to the Governor. He or she is also the Executive Officer of the Senate, in charge of the day-to-day administration of budgeting, personnel, accounting, purchases, contracting and property management.

Chief Sergeant at Arms — The Chief Sergeant-at-Arms, elected by the total Membership of the Senate, is responsible for order on the Senate Floor, and in committees and meetings. He or she is essentially the "chief" of the Senate's internal policing agency. The Chief Sergeant-at-Arms works closely with the California Highway Patrol and the Assembly Sergeants to maintain the security of the Capitol and Senate offices statewide. The Chief Sergeant also oversees various service officers within the house.

2. Limits on Legislative Pensions

Pensions for legislators can be limited or they can be eliminated in their entirety. It is something that can be done by the electorate, and courts upheld the elimination of pensions for the Legislature when the voters enacted Proposition 140 in 1990. Although the portion of the proposition which placed limits on pensions was invalid, the remaining provisions of the measure, dealing with the number of terms of office and legislative expenditures, could be given effect without regard to the invalidity of the provision with respect to pensions, and that provision would be severed.

Notes and Questions

1. One of the most controversial changes to Article IV occurred at the ballot box in 1990, by Proposition 140. Its goal was to impose term limits on legislators and cut their budget by roughly 40%. The ballot measure, after its passage, was deemed to be constitutional, except one provision that attempted to deny pension benefits to currently serving members. The court allowed that provision to act only prospectively. The court's ruling was made in *Legislature v. Eu* (1991) 54 Cal.3d 492.

O. Civil Process Exemption for Legislators

Harmer v. Superior Court of Sacramento County

(1969) 275 Cal.App.2d 345

OPINION

Friedman, J.

Of the four petitioners, three are members of the State Senate and one a member of the Assembly. They seek a writ of prohibition to restrain the Sacramento Superior Court from proceeding against them in a civil lawsuit. They assert the immunity established by article IV, section 14, of the California Constitution: "A member of the Legislature is not subject to civil process during a session of the Legislature or for 5 days before and after a session."

The petitioner-legislators are members of the State Advisory Commission on Indian Affairs. Together with the commission itself, its executive secretary and its nonlegislative members, three of the petitioners were named as defendants in a class action brought in the Sacramento Superior Court on behalf of American Indians residing in California. The lawsuit asserted a violation of the laws requiring open meetings of state agencies (Gov. Code, §§ 11120–11130) and sought an injunction against alleged secret meetings. Summons and complaint in the action were served on these three petitioners on or about April 27, 1969, and a subpoena on the fourth on or about May 5, 1969. Additionally, a notice of deposition and subpoena duces tecum were served on petitioner Harmer on June 18, 1969. The Legislature was in session during these dates and remains in session at this time.

Asserting their constitutional immunity, petitioners moved the superior court to quash the service of summons and the discovery proceedings. The superior court denied the motions. It ordered petitioner Harmer to submit himself to a deposition on August 7, 1969, and allowed him until August 1, 1969, to answer interrogatories. This proceeding was then instituted. The plaintiffs in the lawsuit appear here as real parties in interest. They have filed a general demurrer to the petition.

The State Advisory Commission on Indian Affairs is a statutory body consisting of the Director of Social Welfare, the Director of Public Health, the Director of Education, three members of the Senate and three members of the Assembly. (Gov. Code, §§ 8110–8112.) The chairman is designated by the Governor. (Gov. Code, § 8114.) According to current law, the commission is to go out of existence on October 1, 1969. (Gov. Code, § 8118.) Essentially, the commission's function is to study the problems of Indians in California and to report its findings and recommendations to the Governor and Legislature. (Gov. Code, §§ 8116, 8117.)

Where, as here, a claim of legislative immunity has been made in the trial court and denied, prohibition is a proper remedy. (*Allen v. Superior Court,* 171 Cal. App. 2d 444, 448 [340 P.2d 1030].) Real parties in interest argue that petitioners "waived" their immunity by accepting membership on the State Advisory Commission on Indian Affairs. The argument rests on two assumptions: first, that the exemption in article IV, section 14, is confined to process in those civil actions involving legislative functions; second, that advisory commission membership places the legislator-members in a nonlegislative role or character. Both assumptions are erroneous.

In precise terms article IV, section 14, creates an exemption from civil process without qualification as to the kind or subject matter of the lawsuit. Similar exemptions have been construed to cover civil actions of all kinds, including those involving the legislator's personal affairs. (See *Long v. Ansell*, 293 U.S. 76 [79 L. Ed. 208, 55 S. Ct. 21]; *Fuller v. Barton*, 234 Mich. 540 [208 N.W. 696]; Note, 94 A.L.R. 1470, 1479–1480.) While conveying incidental personal advantage, such immunities are designed to benefit the public by protecting legislators against compelled distraction and interference during the session. (See *Tenney v. Brandhove*, 341 U.S. 367, 373–374, 377 [95 L. Ed. 1019, 1025–1026, 1027, 71 S. Ct. 783].) The California immunity applies to civil process generally and cannot be squeezed by interpretation to a restricted class of lawsuits. (Cf. *Allen v. Superior Court, supra*, 171 Cal. App. 2d 444; *Hancock v. Burns*, 158 Cal. App. 2d 785 [323 P.2d 456].)

The second assumption is equally fallacious. As members of the advisory commission, petitioners have not doffed their legislative character and immunity. A study agency of similar composition and function is the California Commission on Interstate Co-operation. (Gov. Code, §§ 8000–8013.) In 1941 the California Supreme Court held that legislative members of the latter commission were not in violation of the constitutional provision (now found in art. IV, § 13) which prohibits a legislator from holding a nonlegislative office or trust. The court declared: "Where a statute merely makes available new machinery and new methods by which particular legislators may keep themselves informed upon specific problems, it cannot be said to have imposed upon them any new office or trust. The additional duties which rest upon the legislative members of the commission are identical in purpose and kind with those which they already perform. [5] As was said in *People v. Tremaine*, 252 N.Y. 27, 41 [168 N.E. 817], 'The duties of members of the Legislature may be enlarged without making a civil appointment or creating a new office, so long as the duties are such as may be properly attached to the legislative office....' We hold, therefore, that the statute here attacked did not contemplate the conferring of any new office, trust, or employment upon the legislative members of this commission." (*Parker v. Riley*, 18 Cal. 2d 83, 88 [113 P.2d 873, 134 A.L.R. 1405].)

In terms of retention of legislative status, there is no meaningful distinction between Parker v. Riley and the present case. Both commissions are hybrid groups, composed in part of officials of the executive branch and in part of legislators. Both possess a mission and function which are essentially advisory. Both are devoid of administrative functions other than those which forward its prime advisory mission. In neither case do the commission's legislator-members assume a nonlegislative character when engaged in commission activities.

Laws creating an immunity from judicial process, however temporary, inevitably trench upon the judicial function, hence may encounter constitutional objections. (See *Thurmond v. Superior Court*, 66 Cal. 2d 836, 839–840 [59 Cal. Rptr. 273, 427 P.2d 985]; *Granai v. Witters, Longmoore, Akley & Brown* (1963) 123 Vt. 468 [194 A.2d 391].) Because we deal with an immunity created by the State Constitution, real parties in interest give the objection a federal coloration by equating access to the courts with the "due process" concept. By analogy to the Thurmond case, supra, they urge that article IV, section 14, can be sustained only by making its application discretionary.

There are conceivable situations where an immunity of this sort might amount to a denial of due process. This is not one of them. The plaintiffs in the superior court are seeking enforcement of a right conferred by state law to demand open meetings of state boards. (Gov. Code, § 11130, fn. 1, *supra*.) In their lawsuit the commission itself is the only indispensable party; the individual members are proper but not necessary parties. (*Moran v. Board of Medical Examiners*, 32 Cal. 2d 301, 314–315 [196 P.2d 20].) Although, in view of the October 1, 1969, demise of the commission, their inability to serve effective process on the legislator-members occurs during a critical period, it does not bar them from relief.

Moreover, the immunity does not expose private citizens to abuse of governmental power untrammeled by judicial restraint. The commission is advisory only. Although it includes three members of the executive branch, its function is analogous to that of a legislative investigating committee. It does not "govern" in the sense that it executes and administers the laws. It has no power to impinge upon the lives, liberty or property of private citizens. "The positions here created do not measure up to so high a standard. They involve merely the interchange of information, the assembling of data, and the formulation of proposals to be placed before the legislature. Such tasks do not require the exercise of a part of the sovereign power of the state." (*Parker v. Riley, supra*, 18 Cal.2d at p. 87.) A statutory scheme clothing legislators with executive-administrative functions would run afoul of the separation of powers principle and of the prohibition against legislators holding nonlegislative office. (Cal. Const., art. III; art. IV, § 13; *Parker v. Riley, supra*, 18 Cal.2d at p. 88; *Springer v. Philippine Islands*, 277 U.S. 189 [72 L. Ed. 845, 48 S. Ct. 480]; *People v. Tremaine*, 252 N.Y. 27 [168 N.E. 817, 822].) Thus, the specter of legislators wielding executive power while armored in immunity from civil process arouses no constitutional tremors.

Let the writ issue as prayed.

PIERCE, P.J., and REGAN, J., concurred.

Notes and Questions

1. While serving in the legislative session, legislators are exempt from civil service of lawsuits. The purpose is to preclude elected officials from being served while they are taking care of the people's business. The constitutional provision exempting legislators from civil process during the legislative session applies generally and without qualification as to kind or subject matter of a lawsuit and it may not be diluted by interpretation to a restricted class of lawsuits.

2. Based upon this court decision, the exemption from civil process applies regardless of whether the legislator is involved in legislative functions. Is that a correct interpretation? Are there instances you envision for when the immunity should not apply?

P. Publications

1. Legislative Publications

In both the California State Assembly and State Senate, there are three major publications: History (generally published each week), Daily File (published each day they are in session), and Daily Journal (published each day they are in session). The Assembly and Senate Daily Journals are tools that can be used to view the official record of the daily transacted business of the Assembly or Senate.

Contained within the Daily Journals is the following information:

- Members' daily attendance
- Roll Call votes taken on the Floor
- All Parliamentary Issues
- Parliamentary Inquiries

- Points of Order
- Motions
- Rulings by the Chair
- All actions taken by the body or its committees such as committee reports and bill introductions
- First, Second, and Third Readings of Bills
- Explanation of votes, absences, etc.
- Official communications such as communications from the Speaker's Office regarding committee appointments; messages from the Governor (veto messages; proclamation of special sessions); messages from the Senate (bills passed by the Senate; concurrence in assembly amendment; appointments to joint committees)
- Statutorily required reports, etc. to committees
- List of amendments considered
- Text of any document ordered printed in the Journal by the house

Essentially the Assembly and Senate Daily Journals are the official records of the proceedings of each house of the California Legislature. Pursuant to the provisions of Joint Rules 14 and 15, and the State Constitution, Article IV, Sec. 7(b), the Assembly and Senate Daily Journals chronicle the proceedings of the Assembly and Senate as the official record of the Houses.

In looking through this publication, you will likely find the following information:

Attendance Roll Call — The Members' attendance roll call is set forth and shows the time at which the quorum was established. Note that a majority of the membership constitutes a quorum. No official actions may be taken on a bill at any time in the absence of a quorum. A minimum of 41 Members (Assembly) or 21 Members (Senate) is necessary to begin conducting business on the Floor.

Opening Business — The prayer and pledge of allegiance to the Flag are the first orders of business on a Floor Session.

Session Absences — All absences are noted in the official record. Letters requesting a leave of absence are submitted to the Speaker (Assembly) or President pro Tempore (Senate) at least one day prior to the absence.

Explanations of Absence — Letters explaining absences on legislative business are printed in the Journal on the day of the excused absence.

Communications — Communications from the Speaker or Senate Rules Committee relative to the creation of Standing, Select, Joint, or Special Committees, or changes thereto, are printed in the Daily Journal under the Communications heading.

Explanation of Votes — A Member may submit an explanation of vote to the Chief Clerk (Assembly) or Secretary (Senate) for entry in the Daily Journal. The explanation may not exceed 50 words in length and does not need to be submitted on the same day the vote was taken.

Messages from the Senate or Assembly—Actions taken in the Senate or Assembly on both Assembly and Senate measures are reported to this House and entered in the official record.

Introduction of Bills—Bills are placed across the Desk for introduction and their First Reading. This is the first of the three required readings by title pursuant to Article IV, Sec. 8(b) of the state Constitution.

Original Bill Referrals—This order of business ratifies the actions of the Rules Committee relative to the assignment of bills to the appropriate policy committee.

Author's Amendments—An author may amend his or her bill in committee as often as necessary prior to the hearing by submitting "pre-committee" author's amendments to the Desk.

Reports of Standing Committees—Reports of Standing Committees are reported to the Desk and recorded in the Daily Journal.

Adjourn in Memory Motion—Requests that the Assembly or Senate adjourn the day's session out of respect to the memory of a deceased individual (i.e., family member, district official, or state dignitary) must be submitted to the Minute Clerk at the Desk prior to Session. The name of the deceased and his or her city of residence is entered in the Journal.

Adjournment—The adjournment on the last page of the Daily Journal includes the names of all individuals for whom the Assembly or Senate adjourns in respect.

Motions to Re-Refer Bills—Amendments may change the subject matter of a bill, making it more aligned with the jurisdiction of another policy committee. A motion to re-refer a bill or resolution from one committee to another committee can be made during the regular order of business.

Request to Print in Journal—Permission of the House is required to print a statement of clarification or legislative intent in the Journal. There are no limits to the length of text.

Second Reading—All bills favorably reported from committee, with or without amendments (i.e., "Do pass, as amended" or "Do pass"), are placed upon the Second Reading File on the next legislative day, whereupon the recommendations of the committee are normally ratified by the house. The second reading of the bill by title satisfies the second of the three required readings by title pursuant to Article IV, Sec. 8(b) of the State Constitution.

Unfinished Business—Assembly bills which were amended in the Senate or Senate bills which were amended in the Assembly are placed upon the Unfinished Business File for concurrence in amendments when they are returned to the house of origin. The house of origin votes on whether to concur or non-concur in the amendments made by the other house.

Unfinished Business—The Unfinished Business File also includes Motions to Reconsider, Consideration of Governor's Vetoes, Conference Committee Reports, Special Orders of Business, and certain other motions.

Third Reading — Bills are taken up for consideration on the Third Reading File for the last of the three required readings by title pursuant to Article IV, Sec. 8(b) of the state Constitution. This is where the bills are debated upon their merits, and voted upon.

Parliamentary Notes — The previous question may be demanded by five Members and, if sustained, debate is closed and the roll is opened on the question before the body.

Move a Call — A Call of the House may be placed, which delays the announcement of the vote and puts the vote on the measure in a pending status to give Members on either side of the pending question an opportunity to gather additional votes. A call must be dispensed with prior to adjournment of that day's Floor session.

Parliamentary Inquiry — A Member may address a question relative to parliamentary procedure to the Presiding Officer.

Point of Order — A point of order is a parliamentary device used by a Member to bring attention to a possible violation of the Rules. The Presiding Officer rules on the validity of the Point of Order by stating either the point is "well-taken" or "not well-taken."

Consent Calendar — Upon recommendation from the Standing Committee, measures are placed upon the Consent Calendar if they are noncontroversial and have never received a "No" vote. The Consent Calendar process enables the House to take a single vote to pass numerous uncontested bills and resolutions without debate.

Daily Amendments — A complete list of all amendments considered by the house, listed in bill number order with the corresponding Legislative Counsel Request Number (RN), is printed on the last page of each day's Journal. The daily total of measures amended and a cumulative Session total are included at the bottom of the page.

All of these publications, including the Daily Journals, are important for tracking legislative activities in the Assembly and Senate. They should be regularly consulted by those who are actively engaged in legislative advocacy at the State Capitol.

Notes and Questions

1. How are these publications useful to capitol observers? What role does each publication play? How do these publications compare and contrast with those produced by the United States Congress?

2. Legislative Daily Journals

Both houses of the legislature publish a Daily Journal in which the proceedings of the Assembly and Senate are published, such as bill introductions, bill referrals, committee reports, and floor votes. While the Daily Journals set forth relevant information, they are not as comprehensive as the *Congressional Record*, for example, which essentially contains verbatim transcripts of committee hearings and floor sessions.

The contents of the Assembly and Senate Journals are prescribed. They are the proceedings of the respective houses. They are not only required to be kept, but also to be published so that the proceedings of each house shall be made known to the people.

Constitutional amendments shall be entered in the Journals, which means that the amendment must be copied or enrolled on the Journal in full. The identical thing must appear on the Journal, not a refence to it in any way. (*Oakland Paving Company v. Hilton* (1886) 69 Cal. 479.) The Journals required by law to be kept are a record of the proceedings of the houses of the legislature.

Notes and Questions

1. The Journals of the houses of the Legislature are not only required to be kept, but to be published, that the proceedings of each house shall be made known to the people. As the Journals of the Senate and Assembly are records and intended to be such, the obvious meaning of entering a proposed amendment in the Journals is to make such amendment a matter of record. The entry of the proposed amendments furnishes, unless perhaps in the case of its loss or destruction, the only evidence of the contents of the amendment proposed. (*Oakland Paving Co. v. Hilton* (1886) 69 Cal. 479.)

Parkinson v. Johnson

(1911) 160 Cal. 756

OPINION

This is a petition for a writ of *mandamus* to be directed to the respondent, as governor of the state of California, commanding him to cause assembly bill No. 208, passed by both houses of the last session of the legislature, to be certified by the secretary of state as a statute of the state.

The following facts are alleged in the petition: that during the last session of the legislature there originated in the assembly a certain bill known as assembly bill No. 208, entitled, "An act to authorize the personal representatives of James Tuohy, deceased, to bring suit against the state of California"; that on February 16, 1911, said assembly bill passed the assembly of the state of California, and on March 6, 1911, said bill passed the senate of said state; that on March 11, 1911, said assembly bill was presented to and received by respondent as governor of the state of California for his consideration as such governor, at which time said bill had been and was properly enrolled and authenticated as prescribed by law; that said assembly bill has not been approved by respondent and was not returned by him to the assembly of the state of California within ten days (excluding Sundays) after said eleventh day of March, 1911; that said bill was not returned by respondent to the assembly until March 24, 1911, on which date it was returned to it by respondent with his objections, and said objections were thereupon and on said March 24, 1911, entered upon the journal of the assembly; that the said journal of the assembly of said March 24, 1911, contains the following entry.

"Messages from the Governor.

"The following messages from the Governor were received and read.

"'SACRAMENTO, CAL. March 23, 1911

"'To the Assembly of the State of California:

"'I return you herewith without my approval Assembly Bill No. 208 entitled, "An act to authorize the personal representatives of James Tuohy, deceased, to bring suit against the state of California." (Here follow the objections stated by the respondent for declining to approve the bill.) For the reasons given I have vetoed the bill.

"'Respectfully submitted,

"'HIRAM W. JOHNSON,

"'Governor of California.'"

That there is no other or different entry of any objections of the respondent to said assembly bill in the journal of the said assembly; that petitioner has demanded of respondent that, as governor, he cause the secretary of state of California to certify on said assembly bill the fact that said bill was not returned by the governor within ten days (Sundays excepted) after its receipt by him, and that said assembly bill became a law.

Upon these alleged facts the petitioner asks for a mandate to respondent commanding him to cause the fact to be certified on the bill, by the secretary of state, as provided by section 1313 of the Political Code, that said assembly bill had remained with the governor ten days (Sundays excepted) and had therefore become a law.

The answer of respondent to the petition admits all the allegations contained therein excepting those relating to his alleged failure to return the bill to the assembly within ten days (Sundays excepted) after it was presented to him, or that the bill was not returned until March 24, 1911.

These particular allegations are denied, and as a separate answer respondent alleges that the assembly bill in question was received at the office of the governor and receipted for by his private secretary on March 11, 1911; that said bill was returned by said private secretary personally to the assembly within ten days (Sundays excepted) thereafter, to wit, on the afternoon of March 23, 1911, with the message from the governor (referred to in the petition) vetoing it; that at the time said bill was returned — on March 23, 1911 — the assembly was in regular session; that said private secretary was duly recognized by the presiding officer of the assembly, and announced that he was delivering to it a message from the governor, and delivered said message with said bill to the proper officer of the said assembly.

A demurrer to the answer was interposed by the petitioner and the matter is before us after argument on the demurrer and the submission thereof.

The constitution, section 10 of article IV, provides that "each house shall keep a journal of its proceedings, and publish the same; and the yeas and nays of the members of either house, on any question, shall, at the desire of any three members present, be entered on the journal."

Section 16 of article IV of the same constitution provides that "every bill which may have passed the legislature shall before it becomes a law be presented to the governor. If he approves it, he shall sign it; but if not, he shall return it, with his objections, to the house in which it originated, which shall enter such objections upon the journal and proceed to reconsider it. If after such reconsideration, it again passes both houses . . . it shall become a law, notwithstanding the governor's objections. If any bill shall not be returned within ten days after it shall have been presented to him (Sundays excepted) the same shall become a law in like manner as if he had signed it, unless the legislature, by adjournment" etc.

These are the only sections of the constitution having any bearing on the question involved here. There is no provision either constitutional or statutory requiring any record to be kept in the office of the governor respecting bills returned by him to the legislature with his veto thereof; nothing requiring any record to be made of the date of the return of such bills; nor is there any provision which requires any officer of either house of the legislature to make any notation or entry upon a bill returned by the governor as to the date or time when it was returned to the house with his objections thereto, or requiring any entry on the journals of either house respecting the return save what is required by section 16 of the constitution above quoted.

There are three ways in which a bill can become a law by the signature of the governor after its passage by the legislature; by the governor retaining a bill without signing it for ten days (Sundays excepted) after its delivery to him and his causing a certificate of the fact to be made on the bill by the secretary of state and the bill deposited with the laws in the office of said secretary; or by the passage of a bill over the veto of the governor. In all these cases if the act is properly enrolled, authenticated, and deposited in the office of the secretary of state, it is conclusive evidence of the legislative will and courts will not look into the journals of the legislature or permit any other evidence to be submitted to determine whether or how a bill passed. *(People v. Burt,* 43 Cal. 560; *Yolo County* v. *Colgan,* 132 Cal. 265, [84 Am. St. Rep. 41, 64 P. 403]; *People* v. *Harlan,* 133 Cal. 16, [65 P. 9].) So that as to all bills upon which there has been favorable action, due enrollment, authentication, and deposit in the office of the secretary of state of such bill is conclusive evidence of the legislative will.

The bill in question here is not found in the office of the secretary of state authenticated as a law of this state. The petitioner, however, seeks to have the respondent compelled to deposit it there with the authentication of the secretary of state thereon as evidence that it had become a law under section 16 of the constitution through the failure of the governor to return it to the assembly where it originated with his objections thereto within ten days after its presentation to him.

In the absence of such deposit and authentication the position of petitioner in this proceeding is that the entry in the journal of the assembly (which respondent admits in his answer is correctly set forth) shows that the bill was not returned by the governor to the assembly until more than ten days (Sundays excepted) after it had been presented to him; that the journal entry is conclusive evidence of this fact and that parol testimony or extraneous evidence cannot be received to dispute, contradict, or vary such recital; that the facts set forth in the answer constitute an attempt on the part of the respondent to contradict by parol evidence the recital of the assembly journal which under the rule contended for by petitioner he insists may not be done and that the demurrer to the answer for these reasons should be sustained.

This is the only point presented on the demurrer and in our judgment it does not require extended discussion because conceding for present purposes that the position of petitioner is correct — that entries in the assembly journals are conclusive as to matters contained therein — they can only be conclusive as to matters which are actually recited therein and which are specifically required to be entered in those journals.

Now when we come to consider the entry in the journal upon which the petitioner relies and the provisions of section 16 of article IV of the constitution, which is the only section that directs specially what shall be entered in the assembly records when a bill is returned by the governor with his objections thereto, we find that the journal in fact contains no entry or recital of the time when the bill was returned by the governor to the assembly, and further that neither the section of the constitution referred to nor any other section requires any such entry.

All that the assembly journal of March 24, 1911, contains respecting the bill here in question is a recital that "the following messages from the governor were received and read," followed by a *verbatim* copy of the objections contained in the veto message accompanying the bill in question here, and the date of the message — March 23, 1911.

This entry only shows that the message was read to the assembly on the twenty-fourth day of March. The fact that it was returned by the governor on that date, or any other date, is nowhere stated in the journal. It is silent on that subject.

But even if the journal entry could be considered as amounting to a recital that the bill accompanied by the objections of the governor was returned by him to the assembly on the twenty-fourth because it is referred to in the journal of the proceedings of the assembly of that date, such recital would not be conclusive upon the matter.

In order to make the journal entries conclusive there must be some provision of the law which requires such entries to be made therein, and as far as making an entry in the journal, as of the time when a bill with his objections is returned to either house of the legislature by the governor, there is no such provision. There are only two pertinent sections of the constitution respecting journal entries involved here, section 10 and section 16 of article IV. Section 10 requires that each house shall keep a journal of "its proceedings" and the return of a bill without his approval by the governor is not a proceeding of either house of the legislature, so there is nothing in this section referred to which requires such entry. In fact, petitioner does not claim that it does. He relies particularly on section 16, but an examination of that section will show there is nothing contained in it requiring any such entry.

Under our constitution the governor is a component part of the law-making power of the state. To him all bills must be submitted for action before becoming laws, and all that section 16 requires (as far as pertinent here) in discharge of his duty as a part of the legislative branch of the government with respect to such bills is, that if he dis-

approves any of them he must return it to either house within ten days (Sundays excepted) after he receives it, with his objections. When this is done the duty of the
governor is discharged and the duty to be performed by the house where the bill
originated and to which it is returned, arises, and that duty is simply to enter the objections of the executive upon the journal and proceed to consider the bill. There is
not a word in the section which requires that any entry shall be made in the journal
respecting the time when the bill is returned by the governor.

And we would hardly expect to find a provision requiring such an entry and to
which the conclusive evidence rule would apply; the effect of such a provision would
be to make inadvertent and erroneous recitals in the journal of one branch of the
legislative power control the action of the executive as another branch thereof, and
by such recitals defeat the veto power constitutionally vested in the latter, and which
he had in due time properly exercised.

As all acts of the legislature receiving favorable consideration are enrolled, authenticated, and deposited with the secretary of state, and when this is properly done
are conclusive evidence of the legislative will, it is only in extremely rare cases that
it will become necessary to resort elsewhere to ascertain whether an act not so found
in the office of the secretary of state did in fact become a law. This is one of these
rare cases, where the journals of the assembly are resorted to under a claim that there
are recitals therein which are conclusive evidence that the governor failed to return
the bill in question with his veto thereof within the time allowed by the constitution,
and hence it became a law. But, as we have pointed out, there is no provision in the
constitution which requires any such entry of the date of return to be set forth in the
journal of the assembly, and in fact it contains no such entry. If it did it would not
be conclusive, because the conclusive evidence rule can only apply to such entries as
are constitutionally required to be set out in the journal.

On the hearing of this demurrer it was admitted by petitioner, while insisting on
the conclusiveness of the record, that he could not question the truth of the fact set
forth in the answer respecting the return of the bill by the governor on March 23d,
as stated therein.

The demurrer to the answer is overruled, and as the facts set forth in the answer are
in effect admitted to be true by petitioner, it is not necessary to proceed further in this
matter, and therefore the petition for a peremptory writ of mandate is dismissed.

ANGELLOTTI, J., SHAW, J., HENSHAW, J., SLOSS, J., and MELVIN, J., concurred.

Notes and Questions

1. The Daily Journals provide important information regarding the daily proceedings of the California Legislature when they are in session. Where a bill, after having
been passed by the Legislature, had been properly enrolled, authenticated and deposited in the office of the Secretary of State, it having been either signed by the Governor, retained by him without signing and the fact certified to by him, or passed
over his veto, it is conclusive evidence of the legislative will, and courts would not

look to the Journals of the Legislature or permit any other evidence to be submitted in order to determine whether or how the bill passed.

2. There is nothing in Article IV, Section 16 which requires that any entry shall be made in the Journal respecting the time when a bill is returned by the Governor. Where the date on which a bill was returned by the Governor with his disapproval is disputed, evidence outside of entries in the Journal is admissible to establish that fact.

3. The recital in the Journal of the Assembly of a particular date to the effect that "the following messages from the Governor were received and read," followed by a copy of his objections in his veto message accompanying a bill, and the date of the message, only shows that the message was read to the Assembly on the date of the Journal entry, and is not a recital that it was returned by the Governor on that date. *Parkinson v. Johnson* (1911) 160 Cal. 756

4. A branch of the Legislature has power to require and compel attendance of witnesses and the production of documents before it or its duly accredited committees. (*In re Battelle* (1929) 207 Cal. 227.) The State Senate has the power to punish a person for contempt, but such power can only be exercised in strict conformity with the rules of procedure which the laws provide. (*In re Application of Battelle* (1929) 207 Cal. 227.)

5. The Court in *Parkinson* ruled that entries in the assembly Journals are conclusive as to matters contained therein. Specifically, "the conclusive evidence rule can only apply to such entries as are constitutionally required to be set out in the Journal."

6. Where an enacted bill is properly enrolled, authenticated, and deposited in the office of the Secretary of State, it is conclusive evidence of the legislative will, and courts will not look into the Journals of the Legislature or permit any other evidence to be submitted to determine whether or how a bill passed. (*People v. Burt* (1872) 43 Cal. 560; *Yolo County v. Colgan* (1901) 132 Cal. 265.)

3. Validity of Statutes in Journals

The validity of a statute does not depend upon the failure or omission of the Journals to show affirmatively that such requirements were in fact complied with.

Yolo County v. Colgan

(1901) 132 Cal. 265

OPINION

THE COURT.

. . . .

The respondent contends that said statutes were superseded and rendered inoperative by the County Government Act of 1883; or if not, that they were directly repealed, so far as said fees and commissions are concerned, by an act approved February 23, 1893 (Stats. 1893, p. 5), except as to commissions paid to the assessors of the several counties for services in the collection of personal property taxes, as provided by chapter VIII of the Political Code, and except, also, as to the mileage allowed the county treasurers in making settlements with the state, under section 3876 of the same code, and as to which there is no controversy.

The petitioner — appellant here — contends that said repealing act never became a law, because it did not receive, in the senate, the number of votes required by the constitutional provision that "no bill shall become a law without the concurrence of a majority of the members elected to each house."

The court found that the journal of the senate showed that the vote on said bill was, ayes, twenty, noes, three; twenty-one being a majority of the senators elected.

The question whether the validity of a statute duly certified, approved, enrolled, and deposited in the office of the secretary of state can be impeached by a resort to the journals of the legislature has been long controverted, and the conclusions reached in the courts of last resort of the different states are inharmonious and conflicting, and this want of harmony is frequently found in the different decisions in the same state, and this remark is not entirely inapplicable to the state of California.

In *Fowler v. Pierce,* 2 Cal. 165, it was held that the court may go behind the record evidence of a statute, and inquire whether it was passed or approved in accordance with the constitution. The case of *Sherman v. Story,* 30 Cal. 253, decided in 1866, overruled *Fowler v. Pierce, supra,* and it was held that "neither the journals of the legislature, nor the bill as originally introduced, nor the amendments attached to it, nor parol evidence, can be received in order to show that an act of the legislature properly enrolled, authenticated, and deposited with the secretary of state either did not become a law in accordance with the prescribed forms, or did not become a law as enrolled. 89 Am. Dec. 93.

The opinion of the court in that case was delivered by Mr. Justice Sawyer. It is too long to be quoted here, and any attempt at condensation would weaken its force. In it will be found not only cogent arguments in support of the conclusions reached, but many authorities entitled to the highest consideration.

In *Oroville etc. R.R. Co. v. Plumas County,* 37 Cal. 355, the invalidity of an act of the legislature was alleged, upon the ground that its passage was procured by fraud. The court, by Rhodes, J., said "An act of the legislature is not subject to attack on that ground; and it is sufficient on this point to refer to *Sherman v. Story,* 30 Cal. 266." 89 Am. Dec. 93.

In *Harpending v. Haight,* 39 Cal. 189, the question was presented, whether the motive of the mover of a resolution to adjourn the senate was to prevent thereby the executive from returning the bill with his vote. Wallace, J., held the evidence incompetent; citing *Sherman v. Story, supra.* 2 Am. Rep. 432.

In *People v. Burt,* 43 Cal. 560, the court, by Belcher, J., said: "If an act is properly enrolled, authenticated, and deposited with the secretary of state, it is conclusive evidence of the will of the legislature at the time of its passage"; citing *Sherman v. Story, supra.*

In *Oakland Paving Co. v. Hilton,* 69 Cal. 480, a proposed amendment to the constitution was referred to in the journals of the senate and assembly as senate bill No. 10, but was not copied at large in the respective journals. It was held by Thornton,

J., and McKee, J., that the failure to enter the proposed amendment at large in the journals was in violation of section 1 of article XVIII of the constitution, and that the amendment never took effect. The opinion was written by Thornton, J., who said: "There is nothing here in conflict with what is said in *Sherman v. Story, supra.*"

In *People v. Dunn,* 80 Cal. 211, it was contended by the respondent that "every act not shown by the journals to have taken place must be presumed not to have been done." The court said that this contention cannot be upheld by reason or authority, and that the question as to the power of the court to go behind the enrolled bill in order to determine from the journals whether the bill was properly passed, was not presented. *Hale v. McGettigan,* 114 Cal. 112, was similarly disposed of. It was said (pp. 114, 115): "It is, however, unnecessary for us to determine in the present case whether the journals of either branch of the legislature may, under any circumstances, be examined for the purpose of impeaching the validity of an act that has been duly enrolled and deposited with the secretary of state, since we are of the opinion that it does not appear from those journals that the act in question was not constitutionally passed." 13 Am. St. Rep. 118.

It is clear, even upon the authority of those cases which hold that the journals may be looked into to determine whether a bill has been passed in conformity to the requirements of the constitution, that the validity of the statute does not depend upon the failure or omission of the journals to show affirmatively that such requirements were in fact complied with, and hence the correctness of the decisions in *People v. Dunn, supra,* and *Hale v. McGettigan, supra,* cannot be questioned; yet it is equally clear that if the enrolled statute in the office of the secretary of state is conclusive, and unimpeachable by the legislative journals, each of those cases could have been decided with equal propriety upon that ground. These cases have therefore been regarded as somewhat weakening the force of *Sherman v. Story, supra,* and *People v. Burt, supra. Weill v. Kenfield,* 54 Cal. 111, is cited with much confidence by appellant. The report of that case contains no statement of the points or authorities of counsel, nor is any decision of this court, or any other, cited in the opinion. The question we are now considering is not even suggested in it. There was no controversy in that case as to what transpired in the assembly in relation to the passage of the act, it being conceded that only the title and the first few words of the bill were read, the question considered being whether such reading fulfilled the requirement of the constitution in that regard. Here, what transpired in the senate is the very point in controversy, — appellant contending that the journal contains the only competent evidence, while respondent insists that the enrolled act, duly signed, approved, and filed with the secretary of state, is the conclusive evidence that the bill did receive the vote of a majority of the members elected to each house. If it were here conceded that the bill in question received but twenty votes in the senate, *Weill v. Kenfield, supra,* would be in point. Indeed, in such case there could be no controversy.

The learned justice (McKinstry) who wrote the opinion in *Weill v. Kenfield, supra,* in a later case (*People v. Thompson,* 67 Cal. 628), though placing the decision upon a different ground, made some remarks tending strongly to sustain the proposition that the enrolled statute should be held conclusive. That was a petition for a writ of mandate directing the secretary of state to certify that the petitioners had been duly elected as members of Congress in Congressional districts created by the act of 1872, claiming that the act of 1883, under which the election was proclaimed by the governor, was invalid because of non-compliance by the legislature with certain formalities required by the constitution, the petitioners having received a few votes each in the old districts, while the great mass of the people observed the new law and voted in the new districts. The decision was based upon the ground that the proclamation giving notice of the election according to the law must control, whether it was valid or not. It was there said: "Courts of justice in this state take judicial notice, perhaps, of the contents of the journals of the two houses of the legislature; the citizens at large are not required to take legal notice of the entries of the journals. The people had not been actually notified of such entries when the election was held. They had before them (let us assume) the statute of 1883, approved by the governor, and published as statutes are required to be published, and the governor's proclamation. We are asked to decide that all the voters should have inquired whether the statute was invalid by reason of matters of which they had not been notified; that the duty was imposed upon them to make investigation into the history in the legislature of the bill for the act of 1883, and to consider questions as to the validity of the law arising out of the proceedings in the legislature which preceded its final passage."

Here is an actual case practically illustrating the confusion and uncertainty which must inevitably result from the doctrine contended for by appellant.

Appellant also cites *Stevenson v. Colgan,* 91 Cal. 649, and *Popper v. Broderick,* 123 Cal. 456. The first of these cases is distinguished by the court from those cases where it has been held that the court may look into the journals of the legislature for the purpose of determining whether a statute was in fact passed by the requisite vote required by the constitution; but the court said: "While the courts have undoubted power to declare a statute invalid when it appears to them, in the course of judicial action, to be in conflict with the constitution, yet they can only do so when the question arises as a pure question of law, unmixed with matters of fact, the existence of which must be determined upon a trial, and as the result of, it may be, conflicting evidence." This proposition utterly destroys appellant's contention, since whether a bill was passed by a majority vote is a question of fact which could only be established by evidence of what took place in the legislature. In the case of *Popper v. Broderick, supra,* no question here involved was presented or discussed. 25 Am. St. Rep. 230.

From this review of the case in this court it appears that the case of *Sherman v. Story, supra,* has not been followed in some cases where it might have been, the decision being reached upon other grounds; that it has been quoted and followed in two cases, distinguished in another, and that in the only case directly conflicting with it, the opposite doctrine was assumed without discussion, upon conceded facts, and without reference to that case or any other.

We are referred by appellant to *County of San Mateo v. Southern Pacific Co.,* 8 Saw. 238, 294, where the same learned justice who wrote the opinion in *Sherman v.*

Story, supra, afterwards, as United States circuit judge, said: "While we think the case of *Sherman v. Story* correctly decided under the constitution as it then was, we are of the opinion that the change in the constitution requires a change in the rule, and such seems to be the view of the supreme court of California in *Weill v. Kenfield,* 54 Cal. 111"; and cites *Spangler v. Jacoby,* 14 Ill. 297, and *Prescott v. Board of Trustees,* 19 Ill. 326, saying that California adopted the said provision in its present constitution substantially as found in the constitution of Illinois. But this change in the constitution does not affect the rule that the record consisting of the enrolled statute in the office of the secretary of state cannot be impeached by evidence of any fact outside of such record, as was clearly shown in the opinion of the same justice in *Sherman v. Story, supra.* If it could be, then, before it can be determined what the law is in any given case, resort must be had to the journals of the legislature, which are often imperfect and erroneous, and different courts might readily differ in their conclusions as to whether the evidence obtained from the journals did or did not show that the requirements of the constitution had been complied with. We are not bound, however, by this decision of a Federal court, not only because our conclusion upon the question cannot be reviewed by that court, but because the supreme court of the United States has reached a different conclusion. 58 Am. Dec. 571, and note.

    ....

In appellant's brief we find a statement of the amounts directed by the legislature to be raised for state purposes for five fiscal years there named, ending with that of 1897–98, and of the amounts actually collected and paid into the state treasury for the same years, from which it appears that the amount collected exceeds the amount directed to be raised by $1,244,847.54, and the question is asked, "Does not this surplus money belong to the counties?" Whether it does or not is immaterial in this proceeding, as it was not included in petitioner's demand.

Appellant also refers to "An act authorizing the allowance, settlement, and payment of claims of counties against the state," approved March 9, 1893. (Stats. 1893, p. 109.) This statute did not create or fix any fees or charges against the state, but provided for the allowance of fees and commissions which, having been paid into the state treasury, might be allowed in the next settlement. There is no inconsistency between this act and the abolishing act previously passed, since claims which had accrued to the counties prior to the repeal were not affected by it, and besides, "the abolishing act" expressly excepted from its operation certain fees or commissions therein named, to which the later act might properly apply.

Respondent refers to an act approved February 16, 1899 (Stats. 1899, p. 9), to prevent the maintenance of any action for the recovery of the fees and commissions such as are here in question, which provides that "all such actions and proceedings heretofore commenced and now pending, and all such actions or proceedings that may hereafter be instituted, shall be dismissed by the court in which the same may be pending upon its own motion"; but this act excepts the fees and commissions which were excepted by the said "abolishing act." In view of the conclusion reached as to the validity of said "abolishing act," this act need not be considered.

We think the court below did not err in denying the writ, and advise that the judgment appealed from be affirmed.

CHIPMAN, C., and COOPER, C., concurred.

For the reasons given in the foregoing opinion the judgment appealed from is affirmed.

GAROUTTE, J., HENSHAW, J., MCFARLAND, J., VAN DYKE, J., TEMPLE, J., and HARRISON, J., dissented.

Rehearing denied.

Notes and Questions

1. How does this decision comport with the Enrolled Bill Rule? In general, the Journals may be looked into to determine whether a bill has been passed in conformity with the requirements of the Constitution. However, the validity of the statute does not depend upon the failure or omission of the Journals to show affirmatively that such requirements were in fact complied with.

2. The Court found that the Journal of the Senate showed that the vote on the bill was twenty ayes, with twenty-one votes being a majority of the Senators elected. If that is the case, how was the statute validly enacted? Did it actually comply with constitutional requirements?

3. "The law-making power of the state is vested, by the constitution, in the legislature; and while the constitution has prescribed the formalities to be observed in the passage of bills and the creation of statutes, the power to determine whether these formalities have been complied with is necessarily vested in the legislature itself, since, if it were not, it would be powerless to enact a statute. The constitution has not provided that this essential power thus vested in the legislature shall be subject to review by the courts...." (*County of Yolo v. Colgan* (1901) 132 Cal. 265, 274–275.)

4. No Impeachment of Statutes by Journals

The courts have generally determined that the validity of a statute cannot be challenged by a review of the *Daily Journal*. The validity of a statute which has been duly certified, approved, enrolled, and deposited in the office of the secretary of state cannot be impeached by a resort to the Journals of the legislature.

People v. Camp

(1919) 42 Cal.App. 411

OPINION

HART, J. —

On the 16th of October, 1914, defendant, having been convicted by a jury of the crime of "lewd and lascivious conduct with and upon the body of a male child under the age of fourteen years," was sentenced by the superior court of the county of Sacramento to imprisonment in the state prison for the term of fifteen years.

On the twenty-first day of January, 1919, defendant made a motion "that an order be made and entered herein vacating and setting aside the conviction and judgment for want of jurisdiction in said court." An order to show cause was issued and, after a hearing, the motion was by the court denied and the defendant remanded to the custody of the warden of the state prison. The appeal is by the defendant from the order denying said motion.

It is stated in the grounds of appeal that said order is "contrary to law and that said conviction and judgment are void on the face of the record, for want of jurisdiction in said superior court over the subject matter of the action and that said judgment in said action is also void because in excess of the authority of said superior court to the extent that the sentence therein specified exceeds the term of five years."

Defendant was tried and convicted under the provisions of section 288 of the Penal Code, which reads as follows: "Any person who shall willfully and lewdly commit any lewd or lascivious act other than the acts constituting other crimes provided for in part two of this code upon or with the body, or any part or member thereof, of a child under the age of fourteen years, with the intent of arousing, appealing to, or gratifying the lust or passions or sexual desires of such person or of such child, shall be guilty of a felony and shall be imprisoned in the state prison not less than one year."

Appellant urges the following points as grounds for reversal of said order: That said section 288 is void for the following reasons: (1) That the same, after being amended in the senate, was not read at length in the assembly; (2) That it is in violation of section 24 of article IV of the constitution, in that the subject of the act is not expressed in the title, but on the contrary the act itself explicitly negatives and contradicts the subject expressed in the title; (3) That it is in violation of subdivisions 2 and 33 of section 25, article IV, of the constitution; (4) That it operates to deny to the defendant the equal protection of the laws guaranteed him by the fourteenth amendment of the constitution of the United States; (5) That it operates to deprive defendant of his liberty without due process of law, in violation of the fourteenth amendment; (6) That the act is incurably uncertain, vague and unintelligible in that it cannot be ascertained what lewd and lascivious acts are prohibited, as the statute refers to part *two* of the Penal Code, which relates solely to criminal procedure; and that the courts are denied the power to strike out from said section "part two" and substitute "part one"; that so to amend the section is to deprive defendant of his liberty without due process of law, in violation of said fourteenth amendment; (7) That said section and said judgment are in violation of article I, section 6, of the constitution, in that they inflict unusual punishment; (8) That the conduct of which defendant has been convicted is made a misdemeanor by sections 273 and 273g of the Penal Code and is, therefore, expressly excluded from section 288; (9) That section 288 has been repealed by section 28 of the juvenile court law of 1913; (10) That by section 18 of the Penal Code the maximum penalty for a violation of section 288 is five years, which the defendant has served.

Most, if indeed, not all, of the objections to section 288 of the Penal Code urged here on constitutional grounds have been decided adversely to the position of the appellant by the courts. The objections will, nevertheless, be given some notice.

It has been so often held in this state that it is no longer an open question that the validity of a statute, which had been duly certified, enrolled and approved, and deposited in the office of the Secretary of State, cannot be impeached by a resort to the journals of the legislature, or by extrinsic evidence of any character. (*Sherman* v. *Story,* 30 Cal. 253, [89 Am. Dec. 93]; *County of Yolo v. Colgan,* 132 Cal. 265, [84 Am. St. Rep. 41, 64 P. 403]; *Kingsbury v. Nye,* 9 Cal.App. 574, 577, [99 P. 985]. See, also, *De Loach, et al. v. Newton,* 134 Ga. 739, [68 S.E. 708]; *State of Washington v. Jones,* 6 Wn. 452, [23 L.R.A. 340, 34 P. 201]; *Field v. Clark,* 143 U.S. 672, [36 L.Ed. 294, 12 Sup. Ct. Rep. 495, see also Rose's U.S. Notes].)

This point requires no further consideration herein than such as is involved in the citation of these cases.

The title to section 288 of the Penal Code, as it was enacted by the legislature of 1901 (Stats. 1901, p. 630), reads as follows: "An act to amend the Penal Code by adding a new section thereto, to be numbered section two hundred and eighty-two, relating to crimes against children." Thus, it will be observed that the title of the act states generally that the crimes which the section is designed to punish are those perpetrated upon or against children. It was not necessary, to make the act conform to the requirements of the constitution in that respect, to embrace in its title a specification of the nature of the crimes to which the section relates; and the courts of this state have held that such a title as was contained in the act in question, being an amendment of one of the codes, sufficiently expresses the subject of the act as required by section 24 of article IV of the constitution. (See *People v. Dobbins,* 73 Cal. 257, [14 P. 860]; *Ex parte Liddell,* 93 Cal. 633, [29 P. 251]; *People v. Lovren,* 119 Cal. 88, [51 P. 22, 638]; *Jackson v. Baehr,* 138 Cal. 266, [71 P. 167]; *County of Butte v. Merrill,* 141 Cal. 396, 398, [74 P. 1036]; *People v. Oates,* 142 Cal. 12, [75 P. 337]; *People v. Merritt,* 18 Cal.App. 58, [122 P. 839, 844].)

Nor can we perceive any merit in the contention that the act itself contradicts or is in any wise inconsistent with its title. The title, as we have seen, declares that the subject of the act involves certain crimes against children, and the act itself specifically sets forth the acts constituting the crimes to which the title refers. In other words, the title declares in general terms the nature of the legislation of which it is a sort of preamble and that it has relation to certain crimes against children, and the act itself describes or defines the particular kind of act constituting the crime thus intended to be included among those provided for in other sections of the Penal Code against the same class of persons and which define as such crimes acts of a different nature from that constituting the basis of the legislation involved in section 288. It is, therefore, very clear that, when compared to the act itself, no inconsistency between them can be discerned, nor can it be said, when so compared, that the title is misleading or calculated to deceive or convey an erroneous impression as to the subject of the legislation involved in the act.

Section 288 does not involve special legislation within the meaning or contemplation of subdivision 2 of section 25, article IV, of the state constitution. The act applies to all children under fourteen years of age or to all of a class. It has been held time and again that an act of the legislature which applies uniformly upon the whole or any single class of individuals or objects, when the classification is founded upon some natural, intrinsic or constitutional distinction, is a general law. (See cases cited in Treadwell's Constitution, p. 255.) That children or minors constitute a class founded upon a natural or intrinsic distinction and as to whom legislation peculiarly applicable to individuals of their immature years is necessary for their proper protection, are propositions which cannot well be controverted. As to some matters in connection with the welfare of minors, particularly those not beyond or far beyond their infancy, a general law, in the more comprehensive sense of that phrase, could not be made. Section 288 is particularly directed to the prevention and punishment of lewd and lascivious conduct with and upon the bodies of children under fourteen years of age, because, as a rule, it may properly be assumed they are not sufficiently matured mentally to appreciate as fully as older persons the consequences to them, both morally and physically, of such acts of degeneracy, and they, therefore, generally have neither the judgment nor the physical power, which in such cases is often minimized where there is no developed mental power, to protect themselves against the perpetration upon them of such outrages which it is the object of this law to prevent, if it can be done, or to punish where such acts have been done. Such crimes as the one denounced by section 288 are (we think experience shows to be true) ordinarily committed by persons of mature years or who at any rate are old enough to know that the inevitable tendency of conduct so abnormal and utterly diabolical is to corrupt the morals of children and to make them what the perpetrator of such a crime himself is. It was, therefore, quite natural that the people should by their constitution authorize the enactment of laws for the special protection of a class of persons not of sufficient mental and physical development by reason of their youth to protect themselves against those human parasites who make a practice of satiating in a measure their abnormal sexual appetites by that sort of conduct with such minors.

The contention that section 288 denies to persons prosecuted under its provisions the equal protection of the law contrary to the mandates of the first section of the fourteenth amendment of the federal constitution is founded upon the theory that, while said section makes the act therein denounced as criminal a felony, other sections of the Penal Code relating to crimes against children make the acts specified therein misdemeanors only. In support of this argument, counsel refers to sections 272, 273, 273g, and 650 1/2 of said code. None of these sections, however, relates to lewd and lascivious acts *"upon or with the body, or any member thereof, of a child under the age of fourteen years."* But section 273g does relate to such practices in the presence of any child. It provides: "Any person who in the presence of any child indulges in any degrading, lewd, immoral or vicious habits or practices, or who is habitually drunk in the presence of any child in his care, custody or control, is guilty of a misdemeanor." That section was undoubtedly intended to include those cases only where the lewd or immoral conduct is carried on in the presence of children and where the same is not practiced upon or with the body of the child. Furthermore, said section includes all children without regard to their age, while section 288 is confined in its operation to children under the age of fourteen years. Section 650 1/2 makes it a misdemeanor for any person to do certain acts or things in derogation of the rights of property or of the person of an individual, and, among other things, provides that the rights of person are violated and punishable as above indicated when the name of a person is used by another for the accomplishment of lewd or licentious purposes, etc. This section obviously has no bearing upon nor is the subject matter or the object thereof analogous to the crime defined by section 288. The other sections (272 and 273), while prohibiting and penalizing the abuse or misuse of minors, do not relate or refer to acts of lewdness or lasciviousness either with the body of a child or in the presence of children without practicing the same upon or with their bodies. It follows that there is no discrimination involved in our code sections with respect to acts of lewdness or lasciviousness upon or with or in the presence of children. Indeed, there is a marked distinction between the several crimes denounced by the Penal Code for such acts. It is quite true that the crimes referred to may, in a general sense, be said to be correlated, as are robbery and larceny, because of possessing a certain element in common. Both these last-named crimes involve the element of the felonious taking from another his personal property, but they are essentially differentiated by reason of the fact that the stealing in the one case is accomplished by means of force or fear, while in the other a less violent method is resorted to. So, in the case before us. It is true that the act of lewdness or lasciviousness penalized by section 288 involves some of the elements to be found in section 273g. Indeed, it involves some of the elements involved in the crime of rape or the infamous crime against nature, but there are features in those crimes which not only distinguish them one from the other, but which distinguish them from any other crime denounced in our statutes involving acts appertaining, either directly or indirectly, to sexual relations. Upon such distinction it is competent for the legislature to annex a different punishment for the different crimes, and in doing this the legislature will be, and presumptively has always been, governed by the nature of the acts constituting the crime, or, in the case of penal statutes for the prevention of crimes against children, fix the penalty in accordance with the effect that the prohibited acts would naturally have upon that class of persons (and consequently upon society), taking into consideration their age, where that element is important in the determination of such effect, or disregarding the fact of age where it cannot logically or in the nature of the case enter as a factor into the determination of such effect. Of course, no one will question the constitutional authority of the legislature to fix the penalty to suit the crime, or, in other words, to fix different penalties for different crimes, the penalty in each case being measured or fixed according to the nature of the particular crime and its effect upon society. (See *People v. Barbieri*, 33 Cal.App. 770, 780, [166 P. 812]; *Ex parte Selowsky*, 38 Cal.App. 569, [177 P. 301]; *Selowsky v. Superior Court*, 180 Cal. 404, [181 P. 652].) It follows from the foregoing that section 288, either when taken alone or when considered in comparison with the other sections of the Penal Code above named, in no way impinges upon rights guaranteed by the fourteenth amendment of the constitution of the United States, or has the effect of denying to a person prosecuted under its provisions the equal protection of the law or depriving him of his liberty without due process of law. Nor does the section authorize the infliction of unusual punishment within the meaning of the inhibition in that respect of section 6 of article I of the state constitution. (See *Wilkerson v. Utah,* 99 U.S. 130, [25 L.Ed. 345]; *Ex parte Kemmler,* 136 U.S. 436, [34 L.Ed. 519, 10 Sup. Ct. Rep. 930, see also, Rose's U.S. Notes]; *People v. Finley,* 153 Cal. 59, [94 P. 248].)

There is not imparted to section 288 uncertainty or ambiguity or unintelligibleness as to its meaning or intent by reason of the fact that "part two" instead of "part one" is therein erroneously referred to as defining crimes involving in their composition, among other elements, that of lewd or lascivious conduct, which specific conduct is by said section excepted from the operation thereof. Part 2 of the Penal Code relates entirely to the procedure in criminal cases, while part one contains the definition of the several crimes and the penalties annexed thereto. It is, therefore, plainly manifest that the reference by section 288 to "part two" in the connection in which it is therein used was due, not to the intention of the legislature, but to inadvertence or an oversight — a mistake of the printer.

At any rate, it is, as stated, very clear that the legislature did not intend in said section to refer to "part two" of the Penal Code, for such a reference would make the section an absurdity, and it is one of the cardinal rules of statutory construction that, if, by giving to a word or a phrase in a statute its literal meaning, absurd consequences would be the inevitable result, then the literal meaning thereof must be disregarded and such a meaning ascribed thereto, consistent, of course, with the general context and the evident object of the act, as will render the act not only consistent in all its parts, but reasonable in its effect and, therefore, effectual for the purposes for which it was intended. The validity of the identical section was challenged upon precisely the same ground in *People v. Bradford,* 1 Cal.App. 41, [81 P. 712], and the views and the conclusion expressed and arrived at in that case are in harmony with the views above expressed.

Counsel for the defendant contends, however, that the rules of statutory construction which are applied in the Bradford case have application to statutes regulating or defining civil rights and not to penal statutes or legislative acts defining crimes and fixing their penalties, referring to sections 388, 411, 498, 521, and 524 of Sutherland on Statutory Construction, second edition and the case of *Ex parte McNulty,* 77 Cal. 164, [11 Am. St. Rep. 257, 19 P. 237], as supporting that proposition. We fully agree with what is said in the California case named, that "Constructive crimes — crimes built up by courts with the aid of inference, implication and strained interpretation — are repugnant to the spirit and letter of English and American criminal law," but we do not assent to the proposition that that case holds or that Sutherland declares the rule to be that the rules of statutory construction are not, generally, as well applicable to the construction of statutes defining crimes as to the construction of statutes concerning civil rights. There is nothing in the matter of the construction of section 288 but the simple question whether the legislature *intended* to refer therein to a part of the Penal Code which would make said section mean something and what it was obviously intended to mean or to a part of said code which would render the section not only absurd but in truth nonsensical; and manifestly, it requires under the circumstances present here no strained interpretation, nor does it amount to the building up of a "constructive crime," to find that the legislature intended to refer in said section to part one and not to part two of the Penal Code, and that the reference therein to part two is the result of an inadvertence.

There is no merit, so far as the record before us shows, in the point that the "judgment and verdict do not show a violation of section 288 of the Penal Code," and, therefore, "the offense not being within section 288, the superior court had no jurisdiction to sentence the appellant to the state prison." The argument addressed to the support of this point is that, while the said section defines the crime therein denounced as the commission of "any lewd or lascivious act … upon or with the *body* … of a child," etc., the verdict was that defendant was guilty "of the crime of lewd and lascivious conduct with a male child under the age of fourteen years, a felony, as charged in the indictment," and the judgment was in similar phraseology. It will be noticed that neither the verdict nor the judgment stated or declared that the crime of which defendant was convicted was committed "upon and with the *body*," etc.

The indictment upon which the defendant was prosecuted and convicted is not in the record here. We must, therefore, presume, in this collateral attack upon the judgment, that the indictment sufficiently stated the offense defined by section 288 by following substantially and in all essential particulars the language thereof; and so viewing the indictment, the verdict sufficiently finds that the crime denounced by said section was committed by the accused by the use of the general language therein contained, viz.: "*a felony, as charged in the indictment.*" The "judgment" involving the pronouncement of sentence in a criminal case is generally orally rendered and delivered and is usually in informal language, and the law requires it to be no more than that. (Pen. Code, sec. 1202; *People. v. Terrill*, 133 Cal. 120, 123, [65 P. 303].) The record of a criminal action consists of the following papers: 1. The indictment or information, and a copy of the minutes of the plea or demurrer; 2. A copy of the minutes of the trial; 3. The written instructions, etc.; and 4. A copy of the judgment. "The judgment need not and it was not intended that it should repeat anything contained in the papers which precede it, for in view of the fact that they go into the record and make a part of it, such repetition would be idle and serve no useful purpose. The only material parts of a judgment are the statement of the offense for which the defendant has been convicted, omitting therefrom all that is contained in the previous papers and therefore not necessary to be repeated, and the sentence of the court." (Ex *parte Williams*, 89 Cal. 421, 426, 427, [26 P. 887, 889].) If the judgment with sufficient clearness shows that it is the pronouncement of sentence by the court upon the verdict as returned and the penalty imposed by such sentence is authorized by the statute under which the prisoner has been convicted, then the judgment satisfies the demand of the statute in that respect. The mere omission by the court, in passing sentence on the prisoner, to state or describe the offense with technical precision, certainly should not, in reason, be held to have the effect of rendering the judgment of sentence void or even voidable. Of course, all this is upon the assumption that the verdict finds the crime as charged and that the charge, as we are authorized to assume is true here, is correctly described in the indictment. The statement in the judgment that, "Whereas, the said Charles Camp has been duly convicted in this court of the crime of lewd and lascivious conduct with a male child under the age of fourteen years," implies that he has been convicted of the offense shown by the verdict upon which the judgment must necessarily rest, and, therefore, further implies that the offense for which he was sentenced embraced all the vital elements constituting the offense as it is defined by the statute, just as a judgment of sentence for murder upon a verdict convicting the accused of that crime implies, without stating it in the judgment, the unlawful taking of human life deliberately and with malice aforethought. As sustaining the foregoing views, we cite the following cases in addition to those above referred to: *Matter of Ring,* 28 Cal. 248, 253; *Ex parte Gibson,* 31 Cal. 619, [91 Am. Dec. 546]; *Ex parte Raye,* 63 Cal. 491; *People v. Murback,* 64 Cal. 369, 372, [30 P. 608].

There is absolutely no ground for the contention that section 288 has been repealed by section 28 of the so-called juvenile court law. (Stats. 1913, p. 1303.) So much of said section as pertains to the penalty for the offense therein referred to reads as follows: "Any person who shall commit any act or omit the performance of any duty, which act or omission causes or tends to cause, encourage or contribute to the dependency or delinquency of any person under the age of twenty-one years, as defined by any law of this state, or any person who shall, by any act or omission, threats or commands or persuasion, endeavor to induce any such person, under twenty-one years of age, to do or to perform any act or follow any course of conduct, or to so live as would cause or manifestly tend to cause any such person to become, or to remain a dependent or delinquent person, ... shall be punished by a fine not exceeding one thousand dollars, or imprisonment in the county jail for not more than one year, or by both such fine and imprisonment." The design of that law is, so far as a penal statute can go in the accomplishment of so laudable a purpose, to protect minors against those acts and temptations which, if allowed to be practiced and to exist, will surely lead them into habits involving acts of the grossest depravity. Section 3 of the law enumerates and describes eight different acts of omission and commission any or all of which will constitute a minor a dependent person. Section 4 of said act provides that a "delinquent person" is one who violates any law of the state, or any ordinance of any city, town, etc., defining crime and which involves moral turpitude. Among the variety of acts enumerated in section 3 as constituting the dependency of a minor, neither the act of sexual commerce nor that of lewd and lascivious conduct with or upon a minor is specifically or *eo nomine* named or mentioned. There can be no doubt, though, that either or both of the last-mentioned acts upon a minor, under the general language of certain subdivisions of section 3 or that of section 4 of the said law, would properly be construed as acts contributing to the dependency or the delinquency of a minor within the common intent of that law; yet it would hardly with seriousness be contended that the penalty fixed by section 28 of said law was intended to supersede or take the place of the penalty prescribed by section 261 of the Penal Code, defining the crime of rape, where a person is prosecuted and convicted under said code section for the crime of statutory rape — that is, for having sexual intercourse with a female under the age of eighteen years, a minor under the juvenile court law as well as under section 261 of the Penal Code. Nor can such a contention be sustained with respect to the effect of section 28 of the juvenile court law upon section 288 of the Penal Code. Section 28 of the juvenile court law does not repeal section 288 of the code by express language, and we find nothing in its language, either when considered alone or in connection with other provisions of the law to which it belongs, which would justify the conclusion that it does so by implication or thus affects the penalty prescribed by the code section for the distinctive crime by said section defined. In other words, the question here is one of legislative intent, and we perceive nothing in the language of section 28 of the juvenile court law, or in that of any other section of said law, from which it is to be inferred that the legislature intended by said section or by the act of which it is a part to expunge section 288 of the Penal Code or to repeal the penal clause thereof, and this is what the argument of counsel, if sustained, would bring about. The two acts — section 288 of the Penal Code and the juvenile court law, even with its section 28 — can consistently stand together, and when this can be said of two different legislative acts having, in a remote way, some relation to each other as to the general subject matter thereof, then there is no such repugnancy between them as will amount to or operate as a repeal by implication of the earlier act.

The final point urged by appellant is that the court was without jurisdiction to inflict a greater punishment for the violation of section 288 than that of five years. The penalty fixed by section 288 of the Penal Code is, as will be observed, imprisonment "in the state prison not less than one year," no maximum penalty being thereby expressly prescribed. Section 671 of said code reads: "Whenever any person is declared punishable for a crime by imprisonment in the state prison for a term not less than any specified number of years, and no limit to the duration of such imprisonment is declared, the court authorized to pronounce judgment upon such conviction may, in its discretion, sentence such offender to imprisonment during his natural life, or for any number of years not less than that prescribed." The last-named section is obviously a complete answer to the contention of the appellant that the court was without authority to make the penalty in this case greater than that of imprisonment for five years. Counsel insists, however, that section 671 has no application to section 288, but that the maximum punishment under the latter section is fixed by section 18 of said code, which provides: "Except in cases where a different punishment is prescribed by this code, every offense declared to be a felony is punishable by imprisonment in the state prison, not exceeding five years." We are unable to see the force of the argument. Sections 288 and 671 must be read together to ascertain the maximum and the minimum penalties in cases arising under the first-named section. The two together fix the lowest and the highest limits within which the court was authorized to exercise its discretion as to the punishment. Thus, the case here comes within the exception made by section 18, this being as clearly a case "where a different punishment is prescribed" as though both the maximum and minimum penalties were expressly declared in section 288 of the code.

We have now as fully as we have conceived necessary noticed all the general points made by the appellant. We have not discussed the points, though, from all the angles of the argument advanced in support of the appeal or strictly followed the varying ramifications thereof. We have satisfied ourselves, however, that there is no substantial merit in any of the points presented, although they have been ingeniously and with as much force as untenable legal problems may be supported pressed upon us in the brief.

The order appealed from is affirmed.

CHIPMAN, P.J., and BURNETT, J. concurred.

Notes and Questions

1. If the Journal entry declares that a bill has not been properly enrolled pursuant to the state Constitution, how does a member of the public challenge it? In other words, if the Journals cannot be used, by what evidence can someone challenge the proper or improper enactment of a statute?

2. Why did the court determine that the provisions of the act were consistent with the act's title?

Q. Legislative Oversight

A critical role for the legislative branch of government is oversight regarding executive branch activities. Fundamentally, oversight is intended to ensure government accountability and make certain that tax dollars are spent properly and efficiently by the executive branch of state government.

In 2017, Assembly Rules Committee Chairman Ken Cooley released the "2017 Oversight Handbook" for his legislative colleagues. The Legislative Oversight Handbook provides a toolkit and offers useful advice to support legislative committees as they prepare and conduct oversight activities.

According to the Handbook, "Oversight is broadly defined as reviewing, monitoring, and supervising the implementation of public policy." It is intended that these oversight hearings be used to create a "check and balance" to the executive branch and its over two hundred agencies, departments, boards, and commissions that carry out policy. It also allows the legislative branch to ensure that these state agencies are implementing the laws as intended by the Legislature.

In addition, with oversight, the Legislature will be able to review the personnel and budgetary needs of all of the executive branch agencies to determine whether they are utilizing taxpayer dollars properly and efficiently. As might be expected, legislative oversight can take several forms, including private communications, public hearings, the budget process, and legislation. The Legislature also has the Bureau of

State Audits to conduct audits and investigations into the executive branch of state government.

As Assemblyman Cooley opined to his colleagues, "it is quite striking that done well and systematically, oversight can be more impactful than merely passing new laws." There appears to be a renewed sense by the Legislature to exercise its responsibility as a co-equal branch of state government to utilize this oversight function. As an elected branch of government, oversight allows the Legislature to try and have the executive branch reflect the state's priorities with legislative input.

These are essentially two types of oversight hearings that the Legislature can conduct, one that is informational in nature, while the other is investigatory in approach. Informational hearings allow legislators to learn about a particular topic and state agency. These types of hearings also educate other legislators, staff and members of the public who listen to the hearing on television. These usually occur when the Legislature wants to learn more about the subject matter of the hearing.

On the other hand, an investigatory hearing is more of a "fact finding" effort conducted by the Legislature to find out about a particular matter that has previously occurred. This type of hearing is the traditional oversight hearing wherein the Legislature needs to understand what transpired, such as when the Legislature has investigated information technology procurements that went well over budget and the timeline in an effort to appreciate why the procurement was not successful and whether any law changes are required to ensure such a situation does not occur again.

Assemblyman Cooley states that, "to conduct a successful oversight hearing in either case requires a commitment to research." As such, the Handbook that he and his staff developed set forth ways in which the Legislature can successfully carry out these types of oversight hearings. The Handbook contains the following contents that are invaluable to legislators, their staff, and their committees:

- Introduction
- Defining Legislative Oversight
- The Nuts and Bolts of Oversight
- Participants
- Growing Institutional Capacity
- Legislative Rules Governing Oversight Hearings
- Oversight Coordination and Processes
- Office of Legislative Counsel Collaboration for Hearing Preparation
- Oversight Quotes
- Legal Issues Pertinent to Investigative Hearings
- Quick Reference on California Statutory and Other Law
- FAQ Sheet: Rules, Statutes, and Case Law Governing Oversight Hearings
- Rules Governing Legislative Oversight

- Committee Rules Containing Oversight or Investigations Provisions
- Preparation of Briefing Books
- Subpoena Policy

Whether the Legislature is conducting an informational hearing or an investigatory hearing, there must be proper preparation by the legislative branch in which research is thoroughly conducted and the hearing is scripted to ensure that witnesses and documents provide the information that the legislative committee wishes to have released. This requires working with interested parties, interviewing potential witnesses, and conducting thorough research into the topic(s) of the hearing.

Investigatory hearings also require extensive research and preparation. They require fact-finding to be done, and that means knowing which questions to ask of witnesses who will appear before the oversight hearing. This will ensure that the executive branch conducts itself properly and in compliance with the law and the policy that is enumerated by the Legislature. Because of the possibility an investigatory hearing can be adversarial, it is important that the legislative committee act in the highest ethical manner when it acts as the "check" on the executive branch.

Legislators can investigate executive branch agencies and departments, and they can be investigated themselves. The Senate has power to investigate charges of bribery against its own members and, in the exercise thereof, may summon and examine witnesses. (*Ex parte McCarthy* (1866) 29 Cal. 395.)

R. Impeachment by the California Legislature

California's Government Code Title 1, Division 4, Chapter 7, Article 2 provides for impeachment by the California Legislature.

Government Code § 3020 provides that state officers elected on a statewide basis, members of the State Board of Equalization, and judges of state courts are subject to impeachment for misconduct in office. Section 3020.5 states that the Senate, when sitting as the court of impeachment, is a court of record and the officers of the Senate are the officers of the court.

Section 3021 specifies that all impeachments must be by resolution adopted, originated in, and conducted by managers elected by the Assembly. Section 3022 requires that the managers are to prepare articles of impeachment, present them at the bar of the Senate, and prosecute them. The trial is to be before the Senate, sitting as a court of impeachment.

Section 3023 states that, when an officer is impeached by the Assembly for a misdemeanor in office, the articles of impeachment shall be delivered to the President of the Senate. Section 3024 requires the Senate to assign a day for the hearing of the impeachment and inform the Assembly of the date.

Section 3025 requires the Senate President to serve the defendant with a copy of the articles of impeachment with a notice to appear and answer at the appointed time and place. Section 3026 requires the service to be made personally upon the defendant. Section 3027 states that, if the defendant does not appear, then the Senate may assign another day for hearing the impeachment or may proceed to trial and judgment in the absence of the defendant.

Section 3028 provides that, when the defendant appears, then the defendant may object in writing to the sufficiency of the articles of impeachment, or the defendant may answer the articles by an oral plea of not guilty. Section 3029 requires the defendant to answer the articles. If the defendant pleads guilty or refuses to plead, then the Senate must render judgment of conviction against him.

Section 3030 provides that, if the defendant pleads not guilty, then the Senate must try the impeachment at the time it appoints. The plea is then entered upon the Senate Journal. Section 3031 states that the Senate Secretary must administer to all members of the Senate an oath truly and impartially to hear, try, and determine the impeachment. No member of the Senate can act or vote upon the impeachment, or upon any question arising thereon, without having taken such oath.

Section 3032 specifies that the defendant cannot be convicted on impeachment without the concurrence of two-thirds of the members elected. If two-thirds of the members elected do not concur in a conviction, then the defendant must be acquitted. Section 3033 states that, after conviction and at the time appointed by the Senate, the Members of the Senate must pronounce judgment, in the form of a resolution entered upon the Senate Journal.

Section 3034 states, on the adoption of the resolution by a majority of the members present who voted on the question of acquittal or conviction, it becomes the judgment of the Senate. Senate 3035 specifies that the judgment may be that the defendant be suspended, or that the defendant be removed from office and disqualified to hold any office of honor, trust, or profit under the state.

Section 3036 provides that, if judgment of suspension is given, during the continuance of the judgment, the defendant is disqualified from receiving the salary, fees, or emoluments of the office. Section 3037 notes that whenever articles of impeachment against any officer subject to impeachment are presented to the Senate, the officer is temporarily suspended from his or her office and cannot act in his or her official capacity until he or she is acquitted.

Section 3038 specifies that, upon temporary suspension of any officer other than the Governor, the office must at once be temporarily filled by an appointment made by the Governor, with the advice and consent of the Senate. The office is to be filled by the appointee until the acquittal of the party impeached or, in case of his or her removal, until the vacancy is filled at the next election.

Section 3039 provides that, if the Lieutenant Governor is impeached, notice of the impeachment must be immediately given to the Senate by the Assembly in order that another President of the Senate may be chosen. Section 3040 specifies that, if the offense for which the defendant is convicted on impeachment is also the subject of an indictment or information, then the indictment or information is not barred.

Notes and Questions

1. How does the California impeachment process compare with the federal process?

2. Article IV, Section 18 contains the following provisions:

> (a) The Assembly has the sole power of impeachment. Impeachments shall be tried by the Senate. A person may not be convicted unless, by rollcall vote entered in the Journal, two thirds of the membership of the Senate concurs.

> (b) State officers elected on a statewide basis, members of the State Board of Equalization, and judges of state courts are subject to impeachment for misconduct in office. Judgment may extend only to removal from office and disqualification to hold any office under the State, but the person convicted or acquitted remains subject to criminal punishment according to law.

S. Open Government

1. Disclosures

A constitutional enactment providing for access to meetings of public bodies and to the writings of public officials and agencies did not nullify the exemptions from disclosure under the Legislative Open Records Act (LORA) for privileged material and legislator and staff correspondence. The express exemption from LORA's open records policy for correspondence of and to legislative members and their staff is not invalidated by the fact that the correspondence of other state agencies is not similarly exempt.

The state Legislature's response to a LORA record request satisfied the statutory requirement that it justify in writing the withholding of exempt records where the Legislature's response stated that any additional responsive documents in its possession fell within the statutory exemptions and stated that examples of such exemptions were "preliminary draft, notes or legislative memoranda," "correspondence of and to individual members of the Legislature and their staff," and "records the disclosure of which is exempted or prohibited." (*Zumbrun Law Firm v. California Legislature* (2008) 165 Cal.App.4th 1603, review denied.)

2. Does the Legislature Meet in Public or in Private?

California's Constitution, in Article 4, Section 7, deals primarily with the proceedings of the houses and committees of the Legislature. Section 7(c) provides "the proceedings of each house and the committees thereof shall be open and public." Moreover, "the right to attend open and public proceedings includes the right of any person to record by audio or video means any and all parts of the proceedings and to broadcast or otherwise transmit them."

This provision of the state Constitution also allows the Legislature to adopt reasonable rules regulating the placement and use of the equipment for recording or broadcasting the proceedings for the sole purpose of minimizing disruption of the proceedings.

Moreover, the Legislature must provide audiovisual recordings to be made of all proceedings in their entirety and make the recordings public through the Internet within 24 hours after the proceedings have been recessed or adjourned for the day. They also have to maintain an archive of these recordings which must be accessible to the public through the Internet and downloadable for a period of no less than 20 years.

Nonetheless, the Legislature may hold closed sessions, but solely for the following purposes:

- To consider the appointment, employment, evaluation of performance, or dismissal of a public officer or employee, to consider or hear complaints or charges brought against a Member of the Legislature or other public officer or employee, or to establish the classification or compensation of an employee of the Legislature.

- To consider matters affecting the safety and security of Members of the Legislature or its employees or the safety and security of any buildings and grounds used by the Legislature.

- To confer with, or receive advice from, its legal counsel regarding pending or reasonably anticipated litigation, or whether to initiate litigation, when discussion in open session would not protect the interests of the house or committee regarding the litigation.

- A caucus of the Members of the Senate, the Members of the Assembly, or the Members of both houses, which is composed of the members of the same political party, may meet in closed session.

The Legislature must implement these provisions of law by concurrent resolution adopted by rollcall vote entered in the Journal, two-thirds of the membership of each house concurring, or by statute.

Additionally, in the case of a closed session, the Legislature must provide reasonable notice of the closed session, and the purpose of the closed session is to be provided to the public. If there is a conflict between a concurrent resolution and statute, the last adopted or enacted provision prevails.

Bagley-Keene Open Meeting Act

"Bagley-Keene," as it is known in the Capitol community, was adopted in 1967. It implements relevant portions of the California Constitution which declares that "the meetings of public bodies and the writings of public officials and agencies shall be open to public scrutiny." The state Constitution mandates open meetings for state agencies, boards, and commissions.

It is similar to the Brown Act, which applies to meetings at the local government level. The Bagley-Keene Act provides in Government Code § 11120:

It is the public policy of this state that public agencies exist to aid in the conduct of the people's business and the proceedings of public agencies be conducted openly so that the public may remain informed. In enacting this article, the Legislature finds and declares that it is the intent of the law that actions of state agencies be taken openly and that their deliberation be conducted openly.

The people of this state do not yield their sovereignty to the agencies which serve them. The people, in delegating authority, do not give their public servants the right to decide what is good for the people to know and what is not good for them to know. The people insist on remaining informed so that they may retain control over the instruments they have created. This article shall be known and may be cited as the Bagley-Keene Open Meeting Act.

The practical impact of the Bagley-Keene Act is that state agencies and departments must provide members of the public an opportunity to address agenda items in public meetings of the respective state agencies or departments. Before the ability to comment on agenda items, the public must be made aware of any meetings of the state entity.

As a result, notice of state agency or department meetings must be provided to any person who makes such a request in writing at least 10 days in advance of the meetings. Notices must include a specific agenda for meetings, including the items of business to be transacted or discussed, and no item may be added to the agenda subsequent to the notice.

State entities may, however, take action on items of business not on the agenda under certain limited circumstances, most notably upon a determination by a majority vote of the state entity that an emergency situation exists. In addition, the Act forbids a state agency to conduct any meeting or function in any facility prohibiting admittance to any person on the basis of race, religious creed, color, national origin, ancestry, or sex.

There are three critically important aspects of the Bagley-Keene Act to understand that address the following questions: What is a meeting; what is a state body; and what is an action taken? These terms are explained below:

What Is a "Meeting"? (Gov. Code § 11122.5(a))

A "meeting" includes any congregation of a majority of the members of a state body at the same time and place to hear, discuss, or deliberate upon any item that is within the subject matter jurisdiction of the state body to which it pertains.

This can apply to informal gatherings, as well as meetings via video conference or those conducted over the telephone by conference call. Be aware that "serial meetings" count toward this definition. In other words, state agency officials cannot get around the Act's requirements via a series of individual calls or meetings.

What Is a "State Body"? (Gov. Code § 11121)

Every state board, or commission, or similar multimember body of the state that is created by statute or required by law to conduct official meetings is a state body.

In addition, a board, commission, committee, or similar multimember body that exercises any authority of a state body delegated to it by that state body qualifies. Finally, an advisory board, advisory commission, advisory committee, advisory sub-committee, or similar multimember advisory body of a state body created by formal action of the state body and consisting of three or more persons is a state body under the law.

Be aware that the Act's provisions go beyond just the full state body. In other words, this definition applies to advisory committees and other informal bodies that advise state entities. As a result, even a three-person advisory committee to a state department must follow the open meeting laws.

What Is an "Action Taken"? (Gov. Code § 11122)

Action taken means a collective decision made by the members of a state body, a collective commitment or promise by the members of the state body to make a positive or negative decision, or an actual vote by the members of a state body when sitting as a body or entity upon a motion, proposal, resolution, order or similar action.

The easiest example of this provision is a vote taken by a majority of the body's members. But note that the Act's provisions apply even to commitments or promises made by members of the state agency or department.

AG: Caution Regarding "Collective Commitment"

According to the Attorney General, "Conversations that advance or clarify a member's understanding of an issue, or facilitate an agreement or compromise among members, or advance the ultimate resolution of an issue, are all examples of communications that contribute to the development of a concurrence as to action to be taken by the body."

Closed Sessions (Gov. Code § 11126)

Closed sessions can only be held under very limited conditions:

- Appointment, employment, evaluation, or discipline (including dismissal) of a public employee;
- Licensing, honorary degrees, real property negotiations, investments;
- To confer with or receive advice from legal counsel re pending or anticipated litigation

The law has strict requirements regarding notice of closed sessions, what must be disclosed, and what must be subsequently reported in open session.

Remedies for Violation

If the Bagley-Keene Act is violated, the decision of the body may be overturned if challenged within 90 days (Gov. Code § 11130.3). Violations may be stopped or prevented (Gov. Code § 11130). Costs and fees may be awarded (Gov. Code § 11130.5), and criminal misdemeanor penalties may be imposed as well. (Gov. Code § 11130.7.).

3. Legislative Open Meetings Law

The California Legislature is bound by the Legislative Open Meetings Law found in Sections 9027 through 9031 of the Government Code. The major provisions of this Act to be aware of include the following:

Caucuses of the Legislature have full authority to meet in closed session; whereas, state agencies have very limited authority to meet in closed session except for specified exceptions including litigation, personnel actions, etc.

Legislators can meet informally outside of committee meetings and floor sessions to discuss policy so long as no formal action is taken and so long as less than a majority of the body is involved. Staff and other intermediaries working on behalf of members are not counted, and "serial meetings" are not prohibited. (Note that the Bagley-Keene Act prohibits serial meetings and counts staff as board members.)

Legislative leaders can meet with one another and the Governor in private to develop policy proposals so long as the product is brought to an open committee meeting or floor session for adoption. (Note that designees of a state agency engaging in the same activity would usually constitute a "committee" or "advisory body" which must meet in open session.)

This Act is found in Government Code Article 2.2 entitled Open Meetings, which is contained in Sections 9027–9031. Article 2.2 was added to the Government Code in 1989. The following are the key sections impacting the State Legislature:

Gov't Code § 9027

With certain exceptions, all meetings (defined as a gathering of a quorum in one place for the purpose of discussing official matters) of a house of the Legislature or a committee thereof shall be open and public, and all persons shall be permitted to attend the meetings.

Gov't Code § 9028

Any meeting that is required to be open and public can only be held after full and timely notice to the public as provided by the Joint Rules of the Assembly and Senate.

Gov't Code § 9029

A house of the Legislature or a committee may hold a closed session solely for any of the following purposes:

(1) To consider the appointment, employment, evaluation of performance, or dismissal of a public officer or employee, to consider or hear complaints or charges brought against a Member of the Legislature or other public officer or employee, or to establish the classification or compensation of an employee of the Legislature.

(2) To consider matters affecting the safety and security of Members of the Legislature or its employees or the safety and security of any buildings and grounds used by the Legislature.

(3) To confer with, or receive advice from, its legal counsel regarding pending or reasonably anticipated litigation, or whether to initiate litigation, when discussion

in open session would not protect the interests of the house or committee regarding the litigation.

(b) A caucus of the Members of the Senate, the Members of the Assembly, or the Members of both houses, which is composed of members of the same political party, may meet in closed session.

Gov't Code § 9030

Each Member of the Legislature who attends a meeting of the Assembly, the Senate, or any committee or subcommittee, where action is taken in violation of Section 9027, with knowledge of the fact that the meeting is in violation thereof, is guilty of a misdemeanor.

Gov't Code § 9031

Any interested person may commence an action by mandamus, injunction, or declaratory relief for the purpose of stopping or preventing violations or threatened violations of this article by Members of the Legislature or to determine the applicability of this article to actions or threatened future action of a house of the Legislature or a committee thereof.

Notes and Questions

1. Should the Legislature be required to conduct all meetings in public? Are there times when the public should be excluded from a legislative meeting? Is it appropriate to allow party caucuses to discuss public policy issues and specific measures in a closed to the public meeting?

2. A constitutional enactment providing for access to meetings of public bodies and to the writings of public officials and agencies did not nullify the exemptions from disclosure under the Legislative Open Records Act (LORA) for privileged material and legislator and staff correspondence. The express exemption from LORA's open records policy for correspondence of and to legislative members and their staff is not invalidated by the fact that the correspondence of other state agencies is not similarly exempt. (*Zumbrun Law Firm v. California Legislature* (2008) 165 Cal.App.4th 1603, 1620, review denied.)

4. Examining California Legislative Records

Members of the public can examine California legislative records based upon the provisions of the Legislative Open Records Act (LORA), which is found in the California Government Code. LORA was enacted in 1975 to allow public access to legislative records. LORA also limits the public's right to access, inspect and copy these records.

Pursuant to LORA, requests by members of the public must be made in writing and be submitted to either the Senate Committee on Rules or the Assembly Rules Committee, depending upon the location of the documents being requested. The Joint Committee on Rules is charged with the custody of records in the joint custody of the Assembly and Senate.

LORA provides the laws for review, reproduction and access to legislative records, with specified restrictions. Generally, the Rules Committees respond within 3 to 10 days upon receiving written requests for legislative records. If a request is denied, the individual requesting the information is entitled to a written explanation.

Generally, the records may not be removed from the office that is designated for records inspection and must be inspected in the presence of a designated staff member from the Legislature. The public can request copies of records and are charged a nominal amount for the photocopying.

The following categories of legislative records are exempt from mandatory public inspection under Government Code §§ 9072 and 9075:

1. Records prepared before December 2, 1974.

2. Records pertaining to certain claims against the Legislature until they are finally adjudicated or settled, and records pertaining to litigation to which the Legislature is a party until such litigation has been finally adjudicated or settled.

3. Personnel files, medical files, and similar files pertaining to the privacy of individuals.

4. Preliminary drafts, notes, or memoranda among Members and staff, other than committee staff analyses directed to all committee members.

5. Records of individual names and phone numbers of senders and receivers of telephone and telegraph communications.

6. Records of individual transactions for fuel or lubricants for committee leased cars.

7. Communications from private citizens to the Legislature.

8. Records of complaints to the Legislature, its investigations, and its security procedures.

9. Correspondence of Members and their staffs.

10. Correspondence to Members and their staffs on matters other than legislation.

11. Written commentary submitted to a committee on legislation where the commentary (a) was not utilized by the staff of a fiscal committee in the presentation of the analysis of legislation or (b) is otherwise determined by the committee or its staff to be confidential.

12. Records where, based on the facts of the particular case, the Joint Rules Committee believes the public interest served by their nondisclosure clearly outweighs the public interest served by their disclosure.

Members of the public are also allowed to gain access to legislation documents. Government Code § 9080 guarantees public access to legislative committee records concerning legislation. Moreover, legislative committees have adopted written procedures concerning the public inspection of these records.

Generally, interested parties must complete a form stating specifically what legislation records they want to inspect. If those records are not subject to inspection, then they are not released. Otherwise, the committee will arrange for inspection. The records are not removed from the office and are inspected in the presence of committee staff. Copies can be requested, and the public are charged a nominal amount for the photocopying.

Notes and Questions

1. What are some differences and similarities between the Public Records Act, applicable to local jurisdictions, and the Legislative Open Records Act?

T. Proposition 54 and Its Impact on California Government

Proposition 54, which was enacted by the voters at the November 2016 general election, adopted constitutional and statutory changes dealing bill amendments and recordings of legislative proceedings. According to the Attorney General's Ballot Summary, Prop. 54:

> Prohibits Legislature from passing any bill unless published on Internet for 72 hours before vote. Requires Legislature to record its proceedings and post on Internet. Authorizes use of recordings. Fiscal Impact: One-time costs of $1 million to $2 million and ongoing costs of about $1 million annually to record legislative meetings and make videos of those meetings available on the Internet.

Prop. 54, whose title is the "California Legislature Transparency Act," included numerous findings and declarations as part of the ballot measure. For example, those findings included that "It is essential to the maintenance of a democratic society that public business be performed in an open and public manner, and highly desirable that citizens be given the opportunity to fully review every bill and express their views regarding the bill's merits to their elected representatives, before it is passed."

The proponents of Prop. 54 were specifically concerned with "gut-and-amend" bills that contain "last-minute amendments to bills [that] are frequently used to push through political favors without comment or with little advance notice. Moreover, complex bills are often passed before members of the Legislature have any realistic opportunity to review or debate them, resulting in ill-considered legislation."

As a result of the findings, Prop. 54 made several declarations, including that, "to foster disclosure, deliberation, debate, and decorum in our legislative proceedings, to keep our citizens fully informed, and to ensure that legislative proceedings are conducted fairly and openly, our Constitution should guarantee the right of all persons, including members of the press, to freely record legislative proceedings and to broadcast, post, or otherwise transmit those recordings."

In addition, Prop. 54 declared that "the Legislature itself should also be required to make and post audiovisual recordings of all public proceedings to the Internet and to maintain an archive of these recordings, which will be a valuable resource for the public, the press, and the academic community for generations to come. California should also follow the lead of other states that require a 72-hour advance notice period between the time a bill is printed and made available to the public and the time it is put to a vote, allowing an exception only in the case of a true emergency, such as a natural disaster."

Thereafter, Prop. 54 adopted two amendments to the California Constitution, followed by two amendments to the California Government Code. These changes are set forth below:

Article IV, Section 7 was amended to provide (additions are in italics):

(a) Each house shall choose its officers and adopt rules for its proceedings. A majority of the membership constitutes a quorum, but a smaller number may recess from day to day and compel the attendance of absent members.

(b) Each house shall keep and publish a journal of its proceedings. The rollcall vote of the members on a question shall be taken and entered in the journal at the request of 3 members present.

(c) (1) *Except as provided in paragraph (3),* the proceedings of each house and the committees thereof shall be open and public. *The right to attend open and public proceedings includes the right of any person to record by audio or video means any and all parts of the proceedings and to broadcast or otherwise transmit them; provided that the Legislature may adopt reasonable rules pursuant to paragraph (5) regulating the placement and use of the equipment for recording or broadcasting the proceedings for the sole purpose of minimizing disruption of the proceedings. Any aggrieved party shall have standing to challenge said rules in an action for declaratory and injunctive relief, and the Legislature shall have the burden of demonstrating that the rule is reasonable.*

(2) Commencing on January 1 of the second calendar year following the adoption of this paragraph, the Legislature shall also cause audiovisual recordings to be made of all proceedings subject to paragraph (1) in their entirety, shall make such recordings public through the Internet within 24 hours after the proceedings have been recessed or adjourned for the day, and shall maintain an archive of said recordings, which shall be accessible to the public through the Internet and downloadable for a period of no less than 20 years as specified by statute.

(3) Notwithstanding paragraphs (1) and (2), closed sessions may be held solely for any of the following purposes: ...

In addition, Article IV, Section 8 was amended to provide (additions are in italics):

(a) At regular sessions no bill other than the budget bill may be heard or acted on by committee or either house until the 31st day after the bill is introduced unless the house dispenses with this requirement by rollcall vote entered in the journal, three fourths of the membership concurring.

(b) *(1)* The Legislature may make no law except by statute and may enact no statute except by bill. No bill may be passed unless it is read by title on 3 days in each house except that the house may dispense with this requirement by rollcall vote entered in the journal, two thirds of the membership concurring.

(2) No bill may be passed *or ultimately become a statute unless* the bill with *any* amendments has been printed, distributed to the members, *and published on the Internet, in its final form, for at least 72 hours before the vote, except that this notice period may be waived if the Governor has submitted to the Legislature a written statement that dispensing with this notice period for that bill is necessary to address a state of emergency, as defined in paragraph (2) of subdivision (c) of Section 3 of Article XIII B, that has been declared by the Governor, and the house considering the bill thereafter dispenses with the notice period for that bill by a separate rollcall vote entered in the journal, two thirds of the membership concurring, prior to the vote on the bill.*

(3) No bill may be passed unless, by rollcall vote entered in the journal, a majority of the membership of each house concurs.

Government Code § 9026.5 was amended to provide (additions are in italics):

Televised or other audiovisual recordings of public proceedings.

(a) Televised or other audiovisual recordings of the public proceedings of each house of the Legislature and the committees thereof may be used for any legitimate purpose and without the imposition of any fee due to the State or any public agency or public corporation thereof.

(b) The Legislature's costs of complying with paragraph (2) of subdivision (c) of Section 7 and of paragraph (2) of subdivision (b) of Section 8 of Article IV of the California Constitution shall be included as part of the total aggregate expenditures allowed under Section 7.5 of Article IV of the California Constitution.

In addition, Government Code § 10248 was amended to provide (additions are in italics):

Public computer network; required legislative information.

(a) The Legislative Counsel shall, with the advice of the Assembly Committee on Rules and the Senate Committee on Rules, make all of the following information available to the public in electronic form:

(1) The legislative calendar, the schedule of legislative committee hearings, a list of matters pending on the floors of both houses of the Legislature, and a list of the committees of the Legislature and their members.

(2) The text of each bill introduced in each current legislative session, including each amended, enrolled, and chaptered form of each bill.

(3) The bill history of each bill introduced and amended in each current legislative session.

(4) The bill status of each bill introduced and amended in each current legislative session.

(5) All bill analyses prepared by legislative committees in connection with each bill in each current legislative session.

(6) All audiovisual recordings of legislative proceedings that have been caused to be made by the Legislature in accordance with paragraph (2) of subdivision (c) of Section 7 of Article IV of the California Constitution. Each recording shall remain accessible to the public through the Internet and downloadable for a minimum period of 20 years following the date on which the recording was made and shall then be archived in a secure format.

(7) All vote information concerning each bill in each current legislative session.

(8) Any veto message concerning a bill in each current legislative session.

(9) The California Codes.

(10) The California Constitution.

(11) All statutes enacted on or after January 1, 1993.

As a result of the voters' enactment of Prop. 54, the public has a right to record legislative proceedings that they attend, such as with their cell phone or laptop computer. Also, the Legislature must record and promptly make available video audio recordings of legislative proceedings. Finally, final forms of bills must be in print for 3 days before they can be voted upon by legislators on the Floors of the State Assembly and State Senate.

Chapter Five

Qualifications and Elections

A. Oath of Office

Government Code Title 1, Division 4, Chapter 2, Article 4 specifies the oath of office in §§ 1360 to 1369. Article 4 was enacted in 1943. Section 1360 provides that, following any election or appointment and, before any officer enters on the duties of his or her office, he or she must take and subscribe the oath or affirmation that is set forth in Section 3 of Article XX of the Constitution of California.

California's Constitution, in Article 20, Section 3, provides:

> Members of the Legislature, and all public officers and employees, executive, legislative, and judicial, except such inferior officers and employees as may be by law exempted, shall, before they enter upon the duties of their respective offices, take and subscribe the following oath or affirmation:

I, _____, do solemnly swear (or affirm) that I will support and defend the Constitution of the United States and the Constitution of the State of California against all enemies, foreign and domestic; that I will bear true faith and allegiance to the Constitution of the United States and the Constitution of the State of California; that I take this obligation freely, without any mental reservation or purpose of evasion; and that I will well and faithfully discharge the duties upon which I am about to enter.

And I do further swear (or affirm) that I do not advocate, nor am I a member of any party or organization, political or otherwise, that now advocates the overthrow of the Government of the United States or of the State of California by force or violence or other unlawful means; that within the five years immediately preceding the taking of this oath (or affirmation) I have not been a member of any party or organization, political or otherwise, that advocated the overthrow of the Government of the United States or of the State of California by force or violence or other unlawful means except as follows:

   (If no affiliations, write in the words "No Exceptions")

and that during such time as I hold the office of __(name of office)__ I will not advocate nor become a member of any party or organization, political or otherwise, that advocates the overthrow of the Government of the United States or of the State of California by force or violence or other unlawful means.

And no other oath, declaration, or test, shall be required as a qualification for any public office or employment. "Public officer and employee" include every officer and employee of the State, including the University of California, every county, city, city and county, district, and authority, including any department, division, bureau, board, commission, agency, or instrumentality of any of the foregoing.

Government Code § 1362 specifies that the oath may be taken before any officer authorized to administer oaths. Section 1363 requires every oath of office to be certified by the officer before whom it was taken. Thereafter, the officer must file it with specified entities. For example, the oath of all officers elected or appointed for any county must be filed in the office of the county clerk of their respective counties.

Section 1364 provides that it is unlawful to remove a person from an office or position of public trust because that person has not complied with any law, charter, or regulation prescribing an additional test or qualification for such office or position of public trust, other than tests and qualifications provided for under civil service and retirement laws.

In addition, § 1365 notes that it is unlawful for any person having the power of removal from office of any officer to remove or threaten to remove the officer from his office because the officer refuses to require any additional test or qualification, other than the oath prescribed by this article.

Section 1367 prohibits any compensation or reimbursement for expenses incurred from being paid to any officer by any public agency unless he or she has taken and subscribed to the oath or affirmation required by this chapter. Section 1368 makes every person who, while taking and subscribing to the oath or affirmation required by this chapter, and states as true any material matter which he or she knows to be false, guilty of perjury.

Finally, § 1369 specifies that every person having taken and subscribed to the oath or affirmation required by this chapter, who while holding office, advocates or becomes a member of any party or organization, political or otherwise, that advocates the overthrow of the government of the United States by force or violence or other unlawful means, is guilty of a felony.

B. Judging the Qualifications of Members

California Constitution Article IV, Section 5(a)(1) specifies: "Each house of the Legislature shall judge the qualifications and elections of its Members and, by rollcall vote entered in the journal, two-thirds of the membership concurring, may expel a Member." The courts in this state have determined how far that "judgment" goes.

The Legislature also has constitutional power to suspend Members. Also found in Article IV, but in Section 5(a)(2)(A), "each house may suspend a Member by motion or resolution adopted by rollcall vote entered in the journal, two-thirds of the membership concurring. The motion or resolution shall contain findings and declarations setting forth the basis for the suspension."

This section of the state constitution also allows the Legislature to deem the salary and benefits of the Member to be forfeited for all or part of the period of the suspension. A suspended Member cannot exercise any of the rights, privileges, duties, or powers of his or her office, or utilize any resources of the Legislature, during the period the suspension is in effect.

The courts have been clear in deferring to the Legislature on the question of judging the qualifications and giving full respect to the explicit language in the state Constitution. As a result, challenges to whether a Member is entitled to take his or her seat in the Legislature or whether to remain in office are rarely considered by the courts.

Under Article IV, Section 5, the Legislature has sole jurisdiction to determine the qualifications of its members and the sole right to expel them from membership. Accordingly, in an action by a veterans' group to disqualify an Assemblyman from holding office because of his alleged support of North Vietnam against the United States during hostilities, in reliance on Constitution Article VII, providing that no person who advocates the support of a foreign government against the United States in the event of hostilities shall hold any office or employment under the statute, the trial court was found to have properly dismissed the complaint after sustaining defendant's demurrer without leave to amend.

The appellate court ruled that, under the same constitutional principle of separation of powers, plaintiffs were foreclosed from attempts to prohibit the Attorney General or the Secretary of State or the County Registrar from certifying the election results, swearing in, or disbursing money to the Assemblyman, or interfering in the Legislature's determination of the qualifications, fitness and elections of its members. (*California War Veterans for Justice v. Hayden* (1986) 176 Cal.App.3d 982.)

Similarly, a state appeal court ruled that the judiciary lacked jurisdiction to judge the respondent's qualifications to serve as a senator for the 14th Senate District because Constitution Article IV, Section 5(a) vested in the State Senate the sole authority to judge the respondent's qualifications. The California Constitution vests in each house of the Legislature the sole authority to judge the qualifications and elections of a candidate for membership in that house, even when the challenge to the candidate's qualifications is brought prior to the primary election. (*Fuller v. Bowen* (2012) 203 Cal.App.4th 1976.)

More than a hundred years ago, the California Supreme Court ruled that the power conferred upon the Senate by the Constitution to determine the rule of its proceeding and to expel a member is exclusive; the judicial department has no power to revise even the most arbitrary and unfair action of the legislative department. There is no constitutional provision giving persons who have been expelled the right to have a trial and opportunity to be heard in the Senate other than that which they have received. (*French v. Senate of California* (1905) 146 Cal. 604.)

Finally, according to the California Attorney General, election of a member of the Legislature to an incompatible office does not have the effect of removal of the legislator from the legislative office, as only the house of the Legislature has the power to "judge the qualifications of its members" and so to remove a member. (30 Ops.Cal.Atty.Gen. 56.)

As you can see, the state's courts have deferred entirely to the Legislature based upon a clear reading of the state Constitution and the exclusive power of the legislative branch of state government to determine the qualifications of Members of the California Legislature.

Notes and Questions

1. While the Legislature determines whether someone has been properly elected, can you identify an instance where a state court should intervene to either preclude or allow someone to be seated as a Member of the California Legislature?

2. It is the exclusive jurisdiction of the Legislature in regard to a legislator's qualifications as an Assemblymember or Senator. As such, each house of the Legislature, Senate or Assembly, has the sole authority to determine the qualifications of a candidate for office and whether an individual has been duly elected to the Legislature. Once an individual has been sworn into office as having been duly elected to the Legislature, the only means by which that person can be removed is pursuant to the state Constitution with a two-third vote of the respective house of the Legislature.

California War Veterans for Justice v. Hayden

(1986) 176 Cal.App.3d 982

OPINION

McCLOSKY, J.

Appellants California War Veterans for Justice and Mickey R. Conroy appeal from an order (judgment) of dismissal of their complaint for declaratory, injunctive and extraordinary relief. The trial court sustained without leave to amend the demurrers by respondent Tom Hayden, member of the Assembly, 44th District, and respondents John K. Van de Kamp, Attorney General, and March Fong Eu, Secretary of State.

Contentions

Appellants contend that "[t]he court erred in dismissing the complaint without leave to amend" and (2) "[i]f the complaint stated or suggested any cause of action or could have been amended to state a cause of action the court should have allowed plaintiff to amend." They have failed, however, to suggest how they would or could have amended their complaint to state a cause of action.

Facts

Appellants filed their complaint on October 31, 1984. In it they asked that the superior court disqualify Assemblyman Hayden from holding public office because of his "actions in support of North Vietnam against the United States during recent hostilities between these two countries" under article VII, section 9, of the California Constitution. Appellants also sought an injunction prohibiting respondents John K. Van de Kamp, March Fong Eu and Los Angeles County Registrar-Recorder Charles Weissburd from certifying the election results, swearing in, or disbursing money to Mr. Hayden if he were reelected and sought the return to the public treasury of the legislative salary theretofore paid him.

Appellants also prayed for a writ of mandate directing the Attorney General "to carry out his duty to see that the California Constitution is enforced."

Respondent Hayden filed his demurrer to the complaint on February 8, 1985; respondents Van de Kamp and Eu on February 15, 1985.

The trial court sustained both demurrers without leave to amend on March 7, 1985. In sustaining the demurrer of Van de Kamp and Eu, the court held, among other things, that it "has no jurisdiction to force the Secretary of State and Attorney General to perform duties that are exclusively duties of the Assembly" and that "it does not appear that plaintiffs are taxpayers within the meaning of section 526(a) CCP." Sustaining respondent Hayden's demurrer, the court held that jurisdiction over defendant's qualifications as an assemblyman belongs exclusively to the Assembly.

Discussion

I

Appellants contend that "the court erred in dismissing the complaint without leave to amend" and "[i]f the complaint stated or suggested any cause of action or could have been amended to state a cause of action the court should have allowed plaintiff to amend."

"In determining the sufficiency of a complaint against a general demurrer, we consider the demurrer as admitting all material and issuable facts properly pleaded." (*Scott v. City of Indian Wells* (1972) 6 Cal. 3d 541, 549 [99 Cal. Rptr. 745, 492 P.2d 1137]; *King v. Central Bank* (1977) 18 Cal. 3d 840, 843 [135 Cal. Rptr. 771, 558 P.2d 857].) In general, great liberality should be exercised in permitting the plaintiff to amend the complaint. It ordinarily is an abuse of discretion to sustain a demurrer without leave to amend if there is a possibility that the defect can be cured by amendment. (*Lemoge Electric v. County of San Mateo* (1956) 46 Cal. 2d 659, 664 [297 P.2d 638]; *Scott v. City of Indian Wells, supra*, 6 Cal.3d at p. 549.) However, if it does not appear that under applicable substantive law there is any reasonable probability that the defects can be cured, there is no abuse of discretion in sustaining the demurrer without leave to amend for no amendment would change the result. (*Routh v. Quinn* (1942) 20 Cal. 2d 488, 493 [127 P.2d 1].) (*Sackett v. Wyatt* (1973) 32 Cal. App. 3d 592, 603 [108 Cal. Rptr. 219]; see also 5 Witkin, Cal. Procedure (3d ed. 1985) Pleading, § 945, pp. 379–380.)

II

Appellants contend that "Mickey Conroy does pay taxes to the State of California and there are no cases that extend the prohibition created by CCP 526a beyond the governmental divisions enumerated therein."

That question and the question of appellants' standing to sue are questions we need not, and do not, decide in view of the completely dispositive nature of our decision contained in part III of this opinion.

III

Appellants contend that "'[q]uestions relating to interpretations of Statutes are matters of law for the court.' (*Sierra County v. Nevada County* (1908) 155 Cal. 1, 99 P. 371." They also maintain that "[t]he doctrine of separation of powers as set forth in Article III Section 3 ... by itself doesn't prohibit the judiciary from passing on the qualifications of members of the legislature."

Under the California Constitution, as under the federal Constitution and the law of most states, the Legislature has sole jurisdiction to determine the qualifications of its members and the sole right to expel them from membership. Article IV, section 5 provides in pertinent part:

> "Each house shall judge the qualifications and elections of its members and, by rollcall vote entered in the journal, two thirds of the membership concurring, may expel a member."

Article IV, section 5 was adopted on November 8, 1966. Its predecessor statutes, however, contained substantially the same provision.

For over 100 years the California Supreme Court has consistently held that under the Constitution the courts have no jurisdiction to inquire into the qualifications of the members of the Legislature. In its first ruling on this issue, *People v. Metzker* (1874) 47 Cal. 524, the court held that "[i]t is settled beyond controversy, that those words of the Constitution confer upon each house the exclusive power to judge of and determine the qualifications, elections and returns of its own members; ... The Court, therefore, had no jurisdiction of the action." (*Id.*, at pp. 525–526.)

After the adoption of the present California Constitution in 1879, the Supreme Court continued to rule that the judicial branch does not have jurisdiction to determine the membership in the Legislature. In *French v. Senate* (1905) 146 Cal. 604 [80 P. 1031], four members of the state Senate were expelled for malfeasance in office. They petitioned the Supreme Court for writ of mandate to compel the Senate to reinstate them. (*Id.*, at p. 605.) The court sustained a general demurrer to the petition, holding that it had no jurisdiction over the dispute.

"Under our form of government, the judicial department has no power to revise even the most arbitrary and unfair action of the legislative department, or of either house thereof, taken in pursuance of the power committed exclusively to that department by the constitution.... By article III of the constitution it is provided that one department of the state shall not exercise the functions of either of the other departments except as in that instrument, expressly directed and permitted. There is no provision authorizing courts to control, direct, supervise, or forbid, the exercise by either house of the power to expel a member. These powers are functions of the legislative department, and therefore in the exercise of the power thus committed to it the senate is supreme. An attempt by this court to direct or control the legislature, or either house thereof, in the exercise of the power, would be an attempt to exercise legislative functions, which it is expressly forbidden to do." (*Id.*, at pp. 606–607.)

In *Allen v. Lelande* (1912) 164 Cal. 56 [127 P. 643], the court denied a petition for a writ of mandate to order the Los Angeles County Clerk to strike the name of the candidate for the state Assembly from the ballot because of alleged nonresidency, stating "[f]or this court to undertake to try the question of eligibility and to deprive the candidate of any chance to be elected, would simply be to usurp the jurisdiction of the assembly." (*Id.*, at p. 57.)

The California Supreme Court's last decision on the question of whether the judiciary has jurisdiction to determine the qualifications of members of the legislative branch is *In re McGee* (1951) 36 Cal. 2d 592 [226 P.2d 1]. In that case a Democratic candidate challenged the nomination of a Republican candidate who won the nomination of both parties for the Assembly. At that time then extant Elections Code sections 8600 and 8603 (later repealed) provided that any candidate in the primary could contest the nomination of another candidate for the same office by filing an action in the superior court. (*Id.*, at pp. 592–593.)

The Supreme Court in deciding the conflict between the statutes and the Constitution held that the Constitution, under article IV, section 7, "confers exclusive jurisdiction on the Legislature to judge the qualifications and elections of its members." (*In re McGee, supra*, 36 Cal.2d at p. 594.)

The court in *In re McGee, supra*, 36 Cal. 2d 592, also noted that "[t]he overwhelming weight of authority under identical federal and state constitutional provisions is in accord." (*Id.*, at p. 595.)

The parallel provision of the United States Constitution is article I, section 5, which provides in pertinent part: "Each House shall be the Judge of the Elections, Returns, and Qualifications of its own Members, ..." The United States Supreme Court in *Reed v. County Commissioners* (1927) 277 U.S. 376 [72 L. Ed. 924, 48 S. Ct. 531], held that under Article I, section 5, the Senate "is the judge of the elections, returns and qualifications of its members.... It is fully empowered, and may determine such matters without the aid of the House of Representatives or the Executive or Judicial Department." (*Id.*, at p. 388 [72 L.Ed. at p. 926]; see also *Barry v. U.S. ex rel. Cunningham* (1929) 279 U.S. 597 [73 L. Ed. 867, 49 S. Ct. 452].)

Appellants cite 5 Witkin, Summary of California Law (8th ed. 1974) Constitutional Law, section 84, page 3320: "Generally speaking, the Legislature has exclusive constitutional jurisdiction to determine the qualifications of its members. [Citation.] But the power is not unlimited." Witkin cites two limitations. They are: (1) "Conditions violative of First Amendment protections are invalid. (See *Bond v. Floyd* (1966) 385 U.S. 116 ..."; and (2) "Qualifications beyond those specified in the Constitution may not be imposed." (*Powell v. McCormack* (1969) 395 U.S. 486 [23 L. Ed. 2d 491, 89 S. Ct. 1944].) Neither such limitation is involved in the case at bench.

Appellants do not cite *Powell* or *Bond*. They instead cite *Jones v. McCollister* (1958) 159 Cal. App. 2d 708 [324 P.2d 639], as "[t]he one case that speaks of the possible judicial arrogate from the legislature of this power...." Appellants have misread *Jones*. Citing *In re McGee, supra*, 36 Cal. 2d 592,the *Jones* court held: "Finally, as to the office here in issue, the Assembly is the sole and exclusive judge of the 'qualifications, elections, and returns of its members.' (Cal. Const., art IV, § 7; *In re McGee*, 36 Cal. 2d 592 [226 P.2d 1].)" (*Jones v. McCollister, supra*, 159 Cal.App.2d at p. 712.)

Appellants mistakenly rely on article VII, section 9 of the California Constitution which reads in the part pertinent to this case: "Notwithstanding any other provision of this Constitution, no person ... who advocates the support of a foreign government against the United States in the event of hostilities shall: Hold any office or employment under this State, ..."

Appellants contend that this language supersedes all other provisions with which it may conflict. Assuming arguendo that that is true, that does not conflict with, or overcome the constitutional provision that the resolution of the questions of the qualifications and fitness of its members to serve shall be determined exclusively by the legislative house and not by the courts. (Art., IV, § 5.)

Appellant Conroy petitioned the Assembly in 1983 to remove Assemblyman Hayden from office. Appellant did not receive the relief he sought. It is unequivocally clear that under article IV, section 5 of the California Constitution, appellants cannot successfully seek relief in the courts. (*People v. Metzker, supra*, 47 Cal. 524; *French v. Senate, supra*, 146 Cal. 604; *Allen v. Lelande, supra*, 164 Cal. 56; *In re McGee, supra*, 36 Cal. 2d 592.)

Under the same constitutional principle of separation of powers, appellants are foreclosed from attempts to prohibit the Attorney General or the Secretary of State or the County Registrar-Recorder from certifying the election results, swearing in, or disbursing money to Assemblyman Hayden or interfering in the Legislature's determination of the qualifications, fitness and elections of its members.

Appellants, in somewhat incomprehensible language, seem to invite us to issue an advisory opinion. They state in their appellants' opening brief:

> "The court could grant declaratory relief on the issue of Assemblyman Tom Hayden perjured statements on his Affidavit of Nominee, Declaration Of Candidacy to inform the Attorney General that a crime may have been committed, inform the electorite [sic] that Tom Hayden is not qualified to hold office or employment in the State of California, or inform the legislature that Assembly [sic] Tom Hayden is not qualified to hold office and let the legislature take whatever action they deem appropriate.

> "Courts have tradionally [sic] operated with limits to their powers, merely because a court is subject to jurisdictional limits entirely emasculate the jurisdictional power of the court. There are no courts in the 51 jurisdictions that encompass these United States that are of unlimited jurisdictions. If the general rule is unlimited jurisdiction then the exception has devoured the rule."

If that language constitutes an invitation to us to issue an advisory opinion to the Legislature, the executive branch or anyone else, we must decline the invitation, for we have power only to adjudicate actual controversies, not to issue advisory opinions.

IV

Respondent Hayden contends that he is "entitled to damages for having to respond to a frivolous appeal." He seeks damages in the amount of $15,000 or whatever amount the court deems just.

Code of Civil Procedure section 907 provides: "When it appears to the reviewing court that the appeal was frivolous or taken solely for delay, it may add to the costs on appeal such damages as may be just."

The Supreme Court in *In re Marriage of Flaherty* (1982) 31 Cal. 3d 637 [183 Cal. Rptr. 508, 646 P.2d 179], held that an appeal is frivolous either "when it is prosecuted for an improper motive — to harass the respondent or delay the effect of an adverse judgment — or when it indisputedly has no merit — when any reasonable attorney would agree that the appeal is totally and completely without merit. [Citation.]" (*Id.*, at p. 650.)

The law on jurisdiction of the courts to disqualify members of the Legislature is unequivocal. For over 100 years the California Supreme Court has consistently ruled that the Legislature has exclusive jurisdiction. The overwhelming authority of the states of the United States and of the federal law is to the same effect. Appellants raised no meritorious arguments to challenge these holdings.

This appeal, and indeed the whole suit to this stage, might well be viewed by this court as patently frivolous in contrast to simply lacking merit. We are aware that sanctions may properly be imposed in a case even though it involves political controversy. Yet, we are mindful that the chilling effect of sanctions should be avoided wherever possible, especially in a suit involving controversy over political office. Accordingly, the request for sanctions is denied.

The order (judgment) is affirmed.

WOODS, P.J., and ARGUELLES, J., concurred.

Notes and Questions

1. Courts lacked jurisdiction to judge respondent's qualifications to serve as a Senator for the 14th Senate District, because Constitution Article IV, Section 5(a) vested in the State Senate the sole authority to judge the respondent's qualifications. The California Constitution vests in each house of the Legislature the sole authority to judge the qualifications and elections of a candidate for membership in that house, even when the challenge to the candidate's qualifications is brought prior to the primary election. (*Fuller v. Bowen* (2012) 203 Cal.App.4th 1976.)

2. The courts have ruled for more than a hundred years that, under Section 5, the courts do not have jurisdiction to judge whether a candidate for the Legislature has satisfied the requirements specified in Section 5. For example, in *Fuller v. Bowen* (2012) 203 Cal.App.4th 1476, residency requirements were deemed to be the juris-

diction of the legislative branch. Similarly, the court has ruled that only the Legislature has the power to expel a Member from office.

3. The court cites both the California and United States Constitutions as providing the legislative branch with the sole jurisdiction to determine the qualifications of its Members and the sole right to expel them from membership. Do other states follow this approach?

4. The court discussed Article VII, Section 9 of the California Constitution, which reads in the part pertinent to this case: "Notwithstanding any other provision of this Constitution, no person ... who advocates the support of a foreign government against the United States in the event of hostilities shall: Hold any office or employment under this State, ..." It appears to conflict with the Legislature's "sole jurisdiction." However, the court in this case ruled that the provisions do not conflict. What was the basis for the court's ruling?

5. Despite finding that "This appeal, and indeed the whole suit to this stage, might well be viewed by this court as patently frivolous in contrast to simply lacking merit," the court chose not to impose sanctions. Was that the right decision? Why?

Helena Rubenstein International v. Younger

(1977) 71 Cal.App.3d 406

OPINION

POTTER, J.

Helena Rubenstein International, dba People's Lobby, and Joyce Koupal (hereinafter collectively called appellants) appeal from orders of dismissal after trial courts sustained demurrers without leave to amend in the mandamus (2d Civ. No. 45770) and taxpayers' (2d Civ. No. 46036) actions consolidated herein. At issue is the meaning of "convicted" or "conviction" under California law for purposes of exclusion from public office.

On July 27, 1974, the Lieutenant Governor of California, Ed Reinecke, was found guilty of perjury (18 U.S.C. § 1621) by a jury in the United States District Court for the District of Columbia.

On July 29, appellants filed a taxpayers' action (Code Civ. Proc., § 526a) against respondents Reinecke, Controller Houston Flournoy and the State of California to enjoin the payment of Reinecke's salary and to require him to return to the state any compensation received after July 27. Appellants also requested respondent Attorney General Younger to initiate quo warranto proceedings (Code Civ. Proc., § 803) to remove Reinecke from office. Appellants claimed that rendition of the jury verdict disqualified Reinecke from holding office and receiving a salary because the jury verdict constituted a "conviction" under the provision of the California Constitution and implementing legislation providing for exclusion from office of persons "convicted" of perjury.

On that same day, Governor Ronald Reagan requested respondent Attorney General to render "an official written opinion" on the meaning of "conviction" and its effect on Reinecke's status. On August 1, the Attorney General issued his opinion.

The opinion basically concluded that a guilty verdict was not a "conviction" for the purpose of exclusion from public office and that until a judgment was rendered, Reinecke would not be convicted and would be entitled to remain in office and receive his salary. (See 57 Ops.Cal.Atty.Gen. 374 (1974).)

On August 2, the Attorney General informed appellants he would not institute quo warranto proceedings as requested. On August 5, appellants then applied to the Attorney General for leave to sue Reinecke in quo warranto (Code Civ. Proc., § 803; tit. 11, Cal. Admin. Code). Their request was denied on August 12.

The following day, appellants filed with the Supreme Court an original petition for writ of mandate to compel the Attorney General to grant appellants leave to sue Reinecke in quo warranto. In their papers filed with the court, both parties stressed that the issue was one of law. On August 28, the Supreme Court refused to hear the case. It issued an "Order Denying Alternative Writ." The order stated in full: "Petition for writ of mandate denied. This order is final forthwith."

On September 5, appellants filed in the Superior Court of Los Angeles County a petition for writ of mandate involving the identical parties and seeking the same relief as was sought in the Supreme Court. Respondents Reinecke and Attorney General Younger filed answers. The Attorney General also filed a demurrer. On September 16, Judge Lucas sustained the demurrer without leave to amend on the ground that the Supreme Court's denial of the alternative writ of mandate was "a decision on the merits and the matter in this court [was] res judicata." On September 17, appellants filed their appeal (2d Civ. No. 45770) from the ensuing order of dismissal in the mandate proceeding.

On September 27, Reinecke's motions for a judgment of acquittal, a new trial and arrest of judgment were denied by the federal district court. On October 2, Reinecke was sentenced (placed on probation). Upon sentencing, he resigned from all public offices.

On October 21, respondents Reinecke, Flournoy and the State of California demurred and moved to strike portions of appellants' taxpayers' suit. On November 1, Judge Goebel sustained the demurrer without leave to amend on the ground that "[f]or purposes of Article XX, Section 11 of California Constitution and Government Code Sections 1021 and 3000, 'conviction' is as defined in Government Code Section 1770(h), to wit, 'when trial court judgment is entered.'" On November 13, 1974, appellants filed their appeal (2d Civ. No. 46036) from the ensuing order of dismissal of the taxpayers' proceeding.

The sole substantive issue presented here is whether Reinecke was "convicted" within the meaning of the applicable California constitutional provision (former art. XX, § 11) and relevant implementing statutes for the purpose of exclusion from holding public office upon the rendition of the jury verdict, as appellants contend, or the judgment, as respondents contend.

We conclude, for the reasons that follow, that "conviction" so as to exclude from public office does not occur until rendition of judgment following the verdict. We, therefore, affirm the judgments (orders of dismissal) of the trial courts.

<h2 style="text-align:center">Discussion</h2>

Prior to discussing the main issue, we must dispose of two preliminary procedural issues. Respondents contend that the proceedings (1) are moot, and (2) are barred by the doctrine of res judicata. We disagree.

<h3 style="text-align:center">The Proceedings Are Not Moot</h3>

The issue of when a person is "convicted" of a crime for the purpose of exclusion from public office is of general public interest and is likely to recur. Accordingly, these proceedings are not rendered moot by the fact that Reinecke no longer holds the office of Lieutenant Governor. (*Fields v. Eu*, 18 Cal. 3d 322, 325 [134 Cal. Rptr. 367, 556 P.2d 729].)

<h3 style="text-align:center">The Denial of the Writ by the Supreme Court Is Not Res Judicata</h3>

Respondents' contention that the Supreme Court's denial of the writ is res judicata is untenable. In *People v. Medina*, 6 Cal. 3d 484, 491, footnote 6 [99 Cal. Rptr. 630, 492 P.2d 686], our Supreme Court noted that "[t]he denial without opinion of a petition for writ of mandate ... is not res judicata except when the sole possible ground of denial was on the merits or it affirmatively appears that the denial was intended to be on the merits." Here, the Supreme Court summarily denied the petition; it did not issue an alternative writ or order to show cause and did not hear the matter and render a written opinion on the merits. There were other possible reasons for the denial. As a matter of judicial policy, the Supreme Court usually refuses to exercise its original jurisdiction where, as here, the proceeding can be brought in the first instance in a lower court in order "to encourage the filing of petitions for extraordinary writs in the superior court." (*Friends of Mammoth v. Board of Supervisors*, 8 Cal. 3d 247, 269 [104 Cal. Rptr. 761, 502 P.2d 1049].) The order denying the alternative writ merely stated: "Petition for writ of mandate denied. This order is final forthwith." We do not consider this statement "affirmative proof" that the Supreme Court "intended" this denial to be res judicata of the merits of the issues raised.

<h3 style="text-align:center">Reinecke Was Not "Convicted" Until the Judgment Was Entered</h3>

At all times relevant to this proceeding, article XX, section 11 of the California Constitution provided in pertinent part: "Laws shall be made to exclude from office, serving on juries, and from the right of suffrage, persons convicted of bribery, perjury, forgery, malfeasance in office, or other high crimes...." This provision of the 1879 Constitution was originally enacted in the 1849 Constitution as article XI, section 18.

The Legislature has enacted various statutes to implement the exclusion from public office. Government Code section 1021 provides: "A person is disqualified from holding any office upon conviction of designated crimes as specified in the Constitution and laws of the State." Section 3000 of the Government Code states: "An officer forfeits his office upon conviction of designated crimes as specified in the Constitution and laws of the State." Section 1770, as amended in 1971, provides in pertinent part:

> "An office becomes vacant on the happening of any of the following events before the expiration of the term:
>
> "* * *

"(h) His conviction of a felony or of any offense involving a violation of his official duties. An officer shall be deemed to have been convicted under this subdivision when trial court judgment is entered."

Section 1770, subdivision (h) is the only section which purports to define at which point a "conviction" occurs. By its passage, the Legislature has determined that, for the purpose of exclusion, a public officer is "convicted" when a judgment is entered.

Appellants, however, contend that a person stands "convicted" for purposes of exclusion from office as soon as the jury returns a verdict. They assert that the legal meaning of "conviction" was well settled before the adoption of the Constitution in 1879 and, therefore, the language in the constitutional provision must be construed accordingly. Appellants apparently do not directly attack the constitutionality of section 1770, subdivision (h), as amended. Rather, they claim that in order to interpret that section constitutionally, the occurrence of a vacancy for purposes of replacement must be distinguished from the disqualification from office which occurs immediately upon the verdict. We disagree.

. . . .

For purposes of disbarment, however, our Supreme Court has consistently construed "conviction" as requiring a "final judgment," not a verdict. In 1885, the court, in *People v. Treadwell*, 66 Cal. 400, 401 [5 P. 686], held that during the pendency of an appeal, "there is not such a final conviction against the defendant as the law contemplates to justify his removal, ..." and, therefore, disbarment proceedings could not be commenced. This meaning was reaffirmed in 1920 by the court in *In re Riccardi*, 182 Cal. 675 [189 P. 694], construing the same statutes (former Code Civ. Proc., §§ 287–289) providing for disbarment upon "conviction" of a felony involving moral turpitude. In support of its interpretation that a verdict was not sufficient, the court discussed, among other things, the apparent legislative intent, settled construction of the statutes, and the dire collateral consequences of an "absolute" disbarment depriving an attorney of a valuable property right. (*Id.*, at p. 679.)

In *McKannay v. Horton*, 151 Cal. 711 [91 P. 598], the specific question was whether after verdict and judgment, but while an appeal was pending, a person (the mayor) was convicted of a felony for purposes of automatic removal from office within the meaning of identical provisions on vacancy in the San Francisco charter and the state law (former Pol. Code, § 996). The court held he was. The case is authority for the proposition not disputed nor decided herein that "conviction" for purposes of declaring a vacancy occurs as soon as the judgment is entered, despite the pendency of an appeal. The majority stated that it was "not required to decide in this case that the entry of a verdict of guilty constitutes a 'conviction.'" (*Id.*, at p. 718.) However, they describe the removal from office as "a consequence which flows" (*id.*, at p. 720) from the "judgment of conviction" (*ibid.*). But three concurring justices categorically stated that the verdict constitutes a conviction. (*Id.*, at p. 722.)

California constitutional provisions, other than article XX, section 11, employing the terms "convicted" or "conviction" have been construed in California decisions.

In *In re Anderson*, 34 Cal. App. 2d 48 [92 P.2d 1020], the appellate court construed "conviction" as meaning the verdict when used in the constitutional provision empowering the governor to grant pardons "after conviction." The *Anderson* court ruled that conviction in that article should be accorded its "normal popular meaning [the verdict]." (*Id.*, at p. 51.) It distinguished *Riccardi* because of the "peculiar consequences that would follow" (*id.*, at p. 54) if such interpretation were applied in the disbarment situation.

In *Truchon v. Toomey, supra*, 116 Cal. App. 2d 736, the court construed a different constitutional provision (former art. II, § 1) and reached the contrary result that judgment was required. At issue was the meaning of "conviction" for purposes of disfranchisement. The court held that judgment and sentence were necessary before a person was "convicted" within the meaning of the constitutional provision declaring that no person convicted of any infamous crime shall exercise the right of an elector. *Truchon* reviewed authorities in California and elsewhere, including the leading New York case of *People v. Fabian* (1908) 192 N.Y. 443 [85 N.E. 672], and concluded that: (1) conviction had various meanings — the ordinary meaning of verdict and the technical meaning of judgment; and (2) "'[t]he general rule where conviction results in civil penalties and disabilities is that conviction takes the technical meaning of verdict plus judgment.'" (116 Cal.App.2d at p. 745.) *Truchon* distinguished *Anderson*, pointing out there was no real conflict because the philosophy concerning pardons is different from that concerning the imposition of a serious disability.

From the foregoing, we conclude that the terms "convicted" and "conviction" have not had a fixed single meaning in California law. In the context of statutes or constitutional provisions imposing civil penalties or disabilities, they have never been construed to mean the verdict of guilt. Such penalties or disabilities have not been found applicable until at least a court judgment has been entered. The California decisions are in this respect in accord with the weight of authority in other jurisdictions. As the Supreme Court of Oregon recently stated: "Where civil penalties and disabilities are involved ... a large majority of jurisdictions accept the technical meaning of 'conviction' and hold that conviction takes place only after a determination of guilt and a pronouncement of the judgment of the court. [Citations.]" (*Vasquez v. Courtney* (1975) 272 Ore. 477 [537 P.2d 536, 537].)

We consider disqualification from public office a significant civil disability. In California, the right to hold public office has long been recognized as a valuable right of citizenship. In 1869, in *People v. Washington*, 36 Cal. 658, 662, our Supreme Court declared that "[t]he elective franchise and the right to hold public offices constitute the principal political rights of citizens of the several States." In *Carter v. Com. on Qualifications etc.*, 14 Cal. 2d 179, 182 [93 P.2d 140], the court pointed out: "[T]he right to hold public office, either by election or appointment, is one of the valuable rights of citizenship ... *The exercise of this right should not be declared prohibited or curtailed except by plain provisions of law. Ambiguities are to be resolved in favor of eligibility to office....*" (Italics added.) More recently, the high court, citing Carter, has termed the right to hold public office a "fundamental right." (*Zeilenga v. Nelson*, 4 Cal. 3d 716, 720 [94 Cal. Rptr. 602, 484 P.2d 578]; *Fort v. Civil Service Commission*, 61 Cal. 2d 331, 335 [38 Cal. Rptr. 625, 392 P.2d 385].) Thus, any ambiguity in a constitutional provision calling for forfeiture of an existing office and disqualification from holding public office should be resolved in favor of continued eligibility. When this is done, article XX, section 11 of our Constitution, which is ambiguous, can reasonably be construed as authorizing the Legislature to enact legislation providing that forfeiture and exclusion from public office shall be effective upon entry of a judgment of conviction.

Such being the case, cognizance must be taken of the rule stated by our Supreme Court in *Methodist Hosp. of Sacramento v. Saylor*, 5 Cal. 3d 685, 693 [97 Cal. Rptr. 1, 488 P.2d 161], where the court said (quoting *Pacific Indemnity Co. v. Indus. Acc. Com.*, 215 Cal. 461, 464 [11 P.2d 1, 82 A.L.R. 1170]): "'[W]e cannot construe a section of the Constitution as if it were a statute, and adopt our own interpretation without regard to the legislative construction. Where more than one reasonable meaning exists, it is our duty to accept that chosen by the legislature.'"

In *San Francisco v. Industrial Acc. Com.*, 183 Cal. 273 [191 P. 26], a workmen's compensation statute allowing recovery for work-connected "disease" as well as trauma was attacked on the ground that the enabling constitutional provision authorized the Legislature to prescribe such benefits for "injury" only. Our Supreme Court, after reviewing a number of decisions from other jurisdictions construing the word "injury," stated (*id.*, at pp. 279–280):

> "As between these two conflicting lines of decision it is not necessary to determine where the weight of authority lies, or which cases are the better reasoned. If those which give the broader meaning to the word 'injury' do not lay down the better rule, they at least establish this, that it cannot be said that the broader meaning is an impossible or unreasonable one. The situation then, as it presents itself in connection with our constitutional provision, is at least that both by general usage and by the decisions of the courts the word 'injury' may have either of two meanings, and that either is reasonable and possible. In such a situation, *where a constitutional provision may well have either of two meanings, it is a fundamental rule of constitutional construction that, if the legislature has by statute adopted one, its action in this respect is well nigh, if not completely, controlling.* When the legislature has once construed the constitution, for the courts then to place a different construction upon it means that they must declare void the action of the legislature. It is no small matter for one branch of the government to annul the formal exercise by another and coordinate branch of power committed to the latter, and the courts should not and must not annul, as contrary to the constitution, a statute passed by the legislature, unless it can be said of the statute that it positively and certainly is opposed to the constitution. This is elementary. But plainly this cannot be said of a statute which merely adopts one of two reasonable and possible constructions of the constitution...."

"'... Where a statute has been adopted in carrying into effect a constitutional provision, the constitutional provision and statute must both be so construed as to permit the act to stand....'" (Italics added.)

In the case at bench, the Legislature adopted Government Code section 1770, subdivision (h) as part of its duty to carry into effect article XX, section 11. In so doing, it adopted the reasonable meaning that "convicted" signifies the entry of a judgment.

The fact that the constitutional provision herein was mandatory rather than permissive as in *San Francisco* is not significant. Article XX, section 11 provided that the Legislature shall pass laws "to exclude from office ... persons convicted of ... perjury...." Such a provision, while mandatory, is not self-executing. It contemplates and requires legislation to give it effect. (*Taylor v. Madigan*, 53 Cal. App. 3d 943, 951 [126 Cal. Rptr. 376].) The Constitution clearly directs that the responsibility for carrying into effect this provision lies with the Legislature, and not with the courts.

Appellants concede that Government Code section 1770, subdivision (h) appears "at variance" with their claim that rendition of the verdict constitutes "conviction" because it provides that an office becomes vacant at the time the judgment is entered. Appellants claim, however, that the Legislature lacked the power to authorize persons to continue exercising the privileges of public office after a jury verdict of guilty. They cite *Pacific G. & E. Co. v. Industrial Acc. Com.*, 180 Cal. 497, 500 [181 P. 788], for the proposition that terms in a constitution "must be construed in the light of their meaning at the time of the adoption of the [constitutional provision], and cannot be extended by legislative definition, for such extension would, in effect, be an amendment of the constitution, if accepted as authoritative...." Appellants' reliance on *Pacific G. & E. Co.* is misplaced. In contrast to the case at bench, the meaning of the terms there involved was not ambiguous.

The Legislature has enacted three sections in the Government Code which are pertinent to the issue herein as legislation implementing article XX, section 11. All three are in title I, "Public Officers and Employees." Section 1021 provides: "A person is disqualified from holding any office upon conviction of designated crimes as specified in the Constitution and laws of the State." Section 3000 provides that "[a]n officer forfeits his office" under identical circumstances, to wit "conviction . .. as specified in the Constitution and laws of the State." In turn, section 1770 provides that "[a]n office becomes vacant on the happening of any of the following events before the expiration of the term." The subdivisions then list the specified events causing such a vacancy. Until 1971, subdivision (h) simply stated that the vacancy occurs on the "conviction of a felony or any offense involving a violation of his official duties." That year, the Legislature amended the provision to add the following sentence: "An officer shall be deemed to have been convicted under this subdivision when trial court judgment is entered." The legislative intent to construe "convicted" for purposes of a vacancy is patent from the clear language of the amendment.

We must read these three sections together, viewing them in context and harmonizing the whole to ascertain the legislative purpose. It then becomes evident that the Legislature must have intended that an officer would become disqualified, and thereby forfeit his office so as to create a vacancy when judgment was entered following the verdict. It is patent that if the officer is disqualified and has forfeited his office, such office must be vacant. All three events necessarily occur simultaneously.

In summary, the meaning of "convicted" is ambiguous. It has been variously construed by the courts and defined by the Legislature dependent on the context. Where, as here, a civil disability flows as a consequence of the "conviction," the majority and better rule is to require the entry of judgment. In any event, the Legislature has chosen to adopt that meaning for exclusion from public office, and its interpretation is dispositive.

We, therefore, hold, in accord with the Attorney General's opinion (57 Ops.Cal.Atty.Gen. 374, 375 (1974)) that under California law a "conviction" for the purpose of exclusion from public office "consists of a jury verdict or court finding of guilt followed by a judgment upholding and implementing such verdict or finding." Thus, on October 2, 1974, and not before, Lieutenant Governor Reinecke automatically forfeited his office and his rights and powers incident thereto. That forfeiture created a vacancy. Until then, Reinecke was entitled to exercise the powers and privileges of office. He was, therefore, entitled to all the compensation he received.

Accordingly, the orders of dismissal are affirmed.

ALLPORT, Acting P.J., and COBEY, J., concurred.

Notes and Questions

1. As the court explained, the sole substantive issue presented here was whether Reinecke was "convicted" within the meaning of the applicable California constitutional provision (former Article XX, Section 11) and relevant implementing statutes for the purpose of exclusion from holding public office upon the rendition of the jury verdict or the judgment. The court concluded that the term "conviction," at least when it applies to excluding someone from public office, does not occur until rendition of the judgment following the verdict.

2. Nonetheless, with Reinecke having resigned from office, why did the court conclude the proceedings were not moot? Is the notion a legal matter being of general public interest and likely to recur sufficient to overcome the judiciary's general reluctance to address moot legal issues?

3. Was the court's ruling that the issue of when a person is "convicted" of a crime for the purpose of exclusion from public office narrowly construed to address this particular set of facts? Why did the court in this case determine that a "conviction" occurs only when a judgment is entered? Does this conclusion change if the person convicted is not being excluded from public office?

4. The court in this case noted that the Supreme Court had summarily denied the earlier writs, but this court deemed that action to not be res judicata. What was the basis for this holding?

5. The court also noted that in California, as in other jurisdictions, "the word 'conviction' has been used with varying meanings." (*Truchon v. Toomey*, 116 Cal.App.2d 736, 740, 254 P.2d 638.) In fact, the court went so far as to "conclude that the terms 'convicted' and 'conviction' have not had a fixed single meaning in California law." The court spent most of the written opinion reviewing federal and state constitutional and statutory provisions related to "convictions," as well as numerous state and federal court decisions addressing the term. Was all that discussion necessary in order to reach the holding made by the court?

C. Holding More than One Office

As we might imagine, with a full-time Legislature, California state legislators are not allowed to hold any incompatible office. In other words, they cannot hold more than one office at the same time. The purpose is to ensure that legislators fulfill their constitutional duties and not have any potential conflicts of interest while fulfilling those duties because they are serving in an additional or even an incompatible office.

Rich v. Industrial Accident Commission

(1940) 36 Cal.App.2d 628

OPINION

PULLEN, P.J.

This is a review of the findings and award of the Industrial Accident Commission, whereby that body directed that petitioner take nothing on account of his asserted claim for compensation, due to injuries sustained.

The facts are brief and undisputed. At the time of the accident hereinafter referred to, W. P. Rich was a state senator, having been reelected in 1938 for a term of four years. On December 20, 1938, he was notified by Lieutenant Governor George J. Hatfield that he had been appointed a member of a special senate committee to attend the funeral of Senator McColl, to be held in Redding on December 23d. This appointment and all of the activities of this committee occurred after the adjournment of the 1938 session of the legislature sine die and not during any special or subsequent session. Senator Rich accepted the assignment, and in a state car assigned for that purpose, operated by a state employee, he proceeded from his home in Marysville to Redding, where he attended the funeral of his deceased colleague. After the funeral services, as Senator Rich was returning to his home in the same car and operated by the same state employee, the car was overturned, causing serious injury to petitioner.

The question for determination here is whether or not the injury suffered by petitioner occurred in the course of or arising out of his employment as a state senator, or stating it more directly, is attending funerals of fellow senators reasonably incidental to the duties of a state senator?

It is admitted that there was no express legislative or constitutional authority for the appointment of a committee of the senate to attend the funeral of a member of the legislature, although for many years it has been customary for senators to attend funerals after adjournment of the senate as members of a committee designated by the presiding officer of that body, that is by the Lieutenant Governor. It is also admitted that a state senator is an employee within the meaning of the Workmen's Compensation Act (sec. 3351b, Labor Code). Since petitioner is claiming the benefit of that act the burden is placed upon him (Labor Code, sec. 5705) to show that at the time of the injury he was performing services growing out of and incidental to his employment, and that he was acting within the course of his employment. (Sec. 3600, Labor Code.)

While it is true there is no express provision of the law requiring the senate to pay tribute to a deceased member, it has been a custom of long standing to pay such public tribute to a deceased member, thereby upholding the respect and dignity of its office, and it might well be considered a part of its function and duty.

Public money has often been used to erect monuments, commemorating the life of some great man, and bestowing dignity and honor upon the office he once had held. In the city of Sacramento, the state maintains a burying ground where may be interred a person who, at the time of his death, was a state officer or member of the senate or assembly. (Sec. 3596, Pol. Code.) Attendance at funeral rites of a deceased public official by one holding a public position is not alone done as a mark of respect to the deceased and his family but is a tribute to the office he held and tends to maintain a public respect for such office and the government of which it is a part. It would seem, therefore, that the attending of funerals of fellow public officers can, in proper cases, be said to be reasonably included in the duties of a public officer, and in so doing, such public officer is in effect and in law, acting in his official capacity, and especially so when the attending officer was expressly designated by his superior officer to be present in such representative capacity.

Considerable stress is laid upon the fact that the injury to petitioner occurred while the legislature was not in session, and it is urged that the act of a senator in attending a funeral could not be considered as applying directly or indirectly to the business of the legislature, and that the principles laid down in the case of *Special Assembly Interim Committee v. Southard*, 13 Cal. 2d 497 [90 PaCal.2d 304], and *Swing v. Riley*, 13 Cal. 2d 513 [90 PaCal.2d 313], are here decisive.

In the *Southard* case, supra, the court held that neither the senate nor assembly could authorize a committee to act after the legislature had adjourned sine die. In the case of *Swing v. Riley, supra*, the court held that both houses of the legislature acting together by a concurrent resolution did not have the power to appoint a committee to act after the final adjournment of the legislature.

In those two cases the court was considering the legislative functions only of the legislature, and the effect of single house and joint resolutions, and held that such resolutions are not substitutes for the statutory authority necessary to permit legislative committees to subpoena witnesses and to incur expenses after the adjournment of the legislature sine die.

The duties of the committee of which petitioner was a member, did not depend upon the legislative functions of the senate, nor was it an investigating or fact-finding committee. The difference in purpose of an interim committee to find the facts and report back to the legislature, and a committee to pay respect to a deceased member of that branch of our government, is so obviously different that we cannot rest our conclusions upon the cited cases.

While the primary duty of a senator is legislative, there is also imposed upon him other and nonlegislative duties which are incidental to that primary function. Some nonlegislative duties are when a senator is sitting as a member of a court of impeachment, or sitting to receive the returns of the election of a governor, or choosing one for the office of governor in case of a tie vote. In *People v. Blanding*, 63 Cal. 333, it was held the confirmation of appointments by the senate was not a legislative function. Other instances might be readily called to mind; and there is nothing in the cited cases that attempts to deny to the legislature powers other than legislative, or powers incidental thereto.

When the legislature is acting in a nonlegislative capacity, the members thereof are still acting within the scope of their authority and employment.

Nor are these cited cases authority for the proposition that a state senator ceases to be a public officer upon final adjournment of the legislature and prior to the end of the term for which he is elected, or for the proposition that, as a public officer, he does not have any powers whatsoever of any nonlegislative duties, however limited they may be, incidental to his status as a public officer. If such were true, not only would a state senator be denied the right of exercising nonlegislative powers while the legislature was in session, but it would deny to the legislature itself the power by statute to impose post session proper nonlegislative duties upon a state senator.

That members of the legislature are considered officers of the state during their entire term of office is evidenced by certain constitutional limitations, such as accepting other office (art. IV, sec. 19) and their manner of payment of salary. (Art, IV, sec. 23.) The *Interim Committee* cases, *supra*, upon which respondent relies, in fact concede that by statute such power exists to invest in a legislative committee the right to exercise legislative functions subsequent to final adjournment.

While it is true, as contended by respondent, that a public officer's powers may not be enlarged by custom, nevertheless, under the workmen's compensation laws, at least statutory or constitutional duties of a public officer or employee may be enlarged by custom so as to entitle him to compensation benefits. It was held in *San Bernardino County v. Industrial Acc. Com.*, 217 Cal. 618 [20 PaCal.2d 673], that "an employee is in the course of his employment when he does those reasonable things which his contract with his employer, expressly or impliedly, permits him to do"; and *Department of Public Works v. Industrial Acc. Com.*, 128 Cal. App. 128 [16

PaCal.2d 777], is support for the contention that custom may enlarge the scope of employment of public employees. In *Entremont v. Whitsell*, 13 Cal. 2d 290 [89 PaCal.2d 392], the Supreme Court of this state recognizes that the rules of law applicable to workmen's compensation cases may differ from the rules applicable to other types of cases. In other jurisdictions we find the same rule: *City of Alexandria v. McClary*, 167 Va. 199 [188 S.E. 158]; *Grym v. City of Virginia*, 193 Minn. 62 [257 N.W. 661]; *Scrivner v. Franklin School Dist.*, 50 Idaho, 77 [293 P. 666].

If, therefore, we can depend upon the rule that custom may be looked to for a guide we find that the duty involved in this case is one inherent to the public office of state senator. We find it established and has been the custom for many years for members of the senate to pay their tribute of respect to a deceased fellow member or a member of the executive or judicial branch of our government, and for the president of the senate to designate certain members to attend such funerals as officially representing all the other members of the senate.

It therefore appears to us that not only by reason of the rules of the Workmen's Compensation Law but also upon the broad basis that attending funerals of fellow senators, when done by a member especially designated to attend as a representative of that body, is incidental to the duties of the office of a state senator, and that petitioner has fully sustained the burden placed upon him.

Therefore, the injury sustained by petitioner occurred in the course of his employment and in furthering the business of his employer, in the rendering of a service to the memory of, and adding dignity and respect to the office of a deceased officer of the state.

The findings and award of the Industrial Accident Commission are annulled and set aside.

THOMPSON, J., and TUTTLE, J., concurred.

Notes and Questions

1. Members of the Legislature are considered officers of the state during their entire term of office as evidenced by certain constitutional limitations, such as accepting other offices and their manner of payment of salary. The court in this case was addressing whether workers' compensation coverage extended to a state Senator who was attending the funeral of a fellow legislator.

2. The court in this case drew a distinction between prior cases and this dispute based upon whether the activity engaged in dealt with legislative or non-legislative work. In earlier cases, the dispute arose whether committees could be created or conduct legislative business, such as investigations that may involve the subpoena of witnesses, after the legislative session had adjourned. Is the analogy to these cases a correct one when the President of the Senate merely appointed Senators to represent the entire house at a funeral of a former colleague? Does the decision in this case stand upon the distinction that this was not a legislative committee to conduct legislative business? Or is that not relevant to the decision made in this case?

3. If, as the court found, "the duties of the committee of which petitioner was a member, did not depend upon the legislative functions of the senate, nor was it an investigating or fact-finding committee," why was the Senator found to have been involved in work duties for workers' compensation coverage purposes?

4. Is a state legislator only a public officer when the Legislature is in session? Is a distinction made between adjournment of session and the end of a legislator's term?

D. Power of the Legislature

Unlike the U.S. Congress, which possesses only those specific powers delegated to it by the U.S. Constitution, the California Legislature possesses plenary legislative authority except as specifically limited by the California Constitution, and lying at the core of that plenary authority is the power to enact laws.

A state statute passed by the Legislature to place an advisory question on the statewide ballot was held to be a valid exercise of the Legislature's implied power to investigate the necessity to exercise its power to petition for a federal constitutional change, even though the Legislature had already submitted to Congress a call for a national convention to pass an amendment.

The state constitutional provision stating that the Legislature may provide for the selection of committees necessary for the conduct of its business does not implicitly prohibit the Legislature from using advisory ballot measures to determine the electorate's position on whether the Legislature should exercise its power to petition for federal change.

The constitutional provision stating that the Legislature may provide for the selection of committees necessary for the conduct of its business does not implicitly prohibit the Legislature from using advisory ballot measures to determine the electorate's position on whether the Legislature should exercise its power to petition for and participate in federal constitutional change. (*Howard Jarvis Taxpayers Assn. v. Padilla* (2016) 62 Cal.4th 486.)

E. Unique Aspects of California's Electoral System

In California state government, there are nine constitutional offices elected statewide, as well as 120 legislative seats. Constitutional officers are limited to serving two four-year terms in each office. Having to run statewide is a major cost driver in fundraising for these offices. While there are higher campaign contribution limits for these offices, there is still enormous pressure to raise vast sums of money for campaigning up and down the State of California.

For legislative offices, California has 120 elected officials who have lower campaign contribution limits than those candidates for statewide office. Assembly Members have to run for re-election every two years, and State Senators have to run for re-election every four years. They can serve a maximum of 12 years in either house or a combination of both houses. There is always pressure to raise money and actively campaign until their final term in office.

With regard to judicial offices, there are two ways to be a superior court judge in this state, either through appointment by the Governor or by running for the office. For appellate court judgeships, it is by gubernatorial appointment only (i.e., no one can run for such a judgeship), and they are subject to a retention election every 12 years.

Let us take a look at some of the unique aspects of California's electoral system.

Judicial Elections

As opposed to federal judgeships, which are lifetime appointments pursuant to the federal constitution, California judges are generally appointed by the Governor and then subject to confirmation by the JNE Commission and ultimately subject to voter approval through the use of a retention election.

During Governor Jerry Brown's first term, three state Supreme Court justices were removed from office. In June 2018, a Superior Court judge was recalled from office due to the light sentence imposed on a sex offender.

Keep in mind that judges are political in a limited context. For example, the Governor and Legislature provide funding for the courts, including their salaries and their staff. It is not done by an independent body. Also, the Legislature and Governor can obviously change the law and effectively overturn the decisions of the judicial branch. As such, judges are keenly aware of the powers of the other two branches of government and the roles that they play in state government.

California's electoral system is not unique among the states. Individuals run for elected office for a myriad of reasons and the vast majority of them never make it. But judicial elections in this state are limited to trial courts (called the Superior Court) and no one can run for an appellate court seat either on a Court of Appeal or on the state's Supreme Court.

There are three significant measures that have impacted California's electoral system over the past decade. The first is the "top two primary"; the second is the modified term limits law; and the third is the independent redistricting commission. The following is a brief summary of these three measures.

Top Two Primary

Historically, California had followed the regular approach for the June (or sometimes March, when we tried to have an impact on presidential elections) primary by having the top Democrat candidate and the top Republican vote-getter face each other in the November general election. That all changed more than a decade ago when a budget deal resulted in the top two primary system being placed on the statewide ballot and ultimately being adopted by the voters.

As a result, in California, the two candidates who proceed to the November general election are the two candidates with the most votes at the primary. That means that there can be two Democrats facing each other, or two Republicans facing each other, or a Democrat facing a Republican, or a major party candidate facing a third-party candidate.

The intent of this ballot measure, as stated by then-Senator Abel Maldonado and Governor Arnold Schwarzenegger, who advocated for it, is to cause candidates to moderate their positions, because they will have to appeal to a majority of voters in the primary election, rather than wait until the general election.

That intent has not really been borne out by experience so far. In other words, there have been numerous instances where the same party's candidates face each other in both June and November, or where the more conservative or more progressive candidate has still won in the November general election. Time will tell whether this "reform" of the election process will bring the changes desired by its proponents.

Term Limits Law

Prop. 140 in 1990 was adopted by the voters after proponents demonized then-Assembly Speaker Willie Brown, Jr. (the self-anointed "Ayatollah of the Assembly") and got the voters to adopt strict term limits for members of the Legislature. As a result, Assembly terms were limited to three two-year terms, and Senators were limited to two four-year terms.

Such brief term limits meant that legislators were constantly running for office in this state, and public policy issues were not being adequately addressed by legislators in a thoughtful and long-term manner according to critics. The total time in office, for a lifetime, was 14 years, assuming a candidate was successful in getting elected in both houses.

As a result, there were two efforts, the first being unsuccessful, to change the term limits law. According to political pundits, the first measure failed because it was retroactive in its application, meaning that it applied to legislators who were in office at that time, and the state's voters did not like that approach. So that change was rejected by voters.

The second version, and ultimately the successful one, changed the term limits law to allow a maximum of twelve years of service in either house or a combination of the two. The likely reason that this version passed is because it was pitched to voters as reducing the total amount of time that an individual could spend in the Legislature, reducing it from a total of 14 years to a total of 12 years.

The idea behind this change in the term limits law is to allow legislators to serve the entire time in one house, which in theory would bring stability to both houses of the Legislature and allow legislators to look at public policy issues and proposed solutions for a longer period of time and to address these issues with a long-term view, knowing that they may be in the same seat for 12 years and must therefore answer for the votes that they take and the choices they make on addressing policy changes.

There was also talk that legislators would serve on fewer committees, spend more time in their districts, conduct more investigations and oversight activities, and develop long-term expertise in subject matters. The "jury is still out" on whether some of these results will actually happen.

In the meantime, there continues to be the usual complaints from observers of the legislative process, such as that legislators still push through last-minute legislation that has not been properly vetted and that legislators are still moving around with different committee assignments and are not necessarily developing the levels of expertise for which some had hoped.

Independent Redistricting Commission

As with most legislatures around the country, California had long given the job of drawing district lines for the Legislature, congressional seats, and the Board of Equalization to the Legislature itself. As a result, critics claimed that incumbents were always protected in the every-decade process and so challengers had a tougher time taking on long-term incumbents. Also, those in the minority party often complained that legislative district drawing resulted in seats ensuring majority party control with few "toss-up" seats that might change partisan hands.

Eventually, the voters spoke and approved ballot measures that took this job out of the hands of the Legislature and placed the job with the Independent Citizens Commission to draw the political boundaries. The belief of the proponents was that district lines would be drawn in a non-partisan and fair manner that would not ensure protection for incumbents which, in turn, would result in more competitive seats and hoped-for increase in minority party representation.

Since that time, however, Democrats have increased their ranks, and some Republicans have privately complained that they now prefer the earlier approach, which would more likely protect them from losing any more seats in the Legislature.

Finally, as an important aspect of California's electoral system, Prop. 34 provides the law for campaign financing, because it provides contribution limits on funds raised for candidates for state offices, either the Legislature or the nine constitutional offices.

There is one important distinction between federal and state campaign laws in that, in California, corporate contributions can be made. However, at the federal level, they are prohibited and only individual contributions can be made, unless the business has created a political action committee (PAC) that combines individual contributions into the PAC.

Also, in California, state legislators are elected pursuant what is called a "plurality vote in single winner contests," as opposed to ranked-choice voting or multi-winner voting. The same occurs with constitutional officers who are elected on a statewide basis. Some local governments utilize a multi-winner election in which multiple candidates can be elected to the same office (such as the city council). A handful of local jurisdictions utilize a ranked-choice voting system.

States are allowed to determine which particular electoral system they want to use for state offices. For federal offices, they must naturally follow the federal Constitution's requirements.

F. Term Limits Are Constitutional

California enacted its first set of term limits in 1990, which limited senators to two four-year terms and assembly members to four two-year terms. One issue that was raised was whether this was a lifetime limitation, or if a legislator could "sit out" an election and then serve additional terms. However, the courts determined that a lifetime ban is constitutional.

Later, the Legislature placed a measure on the statewide ballot, which the voters approved, so that now a legislator can serve 12 years in either house or in combination of the two houses for a maximum of twelve years. While a legislator could take a "break" from serving in office and then return to office, he or she still cannot serve more than a total of twelve years in state legislative office.

Bates v. Jones
(9th Cir. 1997) 131 F.3d 843, certiorari denied

OPINION

THOMPSON, Circuit Judge:

OVERVIEW

A former state legislator and several of his constituents filed this action, contending the lifetime term limits in California's Proposition 140 violate their federal constitutional rights. After a trial, the district court agreed and enjoined the Proposition's enforcement. The district court stayed its injunction pending appeal.

A divided three-judge panel of this court affirmed the district court. A majority of the active judges of the full court then voted to rehear the case en banc and, to accommodate the parties' interests, we agreed to rehear the case on an expedited basis. We have done so and we now reverse the district court.

FACTS

The facts are set forth in detail in the panel's opinion, see *Jones v. Bates*, 127 F.3d 839 (9th Cir. 1997). We summarize them briefly.

In 1990, California voters approved Proposition 140, an initiative which imposed specific lifetime term limits for state legislators and certain state officers. The Proposition limited state senators to two terms, state assembly members to three terms, and the state governor to two terms. Cal. Const. art. IV, 2(a); art. V, § 2. The Proposition also limited to two terms the Lieutenant Governor, Attorney General, Controller, Secretary of State, Treasurer, Superintendent of Public Instruction, and the members of the Board of Equalization. *Id.* at art. V, § 11; art. IX, § 2; art. XII, § 17. The Proposition declared that the lack of term limits created "unfair incumbent advantages" which "discourage qualified candidates from seeking public office and create a class of career politicians, instead of the citizen representatives envisioned by the Founding Fathers." *Id.* at art. IV, § 1.5. The Proposition stated the term limits were necessary "[t]o restore a free and democratic system of fair elections, and to encourage qualified candidates to seek public office...." *Id.*

In 1991, the state legislature and several individual legislators and constituents challenged before the California Supreme Court the constitutionality of Proposition 140's term limits. On a petition for a writ of mandate, the California Supreme Court concluded that Proposition 140's lifetime term limits did not violate the plaintiffs' federal constitutional rights. See *Legislature v. Eu*, 816 P.2d 1309 (Cal. 1991), cert. denied, 503 U.S. 919 (1992).

Thereafter, in 1995, Tom Bates, a former member of the California Assembly, and a group of his constituents filed the present action, also alleging the lifetime term limits of Proposition 140 are unconstitutional. The district court agreed. See *Bates v. Jones*, 958 F. Supp. 1446 (N.D. Cal. 1997). The district court determined Proposition 140 imposed a severe burden on the plaintiffs' first and fourteenth amendment rights and was not narrowly tailored to advance a compelling state interest. The district court enjoined the enforcement of Proposition 140 but stayed its injunction pending appeal.

A panel of this court, with Judge Sneed dissenting, affirmed the judgement of the district court on other grounds and did not reach the issue whether the term limits are constitutional. *Bates*, 127 F.3d at 844. This en banc review followed.

DISCUSSION

A. Res Judicata

The State presents a strong argument that res judicata bars the plaintiffs from bringing the present action because they are bound by the decision of the California Supreme Court in *Eu*. We conclude, however, that California would apply its public interest exception to the res judicata doctrine and, thus, would reexamine the merits of the constitutional issue.

California recognizes an exception to the doctrine of res judicata when "the public interest requires that relitigation not be foreclosed." *Kopp v. Fair Political Practices Comm'n*, 905 P.2d 1248, 1256 (Cal. 1995) (quotations and citations omitted). When the issue previously litigated involves an issue of public importance and there are unusual circumstances favoring reexamination of the issue, California does not apply preclusive effect to the prior determination. See *id.*; *City of Sacramento v. State*, 785 P.2d 522, 528–29 (Cal. 1990); *Arcadia Unified Sch. Dist. v. State Dep't of Educ.*, 825 P.2d 438, 440–42 (Cal. 1992).

The current case justifies application of the public interest exception. In *Eu*, the California Supreme Court decided to exercise its original jurisdiction on a petition for a writ of mandate, because of the significance and importance of the legal issues raised by the challenge to Proposition 140. As a result, the usual avenues of appellate review were not utilized and the California Supreme Court did not have the benefit of a lower court record. Further, when deciding *Eu*, there was a paucity of case law addressing the validity of term limits. Since *Eu,* the United States Supreme Court has decided two significant cases, shedding light on that issue, *U.S. Term Limits, Inc. v. Thornton,* 514 U.S. 779 (1995), and *Burdick v. Takushi,* 504 U.S. 428 (1992). We conclude that, in the unique circumstances of this case, the public interest exception applies. We therefore consider the merits of the case.

B. Notice

The three-judge panel did not resolve whether Proposition 140 violates the plaintiffs' first and fourteenth amendment rights. Instead, the panel determined Proposition 140 was invalid because the Proposition and the ballot materials did not provide California voters with sufficient notice that the Proposition imposed lifetime rather than consecutive term limits. *Bates,* 127 F.3d at 844. We disagree, and, consistent with the California Supreme Court, we hold that the relevant ballot materials and the surrounding context provided sufficient notice making it clear that Proposition 140 required lifetime bans.

The portion of the Proposition affecting legislators' states: "No Senator may serve more than 2 terms" and "No member of the Assembly may serve more than 3 terms." Nowhere in the Proposition does it state that these bans are less than absolute. As Judge Sneed pointed out in his dissent from the three-judge panel decision, the twenty-second amendment to the Constitution uses similar language: "[n]o person shall be elected to the office of the President more than twice...." There certainly is no confusion that this language imposes a lifetime ban on the office of the President — even though the amendment does not specifically use the term "lifetime."

The surrounding circumstances also clearly indicate the voters had sufficient notice that Proposition 140 imposed lifetime bans. The opposition materials to the Proposition, which were circulated to California voters, clearly state that elected state legislators will be "banned for life" and use "lifetime ban" or similar terminology no less than eleven times. Moreover, when Proposition 140 was submitted to the voters in 1990, there were two competing initiatives on the ballot imposing term limits. In contrast to Proposition 140's lifetime ban, Proposition 131 proposed consecutive term limits. The two propositions received extensive media attention, which was heightened after the California Supreme Court issued a decision five days before the election addressing which of two propositions would govern in the event both were approved. See *Taxpayers to Limit Campaign Spending v. Fair Political Practices Comm.,* 799 P.2d 1220 (Cal. 1990) (specifically addressing Propositions 68 and 73).

Assuming, without deciding, that a federal court may determine whether a state has given adequate notice to its voters in connection with a statewide initiative ballot measure dealing with term limits on state officeholders, we hold that California's notice with regard to Proposition 140 was sufficient.

C. Constitutionality of Proposition 140's Lifetime Term Limit

In *Burdick,* the Supreme Court set forth the analysis we must apply to determine the constitutionality of Proposition 140.

We must weigh "the character and magnitude of the asserted injury to the rights protected by the First and Fourteenth Amendments that the plaintiff seeks to vindicate" against "the precise interests put forward by the State as justifications for the burden imposed by its rule," taking into consideration "the extent to which those interests make it necessary to burden the plaintiff's rights." *Burdick*, 504 U.S. at 434 (quoting *Anderson v. Celebrezze*, 460 U.S. 780, 789 (1983)). If the measure in question severely burdens the plaintiffs' rights, we apply strict scrutiny review. *Burdick*, 504 U.S. at 434. If, however, the law "imposes only 'reasonable, nondiscriminatory restrictions' upon the First and Fourteenth Amendment rights of voters, 'the State's important regulatory interests are generally sufficient to justify' the restrictions." *Id.* (quoting *Anderson*, 460 U.S. at 788).

The rights which the plaintiffs seek to vindicate in this case are the right to vote for the candidate of one's choice and the asserted right of an incumbent to again run for his or her office. Proposition 140's impact on these rights is not severe. As argued by the State, term limits on state officeholders is a neutral candidacy qualification, such as age or residence, which the State certainly has the right to impose. See *Burdick*, 504 U.S. at 433. With regard to incumbents, they may enjoy the incumbency of a single office for a number of years, and, as pointed out by the California Supreme Court, they are not precluded from running for some other state office.

Most important, the lifetime term limits do not constitute a discriminatory restriction. Proposition 140 makes no distinction on the basis of the content of protected expression, party affiliation, or inherently arbitrary factors such as race, religion, or gender. Nor does the Proposition "limit political participation by an identifiable political group whose members share a particular viewpoint, associational preference, or economic status." *Anderson*, 460 U.S. at 793.

Proposition 140's minimal impact on the plaintiffs' rights is justified by the State's legitimate interests. As the Proposition itself states, a lack of term limits may create "unfair incumbent advantages." Long-term entrenched legislators may obtain excessive power which, in turn, may discourage other qualified candidates from running for office or may provide the incumbent with an unfair advantage in winning re-election....

As pointed out by Judge Sneed in his dissent from the three-judge panel opinion, *Thornton* does not provide support for the argument that Proposition 140's term limits are unconstitutional. *Bates*, 127 F.3d at 868 (Sneed, J., dissenting). In *Thornton*, the Court addressed a state's attempt to impose term limits on members of Congress. See *Thornton*, 514 U.S. at 783. The case did not involve a state's amendment of its constitution to impose term limits on state office-holders.

Term limits, like any other qualification for office, unquestionably restrict the ability of voters to vote for whom they wish. On the other hand, such limits may provide for the infusion of fresh ideas and new perspectives, and may decrease the likelihood that representatives will lose touch with their constituents. *Thornton*, 514 U.S. at 837. California voters apparently perceived lifetime term limits for elected state officials as a means to promote democracy by opening up the political process and restoring competitive elections. This was their choice to make. Cf. *Clements v. Fashing*, 457 U.S. 957, 972 (1982).

We hold that Proposition 140's lifetime term limits do not violate the plaintiffs' first and fourteenth amendment rights. The judgement of the district court invalidating Proposition 140 is reversed and its injunction enjoining enforcement of the Proposition is vacated. The stay pending appeal is vacated as moot.

REVERSED.

Notes and Questions

1. A California constitutional amendment establishing term limits for state officeholders did not violate the First and Fourteenth Amendment rights of voters to vote for a candidate of their choice or the asserted right of an incumbent to again run for his or her office. Term limits did not constitute discriminatory restriction, were of minimal impact on plaintiff's rights, and were justified by the state's legitimate interest in avoiding unfair incumbent advantages.

2. The court ruled that the ballot measure gave voters sufficient notice that the proposition imposed lifetime, rather than consecutive, term limits. Official proponents of the ballot measure were entitled to intervention as a right of action, and the Secretary of State did not adequately represent proponents' interests.

3. Prior to this case, the California Supreme Court had already upheld the constitutionality of Prop. 140 and its lifetime term limits provision. How does the court in this case deal with the res judicata argument?

4. What is the basis for the court's decision that voters had sufficient notice that the term limits ban was for an individual's entire lifetime?

5. Why did the court conclude that, "most important, the lifetime term limits do not constitute a discriminatory restriction"?

G. Restrictions on Running for Office

Legislature of the State of California v. Reinecke

(1973) 10 Cal.3d 396

OPINION

WRIGHT, C.J.

In these mandate proceedings we are called upon to resolve the impasse created by the continuing failure of the Legislature to pass legislative and congressional reapportionment bills acceptable to the Governor.

Our first opinion herein was filed on January 18, 1972, when we adopted temporary apportionment plans for the 1972 elections. We concluded that the congressional districts set forth in Assembly Bill No. 16, 1971 First Extraordinary Session, and the existing statutes apportioning the Legislature should be in effect for the 1972 elections.

We retained jurisdiction to draft new reapportionment plans for the elections of 1974 through 1980 in the event the Legislature did not enact valid legislative and congressional reapportionment statutes by the close of its 1972 regular session. (*Legislature v. Reinecke* (1972) 6 Cal.3d 595, 603–604 [99 Cal.Rptr. 481, 492 P.2d 385].)

On May 10, 1972, at the request of the Senate of the State of California, we postponed the time for further court action, stating that "we will not exercise our retained jurisdiction herein if the Legislature, in 1972, enacts valid legislative and congressional reapportionment statutes either during its current regular session or at a special session called for that purpose." (*Legislature v. Reinecke* (1972) 7 Cal.3d 92, 93 [101 Cal.Rptr. 552, 496 P.2d 464].)

The Legislature did not enact reapportionment statutes in 1972 and we were therefore again faced with the necessity of judicial action. On March 23, 1973, we announced our intention to appoint three Special Masters to hold public hearings to permit the presentation of evidence and argument with respect to the possible criteria of reapportionment and of proposed plans to carry out such criteria, to recommend to the court reapportionment plans for possible adoption, and to set forth the criteria underlying the recommended plans and the reasons for the recommendations. We made clear, however, that the Legislature was not foreclosed from enacting reapportionment statutes if it could succeed in doing so. We stated that "If at any time during the proceedings contemplated by this order valid congressional and legislative reapportionment measures are enacted the court will entertain an application to dismiss these proceedings." (*Legislature v. Reinecke* (1973) 9 Cal.3d 166, 168 [107 Cal.Rptr. 18, 507 P.2d 626].)

On May 1, 1973, we appointed the Honorable Martin J. Coughlin, retired Associate Justice of the Court of Appeal, Fourth District, Division One, the Honorable Harold F. Collins, retired Judge of the Superior Court of Los Angeles County, and the Honorable Alvin E. Weinberger, retired Judge of the Superior Court of the City and County of San Francisco, as Special Masters, and we designated Justice Coughlin as Presiding Master. In accord with our order of March 23, 1973, we directed the Masters to present their recommendations to the court not later than August 31, 1973.

The Masters immediately undertook the task assigned to them, and on August 31 they filed their Report and Recommendations (hereinafter Report) with the court. During the course of the Masters' hearings the Legislature passed, but the Governor vetoed, Senate Bill 195, which contained congressional and legislative reapportionment plans. Since the Legislature has recessed for the year, it is now clear that the court has no alternative but to order its own reapportionment plans into effect.

....

We turn to the durational residence requirement of subdivision (c) of section 2 of article IV of the California Constitution. It provides: "A person is ineligible to be a member of the Legislature unless he is an elector and has been a resident of his district for one year, and a citizen of the United States and a resident of California for 3 years, immediately preceding his election." The Masters recognized the problem that might be created by this provision if, as it has now turned out, the new district lines did not exist in time for incumbent candidates and other candidates to select a residence so as to become a resident of a district for a year preceding the election. They recommended that the court "give consideration to an interpretation that the cited section is inapplicable" in such case. (Report, p. 446....) Their recommendation is sound. The constitutional provision contemplates that districts will be established for at least a year before the election, and since they were not so established, the provision by its own terms cannot apply. In the exercise of our equitable powers to fashion remedial techniques in this area of the law (see *Reynolds v. Sims* (1964) 377 U.S. 533, 585 [12 L.Ed.2d 506, 541, 84 S.Ct. 1362]; *Silver v. Brown* (1965) 63 Cal.2d 270, 278 [46 Cal.Rptr. 308, 405 P.2d 132]), we hold that a person is eligible to be a member of the Legislature if he becomes a resident of the district involved by January 28, 1974, the first day for filing the declaration of intention to become a candidate pursuant to Election Code section 25500, and otherwise complies with election law requirements.

In concluding their Report, the Masters stated: "A request has been received from the University of California Institute of Governmental Studies in Berkeley that its facilities be used as a depository of all material lodged with the Masters, with the understanding that the materials received will be safely stored, catalogued and made available for public and scholarly use. It is recommended, when the judgments in these actions become final, that pertinent materials that have been lodged with the Masters be released to the Institute of Governmental Studies for storing and use as requested, upon the conditions noted." (Report, p. 446.) We approve this recommendation and direct that it be carried out.

Since there is no reason to believe that any of the parties to these proceedings will not accede to our holdings herein, no purpose would be served by issuing writs of mandate. The alternative writ of mandate heretofore issued is discharged, and the petitions for writs of mandate are denied. Each party shall bear its own costs in the proceedings herein subsequent to the court's judgment on January 18, 1972.

This judgment is final forthwith.

Notes and Questions

1. What were the seven criteria that the Masters adopted and used in formulating their plans? Which of those criteria were challenged by the parties to this action?

2. What was the basis for the Court to reject the "maintenance of existing relationships between incumbents and their constituencies" as an additional criterion, even after the Court agreed that there are values in maintaining such relationships?

3. Despite finding that the Court was not bound by the Masters' resolutions of the conflicts raised by the parties in the litigation, why did the Court conclude that it should simply approve the districts drawn by the Masters if they appear to reflect reasonable applications of the seven criteria?

4. On what basis, according to the Court's opinion, could the inequalities among groups of electors that occur as a result of reapportioning a legislative body whose

members are elected for staggered four-year terms be addressed? The Court said that "these inequalities flow directly from provisions of the California Constitution...." However, the Court also provided a basis for ignoring this constitutional provision.

5. How did the Court address the "durational residence requirement" that is found in Article IV, Section 2(c)?

6. A provision of the Constitution that makes an individual ineligible to be a member of the Legislature unless he is an elector and has been a resident of his district for one year immediately preceding the election contemplates that districts will be established at least one year before the election and where, under a reapportionment plan, they are not so established, then the constitutional provision cannot apply, according to the Court's decision.

H. Special Elections

Veterans' Finance Committee of 1943 v. Betts

(1961) 55 Cal.2d 397

OPINION

McComb, J.

The Veterans' Finance Committee of 1943 (hereinafter referred to as "petitioner") has petitioned this court for a writ of mandate to compel Bert A. Betts, as Treasurer of the State of California (hereinafter referred to as "respondent"), to cause notice of sale of $100,000,000 principal amount of bonds to be published and to cause said bonds to be prepared and sold, as directed by resolutions of petitioner. Respondent has filed a general demurrer to the petition.

Petitioner is an agency of the State of California created by section 991 of the Military and Veterans Code of this state.

The members of the agency are: Edmund G. Brown, Governor of the State of California; Alan Cranston, State Controller; John E. Carr, Director of Finance; Joseph M. Farber, Director of Veterans Affairs; and respondent.

Chronology

The Legislature of the State of California, at its 1960 First Extraordinary Session, duly adopted a resolution entitled: "Assembly Constitutional Amendment No. 4 — A resolution to propose to the people of the State of California an amendment to the Constitution of the State, by adding to Article XVI thereof a new section to be numbered 21, relating to the issuance of bonds to provide farm and home purchase aid for veterans." (Stats. 1960, 1st Ex. Sess., ch. 12, p. ___, § ___.)

The Legislature at the same session duly adopted the Veterans Bond Act of 1960, constituting article 5h of chapter 6 of division 4 of the Military and Veterans Code of the State of California. (Stats. 1960, 1st Ex. Sess., ch. 50, p. ___, § 1; Stats. 1960, 1st Ex. Sess., ch. 80, p. ___, § 1.)

It was provided in said act that it should take effect upon adoption by the people of an amendment to the Constitution of the State of California approving, adopting, legalizing, ratifying, validating, and making fully and completely effective the Veterans Bond Act of 1960.

The Legislature at its 1960 First Extraordinary Session also duly adopted an act entitled: "An act calling a special election to be consolidated with the Direct Primary Election of 1960 and to provide for the submission to the electors of the State at such consolidated election constitutional amendments adopted by the Legislature at the 1960 First Extraordinary Session, to take effect immediately." (Stats. 1960, 1st Ex. Sess., ch. 12, p. ___; hereinafter referred to as "Chapter 12.")

This act passed both the Assembly and the Senate on April 6, 1960. It was approved by the Governor and filed in the office of the Secretary of State on April 9, 1960.

Section 4 of Chapter 12 reads: "The special election provided for in this act shall be proclaimed, held, conducted, the ballots shall be prepared, marked, collected, counted and canvassed and the results shall be ascertained and the returns thereof made in all respects in accordance with the provisions of the Constitution applicable thereto and the law governing general elections insofar as provisions thereof are applicable to the election provided for in this act."

A special election was held throughout the State of California on June 7, 1960, which special election was consolidated with the direct primary election held on the same date.

Assembly Constitutional Amendment No. 4 was submitted to the electors at the special election and appeared upon the ballot used in the consolidated election.

The Secretary of State distributed ballot pamphlets relating to the measures specified in Chapter 12, including Assembly Constitutional Amendment No. 4, to the county clerk of each county in the state not less than 30 days before the election, and the several county clerks commenced to mail the pamphlets to the voters not less than five days before the election. Distribution of the ballot pamphlets was conducted in all respects in accordance with the provisions of section 1515 of the Elections Code of the State of California.

At the election the people approved and ratified Assembly Constitutional Amendment No. 4 by a majority of the qualified electors voting thereon. 2,254,410 votes were cast in favor of the amendment, and 1,217,808 votes were cast against the amendment. This result was duly certified by the Secretary of State on July 11, 1960.

On December 7, 1960, upon request of the Department of Veterans Affairs of the State of California, supported by a statement of the pertinent plans and projects of the department, and with the approval of the Governor, petitioner adopted its Resolutions I (1960), II (1960), and III (1960).

Petitioner by said Resolution III (1960) determined that it was necessary and desirable to issue bonds authorized under the Veterans Bond Act of 1960 in the aggregate principal amount of $100,000,000 in order to carry such plans and projects into execution. The resolutions directed respondent, among other things, to cause bonds to be prepared, to cause notice of the sale of $100,000,000 principal amount of said bonds to be published, and to cause said bonds to be sold.

Under the terms of the Veterans Bond Act of 1960 and the State General Obligation Bond Law (Gov. Code, § 16720 et seq., as adopted by the Veterans Bond Act of 1960), it is the duty of respondent, as Treasurer of the State of California, to cause notice of sale to be prepared and to cause bonds to be prepared and sold, as directed by petitioner.

Respondent has nevertheless refused to cause notice of such sale to be published and refused to cause bonds to be prepared and sold, as directed.

He bases his refusal upon the ground that Assembly Constitutional Amendment No. 4 was not validly adopted and is not a part of the Constitution of the State of California and that the Veterans Bond Act of 1960 has not been validly ratified and approved, for the reason that no proclamation of the special election called by Chapter 12 was issued by the Governor and no proclamation of the Governor was published in any county of the state prior to the date of the special election.

This is the sole question presented: Was the special election of June 7, 1960, invalid because no proclamation by the Governor was issued and published prior to the holding of the special election?

No.

The courts are reluctant to defeat a fair expression of popular will in an election and will not do so unless so required by the plain mandate of the law.

It is the general rule that any errors or defects claimed to exist in a notice of election will not invalidate the election unless there is some showing that the electors were in fact misled by such defects. (*Ivanhoe Irr. Dist. v. All Parties*, 53 Cal.2d 692, 732 [21], [22] [350 P.2d 69]; *Simpson v. City of Los Angeles*, 40 Cal.2d 271, 277 [2] [253 P.2d 464].)

In the instant case the failure to issue a formal proclamation and publish it did not invalidate the election.

Section 1001 of the Elections Code provides: "At least 30 days before the general election, and at least 70 days before a special state-wide election or a special election to fill a vacancy in the Office of Representative in Congress, State Senator or Member of Assembly, the Governor shall issue an election proclamation, under his hand and the Great Seal of the State, and transmit copies to the boards of supervisors of the counties in which the elections are to be held."

The boards of supervisors must then publish the proclamation in their respective counties, as directed by section 1003 of the Elections Code.

It is essential to the proper exercise of the elective franchise that the voters be informed of the offices to be filled and the measures to be voted upon at any election. Accordingly, where the voters are not bound by law to take notice of the time and the place of holding an election, and the officers to be chosen or measures to be voted upon at such election, a failure to give the statutory notice vitiates the election.

Thus, it has been held that in the case of a special election to fill a vacancy caused by death or resignation, a proclamation is necessary to inform the electors that a vacancy exists and to call on them to fill it, even though the election to fill the vacancy is to be held at the same time and place as a general election. (*People v. Thompson*, 67 Cal. 627, 628 [9 P. 833]; *Kenfield v. Irwin*, 52 Cal. 164, 169; *McKune v. John B. Weller*, 11 Cal. 49, 62 et seq.; *People v. Porter*, 6 Cal. 26, 29.)

The rule is otherwise when the time and the place of holding an election, and the officers to be chosen or measures to be voted upon at such election, are prescribed by law, since the electors are presumed to know the law. Under such circumstances, the proclamation directed to be given by section 1001 of the Elections Code, being merely additional notice to that contained in the statute, is not requisite to the validity of the election. (*People v. Rosborough*, 14 Cal. 180, 188; *People v. Brenham*, 3 Cal. 477, 487.)

The rule is stated in Cooley's Constitutional Limitations, volume 2 (8th ed. 1927), page 1372: "Where, however, both the time and the place of an election are prescribed by law, every voter has a right to take notice of the law, and to deposit his ballot at the time and place appointed, notwithstanding the officer, whose duty it is to give notice of the election, has failed in that duty. The notice to be thus given is only additional to that which the statute itself gives, and is prescribed for the purpose of greater publicity; but the right to hold the election comes from the statute, and not from the official notice."

In the instant case Chapter 12 prescribed the time and the place of the special election and the measures to be voted upon. This constituted notice to the electors, given well in advance of the time set for the election, and the fact that no proclamation by the Governor was issued and published prior to the holding of the election does not affect the validity of the election.

The demurrer is overruled, and it is directed that a writ of mandate be issued forthwith in accordance with petitioner's prayer.

Gibson, C.J., Traynor, J., Schauer, J., Peters, J., White, J., and Dooling, J., concurred.

Notes and Questions

1. Special elections are those called by the Governor in order to fill a vacancy in a state or local office. The Elections Code specifies the dates when the Governor is required to determine the date of election. In case of a special election to fill a vacancy caused by death or resignation, a proclamation is necessary to inform electors that the vacancy exists and to call on them to fill it, though the election to fill the vacancy is to be held at the same time and place as the general election.

2. In this case, the Treasurer took the position that ACA 4 was not validly adopted because "no proclamation of the special election called by Chapter 12 was issued by the Governor and no proclamation of the Governor was published in any county of

the state prior to the date of the special election." The Court simply answered "no" to the claim that the special election was invalid. What was the basis for the Court's ruling that the special election was, in fact, valid?

I. Rules for Resignations and Vacancies

Government Code Title 1, Division 4, Chapter 4 deals with resignations and vacancies. Article 1 concerns resignations and contains §§ 1750 to 1752. Section 1750 requires all resignations to be in writing. A resignation by the Governor or Lt. Governor is made to the Legislature if it is session. If the Legislature is not in session, then it is made to the Secretary of State.

Resignations by all officers commissioned by the Governor are made to the Governor. For Members of the Senate or Assembly, resignations are made to the presiding officers of their respective houses, who are required to immediately transmit the resignation to the Governor. Resignations by all officers of a county or special district not commissioned by the Governor are made to the clerk of the board of supervisors of their respective counties.

Resignations by officers of a superior court are made to the presiding judge. Resignations by officers of a municipal corporation are made to the clerk of the legislative body of their corporation. And resignations by all other appointed officers are made to the body or officer that appointed them.

Section 1750.5 requires the Assembly Speaker or Senate Rules Committee Chair to immediately inform the Governor in writing whenever a resignation has been made to them from any board or commission having members appointed by the Speaker or Senate Rules Committee. Section 1751 specifies that, in all cases not otherwise provided for in this law, a resignation is made by filing the resignation in the office of the Secretary of State.

Under § 1752, for a general law, when a vacancy occurs in the elected mayor position, then the city council may fill that vacancy by appointing a member of the council to the office of mayor.

Government Code Title 1, Division 4, Chapter 4, Article 2 concerns vacancies and contains §§ 1770 to 1782. Section 1770 provides that an office becomes vacant when any of the following occur before the expiration of the term:

- The death of the incumbent
- An adjudication proceeding declaring that the incumbent is physically or mentally incapacitated due to disease, illness, or accident, and that there is reasonable cause to believe that the incumbent will not be able to perform the duties of his or her office for the remainder of his or her term
- His or her resignation
- His or her removal from office

- His or her ceasing to be an inhabitant of the state
- His or her absence from the state without the permission required by law beyond the period allowed by law
- His or her ceasing to discharge the duties of his or her office for the period of three consecutive months, except when prevented by sickness, or when absent from the state with the permission required by law
- His or her conviction of a felony or of any offense involving a violation of his or her official duties
- His or her refusal or neglect to file his or her required oath or bond within the time prescribed
- The decision of a competent tribunal declaring void his or her election or appointment
- The making of an order vacating his or her office or declaring the office vacant when the officer fails to furnish an additional or supplemental bond
- His or her commitment to a hospital or sanitarium by a court of competent jurisdiction as a drug addict, dipsomaniac, inebriate, or stimulant addict
- The incumbent is listed in the Excluded Parties List System [the list maintained and disseminated by the federal General Services Administration containing names of, and other information about, persons who are debarred, suspended, disqualified, or otherwise excluded from participating in a covered transaction, pursuant to federal law]

Section 1770.1 provides that the disqualification from holding office upon conviction or the forfeiture of office upon conviction is neither stayed by the initiation of an appeal from the conviction, nor set aside by the successful prosecution of an appeal from the conviction by the person suffering the conviction.

Section 1770.2 specifies that, upon the entry of a plea of guilty, the entry of a plea of nolo contendere, or the rendering of a verdict of a guilty either by a jury or by the court sitting without a jury of a public offense, the person found guilty is prohibited from assuming the office for which the person is otherwise qualified or is suspended immediately from the office the person holds.

Section 1772 sets forth that, when any office becomes vacant and no mode is provided by law for filling the vacancy, the Governor is required to fill the vacancy by granting a commission, to expire at the end of the next session of the Legislature or at the next election by the people.

Pursuant to § 1773, when a vacancy occurs in the office of Representative to Congress, or in either house of the Legislature, the Governor must, within 14 calendar days after the occurrence of the vacancy, issue a writ of election to fill the vacancy. Under § 1773.5, in addition to any other applicable provision of law, a vacancy occurs in the office of Representative in Congress in the event of his or her disappearance.

Section 1774 requires that, when an office, the appointment to which is vested in the Governor and Senate, either becomes vacant or the term of the incumbent expires, the Governor may appoint a person to the office or reappoint the incumbent after the expiration of the term. Until Senate confirmation of the person, that appointee serves at the pleasure of the Governor.

Under § 1774.5, no person holding an office which is deemed to be vacant may continue to discharge the duties of the office. In addition, the Governor cannot reappoint the person to the same office for a period of 365 days after the time the office has been deemed to be vacant.

Pursuant to § 1775, whenever there is a vacancy in the office of the Superintendent of Public Instruction, the Lieutenant Governor, Secretary of State, Controller, Treasurer, or Attorney General, or on the State Board of Equalization, the Governor is required to nominate a person to fill the vacancy who takes office upon confirmation by a majority of the membership of the Senate and a majority of the membership of the Assembly and who then holds office for the balance of the unexpired term.

In the event the nominee is neither confirmed nor refused confirmation by both the Senate and the Assembly within 90 days of the submission of the nomination, the nominee takes office as if he or she had been confirmed by a majority of the Senate and Assembly. In addition, after a vacancy has occurred in a constitutional office specified in § 1775, and prior to the time the vacancy is filled, the chief deputy to the constitutional officer discharges the duties of the office.

Section 1778 provides that a vacancy in any appointive office on the governing board of a special district is to be filled by appointment by the board of supervisors of the county in which the larger portion of the district is located unless, by the terms of the act under which the district is formed, another method of appointment is expressly provided.

Section 1782 specifies that, whenever a vacancy occurs on a state board or commission, or a seat on a board or commission is abolished by statute, the board or commission must notify the appropriate appointing authority of this occurrence, and the appropriate appointing authority then notifies the person occupying the vacated or abolished seat that the person may no longer serve on the board or commission.

Notes and Questions

1. There are quite a few statutory provisions related to instances where vacancies are created. While the list may not be exhaustive, are there other situations that would warrant a vacancy in a public office from being declared? What would be the basis for including any new situations in this statute?

J. Removal from Office

Government Code Title 1, Division 4, Chapter 7 deals with removal from office. Article 1, containing §§ 3000 to 3003, is on general provisions and was enacted in 1943. Section 3000 provides that an officer forfeits his office upon conviction of designated crimes as specified in the Constitution and laws of the state.

Pursuant to § 3001, any state, county, or city officer who is intoxicated while in discharge of the duties of his or her office, or by reason of intoxication is disqualified for the discharge of, or neglects his or her duties, is guilty of a misdemeanor. On conviction, he or she forfeits the office, and the vacancy is filled in the same manner as if the officer had filed his or her resignation in the proper office.

Under § 3002, whenever the Governor is authorized to appoint a person to an office subject to confirmation by the Senate, and no fixed term has been provided by law for the office, then the Governor may at any time, without cause and without hearing, remove the incumbent from the office and fill the vacancy occasioned by such removal in the same manner as if the officer had filed his or her resignation.

Section 3003 specifies that an elected officer of the state or a city, county, city and county, or district in this state forfeits his or her office upon the conviction of a crime pursuant to the federal or state Stolen Valor Act.

Government Code Title 1, Division 4, Chapter 7, Article 2 concerns impeachment and contains §§ 3020 to 3040. Section 3020 provides that state officers elected on a statewide basis, members of the State Board of Equalization, and judges of state courts are subject to impeachment for misconduct in office. Under § 3020.5, the Senate, when sitting as the court of impeachment, is a court of record. The officers of the Senate are the officers of the court.

Pursuant to § 3021, all impeachments are by resolution adopted, originated in, and conducted by managers elected by the Assembly. Section 3022 specifies that managers prepare articles of impeachment, present them at the bar of the Senate, and prosecute them. The trial is before the Senate, sitting as a court of impeachment. Section 3023 provides that, when an officer is impeached by the Assembly for a misdemeanor in office, the articles of impeachment are delivered to the President of the Senate.

Section 3031 provides that, at the time and place appointed, and before the Senate acts on the impeachment, the Secretary administers to the President of the Senate, and the President of the Senate to each of the members of the Senate present, an oath truly and impartially to hear, try, and determine the impeachment. No member of the Senate can act or vote upon the impeachment, or upon any question arising thereon, without having taken this oath.

Section 3032 specifies that the defendant cannot be convicted on impeachment without the concurrence of two-thirds of the members. If two-thirds of the members elected do not concur in a conviction, the defendant is acquitted. Section 3033 states that, after conviction and at the time appointed by the Senate, the Senate pronounces judgment in the form of a resolution entered upon the Senate Journal.

Under § 3034, on the adoption of the resolution by a majority of the members present who voted on the question of acquittal or conviction, it becomes the judgment of the Senate. Section 3037 specifies that, whenever articles of impeachment against any officer subject to impeachment are presented to the Senate, the officer is temporarily suspended from office and cannot act in his or her official capacity until acquittal.

Pursuant to § 3038, upon temporary suspension of any officer other than the Governor, the office at once can be temporarily filled by an appointment made by the Governor, with the advice and consent of the Senate. The office is filled by the appointee until the acquittal of the party impeached or, in case of his removal, until the vacancy is filled at the next election.

Under § 3039, if the Lieutenant Governor is impeached, notice of the impeachment is immediately given to the Senate by the Assembly in order that another president may be chosen.

Government Code Title 1, Division 4, Chapter 7, Article 3 concerns removal other than by impeachment and contains §§ 3060 to 3075. Section 3060 specifies that an accusation in writing against any officer of a district, county, or city, including any member of the governing board or personnel commission of a school district or any humane officer, for willful or corrupt misconduct in office, may be presented by the grand jury of the county for, or in, which the officer accused is elected or appointed.

Under § 3073, the same proceedings may be had on like grounds for the removal of a district attorney, except that the accusation must be delivered by the foreman of the grand jury to the clerk, and by him to a judge of the Superior Court of the county. The judge appoints a person to act as prosecuting officer in the matter, or places the accusation in the hands of the district attorney of an adjoining county, and requires him or her to conduct the proceedings.

Section 3074 specifies that any officer subject to removal pursuant to this article may be removed from office for willful or corrupt misconduct in office occurring at any time within the six years immediately preceding the presentation of an accusation by the grand jury.

Notes and Questions

1. Are all of these appropriate bases for an elected official to be removed from office? Should all of these provisions require a vote of the electorate? Is it appropriate for a public official to be removed from his or her office without a vote of the same electorate who placed that official in public office?

K. The Citizens Redistricting Commission

The California Citizens Redistricting Commission (CRC) is charged with completing the decennial job of drawing district lines for State Senators, State Assembly Members, U.S. Representatives, and State Board of Equalization Members. The CRC is established in Article XXI of the California Constitution, which deals with the redistricting of the Senate, Assembly, congressional, and Board of Equalization districts every ten years. This article of the state constitution was most recently amended by Proposition 11 on the November 4, 2008 ballot.

Article XXI contains the following three sections:

Section 1 states that, in the year following the year in which the national census is taken under the direction of Congress at the beginning of each decade, the Citizens Redistricting Commission must adjust the boundary lines of the Congressional, State Senatorial, Assembly, and Board of Equalization districts (also known as "redistricting") in conformance with the standards and process set forth in this article of the state Constitution.

Section 2 specifies that the CRC was created no later than December 31 in 2010, and in each year ending in the number zero thereafter. The section provides that the CRC must (1) conduct an open and transparent process enabling full public consideration of and comment on the drawing of district lines; (2) draw district lines according to the redistricting criteria specified in this article; and (3) conduct themselves with integrity and fairness.

The CRC consists of 14 members with specified political party registration. Each commission member is required to be a voter who has been continuously registered in California with the same political party or unaffiliated with a political party and who has not changed political party affiliation for five or more years immediately preceding the date of his or her appointment. The commission must establish single-member districts for the Senate, Assembly, Congress, and State Board of Equalization pursuant to a mapping process using specified criteria.

Section 3 provides that the CRC has the sole legal standing to defend any action regarding a certified final map and that it must inform the Legislature if it determines that funds or other resources provided for the operation of the CRC are not adequate, in which case the Legislature must provide adequate funding to defend any action regarding a certified map.

In addition to these constitutional provisions, California Government Code Title 2, Division 1, Chapter 3.2 deals with the Citizens Redistricting Commission in §§ 8251 to 8253.6. Section 8251 deals with general provisions, and Chapter 3.2 is intended to implement Article XXI of the state Constitution by establishing the process for the selection and governance of the CRC.

The state Auditor randomly selects the first eight members, three who are Democrats, three who are Republicans, and two who are either decline-to-state or are registered with a third party. This occurs after the four legislative leaders exercise their authority to eliminate the names of 24 applicants from the pool of 60 of the most qualified applicants identified by the Auditor. Those eight persons then choose the remaining six members. Together, they are responsible for drawing the new district lines.

Notes and Questions

1. Is the Legislature unable to utilize the decennial census in order to properly draw lines of legislative and congressional districts? Why should this inherently political role be done by an independent commission?

L. The California Citizens Compensation Commission

In 1990, the statewide electorate created the California Citizens Compensation Commission (CCCC) in state government. The voters passed Proposition 112 for the purpose of setting the salaries, as well as the benefits, of California's elected officials. Thereafter, in 2009, the statewide voters also adopted a ballot measure to preclude the CCCC from increasing the salaries of these elected officials during years in which the state has a budget deficit.

The CCCC is comprised of seven members who are appointed by the Governor for 6-year terms. State law requires the CCCC to meet by June 30 each year to decide what changes in compensation and benefits are to be made the following December. As a result, the CCCC's decisions are effective each December.

The CCCC is found in Article III, Section 8 of the California Constitution. Subdivision (a) creates the CCCC and specifies that there are seven members appointed by the Governor and charges the commission to "establish the annual salary and the medical, dental, insurance, and other similar benefits of state officers."

Subdivision (b) specifies the commission's membership, including three public members with specific areas of expertise; two members who have experience in the business community; and two members who are either officers or members of a labor organization.

Subdivision (c) requires the Governor to "strive insofar as practicable to provide a balanced representation of the geographic, gender, racial, and ethnic diversity of the State in appointing commissioners." Subdivision (d) requires the Governor to appoint CCCC members and designate a chairperson. Pursuant to Subdivision (e), current and former officers and employees of the state are ineligible for being appointed to the commission.

Subdivision (f) requires public notice of all CCCC meetings and that these meetings be open to the public. A majority vote of the commission is required to adjust the benefits and salaries of state officers. Subdivision (h) specifies that the commissioners must consider the following factors:

1. The amount of time directly or indirectly related to the performance of the duties, functions, and services of a state officer.

2. The amount of the annual salary and the medical, dental, insurance, and other similar benefits for other elected and appointed officers and officials in the state with comparable responsibilities, the judiciary, and, to the extent practicable, the private sector, recognizing, however, that state officers do not receive, and do not expect to receive, compensation at the same levels as individuals in the private sector with comparable experience and responsibilities.

3. The responsibility and scope of authority of the entity in which the state officer serves.

4. Whether the Director of Finance estimates that there will be a negative balance in the Special Fund for Economic Uncertainties in an amount equal to or greater than 1 percent of estimated General Fund revenues in the current fiscal year.

Subdivision (l) defines the term "state officer" to include the Governor, Lieutenant Governor, Attorney General, Controller, Insurance Commissioner, Secretary of State, Superintendent of Public Instruction, Treasurer, member of the State Board of Equalization, and Member of the Legislature.

Under Subdivision (j), the commissioners are paid for their actual and necessary expenses for performing their duties. Pursuant to Subdivision (k), the Department of Personnel Administration furnishes staff and resources to the commission as needed to perform its duties.

Notes and Questions

1. What is the rationale for an independent commission comprised of non-elected citizens to make decisions about what public officials should be paid? Should this process be done as part of the state budget so that its fiscal considerations can be debated each year?

Chapter Six

Ethics

A. Legislative Code of Ethics

In California's Constitution, Article IV, dealing with the Legislature, there are several sections applicable to ethical conduct. These provisions are found in Sections 4 and 5 of the state Constitution.

Prohibition on Certain Earned Income — Section 4

Section Four prohibits a Member of the Legislature from knowingly receiving any salary, wages, commissions, or other similar earned income from a *lobbyist or lobbying firm*, or from a person who, during the previous 12 months, has been under a contract with the Legislature. While the Legislature is charged with enacting laws that define earned income, the Constitution provides that earned income does not include any community property interest in the income of a spouse.

Any Member who knowingly receives any salary, wages, commissions, or other similar earned income from a *lobbyist employer*, may not, for a period of one year following its receipt, vote upon or make, participate in making, or in any way attempt to use his or her official position to influence an action or decision before the Legislature involving a bill which he or she knows, or has reason to know, would have a direct and significant financial impact on the lobbyist employer and would not impact the public generally or a significant segment of the public in a similar manner.

Prohibition on Honorarium — Section 5

Section Five prohibits any Member of the Legislature from accepting any honorarium, and the Legislature must enact laws that implement this prohibition. In addition, the Legislature must enact laws that ban or strictly limit the acceptance of a gift by a Member of the Legislature from any source if the acceptance of the gift might create a conflict of interest.

Members of the Legislature are prohibited from knowingly accepting any compensation for appearing, agreeing to appear, or taking any other action on behalf of another person before any *state government board or agency*.

If a Member knowingly accepts any compensation for appearing, agreeing to appear, or taking any other action on behalf of another person before any *local government board or agency*, the Member may not, for a period of one year following the acceptance of the compensation, vote upon or make, participate in making, or in any way attempt to use his or her official position to influence an action or decision before the Legislature involving a bill which he or she knows, or has reason to know, would have a direct and significant financial impact on that person and would not impact the public generally or a significant segment of the public in a similar manner.

However, a Member of the Legislature may engage in activities involving a board or agency which are strictly on his or her own behalf, appear in the capacity of an attorney before any court or the Workers' Compensation Appeals Board, or act as an advocate without compensation or make an inquiry for information on behalf of a person before a board or agency

The Legislature is required to enact laws that prohibit a Member of the Legislature whose term of office commences on or after December 3, 1990, from lobbying, for compensation, before the Legislature for 12 months after leaving office.

The Legislature must also enact new laws, and strengthen the enforcement of existing laws, prohibiting Members of the Legislature from engaging in activities or having interests which conflict with the proper discharge of their duties and responsibilities.

In addition, in California's Government Code, there are several code sections that set forth the legislative code of ethics. These statutes were added in 1966 and are found in Title 2, Division 2, Part 1, Chapter 1, Article 2. The provisions of law are summarized below:

Prohibitions on Legislators — Gov't Code § 8920

A Member of the Legislature, state elective or appointive officer, or judge or justice may not, while serving in such a position, have any interest, financial or otherwise, direct or indirect, or engage in any business or transaction or professional activity, or incur any obligation of any nature, that is in substantial conflict with the proper discharge of his or her duties in the public interest and of his responsibilities as prescribed in the laws of this state.

In addition, a Member of the Legislature shall not do any of the following: Accept other employment that he or she has reason to believe will either impair his or her independence of judgment as to his or her official duties or require him or her, or induce him or her, to disclose confidential information acquired by him or her in the course of and by reason of his or her official duties; willfully and knowingly disclose, for pecuniary gain, to any other person, confidential information acquired by him or her in the course of and by reason of his or her official duties or use any such information for the purpose of pecuniary gain; or accept or agree to accept, or be in partnership with any person who accepts or agrees to accept, any employment, fee, or other thing of monetary value, or portion thereof, in consideration of his or her appearing, agreeing to appear, or taking any other action on behalf of another person before any state board or agency.

This does not prohibit a member who is an attorney at law from practicing in that capacity before any court or before the Workers' Compensation Appeals Board and receiving compensation therefor. It also does not prohibit a member from acting as an advocate without compensation or making inquiry for information on behalf of a constituent before a state board or agency, or from engaging in activities on behalf of another which require purely ministerial acts by the board or agency and which in no way require the board or agency to exercise any discretion, or from engaging in activities involving a board or agency which are strictly on his or her own behalf.

A Member of the Legislature may not receive or agree to receive, directly or indirectly, any compensation, reward, or gift from any source except the State of California for any service, advice, assistance or other matter related to the legislative process, except fees for speeches or published works on legislative subjects and except, in connection therewith, reimbursement of expenses for actual expenditures for travel and reasonable subsistence for which payment or reimbursement is not made by the State of California.

A Member of the Legislature may not participate, by voting or any other action, on the floor of either house, in committee, or elsewhere, in the passage or defeat of legislation in which he or she has a personal interest, except in specified circumstances.

Substantial Conflicts with Duties — Gov't Code § 8921

A person subject to this article has an interest that is in substantial conflict with the proper discharge of his or her duties in the public interest and of his or her responsibilities or a personal interest, arising from any situation, within the scope of this article, if he or she has reason to believe or expect that he or she will derive a direct monetary gain or suffer a direct monetary loss, as the case may be, by reason of his or her official activity.

He or she does not have an interest that is in substantial conflict with the proper discharge of his or her duties in the public interest and of his or her responsibilities as prescribed in the laws of this state or a personal interest, arising from any situation, within the scope of this article, if any benefit or detriment accrues to him or her as a member of a business, profession, occupation, or group to no greater extent than any other member of that business, profession, occupation, or group.

Proper Discharge of Duties — Gov't Code § 8922

A person subject to this article is not engaged in any activity that is in substantial conflict with the proper discharge of his or her duties in the public interest and of his or her responsibilities, or does not have a personal interest, arising from any situation, solely by reason of either of the following:

(a) his or her relationship to any potential beneficiary of any situation is one that is defined as a remote interest, or (b) receipt of a campaign contribution, so long as the contribution is not made on the understanding or agreement, in violation of law, that the person's vote, opinion, judgment, or action will be influenced by the contribution.

Employee Prohibition — Gov't Code § 8924

An employee of either house of the Legislature is prohibited, during the time he or she is employed, from committing any act or engaging in any activity prohibited by this article. The provisions of this article that are applicable to a Member of the Legislature are also applicable to any employee of either house of the Legislature. However, this part does not prohibit an employee of either house of the Legislature from serving in an elective or appointive office of a regional or local public agency.

Council on Science and Technology — Gov't Code § 8924.5

The establishment of the California Science and Technology Policy Fellowships as a professional development program is consistent with the Legislature's intent in requesting the creation of the council and is expressly designed to fulfill the council's mission of assisting state policymakers as they face increasingly complex decisions related to science and technology challenges confronting the state in the 21st century.

The services of a California Science and Technology Policy Fellow provided by the California Council on Science and Technology and duly authorized by the Senate Committee on Rules, the Assembly Committee on Rules, or the Joint Committee on Rules are not compensation, a reward, or a gift to a Member of the Legislature.

A California Science and Technology Policy Fellow provided by the California Council on Science and Technology and duly authorized by the Senate Committee on Rules, the Assembly Committee on Rules, or the Joint Committee on Rules is not an employee of either house of the Legislature.

Inducement — Gov't Code § 8925

No person can induce or seek to induce any Member of the Legislature to violate any provision of this law.

Violations — Gov't Code § 8926

Every person who knowingly and willfully violates any provision is guilty of a misdemeanor, and every person who conspires to violate any provision is guilty of a felony.

Notes and Questions

1. Do these Government Code provisions cover all ethical challenges that may be faced by an elected official? If not, what other provisions should be added to the California Government Code?

B. The Role of the Legislative Ethics Committees

Ethics in the California Legislature is an important topic. As such, both houses of the Legislature have their own ethics committees. The Senate has adopted an official Code of Conduct for its members, while the Assembly has not. Nonetheless, both houses have extensive ethics and conflicts of interest rules, and both are bound by constitutional and statutory ethics rules as well.

The Assembly Legislative Ethics Committee consists of six Members of the Assembly who are appointed by the Assembly Speaker. The committee has the power to investigate and make any appropriate findings and recommendations concerning violations of the rules by Assembly Members.

The Committee's authority is set forth in the Standing Rules of the Assembly and in Article 3 (commencing with §8940) of Chapter 1 of Part 1 of Division 2 of Title 2 of the Government Code.

Under the Assembly Rules, any person may file a verified complaint in writing stating the name of the Assembly Member who is alleged to have violated any standard of conduct. The written complaint must set forth the particulars of the alleged violation "with sufficient clarity and detail to enable the committee to make a determination."

The Committee may issue advisory opinions to Assembly Members regarding the standards of conduct and their application and construction to the house's Members. The Committee may also secure an opinion from the Legislative Counsel or it can issue its own opinion. Any committee advisory opinion must be prepared by Committee members or its staff and must be adopted by the Committee.

The Committee is required to conduct twice a year an orientation course on the relevant statutes and regulations governing official conduct of Assembly Members. The Rules Committee actually establishes the course's curriculum. In addition, at least once every two-year session, every Assembly Member and every Assembly employee must take this course. The Committee is also charged with conducting lobbying ethics courses for registered lobbyists.

The Senate Committee on Legislative Ethics is appointed by the Senate Committee on Rules and consists of six Senators. In addition to this Committee, the Rules Committee appoints an ethics ombudsperson to assist in the resolution of potential ethical violations, as well as assist the Senate in providing remedies for retaliatory conduct, to ensure that an informant or complainant does not suffer adverse consequences with respect to his or her employment.

The Senate ombudsperson is accessible to Senators, officers and employees of the Senate, as well as members of the public who wish to provide information or seek guidance about ethical standards or possible violations of standards before filing a formal complaint. All communications are confidential between the informant or complainant and the ombudsperson. The ombudsperson may refer the information to the Rules Committee Chair, the Legislative Ethics Committee Chair, and/or the Secretary of the Senate. In all cases, the identity of the informant or complainant is kept confidential, unless that person consents.

The Senate Committee is required to maintain a public hotline telephone number for purposes of contacting the ombudsperson. The complaints received through the hotline are considered informal complaints, and the existence of the complaints must be kept confidential.

In addition, the Committee must formulate and recommend standards of conduct for Senators, as well as the officers and employees of the Senate in performing their legislative responsibilities. At the request of any Senator, officer or employee of the Senate, the Committee must provide an advisory opinion regarding the standards of conduct of the Senate on the general propriety of past, current or anticipated conduct of that Senator, officer or employee.

The Committee also annually adopts "a clear, informative, and usable manual for the Senate" based on the standards of conduct adopted by the Senate. Similar to its Assembly counterpart, the Committee conducts annual workshops for Senators, officers and employees of the Senate.

At least once every two-year session, each Senator, officer and employee of the Senate has to attend a workshop. Moreover, at least once every two-year session, each Senator has to attend an individual training or review session conducted by the ombudsperson.

Readers should also be aware of two common misconception. The first is that the so-called "revolving door" limitation applies to legislators and staff alike. Under Article IV, Section 5(e) of the state Constitution, "The Legislature shall enact laws that prohibit a Member of the Legislature whose term of office commences on or after December 3, 1990, from lobbying, for compensation, as governed by the Political Reform Act of 1974, before the Legislature for 12 months after leaving office." No such limitation in the state Constitution or statute applies to legislative staff.

In addition, there is a misconception that only a court of law can remove a legislator from office. Under Article IV, Section 5(a)(1) of the state Constitution, "each house of the Legislature shall judge the qualifications and elections of its Members and, by rollcall vote entered in the journal, two-thirds of the membership concurring, may expel a Member." While this has not been used in recent decades, it is an available power to the Legislature.

Ethics will always play an important role in the legislative process. Legislators, staff, lobbyists and those working in and around the State Capitol should be aware of the role of the Assembly and Senate Ethics Committees and the duties and powers of these committees.

Notes and Questions

1. Is the Legislature capable of policing itself (i.e., its Members)? Should the Legislature utilize third parties, or even citizen groups, to review ethics complaints that are lodged against Members of the Legislature? What about complaints filed against legislative staff? How should those complaints be handled?

C. Code of Conduct

The State Senate adopted a "Standards of Conduct" for its house's Members and staff. At this time, the State Assembly has not adopted a similar document. The following is the published Standards:

Senate Standards of Conduct

WHEREAS, Public office is a public trust; and

WHEREAS, That trust is eroded by actions that appear to place the private interests of public officials above the public good; and

WHEREAS, The proper operation of democratic government requires that public officials be independent and impartial, that government policy and decisions be made through the established processes of government, that public officials not use public office to obtain personal benefits, that public officials avoid actions that create the appearance of using public office to obtain a personal benefit, and that the public have confidence in the integrity of its government and public officials; and

WHEREAS, In pursuit of these goals; now, therefore, be it Resolved by the Senate of the State of California, That the Standards of Conduct of the Senate are as follows:

First — Each Senator shall conduct himself or herself so as to justify the high trust reposed in him or her by the people and to promote public confidence in the integrity of the Senate.

Second — A Senator or officer or employee of the Senate shall not engage in un-ethical conduct or tolerate such conduct by others. Each Senator and each officer or employee of the Senate has a responsibility to report any apparent and substantial violation of these standards and to consult with the Senate Committee on Legislative Ethics or, at the option of the individual, the Senate ombudsperson regarding the propriety of any conduct that may violate these standards. Moreover, a Senator or officer or employee of the Senate shall not retaliate against a person who reports a possible violation of these standards or consults about conduct that may violate these standards, or against a person who the Senator, officer, or employee believes made such a report.

Third — Each Senator and each officer or employee of the Senate has an obligation to exercise his or her independent judgment on behalf of the people of California, rather than for personal gain or private benefit. (a) A Senator or officer or employee of the Senate shall not seek or accept anything from anyone that would interfere with the exercise of his or her independent judgment. (b) A Senator or officer or employee of the Senate shall not accept outside employment that is inconsistent with the con-scientious performance of his or her duties. (c) A Senator shall not use the prestige of his or her office, and an officer or employee of the Senate shall not use the status of his or her position, for material or financial gain or private benefit.

Fourth — Each Senator has an obligation to provide energetic and diligent repre-sentation, and each officer or employee of the Senate has an obligation to provide en-ergetic and diligent service on behalf of the Senate, with due consideration for the interests of all of the people of California. (a) Each Senator and each officer or employee of the Senate has an obligation to be informed and prepared, recognizing all sides of an issue. (b) Each Senator and each officer or employee of the Senate, when intervening on behalf of a constituent with any governmental agency, shall make every effort to ensure that decisions affecting any constituent are made on their merits and in a fair and equitable manner. (c) Each Senator shall be accessible to all constituents, making a special effort to attend to the concerns of those who might not otherwise be heard. (d) Each Senator shall fairly characterize the issues confronting the Legislature and accurately inform the public regarding the conduct of his or her office.

Fifth — Each Senator and each officer or employee of the Senate has an obligation to the public and to his or her colleagues to be informed about, and abide by, the rules that govern the proceedings of the Senate and the Legislature. **(a)** Each Senator shall perform his or her duties with courtesy and respect for both colleagues and those who may appear before the Senate. **(b)** In exercising the power of confirmation, each Senator shall act with due regard for the general welfare of the people of California. **(c)** Each Senator and each officer or employee of the Senate, when exercising oversight functions with respect to any governmental agency, shall act in an informed fashion, with attention to the underlying policies being implemented and with due respect for the independence of the agency.

Sixth — Each Senator, and each officer or employee of the Senate, acting in a position of leadership shall exercise his or her power and carry out his or her responsibility so as to enhance reasoned and visible decision-making by the Senate.

Seventh — Each Senator has an obligation to treat each officer or employee of the Senate with fairness and without discrimination, and to ensure that each officer or employee performs only those tasks for which there is a legislative or governmental purpose.

Eighth — Each officer or employee of the Senate has an obligation to perform his or her properly assigned duties using his or her best judgment with diligence and a duty of loyalty to the Senate as an institution.

Ninth — Each Senator and each officer or employee of the Senate has an obligation to make proper use of public funds. **(a)** A Senator or an officer or employee of the Senate shall not use state resources for personal or campaign purposes. **(b)** Each officer or employee of the Senate is free to volunteer for, and participate in, campaign activities on his or her own time, but an officer or employee of the Senate shall not be intimidated, coerced, or compelled, as a condition of continued appointment or employment, to either volunteer time or contribute money to a candidate or campaign. **(c)** A Senator or an officer or employee of the Senate shall not discuss legislative business of any kind while attending or hosting an event at which campaign funds or contributions are solicited, provided, or discussed.

Tenth — Each Senator and each officer or employee of the Senate shall uphold the Constitution of California and the Constitution of the United States, and shall adhere to the spirit and the letter of the laws, rules, and regulations governing officeholder conduct.

Eleventh — Each Senator and each officer or employee of the Senate shall conduct himself or herself in the performance of his or her duties in a manner that does not discredit the Senate.

Twelfth — Each Senator and each officer or employee of the Senate is expected to report to the proper authority any apparent and substantial violation of these standards or related statutes, regulations, or rules, and to consult with the Senate ombudsperson, the Senate Committee on Legislative Ethics, or any other appropriate governmental agency regarding the propriety of any conduct that may violate these standards.

D. Revolving Door Prohibition

There are rules for those leaving government service, which we refer to as the "revolving door" between the public and private sectors. Article IV, Section 5(e) of the California Constitution provides that "the Legislature shall enact laws that prohibit a Member of the Legislature whose term of office commences on or after December 3, 1990, from lobbying, for compensation, as governed by the Political Reform Act of 1974, before the Legislature for 12 months after leaving office."

In addition, Government Code Title 9, Chapter 7, Article 4 concerns the disqualification of former officers and employees. It begins with § 87406(a), which is known as the "the Milton Marks Postgovernment Employment Restrictions Act of 1990."

Section 87406(b)(1) provides that "a Member of the Legislature, for a period of one year after leaving office, shall not, for compensation, act as agent or attorney for, or otherwise represent, any other person by making any formal or informal appearance, or by making any oral or written communication, before the Legislature, any committee or subcommittee thereof, any present Member of the Legislature, or any officer or employee thereof, if the appearance or communication is made for the purpose of influencing legislative action."

In addition, § 87406(b)(2) specifies that "a Member of the Legislature who resigns from office, for a period commencing with the effective date of the resignation and concluding one year after the adjournment sine die of the session in which the resignation occurred, shall not, for compensation, act as agent or attorney for, or otherwise represent, any other person by making any formal or informal appearance, or by making any oral or written communication, before the Legislature, any committee or subcommittee thereof, any present Member of the Legislature, or any officer or employee thereof, if the appearance or communication is made for the purpose of influencing legislative action."

These provisions of the California Government Code are found in the Political Reform Act of 1974, which places restrictions upon legislators and other public officials when they leave government service. Basically, after leaving the Legislature, a former member of the State Senate or State Assembly has a one-year ban on certain activities. The one-year ban on legislators is extended if he or she resigns from office before the expiration of his or her term.

According to the Fair Political Practices Commission, the post-employment activities of a former state legislator are restricted in that the former legislator cannot, for one year, be paid to communicate with their former colleagues in the Legislature in an attempt to influence certain actions or proceedings. If the legislator resigns from office, then the one-year ban begins with the date of the resignation and ends one year after the adjournment sine die of the legislative session in which his or her resignation occurred.

There is also a ban on influencing prospective employers. In other words, a public official is prohibited from making, participating in making, or influencing a governmental decision that directly relates to a prospective employer.

Notes and Questions

1. While the "revolving door" prohibition applies to elected officials, as well as executive branch senior staff, it does not apply to legislative staff. Is that an appropriate exception to the revolving door limitation? What is the justification for not applying this prohibition to legislative staff?

E. Ethics in Government Act

The Ethics in Government Act (EGA) is found in California's Government Code Title 9, which concerns political reform, Chapter 9.5, related to ethics. Section 89500 specifies that the chapter is known as the Ethics in Government Act of 1990. Chapter 9.5 contains the following four articles:

Article 1 Honoraria, §§ 89501–89502

Article 2 Gifts, §§ 89503–89503.5

Article 3 Travel, § 89506

Article 4 Campaign Funds, §§ 89510–89522

Article 1 on honoraria defines the term to mean any payment made in consideration for any speech given, article published, or attendance at any public or private conference, convention, meeting, social event, meal, or like gathering. In addition, § 89510 specifically excludes earned income for personal services which are customarily provided in connection with the practice of a bona fide business, trade, or profession, such as teaching, practicing law, medicine, insurance, real estate, banking, or building contracting, unless the sole or predominant activity of the business, trade, or profession is making speeches.

Section 89502 prohibits any elected state officer, elected officer of a local government agency, or other individual from accepting any honorarium. In addition, no candidate for elective state office, for judicial office, or for elective office in a local government agency shall accept any honorarium.

Article 2 on gifts prohibits any elected state officer, elected officer of a local government agency, or other individual from accepting gifts from any single source in any calendar year with a total value of more than two hundred fifty dollars. In addition, no candidate for elective state office, for judicial office, or for elective office in a local government agency shall accept gifts from any single source in any calendar year with a total value of more than two hundred fifty dollars.

Moreover, no member of a state board or commission or designated employee of a state or local government agency shall accept gifts from any single source in any calendar year with a total value of more than two hundred fifty dollars if the member or employee would be required to report the receipt of income or gifts from that source on his or her statement of economic interests.

However, this section does not apply to a person in his or her capacity as a judge, or to a person in his or her capacity as a part-time member of the governing board of any public institution of higher education unless that position is an elective office.

Finally, this section does not prohibit or limit payments, advances, or reimbursements for travel and related lodging and subsistence permitted, or wedding gifts and gifts exchanged between individuals on birthdays, holidays, and other similar occasions, provided that the gifts exchanged are not substantially disproportionate in value.

This amount of $250 is adjusted annually to reflect changes in the Consumer Price Index. As a result, under current FPPC regulations, the gift limit is over $500.

Article 3 on travel provides that payments, advances, or reimbursements for travel, including actual transportation and related lodging and subsistence that is reasonably related to a legislative or governmental purpose, or to an issue of state, national, or international public policy, are not prohibited or limited by this chapter under specified conditions.

First, there is an exception for travel that is in connection with a speech, if the lodging and subsistence expenses are limited to the day immediately preceding, the day of, and the day immediately following the speech, and the travel is within the United States.

Second, there is an exception for travel that is provided by a government, a governmental agency, a foreign government, a governmental authority, a bona fide public or private educational institution, a nonprofit organization that is exempt from taxation, or by a person domiciled outside the United States who substantially satisfies the requirements for tax-exempt status.

Note that a gift of travel does not include any of the following:

- Travel that is paid for from campaign funds or that is a contribution.
- Travel that is provided by the governmental agency of a local elected officeholder, an elected state officer, member of a state board or commission, or a designated employee.
- Travel that is reasonably necessary in connection with a bona fide business, trade, or profession and that satisfies the criteria for federal income tax deduction for business expenses unless the sole or predominant activity of the business, trade, or profession is making speeches.
- Travel that is excluded from the definition of a gift by any other provision of this law.

Article 4 on campaign funds specifies that a candidate for elective state office may only accept contributions within the limits provided by law. All contributions deposited into the campaign account are deemed to be held in trust for expenses associated with the election of the candidate or for expenses associated with holding office. Section 89511 provides several definitions for terms used in this law.

Section 89512.5 specifies that any expenditure by a committee not subject to the trust imposed by law must be reasonably related to a political, legislative, or governmental purpose of the committee. Any expenditure by a committee that confers a substantial personal benefit on any individual or individuals with authority to approve the expenditure of campaign funds held by the committee must be directly related to a political, legislative, or governmental purpose of the committee.

Section 89513 governs the use of campaign funds for the specific expenditures set forth in that section. Campaign funds may not be used to pay or reimburse the candidate, the elected officer, or any individual or individuals with authority to approve the expenditure of campaign funds held by a committee, or employees or staff of the committee or the elected officer's governmental agency for travel expenses and necessary accommodations except when these expenditures are directly related to a political, legislative, or governmental purpose.

In addition, campaign funds may not be used to pay for or reimburse the cost of professional services unless the services are directly related to a political, legislative, or governmental purpose. Campaign funds cannot be used to pay health-related expenses for a candidate, elected officer, or any individual or individuals with authority to approve the expenditure of campaign funds held by a committee, or members of their households.

Campaign funds cannot be used to pay or reimburse fines, penalties, judgments, or settlements, except in specified circumstances. Other prohibited uses of campaign funds include:

- Campaign, business, or casual clothing generally
- Costs of tickets for entertainment or sporting events
- Personal gifts unless directly related to a government political, legislative, or governmental purpose
- Loans other than to organizations specified
- Penalties, judgments, or settlements for claims of sexual assault, abuse or harassment

Section 89515 allows campaign funds to be used to make donations or loans to bona fide charitable, educational, civic, religious, or similar tax-exempt, nonprofit organizations, where no substantial part of the proceeds will have a material financial effect on the candidate, elected officer, campaign treasurer, or any individual or individuals with authority to approve the expenditure of campaign funds held by a committee, or member of his or her immediate family, and where the donation or loan bears a reasonable relation to a political, legislative, or governmental purpose.

Section 89516 governs the use of campaign funds for vehicle expenses. Section 89517 prohibits campaign funds from being used for payment or reimbursement for the lease of real property or for the purchase, lease, or refurbishment of any appliance or equipment, where the lessee or sublessor is, or the legal title resides, in whole or in part, in a candidate, elected officer, campaign treasurer, or any individual or individuals with authority to approve the expenditure of campaign funds, or member of his or her immediate family.

Section 89518 prohibits campaign funds from being used to compensate a candidate or elected officer for the performance of political, legislative, or governmental activities, except for reimbursement of out-of-pocket expenses incurred for political, legislative, or governmental purposes.

Surplus campaign funds under § 89519 can only be used for the following:

- The payment of outstanding campaign debts or elected officer's expenses.

- The repayment of contributions.

- Donations to a bona fide charitable, educational, civic, religious, or similar tax-exempt, nonprofit organization, where no substantial part of the proceeds will have a material financial effect on the former candidate or elected officer, any member of his or her immediate family, or his or her campaign treasurer.

- Contributions to a political party committee, provided the campaign funds are not used to support or oppose candidates for elective office. However, the campaign funds may be used by a political party committee to conduct partisan voter registration, partisan get-out-the-vote activities, and slate mailers as that term is defined in § 82048.3.

- Contributions to support or oppose a candidate for federal office, a candidate for elective office in a state other than California, or a ballot measure.

- The payment for professional services reasonably required by the committee to assist in the performance of its administrative functions, including payment for attorney's fees and other costs for litigation that arises directly out of a candidate's or elected officer's activities, duties, or status as a candidate or elected officer, including, but not limited to, an action to enjoin defamation, defense of an action brought for a violation of state or local campaign, disclosure, or election laws, or an action from an election contest or recount.

Notes and Questions

1. Are there too many exceptions to the gift laws? Are these laws easy for public officials and their staff to comply with?

F. Prohibitions on Specified Officers

Government Code Title 1, Division 4 deals with public officers and employees. In Article 4 of Chapter 1, there are specified prohibitions applicable to specified officers. Article 4 contains §§ 1090 to 1099. These provisions were enacted in 1943.

Section 1090 prohibits Members of the Legislature, state, county, district, judicial district, and city officers or employees from being financially interested in any contract made by them in their official capacity, or by any entity or board of which they are members. In addition, § 1090 prohibits any state, county, district, judicial district, and city officers or employees from being purchasers at any sale or vendors at any purchase made by them in their official capacity.

In addition, § 1090 prohibits an individual from aiding or abetting a Member of the Legislature or a state, county, district, judicial district, or city officer or employee in violating this law. Section 1090.1 prohibits any officer or employee of the state or any Member of the Legislature from accepting any commission for the placement of insurance on behalf of the state.

Section 1091 specifies when an officer is deemed not to be interested in a contract entered into by a body or board of which the officer is a member within the meaning of this article if the officer has only a remote interest in the contract and if the fact of that interest is disclosed to the body or board of which the officer is a member and noted in its official records, and thereafter the body or board authorizes, approves, or ratifies the contract in good faith by a vote of its membership sufficient for the purpose without counting the vote or votes of the officer or member with the remote interest. The term "remote interest" is defined in this statute.

Under § 1091.1, the prohibition against an interest in contracts is not deemed to prohibit any public officer or member of any public board or commission from sub-dividing lands owned by him or in which he has an interest.

Section 1091.2 specifies that § 1090 does not apply to any contract or grant made by local workforce investment boards created pursuant to the federal Workforce Investment Act of 1998. Section 1091.3 specifies that § 1090 does not apply to any contract or grant made by a county children and families commission created pursuant to the California Children and Families Act of 1998. Section 1091.4 defines "remote interest" to include a person who has a financial interest in a contract if specified conditions are met.

Section 1091.5 details when an officer or employee is not deemed to be interested in a contract. Section 1091.6 specifies that an officer who is also a member of the governing body of an organization that has an interest in, or to which the public agency may transfer an interest in property that the public agency may acquire by eminent domain shall not vote on any matter affecting that organization.

Section 1092 requires that every contract made in violation of any of the provisions of § 1090 may be avoided at the instance of any party, except the officer interested therein. No contract may be avoided because of the interest of an officer therein unless the contract is made in the official capacity of the officer, or by a board or body of which he or she is a member. An action under this section must be commenced within four years after the plaintiff has discovered, or in the exercise of reasonable care should have discovered, a violation.

Section 1093 specifies that the Treasurer and Controller, county and city officers, and their deputies and clerks are prohibited from purchasing or selling, or in any manner receiving for their own or any other person's use or benefit any state, county or city warrants, scrip, orders, demands, claims, or other evidences of indebtedness against the state, or any county or city. In addition, individuals are prohibited from aiding or abetting the Treasurer, Controller, a county or city officer, or their deputy or clerk in violating this statute.

Pursuant to § 1098, any current public officer or employee who willfully and knowingly discloses for pecuniary gain, to any other person, confidential information acquired by him or her in the course of his or her official duties, or uses any such information for the purpose of pecuniary gain, is guilty of a misdemeanor. However, this section does not apply to any disclosure made to any law enforcement agency.

Section 1099 prohibits a public officer including, but not limited to, an appointed or elected member of a governmental board, commission, committee, or other body, from simultaneously holding two public offices that are incompatible. This section specifies that offices are incompatible when any of the following circumstances are present, unless simultaneous holding of the particular offices is compelled or expressly authorized by law:

- Either of the offices may audit, overrule, remove members of, dismiss employees of, or exercise supervisory powers over the other office or body
- Based on the powers and jurisdiction of the offices, there is a possibility of a significant clash of duties or loyalties between the offices
- Public policy considerations make it improper for one person to hold both offices

Pursuant to § 1099, when two public offices are incompatible, a public officer is deemed to have forfeited the first office upon acceding to the second. However, this section does not apply to a position of employment, including a civil service position. And this section does not apply to a governmental body that has only advisory powers. Finally, this section codifies the common law rule prohibiting an individual from holding incompatible public offices.

Notes and Question

1. The intent with these provisions of the Government Code is to prevent self-dealing when an elected official has a financial interest in his or her official duties. Do these statutes sufficiently deal with all possible scenarios for elected officials?

G. Crimes against the Legislative Power

California law contains statutes related to crimes against the "Legislative Power." These provisions are found in Article III, §§ 9050 to 9056, of the California Government Code and are intended to combat crimes against the Legislature and the legislative process.

Section 9050 provides that every person who willfully, and by force or fraud, prevents the Legislature, either of the houses composing the Legislature, or any of its Members from meeting or organizing is guilty of a felony.

Section 9051 provides that every person who willfully disturbs the Legislature, or either of the houses composing the Legislature while it is in session, or who commits any disorderly conduct in the immediate view and presence of either house tending to interrupt its proceedings or impair the respect due to its authority is guilty of a misdemeanor.

Section 9051.5 provides that, as used in this article of the Government Code, "bill or resolution" includes a constitutional amendment.

Section 9052 provides that every person who fraudulently alters the draft of any bill or resolution which has been presented to either of the houses composing the Legislature for passage or adoption, with intent to procure it to be passed or adopted by either house, or certified by the presiding officer of either house, in language different from that intended by the house, is guilty of a felony.

Section 9053 provides that every person who fraudulently alters the enrolled copy of any bill or resolution which has been passed or adopted by the Legislature, with intent to procure it to be approved by the Governor, certified by the Secretary of State, or printed or published by the state in language different from that in which it was passed or adopted by the Legislature is guilty of a felony.

Section 9053.5 provides that every person who intentionally, maliciously, with knowledge of the falsity, and with intent to defame a particular legislator, publishes or causes to be published any writing which purports to be a facsimile of an actual bill or resolution, or any part thereof, of the California Legislature, which is not an exact copy of a bill or resolution, or part thereof, which has been introduced in the Legislature, is guilty of a misdemeanor. This section does not apply to the print media, the electronic media, or to news services.

Section 9054 provides that every person who obtains, or seeks to obtain, money or other things of value from another person upon a pretense, claim, or representation that he or she can or will improperly influence in any manner the action of any member of a legislative body in regard to any vote or legislative matter, is guilty of a felony.

Section 9055 provides that every member of the Legislature convicted of any crime defined in this article, in addition to the punishment prescribed, forfeits his or her office and is forever disqualified from holding any office in the State of California.

Section 9056 provides that any person who secures through his or her influence, knowingly exerted for that purpose, the introduction of any bill, resolution or amendment into the State Legislature and thereafter solicits or accepts from any person other than a person upon whose request he or she secured such introduction, any pay or other valuable consideration for preventing or attempting to prevent, the enactment or adoption of such measure, while it retains its original purpose, is guilty of a crime and upon conviction is punishable by a fine of not exceeding $10,000 or by imprisonment in a county jail for not more than one year, or by both that fine and imprisonment.

Notes and Questions

1. These code sections provide significant criminal penalties for those persons who interfere with the Legislature and its official proceedings. Individuals are pro-

hibited from engaging in conduct that will falsify legislative documents or create inaccurate materials upon which legislators rely. Are these examples of conduct that are appropriate for such criminal penalties? Are there other types of actions that warrant similar criminal penalties?

H. Deal-Making (or Vote Trading) in California's Capitol — Is It Lawful?

We often read about the "wheeling and dealing" among elected officials that occurs in state capitols across this country, even here in California. While some Capitol observers refer to it as deal-making and lawful, others claim it is vote trading and improper or even unlawful. Which one is it?

The key question is whether there is anything improper or unlawful about either a legislator agreeing to vote for one bill because of promises that are made to that legislator, or another legislator or even to the Governor. In other words, does the push and pull, the compromises that are inherent in the lawmaking process, become improper or even unlawful when it occurs among elected officials?

Historically, the courts have been reluctant to examine the internal debates and activities of the legislative branch of government. However, with a claim of improper or possibly illegal activity, would the courts examine these allegations of misconduct?

Most Capitol observers note that, if elected officials are precluded from negotiating over provisions of bills, what will happen in the legislative process? Will it get bogged down? Others have asked whether it is impermissible for legislators to secure tangible benefits for their districts and constituents. While so-called "pork barrel politics" may appear unseemly to some people, does that make it illegal?

Every year in the California State Capitol, there are legislative "deals" between lawmakers or lawmakers and the Governor. With the passage of these deals, there has been private and public debate in and around the Capitol whether such deals violate any federal or state laws.

Let's begin by looking at federal and state laws that may be applicable in determining an answer to these concerns. First, it does not appear that either of the major federal criminal statutes apply in this case:

The Hobbs Act is found at 18 U.S.C. § 1951. According to the U.S. Attorney's Office:

> The Hobbs Act prohibits actual or attempted robbery or extortion affecting interstate or foreign commerce. Section 1951 also proscribes conspiracy to commit robbery or extortion without reference to the conspiracy statute at 18 U.S.C. § 371.

> Although the Hobbs Act was enacted as a statute to combat racketeering in labor-management disputes, the statute is frequently used in connection with cases involving public corruption, commercial disputes, violent criminals and street gangs, and corruption directed at members of labor unions.

There does not appear to be any allegations that there is actual or attempted robbery or extortion in these legislative negotiations. The Hobbs Act would not apply.

The Honest Services Fraud Act is found at 18 U.S.C. § 1346. Honest services fraud is a crime defined in the federal mail and wire fraud statute, which states: "For the purposes of this chapter, the term scheme or artifice to defraud includes a scheme or artifice to deprive another of the intangible right of honest services."

According to Wikipedia, "the statute has been applied by federal prosecutors in cases of public corruption, as well as in cases in which private individuals breached a fiduciary duty to another. In the former, the courts have been divided on the question of whether a state law violation is necessary for honest services fraud to have occurred."

The U.S. Supreme Court has interpreted this statute to only cover "fraudulent schemes to deprive another of honest services through bribes or kickbacks supplied by a third party who ha[s] not been deceived." There does not appear to be any allegation of bribes or kickbacks from a third party occurring in these legislative negotiations. The Honest Services Fraud Act would not apply.

In turning to California law, the state Constitution in Article IV, Section 15 provides: "A person who seeks to influence the vote or action of a member of the Legislature in the member's legislative capacity by bribery, promise of reward, intimidation, or other dishonest means, or a member of the Legislature so influenced, is guilty of a felony."

The California Constitution specifies "a person" who seeks to influence the vote or action of a legislator. This constitutional provision uses Member of the Legislature is three places. Even the legislator who is "so influenced" is guilty of a crime.

However, because this section uses "person" and "member of the Legislature," it appears to be directed at those who are not Members of the Legislature and who try to influence a legislator to act in his or her official capacity. If only non-legislators are affected by this provision, then neither the Governor's nor other legislators' efforts to "influence" another legislator's vote is covered.

California Constitution Article VII, Section 8(b) contains the following provision: "The privilege of free suffrage shall be supported by laws regulating elections and prohibiting, under adequate penalties, all undue influence thereon from power, bribery, tumult, or other improper practice." This provision raises questions of what constitutes "undue influence" and whether legislative negotiations amount to "power, bribery, or other improper practice."

Perhaps one could argue that the chief executive or legislative leaders could impose "undue influence" or "other improper practice" on Members of the Legislature, but that appears to be a stretch.

In turning to California statutes, bribery may be a logical place to start. Bribery is generally defined as an effort to influence a public official in conducting their official work using money or gifts. In legislative negotiations, neither money nor gifts change hands. But let's look at the specific California Penal Code sections that deal with public officers, employees, and legislative officers.

Penal Code § 7 provides the following definition of bribery: "The word 'bribe' signifies anything of value or advantage, present or prospective, or any promise or undertaking to give any, asked, given, or accepted, with a corrupt intent to influence, unlawfully, the person to whom it is given, in his or her action, vote, or opinion, in any public or official capacity."

The law does not require that the bribe is made or received to constitute a crime. However, do legislative negotiations amount to "bribery"? Have the legislators been given something of value? Did the Governor or legislative leaders promise something with a "corrupt intent to influence" other legislators? These are high thresholds to meet and do not appear to be in play with legislative negotiations.

Penal Code §§ 85 and 86 deal specifically with bribery by or of legislators and other elected officials. Penal Code § 85 makes it a felony for any person to give or offer to give a legislator a bribe with a corrupt intent to influence the legislator's vote in an official matter.

Section 85 also prohibits someone from using corrupt means like menace and deceit to coerce a legislator to give or withhold his vote on an issue. Section 85 has been interpreted to include a prohibition against vote trading.

However, this section is premised upon giving a bribe to a legislator. It seems highly unlikely that providing funding for a specific legislative district project, for example, would constitute a bribe. Do legislative leaders or the Governor act with a "corrupt intent" when negotiating with legislators over public policy issues? Bribery is premised upon the elected official receiving a personal financial benefit. No one has argued that is occurring.

Nonetheless, this section has been interpreted to prohibit vote trading. This is because the state's criminal laws not only outlaw bribery and vote-trading, but also "any attempt by menace, deceit, suppression of truth, or any corrupt means, to influence a member in giving or withholding his or her vote." This language appears to be a broad prohibition and could be applicable in these instances.

In addition, using threats or force to compel a public officer to perform an official act could also be prosecuted under Penal Code § 518, which is California's extortion law. This section provides: "Extortion is the obtaining of property from another, with his consent, or the obtaining of an official act of a public officer, induced by a wrongful use of force or fear, or under color of official right." Voting is an official act by a legislator. But are legislative negotiations that induce a vote by wrongful use of fear or under color of an official right permissible?

Similarly, Penal Code § 86 deals with bribes by legislators and makes it a felony for a legislator to ask, receive or agree to receive something of value with a corrupt intent to influence the legislator's vote in an official matter. Section 86 also prohibits a legislator from conditioning his or her vote on that of another legislator.

Here again it appears this Penal Code section deals with bribes and the receipt of personal financial benefit by a legislator. Would the result of these legislative negotiations amount to "bribery"?

The interesting provision is the clause in this section that "prohibits a legislator from conditioning his or her vote on that of another legislator." This implies vote trading with another legislator. In other words, "if you vote for my bill, then I will vote for your bill." But is this what occurs in these legislative negotiations? Is there such an explicit *quid pro quo* involved?

This question leads to an interesting U.S. Court of Appeals for the Ninth Circuit decision that may shed some insight. The case was *Porter v. Bowen*, 496 F.3d 1009 (9th Cir. 2007, and the federal appellate court determined that the First Amendment barred the State of California from closing the 2000 Nader-Gore vote trading websites.

The federal appellate court ruled that the exchange of *political* rather than *personal* benefits rendered the activity protected by the First Amendment, even if the vote exchanges were somehow enforceable. Part of the court's opinion follows:

> Whatever the wisdom of using vote-swapping agreements to communicate these positions, such agreements plainly differ from conventional (and illegal) vote buying, which conveys no message other than the parties' willingness to exchange votes for money (or some other form of private profit). The Supreme Court held in *Brown v. Hartlage*, 456 U.S. 45, 55 (1982), that vote buying may be banned "without trenching on any right of association protected by the First Amendment."

> Vote swapping, however, is more akin to the candidate's pledge in *Brown* to take a pay cut if elected, which the Court concluded was constitutionally protected, than to unprotected vote buying. Like the candidate's pledge, vote swapping involves a "promise to confer some ultimate benefit on the voter, qua ... citizen or member of the general public" — i.e., another person's agreement to vote for a particular candidate. *Id.* at 58–59.

> And unlike vote buying, vote swapping is not an "illegal exchange for *private* profit" since the only benefit a vote swapper can receive is a marginally higher probability that his preferred electoral outcome will come to pass. *Id.* at 55 (emphasis added); cf. Marc Johnandazza, The Other Election Controversy of Y2K: Core First Amendment Values and High-Tech Political Coalitions, 82 Wash. U. L.Q. 143, 221 (2004) ("There can be no ... serious assertion, that anyone entered into a vote-swap arrangement for private profit or any other form of enrichment.").

Without money changing hands (the traditional definition of bribery), it appears the First Amendment protects legislative negotiations. Don't these legislative "deals" amount to "political benefits," which are protected by the First Amendment, rather than "personal benefits," because they do not accrue to the legislator? In the end, these legislators are looking out for what is best for their districts and constituents and do not receive any personal financial benefit.

Do you agree with this analysis?

Chapter Seven

The California Legislative Process

A. Legislative Rules and Procedures by Statute

In California's Government Code, there are several code sections that set forth legislative rules and procedures. These statutes were added by Proposition 24 in 1984 and are found in Title 2, Division 2, Part 1, Chapter 8, Article 3. The provisions of law are summarized below:

Rules — Gov't Code § 9920

Each house of the Legislature must adopt rules for its proceedings for each regular and special session. This is done by resolutions adopted by an affirmative recorded vote of two-thirds of the membership of the respective house. No Assembly or Senate rule can be amended except by resolution adopted by an affirmative recorded vote of two-thirds of the Members of that house.

Any standing rule of either the Assembly or Senate may be suspended temporarily by an affirmative vote of two-thirds of the Members of that house present and voting. Any temporary suspension can apply only to the matter under immediate consideration.

Joint Rules — Gov't Code § 9921

The Senate and Assembly are required to adopt rules for their joint proceedings for each regular and special sessions. This is done by resolution adopted by an affirmative recorded vote of two-thirds of the membership of each house. No joint rule may be amended except by resolution adopted by an affirmative recorded vote of two-thirds of the membership of each house.

The Senate and Assembly may provide for temporary suspension of a joint rule by a single house upon the affirmative recorded vote of two-thirds of the Members of that house. Any temporary suspension can apply only to the matter under immediate consideration.

Standing Committees — Gov't Code § 9922

All standing committees of both the Senate and the Assembly, except the Senate Committee on Rules and the Assembly Committee on Rules, must be created and the size and jurisdiction of each is established through the adoption of or amendment to the rules of the respective houses by resolution with two-thirds of the membership of the house in question concurring in the adoption of the resolution. The standing committee membership must be determined in the specified manner.

<u>Special and Select Committees — Gov't Code § 9923</u>

No special or select committees nor any subcommittee is allowed to be established in either the Senate or the Assembly except by affirmative vote of two-thirds of the Committee on Rules of the house in question. Membership of special or select committees or subcommittees is determined by a two-thirds vote of the membership of the house in question.

<u>Joint Committees — Gov't Code § 9924</u>

No joint committee can be established except by passage of a concurrent resolution with two-thirds of the membership of each house concurring. The membership of each joint committee is to be allocated equally between the Senate and the Assembly and the delegation from each house are chosen pursuant to § 9922.

<u>Member Voting — Gov't Code § 9925</u>

Each house of the Legislature must provide in its rules for appropriate voting procedures on the Floor and in committees or subcommittees. However, no Member is allowed to cast a vote for another Member, nor may any Member be allowed to change his or her vote or add a vote to the roll after the vote is announced without the consent of four-fifths of the membership of the house, nor may any vote be taken in any committee or subcommittee of either house in the absence of a quorum.

B. Legislative Hearings
Allen v. Superior Court of San Diego County
(1959) 171 Cal.App.2d 444

OPINION

MUSSELL, J.

On February 16, 1959, an amended complaint was filed in the Superior Court of San Diego County in which Nate Rosenberg was plaintiff and Bruce F. Allen, petitioner herein, was defendant. In this complaint it was alleged, in substance, that plaintiff appeared in San Diego on October 15, 1958, in response to a subpoena to appear before what was purported to be a Subcommittee on Rackets of the Interim Committee on Judiciary then purporting to be in session at that time and place by virtue of Resolution Number 224 of the California State Assembly; that at said time and place, defendants, Bruce F. Allen and Joseph B. Tracy, did willfully, intentionally, wrongfully and unlawfully assault plaintiff and commit a battery upon his person and did twist and pinch his arm and disarrange his clothing, and did then and there, by means of force and violence, take from plaintiff a certain document, to plaintiff's damage in the sum of $25,000.

Defendant Joseph B. Tracy was not served with process in said action and has not appeared therein. Defendant Bruce F. Allen filed a general and special demurrer in which, inter alia, he raised the question of legislative immunity from civil liability for acts arising out of the performance of legislative functions. The said House Resolution Number 224, the Final Calendar of Legislative Business, Assembly Final History 1958, Regular Budget Session Page 30, and a copy of defendant's letter dated August 7, 1957, establishing the Assembly Interim Committee on Judiciary, Subcommittee on Rackets, were incorporated in the demurrer by reference and made a part thereof. The demurrer was overruled by the trial court on March 27, 1959, and the defendants were granted twenty days from notice within which to answer. On April 8, 1959, Bruce F. Allen filed in this court his petition for a writ of prohibition to require the trial court to desist from further proceeding in said action until further order of this court. An order to show cause was issued herein on April 24, 1959, returnable on May 13, 1959, at which time the matter was argued and it was conceded by Mr. Whelan, counsel for the real party in interest, that the transcript of the testimony and proceedings before the subcommittee at the time involved was considered by the trial court and received in evidence. This transcript and the record before us shows that on October 15, 1958, petitioner Bruce F. Allen was a member of the State Assembly and was Chairman of the Assembly Interim Committee on Judiciary and also Chairman of its Subcommittee on Rackets. Pursuant to House Resolution Number 224 this subcommittee was conducting an investigation in San Diego on subject matter referred to in paragraph 1. (g) of said resolution, which provides as follows:

> "1. The Assembly Standing Committee on Judiciary of the 1957 Regular Session is hereby constituted an interim committee and is authorized and directed to ascertain, study and analyze all facts relating to the system of laws and judicial administration of this State, including but not limited to the following subjects:

> "(g) All provisions of law relating to civil and administrative actions and proceedings and remedies and all laws relating to crimes and the manner of punishment therefor, including capital punishment, and criminal procedure, including all matters relating to county jails, and including the principles of contributory and comparative negligence and the rules of evidence, and all provisions of law relating to the tort liability of the State and its agencies and subdivisions, and uniform acts."

Nate Rosenberg, real party in interest herein, in response to a subpoena, appeared before the said subcommittee and, in response to questions asked by the committee, read from a paper, whereupon the following questions were asked and answers by Rosenberg given:

> "Q. Have you consulted Mr. Whelan with regard to your subpoena to appear before this Committee?

> "A. As a matter of fact, I consulted with him last week when I received the subpoena and that criminal case was in recess for a day because of the illness of one of the defendants, and I hoped that he might be able to be present this morning.

"However, I have consulted with him and retained him under any circumstances, and because of his inability to be here today I refuse to answer the questions.

"Q. Did Mr. Whelan agree to represent you at this hearing?

"A. Yes, sir.

"Q. Well, Mr. Whelan certainly hasn't made any effort to contact this Committee with regard to his representation of you.

"Assemblyman Bradley: I was going to raise that point, Mr. Chairman, and also ask that the Chair examine the document which the witness is referring to.

"The Witness: I don't think you have any authority to examine anything. If the court so orders me to give this paper to anyone, I will. But as you are — I don't believe you have the authority to subpoena any of my personal papers on me, and if the court so orders me to deliver this paper, I will.

"Q. By Chairman Allen: Mr. Rosenberg, you have been sitting here reading from a piece of paper.

"A. That is correct.

"Q. Hand it over.

"A. I refuse to give it to you. You have no authority, I don't believe, to personally search me for any papers.

"Q. You have been sitting here reading in front of this Committee from a piece of paper.

"A. That is correct. If you wish to see —

"Q. Where did you get that piece of paper?

"A. I refuse to answer that question, as I told you, and I will repeat it again, under Section 94.12 of the Penal Code, until the attorney is here.

"Chairman Allen: Mr. Tracy, will you get us that piece of paper?

"The Witness: I don't care what you are. I don't think you have the authority to search me.

"Mr. Tracy: I am so instructed by the Chairman. Let's not have any —

"The Witness: Take your hand off it, and I will give it to him.

"Mr. Tracy: Okay. Thank you."

On the basis of the foregoing questions and statements by Allen as chairman of the committee, Rosenberg filed suit against Allen and Tracy for damages for unlawful assault, battery and for allegedly taking the paper involved from him by force and violence. As noted, the trial court overruled Allen's demurrer to the amended complaint, whereupon Allen filed herein his petition for a writ of prohibition.

The basic question here is whether the trial court erred in overruling the demurrer to the amended complaint in the superior court action.

While the amended complaint alleged an assault and battery and the use of force on plaintiff, the record of what actually took place at the hearing does not, in our opinion, substantiate the charge or constitute an assault and battery or the use of force and violence by petitioner Allen. As chairman of the committee he first asked Rosenberg to hand the paper over and when Rosenberg refused, Allen told Tracy, the Sergeant at Arms, to obtain it. It is conceded by counsel for Rosenberg that there was no physical contact by Allen with Rosenberg and that at the time involved, Allen was sitting behind a desk some distance from Rosenberg. There is nothing in the record to indicate that Allen directed Tracy to commit an assault or battery on Rosenberg or to obtain the paper involved by unlawful means or the use of force.

Where, as here, the demurrer to the amended complaint raised the question of legislative immunity, prohibition is an appropriate remedy to prevent the subjection of the petitioner to the harassment and expense of defending himself in a trial in a civil proceeding. (*People v. Superior Court*, 29 Cal. 2d 754, 756 [178 P.2d 1, 40 A.L.R.2d 919]; 45 Cal.Jur.2d, § 159, p. 513.)

As is said in *Tenney v. Brandhove*, 341 U.S. 367 [71 S. Ct. 783, 95 L.Ed. 1019]: "Legislators are immune from deterrents to the uninhibited discharge of their legislative duty, not for their private indulgence but for the public good. One must not expect uncommon courage even in legislators. The privilege would be of little value if they could be subjected to the cost and inconvenience and distractions of a trial upon a conclusion of the pleader, or to the hazard of a judgment against them based upon a jury's speculation as to motives."

In *Perry v. Meikle*, 102 Cal. App. 2d 602, 605 [228 P.2d 17], it was held that when judicial officers act within their jurisdiction, they are not amenable to any civil action for damages; that no matter what their motives may be, they cannot be inquired into; and that judges of courts of record of superior or general jurisdiction are not liable to civil actions for their judicial acts, even when such acts are in excess of their jurisdiction, and are alleged to have been done maliciously and corruptly.

In *Hardy v. Vial*, 48 Cal. 2d 577, 582 [311 P.2d 494], it was held that the rule of absolute immunity, notwithstanding malice or other sinister motive, is not restricted to public officers who institute or take part in criminal actions; that it has been extended by the federal decisions to all executive public officers when performing within the scope of their power acts which require the exercise of discretion or judgment.

In *Cross v. Tustin*, 165 Cal. App. 2d 146, 150 [331 P.2d 785], it is said that this immunity protects public officers and employees acting within the scope of their duties, even against charges of malicious personal torts, such as libel, slander, and false prosecution. (Citations.)

In *White v. Towers*, 37 Cal. 2d 727, 733 [235 P.2d 209, 28 A.L.R.2d 636], it was held that a public officer is liable for injuries caused by acts done outside the scope of his authority and that the duties of public office include those lying squarely within its scope, those essential to accomplishment of the main purposes for which the office was created, and those which, although only incidental and collateral, serve to promote the accomplishment of the principal purposes.

In *Hancock v. Burns*, 158 Cal. App. 2d 785 [323 P.2d 456], it is stated as follows (syllabus la, lb): "'The Senate Fact Finding Committee on Un-American Activities,' and its individual members, were protected by legislative immunity from suit as a result of their action in recommending that an employer discharge certain employees who refused on constitutional grounds to answer questions before the committee where such action was within the authority conferred on the committee by Senate resolution creating the committee as authorized by Const., art. IV, § 37, and it was proper to sustain without leave to amend a demurrer to the employees' complaint against the committee and its members for damages resulting from loss of their jobs, since the court, in ruling on the demurrer, could take judicial notice of the resolution, which was referred to in the complaint, and could thus determine the immunity of the committee and its members from the face of the complaint and that it was useless to allow amendment."

The court there held, at pages 789, 790, that "Although it is often stated that in considering a demurrer a court is bound to accept the truth of the allegations thereof, this statement may, in certain instances, be modified where, by the nature of the pleading, the court is apprised of the existence of a fact or facts of which it is bound to take judicial notice under the laws of this state. In 39 California Jurisprudence 2d, section 22, under the title 'Facts Judicially Noticed' it is said: '... In determining the sufficiency of a pleading, it may be read as though it included all such facts, though not pleaded, and even when the pleading contains an express allegation to the contrary. But the general rule of pleading that a demurrer admits the facts pleaded has no application to facts of which the court may take judicial notice. Allegations contrary to facts which the court may judicially notice are not admitted by demurrer, but must be disregarded and treated as a nullity.' The complaint here containing, as it does, a reference to Senate Resolution Number 127 would appear well within this rule. The trial court was bound to consider the contents of this Senate resolution."

While it is further stated therein that the Senate resolution there involved could not authorize the commission of a tortious act and that if the committee or its members were charged with the commission of some bodily injury inflicted on another in the course of conducting their hearings, such act could not reasonably be urged to come within the immunity. In the instant case the record does not support a charge of bodily injury on the part of chairman Allen. Courts will take judicial notice of the official acts of the Legislature (Code Civ. Proc., § 1875, subd. 3; *Samish v. Superior Court*, 28 Cal. App. 2d 685, 690 [83 P.2d 305].) In ruling on the demurrer the court can take judicial notice of the resolution under which the hearing involved was conducted.

The reporter's transcript of the proceedings before the committee was received and considered by the trial court in connection with its ruling on the demurrer and admitted in evidence, showing that Rosenberg suffered no bodily injury at the hands of petitioner and that Rosenberg, after telling the Sergeant at Arms to "take your hand off it," stated that he would give it (the paper) to him (Allen), which he did. Allen, as chairman of the committee, was, in our opinion, authorized to demand that the paper be shown to him inasmuch as the witness was referring to it and answering the questions from it. Allen was also authorized to direct the Sergeant at Arms to obtain the paper for inspection. Under these circumstances petitioner herein should not be subjected to the harassment and expense of defending himself in civil proceedings commenced by Rosenberg.

It is claimed by counsel for Rosenberg that the committee had no authority to conduct the hearing involved and was without legal standing. However, it is not the function of the courts to prescribe rigid rules for the Legislature to follow in drafting resolutions establishing investigating committees. That is a matter peculiarly within the realm of the Legislature and its decisions will be accepted by the courts up to the point where their own duty to enforce the constitutionally protected rights of individuals is affected. (*Watkins v. United States*, 354 U.S. 178, 204 [77 S. Ct. 1173, 1 L. Ed. 2d 1273].)

Said Resolution Number 224 contains an avowal of contemplated legislation in respect to several subjects within the scope of prospective legislation and control within the meaning of article IV, section 37, of our state Constitution. The record before us shows that the Interim Committee was lawfully constituted by the assembly with power to conduct the investigation involved. (*In re Battelle*, 207 Cal. 227 [227 P. 725, 65 A.L.R. 1497].)

The demurrer herein should have been sustained without leave to amend and the Superior Court action dismissed. Let the writ of prohibition issue as prayed for in the petition.

GRIFFIN, P.J., and SHEPARD, J., concurred.

Notes and Questions

1. The drafting of resolutions establishing legislative investigating committees is a matter peculiarly within the realm of the Legislature, and its decisions will be accepted by the courts up to the point where their own duty to enforce the constitutionally protected rights of individuals is affected.

2. Is this simply a case of legislative immunity from civil liability for acts arising out of the performance of legislative functions?

3. Why did the court determine that Allen, as chairman of the committee, was legally authorized to demand that the paper be shown to him at this legislative hearing? On what basis did the court decide that Allen had authority to direct the Sergeant at Arms to obtain the paper for inspection from the witness at this legislative hearing?

4. Does the claim in this lawsuit regarding the extent to which a witness can be compelled to testify at a legislative hearing actually amount to an elected official being "subjected to the harassment and expense of defending himself in civil proceedings"?

1. California Legislative Committee Hearings

Committees of the California Legislature can conduct several types of hearings, including bill hearings, investigative or oversight hearings, and informational hearings. Bill hearings are obviously those that are conducted to hear specific bills. Most hearings have a similar purpose, which is to educate the legislators and their staff about the subject matter before them for consideration.

The informational hearings are used to gather information about the subject matter of the hearing, usually in preparation for consideration of legislation in the future. The chair, members or staff of the committee generally come up with the subject matter of the hearing. Sometimes, a hearing will be held prior to the introduction of a bill for the purpose of gathering information the committee can use in shaping legislation.

Another type of hearing is to conduct oversight or investigations, usually of the executive branch of state government. Is there concern about how a program is being administered? Or concern about how a law is being enforced? Some distinguish oversight from investigative hearings wherein there may be an allegation of wrongdoing by a public official in an investigative hearing. A subpoena could be issued, witnesses could be called, and it could be of an adversarial nature, rather than an informative nature.

Finally, there are confirmation hearings, which are generally only held by the State Senate, except for those rare instances when both houses of the Legislature consider a gubernatorial appointment of a constitutional officer. Confirmation hearings are conducted by the Senate Rules Committee to provide "advice and consent" on appointments made.

Informational Hearings

While the subject of informational hearings is not contained in the Assembly Rules or the Senate Rules, there are two applicable rules that are contained in the Joint Rules.

Joint Rule 60 deals with committee hearings. Subdivision (b) provides "A committee may hear the subject matter of a bill or convene for an informational hearing during a period of recess. Four days' notice in the Daily File is required prior to the hearing." Here the rule specifically provides for Assembly and Senate committees to conduct informational hearings.

Joint Rule 62 deals with committee procedures. Subdivision (a) provides "Notice of a hearing on a bill by the committee of first reference in each house, or notice of an informational hearing, shall be published in the Daily File at least four days prior to the hearing. Otherwise, notice shall be published in the Daily File two days prior to the hearing." Here the notice of hearing rule is the same whether the committee is hearing a bill or it is conducting an informational hearing.

Oversight Hearings

Assembly Rule 11.5 provides: "(a) The standing committees of the Assembly created pursuant to Rule 11, with the exception of the Committee on Rules, are hereby constituted Assembly investigating committees and are authorized and directed to conduct oversight hearings and to ascertain, study, and analyze all facts relating to any subjects or matters which the Committee on Rules shall assign to them upon request of the Assembly or upon its own initiative."

In addition, Subdivision (b) of Rule 11.5 specifies: "Each of the Assembly investigating committees consists of the members of the standing committee on the same subject as most recently constituted." Thereafter, Subdivision (d) notes, "In order to prevent duplication and overlapping of studies between the various investigating committees herein created, a committee may not commence the study of any subject or matter not specifically authorized herein or assigned to it unless and until prior written approval thereof has been obtained from the Committee on Rules."

Senate Rule 12.5 provides,

> The General Research Committee is hereby created pursuant to Section 11 of Article IV of the California Constitution, which relates to legislative committees. The committee consists of the 40 Senators, and the President pro Tempore is its chair. The committee is allocated all subjects within the scope of legislative regulation and control, but may not undertake any investigation that another committee has been specifically requested or directed to undertake.
>
> The General Research Committee may act through subcommittees appointed by the Committee on Rules. Each member of the General Research Committee is authorized and directed to receive and investigate requests for legislative action made by individuals or groups and to report thereon to the full committee. The committee and its members shall have and exercise all of the rights, duties, and powers conferred upon investigating committees and their members by the Senate Rules and the Joint Rules of the Senate and Assembly.

In addition, Senate Rule 16 provides for general powers of standing committees and states: "Each standing committee of the Senate to which a proposed law or bill is assigned has full power and authority during the session of the Legislature, or any recess thereof, to make an investigation and study concerning any proposed law or bill as the committee shall determine necessary to enable it to properly act thereon."

Joint Rule 36 provides for investigating committees and specifies that,

> In order to expedite the work of the Legislature, either house, or both houses jointly, may by resolution or statute provide for the appointment of committees to ascertain facts and to make recommendations as to any subject within the scope of legislative regulation or control.
>
> The resolution providing for the appointment of a committee pursuant to this rule shall state the purpose of the committee and the scope of the subject concerning which it is to act, and may authorize it to act either during sessions of the Legislature or, when authorization may lawfully be made, after final adjournment.

In addition, Joint Rule 36 provides: "Every department, commission, board, agency, officer, and employee of the state government, including the Legislative Counsel and the Attorney General and their subordinates, and of every political subdivision, county, city, or public district of or in this state, shall give and furnish to these committees and to their subcommittees upon request information, records, and documents as the committees deem necessary or proper for the achievement of the purposes for which each committee was created."

Joint Rule 37 also provides for the Joint Legislative Budget Committee and that the "committee, with the permission of the appointing authorities of the two houses, may also create subcommittees from its membership, assigning to its subcommittees any study, inquiry, investigation, or hearing that the committee itself has authority to undertake or hold."

Notes and Questions

1. Committees is where most legislative work takes place. Without committees, all bills would be considered just on the Assembly and Senate Floors. Would this be a good outcome?

2. In order to allow greater public participation and "bring the people's business to the people," should legislators be allowed to vote at hearings held outside of the State Capitol?

C. Legislative Floors

1. Conducting Business on the Floors

The California Legislature conducts its business both in policy and fiscal committees, as well as on the Floors of the State Assembly and State Senate. Each house determines its own rules and specifies how business will be handled on their respective Floors. This process of conducting their activities on the Floors is called the "order of business." The processes between the two houses are similar in many regards, but there are some differences as well.

<u>Assembly</u>

Pursuant to Assembly Rule 40(a), the following is the Order of Business of the Assembly:

1. Rollcall

2. Prayer by the Chaplain

3. Reading of the Previous Day's Journal

4. Presentation of Petitions

5. Introduction and Reference of Bills

6. Reports of Committees

7. Messages from the Governor

8. Messages from the Senate

9. Motions and Resolutions

10. Business on the Daily File

11. Announcements

12. Adjournment

Pursuant to Subdivision (b) of Rule 40, with the exception of Special Orders of Business, the Speaker may determine that a different order of business will result in a more expeditious processing of the business of the Assembly by ordering resolutions honoring an individual or an organization, introductions, and adjournments in memory of individuals to be taken up in a different order than that listed in subdivision (a).

In addition, under Assembly Rule 63, the following listing constitutes the order of business of pending legislation on the *Assembly Daily File*:

1. Special Orders of the Day

2. Second Reading, Assembly Bills

3. Second Reading, Senate Bills

4. Unfinished Business

5. Third Reading, Assembly Bills

6. Third Reading, Senate Bills

Senate

Under Senate Rule 4, the Order of Business of the Senate is as follows:

(1) Rollcall

(2) Prayer by the Chaplain

(3) Pledge of Allegiance

(4) Privileges of the Floor

(5) Communications and Petitions

(6) Messages from the Governor

(7) Messages from the Assembly

(8) Reports of Committees

(9) Motions, Resolutions, and Notices

(10) Introduction and First Reading of Bills

(11) Consideration of Daily File:

    (a) Second Reading

    (b) Special Orders

    (c) Unfinished Business

    (d) Third Reading

(12) Announcement of Committee Meetings

(13) Leaves of Absence

(14) Adjournment

There are no additional special rules for the Senate. When a bill is taken up that is not on the *Daily File*, it is done so "without reference to file" (aka WORF). When a bill is subject to a WORF, what the Assembly or Senate is actually doing is "suspending the orders of the day" as set forth in their respective rules providing the Order of Business.

Notes and Questions

1. Who is responsible in the Assembly and Senate to ensure that business is properly conducted on the respective Floors?

2. Making the Houses Run Smoothly

In order to ensure that the two houses of the California Legislature run smoothly, staff play a critical role, especially the two main staff members: The Chief Clerk of the Assembly and the Secretary of the Senate. Both of these individuals wield power as they oversee the California legislative process. The following is a description of the prescribed roles of the Chief Clerk and the Senate Secretary.

<u>Assembly</u>

Under Assembly Rule 32, the Chief Clerk has the following powers, duties and responsibilities:

(a) To keep the bills, papers, and records of the proceedings and actions of the Assembly and to have charge of the publication and distribution of those publications related thereto.

(b) To supervise Assembly employees who are engaged in duties related to subdivision (a).

(c) To act as Parliamentarian of the Assembly and to advise the officers of the Assembly and the Committee on Rules on parliamentary procedure and the Rules of the Assembly when called upon to do so.

(d) To prepare all bills, resolutions, histories, journals, and related publications for printing.

(e) To refuse to permit any bills, papers, or records to be removed from his or her office or out of his or her custody, except upon duly signed receipts from persons authorized.

(f)   To perform other duties that are prescribed by law or the Committee on Rules.

(g) To make technical changes in measures and amendments pending before the Assembly. The Chief Clerk shall notify the Speaker and the author of the measure of any such change.

(h) To compare all bills, ordered or considered engrossed by the Assembly, with the engrossed copies thereof; before they pass out of the possession of the Assembly, to see that each engrossed bill is a true copy of the original, with those amendments that may have been made thereto; and to see that all engrossed bills are reported back in the order in which they were ordered engrossed.

(i) To assist the Committee on Rules, upon its request, in recommending the reference of bills to the appropriate standing committee.

Note that the Assistant Chief Clerk has the powers and performs the duties of the Chief Clerk during his or her absence.

Senate

Under Senate Rule 32, the Senate Secretary has the following powers, duties and responsibilities:

1. It shall be the duty of the Secretary of the Senate to attend every session, call the roll, and read all bills, amendments, and resolutions, and all papers ordered read by the Senate or the Presiding Officer.

2. The Secretary of the Senate shall superintend all printing to be done for the Senate.

3. The Secretary of the Senate shall certify to, and transmit to, the Assembly all bills, joint and concurrent resolutions, constitutional amendments, and papers requiring the concurrence of the Assembly, after their passage or adoption by the Senate.

4. The Secretary of the Senate shall also keep a correct Journal of the proceedings of the Senate, and shall notify the Assembly of the action by the Senate on all matters originating in the Assembly and requiring action on the part of the Senate.

5. The Secretary of the Senate shall have custody of all bills, documents, papers, and records of the Senate and may not permit any of the bills, documents, records, or papers to be taken from the Desk or out of his or her custody by any person, except in the regular course of the business of the Senate.

6. The Secretary of the Senate is the Executive Officer of the Committee on Rules and shall act as its authorized representative in all matters delegated to him or her by the committee.

7. Initiative measures received by the Secretary of the Senate in accordance with §9034 of the Elections Code shall be transmitted to the Committee on Rules and referred by the Committee on Rules to the appropriate committee.

Joint Rules

Under the Joint Rules, there are two provisions relating to records of bills and the roles played by the Assembly Chief Clerk and Senate Secretary:

Joint Rule 19 specifies that the Secretary of the Senate and the Chief Clerk of the Assembly must keep a complete and accurate record of every action taken by the Senate and Assembly on every bill.

Joint Rule 20 provides that the Secretary of the Senate and the Chief Clerk of the Assembly must endorse on every original or engrossed bill a statement of any action taken by the Senate or Assembly concerning the bill.

3. Methods of Voting on the Floors

In the two houses of the California Legislature, there are differences in how voting by legislators is conducted on the Floors of the Assembly and Senate. The main differences are that the Assembly uses an electronic means of recording votes on the Floor, while Senators record their votes with a verbal response to a roll call; and Assembly Members may change their votes under specified circumstances, but Senators cannot do so.

<u>Assembly</u>

Under Assembly Rule 105, the ayes and noes are recorded by the electrical voting system on the final passage of all bills. The names of the legislators and how they cast their votes are entered in the *Assembly Daily Journal*.

Pursuant to Assembly Rule 106, when begun, voting may not be interrupted, except that, before the vote is announced, any legislator may have the total pending vote flashed on the visible vote recorder. Any legislator may move a call of the Assembly after the completion of the roll before the final vote has been announced.

In addition, under Rule 106, prior to adjournment on the same legislative day, and in the absence of any objection, a legislator may instruct the Assembly Chief Clerk to change his or her recorded vote after the vote is announced, so long as the outcome of the final vote on the matter is not changed. The Chief Clerk may record any vote change only after the legislator making the change has announced it to the Assembly.

Under Assembly Rule 107, in a tie vote, the motion or bill fails passage.

<u>Senate</u>

Pursuant to Senate Rule 44, whenever a rollcall is required by the Constitution or rules, or is ordered by the Senate or demanded by three legislators, every legislator within the Senate without debate answers "Aye" or "No" when his or her name is called.

This Rule requires that the names of legislators are called alphabetically. A Senator may not vote or change his or her vote after the announcement of the final vote by the presiding officer. There is an exception for the two party leaders.

Under this Senate Rule, on a legislative day when the President pro Tempore or Minority Floor Leader is in attendance throughout a session, he or she, in the absence of any objection, may instruct the Secretary of the Senate to add his or her vote to any previously announced vote that was taken while he or she was performing the responsibilities of the office of President pro Tempore or Minority Floor Leader, provided the outcome of the vote is not thereby changed.

As explained by Senate Rule 44, the intent of this paragraph is to allow the President pro Tempore and the Minority Floor Leader to carry out the unique and special duties of their offices without losing the opportunity to vote on matters before the Senate.

Chapter Eight

Legislation Generally

A. Operation of Statutes and Resolutions

In California's Government Code, there are several code sections that set forth the operation of statutes and resolutions. These statutes were enacted in 1943 and are found in Title 2, Division 2, Part 1, Chapter 6. The provisions of law are summarized below:

Effective Date of Statutes — Gov't Code § 9600

With the exceptions below, a statute enacted at a regular session goes into effect on January 1 next following a 90-day period from the date of enactment of the statute, and a statute enacted at a special session goes into effect on the 91st day after adjournment of the special session at which the bill was passed.

Statutes calling elections, statutes providing for tax levies or appropriations for the usual current expenses of the state, and urgency statutes go into effect immediately upon their enactment.

Effective Date of Resolutions — Gov't Code § 9602

Every concurrent and joint resolution takes effect upon the filing of it with the Secretary of State.

General Rules of Statutory Construction — Gov't Code § 9603

The general rules for the construction of statutes are contained in the preliminary provisions of the different codes.

Restatements of Statutes — Gov't Code § 9604

When the provisions of one statute are carried into another statute under circumstances in which they are required to be construed as restatements and continuations and not as new enactments, any reference made by any statute, charter or ordinance to such provisions must, unless a contrary intent appears, be deemed a reference to the restatements and continuations.

Repealed Statutes — Gov't Code § 9605

If a section or part of a statute is amended, it is not to be considered as having been repealed and reenacted in the amended form. The portions that are not altered are to be considered as having been the law from the time when those provisions were enacted. The new provisions are to be considered as having been enacted at the time of the amendment. The omitted portions are to be considered as having been repealed at the time of the amendment.

When the same section or part of a statute is amended by two or more acts enacted at the same session, any portion of an earlier one of those successive acts that is omitted from a subsequent act is deemed to have been omitted deliberately and any portion of a statute omitted by an earlier act that is restored in a subsequent act is deemed to have been restored deliberately.

In the absence of any express provision to the contrary in the statute that is enacted last, it is conclusively presumed that the statute which is enacted last is intended to prevail over statutes that are enacted earlier at the same session and, in the absence of any express provision to the contrary in the statute that has a higher chapter number, it is presumed that a statute that has a higher chapter number was intended by the Legislature to prevail over a statute that is enacted at the same session but has a lower chapter number.

Vested Rights — Gov't Code § 9606

Any statute may be repealed at any time, except when vested rights would be impaired. Persons acting under any statute act in contemplation of this power of repeal.

No Revival of Repealed Statutes — Gov't Code § 9607

With the exceptions below, no statute or part of a statute, repealed by another statute, is revived by the repeal of the repealing statute without express words reviving the repealed statute or part of a statute.

If a later enacted statute that deletes or extends the date of termination or repeal of a previously enacted law is chaptered before the date of termination or repeal, the terminated or repealed law is revived when the later enacted statute becomes operative.

Termination or Suspension of Law — Gov't Code § 9608

The termination or suspension of any law creating a criminal offense does not constitute a bar to the indictment or information and punishment of an act already committed in violation of the law that is terminated or suspended, unless the intention to bar the indictment or information and punishment is expressly declared by an applicable provision of law.

Amending a Repealed Statute — Gov't Code § 9609

A statute amending a section of a repealed statute is void.

Fixing Public Salaries — Gov't Code § 9610

The fixing or the authorizing of the fixing of the salary of a state officer or employee by statute is not intended to and does not constitute an appropriation of money for the payment of the salary. The salary is paid only in the event that moneys are made available by another provision of law.

Suspended Provision of Law — Gov't Code § 9611

Whenever a provision of law is temporarily suspended, or is expressly or impliedly modified or repealed by a provision which is declared to be effective for only a limited period of time, the original provisions are not to be deemed repealed. However, upon the expiration of the time of the temporary suspension or the effectiveness of the inconsistent provision, then the original provision has the same force and effect as if the temporary provision had not been enacted.

Military Service Covered — Gov't Code §9612

Whenever the terms United States Army, Army of the United States, United States Navy, or military service appear in a statute, whether singly or any combination of them, the terms are deemed to include the United States Air Force.

B. Enactment of Statutes and Adoption of Resolutions

In California's Government Code, there are several code sections that set forth the enactment of statutes and adoption of resolutions. These statutes were enacted in 1943 and are found in Title 2, Division 2, Part 1, Chapter 5. The provisions of law are summarized below:

Definition of Clerk — Gov't Code §9500

The term "clerk" means the engrossing and enrolling clerk or the employee who performs the duties of engrossing and enrolling clerk when no employee is designated by name.

Definition of Committee — Gov't Code §9501

The term "committee" means the engrossing and enrolling committee of the house ordering the engrossing or enrolling of a bill or other document or the committee of such house which performs the duties of engrossing and enrolling committee when no committee is designated by name.

Enacting Clause — Gov't Code §9501.5

The enacting clause of every law must be "The people of the State of California do enact as follows:".

Engrossing and Enrolling — Gov't Code §9502

All bills and other documents ordered engrossed or enrolled by the Senate or Assembly are to be delivered by the Secretary of the Senate or Chief Clerk of the Assembly to the clerk of the house ordering the engrossment or enrollment.

Delivery to State Printer — Gov't Code §9503

The clerk must deliver the bills and documents without delay, in the order of their receipt, to the State Printer.

Enrolled Copies of Bills — Gov't Code §9504

The State Printer must accept all bills or documents and, without delay, engross or enroll (print) them in the order of their receipt.

Delivery by State Printer — Gov't Code § 9505

The State Printer must deliver the engrossed or enrolled copy of the bill or document, with the original, to the clerk from whom he received the original. The clerk must carefully compare the engrossed or enrolled copy with the original version. If correctly engrossed or enrolled, the individual must report it back with the original version to the committee.

Engrossing of Bills — Gov't Code § 9506

All bills and documents that have been printed must be considered engrossed if no amendments have been made after being printed. The original bill or document is to be delivered to the clerk of the house where it originated. That individual must compare the original with the printed bill or document, and deliver it to the committee for return to the house in the same manner as engrossed bills.

Presentation of Bills — Gov't Code § 9507

If the enrolled copy of a bill or other document is found to be correct, the committee must present it to the proper officers for their signatures. When the officers sign their names, as required by law, it is enrolled.

Transmittal of Enrolled Bills — Gov't Code § 9508

Enrolled bills are required to be transmitted to the Governor for his approval.

Endorsement of Enrolled Bills — Gov't Code § 9509

As soon as an enrolled bill is delivered to the Governor, it must be endorsed as follows: "This bill was received by the Governor this ____ day of ____, 20__." The endorsement must be signed by the private secretary of the Governor or by any other person designated by the Governor whose designation has been reported to the Speaker of the Assembly and the President pro Tempore of the Senate.

Approval by the Governor — Gov't Code § 9510

When the Governor approves a bill, he must affix his name thereto, with the date of signing, and deposit it in the Office of the Secretary of State, where it becomes the official record. Upon the receipt of any bill, the Secretary of State must give it a number, to be known as the chapter number. He numbers each bill in the order in which it is received by him, and the order of numbering is presumed to be the order in which the bills were approved by the Governor.

Two Series of Bill and Resolution Chapter Numbers — Gov't Code § 9510.5

There are two series of bill chapter numbers for each two-year regular session of the Legislature. Bills deposited with the Secretary of State from the beginning of the two-year session through December 31 of the odd-numbered year are to be designated "Statutes of [odd-numbered year], Chapter ____." Bills deposited with the Secretary of State after December 31 of the odd-numbered year are to be designated "Statutes of [even-numbered year], Chapter ____."

Concurrent resolutions, joint resolutions, and proposed constitutional amendments adopted by the Legislature are to be chaptered as resolution chapters with a different series of numbers than those assigned to bills but must otherwise be numbered and designated in the same manner as bills enacted into law.

Appropriations Bills — Gov't Code § 9511

If a bill presented to the Governor contains an item or several items of appropriation, he may object to one or more items while approving other portions of the bill. In such a case, the Governor must append to the bill, at the time of signing it, a statement of the items to which he objects, and the reasons therefor. If the Legislature is in session, the Governor must transmit to the house in which the bill originated a copy of the statement. The items so objected to are to be separately reconsidered in the same manner as bills which have been disapproved by the Governor.

Vetoed Bills — Gov't Code § 9512

When a bill has passed both houses of the Legislature and is returned by the Governor without his signature, and with objections thereto, or if it is a bill containing an item or several items of appropriation which is returned with objections to one or more of the items, and upon reconsideration the bill, item, or items pass both houses by the constitutional majority, the bill, item, or items are then to be authenticated as having become a law by a certificate.

Certificate Attached to Vetoed Bills — Gov't Code § 9513

The certificate is to be attached to the bill, or indorsed on or attached to the copy of the statement of objections. It must be in the following form: "This bill having been returned by the Governor with his objections thereto, and, after reconsideration, having passed both houses by the constitutional majority, has become a law this _____ day of _____, _____"; or, "The following items in the within statement (naming them) having, after reconsideration, passed both houses by the constitutional majority, have become a law this _____ day of _____, _____." A certificate signed by the President of the Senate and the Speaker of the Assembly is a sufficient authentication thereof.

Bills Deposited with Secretary of State — Gov't Code § 9514

The bill or statement authenticated is then to be delivered to the Governor, and by him deposited with the laws in the Office of the Secretary of State. Bills so deposited in the Office of the Secretary of State are to be given a chapter number.

Delivery of Veto Message — Gov't Code § 9515

If, on the day the Governor desires to return a bill without his approval and with his objections thereto, the house in which it originated has adjourned for the day, he may deliver the bill with his message to the Secretary of the Senate if it originated in the Senate, Chief Clerk of the Assembly if it originated in the Assembly, or any member of the house in which it originated. Such delivery is as effectual as though returned when the house was meeting.

Period of Bill Review — Gov't Code § 9516

Every bill which has passed both houses of the Legislature, and has not been returned by the Governor within 12 days, becomes a law. It is authenticated by the Governor and is certified by the Secretary of State in the following form: "This bill having remained with the Governor 12 days, and the Legislature being in session, it has become a law this ____ day of ____, ____." The certificate is to be signed by the Secretary of State and deposited with the laws in his office.

Every bill which has been passed by the Legislature before September 1 of the second calendar year of the biennium of the legislative session, which was in the possession of the Governor on or after September 1, and which has not been returned by the Governor on or before September 30 of that year, thereby becoming a law, is authenticated by the Governor causing the fact to be certified thereon by the Secretary of State in a specified form.

Final Action on the Budget — Gov't Code § 9517

The Legislature must finish its actions on the budget required by the Constitution by June 15th of each year.

Notes and Questions

1. There are provisions of the state Constitution and the Government Code that provide how laws are enacted and resolutions are adopted. Are there additional provisions that could be added to the California Government Code? If so, what would they be?

C. Statute Cannot Conflict with the Constitution

Consulting Engineers and Land Surveyors of California, Inc. v. Professional Engineers in California Government

40 Cal.4th 1016 (2007)

OPINION

MORENO, J.

In *Professional Engineers in California Government v. Kempton* (2007) 40 Cal.4th 1016 [56 Cal.Rptr.3d 814, 155 P.3d 226] (*Kempton*), we held that Proposition 35, which expressly removed a constitutional restriction on the ability of state agencies to contract with private firms for architectural and engineering services on public works projects, also impliedly repealed certain regulatory statutes pertaining to private contracting that were derived from the constitutional provision. The present case involves two participants from *Kempton*. The question presented here is whether a provision of a memorandum of understanding between the state and a state employee union that restricts the use of private contractors for architectural and engineering services by public agencies fatally conflicts with Proposition 35 as we construed that initiative in *Kempton*. We answer that it does and, so, affirm the judgment of the Court of Appeal.

In *Kempton*, Professional Engineers was a plaintiff and appellant, while Consulting Engineers was an intervener and respondent. (*Kempton, supra*, 40 Cal.4th at pp. 1026–1027.)

I. STATEMENT OF THE CASE

A. *Background: Proposition 35*

Proposition 35, entitled the Fair Competition and Taxpayer Savings Act, was passed by the electorate on November 7, 2000. The initiative included both constitutional and statutory provisions. The constitutional provision, California Constitution, article XXII consists of two sections. Section 1 provides in relevant part that the "State of California and all other governmental entities … shall be allowed to contract with qualified private entities for architectural and engineering services for all public works of improvement. The choice and authority to contract shall extend to all phases of project development including permitting and environmental studies, rights-of-way services, design phase services and construction phase services. The choice and authority shall exist without regard to funding sources whether federal, state, regional, local or private, whether or not the project is programmed by a state, regional or local governmental entity, and whether or not the completed project is a part of any State owned or State operated system or facility." (Cal. Const., art. XXII, § 1.) Section 2 provides: "Nothing contained in Article VII of this Constitution shall be construed to limit, restrict or prohibit the State or any other governmental entities, including, but not limited to, cities, counties, cities and counties, school districts and other special districts, local and regional agencies and joint power agencies, from contracting with private entities for the performance of architectural and engineering services." (Cal. Const., art. XXII, § 2.)

Article VII of the state Constitution, referred to in article XXII, section 2 of the state Constitution, establishes the state's merit-based civil service. Prior to the passage of Proposition 35, the courts had interpreted the civil service mandate of article VII as an implied limitation on the use of private contractors that was intended to protect the civil service from political patronage appointments. Article XXII, section 2 thus removed article-VII-based restrictions on contracting with private entities for architectural and engineering services by the State of California.

Proposition 35 also added a new chapter to the Government Code. Additionally, section 5 of the initiative specified: "This initiative may be amended to further its purposes by statute, passed in each house by roll call vote entered in the journal, two-thirds of the membership concurring, and signed by the Governor." (Voter Information Guide, Gen. Elec. (Nov. 7, 2000) text of Prop. 35, § 5, p. 66.)

These provisions (Gov. Code, § 4529.10 et seq.) are not at issue in this case.

. . .

II. ANALYSIS

A. *Introduction*

In its initial briefing, which preceded our decision in *Kempton*, Professional Engineers raised many of the same arguments it had raised in *Kempton*, and which we considered and rejected there. After we issued *Kempton*, we sought supplemental briefing from the parties on its impact on this case. Professional Engineers' supplemental briefs abandon most of its initial arguments and advance arguments that are both new and inconsistent with its previous arguments. Nonetheless, we consider and dispose of these now apparently superseded arguments because this discussion provides the necessary context for discussing the arguments presented in Professional Engineers' supplemental briefs.

B. *Kempton*

Professional Engineers contends that the Legislature's approval of the MOU in which article 24 appears represents a valid exercise of the expanded authority conferred on the Legislature by Proposition 35 to set policy with respect to private contracting by state agencies. This contention is supported by a series of predicate arguments. Professional Engineers argues that the intent of the electorate in enacting Proposition 35 was to expand the power of the Legislature to decide whether to authorize individual agencies to contract with private entities for architectural and engineering services rather than permit the agencies themselves to make those decisions. This argument, in turn, is premised on Professional Engineers' interpretation of the phrase "State of California" in section 1 of article XXII of the state Constitution as referring only to the Legislature. As a corollary, Professional Engineers maintains that any broader construction of that phrase to include executive agencies violates the separation of powers doctrine by shifting legislative authority to set policy regarding private contracting from the Legislature to such agencies. In this same vein, assuming that Proposition 35 did no more than expand legislative authority to set policy for private contracting, Professional Engineers maintains that we, as an appellate court, are required to broadly construe that expansion of authority.

In *Kempton*, we decided whether Proposition 35 impliedly repealed certain statutory regulations on private contracting when it removed the constitutional restriction from which those statutes were derived. Those provisions included Government Code sections 14101, 14130 et seq. and 19130. Each statute incorporated an exception to the general principle that article VII of the state Constitution prohibited the use of private contractors to perform state functions in order to preserve the merit-based civil service system. Those exceptions included the "'nature of the services' rule," the "'new state function' rule," and the "'cost savings exception.'" (*Kempton, supra,* 40 Cal.4th at p. 1033.)

We concluded that Proposition 35 impliedly repealed these statutes when it expressly repealed the constitutional restriction judicially construed from article VII of the state Constitution because the provisions of Proposition 35, authorizing private contracting free of article VII's restrictions, "cannot be reconciled with the existing statutes that authorize private contracting by Caltrans of architectural and engineering services, subject to conditions derived from the exceptions to article VII's rule generally restricting such contracting. That rule has been abrogated by Proposition 35 and if the rule no longer has any force, neither should its exceptions." (*Kempton, supra,* 40 Cal.4th at p. 1041.)

In light of this conclusion, we rejected Professional Engineers' argument that the purpose of Proposition 35 was merely to remove the constitutional restriction on the *Legislature's* plenary authority to regulate private contracting based on its assertion that reference to the "State of California" in California Constitution, article XXII was to the Legislature alone. We pointed out that, constitutionally, the legislative power in California is shared by the Legislature and the electorate acting through its powers of initiative and referendum, not exclusively exercised by the Legislature. (*Kempton, supra*, 40 Cal.4th at p. 1042.)

Then, because applying "fundamental principles of construction, applicable equally to constitutional provisions, statutes and initiatives, require[s] us to give words in such texts their ordinary meanings" we concluded that "the phrase 'State of California,' as it refers to state government, includes all three branches — legislative, executive and judicial. (See Cal. Const., art. III, § 3.) Thus, section 1, in tandem with section 2, of article XXII grants all three branches of government the authority to contract with private entities for architectural and engineering services unimpeded by article VII restrictions." (*Kempton, supra*, 40 Cal.4th at p. 1043.)

We next considered and rejected Professional Engineers' separation of powers argument. "[Our] interpretation of Proposition 35 does not endorse a shift of policy-making powers from the legislative branch to executive branch agencies. Rather, it recognizes that there has been a policy determination, made by a constitutionally empowered legislative entity, the electorate acting through its initiative power, to permit those agencies to contract for architectural and engineering services free of article-VII-derived limitations." (*Kempton, supra*, 40 Cal.4th at pp. 1044–1045.)

Professional Engineers renews these arguments in the different context of this case. Professional Engineers argues that the conclusion of the Court of Appeal that article 24 violated Proposition 35 interferes with the Legislature's prerogative to set policy in the realm of private contracting and, by "give[ing] the Legislature's plenary power to individual state department[s] ... violate[s] the separation of powers doctrine."

As in *Kempton*, Professional Engineers erroneously assumes that the Legislature not only has plenary, but *exclusive*, authority to set state policy for private contracting when, in fact, that authority is shared by the electorate. It was the electorate, not the Court of Appeal in this case, that removed California Constitution, article VII's restriction on private contracting and statutory exceptions to that restriction in order to permit the unfettered use of private entities for architectural and engineering services should the agency choose to exercise its authority to do so. (*Kempton, supra*, 40 Cal.4th at pp. 1037–1039.) Further, the electorate also chose to limit the Legislature's ability to set policy in this area by providing that amendments to the initiative must further the purposes of the initiative and be passed by a two-thirds majority of each house. (Prop. 35, § 5.) Such a limitation is well within the power of the electorate. (*Amwest Surety Ins. Co. v. Wilson* (1995) 11 Cal.4th 1243, 1251 [48 Cal.Rptr.2d 12, 906 P.2d 1112].) These legislative choices by the electorate are entitled to the same deference by the courts as enactments of the Legislature. (*Kempton, supra*, 40 Cal.4th at pp. 1042–1043.)

Therefore, the question is not the Legislature's authority to set policy in this area but whether the Legislature's actions are consistent with Proposition 35. It is to that question we turn.

C. *Article 24 As a Self-imposed Legislative Restriction on Private Contracting*

Professional Engineers asserts: "Proposition 35 grants authority to the Legislature to choose to contract out under circumstances that were previously restricted by Article VII. Accordingly, Proposition 35 authorizes the Legislature to choose to voluntarily approve the alleged contracting out restrictions reflected in Article 24." Elaborating on this assertion, Professional Engineers explains: "Specifically, because Proposition 35 *permits* the Legislature [to] choose contracting out policies and procedures for the State, contracting out is not mandated. Thus, choosing to voluntarily restrict contracting does not change or amend the grant of authority given by the initiative and the Legislature's contracting out policy choice reflected in Article 24 is consistent with Proposition 35's grant of authority."

Consulting Engineers counters that, because approval of the MOU was a legislative amendment to the initiative, it failed to comply with section 5 of Proposition 35, which permits such amendment only to "further [the] purposes" of Proposition 35 and which requires a two-thirds vote of each house. (Voter Information Guide, Gen. Elec. (Nov. 7, 2000) text of Prop. 35, § 5, p. 66.) We do not agree that the MOU was, or could have been, an amendment of the initiative. The operative principle applicable here is that the Legislature cannot take action, whether by statute or MOU, that contravenes a constitutional provision. (See *California State Personnel Bd. v. California State Employees Assn., Local 1000, SEIU, AFL-CIO* (2005) 36 Cal.4th 758, 774 [31 Cal.Rptr.3d 201, 115 P.3d 506] ["In adopting the constitutional merit principle, California voters made clear their intent that permanent civil service appointments and promotions be made solely on the basis of merit. No matter what discretion the Legislature has purported to give or withdraw from appointing powers, it does not have a free hand to approve MOU's or enact statutes that flout this mandate"]; *County of Fresno v. State of California* (1991) 53 Cal.3d 482, 493 [280 Cal.Rptr. 92, 808 P.2d 235] ["''legislation must be subordinate to the constitutional provision, and in furtherance of its purpose, and must not in any particular attempt to narrow or embarrass it'''"].)

Article 24 revives some of the restrictions on the ability of state agencies to enter into private contracts for architectural and engineering services contained in the statutes that we held in *Kempton* were impliedly repealed by Proposition 35. For example, article 24, paragraph B proposes a limitation upon private contracting "[e]xcept in extremely unusual or urgent, time-limited circumstances," or if otherwise required by "law, Federal mandate, or court decisions/orders...." The "time-limited circumstances" language echoes language in Government Code section 14101, which authorizes private contracting if "obtainable staff is unable to perform the particular work within the time the public interest requires such work to be done." (Gov. Code, § 14101.) Similarly, Government Code section 14130 permits private contracting by Caltrans "whenever the department is inadequately staffed to satisfactorily carry out its program of project study reports, project development, surveying, and construction inspection in a timely and effective manner." (Gov. Code, § 14130, subd. (b).) In both article 24 and these statutes, then, the availability of private contracting is tied to the inability of the agency to perform its functions in a timely manner using state employees. In *Kempton* we concluded that both Government Code sections 14101 and 14130 were derived from California Constitution, article VII restrictions on private contracting and were impliedly repealed by Proposition 35. (*Kempton, supra*, 40 Cal.4th at pp. 1037–1041.)

We reached the same conclusion with respect to Government Code section 19130. (*Kempton, supra*, 40 Cal.4th at pp. 1037–1041.) Among the provisions of that statute is the requirement that such contracts not displace civil service employees. "The term 'displacement' includes layoff, demotion, involuntary transfer to a new class, involuntary transfer to a new location requiring a change of residence, and time base reductions." (Gov. Code, § 19130, subd. (a)(3).) A similar requirement is found in Government Code section 14131: "Services contracted for shall not cause the displacement of any permanent, temporary, or part-time employee of the department. [¶] For purposes of this section, 'displacement' means layoff, demotion, involuntary transfer to a new class, or involuntary transfer to a new work location requiring the employee to change his or her place of residence in order to be able to continue in his or her job classification." Paragraph E of article 24 similarly limits the use of private contracting where it would cause displacement of Unit 9 employees and defines displacement in much the same language as the statutes quoted above: "Displacement includes layoff, involuntary demotion, involuntary transfer to a new class, involuntary transfer to a new location requiring a change of residence, and time base reductions."

In short, the limitations on private contracting by public agencies imposed by article 24 reflect the spirit and to some extent the letter of those California Constitution, article-VII-derived statutes that we held in *Kempton* had been impliedly repealed by Proposition 35. Thus, legislative approval of the MOU, in addition to not complying with section 5 of Proposition 35, violates the constitutional mandate of article XXII of the California Constitution, which abolished article VII's restrictions on the ability of agencies to use private contractors for architectural and engineering services.

D. *Article 24 As a Self-imposed Executive Restriction on Private Contracting*

As noted, following our decision in *Kempton*, we sought supplemental briefing from the parties on the impact of that decision on this case. In its supplemental briefing, Professional Engineers performs a volte-face. While maintaining that article 24 represents a legitimate policy choice regarding private contracting, it abandons its claim that the Legislature was empowered by Proposition 35 to make this choice and now maintains that this authority resides in the executive branch. Indeed, Professional Engineers now contends that the Legislature was not required to approve the MOU that contained article 24 at all. Professional Engineers also attempts to characterize article 24 as nothing more than a mechanism for gathering and analyzing data pertaining to private contracting, and specifically asserts that article 24 does not authorize termination of such contracts, now or in the future. Additionally, Professional Engineers maintains that article 24 does not contain the kind of article VII restrictions that we discussed in *Kempton* because the purpose of article 24 is not to promote the merit-based civil service system as was the judicially construed purpose of the article VII restrictions. We reject these arguments.

Professional Engineers' attempt to locate the authority for the restrictions on private contracting found in article 24 in the executive branch rather than the Legislature founders on two points. First, as we made clear in *Kempton*, Proposition 35 applies equally to all three branches of government: executive, legislative and judicial. (*Kempton, supra*, 40 Cal.4th at p. 1042.) Thus, executive branch agencies are no more at liberty to violate California Constitution, article XXII by reviving California Constitution, article-VII-based restrictions under the guise of collective bargaining than is the Legislature. Second, as we demonstrated in the prior part, the restrictions imposed by article 24 on the use of private contractors appear to be based on the California Constitution, article-VII-derived statutes that we concluded in *Kempton* had been impliedly repealed by Proposition 35. Professional Engineers' assertion that the purpose of article 24, unlike the judicially construed article VII restriction, is not to promote the merit-based civil service system draws a distinction without a difference. We agree with the Court of Appeal majority that "[t]he effect of [article 24] is to restrict the ability of state authorities to freely contract out [architectural and] engineering services," and that, therefore, article 24 "contravenes the goals of the Proposition 35 and thwarts the intent of the electorate."

In their supplemental brief, the leadership of the Legislature as amici curiae, argues that this reasoning converts the discretion of executive agencies to use private firms for architectural and engineering services to a mandate. This is the same argument made by the dissenting justice in the Court of Appeal who characterized the majority's holding as requiring the state to contract with private entities for architectural and engineering services. This is not accurate. Our holding does not compel state agencies to enter into such contracts. Under Proposition 35, state agencies have the choice and authority to use private contractors so, clearly, they can choose not to if they conclude that a particular public works project can be more efficiently performed by civil service employees. Moreover, Proposition 35 does not preclude state agencies from imposing conditions consistent with Proposition 35 on private contractors that perform such work. What the state may not do is to impair an individual agency's choice to engage in private contracting in derogation of the authority conferred on it by Proposition 35. Neither the Governor nor the Legislature, separately or jointly, can undo by MOU what the electorate enacted through Proposition 35.

Like the Court of Appeal, we also reject Professional Engineers' attempts to recast the purpose of article 24 as merely an innocuous mechanism for gathering and analyzing data on private contracting. The plain language of article 24 — allowing as it does for termination of private contracts and clearly serving to protect the interests of state employees — belies this interpretation. As the Court of Appeal majority noted, "By any measure, [article 24 imposes] significant restrictions on the ability of a state entity to contract out for architectural and engineering services on public works projects now and in the future."

Lastly, we note Professional Engineers' curious argument that, because by its terms article 24 "is not triggered when contracting out is recognized or required by law," and Proposition 35 now allows such private contracting, article 24's preference for using state employees "does not violate Proposition 35 because that preference does not apply when the 'law' and 'court decisions' (such as the *Kempton* decision) 'recognize' contracting out." This argument appears to amount to a concession that any provisions of article 24 in conflict with Proposition 35 as we construed that initiative in *Kempton* are a nullity.

III. CONCLUSION

We affirm the judgment of the Court of Appeal.

George, C. J., and Kennard, J., Baxter, J., Werdegar, J., Chin, J., and Corrigan, J., concurred.

Notes and Questions

1. Perhaps an obvious statement, but a statute cannot conflict with either the federal or state Constitutions. In our hierarchy of laws, the Constitution is the highest law of the land, followed by statutes, and ending with regulations. As such, neither a statute nor a regulation can conflict with the Constitution.

2. As a result, the Legislature cannot act by enacting a statute that contravenes a constitutional provision. This may be an obvious outcome, but sometimes, the legislative branch decides to pursue legislation that attempts to test the limits of their authority to enact legislation. In other instances, legislation may contravene the will of the voters as they have determined through the use of direct democracy (i.e., the initiative).

3. The specific issue before this Court was "whether a provision of a memorandum of understanding between the state and a state employee union that restricts the use of private contractors for architectural and engineering services by public agencies fatally conflicts with Proposition 35." The Court held that the MOU did conflict with the voters' will.

4. The public employee union argued that the phrase "State of California" was limited to just the legislative branch of state government. However, the appellate Court ruled that this phrase actually refers to the state government, including all three branches — legislative, executive and judicial. As a result of this determination, the Court held that Prop. 35 (as embodied in Article XXII) grants all three branches of government the authority to contract with private entities for architectural and engineering services.

5. The Court rejected the public employee union's separation of powers argument because, as a result of the voters' adoption of Prop. 35, there is not a shift of policy-making powers from the legislative branch to executive branch agencies.

6. The Court summarily rejected the argument that the MOU entered into between the State of California and the public employee union was, or could have been, an amendment of the initiative. The Legislature had approved the MOU. The Court held, "The operative principle applicable here is that the Legislature cannot take action, whether by statute or MOU, that contravenes a constitutional provision."

7. What were the two reasons the Court cited to explain why the Professional Engineers' attempt to locate the authority for the Article XXIV restrictions on private contracting in the executive branch rather than the Legislature?

D. Changing the Words of a Statute

Changing the words of an existing statute is done by a bill that amends the existing statute, one of the three permitted methods of dealing with statutes. The Legislature can add, amend or repeal a statute. By changing the words of an existing statute, the Legislature is amending the existing law so that it comports with the desired intent of changing the statutory language.

Lundquist v. Lundstrom

(1928) 94 Cal.App. 109

OPINION

BEAUMONT, J., pro tem.

This is an appeal from a judgment of nonsuit. The action was for damages resulting from the alleged negligent operation by defendants of an automobile in the city of Los Angeles on May 14, 1925. There are four defendants: (1) Marcus Lundstrom, a minor; (2) his mother, Mrs W.N. Lundstrom, who signed his application for a driver's license; (3) Gilbert Talbot, a minor, and (4) his mother, Alma Talbot, who signed her son's application for an operator's license. Marcus Lundstrom owned the automobile, but at the time of injury to plaintiff Mrs. Lundquist, defendant Gilbert Talbot was driving. This was with the consent of the owner, who was seated in the machine. As the automobile approached a street intersection, Mrs. Lundquist and her daughter were attempting to cross the street in the course of the approaching machine. They were coming toward the path of the automobile from the right. The driver, Talbot, according to his own statement, did not see them. The daughter, observing the approaching machine, returned to a place of safety on the curb. Marcus Lundstrom, observing Mrs. Lundquist in a position of danger, shouted, "Look out, there is a lady!" Talbot, the driver, thinking she was coming from the left, turned the machine to the right and struck the plaintiff, Mrs. Lundquist. Each of the above-mentioned minors held a state operator's license. Upon the resting of plaintiff's case, motion for nonsuit was made on behalf of Mrs. Lundstrom, on the ground that, as she had been made a defendant solely because she had made application for a driver's license for her son, and the evidence showed conclusively that her son was not driving the automobile at the time the injury occurred, no liability attached to her. The motion was granted. A verdict was rendered for plaintiff against all defendants except Mrs. Lundstrom, in whose favor a judgment of nonsuit was entered.

In *Bosse v. Marye,* 80 Cal.App. 109 [250 P. 693], Claudine Spreckels, a minor, had been issued, upon the written request of her father, a license to operate a motor vehicle. She invited Helen Marye, also a minor, to drive her automobile. While Miss Marye, who did not hold an operator's license, was driving, the machine collided with and injured Louis Bosse, the plaintiff. In an action for damages, plaintiff alleged negligent operation of said automobile. A verdict was rendered against said Rudolph Spreckels. The court made a distinction upon appeal by Spreckels between "operating" and "driving" an automobile, saying: "The liability of a parent, under the statute is not limited, however, to negligent acts of the minor resulting from 'driving' an automobile, the statute employing the broader term, 'operating or driving,' showing a clear intention to include within such liability any negligent act which is the direct result of the privilege extended by the statute to said minor under his or her operator's license *to operate* an automobile on the public highway. (Italics ours.) 'To drive' is defined as meaning, 'to impel the motion and quicken'; whereas 'to operate' means, 'to direct or superintend.' Century Dictionary."

The liability of the parent in *Bosse v. Marye* was determined upon construction of the Statutes of 1919. (Sec. 14, am. sec. 24, pp. 223, 224, 225.) The Motor Vehicle Act then provided that "any negligence of a minor, so licensed, in operating or driving a motor vehicle upon the public highway, whether a chauffeur or operator, shall be imputed to the person or persons who shall have signed the application of such minor for such license, which person or persons shall be jointly and severally liable with such minor for any damages caused by such negligence." The Motor Vehicle Act of 1923, upon which the claim of liability of the parent in the present case is based, has been materially changed from that of 1919. The 1923 act (Stats. 1923, p. 531, sec. 58) declares that it shall be unlawful for any person to drive any motor vehicle upon any public highway unless licensed or exempt under the act. Section 62 (a) provides for the granting of the application. Section 62 (b) of the same act is as follows: "Any negligence of a minor so licensed in *driving* (italics ours) a motor vehicle upon a public highway shall be imputed to the person or persons who shall have signed the application of such minor for said license, which person or persons shall be jointly and severally liable with such minor for any damages caused by such negligence."

A change of legislative purpose is to be presumed from a material change in the wording of a statute. (*McCarthy v. Board of Fire Commissioners,* 37 Cal.App. 495 [174 P. 402]; *Thomas v. Joplin,* 14 Cal.App. 662 [112 P. 729].) That there is a difference in the meaning of the words "drive" and "operate" is clearly pointed out in *Bosse v. Marye, supra.* It is elementary that the legislature is presumed to know the meaning of language.

We must assume, therefore, that it was the intention of the legislature to limit the imputation of negligence, as provided by this act (Motor Vehicle Act of 1923) to that resulting from the actual *driving,* for the more comprehensive word "operating" is eliminated, leaving only the word "driving," instead of "operating or driving."

The claim against respondent in this case is grounded on the statute. (Motor Vehicle Act 1923.) No liability could attach to her unless it is shown that the car which caused the injury to appellant was being driven under authority of the license of Marcus Lundstrom. The signing of the application, the issuance of the license and the alleged driving of the motor vehicle under the authority of the license are the basis of the action against Mrs. Lundstrom, coupled, of course, with the alleged negligence and resultant injuries. It cannot be successfully claimed that the automobile was being driven under the authority of Marcus Lundstrom's license. The evidence shows that at the very time of the accident the driver himself, Gilbert Talbot, held a state license to drive a motor vehicle. It will not be presumed that he was driving in violation of the provisions of section 58 of the Motor Vehicle Act, but on the other hand, that as a licensee of the state, he was acting under authority of his own license. We are convinced that the action of the trial court in granting the motion for nonsuit was without error. The judgment is affirmed.

Tyler, P.J., and Knight, J., concurred.

Notes and Questions

1. Was this a case of simple statutory construction? According to the court, there is a presumption of change of legislative purpose arising from a material change in the wording of a statute. The Legislature is presumed to know the meaning of language that they use in legislation. This presumption of change of legislative purpose arises due to a material change in the wording of a statute, which also means that the Legislature must enact substantive, rather than technical, amendments to a statute in order for the presumption to be invoked. This case appears to hinge on the difference in the meaning of the words "drive" and "operate."

Pierce v. Riley

(1937) 21 Cal.App.2d 513

OPINION

The Court.

This is an appeal from a judgment denying a petition for a writ of mandamus and dismissing the proceeding. The writ was sought to compel the state controller to draw a warrant for the petitioner's increase of salary as secretary of the state board of equalization on the theory that his salary was fixed by the board according to the provisions of section 3692, subdivision 12, of the Political Code as amended in 1933. (Stats. 1933, p. 2689.) The respondent contends that the salary which was allowed the secretary by the board was not "effectual and payable" until it was first approved by the department of finance as required by section 675b, now section 675.1, of the Political Code, which approval of the increased portion of his salary was never procured. This proceeding depends upon the construction of the two sections of the code above mentioned, as they then existed.

The petitioner has been secretary of the state board of equalization for several years past. In 1917 his salary was fixed by section 3700a of the Political Code at $4,000 per year. In 1931 section 3700a was repealed. At the same time section 3692 of the Political Code, relating to the powers of the board of equalization, was amended so that subdivision 12 thereof then provided:

"The powers and duties of the state board of equalization are as follows: * * *

"12. To appoint a secretary, prescribe and enforce his duties. The secretary shall hold his office during the pleasure of the board and shall receive such compensation as may be prescribed by the board with the approval of the department of finance."

This amendment was approved June 9, 1931, and took effect August 14, 1931. (Stats. 1931, p. 1434.) Pursuant to that amendment the salary of the secretary was fixed and approved at $6,600 per year.

At the same time the last-mentioned amendment of the code was enacted, section 675b of the Political Code was also adopted. It was approved May 15, 1931, but it took effect August 14, 1931, at the same time the amendment to section 3692 also took effect. (Stats. 1931, p. 843.) Section 675b provided:

"Whenever any state department, board, commission, court or officer fixes the salary or compensation of an employee or officer, which salary is payable out of state funds, the salary shall be subject to the approval of the state department of finance before it becomes effective and payable."

In 1933, subdivision 12 of section 3692 of the Political Code was again amended by omitting therefrom the phrase with relation to the secretary's salary, "with the approval of the department of finance". That section now reads:

"The powers and duties of the state board of equalization are as follows: * * *

"12. To appoint its secretary, prescribe and enforce his duties. The secretary shall hold his office during the pleasure of the board and shall receive such compensation as may be prescribed by the board."

January 7, 1935, the board of equalization reduced the salary of the secretary to $5,000 per year, which change in his salary was duly approved by the department of finance. But at a meeting on August 7, 1935, the board of equalization, effective August 1, 1935, again increased his salary to the former amount of $6,600 per year, which was payable in equal monthly instalments. This last-mentioned action of the board of equalization, which increased the secretary's salary to the amount of $1600 per year over the preceding fixed salary of $5,000 per year, was not approved by the department of finance. The former fixed and approved salary of $5,000 has been fully paid. After having served as secretary for the period of one year following the last-mentioned increase of salary, the secretary demanded of the state controller the issuing of a warrant in his favor for the increased amount of his salary to August 1, 1936, in the sum of $1600, which was refused. The last-mentioned sum is all that is involved in this proceeding. This petition for a writ of mandamus was then filed in the Superior Court of Sacramento County. The writ was denied, and a judgment was rendered dismissing the proceeding. From that judgment this appeal was perfected.

The questions to be determined are whether the amendment to section 3692, subdivision 12, in 1933, eliminating therefrom the phrase "with the approval of the department of finance" constitutes a special statute which is controlling over the general provisions of section 675b, now 675.1, of the Political Code, with respect to the necessity of procuring the approval of the department of finance before the salary of the secretary which has been fixed by the board of equalization becomes "effective and payable", and whether section 675b of the Political Code was unconstitutional and void for the reason that the subject of the regulation and approval of salaries by the department of finance was not expressed in the title to the act as required by article IV, section 24, of the Constitution of California.

It will be observed that prior to the amendment of section 3692, subdivision 12, of the Political Code in 1933, both that section and the provisions of section 675b of the Political Code required the approval of the department of finance before the secretary's salary became effective and payable.

It is urged by the petitioner that the act of the legislature amending section 3692, subdivision 12, in 1933 by eliminating the phrase, "with the approval of the department of finance", and by adding thereto the mandatory language that the secretary "shall receive such compensation as may be prescribed by the board" clearly indicates that it was the intention of the legislature to exempt from the law authorizing the fixing of the secretary's salary the necessity of procuring the approval of the department of finance. It is also asserted that section 675b, as it then existed, was unconstitutional and void for the reason above mentioned.

On the contrary, the respondent argues that the elimination of the approval clause of the special statute merely left the general law, which was then found in section 675b, applicable, and that it must be presumed on the principle of upholding both statutes, if they may be reasonably reconciled, that the legislature knew the provision with relation to the approval of the salary by the department of finance, which was found in both sections, was merely cumulative and unnecessary.

The principles applicable to the construction of statutes which are adopted at the same time and which apply to the same subject-matter are so closely related that it is often difficult to determine which one is controlling. The solution of the problem frequently turns upon the application of these well-known rules to ascertain if possible the intention of the legislature with relation to the statutes in question.

We have concluded that the amendment of section 3692, subdivision 12, of the Political Code in 1933, eliminating therefrom the phrase "with the approval of the department of finance" was intended by the legislature to and had the effect of relieving the board of equalization from the necessity of securing the approval of the department of finance of the secretary's salary which was fixed by the board subsequent to that amendment, and that his salary fixed by the board pursuant to that amended statute thereafter became effective and payable without the approval of the department of finance.

It is true that statutes which are in pari materia should be construed together and reconciled so as to uphold both of them if it is reasonably possible to do so. This is especially true when such statutes are enacted at the same time, or at the same session of the legislature or when they become effective on the same date. (59 C.J. 1053, sec. 622.) Even when one such statute merely deals generally with a particular subject while the other legislates specially upon the same subject with greater detail and particularity, the two should be reconciled and construed so as to uphold both of them if possible. (*Cohn v. Isensee*, 45 Cal. App. 531 [188 P. 279].) Section 675b of the Political Code, which was applicable generally to the necessity of procuring the approval of salaries of officers fixed by certain departments did not permanently lose its effectiveness with respect to the salary of the secretary of the board of equalization merely because that approval was also required by the provisions of the special enactment of section 3692, subdivision 12. Upon the repeal or amendment of the last-mentioned section, the general provisions of section 675b with respect to that subject might be set in motion and become effective in that regard if it were valid. (*Seattle Coal & Transp. Co. v. Thomas*, 57 Cal. 197; *Lewis v. County Clerk of Santa Clara County*, 55 Cal. 604; *Ex parte Williamson*, 116 Wash. 560 [200 P. 329]; *County of Ventura v. Barry*, 202 Cal. 550 [262 P. 1081].)

But in the present proceeding the following circumstances furnish very persuasive evidence that the legislature did not intend to subject the payment of the salary of the secretary of the board of equalization to the approval clause of the general enactment of section 675b of the Political Code. When the last-mentioned section was approved May 15, 1931, the salary of the secretary was then statutory. It was then definitely fixed by section 3700a of the Political Code at $4,000 per year. Section 675b did not assume to apply to salaries of officers which were then definitely fixed by statute. It purports to apply only to salaries fixed by "state departments, boards, commissions, courts or officers". It is true that section 3692, which authorized the board of equalization to fix the secretary's salary was later approved on June 9, 1931, and that it took effect upon the same date when section 675b became effective.

It is not conclusive of this problem, but it is recognized as a rule of construction in determining which act is controlling under such circumstances, that the statute last approved particularly if it be a special act applicable to a particular subject, will be controlling over one which was previously approved, on the theory that it is the latest utterance of the legislature. (*County of Mariposa v. County of Madera*, 142 Cal. 50, 55 [75 P. 572]; *Ex parte Sohncke*, 148 Cal. 262 [82 P. 956, 113 Am.St.Rep. 236, 7 Ann. Cas. 475, 2 L.R.A. (N. S.) 813].) In the present case it is evident that section 3692, subdivision 12, is a special act applying only to the duties and salary of a particular officer, while section 675b is general in its nature. The rule of construction is established that a special statute ordinarily has precedence over a general act of the legislature. Moreover, it seems clear that by deliberately amending section 3692, subdivision 12, by omitting the language "with the approval of the department of finance", the legislature intended to relieve that statute of the approval clause. (*Shearer v. Flannery*, 68 Cal. App. 91, 94 [228 P. 549]; *United States v. Prentis*, 182 Fed. 894; *United States v. One Ice Box*, 37 Fed.2d 120; *San Marcos Baptist Academy v. Burgess* (Tex. Civ. App.) 292 S.W. 626.)

We must assume the legislature had some definite purpose in view in amending the last-mentioned section. The only reasonable result to be attained by that amendment was to relieve the statute of the approval clause. If this statute was deemed to be merely cumulative in its effect with that of section 675b it would appear to be idle and useless to amend one of them, for it certainly did no harm to leave it as it previously existed. The strongest circumstance indicating that the legislature intended by the amendment of section 3692 to relieve it of the approval clause is that this intention would furnish a reasonable purpose and design for the change in the law. Otherwise it was useless and idle to modify the statute. We must assume the legislature had a purpose and design in amending that statute. (*People v. Weitzel*, 201 Cal. 116, 118 [255 P. 792, 52 A.L.R. 811].) In the case last cited it is said in that regard:

> "'Where changes have been introduced by amendment, it is not to be assumed that they were without design; usually an intent to change the law is inferred.' (*In re Segregation of School District No. 58*, 34 Idaho, 222 [200 P. 138].) In *Rieger v. Harrington*, 102 Or. 603 [203 P. 576, 580], it was said: 'By amending that statute, the legislature demonstrated an intent to change the pre-existing law, and the presumption must be that it was intended to change the meaning of the statute in all the particulars wherein there is a material change in the language of the amended act.' To the same effect are the following authorities: *Springfield Co. v. Walton*, 95 Mo. App. 256 [69 S.W. 477]; *Duff v. Karr*, 91 Mo. App. 16; *Pierce v. County of Solano*, 62 Cal. App. 465, 469 [217 P. 545]; *Shearer v. Flannery*, 68 Cal. App. 91, 94 [228 P. 549]."

In *Lundquist v. Lundstrom*, 94 Cal. App. 109, 112 [270 P. 696], it was also held that the legislature must be presumed to have intended to change the effect of a statute by an amendment which deliberately and clearly changes the language substantially.

There is another reason which precludes us from holding that the general provisions of section 675b of the Political Code, as it existed after the amendment of section 3692 in 1933, were not controlling with respect to the necessity of procuring an approval of the salary of the secretary which was fixed at $6,600 on August 1, 1935. We are persuaded that section 675b was unconstitutional and void for the reason that its title contained no reference to the authority of the department of finance to regulate, control or approve salaries of officers. The title to the act merely declared that it was enacted to amend certain sections of the Political Code and to add other sections, including section 675b, "relating to the department of finance". This title gave no intimation that authority was to be conferred upon that department to regulate or approve salaries of officers. Prior to the adoption of that section the department of finance had no such authority. For the reason that the title to section 675b was defective and fails to conform to the mandate of article IV, section 24, of the

Constitution of California it was void and may therefore not control the provisions of the special act with regulation to the secretary's salary contained in section 3692, subdivision 12, of the Political Code. The unconstitutionality of section 675b, because of the defective title thereto, was evidently recognized by the legislature by the subsequent repeal of the last-mentioned section in 1935 and the adoption of a new section in lieu thereof, designated as section 675.1 of the Political Code. (Stats. 1935, p. 404.) This last-mentioned enactment, however, does not affect this proceeding because it was adopted after the petitioner's claim accrued.

It is true that the title to an act should be liberally construed so as to uphold the statute if a reasonable reference to the subject-matter included therein may be ascertained from the language employed, and that it is not necessary to embrace in the title every detail of the subjects of the enactment. (*Hecke v. Riley*, 209 Cal. 767, 775 [290 P. 451].) It is there said:

> "It is now well settled 'that the constitutional provision requiring the subject of the act to be expressed in its title must be liberally construed, and that all that is required to be contained therein in order to meet the constitutional requirement is a reasonably intelligent reference to the subject to which the legislation of the act is to be addressed. It is not necessary that it should 'embrace an abstract or catalogue of its contents'. (*Estate of McPhee*, 154 Cal. 385, 389 [97 P. 878, 880].)"

In the *Hecke case, supra*, the title, which was held to adequately comply with the Constitution, after specifying certain sections of the Political Code which were amended, then recites that the provisions are "relating to the department of agriculture and the division of land settlement thereof". (Stats. 1929, p. 677.) These amendments merely modified the provisions of an act creating the department of agriculture of the state and designating the duties of the director of agriculture (Stats. 1919, p. 542; 1 Deering's General Laws of 1931, p. 40, Act 113), with relation to the state land settlement division thereof. The general powers of that division then existed by virtue of the Department of Agriculture Act. The amendments affected only such general authority. Reference in the title to the "department of agriculture and the division of land settlement" was therefore held to be adequate. But in the present case the effort to confer upon the department of finance for the first time in section 675b of the Political Code the authority to regulate and approve all salaries fixed by "departments, boards, commissions, courts or officers" was entirely foreign to any powers previously possessed by the department of finance. That department had previously been authorized by statute to audit all claims, but it had not been permitted to regulate or approve the fixing of any salaries. These added duties are so distinct from the former duties of the department that the title to section 675b would be entirely misleading with regard to the proposed legislation. We are therefore of the opinion that section was unconstitutional and void.

For the foregoing reasons the judgment should be reversed. It is so ordered. The court is directed to grant the writ of mandamus requiring the state controller to issue a warrant in favor of the petitioner in the sum of $1600 as prayed for.

Notes and Questions

1. The Legislature is presumed to have intended to change the effect of a statute by an amendment which deliberately and clearly changes the language substantially. This would seem an obvious outcome, but nonetheless is an important rule of the lawmaking process. If the Legislature intends to change a statute, then it must do so by making a substantive change to the statutory language.

2. How did the court address the question of whether eliminating the phrase "with the approval of the department of finance" constituted a special statute which was controlling over a general provision of law? What evidence did the court cite to conclude that the Legislature did not intend to subject the payment of the salary of the secretary of the Board of Equalization to the approval clause involving the Department of Finance?

E. Authority to Repeal Laws

Just as the legislature has the authority to adopt laws, it also has authority to repeal laws. This is implicit in the lawmaking process. By means of passing a bill, the Legislature can add, amend or repeal a statute. Repealing a statute requires a bill to be enacted and signed into law by the Governor.

Notes and Questions

1. A corollary of the legislative power to make new laws is the power to abrogate existing ones. In other words, what the Legislature has enacted, it may repeal. At the core of the legislative power is the authority to make laws. The legislative power that the state Constitution vests is plenary.

2. Under the legislative power of the state Constitution, the entire lawmaking authority of the state, except the people's right of initiative and referendum, is vested in the Legislature, and that body may exercise any and all legislative powers which are not expressly or by necessary implication denied to it by the Constitution. Only where the state Constitution withdraws legislative power will the state Supreme Court conclude an enactment is invalid for want of authority. (*California Redevelopment Association v. Matosantos* (2011) 53 Cal.4th 231.)

F. Legislative Findings

On occasion, the Legislature employs the use of findings and declarations to express its intent in enacting a law. These findings are intended to express the intent of the Legislature in enacting the law so that guidance is provided to both those who are regulated by the law and those who are enforcing and interpreting the law. The courts historically rely upon these findings in order to properly ascertain the intent of the Legislature.

The courts often defer to these legislative findings and give them the respect they are entitled to, as the legislative branch is charged with the lawmaking function, and these legislative findings are appropriate to ensure that the bill's provisions are interpreted and enforced as intended by the Legislature.

1. Are Legislative Findings and Declarations Necessary in Legislation?

On occasion, when we review California bills, we come across legislative findings and declarations in these measures. Why are they used and are they necessary? There are basically two schools of thought among bill drafters.

But first, what are they? Bills sometimes contain the equivalent of a "preamble," or a declaration of purpose. This preamble to a bill usually consists of statements of legislative intent. In California, we call these "legislative findings and declarations." The general purpose of this language is to explain the purpose or the intent of the Legislature in enacting the particular statute.

Are they necessary? That depends. There are those who believe these statements of purpose, or legislative findings and declarations, can assist the courts in interpreting any ambiguous terms found in the statute.

Our state's statutes sometimes have ambiguities, and courts must look to the legislative history to determine what those statutory words were intended to mean. While statute's plain reading is generally to be followed, at times, that may not be so easy, and courts will have to rely upon the limited evidence of legislative intent that is available for California legislation. One of those pieces of evidence could come from the bill itself—the legislative findings and declarations.

Based upon this point of view, use of legislative findings may provide a reviewing court with a "roadmap" that will assist the court in its analysis of the statutory language. This viewpoint also advocates for the judicial branch to provide deference to the legislative body's determination regarding the need for the bill and, as a matter of separation of powers, a bill's explicit rationale helps ensure that a court does not have to go on a "fishing expedition" among other forms of extrinsic aids to determine what the legislature intended.

What might this language look like? The following is an example from a California bill:

The Legislature finds and declares all of the following:

(a) According to a December 6, 2017, report by the Legislative Analyst's Office entitled, "Improving In-Prison Rehabilitation Programs," California state prisons house nearly 130,000 inmates.

(b) While incarcerated in prison, inmates often participate in various rehabilitation programs that seek to improve the likelihood that inmates will lead a productive, crime-free life upon release from prison by addressing the underlying factors that led to their criminal activity.

(c) The Department of Corrections and Rehabilitation offers inmates various rehabilitation programs while they are in prison, including education and substance use disorder treatment programs. The primary goal of those programs is to reduce recidivism — the number of inmates who reoffend after they are released from prison.

On the other hand, there are those who believe that a well-drafted bill should not require any extraneous statement within itself of what it seeks to accomplish or the reasons prompting its enactment. For example, according to the South Dakota Legislative Counsel, "A declaration of purpose is strongly discouraged and is rarely useful. A well drafted bill should not need a declaration of purpose. However, if a statement of policy or purpose is to be included, it is ordinarily the first section of the bill and should be short and concise. An improperly worded statement of purpose may cause serious problems of judicial interpretation."

Based upon this viewpoint, language stating the purpose of a bill or recital of facts upon which a bill is predicated should not be included as a matter of course. However, in some circumstances, purpose language may be useful in upholding a bill against constitutional attack after enactment or to give meaning to a provision for liberal construction. In those circumstances, appropriate language may be included in a bill.

Notes and Questions

1. The determination of whether a program at issue serves a public purpose is generally vested in the Legislature. Though not binding on the courts, legislative findings are given great weight and will be upheld unless they are found to be unreasonable and arbitrary.

2. Because legislative power is practically absolute, constitutional limitations on legislative power are strictly construed and may not be given effect as against the general power of the Legislature unless such limitations clearly inhibit the act in question. (*Foundation for Taxpayer and Consumer Rights v. Garamendi* (2005) 132 Cal.App.4th 1354.)

G. Inability to Enact Laws that Tie Future Legislatures

A popular saying is that the "Legislature cannot bind future Legislatures." This statement is rooted in the fact that a future Legislature can amend an existing statute and, as a result, there is no ability to bind the hands of a future Legislature. A Legislature the following year or many years after a law has been enacted can amend or repeal that statute. Because a future Legislature can make changes to or repeal an existing statute, we know that a current Legislature is unable to enact any laws that tie future Legislatures.

United Milk Producers of California v. Cecil

(1941) 47 Cal.App.2d 758

OPINION

Tuttle, J.

Petitioners seek by writ of mandate to compel respondent Director of Agriculture of California to forthwith rescind and revoke an order made by him denying milk distributors' licenses to them, and also to compel said director to issue to each of petitioners such licenses for the year 1941. An alternative writ was issued by this court, and a demurrer to said petition was filed by the Attorney General on behalf of respondents. All parties agree that the petition sets forth all necessary facts, and that decision of this court upon the demurrer will dispose of the entire litigation.

Under the provisions of section 737.11 of the Agricultural Code, orders to show cause were issued by the Director of Agriculture (hereinafter referred to as the "Director"), why petitioners' licenses should not be revoked. A hearing was had, at which petitioners both appeared. Oral and documentary evidence was introduced, the transcript of said hearing being some two hundred pages in length. Upon the conclusion of said hearing, the order under attack here was made and entered.

The refusal to grant a license, or the suspension or revocation of a license may occur "when he (the 'Director') is satisfied that any applicant or licensee has violated any provision of this chapter (div. IV, chapter 10, Agricultural Code), or any provision of any stabilization and marketing plan formulated under the provisions of this chapter." (Agricultural Code, section 737.11.) No exception is taken by petitioners to the facts found by the "Director." Such findings are very exhaustive, and take up some eighteen pages of the petition. It may thus be properly concluded that the facts found were proven at said hearing. The order of revocation was not absolute, it being provided "that such application of said respondent, The Borden Company, may be renewed upon presentation of satisfactory evidence to the Director of Agriculture that said contract between it and United Milk Producers of California, dated August 1, 1940, has been terminated and abandoned, and that said, The Borden Company has paid to the individual producer-members and to all other producers from whom it has received fluid milk since August 1, 1940, the full, applicable minimum prices therefor as established under the stabilization and marketing plan or plans effective during said time."

As we view the several contentions of the parties, the real question is whether or not the "Director" has authority, under the Milk Control Act (Agricultural Code of California, chapter 10, div. IV), to fix the minimum price which must be paid to its members by cooperative marketing associations organized under the provisions of division VI, chapter 4 of said code. The litigants appear to concede that if the Milk Control Act governs the situation, the order under attack must be sustained. It is admitted by petitioners that the individual producers who constitute United Milk Producers (hereinafter referred to as "United"), for a number of months prior to, and also at the time of said hearing, did not receive the minimum price for their milk prescribed and fixed by the "Director". This was held by the "Director" to constitute a violation of the law and regulations made pursuant thereto. The exact nature of the controversy, and the conflicting views in respect thereto, are thus aptly summarized by petitioners in their reply brief:

> "As pointed out at the argument, the above contention of respondents assumes the point in issue. The question is whether the Milk Control Act requires that the equivalent of the Directors' control prices be paid in all cases, or whether under the laws of the State there is an exception applicable to cooperatives.... Respondents, however, contend that all cooperative-distributors, without exception, are required by the Milk Control Act to return to their members at least the control prices. If a cooperative is unable to return the equivalent of these prices, presumably it must go out of the distributing business. This, we submit, is something which, if it is to be said, should be said by the legislature, and not by the courts. The statute does not expressly say that cooperatives must go out of the distributing business under these circumstances, and a provision of this kind, we submit, should not go into the statute by implication."

....

Petitioners strongly rely upon section 1219 of the Agricultural Code, which is a portion of the law dealing with cooperative marketing associations. Said section reads as follows:

> "The general corporation laws of this state and all powers and rights thereunder, shall apply to the associations organized hereunder, except where such provisions are in conflict with or inconsistent with the express provisions of this chapter."

They argue that the foregoing section establishes a rule of construction which must control here. It will be noted, however, that it has reference only to "the general corporation laws of this state." The inconsistency and conflict here do not come from such laws, but from the Agricultural Code. There is therefore no rule of construction laid down for our guidance.

Furthermore, it is the general rule that one legislature cannot enact irrepealable legislation or limit or restrict its own power or the power of its successors as to the repeal of statutes, and an act of one legislature is not binding upon, and does not tie the hands of future legislatures. (59 C.J., sec. 500, pages 899, 900). In Lewis' Sutherland Statutory Construction, vol. 1, sec. 244, pages 456, 457, the rule is thus stated:

> "Every legislative body may modify or abolish the acts passed by itself or its predecessors. This power of repeal may be exercised at the same session at which the original act was passed; and even while a bill is in its progress and before it becomes a law. The legislature cannot bind a future legislature to a particular mode of repeal. It cannot declare in advance the intent of subsequent legislatures or the effect of subsequent legislation upon existing statutes."

In the same volume, section 247, pages 461–464, it is said:

"Such repeals are recognized as intended by the legislature, and its intention to repeal is ascertained as the legislative intent is ascertained in other respects, when not expressly declared, by construction. An implied repeal results from some enactment the terms and necessary operation of which cannot be harmonized with the terms and necessary effect of an earlier act. In such case the later law prevails as the last expression of the legislative will; therefore, the former law is constructively repealed, since it cannot be supposed that the law-making power intends to enact or continue in force laws which are contradictions. The repugnancy being ascertained, the later act or provision in date or position has full force, and displaces by repeal whatever in the precedent law is inconsistent with it. Subsequent legislation repeals previous inconsistent legislation whether it expressly declares such repeal or not. In the nature of things, it would be so, not only on the theory of intention, but because contradictions cannot stand together. The intention to repeal, however, will not be presumed, nor the effect of repeal admitted, unless the inconsistency is unavoidable, and only to the extent of the repugnance."

It must be apparent that the Cooperative Marketing Act, passed several years prior to the Milk Control Act, was inconsistent with the latter. Under the Marketing Act, the members were permitted to enter such marketing contracts as they wished, and to distribute the proceeds from the sale of milk among themselves, after deducting necessary expenses. On the other hand, the Milk Control Act gives authority to the "Director" to fix the minimum amount which a producer may receive for his milk. In this connection the word "price" is used in the latter act. Considering the act in its entirety, we think the legislature did not use that word in a technical sense, and that it can be reasonably construed to include any return which is received by the producer from the distributor in the marketing of his product. It is therefore our conclusion that the Cooperative Marketing Act, in respect to the particulars mentioned, was impliedly repealed by the Milk Control Act, and that cooperative marketing associations are distributors for their members, and therefore subject to its operation and control.

Petitioners, in attempting to show lack of legislative intent to repeal, point out that a cooperative, from the very nature of its organization, cannot return the price fixed by the "Director" for milk, if its net returns are less than such price; that in cooperatives, the producer-member is the owner, and that he receives the profits from its marketing activities, and should therefore bear any loss. It must be assumed that the foregoing effect upon cooperative organizations must have been foreseen by the legislature, but that they considered that the health and general welfare of the people as a whole were paramount over such matters as the internal management of such associations, and their customary method of operation. The proof of a legislative intent to make the Milk Control Act all-inclusive is so apparent and strong that considerations of the foregoing nature must give way before it. By its very terms the act covered the distribution by "United." The burden was therefore upon "United" to show that it was excepted from the enactment. This burden, as we have indicated, they have failed to sustain.

The authorities relied upon by petitioners are practically all directed toward the use and meaning of the word "price" in the Milk Control Act. It is contended that the use of that word indicates an intent to exclude cooperatives from its operation. They state:

> "We assume that respondents will contend that the term 'price', as used in the Milk Control Act and in the marketing and stabilization plan, must be given a broader and more inclusive meaning than its ordinary sense in order to effect the purpose of the Act by assuring all producers a minimum return for their milk. We point out, however, that if the term were given this broad construction, the director would be authorized to fix not only the minimum return which Borden must make to United under the agency contract, but also the minimum return which every cooperative-distributor must make to its members. In no event could the term 'price' be given a broad meaning to cover the one situation and a different and narrower meaning to exclude the other."

They rely chiefly upon the case of *Green v. Milk Control Commission* (1940), 340 Pa. 1, 10 [16 Atl. (2d) 9, 10], where it is said:

> "The principal guiding to decision is this: The power and authority to be exercised by administrative commissions must be conferred by legislative language clear and unmistakable.... With the principle stated before us, turning to the law embodying the powers of the Milk Control Commission, we find nothing said about milk shipped to dealers on consignment. It speaks of the 'purchase' of milk by dealers, its 'delivery and sale' to them; it uses the words 'buy', 'purchase', 'prices', 'bought or sold', 'sell or buy.' The words 'consign' or 'consignment' nowhere appear. We are asked by the Commonwealth to interpolate these words into the Act. This we cannot do without violating the important principle to which we have adverted. If the legislature desires to change the law, this can shortly be demonstrated by an amendment at the coming session, writing into the Act a provision covering milk sent to dealers on consignment."

As stated above, we are of the opinion that the word mentioned was used in a broader sense, and that, under the statute, any producer, irrespective of how he places his milk upon the market, must receive the minimum amount fixed by the "Director." We accept the view of the dissenting opinion in the Green case, wherein the following language is used:

> "Plaintiffs are a handful of dealers who have contrived an ingenious scheme by which, although for all practical purposes transactions in the business are carried on as before, a new relationship, from a legalistic standpoint, is imposed upon the contracting parties. Instead of producers selling to dealers and the latter in turn to consumers, a form of agreement between producers

and dealers has now been prepared whereby the dealer calls himself a 'factor'" (agent), "the milk is said to be 'consigned' to the 'factor'" (agent), "the title is to remain in the producer until the milk is sold 'whereupon it shall pass directly from producer to the person purchasing same....' The obvious purpose of this device" (as in the proceeding at bar) "is to enable the plaintiffs to obtain milk from producers at prices lower than those fixed by the Milk Control Commission. If they succeed in this attempt the force of competition will naturally compel the entire industry to adopt the same arrangement, so that price-fixing by the Commission will become a nullity, the Milk Control Law will be effectively torpedoed, and the industry will be reduced to the condition which the Act was designed to remedy.... The Act is not primarily aimed at *what the dealer or consumer shall pay, but what the producer shall receive....* The majority opinion stresses the fact that the Milk Control Law uses only the words 'buy,' 'purchase,' 'prices,' etc.; from this it is argued that consignment transactions are not within the purview of the act. It has already been pointed out that these 'consignment' agreements" (just as does the contract between the petitioners in the instant case) "necessarily involve also sales somewhere down the line, and that the Commission is empowered to fix the minimum price to be charged in such sales and to prevent the price thus fixed from being undermined by the device of paying commissions to so-called 'factors' or by any similar scheme. But there is high authority even for the broader proposition that the 'consignment' phase of the transaction is itself directly subject to the power of the Commission irrespective of any subsequent sales of milk by the 'factor' (agent). In *United States v. Rock Royal Co-Operative, Inc.*, 307 U.S. 533, 579, 580 [59 S. Ct. 993, 83 L. Ed. 1446], the Court construed the word 'purchased' in the Agricultural Marketing Agreement Act of 1937, 7 U.S.C.A. § 601, et seq., as being not confined merely to technical 'sales,' but as having the more general meaning of 'acquired for marketing.' So, here, since the act defines a dealer not only as one who 'purchases' but also one who 'handles' milk, [in section 735.3(f), California Agricultural Code 'distributor' is defined as anyone 'who purchases or handles fluid milk or fluid cream for sale'] the power to fix 'prices' as between producer and dealer properly includes the power to regulate the terms of transactions by which the milk is merely 'acquired' by the dealer 'for marketing,' or, in other words, 'consigned,' instead of being 'bought' outright by him, and particularly to prescribe the amount of commissions, if any to be allowed in such cases.

"*Having regard,* then *to the fundamental purpose* of the Milk Control Law and the *necessity of judicially implementing* its provisions for the welfare of the people of the Commonwealth, especially the children, the *act,* in my opinion *should not be emasculated by unduly technical construction.*" (Italics ours.)

It is urged by petitioners that in the 1941 session of the legislature, proposed amendments to the Milk Control Act which would have included cooperatives within its scope, failed of passage. Thus, they say, the legislature must have intended, when the original act was passed, to exclude cooperatives from its scope. While this may be some evidence of legislative intent, it can be argued with equal force, that the omission to include the amendments was due to the fact that the legislature considered that the bill already included cooperatives, and that such amendments would be mere surplusage.

We have examined the other authorities cited by petitioners, but find nothing in them which is controlling. When it comes to a question of legislative intent, that matter must be decided from the peculiar facts and circumstances of each enactment.

The parties devote considerable time to the discussion of the question whether or not the contract between petitioners was one of agency or one under which "Borden" actually purchased the milk from "United." We do not deem it necessary to discuss that phase of the matter. We have shown that "United" was subject to the provisions of the Milk Control Act. If "Borden" was its agent, as petitioners contend, they were in exactly the same predicament as their principal, and violated the Milk Control Act, as the member-producers of "United" did not receive the minimum amount fixed by the "Director" as the price of the milk.

In conclusion, we hold that there was ample evidence before the "Director" to sustain the order in question.

The demurrer to the petition is sustained and the writ denied, respondents to recover their costs.

THOMPSON, Acting P.J., concurred.

Notes and Questions

1. Generally, the Legislature cannot enact irrepealable legislation or limit or restrict its own power or the power of its successors regarding the ability to repeal statutes. Specifically, an act of one Legislature is not binding upon and does not tie the hands of future Legislatures. Moreover, the Legislature cannot bind a future Legislature to a particular mode of repeal and cannot declare in advance the intent of subsequent Legislatures or the effect of subsequent legislation upon existing statutes.

2. What was the basis for the court's ruling that there was a "clear indication" that the Legislature intended to include all associations within the scope of the Act?

3. As the court explained, "it is the general rule that one legislature cannot enact irrepealable legislation or limit or restrict its own power or the power of its successors as to the repeal of statutes, and an act of one legislature is not binding upon, and does not tie the hands of future legislatures. (59 C.J., sec. 500, pages 899, 900)."

4. Moreover, in Lewis' Sutherland Statutory Construction, vol. 1, sec. 244, pages 456, 457, the rule was described in the following manner: "Every legislative body may modify or abolish the acts passed by itself or its predecessors. This power of repeal may be exercised at the same session at which the original act was passed; and even while a bill is in its progress and before it becomes a law. The legislature cannot bind a future legislature to a particular mode of repeal. It cannot declare in advance the

intent of subsequent legislatures or the effect of subsequent legislation upon existing statutes."

5. Why did the court reject the petitioners' argument that, in the 1941 session of the Legislature, proposed amendments to the Milk Control Act which would have included cooperatives within its scope, failed passage and therefore the Legislature must have intended, when the original act was passed, to exclude cooperatives from its scope?

H. Retroactive Laws

A retroactive law is one that is enacted by the Legislature that goes back in time, meaning it adds to, changes or repeals a law prior to the year in which the current bill is enacted. In other words, a retroactive law enacted in the 2020 Legislative Session is one that has effect prior to the 2020 calendar year.

For example, a bill affecting the state's Revenue & Taxation Code could be enacted by the Legislature during its 2020 Session, but the new law impacts a 2019 or 2018 tax year. The basic rule is that retroactive law changes are permissible if the Legislature states a public purpose why the law must have retroactive effect.

Retroactive changes to criminal laws (i.e., the California Penal Code) are generally prohibited where they make an act criminal after someone has engaged in the particular conduct that is now being prohibited.

1. Retroactivity of California Statutes

In California, as in most states, a statute is presumed to operate prospectively. (*Quarry v. Doe I* (2012) 53 Cal.4th 945, 955.) In construing statutes, there is a presumption against retroactive application unless the Legislature plainly has directed otherwise by means of express language of retroactivity or other sources that provide a clear and unavoidable implication that the Legislature intended retroactive application of the statute. (*Id.*)

In addition, a statute should be construed to preserve its constitutionality. (*In re York* (1995) 9 Cal.4th 1133, 1152.) The burden of establishing the unconstitutionality of a statute rests on the party attacking it, and courts may not declare a legislative classification invalid unless, viewed in the light of facts made known or generally assumed, it is of a character that precludes the assumption that the classification rests upon some rational basis within the knowledge and experience of the legislators. (*Id.*)

The California Civil Code includes a specific codification of this general principle by stating in Section 3, "No part of this Code is retroactive, unless expressly so declared." Moreover, the presumption against retroactivity applies with particular force to laws creating new obligations, imposing new duties, or exacting new penalties because of past transactions. (*In re Marriage of Reuling* (1994) 23 Cal.App.4th 1428, 1439.)

Based upon recent decisions by the California Supreme Court, the general rule in this state is that, if the Legislature clearly indicated its intent that an amendment to a statute is to be applied retroactively, then a court generally must honor that intent unless there is a constitutional objection to doing so. "The presumption against statutory retroactivity has consistently been explained by reference to the unfairness of imposing new burdens on persons after the fact." (*Landgraf v. USI Film Products* (1994) 511 U.S. 244, 270.)

This is not to say that a statute may never apply retroactively. "[A] statute's retroactivity is, in the first instance, a policy determination for the Legislature and one to which courts defer absent 'some constitutional objection' to retroactivity." (*Myers v. Philip Morris Companies, Inc.* (2002) 28 Cal.4th 828, 841.) As such, the basic rule in California is that "a statute may be applied retroactively only if it contains express language of retroactivity or if other sources provide a clear and unavoidable implication that the Legislature intended retroactive application." (*Id.*)

The California Supreme Court has made the statement that "where a statute provides that it clarifies or declares existing law, '[i]t is obvious that such a provision is indicative of a legislative intent that the amendment applies to all existing causes of action from the date of its enactment. In accordance with the general rules of statutory construction, we must give effect to this intention unless there is some constitutional objection thereto'." *Western Security Bank v. Superior Court* (1997) 15 Cal.4th 232, 244.)

California courts look to the text of the bill and legislative materials to determine whether the later enacted bill made a change in the law or whether the later enacted bill clarified existing law. If the bill represents a clarification of existing law, then the bill is applied to all instances, both retroactively and prospectively. If the bill enacts a change in the law, then the court looks to determine whether the Legislature intended for the law change to be applied retroactively. In this regard, the court basically asks, did the Legislature make a clear intent to apply the amendment retroactively?

As a result of these appellate court decisions, three main points can provide guidance to lawmakers and bill drafters when attempting to make retroactive changes to California statutes:

1. Did the Legislature enact the change in law promptly after the adverse court decision? In most instances, the legislative change needs to be made within a few months of the court decision.

2. Has the Supreme Court rendered a final decision? If yes, then the legislative enactment is most likely to be deemed only prospective in application.

3. Is there some amount of ambiguity in the statute that was amended? The courts are usually more inclined to allow a retroactive law change when an ambiguous statute was amended by the Legislature.

Based upon these appellate court decisions and the guidance issued, the Legislature does have the authority to declare that certain statutory changes can be applied retroactively, but only in certain specified instances. The most important point is that the California Supreme Court must not have ruled on the statute in question. Otherwise, the Legislature can only make a prospective change in the law.

Notes and Questions

1. A retroactive law is one that relates back to a previous transaction and gives it some legal effect that is different from that which it had under the law when it occurred. (*Ware v. Heller* (1944) 63 Cal.App.2d 817.) Why is retroactivity important when drafting legislation?

I. Weighing Competing Interests

As part of the lawmaking process, the Legislature is forced to weight competing interests when enacting new laws or changes to existing laws. These interests can often represent significant political players in the state legislative process who attempt to exert influence on elected officials and their staff while legislation is debated by members of the Assembly and Senate.

People v. Bunn

(2002) 27 Cal.4th 1

OPINION

BAXTER, J.

In 1994 and thereafter, the Legislature established and amended a special supplementary statute of limitations for certain sex crimes against minors. (Pen. Code, § 803, subd. (g) (section 803(g)).)

Under specified circumstances, the 1994 law, as more recently refined, revives the limitations period for such offenses after the usual statute of limitations has expired, even if both the crime, and expiration of the usual limitations period, occurred before 1994. We found that these retroactive features did not offend either ex post facto or due process principles in *People v. Frazer* (1999) 21 Cal.4th 737 (*Frazer*) (cert. den. *sub nom. Frazer v. California* (2000) 529 U.S. 1108, rehg. den. (2000) 530 U.S. 1284).

We granted review in this case and its companion, *People v. King* (Jan. 10, 2002, S085942) ___ Cal.4th ___ (*King*), to consider an additional narrow issue presented by this legislation. In 1996 and 1997, section 803(g) was amended to authorize, in certain circumstances, the filing of a molestation charge even where an accusatory pleading involving the same offense was previously dismissed as time-barred by the courts. The question is whether, and to what extent, the separation of powers clause of the California Constitution (art. III, § 3) precludes application of such a refiling provision.

Following *Plaut v. Spendthrift Farm, Inc.* (1995) 514 U.S. 211 (*Plaut*), which we find both consistent with California law and persuasive for state separation of powers purposes, we conclude that refiling legislation cannot be applied retroactively to reopen court cases that had already been dismissed, if the dismissals had become final judgments, under the law of finality which then pertained, before the refiling provision became effective. In this sense, and for separation of powers purposes, such prior judgments are sacrosanct. On the other hand, as *Plaut* itself explained, any dismissal that was already subject to a particular refiling law at the time the dismissal was entered or finally upheld cannot, to that extent, be deemed a final judgment immune from legislative interference. Hence, the refiling provision, as it existed at the time the dismissal was entered or finally upheld, may constitutionally permit reopening of the case.

As demonstrated here and in *King, supra*, ___ Cal.4th ___, the relevant statutory provisions survive separation of powers scrutiny depending upon the particular circumstances of the case. In the present matter, the reinstituted complaint satisfied the requirements of the 1996 refiling provision that was already in effect when the Court of Appeal finally upheld the prior dismissal. Hence, prosecution of the instant case under the refiled complaint is not barred by the separation of powers clause. We reach the opposite conclusion, however, and do find a constitutional violation in *King*. There, the complaint was refiled under conditions that complied only with the 1997 version of section 803(g) not yet in effect when the prior judgment dismissing the same counts became final.

   ....

II. DISCUSSION

The California Constitution establishes a system of state government in which power is divided among three coequal branches (Cal. Const., art. IV, § 1 [legislative power]; Cal. Const., art. V, § 1 [executive power]; Cal. Const., art. VI, § 1 [judicial power]), and further states that those charged with the exercise of one power may not exercise any other (Cal. Const., art. III, § 3). Notwithstanding these principles, it is well understood that the branches share common boundaries (*Hustedt v. Workers' Comp. Appeals Bd.* (1981) 30 Cal.3d 329, 338), and no sharp line between their operations exists. (*Superior Court v. County of Mendocino* (1996) 13 Cal.4th 45, 52 (*Mendocino*); see *Davis v. Municipal Court* (1988) 46 Cal.3d 64, 76 (*Davis*) [" 'From the beginning, each branch has exercised all three kinds of powers' "].)

Indeed, the "sensitive balance" underlying the tripartite system of government assumes a certain degree of mutual oversight and influence. (*Harbor v. Deukmejian* (1987) 43 Cal.3d 1078, 1086; see *Mendocino, supra*, 13 Cal.4th 45, 53 ["the judiciary passes upon the constitutional validity of legislative and executive actions, the Legislature enacts statutes that govern the procedures and evidentiary rules applicable in judicial and executive proceedings, and the Governor appoints judges and participates in the legislative process through the veto power"].)

Despite this interdependence, the Constitution does vest each branch with certain "core" (*Carmel Valley Fire Protection Dist. v. State of California* (2001) 25 Cal.4th 287, 297 (*Carmel*)) or "essential" (*Butt v. State of California* (1992) 4 Cal.4th 668, 700, fn. 26) functions that may not be usurped by another branch.

We focus here on the constitutional roles of the Legislature and the judiciary, particularly with respect to criminal statutes of limitation and judgments of dismissal obtained thereunder.

The Legislature is charged, among other things, with "mak[ing] law ... by statute." (Cal. Const., art. IV, § 8, subd. (b).) This essential function embraces the far-reaching power to weigh competing interests and determine social policy. (*Carmel, supra*, 25 Cal.4th 287, 299; *Connecticut Indemnity Co. v. Superior Court* (2000) 23 Cal.4th 807, 814; see *Nougues v. Douglass* (1857) 7 Cal. 65, 70 [describing the legislative power as the "creative element" of government].)

Such nuanced determinations underlie the existence and nature of any statutory time bar in criminal cases. (See *Frazer, supra*, 21 Cal.4th 737, 758 & fn. 19 [noting that criminal statutes of limitation are "an optional form of 'legislative grace,'" and that they are not constitutionally compelled]; *id.* at p. 770 [indicating that such laws carefully balance society's interest in repose against the need to prosecute crime].) No less the product of competing policy choices is the decision to make any statute retroactive (*Evangelatos v. Superior Court* (1988) 44 Cal.3d 1188, 1206), and the enactment of rules regulating the dismissal and refiling of criminal counts. (E.g., §§ 999 [permitting reprosecution of an offense following an order setting aside an indictment or information as defined in the statute], 1010 [contemplating orders directing the filing of a new information after a demurrer is sustained and the action is dismissed as defined in the statute], 1387, subd. (a) [permitting reprosecution of a felony following one prior order terminating the action as defined in the statute], 1387.1, subd. (a) [allowing the refiling of a violent felony charge following two prior dismissals as defined in the statute].)

Quite distinct from the broad power to pass laws is the essential power of the judiciary to resolve "specific controversies" between parties. (*Mandel v. Myers* (1981) 29 Cal.3d 531, 547 (*Mandel*).) In such proceedings, existing laws, like criminal statutes of limitation, are interpreted and applied. (See *California Teachers Assn. v. Governing Bd. of Rialto Unified School Dist.* (1997) 14 Cal.4th 627, 632–633 (*California Teachers*) [describing the judicial role of construing statutes consistent with their plain meaning and other indicia of legislative intent]; *Marin Water etc. Co. v. Railroad Com.* (1916) 171 Cal. 706, 712 [noting that judicial controversies are resolved under "'laws supposed already to exist'"].)

The courts also decide on an appropriate case-by-case basis whether constitutional, jurisdictional, or tactical concerns bar enforcement of criminal statutes of limitation. (See, e.g., *Frazer, supra*, 21 Cal.4th 737, 754–775 [rejecting ex post facto and due process challenges to § 803(g)]; *People v. Williams* (1999) 21 Cal.4th 335, 341–346 [limiting the circumstances under which criminal statutes of limitation may be forfeited]; *Cowan v. Superior Court* (1996) 14 Cal.4th 367, 373–374 [holding that such statutes do not implicate fundamental subject matter jurisdiction].) In general, the "power to dispose" of criminal charges belongs to the judiciary. (*People v. Birks* (1998) 19 Cal.4th 108, 136, italics omitted; see *People v. Superior Court (Romero)* (1996) 13 Cal.4th 497, 512.)

The separation of powers doctrine protects each branch's core constitutional functions from lateral attack by another branch. As noted, however, this does not mean that the activities of one branch are entirely immune from regulation or oversight by another. We have regularly approved legislation affecting matters over which the judiciary has inherent power and control. (See, e.g., *Obrien v. Jones* (2000) 23 Cal.4th

40, 47–57 [statute changing the Supreme Court's authority to appoint State Bar Court judges]; *Mendocino, supra,* 13 Cal.4th 45, 58–66 [statute designating unpaid furlough days on which trial courts shall not be in session]; *Solberg v. Superior Court* (1977) 19 Cal.3d 182, 191–204 [statute allowing trial judges to be peremptorily disqualified by litigants]; *In re McKinney* (1968) 70 Cal.2d 8, 10–13 [statute fixing the punishment for witnesses found in contempt of court].) As long as such enactments do not "'defeat or materially impair'" the constitutional functions of the courts, a "'reasonable'" degree of regulation is allowed. (*Mendocino, supra,* 13 Cal.4th at p. 58.)

Nevertheless, the separation of powers doctrine prohibits the Legislature "from arrogating to itself core functions of the executive or judicial branch." (*Carmel, supra,* 25 Cal.4th 287, 298.) No branch of government can exercise "'the *complete* power constitutionally vested in another.'" (*Ibid.,* quoting *Younger v. Superior Court* (1978) 21 Cal.3d 102, 117; original italics.) The Constitution thereby seeks to avoid both the "concentration of power in a single branch of government," and the "overreaching" by one branch against the others. (*Kasler v. Lockyer* (2000) 23 Cal.4th 472, 495; see *Davis, supra,* 46 Cal.3d 64, 76 [noting that the doctrine prevents "'the combination in the hands of a single person or group of the basic or fundamental powers of government'"].)

Regarding the core functions discussed above, separation of powers principles compel courts to effectuate the purpose of enactments (*California Teachers, supra,* 14 Cal.4th 627, 632), and limit judicial efforts to rewrite statutes even where drafting or constitutional problems may appear. (*People v. Garcia* (1999) 21 Cal.4th 1, 14; *Kopp v. Fair Pol. Practices Com.* (1995) 11 Cal.4th 607, 660–661.) The judiciary may be asked to decide whether a statute is arbitrary or unreasonable for constitutional purposes (e.g., *Frazer, supra,* 21 Cal.4th 737, 773), but no inquiry into the "wisdom" of underlying policy choices is made. (*Lockard v. City of Los Angeles* (1949) 33 Cal.2d 453, 461.)

By the same token, direct legislative influence over the outcome of judicial proceedings is constitutionally constrained. Thus, it has been said that the Legislature cannot "interpret" a statute or otherwise bind the courts with a post hoc "declaration" of legislative intent. (*Hunt v. Superior Court* (1999) 21 Cal.4th 984, 1007 (*Hunt*).) Separation of powers principles do not preclude the Legislature from amending a statute and applying the change to both pending and future cases, though any such law cannot "readjudicat[e]" or otherwise "disregard" judgments that are already "final." (*Mandel, supra,* 29 Cal.3d 531, 547; see *id.* at pp. 545–551 [rejecting legislative attempt, as part of state budget process, to review the merits of an attorney fee award previously entered against the state and affirmed on appeal]; *Hunt, supra,* 21 Cal.4th at p. 1008 [indicating that judgments do not become final for separation of powers purposes until both the trial and appellate process is complete, and the case is no longer pending in the courts].)

Here, as below, defendant claims section 803(g) thwarts final judgments insofar as it allows the People to timely refile, as part of the 1997 complaint, six molestation counts that were previously included in the 1995 complaint and dismissed under *Bunn I, supra,* 53 Cal.App.4th 227. Defendant observes that similar concerns were addressed for federal separation of powers purposes in *Plaut, supra,* 514 U.S. 211, and suggests the latter decision should guide our resolution of his analogous state law claim. For reasons explained below, we agree that *Plaut*'s analytical framework applies here. However, contrary to what defendant assumes, careful examination of *Plaut* reveals that the instant prosecution is not constitutionally flawed.

Plaut concerned a civil action filed in federal district court in 1987 alleging the fraudulent sale of securities in 1983 and 1984 in violation of substantive federal law. (See Securities Exchange Act of 1934 (the SEC Act), § 10(b), 15 U.S.C. § 78j(b) (section 10(b) of the SEC Act).) From the time the alleged fraud occurred through the time the *Plaut* suit was filed, federal courts were required to "borrow" the analogous state statute of limitations in the jurisdiction in which such actions were pending. The defendant in *Plaut* moved to dismiss the complaint because it was filed more than three years after the alleged fraud occurred, and because it was allegedly untimely under applicable state law. The plaintiffs countered that the three-year state law period had not expired because it ran from the time the alleged fraud was, or should have been, discovered. (*Plaut, supra*, 514 U.S. 211, 213; see *id.* at pp. 249–250 (dis. opn. of Stevens, J.).)

On June 20, 1991, before the district court resolved the timeliness issue argued by the parties in *Plaut*, the United States Supreme Court changed the controlling law and decided *Lampf v. Gilbertson* (1991) 501 U.S. 350 (*Lampf*). In *Lampf*, the court adopted a uniform federal limitations rule requiring actions under section 10(b) of the SEC Act to commence within one year of the time the violation was discovered, and within three years of the time the violation occurred. Moreover, this new rule applied in *Lampf* itself, and in all cases then pending under section 10(b) of the SEC Act. The effect was to retroactively shorten the statute of limitations in actions which, like *Plaut*, were not necessarily time-barred under pre-*Lampf* law. Based on *Lampf*, the district court determined that the complaint in *Plaut* was untimely, and the case was dismissed on August 13, 1991. The decision became final on September 12, 1991. (*Plaut, supra*, 514 U.S. 211, 214; see *id.* at pp. 250–251 (dis. opn. of Stevens, J.).)

Congress promptly responded to *Lampf, supra*, 501 U.S. 350, by passing section 27A of the SEC Act, which became effective December 19, 1991. (15 U.S.C. § 78aa-1 (section 27A).) This provision did not affect *Lampf* insofar as it established a uniform federal limitations period in actions filed under section 10(b) of the SEC Act after *Lampf*. However, through section 27A, Congress repudiated the high court's decision to apply *Lampf* retroactively, and restored the pre-*Lampf* limitations rule in two kinds of actions commenced before June 20, 1991, when *Lampf* was filed: (1) cases which were still pending on December 19, 1991, when section 27A took effect, and (2) cases which were dismissed as time-barred between June 20 and December 19, 1991, and which were timely when filed. By its terms, section 27A allowed plaintiffs to seek reinstatement of dismissed actions no more than 60 days after the statute took effect. (*Plaut, supra*, 514 U.S. 211, 214–215; see *id.* at p. 251 (dis. opn. of Stevens, J.).)

Complying with all statutory requirements, the plaintiffs in *Plaut* moved to reinstate their lawsuit under section 27A of the SEC Act. The district court denied the request on the ground the statute violated separation of powers principles insofar as it contemplated the reinstatement of actions that had been dismissed as time-barred under *Lampf*. The ruling was upheld on appeal. The United States Supreme Court affirmed.

(*Plaut, supra*, 514 U.S. 211, 215, 240.) According to *Plaut* at pages 217–218, Congress "exceeded its authority by requiring the federal courts to exercise '[t]he judicial Power of the United States,' U.S. Const., Art. III, § 1, in a manner repugnant to the text, structure, and traditions of Article III."

The high court started from the premise that, under the United States Constitution's tripartite system of government, there exists a judicial branch separate and independent from the legislative branch. (*Plaut, supra*, 515 U.S. 211, 221.) The court noted that while the legislature makes and prescribes the law (*id.* at p. 222), the essential function of the judiciary is to interpret statutes (*id.* at p. 222), and to decide individual cases and controversies arising thereunder (*id.* at pp. 218–219).

Plaut also observed that the balance created by this constitutional division between the legislative and judicial departments serves in large part to prevent "interference with the final judgments of courts." (*Plaut, supra*, 514 U.S. 211, 223; see *id.* at pp. 221, 222.) In an extensive historical discussion, the high court emphasized the Framers' interest in eliminating the colonial practice by which assemblies and legislatures either functioned as equitable courts of last resort, hearing original actions and providing appellate review of judicial decisions, or enacted special bills to vacate judgments and order new trials or appeals. (*Id.* at pp. 219–225.)

Against this backdrop, *Plaut, supra*, 514 U.S. 211, declared, in almost talismanic form, that Congress lacks the power to "reopen" (*id.* at pp. 219, 234, 240), "correct" (*id.* at p. 219), "'reverse'" (*id.* at pp. 220, 222, 225), "revise" (*id.* at pp. 226, 233), "vacate" (*id.* at p. 224), or "annul" (*ibid.*) final court judgments. The controlling separation of powers principle was stated as follows: "Having achieved finality, … a judicial decision becomes the last word of the judicial department with regard to a particular case or controversy, and Congress may not declare by retroactive legislation that the law applicable *to that very case* was something other than what the courts said it was." (*Id.* at p. 227, original italics.)

In *Plaut*, both the plaintiffs and the court minority raised various arguments in an attempt to exempt section 27A of the SEC Act from the foregoing rule. All were unsuccessful. For example, the *Plaut* majority rejected any suggestion that judgments of dismissal enforcing a statute of limitations are "uniquely subject to congressional nullification." (*Plaut, supra*, 514 U.S. 211, 228.) The court observed that whether an action was dismissed on statute of limitation grounds or for some other reason — such as failure to state a claim, to prove substantive liability, or to prosecute — it has, for separation of powers purposes, the same conclusive effect under procedural rules governing actions filed in federal court. *Plaut* saw no reason to depart from such "statutory and judge made" rules of finality for constitutional purposes, or to otherwise forgo separation of powers protection for judgments that "rested on the bar of a statute of limitations." (*Ibid.*)

In a related vein, *Plaut* determined that the judgments covered by section 27A of the SEC Act were not vulnerable to legislative attack simply because the actions had previously been dismissed under a limitations period created by the court itself in

Lampf, supra, 501 U.S. 350, rather than by Congress. Indeed, *Plaut* admonished, the operative separation of powers rule was neither triggered nor affected by congressional disagreement with the substantive reasoning of *Lampf.* According to *Plaut,* the constitutionality of section 27(A) concerned, "not the validity or even the source of the legal rule that produced the Article III judgments, but rather the immunity from legislative abrogation of those judgments themselves. The separation-of-powers question before us has nothing to do with *Lampf....*" (*Plaut, supra,* 514 U.S. 211, 230; see *id.* at p. 228 [noting that the separation of powers doctrine is violated "when an individual final judgment is legislatively rescinded for even the *very best* of reasons, such as the legislature's genuine conviction ... that the judgment was wrong"], original italics.)

Moreover, notwithstanding the constitutional protection afforded final judgments on an individual basis, section 27A of the SEC Act did not somehow escape separation of powers scrutiny merely because the reopening provision affected "a whole class of cases." (*Plaut, supra,* 514 U.S. 211, 227.) The court reiterated that a separation of powers violation occurs when postjudgment legislation deprives court decisions "of the conclusive effect that they had when they were announced." (*Id.* at p. 228.) Thus, whether a statute targets particular suits or parties, or whether it purports to apply more generally like section 27A, the critical factor for separation of powers purposes is whether such impermissible legislative interference with final judgments has occurred. (*Plaut, supra,* 514 U.S. at p. 228; see *id.* at p. 238 [confirming that a separation of powers violation does not require any "'singling out'" of individual court cases].)

Notwithstanding the foregoing analysis, the circumstances under which a judgment achieves finality and is therefore immune from legislative interference are clearly limited under *Plaut.* First, the high court included in the constitutionally protected category only those decisions that represent "*the final word* of the [judicial] department as a whole," as expressed by "*the last court in the hierarchy that rules on the case.*" (*Plaut, supra,* 514 U.S. 211, 227, italics added.) *Plaut* explained that because the judicial branch consists of both inferior and reviewing courts, a judgment has no conclusive effect until — under procedural statutes and rules then in existence — either the time for appealing an inferior court decision has expired, or such an appeal has been pursued and the review process is complete. (*Ibid.*) For this reason, *Plaut* observed, separation of powers principles are not implicated, and an inferior court decision has not been impermissibly revised, where a reviewing court applies a new retroactive statute to cases "still [pending] on appeal." (*Id.* at p. 226; see *id.* at p. 233, fn. 7.) Under such circumstances, no final judgment was obtained for federal constitutional purposes before the substantive law changed.

Second, *Plaut* established that statutory limitations on the conclusive effect of judgments are not impermissibly retroactive and can constitutionally be applied as long as they were already in existence when the judiciary gave its "last word" in the particular case. (*Plaut, supra,* 514 U.S. 211, 227.) Stated differently, the high court found nothing to prevent Congress from authorizing or requiring the reinstatement of a dismissed action where the prior judgment otherwise becomes final for separation of powers purposes *after* the law's effective date. (*Id.* at p. 234.)

Plaut's reasoning on this core point was clear: "The relevant retroactivity, of course, consists not of the requirement that there be set aside a judgment that has been rendered prior to its being set aside — for example, a statute passed today which says that all default judgments rendered in the future may be reopened within 90 days after their entry. In that sense, all requirements to reopen are 'retroactive,' and the designation is superfluous. Nothing we say today precludes a law such as that. *The finality that a court can pronounce is no more than what the law in existence at the time of judgment will permit it to pronounce. If the law then applicable says that the judgment may be reopened for certain reasons, that limitation is built into the judgment itself, and its finality is so conditioned.*" (*Plaut, supra,* 514 U.S. 211, 234, original italics omitted and new italics added.)

In *Plaut* itself, the challenged provision could not constitutionally be applied because it was not "built into" the judgment of dismissal for which reopening was sought. Specifically, the high court invalidated section 27A of the SEC Act insofar as it contemplated the reinstatement of actions which had been dismissed as time-barred and reduced to final judgment *before* the statute's effective date. Under *Plaut*'s separation of powers analysis, Congress was without power to subject judgments of dismissal to a retroactive reopening provision not in existence when those judgments achieved conclusive effect. (*Plaut, supra,* 514 U.S. 211, 225, 227, 234, 240.)

We find *Plaut* persuasive for purposes of interpreting California's separation of powers clause. (See *Mendocino, supra,* 13 Cal.4th 45, 53 [citing *Plaut, supra,* 514 U.S. 211, as support for the state separation of powers prohibition against statutes that "readjudicate" cases already resolved by "final" judgment].) Consistent with the California principles and authorities discussed above, *Plaut* properly preserves and balances the respective "core functions" of the two branches. (*Carmel, supra,* 25 Cal.4th 287, 298.) On the one hand, *Plaut* recognizes the core judicial power to resolve "specific controversies" (*Mandel, supra,* 29 Cal.3d 531, 547) between parties by judgments that are "final" under laws then extant (*ibid.*), and holds such final dispositions inviolate from legislative "disregard" (*ibid.*). On the other hand, *Plaut* acknowledges the paramount legislative power to "make" law by statute (Cal. Const., art. IV, § 8, subd. (b)), to apply new laws to all cases still pending at either the trial or the appellate level (*Hunt, supra,* 21 Cal.4th 984, 1008), and to regulate, within reasonable limits, the practices and procedures by which judicial matters are to be resolved. (*Mendocino, supra,* 13 Cal.4th 45, 58.) When the finality of a judicial determination is limited or conditioned by the terms of a general statute already in effect when the determination is made, application of the statute according to its terms is but a "'reasonable,'" and therefore permissible, legislative restriction upon the constitutional function of the judiciary; it does not "'defeat or materially impair'" that function. (*Ibid.*) Because we therefore conclude that *Plaut, supra,* 514 U.S. 211, is in clear conformity with California law, we follow it here.

. . . .

We therefore hold that a refiling provision like section 803(g) cannot be retroactively applied to subvert judgments that became final before the provision took effect, and before the law of finality changed. This ban applies even where lawmakers have acted for "the very best of reasons" (*Plaut, supra*, 514 U.S. 211, 228, italics omitted), and whether or not legislative disagreement with the "legal rule" underlying the judgment has been expressed (*id.* at p. 230). By the same token, a judgment is not final for separation of powers purposes, and reopening of the case can occur, under the specific terms of refiling legislation already in effect when the judicial branch completed its review and ultimately decided the case. Such nonretroactive limitations on judgment finality are constitutionally allowed.

We have seen that since it was first amended in 1996, section 803(g) has continuously offered the People a new opportunity to prosecute child sex crimes that were previously charged under prior versions of the statute but dismissed by the courts. Both the 1996 and 1997 laws authorize the "refiling" and "revival" of otherwise time-barred counts. However, the precise conditions under which prosecutors may refile depend upon which version of section 803(g) is involved. For example, the 1996 law required, among other things, the refiling of complaints "on or before June 30, 1997." (Former § 803(g)(3)(B)(ii) (1996 version).) The 1997 law — in addition to other changes and conditions — extends the refiling period to a point "no later than 180 days after" finality of an authoritative high court decision upholding retroactive application of the statute, namely, *Frazer, supra*, 21 Cal.4th 737. (§ 803(g)(3)(A)(iv).)

To the extent neither the 1996 nor the 1997 refiling provision was in effect when a prior judgment of dismissal under section 803(g) became final within the meaning of *Plaut, supra*, 514 U.S. 211, 227, 234, the state separation of powers doctrine bars reliance on either provision to recharge a molestation defendant with the same crimes. Such a scenario is indistinguishable from the circumstances that gave rise to a separation of powers violation in *Plaut* itself.

Constitutional problems also arise where the prior dismissal was entered or finally upheld when one version of section 803(g) was in effect (e.g., the 1996 refiling provision), but the reinstituted complaint complies only with a later version (e.g., the 1997 refiling provision) which became effective after the prior dismissal was entered or finally upheld. In that circumstance, use of the later law constitutes an impermissible retroactive attack on a judgment constitutionally subject to reopening only under the earlier law. (Cf. [*Ex parte*] *Jenkins, supra*, 723 So.2d 649, 655–658 (lead opn. of See, J.).) It is on this basis that we disallow reprosecution of the defendant in the companion case of *King, supra*, ___ Cal.4th ___.

In the present case, the pertinent facts are materially distinct from those in *King*, and we therefore reach the opposite result. Dismissal of the 1995 complaint against defendant Bunn did not become final for constitutional purposes until judicial review in *Bunn I, supra*, 53 Cal.App.4th 227, was complete. Both in February 1997, when the decision in *Bunn I* was filed, and in May 1997, when review in *Bunn I* was denied, the 1996 version of section 803(g) was in effect, including the refiling provision contained in former section 803(g)(3)(B)(ii) (1996 version).

The 1997 complaint now challenged by defendant satisfies all requirements of former section 803(g)(3)(B)(ii) (1996 version), as follows: (1) the victim reported the

crimes to law enforcement officials "between January 1, 1994, and January 1, 1997,"
(2) the 1995 complaint was filed within one year of the report "but was dismissed,"
and (3) the same crimes were recharged as part of the 1997 complaint "on ... June
30, 1997." (*Ibid.*) Because the 1996 law permits refiling under these statutory conditions, and because these conditions were incorporated into the judgment when it
otherwise became final in *Bunn I, supra,* 53 Cal.App.4th 227, prosecutorial use of
the 1996 refiling provision does not retroactively reopen the case or violate the constitutional rules we have discussed. (*Plaut, supra,* 514 U.S. 211, 234; cf. *Jenkins, supra,*
723 So.2d 649, 658–660 (lead opn. of See, J.).)

Accordingly, the correct result was reached on appeal in the present case. On the
one hand, the Court of Appeal failed to consider either the concept of judgment finality in *Plaut, supra,* 514 U.S. 211, or the effect of the 1996 refiling provision on defendant's separation of powers claim. On the other hand, the Court of Appeal properly
allowed reinstatement of the six molestation counts dismissed in *Bunn I, supra,* 53
Cal.App.4th 227, and properly declined to uphold the superior court's dismissal of
the information on separation of powers grounds.

III. DISPOSITION

The judgment of the Court of Appeal is affirmed.

George, C.J., Kennard, J., Werdegar, J., Chin, J., and Moreno, J., concurred.

Notes and Questions

1. The Legislature's essential function under the state Constitution of making law
by statute embraces the far-reaching power to weigh competing interests and determine social policy, according to the Court in this case. The existence and nature of
any statutory time bar in criminal cases, the decision to make any statute retroactive,
and the enactment of rules regulating the dismissal and refiling of criminal counts
are products of competing policy choices which are within the Legislature's essential
function of making law.

2. If the Court already determined that the retroactive application of the amended
statute did not violate the ex post facto prohibition nor did it raise due process concerns, why did the Court consider an argument based upon the separation of powers
doctrine?

3. The Court spent most of its opinion discussing the U.S. Supreme Court's *Plaut*
decision, but also reviewed in great detail the underlying statute and its different versions
as the Legislature amended the law. Did this case depend on the separation of powers
doctrine for its decision? Or did the case actually hinge on statutory interpretation?

4. The California Supreme Court ultimately concluded "that refiling legislation
cannot be applied retroactively to reopen court cases that had already been dismissed,
if the dismissals had become final judgments, under the law of finality which then
pertained, before the refiling provision became effective." The basis for its conclusion
is grounded in separation of powers, essentially stating that final court judgments
are "sacrosanct." Nonetheless, the Court also stated, "On the other hand, as *Plaut*

itself explained, any dismissal that was already subject to a particular refiling law at the time the dismissal was entered or finally upheld cannot, to that extent, be deemed a final judgment immune from legislative interference."

5. How does the Court interpret the inclusion or lack of express statements of "retroactivity" and "revival" language in a statute?

6. The Court described the separation of powers doctrine in California as the state Constitution vesting each of the three branches of government with certain "core" (*Carmel Valley Fire Protection Dist. v. State of California* (2001) 25 Cal.4th 287, 297) or "essential" (*Butt v. State of California* (1992) 4 Cal.4th 668, 700, fn. 26) functions that may not be usurped by another branch. Do the terms "core" and "essential" provide sufficient guidance to the other branches of government to know when an activity would violate the doctrine?

7. The California Supreme Court, in explaining the limitation on the legislative branch, cited the following excerpt from the U.S. Supreme Court decision in *Plaut*: "Having achieved finality, ... a judicial decision becomes the last word of the judicial department with regard to a particular case or controversy, and Congress may not declare by retroactive legislation that the law applicable *to that very case* was something other than what the courts said it was." (*Quoting Plaut, 514 U.S.* at 227, original italics.)

8. What were the two main circumstances that the Court cited when a judgment achieves finality and is immune from legislative interference under *Plaut*?

9. Did it matter to the California court that *Plaut*'s constitutional analysis had been adopted by the high courts of other states?

J. Allowance of Time for a Referendum

The law allows sufficient time for the people to consider repeal of legislation before it takes effect on January 1 of the year following a bill's enactment. In other words, once the Legislature adjourns in early fall, and the Governor acts on legislation sent to his or her desk, then there are roughly 90 days until January 1.

Certain measures that take effect immediately when the Governor signs them are not subject to a referendum. These four types of measures are set forth in the state Constitution. Hence, all other bills are subject to referendum before they take effect on January 1. Therefore, time is allowed for a referendum to be pursued.

Busch v. Turner

(1945) 26 Cal.2d 817

OPINION

GIBSON, C.J.

Petitioner, the District Attorney of Lake County, asks a writ of mandate to compel respondent, the auditor of that county, to pay petitioner's salary at the rate of $2,400 a year from and after January 25, 1945, rather than at the rate of $1,800 a year, the amount which petitioner received prior to January 25. There is no dispute as to the facts, and the matter was submitted upon respondent's demurrer to the petition.

Petitioner was elected on August 25, 1942, for the term beginning in January, 1943, and ending in January, 1947. Prior to August, 1943, his salary was fixed at $1,800 a year by section 4280 of the Political Code. In 1943 the Legislature amended this section to increase the salary of the District Attorney of Lake County to $2,400 a year. The statute was silent with respect to its applicability to incumbents. At this time, however, section 5 of article XI of the California Constitution provided, in part: "The compensation of any county, township or municipal officer shall not be increased after his election or during his term of office...." Accordingly, petitioner did not then receive an increase.

In 1944 section 5 of article XI was amended to read, in part: "The Legislature by a two-thirds vote of the members of each House may suspend the provision hereof prohibiting the increase of compensation of any county, township or municipal officer after his election or during his term of office for any period during which the United States is engaged in war and for one year after the termination of hostilities therein as proclaimed by the President of the United States."

Pursuant to the constitutional amendment the Legislature passed chapter 5, Statutes of 1945, suspending the prohibition against salary increases in section 5 of article XI "for the period commencing upon the effective date of this act and continuing until six months after hostilities terminate in each of the wars in which the United States is now engaged." The act was declared to be an urgency measure and to go into effect immediately. It was approved by the Governor on January 24, 1945.

Thereafter petitioner demanded payment of his salary at the increased rate provided by the 1943 legislation. Respondent, however, refused to issue warrants including the increase and petitioner received his salary for the months of January and February, 1945, at the rate fixed prior to 1943. He thereupon instituted this proceeding for a writ of mandate ordering respondent to deliver a warrant for the balance assertedly due, representing the amount of the increase, for the period beginning January 25, 1945, and ending January 31, 1945, and for the month of February, 1945.

Subsequent to the institution of this proceeding the Legislature, by chapter 417 of the Statutes of 1945, again amended section 4280 of the Political Code fixing the salary of the District Attorney of Lake County at $2,400 per year and specifically stating that this compensation shall be paid to incumbents. Although this amendment, not effective until September 15, 1945, does not directly govern the problems raised herein, it does afford some indication of a general legislative intent to make the salary increase applicable to incumbents. (Cf. *Standard Oil Co. v. Johnson*, 24 Cal.2d 40, 48–49 [147 P.2d 577]; *Union League Club v. Johnson*, 18 Cal.2d 275, 278–279 [115 P.2d 425].)

The 1943 legislation was sufficiently broad in its terms to include incumbents and it is clear that the prohibition in section 5 of article XI constituted the sole reason precluding petitioner from receiving an increase of salary in that year. Petitioner contends that this prohibition was removed by the constitutional amendment in 1944 together with the subsequent enactment of chapter 5 of the Statutes of 1945, thus permitting section 4280 of the Political Code, as amended in 1943 to become immediately effective on January 24, 1945.

Although no decision considering the precise point has been found, section 5 of article XI as it read before the 1944 amendment has frequently been applied to statutes increasing compensation but containing no specific indication of the Legislature's intention with respect to incumbents. It was determined that such a statute is to be held in abeyance until the next term of office, leaving the former law in effect as to the incumbent. (*Smith v. Mathews*, 155 Cal. 752 [103 P. 199]; *Regan v. County of San Mateo*, 14 Cal.2d 713 [97 P.2d 231]; *Galeener v. Honeycutt*, 173 Cal. 100 [159 P. 595]; *Rice v. National City*, 132 Cal. 354 [64 P. 580]; see *Cline v. Lewis*, 175 Cal. 315, 318–319 [165 P. 915]; *Harrison v. Colgan*, 148 Cal. 69 [82 P. 674]; *Kilroy v. Whitmore*, 115 Cal.App. 43, 48 [300 P. 851]; *Shay v. Roth*, 64 Cal.App. 314, 323 [221 P. 967]; *Williams v. Garey*, 19 Cal.App. 769, 771 [127 P. 824].) It was reasoned that until the next term of office commenced, there was no subject upon which the statute could constitutionally operate, and that in order to harmonize the statute with the Constitution in so far as possible, it should be held that the Legislature intended to postpone the operation of the statute until the expiration of the incumbent's term of office. (See *Smith v. Mathews, supra*, 155 Cal. at p. 757; *Harrison v. Colgan, supra*, 148 Cal. at p. 73.) These decisions, therefore, represent a specific application of the general principle that statutes will be construed, if their language permits, so as to avoid unconstitutionality. The court thus held, in substance, that the Legislature intended the statutes to be operative at the earliest time the Constitution would permit, but not before. As said in the concurring opinion in the Smith case (155 Cal. at p. 762), such laws "are construed to be intended only for prospective operation and hence not void, but only in abeyance *until the conditions occur to which they can apply with effect....* The old law stands and controls the right to compensation *until the time arrives at which, by the constitution, the new law is permitted to supersede it....*" (Italics added.) Similarly, as expressed in *Shay v. Roth*, 64 Cal.App. 314, 323 [221 P. 967], the law "is held in abeyance until the incumbency of an officer upon whom the increase may constitutionally operate."

Although it is true that most of the decisions referred to the expiration of the incumbent's term of office as the effective date intended by the Legislature, it must be recognized that at the time those opinions were written this was the earliest date or "condition" upon which a statute increasing salaries could constitutionally operate, and, therefore, it was perfectly natural for the courts to designate it as representing the legislative intent. There was then no occasion for the courts to consider what construction should be given such a statute in the event that the constitutional prohibition as to incumbents was removed by a constitutional amendment; the question was not passed upon in any of the decisions; and, therefore, they are not authority here in so far as they may suggest that the Legislature could not have intended to give increases to incumbents in the event of such a contingency. (Cf. *Hobart v. Hobart*

Estate Co., ante, p. 412, 445 [159 P.2d 958]; *Maguire v. Hibernia S. & L. Soc.,* 23 Cal.2d 719, 730 [146 P.2d 673, 151 A.L.R. 1062].)

As asserted by petitioner, the statements in the Shay case and the concurring opinion in the Smith case more accurately express the principle applied in the decisions. A statute purporting, in general terms, to increase salaries would ordinarily be construed to include incumbents, and but for the constitutional bar it would do so. When the prohibition of the Constitution ceases to operate, there is no longer any reason to limit the statute, and its literal meaning may be carried out in full. The reason why the prohibition ceases to operate is entirely immaterial, whether it is because of expiration of the period designated in the Constitution or because of an amendment changing the Constitution. We hold, therefore, that the 1943 act increasing the salary of the District Attorney of Lake County was intended to take effect as soon as it lawfully could, including the contingency of a constitutional amendment permitting an operative date earlier than would have been permissible under the Constitution as it existed in 1943.

There appears to be no constitutional objection to such an interpretation. Although the taking effect of the act as to incumbents would thus depend upon the happening of a contingency, namely, passage of a constitutional amendment, it has been held in many states that a statute which is expressly made contingent upon the adoption of a constitutional amendment is valid even where, as here, the Legislature would have had no power so to act in absence of the amendment. (*Alabam's Freight Co. v. Hunt,* 29 Ariz. 419 [242 P. 658]; *State v. Hecker,* 109 Ore. 520 [221 P. 808]; *State v. Rathie,* 101 Ore. 339 [199 P. 169, 200 P. 790]; *In re Opinions of the Justices,* 227 Ala. 291 [149 So. 776]; *Fry v. Rosen,* 207 Ind. 409 [189 N.E. 375]; *Pratt v. Allen* (1839), 13 Conn. 119; see *Druggan v. Anderson,* 269 U.S. 36 [46 S.Ct. 14, 70 L.Ed. 151]; 16 C.J.S. 97–98; cf. *State v. Smith,* 335 Mo. 840 [74 S.W.2d 27].) Cases to the contrary have been found in only one jurisdiction. (*In re Opinion of the Justices,* 132 Me. 519 [174 A. 845]; *In re Opinion of the Justices,* 137 Me. 350 [19 A.2d 53].) Although this problem apparently has not been decided heretofore in California, it has been held that the effective date of a statute may be made contingent upon a future event. (*Ex parte Beck,* 162 Cal. 701, 706–708 [124 P. 543]; see *Ogle v. Eckel,* 49 Cal.App.2d 599, 606 [122 P.2d 67]; *People v. High School District,* 62 Cal.App. 67, 71 [216 P. 959].) It may also be noted that the former State Liquor Control Act, passed and approved by the Governor in June, 1933, was expressly declared to take effect "If and when it shall become lawful under the Constitution and laws of the United States" to manufacture and sell intoxicating liquors for beverage purposes, whereas the 21st Amendment was not proclaimed ratified until December 5, 1933. (Cal. Stats., 1933, ch. 658, p. 1697, § 39.)

The case of *County of Fresno v. Brix Estate Co.,* 194 Cal. 85 [226 P. 77], is not controlling. There a state act authorized cities and counties to eradicate animal pests. A county board of supervisors adopted a resolution relating thereto after passage of the state act but prior to its effective date. The court held that the board of supervisors had no power to pass the resolution in anticipation of the effective date of the act, since, said the court, the referendum provisions of the Constitution made it uncertain that the act would become effective. Whatever may be the law with respect to the power of a county board of supervisors to adopt resolutions to be effective upon the occurring of uncertain events, it is clear from the foregoing authorities that the Legislature does have such power.

The case of *Banaz v. Smith*, 133 Cal. 102, 104 [65 P. 309], cited by respondent, is not contrary to petitioner's position. It was there stated that if a statute is void from the beginning, a subsequent amendment to the Constitution does not give life to the statute unless the amendment expressly so provides. Such a situation is not presented here. The 1943 legislation was at no time in violation of the Constitution if interpreted as not intended to apply to incumbents until removal of the constitutional prohibition — such an interpretation is in recognition of, not in contravention of, the Constitution.

It follows, therefore, that chapter 5 of the 1945 statutes, together with the constitutional amendment adopted in 1944, operated to advance the effective date of the 1943 act, thereby granting petitioner an increase of salary as of the effective date of the 1945 act.

Respondent contends, next, that the urgency clause of the 1945 statute is invalid as to petitioner under section 1 of article IV of the California Constitution which provides, in part, that "no measure creating or abolishing any office or changing the salary, term or duties of any officer ... shall be construed to be an urgency measure." Respondent argues that if the 1945 act is given the effect for which petitioner contends, it would constitute a measure changing his salary. The statute, however, does not by its terms change salaries — it purports merely to exercise the authority granted the Legislature by the 1944 amendment to suspend temporarily the prohibition contained in section 5 of article XI. The increase in salary of the District Attorney of Lake County was made by the legislation of 1943, and although passage of the 1945 act constituted the final event making the increase applicable to petitioner, this only resulted indirectly from removal of the constitutional prohibition.

Since the act does not directly purport to change salaries, we may properly consider it in light of the purposes underlying the rules governing urgency measures as set forth in section 1 of article IV of the Constitution. These are included as a part of the referendum provisions adopted by the people in 1911. It is there stated that referendum petitions may be presented to the Secretary of State within ninety days after the final adjournment of the Legislature, and that no act passed shall go into effect until ninety days after the final adjournment of the session at which it was passed, with exceptions being made to certain types of legislation including urgency measures. Prior to the adoption of the referendum system, the Constitution contained no provision precluding immediate operation of statutes, and the effective dates of the statutes were determined by the Legislature. (23 Cal.Jur. 621; see Pol. Code, § 323, as it read before its amendment in 1929.) The obvious purpose of placing the ninety-day limitation in the Constitution was to give the people "an opportunity ... to express their judgment as to the merits" of a statute by filing a referendum petition. (*McClure v. Nye*, 22 Cal.App. 248, 251 [133 P. 1145]; see 59 C.J. 1149; cf. *Solomon v. Alexander*,

161 Cal. 23, 27 [118 P. 217] (referendum provision in a city charter).) Thus, in declaring that measures changing salaries are not to be construed as urgency measures, the people in substance reserved the right to an opportunity to pass upon such laws before the taking effect thereof.

In the present case, however, this purpose has been completely fulfilled, and there remains no reason to delay the effective date of the 1945 act. The people have already passed upon it, since they specifically authorized it by adopting the 1944 amendment to section 5 of article XI of the Constitution. The 1945 act, with one unimportant exception relating to the date of termination of the period of suspension, strictly follows the authority granted by the 1944 amendment. It is clear that this amendment was adopted in view of the present war and contemplated action by the Legislature with respect thereto. It would be unreasonable to hold that the people, having directly authorized the statute, would wish to pass upon it again under the referendum provisions.

We conclude, therefore, that the 1945 act took effect immediately upon its approval by the Governor.

The peremptory writ is granted.

Shenk, J., Carter, J., Traynor, J., Schauer, J., and *Spence, J.,* concurred.

Notes and Questions

1. The purpose of the state Constitution that legislation with certain specified exceptions should not go into effect until 90 days after final adjournment of the session at which it was adopted was to give the people an opportunity to express their judgment as to the merits of a statute by filing a referendum petition. The effective date of a statute may be made contingent upon a future event.

2. What was the basis for the Court ruling that there was legislative intent to make the salary increase applicable to incumbents?

3. How did the Court address the issue raised by Article IV, Section 1 of the state Constitution that provides, in part, that "no measure creating or abolishing any office or changing the salary, term or duties of any officer … shall be construed to be an urgency measure"?

4. The Court provides important historical insight into the referendum process, which was adopted in 1911 by a vote of the state's electorate in adding provisions to Article II of the California Constitution. "It is there stated that referendum petitions may be presented to the Secretary of State within ninety days after the final adjournment of the Legislature, and that no act passed shall go into effect until ninety days after the final adjournment of the session at which it was passed, with exceptions being made to certain types of legislation including urgency measures." As the Court noted, prior to 1911, the state Constitution did not contain any provision related to urgency clauses. The Court also explained that "The obvious purpose of placing the ninety-day limitation in the Constitution was to give the people 'an opportunity … to express their judgment as to the merits' of a statute by filing a referendum petition."

K. Power to Eliminate Existing Laws

Existing laws are subject to repeal by the Legislature and Governor. The Legislature, as part of its lawmaking authority, has the power to eliminate existing laws as well. The legislative power that the state Constitution vests is plenary and a corollary of the legislative power to make new laws is the power to abrogate existing ones.

Courts start from the premise that the Legislature possesses the full extent of the legislative power and its enactments are authorized exercises of that power, and only where the state Constitution withdraws legislative power will courts conclude an enactment is invalid for want of authority. The reenactment rule's purpose is to make sure legislators are not operating in the blind when they amend legislation and to make sure the public can become apprised of changes in the law.

Gillette Company v. Franchise Tax Board

(2015) 62 Cal.4th 468

OPINION

CORRIGAN, J.

Here we consider how California calculates income taxes on multistate businesses. In 1974, California joined the Multistate Tax Compact (Multistate Tax Com., Model Multistate Tax Compact (Aug. 4, 1967)) (Compact), which contained an apportionment formula and permitted a taxpayer election between the Compact's formula and any other formula provided by state law. (Rev. & Tax. Code, former § 38001 et seq., enacted by Stats. 1974, ch. 93, § 3, p. 193 and repealed by Stats. 2012, ch. 37, § 3.) The Legislature later amended the Revenue and Taxation Code to specify a different apportionment formula that "shall" apply "[n]otwithstanding" the Compact's provisions. (Rev. & Tax. Code, § 25128, subd. (a) (section 25128(a)).) Taxpayers here contend they remain entitled to elect between the new statutory formula and that contained in the Compact. We conclude the Legislature may properly preclude a taxpayer from relying on the Compact's election provision.

. . . .

II. DISCUSSION

The FTB contends section 25128(a)'s new apportionment formula should control, arguing that when member states entered the Compact their intent "was to allow them to change their state laws to establish alternate mandatory apportionment formulas." Taxpayers do not dispute that the Legislature has authority to enact an alternate formula. They argue instead that the Compact explicitly permits election and the Legislature is bound to allow it. This case turns on whether the Legislature is so bound. We conclude it is not and California's statutory formula governs.

A. The Compact Constitutes State Law

Taxpayers recognize that the Compact does not have the force of federal law. It was never ratified by Congress as required under the compact clause. (See U.S. Const., art. I, § 10, cl. 3.) Even so, the United States Supreme Court held in *U.S. Steel* that states could enter into an agreement with each other without such ratification so long as the agreement was not "'directed to the formation of any combination tending to the increase of political power in the States, which may encroach upon or interfere with the just supremacy of the United States.'" (*U.S. Steel,* [*Corp. v. Multistate Tax Comm'n*], *supra,* 434 U.S. at p. 468, quoting *Virginia v. Tennessee* (1893) 148 U.S. 503, 519 [37 L.Ed. 537, 13 S.Ct. 728].) *U.S. Steel* concluded the Compact did not run afoul of the compact clause: "[T]he test is whether the Compact enhances state power *quoad* the National Government. This pact does not purport to authorize the member States to exercise any powers they could not exercise in its absence. Nor is there any delegation of sovereign power to the Commission; each State retains complete freedom to adopt or reject the rules and regulations of the Commission. Moreover, as noted above, each State is free to withdraw at any time." (*U.S. Steel,* at p. 473.)

The Legislature ordinarily has authority to repeal or modify any enactment. "[T]he legislative power the state Constitution vests is plenary," and "[a] corollary of the legislative power to make new laws is the power to abrogate existing ones. What the Legislature has enacted, it may repeal." (*California Redevelopment Assn. v. Matosantos* (2011) 53 Cal.4th 231, 254, 255 [135 Cal.Rptr.3d 683, 267 P.3d 580]; see Cal. Const., art. IV, § 1.) "We thus start from the premise that the Legislature possesses the full extent of the legislative power and its enactments are authorized exercises of that power. Only where the state Constitution withdraws legislative power will we conclude an enactment is invalid for want of authority." (*Matosantos,* at p. 254.) Similarly, "the Legislature is supreme in the field of taxation, and the provisions on taxation in the state Constitution are a limitation on the power of the Legislature rather than a grant to it." (*Delaney v. Lowery* (1944) 25 Cal.2d 561, 568 [154 P.2d 674]; see *Santa Clara County Local Transportation Authority v. Guardino* (1995) 11 Cal.4th 220, 247 [45 Cal.Rptr.2d 207, 902 P.2d 225].)

Taxpayers acknowledge the lack of congressional approval but argue "interstate compacts (approved or not) take precedence over other state laws" because "they are both contracts and binding reciprocal statutes among sovereign states." Taxpayers thus contend section 25128 violates the contract clauses of the federal and state Constitutions because it impairs an obligation created by an interstate compact. (See U.S. Const., art. I, § 10, cl. 1; Cal. Const., art. I, § 9.) We need not decide whether an interstate compact not approved by Congress necessarily takes precedence over other state law. Instead, we evaluate whether this Compact is a binding contract among its members. We conclude it is not.

    . . . .

C. The Reenactment Rule Does Not Bar the Legislature's Amendment of Section 25128

Taxpayers alternatively argue that the Legislature's amendment of section 25128 is invalid because it violates the reenactment rule. That rule derives from article IV, section 9 of our Constitution, stating: "A statute shall embrace but one subject, which shall be expressed in its title. If a statute embraces a subject not expressed in its title, only the part not expressed is void. A statute may not be amended by reference to its title. *A section of a statute may not be amended unless the section is re-enacted as amended.*" (Italics added.) One purpose of this provision "is to 'make sure legislators are not operating in the blind when they amend legislation, and to make sure the public can become apprised of changes in the law.'" (*St. John's Well Child & Family Center v. Schwarzenegger* (2010) 50 Cal.4th 960, 983, fn. 20 [116 Cal.Rptr.3d 195, 239 P.3d 651]; see *Hellman v. Shoulters* (1896) 114 Cal. 136, 152 [45 P. 1057] (*Hellman*).)

Generally, the reenactment rule does not apply to statutes that act to "amend" others only by implication. (*Hellman, supra,* 114 Cal. at p. 152.) We reasoned long ago in *Hellman*: "To say that every statute which thus affects the operation of another is therefore an amendment of it would introduce into the law an element of uncertainty which no one can estimate. It is impossible for the wisest legislator to know in advance how every statute proposed would affect the operation of existing laws." (*Ibid.*) The Legislature's 1993 amendment of section 25128 replaced the equal-weighted UDITPA apportionment formula with a different formula double-counting the sales factor. This amendment expressly referenced the Compact, stating that it applied "[n]otwithstanding Section 38006...." (§ 25128(a) as amended by Stats. 1993, ch. 946, § 1, p. 5441.) Although Taxpayers note that the legislative bill *analyses* of the amendment did not refer to the Compact or the election provision expressly, reference to the Compact in section 25128(a) itself is strong evidence that the Legislature acted with the Compact in mind. "Even without a reenactment, the legislators and the public have been reasonably notified of the changes in the law." (*White v. State of California* (2001) 88 Cal.App.4th 298, 315 [105 Cal.Rptr.2d 714]; see *Brosnahan v. Brown* (1982) 32 Cal.3d 236, 256–257 [186 Cal.Rptr. 30, 651 P.2d 274].) So too here. Even without a reenactment of section 38006 to eliminate the election language, the amendment of section 25128 did not violate the reenactment rule.

D. The Legislature Intended to Supersede the Compact's Election Provision

Having concluded the Legislature had the unilateral *authority* to eliminate the Compact's election provision, we must determine whether it *intended* to do so. Taxpayers suggest it did not, arguing that the Legislature intended section 25128's double-sales factor formula to apply only "if the Compact Formula is not elected."

Both the language of section 25128 and its legislative history defeat such a claim. First, section 25128(a) explicitly provides that "*all business income shall be apportioned to this state by*" using the formula it sets out, "[n]otwithstanding Section 38006 [i.e., the Compact]...." (Italics added.) There is no ambiguity in this language. The Assembly Committee on Revenue and Taxation's analysis of the bill explained the need for the amendment: "California and most other states have used an equal weighted three-factor apportionment formula for many years. This formula has been retained largely out of a belief that uniformity among states is the best way to ensure that corporations are not subject to double taxation or that some income 'falls through the crack'. While any apportionment formula may be somewhat arbitrary, supporters of the current system argue that it is still in California's best interest to remain uniform with other states. However, while uniformity in apportionment methods existed between states in the 1960's and may still be a desirable principle, this uniformity has been eroded significantly in recent years by the actions of other states. Currently twenty-five other states at least provide an option to certain taxpayers to place an additional weight on the sales factor in their apportionment formulas [citation]. Proponents believe that California's continued reliance upon the three-factor apportionment system results in discriminatory taxation against California-based companies, particularly given the additional weight given to sales factors by other states." (Assem. Com. on Revenue & Taxation, analysis of Sen. Bill No. 1176 (1993–1994 Reg. Sess.) as introduced Mar. 5, 1993, pp. 1–2; see also Sen. Com. on Revenue & Taxation, analysis of Sen. Bill No. 1176 (1993–1994 Reg. Sess.) as introduced Mar. 5, 1993, p. 2.) In light of the statute's language and this legislative history, there is no credible argument that the Legislature intended to retain the Compact's election provision.

III. DISPOSITION

The Court of Appeal's judgment is reversed.

CANTIL-SAKAUYE, C.J., WERDEGAR, J., LIU, J., CUÉLLAR, J., KRUGER, J., and MURRAY, J., concurred.

Notes and Questions

1. One purpose of the constitutional provisions stating that a section of a statute may not be amended unless the section is re-enacted as amended is to make sure legislators are not operating in the blind when they amend legislation, and to make sure the public can become apprised of changes to the law. Generally, the reenactment rule does not apply to statutes that act to "amend" others only by implication.

2. What are the features attributable to the Multistate Tax Commission? Why would a state want to adopt the Multistage Tax Compact?

3. The first appellate court decision in this case ruled that the Legislature could not unilaterally repudiate mandatory terms of the Tax Compact. The high Court rejected this holding. Even the taxpayers challenging the Franchise Tax Board's position acknowledged that the Legislature has authority to enact an alternate formula for taxing multinational corporations.

4. The taxpayers in this case argued unsuccessfully that "interstate compacts (approved or not) take precedence over other state laws" because "they are both contracts and binding reciprocal statutes among sovereign states." However, the Court in this case did not find a violation of either the state or federal constitutional Contract Clause provisions. What was the basis for this holding?

5. What is the practical effect of the Court's ruling that an interstate compact not approved by Congress necessarily takes precedence over other state law? Did the Court find that the Multistate Tax Compact satisfied any of the indicia of binding interstate compacts? What are those indicia and how did the Court view them in this case? What was the basis for the Court's view that the Tax Compact was more akin to a model or uniform act as opposed to a binding compact?

6. Why did the Court rule that the Multistate Tax Commission was not "a joint regulatory organization"? What is the significance of this determination?

7. The Court reviewed California's "reenactment rule" and explained, "One purpose of this provision 'is to "make sure legislators are not operating in the blind when they amend legislation, and to make sure the public can become apprised of changes in the law.""'" This amendment expressly referenced the Compact, stating that it applied "[n]otwithstanding Section 38006...." Even without a reenactment of § 38006 to eliminate the election language, the amendment of § 25128 did not violate the reenactment rule.

L. General v. Special Laws

Under the constitutional prohibition on special legislation, a law is "general" when it applies equally to all persons in a class founded upon some natural, intrinsic or constitutional distinction, and it is "special" if it confers particular privileges or imposes peculiar disabilities or burdensome conditions in the exercise of a common right upon a class of persons arbitrarily selected from the general body of those who stand in precisely the same relation to the subject of the law.

The test for determining whether a statutory classification violates the constitutional provision stating that a "local or special statute is invalid in any case if a general statute can be made applicable" is substantially the same as that used to determine constitutionality under the Equal Protection Clause. The constitutional prohibition on special legislation does not preclude legislative classification but only requires that the classification be reasonable. (*Law School Admission Council, Inc. v. State* (2014) 222 Cal.App.4th 1265, review denied.)

1. General versus Special Statutes in California

Most Capitol observers do not often come across bills that delineate between general or special statutes. What is a general statute versus a special statute?

A general statute is essentially a law that pertains uniformly to an entire community or all persons generally. On the other hand, a special statute is essentially a law that applies to a particular person, place, or interest. California law provides for both types of statutes.

California's Constitution in Article IV, Section 16, provides "(a) All laws of a general nature have uniform operation. (b) A local or special statute is invalid in any case if a general statute can be made applicable." As a result, general statutes are the main type, and they apply uniformly by their language; however, special statutes can be pursued so long as a general statute would not apply in the particular circumstance.

Working with the bill author, the Office of Legislative Counsel will make a determination whether a special statute will pass constitutional muster and, if so, how the bill must be drafted. The initial determination is whether the proposed legislation can be addressed by a bill of general application. If not, then a special law would be required.

With a special statute bill, a reader may see the following language in the measure:

> The Legislature finds and declares that a special law is necessary and that a general law cannot be made applicable within the meaning of Section 16 of Article IV of the California Constitution because of ___.

Thereafter, the bill must contain an explanation of the special nature of the bill and why a bill of general application will not work in these particular circumstances. An example of this explanatory language could be (taken from a prior bill):

> The unique island location of the City of Coronado and its proximity to large military installations requires a special law. In addition, the complexities of amending a general plan and a local coastal plan for the City of Coronado will take significantly longer than six months. As a result, a general law cannot be made applicable.

Although special statutes are not common, being aware of the general rules can be helpful when you need such a bill.

Notes and Questions

1. In most instances, legislation is general in its application, because most statutes apply equally to all persons, for example. However, there are instances each year when the Legislature must enact a special statute, which is designed for a particular geographic area of the state.

M. Severability

When a provision of an existing law is found to be unconstitutional, the unlawful provision can be severed from the rest of the law so that the remaining provisions of the law remain valid and intact. There are instances, however, when an entire law is ruled invalid and no part of it can be severed. Severability is a key consideration when a law is ruled unconstitutional.

The test of severability is whether invalid parts of the statute can be severed from otherwise valid parts without destroying the statutory scheme or utility of the remaining provisions.

1. Severability or Savings Clauses

On occasion, a reader may come across a severability or savings clause contained in a California bill. Basically, a severability clause is a statement by the Legislature that, if a part of a law that is enacted is subsequently held to be unconstitutional, then the unconstitutional provision(s) does not invalidate the rest of the law.

It is a type of savings clause in that it "saves" parts of a law if any other parts of the law are invalidated by court action. Some states have a general severability clause applicable across all statutes.

So, the general rule developed and applied by the courts is that, if a portion of a statute is invalid or unconstitutional, then the remaining portions of the statute are valid and enforceable if they stand on their own. On the other hand, if the remaining portions are completely dependent on the stricken portions, then the remaining portions are also invalid.

Why are severability or savings clauses used? Sometimes the legislature wants a statute to either stand or fall on its own. To avoid a court interpretation that might allow a statute to continue remaining in force after a portion of the statute has been invalidated, a bill drafter may insert a non-severability clause at or near the end of the bill.

As a general rule, a bill drafter should only use a severability clause when there is a possibility of a statute being partially invalidated and it is not clear that the intention of the Legislature is that the bill be severed. However, others believe a severability clause is unnecessary for legal purposes, because the courts have repeatedly ruled that, regardless of the presence or absence of a severability clause in a statute, the courts will sever invalid portions from an otherwise valid law whenever possible.

In other words, some observers argue that a severability clause ordinarily is not necessary, because both statutes and common law make statutory provisions severable. Nonetheless, we find these provisions scattered throughout California laws. Even the state Constitution utilizes such a provision. For example, Article I, Section 31(h) provides, in part, that "Any provision held invalid shall be severable from the remaining portions of this section." Similarly, Article X B, Section 16 specifies that, "and to this end, the provisions of this article are severable."

In addition, numerous California statutes contain severability clauses. For example, Government Code § 9906, which is entitled "Severability," provides the following: "If any provision of this chapter, or the application of any such provision to any person or circumstances, shall be held invalid, the remainder of this chapter to the extent it can be given effect, or the application of such provision to persons or circumstances other than those as to which it is held invalid, shall not be affected thereby, and to this end the provisions of this chapter are severable."

Additional examples of some of the standardized language found in California legislation include:

> The provisions of this bill are severable. If any provision of this bill or its application is held invalid, that invalidity shall not affect other provisions or applications that can be given effect without the invalid provision or application.

> If any provision of this act or the application thereof to any person or circumstance is held invalid for any reason in a court of competent jurisdiction, the invalidity shall not affect other provisions or any other application of this act which can be given effect without the invalid provision or application, and for this purpose the provisions of this act are declared severable.

Because some courts have given some weight to the inclusion of a severability clause in specific statutes, a severability clause is occasionally included in a measure, especially in long or controversial bills or when a legislator specifically requests its inclusion in a bill. But such clauses are not necessary in most legislation.

Manning v. Municipal County

(1982) 132 Cal.App.3d 825

OPINION

ROUSE, Acting P.J.

Defendant, Gail Manning, was charged by a first amended complaint, filed in the municipal court, which alleged a violation of section 316 of the Penal Code in that she "did willfully and unlawfully keep a house used for the purpose of assignation or prostitution, and did let rooms, apartments, or tenements, knowing that it [sic] was to be used for the purpose of assignation or prostitution." She demurred to the complaint, contending, inter alia, that section 316 was unconstitutional because it was overbroad and void for vagueness. The municipal court overruled the demurrer, and defendant then sought a peremptory writ of mandamus or prohibition from the superior court to compel the municipal court to sustain the demurrer. The superior court denied her such relief and now she has appealed from the order of denial.

Defendant claims that section 316 is so worded that its enforcement could infringe upon an individual's constitutional right to privacy. To the extent that the statute prohibits conduct described as an "assignation," we agree.

If a statute is worded in such a manner that its enforcement could infringe upon the exercise of a First Amendment right, then that statute must be held void for overbreadth even though the statute also prohibits conduct which is not protected by the First Amendment and which could properly be prohibited pursuant to a reasonable exercise of the police power. (*Alford v. Municipal Court* (1972) 26 Cal. App. 3d 244, 247–248 [102 Cal. Rptr. 667].) In the case of *In re Bell* (1942) 19 Cal. 2d 488, 496 [122 P.2d 22], the California Supreme Court observed that "It is not the function of the court to determine whether the restrictions imposed by the legislation can be validly applied to the facts of a particular case.... Language prohibiting conduct that may be prohibited and conduct that may not affords no reasonably ascertainable standard of guilt and is therefore too uncertain and vague to be enforced. [Citations.] A conviction based upon such a statute cannot stand even though the acts of misconduct in the particular case could be validly prohibited by properly drafted legislation. [Citations.]" (To the same effect, see *In re Porterfield* (1946) 28 Cal. 2d 91, 115 [168 P.2d 706, 167 A.L.R. 675]; *Rees v. City of Palm Springs* (1961) 188 Cal. App. 2d 339, 347 [10 Cal. Rptr. 386].)

A statute which either forbids or requires the doing of an act in terms so vague that men of common intelligence must necessarily guess at its meaning and differ as to its application is in violation of the first essential of due process of law. (*Connally v. General Const. Co.* (1926) 269 U.S. 385, 391 [70 L. Ed. 322, 328, 46 S. Ct. 126]; *Katzev v. County of Los Angeles* (1959) 52 Cal. 2d 360, 370 [341 P.2d 310]; *Mandel v. Municipal Court* (1969) 276 Cal. App. 2d 649, 660 [81 Cal. Rptr. 173].)

Section 316 was enacted in 1872 and has been amended once, during the 1873–1874 session of the state Legislature. (Code Amend. 1873–1874, ch. 614, §26, p. 430.) We must assume that, in those times, the word "assignation," as set forth in the statute, was generally understood to denote conduct involving the commercial exploitation of illicit sexual activities. However, we believe that the use of the word for such purpose, in today's world, would fall far short of its mark. The present definition of "assignation" is sufficiently uncertain as to make it unlikely that an average individual, desirous of avoiding prosecution under section 316, would have any clear idea of what conduct fell within the purview of that term.

Webster's Seventh New Collegiate Dictionary (1971), at pages 53, 953, defines "assignation" as "1: the act of assigning or the assignment made; esp.: Allotment 2: Tryst." The word "tryst" is defined as "1: an agreement (as between lovers) to meet 2: an appointed meeting or meeting place." Nothing in these definitions suggests conduct which is immoral, let alone illegal. Since the state has no legitimate interest in prohibiting even lewd and dissolute sexual conduct unless it occurs within the presence of individuals who might be offended by it (*Pryor v. Municipal Court* (1979) 25 Cal. 3d 238, 256–257 [158 Cal. Rptr. 330, 599 P.2d 636]), then it is obvious that it has even less interest in prohibiting a lover's tryst occurring within the privacy of an individual's apartment or hotel room.

We conclude that the word "assignation," as used in section 316, is too vague to give notice to a potential offender of the conduct to be avoided; also, such vagueness allows for the exercise by the police of unfettered discretion to determine for themselves what conduct shall be deemed to constitute an "assignation." (See *Papachristou v. City of Jacksonville* (1972) 405 U.S. 156, 168–170 [31 L. Ed. 2d 110, 119–120, 92 S. Ct. 839].)

The principle is well established that we should not pronounce a statute unconstitutional unless such result is necessary to the proper disposition of a cause. (*Mandel v. Hodges* (1976) 54 Cal. App. 3d 596, 618–619 [127 Cal. Rptr. 244, 90 A.L.R.3d 728].) Even when such a result is indicated, an unconstitutional enactment may be upheld in part if it can be said that such part is complete in itself and would have been adopted by the Legislature had that body foreseen the partial invalidity of the statute. (*O'Kane v. Catuira* (1963) 212 Cal. App. 2d 131, 141 [27 Cal. Rptr. 818, 94 A.L.R.2d 487].) Unconstitutional provisions will not vitiate an entire act unless they enter so entirely into the scope and design of the law that it would be impossible to maintain it without the invalid provisions. (*In re King* (1970) 3 Cal. 3d 226, 237 [90 Cal. Rptr. 15, 474 P.2d 983]; *Davis v. Municipal Court* (1966) 243 Cal. App. 2d 55, 59 [52 Cal. Rptr. 189].) The test of severability is whether the invalid parts of a statute can be severed from the otherwise valid parts without destroying the statutory scheme or utility of the remaining provisions. (*Dillon v. Municipal Court* (1971) 4 Cal. 3d 860, 872 [94 Cal. Rptr. 77, 484 P.2d 945]; *Blumenthal v. Board of Medical Examiners* (1962) 57 Cal. 2d 228, 238 [18 Cal. Rptr. 501, 368 P.2d 101].)

Here, under settled rules of statutory construction, the portions of the statute which prohibit prostitution appear readily severable from those which prohibit conduct described as "assignation"; thus, we cannot accept defendant's contention that the entire statute must be declared unconstitutional. However, in this instance, the question of whether the prosecution could have lawfully proceeded against defendant solely on the charge of engaging in conduct furthering prostitution is not before us. The prosecutor declined to follow the trial court's suggestion that he delete from the complaint all references to "assignation" and proceed against defendant solely on those portions of the statute referring to "prostitution." Instead, the prosecutor insisted upon continuing to charge violations of both portions of the statute, thereby forcing the matter through a laborious appellate process to this predictable result.

The purported appeal from the order denying plaintiff's motion to strike the district attorney's return is dismissed. The order denying the petition for writ of mandate/prohibition is reversed, and the trial court is directed to issue a writ of mandate compelling defendant municipal court to sustain the demurrer to the complaint which charges plaintiff with violating section 316.

MILLER, J., and SMITH, J., concurred.

Notes and Questions

1. The court noted an important exception when stating that if a statute is worded in such a manner that its enforcement could infringe upon the exercise of a First Amendment right, then that statute must be held void for overbreadth even though the statute also prohibits conduct which is not protected by the First Amendment and which could properly be prohibited pursuant to a reasonable exercise of the police power. (*Alford v. Municipal Court* (1972) 26 Cal.App.3d 244.)

2. What is the impact of the court's distinction between the present definition of "assignation" and the definition likely in effect when the statute was adopted by the Legislature?

3. The court provided an important explanation regrading severability: Unconstitutional provisions will not vitiate an entire act unless they enter so entirely into the scope and design of the law that it would be impossible to maintain it without the invalid provisions. (*In re King* (1970) 3 Cal.3d 226, 237.) The test of severability is whether the invalid parts of a statute can be severed from the otherwise valid parts without destroying the statutory scheme or utility of the remaining provisions. (*Dillon v. Municipal Court* (1971) 4 Cal.3d 860, 872.)

4. Is a severability analysis premised on statutory construction?

N. Purpose of Reenactment Rule

The "reenactment rule" essentially means that the legislature reenacts an entire code section even when simply amending a word or two of that code section. As a result, the enactment of a bill results in the reenactment of the existing code section.

The purpose of this rule is to ensure that legislators and the public understand the context of the statutory changes.

One purpose of the constitutional provisions stating that a section of a statute may not be amended unless the section is reenacted as amended is to make sure legislators are not operating in the blind when they amend legislation, and to make sure the public can become apprised of changes to the law. Generally, the reenactment rule does not apply to statutes that act to "amend" others only by implication. (*Gillette Co. v. Franchise Tax Board* (2015) 62 Cal.4th 468.)

1. California's Reenactment Rule

California's Constitution, in Article IV, Section 9, provides "A section of a statute may not be amended unless the section is re-enacted as amended." What does that mean?

According to the courts, the purpose of the constitutional reenactment rule, which prohibits amending a section of statute unless the section is reenacted as amended, is "to avoid enactment of statutes in terms so blind that legislators themselves are deceived in regard to their effect." The rule applies to bills which are amending some former act.

However, the reenactment rule does not apply to the addition of new code sections or enactment of entirely independent acts that impliedly affect other code sections. In other words, when adding a new code section, the Legislature is not required to reenact other code sections that were affected by the change.

There have been a number of court decisions addressing the reenactment rule. At least one court has opined that non-substantive amendments cannot serve to reenact substantive provisions of an invalid statute. (See *People v. Barros* (2012) 209 Cal.App.4th 1581, 1590.) The court said that the bill that made a "nonsubstantive technical amendment to [an invalid statute] as it continued to appear in the annotated codes," could likely not have "served to reenact the substantive provisions" of the invalid statute.

In *Gillette Company v. Franchise Tax Board* (2015) 62 Cal.4th 468, the court addressed whether California Revenue and Taxation Code § 25128 violated the reenactment rule of the California Constitution. One purpose of that provision is to ensure that legislators are aware of statutory changes when they adopt legislation and to ensure that the public was apprised of changes in the law.

On this issue, the Court found that, even without reenactment of CRTC § 38006 to address the change, the Legislature and the public were reasonably notified of the changes in the law because the amendment to § 25128 requiring the use of the double-weighted sales factor "expressly referenced the Compact, stating that it applied '[n]otwithstanding § 38006....'"

Under this provision of the state constitution, the Legislature is required to reenact a code section when it amends that particular code section. In reviewing the contents of a bill that amends a code section, this rule also ensures that the bill reader can easily identify what changes are proposed by the bill because, in amending a code section, the bill sets forth the changes within the context of the current statute.

Notes and Questions

1. The purpose of the reenactment rule is to avoid the enactment of statutes in terms so blind that the legislative body is deceived in regard to their effect, and the public, from the difficulty of making the necessary examination and comparison, and fails to become apprised of the changes made in the laws. (*County of San Diego v. Commission on State Mandates* (2016) 212 Cal.Rptr.3d 259.)

2. A statute declares law and, if enacted by the Legislature, must be initiated by a bill passed with certain formalities and presented to the Governor for signature. Resolutions serve to express the views of the resolving body. A resolution does not require the same formality of enactment as a statute and is not presented to the Governor for approval. A resolution, as distinct from a statute, is essentially an enactment which only declares a public purpose and does not establish means to accomplish that purpose. (*American Federation of Labor v. Eu* (1984) 36 Cal.3d 687.) Because a resolution does not state law, the reenactment rule does not apply to resolutions.

O. The Enrolled Bill Rule in California

In general, the judicial branch is loath to review the record keeping practices of the Legislature to determine the validity of statutes. This limitation on judicial inquiry is known as the "Enrolled Bill Rule," and this legal doctrine holds that, if an act of the Legislature is "properly enrolled, authenticated and filed," then it is presumed that "all of the steps required for its passage were properly taken," and "even the journal of the Legislature is not available to impeach it."

Based upon the California Constitution's enumerated separation of powers doctrine, the reasoning behind this judicial limitation is that the judicial branch should not impinge on the constitutionally enumerated power of the legislative branch to govern its internal affairs. Despite some critics of this legal principle, as recently as 2009, courts have concluded that this rule is still "in full effect in California."

Capitol observers note that the Enrolled Bill Rule is part of the governing rules between the legislative and judicial branches of state government and ensures that legislative rules and procedures are respected by the judiciary. Basically, when a legal question is raised with a court whether a bill was passed by the Legislature and sent to the Governor's desk, the legal inquiry is whether the requirements of California's Constitution, found in Article IV, Section 8(b), where complied with by the legislative branch.

The provisions of Section 8(b) include that (1) each bill be read by title on three days in each house unless the house dispenses with the requirement by rollcall vote entered in the Journal and (2) no bills are to be passed unless the bill with amendments has been printed and distributed to the members. If these constitutional requirements were not met, then a court could invalidate a statute passed by the Legislature.

Existing state case law provides that, once a bill has been authenticated and enacted, it would violate the separation of powers doctrine found in the state Constitution, Article III, for a court to use extrinsic evidence to determine that the Legislature failed to satisfy the constitutional requirements for enacting a statute.

Almost 100 years ago, the California Supreme Court ruled in *Taylor v. Legislature* (1927) 201 Cal. 327, 332, that "a statute, properly enrolled and authenticated, conclusively establishes not only the contents of the law but the due performance of all steps requisite to its passage by the legislature. This is the general law and has long been the rule of decision in this state."

This principle, known as the Enrolled Bill Rule, was described by the court in 1927 as having "long been the rule of decision in this state," in that the rule was first articulated by the California Supreme Court in *Sherman v. Story* (1866) 30 Cal. 253. In that 1866 decision, the Court refused to consider uncontradicted legislative journals and oral testimony alleging that certain proposed amendments that were rejected in the Assembly were nonetheless, and apparently mistakenly, incorporated into the act by the enrolling clerk of the Senate.

Thereafter, in *County of Yolo v. Colgan* (1901) 132 Cal. 265, the California Supreme Court rejected a claim that, based on an entry in the *Senate Daily Journal*, a statute had not received the requisite number of votes for passage and was thus invalid; in so ruling, the Court cited the separation of powers doctrine, concluding that "while the constitution has prescribed the formalities to be observed in the passage of bills and the creation of statutes, the power to determine whether these formalities have been complied with is necessarily vested in the legislature itself...."

In addition, in *Planned Parenthood Affiliates v. Swoap* (1985) 173 Cal.App.3d 1187, a conference committee on the annual Budget Bill proposed to each house a version of the Budget Bill that excluded a provision, Section 33.35, and the conference committee proposal was approved by the Senate and Assembly and duly enacted into law. Notwithstanding the discovery that, due to staff error, Section 33.35 had not in fact been removed from the Budget Bill proposal, the court ruled that it lacked the power to strike the section from the enacted Budget Bill.

Citing the "salutary principle [that] has long been established in California that the judicial branch may not go behind the record evidence of a statute," the court ruled that because Section 33.35 received the necessary approval of each house of the Legislature and was "duly enrolled and approved by the Governor," it could not be impeached by extrinsic evidence.

Nonetheless, the California courts have identified one exception to the Enrolled Bill Rule. That exception was discussed at length in *People ex rel. Levin v. County of Santa Clara* (1951) 37 Cal.2d 335, a case in which a defect in the local adoption of charter amendments was evidenced by a recitation on the face of a resolution adopted by the Legislature addressing that local enactment. In *Levin*, the Court cited the general principle that, "when an act of the Legislature is valid on its face, properly enrolled, authenticated and filed, it is conclusively presumed that all of the steps required for its passage have been properly taken; even the journal of the Legislature is not available to impeach it."

The Court then engaged in a discussion of case law and treatises reviewing the scope of the Enrolled Bill Rule, concluding as follows: "Thus the holding is that if irregularity in the proceedings by the local authorities appears on the face of the legislative resolution, the approval by the Legislature is not conclusive, as it would be, if it was not revealed by the resolution." In *Levin*, the court deemed this exception to the Enrolled Bill Rule to apply for the reason that the procedural defect in the local adoption of charter amendments was evidenced on the face of the resolution adopted by the Legislature.

Notes and Questions

1. Is the Enrolled Bill Rule premised on the separation of powers doctrine?

2. Do the courts in California apply the Enrolled Bill Rule too strictly? In other words, are there really any viable challenges to the Legislature's enactment of a statute based upon whether the legislative process as embodied in Article IV of the state Constitution was followed?

Chapter Nine

Bills, Resolutions, and Constitutional Amendments

A. Bills

1. What Is a Bill?

What is a "bill"? Although the term "bill" is mentioned more than two dozen times in the California Constitution, the word is actually not defined in this document. It is also not defined in the California Government Code.

A traditional definition of a bill is simply proposed legislation that is considered by a legislative body. Of course, a bill does not become law until it has been passed by the legislative branch and approved by the executive branch. Bills only apply to the Legislature. In the two dozen states that have direct democracy, including California, the people can enact statutes, but only by initiative.

California's Legislative Counsel defines a bill as "A proposed law, introduced during a session for consideration by the Legislature, and identified numerically in order of presentation; also, a reference that may include joint and concurrent resolutions and constitutional amendments."

Pursuant to the state Constitution, the use of bills is granted solely to the legislative branch of state government. Article IV, Section 8(b)(1) provides: "The Legislature may make no law except by statute and may enact no statute except by bill." Hence, the lawmaking process requires the use of bills.

A few other state constitutional provisions apply to bills, including Section 8(b)(3), which states "No bill may be passed unless, by rollcall vote entered in the journal, a majority of the membership of each house concurs." Section 10(a) requires that "(a) Each bill passed by the Legislature shall be presented to the Governor." And Section 12 deals with budget bills.

As set forth in Article IV, which deals with the legislative branch of state government and sets forth the general legislative process, a bill is required to create a law (a statute). And it is the document that the Legislature uses to create a statute.

2. Bills to Be Read on Three Separate Days

The state Constitution requires bills to be read on three separate occasions as a means of alerting the public to the legislation and the changes that the Legislature is contemplating. The first reading is when the bill is introduced. The second reading is when the bill has been amended or passed out of a committee. The third reading occurs when the bill is ready for debate and vote on the floor of the legislature.

3. The Three Readings of a Bill

The California Constitution requires a bill to be "read" three times before it can be debated and voted upon by either house. A "reading" of a bill in the Assembly or Senate is defined as being the presentation of the bill before the house by reading the bill's number, author and title. Each time the bill is read, those three provisions are read aloud on the Floor by the Reading Clerk in either the Senate or Assembly.

There is a misconception that the three constitutionally-required readings of bills are the same. In fact, each is for a different purpose. First reading occurs upon introduction of the bill. Second reading occurs after a bill has been reported to the floor from committee (with or without amendments). Third reading occurs when the measure is about to be taken up on the floor of either house for final passage. Note that the three readings requirement can be suspended by a 2/3 vote in either house pursuant to the state Constitution.

First Reading — The first reading of the bill takes place when it is actually introduced in either house. The bill is placed "across the desk (of the Assembly or Senate)" which is the official act of introducing a bill in the Legislature. In the Assembly, the Chief Clerk or his or her representative at the Assembly Desk receives the measure. In the Senate, the Secretary of the Senate or his or her representative takes the bill.

The bill is given a bill number upon introduction. Once a bill passes over to the other house for consideration, it is simply read for the first time. Introduced bills are noted in the *Assembly Daily File* or the *Senate Daily File*, but there is no "first reading" portion of either *Daily File*. No floor analysis is prepared of the introduced bill.

Second Reading — The second reading of the bill takes place after the bill has been reported out of committee, either the policy or fiscal committee, to the Floor of either the Assembly or Senate. This process occurs whether the bill has been amended or not. Also, a bill can be on Second Reading several times, such as when the bill has been reported out of the policy committee and then again after being reported out of the fiscal committee.

There is a Second Reading portion in both the Assembly and Senate *Daily Files*. This portion lists by file number (assigned to each bill once it has been listed in the *File*) each bill that has been reported out of committee to the floor. The general rule is that a bill remains on the Second Reading File for one day before moving to the Third Reading File. No floor analysis is prepared for the Second Reading file bills.

Readers should be aware that the file numbers assigned to bills in the *Daily File* change each day as all the bills get processed and move onto or off of the *Daily File*.

Generally, bills are taken up on the Assembly or Senate Floors in file item order, unless some special reason exists to do otherwise. And, when the presiding officer announces a bill for consideration, it is usually referred to by its file number.

Third Reading—The third reading of the bill takes place when the bill is about to be taken up for consideration (i.e., presentation, debate and vote) on either the Assembly Floor or the Senate Floor for final passage. There is a Third Reading portion in both the Assembly and Senate *Daily Files*.

This portion lists by file number each bill that is eligible to be taken up for a final vote on either Floor. A Third Reading Analysis is prepared for bills eligible for consideration on either the Assembly or Senate Floors. This analysis of the bill generally provides an explanation of existing law, what this bill does to existing law, any amendments, a listing of supporters and opponents, etc.

Unfinished Business File—Both the *Assembly Daily File* and the *Senate Daily File* contain a portion titled "Unfinished Business," which is the section that contains bills that have returned to their house of origin from the other house and await a concurrence vote due to amendments that were made to the bill by the other house.

This section of the *Daily File* also contains bills that were vetoed by the Governor. They remain on the *Daily File* for a 60-day period after the gubernatorial veto. Thereafter, unless voted upon, they are removed from the *Daily File* and can no longer be considered.

Inactive File—The other section of the *Daily File* to be aware of is for bills that made it to the Floor of either the Assembly or the Senate, but for whatever reason, the bill's author does not want to proceed with the measure. Bills that have failed passage can be moved to the Inactive File upon request of the bill's author. If an author has moved a bill to the Inactive File, he or she can remove it from the Inactive File at a later date with public notice.

Floor Managers—While the bill's author presents his or her bill on the Floor of the bill's house of origin (i.e., Assembly Bill presented by the Assembly Member or Senate Bill presented by the Senator), that is not the case in the other house. In other words, Assembly Members cannot present their bills for consideration and debate on the Senate Floor and, similarly, Senators cannot present their bills for consideration and debate on the Assembly Floor.

So, while a bill's author is responsible for taking up his or her measure on their own Floor, a "floor manager" for that bill is required in the other house. A Member of the other house designated by the bill's author when the bill is considered by the other house is deemed the bill's floor manager. In years past, this Member was referred to as the "floor jockey," but this term is no longer used. The Member's name who is the Floor Manager in the other house appears in parentheses after the bill author's name in the Second or Third Reading portion of the *Daily File*.

WORFs—According to the rules, bills that are not listed on the *Daily File* can only be taken up with either unanimous consent of the house's members or by suspending the rules. A bill that is not listed on the *Daily File*, but which is taken up nonetheless, is referred to as a "WORF." The process of taking up a WORF bill is to take the measure up "without reference to file" (WORF). In order to do so, a vote of a majority of the house's membership (41 in the Assembly and 21 in the Senate) is required to take up a bill without reference to file.

People v. Dunn

(1889) 80 Cal. 211

OPINION

WORKS, J.

This is an application for a writ of *mandamus* to compel the respondent, as controller of state, to issue his warrant for certain moneys which the relators claim should be paid out of the appropriation contained in the act of the legislature, entitled "An act to provide a permanent site for the California Home for the Care and Training of Feeble-minded Children, to erect suitable buildings thereon, and making an appropriation therefor." (Stats. 1889, p. 69.)

The respondent resists the claim of the petitioners, on the ground that the said statute is unconstitutional and void, for five reasons, set forth in his return to the alternative writ, as follows: —

"1. Said bill was not read on three several days in the senate prior to its final passage, nor was it declared to be a case of urgency.

"2. Said alleged law was introduced, known in its various stages in the legislature, and passed as senate bill No. 194, which said bill was put upon its final passage in the assembly after it had been amended in its title, and in all its sections save section 5, and before and without being printed with the amendments thereto for the use of the members, in violation of article 1, section 15, of the constitution of this state.

"3. Said bill was not read at length upon its final passage, in violation of article 1, section 15, of the constitution of this state.

"4. Said bill or law is void, as it delegates legislative powers and functions to a board of trustees aided by two "citizens, the two bodies forming a commission clothed with legislative powers and functions.

"5 Said bill or law is void on its face. It is not a general appropriation bill, and does contain more than one item of appropriation, and that for more than one single and certain purpose, wherefor the' respondent prays that the writ be discharged, and that he go hence with his cost."

The claim of the respondent is, that the journals of the two houses of the legislature do not show affirmatively that the bill was read three several times in the senate, that it was printed with its amendments before its final passage, or that it was read at length upon its final passage, as required by the constitution. (Art. 1, sec. 1, and art. 4, sec. 15.)

The point made and relied upon is, that it must affirmatively appear from the journals of the two houses that every act required to be done in the enactment of a law has been done, and that in the absence of such a showing, it must be presumed that such acts were not done.

In support of this contention counsel cite Constitution, art. 4, secs. 10, 15, 16, 28; art. 18, sec. 1; Pol. Code, secs. 240, 256, 257; *Gardner* v. *The Collector,* 6 Wall. 499; *Santa Clara Railroad Tax Case,* 9 Saw. 226, 227; *Spangler* v. *Jacoby,* 14 Ill. 298; *Weill* v. *Kenfield,* 54 Cal. 111; *Oakland Paving Company* v. *Hilton,* 69 Cal. 481; *Indiana Canal Co.* v. *Potts,* 7 Ind. 681; *Madison* v. *Baker,* 80 Ind. 374.

The case does not present the question as to the power of this court to go behind the enrolled bill in order to determine from the journals of the two houses whether the bill was properly passed or not. The respondent does not stop with the contention that the journals may be looked to in order to determine this question. His position is, that as the two houses of the legislature are required to keep journals of their proceedings, every act not shown by such journals to have taken place must be presumed not to have been done. His position cannot be upheld by reason or authority. It is uniformly repudiated even in those states in which it is held that the journals may be looked to as against the enrolled bill. (*Larrison* v. *Peoria etc. Railroad Co.,* 77 Ill. 11; Cooley's Constitutional Limitations, 164; *Minnesota* v. *City of Hastings,* 24 Minn. 78; *Miller* v. *State,* 3 Ohio St. 476; *Illinois* v. *Illinois Central Railroad Co.,* 33 Fed. Rep. 760.) For these reasons we think the objections to the law, on the ground that it was not legally passed, are not well taken.

Nor do we think there is any force in the objection that, by providing that certain persons should select the site for the building proposed to be constructed, the act attempted to delegate legislative functions and powers. To hold that such a power could not be vested in persons named in the act would be an unreasonably strict application of the rule that legislative functions cannot be delegated. The mere act of selecting a site to be purchased was not a legislative act. (*State* v. *Chicago M. & St. P. Railway Co.,* 38 Minn. 281.)

The last objection, viz., that the bill is not a general appropriation bill, and contains more than one item of appropriation for more than one single purpose, is equally groundless. There is but one appropriation in the act for one purpose. The object and purpose of the appropriation is to supply a permanent location for a home for feeble-minded children. It was not necessary that there should have been a separate appropriation for the purchase of the land, another for the erection of the building, another for the construction of fences, and another for each improvement necessary to the proper completion of the proposed work. Section 34, article 4, of the constitution, which is relied upon to support this objection to the law, cannot be given any such unreasonable construction.

The relators are entitled to a peremptory writ, as prayed for, and the same will be issued.

BEATTY, C.J., FOX, J., PATERSON, J., and MCFARLAND, J., concurred.

Notes and Questions

1. What were the five grounds on which the respondent claimed that the statute is unconstitutional?

2. The bill making the appropriation had not been read on three separate days in either the senate or the assembly, as required by the Constitution, but it is not necessary that the legislative Journals show affirmatively that a bill and its amendments were read as required by the Constitution. In the absence of a record, not required by the Constitution to be kept, it would be presumed that in the passage of a bill that the legislature complied with all constitutional requirements.

B. Authentication of Legislative Acts

All legislative acts must be authenticated in order to take proper effect. Legislative acts are authenticated by the Senate Secretary or his or her designee, the Assembly Chief Clerk or his or her designee, and the Governor's legislative deputy. Legislative acts also go through processes called engrossment and enrollment to ensure that they have been properly through the legislative process.

Notes and Questions

1. An act authenticated by the signatures of the Secretary of the Senate and the Clerk of the Assembly, the President of the Senate and Speaker of the House, approved by the Governor and deposited in the office of the Secretary of State must be regarded as the record. (*Sherman v. Story* (1866) 30 Cal. 253.)

C. "Spot Bills" in the California Legislature

During the first two months of the California Legislative Session, over 2,500 bills are usually introduced. Hundreds of those bills are "spot bills" or "intent bills." What are they and why are they used?

Defined

As described by the Legislative Counsel, a "spot bill" is one that does not make any substantive change to existing law, "and would not otherwise affect the ongoing operations of state or local government." An "intent bill" is one that merely makes a statement of legislative intent.

In both instances, these bills upon introduction are merely placeholders for future language. They do not make any substantive changes to existing law. By the rules of the Assembly and Senate, spot bills or intent bills may not be referred to a policy committee unless and until the bill is amended to make a substantive change in the law.

Their Use

Now that we understand what they are, why are they used? Because the California Legislative Session is dependent upon its deadlines, including a deadline for introducing bills, sometimes legislators do not have their bill proposals fully prepared by that time. As such, they need to introduce a "placeholder" bill and then develop or finalize their substantive bill language.

Rules

While there are not specific rules for spot bills in the Senate Rules or the Joint Rules, there is one in the Assembly Rules. AR 51.5 reads as follows:

Spot Bills

51.5. A bill that upon introduction makes no substantive change in or addition to existing law, and would not otherwise affect the ongoing operations of state or local government, except a bill stating legislative intent to make necessary statutory changes to implement the Budget Bill, may not be referred to a committee by the Committee on Rules. If the author subsequently proposes to the Committee on Rules to make substantive changes in the bill as introduced, the Committee on Rules may refer the bill to a committee, together with the proposed changes for consideration as author's amendments. A vote on passage of the bill may not be taken, however, until the bill with its amendments, if adopted, has been in print for at least 15 days.

From the 2019 Legislative Session, the following are examples of a spot bill and an intent bill:

Example of a Spot Bill

SB 362, as introduced, Roth. Legal remedies.

Existing law encompasses provisions pertaining to the civil law of the state, including laws concerning persons, property, and obligations, among other subjects. Existing law provides for relief or remedy for violation of private rights and to secure observance of those rights. Existing law prohibits specific or preventative relief in cases, except as specified. This bill would make non-substantive changes to those provisions.

DIGEST KEY

Vote: majority Appropriation: no Fiscal Committee: no Local Program: no

THE PEOPLE OF THE STATE OF CALIFORNIA DO ENACT AS FOL-LOWS:

SECTION 1.

Section 3274 of the Civil Code is amended to read:

3274. As a general rule, compensation is the relief or remedy provided by the law of this ~~State~~ *state* for the violation of private ~~rights,~~ *rights* and the means of securing their ~~observance; and specific~~ *observance. Specific* and preventive relief may be given in no other cases than those specified in this ~~Part of the Civil Code~~ *part*.

Example of an Intent Bill

> AB 106, as introduced, Ting. Budget Act of 2019.
>
> This bill would express the intent of the Legislature to enact statutory changes relating to the Budget Act of 2019.
>
> DIGEST KEY
>
> Vote: majority Appropriation: no Fiscal Committee: no Local Program: no
>
> THE PEOPLE OF THE STATE OF CALIFORNIA DO ENACT AS FOLLOWS:
>
> SECTION 1.
>
> It is the intent of the Legislature to enact statutory changes relating to the Budget Act of 2019.

Assembly Process

In the Assembly, a deadline is specified each year, which is set a few weeks after the bill introduction deadline. That deadline is to get amendments to spot or intent bills to the Committee on Rules. Once the Rules Committee reviews the proposed amendments, the Rules Committee refers the bill and its amendments to the relevant policy committee. Thereafter, the committee processes the amendments to the bill.

Senate Process

In the Senate, there is no deadline specified for getting amendments to the Rules Committee. However, those amendments must be submitted within sufficient time for the Rules Committee to refer to the amended bill to committee for a hearing before the relevant deadline. The bill's amendments are submitted to the Committee on Rules, and the Rules Committee makes the amendments to the bill. Thereafter, the bill is referred to the relevant policy committee.

2019 Data

In the State Assembly in 2019, there were 1,799 bills introduced by the deadline, with over 600 of those measures being spot bills or about 1/3 of the introduced bills. Amendments to nearly 500 of those spot bills were submitted by the deadline.

In the State Senate this year, there were 777 bills introduced by the deadline, including 231 spot bills, or roughly 30% of the measures introduced.

Notes and Questions

1. What is the most common reason for a legislator to introduce a "spot" bill? Does a spot bill satisfy the public's view of transparency in the legislative process?

2. These types of bills are commonly introduced at the start of each legislative session in order for legislators to have so-called "placeholder bills" in which no substantive language is contained. The purpose of spot bills is to essentially hold a place in the legislative process for a legislator to later amend his or her substantive language into the measure. As such, the spot bills are of a temporary nature until substantive amendments can be ascertained and inserted into the bill.

Howard Jarvis Taxpayers Association v. Bowen

(2013) 212 Cal.App.4th 129

OPINION

RAYE, P.J.

The narrow, but potentially recurring and important, question we address in these writ proceedings is whether the California Constitution, as amended by the voters in 2010, allows the Legislature to identify blank bills with an assigned number but no substance (so-called "spot bills") in the budget bill, pass the budget, and thereafter add content to the placeholder and approve it by a majority vote as urgency legislation. (Cal. Const., art. IV, § 12, subds. (d) & (e).) We conclude that spot bills which remain empty of content at the time the budget is passed are not bills that can be identified within the meaning of article IV, section 12, subdivision (e)(2) of the California Constitution and enacted as urgency legislation by a mere majority vote.

According to the California State Legislature Glossary, a spot bill is "[a] bill that amends a code section in a nonsubstantive way. A spot bill may be introduced to ensure that a germane vehicle will be available at a later date. Assembly Rules provide that a spot bill cannot be referred to a committee by the Rules Committee without substantive amendments." (Legis. Counsel, *A Guide for Accessing California Legislative Information on the Internet, Appendix B: Glossary of Legislative Terms,* <http://www.leginfo.ca.gov/guide.html# S> [as of Jan. 10, 2013].)

FACTUAL AND LEGAL CONTEXT

The requests for judicial notice filed by petitioners and real party in interest Legislature of the State of California are granted.

Prior to the 2010 amendments to the California Constitution, a two-thirds supermajority of the Legislature was required to pass an annual budget. (Cal. Const., art. IV, former § 12.) Through an initiative measure on the November 2, 2010, ballot, however, the voters passed the "On-Time Budget Act of 2010," thereby amending article IV, section 12 of the California Constitution (hereafter art. IV, § 12). At issue in these proceedings is the language set forth in article IV, section 12, subdivisions (d) and (e)(2).

Subdivision (d) of article IV, section 12 states: "No bill except the budget bill may contain more than one item of appropriation, and that for one certain, expressed purpose. Appropriations from the General Fund of the State, except appropriations for the public schools *and appropriations in the budget bill and in other bills providing for appropriations related to the budget bill,* are void unless passed in each house by rollcall vote entered in the journal, two-thirds of the membership concurring." (Language added by 2010 amend. in italics.)

Subdivision (e)(2) of article IV, section 12 further explains: "For purposes of this section, 'other bills providing for appropriations related to the budget bill' shall consist only of bills identified as related to the budget in the budget bill passed by the Legislature."

In February 2012 there were 80 spot bills on the legislative docket: Assembly Bill Nos. 1464, 1465, 1466, 1467, 1468, 1469, 1470, 1471, 1472, 1473, 1474, 1475, 1476,

1477, 1478, 1479, 1480, 1481, 1482, 1483, 1484, 1485, 1486, 1487, 1488, 1489, 1490, 1491, 1492, 1493, 1494, 1495, 1496, 1497, 1498, 1499, 1500, 1501, 1502, and 1503; and Senate Bill Nos. 1004, 1005, 1006, 1007, 1008, 1009, 1010, 1011, 1012, 1013, 1014, 1015, 1016, 1017, 1018, 1019, 1020, 1021, 1022, 1023, 1024, 1025, 1026, 1027, 1028, 1029, 1030, 1031, 1032, 1033, 1034, 1035, 1036, 1037, 1038, 1039, 1040, 1041, 1042, and 1043. Each of these bills was assigned a number but was otherwise empty of content. Indeed, their purpose is to reserve a spot on the legislative calendar. Each blank bill contains the same place-saving 18 words: "It is the intent of the Legislature to enact statutory changes relating to the Budget Act of 2012." One of these blank bills is at the center of the current controversy — Assembly Bill No. 1499.

The Committee on Budget introduced Assembly Bill No. 1499 on January 10, 2012. (Assem. Bill No. 1499 (2011–2012 Reg. Sess.) as introduced Jan. 10, 2012.) It reiterates the language that appears in each of the other spot bills: "The people of the State of California do enact as follows: SECTION 1. It is the intent of the Legislature to enact statutory changes relating to the Budget Act of 2012." The Legislative Counsel's Digest states, in part: "Vote: majority. Appropriation: no. Fiscal committee: no. State-mandated local program: no." (Legis. Counsel's Dig., Assem. Bill No. 1499, *supra*, as introduced Jan. 10, 2012.) It was read on January 10, March 19, and March 22, 2012, passed by the Assembly, and ordered to the Senate. (Complete Bill Hist., Assem. Bill No. 1499, *supra*, at <http://www.leginfo.ca.gov/pub/11–12/bill/asm/ab_1451–1500/ab_1499_bill_20120627_history.html> [as of Jan. 10, 2013].)

The budget bill, Assembly Bill No. 1464, was enacted on June 15, 2012, by a majority vote of the Legislature. (Stats.2012, ch. 21, § 39.00; see complete Bill Hist., Assem. Bill No. 1499, *supra*, at <http://www.leginfo.ca.gov/pub/11–12/bill/asm/ab_1451–1500/ab_1499_bill_20120627_history.html> [as of Jan. 10, 2013].) The budget bill states: "The Legislature hereby finds and declares that the following bills are other bills providing for appropriations related to the Budget Bill within the meaning of subdivision (e) of Section 12 of Article IV of the California Constitution: ... AB 1499...." (Stats.2012, ch. 21, § 39.00.)

Ten days later the Legislature, again by majority vote, added substance to the otherwise empty Assembly Bill No. 1499. (Assem. Bill No. 1499, *supra*, as amended June 25, 2012.) The Legislative Counsel's Digest was amended to read, in part: "Appropriation: yes. Fiscal committee: yes." (Legis. Counsel's Dig., Assem. Bill No. 1499, *supra*, as amended June 25, 2012.) As of June 25, 2012, Assembly Bill No. 1499 read:

"The *people of the State of California do enact as follows:*

"*SECTION 1. (a) The Legislature finds and declares that bond measures and constitutional amendments should have priority on the ballot because of the profound and lasting impact these measures can have on our state. Bond measures create debts against the state treasury that obligate the resources of future Californians. Constitutional amendments make changes to our state's fundamental principles and protections. In recognition of their significance, bond measures and constitutional amendments should be placed at the top of the ballot to ensure that the voters can carefully weigh the consequences of these important measures.*

"(b) The Legislature further finds and declares that the Secretary of State has received funding in the Budget Act of 2012, and an appropriation contained herein, to provide direction to counties regarding the preparation of ballots, and to prepare the ballot pamphlet, in a manner that is consistent with the changes to the Elections Code provided by this act.

"SEC. 2. Section 13115 of the Elections Code is amended to read:

"13115. The order in which all state measures that are to be submitted to the voters shall appear upon the ballot is as follows:

"(a) Bond measures, *including those proposed by initiative,* in the order in which they qualify.

"(b) Constitutional amendments, *including those proposed by initiative,* in the order in which they qualify.

"(c) *Legislative* measures, *other than those described in subdivision (a) or (b),* in the order in which they are approved by the Legislature.

"(d) Initiative measures, *other than those described in subdivision (a) or (b),* in the order in which they qualify.

"(e) Referendum measures, in the order in which they qualify.

"SEC. 3. The sum of one thousand dollars ($1,000) is hereby appropriated from the General Fund to the Secretary of State to implement the requirements of this act.

"SEC. 4. This act is a bill providing for appropriations related to the Budget Bill within the meaning of subdivision (e) of Section 12 of Article IV of the California Constitution, has been identified as related to the budget in the Budget Bill, and shall take effect immediately." (Assem. Bill No. 1499, *supra,* as amended June 25, 2012.)

The following day, June 26, it was passed from committee. And the next day, June 27, Assembly rules were suspended, the Senate amendments were concurred in, and the bill was enrolled and presented to the Governor, signed by the Governor, and chaptered by the Secretary of State. (Complete Bill Hist., Assem. Bill No. 1499, *supra,* at <http://www.leginfo.ca.gov/pub/11–12/bill/asm/ab_1451–1500/ab_1499_bill_201 20627_history.html> [as of Jan. 10, 2013]; Stats.2012, ch. 30.)

As a result of the legislation, the Secretary of State was prepared to place Governor Brown's initiative to increase taxes first on the ballot for the November 2012 general election and identified as Proposition 30.

The Superior Court denied the Howard Jarvis Taxpayers Association and Jon Coupal's petition for a writ of mandate seeking an order to restore the ordering of ballot initiatives on the ballot prior to the enactment of Assembly Bill No. 1499. (Our *Children, Our Future v. Debra Bowen* (Super. Ct. Sacramento County, 2012, No. 34-

2012-80001194).) On July 9, 2012, petitioners filed the petition for a writ of mandate or other extraordinary relief in the instant case and requested a stay ordering the Secretary of State to desist and refrain from taking any further action relative to the numbering of the ballot measures, which was set to occur the following day. On July 10, 2012, we issued the alternative writ but denied the stay request. On July 30, 2012, and August 6, 2012, the Legislature, the Secretary of State, and Thomas A. Willis, the proponent of The Schools and Local Public Safety Protection Act of 2012 (Proposition 30), filed returns to the petition.

Respondent Debra Bowen and real party in interest Thomas A. Willis take no position on the constitutionality of Assembly Bill No. 1499. Their returns discuss the propriety of the stay. Thus, we refer to the Legislature as the sole real party in interest throughout this opinion.

DISCUSSION

I

The Legislature urges us to dismiss the writ proceedings as moot because the petition does not present a justiciable controversy. Since it is now too late to grant petitioners the relief they seek, that is, the reordering of the ballot propositions on the November 6, 2012, ballots, the Legislature concludes there is no likelihood the instant dispute will ever recur and we should dismiss the petition without reaching the merits of the constitutional challenge. The Legislature fails to properly characterize the narrow, but dispositive, question before us. Properly understood, the constitutional issue we resolve is one that is "'likely to recur ... yet evade review'" and is "'of continuing public interest.'" (*Howard Jarvis Taxpayers Assn. v. Bowen* (2011) 192 Cal.App.4th 110, 120, 120 Cal.Rptr.3d 865 (*Howard Jarvis I*).) We therefore exercise our discretion to address the constitutionality of Assembly Bill No. 1499.

The issue is neither as broad as petitioners contend nor as narrow as the Legislature asserts. Petitioners would have us decide whether the $1,000 appropriation was a sham and whether the Legislature has violated article IV, section 12 by finding the amendment to the Elections Code reordering ballots is "related to the budget." (Art. IV, § 12, subd. (e)(2).) But cognizant of the "appropriate role of the judiciary in a tripartite system of government" (*Schabarum v. California Legislature* (1998) 60 Cal.App.4th 1205, 1213, 70 Cal.Rptr.2d 745 (*Schabarum*)), we need not decide either of these two issues in this case.

We telegraphed the dispositive constitutional inquiry at the top of our opinion. Put another way, the question is whether the Legislature violated the meaning of article IV, section 12, subdivision (e)(2) by passing a budget with empty bills and identifying them by number, but only after the budget was passed filling them with substantive content. In its simplest formulation, the issue is whether a spot bill is a bill within the meaning of subdivision (e)(2).

This issue is justiciable precisely because it is likely to recur and it is within the most basic duty of a court to decide. "[I]t is well established that it is a judicial function to interpret the law, including the Constitution, and, when appropriately presented in a case or controversy, to declare when an act of the Legislature or the executive is beyond the constitutional authority vested in those branches." (*Schabarum, supra,* 60 Cal.App.4th at p. 1213, 70 Cal.Rptr.2d 745.) Although Proposition 30's fate was determined on November 6, 2012, the legislative practice of reserving spots for legislative content after a budget bill is passed has a long history and is very likely to continue well after Proposition 30's fate was sealed. It is up to the judiciary to carefully review the meaning of the words chosen by the voters to amend their Constitution, and it is a matter of utmost public interest whether the representatives of the people are subscribing to the letter and the spirit of Proposition 25, the constitutional amendment to the budgeting process at issue in these proceedings. (Prop. 25, as approved by voters, Gen. Elec. (Nov. 2, 2010).)

II

The Legislature insists that we must presume the constitutionality of decisions made by the two other branches of government. In the Legislature's view, we are not at liberty to interfere with a legislative decision "unless it is palpably arbitrary, that is, unless no rational set of facts supports that decision." (*Schabarum, supra,* 60 Cal.App.4th at p. 1227, 70 Cal.Rptr.2d 745.) Indeed, there is no question that the scope of judicial review is limited and derives from the venerable dispersion of power among the three coordinate branches of our government. (*Ibid.*)

As we explained in *Schabarum,* "The people, in their Constitution, may place restrictions upon the exercise of the legislative power by the Legislature but the courts may not do so without violating the fundamental separation of powers doctrine. Judicial application of clear and unequivocal constitutional restrictions on the Legislature's authority merely enforces the people's exercise of the right to place restrictions upon the Legislature. On the other hand, legislative restraint imposed through judicial interpretation of less than unequivocal language would inevitably lead to inappropriate judicial interference with the prerogatives of a coordinate branch of government. Accordingly, the only judicial standard commensurate with the separation of powers doctrine is one of strict construction to ensure that restrictions on the Legislature are in fact imposed by the people rather than by the courts in the guise of interpretation." (*Schabarum, supra,* 60 Cal.App.4th at p. 1218, 70 Cal.Rptr.2d 745.)

The Legislature's view of our role presupposes that we are reviewing a legislative decision rather than interpreting the meaning of the constitutional amendment enacted through the initiative process. Because our task is to construe the meaning of the Constitution, the rules guiding our task are well established. The overarching goal is to interpret the words so as to effectuate the electorate's intent, a project no different from attempting to effectuate the Legislature's intent in enacting a statute. We begin with the plain meaning of the words we seek to understand in the context of the entire law in which they appear. (*People v. Elliot* (2005) 37 Cal.4th 453, 478, 35 Cal.Rptr.3d 759, 122 P.3d 968.) Only if the plain meaning is obscured should we look to extrinsic aids such as the purpose of the amendment, the evil to be remedied, the policy to be achieved, and the analyses and arguments contained in the official ballot pamphlet to resolve the ambiguity. (*Howard Jarvis I, supra,* 192 Cal.App.4th at p. 122, 120 Cal.Rptr.3d 865.)

We turn then, as we must, to the words of the initiative that fundamentally changed the budgetary process. As we quoted above, article IV, section 12, subdivision (d) allows the Legislature to pass a budget by a simple majority rather than a two-thirds supermajority. In the background analysis in the Voter Information Guide, the Legislative Analyst explained: "Certain budget actions, such as a decision to change the services that a state department is mandated to provide, require changing state law. These changes often are included in 'trailer bills' that accompany passage of the budget each year." (Voter Information Guide, Gen. Elec. (Nov. 2, 2010) analysis of Prop. 25 by the Legis. Analyst, p. 52.) According to the Legislative Analyst, the lower vote requirement prescribed by Proposition 25 would also apply to trailer bills. (Voter Information Guide, at p. 53.)

We must scrutinize the meaning of two phrases limiting the Legislature's power to enact trailer bills by a majority vote. The Constitution states the general rule that appropriations must be approved by a supermajority vote. (Art. IV, §12, subd. (d).) The Constitution also provides that a statute enacted at a regular session is not effective until January 1 next following a 90-day period from the date of its enactment unless it is an urgency statute approved by a supermajority vote, a statute calling an election, or a statute providing for tax levies or appropriations for the usual current expenses of the state (the budget bill). (Cal. Const., art. IV, §8, subd. (c).) Assembly Bill No. 1499, the trailer bill here at issue, which was passed by majority vote, could not have become effective immediately and thus operative during the November 2012 general election had it not contained an appropriation and were it not for article IV, section 12, subdivision (d), which permits "appropriations in the budget bill and in other bills providing for appropriations related to the budget bill" to be passed by majority vote. The electorate recognized the need for trailer bills but restricted the Legislature's ability to pass the trailer bills by a mere majority to those appropriations "related to the budget bill." (*Ibid.*)

The electorate further limited the Legislature's opportunity to avoid the two-thirds vote requirement by expressly defining the trailer bills that would qualify for the exception. Subdivision (e)(2) of article IV, section 12 constricts the number of trailer bills by imposition of a time limitation. "For purposes of this section, 'other bills providing for appropriations related to the budget bill' shall consist only of bills identified as related to the budget in the budget bill passed by the Legislature." (Art. IV, §12, subd. (e)(2).) Thus, the bills must not only be related to the budget bill, but they must be identified at the time the budget bill is passed by the Legislature.

The Legislature argues that it complied with these constitutional requirements by appropriating $1,000 to the Secretary of State to pay for expenses, by finding that Assembly Bill No. 1499 is related to the budget, and by identifying Assembly Bill No. 1499 at the time the budget bill was passed and designating it by number in the budget bill. The problem, of course, is that Assembly Bill No. 1499 was nothing but a number, a placeholder, an empty vessel at the time the budget bill was passed. What was later to become the substantive content of Assembly Bill No. 1499 was not contained in the bill at the time it was passed. Did the electorate intend to allow the Legislature to amend spot bills after the budget bill is passed by a mere majority vote as urgency legislation? The answer resides in the plain language of article IV, section 12, subdivision (e)(2).

First is the common-sense notion that if the electorate intended to allow the Legislature to enact trailer bills by a majority vote after passing the budget bill, subdivision (e)(2) of article IV, section 12 is superfluous. Subdivision (d) of article IV, section 12 requires the subject matter of the trailer bill to be budget related. But subdivision (e)(2) further limits the trailer bills that can be enacted as urgency legislation by a simple majority vote by compelling the Legislature to identify those bills in the budget bill itself. If, as the Legislature suggests, it can comply with subdivision (e)(2) with a mere reference to blank bills, then subdivision (e)(2) does not perform any function of limiting the bills to those related to the budget at the time the budget is passed, but instead sets up a shell game whereby the Legislature can identify nothing more than a bill number in the budget bill, pass it, and only then add substance to the bill. We will not presume the electorate intended subdivision (e)(2) to create such a transparent loophole in the budgeting process.

Second, the meanings of the two key words, "identified" and "bills," used in article IV, section 12, subdivision (e)(2) belie the interpretation suggested by the Legislature. According to the Encarta World English Dictionary (1999) page 894, to identify means "to recognize somebody or something and to be able to say who or what he, she, or it is." According to the American Heritage Dictionary, Second College Edition, to identify is "[t]o ascertain the origin, nature, or definitive characteristics of." (American Heritage Dict. (2d college ed. 1985) p. 639.) The mere number of a bill does not allow legislators or voters to recognize what the bill really is, or to ascertain any of its definitive characteristics. Thus, to refer to a spot bill number is not to "identify" the bill because the content remains a secret to be disclosed only after the budget bill is passed. Yet subdivision (e)(2) clearly demands that the bill be identified at the time the bill is passed.

Moreover, the term "spot bills" is a misnomer because a spot bill does not meet the definition of a bill at all. According to the Legislature in its "Overview of Legislative Process" (<http://www.leginfo.ca.gov/bil2lawx.html> [as of Jan. 10, 2013]), "All legislation begins as an idea or concept. Ideas and concepts can come from a variety of sources. The process begins when a Senator or Assembly Member decides to author a bill." A spot bill, however, does not contain an idea or concept. Rather, it reserves a spot for a later conceived idea or concept, thereby defeating the electorate's intent to pinpoint the idea or concept at the time the budget is passed. Similarly, according to Merriam-Webster's Collegiate Dictionary (11th ed. 2006) at page 121 and the American Heritage Dictionary, *supra*, at page 178, a bill is a "draft of a law presented to a legislature for enactment" and a "draft of a proposed law presented for approval to the legislative body," respectively. A spot bill contains no "draft of a law." Very simply, a designated number does not constitute a bill within the meaning of article IV, section 12, subdivision (e)(2).

We therefore conclude that article IV, section 12 does not allow the Legislature to name empty spot bills in the budget bill and only after the budget bill is passed to fill those placeholders with content as urgency legislation. The Legislature's practice of identifying spot bills defeats the very purpose of article IV, section 12, subdivision (e)(2) to limit budget legislation to bills that appear in the budget bill by doing violence to the meaning of both "identified" and "bills." We resolve this narrow issue of constitutional interpretation because it is likely to recur during future efforts to pass an annual budget. In deference to our coordinate branches of government, we defer other questions related to "appropriations" and whether a bill is "related to the budget" to future cases in which those issues are necessary for resolution.

DISPOSITION

Petitioners' prayer for relief is narrowly tailored to a request for a writ of mandate ordering respondent Secretary of State to reorder the propositions on the November ballot, relief we can no longer provide.

Notes and Questions

1. For measures to be "bills identified as related to the budget in the budget bill" within the meaning of the constitutional provision excluding such identified bills from the supermajority vote requirement for appropriations, the bills must not only be related to the budget bill, but also they must be identified at the time the budget bill is passed by the Legislature.

2. "Spot bills" that contain no substance when the budget bill is passed are not "bills identified as related to the budget in the budget bill" within the meaning of the constitutional provision, even if the budget bill refers to the spot bills by number. (*Howard Jarvis Taxpayers Assn. v. Bowen* (2013) 212 Cal.App.4th 12.)

3. The court in this case concluded that "spot bills which remain empty of content at the time the budget is passed are not bills that can be identified within the meaning of article IV, section 12, subdivision (e)(2) of the California Constitution and enacted as urgency legislation by a mere majority vote." This ruling is based upon the court's view that a spot bill is not a bill within the meaning of subdivision (e)(2) in the above circumstance.

4. What was the basis for the Legislature's argument that the issue before the court was moot? Why did the court reject the Legislature's argument?

5. "The only judicial standard commensurate with the separation of powers doctrine is one of strict construction to ensure that restrictions on the Legislature are in fact imposed by the people rather than by the courts in the guise of interpretation." (*Schabarum*, 60 Cal.App.4th at 1218.)

6. The Legislature argued that the electorate intended to allow the Legislature to amend spot bills after the budget bill is passed by a mere majority vote as urgency legislation. The court rejected that interpretation for two major reasons. What were they?

7. What is the impact of the court's determination that a "spot bill" is not a bill at all?

D. Amendments

1. Types of Bill Amendments

In the California Legislature, there are several types of amendments that can be made to measures, including bills, resolutions and constitutional amendments. To begin, an amendment is defined by Legislative Counsel as an alteration to a bill, motion, resolution, or clause by adding, changing, substituting, or omitting language.

In order to adopt an amendment to any measure, that amendment must be submitted to Legislative Counsel for drafting. Essentially, there are three ways to make amendments to measures: author's amendments, committee amendments, and floor amendments.

Author's Amendments

Upon request of the author of a measure, the chairperson of the committee to which the measure (bill, resolution or constitutional amendment) has been referred may report to the full house (i.e., the Assembly or Senate) with the recommendation that amendments submitted by the author be adopted and the measure be reprinted as amended and re-referred to that committee.

There are several instances where an author may make "author's amendments" to his or her measure:

- Before a committee hearing — Amendments submitted by the author of the measure to the committee and submitted to the Senate or Assembly Desk by the chair of the committee to which the measure has been referred are allowed pursuant to individual committee rules. Author's amendments are permitted without the benefit of a committee hearing and recommendation.

- At a committee hearing or on the Floor — Amendments in committee or on the Floor that are supported by the author can be made to a measure.

Committee Amendments

In addition, there are "committee amendments," which are amendments proposed by a committee or a committee member in a committee hearing. Such amendments are adopted by roll call vote of the committee. They may or may not be hostile to the author.

Committee amendments to bills are considered upon their second reading, and the amendments may be adopted by a majority vote of the Members present and voting. Assembly and Senate bills amended on second reading by committee amendments are usually ordered reprinted and returned to the second reading file.

Committee amendments must be prepared, or approved as to form, by the Legislative Counsel. A specified number of copies of the committee amendments to measures are delivered to the Assembly Chief Clerk's or Senate Secretary's Desk.

Floor Amendments

Any Member may move to amend a measure during its second or third reading, and that motion to amend may be adopted by a majority vote of the Members present and voting. Amendments to a measure offered from the Floor, except committee amendments reported with them, amendments offered with a motion to amend and re-refer a measure to committee, amendments deleting any number of words, or amendments previously printed in the *Daily Journal*, are not in order unless a copy of the proposed amendments has been placed upon the desks of the Members on the Floor.

A copy of a measure that has been amended only to add coauthors is not required to be placed upon the desks of the Members. Amendments offered from the Floor during a measure's second or third reading must be prepared, or approved as to form, by the Legislative Counsel. Thereafter, a specified number of copies of the proposed amendments must be delivered to the Assembly Chief Clerk's or Senate Secretary's Desk.

Amendments from the Floor during a measure's second or third reading that would make a substantive change to it must be submitted to the Assembly or Senate Desk by the time of adjournment on the business day before the start of session on the legislative day at which the amendments are to be considered. After the amendments are submitted to the Desk, an analysis is prepared by the committee of origin and a copy of that analysis is distributed to each Member prior to the beginning of debate on adoption of the proposed amendments.

Any measure amended on the second or third reading file is then ordered reprinted and returned to the third reading file, and may not be acted on until the measure, as amended, has been on the *Daily File* for a specified period (depending on Senate or Assembly rules). This requirement does not apply to a bill that is amended to add or delete an urgency clause or to a bill that is amended to make statutory changes to implement the Budget Bill.

Under the Joint Rules, an amendment must relate to the same subject as the original bill, constitutional amendment, or resolution under consideration by the respective house. An amendment is not in order when all that would be done to the measure is the addition of a coauthor or coauthors, unless the Committee on Rules of the house in which the amendment is offered grants prior approval.

Under Assembly Rule 77.2, the Speaker may re-refer a bill to a committee for two reasons: amendments adopted on the Assembly Floor include policy not previously heard in an Assembly committee, or a bill returned to the Assembly for concurrence in Senate amendments contains policy not previously heard in an Assembly committee.

Under Senate Rule 29.10, floor amendments to Assembly Bills are handled based upon the policy committee's analysis of the floor amendments. If the floor amendments are marked "re-write" or "new bill," then special rules apply. If the analysis is marked "re-write," but the subject matter of the amendments is germane to the previous version of the bill, the measure is sent back to the Committee on Rules for consideration on re-referral.

If the Rules Committee re-refers the bill to a standing committee, the standing committee may (1) hold the bill, (2) return the bill as approved by the committee to the Senate Floor, or (3) re-refer the bill to the fiscal committee pursuant to Joint Rule 10.5. Committees may amend these bills as floor amendments only, and only during the time that amending on the Senate Floor is permitted.

If the analysis is marked "new bill," then the bill is withdrawn from the Senate Floor and sent to the Rules Committee. The Committee on Rules may either (1) hold the bill or (2) refer the bill to the appropriate standing committee, subject to all Senate Rules and Joint Rules applicable for hearing of bills.

Other Amendments

While amendments to measures can be made in one of the three specified manners previously discussed, Capitol observers hear about two other types of amendments as well. There are "hostile amendments," which can be made at either a committee hearing or on the Floor. Amendments proposed by another Member in Committee or on the Floor that are not supported by the bill's author are considered to be "hostile."

In addition, there are "gut and amend" amendments in which amendments to a measure remove the current contents in their entirety and replace them with different provisions. This last type of amendment does raise the issue of germaneness, which refers to whether a proposed amendment is relevant to the subject matter currently contained in the measure.

However, while Legislative Counsel may opine on the issue of germaneness, the determination of germaneness is decided by the Presiding Officer and, ultimately, subject to an appeal to the membership of the house. As a result, a majority of the Members of the Assembly or Senate determines whether amendments to a measure are germane or not.

2. Technical Amendments

In the California Legislature, there are technical and substantive amendments that are made to bills, whether by the bill's author or by the committee or Floor considering the particular measure. While substantive amendments deal with the core of the bill, there are also important technical amendments that need to be made to legislation sometimes to ensure that the bills are properly enacted into statutes.

According to California's Legislative Counsel, an amendment is a proposal to change the text of a bill after it has been introduced. Amendments must be submitted to the Legislative Counsel for drafting or approval. The use of chaptering amendments, double-jointing language, and contingent enactment language is often misunderstood in the legislative process. These generally are used when measures are in conflict.

In such cases, the Legislative Counsel send the authors a "conflict notification" which identifies the measures that appear to be in conflict with each other. Pursuant to this notification, "a conflict exists when two or more bills and/or constitutional amendments amend, add, repeal, or amend and renumber the same section, article, chapter, division, tittle, or heading."

Chaptering-Out Amendments

Chaptering out refers to when provisions of one chaptered bill amend the same code section(s) as another chaptered bill does. The bill with the higher chapter number prevails over the lower chapter number bill. Chaptering out can be avoided with the adoption of "double jointing" amendments to a bill prior to passage by both houses of the Legislature and signature by the Governor.

Double-Jointing Amendments

Double-jointing requires technical amendments prepared by Legislative Counsel that will prevent the amended bill from "chaptering out" the provisions of another bill when both bills amend the same code section. According to Legislative Counsel, "double-jointing amendments to a bill provide that the amended bill does not override the provisions of another bill, where both bills propose to amend the same section of law."

Unlike contingent enactment, double-jointing is not driven primarily by policy considerations. Rather, double-jointing is a solution to the technical problem known as "chaptering out." Government Code § 9605 provides that, when two or more bills amending the same code section are passed by the Legislature and signed by the Governor, the changes made by the bill with the higher chapter number (i.e., the one signed last by the Governor) prevails over the changes made by the bill with the lower chapter number.

This will occur unless the bill with the higher chapter number contains a provision to the contrary. If a bill with the higher chapter number does not contain language addressing this situation, its changes will supersede (called "chapter out") the changes made to the same code section by the bill with the lower chapter number. Double-jointing amendments are used to prevent this chaptering-out problem from occurring by allowing all of the changes to a code section proposed by two or more bills to take effect. The double-jointing language must occur in both measures in order to be effective.

Contingent Enactment Amendments

Observers should also be aware of "contingent enactment language," which is language that connects two bills so that one bill will not become operative unless the other bill also takes effect.

An example of this language was contained in AB 1676 from the 2016 Session:

> SEC. 3. Section 2.5 of this bill incorporates amendments to Section 1197.5 of the Labor Code proposed by both this bill and Senate Bill 1063. It shall only become operative if (1) both bills are enacted and become effective on or before January 1, 2017, (2) each bill amends Section 1197.5 of the Labor Code, and (3) this bill is enacted after Senate Bill 1063, in which case Section 2 of this bill shall not become operative.

How is contingent enactment language distinguished from double-jointing language? Contingent enactment language connects two bills such that one bill does not become operative unless another bill also takes effect, even if it has passed both houses and is signed by the Governor. Generally, contingent enactment language is used for policy reasons rather than to resolve technical issues. Contingency enactment language makes the policy goals contained in one bill dependent upon the policy goals contained in another bill.

On the other hand, double-jointing occurs when two bills amend the same code section but in different ways and the Legislature wants both bills to be enacted. In such a case, technical amendments are drafted which add provisions to the bill that would make all of the changes in a section of a code if each bill is chaptered. Double-jointing prevents the problem of chaptering out.

3. Amendments to a Statute

A statute may be amended by a bill that is enacted by the Legislature and signed into law by the Governor. Amendments can also be made to statutes by initiative measures proposed by the people and adopted at a statewide election.

People v. Chenze

(2002) 97 Cal.App.4th 521

OPINION

O'LEARY, J. —

Steven Allen Chenze appeals his felony conviction for battery on a custodial officer under Penal Code section 243.1. He contends section 243.1 was impliedly repealed by an amendment to section 243, which provides that a battery on a custodial officer is a misdemeanor (§ 243, subd. (b)); but if injury is inflicted, it may be sentenced as a misdemeanor or a felony (§ 243, subd. (c)(1)). He also complains the evidence was insufficient, the jury instructions were inadequate, and his counsel was incompetent. We reject his contentions and affirm.

....

I

Chenze contends he was improperly charged with violating section 243.1 because it was impliedly repealed by the subsequent amendment of section 243. In the alternative, he argues section 243 is the more specific statute and hence the only one under which he could be charged. We reject his contentions.

Chenze was charged with, and convicted of, violating section 243.1. That section was originally enacted in 1976 and provides that any battery on a custodial officer is a felony. Section 243 also sets forth punishments for battery. It provides a battery is generally punished as a simple misdemeanor (§ 243, subd. (a)), but also specifies more severe punishment for battery against various public safety officers. As amended in 1982 by Assembly Bill No. 3276 (1982–1983 Reg. Sess., hereafter AB 3276), which added custodial officers to the list of special victims (Stats. 1982, ch. 1353, § 2, p. 5048), section 243, subdivision (b), makes a battery against a custodial officer a misdemeanor subject to up to one year in county jail, and 243, subdivision (c)(1), makes the offense a wobbler — i.e., punishable as a misdemeanor or felony — if injury is inflicted.

Chenze argues that section 243.1 and section 243, as amended in 1982 by AB 3276, are in irreconcilable conflict. The older statute, section 243.1, provides that any battery against a custodial officer is a felony. But the more recent statute permits felony treatment only if injury is inflicted (§ 243, subd. (c)(1)). The 1982 amendment to section 243 does not effect an implied repeal of section 243.1.

> [2] "In recognition of the courts' constitutional role to construe, not write, statutes, "'[a]ll presumptions are against a repeal by implication.'" 'It is the duty of this court to harmonize statutes on the same subject [citations], giving effect to all parts of all statutes if possible [citation].' '[W]e will find an implied repeal "only when there is no rational basis for harmonizing the two potentially conflicting statutes [citation], and the statutes are 'irreconcilable, clearly repugnant, and so inconsistent that the two cannot have concurrent operation.'"' [¶] Significantly, whether the canon invoked is that the specific statute prevails over the general or that the latest statutory expression prevails, such canons share the requirement that the enforcement of one duly enacted statute at the expense of another on the same subject only applies when the two statutes cannot be reconciled. Restraint of judicial trespass into the legislative province is no doubt the reason for the rule that a judicially determined repeal requires a repugnancy between the two statutes that prevents their concurrent operation — a restraint that has constitutional underpinnings premised on the separation of powers." (*Medical Board v. Superior Court* (2001) 88 Cal. App. 4th 1001, 1013–1014, fns. omitted.)

The statutes are not in irreconcilable conflict as Chenze suggests. *In re Rochelle B.* (1996) 49 Cal. App. 4th 1212, discusses some of the legislative history of both provisions. The court noted that section 243.1 was part of legislation introduced to include airport officers within the definition of peace officers for purposes of enhanced punishment for batteries committed against them "and separately to provide similar increased punishment for a new crime of battery committed against 'custodial officers.' [Citation.]" (*Id.* at p. 1216.) When section 243 was amended in 1982 to include custodial officers among its special battery victims, "a report of the Assembly Committee on Criminal Justice suggested the bill 'should be amended to delete Section 243.1 of the Penal Code which is a special section referring only to custodial officers,' apparently to avoid the resulting duplication in provisions setting out aggravated penalties for batteries against 'custodial officers.' [Citation.] This suggestion was evidently ignored, with the result that two separate statutes now provide somewhat different punishments for batteries against custodial officers." (*Id.* at p. 1217, fn. omitted.)

We have obtained, and take judicial notice of, additional legislative history materials concerning AB 3276. An enrolled bill report recommending the Governor sign AB 3276, prepared by the California Youth and Adult Correctional Agency (Enrolled Bill Rep. on AB 3276 (1982 Reg. Sess.) September 20, 1982), explained the aim of the amendment was to "make the punishment for committing battery (when no injury or minor injury is inflicted) on a custodial officer the same as committing battery (when no injury or minor injury is inflicted) on a peace officer, fire fighter, or emergency medical staff." (*Id.* at p. 1.) The enrolled report's analysis explains, "According to the bill's sponsors, simple battery charges against custodial officers are rarely pursued by local prosecutors because the present law only provides for felony charges with imprisonment in a state prison. Thus, these violators are rarely, if ever, punished. By providing for the option of county jail and/or fine for such violations, proponents hope that simple battery charges will be prosecuted more vigorously. Felony battery charges can still be pursued for the more serious cases." (*Id.* at p. 2.)

In view of the fact that the Legislature amended section 243 to include custodial officers when it was aware of section 243.1, it is apparent the Legislature intended to give prosecutors a full panoply of prosecutorial options for a battery on a custodial officer. Under section 243, the offense may be punished as a misdemeanor (§ 243, subd. (b)), or a misdemeanor or felony if injury is inflicted (§ 243, subd. (c)(1)). But the Legislature also apparently envisioned that there might be circumstances under which no or only slight injury was inflicted, but felony charges would nonetheless still be appropriate. Accordingly, it did not repeal section 243.1, and has very recently amended it. Senate Bill No. 205 (SB 205), passed in September 2001 and signed by the Governor in October, made numerous nonsubstantive changes to clarify and update some 77 sections of 8 different codes. (Stats. 2001, ch. 854.) With respect to section 243.1, SB 205 changed the word "his" to "his or her." (Stats. 2001, ch. 854, § 24.) Although this was a minor amendment, it is not without significance because "[w]e does not presume that the Legislature performs idle acts...." (*Shoemaker v. Myers* (1990) 52 Cal. 3d 1, 22.) "The amendment of a statute ordinarily has the legal effect of reenacting (thus enacting) the statute as amended, including its unamended portions." (*People v. Scott* (1987) 194 Cal. App. 3d 550, 554; see Gov. Code, § 9605 [when statute is amended "portions which are not altered are to be considered as having been the law from the time when they were enacted...."].)

Chenze takes umbrage with the notion that under section 243.1 all batteries on a custodial officer may be punished as felonies, but under section 243 only those in which injury is inflicted may. [3] But "[i]t is axiomatic the Legislature may criminalize the same conduct in different ways. [Citations.]" (*People v. Superior Court (Caswell)* (1988) 46 Cal. 3d 381, 395.) The prosecutor has discretion to proceed under either of two statutes that proscribe the same conduct, but which prescribe different penalties. (*United States v. Batchelder* (1979) 442 U.S. 114, 123–125.)

Nor can Chenze find relief in the specific statute versus general statute distinction. He argues that section 243 is the "specific" statute because it distinguishes between the severity of a battery. If there is no injury, the offense is a misdemeanor; if there is injury, the offense is a wobbler. Section 243.1, he urges, is the "general" statute because it makes no distinction in severity — all batteries on custodial officers are felonies. Otherwise, the elements of both statutes are the same. Chenze points out that a violation of section 243, subdivisions (b) or (c) will always result in a violation of section 243.1. But the reverse is true as well. A violation of section 243.1, will always result in a violation of section 243, subdivisions (b) or (c). Thus, it is unclear where the distinction gets him.

Furthermore, the specific-statute-prevails-over-general-statute principle will not be applied when it appears the Legislature intended that prosecution under the general statute remains available in appropriate cases even though a more specific statute has been adopted. (*Mitchell v. Superior Court* (1989) 49 Cal. 3d 1230, 1250; *People v. Woods* (1986) 177 Cal. App. 3d 327, 333–334.) As already noted, the two statutes can be harmonized. (*People v. Price* (1991) 1 Cal. 4th 324, 385 ["Two statutes dealing with the same subject are given concurrent effect if they can be harmonized, even though one is specific and the other general"].) It is apparent the Legislature intended prosecution under section 243.1 remain an option because it did not repeal the section and has recently amended it.

The judgment is affirmed.

Notes and Questions

1. The principle that the specific statute prevails over the general statute will not be applied when it appears that the Legislature intended that prosecution under the general statute remains available in appropriate cases even though a more specific statute has been adopted. The amendment of a statute ordinarily has the legal effect of reenacting, and thus enacting, the statute as amended, including its unamended portions.

2. A court is likely to find an implied repeal of a statute only when there is no rational basis for harmonizing the two potentially conflicting statutes and the statutes are irreconcilable, clearly repugnant, and so inconsistent that the two cannot have concurrent operation.

3. What does "implied repeal" refer to in the legislative context?

4. The court decision rests on the court's determination that statutes which are not in irreconcilable conflict have the result of not implicating the implied repeal doctrine. Does the Legislature have clear guidance regarding what an "irreconcilable conflict" is?

5. The court also holds that statutes dealing with the same subject matter can remain in effect if they are "harmonized." What does that mean?

6. Why did the court reject Chenze's argument about the specific statute versus general statute distinction?

4. Definition of an Amendment

An amendment may be defined "as a legislative act designed to change some prior and existing law by adding or taking from it some particular provision. A provision which operates to repeal by implication a portion of a prior statute is not, properly speaking, an amendment. *Nor is an act which adds new sections to a code or statute an amendment* within the meaning of the provisions requiring that acts or sections revised or amended shall be re-enacted and published at length as revised or amended." (23 Cal.Jur. p. 680, § 71; emphasis added.)

Notes and Questions

1. The general rule regarding amendments is that an amendment of an act operates as a repeal of its provisions to the extent that they are changed by and rendered repugnant to the amending act. (*California Employment Commission v. Arrow Mill Company* (1941) 45 Cal.App.2d 668.)

2. An amendment can be made to both a statute and a bill. An amendment is simply a change. An amendment to a bill is a change in the bill's language, while an amendment to a statute is a change in the existing statutory provision in one of the nearly 30 codes. An amendment is a legislative act that is designed to change some prior and existing law by adding or taking from it some particular provision. (*Assets Reconstruction Corporation v. Munson* (1947) 81 Cal.App.2d 363.)

5. Impact of Amendments

Estate of Cottle

(1983) 148 Cal.App.3d 1023

OPINION

MILLER, J.

Kenneth Cory, State Controller (Controller), appeals from a decision of the superior court overruling his objection to the amended report of the inheritance tax referee with respect to the estate of Dorothy T. Cottle (Cottle). The sole issue presented on appeal is whether the provisions of Revenue and Taxation Code section 13957 (section 13957) are operative for the estates of persons dying after December 31, 1974.

Cottle died on December 7, 1981. The original report of the inheritance tax referee reported total tax due the state in the amount of $1,691,614.04. The executor, Harry J. Kaplan, objected to that report on the ground that the referee had not valued the principal asset of the estate, approximately 70 acres of land, under the provisions of section 13957 although the executor had requested such valuation. After a hearing, the court ruled that the provisions of section 13957 apply to the estates of persons dying both before and after December 31, 1974, and ordered the referee to value the property in accordance with that section.

The referee thereafter filed an amended report, valuing the property pursuant to section 13957 and reporting total tax due the state in the amount of $380,412. The Controller objected to the amended report on the ground that the provisions of section 13957 are not operative for the estates of persons dying after December 31, 1974. The objection was overruled and this appeal followed.

Section 13957, prescribing an optional method of valuing properties subject to open-space restrictions under the Williamson Act (Gov. Code, § 51200 et seq.), was added to the Revenue and Taxation Code by the Statutes of 1970, chapter 1453, section 1. Chapter 1453 contained three sections, the full text of which are set forth in the margin. Section 2 thereof declared the legislative intent that section 13957 be operative only during a transitional period, and section 3 provided that the act would not be operative for the estates of any persons dying after December 31, 1974 (hereafter the expiration date).

In 1973 section 13957 was amended to change the word "appraiser" to the word "referee." (Stats. 1973, ch. 78, § 9, p. 135.) Chapter 78 contained 25 sections and was entitled "[a]n act relating to the maintenance of various codes...." It amended various provisions of the Public Utilities Code, the Revenue and Taxation Code and the Vehicle Code. The executor argues, and the court below apparently agreed, that because section 3 of chapter 1453 was not repeated in chapter 78, it was repealed. We do not agree and accordingly reverse the order overruling the objection to the amended report.

The Controller contends that chapter 78 in no way affected section 3 of chapter 1453, and that the legislative intent, which was to make no substantive changes in the law in enacting chapter 78, supports that construction. The executor contends that in enacting chapter 78, the Legislature amended section 13957 and expressly omitted therefrom the expiration date, thereby repealing the expiration date; that article IV, section 9 of the California Constitution and Government Code section 9605 require that construction; and that the legislative intent was not to make only non-substantive changes through the enactment of chapter 78.

The executor erroneously treats chapter 1453 as only one section, section 13957 of the Revenue and Taxation Code. Chapter 1453 actually consisted of three sections. ... Section 1 of that chapter did add section 13957 to the Revenue and Taxation Code. Sections 2 and 3, declaring legislative intent and providing for the expiration date, respectively, were uncodified provisions. They were not made part of the Revenue and Taxation Code. Section 9 of chapter 78 amended only section 13957 of the Revenue and Taxation Code, which had been added by section 1 of chapter 1453. It did not affect the uncodified provisions contained in sections 2 and 3 of that chapter.

Neither article IV, section 9 of the Constitution nor Government Code section 9605 requires a different result.

Article IV, section 9 provides in relevant part "[a] section of a statute may not be amended unless the section is re-enacted as amended." In construing a similar provision of former article IV, section 24 of the Constitution, the court in *People v. Western Fruit Growers* (1943) 22 Cal. 2d 494, 501 [140 P.2d 13], held that "[T]he Legislature may use either an existing statute or a section of it as the basis for changing an existing law. The decision as to which unit shall be used is one to be made by the Legislature in its discretion.... The determination of the Legislature will not be questioned by the courts...." The language in the title and in each section of a new enactment may often disclose which unit, act or section, the Legislature used. (*Id.*, at p. 502.) Where the only portion of an act which is amended is one section thereof, all the Constitution requires is that the whole of that section be reenacted and published as amended. (*Estate of Campbell* (1904) 143 Cal. 623, 627 [77 P. 674] [also construing former art. IV, § 24 of the Constitution].)

Here, chapter 78 was declared in its title to be an act relating to the maintenance of various codes. (Stats. 1973, ch. 78, p. 133.) Section 9 recited that it amended section 13957 of the Revenue and Taxation Code. (*Id.*, at p. 135.) Section 13957 was reenacted as amended. The unit the Legislature chose to amend was one section of a code, not the entire act contained in chapter 1453. Thus, it did not repeal sections 2 and 3 of chapter 1453 in enacting chapter 78.

Government Code section 9605 is equally unavailing to the executor. It provides in relevant part that "Where a section or part of a statute is amended, *it* is not to be considered as having been repealed and reenacted in the amended form. The portions which are not altered are to be considered as having been the law from the time when they were enacted; the new provisions are to be considered as having been enacted at the time of the amendment; and the omitted portions are to be considered as having been repealed at the time of the amendment." (Italics added.) The executor deems the pronoun "it" in the first sentence of this section to apply to the antecedent "statute," as opposed to applying to the antecedent "section" or "part." Such an interpretation would lead to absurd results, for every time the Legislature sought to amend a section of a code it would be required to restate all sections of the act which had enacted the section in question, a task which would often encompass dozens of sections and obviously be unmanageable for the legislative body.

A statute should be interpreted to produce a result which is reasonable. (*Ivens v. Simon* (1963) 212 Cal. App. 2d 177, 181 [27 Cal. Rptr. 801].) [4] We therefore hold that Government Code section 9605, correctly read, provides that if a section of a statute is amended and a portion of the section is omitted, that portion is repealed. It does not require that an amendment of one section of a statute result in the repeal of all other sections of the original enacting statute which are not restated in the amendatory act.

The executor seeks to rely upon *Rudley v. Tobias* (1948) 84 Cal. App. 2d 454 [190 P.2d 984], and *Shearer v. Flannery* (1924) 68 Cal. App. 91 [228 P. 549]. Neither is supportive of his position. In both cases an amendment was made to one section of a code and omitted portions were deemed repealed. The amendments did not repeal provisions of law which had not been part of the former or predecessor code sections involved.

Finally, an examination of legislative intent discloses that chapter 78 was not intended to repeal the expiration date set forth in chapter 1453. The Thirteenth Report on Legislation Necessary to Maintain the Codes submitted to the Legislature by the Office of the Legislative Counsel, pursuant to Government Code section 10242, on December 31, 1972, recommended, inter alia, that the term "appraiser" be changed to "referee" in sections 13957, 14533 and 16537 of the Revenue and Taxation Code (at p. 19). The report described the recommendations contained therein as "for non-substantive changes in the statutes." (*Id.*, at p. 2.) Such recommendations comport with the requirement of Government Code section 10242 that "The Legislative Counsel shall advise the Legislature from time to time as to legislation necessary to maintain the codes…. Such recommendations shall include such restatement *without substantive change* as will best serve clearly and correctly to express the existing provisions of the law." (Italics added.)

Chapter 78 was enacted in 1973. The Fourteenth Report on Legislation Necessary to Maintain the Codes (Office of the Legislative Counsel, Mar. 31, 1974, p. 3) reported that chapter 78 of the 1973 Statutes was one of the bills enacted for correction of errors specified in the prior report. Thus, it is clear that chapter 78 was intended to change only the term "appraiser" to "referee" in section 13957 as part of a routine code maintenance bill, not to bring about any substantive change such as the repeal of the expiration date set forth in section 3 of chapter 1453.

The order overruling the Controller's objection to the amended report of the inheritance tax referee is reversed and the cause is remanded for further proceedings consistent with the views expressed herein.

ROUSE, Acting P.J., and SMITH, J., concurred.

Notes and Questions

1. The Government Code (in § 9605) does not require that an amendment of one section of a statute result in repeal of all other sections of the original enacting statute which are not restated in the amending act. Otherwise, the court explained, "such an interpretation would lead to absurd results, for every time the Legislature sought to amend a section of a code it would be required to restate all sections of the act which had enacted the section in question, a task which would often encompass dozens of sections and obviously be unmanageable for the legislative body."

2. The court also explained that, when an amendment was made to one section of a code and omitted some portions of that section, those omitted portions were deemed repealed. In addition, any amendments that did not repeal provisions of law which had not been part of the former or predecessor code sections involved are deemed to not have been made.

6. Multiple Amendments in a Single Bill

Californians for an Open Primary v. McPherson

(2006) 38 Cal.4th 735

OPINION

GEORGE, C.J.

We granted review to address an issue of first impression: the proper interpretation of California Constitution, article XVIII, section 1 (article XVIII, section 1), which requires in its second sentence that when the Legislature proposes an amendment of the state Constitution, "[e]ach amendment shall be so prepared and submitted that it can be voted on separately."

We conclude, as did the Court of Appeal below, and consistent with our provision's language and history and more than a century of out-of-state decisions construing the essentially identical provisions of nearly 30 other state constitutions, that the separate-vote provision is a *limitation* upon legislative power to submit constitutional amendments to the voters.

We disagree, however, with the Court of Appeal below, concerning the applicable test for determining whether, in a given case, the Legislature's submission of constitutional changes in a single measure violates article XVIII, section 1. In addressing that question, the Court of Appeal followed a minority rule that recently was reinvigorated by *Armatta v. Kitzhaber* (1998) 327 Ore. 250 [959 P.2d 49] (*Armatta*) — a decision in which the Oregon Supreme Court construed its state's separate-vote provision as establishing a test different from *and stricter than* the traditional test employed by courts under a related constitutional provision also found in most state constitutions — the "single subject rule" (see Cal. Const., art. II, §8, subd. (d); *id.*, art. IV, § 9). Unlike the Oregon court and a few other courts that have followed *Armatta* under their respective state constitutions, we find no basis in the history of the California Constitution for such a conclusion, and hence we shall follow the approach that is, and has been, the majority rule for nearly 130 years: the separate-vote provision should be construed consistent with its kindred provision, the single subject provision.

So, construing the separate-vote provision of article XVIII, section 1, we conclude that the Legislature's proposed submission, in a single constitutional amendment, of two changes to the state Constitution that are not germane to a common theme, purpose, or subject, violated the constitutional separate-vote requirement. Accordingly, we affirm this aspect of the judgment rendered by the Court of Appeal, although for reasons different from those relied upon by that court.

We also address the question of remedy. The Court of Appeal, by a two-to-one vote, ordered the Secretary of State to separate the two proposed constitutional changes at issue in this matter into two measures for submission to the voters. When ruling upon this matter in the weeks preceding the November 2004 general election (and only days before the deadline for the printing of ballot materials), we declined to disturb the Court of Appeal's order, and the voters of this state subsequently adopted each separate constitutional amendment. Although we conclude that the Court of Appeal erred by ordering bifurcation, we find it unnecessary and inappropriate to invalidate either of these separately submitted and approved constitutional amendments.

I

. . . .

II

Article XVIII, addressing the subject of amending and revising the Constitution, is comprised of four sections. The first section — the second sentence of which we must construe in this case — provides: "The Legislature by rollcall vote entered in the journal, two-thirds of the membership of each house concurring, may propose an amendment or revision of the Constitution and in the same manner may amend or withdraw its proposal. *Each amendment shall be so prepared and submitted that it can be voted on separately.*" (Art. XVIII, § 1, italics added.) Although this provision (hereafter sometimes referred to as the separate-vote provision) — or one essentially identical to it — has existed in this article since it was added to our Constitution in 1879, no California decision has defined the scope of the provision.

The next three sections of article XVIII address related matters. Section 2 concerns revision by a Constitutional Convention. It provides: "The Legislature by rollcall vote entered in the journal, two-thirds of the membership of each house concurring, may submit at a general election the question whether to call a convention to revise the Constitution. If the majority vote yes on that question, within 6 months the Legislature shall provide for the convention. Delegates to a constitutional convention shall be voters elected from districts as nearly equal in population as may be practicable." (Cal. Const., art. XVIII, § 2.) Section 3 of article XVIII of the Constitution simply confirms what already is stated in the state Constitution, article II, section 8, subdivision (b), by providing: "The electors may amend the Constitution by initiative." Section 4 specifies, among other things, the effective date of amendments or revisions. It provides: "A proposed amendment or revision shall be submitted to the electors and if approved by a majority of votes thereon takes effect the day after the election unless the measure provides otherwise. If provisions of 2 or more measures approved at the same election conflict, those of the measure receiving the highest affirmative vote shall prevail." (*Id.*, art. XVIII, § 4.)

A

On its face, the separate-vote provision appears to *limit* legislative power. The Legislature, however, insists that this provision in fact has a different and quite opposite purpose and effect. It argues that instead of limiting legislative authority to package disparate proposed changes in a single measure, the separate-vote provision actually guarantees that however the Legislature deems it appropriate to combine or separate proposed changes, those changes will be submitted to the voters in the chosen manner. Specifically, the Legislature asserts that the word "amendment" in the second sentence of article XVIII, section 1 "has always been" construed to "mean a Senate Constitutional Amendment ... or an Assembly Constitutional Amendment, with the resulting assurance that when more than one [Senate Constitutional Amendment] or [Assembly Constitutional Amendment] appears on the same ballot each such legislative constitutional amendment will be prepared and submitted so that it 'can be voted on separately.'" The Legislature concludes: "*Pursuant to this ... view of* [article XVIII,] *section 1, the Legislature, by two-thirds vote of each house, is free to combine disparate substantive changes within a single legislative constitutional amendment for submission to the people.... The 'separate vote' requirement guarantees that neither the Executive* [that is, the Secretary of State] *nor succeeding legislative majorities may interfere with these determinations.*" (Italics added.) In other words, as Californians for an Open Primary observes, the Legislature views the separate-vote provision as not a limitation upon itself, but instead as a restraint upon hypothetical "renegade Secretaries of State" who might take it upon themselves either to combine separate measures that the Legislature has determined should be submitted to the voters separately, or to separate measures that the Legislature has determined should be submitted to the voters as a package.

As explained below, we do not find support for the Legislature's view in the language of the second sentence of article XVIII, section 1, or in the provision's history or the case law construing that provision or similar provisions in the charters of our sister states. Nor, contrary to the Legislature's position, do we find support for its construction of the provision in past legislative constitutional amendment measures adopted by the electorate, or in the circumstance that, since 1962, the Legislature has had authority to propose not only amendments to the Constitution, but revisions as well.

1

We first review the text of the provision. Its first sentence, addressing the power to propose a constitutional amendment or revision, is directed expressly to "the Legislature." The second sentence, which we must construe in the present case (providing that "[e]ach amendment shall be so prepared and submitted that it can be voted on separately") also appears to be directed to the Legislature. There is no indication in the language of the provision that the second sentence was directed toward an unidentified entity within the executive branch, such as the Secretary of State.

The Legislature insists nevertheless that the word "amendment" in the second sentence of article XVIII, section 1 (the separate-vote provision) means or refers to the legislative *vehicle* employed by the Legislature, that is, a resolution proposing a Senate Constitutional Amendment or an Assembly Constitutional Amendment. We note, however, that the same word ("amendment") also appears in the first sentence of section 1 of article XVIII. In that context it is clear the word refers not to the legislative *vehicle* for proposing a change, but instead to the *substantive content* of such a proposal. Although it is possible that the word "amendment" might be employed in a different sense in the second sentence of article XVIII, section 1, as explained below there is no evidence that the drafters or the electorate in 1879 or thereafter ever so intended, or that they even contemplated the construction that the Legislature now places upon the provision.

In another respect we find the language used in the provision to be at odds with the Legislature's interpretation. The provision's use of the word "submitted" ("[e]ach amendment shall be so prepared and *submitted* that it can be voted on separately" (art. XVIII, § 1, italics added)) seems most naturally to refer to the Legislature, and not to an entity such as the Secretary of State. Even though the Legislature does not itself physically "submit" anything to the voters, section 2 of the same article states that "the Legislature ... may submit" (*id.*, § 2) to the voters a call for a constitutional convention — thereby demonstrating that, insofar as this article of the Constitution is concerned, the word "submit" must be understood to cover the general process of placing a legislative proposal before the voters.

2

Mindful of the admonitions set forth by Justice Landau in his article, *A Judge's Perspective on the Use and Misuse of History in State Constitutional Interpretation* (2004) 38 Val.U. L.Rev. 451 (Landau), we next review the history of California's separate-vote provision. Former article X of the 1849 Constitution set forth the procedures for the Legislature to propose one or more amendments to the Constitution (*id.*, § 1), or to revise the entire Constitution (*id.*, § 2). Former article X, section 1 allowed the Legislature to propose a constitutional amendment based upon a majority vote of both houses of two successive legislative sessions, but it placed no limitation upon the manner in which the submission was to be made to the electorate. Indeed, the former provision did the opposite: it made it the "duty of the Legislature to submit such proposed amendment or amendments to the people, *in such manner* and at such time *as the Legislature shall prescribe.*" (Cal. Const. of 1849, art. X, § 1, italics added.)

....

In addition, in view of the introductory phrase included in article XVIII as adopted in 1879 ("it shall be the duty of the Legislature to submit") — a phrase that appeared in some form in almost every other constitution of the day — it seems highly improbable that the drafters viewed the following sentence, which contained the separate-vote provision, as imposing a limitation on any entity other than the Legislature.

3

We next review our case law's interpretation of the separate-vote provision of article XVIII, section 1. This court has addressed the provision only once, in *Wright v. Jordan* (1923) 192 Cal. 704 [221 P. 915] (*Wright*). As explained below, in doing so we repeatedly characterized the provision as imposing a "limitation" upon the Legislature, and not, as the Legislature now argues, a protection of a legislative prerogative and/or a limitation upon the Secretary of State.

The petitioner in *Wright* (the City Clerk of San Diego) sued the Secretary of State (Frank C. Jordan) to compel him to recognize and file the results of an election concerning the consolidation of the City of San Diego and the City of East San Diego. (*Wright, supra*, 192 Cal. 704, 706.) Secretary of State Jordan refused to take this action on the ground that the statute under which the consolidation election had proceeded was unconstitutional because, he asserted, it in turn was based upon an improperly adopted amendment to article XI, former section 8 1/2, subdivision 7 of the Constitution. That constitutional amendment (governing consolidation elections) earlier had been adopted by the electorate as a constitutional *initiative* under the power conferred upon the voters by constitutional amendment in 1911. The Secretary of State argued in *Wright* that the prior amendment to article XI, former section 8 1/2, subdivision 7, was void because it had not been adopted "in the manner required by the provisions of section 1 of article XVIII" (*Wright, supra*, 192 Cal. at p. 711) —

that is, in the manner required of *legislative* constitutional amendments. In rejecting the Secretary of State's argument, this court in *Wright* quoted article XVIII, section 1's separate-vote provision and then noted that, with regard to the people's authority to adopt constitutional amendments through the *initiative* process, "no such limitation as is embodied in the provisions of section 1 of article XVIII ... can be found." (*Wright, supra*, 192 Cal. at p. 711.) The court in *Wright* twice more characterized section 1 of article XVIII as setting forth a "limitation" (*Wright, supra*, 192 Cal. at p. 711), and thereafter acknowledged that the amendment to article XI, former section 8 1/2, subdivision 7 "effectuate[d] changes in several already existing articles, sections, and clauses of the constitution, and ... these [were] not presented in the form of separate amendments." (*Wright, supra*, 192 Cal. at p. 712.) Nevertheless, the court reiterated, there had been no need to comply with article XVIII section 1's separate-vote requirement, because, again, that requirement did not apply to amendments proposed by initiative. (*Wright, supra*, 192 Cal. at p. 712.)

Thereafter, the court commented in dictum that even if the prior constitutional amendment had been proposed to the electorate not as an initiative measure but instead by the Legislature, the prior amendment may have satisfied the separate-vote requirement: "[W]e are not at all satisfied that under a liberal interpretation of section 1 of article XVIII of the constitution the legislature might not have itself proposed and presented to the people for their adoption in the form of a single amendment to the constitution the precise measure embodied in this initiative amendment, even though its effect might be to change or abrogate other portions of the constitution not embodied in the particular article thereof thus sought to be amended." (*Wright, supra*, 192 Cal. 704, 712–713.)

We conclude, contrary to the Legislature's suggestion, that *Wright, supra*, 192 Cal. 704, far from supporting the Legislature's interpretation of the separate-vote provision, does the opposite and supports the view that the provision imposes a limitation upon the Legislature.

    . . . .

5

The Legislature insists, nevertheless, that its view — that the separate-vote provision protects the Legislature's right to package constitutional amendment measures as it sees fit — is supported by (i) contemporaneous and ongoing practices, and (ii) the circumstance that, since 1962, the Legislature has had authority to propose not only constitutional amendments, but also constitutional revisions. As explained below, we are not persuaded.

a

The Legislature cites approximately 30 constitutional amendment measures that it submitted to the electorate between 1892 and 2004, and argues that many if not most of those measures would have failed the strict test proposed below by the Court of Appeal. This circumstance, according to the Legislature, demonstrates the propriety of its own interpretation of the separate-vote provision.

We agree generally that long-established and adhered-to practice with regard to a constitutional provision informs a court's interpretation of such a provision. (E.g., *People v. Southern Pac. Co.* (1930) 209 Cal. 578, 595 [290 P. 25] ["'contemporaneous and long continued construction'" of a constitutional provision "'by the legislature is entitled to great deference'"].) Indeed, early out-of-state cases so proceeded in arriving at a lenient and accommodating—rather than a narrow and strict—construction of their own separate-vote provisions. (E.g., *State v. Timme* (1882) 54 Wis. 318 [11 N.W. 785, 791–793] (*Timme*).) On the facts of the present case, however, we find the Legislature's argument unpersuasive.

The Legislature cites nothing to suggest that, at any time prior to the commencement of this litigation, the Legislature—by rule, legal opinion, or otherwise—actually held the presently stated view of the constitutional provision. Moreover, as the Court of Appeal below observed, "we do not know that any of [the Legislature's] examples [of prior constitutional amendment measures] violate section 1 for no cases have been brought to test them." In any event, even assuming that, as the Legislature suggests, some of the prior legislative constitutional amendment measures that were adopted by the electorate might have failed the strict separate-vote test endorsed by the Court of Appeal below, as we shall explain *post*, part II.B.3, we do not endorse that strict test or anything like it. The Legislature does not argue that any prior measure cited would fail under scrutiny of the separate-vote provision as we shall construe it in this case.

In conclusion on this point—and contrary to the Legislature's argument based upon past practices—we find it highly improbable that, despite every other jurisdiction's long-standing view of the separate-vote provision as a *limitation* upon the Legislature's authority to submit proposed constitutional amendments, California's drafters, electors, and Legislature ever did (or reasonably could) view our own provision otherwise.

b

The Legislature argues that, even if, for the first eight decades of its existence, the separate-vote provision in California (like the essentially identical provision in numerous other jurisdictions) operated as a limitation upon the Legislature, that restraint effectively and silently was abrogated when, in 1962, the electorate amended the first sentence of article XVIII, section 1—or at least when, in 1970, the electorate adopted the present version of article XVIII, section 1. In order to address the Legislature's contention, we must in some detail review the history upon which it relies.

Like many other states in the late 1950's and early 1960's, the California Legislature in 1956 authorized and thereafter appointed a Citizens Legislative Advisory Commission to make recommendations for legislative improvement and reform. (See, e.g., Advisory Com., Final Rep. to Cal. Leg. and Citizens of Cal. (Mar. 1962), p. 9.) One of the major recommendations of the Advisory Commission was that the Constitution should be changed to allow for the Legislature to propose not only amendments or the calling of a constitutional convention to revise the charter, but also to permit the Legislature to propose a wholesale or partial constitutional revision without the need to call a constitutional convention. (*Id.*, at pp. 42–44.) The Legislature agreed with this recommendation and in resolution chapter 222 (Assem. Const. Amend. No. 14, Stats. 1961 (1961 Reg. Sess.) res. ch. 222, pp. 5013–5014) proposed to alter the *first* sentence of then-existing article XVIII, section 1, by allowing the Legislature to propose not only amendments to the Constitution, but also revisions. The resulting measure was submitted to the electorate at the November 1962 general election as Proposition 7. The ballot materials submitted to the voters concerning that matter did not suggest that the proposed amendment in any manner would change the meaning or effect of the unaltered *second* sentence of the section — the sentence at issue in this case, which is directed exclusively to the question of legislative proposals for *amendment* to the Constitution and which contains the separate-vote provision.

Prior case law had established that pursuant to article XVIII, section 1, as adopted in 1879, the Legislature had authority to propose only amendments to the Constitution and not revisions. (*Livermore v. Waite* (1894) 102 Cal. 113, 118 [36 P. 424] (*Livermore*); see also *McFadden v. Jordan* (1948) 32 Cal.2d 330, 333–334 [196 P.2d 787] [the people have no authority to propose constitutional revision by initiative].)

The ballot pamphlet supplied to the electorate included the following analysis by the Legislative Counsel, highlighting the difference between a constitutional amendment and a revision: "This measure [that is, Proposition 7] … would authorize the Legislature by a vote of two-thirds of the members elected to each house to propose complete or partial 'revisions' of the Constitution for approval or rejection by the people. Under existing provisions, the Legislature can only propose *'amendments,' that is[,] measures which propose changes specific and limited in nature. 'Revisions,' i.e., proposals which involve broad changes in all or a substantial part of the Constitution*, can presently be proposed only by convening a constitutional convention." (Ballot Pamp., Gen. Elec. (Nov. 6, 1962) analysis of Prop. 7, p. 13, italics added.)

Specifically, even after amendment of article XVIII, section 1, in 1962, the second sentence of that section *continued* to read, as it had since 1879: "Should more amendments than one be submitted at the same election they shall be so prepared and distinguished, by numbers or otherwise, that each can be voted on separately." (1 Stats. 1963, p. ciii.)

Thereafter, in 1963, the Legislature appointed a Constitution Revision Commission (Revision Commission), which undertook to analyze and propose to the Legislature revisions to the entire state Constitution. (See generally Sumner, *Constitution Revision by Commission in California* (1972) 1 Western St.U. L.Rev. 48.) Based upon the Revision Commission's recommendations, the Legislature in 1966 invoked its new power to propose revision of the Constitution and submitted for the electorate's approval resolution chapter 139 (Assem. Const. Amend. No. 13, Stats. 1966, 1st Ex. Sess. 1966, res. ch. 139, pp. 960–982) (hereafter Resolution 139) — an omnibus proposed revision of articles III, IV, V, VI, VII, VIII, XIII, and XXII of the Constitution. Prior to setting forth the various proposed changes, Resolution 139 provided: "*Resolved by the Assembly, the Senate concurring*, That the Legislature of the State of California … hereby proposes to the people of the State of California that portions of the Constitution of the state be *revised* as follows: …" (Assem. Const. Amend. No. 13,

Stats. 1966, 1st Ex. Sess. 1966, res. ch. 139, p. 960, second italics added.) Thereafter Resolution 139 set forth the Legislature's proposed amendments (including numerous repeals, modifications, and additions) to the eight disparate articles mentioned above.

Consistent with the Legislature's characterization of Resolution 139 as a proposed revision of the Constitution, the Attorney General's ballot title for the measure commenced as follows: "Constitutional Revision. Legislative Constitutional amendment. ..." (Ballot Pamp., Gen. Elec. (Nov. 8, 1966) analysis of Prop. 1-a, p. 1.) The Secretary of State designated this omnibus measure as Proposition 1-a (*ibid.*), and the electorate adopted it at the November 1966 general election.

. . . .

For different reasons we reach the same conclusion with respect to Proposition 16 on the November 1970 ballot, which resulted in the present version of article XVIII, section 1. As noted above, that measure was characterized by the Legislature in Resolution 187 as an amendment; the Attorney General titled the resulting proposition as such, and the voters adopted that proposition as such without any reason to believe that in doing so they were endorsing a new or changed meaning for the separate-vote provision. Although Proposition 16, presented as an amendment and not as a partial revision, *was* subject to the separate-vote provision — and although, as the Legislature suggests, that measure might have violated the separate-vote provision if judged under the strict test proposed by the Court of Appeal below — we shall, for reasons explained *post*, part II.B.3, reject the exacting test applied by the lower court. Under the test that we shall confirm in this case — essentially the same test employed by the vast majority of our sister-state jurisdictions for approximately 125 years — 1970's Proposition 16 is not called into question under the separate-vote provision of article XVIII, section 1.

The Legislature, after describing the changes made by Proposition 16, asserts that "[i]n a loose sense these changes all relate to elections. They are not, however, 'functionally related.'" But even assuming, as the Legislature asserts, that the various changes proposed in Proposition 16 were not "functionally related," as we shall explain *post*, part II.2.c, they did not need be. Moreover, the provisions of that measure not only were related to the general subject of elections (as the Legislature concedes), they shared a more focused commonality: each change in article XVIII and in former article IV, section 24, subdivision (a) of the Constitution (present Cal. Const., art. n, § 10, subd. (a)) related to election procedures for amending and revising the Constitution. As we shall explain *post*, part II.2.C, it is sufficient, under the separate-vote requirement, that provisions be *reasonably germane* to a common theme, purpose, or subject — and all parts of Proposition 16 clearly were reasonably germane to the subject of amending and revising the Constitution.

In conclusion on this point, we find no support in the language or history of the separate-vote provision, or in any of numerous decisions of our sister states construing their own essentially identical provisions, that would lead us to adopt the Legislature's construction of article XVIII, section 1, as protecting an asserted legislative right to combine into one package disparate and unrelated changes to the Constitution. Nor can we agree with the Legislature that, in light of its ability, since 1962, to propose *revisions* as well as amendments, the limitation upon legislatively proposed *amendments* imposed by the separate-vote provision no longer is relevant or effective. The provision's words and history, its construction by the Revision Commission, and the uniform construction of such provisions in other jurisdictions instead reveals that it was intended to be, and remains, a limitation upon the power of the Legislature to submit constitutional amendments to the voters.

Because, as noted above, the Legislature presented Resolution 103 as an amendment and not as a "revision" or "partial revision," we need not address the problem of defining the contours of those terms. Furthermore, as the parties observed at oral argument, the definitional issue, which is not fully briefed in this case, is a potentially difficult one.

We next consider the nature and scope of that limitation, and the test to be applied in discerning whether a violation of the separate-vote provision has occurred.

B

Although we reject the Legislature's interpretation of article XVIII, section 1, and find instead that the provision restricts legislative authority to submit disparate proposed constitutional changes in a single measure, as further explained we also disagree with the position taken by Californians for an Open Primary in its briefs, and the Court of Appeal below, that we should endorse a recent trend commenced by the Oregon Supreme Court in *Armatta, supra,* 959 P.2d 49, and construe our separate-vote provision as requiring a test different from *and stricter than* the traditional test employed under the related constitutional single subject rule. For the reasons that follow, we find no basis for that position in the words of our Constitution's separate-vote provision or in the history of our charter. We also find no rationale for concluding — as we would have to, were we to construe the provision as proposed — that the Constitution should be interpreted in a manner that would impose a restraint upon the *Legislature's* power to submit constitutional amendments to the voters greater than that imposed upon the *people* through the initiative process.

Instead, we shall adopt the approach that is, and has been, the majority rule in our sister state jurisdictions for approximately 125 years: the separate-vote provision should be construed consistently with its kindred provision, the single subject rule. We already have rejected, in part II.1, the Legislature's argument that the word "amendment" in article XVIII, section 1 ("[e]ach amendment shall be so prepared and submitted that it can be voted on separately") refers to the legislative *vehicle* (the resolution proposing the constitutional amendment) by which the Legislature transmits a proposed amendment to the Secretary of State for eventual submission on the ballot. We shall explain below that the word "amendment" as used in the provision refers to a substantive change or group of substantive changes that are *reasonably germane* to a common theme, purpose, or subject. If (as in this case) the Legislature proposes to the electorate in such a resolution that the Constitution should be amended in a manner that presents in a single measure substantive changes that are not reasonably germane to a common theme, purpose, or subject, the presentation of such a single measure to the voters as an amendment will violate the separate-vote provision found in the second sentence of article XVIII, section 1.

1

The California Constitution, like that of most states, long has contained not only the separate-vote provision at issue in this case, but also a related "single subject" provision. Indeed, California has two single subject provisions: one, which has existed in the California Constitution since 1849, requires that *statutes* "embrace but one subject" (Cal. Const., art. IV, §9); the other, added to the Constitution in 1948, extends that rule to *initiatives* proposing either statutory or constitutional changes. (Cal. Const., art. II, §8, subd. (d) ["An initiative measure embracing more than one subject may not be submitted to the electors or have any effect"].)

Although we have not previously construed our own separate-vote provision (except in the dictum of *Wright, supra*, 192 Cal. 704, 712–713 …), we long have construed our two single subject provisions in an accommodating and lenient manner so as not to unduly restrict the Legislature's or the people's right to package provisions in a single bill or initiative. (E.g., *Fair Political Practices Com. v. Superior Court* (1979) 25 Cal.3d 33, 39 [157 Cal.Rptr. 855, 599 P.2d 46] *(Fair Political Practices Commission); Perry v. Jordan* (1949) 34 Cal.2d 87, 92–93 [207 P.2d 47], and cases cited [construing identically the statutory and initiative versions of the constitutional single subject provisions].) We have found the single subject rules to have been satisfied so long as challenged provisions meet the test of being *reasonably germane* to a common theme, purpose, or subject. (*Senate of the State of Cal. v. Jones* (1999) 21 Cal.4th 1142, 1157 [90 Cal.Rptr.2d 810, 988 P.2d 1089] *(Jones); Legislature v. Eu* (1991) 54 Cal.3d 492, 512 [286 Cal.Rptr. 283, 816 P.2d 1309] *(Eu); Brosnahan v. Brown* (1982) 32 Cal.3d 236, 243–253 [186 Cal.Rptr. 30, 651 P.2d 274] *(Brosnahan); Harbor v. Deukmejian* (1987) 43 Cal.3d 1078, 1099 [240 Cal.Rptr. 569, 742 P.2d 1290]; *Perry, supra*, 34 Cal.2d at pp. 92–93.)

In setting forth the "reasonably germane" test, several of our prior decisions have stated or repeated language suggesting the standard requires that each of a measure's parts be reasonably germane *to one another* as well as reasonably germane *to a common theme, purpose, or subject*. (See, e.g., *Brosnahan, supra*, 32 Cal.3d 236, 245 ["'an initiative measure does not violate the single-subject requirement if … all of its parts are "reasonably germane" to each other,' and to the general purpose or object of the initiative" (italics omitted)]; *Eu, supra*, 54 Cal.3d 492, 512, quoting *Brosnahan; Jones, supra*, 21 Cal.4th 1142, 1157, quoting *Eu*.) In *applying* the reasonably germane test, however, our decisions uniformly have considered only whether each of the parts of a measure is reasonably germane to a common theme, purpose, or subject, and have not *separately* or *additionally* required that each part also be reasonably germane to one another. (See, e.g., *Eu, supra*, 54 Cal.3d at pp. 512–514; *Brosnahan, supra*, 32 Cal.3d at pp. 245–253; *Fair Political Practices Commission, supra*, 25 Cal.3d 33, 38–43; see also *Jones, supra*, 21 Cal.4th at p. 1158 ['The single-subject rule … simply precludes drafters from combining, in a single [measure], provisions that are not reasonably germane to a common theme or purpose" (italics omitted)].) The governing decisions' consistent application of the standard suggests that a measure's separate provisions have been considered to be reasonably germane *to each other* within the meaning of the standard so long as *all* of the provisions are reasonably germane to a single common theme, purpose, or subject. For clarity and simplicity, we believe it is appropriate to describe the test, as set forth in the text above, as simply requiring that the separate provisions of a measure be reasonably germane to a common theme, purpose, or subject. (At the same time, of course, our decisions also establish that the single subject provision "obviously forbids joining disparate provisions which appear germane only to topics of excessive generality such as 'government' or 'public welfare.'" [*Brosnahan, supra,* 32 Cal.3d at p. 253; see, e.g., *Jones, supra,* 21 Cal.4th at pp. 1161–1162.].)

Most of our sister states have similarly and leniently construed their own single subject provisions. And, significantly, for more than a century a clear majority of the nearly 30 other jurisdictions that have a separate-vote provision similar to ours have similarly construed their separate-vote provisions, upholding amendments against challenges so long as the measure's provisions are *reasonably germane* to a common theme, purpose, or subject. See, e.g., Dubois Feeney, Lawmaking by Initiative (1998) page 138; but see Lowenstein, *Initiatives and the New Single Subject Rule* (2002) 1 Elec. L.J. 35 (criticizing recent decisions, some of which employ a more exacting single subject test and find violations of states' single subject provisions and/or separate-vote provisions); Miller, *Courts as Watchdogs of the Washington State Initiative Process* (2001) 24 Seattle U. L.Rev. 1053, 1079–1083 (noting with approval the same recent cases).

. . . .

III

The Legislature does not argue that Resolution 103's two provisions—the primary elections provision (amending California Constitution, article II by adding a new section 5, subdivision (b)), and the state property/bonds repayment provision (amending California Constitution, article III by adding a new section 9)—satisfy the traditional single subject provision test that, as we confirm today, also governs the separate-vote provision of article XVIII, section 1. Nor could the Legislature so contend; patently, the two provisions are not reasonably germane to a common theme, purpose, or subject. Accordingly, we agree with the Court of Appeal's conclusion (although for reasons different from those relied upon by that court) that the Legislature's proposed submission to the electorate of both provisions in a single measure as proposed in Resolution 103 violated the separate-vote provision of article XVIII, section 1.

IV

As demonstrated by the out-of-state cases discussed above, the normal remedy for violation of the separate-vote provision has been either (1) a preelection order barring submission of the measure to the voters in a single package, or (2) postelection invalidation of a measure that improperly was submitted to the voters in a single package. In the present case, as noted earlier, the Court of Appeal devised an alternative remedy: it rejected, by a two-to-one vote, the assertion of Californians for an Open Primary that Proposition 60 should be stricken from the ballot, and instead issued a peremptory writ of mandate directing the Secretary of State to bifurcate the two provisions and submit them to the voters separately. Also, as noted above, after we granted review in this matter, and in light of the then-impending election and ballot preparation deadlines, we rejected the request of Californians for an Open Primary for a stay, instead ordering the Secretary of State to place Resolution 103 on the November 2004 ballot "in the manner directed by the Court of Appeal" — that is, as Propositions 60 (the primary elections provision) and 60A (the state property/bonds repayment provision). Thereafter the voters at the November 2004 election, while rejecting Proposition 62, enacted both Propositions 60 and 60A.

Californians for an Open Primary observes that the resulting bifurcated provisions that were placed on the ballot proposed two constitutional amendments, neither of which, standing alone, had received the approval of two-thirds of each house of the Legislature as required by the first sentence of the first section of article XVIII. Californians for an Open Primary argues: "[Resolution 103] was the product of coalition-building in the Legislature.... [I]t is not at all clear that the requisite two-thirds majority of each house would have supported the separate submission to the voters of Propositions 60 and 60A. Most importantly, *nobody in the Legislature ever proposed that Proposition 60 or 60A be submitted to the voters separately for their approval.*" Relying upon our observation in *Livermore, supra,* 102 Cal. 113, 117–118, that "the power of the legislature to initiate any change in the existing organic law ... is to be strictly construed under the limitations by which it has been conferred" and "cannot be ... enlarged beyond these terms," Californians for an Open Primary argues that because the two amendments were not separately approved by the Legislature, they must be invalidated now, even though the voters enacted each separately in November 2004. In other words, whereas in its petition for a writ of mandate filed prior to the November 2004 election, Californians for an Open Primary originally sought to have the combined measure withheld from the ballot, it now argues that bifurcation was improper and that the appropriate postelection remedy is to invalidate both Propositions 60 and 60A.

The Legislature, in its opening brief filed prior to the November 2004 election, also questions the propriety of the Court of Appeal's bifurcation remedy, arguing that even though it had "acquiesced in this remedy in order to permit deliberative review in this court," as a general matter, bifurcation is "highly problematic." The Legislature asserted: "Even when done by court order, such dissection of a measure adopted by the Legislature is inappropriate absent some express statement by the Legislature that it would prefer this alternative to barring the measure from the ballot altogether." Subsequently, after the defeat of Proposition 62 and the adoption of both Propositions 60 and 60A, the Legislature modified its position, arguing in its reply brief that assuming Resolution 103 violated the separate-vote provision, "the goal of article XVIII, section 1 was met when the 'amendments' were separately voted upon by the people, which happened when the voters overwhelmingly approved each measure." Accordingly, the Legislature asserts, "[a]lthough court-mandated bifurcation of a legislative proposal is generally not favored, this remedy was appropriate in the unique circumstances presented here."

We conclude that the Court of Appeal erred in bifurcating the two measures. Nothing in the language or history of article XVIII generally, or of the separate-vote provision in particular, suggests that a violation of the provision should be remedied by bifurcation of proposed amendments and the presentation of those matters to the electorate in separate measures. Nor do we discern in our case law, or in that of any other jurisdiction, any suggestion that bifurcation is an appropriate remedy in such a circumstance. Finally, we find it instructive that the analogous initiative single subject provision (Cal. Const., art. n, §8, subd. (d)) precludes the related remedy of severance. (See *Jones, supra*, 21 Cal.4th at p. 1168 ["when an initiative measure violates the single-subject rule, severance is not an available remedy"]; see also *California Trial Lawyers Assn. v. Eu* (1988) 200 Cal.App.3d 351, 361–362 [245 Cal.Rptr. 916] [concluding the same].)

As observed earlier, the provision states: "An initiative measure embracing more than one subject may not be submitted to the electors or have any effect." (Cal. Const., art II, §8, subd. (d).) By contrast, the *legislative* single subject and title provision contains an express severance clause.

Indeed, allowing bifurcation of a measure that violates the separate-vote provision would permit — if not encourage — logrolling-type manipulations that in turn would frustrate one purpose of the separate-vote provision. If, for example, it were known in advance that bifurcation was a potential and permissible remedy, factions within the Legislature, none of which on its own could garner a two-thirds vote for a particular amendment, might join forces by agreeing to present disparate proposed amendments in a single measure, knowing that a court likely would find a separate-vote violation but thereafter could order the provisions bifurcated and presented separately to the electorate as discrete amendments. In this manner, legislators constituting less than two-thirds of each house could place such measures before the voters in violation of the rule set forth in the first sentence of article XVIII, section 1. Our conclusion that bifurcation is not a remedy for violation of the separate-vote provision avoids creating such incentives or facilitating such manipulations.

Justice Davis, dissenting on this issue in the Court of Appeal below, made the same point as follows: "In future cases, the majority's remedy would allow a faction of those voting for a conjoined set of amendments to accomplish with stealth what could not be secured through the legislative process; namely the separate enactment of an amendment. Those members and their allies could do so by later persuading the Secretary [of State] or the judiciary to extract their favored amendment for individual consideration. [The majority's proposed] remedy should not be invoked in the context of the fundamental organic law of the state, where the Legislature must comply strictly with the procedure for amendment."

V

Although we conclude that the Court of Appeal erred in directing the Secretary of State to bifurcate the two measures and place them on the ballot, we conclude that under the unusual circumstances of this case, it would be inappropriate to invalidate the two approved measures, each of which, as noted, subsequently was separately approved by the voters after this court, in the face of the then impending election, declined to stay the Court of Appeal's bifurcation order. (Cf. *Assembly v. Deukmejian* (1982) 30 Cal.3d 638, 652, 669 [180 Cal.Rptr. 297, 639 P.2d 939] [refusing, under the "unusual and unique circumstances" there presented, to invalidate redistricting referendum petitions that clearly violated the Elections Code, and ordering the use of redistricting plans that had been stayed by the referendum, because doing so "minimize[d] the potential disruption of the electoral process" (italics omitted)].)

The potential for manipulation of the process that we described at the close of part IV, *ante*, manifestly did not occur here. There is no basis upon which to conclude that any legislator could have, or did, anticipate the Court of Appeal's adoption of its novel bifurcation remedy. Indeed, as the briefing in this matter discloses, the Legislature was surprised by, and strenuously objected to, the solution imposed by that court.

In light of the absence of any prior definitive California ruling with regard to either the scope of the separate-vote provision or the remedy for its violation, and in light of the circumstance that the two proposed amendments ultimately *were* separately submitted to the voters and separately adopted as Propositions 60 and 60A after the electorate was afforded an opportunity to consider the arguments for and against each measure, we do not invalidate those constitutional amendments.

VI

For the reasons discussed above, the judgment of the Court of Appeal is vacated and the matter is remanded to the Court of Appeal with directions to discharge the alternative writ and to deny the request that a peremptory writ issue to invalidate Propositions 60 and 60A. Each party shall bear its own costs in this proceeding.

KENNARD, J., BAXTER, J., CHIN, J., and CORRIGAN, J., concurred.

Notes and Questions

1. This was the first appellate court decision to address the constitutional provision that "[e]ach amendment shall be so prepared and submitted that it can be voted on separately" when the Legislature places a constitutional amendment on the ballot. The Court held, "We conclude, as did the Court of Appeal below, and consistent with our provision's language and history and more than a century of out-of-state decisions construing the essentially identical provisions of nearly 30 other state constitutions, that the separate-vote provision is a *limitation* upon legislative power to submit constitutional amendments to the voters. We disagree, however, with the Court of Appeal below, concerning the applicable test for determining whether, in a given case, the Legislature's submission of constitutional changes in a single measure violates article XVIII, section 1."

2. What is the distinction between the state Constitution's "single subject rule" and the requirement that "each amendment shall be so prepared and submitted that it can be voted on separately"? How did the Legislature argue its point of view on the "separate vote" provision of the Constitution? How did the Court respond to the

Legislature's argument on this point? Note that the separate vote requirement found in Article XVIII, Section 1 does not apply to voter-submitted initiative measures. As the Court explained, "In California, by contrast, the separate-vote provision applies only to legislative proposals for constitutional amendment, and does not govern initiative proposals for constitutional amendment." In light of California's single subject rule, is there any legal significance to this limitation?

3. The state Supreme Court defines "germane" to require a common theme, purpose, or subject. The Court of Appeal ruled in the same manner, but simply split the two provisions of the proposed ballot measure and placed them on the general election statewide ballot. Even though the Supreme Court ruled that the Court of Appeal was incorrect in bifurcating the two issues contained in the legislatively-approved constitutional amendment, the high Court did not invalidate either or both of the measures. Why did it not do so?

4. Were you persuaded by the Court's recounting of the history from the Constitutional Convention — that is, the apparently unchallenged view among the delegates that the 1849 Constitution's corresponding provision allowing the Legislature unfettered discretion to prescribe the "manner" of submission should be rejected in favor of an approach limiting that discretion by imposing a separate-vote requirement essentially identical to that adopted by most other states in the intervening decades?

5. Why did the Court not agree with the Legislature's argument that the approximately 30 constitutional amendment measures that the Legislature had submitted to the electorate between 1892 and 2004 would have failed the strict test proposed by the Court of Appeal?

6. In the Court's lengthy description of the development of the state Constitution's provisions at issue in this case was the following nugget: "The history described above demonstrates that the Legislature, after the 1962 amendment expanding its authority to propose constitutional changes amounting to revisions, decided — over the contrary recommendation of the Revision Commission — to *retain* the separate-vote provision. There is no evidence that the Legislature at that time or thereafter considered the separate-vote provision to have metamorphosed from what the Revision Commission in 1967 aptly characterized as a 'restriction' and 'limitation' upon the Legislature's authority to package disparate amendments in a single measure, into the opposite — protection for an asserted legislative prerogative to package disparate proposed changes in a single measure as it wishes." How did the Court utilize this information in its decision?

7. If the Supreme Court "confirmed" the test which it described as "essentially the same test employed by the vast majority of our sister-state jurisdictions for approximately 125 years," why did the Court of Appeal not apply it? What test did the Court of Appeal utilize instead?

8. The Court held that the separate-vote provision should be construed consistently with its kindred provision, the single subject rule. What were the stated reasons that the California Supreme Court did not follow the Oregon Supreme Court's *Armatta* decision?

9. In describing the single subject rule, and now the companion separate vote provision, the Court described that it has "long construed our two single subject provisions in an accommodating and lenient manner so as not to unduly restrict the Legislature's or the people's right to package provisions in a single bill or initiative." The Court further explained that "we have found the single subject rules to have been satisfied so long as challenged provisions meet the test of being *reasonably germane* to a common theme, purpose, or subject." Note that the Court also clarified a point with this test: "and have not *separately* or *additionally* required that each part also be reasonably germane to one another."

10. The Court distinguished the California single subject rule (where provisions are reasonably germane to a common theme, purpose, or subject) from what is described as a stricter standard as one "requiring a showing of 'close' or 'functional' relatedness" Does the stricter standard provide sufficient guidance to legislators in drafting legislation or to the people in drafting ballot initiatives?

11. Why did the Supreme Court conclude that the Court of Appeal erred in bifurcating the two measures?

12. The high Court in this case explained an important distinction between the single subject provisions: "An initiative measure embracing more than one subject may not be submitted to the electors or have any effect" pursuant to the state Constitution under Article II, Section 8(d). On the other hand, the Court noted that, "By contrast, the *legislative* single subject and title provision contains an express severance clause."

E. Conflicting Sections Taking Effect at the Same Time

If sections of the law conflict at the same time, that is, during the same legislative session, then the last enacted bill takes effect over the earlier enacted measure. This issue only occurs when there are conflicting sections of law taking effect at the same time.

Kalina v. San Mateo Community College District

(1982) 132 Cal.App.3d 48

OPINION

SMITH, J.

Appellant Michelle Kalina, a certificated community college instructor, appeals from a judgment denying her petition for writ of mandate to compel respondents, the San Mateo Community College District and the Governing Board of the San Mateo Community College District, to classify her as a probationary employee pursuant to Education Code section 87482 and to compensate her for any damages caused by respondents' failure to classify her properly.

The principal issue in this case concerns the construction and applicability of Education Code sections 87481 and 87482.

Facts

Appellant was first employed by respondent college district as a temporary employee to teach 12 units in the fall 1976 semester. She was subsequently employed as a full-time temporary employee for the spring 1977 semester as well as the fall and spring semesters of the 1977–1978 school year, teaching 15 units per semester, for the purpose of replacing instructors on leave. Although appellant was hired to teach 14 units in the fall of the 1978–1979 school year, respondent college district offered her only a 3-unit teaching assignment for the spring of that year, thus restricting her to 60 percent or less of a full-time teaching assignment in an apparent attempt to prevent her from acquiring vested rights as a probationary employee under section 87482.

Discussion

Appellant's principal contention is that, since she was employed by respondent college district as a temporary employee in the fall of 1976, teaching more than 60 percent of a full-time assignment, and as a temporary sabbatical replacement in the spring of 1977 teaching full-time, pursuant to Education Code section 87482, respondent college district was required to classify her as a contract or probationary employee (see Ed. Code, § 87602, subd. (a)) when it rehired her full-time for the 1977–1978 school year. On the other hand, respondents argue that this controversy is governed exclusively by section 87481 and maintain that, since appellant was not hired to fill vacant positions, under this section she was not entitled to probationary status when she was rehired for the 1977–1978 school year.

Prior to the reorganization of the Education Code in 1976 with the enactment of Statutes 1976, chapters 1010 and 1011, provisions governing community colleges might be found dispersed throughout the Education Code. While some code sections referred specifically to community colleges, others did not, and it became necessary that the courts determine which provisions pertaining generally to "school districts" applied only to the K-12 system and which also encompassed the community college system. (See, generally, Final Report of the Ad Hoc Advisory Committee, Plan for the Reorganization of the Education Code (Feb. 1975) pp. 7–11, 21–23.)

The employment classification system for public educational institutions in effect prior to the reorganization of the Education Code was characterized by one court as "complex and obscure" and governed by inconsistent provisions. (*Santa Barbara Federation of Teachers v. Santa Barbara High Sch. Dist.* (1977) 76 Cal. App. 3d 223, 228 [142 Cal. Rptr. 749].) This court, in *Covino v. Governing Board* (1977) 76 Cal. App. 3d 314, 320–321 [142 Cal. Rptr. 812], recognized such inconsistency between former Education Code sections 13337.3 and 13337.5, the predecessor statutes to sections 87481 and 87482 respectively. There, we held that former section 13337.3 applied only to the K-12 system while the employment of community college instructors was governed by section 13337.5. (*Id* at pp. 321–322.)

In its final report submitted to the Assembly Committee on Education, the advisory committee appointed to study the reorganization of the Education Code also recognized that former sections 13337.3 and 13337.5 appeared to be at least in part conflicting and recommended that 13337.3 be reenacted solely under the division governing the K-12 system and that it not be reenacted under the division pertaining to community colleges. (Final Report of the Ad Hoc Advisory Committee, supra, pp. 31–32, 39, E 24–25; see also Final Report of the Review Committee on the Plan to Reorganize the Education Code (Feb. 1975) pp. 5–7, 42–43.) The Legislature, however, chose not to follow this recommendation and reenacted both former sections 13337.3 and 13337.5 under the division pertaining to community colleges as sections 87481 and 87482 respectively.

It is a cardinal rule of statutory construction that statutes relating to the same subject matter must be read together and reconciled whenever possible to avoid nullification of one statute by another. (See *Fuentes v. Workers' Comp. Appeals Bd.* (1976) 16 Cal. 3d 1, 6–7 [128 Cal. Rptr. 673, 547 P.2d 449]; *Organization of Deputy Sheriffs v. County of San Mateo* (1975) 48 Cal. App. 3d 331, 340 [122 Cal.Rptr. 210]). The statutes in the instant case can only be reconciled if, to the extent section 87482 appears inconsistent with section 87481, it is read as a subdivision of that section.

Thus, as applied to the instant case, we read section 87481 as concerned with the employment of certificated instructors to replace persons on leave and the classification of such instructors as temporary employees, subject to the limitation contained in the second paragraph pertaining to the reemployment of such persons to fill vacant positions. As we interpret it, section 87482 contains a further limitation upon the classification of such employees, prohibiting the community colleges from classifying as temporary instructors those persons employed for more than two semesters or quarters within a period of three consecutive years. (See 62 Ops.Cal.Atty.Gen. 49 (1979).)

Pointing to Education Code section 3 which provides that "[t]he provisions of this code, insofar as they are substantially the same as existing statutory provisions relating to the same subject matter, shall be construed as restatements and continuations, and not as new enactments," respondents submit that sections 87481 and 87482 should be interpreted as reenactments of predecessor statutes. They urge that the interpretation of section 87842 is governed by *Santa Barbara Federation of Teachers v. Santa Barbara High Sch. Dist., supra,* 76 Cal. 3d 223 at page 235 which, in interpreting the term "vacant" of former section 13337.3, the predecessor to section 87481, concluded that school districts might continue indefinitely to hire instructors as temporary employees so long as it might be shown that the number of temporary employees hired did not exceed the number of regular and probationary staff on leave or experiencing long term illness. Respondents maintain that this interpretation cannot reasonably be reconciled with section 87482.

Section 87481, however, applies to community colleges while former section 13337.3 applied to the K-12 system. Section 3 of the reorganized Education Code therefore does not apply. (See *Covino v. Governing Board, supra,* 76 Cal. App. 3d 314, 322.)

Moreover, respondents have overlooked the rule of statutory construction that where specific provisions of different sections of a chapter or article which were intended to take effect at the same time are found to be partially or totally conflicting, the provisions of the section last in numerical order must prevail, unless such construction is inconsistent with the intent of that chapter or article. (See *Hartford Acc. etc. Co. v. City of Tulare* (1947) 30 Cal. 2d 832, 835 [186 P.2d 121]; *People v. Moroney* (1944) 24 Cal. 2d 638, 645 [150 P.2d 888]; *Sanders v. County of Yuba* (1967) 247 Cal. App. 2d 748, 751 [55 Cal. Rptr. 852]; Civ. Code, §23.6.)

To hold, as respondents urge, that section 87481 exclusively controls the instant case would effectively strike a major portion of section 87482, specifically paragraph three. This construction would do violence to a clearly stated legislative intent.

For the foregoing reasons, we hold that the provisions of the third paragraph of section 87482, as a further limitation on the provisions of section 87481, governs the present controversy. Our holding is in harmony with the general policy of the teacher classification system to afford teachers some measure of employment security. (*Curtis v. San Mateo Junior College Dist.* (1972) 28 Cal. App. 3d 161, 165 [103 Cal. Rptr. 33].) Moreover, because temporary employees are not afforded certain important procedural rights enjoyed by probationary and regular employees, the courts have strictly interpreted the statutes authorizing their employment. (See *Balen v. Peralta Junior College Dist., supra*, 11 Cal. 3d 821, 826; *Santa Barbara Federation of Teachers v. Santa Barbara High Sch. Dist., supra*, 76 Cal. App. 3d 223, 228, 240.) While it is also the policy of the law authorizing temporary employment of teachers to permit flexibility in teacher assignments and to prevent overstaffing (see *Santa Barbara Federation of Teachers, supra*, at pp. 232–234; *Centinela Valley Secondary Teachers Assn. v. Centinela Valley Union High Sch. Dist.* (1974) 37 Cal. App. 3d 35, 41 [112 Cal.Rptr. 27]), our holding does not in any meaningful way impair such flexibility, for, under section 87482 authorizing the indefinite hiring of temporary employees for 60 percent or less of full-time assignments, community college districts retain considerable control over the hiring of temporary and probationary staff.

We find no merit in respondents' argument that appellant's employment contract providing that she would at all times be classified as a temporary employee should be deemed controlling. Both statutory and case law prohibit the waiver of benefits afforded by the tenure law. (§87485; *Covino v. Governing Board, supra*, 76 Cal. App. 3d 314, 322–323.)

The judgment is reversed.

ROUSE, Acting P.J., and MILLER, J., concurred.

Notes and Questions

1. Where specific provisions of a different section of a chapter or article which were intended to take effect at the same time are found to be partially or totally conflicting, then provisions of the section last in numerical order must prevail, unless

such construction is inconsistent with the intent of that chapter or article. The court properly explained the applicable rule.

F. Bill Amendments in General

The legislative power that the state Constitution vests is plenary, and a corollary of the legislative power to make new laws is the power to abrogate existing ones. Courts start from the premise that the Legislature possesses the full extent of the legislative power and that its enactments are authorized exercises of that power, and only where the state Constitution withdraws legislative power will courts conclude an enactment is invalid for want of authority. The reenactment rule's purpose is to make sure legislators are not operating in the blind when they amend legislation and to make sure the public can become apprised of changes in the law.

One purpose of the constitutional provisions stating that a section of a statute may not be amended unless the section is re-enacted as amended is to make sure legislators are not operating in the blind when they amend legislation, and to make sure the public can become apprised of changes to the law. Generally, the reenactment rule does not apply to statutes that act to "amend" others only by implication. (*Gillette Co. v. Franchise Tax Board* (2015) 62 Cal.4th 468, certiorari denied.)

G. Resolutions

1. What Is a Resolution?

What is a "resolution"? Although resolutions and concurrent resolutions are mentioned several times in Article IV of the California Constitution, neither term is defined in that document. There also is not a definition for either term in the Government Code. A traditional definition of a resolution is a written motion that is considered for adoption by a legislative body.

Fundamentally, a resolution is a written measure that expresses the will of the Legislature. As opposed to a bill, once adopted, a resolution does not have the force or effect of law. In California, there are several types of resolutions. California's Legislative Counsel provides definitions for concurrent and joint resolutions as follows:

Joint Resolution

A resolution expressing the Legislature's opinion about a matter within the jurisdiction of the federal government, which is forwarded to Congress for its information. Requires the approval of both Assembly and Senate but does not require signature of the Governor. The Senate version uses the acronym SJR, while the Assembly version uses AJR.

There is also a house resolution and a memorial resolution. A memorial resolution is one used to convey the sympathy of the Legislature on the passing of a constituent or dignitary. A house resolution is used to adopt rules for the individual house. They involve the internal business of a single house of the Legislature, and they only require passage in that particular house. The Assembly version uses the acronym HR, while the Senate version uses SR.

Concurrent Resolution

A concurrent resolution is a measure introduced in one house that, if approved, must be sent to the other house for approval. It requests action or states the Legislature's position on an issue. The Governor's signature is not required. These measures usually involve the internal business of the Legislature. The Assembly version uses the acronym ACR, while the Senate version uses SCR.

A concurrent resolution is one that is adopted by both the Assembly and the Senate in order to take effect. The resolution does not have any force or effect of law, because it is merely a statement of the Legislature's intent regarding a topic, such as a rule for proceedings.

Swing v. Riley

(1939) 13 Cal.2d 513

OPINION

THE COURT.

This proceeding is companion to the matter of the *Special Assembly Interim Committee v. Southard*, L.A. No. 16753. A rehearing was granted herein for the reason set forth in the opinion filed this day (*ante*, p. 497 [90 PaCal.2d 304]), in that matter. For the reasons stated therein the opinion of this court on the former hearing is adopted as the opinion of the court on rehearing, as follows:

"The present petition … involves several additional points not involved in L.A. No. 16753.

"The state senate at its fifty-second session, just prior to the adjournment of that session sine die on May 28, 1937, duly passed a single house resolution reciting the need for regulation of the manufacture, sale and disposition of alcoholic beverages 'in the interest of the moral, social and economic welfare of the people and in the interest of the temperate use of such beverages', and the helpfulness of a 'study of the problems relating to such matters … in the drafting of legislation and rules and regulations designed to accomplish such purposes', and creating a committee of five of its members with power and authority 'to make a full, complete study and investigation of all matters relating to the manufacture, sale and disposition of alcoholic beverages within this state … in relation to the issuance of licenses and the enforcement of laws, rules and regulations concerning such business'. The committee was given full power to subpoena witnesses and to compel the giving of testimony. It was given leave 'to sit during the sessions of the senate, and/or during recess and at such times and at such place or places as the committee may determine' and was directed to 'report to the Senate at the next regular session of the Legislature its findings and recommendations …' The resolution also provided that 'the sum of $2000 … is hereby set aside and made available for the purpose of defraying the expenses of such committee and the members thereof, other than that required by law to be paid from the legislative help fund. Said sum to be paid from the contingent fund of the Senate and the State Controller is hereby authorized and directed to draw his warrants in favor of the person or persons entitled thereto for such expenditures as may be certified to him from time to time by the chairman of said committee, and the State Treasurer is hereby authorized and directed to pay the same.'

"Thereafter the committee was duly selected and petitioner Swing was appointed chairman thereof. Thereafter the committee proceeded to meet for the purpose of performing the functions delegated to it.

"In January of 1938, the governor, pursuant to the powers conferred upon him by article V, section 9, of the Constitution, called a special session of the legislature. It is conceded that in the proclamation calling the special session there was no mention of legislative committees generally, nor of the committee here involved specifically. The proclamation was likewise silent as to the subject-matter delegated to this committee for study and report. At this special session the legislature by concurrent resolution passed assembly concurrent resolution 18 (chap. 27 of Resolutions, Extra Session, 1938). This resolution should be quoted in full. It provides:

"'WHEREAS, Several interim committees have been established by single house and concurrent resolutions; and

"'WHEREAS, It is desired to supplement and affirm such single house and concurrent resolutions; now, therefore, be it

"'Resolved by the Assembly of the State of California, the Senate thereof concurring, That all Assembly and Senate single house and concurrent resolutions heretofore passed at the regular session of the Fifty-second Legislature and heretofore and hereafter passed at the first extra session of the Fifty-second Legislature, are hereby validated, affirmed and authorized, and the committees established and to be established thereunder are hereby authorized to exercise all the powers and perform all the duties vested in them and imposed upon them by the particular resolution under which the committee or committees are established.'

"Prior to the adoption of this concurrent resolution certain incidental expenses were incurred by the committee. Other expenses were incurred after the adoption of the concurrent resolution. The chairman of the committee duly certified these expenditures to the respondent controller. The controller refused to draw warrants for the claims on the grounds that 'interim committees cannot be established by single house resolution with power to function after the adjournment of the Legislature', and that the concurrent resolution was also ineffectual as a valid authorization for the creation of the committee. Petitioners thereupon brought this proceeding in mandamus to compel the issuance of the warrants.

"In so far as the petition involves the question as to whether either house of the legislature by single house resolution may lawfully create a fact finding interim-committee with authority to function after adjournment of the legislature sine die, that question need not be discussed in this opinion. The identical question was answered in the negative in L.A. No. 16753 (*ante*, p. 497 [90 PaCal.2d 304]), this day decided. For the reasons therein stated, and upon the authority of that case, it must be held that the senate resolution of May 28, 1937, was legally insufficient to authorize the committee to incur the expenditures here involved.

"Petitioners contend that, even if it be held that the assembly cannot lawfully create committees with authority to sit after adjournment, for the reason that the assembly is not a continuing body because all of its members are elected each two years, such rule has no application to the senate where only one-half of the membership is elected every two years. It is contended that for this reason the senate must be held to be a continuing body, with power to appoint its committees with authority to sit after adjournment. In this connection petitioners rely on *McGrain v. Daugherty*, 273 U.S. 135 [47 S.Ct. 319, 71 L.Ed. 580, 50 A.L.R. 1].

"To this contention there are two answers. In the first place the legal basis of the rule holding that a single house resolution is ineffectual to authorize a committee to function after adjournment is that upon adjournment sine die all legislative power of both houses terminates, including the auxiliary power of functioning through legislative committees. In the second place, even if we were inclined to follow the holding of the Daugherty case, supra, the rule of that case would not be applicable here. As was pointed out in the assembly committee case, L.A. No. 16753 (*ante*, p. 497 [90 PaCal.2d 304]), in the *Daugherty* case the United States Supreme Court held that senate interim committees could lawfully sit after adjournment for the reason that the senate is a continuing body, two-thirds of its membership at each new session of congress consisting of holdover senators. The United States Supreme Court intimated that this rule probably did not apply to the house of representatives whose entire membership is elected anew each two years. Apparently, the theory of the *Daugherty* case is that a senate interim committee when it reports back to the senate will be reporting back to a body whose membership consists of at least two-thirds of the members that originally appointed the committee. The California senate cannot be held to be a continuing body under any such theory. Article IV, section 8, of the Constitution provides that 'A majority of each house shall constitute a quorum to do business ...' As already pointed out fifty per cent of the senators are elected anew each two years. It follows that since fifty per cent of the senate membership at each regular session is newly elected, there is not present a 'majority' of the membership of the body that originally appointed the committee.

"Petitioners next rely on the concurrent resolution passed at the special session, purporting to validate, affirm and authorize the prior action of the senate in creating the committee here involved. This resolution, in our opinion, was ineffectual for the purpose for which it was passed.

"If it be assumed that by concurrent resolution the legislature could validly create an interim fact finding committee with power to sit after adjournment sine die (and could therefore validate by subsequent resolution a committee improperly appointed in the first instance) we have grave doubts that such a concurrent resolution could be constitutionally passed at a special session when the subject-matter contained in the resolution is not mentioned in the governor's proclamation calling the special session. Article V, section 9, of the Constitution provides that the legislature at special session 'shall have no power to legislate on any subjects other than those specified in the proclamation …'. This constitutes a prohibition against exercising legislative powers at a special session except in considering matters included within the call. The work of legislative committees is subsidiary and auxiliary to the legislative functions of each house. If the legislature cannot directly legislate on matters not included within the call, then it cannot exercise dependent or subsidiary powers derived solely from the direct power to legislate. This problem was exhaustively considered and discussed in *Ex parte Wolters*, 64 Tex. Cr. R. 238 [144 S.W. 531, 535, Ann. Cas. 1916B, 1071], where it was held that the legislative power to create legislative committees by single house or concurrent resolution at a special session was necessarily limited to the creation of committees to consider legislation within the governor's call. (See, also, *Gilbreath v. Willett*, 148 Tenn. 92 [251 S.W. 910, 28 A.L.R. 1147].) In *People v. Curry*, 130 Cal. 82 [62 P. 516], it was held that the legislature in special session by concurrent resolution had no power to propose a constitutional amendment on a subject not included within the governor's call. The court pointed out that (p. 89): 'It may be admitted that proposing constitutional amendments is not legislation … but it is nevertheless performing a legislative function.' The same reasoning is applicable to the appointment of legislative committees.

"Another and complete answer to this contention is that we are of the opinion that under our Constitution the legislature has no power by concurrent resolution to create a committee with power to sit after adjournment sine die. As far as the question of power is concerned there is no difference in this regard between a single house and a concurrent resolution. It is true that on this subject there is a conflict of authority. The cases both ways are noted in the assembly committee case, L.A. No. 16753 (*ante*, p. 497 [90 PaCal.2d 304]). As was pointed out in the assembly committee opinion, several of the cases holding that by a concurrent resolution the legislature may validly create an interim committee, are in fact not authority for that holding, for the reason that in the particular jurisdiction there is no legal distinction between a concurrent resolution and a statute, both requiring the governor's signature. The reasoning of the several cases holding that a concurrent resolution is ineffectual to validly create such a committee seems to us to be unanswerable. If such a committee cannot lawfully be created by single house resolution (and on this point all state courts agree) it cannot be created by concurrent resolution. Every argument fully set forth in the assembly committee case, L.A. No. 16753 (*ante*, p. 497 [90 PaCal.2d 304]) is equally applicable here. Legislative powers of the legislature cease upon adjournment sine die. Such powers cannot be continued after adjournment by either single house or concurrent resolution. The power to investigate by committees is subsidiary to the legislative power. When the main power ceases, the auxiliary power dies with it. If such committee or commission is to function lawfully after adjournment it can be created only by statute.

"Petitioners' last argument is that if a statute is required to validly create such a committee, such a statute was in fact passed in reference to the committee here involved. In this connection petitioners rely on two statutes. The first of these is the 1935 Budget Act (Stats. 1935, chap. 341, p. 1176) which provides in part as follows:

"'Item 3. For contingent expenses of Senate for fifty-second session and interim committees thereof, twenty thousand dollars.'

"The second statute relied upon is the Appropriation Act of 1937 (Stats. 1937, chap. 23, p. 91) which provides in part as follows:

"'SECTION 1. The sum of twenty thousand dollars is hereby appropriated out of any money in the State treasury, not otherwise appropriated, for contingent expenses of the Senate, for fifty-second session and interim committees thereof to be expended for such purposes and in such manner as the Senate shall by resolution direct. This appropriation shall be available without regard to fiscal years.

"'Sec. 2. Inasmuch as this act provides an appropriation for the usual current expenses of the State, it is hereby declared an urgency measure and shall, under the provisions of article IV, section 2, of the Constitution, take effect immediately.'

"In their opening brief petitioners contend that these statutes constitute 'statutory recognition and validation of the instant committee'. (Pet. Op. Brief, p. 29.) In their closing brief petitioners concede that the statutes cannot be considered 'technically' as validating statutes, because they were passed before the committee was created. (Pet. Reply Brief, p. 74.)

"It is quite clear that these statutes in no way constitute a statutory recognition of interim committees generally, or of the committee here involved specifically. The provisions for expenses contained in these statutes obviously contemplated the creation of valid and legal interim committees. It cannot logically be argued that in passing these statutes (one over two years, the other over two months, before the committee here involved was created) the legislature had in mind that interim committees would thereafter be unlawfully created by resolution, and that this was an attempt to 'validate' or 'authorize' them in advance. The statutes are of no legal significance in this case.

"The other points involved have all been discussed in the assembly committee case, L.A. No. 16753 (*ante*, p. 497 [90 PaCal.2d 304]), and need not be discussed in this opinion."

For the foregoing reasons the alternative writ of mandate heretofore issued is discharged, and the application for a peremptory writ is denied.

Notes and Questions

1. A concurrent resolution of the Legislature, passed at a special session, and purporting to validate, affirm and authorize the prior action of the Senate in creating an interim committee to sit after adjournment sine die, was ineffective for that purpose.

If an interim committee appointed by the Legislature is to function lawfully after adjournment of the Legislature, it can be created only by statute.

2. The Court also ruled that the one-house (Senate) resolution was legally insufficient to authorize the committee to incur the expenditures that it had incurred.

3. Is this Court decision based entirely on the fact that a single house resolution is ineffectual to authorize a committee to function after adjournment because, upon adjournment sine die, all legislative power of both houses terminates, including the auxiliary power of functioning through legislative committees?

4. Why did the Court determine that the California Senate cannot be held to be a continuing body? What theory was advanced to seek such a determination?

5. After ruling that under the state Constitution the Legislature does not have the power by concurrent resolution to create a committee with power to sit after adjournment sine die, did the Court find any difference between a single house and a concurrent resolution? What would be the basis of such an argument?

H. Constitutional Amendments

1. What Is a Constitutional Amendment?

Although California's Constitution provides for the amendment of this document, the Constitution does not define this term. A traditional definition of a constitutional amendment is a modification to an existing constitution.

California's Legislative Counsel defines a constitutional amendment as "a resolution proposing a change to the California Constitution. It may be presented by the Legislature or by initiative, and is adopted upon voter approval at a statewide election."

In California, there is a legal distinction between "amending" the Constitution and "revising" it. There is not a definition in the Constitution to distinguish between the two types of modifications to the state's Constitution, but the courts have defined the difference. Article XVIII of the California Constitution sets forth amending and revising this document.

In Section 1, the Legislature is granted the ability to propose either an amendment or a revision to the Constitution. Both a proposed amendment and revision require a vote of the people. If a revision is requested by the Legislature, and the voters approved, then a constitutional convention must be convened. In Section 3, however, only the people are allowed to amend the Constitution.

For constitutional amendments in California, there are two methods: those proposed by the Legislature and those proposed by the people.

<u>By the Legislature</u>

For constitutional amendments proposed by the Legislature, they are mentioned just once in Article IV, Section 8.5, which includes a provision for a "constitutional amendment proposed by the Legislature." Again, the term is not defined anywhere in the state's Constitution.

Thereafter, in Article 18, Section 1, "The Legislature by rollcall vote entered in the journal, two-thirds of the membership of each house concurring, may propose an amendment or revision of the Constitution and in the same manner may amend or withdraw its proposal. Each amendment shall be so prepared and submitted that it can be voted on separately."

As a result, the Legislature can propose amendments to the California Constitution, so long as both the Assembly and Senate vote by a 2/3 majority to place the proposal on the statewide ballot (note that the Governor does not have a formal role in the adoption of proposed amendments), but the constitutional amendments are subject to a majority vote approval of the people for adoption.

<u>By the People</u>

For constitutional amendments proposed by the people, the process is set forth in Article II, Section 8, which provides:

> (a) The initiative is the power of the electors to propose statutes and amendments to the Constitution and to adopt or reject them.

> (b) An initiative measure may be proposed by presenting to the Secretary of State a petition that sets forth the text of the proposed statute or amendment to the Constitution and is certified to have been signed by electors equal in number to 5 percent in the case of a statute, and 8 percent in the case of an amendment to the Constitution, of the votes for all candidates for Governor at the last gubernatorial election.

As a result, the state's electorate can propose and adopt amendments to the California Constitution without approval by the Legislature or Governor. Just like with amendments proposed by the Legislature, those proposed by the people are subject to a majority vote approval of the electorate for adoption.

2. Amending v. Revising the Constitution

Article XVIII, which deals with amending and revising the constitution, was added to the California Constitution by Proposition 6 on the November 3, 1970 ballot. It contains the following four sections.

Section 1 — The Legislature by rollcall vote entered in the journal, two-thirds of the membership of each house concurring, may propose an amendment or revision of the Constitution and in the same manner may amend or withdraw its proposal. Each amendment shall be so prepared and submitted that it can be voted on separately.

Section 2 — The Legislature by rollcall vote entered in the journal, two-thirds of the membership of each house concurring, may submit at a general election the question whether to call a convention to revise the Constitution. If the majority vote yes on that question, within six months, the Legislature shall provide for the convention.

Delegates to a constitutional convention shall be voters elected from districts as nearly equal in population as may be practicable.

Section 3 — The electors may amend the Constitution by initiative.

Section 4 — A proposed amendment or revision shall be submitted to the electors and, if approved by a majority of votes cast thereon, takes effect on the fifth day after the Secretary of State files the statement of the vote for the election at which the measure is voted on, but the measure may provide that it becomes operative after its effective date. If provisions of two or more measures approved at the same election conflict, the provisions of the measure receiving the highest number of affirmative votes shall prevail.

Based upon these provisions, an amendment to the state Constitution requires passage of a state ballot measure approved by a majority vote of the state's electorate. These ballot propositions can be proposed by legislators or voters. For voters to place an amendment on the ballot, they must obtain signatures from voters that are equal to 8% of the votes cast in the last gubernatorial election, which is actually one of the lowest thresholds of any state in the nation. Section 3 of Article 18 provides that the electors may amend the Constitution by initiative.

The California Constitution may also be amended or revised by the state Legislature, as well as by the electorate. While the voters can approve a constitutional initiative on the statewide ballot, the Legislature can place a constitutional amendment on the statewide ballot. This process is allowed pursuant to Article XVIII, which provides specific rules for amending and revising the California Constitution.

Although California's initiative process has been criticized for being "too easy" to place a measure on the ballot for the people to adopt, it is important for both voters and the Legislature to have the power to amend or revise the state Constitution. Although the electorate must always have the option to place a measure on the ballot, so too should the Legislature to ensure that potential amendments or revisions to the California Constitution get appropriate consideration by the lawmaking body for the state.

3. Standing to Challenge a Constitutional Amendment

Not everyone has standing (or the legal authority) to file a lawsuit to challenge an amendment to the state's Constitution. As a general rule, "standing" is a legal concept to ascertain whether an individual or group has the legal authority to go to court to challenge the lawfulness of a constitutional amendment proposed by the people.

Rippon v. Bowen

(2008) 160 Cal.App.4th 1308

OPINION

Cooper, P.J.

California voters passed Proposition 140 in November 1990, and thereby limited the Legislature's budget and imposed lifetime term limits and pension restrictions for state legislators and other state officers. (*Legislature v. Eu* (1991) 54 Cal.3d 492, 502, 506 (*Eu*).) The purpose of the initiative was that incumbent advantages "discourage qualified candidates from seeking public office and create a class of career politicians, instead of the citizen representatives envisioned by the Founding Fathers." (*Id.* at p. 501.) In this appeal, appellants revisit a constitutional challenge to Proposition 140 raised shortly after its passage; they argue Proposition 140 revised the California Constitution and is therefore invalid.

Except for the pension restrictions, our Supreme Court and an en banc panel of the Ninth Circuit upheld the constitutionality of Proposition 140. (*Eu, supra,* 54 Cal.3d 492; *Bates v. Jones* (9th Cir. 1997) 131 F.3d 843 (*Bates*).) In *Eu*, our high court concluded "the basic and fundamental structure of the Legislature as a representative branch of government is left substantially unchanged by Proposition 140. Term and budgetary limitations may affect and alter the particular legislators and staff who participate in the legislative process, but the process itself should remain essentially as previously contemplated by our Constitution." (*Eu*, at p. 508.) Therefore, the high court concluded that Proposition 140 amended the California Constitution; it did not revise the California Constitution, precisely the issue in this case. (*Eu*, at pp. 510–511.) Following *Eu*, we affirm the judgment on the pleadings.

   . . . .

I. Distinction Between an Amendment and a Revision

Article XVIII of the California Constitution allows for amendment of the Constitution by the Legislature, or initiative and revision of the Constitution by the Legislature, or a constitutional convention. There is no other method for revising or amending the Constitution. (*Livermore v. Waite* (1894) 102 Cal. 113, 117 (*Livermore*).) Relevant here, the Constitution may be revised only through a constitutional convention and popular ratification or legislative submission of the measure to the people. (*McFadden v. Jordan* (1948) 32 Cal.2d 330, 334 (*McFadden*); *California Assn. of Retail Tobacconists v. State of California* (2003) 109 CalApp.4th 792, 833 (*California Tobacconists*).)

"'[A]mendment' implies such an addition or change within the lines of the original instrument as will effect an improvement, or better carry out the purpose for which it was framed." (*Livermore, supra,* 102 Cal. at pp. 118–119.) The "revision/amendment analysis has a dual aspect, requiring us to examine both the quantitative and qualitative effects of the measure on our constitutional scheme. Substantial changes in either respect could amount to a revision." (*Raven v. Deukmejian* (1990) 52 Cal.3d 336, 350 (*Raven*).) "[A]n enactment which is so extensive in its provisions as to change directly the 'substantial entirety' of the Constitution by the deletion or alteration of numerous existing provisions may well constitute a revision thereof. However, even a relatively simple enactment may accomplish such far reaching changes in the nature of our basic governmental plan as to amount to a revision also." (*Amador Valley Joint Union High Sch. Dist. v. State Bd. of Equalization* (1978) 22 Cal.3d 208, 223 (*Amador*).)

A. Examples of Constitutional Amendments

In *Amador, supra*, 22 Cal.3d 208, our high court considered Proposition 13 on the June 1978 ballot. The proposition imposed a limitation on the tax rate applicable to real property, restricted the assessed value of real property, limited the method of changes to state taxes, and imposed a restriction on local taxes. (*Amador*, at p. 220.) The high court rejected the argument that the proposition revised rather than amended the Constitution. (*Id.* at pp. 227–228.) Although there would be "substantial changes in the operation of the former system of taxation," the changes did not constitute a constitutional revision. (*Id.* at p. 228.)

Similarly, in *Brosnahan v. Brown* (1982) 32 Cal.3d 236 (*Brosnahan*), the court concluded that the "Victims' Bill of Rights" (Prop. 8 in 1982) did not constitute a revision of the Constitution. "[W]hile Proposition 8 does accomplish substantial changes in our criminal justice system, even in combination these changes fall considerably short of constituting such far reaching changes in the nature of our *basic governmental plan* as to amount to a revision...." (*Brosnahan*, at p. 260.) The court rejected the petitioners' "wholly conjectural" predictions. (*Id.* at p. 261.) "[N]othing contained in Proposition 8 necessarily or inevitably will alter the basic governmental framework set forth in our Constitution. It follows that Proposition 8 did not accomplish a 'revision' of the Constitution within the meaning of article XVIII." (*Ibid.*) The high court later rejected a subsequent challenge to a portion of Proposition 8 finding that *Brosnahan* "necessarily encompassed a conclusion that [the portion] was properly adopted through the amendment procedure." (*In re Lance W.* (1985) 37 Cal.3d 873, 891.)

B. Examples of Constitutional Revisions

In *McFadden, supra*, 32 Cal.2d 330, a proposed measure sought to add a new article to the constitution "to consist of 12 separate sections (actually in the nature of separate articles) divided into some 208 subsections (actually in the nature of sections) set forth in more than 21,000 words." (*Id.* at p. 334.) In comparison, the Constitution at that time "contain[ed] 25 articles divided into some 347 sections expressed in approximately 55,000 words." (*Ibid.*) The new measure would have altered substantially at least 15 of 25 articles in the constitution and introduced at least four new topics. (*Id.* at p. 345.) The court found the proposed change to constitute an invalid constitutional revision.

Raven, supra, 52 Cal.3d 336, concerned the "Crime Victims Justice Reform Act" (Prop. 115 approved by the voters in June 1990). The court concluded that the following provision constituted a qualitative constitutional revision and was therefore invalid: "certain enumerated criminal law rights shall be construed consistently with the United States Constitution, and shall not be construed to afford greater rights to criminal or juvenile defendants than afforded by the federal Constitution." (*Raven*, at pp. 342–343.)

The high court reasoned that the enactment effected a far-reaching change in the nature of basic government because it "would vest all judicial *interpretive* power, as to fundamental criminal defense rights, in the United States Supreme Court. From a qualitative standpoint, the effect of Proposition 115 is devastating." (*Raven, supra*, 52

Cal.3d at p. 352.) "California courts in criminal cases would no longer have authority to interpret the state Constitution in a manner more protective of defendants' rights than extended by the federal Constitution, as construed by the United States Supreme Court." (*Ibid.*) "Proposition 115 not only unduly restricts judicial power, but it does so in a way which severely limits the independent force and effect of the California Constitution." (*Id.* at p. 353.) Proposition 115 "substantially alters the preexisting constitutional scheme or framework heretofore extensively and repeatedly used by courts in interpreting and enforcing state constitutional protections. It directly contradicts the well-established jurisprudential principle that, 'The judiciary, from the very nature of its powers and means given it by the Constitution, must possess the right to construe the Constitution in the last resort....'" (*Raven*, at p. 354.) The provision "vests a critical portion of state judicial power in the United States Supreme Court, certainly a fundamental change in our preexisting governmental plan." (*Id.* at p. 355.)

II. Eu *Bars This Lawsuit*

A. Eu *Holds That Proposition 140 Did Not Revise the California Constitution*

Our high court analyzed whether Proposition 140 constituted a constitutional amendment or a constitutional revision in *Eu, supra*, 54 Cal.3d 492. The Legislature along with individual legislators, citizens, voters, and taxpayers challenged the constitutionality of Proposition 140. Petitioners argued that Proposition 140 effected a constitutional revision, the identical argument made in the present case. (*Eu*, at p. 506.) Specifically, petitioners argued, "'Weakened by budget cuts and harsh term limits, the Legislature will be unable to discharge its traditional duties of policymaker, keeper of the purse, and counterweight to the executive branch in the way the Constitution intends. The result is a change so profound in the structure of our government that it constitutes a revision....'" (*Id.* at p. 507.)

The high court rejected these arguments and instead found "the basic and fundamental structure of the Legislature as a representative branch of government is left substantially unchanged by Proposition 140. Term and budgetary limitations may affect and alter the particular legislators and staff who participate in the legislative process, but the process itself should remain essentially as previously contemplated by our Constitution." (*Eu, supra*, 54 Cal.3d at p. 508.) "Proposition 140 on its face does not affect either the structure or the foundational powers of the Legislature, which remains free to enact whatever laws it deems appropriate. The challenged measure alters neither the content of those laws nor the process by which they are adopted. No legislative power is diminished or delegated to other persons or agencies. The relationships between the three governmental branches, and their respective powers, remain untouched." (*Id.* at p. 509.)

The court concluded, in a paragraph emphasized by appellants that "although the immediate foreseeable effects of the foregoing term and budgetary limitations are indeed substantial (primarily, the eventual loss of experienced legislators and some support staff), the assertedly momentous consequences to our governmental scheme are largely *speculative* ones, dependent on a number of as yet unproved premises." (*Eu*, *supra*, 54 Cal.3d at p. 509.) "Petitioners assume, for example, that the eventual loss of experienced legislators, and the arrival of their relatively unseasoned replacements, will irreparably hinder and damage the legislative process. Yet respondents argue with equal conviction that Proposition 140's term limitations will free the entire process from the control of assertedly entrenched, apathetic, veteran incumbents, thereby allowing fresh creative energies to flourish free of vested, self-serving legislative interests." (*Ibid.*)

The court then instructed that the speculative nature of the petitioners' arguments demonstrated that a revision did not appear from the face of the challenged provision. "We are in no position to resolve the controversy between the parties regarding the long-term consequences of Proposition 140, for the future effects of that measure on our 'basic governmental plan' are simply unfathomable at this time. Indeed, that very uncertainty inhibits us from holding that a constitutional revision has occurred in this case. Our prior decisions have made it clear that to find such a revision, it must *necessarily or inevitably appear from the face* of the challenged provision that the measure will substantially alter the basic governmental framework set forth in our Constitution." (*Eu, supra*, 54 Cal.3d at p. 510.)

Justice Mosk disagreed with the conclusion of the majority, but applied the same test. He concluded, "Proposition 140 amounts to an unconstitutional revision of the state charter *on its face* and, as a result, is invalid." (*Eu, supra*, 54 Cal.3d at p. 538, italics added.) "Manifestly, Proposition 140 amounts to an unconstitutional revision because of its significant effect on the Legislature." (*Id.* at p. 543.) "[T]he Legislature is a fundamental component of the state constitutional system." (*Ibid.*) "[T]he Legislature must be deemed fundamentally altered by any substantial change in its nature or character" and the change that would be effected by Proposition 140 is substantial. (*Eu*, at p. 543.) Justice Mosk explained: "The majority conclude to the contrary. They reason that Proposition 140's possible future consequences for the Legislature are not dispositive. I agree. They also reason that the initiative does not affect the Legislature's constitutional structure or powers. Again, I agree. But ... a judiciary comprising laypersons is fundamentally different from one made up of jurists — even if its structure and powers are the same. Similarly, a Legislature of 'citizens' is fundamentally different from one of 'politicians.'" (*Id.* at p. 544.)

B. Eu Controls This Case

We are bound by the ruling in *Eu*. (*Auto Equity Sales, Inc. v. Superior Court* (1962) 57 Cal.2d 450, 455.) The high court held that Proposition 140 does not revise the basic form of government. It is a constitutional amendment, not a constitutional revision. (*Id.* at pp. 510–511.) That conclusion is dispositive of appellants' case. Under *Eu*, "[f]or a revision to be found, 'it must *necessarily or inevitably appear from the face* of the challenged provision that the measure will substantially alter the basic governmental framework set forth in our Constitution. [Citations.]'" (*Id.* at p. 510; see also *California Tobacconists, supra*, 109 Cal.App.4th at p. 834.) If it does not necessarily or inevitably appear from the face of an initiative that the provisions will substantially alter the basic governmental framework, the change is not a revision to the constitution. (See *California Tobacconists*, at p. 834.)

Because the predictions in *Eu* were speculative, it showed that nothing contained in the proposition "'necessarily or inevitably'" altered the basic governmental framework. (See *Brosnahan, supra*, 32 Cal.3d at p. 261.) The speculative nature of the arguments was relevant to determining whether the proposition was an amendment; it was not an invitation to subsequently mount an identical challenge to the initiative. Appellants misinterpret *Eu* by erroneously concluding that the speculative nature of the petitioners' arguments left room for a subsequent challenge to the constitutionality of the initiative on the ground that it is a revision. Under appellants' theory, there would be no limit to the number of times the revision/amendment analysis could be revisited. Amend and revise connote procedures, (*McFadden, supra*, 32 Cal.2d at p. 347), and an initiative is either one or the other, regardless of the passage of time since the enactment of the initiative.

Appellants argue that we should apply the public interest exception to res judicata. The argument is tantamount to an acknowledgement that the issues in this case already have been litigated. The doctrine of res judicata applies to preclude "the relitigation of certain matters which have been resolved in a prior proceeding under certain circumstances. [Citation.]" (*Brinton v. Bankers Pension Services, Inc.* (1999) 76 Cal.App.4th 550, 556.) Appellants argue that we should apply the exception to the doctrine of res judicata that "'when the issue is a question of law rather than of fact, the prior determination is not conclusive either if injustice would result or if the public interest requires that relitigation not be foreclosed. [Citations.]'" (*City of Sacramento v. State of California* (1990) 50 Cal.3d 51, 64.)

The Ninth Circuit applied the public interest exception to res judicata to reconsider the constitutionality of Proposition 140 after *Eu*. (*Bates, supra*, 131 F.3d at pp. 845–846.) We need not decide if unusual circumstances are present here to warrant applying *a second time* the public interest exception to res judicata because even if appellants were allowed to relitigate the issue, we are bound by the holding of our Supreme Court. (*Auto Equity Sales, Inc. v. Superior Court, supra*, "57 Cal.2d at p. 455.)

This is not a case, like those cited by appellants, where the law has changed since it was first considered or where the law arose from an emergency situation and should be deemed terminated once the emergency abated. (See, e.g., *Palermo v. Stockton Theatres, Inc.* (1948) 32 Cal.2d 53; *Chastleton Corp. v. Sinclair* (1924) 264 U.S. 543; but see *Santa Monica Beach, Ltd. v. Superior Court* (1999) 19 Cal.4th 952, 1005.) Proposition 140 is the same and the arguments appellants raise are the same as those raised in *Eu*.

C. The Passage of Time Does Not Alter the Nature of the Challenge

Appellants characterize their challenge as an "as applied" challenge to the constitutionality of Proposition 140. According to their opening brief, appellants "allege that Proposition 140 as applied has achieved a qualitative change in our Constitution; it has altered the basic form of our government."

Notwithstanding appellants' "as applied" label, the challenge is the same facial challenge as that made in *Eu*, and the relief sought is the invalidation of the entire initiative. The complaint attacks Proposition 140 because of its effects on the California Legislature. For example, appellants support the claim that Proposition 140 resulted in a change to our form of government with the following statements: "[t]he effect of Proposition 140 has been to dramatically reduce the role of the legislative branch and increase the powers vested in the executive branch and the governor. Proposition 140 has fundamentally altered the relationship between the separate branches of government; it has ceded constitutionally vested roles, functions and powers from the legislative branch to the executive branch and other entities. Proposition 140 has subordinated the constitutional role assumed by the legislative branch in our governmental scheme and substantially altered California's preexisting constitutional framework."

Appellants' challenge is not "as applied" even though they characterize it as such. First, and most significantly, the question of whether an initiative constitutes an amendment or a revision requires analysis of the statute on its face. The purported "as applied" challenge is inconsistent with the test for a constitutional revision that "must *necessarily or inevitably appear from the face* of the challenged provision." (*Eu, supra,* 54 Cal.3d at p. 510.) Therefore, their label simply applies the wrong test to analyze the question they ask.

Second, appellants allege no particularized injury that as applied to them in particular deprived them of a right. Instead, they argue for example that they "seek to undo the damaging effects caused by Proposition 140's legislative term limits on California." They seek to assist all legislatures [sic] who are currently subject to term limits to run for office. According to them, "even if Appellants prevail on this appeal, it will be of no consequence to those legislators now facing term limits and their constituents unless Appellants prevail quickly." They do not seek to prevent a specific application of any provision enacted pursuant to Proposition 140, but instead seek to invalidate the initiative as a whole.

Third, the so-called "as applied" test appellants propose — to reevaluate the initiative "in light of the actual qualitative consequences now known to have been caused by the initiative" — raises a question with respect to the role of the judiciary in deciding, 17 years after the passage of an initiative, the wisdom of an initiative enacted by the People. It is the court's role and obligation to decide if an act is unconstitutional. (*Schabarum* [*v. California Legislature*], *supra,* 60 Cal.App.4th at p. 1213.) That is what the Supreme Court did in *Eu.*

But, in *Eu,* the court eschewed opining on petitioners' arguments that "the eventual loss of experienced legislators, and the arrival of their relatively unseasoned replacements, will irreparably hinder and damage the legislative process" and respondents' counterarguments that "Proposition 140's term limitations will free the entire process from the control assertedly entrenched, apathetic, veteran incumbents, thereby allowing fresh creative energies to flourish free of vested, self-serving legislative interests." (*Eu, supra,* 54 Cal.3d at p. 509.) The same effects were described pejoratively by petitioners in *Eu* and laudably by respondents in *Eu.* Our high court, however, narrowed its analysis to the constitutional question before it — whether it "*necessarily or inevitably appear from the face* of the challenged provision that the measure will substantially alter the basic governmental framework set forth in our Constitution."

(*Id.* at p. 510.) In his dissent, Justice Mosk made clear that the question was whether the change from a "Legislature of 'politicians,' to one that prohibits such a result" was the question, not the "wisdom" of the initiative. (*Id.* at p. 542.)

To look beyond changes to the Legislature that "necessarily and inevitably" appear on the face of the initiative takes us uncomfortably close to a political question. The political question doctrine "'excludes from judicial review those controversies which revolve around policy choices and value determinations constitutionally committed for resolution to the [legislative and executive branches].'" (*Schabarum, supra,* 60 Cal.App.4th at p. 1213.) We need not conclusively determine whether "an as applied" challenge based on "qualitative effects" of Proposition 140 in its 17 years of existence amounts to a political question, because it is, as explained, the wrong test. The correct test is a facial one, and that test has already been applied by our high court. (*Eu, supra,* 54 Cal.3d at p. 510.)

In *Eu,* the high court made clear what appellants could do if the then speculative predictions were borne out: "If, as petitioners predict, Proposition 140 ultimately produces grave, undesirable consequences to our governmental plan, the Legislature (Cal. Const., art. XVIII, Sec. 1) or the people (*id.,* art. XVIII, Sec.3) are empowered to propose a new constitutional amendment to correct the situation." (*Eu, supra,* 54 Cal.3d. at p. 512.) Those avenues remain available.

D. Appellants' Do Not Challenge a Particular Interpretation or Application of Proposition 140

It is true that our Supreme Court has stressed that analysis of the amendment/ revision distinction is not tantamount to an "'Analysis of the problems which may arise respecting the interpretation or application of particular provisions of the act.'" (*Amador, supra,* 22 Cal.3d at p. 219.) Analysis of particular problems "'should be deferred for future cases in which those provisions are more directly challenged.'" (*Ibid.*) Here appellants do not seek the interpretation of any particular provision of Proposition 140, but instead seek to invalidate the entire proposition based on their allegations that it revised the Constitution.

This is not a case where appellants challenge a particular provision enacted by Proposition 140. *Schabarum, supra,* 60 Cal.App.4th 1205, is an example of such a case. It involved a challenge to article IV, section 7.5 of the California Constitution, which was enacted as part of Proposition 140. In that case, the court considered "whether the funds budgeted for the Legislative Counsel Bureau must be included in the budget of the Legislature for purposes of constitutional spending limitations." (*Schabarum,* at p. 1211.) The majority held that excluding the budget for the Legislative Counsel from the Legislature's spending cap was not unconstitutional. (*Id.* at pp. 1227, 1230.)

In contrast to *Schabarum,* which involved a challenge to a specific substantive change caused by the initiative, the issue appellants seek to litigate — whether Proposition 140 constitutes a revision — is identical to the issue decided in *Eu.* While appellants allege they now have more conclusive evidence than that presented to our high court in *Eu*, that evidence is irrelevant to determine whether it appeared from the face of the initiative that, the initiative necessarily and inevitably changed the basic form of government. Nor does the existence of additional evidence relating to the role of the Legislature transform a facial attack on Proposition 140 into an "as applied" constitutional challenge.

We do not hold that appellants cannot challenge a specific provision by raising either a facial or an as applied challenge. We hold only that the question of whether Proposition 140 constitutes an amendment or a revision was already decided in *Eu* and forecloses appellants' current challenge. The trial court correctly granted the Secretary of State's motion for judgment on the pleadings.

DISPOSITION

The judgment is affirmed. Respondents are entitled to costs on appeal.

Notes and Questions

1. Voters and former state legislators had standing to raise a facial challenge to a state constitutional amendment imposing budget and term limits on state legislators. The challenge did not call for an advisory opinion, because a successful challenge would affect the plaintiffs' ability to run for office and to vote for termed out legislators.

2. The court in this case looked at the question whether Proposition 140 revised the California Constitution and was therefore invalid, or whether it was a permissible amendment to the state Constitution.

3. The appellants in this case unsuccessfully argued that a constitutional revision occurred because the initiative fundamentally changed the structure of government and altered the balance of power between the executive and legislative branches of government. They also argued, which the court rejected, that Proposition 140 rendered the Legislature unable to competently perform its essential legislative function.

4. The court addressed a procedural issue (whether the appellants had standing to maintain the action) and a substantive issue (whether this case was barred by stare decisis because the California Supreme Court already has held that Proposition 140 does not effect a revision to the California Constitution). How did the court ultimately rule on both issues?

5. The court's opinion helpfully provided a number of cases that provide examples of the difference between a constitutional amendment and a constitutional revision. Ultimately, the court ruled that "Proposition 140 on its face does not affect either the structure or the foundational powers of the Legislature, which remains free to enact whatever laws it deems appropriate. The challenged measure alters neither the content of those laws nor the process by which they are adopted. No legislative power is diminished or delegated to other persons or agencies. The relationships between the three governmental branches, and their respective powers, remain untouched." (*Eu*, 54 Cal.3d at p. 509.)

6. The court explained that prior state court decisions have made it clear that to find a constitutional revision, it must "*necessarily or inevitably appear from the face*

of the challenged provision that the measure will substantially alter the basic governmental framework set forth in our Constitution." (Quoting *Eu*, 54 Cal.3d at p. 510.)

7. Ultimately, the court determined that it was bound by the ruling in *Eu*. Why did the court decide that the conclusion under *Eu* was dispositive of appellants' case?

8. Why did the court reject the appellants' argument that the court should apply the public interest exception to res judicata?

9. Should the court have decided this case by invoking the political question doctrine? Why did it choose not to do so?

Chapter Ten

Special Rules for Legislation

A. Urgency Clauses

1. What Is an Urgency Clause?

Bills signed into law by the Governor that contain an urgency clause become urgency statutes or urgency clause statutes. California Constitution Article IV, Section 8 deals with urgency statutes. Section 8(c)(3) provides that urgency clause bills go into effect immediately upon their enactment. That is the major distinction between a regular bill and an urgency clause bill. The regular bill takes effect on the following January 1 (or later) while the urgency clause bill takes effect immediately.

What determines an urgency? Section 8(d) specifies that "urgency statutes are those necessary for immediate preservation of the public peace, health, or safety." Because of this definition, an urgency measure must contain an urgency clause which specifies why the bill qualifies for this special status based upon this definition.

In this regard, Section 8(d) requires that "a statement of facts constituting the necessity shall be set forth in one section of the bill. In each house the section and the bill shall be passed separately, each by rollcall vote entered in the journal, two-thirds of the membership concurring." Not only is the urgency clause required with the relevant explanation, but also the Legislature must vote on the urgency clause itself.

Finally, Section 8(d) provides that "an urgency statute may not create or abolish any office or change the salary, term, or duties of any office, or grant any franchise or special privilege, or create any vested right or interest." As a result, these types of bills are simply not allowed to contain an urgency clause and may not be enacted as an urgency statute.

Due to these constitutional provisions, the two major distinctions with an urgency clause statute, as opposed to a regular statute, are the vote threshold requirement and the effective date. Instead of the usual simple majority vote required of most bills to pass, an urgency clause statute requires a super-majority vote on both floors of the California Legislature.

In addition, urgency statutes once enacted are effective the day they are chaptered, rather than January 1 of the following year (absent a statutory operative date otherwise specified). There is also a floor requirement that there be two separate votes by legislators — one on the urgency clause itself and one on the bill in chief.

Notes and Questions

1. Urgency bills are those that are deemed to be urgency by the Legislature and contain an "urgency clause" in which the Legislature provides a statement of facts that constitute the urgency and the need for the bill to take immediate effect. Urgency measures must contain an urgency clause and must be passed by a 2/3 majority of both houses of the Legislature.

2. Concerning urgency clause statutes, the courts have historically upheld the determinations made by the Legislature. In other words, courts generally defer to the Legislature's judgment contained in the urgency clause. The only time a court will reject an urgency clause is when it "appears clearly and affirmatively from the Legislature's statement of facts that a public necessity does not exist." (*Stockburger v. Jordan* (1938) 10 Cal.2d 636, 642.)

3. Furthermore, the *Stockburger* Court went on to say that "The Legislature having determined by the declaration contained in said act that the enactment of said statute was necessary for the immediate preservation of the public peace, health and safety, and the determination of the legislature of the existence of such necessity being conclusive upon the courts, we are precluded in these proceedings from further questioning the necessity for such legislation." (*Stockburger,*10 Cal.2d at 643.)

4. The fact that several of the Senators who voted to declare a bill a case of urgency afterwards voted against the bill on its final passage has been held to be immaterial. Under Constitution Article IV, Section 15, a dispending resolution adopted by two-thirds vote of the Senate, declaring that a number of specified bills "present cases of urgency" and that the provision of the Constitution "requiring that the bill be read on three separate days in each house is hereby dispensed with" is not objectionable upon the ground that it includes other bills as well as the one brought in question. (*People ex rel. Scearce v. County of Glenn* (1893) 1001 Cal. 419.)

5. The California Constitution provides four types of statutes that are not subject to a referendum. For example, an urgency statute avoids the threat of a referendum. In *Davis v. Los Angeles County* (1938) 12 Cal.2d 412, the court ruled that it would not interfere with the Legislature's determination that a measure required an urgency clause.

2. Statement of Facts in Urgency Clauses

An urgency bill must contain an urgency clause. The urgency clause contains a statement of facts made by the Legislature setting forth or explaining the urgent nature of the necessary law change(s). This statement of facts must be included in any measure in which the Legislature desires a measure to take immediate effect.

Davis v. County of Los Angeles

12 Cal.2d 412

OPINION

SHENK, J.

By this action for an injunction and declaratory relief the plaintiff sought to test the validity of the emergency clause of Statutes of 1937, page 153. That act repealed the act of 1929 (Stats. 1929, p. 357), which provided for the payment of retirement compensation to teachers and other employees. The act of 1929 was declared unconstitutional in *Los Angeles City School Dist. v. Griffin*, 3 Cal.2d 651 [46 PaCal.2d 141].

The 1937 enactment presented a different plan or method for adopting a pension and retirement system in the school districts throughout the state. Section 5.1100 thereby added to the School Code, provides that in any school district in which the employees are not entitled to the benefits of a pension or retirement system maintained by a city, city and county, or county, the governing board of the district shall have power in its discretion to submit, and upon a petition duly signed and filed as prescribed it must submit, to the qualified electors of the district "the proposition of establishing a plan for a district retirement salary under the provisions of this article", to be paid to teachers and such other employees as the board may determine.

By section 5.1101 "the proposition of establishing such plan may be submitted to the electors of the district at any general or special election", also authorizing the governing bodies to call and hold elections for such purpose. The same section permits the consolidation of elections where "the governing board calling such an election is the governing board of more than one school district and calls elections in two or more districts to submit to the electors of the respective districts, on the same day, in the same territory, or in territory which is in part the same, the question whether a district retirement plan shall be established in such respective districts". Other particulars are specified including requirements for posting and publishing notice of the election. The form of ballot is prescribed. A majority vote favorable to the proposition bestows upon the board the power and imposes upon it the duty of establishing a district retirement salary for teachers and employees.

Section 5.1102 designates the teachers and employees who shall be bound by the burdens and benefits of the plan.

Before formulating the plan, the board must, pursuant to section 5.1103, and after inquiry and hearing, find rates of contribution which are substantially in accordance with the more recent generally prevailing rates of such contributions in established retirement systems of public institutions, and determine that such plan is in accordance with sound business practice and recognized actuarial methods. This section establishes minimum and maximum retirement salary payments. It also requires the levy and collection of district taxes to provide funds for the retirement payments.

Section 5.1104 specifies the period of service and minimum age limits of a beneficiary of the system, with certain exceptions in cases of disability. Section 5.1105 provides for a "retired list". Section 5.1106 gives to the governing boards general rule-making power in aid of the provisions of the act. A "District Retirement Fund" is defined by section 5.1107, a record of which is required to be kept upon the books of the auditor and county treasurer. It includes contributions received from teachers and employees and moneys from all other sources properly allocable to the fund. By the same section members of governing boards are charged with the performance of such duties and responsibilities without additional compensation. Also serving without compensation is a district retirement board (section 5.1108) composed of not less than three nor more than seven members, upon which the governing board, the teachers and other employees in the district shall be represented, to be selected by them by secret ballot, and of which the county treasurer shall be ex officio a member. Section 5.1109 places in the charge and control of the district retirement board, the district retirement fund and the payment of all retirement salaries and annuities. This board is also charged with the investment and management of the fund. The attorney for the governing board of the district is directed to act as attorney for the district retirement board without additional compensation. Securities purchased are to be deposited with the county treasurer for safekeeping. The same section provides that the duties reposed by the act in "the county treasurer shall be deemed a part of his official duties, for the faithful performance of which he shall be liable upon his official bond". The county auditor is required to audit the accounts of the district retirement board at least once a year and report upon the financial condition thereof to the governing board of the district.

Sections 5.1110 and 5.1111 indicate that the plan is not intended to displace retirement salaries otherwise provided by law but is in addition thereto.

In a separate section of the act the legislature declared the immediate effect of the act as an urgency measure necessary for the preservation of the public peace, health and safety. The section also contains a statement of the facts deemed to constitute the necessity.

The act was approved by the Governor on April 22, 1937. Immediately following its approval the board of education of the city of Los Angeles, as the governing board of the city elementary school district, the city high school district, and the city junior college district, voted to call an election to be held on May 4, 1937, for the purpose of submitting to the electors of those districts the proposition of establishing a retirement plan as authorized by the act. The board thereby also voted to consolidate the election for such purpose with a general municipal election theretofore called for the same day. Notice of the call was given as prescribed. At the elections the proposition was submitted to the voters in the three districts, and passed by a large majority vote.

On August 5, 1937, the board adopted rules and regulations for a retirement plan pursuant to the act and subsequently filed with the superintendent of schools its retirement budget requirements, including $451,490 for the elementary school district, $510,380 for the high school district, and $19,630 for the junior college district, a total of $981,500. On September 1, 1937, the board of supervisors accordingly set the appropriate tax rate for each of said districts and levied the same upon the taxable property in the respective districts.

A petition that the act be referred to a vote of the people of the state was not filed.

The plaintiff herein, owner of property in the three districts, sought a declaration of the invalidity of the proceedings purporting to levy the tax to raise retirement funds pursuant to the act and the plan. The trial court found favorably as to the validity and constitutionality of the act and the emergency clause giving it immediate effect; further that any irregularity in the call and conduct of the election of May 4th did not affect the result. The plaintiff appealed from the judgment entered pursuant to those findings.

The plaintiff attacks the validity of the urgency clause and contends that in any event the act did not become effective on April 22, 1937; and consequently, that the election of May 4, 1937, was a nullity.

Section 1 of article IV of the state Constitution vests legislative power in the senate and assembly, but reserves to the people the powers of the initiative and referendum. An act passed by the legislature does not become effective until 90 days after the final adjournment of the legislative session at which the act was passed. Exceptions are acts calling elections, acts providing for tax levies or appropriations for the usual current expenses of the state, and urgency measures necessary for the immediate preservation of the public peace, health or safety, passed by a two-thirds vote of all members elected to each house.

The Constitution provides: "Whenever it is deemed necessary for the immediate preservation of the public peace, health or safety that a law shall go into immediate effect, a statement of the facts constituting such necessity shall be set forth in one section of the act, which section shall be passed only upon a yea and nay vote, upon a separate roll call thereon; provided, however, that no measure creating or abolishing any office or changing the salary, term or duties of any officer, or granting any franchise or special privilege, or creating any vested right or interest, shall be construed to be an urgency measure. Any law so passed by the legislature and declared to be an urgency measure shall go into immediate effect."

Section 3 of the act here in question contains the following statement of facts deemed by the legislature to constitute the necessity: "The School Code was amended by the Legislature at its 1935 session to permit governing boards of school districts to discharge teachers who have reached the age of sixty-five years, which amendment will become effective September 1, 1937. Many boards of education desire to take advantage of the provisions of said amendment, and to avoid the hardships which will follow the discharge of many teachers aged sixty-five years or more and to avoid the possibility of placing such teachers and their families and dependents on relief rolls of their respective counties, such boards desire to establish district retirement plans for their employees, as authorized herein. This act requires that the establishment of such plan be submitted to the vote of the people of the school district, and many municipal and school district elections are to be held during the months of April and May, 1937, at which such propositions can be submitted to the voters of the respective districts, at a large saving to the taxpayers of the respective districts."

The plaintiff contends that the foregoing statement does not show any necessity for the preservation of the public peace, health or safety, and for that reason the urgency declaration was ineffective as such.

It is urged by the defendants that a sufficient answer to all of the grounds of the plaintiff's opposition to the effectiveness of the legislation as an urgency measure is that the act is not self-executing but is rather an enabling act and requires an election to be called and held in the district to be affected thereby before the powers to be exercised thereunder are vested in the appropriate body. The argument that the urgency clause of the act, if effective, cuts off unwarrantedly the power to exercise the referendum loses much of its power for the reason that the voters still must register their assent to be bound by the act. But we need not rest our conclusion that the act was effective urgency legislation upon that observation.

It is apparent that there is a conflict in the authorities on the question whether a legislative declaration of urgency is binding on the courts. It has been held by some courts, and probably by the weight of authority, that the declaration of the existence of the emergency or necessity is exclusively within the exercise of the legislative function, and if the prescribed procedure has been followed the law is immediately effective and the declaration is not subject to review in the courts. (*Kadderly v. City of Portland,* 44 Or. 118 [74 P. 710, 75 P. 222]; *City of Roanoke v. Elliott,* 123 Va. 393 [96 S.E. 819]; *Orrick v. City of Ft. Worth,* 52 Tex. Civ. App. 308 [114 S.W. 677]; *Joplin v. Ten Brook,* 124 Or. 36 [263 P. 893, 894]; *Simpson v. Winegar,* 122 Or. 297 [258 P. 562]; *State v. Kennedy,* 132 Ohio St. 510 [9 N.E. (2d) 278, 110 A.L.R. 1428]; *Hill v. Taylor,* 264 Ky. 708 [95 S.W. (2d) 566]; *Hutchens v. Jackson,* 37 N. M. 325 [23 PaCal.2d 355].) The basis for the foregoing conclusion is that the law makers in the process of enacting laws must pass upon all questions of expediency, necessity and fact connected therewith (see, also, *Stevenson v. Colgan,* 91 Cal. 649 [27 P. 1089, 25 Am.St.Rep. 230, 14 L.R.A. 459]), "and must, therefore, determine whether a given law is necessary for the preservation of the public peace, health and safety. It has always been the rule, and is now everywhere understood, that the judgment of the legislative and executive departments as to the wisdom, expediency or necessity of any given law is conclusive on the courts and cannot be reviewed or called in question by them. It is the duty of the courts, after a law has been enacted, to determine in a proper proceeding whether it conflicts with the fundamental law, and to construe and interpret it so as to ascertain the rights of the parties litigant. The powers of the courts do not extend to the mere question of expediency or necessity, but, as said by Mr. Justice Brewer, 'they are wrought out and fought out in the legislature and before the people. Here the single question is one of power. We make no laws. We change no constitutions. We inaugurate no policy. When the legislature enacts a law, the only question which we can decide is whether the limitations of the Constitution have been infringed upon'. (Prohibitory Am. Cas., 24 Kan. 700, 706.) The amendment excepts such laws as may be necessary for a certain purpose. The existence of such necessity is therefore a question of fact, and the authority to determine such fact must rest somewhere. The Constitution does not confer it upon any tribunal. It must therefore necessarily reside with that department of the government which is called upon to exercise the power. It is a question of which the legislature alone must be the judge, and, when it decides the fact to exist, its action is final ... (citing cases)." (*Kadderly v. City of Portland, supra.*)

The view opposed to the foregoing, expressed in the case of *State v. Meath*, 84 Wash. 302, 304 [147 P. 11] (see, also, *State v. Hinkle*, 116 Wash. 1 [198 P. 535]; *State v. Hutchinson*, 173 Wash. 72 [21 PaCal.2d 514]; *State v. Martin*, 173 Wash. 249 [23 PaCal.2d 1, 4]), leans toward a policy which would accord the greatest effectiveness to the exercise of the right of referendum. (For further discussion and citation of cases see *Hutchens v. Jackson, supra*, and note, 7 A.L.R. 519 et seq.)

It is unnecessary to enter upon a further analysis of the cases in other jurisdictions supporting the divergent views. In this state in *Stevenson v. Colgan, supra*, at page 652, it was said: "The authority and duty to ascertain the facts which ought to control legislative action are, from the necessity of the case, devolved by the Constitution upon those to whom it has given the power to legislate, and their decision that the facts exist is conclusive upon the court, in the absence of an explicit provision in the Constitution giving the judiciary the right to review such action." The reasoning of the case of *Kadderly v. City of Portland, supra*, as applied to statements of necessity in urgency measures, is reflected in the early decisions of this court. (*Franklin v. State Board of Examiners*, 23 Cal. 1; *People v. Pacheco*, 27 Cal. 175, 176, 221.) There is nothing to the contrary to be inferred from *In re Hoffman*, 155 Cal. 114 [99 P. 517, 132 Am.St.Rep. 75]. That case involved a purported urgency ordinance of the city of Los Angeles regulating the sale of milk and cream. As indicated in *Joplin v. Ten Brook*, 124 Or. 36 [263 P. 893, 895], restrictions may be imposed upon the power exercised by a city legislative body to declare the urgency nature of an ordinance which are not imposed by the Constitution upon the state legislature. In the same category as the Hoffman case are the cases of *Los Angeles G. & E. Corp. v. City of Los Angeles*, 163 Cal. 621, 629 [126 P. 594], and *Morgan v. City of Long Beach*, 57 Cal.App. 134 [207 P. 53].

Since the adoption by the people in 1911 of section 1, article IV of the Constitution, reserving the powers of the initiative and the referendum, the courts have nevertheless adhered to the fundamental philosophy that questions of fact, necessity and expediency are for the legislature. It has been felt that the requirement for a statement of the facts constituting the necessity in emergency legislation does not modify the principle nor bestow upon the judiciary power to declare the declaration invalid unless it "appears clearly and affirmatively from the legislature's statement of facts that a public necessity does not exist". (*Stockburger v. Jordan*, 10 Cal.2d 636 [76 PaCal.2d 671], citing *Hollister v. Kingsbury*, 129 Cal.App. 420 [18 PaCal.2d 1006], and *In re McDermott*, 180 Cal. 783 [183 P. 437].) Thus in the *Stockburger* case it was also said: "The legislature having determined by the declaration contained in said act that the enactment of said statute was necessary for the immediate preservation of the public peace, health and safety, and the determination of the legislature of the existence of such necessity being conclusive upon the courts, we are precluded in these proceedings from further questioning the necessity for such legislation."

There is no clear and affirmative showing on the face of the statement of facts included in the present act such as would justify this court in concluding that the legislative declaration of the existence of a public necessity was invalid. Certainly, it is not for the court to say that, since the previous act of 1929 was declared unconstitutional, and since an act passed in 1935 (Stats. 1935, p. 1881) divested teachers attaining age of 65 of their permanent tenure from and after September 1, 1937, the acute situation indicated in the statement with respect to teachers expecting retirement has not arisen. That such a situation has or might have a direct bearing upon the public health, peace and safety, cannot be doubted. Nor may we conclude that an early vote by the electors on the proposition to authorize the establishment of a retirement plan would not serve an immediate necessity involving the public health, peace and safety in addition to affording the opportunity for public economy obtained by consolidating the elections provided for with general elections already called.

If there is any doubt as to whether the facts do or do not state a case of immediate necessity, that doubt should be resolved in favor of the legislative declaration (*Naudzius v. Lahr*, 253 Mich. 216 [234 N.W. 581, 585 [74 A.L.R. 1189]); or, as it has otherwise been stated, "if fair-minded and intelligent men might reasonably differ as to the sufficiency and truth of the fact assigned for placing the act in effect immediately upon its passage, the courts are concluded by the finding" (*Jumper v. McCollum*, 179 Ark. 837 [18 S.W. (2d) 359, 361], and cases referred to); or, if the legislature "states facts constituting an emergency so that its action cannot be said to be arbitrary, courts cannot say that it has not performed its constitutional duty, even though they may disagree with the legislature as to the sufficiency of declared facts to constitute a sufficient reason for immediate action". (*Baker v. Hill*, 180 Ark. 387 [21 S.W. (2d) 867, 868].)

We are brought then to a consideration of the question whether the act creates any office or changes the salary or duties of any officer, or creates any vested right or interest so as to defeat the immediate effectiveness thereof.

The plaintiff contends that "additional burdens are placed upon" the school board, the county treasurer, county auditor, county school superintendent and the county counsel by the new provisions of the School Code; that the duties of the officers and boards are enlarged and increased by the provisions of the statute, and that section 5.1108 creates the offices of members of a district retirement board. A sufficient answer to these contentions would seem to be that until the election authorized by the act has resulted in favor of the adoption of the proposition to establish a retirement plan, none of the provisions of the act controls or governs in the district or districts. If the election is not held in any school district in the state, then the act would have no more effect upon the duties of officers or otherwise than if it had never been passed.

In support of her contention that the additional duties devolving upon the school board, the county treasurer, auditor, school superintendent and counsel effect a "change" in their respective duties, the plaintiff relies on the recent decision of this court in *Stockburger v. Jordan, supra.* That case involved the validity of the urgency declaration purporting to give immediate effect to chapter 304 of Statutes of 1937 (p. 665), which related to the development, production, and disposition of oil, gas and other hydro-carbon substances from state-owned tide and submerged lands at Huntington Beach. The act purported to vest immediately in the director of finance the power and duty to secure the development, extraction, removal and sale of oil and gas, to acquire by condemnation or otherwise property necessary for government access to the lands, and if the oil lands be leased to others, to dispose of leases thereof for production purposes, or to obtain the immediate drilling thereof if bids for leases are not received. When, in that case, this court concluded that such a material and substantial addition to the duties of the director of finance was a "change" of duties within the meaning of the pertinent constitutional section, it was not intended that it should be inferred therefrom that every addition to the duties devolving upon public officers should be deemed to constitute a "change" of duties. The definition of "change of duties" adopted in that case was not intended to embrace such additional duties imposed by law the performance of which would naturally devolve upon the officer had no express mention thereof been made in the act, and as otherwise would be incidental to his office. Obviously, such was not the situation in the *Stockburger* case. The new and special character of the additional duties imposed upon the director of finance under the act involved in that case was entirely foreign to the duties theretofore devolving upon him by law.

Inasmuch as the provisions of the act or the code sections do not impose undue or material and substantial additional burdens or duties upon the officers mentioned, different in nature from those already required of them by law, we conclude that such provisions did not produce a "change" either in the salary or duties of those officers.

The act does not create any vested right or interest, if for no other reason than that claims to pension, whether inchoate or vested, cannot arise under its provisions until the electors vote to authorize the establishment of a plan, and the plan is accordingly formulated and put into effect. It is therefore not necessary at this time to determine the nature of that right.

The act is not special or "class" legislation, nor does it lack uniformity of operation. It is a general law applicable throughout the state for the benefit of every school district whose electors vote to take advantage of its provisions.

The act does not delegate to boards of education legislative functions. Acting within its recognized powers, the legislature has provided for delegation to the boards of governors of only the administrative duties to establish the details of the plans for retirement pensions subject to the limitations and requirements prescribed by the act. That such plans must differ in each section of the state, in accordance with its needs, or even within different districts in the same section of the state, must be obvious. The legislature was acting within its proper function in delegating to the local governing boards the discretion to formulate the details of a retirement plan pertaining to such matters as determining what persons are within the class entitled to benefit under the law, what are the recent generally prevailing rates of contribution in public institutions and the rate to be adopted based thereon, and what are the sound business practices and actuarial methods and the introduction and application thereof in the plan to be adopted. The delegation by the legislature of the performance of such duties guided by the rules prescribed is not unlawful. (*Tarpey v. McClure*, 190 Cal. 593, 600 [213 P. 983]; *People v. Monterey Fish Products Co.*, 195 Cal. 548, 558 [234 P. 398, 38 A.L.R. 1186]; 5 Cal.Jur. 679, 681.)

Differences which may result from methods of administration depending upon differences for instance in population, do not create any unlawful discrimination. (*Grigsby v. King*, 202 Cal. 299 [260 P. 789]; *Morris v. Board of Education*, 119 Cal.App. 750 [7 PaCal.2d 364, 8 PaCal.2d 502].)

Finally the plaintiff contends that certain irregularities occurred in the call and conduct of the election of May 4, 1937, which avoided the proceedings and resulted in an invalid tax for the purposes of the plan established by the Board of Education. Of the three districts mentioned herein, the elementary school district of Los Angeles city is the smallest in area; the high school district is the next larger and the junior college district is the largest. However, the elementary school district is embraced entirely within the high school district, and the high school district is within the junior college district. The Board of Education submitted to the voters in all three districts the following proposition: "Shall the governing board of the Los Angeles City School District of Los Angeles County, Los Angeles City High School District of Los Angeles County, and Los Angeles Junior College District of Los Angeles County be authorized to establish a plan for a district retirement salary for the teachers and such other employees of such districts as such governing board may determine." The submission to the electors of the proposition in the form stated was in accordance with section 5.1101, added to the School Code, permitting consolidation of elections for several districts when the same board is the governing board of more than one district, and prescribing the wording of the proposition to be submitted accordingly which is substantially identical with that drafted by the board and submitted at the election of May 4th. The facts shown in the record bearing upon the plaintiff's contention that irregularities existed have been examined. It appears that 95 per cent of the registered voters live in the territory comprising the elementary school district, and therefore in territory which is common to all three districts. At the election 206,353 votes were cast in favor of the proposition, and 84,178 against it. In the precincts outside the elementary school district a total of 2,673 votes was cast, 675 of which were unfavorable to the proposition. It may not be supposed that those voting favorably to the establishment of a plan for all three districts would so have registered their choice if they had been in favor of establishing a plan for only one district. The manner of submitting the proposition was not contrary to the act. The legislature might well have contemplated that boards of education could properly determine that such a plan should encompass all three such districts governed by one board, or none at all.

These facts and considerations also support the finding of the trial court that misdescription of outlying precincts in the notice of election did not mislead the voters, was immaterial and did not affect the result of the election. Such alleged error related to merely directory provisions. Technical errors or irregularities arising in carrying out directory provisions which do not affect the result will not avoid the election. (*Rideout v. City of Los Angeles*, 185 Cal. 426, 430 [197 P. 74]; *East Bay Mun. Utility Dist. v. Hadsell*, 196 Cal. 725 [239 P. 38].) The trial court's finding was a proper application of the policy that an election will not be declared a nullity, if upon any reasonable basis such a result can be avoided.

The judgment of the trial court denying to the plaintiff the relief sought by her is affirmed.

CURTIS, J., LANGDON, J., WASTE, C.J., and SEAWELL, J., concurred.

Notes and Questions

1. Where there is any doubt as to whether the statement of facts constituting the necessity in emergency legislation states a case of immediate necessity, the doubt should be resolved in favor of the legislative declaration. The requirement that emergency legislation contain a statement of the facts constituting the necessity does not empower the judiciary to declare the declaration invalid, unless it appears clearly and affirmatively from the statement of facts that a public necessity does not exist. A legislative declaration of urgency is binding on the courts.

2. The judgment of the Legislature is normally considered to be final. When courts examine urgency measures, they normally consider the statement of facts contained in the urgency clause to be final. In other words, the judicial branch of state government will generally defer to the legislative branch's judgment in deciding whether there is a threat to the public health or safety and therefore a bill must take effect immediately. That deference afforded to the Legislature means that a court will usually not overturn the Legislature's judgment, which must normally be considered final.

3. When the Legislature has determined the necessity of an urgency measure as authorized by the Constitution, the Legislature's judgment is final, unless no declaration of facts constituting the urgency or a clearly insufficient declaration is included. (*In re Livingston* (1938) 10 Cal.2d 730.)

4. Note how the Court in this case referred to it as "the emergency clause."

5. The Court noted that the legislation (i.e., the act) contained an urgency clause along with "a statement of the facts deemed to constitute the necessity." The plaintiff in the case attacked the validity of the urgency clause, basically arguing that the statement did not demonstrate the requisite necessity. How did the Court address the plaintiff's argument?

6. What is the explanation of the Court that it is not for them to determine the validity of the statement? Based upon this rationale, should the same approach be applied if a plaintiff challenged the Legislature's determination that an act constituted a "special statute" (rather than a general statute) under the state Constitution?

7. Why did the Court not find a violation that the act creates any office or changes the salary or duties of any officer, or creates any vested right or interest so as to defeat

the immediate effectiveness thereof? What test did the Court set forth as to whether an act produced a "change" in either the salary or duties of a public officer?

3. Immediate Effect of an Urgency Bill

Simply stated, the California Constitution specifically provides that an urgency bill takes effect immediately and so, once such a measure has been signed into law by the Governor, then the measure takes immediate effect on the day it has been chaptered with the Secretary of State's Office.

Notes and Questions

1. A "three strikes" statute was effective immediately when it was signed by the Governor and transmitted to the Secretary of State and, thus, it applied to a defendant who was arrested approximately seven and one-half hours later on the same date, despite the contention that the term "immediately" in the statute meant the next day. (*People v. Cargill* (1995) 38 Cal.App.4th 1551, rehearing denied, review denied.)

B. Effective and Operative Dates

There is often confusion regarding effective versus operative dates. Specifically, Capitol observers often inquire when a statute actually "takes effect." When it takes effect can be different than when the statute is operative.

January 1 following the year a bill is enacted is the most common effective date and is basically the "default" effective date, unless the statute specifies something different. A common definition of "effective date" is when the new law is "on the books." A common definition of "operative date" is when the new law becomes operative (which commonly, but mistakenly, is described as when the new law is "in effect").

Any bill can specify a delayed effective date. There are certain types of bills that are deemed to be in effect upon enactment (i.e., when the Governor signed them and the Secretary of State assigns a chapter number). Therefore, unless the bill calls an election, contains an urgency clause, or is a budget-related or tax levy measure, one can presume the effective date of a new law is January 1 of the following year.

What about operative dates? An operative date is distinguished from an effective date. "A statute may be worded so as to provide for an operative date other than its effective date." (28 Ops.Atty.Gen. 20 (1956).) An operative date, therefore, may be the same as the effective date, or it may be different than the effective date.

According to a decision of the Court of Appeal in California, "unlike a statute's effective date, which is determined according to immutable rules written into the state constitution, its operative date, the date upon which the directives of the statute are actually implemented, is set by the Legislature in its discretion." (*People v. Verba* (2012) 210 Cal.App.4th 991.)

By way of background, in the California Legislature, certain bills take effect immediately upon the Governor signing the bill and the measure being chaptered by the Secretary of State. These are measures containing urgency clauses or tax levies, as well as bills calling an election.

The general rule for the effective dates of statutes is found in the California Constitution, Article IV, Section 9(c). That section provides:

> (c)(1) Except as provided in paragraphs (2) and (3) of this subdivision, a statute enacted at a regular session shall go into effect on January 1 next following a 90-day period from the date of enactment of the statute and a statute enacted at a special session shall go into effect on the 91st day after adjournment of the special session at which the bill was passed.

> (2) A statute, other than a statute establishing or changing boundaries of any legislative, congressional, or other election district, enacted by a bill passed by the Legislature on or before the date the Legislature adjourns for a joint recess to reconvene in the second calendar year of the biennium of the legislative session, and in the possession of the Governor after that date, shall go into effect on January 1 next following the enactment date of the statute unless, before January 1, a copy of a referendum petition affecting the statute is submitted to the Attorney General pursuant to subdivision (d) of Section 10 of Article II, in which event the statute shall go into effect on the 91st day after the enactment date unless the petition has been presented to the Secretary of State pursuant to subdivision (b) of Section 9 of Article II.

> (3) Statutes calling elections, statutes providing for tax levies or appropriations for the usual current expenses of the State, and urgency statutes shall go into effect immediately upon their enactment.

Chapter 6 of the California Government Code also deals with the operation of statutes and resolutions. The general rule concerning the effective dates of statutes is found in § 9600(a), which provides that a statute enacted at a regular session shall go into effect on January 1 next following a 90-day period from the date of enactment of the statute and a statute, enacted at a special session shall go into effect on the 91st day after adjournment of the special session at which the bill was passed.

The exceptions to this general rule are found in § 9600(b) of the Government Code, which provides that statutes calling elections, statutes providing for tax levies or appropriations for the usual current expenses of the state, and urgency statutes shall go into effect immediately upon their enactment.

One should also be aware of Government Code § 17580, which provides:

> No bill, except a bill containing an urgency clause, introduced or amended on or after January 1, 1989, that mandates a new program or higher level of service requiring reimbursement of local agencies or school districts pursuant to Section 6 of Article XIII B of the California Constitution shall become operative until the July 1 following the date on which the bill takes effect, unless the bill specifically makes this section inapplicable or contains an ap-

propriation for the reimbursement or a specification that reimbursement be made pursuant to Section 17610.

Under these rules, for example, a non-urgency bill passed on September 5, 2019, would take effect on January 1, 2020. A non-urgency measure, however, that is enacted in the second year of the two-year session would go into effect on January 1 following a 90-day period from the date of enactment. By contrast, statutes enacted at a special session take effect on the 91st day after the adjournment of the special session at which they were passed.

The delays in the effective dates of the statutes enacted at regular and special sessions provide a 90-day interval between the enactment and the effective date of the statute as is required by the Constitution in order to permit the circulation and presentation of a referendum petition requesting that the statute, or a part of it, be submitted to the electorate.

Notes and Questions

1. This is a commonly misunderstood area of the law — the difference between an operative date and an effective date. When does a statute become effective? Its effective date is when the bill's provisions actually are "on the books," that is, when they are in the code book. This is distinguished from when the bill becomes operative. A statute has no force whatever until it goes into effect pursuant to the law relating to legislative enactments, and it speaks from the date it takes effect and not before. (*Kennelly v. Lowery* (1944) 64 Cal.App.2d 903.)

1. Operative Date Specified and Urgency Clauses

When a measure becomes operative is determined by specific language contained in the statute, if there is a specified operative date. Otherwise, the default rule is the effective date, which is generally January 1 following the date the bill was signed into law. With regard to urgency clauses, the effective date is the date the measure was chaptered into law; however, an urgency clause can have as its operative date either the date the bill was chaptered or a later specified operative date.

Enactment of a law on its effective date only means that it cannot be changed except by the legislative process. The rights of individuals under its provisions are not substantially affected until the provision operates as law. The Legislature's power to enact laws includes the power to fix a future date on which the act will become operative (i.e., to establish an operative date for a statute that is later than its effective date).

A statute's operative date is the date upon which directives of a statute may be actually implemented, whereas the statute's effective date is considered that date upon which the statute came into being as existing law. The Legislature's determination of urgency in enactment of the statute is final, and the courts will not interfere with that determination unless no declaration of facts constituting the emergency is included in the act or unless the statement of facts is so clearly insufficient as to leave no reasonable doubt that urgency does not exist.

Courts cannot say that the Legislature has not performed its constitutional duty, even when they may disagree with the Legislature about whether declared facts constitute sufficient reason for immediate action. Under the state constitutional requirements for urgency measures, a second roll call vote was not needed to approve the urgency clause of a bill reducing the percentage of days of pre-conviction confinement even though the bill returned to its house of origin in drastically amended form.

People v. Camba

(1996) 50 Cal.App.4th 857

OPINION

A. Enactment as an Urgency Measure.

Appellant's claim that the urgency provision of section 2933.1 cannot be given recognition is based upon article IV, section 8, subdivision (d) of the California Constitution, which provides: "Urgency statutes are those necessary for immediate preservation of the public peace, health, or safety. A statement of facts constituting the necessity shall be set forth in one section of the bill. In each house, the section and the bill shall be passed separately, each by rollcall vote entered in the journal, two thirds of the membership concurring...."

If the urgency clause of legislation is found constitutionally unsound, the remainder of the statute is nonetheless valid, and it takes effect "at the regular time appointed by law. [Citations.]" (*People v. Phillips* (1946) 76 Cal. App. 2d 515, 521 [173 P.2d 392].)

Appellant insists that when the history of the legislation is considered, the urgency clause was not properly passed by a separate roll call vote of each house of the Legislature, and the urgency statement was "no longer relevant" when it was enacted.

We are severely constrained in our review of the section 2933.1 urgency clause.

"Authority is conferred upon the legislature to determine when urgency measures are necessary, and when such necessity has been determined as provided by the Constitution, the judgment of the legislature is final, and will not be interfered with by the courts unless no declaration of facts constituting such emergency is included in the act or unless the statement of facts is so clearly insufficient as to leave no reasonable doubt that the urgency does not exist. (*Hollister v. Kingsbury* [(1933)] 129 Cal. App. 420 [18 Pac. (2d) 1006].)" (*Livingston v. Robinson* (1938) 10 Cal. 2d 730, 740 [76 P.2d 1192]; see also *Davis v. County of Los Angeles* (1938) 12 Cal. 2d 412, 420–421 [84 P.2d 1034].) "The recitals of necessity and public interest in legislation must be given great weight and every presumption made in favor of their constitutionality (*Monterey County Flood Control & Water Conservation Dist. v. Hughes* [(1962)] 201 Cal. App. 2d 197, 209 [20 Cal.Rptr. 252])." (*Azevedo v. Jordan* (1965) 237 Cal. App. 2d 521, 526 [47 Cal. Rptr. 125].)

We find no procedural defect in the legislative approval of the Assembly Bill No. 2716, 1993–1994 Regular Session, September 21, 1994, urgency provision. In the form originally passed in the Assembly, both Assembly Bill No. 2716 and a statement of urgency were separately approved by roll call votes, but neither the bill nor the urgency clause attached to it were then related to reform of prison credits. When the bill was amended in the Senate to add Penal Code section 2933.1, the urgency section was revised to refer to the need to protect the public from the early release of repeat offenders — a statement apparently taken from legislation which had been considered but not enacted the year before — and again both were approved by separate roll call votes. Upon the return of Assembly Bill No. 2716 to the Assembly, the Senate amendments adding section 2933.1 to the Penal Code "and declaring the urgency thereof, to take effect immediately," were passed by a single concurrence roll call vote of more than two-thirds of the membership, apparently in accordance with the Joint Assembly and Senate Rules.

Nothing more is demanded by the Constitution for mere concurrence in amendments to a bill which was already separately passed by each house as an urgency measure.

"'[T]he California Constitution is a limitation or restriction on the powers of the Legislature. [Citations.] Two important consequences flow from this fact. First, ... that body may exercise any and all legislative powers which are not expressly or by necessary implication denied to it by the Constitution. [Citations.] ... [¶] Secondly, all intendments favor the exercise of the Legislature's plenary authority: "If there is any doubt as to the Legislature's power to act in any given case, the doubt should be resolved in favor of the Legislature's action. Such restrictions and limitations [imposed by the Constitution] are to be construed strictly, and are not to be extended to include matters not covered by the language used." [Citations.]' [Citations.]" (*California State Employees' Assn. v. State of California* (1988) 199 Cal. App. 3d 840, 845–846 [245 Cal. Rptr. 232]; see also *County of Los Angeles v. Sasaki* (1994) 23 Cal. App. 4th 1442, 1453 [29 Cal. Rptr. 2d 103]; *State Bd. of Education v. Honig* (1993) 13 Cal. App. 4th 720, 755 [16 Cal. Rptr. 2d 727].) [2d] As we read article IV, section 8, subdivision (d), each house must approve in two separate votes any bill and its accompanying urgency section. (See Ops. Cal. Legis. Counsel, No. 12227 (Apr. 29, 1957) 2 Assem. J. (1957 Reg. Sess.) pp. 3663–3664.) That was done with Assembly Bill No. 2716, 1993–1994 Regular Session, September 21, 1994, and although the bill subsequently returned in amended form to the house of origin, the single roll call vote concurring in the amendments and the urgency section was valid. Article IV, section 8, subdivision (d) does not require a second separate roll call approval of the urgency section of a single bill, even one, such as Assembly Bill No. 2716, 1993–1994 Regular Session, September 21, 1994, drastically altered by amendments. We cannot impose a restriction upon legislative authority which has not been clearly expressed by the Constitution.

We also find no flaw in the legislative determination of urgency in the enactment of Assembly Bill No. 2716, 1993–1994 Regular Session, September 21, 1994, to protect the public from repeat offenders who would otherwise be released, even though as ultimately enacted Assembly Bill No. 2716 applied to all violent felony offenders. "'[I]f the legislature "states facts constituting an emergency so that its action cannot be said to be arbitrary, courts cannot say that it has not performed its constitutional duty, even though they may disagree with the legislature as to the sufficiency of declared facts to constitute a sufficient reason for immediate action." (*Baker v. Hill* [(1929)] 180 Ark. 387 [21 S.W.2d 867, 868].)' (*Davis v. County of Los Angeles, supra,* 12 Cal.2d at pp. 422–423.)" (*Behneman v. Alameda-Contra Costa Transit Dist.* (1960) 182 Cal. App. 2d 687, 692 [6 Cal. Rptr. 382].) Given our exceedingly limited reviewing function, we must conclude that the mistaken reference to repeat, rather than all, offenders does not render erroneous the Legislature's finding and declaration of the need to protect the public by immediately implementing the credit reduction scheme of section 2933.1 to forestall the early release of dangerous criminals under previously existing law.

B. Effective Date of the Statute.

Even if the urgency clause of section 2933.1 is found valid, appellant argues that the operative date of the statute was still January 1, 1995. He relies upon subdivision (d) of section 2933.1, which specifies: "This section shall only apply to offenses ... that are committed on or after the date on which this section becomes *operative.*" (Italics added.) Appellant maintains that use of the word "operative" in subdivision (d) of section 2933.1, rather than effective, indicates a legislative intent to delay the implementation of the reduction of sentence credits to avoid the confusion in the courts — and associated miscalculation of credits — inevitable with an immediate change in the law. We disagree.

"'Under the California Constitution, a statute enacted at a regular session of the Legislature generally becomes effective on January 1 of the year following its enactment except where the statute is passed as an urgency measure and becomes effective sooner. [Citation.] In the usual situation, the "effective" and "operative" dates are one and the same, and with regard to ex post facto restrictions, a statute has no force and effect until such effective-operative date. [Citation.]' (*People v. Henderson* (1980) 107 Cal. App. 3d 475, 488 [166 Cal. Rptr. 20].) [¶] In some instances, the Legislature may provide for different effective and operative dates. (*Cline v. Lewis* (1917) 175 Cal. 315, 318 [165 P. 915]; 57 Ops.Cal.Atty.Gen. 451, 454 (1974).) '[T]he operative date is the date upon which the directives of the statute may be actually implemented. The effective date, then, is considered that date upon which the statute came into being as an existing law.' (*People v. McCaskey* (1985) 170 Cal. App. 3d 411, 416 [216 Cal. Rptr. 54]; see also *People v. Righthouse* (1937) 10 Cal. 2d 86, 88 [72 P.2d 867].)" (*People v. Jenkins* (1995) 35 Cal. App. 4th 669, 673–674 [41 Cal. Rptr. 2d 502].)

"'An enactment is a law on its effective date only in the sense that it cannot be changed except by legislative process; the rights of individuals under its provisions are not substantially affected until the provision operates as law.' ([*People v. Henderson* (1980) 107 Cal. App. 3d 475,] 488 [166 Cal. Rptr. 20].) ... [T]he courts have recognized the power of the Legislature to establish an operative date later than the effective date.... [Citation.]" (*Estate of Martin* (1983) 150 Cal. App. 3d 1, 3–4 [197 Cal. Rptr. 261].) "'[T]he power to enact laws includes the power to fix a future date on which the act will become operative. [Citations.]' [Citation.]" (*Johnston v. Alexis* (1984) 153 Cal. App. 3d 33, 40 [199 Cal. Rptr. 909].) Our task is to ascertain and promote the legislative intent of the enactment. (*Id.* at p. 41.)

With the enactment of section 2933.1 the Legislature did not specify different effective and operative dates, or otherwise postpone implementation of the law until occurrence of a contingency, as with the restitution statutes found to have delayed legal effects in *People v. Palomar* (1985) 171 Cal. App. 3d 131, 135–136 [214 Cal. Rptr. 785], and *People v. McCaskey* (1985) 170 Cal. App. 3d 411, 418 [216 Cal. Rptr. 54]. Section 2933.1, subdivision (d) merely provides that offenses committed before the "operative" date of the statute are excluded from the credit reduction scheme; it does not defer the operative date of the law. We find nothing in the statute which indicates a legislative intent that it is to become operative later than as provided in the valid urgency provision. (*People v. Jenkins, supra,* 35 Cal.App.4th at p. 675.) To the contrary, the statement of urgency found in Assembly Bill No. 2716, 1993–1994 Regular Session, September 21, 1994, conflicts with any delayed implementation of the statute. We do not consider the Legislative Committee Analysis of unrelated legislation in 1996, prepared nearly two years later — and which refers to sentences for crimes committed after January 1, 1995, as incurring the 15 percent credit limit of section 2933.1 — persuasive in determining the operative date of the statute. (*Peralta Community College Dist. v. Fair Employment & Housing Com.* (1990) 52 Cal. 3d 40, 52 [276 Cal. Rptr. 114, 801 P.2d 357].) We also do not think any postponement of operation of the statute was necessary to prepare the trial courts for the change in credit calculations, a relatively simplistic and straightforward task. We conclude that section 2933.1 was operative, as expressly provided, when it was enacted on September 21, 1994, and was properly applied to appellant's sentence by the trial court. The judgment is affirmed.

Notes and Questions

1. The Legislature has the power to enact urgency statutes so long as those measures comply with the constitutional requirements. The Legislature must demonstrate in the bill that there is a necessity, and the courts are unlikely to disturb the determination made by the Legislature. The only basis, according to this decision, is if the bill does not contain any declaration of facts constituting the specified emergency or that the declaration is clearly insufficient to justify the alleged necessity.

2. The appellant argued that the history of the legislation demonstrates that the urgency clause was not properly passed by a separate roll call vote of each house of the Legislature. On what basis did the court disagree with this argument?

3. As the court explained, "Upon the return of Assembly Bill No. 2716 to the Assembly, the Senate amendments adding section 2933.1 to the Penal Code 'and declaring the urgency thereof, to take effect immediately,' were passed by a single concurrence roll call vote of more than two-thirds of the membership, apparently in accordance with the Joint Assembly and Senate Rules." Based upon this statement of fact, why did the court rule that the Legislature had complied with the constitutional requirement?

4. In this case, the plaintiff argued that, when the bill returned from the Senate with amendments to the Assembly for a final concurrence floor vote, only one vote

was taken on the Assembly Floor. That single vote embodied both the vote on the floor and the vote on the urgency clause. The court did not find a violation of the constitutional requirement because, when the bill passed its house of origin (i.e., the Assembly), two separate votes were taken at that time. Therefore, the constitutional requirement was met when the Assembly first voted on the bill.

5. The court also discussed the difference between an operative date of a statute and an effective date. Even though the statute used the word "operative" in subdivision (d) of § 2933.1, rather than effective, why did the court not agree that this was an indication of legislative intent to delay the implementation of the statute's provisions?

2. Effective v. Operatives Dates

In most circumstances and with most bills, the effective date and the operative date are the same. However, these dates are separate and distinct, and those who must comply with a new law's provisions should understand the difference in case the bill that enacted the new law specifies different dates.

People v. Jenkins

(1995) 35 Cal.App.4th 669

OPINION

YEGAN, J.

Donald Wayne Jenkins appeals from a trial court finding that he is a mentally disordered offender (MDO) within the meaning of Penal Code section 2962. We affirm and reject appellant's argument that the MDO statutory scheme, as applied, violates the ex post facto clauses of the federal and state constitutions. We explain the differences between date of enactment, effective date and operative date and hold that the MDO statutes apply to persons convicted and imprisoned for certain crimes committed after the statutory scheme's effective date, January 1, 1986. (§ 2980.)

Facts and Procedural History

On February 21, 1986, appellant strangled Yolanda Gallagher to death. He was charged with murder, found incompetent to stand trial, and sent to Patton State Hospital. (§ 1370.01, subd. (a)(1).) In 1988 appellant regained his mental competency and pled guilty to voluntary manslaughter. The trial court sentenced him to state prison for 11 years.

Prior to his release from prison the Department of Corrections determined that appellant was an MDO and required treatment by the State Department of Mental Health. (§ 2962, subd. (d)(1).) Appellant refused to sign parole conditions placing him in the custody of the State Department of Mental Health. Parole was revoked and his release date was extended to June 24, 1993.

On June 15, 1993, appellant was reevaluated and again certified as an MDO. Appellant signed his parole conditions and was released to Atascadero State Hospital for treatment. He thereafter challenged the involuntary commitment. (§ 2966, subd. (a).) On October 19, 1993, the Board of Prison Terms conducted a hearing and found that he met the MDO criteria set forth in section 2962.

Appellant filed a petition for a trial de novo and waived his right to a jury. (§ 2966, subd. (b).) Prior to trial, appellant moved to dismiss on the ground that the MDO statute, as applied to him, was ex post facto. The trial court denied the motion and, on substantial evidence, found that appellant was an MDO. This appeal followed.

Ex Post Facto Rule

"An ex post facto law is a retrospective statute applying to crimes committed before its enactment, and substantially injuring the accused. The Constitutions prohibit the passage of such laws (U.S. Const., Art. I, §§ 9, 10; Cal. Const., Art. I, § 9)...." (7 Witkin, Summary of Cal. Law (9th ed. 1988) Constitutional Law, § 419, p. 601.) If a crime is committed before the "effective date" of a statute and the statute retroactively increases the punishment for the crime or eliminates a defense, the statute violates the ex post facto clauses. (See also *Tapia v. Superior Court* (1991) 53 Cal. 3d 282, 298 [279 Cal. Rptr. 592, 807 P.2d 434]; *Collins v. Youngblood* (1990) 497 U.S. 37, 42 [111 L. Ed. 2d 30, 38–39, 110 S. Ct. 2715].)

Legislative History

The MDO statutes were enacted October 1, 1985, and became operative July 1, 1986. (Stats. 1985, ch. 1419, § 1, p. 5011.) The effective date of the statute, codified as section 2960, was January 1, 1986. Section 2960, subdivision (j) provided: "The amendments to this section made in the first year of the 1985–86 Regular Session apply to persons incarcerated before, as well as after, the effective date of those amendments." In 1986, the Legislature recodified the MDO statutory scheme to give it separate section numbers. (§§ 2962–2980; Stats. 1986, ch. 858, p. 2951.) Section 2980 then provided that "[t]his article applies to persons *incarcerated before, as well as after January 1, 1986.* (Italics added.)

In *People v. Gibson, supra,* 204 Cal. App. 3d 1425, we held that the MDO statutory scheme was ex post facto as applied to Gibson. Gibson was convicted of forcible rape in 1983, sentenced to state prison, and became eligible for parole in 1986. Instead of being released, he was certified as an MDO and required to accept inpatient treatment through the State Department of Mental Health. We concluded that " ... the retroactive application of the MDO provisions to persons whose crimes were committed prior to their *effective date* violates the ex post facto clauses of the United States and California Constitutions because the provisions: (1) are applicable only to persons who were convicted for certain crimes and *who are still serving their terms of imprisonment on the operative date of the legislation* (§ 2962)...." (*Id.,* at pp. 1434–1435, italics added.)

In 1989 the Legislature passed an urgency measure in response to *People v. Gibson.* It declared: "This act is an urgency statute necessary for the immediate preservation of the public peace, health, or safety within the meaning of Article IV of the Constitution and shall go into immediate effect.... [¶] ... In order to keep the mentally disordered offender program in effect for those persons who committed their crimes on or after January 1, 1986, it is necessary that this act take effect immediately." (Stats. 1989, ch. 228, § 8, p. 1258.) Section 2980 was amended to provide that "[t]his article applies to persons who committed their crimes on and after January 1, 1986." (Stats. 1989, ch. 228, § 5, p. 1256.)

Enactment Date, Effective Date, and Operative Date

Appellant claims that the MDO statutory scheme, as applied, is ex post facto because he committed the homicide before the statute's operative date, July 1, 1986. The argument is without merit.

"Under the California Constitution, a statute enacted at a regular session of the Legislature generally becomes effective on January 1 of the year following its enactment except where the statute is passed as an urgency measure and becomes effective sooner. [Citation.] In the usual situation, the 'effective' and 'operative' dates are one and the same, and with regard to ex post facto restrictions, a statute has no force and effect until such effective-operative date. [Citation.]" (*People v. Henderson* (1980) 107 Cal. App. 3d 475, 488 [166 Cal. Rptr. 20].)

In some instances, the Legislature may provide for different effective and operative dates. (*Cline v. Lewis* (1917) 175 Cal. 315, 318 [165 P. 915]; 57 Ops.Cal.Atty.Gen. 451, 454 (1974).) "[T]he operative date is the date upon which the directives of the statute may be actually implemented. The effective date, then, is considered that date upon which the statute came into being as an existing law." (*People v. McCaskey* (1985) 170 Cal. App. 3d 411, 416 [216 Cal. Rptr. 54]; see also *People v. Righthouse* (1937) 10 Cal. 2d 86, 88 [72 P.2d 867].)

As indicated, the MDO statutes were enacted in 1985 and became effective January 1, 1986. Although the statutory scheme had a July 1, 1986, operative date for purposes of MDO commitments, it applied to persons who committed certain crimes on or after January 1, 1986, and later imprisoned therefore.

As previously indicated, in *People v. Gibson, supra*, 204 Cal. App. 3d 1425, we held that the Legislature could not retroactively extend the MDO statutory scheme to crimes committed before its enactment. The first sentence of the opinion stated that the MDO legislation was "effective July 1, 1986." (*Id.*, at p. 1429.) Because Gibson's offense was committed in 1983, the distinctions between enactment date, effective date, and operative date were not determinative. We did, however, conclude that section 2980, which applied to persons incarcerated before January 1, 1986, was ex post facto because "[i]t is ... expressly retroactive to persons whose crimes ... were committed *prior to the enactment* of the Legislature so long as they had not earlier been released on parole. [Fn. omitted.]" (204 Cal.App.3d at p. 1430, italics added.) Our use of the terms "enactment" and "effective date" was imprecise.

Here, appellant committed the offense more than a month after the effective date of the MDO statutory scheme. The trial court correctly found that the MDO statutory scheme, as enacted and presently amended, did not violate the ex post facto clauses of the United States and California Constitutions.

Legislative Intent

Appellant's reliance on *People v. McCaskey, supra,* 170 Cal. App. 3d 411 (amendment of Gov. Code, § 13967 restitution statute) and *People v. Palomar* (1985) 171 Cal. App. 3d 131 [214 Cal. Rptr. 785] (enactment of § 1202.4 restitution statute) does not compel a different result. There the defendants committed the offenses after the enactment of the legislation but before the operative date. The Legislature, in delaying the operative date of the statute, provided that the operative clause would apply to all aspects of the statute. "The Legislature may specify the legal effects to be attached to the operative clause. For example, it may specify that a statute will become operative upon the occurrence of a contingency [citation] or it may specify that some part of a statute will become operative at a date after the date the statute takes effect. [Citation.]" (*People v. Palomar, supra,* 171 Cal.App.3d at p. 135, fn. 5.)

Not so here. The Legislature provided that the MDO statutory scheme applied to prisoners already incarcerated and new prisoners committing certain crimes before the July 1, 1986, operative date. Section 2960, as enacted in 1985, stated in pertinent part: "(a) The Legislature finds that there are prisoners who have a treatable, severe mental disorder which caused, was one of the causes of, or was an aggravating factor in the commission of the crime for which they were incarcerated. Secondly, the Legislature finds that if the severe mental disorders of those prisoners are not in remission or cannot be kept in remission at the time of their parole or upon termination of parole, there is a danger to society, and the state has a compelling interest in protecting the public. Thirdly, the Legislature finds that in order to protect the public from those persons it is necessary to provide mental health treatment until the severe mental disorder which was one of the causes of or was an aggravating factor in the person's prior criminal behavior is in remission and can be kept in remission. [¶] The Legislature further finds and declares the Department of Corrections should evaluate each prisoner for severe mental disorders during the first year of the prisoner's sentence, and that severely mentally disordered prisoners should be provided with an appropriate level of mental health treatment while in prison and when returned to the community." (Stats. 1985, ch. 1419, § 1.)

In determining the legal effect to be given an enactment that contains different effective and operative dates, the court must ascertain and promote the legislative intent of the enactment. (*Johnston v. Alexis* (1984) 153 Cal. App. 3d 33, 41 [199 Cal. Rptr. 909].) The legislative findings, original enactment, and subsequent amendments demonstrate that the MDO statutory scheme was intended to apply to persons imprisoned for certain crimes committed on or after January 1, 1986.

"[I]t is our duty to uphold [the] statute unless its unconstitutionality clearly, positively, and unmistakably appears; all presumptions and intendments favor its validity. [Citations.]" (*Mills v. Superior Court* (1986) 42 Cal. 3d 951, 957 [232 Cal. Rptr. 141, 728 P.2d 211].) To be an ex post facto law, the enactment must be retrospective, that is, it must apply to events occurring before its existence and cause the defendant disadvantage. (*Weaver v. Graham* (1981) 450 U.S. 24, 28–29 [67 L. Ed. 2d 17, 23, 101 S. Ct. 960].) We conclude that the MDO statutory scheme, as enacted and presently amended, is not an ex post facto for an offense committed on February 21, 1986. The judgment is affirmed.

STONE (S.J.), P.J., and GILBERT, J., concurred.

Notes and Questions

1. Under the California Constitution, a statute enacted at a regular session generally becomes effective on January 1 of the year following its enactment except where the statute is passed as an urgency measure and becomes effective sooner. In some instances, the legislature may provide for different effective and operative dates for a statute.

2. The operative date of the statute is the date upon which directives of the statute may be actually implemented. The effective date of the statute is the date upon which the statute came into being as existing law. In determining legal effect to be given an enactment that contains a different effective and operative date, a court must ascertain and promote the legislative intent of the enactment.

3. Although statutes providing for tax levies must go into effect immediately upon their enactment pursuant to Constitution Article IV, Section 8(c)(2), such requirement imposes no greater barrier to a postponed operative date in the case of a tax levy than in the case of any other type of statute. Thus, the Legislature was empowered to delay substantive application of an inheritance tax statute until January 1 of the following year. (*Estate of Nicoletti* (1982) 129 Cal.App.3d 475.)

4. The court addressed the differences between date of enactment, effective date and operative date of a statute in the context of an alleged ex post facto law. How did it define each of these three terms?

5. The case also dealt with an urgency clause statute. How did the court address that issue?

6. As the court notes in its decision, "In some instances, the Legislature may provide for different effective and operative dates. (*Cline v. Lewis* (1917) 175 Cal. 315, 318.)" And the court offered the usual definition of these two terms: "'[T]he operative date is the date upon which the directives of the statute may be actually implemented. The effective date, then, is considered that date upon which the statute came into being as an existing law.' (*People v. McCaskey* (1985) 170 Cal.App.3d 411, 416....)"

7. What is the importance of the court's acknowledgment that, in its prior opinion, "Our use of the terms 'enactment' and 'effective date' was imprecise"?

3. Legislature Can Set Operative Date

A statute's effective date is by operation or law. It is either January 1 when the new law comes on the books, or it is when the bill was chaptered because it has an urgency clause. On the other hand, an operative date can be specified by the Legislature at some point in the future. Why might the Legislature want to set an operative date different than its effective date? The most likely reason would be to allow the regulator (e.g., a state agency) or the regulated community to have sufficient time before the law takes effect.

For example, the Legislature may recognize that it will take a year or more to adopt regulations to implement a new statutory scheme. As such, they may delay the operative date a law is to be enforced in order for the regulatory agency to adopt the required new regulations and to provide the regulated community a specified amount of time to adopt its operations to comply with the new regulations. As such, the Legislature may push back the new law's operative date for a year or more.

People v. Verba

(2012) 210 Cal.App.4th 991,
rehearing denied, review denied

OPINION

Defendants who committed their crimes on or after October 1, 2011 are eligible for presentence conduct credits calculated on the basis of two days of conduct credit for every two days of actual custody. (Pen.Code, § 4019, subds. (b), (c) & (f).) Defendants who committed their crimes prior to October 1, 2011 are eligible for conduct credits at the previous rate of two days for every four days in custody. (§ 4019, subd. (h).) Appellant, who committed his crime in April 2010, contends that affording him a lower level of conduct credits solely because he committed his crime prior to October 1, 2011 violates his constitutional right to the equal protection of the laws. We conclude that the right to equal protection does not prevent the Legislature from limiting the increased level of presentence conduct credits to detainees who committed their crimes on or after the October 1, 2011 operative date of the statute. We therefore uphold appellant's sentence.

All statutory references are to the Penal Code.

FACTS AND PROCEEDINGS BELOW

In August 2011, the trial court sentenced Mark Verba for the crime of failing to register as a sex offender in April 2010. A defendant is entitled to accrue presentence custody credits under section 2900.5 and conduct credits under section 4019, subdivisions (b) and (c), for the period of incarceration prior to sentencing. In sentencing Verba, the trial court awarded him two days of conduct credit for every four days he spent in presentence custody under section 4019, subdivisions (b) and (c), as amended by Senate Bill No. 76 which became effective in September 2010. (Stats.2010, ch. 426, §§ 2, 5.) Under this formula, Verba received 182 days of presentence custody credit consisting of 122 actual days in custody and 60 days of conduct credit.

The previous limit on conduct credits to persons required to register as sex offenders of two days for every six days of custody (Stats.2009, 3d Ex.Sess., ch. 28, § 50) was eliminated in 2010. (Stats.2010, ch. 426, § 2.)

While Verba was in presentence custody, the Legislature amended section 4019, subdivisions (b) and (c), to provide that "a term of four days will be deemed to have been served for every two days spent in actual custody." (§ 4019, subd. (f).) The statute containing this amendment became effective on June 30, 2011 (Stats.2011, ch. 39, §§ 53, 73) but the amendment was expressly made operative only as to "prisoners who are confined … for a crime committed on or after October 1, 2011." (§ 4019, subd. (h), added by A.B. No. 117, Stats.2011, ch. 39, § 53; referred to hereafter as the "October 1 amendment.") Because Verba committed his crime in April 2010, he was not entitled to the new level of conduct credit.

Verba contends that making the new level of conduct credit operative on a date after the effective date of the statute violates his right to the equal protection of the laws as guaranteed by the Fourteenth Amendment of the federal Constitution and article I, section 7 of the California Constitution. To remedy this constitutional infirmity, he argues, the new level of conduct credit should apply to all defendants who were inmates on the statute's effective date, June 30, 2011.

DISCUSSION

I. VERBA'S CHALLENGE TO THE OCTOBER 1 AMENDMENT IS NOT BARRED BY SECTION 1237.1

We disagree with the Attorney General's contention that section 1237.1 bars Verba's challenge to the constitutionality of the October 1 amendment. Section 1237.1 states in relevant part: "No appeal shall be taken by the defendant from a judgment of conviction on the ground of an error in the calculation of presentence custody credits, unless the defendant first presents the claim in the trial court at the time of sentencing[.]"

Section 1237.1 does not apply here. Verba does not contend that the court erred in calculating his custody credits under the version of section 4019 in effect at the time.

II. THE OCTOBER 1 OPERATIVE DATE OF THE STATUTE DOES NOT VIOLATE VERBA'S RIGHT TO THE EQUAL PROTECTION OF THE LAWS

Under the October 1 amendment, if A commits a crime on September 30, 2011 and B commits a crime on October 2, 2011, A will receive a lower level of conduct credits than B, even if their time in custody begins on the same day, e.g., October 3, 2011, because A committed his crime before October 1, 2011 and B committed his crime "on or after October 1, 2011." (§ 4019, subd. (h), as amended by Stats.2011, ch. 39, § 53.)

We are asked to decide whether this sentencing scheme creates a classification that affects two similarly situated groups in an unequal manner (*Cooley v. Superior Court* (2002) 29 Cal.4th 228, 253, 127 Cal.Rptr.2d 177, 57 P.3d 654), and, if so, whether the classification "is supported by a rational and legitimate state interest." (*In re Kapperman* (1974) 11 Cal.3d 542, 546, 114 Cal.Rptr. 97, 522 P.2d 657.)

A. Inmates Who Committed Their Crimes Before and After October 1, 2011 Are Similarly Situated for Purposes of The Statute That Increased the Level of Conduct Credit

Verba contends that he is a member of the class of defendants in presentence custody who committed their crimes prior to October 1, 2011 to whom the Legislature denied a benefit, four days of credit for every two days of actual time served, which it granted to defendants in presentence custody who committed crimes on or after October 1, 2011.

Respondent argues that inmates who served time before and after the October 1 operative date of the amendment are not similarly situated with respect to the purpose of increasing conduct credit in order to provide inmates with incentives to engage in productive work and maintain good conduct while they are in custody. (People *v. Brown* (2012) 54 Cal.4th 314, 328–329, 142 Cal.Rptr.3d 824, 278 P.3d 1182.) These incentives for good behavior, respondent argues, "are not served by rewarding prisoners who served time before the incentives took effect and thus could not have modified their behavior in response." (*Ibid.*) (See also *In re Strick* (1983) 148 Cal.App.3d 906, 913, 196 Cal.Rptr. 293 ["it is impossible to influence behavior after it has occurred"].)

This argument fails and *Brown* and *Strick* are not on point because in this instance the legislative purpose for increasing the level of conduct credits was not to provide inmates with incentives for better behavior in custody. Indeed, the Legislature made no change in the behavior required to earn conduct credit. Rather, the increased conduct credits were enacted "as part of a larger measure intended to save the state money by releasing eligible prisoners early to reduce jail and prison populations and by emphasizing programs designed to prevent recidivism." (*People v. Lara* (2012) 54 Cal.4th 896, 902, 144 Cal.Rptr.3d 169, 281 P.3d 72; and see *People v. Garcia* (2012) 209 Cal.App.4th 530, 534–541, 147 Cal.Rptr.3d 221 [summarizing the back-and-forth changes in the levels of conduct credits between 2009 and 2011].)

We agree with Verba that with respect to the awarding of conduct credits under section 4019 he is similarly situated with persons whose offenses were committed on or after October 1, 2011. Defendants who committed offenses and earned conduct credit before the operative date of the statute are treated more harshly than those who committed the same crimes and earned conduct credit on or after October 1, 2011. The two groups are similarly situated in the sense that they committed the same offenses but are treated differently in terms of earning conduct credit based solely on the dates their crimes were committed. For purposes of receiving conduct credit, nothing distinguishes the status of a prisoner whose crime was committed after October 1, 2011, from one whose crime was committed before that date.

B. A Statute's Operational Date Requires A Rational Basis

Verba's equal protection claim requires us to distinguish between a statute's effective date, "'the date upon which the statute came into being as an existing law'" and its operative date, "'the date upon which the directives of the statute may be actually implemented.'" (*Preston v. State Bd. of Equalization* (2001) 25 Cal.4th 197, 223, 105 Cal.Rptr.2d 407, 19 P.3d 1148.)

As respondent points out, courts have long held that "'[t]he 14th Amendment does not forbid statutes and statutory changes to have a beginning, and thus to discriminate between the rights of an earlier and later time.'" (*People v. Floyd* (2003) 31 Cal.4th 179, 191, 1 Cal.Rptr.3d 885, 72 P.3d 820, quoting Justice Holmes in *Sperry*

& Hutchinson Co. v. Rhodes (1911) 220 U.S. 502, 505, 31 S.Ct. 490, 55 L.Ed. 561; accord *People v. Lynch* (2012) 209 Cal.App.4th 353, 359, 146 Cal.Rptr.3d 811.) In other words, the practical necessity that a statutory change has a beginning provides a rational basis for classifications that fall on either side of the statute's effective date.

This rationale does not apply to the operative date of a statute, however. Unlike a statute's effective date, which is determined according to immutable rules written into the state constitution (Cal. Const., art. IV, § 8), its operative date, the date upon which the directives of the statute are actually implemented, is set by the Legislature in its discretion. (*Preston v. State Bd. of Equalization, supra,* 25 Cal.4th at p. 223, 105 Cal.Rptr.2d 407, 19 P.3d 1148.) The exercise of that discretion is subject to rational basis review. (*Carson Redevelopment Agency v. Wolf* (1979) 99 Cal.App.3d 239, 243, 245, 160 Cal.Rptr. 213; but see dictum in *People v. Lynch, supra,* 209 Cal.App.4th at p. 359, 146 Cal.Rptr.3d 811 [distinction between effective and operative dates of Proposition 36 "was irrelevant to the Supreme Court's analysis" in *People v. Floyd*].)

C. Rational Bases Exist for The October 1 Operative Date

We can envision several legitimate reasons for making the increased level of pre-sentence conduct credit applicable only to those who commit their crimes on or after October 1, 2011.

As noted above, the Legislature's decision to increase the amount of presentence conduct a defendant could earn "was intended to save the state money." (*People v. Lara, supra,* 54 Cal.4th at p. 902, 144 Cal.Rptr.3d 169, 281 P.3d 72.) The Legislature may have decided that the nature and scope of the fiscal emergency required granting an increase in the level of conduct credits but only at a time after the effective date of the amendments. A slightly delayed operative date, the Legislature may have be-lieved, struck a proper, rational balance between the state's fiscal concerns and its public safety interests.

A related justification for the prospective application of increased conduct credits lies in the Legislature's right to control the risk of new legislation by limiting its ap-plication. "Requiring the Legislature to apply retroactively any change in the law ben-efitting criminal defendants imposes unnecessary additional burdens on the already difficult task of fashioning a criminal justice system that protects the public and re-habilitates criminals." (*People v. Lynch, supra,* 209 Cal.App.4th at p. 361, 146 Cal.Rptr.3d 811.)

In addition, the Legislature could have rationally believed that by tying the increased level of conduct credits to crimes committed on or after a future date, it was preserving the deterrent effect of the criminal law as to those crimes committed before that date. (*People v. Floyd, supra,* 31 Cal.4th at p. 190, 1 Cal.Rptr.3d 885, 72 P.3d 820; *In re Kap-perman, supra,* 11 Cal.3d at p. 546, 114 Cal.Rptr. 97, 522 P.2d 657.) To reward an in-mate with enhanced conduct credits, even for time spent in presentence custody after the effective date of the statute, arguably weakens the deterrent effect of the law as it stood when the inmate committed the crime. We see nothing irrational or implausible in a legislative conclusion that individuals should be punished in accordance with the sanctions and given the rewards in effect at the time they committed their offense. Such a punishment scheme also avoids "sentencing delays and other manipulations." (*People v. Floyd, supra,* 31 Cal.4th at p. 191, 1 Cal.Rptr.3d 885, 72 P.3d 820.)

We acknowledge that most all statutory dates and time periods are "somewhat arbitrary" in the sense that other dates and time periods might have been chosen. (*People v. Willis* (1978) 84 Cal.App.3d 952, 956, 149 Cal.Rptr. 301.) In California, with some exceptions, statutes enacted by the Legislature in one year take effect on January 1 of the following year. (Cal. Const., art. IV, § 8, subd. (c)(2).) There is no compelling reason for making January 1 the effective date. Statutes could, for example, just as well take effect 40 days after their passage or on the following July 4 or 90 days after the legislature adjourns. (See 2 Sutherland Statutory Construction (7th ed.2009) § 33:2, pp. 2–6.)

DISPOSITION

The judgment is affirmed.

We concur: CHANEY, and JOHNSON, JJ.

Notes and Questions

1. Unlike a statute's effective date, which is determined according to immutable rules written into the state Constitution, its operative date is the date upon which the directives of the statute are actually implemented, and is set by the Legislature in its discretion.

2. The court agreed that the criminal defendant was being treated differently than those who committed similar crimes after the new law went into effect. Nonetheless, it did not view this as a violation of his constitutional right to the equal protection of the laws. Why? What was the rational basis cited?

3. The statute that made changes to the law became effective (i.e., on the books) on June 30, 2011, but the amendment was expressly made operative for specified prisoners on or after October 1, 2011. The court said a statute's operative date "requires a rational basis" in order to not violate someone's equal protection claim. The court defined these two dates in the following manner: A statute's effective date, "'the date upon which the statute came into being as an existing law'" and its operative date, "'the date upon which the directives of the statute may be actually implemented.'"

4. The court also made the following observation: "We acknowledge that most all statutory dates and time periods are 'somewhat arbitrary' in the sense that other dates and time periods might have been chosen." What is the significance of this acknowledgement?

4. Retroactive Effect of a Bill

Although it does not occur very often, the Legislature can make a bill have a retroactive effect. While there are constitutional prohibitions against ex post facto laws, other laws can be made retroactive if the Legislature determines that there is a sufficient need to do so.

An example of such a bill in the California Legislature has been when the U.S. Congress has enacted tax law changes to the federal Internal Revenue Code and California tax law conforms to those federal tax law changes even though they apply to prior tax years.

Industrial Indemnity Company v. Workers' Compensation Appeals Board

(1978) 85 Cal.App.3d 1028

OPINION

Thompson, J.

We have consolidated these petitions for writ of review because they involve the identical question. Each seeks reversal of a Workers' Compensation Appeals Board (WCAB) determination that an amendment to Labor Code section 139.5 is applicable to require rehabilitation benefits to workers injured prior to the effective date of the amendment. We conclude that the WCAB has given an impermissibly retroactive application to the statute. Accordingly, we reverse the determinations of the board. Although section 139.5 was further amended in the 1976 legislative session to specify that the earlier amendment is not to be applied to workers injured prior to its effective date, we publish this opinion because we are informed that a significant number of cases involving the issue are pending.

As enacted in 1965, Labor Code section 139.5 created a system for initiation of rehabilitation plans by employers and insurance carriers, for state approval of plans so initiated, and for the payment of special benefits to injured workers who participate in a rehabilitation plan. The 1965 version of section 139.5 provided that the initiation of a plan was voluntary and not compulsory on the part of the employer or insurance carrier and that participation by an injured worker in a plan that had been initiated was also voluntary on his part. (See *Moyer v. Workmen's Comp. Appeals Bd.* (1973) 10 Cal. 3d 222, 226, fn. 1 [110 Cal. Rptr. 144, 514 P.2d 1224].)

Effective January 1, 1975, Labor Code section 139.5 was amended. The amended version calls for rehabilitation benefits "When a qualified injured workman chooses to enroll in a rehabilitation program" and eliminates the prior statutory language to the effect that initiation of a rehabilitation program was not required of an employer or its insurance carrier but rather was voluntary.

While employed by employers who had not initiated a rehabilitation plan, and whose insurers had not done so, Norman L. Duncan and Thomas F. Brown suffered industrially connected injury prior to January 1, 1975. After that date, each sought rehabilitation benefits. After a hearing before the board, the WCAB concluded that Duncan and Brown were entitled to the benefits they sought. We issued our writ of review bringing the matters to this court.

Subject to circumstances which indicate a legislative intent to the contrary, "the law in force at the time of the injury is to be taken as the measure of the injured person's right of recovery" in workers' compensation. That principle follows from the proposition that "'the industrial injury is the basis for any compensation award.'" (*Aetna Cas. & Surety Co. v. Ind. Acc. Com.* (1947) 30 Cal. 2d 388, 392–393 [182 P.2d 159]; *State Comp. Ins. Fund v. Workers' Comp. Appeals Bd. (Silva)* (1977) 71 Cal. App. 3d 133, 136 [139 Cal. Rptr. 410].) Hence statutory change in workers' compensation which is "substantive in character" i.e., that which "enlarge[s] [or diminishes] the employee's existing rights and the employer's corresponding obligations" does not act retrospectively absent a clear showing of legislative intent that it should do so. (*Aetna Cas. & Surety Co. v. Ind. Acc. Com., supra*, 30 Cal.2d at pp. 392–393; *State of California v. Ind. Acc. Com. (Erickson)* (1975) 48 Cal. 2d 355, 361–363 [310 P.2d 1].)

Legislative intent calling for retroactive operation of a statutory change may be found in such factors as context, the objective of the legislation, the evils to which it is addressed, the social history of the times and legislation upon the same subject, the public policy enunciated or vindicated by the enactment, and the effect of the particular legislation upon the entire statutory scheme of which it is a party. (*In re Marriage of Bouquet* (1976) 16 Cal. 3d 583, 587 [128 Cal. Rptr. 427, 546 P.2d 1371]; *Harrison v. Workmen's Comp. Appeals Bd.* (1974) 44 Cal. App. 3d 197, 205–206 [118 Cal.Rptr. 508] — retrospective application of amendment required to achieve statutory objective of ameliorating the procedural morass in multiple defendant WCAB cases.)

Here the amendment to Labor Code section 139.5 effective in 1975 substantially enlarged employee rights. Where previously an injured worker was entitled to rehabilitation benefits only if his employer or its insurance carrier had voluntarily initiated a rehabilitation plan, the 1975 change granted the benefits solely at the employee's option irrespective of whether the employer or its carrier had voluntarily initiated a plan.

Here we can find nothing which points to a legislative intent that the 1975 amendment should act retrospectively. The amendment unquestionably represents progress in promoting the highly desirable objective of rehabilitating the industrially disabled. The increased benefits to the seriously injured employee considered by our Supreme Court in Aetna and the amelioration by the Subsequent Injuries Fund of financial burden upon employers obligated to pay benefits for silicosis caused in part by employment by others before the high court in Erickson also, both represented legislation of a commendable social objective. Yet in each case our Supreme Court held the enactments to be prospective only in their operation. Something more than a desirable social objective served by the legislation is thus required if we are to infer a legislative intent of retroactivity. We perceive that factor to be the necessity of retroactivity to the purpose of the legislation or some factor extraneous to the purpose alone which leads to the same conclusion. Retrospective operation is not necessary to the rehabilitative purpose of the statute. Legislative action of the 1976 session (Stats. 1976, ch. 428, § 1, p. 1095) which specifies that the 1975 expanded rehabilitation benefits "shall [not] apply to any injured employee whose injury occurred prior to January 1, 1975" is indicative of a legislative finding of lack of that necessity. Prospective operation limits the class of persons entitled to the benefits but does not inhibit the operation of the expanded program. We have not been able to find, and counsel have not pointed us to, any other factor which indicates a legislative intent that the amendment which we here consider should be given retroactive effect.

The board and the applicants rely upon cases such as *Jenkins v. Workmen's Comp. Appeals Bd.* (1973) 31 Cal. App. 3d 259 [107 Cal. Rptr. 130], and *State Comp. Ins. Fund v. Workers' Comp. Appeals Bd. (Silva), supra,* 71 Cal. App. 3d 133. Those cases are distinguished from the case at bench by the proposition that they either involve rights accruing after the statutory change so that application of the amendment to the particular case is in fact a prospective application (*Jenkins*) or involve a change in the manner of satisfying a right already existing before the statutory change (*Silva*). In contrast, the applicants in the case at bench had no right to rehabilitation benefits before the 1975 amendment absent their employers' or their employers' carriers' voluntary adoption of a rehabilitation plan.

The orders of the Workers' Compensation Appeals Board are reversed.

LILLIE, Acting P.J., and HANSON, J., concurred.

Notes and Questions

1. The guidelines to be followed in determining whether a statute imposing civil penalties should or should not be applied retroactively are (1) a presumption that legislative changes do not apply retroactively in the absence of clear legislative intent, (2) a presumption that the purpose of the change would not often attain significant advancement by retroactive application, (3) the possible constitutional objections in the case of ex post facto punishment, (4) the doubt as to the constitutionality of retroactive application, and (5) the retroactive imposition of increased liabilities should be carefully avoided. (*Western & Southern Life Insurance Company v. State Board of Equalization* (1946) 4 Cal.App.3d 21.)

2. The Legislature amended the statute at issue in this case to make clear that the earlier change in the law was not to be applied to workers injured prior to its effective date. Nonetheless, the court issued its opinion and held that "the WCAB has given an impermissibly retroactive application to the statute." Why did the court issue its opinion despite the change in the law by the Legislature?

3. As the court noted, "Legislative intent calling for retroactive operation of a statutory change may be found in such factors as context, the objective of the legislation, the evils to which it is addressed, the social history of the times and legislation upon the same subject, the public policy enunciated or vindicated by the enactment, and the effect of the particular legislation upon the entire statutory scheme of which it is a party." (Citing *In re Marriage of Bouquet* (1976) 16 Cal. 3d 583, 587.)

5. Effect of Postponing the Operative Date

The practical effect of postponing a law's operative date is to postpone when the new law can be enforced or relied upon. Until that date, the law has not taken effect, even though the new law is "on the books" and is part of the state statutes found in one of the numerous Codes.

Notes and Questions

1. The postponement of the operative date of the legislation does not necessarily mean that the Legislature intended to limit its application to transactions occurring after that date. Although the effective date of a statute, the date upon which the statute came into being as an existing law, and its operative date, the date upon which the directives of the statute may be actually implemented, are often the same, the Legislature may postpone the operation of certain statutes until a later time. (*People v. Alford* (2007) 42 Cal.4th 749.)

C. Gubernatorial Bill Actions

1. A Look at the Governor's Powers

The purpose of this section is to examine the constitutional provisions related to California's Governor and some of the published appellate court decisions that provide insights into how these provisions are interpreted by the courts.

Article V focuses on the executive branch of state government, and our focus is on the chief executive of the state — the Governor. These constitutional provisions set forth the role and the authority of the Governor, and there are a number of appellate court decisions that provide guidance in the interpretation of these specific provisions.

Article V of the California Constitution deals with the executive branch of government — not only the Governor, but also other constitutional officers. Here are some interesting provisions related to the executive branch found in the state Constitution (along with the relevant section):

The executive power of the state is vested in the Governor, and he or she must see that the law is faithfully executed. (Section 1)

The Governor and the other constitutional officers are elected every four years at the same time and place as Assembly Members. The constitutional officers take their office on the Monday after January 1 following their election, which was Monday, January 7, 2019, for those elected in the November 2018 general election. (Section 2)

Both the Governor and Lt. Governor, in order to hold office, must have been a U.S. citizen and resident of California for the 5 years preceding their election and are limited to 2 terms. (Sections 2 and 9)

Just like the U.S. President, the Governor must report to the Legislature each year on the condition of the state. This is called the "State of the State" address. The Governor may, but is not required to, make recommendations to the Legislature at that time. (Section 3)

If there is a vacancy in any constitutional office, the Governor must nominate a person to fill that vacancy. The nominee can only take office upon being confirmed by majority vote of the Senate and Assembly. If the nominee is neither confirmed nor refused confirmation by both houses within 90 days, then he or she takes office as if there had been a confirmation vote. (Section 5)

The Governor has the authority to assign and reorganize executive officers, agencies and their employees. This authority is set forth in statute, and they are called GRPs — Governor's Reorganization Plans. They take effect unless the Legislature rejects the GRP. However, this authority does not extend to the Legislature or the other constitutional officers (i.e., the Governor cannot reorganize their offices and employees). (Section 6)

The Governor is the state militia's commander in chief, and he or she has the authority to use the militia to execute the laws. (Section 7)

The Governor has the authority to grant reprieves, pardons and commutations after an individual's sentence. But this power does not extend to a case of impeachment. If this power is used, the Governor has to report it to the Legislature in each instance, and the report must contain the pertinent facts and reasons that he or she used to grant the reprieve, pardon or commutation.

In the case of an individual who has two or more felony convictions, the Governor can only grant a pardon or commutation if a majority of the state Supreme Court agrees with his or her decision. (Section 8) You might have read of several instances in late 2018, for example, where the Governor petitioned the Supreme Court to review several pardon requests. And, for the first time, several were rejected.

The Governor also has the authority (limited to 30 days) to review grants of parole for those convicted of murder, but his or her review to affirm, modify or reverse the parole decision must be limited to the same factors which the parole authority considered. Here, too, the Governor's decision must be reported to the Legislature. (Section 8)

The Lt. Governor is the President of the Senate, but he or she only has the power to cast a vote when there is a tie of 20–20 in the 40-member Senate. (Section 9) This is why the Senate President pro Tempore is in charge of the day-to-day operations of the State Senate.

Although they are elected separately (i.e., not on a joint ticket like the U.S. President and Vice President), the Lt. Governor becomes the Governor when a vacancy occurs. Nonetheless, the Lt. Governor also becomes Acting Governor whenever the Governor is out of state, has a temporary disability or during impeachment proceedings. (Section 10) By statute, when the Governor and Lt. Governor are absent from the state, then the Senate President pro Tempore becomes Acting Governor.

Notes and Questions

1. The Governor's authority to act on legislation is a power exclusive to the executive branch of state government. That means that neither of the other two branches

of government can exercise the gubernatorial power concerning bills. Of course, if a bill is vetoed by the Governor, the Legislature can attempt to override the Governor's veto, which would require a 2/3 majority vote of both houses (i.e., the Senate and the Assembly).

2. The state's electorate also has the ability to attempt to override the Governor's signature of a bill, by pursuing a referendum to seek the voters' repeal of an adopted law. Otherwise, the power of bills rests with the Governor.

3. The Governor has exclusive discretion to sign or veto bills passed by the Legislature and he also has the power to reduce or eliminate one or more items of appropriations. (*California State Employees Association v. State* (1973) 32 Cal.App.3d 103.)

2. What Can California's Governor Do with Legislation on the Desk?

When a bill is passed by the Legislature and sent to the Governor, there are three actions that can occur: (1) sign the bill into law; (2) veto the bill; or (3) allow the bill to become law without a signature ("pocket signature"). The options available to the Governor can be found in Section 10 of Article IV of the California Constitution. Let us examine each of the options in turn:

Signature by the Governor

Section 10(a) provides in part: "Each bill passed by the Legislature shall be presented to the Governor. It becomes a statute if it is signed by the Governor." In general, the Governor has 12 days in which to act on a bill sent to him or her from the Legislature, except those measures received after the Legislature has adjourned for the year. That 12-day period begins once the bill has been "presented" to the Governor, not the day that the bill passed the Senate or Assembly.

The 12-day "signing" period is applicable to all bills that are presented to the Governor twelve or more days prior to the date the Legislature adjourns for a joint recess in the first year of the two-year session, and on or before August 20th of the second year of the Session. The applicable calendar date in the first year is based on the date both houses of the Legislature "consent" to adjourn for the interim recess and is subject to change. This date is set forth in the Joint Rules of the Assembly and Senate, which are adopted for each two-year legislative session.

Section 10(b)(2) provides: "Any bill passed by the Legislature before September 1 of the second calendar year of the biennium of the legislative session and in the possession of the Governor on or after September 1 that is not returned on or before September 30 of that year becomes a statute." As a result of this provision, the Governor has 30 days to act upon measures sent to the Governor's Desk at the end of each legislative year.

The recess date (which is August 31) in the second year of the two-year Session is fixed by the state Constitution. Bills that are passed before September 1 in the second year of the session and which are in the Governor's possession on or after

September 1 must be signed or vetoed by September 30th of that year or they become a statute without his or her signature.

Any bill passed by the Legislature at a special session, which is in the Governor's possession on or after the adjournment date of the special session, becomes law unless the Governor vetoes the bill within 12 days by returning the vetoed bill to the office of the Secretary of the Senate or the Chief Clerk of the Assembly.

When the Governor approves a bill, he or she signs it, dates it and deposits it with the Secretary of State. This copy is the official record and law of the state. The Secretary of State assigns the bill a number known as the "chapter number." The bills are numbered consecutively in the order in which they are received, and the resulting sequence is presumed to be the order in which the bills were approved by the Governor.

There is only one sequence of chapter numbers maintained for each year of the regular session of the Legislature. As a result, the numbers do not continue in the second year of the Session. In addition, a separate set of chapter numbers is maintained for each special session.

Veto by the Governor

Section 10(a) provides in part: "The Governor may veto it by returning it with any objections to the house of origin, which shall enter the objections in the journal and proceed to reconsider it. If each house then passes the bill by rollcall vote entered in the journal, two-thirds of the membership concurring, it becomes a statute."

When the Governor vetoes a bill, he or she returns it, with his or her objections to the bill, to the house of origin. The house of origin may consider the veto immediately or place it on the "unfinished business file." The Legislature has 60 calendar days, with days in joint recess excluded, to act upon the vetoed bill. If no action has been taken during this time, then the measure is removed from the file and the veto is effective.

Veto overrides are rare. The Legislature has not overridden a Governor's veto since 1979. The result of sustaining the Governor's veto or failing to consider it in the time allotted is to "kill" the bill or to reduce or eliminate the appropriation as recommended by the Governor. If two-thirds of the elected Members of each house disagree with the Governor, the bill as passed by the Legislature becomes law notwithstanding his or her objections.

When the Legislature successfully overrides a Governor's veto, the bill or items of appropriation are authenticated as having become law by a certificate. The bill or statement so authenticated is then delivered to the Governor, and by him or her deposited with the laws in the office of the Secretary of State. Bills deposited in the office of the Secretary of State are given a chapter number in the same manner as bills approved by the Governor.

Line-Item Vetoes

Section 10(e) provides: "The Governor may reduce or eliminate one or more items of appropriation while approving other portions of a bill. The Governor shall append to the bill a statement of the items reduced or eliminated with the reasons for the action. The Governor shall transmit to the house originating the bill a copy of the statement and reasons. Items reduced or eliminated shall be separately reconsidered and may be passed over the Governor's veto in the same manner as bills."

If a bill presented to the Governor contains one or several items of appropriation, he or she may eliminate or reduce any or all of those items while approving the other portions of the bill. When the Governor utilizes this "item veto," he or she appends to the bill, at the time of signing it, a statement of the items to which he or she objects and his or her reasons therefor.

A copy of this statement is then transmitted to the house in which the bill originated. The items then may be separately reconsidered and the vetoes sustained or overridden in the same manner as bills which have been vetoed by the Governor.

Allowed to Become Law without the Governor's Signature

Section (10)(b)(1) provides: "Any bill, other than a bill which would establish or change boundaries of any legislative, congressional, or other election district, passed by the Legislature on or before the date the Legislature adjourns for a joint recess to reconvene in the second calendar year of the biennium of the legislative session, and in the possession of the Governor after that date, that is not returned within 30 days after that date becomes a statute." As mentioned previously, bills passed at the conclusion of the legislative year can be considered for 30 days by the Governor.

Section (10)(b)(3) provides: "Any other bill presented to the Governor that is not returned within 12 days becomes a statute." Except for bills sent to the Governor at the end of the legislative year, the Governor must act upon measures within 12 days of receiving them from the legislature.

California has a "pocket signature" rule. If the Governor does not act on the measure within the allotted time, then the bill becomes law without his or her signature. Compare this to the language contained in Article 1, Section 7 of the federal Constitution:

> ... If any Bill shall not be returned by the President within ten Days (Sundays excepted) after it shall have been presented to him, the Same shall be a Law, in like Manner as if he had signed it, unless the Congress by their Adjournment prevent its Return, in which Case it shall not be a Law.

3. Limit on Governor's Power

The Governor in this state has three options when a bill reaches his or her desk — sign the bill; veto the bill; or allow the bill to become law without his or her signature. While there is this grant of authority, it also places limits on the Governor's power. For example, the Governor cannot simply withhold action on a bill.

Also, the Governor's line-item veto authority only applies to individual appropriations of funds and not the remaining provisions of a bill that contains both an appropriation and a statutory change. And, finally, the Governor cannot "line-item" provisions of a bill that he or she may object to. In other words, the Governor must sign or veto the entire bill, not a portion of it.

Harbor v. Deukmejian

(1987) 43 Cal.3d 1078, rehearing denied

OPINION

Mosk, J.

In this case, we consider two issues of constitutional significance. The first relates to the limitation imposed by article IV, section 10 of the California Constitution on the Governor's power to veto legislation, and the second to the limitations placed on the Legislature by California Constitution, article IV, section 9, which provides that a "statute shall embrace but one subject, which shall be expressed in its title."

On June 15, 1984, the Legislature enacted a budget for the 1984–1985 fiscal year (Budget Act). (Stats. 1984, ch. 258, p. 874 et seq.) One item of the budget (5180-101-001(a), sched. 10.04.005) was an appropriation for aid to families with dependent children (AFDC) for over $1.5 billion.

Ten days later, the Legislature passed Senate Bill No. 1379 (Stats. 1984, ch. 268, p. 1302 et seq.; hereinafter Bill 1379). Bill 1379, according to its title, related to "fiscal affairs, making an appropriation therefor." It was not to become operative unless the Budget Act was also passed (*id.*, § 70, p. 1407) and it was declared to be an urgency measure because it would provide "necessary statutory adjustments to implement" the Budget Act (*id.*, § 71, p. 1407).

Bill 1379 contains 71 sections enacting, amending, and repealing numerous provisions in numerous codes. Among these is section 45.5 of Bill 1379 (hereafter section 45.5), which amends section 11056 of the Welfare and Institutions Code to allow AFDC benefits to be paid under certain circumstances from the time application for such benefits is made rather than from the date the application is processed by the State Department of Social Services (department), as was the case before the amendment. The director of the department is required by the section to adopt regulations to implement its provisions within 30 days after enactment of Bill 1379. (Stats 1984, ch. 268, § 45.5, p. 1383.)

In approving the budget, the Governor reduced the item containing the AFDC allotment by $9,776,000. (Stats. 1984, ch. 258, item. 5180-101-001, sched. 10.04.005, p. 847.) In his message relating to the reduction, the Governor stated that this sum was an "augmentation" to the item for AFDC "that would have reversed current State policy and regulations regarding the effective date of the first ... [AFDC] aid payment." (*Id.*)

Two days later, he approved Bill 1379, but purported to veto section 45.5. (Stats. 1984, ch. 268, p. 1304.) His explanation for the veto was as follows: "I have made a number of reductions in appropriations and sections contained in the Budget Act. In order to fully implement my actions, I must also make conforming changes in this bill.... I have reduced ... [the AFDC appropriation in the Budget Act] by $9,776,000 ... to maintain current policies regarding the effective date of aid.... The elimination of this section conforms to my actions on the Budget." (*Ibid.*)

The director of the department refused to adopt regulations to implement section 45.5, as required therein, on the ground that the Governor's veto of the section was valid. Thereafter, three individuals who had applied for AFDC grants toward the end of August or the beginning of September 1984, and who claimed they had lost benefits due to the department's failure to implement section 45.5, and a coalition of welfare rights organizations, filed a petition for a writ of mandate. They sought to compel the director to adopt regulations to implement section 45.5 and to recompute the amount of benefits due all AFDC recipients whose applications were pending on July 1, 1984, and thereafter in accordance with the section.

The petition asserted that the Governor's veto was ineffective because his veto power did not extend to disapproving parts of bills which were not appropriation measures, and that section 45.5 was not such a measure. Petitioners joined in the action the Governor, the director of the department, and the Department of Finance and its director. The petition was initially filed in the Court of Appeal, which denied it without opinion. We granted a hearing from the denial and retransferred the matter to that court with directions to issue an alternative writ. The court's opinion following issuance of the writ supported the position of respondents. The Court of Appeal denied a peremptory writ and we granted review.

Validity of the Governor's Veto

The California Constitution declares that the legislative power of the state is vested in the Legislature (art. IV, § 1) and the executive power in the Governor (art. VI, § 1). Unless permitted by the Constitution, the Governor may not exercise legislative powers. (Art. III, § 3.) He may veto a bill "by returning it with any objections to the house of origin," and it will become law only if "each house then passes the bill by rollcall vote … two thirds of the membership concurring…." If the Governor fails to act within a certain period of time, the measure becomes law without his signature. (Art. IV, § 10, subd. (a).) The Governor's veto power is more extensive with regard to appropriations. He may "reduce or eliminate one or more items of appropriation while approving other portions of a bill." Such items may be passed over his veto in the same manner as vetoed bills. (Art. IV, § 10, subd. (b).)

Petitioners assert that, in vetoing legislation, the Governor acts in a legislative capacity, and that in order to preserve the system of checks and balances upon which our government is founded, he may exercise legislative power only in the manner expressly authorized by the Constitution. Since that document only authorizes the Governor to veto a "bill" or to reduce or eliminate "items of appropriation" the Governor may not veto part of a bill which is not an "item of appropriation." Section 45.5 is a substantive measure and cannot be so characterized, and it is only one provision of a bill rather than a "bill." Therefore, the Governor's attempted veto of that provision is invalid.

Respondents also rely on the separation of powers doctrine as the basis for their assertion that the Governor's veto of section 45.5 should be upheld. The purpose of the veto power is to circumscribe the power of the legislative branch, and, they assert, the Governor's veto authority must be liberally construed in order to preserve the separation of powers between the executive and legislative branches of government. To this end, the breadth of that power must relate to the nature of legislation which has been presented to the Governor for approval. Here, claim respondents, the Legislature attempted to circumvent the Governor's power to disapprove legislation by separating in different bills the amount necessary to fund the program mandated by section 45.5 (the $9,776,000 allegedly included in the budget as part of the lump sum AFDC appropriation and the federal funds to implement the program) from the purpose of the appropriation, as set forth in section 45.5. By reducing the item in the budget for AFDC in the amount required to support the section 45.5 program and vetoing the section, the Governor was properly exercising the power granted to him in article IV, section 10, subdivision (b), to reduce items of appropriation.

For the reasons stated below, we shall conclude that petitioners' position must prevail on this issue.

. . . .

This court recognized that the Governor was prohibited from selectively vetoing general legislation in *Lukens v. Nye* (1909) 156 Cal. 498 [105 P. 593]. There, the Legislature enacted a measure appropriating money to pay a claim against the state. Before approving the bill, the Governor informed the assignees of the claim that the amount allowed was excessive, and that he would not approve the bill unless plaintiffs would agree to accept a lesser sum. Plaintiffs agreed, and sued for the full amount after the measure was approved.

We held for plaintiffs, stating that in exercising the veto power the Governor acts as a "legislative instrumentality," and as a special agent with limited powers, and that he may therefore act only as the Constitution allows. Except for a bill containing several items of appropriation, he may not modify or change the effect of a proposed law "or ... do anything concerning it except to approve or disapprove it as a whole." Thus, "[i]n the case of a bill containing several items of appropriation of money, he may approve one or more of them, and object to the others. [Citation.] In no other case is he empowered to modify or change the effect of a proposed law, or to do anything concerning it except to approve or disapprove it as a whole." (156 Cal. 498 at pp. 501–503.) We cited *Lukens* with approval in *California Mfrs. Assn. v. Public Utilities Com.* (1979) 24 Cal. 3d 836, 847–848 [157 Cal. Rptr. 676, 598 P.2d 836].)

The same principle was expressed in a recent Colorado case on the basis of a constitutional provision similar to article III, section 3 of the California Constitution. The Colorado Supreme Court held that the grant of the veto to the Governor was a grant of legislative power, and an exception to the separation of powers otherwise required by the Constitution. Therefore, the veto power could be exercised "only when clearly authorized by the constitution, and the language conferring it is to be strictly construed." (*Colorado General Assembly v. Lamm* (Colo. 1985) 704 P.2d 1371, 1385–1386.)

Respondents assert that the statements from Lukens, supra, 156 Cal. 498, regarding the Governor's veto power are dicta since the Governor did not attempt to exercise his veto in that case but, rather, made a private agreement to reduce an appropriation. Even so, the principles set forth there are clearly correct. As we have seen, article III, section 3 provides that one branch of government may not exercise the powers granted to another "except as permitted by this Constitution." Case law, commentators, and historians have long recognized that in exercising the veto the Governor acts in a legislative capacity. (See e.g., *La Abra Silver Mining Co. v. U.S.* (1899) 175 U.S. 423, 453 [44 L. Ed. 223, 233–234, 20 S. Ct. 168]; *State v. Holder, supra*, 23 So. 643, 645; *Colorado General Assembly v. Lamm, supra*, 704 P.2d 1371, 1382; 1 Bryce, The American Commonwealth (1913) p. 57; Wilson, Congressional Government (1973) p. 53; Zinn, 12 F.R.D. 207, 214–215.) It is not coincidental that from the first Constitution of this state in 1849, and in the United States Constitution as well, the executive's power to veto legislation has appeared in the legislative article.

It follows that in exercising the power of the veto the Governor may act only as permitted by the Constitution. That authority is to veto a "bill" (art. IV, § 10, subd. (a)) or to "reduce or eliminate one or more items of appropriation" (*id.*, subd. (b)).

The Governor did not veto Bill 1379, but purported to disapprove only section 45.5 thereof, and we must decide, therefore, whether the veto was justified on the ground that section 45.5 is an "item of appropriation." The term has been defined in various ways. *Wood v. Riley, supra*, 192 Cal. 293, 303, defines it as "a specific setting aside of an amount, not exceeding a definite sum, for the payment of certain particular claims or demands ... not otherwise expressly provided for in the appropriation bill." It "adds an additional amount to the funds already provided." In *Bengzon* [*v. Secretary of Justice*] the term was described as a bill whose "primary and specific aim ... is to make appropriations of money from the public treasury." (299 U.S. 410 at p. 413 [81 L. Ed. 312 at p. 314].) Other cases employ somewhat different definitions (e.g., *Jessen Associates, Inc. v. Bullock* (Tex. 1975) 531 S.W.2d 593, 599 ["setting aside or dedicating of funds for a specified purpose"]; *Commonwealth v. Dodson* (1940) 176 Va. 281 [11 S.E.2d 120, 127] ["an indivisible sum of money dedicated to a stated purpose"]).

We do not see how it can be seriously claimed that section 45.5 qualifies as an item of appropriation under any of these definitions. It does not set aside money for the payment of any claim and makes no appropriation from the public treasury, nor does it add any additional amount to funds already provided for. Its effect is substantive. Like thousands of other statutes, it directs that a department of government act in a particular manner with regard to certain matters. Although as is common with countless other measures, the direction contained therein will require the expenditure of funds from the treasury, this does not transform a substantive measure to an item of appropriation. We agree with petitioners that section 45.5 only expresses the Legislature's intention that the AFDC appropriation, whatever its amount, must be used to provide benefits to recipients from the date of application under certain circumstances.

Respondents' arguments to the contrary are not convincing. They claim that section 45.5 is in reality part of an "item of appropriation." Such an item consists of two indivisible parts: the sum appropriated and its purpose. (Citing *Wood v. Riley, supra*,

192 Cal. 293.) The "normal" form of appropriation, according to respondents, is to combine the substantive provisions which will require the expenditure of funds with the appropriation for that purpose in one bill, and the measure is then subject to the veto as to both purpose and funding. Here, the Legislature attempted to evade a veto by separating these indivisible parts, placing the appropriation in the budget bill, and its purpose in a separate measure. The Governor's veto of section 45.5 was a proper response to the Legislature's attempt to violate the system of checks and balances.

We cannot agree, however, that the appropriation and its purpose were set forth in separate measures. Both were specified in the Budget Act, that is, over $1.5 billion was appropriated for the purpose of funding AFDC. The Governor is bound by this "purpose" as set forth in the budget. If the Legislature chooses to budget by a lump sum appropriation, he may eliminate or reduce the amount available for the purpose as set forth therein. Here, the Governor not only reduced the "item of appropriation" as set forth in the budget, but he divided it into its supposed component parts, assigned a purpose and amount to the part he disapproved, reduced the total by that amount, and attempted to veto a portion of a substantive bill which he claims contains the "subject of the appropriation." We are aware of no authority which even remotely supports the attempted exercise of the veto in this manner.

Respondents place primary reliance on *Wood v. Riley, supra*, 192 Cal. 293. That case was decided one year after the Constitution was amended in 1922 to allow the Governor to reduce as well as eliminate "items of appropriation." There, the Legislature added a proviso to the budget bill requiring the State Controller to transfer 1 percent of a lump sum appropriation to a government department for a certain purpose, at the request of the Director of Education. The Governor vetoed the proviso, and the Director of Education, claiming that the veto was ineffective, filed suit against the Controller to transfer the funds from the larger appropriation. The veto was upheld on the ground that the proviso was an "item of appropriation."

Respondents point to several statements in the opinion to the effect that the Legislature had attempted to evade the Governor's veto power by the manner in which it set forth the appropriation. The opinion comments that had the Legislature made an express appropriation of the amount and for the purposes set forth in the proviso, the Governor would have vetoed it. If the provision were immune from the veto the Legislature might "by indirection, defeat the purpose of the constitutional amendment giving the Governor power to control the expenditures of the state, when it could not accomplish that purpose directly or by an express provision in appropriation bills.... The point of this decision is that the legislature attempted to make an appropriation ... in such way as to circumvent the veto power of the Governor. Under the constitution of the state ... he had the power to eliminate the item...." (192 Cal. 293 at pp. 305–306.)

The present case is similar to *Wood*, according to respondents, because here, too, the Legislature has attempted to avoid the veto power of the Governor. In order to prevent the evasion, the term "item of appropriation" as used in the Constitution should be interpreted to include a measure like section 45.5. As we point out above, however, no definition of that term — including the one employed in *Wood* itself — can reasonably embrace a provision like section 45.5, which does not set aside a sum of money to be paid from the public treasury. The fact that in *Wood* the term "item of appropriation" was construed in such a way as to facilitate the Governor's power to veto a portion of the budget bill which could reasonably be encompassed within the meaning of that term does not provide authority for holding, as respondents suggest, that the Governor may veto part of a general bill — a power denied him by the Constitution — in order to foil an alleged legislative attempt to evade the veto.

Another theory advanced by respondents to support the validity of the veto of section 45.5 is that even if the section is not deemed to be an "item of appropriation," the Governor acted properly because the section, standing alone, is a "bill" for the purpose of determining the scope of the veto power. The argument is as follows: although section 45.5 is purportedly part of Bill 1379, the bill in fact includes provisions relating to many different subjects; a multisubject bill violates article IV, section 9 of the Constitution; when such a bill is presented to the Governor, he may exercise his veto on a subject-by-subject basis; since section 45.5 amounts to legislation on a separate subject, the section is a "bill" for the purpose of the Governor's veto; ergo, by vetoing the section, he vetoed a "bill," as he is authorized to do by the Constitution.

Again, respondents' claim has no support in either the Constitution or case law.

While one or more subjects may be referred to in a single bill, the term "bill" is not synonymous with "subject." A bill is the "draft of a proposed law from the time of its introduction in a legislative house through all the various stages in both houses." (Black's Law Dict. (5th ed. 1979) p. 152.)

Not only would we be violating the plain words of the Constitution if we were to adopt the unwarranted definition proposed by respondents, but we would place an intolerable burden on the relations between the executive and legislative branches of government. If, as respondents suggest, the Governor has the power to exercise his veto as to any portion of a substantive bill which in his view constitutes a "subject," the result would be a continual conflict between the Governor and the Legislature over whether the scope of the veto power was exceeded because the Governor failed to confine his disapproval to a single subject encompassed in a bill. We find it ironic that respondents themselves concede that it is very difficult to define the term "subject" as used in the constitutional provision.

We reject, therefore, respondents' claim that the Governor should be empowered to make a determination as to how many subjects are contained in a bill presented to him for signature, and to veto parts of a bill which he determines constitute a separate subject therein.

Before we reach the issue whether Bill 1379 violates the single subject provision of article IV, section 9 of our Constitution, we consider an interesting argument made by respondents as to the relationship between that provision and the veto power. In construing the provisions of the Constitution each must be "read in the context of the other provisions ... bearing on the same subject. [Citation.] The goal ... is to harmonize all related provisions if it is reasonably possible to do so without distorting their apparent meaning, and in doing so to give effect to the scheme as a whole." (*Fields v. Eu* (1976) 18 Cal. 3d 322, 328 [134 Cal. Rptr. 367, 556 P.2d 729].)

In the present case, argue respondents, the one subject rule and the veto power are related to one another in that the Governor has the power to veto bills (art. IV, § 10), and a bill may not contain more than one subject (art. IV, § 9). This relationship is evident on a pragmatic level since the broader the meaning given to the term "one subject" in the Constitution, the narrower is the power of the Governor to veto legislation. The Governor must accept all of the provisions of a nonappropriation bill or disapprove the whole measure, and the greater the range of matters that can be included in a bill, the more difficult a veto decision becomes. Even if a liberal construction of the word "subject" might be appropriate for deciding whether a bill violates the single subject rule in the absence of a veto, where, as here, the Governor has vetoed a provision which he claims violates the rule, liberal construction would be unjustified because it would diminish the effect of the Governor's veto power and violate the maxims of constitutional interpretation recited above.

This appears to be a matter of first impression in California, although a few cases from other jurisdictions have related the efficacy of the Governor's veto power to the scope of the single subject rule. (*Turner v. Wright* (1957) 11 Ill. 2d 161 [142 N.E.2d 84, 90]; *Commonwealth v. Barnett* (1901) 199 Pa. 161 [48 A. 976, 977]; see *State v. Henry* (1935) 82 Wis.2d 679 [260 N.W. 486, 492, 99 A.L.R. 1267].) As we shall see, the primary purpose of the one subject rule is the regulation of legislative procedures: the avoidance of logrolling by legislators in the enactment of laws. (Ruud, One-Subject Rule (1958) 42 Minn.L.Rev. 389, 391, hereinafter referred to as Ruud.) The veto power, on the other hand, provides the executive with a defense against the power of the Legislature. (*Thirteenth Guam Legislature v. Bordallo, supra*, 430 F. Supp. 405, 409.) There is no evidence that the framers of our Constitution recognized a relationship between the two provisions. The single subject rule was adopted without debate in the Constitutional Convention which led to the adoption of the Constitution of 1849. (Debates & Proceedings, Cal. Const. Convention 1849, p. 90.) During the 1879 Constitutional Convention the purpose of the provision was stated to be "to prevent collusion in a legislative body; to prevent the passage of what are called omnibus bills — uniting various interests in order to get them passed." (Debates & Proceedings, Cal. Const. Convention 1878–1879, p. 798.) There is some doubt, therefore, whether in a historical sense at least, the single subject rule and the veto power bear on the "same subject" and are "related provisions" which must be harmonized in order to give effect to a constitutional scheme as a whole. (*Fields v. Eu, supra*, 18 Cal. 3d 322, 328.)

Nevertheless, it cannot be denied that as a practical matter the broader the definition ascribed to the term "one subject" in the Constitution, the more circumscribed is the Governor's power to veto legislation. The problem is intriguing and would warrant discussion and analysis in an appropriate case. In the present case, however, we shall conclude that Bill 1379 violates the single subject rule on the basis of the settled rules established in a nonveto context; we have no occasion, therefore to decide whether, as respondents urge, the single subject rule should be strictly construed when the Governor has vetoed a bill which he alleges violates the rule.

Validity of Bill 1379

Petitioners argue that we should not consider the question of the validity of Bill 1379 because respondents did not timely raise in the Court of Appeal their claim that the bill violates the single subject provision of the Constitution (Cal. Rules of Court, rule 28(a)), and that respondents have no standing to raise the issue. We disagree on both counts.

The alleged violation of the single subject rule was raised by respondents in the Court of Appeal in their answer to the amicus curiae brief filed by the California Legislature, and again in response to the alternative writ of mandate issued by the Court of Appeal following our remand to that court.

As to the issue of standing, petitioners assert that the Governor may not claim that section 45.5 is invalid on single subject grounds because he does not have the power to veto legislation based on his opinion that it is unconstitutional. The rules relating to "standing" refer to a plaintiff's ability to challenge the constitutionality of a statute if he is not injured by its operation. (5 Witkin, Summary of Cal. Law (8th ed. 1974) § 44, p. 3282.) The Governor is not a plaintiff in this proceeding but a respondent and his assertion that section 45.5 violates the single subject rule is employed as a matter of defense to petitioner's claim that the measure is valid and his veto ineffective. The issue raised by respondents is of great public importance, the matter has been fully briefed by the parties, and petitioners have cited no authority which requires us to postpone consideration of the matter until, as they suggest, a taxpayer challenges the constitutionality of Bill 1379 on the ground that it violates the single subject rule.

We come, then, to the merits of the question whether Bill 1379 violates article IV, section 9 of the Constitution. It provides, as we have seen, that a "statute shall embrace but one subject, which shall be expressed in its title." This provision has its origin in the Constitution of 1849. (Art. IV, § 25.)

Petitioners' argument that Bill 1379 does not violate the single subject rule is based on a simple premise: they deny that the provision sets forth an independent requirement that a bill must be confined to one subject and assert that a statute complies with the Constitution even if it includes numerous unrelated subjects so long as they are all germane to the title of the act. The problem with this claim is that it reads the single subject provision out of the Constitution and substitutes for it a provision that a statute with multiple subjects complies with section 9 so long as those subjects are included within the title.

Contrary to petitioners' assertion, the two aspects of section 9 relating to the subject of an act and its title are independent provisions which serve separate purposes. A statute must comply with both the requirement that it be confined to one subject and with the command that this one subject be expressed in its title. (See 1A Suther-land, Statutory Construction (1985 rev. ed.) § 17.01, p. 1; Ruud at p. 391.)

The single subject clause has as its "primary and universally recognized purpose" the prevention of log-rolling by the Legislature, i.e., combining several proposals in a single bill so that legislators, by combining their votes, obtain a majority for a measure which would not have been approved if divided into separate bills. (Ruud at p. 391.) As of 1982, the constitutions of 41 states included a single subject requirement. (1A Sutherland, op. cit., *supra*, at pp. 1–2.) The purpose of the requirement that the single subject of a bill shall be expressed in its title is to prevent misleading or inaccurate titles so that legislators and the public are afforded reasonable notice of the contents of a statute. (See e.g., *Ex parte Liddell* (1892) 93 Cal. 633, 635–656 [29 P. 251]; *Abeel v. Clark* (1890) 84 Cal. 226, 228 [24 P. 383].)

The authorities cited by petitioners for the proposition that compliance with the title requirement satisfies section 9 do not support their claim. They call for a liberal construction of section 9 so that it does not become a "loophole of escape from, or a means for the destruction of legitimate legislation" (*Heron v. Riley* (1930) 209 Cal. 507, 510 [289 P. 160]), but they do not suggest that an accurate title alone will comply with the single subject rule. For the most part, the cases they cite involve a challenge only to the appropriateness of the title of a statute (e.g., *Heron v. Riley, supra*, 209 Cal. 507, 512–514; *Ex parte Hallawell* (1909) 155 Cal. 112, 113–114 [99 P. 490]; *Estate of McPhee* (1908) 154 Cal. 385, 389 [97 P. 878]; *Ex parte Liddell, supra*, 93 Cal. 633, 635; *Abeel v. Clark, supra*, 86 Cal. 226, 228), although a few relate also to the single subject rule, and these evaluate the merits of both the single subject and title requirements (e.g., *Robinson v. Kerrigan* (1907) 151 Cal. 40, 50–51 [90 P. 129]).

A few cases have held statutes unconstitutional on the basis that they violated the single subject rule in addition to the title requirement. (E.g., *In re Werner* (1900) 129 Cal. 567, 572–575 [62 P. 97]; *People v. Parks* (1881) 58 Cal. 624, 638–640; see *Hill v. Board of Supervisors* (1917) 176 Cal. 84, 87 [167 P. 514] [overruled on other grounds in *Simpson v. Hite* (1950) 36 Cal.2d 125, 131 (222 P.2d 225)]; cf. *Planned Parenthood Affiliates v. Swoap* (1985) 173 Cal. App. 3d 1187, 1196–1201 [219 Cal. Rptr. 664].)

Bill 1379 amends, repeals, or adds approximately 150 sections contained in more than 20 codes and legislative acts. Its title describes the measure as "relating to fiscal affairs, making an appropriation therefor, and declaring the urgency thereof to take effect immediately." (Stats. 1984, ch. 268, p. 1302.) Respondents characterize the measure as a "trailer bill" which "trails" the budget bill and is closely related to it. Both bills follow the same legislative path, and are reviewed by the same legislative committees on the same time schedule. Section 71 of the bill provides that it is an urgency measure to take effect immediately and that it provides "necessary statutory adjustments to implement the Budget Act of 1984." (*Id.* at p. 1408.)

Many cases which discuss the single subject rule combine its expression with the requirement that the single subject of the enactment must be stated in its title even though, as we note above, each aspect of the constitutional provision declares a separate requirement with an independent purpose. This combination is natural in view of the fact that both requirements appear in a single sentence and are related to one another.

Here, however, respondents' main concern is that the text of Bill 1379 contains more than one subject. *Evans v. Superior Court* (1932) 215 Cal. 58 [8 P.2d 467], although decided more than half a century ago, remains the leading authority on the construction of section 9 of article IV of the Constitution. In that case, the Legislature adopted the entire Probate Code in one enactment with a title declaring that it was an "act to revise and consolidate the law relating to probate ... to repeal certain provisions of law therein revised and consolidated and therein specified; and to establish a Probate Code." This court held that the act contained only one subject, and that that subject was expressed in its title.

The opinion, like those before and after it, confirms the liberal construction to be accorded the single subject rule. It states the following principles as the basis of its holding: "Numerous provisions, having one general object, if fairly indicated in the title, may be united in one act. Provisions governing projects so related and interdependent as to constitute a single scheme may be properly included within a single act. [Citation.] The legislature may insert in a single act all legislation germane to the general subject as expressed in its title and within the field of legislation suggested thereby. [Citation.] Provisions which are logically germane to the title of the act and are included within its scope may be united. The general purpose of a statute being declared, the details provided for its accomplishment will be regarded as necessary incidents. [Citations.] ... A provision which conduces to the act, or which is auxiliary to and promotive of its main purpose, or has a necessary and natural connection with such purpose is germane within the rule." (215 Cal. at pp. 62–63.)

In analyzing petitioners' contentions, it is helpful to consider decisions of this court which have applied the single subject rule in a context independent of the title requirement. In 1948, California adopted a single subject constitutional provision applicable to initiatives. It states that an initiative measure embracing more than one subject may not be submitted to the electors or have any effect (Cal. Const., art. II, § 8, subd. (d)), and it does not incorporate in the same sentence the requirement that the subject must be expressed in the title; nor does it contain a provision for severance in the event more than one subject is included in the measure. Shortly after the adoption of this provision, it was held that the same principles apply to the single subject rule relating to initiatives as to legislative enactments. (*Perry v. Jordan* (1949) 34 Cal. 2d 87, 92–93 [207 P.2d 47].) The single subject rule as applied to the initiative has the dual purpose of avoiding logrolling and voter confusion. (*Amador Valley Joint Union High Sch. Dist. v. State Bd. of Equalization* (1978) 22 Cal. 3d 208, 231 [149 Cal. Rptr. 239, 583 P.2d 1281].)

In three recent cases, we have relied on the rules laid down in *Evans, supra,* 215 Cal. 58, to uphold initiative measures challenged on the ground that they embraced more than one subject. (*Amador Valley Joint Union High School Dist. v. State Board of Equalization, supra,* 22 Cal. 3d 208, 229–232; *Fair Political Practices Com. v. Superior*

Court (1979) 25 Cal. 3d 33, 37–43 [157 Cal. Rptr. 855, 599 P.2d 46]; hereinafter *FPPC*; *Brosnahan v. Brown* (1982) 32 Cal. 3d 236, 245–253 [186 Cal. Rptr. 30, 651 P.2d 274].) In each of these decisions, we held that the measures involved complied with Evans in that their provisions were "reasonably germane" to the object of the act. As additional support for its conclusion, *Amador* held that the constitutional initiative involved there contained provisions which were "'functionally related in furtherance of … a common underlying purpose.'" (22 Cal.3d at p. 230.) The initiative changed the previous system of real property taxation and imposed limitations on the assessment and taxing power of local and state government.

The following year, we were faced with another single subject challenge in FPPC. The measure in that case concerned "elections and different methods for preventing corruption and undue influence in political campaigns and governmental activities." (25 Cal.3d at p. 37.) Again, we upheld the initiative concluding that its provisions were "reasonably germane" to the subject of political practices.

In the last of these cases, *Brosnahan*, a majority of this court rejected the claim that the single subject rule requires that a measure meet both the "reasonably germane" and "functionally related" tests, and held that either standard would satisfy the constitutional requirement. The initiative measure in that case had as its aim the accomplishment of changes in the criminal justice system for the purpose of protecting the rights of victims of crime. The majority concluded that it did not violate the rule because "[e]ach of its several facets bears a common concern, 'general object' or 'general subject,' promoting the rights of actual or potential crime victims." (32 Cal.3d at p. 247.)

In a statement which is important to the resolution of the issue before us, the majority observed that proponents of initiative measures do not have "blank checks to draft measures containing unduly diverse or extensive provisions bearing no reasonable relationship to each other or to the general object which is sought to be promoted. The single subject rule indeed is a constitutional safeguard adopted to protect against multifaceted measures of undue scope. For example, the rule obviously forbids joining disparate provisions which appear germane only to topics of excessive generality such as 'government' or 'public welfare.'" However, we concluded that the initiative sustained fairly disclosed a "reasonable and common-sense relationship among their various components in furtherance of a common purpose." (32 Cal.3d at p. 253.) The decision commanded a bare four-to-three majority (dis. opn. by Bird, C. J.; Mosk, J., filed a separate dis. opn. joined by Broussard, J.), but all seven justices agreed that subjects of "excessive generality" would violate the purpose and intent of the single subject rule.

In sum, these cases hold that a measure complies with the rule if its provisions are either functionally related to one another or are reasonably germane to one another or the objects of the enactment.

Bill 1379 complies with none of these standards. Petitioners do not claim that the provisions of the bill are either functionally related or germane to one another, and examination reveals that there is no apparent relationship among its various sections.

A few examples will suffice: section 0.2 amends a provision of the Business and Professions Code to require that before transmitting a fiscal impact report to the Legislature, agencies within the Department of Consumer Affairs must submit it to the director of the department (Stats. 1984, ch. 268, p. 1306). Section 0.4 amends the same code to provide that the Contractors' State License Board may disclose to the public general information regarding complaints filed against licensees (ibid.); section 28.4 amends the Military and Veterans Code to provide that a veterans' home may be appointed guardian of the estate of a veteran (id. at p. 1352); section 66.7 permits concession contracts for state parks to exceed 20 years (id. at p. 1405).

Our second inquiry is whether the provisions of Bill 1379 can be fairly characterized as "reasonably germane" to the objects of the measure. Petitioners suggest that the subject of Bill 1379 is "fiscal affairs," as stated in its title, and that its object is "to make statutory adjustments which relate to the ongoing allocation of state funds appropriated annually in the budget bill, within the state programs so funded." Section 45.5 comes within this object because it "affects the cost of the state's AFDC program."

We understand this somewhat cryptic analysis to mean that the goal of Bill 1379 is to reflect matters encompassed in the budget bill, and that since the cost of the program mandated by section 45.5 affects the amounts appropriated in the budget, its provisions are conducive to that goal and therefore in compliance with the single subject rule.

Our unanimous determination in *Brosnahan, supra*, 32 Cal. 3d 236, that a bill which encompasses matters of "excessive generality" violates the purpose and intent of the single subject rule is applicable to this assertion. "Fiscal affairs" as the subject of Bill 1379 and "statutory adjustments" to the budget as its object suffer from the same defect. They are too broad in scope if, as petitioners appear to claim, they encompass any substantive measure which has an effect on the budget. The number and scope of topics germane to "fiscal affairs" in this sense is virtually unlimited. If petitioners' position were accepted, a substantial portion of the many thousand statutes adopted during each legislative session could be included in a single measure even though their provisions had no relationship to one another or to any single object except that they would have some effect on the state's expenditures as reflected in the budget bill. This would effectively read the single subject rule out of the Constitution. We hold, therefore, that Bill 1379 is invalid as a violation of article IV, section 9 of the California Constitution.

Disposition

We next consider the difficult question of the effect of our ruling that the Governor's veto of section 45.5 was invalid and that Bill 1379 violates the single subject rule. It is clear from what we have said above that our holding in these respects does not constitute a new rule of law. We recognize, of course, that ordinarily a judicial decision which does not establish a new rule applies retroactively, and it is only if a ruling is new law that the issue of prospective operation arises. At most, our decision applies existing precedent to a distinct fact situation, a circumstance that does not readily overcome the presumption of retroactivity. (*People v. Guerra* (1984) 37 Cal.

3d 385, 399 [208 Cal. Rptr. 162, 690 P.2d 635].) Nevertheless, we hold that our determination as to both rulings in this case is to be applied prospectively only.

With regard to our conclusion that Bill 1379 violates the single subject rule, it is appropriate to consider that the rule regulates internal procedures of the Legislature and its violation has little or no effect on individual rights or vested property interests; that is, of course, the usual objection raised when the issue of potential retroactive application of a court decision arises.

In addition, retroactive application of our ruling in this instance would have serious consequences far beyond the question of the validity of section 45.5. It would mean not only that the many provisions contained in Bill 1379 in addition to section 45.5 are invalid, but the door would be opened to a challenge to numerous other provisions of substantive law contained in prior so-called budget implementation acts. According to the Legislative Counsel's office, the practice of enacting budget implementation bills began in the 1978–1979 fiscal year. Between that time and the enactment of Bill 1379 in 1984, several such bills were passed to make "adjustments" to the budget. A cursory examination of some of these measures reveals that they suffer from the same defect as Bill 1379, i.e., they combine in a single bill numerous provisions which have no relationship to one another, nor are they reasonably germane to the object of the bill, except in the broad sense that we hold improper. Thus, an undetermined but substantial number of provisions in prior budget implementation bills would be subject to challenge. Finally, respondents themselves urge that our holding as to the single subject rule be made prospective in order to avoid the "devastating" effects of retroactivity. (Cf. *Sumner v. Workers' Comp. Appeals Bd.* (1983) 33 Cal. 3d 965, 972 [191 Cal. Rptr. 811, 663 P.2d 534].)

In view of this conclusion, we hold also that our determination as to the Governor's veto power should not apply to section 45.5. The Governor would clearly have had the power to veto section 45.5 if it had been passed by the Legislature as a separate bill. His inability to do so was frustrated by the Legislature's unlawful inclusion of the section in a multisubject bill. In these circumstances, an evenhanded respect for the executive and legislative branches of government leads us to invoke an exception to the general rule of retroactivity (see *Forster Shipbuilding Co. v. County of Los Angeles* (1960) 54 Cal. 2d 450, 458–459 [6 Cal. Rptr. 24, 353 P.2d 736]) so as to achieve a result that most closely conforms to the outcome that would have occurred if both the Legislature and the Governor had complied with the law. Accordingly, the Governor's veto of section 45.5 will not be invalidated and only that section of Bill 1379 will be rendered inoperative.

Petitioners also seek attorney fees under the "private attorney general" doctrine embodied in section 1021.5 of the Code of Civil Procedure. We believe they are entitled to such an award, even though their named clients have not personally benefitted. They are the "successful" party in that the impact of our decision is to vindicate the principle upon which they brought this action, i.e., that the Governor's power to veto legislation cannot be exercised to invalidate part of a bill which is not part of an appropriation bill. (*Folsom v. Butte County Assn. of Governments* (1982) 32 Cal.

3d 668, 684–685 [186 Cal. Rptr. 589, 652 P.2d 437].) Our decision will result in enforcement of an important right affecting the public interest, conferring a "significant benefit" on the general public in clarifying the extent of the Governor's veto power and emphasizing the inviolability by the Legislature of the one-subject rule. It is obvious that private enforcement to give effect to section 45.5 was necessary since the director of the department refused to promulgate regulations to implement the section. Because this proceeding originated in the Court of Appeal, we cannot remand the matter to the trial court to determine the appropriate amount of attorney fees. We shall, therefore, direct the Court of Appeal to determine and award such fees.

The judgment of the Court of Appeal is affirmed insofar as it denies the petition for a peremptory writ of mandate. The cause is transferred to the Court of Appeal with instructions to award reasonable attorney fees to petitioners.

LUCAS, C.J., BROUSSARD, J., PANELLI, J., ARGUELLES, J., EAGLESON J., and KAUFMAN, J., concurred.

Notes and Questions

1. The Governor is not empowered to decide as to how many subjects are contained in a bill presented to him for signature and to veto parts of a bill which he determines constitute separate subjects.

2. This case involved two major constitutional issues: The Governor's power to veto legislation and the single subject rule as it applies to legislation (as opposed to initiatives, although the courts treat the rule the same for both forms of lawmaking in this state).

3. Clearly the Governor acts in a legislative capacity when he or she signs or vetoes legislation. Do you agree that the Governor's role in the legislative process should be narrowly construed? If so, why? Do you view the role of veto power as part of the system of checks and balances?

4. The Court rejected the effort to permit the Governor from picking and choosing among the various provisions of a substantive measure. Why did the Court make this ruling?

5. What is the significance of the Court's statement that, "It is not coincidental that from the first Constitution of this state in 1849, and in the United States Constitution as well, the executive's power to veto legislation has appeared in the legislative article"?

6. The Court in this case rejected claims that § 45.5 qualifies as an item of appropriation under any definitions used previously. "It does not set aside money for the payment of any claim and makes no appropriation from the public treasury, nor does it add any additional amount to funds already provided for. Its effect is substantive. Like thousands of other statutes, it directs that a department of government act in a particular manner...." What is the impact of this statement?

7. The Court relied upon Black's Law Dictionary to find a definition of the term "bill," even though neither the California Constitution nor the Government Code provides a definition. Is the following an appropriate definition: "A bill is the 'draft

of a proposed law from the time of its introduction in a legislative house through all the various stages in both houses'? (Black's Law Dict. (5th ed. 1979) p. 152.)"

8. What do you think about the Court's discussion examining whether there is a legal relationship between "the efficacy of the Governor's veto power to the scope of the single subject rule"? The Court did note that "There is no evidence that the framers of our Constitution recognized a relationship between the two provisions."

9. In addition, the Court discussed whether the subject of an act and its title are independent provisions which serve separate purposes or if they should be read together. The Court turned to a legal commentary to state, "A statute must comply with both the requirement that it be confined to one subject and with the command that this one subject be expressed in its title. (See 1A Sutherland, Statutory Construction (1985 rev. ed.) § 17.01, p. 1; Ruud at p. 391.)"

10. Another issue addressed by the Court decision was instances in which statutes have been held unconstitutional on the basis that they violated the single subject rule in addition to the title requirement. The Court characterized these cases as holding that "a measure complies with the rule if its provisions are either functionally related to one another or are reasonably germane to one another or the objects of the enactment."

11. The Court concluded with a discussion about the petitioners' motion for attorney fees under the "private attorney general" doctrine embodied in § 1021.5 of the Code of Civil Procedure. Why did the Court believe the petitioners were entitled to such an award?

4. Presentation of Bills to the Governor

In order for the Governor to act on a bill, it must be "presented" to the Governor for final consideration. This means the Governor must have the actual bill before him or her in order to either sign or veto the measure. There has been litigation over whether the Legislature can withdraw a bill from the Governor's desk, and the courts have generally ruled that they may, even though the official records may reflect that the bill was "presented" to the Governor's office. The courts view the presentation as having occurred when the Governor acts on the bill.

De Asis v. Department of Motor Vehicles

(2003) 112 Cal.App.4th 593

OPINION

SCOTLAND, P.J.

During the 2001–2002 Regular Session of the Legislature, both the Assembly and the Senate passed Assembly Bill No. 60 to allow aliens who do not have a Social Security number to obtain a California driver's license or a California identification card if they have petitioned, or are the beneficiaries of a petition, for lawful immigration status or an extension of legal presence in the United States. Assembly Bill

No. 60 was sent to enrollment on September 14, 2001, and, plaintiff alleges, the bill went to the Governor on October 2, 2001. Soon thereafter, the Chief Clerk of the Assembly retrieved Assembly Bill No. 60 from the Governor's Office and returned it to the Legislature, where it was withdrawn from enrollment and placed in the Legislature's inactive file on motion of the bill's author. The following year, the Legislature returned Assembly Bill No. 60 to enrollment and sent it to the Governor, after which he vetoed the legislation.

Prior to the Governor's veto, plaintiff Mary Grace O. De Asis, whose application for a California identification card was denied because she did not have a Social Security number, filed a petition for writ of mandate and complaint for declaratory and injunctive relief, alleging that Assembly Bill No. 60 became law by virtue of the Governor's failure to approve or veto the bill in a timely manner after it was sent to him on October 2, 2001. (Cal. Const., art. IV, § 10, subd. (b)(1).) Thus, she sought to compel the Department of Motor Vehicles and its director (DMV) to implement Assembly Bill No. 60.

When the Governor allows a bill to become law without his signature, he is required to authenticate the bill by causing the Secretary of State to certify that fact and deposit it with the laws in the Office of the Secretary of State. (*Parkinson v. Johnson* (1911) 160 Cal. 756, 761 [117 P. 1057]; see Gov. Code, § 9516.) When a bill is properly enrolled, authenticated, and deposited in the Office of the Secretary of State, it becomes conclusive evidence of the enactment of the bill. (*Parkinson v. Johnson, supra,* 160 Cal. at p. 761.) The requirement that he cause the bill to be authenticated and deposited with the Secretary of State is mandatory and may be compelled by writ of mandate. (*Harpending v. Haight* (1870) 39 Cal. 189, 209–213.) But plaintiff does not seek mandate against the Governor. Instead, she seeks to compel a state agency, DMV, to look beyond the duly authenticated laws on deposit in the Office of the Secretary of State, to look into the legislative process, and to determine for itself that a bill has become law. Because DMV does not contend that it is not a proper party or that the Governor is an indispensable party, we do not address such questions.

Finding that the Chief Clerk of the Assembly retrieved Assembly Bill No. 60 "shortly after" it was enrolled on September 14, 2001, thereby "cut[ting] short the presentation period ... provide[d] to the Governor for considering legislation," the trial court concluded that Assembly Bill No. 60 did not become law as plaintiff claimed. Hence, the court sustained DMV's demurrer without leave to amend and entered a judgment of dismissal.

For reasons that follow, we reject plaintiff's claims on appeal.

As we will explain, when the Legislature and the Governor acquiesce in the retrieval of a bill after enrollment but before expiration of the 30-day time period allotted to the Governor to deliberate on the bill, courts will not interfere with that decision. And since such retrieval deprives the Governor of the full period in which to deliberate on the bill, it cannot become law without the Governor's signature because the bill has not been presented to the Governor within the meaning of article IV, section 10 of California's Constitution.

Accordingly, the trial court correctly concluded that Assembly Bill No. 60 did not become law, and we shall affirm the judgment of dismissal.

BACKGROUND

When Assembly Bill No. 60 was introduced, the law required an application for a California driver's license or California identification card to include the Social Security number of the applicant. (Veh. Code, §§ 1653.5, 12800, 12801.) Accordingly, a person who did not have a Social Security number could not obtain a California driver's license or California identification card.

Federal regulations provide that a Social Security number can be assigned only to a United States citizen, or an "alien lawfully admitted to the United States for permanent residence or under other authority of law permitting [the alien] to work in the United States," or an "alien who is legally in the United States ... for a valid nonwork purpose." (20 C.F.R. § 422.104(a) (2001).)

Assembly Bill No. 60 would have enabled some persons who cannot obtain a Social Security number to obtain a California driver's license or California identification card by using an alternative form of identifier.

DMV asks us to take judicial notice of excerpts from the Assembly Daily Journal for the 2001–2002 Regular Session of the Legislature, the Complete Bill History for Assembly Bill No. 60, and an excerpt from The Constitution of the State of California, edited by Edward F. Treadwell (5th ed. 1923). The request is proper because we may take judicial notice of the public and private official acts of the legislative, executive, and judicial departments of this state. (*Davis v. Whidden* (1897) 117 Cal. 618, 623 [49 P. 766]; Evid. Code, § 452.) We also may always resort to appropriate books and documents of reference for our aid in resolving issues. (Davis *v. Whidden, supra,* 117 Cal. at p. 623.) Plaintiff opposes the request, asserting the materials are irrelevant. However, in taking judicial notice, we do not thereby determine that the materials necessarily are relevant. That is a matter we must consider in addressing the issues presented on appeal. Hence, we grant the request for judicial notice.

The complete bill history prepared by the Assembly reflects that Assembly Bill No. 60 was approved by the Assembly and sent to the Senate on June 7, 2001. Assembly Bill No. 60 was approved by the Senate with amendments on September 14, 2001, and that same date the bill was sent for enrollment after the Assembly concurred in the Senate's amendments. The complete bill history does not reflect that Assembly Bill No. 60 was actually presented to the Governor. Rather, the next entry on January 14, 2002, shows that the bill was withdrawn from enrollment and placed in the inactive file upon motion of its author.

On August 20, 2002, the Legislature withdrew Assembly Bill No. 60 from the inactive file and returned the bill to enrollment. Sometime thereafter, Assembly Bill No. 60 was presented to the Governor, who vetoed the bill on September 30, 2002.

In her complaint, plaintiff alleges that on September 15, 2001, after both houses had approved Assembly Bill No. 60, the Legislature adjourned for a joint recess to reconvene in 2002. She further alleges, on information and belief, the following: (1)

on or about October 2, 2001, Assembly Bill No. 60 was enrolled and sent to the Governor; (2) the Chief Clerk of the Assembly "then retrieved [the bill] from the Governor's desk and returned it to the Legislature"; and (3) the asserted reason for retrieving Assembly Bill No. 60 was not based upon "any clerical error," but because "the bill was mistakenly sent to the Governor."

Plaintiff suggests Assembly Bill No. 60 was withdrawn from enrollment at the request of Governor Davis because he wanted, in her words, "to avoid having to sign or veto the bill." For this proposition, plaintiff quotes journalists' claims that the Governor wanted to "'toughen up the identification requirements in [the] bill'" but did not want to have to veto it "'because a veto would have alienated Latino voters.'" However, these suggestions are not supported by the appellate record, to which we are bound.

The complaint alleges that the retrieval of Assembly Bill No. 60 from the Governor was ineffectual because the Chief Clerk of the Assembly lacked the authority to do so. It follows, the complaint claims, that when the Governor failed to act upon the bill in the 30-day time period allotted by the Constitution, it automatically became law. (Cal. Const., art. IV, § 10, subd. (b)(1).)

DISCUSSION

Article IV, section 10, subdivision (a) of California's Constitution provides: "Each bill passed by the Legislature shall be presented to the Governor. It becomes a statute if it is signed by the Governor. The Governor may veto it by returning it with any objections to the house of origin, which shall enter the objections in the journal and proceed to reconsider it. If each house then passes the bill by rollcall vote entered in the journal, two thirds of the membership concurring, it becomes a statute."

Article IV, section 10, subdivision (b)(1) of California's Constitution provides: "Any bill, other than a bill which would establish or change boundaries of any legislative, congressional, or other election district, passed by the Legislature on or before the date the Legislature adjourns for a joint recess to reconvene in the second calendar year of the biennium of the legislative session, and in the possession of the Governor after that date, that is not returned within 30 days after that date becomes a statute."

As we have noted, plaintiff claims that Assembly Bill No. 60 was sent to the Governor on or about October 2, 2001, that the Chief Clerk of the Assembly had no authority thereafter to retrieve the bill, and that when the Governor neither signed nor vetoed Assembly Bill No. 60 within 30 days of October 2, 2001, the measure automatically became law.

DMV notes there is nothing in the record to establish that Assembly Bill No. 60 "had *ever* been presented to the Governor" before it was withdrawn from enrollment. Nevertheless, DMV goes on to address the merits of plaintiff's claim, assuming that Assembly Bill No. 60 in fact went to the Governor prior to its retrieval by the Chief Clerk of the Assembly. So, shall we. For purposes of demurrer, we will accept plaintiff's factual allegations as true. The issue presented is whether those factual allegations, if true, establish a cause of action upon which relief may be granted.

A

We begin our analysis by noting that the Governor acquiesced in the retrieval of Assembly Bill No. 60. Therefore, we are not concerned with whether the Legislature can compel the Governor to allow retrieval of a bill that has been sent to him and, if so, the circumstances in which, or the formalities by which, the Legislature could do so. The Legislature also acquiesced in the retrieval of the bill. Thus, both parties to the lawmaking function acquiesced in the retrieval of the bill, neither of them asserts that retrieval was ineffective or that presentation to the Governor was complete, and neither of them maintains that Assembly Bill No. 60 became law by the passage of time.

In this case, we are confronted with a private person's claim that, regardless of the views of the Governor and the Legislature, Assembly Bill No. 60 became law without the Governor's approval. We cannot agree.

B

Plaintiff's claim for relief is premised upon her argument that the retrieval of Assembly Bill No. 60 by the Chief Clerk of the Assembly (Chief Clerk) was ineffectual because he had no authority to take the bill back once it was sent to the Governor by the Legislature. Consequently, she contends, the constitutional deadline for the Governor to act on the bill remained in effect.

Plaintiff concedes that, in some instances, the Chief Clerk does have authority to retrieve a bill from the Governor's Office. Her argument is not that the Chief Clerk lacks all authority to retrieve a bill, but that his reason for doing so in this instance was insufficient. Thus, plaintiff wants the court to determine, as a question of fact, whether the Chief Clerk's action was within his authority. We decline the invitation.

"The law-making power of the state is vested, by the constitution, in the legislature; and while the constitution has prescribed the formalities to be observed in the passage of bills and the creation of statutes, the power to determine whether these formalities have been complied with is necessarily vested in the legislature itself, since, if it were not, it would be powerless to enact a statute. The constitution has not provided that this essential power thus vested in the legislature shall be subject to review by the courts, while it has expressly provided that no person charged with the exercise of powers properly belonging to one of the three departments — the legislative, executive, and judicial — into which the powers of the government are divided, shall exercise any functions appertaining to either of the others." (*County of Yolo v. Colgan* (1901) 132 Cal. 265, 274–275 [64 P. 403].)

Since the Legislature is vested with the exclusive authority to determine whether the formalities for enactment of a statute have been fulfilled, it follows that a court cannot retry, as a question of fact, the Legislature's determinations. "The authority and duty to ascertain the facts which ought to control legislative action are, from the necessity of the case, devolved by the constitution upon those to whom it has given the power to legislate, and their decision that the facts exist is conclusive upon the courts, in the absence of an explicit provision in the constitution giving the judiciary the right to review such action." (*Stevenson v. Colgan* (1891) 91 Cal. 649, 652 [27 P. 1089]; see also *County of Yolo v. Colgan, supra,* 132 Cal. at p. 271.)

The Legislature does not contend that Assembly Bill No. 60 was presented to the Governor in 2001. Rather, Assembly records reflect that, after the retrieval of the bill, on motion of the author and with unanimous consent, the bill was withdrawn from engrossing and enrolling and was sent to the inactive file. Later, in August 2002, the bill was withdrawn from the inactive file and returned to enrollment, and was then presented to the Governor. By these actions, the Legislature necessarily determined that the retrieval of the bill by the Chief Clerk was proper and effectual. It is not competent for a court to retry that determination as a question of fact.

C

Nonetheless, plaintiff suggests that, once a bill is presented to the Governor, he "cannot give up his opportunity to consider the bill," i.e., allow the Legislature to retrieve it. We disagree for reasons akin to those expressed in *Eber Bros. Wine Liquor Corporation v. United States* (1964) 167 Ct.Cl. 665, 337 F.2d 624 (hereafter *Eber Bros.*).

The court in *Eber Bros.* was called upon to interpret when a bill passed by Congress was presented to the President for his consideration and, thus, whether the bill became law because the President failed to veto it within the time prescribed by the Constitution. (*Eber Bros., supra,* 337 F.2d at p. 625.) The government asserted that when Congress sent the bill to the President while he was out of the country, it was not presented to him until his return. The plaintiff took the position that "bills are customarily presented to the President through delivery to the White House" and that without an explicit agreement between the legislative and executive branches, "that practice cannot be altered...." (*Id.* at p. 626.)

Ruling in the government's favor, the court reasoned that, while either the President or Congress could insist that certain formalities attend the presentation of a bill to the President, "[w]ithin the constitutional scheme, there is large leeway, through mutual arrangement and understanding, for the President and Congress to accommodate each other's needs and interests." (*Eber Bros., supra,* 337 F.2d at p. 629.) The court concluded that "presentation can be made in any agreed manner or in a form established by one party in which the other acquiesces...." (*Ibid.*)

Here, neither the Governor nor the Legislature maintains that the retrieval of Assembly Bill No. 60 by the Chief Clerk was ineffectual or that the presentation requirement (see pt. D, *post*) was fulfilled. Both of the parties to the lawmaking function, the Legislature and the Governor, acquiesced in the action of the Chief Clerk. Unless the Constitution expressly requires otherwise, a court should not interfere with the means by which the Governor and the Legislature accommodate each other's needs and interests.

Because the Constitution does not expressly prohibit the retrieval of a bill once it has been sent to the Governor, and since the Governor and the Legislature acquiesced in the retrieval of Assembly Bill No. 60, we should not hold that the retrieval was ineffectual.

D

In any event, we conclude that Assembly Bill No. 60 did not become law based upon the Governor's inaction because it was not left with him for the period allotted to him to act upon the legislation.

In *Harpending v. Haight, supra,* 39 Cal. 189, the California Supreme Court addressed what is required to effectuate a "return" of a bill to the house of origin. It concluded: "There can be no doubt whatever of the meaning of the word 'return,' as used in this connection in [former article IV, section 17 (now article IV, section 10) of California's] Constitution. As applicable to the bill itself, it is equivalent to the word 'presented,' as previously used in the same sentence. The bill must, before it becomes a law, be 'presented to the Governor.' It might be merely exhibited to that officer; and even if it should be immediately thereafter taken away or withdrawn, it might be contended that it had, nevertheless, been 'presented' within the very letter of the Constitution. But when we come to reflect that the only purpose for which the bill is to be 'presented to the Governor' is to afford him an opportunity to deliberately consider its provisions and prepare his objections, if any he have, to its passage, we would instinctively reject such a presentation as being fictitious — merely spurious — and certainly not that one contemplated by the Constitution, because it would defeat, rather than promote, the very object intended." (*Id.* at pp. 198–199.)

In other words, a bill is not presented to the Governor unless it is in the physical possession of the Governor for a period of time, not more than 30 days, necessary to permit the Governor to deliberate on the bill (the presentation period). The Governor's act of returning a bill to the Legislature is "a step taken by which his own time for deliberation is ended, and … the bill itself [is] put beyond the [Governor's] possession." (*Harpending v. Haight, supra,* 39 Cal. at p. 199.)

Plaintiff concedes that shortly after Assembly Bill No. 60 was sent to the Governor, the Chief Clerk retrieved it from the Governor's Office and returned it to the Legislature. Because the bill was not left in the Governor's possession for the presentation period, it follows from the decision in *Harpending v. Haight, supra,* 39 Cal. 189, that Assembly Bill No. 60 was not presented to the Governor within the meaning of the Constitution.

Plaintiff would have this court indulge in a fiction that the presentment requirement was satisfied, because, in her view, the Chief Clerk lacked authority to retrieve the bill from the Governor. However, regardless of whether he had the authority to retrieve the bill, the fact is that he did so.

The Chief Clerk is an employee of the Legislature who is charged with carrying out legislative directions. (Gov. Code, §§ 9171, 9191.) When directed by the Legislature to present a bill to the Governor, he must do so by taking the bill to the Governor and leaving it in the Governor's possession. (*Harpending v. Haight, supra,* 39 Cal. at pp. 198–199.) By failing to leave Assembly Bill No. 60 in the Governor's possession for the presentment period, the Chief Clerk did not present the bill to the Governor as required by the Constitution.

E

Plaintiff's position would have severe consequences if it were accepted. Since plaintiff concedes that the Chief Clerk has some authority to retrieve a bill after it has been sent to the Governor, to conclude that a court may later second-guess the Chief Clerk's reasons for doing so would place the initial onus on the Governor. Thus, when the Chief Clerk asks to retrieve a bill, the Governor would be required to inquire and assess the sufficiency of the reasons for the request. If the Governor finds that the reasons are sufficient and permits retrieval, he could later be hailed into court to defend his decision. If the court finds that the reasons were insufficient, then the Governor will have been denied the constitutional power to review the bill to determine whether he has objections to its passage. The Governor should not be cut out of the constitutional process through such after-the-fact judicial second-guessing.

The answer is simple.

When the Chief Clerk retrieves a bill from the Governor, he thereby curtails the presentation period required by the Constitution. (*Harpending v. Haight, supra,* 39 Cal. at pp. 198–199.) If the Legislature determines that the retrieval was inappropriate, it can direct the Chief Clerk to promptly fulfill the presentation requirement by providing the Governor with the full period for review of the bill. If the Legislature acquiesces in the retrieval of the bill, then courts should not second-guess that determination. This procedure is efficacious and adds certainty to the law. Most importantly, it leaves the lawmaking authority, including the power to determine whether formalities for enactment of a law have been fulfilled, in the body that is exclusively vested with that authority by the Constitution. (*County of Yolo v. Colgan, supra,* 132 Cal. at p. 275; *Stevenson v. Colgan, supra,* 91 Cal. at p. 652.)

F

For the reasons stated above, the trial court properly dismissed plaintiff's lawsuit.

DISPOSITION

The judgment is affirmed.

RAYE, J., and ROBIE, J., concurred.

Appellant's petition for review by the Supreme Court was denied December 23, 2003.

Notes and Questions

1. Since the Legislature is vested with the exclusive authority to determine whether the formalities for enactment of a statute have been fulfilled, it follows that a court cannot retry, as a question of fact, the Legislature's determinations. The lawmaking power of the state is vested in the legislature.

2. While the Constitution has prescribed the formalities to be observed in the passage of bills and the creation of statutes, the power to determine whether these formalities have been complied with is necessarily vested in the legislature itself since, if it were not, it would be powerless to enact a statute.

3. When the Chief Clerk of the Assembly retrieves a bill from the Governor, he thereby curtails the presentation period required by the Constitution. If the Legislature determines retrieval was inappropriate, it can direct the Chief Clerk to promptly fulfill the presentation requirement by providing the Governor with the full period for review of the bill, and courts should not second-guess that determination. A bill is not presented to the Governor unless it is in the physical possession of the Governor for a period of time, not more than 30 days, necessary to permit the Governor to deliberate on the bill.

4. The Governor's act of returning the bill to the Legislature ends his own time for deliberation, and the bill itself is put beyond the Governor's possession. The Legislature may retrieve a bill after it has been presented to the Governor. Where Assembly records reflected that, after retrieval of the bill from the Governor, on motion of its author and with unanimous consent, the bill was withdrawn from engrossing and enrolling and was sent to the inactive file, it was later withdrawn from the inactive file and returned to enrollment and was presented to the Governor at that time.

5. When the Governor allows a bill to become law without his signature, he is required to authenticate the bill by causing the Secretary of State to certify that fact and deposit it with the laws in the office of the Secretary of State.

6. Instead of seeking, for example, a writ of mandamus against the Legislature, Governor, or even the Secretary of State, with whom laws are filed, the plaintiff sought to compel a state agency, DMV, "to look beyond the duly authenticated laws on deposit in the Office of the Secretary of State, to look into the legislative process, and to determine for itself that a bill has become law." Did the plaintiff err in choosing to sue the DMV?

7. The court noted several times in its opinion that the Legislature and the Governor acquiesced in the retrieval of AB 60 after enrollment, but before expiration of the 30-day time period allotted to the Governor to deliberate on the bill. In this instance, the court held that the judiciary will not interfere with that decision. What if the Governor did not "acquiesce"? Could the Legislature still demand the bill be returned? Should both houses be required to request a bill be returned, or only the house of origin (which is the current practice)? The court said, "Therefore, we are not concerned with whether the Legislature can compel the Governor to allow retrieval of a bill that has been sent to him and, if so, the circumstances in which, or the formalities by which, the Legislature could do so." It left this question open for a future dispute.

8. The court noted that the plaintiff alleged that the retrieval of AB 60 from the Governor was ineffectual because the Chief Clerk of the Assembly lacked the authority to do so. How did the court respond to this claim by the plaintiff?

9. "Plaintiff concedes that, in some instances, the Chief Clerk does have authority to retrieve a bill from the Governor's Office." Did this position by the plaintiff hurt her claim?

10. "By these actions, the Legislature necessarily determined that the retrieval of the bill by the Chief Clerk was proper and effectual. It is not competent for a court

to retry that determination as a question of fact.... Because the Constitution does not expressly prohibit the retrieval of a bill once it has been sent to the Governor, and since the Governor and the Legislature acquiesced in the retrieval of Assembly Bill No. 60, we should not hold that the retrieval was ineffectual." Based on this reasoning, is this case premised upon the Legislature's plenary authority in making laws or upon the separation of powers doctrine?

11. According to the court, "Plaintiff's position would have severe consequences if it were accepted." What are some of those consequences according to the court?

12. When the Governor allows a bill to become law without his signature, he is required to authenticate the bill by causing the Secretary of State to certify that fact and deposit it with the laws in the office of the Secretary of State. For this purpose, the bill is treated as if the Governor had signed the measure into law.

13. The court placed a great deal of emphasis on the fact that the Legislature and the Governor acquiesced in the retrieval of the bill after enrollment but before expiration of the 30-day time period allotted to the Governor to deliberate on the bill. Should the courts not interfere with that decision in all instances? If so, how could a court determine whether the constitutional requirements are met? Would members of the public be without any recourse to challenge the actions of the Legislature?

5. Governor's Actions on Bills

Where a bill, after having been passed by the Legislature, had been properly enrolled, authenticated and deposited in the office of the Secretary of State, it having been either signed by the Governor, retained by him without signing and the fact certified by him, or passed over his veto, it is conclusive evidence of the legislative will, and courts do not look to the Journals of the Legislature or permit any other evidence to be submitted in order to determine whether or how the bill passed.

Parkinson v. Johnson

(1911) 160 Cal. 756

OPINION

Lorigan, J.

This is a petition for a writ of *mandamus* to be directed to the respondent, as governor of the state of California, commanding him to cause assembly bill No. 208, passed by both houses of the last session of the legislature, to be certified by the secretary of state as a statute of the state.

The following facts are alleged in the petition: that during the last session of the legislature there originated in the assembly a certain bill known as assembly bill No. 208, entitled, "An act to authorize the personal representatives of James Tuohy, deceased, to bring suit against the state of California"; that on February 16, 1911, said assembly bill passed the assembly of the state of California, and on March 6, 1911, said bill passed the senate of said state; that on March 11, 1911, said assembly bill was presented to and received by respondent as governor of the state of California for his consideration as such governor, at which time said bill had been and was properly enrolled and authenticated as prescribed by law; that said assembly bill has not been approved by respondent and was not returned by him to the assembly of the state of California within ten days (excluding Sundays) after said eleventh day of March, 1911; that said bill was not returned by respondent to the assembly until March 24, 1911, on which date it was returned to it by respondent with his objections, and said objections were thereupon and on said March 24, 1911, entered upon the journal of the assembly; that the said journal of the assembly of said March 24, 1911, contains the following entry.

"Messages from the Governor.

"The following messages from the Governor were received and read.

"'Sacramento, Cal. March 23, 1911

"'To the Assembly of the State of California:

"'To return you herewith without my approval Assembly Bill No. 208 entitled, "An act to authorize the personal representatives of James Tuohy, deceased, to bring suit against the state of California." (Here follow the objections stated by the respondent for declining to approve the bill.) For the reasons given I have vetoed the bill.

"'Respectfully submitted,

"'Hiram W. Johnson,

"'Governor of California.'"

That there is no other or different entry of any objections of the respondent to said assembly bill in the journal of the said assembly; that petitioner has demanded of respondent that, as governor, he cause the secretary of state of California to certify on said assembly bill the fact that said bill was not returned by the governor within ten days (Sundays excepted) after its receipt by him, and that said assembly bill became a law.

Upon these alleged facts the petitioner asks for a mandate to respondent commanding him to cause the fact to be certified on the bill, by the secretary of state, as provided by section 1313 of the Political Code, that said assembly bill had remained with the governor ten days (Sundays excepted) and had therefore become a law.

The answer of respondent to the petition admits all the allegations contained therein excepting those relating to his alleged failure to return the bill to the assembly within ten days (Sundays excepted) after it was presented to him, or that the bill was not returned until March 24, 1911.

These particular allegations are denied, and as a separate answer respondent alleges that the assembly bill in question was received at the office of the governor and receipted for by his private secretary on March 11, 1911; that said bill was returned by said private secretary personally to the assembly within ten days (Sundays excepted) thereafter, to wit, on the afternoon of March 23, 1911, with the message from the governor (referred to in the petition) vetoing it; that at the time said bill was returned — on March 23, 1911 — the assembly was in regular session; that said private secretary was duly recognized by the presiding officer of the assembly, and announced that he was delivering to it a message from the governor, and delivered said message with said bill to the proper officer of the said assembly.

A demurrer to the answer was interposed by the petitioner and the matter is before us after argument on the demurrer and the submission thereof.

The constitution, section 10 of article IV, provides that "each house shall keep a journal of its proceedings, and publish the *same;* and the yeas and nays of the members of either house, on any question, shall, at the desire of any three members present, be entered on the journal."

Section 16 of article IV of the same constitution provides that "every bill which may have passed the legislature shall before it becomes a law be presented to the governor. If he approves it, he shall sign *it;* but if not, he shall return it, with his objections, to the house in which it originated, which shall enter such objections upon the journal and proceed to reconsider it. If after such reconsideration, it again passes both houses ... it shall become a law, notwithstanding the governor's objections. If any bill shall not be returned within ten days after it shall have been presented to him (Sundays excepted) the same shall become a law in like manner as if he had signed it, unless the legislature, by adjournment" etc.

These are the only sections of the constitution having any bearing on the question involved here. There is no provision either constitutional or statutory requiring any record to be kept in the office of the governor respecting bills returned by him to the legislature with his veto thereof; nothing requiring any record to be made of the date of the return of such bills; nor is there any provision which requires any officer of either house of the legislature to make any notation or entry upon a bill returned by the governor as to the date or time when it was returned to the house with his objections thereto, or requiring any entry on the journals of either house respecting the return save what is required by section 16 of the constitution above quoted.

There are three ways in which a bill can become a law — by the signature of the governor after its passage by the legislature; by the governor retaining a bill without signing it for ten days (Sundays excepted) after its delivery to him and his causing a certificate of the fact to be made on the bill by the secretary of state and the bill deposited with the laws in the office of said secretary; or by the passage of a bill over the veto of the governor. In all these cases if the act is properly enrolled, authenticated, and deposited in the office of the secretary of state, it is conclusive evidence of the legislative will and courts will not look into the journals of the legislature or permit any other evidence to be submitted to determine whether or how a bill passed. *(People v. Burt,* 43 Cal. 560; *Yolo County* v. *Colgan,* 132 Cal. 265, [84 Am. St. Rep. 41, 64 Pac. 403]; *People* v. *Harlan,* 133 Cal. 16, [65 Pac. 9].) So that as to all bills upon which there has been favorable action, due enrollment, authentication, and deposit in the office of the secretary of state of such bill is conclusive evidence of the legislative will.

The bill in question here is not found in the office of the secretary of state authenticated as a law of this state. The petitioner, however, seeks to have the respondent compelled to deposit it there with the authentication of the secretary of state thereon as evidence that it had become a law under section 16 of the constitution through the failure of the governor to return it to the assembly where it originated with his objections thereto within ten days after its presentation to him.

In the absence of such deposit and authentication the position of petitioner in this proceeding is that the entry in the journal of the assembly (which respondent admits in his answer is correctly set forth) shows that the bill was not returned by the governor to the assembly until more than ten days (Sundays excepted) after it had been presented to him; that the journal entry is conclusive evidence of this fact and that parol testimony or extraneous evidence cannot be received to dispute, contradict, or vary such recital; that the facts set forth in the answer constitute an attempt on the part of the respondent to contradict by parol evidence the recital of the assembly journal which under the rule contended for by petitioner he insists may not be done and that the demurrer to the answer for these reasons should be sustained.

This is the only point presented on the demurrer and in our judgment it does not require extended discussion because conceding for present purposes that the position of petitioner is correct — that entries in the assembly journals are conclusive as to matters contained therein — they can only be conclusive as to matters which are actually recited therein and which are specifically required to be entered in those journals.

Now when we come to consider the entry in the journal upon which the petitioner relies and the provisions of section 16 of article IV of the constitution, which is the only section that directs specially what shall be entered in the assembly records when a bill is returned by the governor with his objections thereto, we find that the journal in fact contains no entry or recital of the time when the bill was returned by the governor to the assembly, and further that neither the section of the constitution referred to nor any other section requires any such entry.

All that the assembly journal of March 24, 1911, contains respecting the bill here in question is a recital that "the following messages from the governor were received and read," followed by a *verbatim* copy of the objections contained in the veto message accompanying the bill in question here, and the date of the message — March 23, 1911.

This entry only shows that the message was read to the assembly on the twenty-fourth day of March. The fact that it was returned by the governor on that date, or any other date, is nowhere stated in the journal. It is silent on that subject.

But even if the journal entry could be considered as amounting to a recital that the bill accompanied by the objections of the governor was returned by him to the assembly on the twenty-fourth because it is referred to in the journal of the proceedings of the assembly of that date, such recital would not be conclusive upon the matter.

In order to make the journal entries conclusive there must be some provision of the law which requires such entries to be made therein, and as far as making an entry in the journal, as of the time when a bill with his objections is returned to either house of the legislature by the governor, there is no such provision. There are only two pertinent sections of the constitution respecting journal entries involved here, section 10 and section 16 of article IV. Section 10 requires that each house shall keep a journal of "its proceedings" and the return of a bill without his approval by the governor is not a proceeding of either house of the legislature, so there is nothing in this section referred to which requires such entry. In fact, petitioner does not claim that it does. He relies particularly on section 16, but an examination of that section will show there is nothing contained in it requiring any such entry.

Under our constitution the governor is a component part of the law-making power of the state. To him all bills must be submitted for action before becoming laws, and all that section 16 requires (as far as pertinent here) in discharge of his duty as a part of the legislative branch of the government with respect to such bills is, that if he disapproves any of them he must return it to either house within ten days (Sundays excepted) after he receives it, with his objections. When this is done the duty of the governor is discharged and the duty to be performed by the house where the bill originated and to which it is returned, arises, and that duty is simply to enter the objections of the executive upon the journal and proceed to consider the bill. There is not a word in the section which requires that any entry shall be made in the journal respecting the time when the bill is returned by the governor.

And we would hardly expect to find a provision requiring such an entry and to which the conclusive evidence rule would apply; the effect of such a provision would be to make inadvertent and erroneous recitals in the journal of one branch of the legislative power control the action of the executive as another branch thereof, and by such recitals defeat the veto power constitutionally vested in the latter, and which he had in due time properly exercised.

As all acts of the legislature receiving favorable consideration are enrolled, authenticated, and deposited with the secretary of state, and when this is properly done are conclusive evidence of the legislative will, it is only in extremely rare eases that it will become necessary to resort elsewhere to ascertain whether an act not so found in the office of. the secretary of state did in fact become a law. This is one of these rare cases, where the journals of the assembly are resorted to under a claim that there are recitals therein which are conclusive evidence that the governor failed to return the bill in question with his veto thereof within the time allowed by the constitution, and hence it became a law. But, as we have pointed out, there is no provision in the constitution which requires any such entry of the date of return to be set forth in the journal of the assembly, and in fact it contains no such entry. If it did it would not be conclusive, because the conclusive evidence rule can only apply to such entries as are constitutionally required to be set out in the journal.

On the hearing of this demurrer it was admitted by petitioner, while insisting on the conclusiveness of the record, that he could not question the truth of the fact set forth in the answer respecting the return of the bill by the governor on March 23d, as stated therein.

The demurrer to the answer is overruled, and as the facts set forth in the answer are in effect admitted to be true by petitioner, it is not necessary to proceed further in this matter, and therefore the petition for a peremptory writ of mandate is dismissed.

ANGELLOTTI, J., SHAW, J., HENSHAW, J., SLOSS, J., and MELVIN, J., concurred.

Notes and Questions

1. In this case, the Court made clear that the conclusive evidence rule can only apply to such entries as are constitutionally required to be set out in the Journal. The Journal did contain the Governor's veto, but not when the bill was delivered to the Governor and therefore began the time period in which the Governor was required to act on the bill or else it would become law without his signature. Was this the correct outcome?

2. "There is no provision either constitutional or statutory requiring any record to be kept in the office of the governor respecting bills returned by him to the legislature with his veto thereof." Do you recall the courts citing repeatedly the Legislature's plenary lawmaking authority? Is this case an extension of that theory — that, because there is not a prohibition, the Journals can set forth any information, except that which is clearly prohibited in the state's Constitution? The Court goes on to explain, "we find that the journal in fact contains no entry or recital of the time when the bill was returned by the governor to the assembly, and further that neither the section of the constitution referred to nor any other section requires any such entry."

6. Bills Becoming Law without Governor's Signature

In California, there is a pocket signature rule, which means that, if the Governor does not act within a specified period of time concerning a bill on his or her desk, then the bill becomes law automatically without the Governor's signature. No official action is required by the Governor. Rather, the bill simply becomes law without the Governor's signature because he or she did not act on it by signing it or vetoing it.

Notes and Questions

1. Budget bills that substantively change existing law violate the single subject rule, because a substantive bill making a change to existing law can be vetoed in its entirety by the Governor, and incorporating such a bill into a budget bill makes it impossible for the Governor to properly exercise his veto. The legislative power is circumscribed by the requirement that the legislative acts be bicamerally enacted and presented to the head of the executive branch for approval or veto.

2. A bill making an appropriation of zero dollars is not a substantive act but is simply an act of non-appropriation which, by operation of the statute, has the automatic legal effect of freeing local agencies from the obligation to implement the mandate for that year. When there is a lump sum appropriation intended for multiple purposes, but does not specifically allocate amounts to each of these purposes, the Governor may use the line-item veto to reduce the lump sum amount, but the Governor may not attribute the amount of the reduction to a specific purpose.

3. The constitutional provision requiring the Legislature to either fund or suspend local agency mandates does not prohibit the Governor from applying the line-item veto to reduce an appropriation funding a local agency mandate to zero. When the Governor exercises the power of the veto, he is acting in a legislative capacity, and he may only act as permitted by the Constitution. The Governor possesses the constitutional authority to reduce or eliminate an item of appropriation in the budget bill passed by the Legislature.

4. The Legislature cannot shield an appropriation from the Governor's line-item veto simply by not using the language of appropriation in the budget bill. The legislative power is circumscribed by the requirement that legislative acts be bicamerally enacted and presented to the head of the executive branch for approval or veto.

D. Repealed Measures

The legislative power that the state Constitution vests is plenary, and a corollary of the legislative power to make new laws is the power to abrogate existing ones. Courts start from the premise that the Legislature possesses the full extent of the legislative power and its enactments are authorized exercises of that power, and only where the state Constitution withdraws legislative power will courts conclude an enactment is invalid for want of authority.

The reenactment rule's purpose is to make sure legislators are not operating in the blind when they amend legislation and to make sure the public can become apprised of changes in the law. (*Gillette Company v. Franchise Tax Board* (2015) 62 Cal.4th 468, certiorari denied.)

1. Implied Repeal of a Statute

The principle that the specific statute prevails over the general statute will not be applied when it appears that the Legislature intended that the prosecution under the general statute remains available in appropriate cases even though a more specific statute has been adopted.

The court of appeal will find an implied repeal of a statute only when there is no rational basis for harmonizing the two potentially conflicting statutes and the statutes are irreconcilable, clearly repugnant, and so inconsistent that the two cannot have concurrent operation. The amendment of a statute ordinarily has the legal effect of reenacting, and thus enacting, the statute as amended, including its unamended portions. (*People v. Chenze* (2002) 97 Cal.App.4th 521.)

2. Impact of Repeal on Pending Actions

Because the Legislature can repeal existing statutes, on occasion, parties to litigation and the courts are faced with the question of what, if any, impact is there of the repealed legislation on a pending lawsuit? Do the parties to this lawsuit and the trial court judge apply the old law that was in effect prior to it being repealed? Or must they consider the action in light of the fact that the statute is no longer on the books?

Traub v. Edwards

(1940) 38 Cal.App.2d 719

OPINION

SPENCE, J.

Defendant appeals from a judgment entered in favor of plaintiff in this action for damages for the alleged alienation of the affections of plaintiff's husband.

Said action was filed in 1938 and the judgment was entered in 1939. The notice of appeal was filed on September 15, 1939, and certain code amendments thereafter took effect on September 19, 1939. This appeal is presented on the judgment roll alone and no question is discussed in the briefs other than that of the effect of said code amendments upon actions for alienation of affections pending on September 19, 1939.

Defendant contends that "plaintiff's cause of action was destroyed by the repeal of the statute on which her cause of action depended". Defendant quotes the language found in *Krause v. Rarity*, 210 Cal. 644 at page 652 as follows [293 P. 62, 77 A.L.R. 1327]: "By those cases the rule obtaining elsewhere has become thoroughly established in the law of this state that when a right of action does not exist at common law, but depends solely upon a statute, the repeal of the statute destroys the right unless the right has been reduced to final judgment or unless the repealing statute contains a saving clause protecting the right in a pending litigation."

Defendant then argues: First, that the right of action for the alienation of the affections of a husband did not exist at common law but was created by subdivision 1 of section 49 of the Civil Code as it existed prior to September 19, 1939 (*Humphrey v. Pope*, 122 Cal. 253 [54 P. 847]; 13 Cal.Jur. 901); second, that plaintiff's right of action had not been reduced to final judgment and her action was still pending when the previously existing provisions of subdivision 1 of said section 49 relating to alienation of affections were repealed on September 19, 1939; and third, that there was no "saving clause in the repealing statute protecting plaintiff's right". It is upon these three points that defendant bases her contention that plaintiff's cause of action "was destroyed by the repeal of the statute" and that the judgment should therefore be reversed. Plaintiff apparently concedes the soundness of the first two points but contends that there was a saving clause and that there is therefore no foundation for defendant's contention. Before considering the code amendments which went into effect in 1939, we deem it appropriate to set forth certain general principles which we believe are applicable here.

When it is the purpose of the legislature to repeal a statute and to save the rights of litigants in pending actions based upon such statute, such purpose may be accomplished by including an express saving clause in the repealing act. But such rights may likewise be saved by any act passed at the same session of the legislature showing that the legislature intended that the rights of litigants in pending actions should be saved. (Black on Interpretation of Laws, 2d ed., pp. 424 and 425.) It is not essential that there be an express saving clause (*Gorley v. Sewell*, 77 Ind. 316; *Commonwealth v. Mortgage Trust Co.*, 227 Pa. 163 [76 P. 5]), or that the intention to save the rights of litigants in pending actions appear in the repealing act itself. (*Baltimore & Ohio R. Co. v. Pittsburgh W. K. R. Co.*, 17 W. Va. 812.) These principles are clearly set forth in the text above cited where it is said on page 424, "An express saving clause in a repealing statute is not required in order to prevent the destruction of rights existing under the former statute, if the intention to preserve and continue such rights is otherwise clearly apparent. Thus, if it can be gathered from any act on the same subject passed by the legislature at the same session that it was the legislative intent that pending proceedings should be saved, it will be sufficient to effect that purpose."

There is no conflict between the general principles above set forth and the decision in *Krause v. Rarity, supra*. The above-quoted language from the opinion in that case was used in a general discussion of the subject and not in relation to a situation such as is presented here. Language similar to that quoted above had been used in a previous opinion of the supreme court of appeals of West Virginia and was considered by that court in its later decision in *Baltimore & Ohio R. Co. v. Pittsburgh W. K. R. Co., supra*, where it said at page 879, "The language used by this court in *Currans v. Owens* [15 W. Va. 208], that the legislative intent in such cases must be gathered from the repealing act itself, must be understood as applying to the circumstances of that case. In that case there was no act passed at the session of the legislature referred to upon the subject, except the act containing the repealing section; and the legislative intent was in that case necessarily gathered from the repealing act itself."

We now turn to the situation presented by the legislation enacted at the 1939 session of the legislature. Three chapters of the statutes of that year have a bearing upon the subject under discussion. By chapter 128, section 49, of the Civil Code was amended so as to eliminate therefrom the provisions relating to alienation of affections and a new section, being section 43.5 of the Civil Code, was added to provide in part, "No cause of action arises for: (a) Alienation of affection." By chapter 129, which was filed with the secretary of state on the same day, a new section, being section 341.5 of the Code of Civil Procedure, was added to provide that "An action upon any cause of action arising before the effective date of this section from … alienation of affections . .. must be commenced within sixty days after the effective date of this section, but this provision does not revive an action the time for the commencement of which has expired prior to the effective date hereof." More than two months later, chapter 1103 was filed with the secretary of state. By this last-mentioned chapter, said section 49 of the Civil Code was amended and said section 341.5 of the Code of Civil Procedure was amended. The wording of said chapter 1103 was in all respects similar to the wording found in said chapters 128 and 129 in so far as it related to the subject of alienation of affections. Said three chapters went into effect on the same day, September 19, 1939.

It is apparent from what has been said that there was no express saving clause in any of said chapters, expressly saving to litigants any rights which had theretofore arisen under the repealed portions of section 49 of the Civil Code relating to alienation of affections. It is equally apparent, however, that it was the intention of the legislature to save such rights provided that actions to enforce such rights were commenced within sixty days from and after the effective date of said chapters. In the last analysis the question is one of the intentions of the legislature and we believe that the intention to save such rights was clearly manifested by the portions of chapters 129 and 1103 dealing with section 341.5 of the Code of Civil Procedure. While it is true that these provisions related directly to new actions rather than to pending actions, the legislature could not have intended to preserve the rights of litigants whose actions had not then been filed and to destroy the rights of those whose actions had already been filed and were pending.

The judgment is affirmed.

NOURSE, P.J., and STURTEVANT, J., concurred.

Notes and Questions

1. The purpose of repealing a statute and yet saving rights of litigants in pending actions, based upon the statute, may be accomplished either by including an express saving clause in the repealing act or by an act passed at the same session of the Legislature showing the intention that the rights of litigants in pending actions be saved, without the necessity of an express saving clause or an expression of such intention in the repealing act itself.

2. In this case, there was no express saving clause in any of the three acts that would have expressly saved litigants any rights which had arisen under the now repealed portions of the Civil Code relating to the claim of alienation of affections.

3. Retroactive Application of Repealed Acts

Under California law, absent a saving clause, repeals of statutory enactments must apply retroactively to pending cases.

Palmer v. Stassinos

(N.D. Cal. 2005) 419 F.Supp.2d 1151

OPINION

WHYTE, District Judge

Defendants in the three cases captioned above seek reconsideration of this court's December 14, 2004, consolidated order on two grounds: (1) the enactment of Proposition 64 applies retroactively to deprive Palmer of all standing to sue under California's unfair competition law ("UCL"); (2) the statutory remedies provided in Cal. Civil Code § 1719 are not "mandatory and exclusive." On this second ground, plaintiff seeks reconsideration of the court's determination that pre-judgment interest is not permitted in addition to statutory remedies and that those statutory remedies are not intended to do away with remedies not addressed by the parties, in particular, contractual remedies, attorney's fees, and post-judgment interest.

....

II. ANALYSIS

A. Clarification

1. "Exclusive and Mandatory" Remedy

As set forth in its December 14, 2004, order, the court held that double recovery was prohibited and that the collection of both the statutory damages provided under § 1719 and pre-judgment interest would result in double recovery against debt collectors. Defendants contend that the court's order was stated so broadly that additional types of recovery (i.e., attorney's fees, post-judgment interest, contractual remedies) would be precluded.

The court stated that the statutory damages in § 1719 were "exclusive and mandatory." Its determination was made in light of the parties' dispute over whether defendants were entitled to both pre-judgment interest and statutory damages on bad checks. The court concluded that § 1719 provided for a mandatory remedy and, because the legislature enacted a new remedy, that mandatory remedy was exclusive. Defendants argue that the legislature's enactment of the relevant provisions of § 1719 was merely a clarification of the existing statutory remedy and not intended to supplant any relief available under California's statutory scheme including pre-judgment interest, post-judgment interest, and, in some instances contractual damages and attorney's fees.

The court finds unpersuasive defendants' arguments for reconsideration of its ruling that pre-judgment interest is not permitted in light of the remedies provided in § 1719. However, with regard to attorney's fees, post-judgment interest and contractual damages, the court clarifies that its analysis of § 1719 was not intended to address or preclude recovery of such relief.

2. Impact on Default Judgments

Defendant Stassinos complains that the court failed to address the impact of its rulings on default judgments awarded by the state courts providing for both pre-judgment interest and statutory remedies under § 1719. The court noted in its order at footnote 7 that it need not address the issue of the effect on any default judgment awarded by any state court because defendants never collected any such amounts from plaintiffs. No default judgment entered in favor of Stassinos is at issue in this case, and the court declines, as it did before, to issue an advisory opinion as to the effect of its ruling on any other cases.

B. Proposition 64

On the [sic] November 2, 2004, after the court had issued its order granting in part and denying in part defendants' motion to dismiss, the voters in California passed Proposition 64. Proposition 64, which became effective the day after its approval by the electorate, *see* Cal. Const., art. II, § 10, subd. (a), limits the standing of plaintiffs to sue under the UCL. It eliminated the provision of Cal. Bus. Prof. Code § 17204 authorizing initiation of a complaint by "any person acting for the interests of itself, its members, or the general public," substituting a provision for enforcement only by "any person who has suffered injury in fact and has lost money or property as a result of such unfair competition." Cal. Bus. Prof. Code § 17204 (2005). Proposition 64 also amended § 17203, which deals with injunctive relief. This section now provides that a private person "may pursue representative claims or relief on behalf of others only if the claimant meets the standing requirements of Section 17203 and complies with Section 382 of the Code of Civil Procedure," which governs class actions. Cal. Bus. Prof. Code § 17203. The amended statute thus bars representative actions that cannot meet the class certification requirements imposed by Cal. Civ. Proc. Code § 382. Cal. Bus. Prof. Code § 17203.

Proposition 64 makes clear that, in order to sue for injunctive relief under California's unfair business practices laws, a party must have "suffered injury in fact and [have] lost money or property as a result of such unfair competition." *Id.* § 17204. In addition, Proposition 64 allows representative actions for injunctive relief only if a claimant meets the section's standing requirements and the class being represented meets the California class action lawsuit standards set forth in Cal. Civ. Proc. Code § 382. *See* Cal. Bus. Prof. Code § 17535.

It is undisputed that plaintiff did not lose money or property as a result of the unfair competition activities alleged in these actions, nor has she suffered any other cognizable injury in fact. Defendants ask this court to reconsider its ruling as to whether plaintiff's UCL claims must be dismissed for lack of standing following the passage of Proposition 64.

The retroactivity of Proposition 64 is now hotly contested in California state courts. In April 2005 the California Supreme Court granted review in five of the cases in which the Proposition 64 retroactivity question has been raised. All five cases involve California Court of Appeal opinions: *Californians for Disability Rights v. Mervyn's, LLC,* 126 Cal. App. 4th 386 (2005); *Benson v. Kwikset,* 126 Cal. App. 4th 887 (2005); *Branick v. Downey Sav. Loans Ass'n,* 126 Cal. App. 4th 828 (2005); *Bivens v. Corel Corp.,* 126 Cal. App. 4th 1392 24 Cal.Rptr.3d 847 (2005); *Lytwyn v. Fry's Electronics, Inc.,* 126 Cal. App. 4th 1455 (2005). These courts of appeal decisions have since been depublished pending review by the California Supreme Court and are no longer citable authority. *See* Cal. Rules of Court 976(d), 977(a). In spite of the California Supreme Court's intention to address this issue, defendants seek this court's reconsideration of whether plaintiff's UCL causes of action should be dismissed entirely for lack of standing. Because plaintiff continues to press forward with her cases and now has moved for class certification in *Palmer v. Stassinos* and *Palmer v. Far West,* the court finds that it is appropriate to rule on this matter, rather than awaiting a California Supreme Court determination.

When reviewing issues of state law, a federal court is "bound to follow the decisions of a state's highest court in interpreting that state's law." *Olympic Sports Prod. v. Universal Athletic Sales Co.,* 760 F. 2d 910, 912–13 (9th Cir. 1986) (citing *Aydin Corp. v. Loral Corp.,* 718 F. 2d 897, 904 (9th Cir. 1983)). A federal court should apply state law as it believes the highest court of the State would apply it. *See Jones-Hamilton Co. v. Beazer Materials Servs., Inc.,* 973 F.2d 688, 692 (9th Cir. 1992).

Litigants in this case generally advance the same arguments as litigants in other cases in which the retroactive application the Proposition 64 is a central issue. Plaintiff urges that, in the absence of clear voter intent, the court should apply the usual presumption that statutory enactments do not operate retroactively. *Evangelatos v. Superior Court,* 44 Cal. 3d 1188, 1208 (1988) ("[B]oth this court and the Courts of Appeal have generally commenced analysis of the question of whether a statute applies retroactively with a restatement of the fundamental principle that 'legislative enactments are generally presumed to operate prospectively and not retroactively unless the Legislature expresses a different intention.'"). Defendants assert that the materials advocating support of Proposition 64 demonstrate that California voters clearly intended for Proposition 64 to apply retroactively.

The court need not determine whether the legislative intent is clear. As one defendant argues, Proposition 64 falls squarely within a rule on repeal of statutes: absent a savings clause, repeals of statutory enactments must apply retroactively to pending cases. Cal. Gov't Code § 9606. The California Supreme Court explained the application of § 9606 notwithstanding customary presumption against retroactivity in *Callet v. Alioto,* 210 Cal. 65 (1930). However, under Gov't Code § 9606, this presumption does not apply when a statutory enactment repeals a statute that provides a purely statutory cause of action. Gov't Code § 9606 provides that "[a]ny statute may be repealed at any time, except when vested rights would be impaired. Persons acting under any statute act in contemplation of this power of repeal." The California Supreme Court explained the rule and its application — despite the general presumption against retroactivity — in *Callet*:

> It is too well settled to require citation of authority, that in the absence of a clearly expressed intention to the contrary, every statute will be construed so as not to affect pending causes of action. Or, as the rule is generally stated, every statute will be construed to operate prospectively and will not be given a retrospective effect, unless the intention that it should have that effect is clearly expressed. It is also a general rule, subject to certain limitations not necessary to discuss here, that a cause of action or remedy dependent on a statute falls with a repeal of the statute, even after the action thereon is pending, in the absence of a saving clause in the repealing statute. The justification for this rule is that all statutory remedies are pursued with full realization that the legislature may abolish the right to recover at any time. (Sec. 327, Pol. Code.) [the predecessor to Gov. Code § 9606.] ... This rule only applies when the right in question is a statutory right and does not apply to an existing right of action which has accrued to a person under the rules of the common law, or by virtue of a statute codifying the common law. In such a case, it is generally stated, that the cause of action is a vested property right which may not be impaired by legislation. In other words, the repeal of such

a statute or of such a right, should not be construed to affect existing causes of action.

210 Cal. at 67–68 (citations to cases omitted).

The rule was more recently applied in *Governing Board v. Mann,* 18 Cal. 3d 819 (1977), wherein the California Supreme Court held that a legislative enactment repealed a certain law. The plaintiff argued, as plaintiffs argue here, that even if the law was repealed, it should not apply retroactively to plaintiff's lawsuit based on the traditional rule that statutory enactments are generally presumed to have prospective effect. The Supreme Court rejected the argument: "Although the courts normally construe statutes to operate prospectively, the courts correlatively hold under the common law that when a pending action rests solely on a statutory basis, and when no rights have vested under the statute, a repeal of [the] statute without a saving clause will terminate all pending actions based thereon." *Id.* at 6–7 (internal quotation marks and citation omitted). The justification for this rule is that all statutory remedies are pursued with full realization that the legislature may abolish the right to recover at any time. *Younger v. Superior Court,* 21 Cal. 3d 102, 109 (1978).

Plaintiff contends that the rule that the repeal of statutes operates retrospectively does not apply here (1) because Proposition 64 added standing requirements rather than repealing rights under the UCL, and (2) because the UCL is "derived from" common law. However, these arguments are unavailing. First, it is clear that the amendments to the UCL pursuant to Proposition 64 enacted at least a limited repeal of "private attorney general" standing within the UCL in spite of the use of the word "amends" in the text of the proposition itself. Second, California courts have repeatedly found that UCL torts cannot be equated with their common law ancestors. *See, e.g., Bank of the W. v. Superior Court,* 2 Cal. 4th 1254, 1264 (1992); *Kraus v. Trinity Mgmt. Servs., Inc.,* 23 Cal. 4th 1245, 1263–64 (2000).

Plaintiff, in addition, contends that *Myers v. Philip Morris Cos., Inc.,* 28 Cal. 4th 828, 839–48 (2002), demonstrates that the California Supreme Court will apply the presumption against retroactive application to a statutory repeal. In that case, the California Supreme Court addressed whether 1998 legislation that repealed a statute creating immunity for tobacco manufacturers had retroactive effect, deciding that, absent clear legislative intent, it did not. *Id.* at 843. Addressing this argument, Judge Charles R. Breyer of this court distinguished the repeal at issue in *Myers* from the type of repeal at issue with regard to Proposition 64:

> *Myers,* however, involved the repeal of a statutory affirmative defense. The rule articulated in *Mann* and *Callet* applies to statutory causes of action or remedies. This distinction, of course, makes sense: it is one thing to retroactively repeal the right to recover money from someone, it is quite another to retroactively make conduct unlawful that was lawful at the time it occurred.

Envtl. Prot. Info. Ctr. v. United States Fish Wildlife Serv., 2005 U.S. Dist. LEXIS 7200, 16–17 (N.D. Cal., Apr. 22, 2005). *Myers,* therefore, does not suggest that the California Supreme Court will find Proposition 64 to be purely prospective.

Further, plaintiff asserts that the California Business and Professions Code contains a general savings clause:

> No action or proceeding commenced before this code takes effect, and no right accrued, is affected by the provisions of this code, but all procedure thereafter taken therein shall conform to the provisions of this code so far as possible.

Cal. Bus. Prof. Code § 4. This general savings clause, according to plaintiff, applies to Proposition 64 by virtue of Bus. Prof. Code § 12, which provides "[w]henever such reference is made to any portion of this code or any other law of this State, such reference shall apply to all amendments and additions thereto now or hereafter made." Thus, plaintiffs contend that all amendments to the UCL fall under the exception stated in *Callet* and *Mann* that statutory repeal is retroactive unless there is a savings clause.

In support of her argument, plaintiff cites *Peterson v. Bell* in which the California Supreme Court held that "a general savings clause in the general body of the law is as effective as a special savings clause in a particular section." 211 Cal. 461, 475 (1931). Plaintiff also relies on *Sobey v. Molony* for the proposition that section 4 was "intended to cover situations, either where the codification made a substantial change in the law, or where the legislature at that or subsequent sessions amended the law in a substantial manner." *See* 40 Cal. App. 2d 381, 388 (1940). However, the *Sobey* court's statements were made in the context of its determination that "[i]n codifying the law the code commission and the legislature avoided, wherever possible any substantive change in existing law." *Id.* at 384. The change at issue here is not a codification of the law, rather a change in the statutory provision. Section 4 does not appear to operate as a savings clause to alterations to statutes already enacted.

Finally, plaintiff cites to a Ninth Circuit opinion which, when considering a similarly phrased section in the California Corporations Code, stated without further analysis that that section casts doubt on the retroactivity of the code amendments at issue. *Koster v. Warren,* 297 F.2d 418, 420 (9th Cir. 1961) ("In the first place, the Corporations Code itself, §§ 4 and 9, casts doubt on the applicability of the code amendments to pending actions."). Nevertheless, despite this *dicta,* this court believes, based on *Mann* and *Callet,* that the California Supreme Court will find Proposition 64 to apply to pending actions. Accordingly, it dismisses plaintiff's UCL causes of action for lack of standing.

III. ORDER

For the foregoing reasons, the court clarifies its December 14, 2004, consolidated order as set forth above and dismisses plaintiff's UCL causes of action for lack of standing.

Notes and Questions

1. Is it easy to ascertain a statute's savings clause? Should the general rule be that repeal of a statute is retroactive? What would be the purpose of such a rule?

2. One claim in this case was that the Legislature's enactment of relevant provisions of § 1719 was simply clarifying existing law, rather than intended to supplant any relief available. How did the court respond to this claim?

3. As the court noted, there is a general rule that, in the absence of clear voter intent, the court should apply the usual presumption that statutory enactments do not operate retroactively. (*Evangelatos v. Superior Court* (1988) 44 Cal. 3d 1188, 1208.)

4. The court also cited Government Code § 9606 which provides that, absent a savings clause, repeals of statutory enactments must apply retroactively to pending cases. How did the court use this provision of California statutory law in this case?

5. The court held that "The rule articulated in *Mann* and *Callet* applies to statutory causes of action or remedies. This distinction, of course, makes sense: it is one thing to retroactively repeal the right to recover money from someone, it is quite another to retroactively make conduct unlawful that was lawful at the time it occurred." Do you agree with this distinction?

E. Single Subject Rule

1. California Legislation and the Single Subject Rule

Many Capitol observers are aware of the single subject rule. Some know that the California Constitution, in Article II, Section 8(d), provides that "an initiative measure embracing more than one subject may not be submitted to the electors or have any effect." But does a similar rule exist for bills considered by the California Legislature?

The single subject rule is found in several state constitutions in this country, providing that some or all legislation may only deal with one main issue. The general idea is to ensure that measures are not overly complex or that they may possibly confuse or "hide" provisions in a multi-faceted measure. Some have argued the single subject rule also precludes combining popular and unpopular unrelated provisions in one omnibus measure.

In California, there is a single subject rule for legislation that is considered by the Legislature. Article IV, Section 9, of the state Constitution provides "A statute shall embrace but one subject, which shall be expressed in its title. If a statute embraces a subject not expressed in its title, only the part not expressed is void. A statute may not be amended by reference to its title. A section of a statute may not be amended unless the section is re-enacted as amended."

Section 9's language is similar to that which is applicable to initiatives placed on the ballot before the statewide electorate. In both instances, the rule essentially provides that neither an initiative nor a bill may embrace more than one subject.

While the section of the state Constitution dealing with initiatives speaks only to the single subject rule, the section of the state Constitution dealing with legislation encompasses several provisions. Its first clause provides the single subject rule. In addition, it requires the bill's title to accurately reflect the subject of the bill and makes void any subject contained in the bill that is not expressed in the bill's title.

It was in 1948 that the California Constitution was amended to add the single subject rule for initiatives. The following year, the California Supreme Court ruled that the single subject rule applicable to initiatives was to be construed in the same manner as Article IV, Section 9. The provision applicable to legislation had long been in effect by that time. The single subject rule is generally "to be construed liberally to uphold proper legislation, all parts of which are reasonably germane."

There are a number of cases that have interpreted and applied the single subject rule as it applies to legislation. The main case is *Harbor v. Deukmejian* (1987) 43 Cal.3d 1078, which was decided by the California Supreme Court. The Court explained that "the single subject clause has as its 'primary and universally recognized purpose' the prevention of log-rolling by the Legislature, i.e., combining several proposals in a single bill so that legislators, by combining their votes, obtain a majority for a measure which would not have been approved if divided into separate bills."

The Court further explained that, "as of 1982, the constitutions of 41 states included a single subject requirement. The purpose of the requirement that the single subject of a bill shall be expressed in its title is to prevent misleading or inaccurate titles so that legislators and the public are afforded reasonable notice of the contents of a statute."

The Court also stated that the cases interpreting Article IV, Section 9 "hold that a measure complies with the rule if its provisions are either functionally related to one another or are reasonably germane to one another or the objects of the enactment."

California legislation is bound by a single subject rule, and there is guidance from the state Supreme Court regarding how that rule is to be applied when bills are considered by the Legislature.

Notes and Questions

1. A statute must comply with both the requirement that it be confined to one subject and with the requirement that this one subject be expressed in the bill's title. To minimize judicial interference in legislative branch activities, the decisions have been that courts must construe the single subject rule liberally.

2. For the legislative single subject rule, the courts have ruled that provisions of a single bill must be "reasonably germane" to the title of the bill. This has been the de-

termination in cases including *Raven v. Deukmejian* (1990) 52 Cal.3d 336, *Harbor v. Deukmejian* (1987) 43 Cal.3d 1078, and *Brosnahan v. Brown* (1982) 32 Cal.3d 236. *Harbor* actually found a violation of the single subject rule had occurred.

3. The constitutional single subject rule for statutes is to be liberally construed to uphold proper legislation and not to be used to invalidate legitimate legislation. The constitutional requirement that the single subject of a legislative bill shall be expressed in its title is to prevent misleading or inaccurate titles so that legislators and the public are afforded reasonable notice of the contents of a statute. (*Marathon Entertainment, Inc. v. Blasi* (2008) 42 Cal.4th 974, rehearing denied.)

2. Germane Provisions

It is the title of an act that defines the "subject" to which the substance of its provisions must be germane. The courts have also ruled that the provisions must be reasonably related to the subject matter contained in the title. In other words, the courts in California have generally ruled that being "germane" means the bill's provisions are "reasonably related."

3. Determining Whether Amendments Are Germane

In the California Legislature, as with several other legislative bodies around the country, there is an initial question regarding whether amendments to existing bills must be "germane" to the subject matter of the existing bill. As described in legislative glossaries, "germane" refers to whether a proposed amendment is relevant to the subject matter in the bill.

In California, the Office of the Legislative Counsel may opine on germaneness, but the determination of germaneness is decided by the Presiding Officer of either the State Assembly or State Senate, subject to an appeal to the membership. In other words, the ultimate determination of whether amendments are germane to an existing bill rests with the legislators in either house. Each house of the Legislature has rules related to determining whether amendments are germane.

Assembly

There are several rules in the State Assembly regarding the issue of "germane" bills regarding their subject matter. Pursuant to Assembly Rule 47(d), the Committee on Budget may introduce a bill that is germane to any subject within the jurisdiction of the committee in the same manner as any Assembly Member. Any other standing committee may introduce a total of five bills in each year of a biennial session that are germane to any subject within the proper consideration of that committee.

Under Assembly Rule 92, titled Amendment to Be Germane, provides that an amendment to any bill, other than a bill stating legislative intent to make necessary statutory changes to implement the Budget Bill, whether reported by a committee or offered by an Assembly Member, is not in order when the amendment relates to a different subject than, is intended to accomplish a different purpose than, or requires a title essentially different than, the original bill.

Furthermore, Rule 92 states that a motion or proposition on a subject different from that under consideration may not be admitted as an amendment. An amendment is not in order that changes the original number of any bill.

Senate

Under Senate Rule 23(a), similar to its Assembly counterpart, an Introduction of Bills by a Committee standing committee may introduce a bill that is germane to any subject within the proper consideration of the committee in the same manner as any Senator. Under Subdivision (b), a committee may amend into a bill related provisions that are germane to the subject and embraced within the title and, with the consent of the author, may constitute that bill a committee bill.

Under Subdivision (e), there is a distinction drawn with amendments to rewrite a bill. The first inquiry is whether the amendment is germane to the previous version of the bill, but adds a new subject to the bill that is different from, but related to, the contents of the bill. Subdivision (f) acknowledges new bills when an amendment creates a new bill if the amendment changes the subject of the bill to a new or different subject.

Senate Rule 38.5 requires every amendment proposed to be germane. In order to be germane, an amendment must relate to the same subject as the original bill, resolution, or other question under consideration. A point of order may be raised that the proposed amendment or an amendment now in the bill, resolution, or other question under consideration is not germane, so long as the question is within control of the body.

In that case, Rule 38.5 provides the President pro Tempore must decide whether the point of order is well taken. In the absence of the President pro Tempore, the Vice Chair of the Committee on Rules decides whether the point of order is well taken. If, in the opinion of the President pro Tempore or the Vice Chair of the Committee on Rules, the point of order is well taken, the question of germaneness is referred to the Committee on Rules for determination.

Thereafter, the Committee on Rules must make its determination by the following legislative day. If the point of order is raised and referral is made on the last legislative day preceding a joint recess, the Committee on Rules makes its determination before adjourning for the recess. The matter remains on file until the determination is made.

Finally, if, upon consideration of the matter, the Committee on Rules determines that the amendment is not germane, then the bill, resolution, or other question is stricken from the *Daily File* and may not be acted upon during the remainder of the session, provided that the author of a bill, resolution, or other question must be given the opportunity to amend the bill, resolution, or other question to delete the portions that are not germane. If that occurs, then the bill, resolution, or other question may continue to be acted upon. If the Committee on Rules determines that the amendment is germane, the bill, resolution, or other question may be acted upon by the house.

Tomra Pacific, Inc. v. Chiang

(2011) 199 Cal.App.4th 463, rehearing denied

OPINION

SEPULVEDA, J. —

At issue is the legality of $519 million in loans between state funds to help balance the state budget during times of fiscal crisis. We conclude that the loans are lawful. The loan provisions, contained in annual budget bills, are germane to the subject of appropriations and thus do not violate the single-subject rule prohibiting legislation having multiple subjects. (Cal. Const., art. IV, § 9.) Nor do the loans interfere with the lending fund's regulatory purpose or object. (Gov. Code, § 16310, subd. (a).) We affirm the trial court order denying petitions for a writ of mandate seeking compelled repayment of the loans.

. . . .

F. Executive and legislative efforts to address the Recycling Fund deficit

Upon learning of the projected deficit in the Recycling Fund in May 2009, the Governor proposed restructuring the program to address its fiscal problems. The Legislature rejected the proposal and enacted its own in September 2009 but the Governor vetoed it. A resolution was reached in March 2010. The Legislature passed — and the Governor signed — emergency legislation that returned the Recycling Fund to solvency. (Stats. 2009, 8th Ex. Sess. 2009–2010, ch. 5.) The legislation suspended some program expenditures that were otherwise required for public education and grants, accelerated redemption payments due from distributors, and reduced some incentive payments and subsidies. These changes saved millions of dollars. The Recycling Fund also received $28.9 million in repayment of its prior loans to the General Fund and a loan of $8.25 million from a special fund. (CalRecycle, Quarterly Report on Status of the Beverage Container Recycling Fund (Apr. 8, 2011) (CalRecycle April 2011 Status Report) <http://www.calrecycle.ca.gov/BevContainer/RecycleFund/2011/AprStatus.pdf> [as of Sept. 22, 2011].) The Legislature also amended the Recycling Act in March 2009 to declare "that the maintenance of the fund is of the utmost importance to the state and that it is essential that any money in the fund be used solely for the purposes authorized in this division and should not be used, loaned, or transferred for any other purpose." (Pub. Resources Code, § 14580, subd. (e).)

. . . .

III. DISCUSSION

A. Budget act loans from one state fund to others did not violate the single-subject rule

The California Constitution provides: "A statute shall embrace but one subject, which shall be expressed in its title. If a statute embraces a subject not expressed in its title, only the part not expressed is void." (Cal. Const., art. IV, § 9.) Budget bills appropriate funds for expenditure and are authorized to contain more than one item of appropriation. (Cal. Const., art. IV, § 12.) In 2002, the Legislature enacted legislation "making appropriations for the support of the government of the State of California and for several public purposes" entitled "Budget Act of 2002." (Stats. 2002, ch. 379, p. 1472.) The Budget Act of 2002 included numerous items, including $2.6 billion in loans and transfers from special funds to the General Fund. (Legis. Analyst, Cal. Spending Plan 2002–03, ch. 3.) Among these was an item authorizing a loan from the Recycling Fund to the General Fund in an amount ultimately set at $188 million.

The Chamber of Commerce Plaintiffs argue that the loan from the Recycling Fund to the General Fund in the Budget Act of 2002, and similar loans in subsequent budget bills, violates the single-subject rule embodied in article IV, section 9 of the California Constitution by containing multiple subjects — the proper subject of appropriations for the support of state government and the separate subject of loans between state funds, which is a subject not expressed in the bills' titles. Plaintiffs are correct in pointing out that "[a] statute must comply with both the requirement that it be confined to one subject and with the command that this one subject be expressed in its title." (*Harbor v. Deukmejian* (1987) 43 Cal.3d 1078, 1096 [240 Cal.Rptr. 569, 742 P.2d 1290].) Plaintiffs are incorrect, however, in their assertion that the budget bills at issue here violated these requirements.

1. The loan provisions are cognate and germane to the subject matter designated by the budget bill title: appropriations

"The single subject clause has as its 'primary and universally recognized purpose' the prevention of log-rolling by the Legislature, i.e., combining several proposals in a single bill so that legislators, by combining their votes, obtain a majority for a measure which would not have been approved if divided into separate bills. [Citation.] ... The purpose of the requirement that the single subject of a bill shall be expressed in its title is to prevent misleading or inaccurate titles so that legislators and the public are afforded reasonable notice of the contents of a statute." (*Harbor v. Deukmejian, supra*, 43 Cal.3d at p. 1096.)

"[T]he single-subject rule 'is to be liberally construed to uphold proper legislation and not used to invalidate legitimate legislation.' [Citations.] The Legislature may combine in a single act numerous provisions "'governing projects so related and interdependent as to constitute a single scheme,'" and provisions auxiliary to the scheme's execution may be adopted as part of that single package. [Citation.] The act's title 'need not contain either an index or an abstract of its provisions. The constitutional mandate [citation] is satisfied if the provisions themselves are cognate and germane to the subject matter designated by the title, and if the title intelligently refers the reader to the subject to which the act applies, and suggests the field of legislation which the text includes.'" (*Marathon Entertainment, Inc. v. Blasi* (2008) 42 Cal.4th 974, 988–989 [70 Cal.Rptr.3d 727, 174 P.3d 741].) In short, legislation complies with the single-subject rule "if its provisions are either functionally related to one another or are reasonably germane to one another or the objects of the enactment." (*Harbor v. Deukmejian, supra,* 43 Cal.3d at p. 1100.)

The challenged provisions in the budget bills lending money from a special fund to the General Fund are functionally related to expenditures from the General Fund, and are reasonably germane to each other and the objects of the enactments, which are appropriations for the support of state government. Transfers and loans between funds are integral parts of government finance and, indeed, of any organization that handles large sums of money. (See *Service Employees Internat. Union, Local 1000 v. Brown* (2011) 197 Cal.App.4th 252, 268, fn. 8 [128 Cal.Rptr.3d 711] [interfund loans "have become an integral component of the budgetary calculus"].) The movement of money from one fund with a surplus to another with a deficit fosters efficient appropriation and sound financial management.

The Recycling Fund itself has been a recipient of interfund loans, receiving loans from other funds in its early years and more recently when it faced an unexpected deficit. As we noted earlier, the Recycling Fund borrowed about $43 million to maintain its solvency during the early 1990's. In the fiscal year 2009–2010 budget, the Legislature approved an $8.25 million loan from a special fund to the Recycling Fund, which helped return the Recycling Fund to solvency and end the disputed processing payment and fee reductions. (CalRecycle April 2011 Status Report.)

Appropriations and interfund loans are not separate subjects but are intricately intertwined.

A legislative provision is "germane" for purposes of the single-subject rule if it is "auxiliary to and promotive of the main purpose of the act or has a necessary and natural connection with that purpose...." (*Metropolitan Water Dist. v. Marquardt* (1963) 59 Cal.2d 159, 172–173 [28 Cal.Rptr. 724, 379 P.2d 28].) The loan provisions at issue here both promote the main purpose of the act (appropriations for the support of the government and public functions) and have a natural connection with that purpose.

2. The loan provisions are not disguised efforts at changing existing statutes or agency authority

The Chamber of Commerce Plaintiffs argue that the budget bill loans' provisions are "substantive in nature" and meant to divert money from the Recycling Act's statutory purposes related to beverage container recycling to unauthorized uses. Although it is true that budget bills are "particularly susceptible to abuse" of the single-subject rule and have sometimes been used as vehicles for substantive policy changes, we see no evidence of that here. (*Planned Parenthood Affiliates v. Swoop* (1985) 173 Cal.App.3d 1187, 1198 [219 Cal.Rptr. 664] (*Planned Parenthood*).)

Our Supreme Court has observed that the single-subject rule was adopted to cure "an abuse [that] had grown up, which consisted in attaching to a bill dealing with one matter of legislation a clause entirely foreign to that subject-matter, to the end that, hidden under the cloak of the meritorious legislation, the obnoxious measure might 'ride through.'" (*Ex parte Hallawell* (1909) 155 Cal. 112, 114 [99 P. 490].) "'History tells us that the general appropriation bill presents a special temptation for the attachment of riders. It is a necessary and often popular bill which is certain of passage. If a rider can be attached to it, the rider can be adopted on the merits of the general appropriation bill without having to depend on its own merits for adoption.'" (*Planned Parenthood, supra,* 173 Cal.App.3d at p. 1198.) But this case does not concern unrelated riders attached to a budget bill and, contrary to plaintiffs' claim, bears no resemblance to *Planned Parenthood.*

In *Planned Parenthood,* the Legislature adopted a budget bill provision that effectively amended existing statutes to prohibit the state Office of Family Planning from making state funds available to any clinic that performs, promotes, or advertises abortion. (*Planned Parenthood, supra,* 173 Cal.App.3d at p. 1191.) This Court of Appeal found the provision unconstitutional under the single-subject rule because the provision changed the substantive authority of a state agency, which was a subject materially distinct from the subject of appropriations. (*Id.* at pp. 1201–1202.) A number of cases have found violations of the single-subject rule where "a substantive policy change 'masquerad[es] as [a] Budget Act provision.'" (*Professional Engineers in California Government v. Schwarzenegger* (2010) 50 Cal.4th 989, 1049–1050 & fn. 37 [116 Cal.Rptr.3d 480, 239 P.3d 1186] [collecting cases] (*Professional Engineers*).) This is not such a case.

This case is closer to a recent California Supreme Court case that upheld a budget bill provision against a claim that the provision violated the single-subject rule. (*Professional Engineers, supra,* 50 Cal.4th at pp. 1049–1051.) In *Professional Engineers,* the Legislature adopted a provision in the Budget Act of 2008 reducing the appropriations for state employee compensation and authorizing the use of furlough plans as a means of achieving the reduction. (*Professional Engineers,* at pp. 1044, 1049.) The plaintiffs there argued that the furlough plan provision violated the single-subject rule, and our high court rejected the argument. (*Id.* at p. 1049.) The court contrasted the case before it with *Planned Parenthood, supra,* 173 Cal.App.3d 1187 and similar cases, noting that the furlough provision was related to appropriations and "does not substantively amend or change any existing statutory provision or expand or restrict the substantive authority of any state agency." (*Professional Engineers,* at pp. 1049–1050.)

The loans from the Recycling Fund to the General Fund are likewise related to appropriations and do not change existing statutes or agency authority.

The Chamber of Commerce Plaintiffs claim otherwise and insist that the loan provisions changed two sections of the Public Resources Code: (1) section 14580, subdivision (a)(1), which provides that redemption payments and other revenue shall be deposited in the Recycling Fund and that money in the fund is "continuously appropriated" to CalRecycle for the payment of refund values and processor administrative fees and (2) former section 14581, subdivision (a)(7)(B), which provided that, "[s]ubject to the availability of funds," processing fee revenues are "continuously appropriated" to CalRecycle for processing payments. Plaintiffs argue that the budget bill loan provisions effectively amend these code provisions by directing Recycling Fund money elsewhere. We disagree.

The budget bill loan provisions authorized loans of Recycling Fund balance surpluses, not diversions of revenue nor a cancellation of appropriations to the recycling program. Redemption payments, processing fees, and other revenue continued to be deposited in the Recycling Fund and appropriated to the payment of refund values, processor administrative fees, and processing payments. Refund values and processor administrative fees under Public Resources Code former section 14580, subdivision (a)(1) were not impacted by the loans. Those payments were always paid in full, even when an unforeseen deficit occurred in the Recycling Fund and temporary reductions in other aspects of the recycling program were imposed. Processing fee revenue from manufacturers under Public Resources Code section 14581, subdivision (a)(7)(B) also continued to be appropriated to processing payments. Manufacturers paid more in processing fees when the Recycling Fund experienced a deficit in 2009 and their subsidy was reduced, but all manufacturer processing fees remained appropriated to processing payments.

Even if there were some impact on processing fee appropriations under Public Resources Code section 14581, subdivision (a)(7)(B), any impact was an unforeseen consequence of borrowing money from the fund. Lending money from one fund to another was germane to appropriations and was not a purposeful change to the statute or agency authority extraneous to appropriations. The Legislature did not direct money away from the Recycling Fund with the intention or effect of reducing Cal-Recycle appropriations or rendering CalRecycle unable to function. At the time each budget bill was enacted, the Recycling Fund had a balance surplus. The fund's deficit in fiscal year 2009–2010 was the unexpected result of market changes that increased expenditures and reduced revenues, and flaws in CalRecycle's projections that overstated the fund's balance. It is argued that the budget bill loans were excessive given later developments. The point is debatable but the debate is irrelevant to our consideration of the single-subject rule. The single-subject rule does not demand legislative foresight, only legislative focus. The loan provisions were properly focused on the single subject of appropriations and were not disguised efforts at changing existing statutes or agency authority "hidden under the cloak" of lawful appropriations. (*Ex parte Hallawell, supra,* 155 Cal. at p. 114.) The loan provisions concerned only the one subject of appropriations to support the annual budget, not more than one subject, and therefore do not violate the single-subject rule.

3. The budget bill loans did not convert regulatory processing fees into taxes

The Chamber of Commerce Plaintiffs allege that the budget bills are not properly focused upon the single subject of appropriations because the bills' loan provisions effectively impose a tax upon beverage manufacturers by diverting fees the manufacturers pay into the Recycling Fund for regulatory functions into funds used for general revenue purposes. A tax, plaintiffs argue, is not an appropriation and therefore offends the constitutional single-subject rule. (Cal. Const., art. IV, § 9.) We reject the argument. Regulatory fees paid into the Recycling Fund were not converted into taxes when the Recycling Fund made loans to the General Fund.

As discussed previously, the Recycling Act imposes processing fees upon beverage manufacturers, which partially fund processing payments made to recyclers and processors to encourage the recycling of glass and plastic beverage containers that have low scrap value. (Pub. Resources Code, §§ 14518.5, 14573, subd. (a)(3), 14573.5, subd. (a)(3), 14575, subd. (e)(1).) A processing fee is imposed upon manufacturers who use container materials with recycle costs that exceed their scrap value under the "polluter-pays" principle, which encourages manufacturers to switch to materials that have a lower cost of recycling. The manufacturer processing fee is statutorily capped at 65 percent of the cost of the processing payment. (Pub. Resources Code, § 14575, subd. (e)(1)(I).)

The Chamber of Commerce Plaintiffs allege in their complaint that "[t]he processing fees paid by beverage manufacturers are not being used for regulatory purposes but instead to fund general government purposes through the General Fund. As such, the manufacturer's processing fee is a tax." On appeal, these plaintiffs suggest that redemption payments made by consumers are also being converted to taxes but that claim was not alleged in the complaint nor raised in the memorandum supporting the petition for a writ of mandate, and therefore is not a proper subject for this appeal. The relevant question is whether the processing fee is a tax, as plaintiffs allege. We conclude that the processing fee is a regulatory fee, not a tax.

"In general, taxes are imposed for revenue purposes, rather than in return for a specific benefit conferred or privilege granted." (*Sinclair Paint Co. v. State Bd. of Equalization* (1997) 15 Cal.4th 866, 874 [64 Cal.Rptr.2d 447, 937 P.2d 1350] (*Sinclair Paint*).) Fees are imposed to support regulatory activities or "to defray the actual or anticipated adverse effects of various business operations." (*Id.* at pp. 876–877.) But the word "'tax' has no fixed meaning, and … the distinction between taxes and fees is frequently 'blurred,' taking on different meanings in different contexts." (*Id.* at p. 874.) The California Supreme Court has therefore set out guidelines for determining whether a denominated fee is, in fact, a bona fide regulatory fee and not a disguised tax. (*Id.* at pp. 873–881.) In *Sinclair Paint*, a plaintiff complained that a fee enacted by majority vote of the Legislature was, in effect, a tax, and unconstitutional because taxes require a two-thirds vote of the Legislature. (*Id.* at p. 870; Cal. Const., art. XIII A, § 3.) Plaintiffs here base their constitutional challenge upon the single-subject rule (Cal. Const., art. IV, § 9), but *Sinclair Paint* is instructive in distinguishing fees from taxes.

In *Sinclair Paint*, the court reviewed a statute enacted by the Legislature to address childhood lead poisoning. (*Sinclair Paint, supra,* 15 Cal.4th at p. 870; Health & Saf. Code, § 105275 et seq.) The statute established a program to provide medical evaluation and services for children who were deemed potential victims of lead poisoning. (*Sinclair Paint, supra,* at p. 870.) The program was funded by fees assessed on paint manufacturers and other contributors to environmental lead contamination. (*Ibid.*) A paint manufacturer alleged that the fees were really taxes, and unauthorized because they were not enacted by a two-thirds majority vote. (Cal. Const., art. XIII A, § 3; *Sinclair Paint, supra,* at p. 870.) The California Supreme Court held that the statute "imposed bona fide regulatory fees, not taxes, because the Legislature imposed the fees to mitigate the actual or anticipated adverse effects of the fee payers' operations." (*Sinclair Paint, supra,* at p. 870.) The court explained that the government may charge fees ""in connection with regulatory activities which fees do not exceed the reasonable cost of providing services necessary to the activity for which the fee is charged and which are not levied for unrelated revenue purposes.""' (*Id.* at p. 876, quoting *Pennell v. City of San Jose* (1986) 42 Cal.3d 365, 375 [228 Cal.Rptr. 726, 721 P.2d 1111].)

The Chamber of Commerce Plaintiffs concede that the processing fee imposed upon beverage manufacturers meets the first criterion of *Sinclair Paint* because the fee is regulatory in nature and is limited to the costs of the service or program. Plaintiffs contend that the processing fee fails the second criterion of *Sinclair Paint,* asserting that the fee is imposed for unrelated revenue purposes. We reject the contention. The fee is levied upon beverage manufacturers as a partial contribution to the processing payment made to recyclers and processors for recycling the manufacturers' containers. The processing fee is a regulatory fee and not a tax because the fee is collected to mitigate the adverse effects of the fee payers' operations and not for unrelated revenue purposes. (*Sinclair Paint, supra,* 15 Cal.4th at pp. 870, 876.)

Chamber of Commerce Plaintiffs do not dispute this statutory framework but argue that processing fees, although initially *collected* for regulatory purposes, were *diverted* to other purposes when the Legislature put Recycling Fund money into the General Fund, where it was used for general revenue purposes unrelated to recycling. The argument would have more force if the diversion plaintiffs decry were a permanent diversion of Recycling Fund money to the General Fund. Plaintiffs often put quotation marks around the word "loan" when describing the fund transfers, implying that the transfers are actually permanent diversions. The record does not support that view. Each of the challenged budget bills expressly provides that the transfer of funds from the Recycling Fund to the General Fund is a loan that will be fully repaid with interest. As of July 2011, roughly $148 million has been repaid, representing over 28 percent of the aggregate loan amount, and further repayment is included in the Governor's budget for the next fiscal year. (CalRecycle July 2011 Status Report; CalRecycle April 2011 Status Report.) The fund transfers are loans, not permanent diversions. We reject plaintiffs' position that a regulatory fee becomes a tax when the regulatory fund lends money to the General Fund. The budget bills did not enact a tax and did not violate the single-subject rule.

B. The loans from the Recycling Fund did not interfere with the object for which the Recycling Fund was created

All plaintiffs, both the Chamber of Commerce Plaintiffs and the Recycling Center Plaintiffs, contend that the loans from the Recycling Fund to the General Fund and the Air Pollution Control Fund adversely affected recycling programs and interfered with the object for which the Recycling Fund was created. We find insufficient evidence of interference with the Recycling Fund's regulatory object of promoting beverage container recycling.

1. Government Code section 16310 establishes the relevant standard for determining the lawfulness of interfund loans

For over a century, California statutory law has permitted a loan from a special fund to the General Fund provided the loan does not interfere with the object for which the special fund was created. (Gov. Code, § 16310; see *California Medical Assn.* [*v. Brown*], *supra,* 193 Cal.App.4th at pp. 1456–1457 [discussing former Pol. Code, § 444].) Our Supreme Court has recognized that the Legislature may enact an appropriations bill that transfers "a special fund reserve temporarily from one purpose to another" provided the transfer does not interfere "with the objects for which such fund was created." (*Daugherty v. Riley, supra,* 1 Cal.2d at p. 309.) Recently, this district Court of Appeal stated that "money in special funds [may] be loaned to shore up the General Fund" subject to the specified statutory conditions of Government Code section 16310: "exhaustion of the General Fund, no interference with the object for which the special fund was created, [and] return of the money as soon as feasible." (*California Medical Assn., supra,* at p. 1458.) In accordance with that principle, the court in *California Medical Assn.* upheld the legality of a 2008 budget bill loan of $6 million to the General Fund from a special fund regulating physicians. (*Id.* at pp. 1455–1466.)

In enacting the budget bills at issue here, the Legislature acknowledged the principle that interfund loans should not interfere with a fund's purpose. The 2002 budget bill authorized a loan from the Recycling Fund to the General Fund, set a date for repayment, and stated: "It is the intent of the Legislature that the repayment is made so as to ensure that the programs supported by this fund are not adversely affected by the loan." The 2002 budget bill also authorized the Director of Finance to transfer some of the loan proceeds back to the Recycling Fund during the 2002–2003 fiscal year as necessary to meet the Recycling Fund's cashflow needs, with all unused loan money reverting to the General Fund at fiscal yearend. Similar statements were included in later budget bills authorizing loans from the Recycling Fund.

Plaintiffs argue that these budget bill statements "expand the mandate contained in Government Code section 16310" setting limits on interfund loans. Government Code section 16310, subdivision (a) prohibits "any transfer that will interfere with the object" for which the Recycling Fund was created. Plaintiffs insist that the budget bill provisions set a more stringent standard that prohibits any transfer that "adversely affects" Recycling Fund programs. The argument differs from the position taken below by the Recycling Center Plaintiffs, where they asserted in their petition and supporting memorandum that the budget bills' statements were "consistent" with Government Code section 16310, rather than more expansive. The Chamber of Commerce Plaintiffs were vague on this point in their petition but they did assert in their supporting memorandum — in the closing footnote — that the budget bills' statements created a mandatory duty to ensure that the Recycling Fund programs were not adversely affected. That argument gained momentum on appeal, where all plaintiffs proposed in their briefing to this court that the budget bills impose a mandatory duty to ensure that the Recycling Fund programs are not adversely affected by the interfund loans. Plaintiffs are now united in asserting that the budget bill provisions go beyond Government Code section 16310's prohibition of interfund loans that interfere with a regulatory fund's purpose and prohibit any loan that "adversely affects" Recycling

Fund programs. It is an argument largely ignored by the state, which concerns itself with demonstrating that the loans satisfy the standard articulated by Government Code section 16310.

At oral argument, counsel for the Recycling Center Plaintiffs suggested that the state's failure to offer a direct refutation of their claim that the budget bills imposed a mandatory duty apart from, and greater than, the duty imposed by Government Code section 16310 was a "waiver." There is no waiver. The state's position is, and always has been, that Government Code section 16310 sets the standard for the legality of interfund loans and that the loans at issue here satisfy that standard. That position is not forfeited by the state's failure to address an alternative standard proposed by plaintiffs. Nor do we accept the suggestion made at oral argument that plaintiffs are entitled to submit supplemental briefing on the question of whether the budget bill provisions created a mandatory duty more stringent than any duty imposed by Government Code section 16310. (Gov. Code, § 68081.) Plaintiffs raised the issue in their briefing on appeal and had a full opportunity to address it. (*People v. Alice* (2007) 41 Cal.4th 668, 677 [61 Cal.Rptr.3d 648, 161 P.3d 163].) The issue requires no additional briefing.

We conclude that the budget bills do not create a mandatory duty to ensure that Recycling Fund programs are not adversely affected by the interfund loans. Precatory statements of intent, like the ones contained in the budget bills, do not impose an affirmative duty enforceable through a writ of mandate. (*Shamsian v. Department of Conservation* (2006) 136 Cal.App.4th 621, 640–641 [39 Cal.Rptr.3d 62]; accord, *Common Cause v. Board of Supervisors* (1989) 49 Cal.3d 432, 444 [261 Cal.Rptr. 574, 777 P.2d 610].) Essential to the issuance of a writ of mandate is "[a] clear, present and usually ministerial duty upon the part of the respondent." (*Shamsian, supra,* at p. 640.) The budget bills' statement that "repayment is made so as to ensure that the programs supported by this fund are not adversely affected by the loan" is a general statement of intent, not the adoption of a clear and present duty to act in a particular manner. Similar statements of intent to repay loans are routinely included in budget bills. (See *California Medical Assn., supra,* 193 Cal.App.4th at p. 1452 [2008 budget bill provides for repayment "'so as to ensure that the programs supported by the Contingent Fund of the Medical Board of California are not adversely affected by the loan'"].) No mandatory duty enforceable by a writ of mandate is created by such general statements in budget bills.

Even if some mandatory duty were extrapolated from these general statements in the budget bills, that duty must be read in light of Government Code section 16310. When read in the proper light, the budget bills' stated concern that the Recycling Fund not be adversely affected by the loans appears to be no more than an acknowledgement of Government Code section 16310's limitation on interfund loans that interfere with a fund's purpose rather than, as plaintiffs argue, a departure from the statutory standard to a stricter limitation on interfund loans.

Plaintiffs have also misread the budget bill provision that allows the Director of Finance to transfer some of the loan proceeds back to the Recycling Fund to meet the fund's monthly cashflow needs. This provision allowed for temporary transfers during the fiscal year covered by the budget bill with all unused loan money reverting to the General Fund at the end of the fiscal year. Effectively, the provision protected the Recycling Fund from month-to-month cashflow problems that could arise from a large lump-sum payment of the loan at the start of the fiscal year. The provision does not mandate transfers and does not apply beyond the relevant fiscal year.

The guiding standard is the one established by Government Code section 16310 and the cases interpreting its limitation on interfund loans. Plaintiffs' evidence of alleged adverse effects on Recycling Fund programs is therefore immaterial. The relevant question is whether the loans from the Recycling Fund interfered with the object for which the Recycling Fund was created. (Gov. Code, § 16310; *Daugherty v. Riley, supra,* 1 Cal.2d at p. 309.)

Recently, this district Court of Appeal was faced with a similar question when it considered whether a loan from the Contingent Fund of the Medical Board of California interfered with the object of the fund. The medical board licenses physicians, investigates complaints against physicians, and disciplines those found guilty of violating the law. (Bus. & Prof. Code, § 2004; *California Medical Assn., supra,* 193 Cal.App.4th at p. 1453.) The medical board collects license fees from physicians, which are held in the contingent fund and used to support the medical board's regulatory operations. (193 Cal.App.4th at p. 1453.) In the 2008 budget bill, the Legislature approved a $6 million loan from the contingent fund to the General Fund. (*Id.* at p. 1452.) An association of physicians challenged the legality of the loan with a petition for a writ of mandate directing that the money be returned. (*Ibid.*) Denial of the petition was affirmed on appeal. (*Id.* at p. 1466.)

The court rejected the plaintiffs' claim that the loan interfered with the object for which the special fund was created and held that the loan was authorized under Government Code section 16310. (*California Medical Assn., supra,* 193 Cal.App.4th at pp. 1455–1466.) In so holding, the court found no "evidence indicat[ing] that the loan in question has compromised the Medical Board's regulatory mission." (*Id.* at p. 1464.) The record showed that a surplus remained in the contingent fund after extending the loan to the General Fund, and a medical board budget analyst declared that the loan had no material effect on the medical board's ability to perform its statutory obligations of licensing physicians and enforcing the law. (*Id.* at p. 1455.) The court acknowledged that the loan may have resulted in physicians paying higher license fees because fees are statutorily set to provide a certain fund balance, and the loan reduced the fund balance. (*Id.* at p. 1459.) This effect, however, was not an interference with the *object* of the fund that would invalidate the loan, the court found. (*Ibid.*) The court reasoned that the fund was not created to set the amount of license fees but to regulate physicians — and that object was not impaired by the loan. "The Contingent Fund exists, broadly speaking, to enable the regulation of California physicians. Because the loan has not hindered performance of the Medical Board's regulatory responsibilities, it has not interfered with the purpose for which the Contingent Fund was 'created.'" (*Ibid.*)

The *California Medical Assn.* case is instructive in noting that not every negative impact occasioned by an interfund loan constitutes an interference with the object of the fund that invalidates the loan. A practical approach is necessary, one that protects regulatory operations while allowing the state sufficient "flexibility to balance its budget." (*California Medical Assn., supra,* 193 Cal.App.4th at p. 1465.)

....

We recognize that convenience zone recycling center operators and their employees have suffered financial troubles, and we do not minimize their difficulties. But these are difficult times, and the Legislature must make difficult choices when balancing the budget during a recession. The Legislature must also, of course, make lawful choices — regardless of financial expediency. It is the judiciary's task to hold the Legislature to account on that matter. We have scrutinized the record and are satisfied that the Legislature acted lawfully here. The loans from the Recycling Fund did not interfere with the object for which the Recycling Fund was created and were therefore lawful. (Gov. Code, § 16310; *Daugherty v. Riley, supra,* 1 Cal.2d at p. 309.)

IV. DISPOSITION

The order denying petitions for a writ of mandate is affirmed.

REARDON, Acting P. J., and RIVERA, J., concurred.

Notes and Questions

1. A legislative provision is germane for purposes of the single subject rule if it is auxiliary to and promotes the main purpose of the act or has a necessary and natural connection with that purpose. Legislation complies with the single subject rule if its provisions are either functionally related to one another or are reasonably germane to one another or the objects of the enactment.

2. The single subject rule is satisfied if the provisions of the act are cognate and germane to the subject matter designated by the title, if the title intelligently refers the reader to the subject to which the act applies and suggests the field of legislation which the text includes.

3. The Legislature may combine in a single act numerous provisions governing projects so related and interdependent as to constitute a single scheme, and provisions auxiliary to the scheme's execution may be adopted as part of that single package. The single subject rule is to be liberally construed to uphold proper legislation and not used to invalidate legitimate legislation. A statute must comply with both the requirement that it be confined to one subject and with the command that one subject be expressed in its title.

4. The single subject clause has as its primary and universally recognized purpose the prevention of log-rolling by the Legislature (i.e., combining several proposals in a single bill so that legislators, by combining their votes, obtain a majority for a measure which would not have been approved if divided into separate bills).

5. There were quite a few claims made by two different sets of plaintiffs. In both instances, the parties sought a declaration that the loans from the Recycling Fund to another special fund and the General Fund were illegal. Existing California law, found in Government Code § 16310(a), prohibits "any transfer that will interfere with the object for which a special fund was created." How did the court respond to this provision of statutory law?

6. One set of plaintiffs also argued that the loans violated the state Constitution's single subject rule. The plaintiffs argued that loans could not be contained in budget bills because they were different subjects. The court ruled differently. What was the justification that the court used to make its determination?

7. What is the impact of the bill's title, "appropriations," for purposes of the single subject rule? What are examples of budget items that would be "intricately intertwined"?

8. How did the court contrast the *Planned Parenthood* and *Professional Engineers* cases?

9. "The single-subject rule does not demand legislative foresight, only legislative focus." What does this statement by the court mean?

10. What was the importance of distinguishing the budget bill loans between a regulatory processing fee versus a tax? How does the court discern "whether a denominated fee is, in fact, a bona fide regulatory fee and not a disguised tax"?

4. Construing the Single Subject Rule

To minimize judicial interference in legislative branch activities, the decisions have been that courts must construe the single subject rule liberally. The general rule is that a bill will comply with the rule if the bill's provisions are either functionally related to one another or are reasonably germane to one another or the objects of the enactment.

Notes and Questions

1. To minimize judicial interference in legislative branch activities, courts must construe a constitutional provision requiring that a statute embrace but one subject liberally. A provision is deemed germane to other provisions in a statute if it would support a determination that the statute complies with the single subject rule providing that the statute must embrace but one subject.

Chapter Eleven

State Budget and Fiscal Legislation

A. Overview of the California Budget Process

The state budget process on paper is similar to the legislative process; however, it can be different in practical terms. The full budget committees of the Senate and Assembly act mostly as the final arbiter of their respective houses when it comes to finalizing the actions of their subcommittees.

Parts of the Budget

The following are the main parts of the California state budget:

Budget Bill — This contains the appropriations and "Budget Bill Language." Note that only a Budget Bill can contain multiple appropriations. It requires a majority vote for passage, and the bill takes effect immediately.

"Budget Bill Jr." — This is the bill that amends the main Budget Bill.

Trailer Bill — This bill makes the statutory changes needed to implement the budget. It is the same as any other bill, but it takes effect immediately with a majority vote if it contains an appropriation related to the budget bill and is listed as a "trailer bill" in the budget bill.

Supplemental Report — This is a separate report that requests specific actions from state agencies and departments. It does not have the force of law.

Timing

Keep in mind the following three dates:

January 10 — Constitutional Requirement for Governor to propose the budget.

June 15 — Constitutional Requirement for Legislature to pass the budget.

July 1 — Fiscal Year begins.

The Assembly Budget Committee and the Senate Budget and Fiscal Review Committee are charged with adopting the state budget and the respective trailer bills. Once the Governor's budget proposal is released by January 10, both budget committees' staff prepare a summary overview of the Governor's budget; a similar document is prepared by the Legislative Analyst Office (LAO).

In early March, the Assembly and Senate subcommittees begin holding hearings and taking testimony from the Department of Finance (DOF), LAO, respective state agencies and departments, and members of the public. This is a critical time to advocate for your client's position on specific budget requests. Most of the work on the budget occurs at the subcommittee level.

Prior to these hearings, the budget committee staff members examine the budget proposals and prepare agendas that include an explanation of the Governor's budget proposals and the staff's recommendations whether to accept, modify, hold open, or reject the budget proposals. Sometimes the Governor's budget proposals are "held open" for further discussions. The minority party staff prepare similar information for their members.

By the time the Governor's May Revise of the budget is released in mid-May, after April tax receipts are known, the subcommittees must conclude their deliberations within two weeks or so. As such, it is hard for the public to have much more input unless there is an entirely new budget proposal. As a result, it is important that communication be done early in the budget process.

Reconciling Differences

Differences between the actions of the Assembly and Senate are usually handled by a two-house conference committee. The procedural requirements have sometimes been waived due to time constraints for establishing the budget conference committee. The Assembly and Senate rotate the chairmanship of the conference committee each year.

This process is supposed to address the differences between the versions of the budget adopted by the Senate and Assembly. While the conference committee is open to the public and usually broadcast on California Channel, usually there is no public testimony taken. Instead, advocates rely upon budget conferees to advocate for a position adopted by one house.

The three Assembly Members and three Senators (4 Democrats and 2 Republicans) hear from the DOF and the LAO and deliberate among themselves. The conference committee will sometimes make changes known as "conference compromises." After that, they will finalize the remaining items and close out the budget.

Thereafter, both houses will vote on the conference report, and they will pass budget trailer bills. Again, once the budget is on the floor, there is little opportunity to make changes. Sometimes there will be an opportunity to modify policy language contained in a trailer bill, or some budget line items are modified in a "budget junior" bill.

Preparing the Budget

State departments must submit their budget proposals to their respective agencies, who in turn submit their proposals to the Department of Finance. This occurs in the early fall. After the DOF makes its recommendations, the Governor and his staff will make final determinations in consultation with DOF in time for release of the Governor's budget by the January 10 deadline.

The Governor's budget is on the DOF website under the E-BUDGET tab. The budget is over 1,300 pages in length and contains the details of the Governor's proposed budget spending for the upcoming fiscal year. Each budget item is assigned a 10-digit code and includes the state department, purpose and funding source.

The legislative budget subcommittees (which are known by numbers in both the Assembly and Senate) have the following subject matter jurisdictions:

Education (Senate Subcmte #1 and Assembly Subcmte #2)

Resources, Environment, and Transportation (Senate Subcmte #2 and Assembly Subcmte #3)

Health and Human Services (Senate Subcmte #3 and Assembly Subcmte #1)

State Government (Senate Subcmte #4 and Assembly Subcmte #4)

Public Safety and Judiciary (Senate Subcmte #5 and Assembly Subcmte #5)

Budget Phases

State agencies submit "budget change proposals," often referred to as BCPs, which contain proposed expenditures and budget changes to existing levels of service that are used to prepare the Governor's budget. These BCPs can be reviewed on the DOF website.

This is distinguished from a "deficiency" request, wherein an agency or department has an unanticipated increase in its costs (regardless of reason) that exceed the funding that was appropriated for the agency or department in the state budget. In these cases, the agency or department will request a deficiency appropriation in separate legislation.

Budget control language (BCL) is language contained in the budget bill that provides conditions on the use of a specific appropriation contained in the budget.

There are also "Finance Letters" which are proposals made by the Director of Finance to the chairs of the budget committees in each house to amend the Budget Bill and the Governor's Budget from the form submitted by January 10 in order to reflect a revised plan of expenditure.

The six distinct phases of the budget process:

Phase 1: Study Phase (November–February)

Phase 2: Public Participation/Listening Phase (March–Mid-May)

Phase 3: Action Phase (Mid-May to End of May)

Phase 4: Negotiation Phase (June 1–June 10)

Phase 5: Vote and Signing Phase (June 15–June 27)

Phase 6: Follow-up and Clean-up Phase (July–September)

B. California's Balanced Budget Requirement

Does California have to adopt a "balanced budget"? The short answer is yes. But there are several interesting aspects to this requirement.

Existing provisions of the California Constitution were interpreted to require a balanced budget. For example, Article IV, Section 12(a) requires the Governor to submit a budget by January 10 and, "if recommended expenditures exceed estimated revenues, the Governor shall recommend the sources from which the additional revenues should be provided." This constitutional provision was deemed to at least require the Governor to submit a balanced budget.

In addition, Article XVI, Section 1 limits the Legislature's ability to incur debt of more than $300,000 unless the Legislature passes by a 2/3 vote a measure that is adopted by the electorate. This constitutional provision was deemed to preclude the Legislature from adopting a budget that would create debt or liability in excess of $300,000 to the state.

And since 1983, Government Code § 13337.5 has required a balanced budget. This statute provides: "The annual Budget Act shall not provide for projected expenditures in excess of projected revenues. Further, it is the intention of the Legislature that in the event, after enactment of the Budget Act, revised estimates of expected revenues or expenditures, or both, show that expenditures will exceed estimated revenues, expenditures should be reduced or revenues increased, or both, to ensure that actual expenditures do not exceed actual revenues for that fiscal year."

The issue was finally settled with an amendment to Article IV, Section 12, when subdivision (g) was added, which reads: "(g) For the 2004–05 fiscal year, or any subsequent fiscal year, the Legislature may not send to the Governor for consideration, nor may the Governor sign into law, a budget bill that would appropriate from the General Fund, for that fiscal year, a total amount that, when combined with all appropriations from the General Fund for that fiscal year made as of the date of the budget bill's passage, and the amount of any General Fund moneys transferred to the Budget Stabilization Account for that fiscal year pursuant to Section 20 of Article XVI, exceeds General Fund revenues for that fiscal year estimated as of the date of the budget bill's passage. That estimate of General Fund revenues shall be set forth in the budget bill passed by the Legislature."

As such, the balanced budget requirement is a constitutional mandate that applies equally to both the legislative and executive branches of government. The Legislature is prohibited from sending the Governor an unbalanced budget, and the Governor is prohibited from signing an unbalanced budget. Of course, this leads to other questions, such as: How is "balanced" determined and who gets to decide if the budget is "balanced"?

Per the California Constitution and an appellate court decision, the determination is made based upon what is contained in the budget bill. In other words, the budget bill contains both the listing of expenditures as well as the estimate of revenues for the forthcoming fiscal year. That means the determination is up to the legislative and executive branches of government.

This was confirmed by the Third District Court of Appeal in its *Steinberg v. Chiang*, (2014) 223 Cal.App.4th 338, decision issued in 2014. The previous State Controller, John Chiang, argued that, in his audit capacity, he could determine whether the budget was balanced and, for purposes of the 2011 state budget, he claimed it was not balanced at the time the Legislature sent the budget bill to the Governor. The appellate court unanimously disagreed.

The trial court and then the appellate court concluded that the Legislature complies with the constitutional provision for a balanced budget when it enacts a budget bill in which its revenue estimates for the coming fiscal year exceed the total of existing appropriations for the fiscal year, new appropriations proposed in the budget bill for the fiscal year, and any transfer to the reserve fund. At that point, the Controller does not have the authority to make an independent assessment that the budget bill is not in fact balanced, because it relies on revenues not yet authorized in existing law or in enrolled legislation.

The Legislature successfully sought and received a declaration by the court that the Legislature complies with the balanced budget provision of the state Constitution when it passes a budget bill in which appropriations (and monies transferred to the reserve account) do not exceed the legislative estimate of revenues. So the Legislature sets forth its revenue estimate in the state budget bill, and that estimate will essentially not be subject to review by a constitutional officer or a court. In fact, the appellate court specifically found that the Controller cannot second-guess revenue estimates.

The court stated, "All that the balanced budget provision prescribes for the budget bill is inclusion of a legislative estimate of revenues 'made as of the date of the budget bill's passage' that exceeds the combination of the total amount of appropriations in the bill, the existing appropriations for the upcoming fiscal year, and transfers to the reserve fund." The appellate court went on to explain that "the balanced budget provision does not prescribe the manner in which the Legislature must calculate this estimate, the nature of the revenue sources the Legislature may or may not take into account, or any role for the Controller in overseeing the estimate."

In addition, the court ruled that the state's Constitution does not require budget trailer bills to be enrolled and sent to the Governor for signature before the constitutional deadline of June 15. The court also expressly addressed the issue of estimates on the receipt of federal funds: "Indeed, the Controller overlooks the extent to which California balances its budget with federal funds, the authorization for which is entirely outside the control of the Legislature (and the predicted total of which bespeaks more legislative artistry than accounting skills)."

Hence, even though the Controller alleged that there may be "phantom revenues included in the budget bill's estimate," the appellate court ruled that "it would amount to 'inappropriate judicial interference with the prerogatives of a coordinate branch of government' to endorse his [the Controller's] intrusion into the budget process under 'the guise of interpretation'." The court then addressed the obvious question how to enforce the balanced budget requirement.

Here the court ruled that "The Governor can enforce it either through vetoing the budget as a whole or exercising his power to veto line items to bring appropriations in balance with accurate revenues." As such, it is essentially the Legislature that enacts what it designates as a balanced budget, with a check from the Governor through his or her use of the blue pencil. It also means that the Legislature can adopt a "balanced budget" based upon its determination that federal funds or new revenues are forthcoming, even though there is no guarantee of receipt of those funds.

Notes and Questions

1. A perennial issue before the California Legislature is whether they have to adopt an actual balanced budget by June 15. Fundamentally, the answer is that, "on paper," they have to do so. The reality is that the revenues anticipated to be received the state are simply an estimate. While it is an educated estimate, it is still a guess. As such, should courts hold the Legislature responsible for not properly estimating revenue for the forthcoming fiscal year?

C. Budget Bills and Line-Item Vetoes

One of the most important bills that is considered each year by the legislative and executive branches of state government is the enactment of the annual budget bill. The 2020–21 state budget expended over $220 billion of state, federal and special funds. The executive branch of government gets "two bites at the apple"—at the beginning of the annual budget process when the Governor first proposed, the state's expenditure plan and then again at the end of the process when the Governor gets to sign or veto the budget bill and consider individual appropriations of state dollars. The line-item veto authority provides extra power to the state's Governor when he or she is negotiating the budget.

Budget bills that substantively change existing law violate the single subject rule, because a substantive bill making a change to existing law can be vetoed in its entirety by the Governor and incorporating such a bill into a budget bill makes it impossible for the Governor to properly exercise his veto. The legislative power is circumscribed by the requirement that the legislative acts be bicamerally enacted and presented to the head of the executive branch for approval or veto.

A bill making an appropriation of zero dollars is not a substantive act but is simply an act of non-appropriation which, by operation of statute, has the automatic legal effect of freeing local agencies from the obligation to implement the mandate for that year. When there is a lump sum appropriation intended for multiple purposes, but does not specifically allocate amounts to each of these purposes, the Governor may use the line-item veto to reduce the lump sum amount, but the Governor may not attribute the amount of the reduction to a specific purpose.

The constitutional provision requiring the Legislature to either fund or suspend local agency mandates does not prohibit the Governor from applying the line-item veto to reduce an appropriation funding a local agency mandate to zero. When the Governor exercises the power of the veto, he is acting in a legislative capacity, and he may only act as permitted by the Constitution.

The Governor possesses the constitutional authority to reduce or eliminate an item of appropriation in the budget bill passed by the legislature. The Legislature cannot shield an appropriation from the Governor's line-item veto simply by not using the language of appropriation in the budget bill. (*California School Boards Association v. Brown* (2011) 192 Cal.App.4th 1507, review denied.)

Notes and Questions

1. The power to appropriate public funds belongs exclusively to the Legislature. The line-item veto does not confer the power to selectively veto general legislation. As a result, the Governor has no authority to veto part of a bill that is not an item of appropriation.

2. In *St. John's Well Child and Family Center v. Schwarzenegger* (2010) 50 Cal.4th 960, the Court ruled that the Governor's line-item veto authority extends to instances where a previously-enacted appropriation is presented again to the Governor. The Governor did not exceed his powers by using his line-item veto authority to further reduce funding levels set forth in midyear reductions.

D. Limitation on Budget Bills

The budget bill is the only measure authorized under law to have multiple appropriations and not have to comply with the single subject rule. Nonetheless, there are several constitutional provisions that set forth the rules for consideration and adoption of budget bills in this state.

California Labor Federation v. Occupational Safety and Health Standards Board

(1992) 5 Cal.App.4th 985, rehearing denied

OPINION

SMITH, J.

We are called upon here to determine the constitutionality of provisions of the state Budget Act which purport to limit the amounts the state will pay towards a certain category of attorney fee awards against state agencies. We conclude that the challenged provisions violate the single subject rule set forth in section 9 of article IV of the California Constitution, and are therefore void.

I. BACKGROUND

Petitioners brought this original proceeding for a writ of mandate compelling respondent California Occupational Safety and Health Standards Board to incorporate in the California Occupational Health and Safety Act (Cal/OSHA) plan certain health and safety provisions adopted in Proposition 65, the Safe Drinking Water and Toxic Enforcement Act of 1986. We granted the relief requested. (California *Lab. Federation v. Occupational Safety Health Stds. Bd.* (1990) 221 Cal.App.3d 1547, 1559 [271 Cal.Rptr. 310], review den.) Thereafter, petitioners moved under Code of Civil Procedure section 1021.5 (hereinafter cited as section 1021.5) for an award of some $234,373.10 in attorney fees and costs. We awarded $114,266.25 in fees and $2,820.30 in costs, and directed respondent to pay these sums "forthwith."

When petitioners sought payment, a budget analyst for the Department of Industrial Relations advised counsel by letter that the state would not pay the full award: "The State of California has established a Budget Appropriation for payment of attorney's fees awarded pursuant to [section 1021.5] with a $125 cap on the hourly fee payable. The court's award of $114,226.25 [*sic*] was reduced to $55,422.75 in compliance with the hourly rate cap requirement for 1021.5 cases." In order to receive any payment at all, petitioners would have to execute releases discharging the state from any further liability.

… Petitioners brought this motion to enforce the award as made, seeking an order requiring respondent to pay the full amount awarded. They contend that the budget provisions on which the state relies are void because they effect an amendment of existing law in violation of the single subject rule.

In passing, respondent questions whether we have jurisdiction to determine the motion. A court issuing a writ of mandate has the inherent continuing power "'to make any orders necessary and proper for the complete enforcement of the writ.'" (*King v. Woods* (1983) 144 Cal.App.3d 571, 578 [192 Cal.Rptr. 724]; *Professional Engineers in Cal. Government v. State Personnel Bd.* (1980) 114 Cal.App.3d 101, 109 [170 Cal.Rptr. 547]; see *County of Inyo v. City of Los Angeles* (1977) 71 Cal.App.3d 185, 205 [139 Cal.Rptr. 396]; *County of Inyo v. City of Los Angeles* (1976) 61 Cal.App.3d 91, 95 [132 Cal.Rptr. 167].) The court has the distinct power to award "damages and costs," and the award "may be enforced in the manner provided for money judgments generally." (Code Civ. Proc., § 1095; see Cal. Civil Writ Practice (Cont.Ed.Bar 2d ed. 1987), § 11.6, p. 455.) We have the further power "[t]o compels obedience to [our] judgments…." (Code Civ. Proc., § 128, subd. (a)(4).) In the absence of prescribed procedures for doing so, "any suitable process or mode of proceeding may be adopted which may appear most conformable to the spirit of this code," i.e., the Code of Civil Procedure. (*Id.,* § 187.) We discern no basis for doubting our jurisdiction.

II. ANALYSIS

A. *Introduction*

The controversy before us is one of considerable delicacy, arising as it does in the sometimes turbulent region where the legislative and judicial spheres come into close contact. In making the present award, we did no more than carry out the legislative directive of section 1021.5 that we reward litigants in certain cases by granting a reasonable attorney fee. We are now called upon to consider the effect of budget provisions by which the Legislature sought to restrict the right thus granted. In addressing this question, we must consider the paramount command of the California Constitution that the Legislature may not use the Budget Act to expressly or impliedly amend or repeal existing substantive statutes.

This case raises no question concerning the Legislature's substantive power to limit or control attorney fee awards against the state. In *Mandel v. Myers* (1981) 29 Cal.3d 531, 550–551 [174 Cal.Rptr. 841, 629 P.2d 935], the Supreme Court pointed out several means by which the Legislature might accomplish such a result through properly enacted statutes. One of the strategies noted is similar in substance to the provisions in question here, i.e., "establish[ing] a fixed or maximum hourly rate of recovery for attorney services...." (*Id.* at p. 551.) There is no occasion here to question the Legislature's competence to enact such a limitation. The sole issue is the lawfulness, in light of the single subject rule, of a "cap" on fee awards *enacted as part of the Budget Act.*

B. *Single Subject Rule*

Article IV, section 9 of the California Constitution (hereafter article IV, section 9) requires that every statute "embrace but one subject, which shall be expressed in its title." This requirement grew out of an abhorrence of "log-rolling," "pork barrel politics," and legislation by "riders" — all variations on the parliamentary tactic of combining unrelated provisions in a single bill in order to secure their enactment. A "rider," for example, "'consisted in attaching to a bill dealing with one matter of legislation a clause entirely foreign to that subject matter, to the end that, hidden under the cloak of the meritorious legislation, the obnoxious measure might "ride through." Such "riders" ... not infrequently embraced ill-digested and pernicious legislation, relief bills, private appropriation measures, and the like, which would not have carried if the legislative mind had been directed to them. It was to cure this evil that the constitution made it mandatory that a bill should embrace but one subject-matter, and to meet the case of such a "rider" actually slipping through, declared that any matter foreign to the title of the bill should be held void.'" (*Planned Parenthood Affiliates v. Swoap* (1985) 173 Cal.App.3d 1187, 1196 [219 Cal.Rptr. 664] (hereinafter cited as *Swoap*), quoting *Ex parte Hallawell* (1909) 155 Cal. 112, 114 [99 P. 490].)

The Budget Act is a complex measure whose passage is essential, and as such is "particularly susceptible to abuse" of the kind just described. (*Swoap, supra,* 173 Cal.App.3d at p. 1198.) It is, therefore, fully subject to scrutiny under the single subject rule. (*Id.* at pp. 1198–1199.) Its "subject" is the appropriation of funds for government operations, and it cannot constitutionally be employed to expand a state agency's authority, or to "substantively amend and chang[e] existing statute law." (*Id.* at p. 1199, quoting *Association for Retarded Citizens v. Department of Developmental Services* (1985) 38 Cal.3d 384, 394 [211 Cal.Rptr. 758, 696 P.2d 150], quoting 64 Ops.Cal.Atty.Gen. 910, 917 (1981); internal quotation marks omitted.) Whether it effects an amendment of existing law for purposes of this prohibition "is determined not by title alone, or by declarations in the new act that it purports to amend existing law. On the contrary, it is determined by an examination and comparison of its provisions with existing law. If its aim is to clarify or correct uncertainties which arose from the enforcement of the existing law, or to reach situations which were not covered by the original statute, the act is amendatory, even though in its wording it does not purport to amend the language of the prior act." (*Ibid.,* quoting *Franchise Tax Bd. v. Cory* (1978) 80 Cal.App.3d 772, 777 [145 Cal.Rptr. 819], quoting *Balian Ice Cream v. Arden Farms Co.* (S.D.Cal. 1950) 94 F. Supp. 796, 798–799, italics and internal quotation marks omitted.)

"A statute shall embrace but one subject, which shall be expressed in its title. If a statute embraces a subject not expressed in its title, only the part not expressed is void. A statute may not be amended by reference to its title. A section of a statute may not be amended unless the section is re-enacted as amended." (Art. IV, § 9.)

C. *Budget Act Provisions*

We are called upon here to apply the principles of article IV, section 9 to provisions of the Budget Act purporting to limit the payment of fee awards under section 1021.5 Section 5 of the Budget Act provides that no award may be paid except as "[s]pecifically authorized and set forth in an item or section of this act." Item 9810-001-001 purports to (1) place a cap of $125 per hour on fee award payments, and (2) condition payment on acceptance of this amount "in full and final satisfaction" of the fee claim.

In all pertinent respects, the Budget Acts of 1990 and 1991 are identical, and we therefore refer to them without distinction as the "Budget Act."

Section 5.00 provides as follows:

"(a) No funds appropriated by this act or appropriated under any other statute may be used to pay attorney's fees in actions arising in state courts unless payment of the fees is:

"(1) Specifically authorized and set forth in an item or section of this act;

"(2) Expressly authorized by a statutory provision other than Section 1021.5 of the Code of Civil Procedure; or

"(3) Awarded by a federal court pursuant to federal law expressly authorizing attorney's fees.

"(b) This section shall not be construed as making an appropriation of funds for the payment of court-awarded attorney's fees." (Stats. 1991, ch. 118, § 5.00, No. 4 West's Cal. Legis. Service, p. 1124; Stats. 1990, ch. 467, § 5.00, No. 9 West's Cal. Legis. Service, pp. 2272–2273.)

Item 9810-001-001 provides:

"For payment of specified attorney's fee claims, settlements, compromises, and judgments arising from actions in state courts against the state, its officers, and officers and employees of state agencies, departments, boards, bureaus, or commissions, supported by the General Fund. 1,445,000.

"Schedule:

"(a) Payment of Specified Attorney's Fees.......... 1,505,000

"(b) Trigger reduction................................ –60,000

"Provisions:

"1. Expenditures from this item shall be made by the Controller, subject to the approval of the Department of Finance, and shall be charged to the fiscal year in which the disbursement is issued.

"2. Payments from this item shall only be made for state court actions filed pursuant to Section 1021.5 of the Code of Civil Procedure, the 'private attorney general' doctrine, or the 'substantial benefit' doctrine. Payments for state court actions shall not exceed the maximum hourly rate specified in Budget Act Item 9810-001-001 that was in effect on the date the judgment is entered or the date of the settlement agreement for attorney's fees. In no event shall the rate exceed $125 per hour.

"3. No payment shall be made by the Controller from this item except in full and final satisfaction of the claim, settlement, compromise, or judgment for attorney's fees incurred in connection with a single action.

"4. The Director of Finance shall notify the Chairperson of the Joint Legislative Budget Committee and the chairperson of the fiscal committees in each house when funds from this item have been exhausted, or when there are insufficient funds to satisfy a claim completely. This report shall list the known unsatisfied claims, and the amount of each of these claims." (Stats. 1991, ch. 118, No. 4 West's Cal. Legis. Service, pp. 1115–1116; see Stats. 1990, ch. 467, No. 9 West's Cal. Legis. Service, pp. 2262–2263.)

The question before us is whether these provisions are "amendatory" for purposes of the rule that the Budget Act may not be utilized to amend existing statutory law. Despite the fact that some such restrictions have been included in the Budget Act for at least 10 years, no published decision has yet faced the issue whether the restrictions survive scrutiny under the single subject rule. In *Swoap, supra,* we ourselves declined to reach the issue, characterizing it as a problem of enforcement not then before us. (173 Cal.App.3d 1187, 1202, fn. 12, citing *Committee to Defend Reproductive Rights v. Cory* (1982) 132 Cal.App.3d 852, 859 [145 Cal.Rptr. 819].) Other courts have not reached the issue because they determined that the awards before them fell outside the terms of the budget restrictions. (E.g., *Green v. Obledo* (1984) 161 Cal.App.3d 678 [207 Cal.Rptr. 830], cert. den. (1985) 474 U.S. 819 [88 L.Ed.2d 54, 106 S.Ct. 67] [award based on federal law]; *Coalition for Economic Survival v. Deukmejian* (1985) 171 Cal.App.3d 954 [217 Cal.Rptr. 621] [same]; see *Filipino Accountants' Assn. v. State Bd. of Accountancy* (1984) 155 Cal.App.3d 1023 [204 Cal.Rptr. 913].) And one court held the restrictions ineffective as against an award made before their adoption, finding them to constitute an impermissible legislative readjudication of a final judgment. (*Serrano v. Priest* (1982) 131 Cal.App.3d 188, 200–201 [182 Cal.Rptr. 387].)

In *Estate of Cirone* (1987) 189 Cal.App.3d 1280 [234 Cal.Rptr. 749], review denied, similar budget restrictions were upheld as against a contention that they violated the separation of powers. However, the decision nowhere acknowledged, let alone decided, the possible applicability of the single subject rule.

"[I]t is axiomatic that 'cases are not authority for propositions not considered therein.'" (*Isbell v. County of Sonoma* (1978) 21 Cal.3d 61, 73 [145 Cal.Rptr. 368, 577 P.2d 188], cert. den. 439 U.S. 996 [58 L.Ed.2d 669, 99 S.Ct. 597], quoting *Worthley v. Worthley* (1955) 44 Cal.2d 465, 472 [283 P.2d 19].) Since *Cirone* is addressed solely to the question of separation of powers, its authority as precedent is limited to its holding on that question, and it has no bearing on the issue before us. (See *Worthley v. Worthley, supra,* 44 Cal.2d at p. 472.)

D. *Amendatory Enactment*

To determine whether the budget restrictions effect an impermissible amendment, we must examine existing law concerning fee awards of the kind made here.

Section 1021.5 permits a prevailing party to recover attorney fees where certain criteria are met and the action "has resulted in the enforcement of an important right affecting the public interest...." This is a "codification of the 'private attorney general' attorney fee doctrine that had been developed in numerous prior judicial decisions." (*Woodland Hills Residents Assn., Inc. v. City Council* (1979) 23 Cal.3d 917, 933 [154 Cal.Rptr. 503, 593 P.2d 200].) Its enactment "in significant measure ... was an explicit reaction" to *Alyeska Pipeline Co. v. Wilderness Society* (1975) 421 U.S. 240 [44 L.Ed.2d 141, 95 S.Ct. 1612], in which the United States Supreme Court held that federal courts could not award fees on a private attorney general theory without statutory authorization. (*Woodland Hills Residents Assn., Inc. v. City Council, supra,* 23 Cal.3d at p. 934.) Section 1021.5 is "a legislative declaration that, in California, courts do enjoy the authority—exercised in numerous pre-*Alyeska* federal decisions—to award attorney fees on a private attorney general theory." (23 Cal.3d at p. 934.)

> "Upon motion, a court may award attorneys' fees to a successful party against one or more opposing parties in any action which has resulted in the enforcement of an important right affecting the public interest if: (a) a significant benefit, whether pecuniary or nonpecuniary, has been conferred on the general public or a large class of persons, (b) the necessity and financial burden of private enforcement are such as to make the award appropriate, and (c) such fees should not in the interest of justice be paid out of the recovery, if any. With respect to actions involving public entities, this section applies to allowances against, but not in favor of, public entities, and no claim shall be required to be filed therefor." (§ 1021.5)

These "prior judicial decisions" were mostly federal. California case law did not confirm the availability of a private attorney general theory until scant days after section 1021.5 was signed into law (but several months before it took effect), when the Supreme Court held that courts possessed inherent equitable power to award fees on such a theory, at least where the action vindicated a public policy with a constitutional basis. (*Serrano v. Priest* (1977) 20 Cal.3d 25, 46–47 [569 P.2d 1303]; see *Woodland Hills Residents Assn., Inc. v. City Council, supra,* 23 Cal.3d 917, 925.)

Section 1021.5 contains no express limitation on the size of the award, but has been universally understood to permit a "reasonable" award in light of factors derived from the statute's history and purpose. (*Serrano v. Unruh* (1982) 32 Cal.3d 621, 635, 639 [652 P.2d 985]; see *Sokolow v. County of San Mateo* (1989) 213 Cal.App.3d 231, 249, 250 [261 Cal.Rptr. 520], review den.; *Citizens Against Rent Control v. City of Berkeley* (1986) 181 Cal.App.3d 213, 232–233, 236 [226 Cal.Rptr. 265].) The Budget Act provisions in question here, on the other hand, impose what the state itself refers to as a "cap" on the hourly rate which will be paid. Coupled with the requirement that the recipient waive any amounts exceeding this "cap," the provisions impose what amounts to a mandatory numerical ceiling on the fees which may be recovered.

Quoting from *Estate of Cirone, supra,* respondent suggests that the cap is really something less than that because the fee recipient need not accept the reduced sum: "It is up to [the recipient] to decide whether to accept the payment on the terms or conditions offered by the Legislature or whether to refuse payment in hopes of a greater appropriation in the future." (189 Cal.App.3d at p. 1292.) We fail to see how the ability to "hope" for full payment dispels the mandatory character of the invitation. On the contrary, a person relegated to a mere "hope" experiences the essence of legal powerlessness. Insofar as the budget provisions here may be viewed as having that effect, they conflict with section 1021.5, which grants a *right* to a reasonable fee as fixed by a court.

In *Swoap, supra,* 173 Cal.App.3d 1187, we held invalid a budget provision purporting to withhold family planning funds from organizations which promoted abortion services. (173 Cal.App.3d at p. 1191, fn. 1.) We compared this restriction to existing statutes providing for family planning education, training, and services, and to regulations, promulgated under those statutes, requiring that clients be advised of all possible family planning options. (Id. at p. 1200.) We concluded that the budget restriction was impermissibly amendatory, for even if it did not flatly contradict the family planning statutes it sought to "clarify" them, and to "impose substantive conditions that nowhere appear in existing law." (*Id.* at p. 1201.)

As noted, section 1021.5 contains an implicit "cap" of its own, i.e., a party may only recover a "reasonable" fee, and no more. (See *Serrano v. Unruh, supra,* 32 Cal.3d 621, 635.) The budget restrictions purport to impose a wholly different cap based on a flat maximum hourly rate. This appears to be a markedly different substantive measure, and one which will in many cases be irreconcilable with the grant of a "reasonable" fee.

Respondent contends, however, that the existing limitation to a reasonable fee is not "statutory" but a mere judicial *interpretation* of section 1021.5; therefore, respondent asserts, the budget provisions do not affect "existing *statutory* law." We question the implicit premise that the distinction between statutory and court-made law plays the crucial role respondent would give it. However, we need not thoroughly explore that premise because we find the existing limitation to a "reasonable" award to be as much a matter of "statutory law" as anything explicitly stated in section 1021.5.

"'[W]hatever is necessarily implied in a statute is as much part of it as that which is expressed.'" (*Welfare Rights Organization v. Crisan* (1983) 33 Cal.3d 766, 771 [190 Cal.Rptr. 919, 661 P.2d 1073, 31 A.L.R.4th 1214], quoting *Johnston v. Baker* (1914) 167 Cal. 260, 264 [139 P. 86].)

The limitation to a reasonable fee is so inherent and essential to section 1021.5 that it must be considered "necessarily implied." The statute limits fee awards to a "reasonable" sum as surely as if it said so. The budget provisions purporting to impose a different limitation seek to effect an outright alteration of section 1021.5 as drawn.

The apparent reason for striking down "amendatory" budget provisions is that they have a *substantive* effect, whereas the sole "subject" of the Budget Act is the enactment of *fiscal* policy. The rationale, again, is that such proposals should be separately presented and considered, in order to attract the distinct attention of the legislative mind. For these purposes any amendment of existing law, other than fiscal law, would seem to be a "substantive" enactment.

Furthermore, as we stated in *Swoap*, a Budget Act provision is impermissibly amendatory not only if it alters existing statutory law but also if "its aim is to clarify or correct uncertainties which arose from the enforcement of the existing law." (*Swoap, supra,* 173 Cal.App.3d 1187, 1199, citations and internal quotation marks omitted.) If section 1021.5 is viewed as ambiguous with respect to the amount of fees allowed, the provisions here are amendatory for purporting to supersede the judicial resolution of that ambiguity with a legislative "clarification" set forth as an appropriation. The challenged provisions are amendatory in that sense and in the sense that they impose "substantive conditions that nowhere appear in existing law." (173 Cal.App.3d at p. 1201, fn. omitted.)

In *Committee to Defend Reproductive Rights v. Cory, supra,* 132 Cal.App.3d 852, the court remarked in passing that similar budget restrictions "cannot be read as an amendment by implication of Code of Civil Procedure section 1021.5" (132 Cal.App.3d at p. 859.) This statement was followed immediately by a citation to article IV, section 9 — the Constitution's single subject rule. (132 Cal.App.3d 859) We do not understand the quoted remark to mean that the budget restrictions could not be understood as amendatory, but rather that they could not be *permitted* to have that effect consistent with the single subject rule. In short, the court anticipated our holding today, without actually reaching the issue.

We reiterate that the Legislature is presumptively free to limit attorney fee awards under section 1021.5 What the Legislature may *not* do is grant a substantive right to fees, as it has done in section 1021.5, and then retract or impair the right thus granted through amendments masquerading as Budget Act provisions. To hold otherwise would deny the people the legislative accountability they sought to secure by adopting article IV, section 9 of the state Constitution. The provisions under scrutiny violate the single subject rule and are void.

Although we do not reach the issue, we note that the Budget Act restrictions may also be amendatory of existing statutes concerning cost awards against the State. For some purposes, at least, a fee award under section 1021.5 is an item of "costs." (See

Code Civ. Proc., § 1033.5, subd. (a)(10)(B) [fees awarded pursuant to statute are costs]; *T.E.D. Bearing Co. v. Walter E. Heller Co.* (1974) 38 Cal.App.3d 59, 62 [112 Cal.Rptr. 910] [same]; *Plumbing etc. Employers Council v. Quillin* (1976) 64 Cal.App.3d 215, 220 [134 Cal.Rptr. 332] [marshalling cases]; *Committee to Defend Reproductive Rights v. Cory, supra,* 132 Cal.App.3d 852, 858 [petitioners were "entitled to recover . . . costs . . . , including reasonable attorneys' fees. . . ."] (fn. omitted); *Swoap, supra,* 173 Cal.App.3d 1187, 1202 [same]; Gov. Code, § 800 [authorizing fee award in certain cases "in addition to . . . other costs"].) At least in general, cost awards "must be paid out of the appropriation for the support of the agency on whose behalf the State appeared." (Code Civ. Proc., § 1028; compare *id.,* § 1095 [losing public entity in mandate proceedings must pay costs "as other claims against the public entity are paid," and a cost award "may be enforced in the manner provided for money judgments generally"]; see Gov. Code, § 965.2 ["The Controller shall draw a warrant for the payment of any final judgment or settlement against the state whenever the Director of Finance certifies that a sufficient appropriation for the payment of such judgment or settlement exists."].)

III. RELIEF

Respondent seems to contend that whether or not the budget provisions are void, this court cannot direct payment of the full award because to do so would infringe legislative prerogatives and transgress the separation of powers. While we recognize the delicacy of the problem presented, we are satisfied that we can grant the relief requested by petitioners without impermissibly invading the domain of the Legislature.

"[T]he separation of powers doctrine has generally been viewed as prohibiting a court from directly ordering the Legislature to enact a specific appropriation, [but] it is equally well established that once funds have already been appropriated by legislative action, a court transgresses no constitutional principle when it orders the State Controller or other similar official to make appropriate expenditures from such funds." (*Mandel v. Myers, supra,* 29 Cal.3d 531, 540.) Here, funds have been appropriated for the payment of attorney fee awards under section 1021.5, but payment has been made subject to certain conditions which, as we have held, are void. The funds in question "have already been appropriated by legislative action" for the very purpose here contemplated. Accordingly, we transgress no constitutional principle by directing payment of the award without regard to the impermissible restrictions.

In accord with petitioners' request, we "order *respondent* to comply fully with this court's Order . . . by paying forthwith the amount of $117,086.55." (Italics added.) We retain jurisdiction (1) to enforce this order as may be necessary, (2) to determine whether a further award of attorney fees can and should be allowed, and if so in what amount, in connection with work performed by petitioners' counsel in seeking to enforce the original award, and (3) to consider such other matters as may be necessary and proper.

KLINE, P.J., and PETERSON, J., concurred.

A petition for a rehearing was denied May 21, 1992.

Notes and Questions

1. The budget is fully subject to scrutiny under the single subject rule, and its subject is the appropriation of funds for government operations, and it cannot constitutionally be employed to expand a state agency's authority or to substantively amend and change an existing statute. Instead, that is the role of the budget "trailer bills," which trail the adoption of the main budget bill and make any statutory changes to implement the budget.

2. According to the court, the sole issue in this case was the lawfulness, in light of the single subject rule, of a "cap" on fee awards that was enacted as part of the Budget Act. In examining the answer to this issue, the court explained that the "subject" of the Budget Act is the appropriation of funds for operating state government. On the other hand, the court ruled, the Budget Act cannot lawfully be used to expand a state agency's authority, nor can it be used to substantively amend and change existing statutes.

3. The court went on to declare that CCP § 1021.5 does not contain any express limitation on the size of an attorneys' fee award. In fact, according to the court, the section "has been universally understood to permit a 'reasonable' award in light of factors derived from the statute's history and purpose. (*Serrano v. Unruh* (1982) 32 Cal.3d 621, 635, 639.)"

4. What was the impact on the court in finding that § 1021.5 could be viewed as ambiguous with respect to the amount of fees allowed? Did the court distinguish between a "legislative clarification" of a statute and an "amendment"?

E. Legislature Can Create Offices without Funding

While the Governor has the power to reorganize executive branch offices through the use of a Governor's Reorganization Plan (GRP), the Legislature can create offices by adoption of a statute. Assuming such a bill gets signed into law by the Governor, then an office can be created. Under separate legislation, usually in the budget bill, funding for such a newly-created office would occur. Simply creating a new office does not mandate funding of that office by the Legislature.

Brown v. Superior Court of Sacramento

(1982) 33 Cal.3d 242

OPINION

NEWMAN, J.

The Court of Appeal system in California was expanded significantly by a statute the Legislature passed and the Governor approved during September 1981. The statute went into effect on January 1, 1982. (Stats. 1981, ch. 959.)

On February 26, 1982, via permanent injunction, Judge Fogerty — sitting by assignment on the Sacramento Superior Court — held the statute unconstitutional. He ordered that (1) the Governor refrain from appointing new judges, (2) the Controller refrain from disbursing funds for carrying out the statutory scheme, and (3) the Administrative Director of the Courts refrain from allocating appropriated moneys for that purpose.

The question now is whether we should vacate that injunction. The challenged statute (ch. 959) in its six sections:

1. Adds a fifth division of three judges to the First Appellate District in San Francisco.

2. Adds sixth and seventh divisions of three judges to the Second Appellate District. One new division is in Los Angeles; the other, in Santa Barbara.

3. Adds a third division of four judges to the Fourth Appellate District. The number of judges in the first division, at San Diego, is increased from five to six; at San Bernardino in the second division the number is decreased from five to four. The judges of the new third division are to sit in Orange County.

4. Adds two judges to the Fifth Appellate District in Fresno.

5. Creates a three-judge Sixth Appellate District in San Jose.

6. Declares that money for the Orange County division's judges and staff is to come from existing resources and the 1981 Budget Act, articulates a legislative intent that financing of that division's library and equipment "be achieved by local funding or public or private donation," and proscribes the use of other funds for the library and equipment.

The Legislature's power to enact the first five sections has not been challenged because article VI, section 3 of the California Constitution provides: "The Legislature shall divide the State into districts each containing a court of appeal with one or more divisions. Each division consists of a presiding justice and 2 or more associate justices...." During the proceedings below, however, Judge Fogerty concluded that chapter 959's section 6 (see our fn. 1) was unconstitutional.

How This Case Arose

In December 1981 Thomas Martin and Thomas Tweedy, taxpayers (and real parties in interest here), sued and in an amended complaint filed on December 29 advanced arguments to support their request that implementation of chapter 959 be enjoined. Judge Fogerty in his order of February 26, 1982, recites: "The cause was submitted upon the pleadings, upon judicial notice imparted by documents placed in the record and upon the transcribed oral arguments of counsel. The Court has concluded (1) that there is no question of fact before the Court; (2) that Chapter 959, California Statutes of 1981, is unconstitutional and void."

In S.F. No. 24403 here the petitioners are the Governor and the Controller. In S.F. 24405 the petitioner is the Administrative Officer of the Courts. They seek mandate to compel respondent court to vacate the injunction.

The Basis of the Injunction

Judge Fogerty's opinion, dated February 17, 1982, reads in part as follows: "A Court clearly cannot function without a library or equipment. Nor should the Court be in a position where it must solicit and accept donations, whether public or private. [¶] The concept of a tripartite government with its doctrine of separation of powers has been violated by this legislative enactment [chapter 959]. The independence of the judiciary is sacrosanct.... [Citation.] [¶] The legislature, through its enactment, has impinged upon the efficient operation of the court, and has thereby violated Article 3, Section 3 of the California Constitution. Furthermore, a statute which requires a state court to finance its necessary operations from donations threatens the integrity of the judicial process and the reputation for impartiality which is indispensable to the judicial functions. [¶] Finally, this Court concludes that the unconstitutional funding provisions cannot be severed from the statute as a whole.... It would ... be beyond the jurisdiction of this Court to attempt to rewrite the statute to determine which of the new divisions would stand or fall. Nor can this Court merely strike the limitation thereby requiring the State to fund a program where an insufficient budget has been allocated. [¶] ... [T]his Court can review and act only on what is before it. The fact that in the future the legislature may be able to rewrite the statute to then make it constitutional is not a factor to be considered by this Court."

On June 30 this year, perhaps in response to Judge Fogerty's concerns, the Legislature included the following provision in its 1982 Budget Act (Stats. 1982, ch. 326, item 0250-490, provision 2): "Notwithstanding Section 6 of Chapter 959 [see fn. 1, ante] ... $209,480 ... is expressly allocated to fund the library and equipment for Division Three of the Fourth Appellate District (the division holding sessions in Orange County)." That is to say, no longer was there any intent that financing of that library and equipment "be achieved by local funding or public or private donation...."

Thus, it appears that the Fogerty injunction, challenged here, reflected the judge's concerns regarding a statutory restriction that no longer exists. Deemed temporary when enacted (see fn. 1, *ante*), that restriction in toto was superseded by the 1982 Budget Act. So, we need not consider whether he correctly concluded that in 1981, because of its section 6, the Legislature passed "a statute which violated the California Constitution...."

He stressed, though, that his ruling was "dispositive without regard to other significant problems raised in this litigation." Therefore, we proceed to examine those problems, as they have been identified and discussed in the briefs of the parties and amici and during oral argument.

Other Significant Issues

Article XVI, section 7 of our state's Constitution prescribes: "Money may be drawn from the Treasury only through appropriation made by law...." For fiscal year 1982–1983 the Legislature has appropriated $36,015,838 "[f]or support of Judiciary, Judicial

Council" including specifically $20,964,632 for the Courts of Appeal. Further, the *amounts appropriated … are intended to fully fund all of the judgeships and places of sitting created by Chapter 959 of the Statutes of 1981."* (Italics added.)

Notwithstanding that brief but unambiguous legislative pronouncement, real parties contend that no such funds have legally been appropriated and that the superior court's injunction accordingly should stay in effect.

Why might the pertinent 1982–1983 appropriation be invalid? Because, say real parties, chapter 959 either was void ab initio or become void on January 1, 1982, its effective date. We discuss first the latter contention.

It is conceded in this case that real parties' complaint would have been groundless if chapter 959's effective date had been July 1, 1982. But the Legislature's choice of January 1 instead of July 1, it is argued, was fatal since on that day the Governor, the Controller, and the courts' Administrative Director were endowed with powers they could not exercise because, allegedly, the Legislature had provided no money.

Real parties cite no precedents. They maintain, though, that their view is supported by article IV, section 12 of the Constitution and, particularly, by the pronouncement in section 12, subdivision (d) that "[a]ppropriations … are void unless passed in each house by rollcall vote … two thirds of the membership concurring." Chapter 959 did not receive a two-thirds vote.

Nowhere in the words of the Constitution or in California legislative annals or in juridical opinions can we discover any overriding rule that the Legislature may not, without funding the initial fiscal year, create agencies or offices, including courts and judgeships. On the contrary, in this century the remarkable, nationwide development of budgeting-and-appropriating powers evidences a basic concern that laws which "authorize" be distinguished from those which "appropriate." Legislatures first decide whether a need for a new agency or office seems established; they then decide whether and how to prescribe the funding.

During the first half of this year none of the chapter 959 judgeships was filled, and no new court was inaugurated. As of July 1, though, funding that indisputably meets the constitutional tests of adequacy had been provided. Whatever might have been a problem had the Governor, the Controller, or the courts' Administrative Director taken action during the first six months, in fact they took no action. As of now, no longer is there a problem. Pursuant to article VI, section 3 (quoted above), once again the Legislature (via ch. 959) has "divide[d] the State into districts each containing a court of appeal with one or more divisions … consist[ing] of a presiding justice and 2 or more associate justices." Further, pursuant to section 12, subdivision (c) of article IV the 1982 Budget Act "fully [funds] all of the judgeships and places of sitting created by Chapter 959".… Nothing else is required.

The suggestion that chapter 959 was void ab initio (i.e., from its date of enactment) is based on the clause in article IV, section 12, subdivision (d) that provides: "Appropriations … are void unless passed in each house by rollcall vote … two thirds of the membership concurring." Real parties argue that chapter 959, passed by less than a two-thirds vote, contained implied appropriations and that thus the whole chapter is void.

The only reference to money in chapter 959, however, appears in its section 6, the Orange County library-and-equipment clause. We concluded above that the restrictions there were superseded by the 1982 Budget Act. No words in chapter 959 curtail a subsequently created authority to make expenditures from current appropriations. Section 6 itself dealt only with the 1981–1982 budget; it stressed that "funding for [Orange County] support staff [should] be provided from existing resources, and funding for the four judges … is provided in the [1981] Budget Act."

Nonetheless as to judges, it is argued, the separation of powers doctrine commands that — once appointed — judges are entitled to their salaries.... Again, we stress that no chapter 959 judges have been appointed. If any had been, though, it appears that a claim for salary would have involved not only chapter 959 but also Government Code section 68200 et seq., which fix base salaries for all Supreme Court and Court of Appeal justices and judges in trial courts of record. Those Government Code sections apparently were approved by vote of 25 Senators, 2 short of the two-thirds required for appropriation bills. (Stats. 1976, ch. 1183, §§ 1–3 (Assem. Bill No. 3844); 9 Sen. J. (1975–1976 Reg. Sess.) p. 16794.) Yet clearly those sections and like laws are valid. Thus, even were it regarded as a law that sets judges' salaries, chapter 959 did not need a two-thirds vote.

Real parties urge that "a proposal establishing a new state agency and appropriating its initial support funds entails not only an appropriation 'for the ensuing fiscal year' within the meaning of Art. IV, sec. 12, subd. (a), but also for an indeterminate number of fiscal years thereafter." Without further legislative action, though, even special appropriations for starting a new agency would not fund its operation in later years. Moreover, no clause in the Constitution extends to laws that create new agencies or offices the two-thirds requirement the people have prescribed for appropriations (art. IV, § 12, subd. (d)), urgency statutes (art. IV, § 8, subd. (d)), and a limited listing of certain laws on taxation and other matters (e.g., art. XIII A, § 3; art. IV, § 4). Absent such a clause, the obvious implication is that agency- and office-creating statutes indeed may be passed by simple majority, separately from whatever budget or appropriation act is needed for implementation.

Real parties suggest that the initial costs of an agency are not "usual current expenses" to which budget acts assertedly are confined. (See Const., art. IV, § 8, subd. (c)(2) (appropriations for usual current expenses take immediate effect); McClure v. Nye (1913) 22 Cal.App. 248 [133 P. 1145] (appropriations to construct buildings were not for usual current expenses and did not take immediate effect).) Yet the budget bill must itemize "expenditures" (art. IV, § 12, subd. (c)), including capital outlays, whether or not they are usual and current. And both the 1981 and the 1982 Budget Acts include urgency clauses, seemingly to assure their taking immediate effect without reliance on the "usual current expenses" reference in article IV, section 8, subdivision (c)(2). (See Stats. 1981, ch. 99, § 36.00; Stats. 1982, ch. 326, § 36.00.)

Petitioners cite a precedent for creating appellate judgeships by a statute that specifies no appropriation for their support. Item 17 of the 1973 Budget Act (Stats. 1973, ch. 129) appropriated a lump sum for appellate courts and added a proviso "that $72,000 of the funds appropriated in this item shall not be expended unless legislation is enacted during the 1973–74 Regular Session establishing an additional judgeship for the Third Appellate District." When that law was enacted Government Code section 69103 declared, "The Court of Appeal for the Third Appellate District consists of one division having four judges and shall hold its regular sessions at Sacramento." Later, on October 2, 1973, section 69103 was amended to provide that, until January 15, 1975, the Third Appellate District should have six judges and, on and after that date, seven. (Stats. 1973, ch. 1124.) Section 4 of the amending chapter provided "Notwithstanding the provisions of Item 17 of the Budget Act of 1973, the seventy-two thousand dollars ($72,000) reserved by that item for an additional judgeship in the Third Appellate District of the Court of Appeal may be expended for more than one additional judgeship for that district."

Is that relaxation of the previously imposed budgetary restriction distinguishable from the legislative history here? We think not, for in 1973 the Legislature patently did not treat chapter 1124 as an appropriation bill. In its final paragraph, the Legislative Counsel's Digest of the last-amended version of Senate Bill No. 1149 (which became ch. 1124) reads: "*Vote: majority. Appropriation: no.* Fiscal committee: yes...." (Italics added.) Though chapter 1124 in fact passed both houses with more than a two-thirds vote (see 5 Assem.J. (1973 Reg. Sess.) p. 8880; 4 Sen.J. (1973 Reg. Sess.) pp. 6754–6755), that digest reflects the Legislative Counsel's opinion that the bill contained no appropriation. The Legislature's creation — with no contemporaneous appropriation — of three new judgeships in 1973 (ch. 1124) and many new judgeships and appellate courts in 1981 (ch. 959) raises a "strong presumption" that accompanying appropriations were not constitutionally required. (See *Methodist Hosp. of Sacramento v. Saylor* (1971) 5 Cal.3d 685, 692 [97 Cal.Rptr. 1, 488 P.2d 161] (referring to a "settled principle of construction, i.e., the strong presumption in favor of the Legislature's interpretation of a provision of the Constitution"); cf. *San Jose Mercury-News v. Municipal Court* (1982) 30 Cal.3d 498, 514 [179 Cal.Rptr. 772, 638 P.2d 655].)

Finally, by our clerk's letter of July 8, 1982, real parties were invited to comment on the effect of the 1982 Budget Act in this case. In response they have argued that the absence of appropriations in chapter 959 and a claimed absence of appropriations for new judgeships and courts in the 1981 Budget Act made that chapter void ab initio, incapable of being revived by the 1982 Budget Act. They invoke the principle that "[a]n act of the legislature which is in conflict with the constitution is no statute at all." (*Reclamation District v. Superior Court* (1916) 171 Cal. 672, 676 [154 P. 845]; see *Norton v. Shelby County* (1886) 118 U.S. 425, 442 [30 L.Ed. 178, 186, 6 S.Ct. 1121].)

They concede exceptions to the principle, and properly they note the inapplicability here of one exception: the giving of limited effect to a void statute in order to protect rights created by innocent reliance on its validity. (See *Chicot County Dist. v. Bank*

(1940) 308 U.S. 371, 374 [84 L.Ed. 329, 332–333, 60 S.Ct. 317].) Rights have not intervened here because the new divisions are not now established, the new judgeships not yet filled.

Real parties then identify, but puzzlingly fail to discuss, another exception: "[A] partially invalid statute may be validated by later legislation." That exception applies here. Real parties concede, for instance, that the 1982 Budget Act validly superseded chapter 959's section 6 (see above). Why then would the first five sections still be invalid? Not because of what those sections say, it is argued, but because of what they fail to say; namely, that funds are available for spending.

We hold that the 1982 Budget Act cures the alleged omission and renders the chapter fully operative. In point is *County of Los Angeles v. Jones* (1936) 6 Cal.2d 695 [59 P.2d 489], for example, where the Legislature enacted amendments (Stats. 1935, ch. 729, p. 1999) to sections of the Assessment Bond Refunding Act of 1933 (Stats. 1933, ch. 749, p. 1915) in response to a decision holding the act unconstitutional (*County of Los Angeles v. Rockhold* (1935) 3 Cal.2d 192 [44 P.2d 340, 100 A.L.R. 149]). Ruling the amendments valid, this court rejected the contention that they were void simply because the law they modified had been declared unconstitutional. (*County of Los Angeles v. Jones, supra,* 6 Cal.2d at p. 708.)

Conclusion

Chapter 959 was a proper exercise of the Legislature's power to establish additional courts of appeal and judgeships. We need not decide whether judgeships could have been filled or courts started up before passage of the 1982 Budget Act. That act now has become law, and implementation of chapter 959 thus is lawful.

Let a peremptory writ issue, ordering respondent to vacate its judgment against petitioners and to enter judgment against real parties in interest.

REYNOSO, ACTING C.J., BROWN (GERALD), J., and WHITE, J., concurred.

Notes and Questions

1. The Legislature is not precluded from creating agencies or offices, including courts and judgeships, without funding the initial fiscal year, but rather the Legislature first decides whether the need for the new agency or office seems established and then decides whether and how to prescribe the funding. Why might the Legislature want to create an office without providing it funding to operate?

2. The main holding of the decision provides that, "Nowhere in the words of the Constitution or in California legislative annals or in juridical opinions can we discover any overriding rule that the Legislature may not, without funding the initial fiscal year, create agencies or offices, including courts and judgeships. On the contrary, in this century the remarkable, nationwide development of budgeting-and-appropriating powers evidences a basic concern that laws which 'authorize' be distinguished from those which 'appropriate.' Legislatures first decide whether a need for a new agency or office seems established; they then decide whether and how to prescribe the funding."

3. Why was the statute at issue alleged to have had an appropriation and therefore needed a 2/3 vote for passage? How did the Court address this argument?

F. Appropriations Bills and the Reenactment Rule

In *Wood v. Riley* (1923) 192 Cal. 293, the court actually defined the term appropriation when it described such a bill as "an act by which a named sum of money has been set apart in the treasury and devoted to the payment of a particular claim or demand." Otherwise, this term is not defined in the state Constitution nor in the Government Code.

American Lung Association v. Wilson

(1996) 51 Cal.App.4th 743

OPINION

Davis, J.

In these two consolidated appeals, we conclude that a portion of Assembly Bill No. 816 (1993–1994 Reg. Sess.) (Stats. 1994, ch. 195) is a legally invalid legislative enactment. The portion of Assembly Bill No. 816 at issue is an appropriations measure that the defendants (collectively, the State) maintain substantively amends Proposition 99 (the 1988 tobacco tax initiative measure). As we explain, this portion of Assembly Bill No. 816 is at odds with Proposition 99 as originally enacted, and, if this part of Assembly Bill No. 816 is construed as a substantive amendment of Proposition 99, it is at odds with the reenactment rule of article IV, section 9 of the California Constitution. In light of our analysis, we affirm the judgment.

Background

Proposition 99, the Tobacco Tax and Health Protection Act of 1988 (the Act), is an initiative measure approved by the voters in November 1988. (Rev. & Tax. Code, § 30121 et seq.; all further undesignated section references are to the Revenue and Taxation Code unless otherwise noted.) The Act imposes additional taxes on cigarette and tobacco product distributors. (§ 30123.) For example, the Act imposes an additional excise tax of 25 cents on a standard pack of cigarettes. (§ 30123, subd. (a).) The Act creates a Cigarette and Tobacco Products Surtax Fund in the state treasury and deposits its taxes into that fund. (§ 30122, subd. (a).)

The Cigarette and Tobacco Products Surtax Fund (the Fund) consists of six separate accounts: the health education account; the hospital services account; the physician services account; the research account; the public resources account; and the unallocated account. (§ 30122, subd. (b).) The accounts at issue here are the health education account and the research account. Pursuant to section 30124, subdivision (b), 20 percent of the moneys deposited in the Fund are to be allocated to the health education account and 5 percent are to be allocated to the research account. Pursuant to section 30122, subdivision (b), the health education account is available only for "appropriation for programs for the prevention and reduction of tobacco use, primarily among children, through school and community health education programs"; and the research account is available only for "appropriation for tobacco-related disease research." Under section 30122, subdivision (b), the hospital services account and the physician services account are to be used to pay for medical care for indigents (such care does not have to be tobacco related). (§ 30122, subd. (a).)

The Legislature, through the part of Assembly Bill No. 816 before us, made certain appropriations from the health education account and the research account for the 1994–1995 and the 1995–1996 fiscal years; these appropriations are challenged here by, among others, the American Lung Association and Americans for Nonsmokers' Rights. (Stats. 1994, ch. 195, § 53, subds. (b)(3) & (5), (j), (k), (l), (m), (n), (o), & (p); *id.* § 54, subds. (b)(3) & (5), (k), (l), (m), (n), & (o).)

For purposes of appellate review, the State has conceded that the challenged appropriations from the health education account and the research account were not spent on the health education programs and research subjects mandated by section 30122, subdivision (b). Instead, these appropriations were used to pay for medical services for indigents, primarily children. Thus, the State has conceded that it has appropriated moneys from the health education account and the research account, through Assembly Bill No. 816, in ways that would violate the Act as passed by the voters. These challenged appropriations have also apparently reduced the percentages of the Fund going to the health education account and to the research account and increased the percentages of the Fund going to the accounts covering medical services for indigents; this would violate section 30124, subdivision (b) specifying that 20 percent of the Fund is to go to the health education account and 5 percent to the research account.

The State contends, however, that it has substantively amended the Act via Assembly Bill No. 816, and that the challenged appropriations are proper in light of this amendment. Section 30130 allows the Legislature to amend the Act by a four-fifths vote of each house. Assembly Bill No. 816 met this vote requirement. Section 30130 also requires that "[a]ll amendments … be consistent with [the Act's] purposes." (§ 30130.)

Discussion

The challenged language in Assembly Bill No. 816 follows a particular format, an example of which is as follows:

> "SEC. 53. For the 1994–95 fiscal year, the sum of three hundred ninety-six million one hundred fifty-eight thousand dollars ($396,158,000) is appropriated from the Cigarette and Tobacco Products Surtax Fund … according to the following schedule: * * *
>
> "(b) Seventy million eight hundred ninety-nine thousand dollars ($70,899,000) from the Health Education Account to the State Department

of Health Services, as follows: [Partly to pay for certain medical care programs for indigents]. * * *

"(m) Five million dollars ($5,000,000) from the Research Account [to a medical care program for indigents]. * * *

"(p) Eleven million dollars ($11,000,000) from the research account [to another medical care program for indigents]." (See Stats. 1994, ch. 195, § 53, subds. (b)(3) & (5), (j), (k), (l), (m), (n), (o), & (p).) Similar language is used in Assembly Bill No. 816 to cover the 1995–1996 fiscal year. (Stats. 1994, ch. 195, § 54, subds. (b)(3) & (5), (k), (l), (m), (n), & (o).)

Viewed simply as an appropriations measure, Assembly Bill No. 816 is legally invalid because an appropriations statute naturally must align with the substantive legislation which authorizes the appropriation. As we have noted, Assembly Bill No. 816 does not align with section 30122, subdivision (b) (specifying how the account funds must be spent) or with section 30124, subdivision (b) (specifying the percentages of the Fund each account is to receive). Sections 30122, subdivision (b) and 30124, subdivision (b) are substantive provisions of the Act authorizing appropriations.

The State argues, however, that Assembly Bill No. 816 constitutes an attempt by the Legislature to amend the Act substantively and that this amendment is consistent with the purposes of the Act. The Legislature is permitted to amend the Act, so long as the amendment receives the required four-fifths votes and is consistent with the purposes of the Act. (§ 30130; Cal. Const., art. II, § 10, subd. (c).) In effect, the State argues that Assembly Bill No. 816 has amended the account percentages set forth in section 30124, subdivision (b) by reducing the percentages of the Fund going to the health education and the research accounts and increasing the percentages of the Fund going to the accounts covering medical services for indigents. As the starting point for this argument, the State notes that the Legislature passed Assembly Bill No. 816 by meeting the four-fifths vote requirement of section 30130. This view is supported by language appearing in the legislative history which described Assembly Bill No. 816 as an "Urgency statute. 4/5 vote required (Amends Proposition 99)." (Proposed Conf. Rep. No. 1 Assem. Bill No. 816 (1993–1994 Reg. Sess.) July 6, 1994, p. 1.) As we shall explain, if Assembly Bill No. 816 constitutes an attempt to substantively amend the Act, it runs afoul of the reenactment rule.

The reenactment rule is set forth in article IV, section 9 of the California Constitution, which provides in pertinent part: "A statute may not be amended by reference to its title. A section of a statute may not be amended unless the section is reenacted as amended."

The purpose of the reenactment rule was explained a century ago in *Hellman v. Shoulters* (1896) 114 Cal. 136 [45 P. 1057] (*Hellman*). That purpose is to avoid "'the enactment of statutes in terms so blind that legislators themselves [are] sometimes deceived in regard to their effect, and the public, from the difficulty of making the necessary examination and comparison, fail[s] to become appraised [sic] of the changes made in the laws.'" (*Hellman, supra*, 114 Cal. at p. 152; *Huening v. Eu* (1991) 231 Cal. App. 3d 766, 773 [282 Cal. Rptr. 664].)

As noted, the State argues that Assembly Bill No. 816's redirection of funds amended section 30124, subdivision (b) by reducing the 20 percent allocation to the health education account and the 5 percent allocation to the research account and correspondingly increasing the percentage allocations to the accounts covering medical services for indigents.

However, if one looks for these changes to section 30124, subdivision (b) in the logical spot — in the section itself — they will be disappointed. Section 30124, subdivision (b) reads exactly the same after Assembly Bill No. 816 as it did before Assembly Bill No. 816. In short, section 30124, subdivision (b), with its purported amendments from Assembly Bill No. 816, was not reenacted with those amendments. The reenactment rule "applies clearly to acts which are in terms … amendatory of some former act." (*Pennie v. Reis* (1889) 80 Cal. 266, 270 [22 P. 176].) Under the State's argument, Assembly Bill No. 816 amended section 30124, subdivision (b) through the stated redirections from the health education and research accounts to the medical programs for indigents. Under this argument, then, Assembly Bill No. 816 was "in terms … amendatory of some former act," and as such, in violation of the reenactment rule.

The State contends the reenactment rule applies only where a statute is amended by striking out or inserting certain words, phrases or clauses. (See *Fletcher v. Prather* (1894) 102 Cal. 413, 418 [36 P. 658]; *Hellman, supra*, 114 Cal. at pp. 152–153; *People v. Western Fruit Growers* (1943) 22 Cal. 2d 494, 500–501 [140 P.2d 13]; see also *Yoshisato v. Superior Court* (1992) 2 Cal. 4th 978, 989–990 [9 Cal. Rptr. 2d 102, 831 P.2d 327].) The key to the reenactment rule's applicability, however, does not turn on a particular method of amendment but on whether legislators and the public have been reasonably notified of direct changes in the law. (*Hellman, supra*, 114 Cal. at p. 152; *Huening v. Eu, supra*, 231 Cal.App.3d at p. 773; see *Harbor v. Deukmejian* (1987) 43 Cal. 3d 1078, 1096 [240 Cal. Rptr. 569, 742 P.2d 1290].) In fact, neither *Fletcher* (upon which *Western Fruit Growers* relies) nor *Hellman* takes such a limited approach. *Fletcher* notes that an act "might be" amended in these ways, while *Hellman* mentions these methods simply in passing. (*Fletcher, supra*, 102 Cal. 413; *Hellman, supra*, 114 Cal. 136)

This limited view of the reenactment rule, moreover, flies in the face of public policy, good government and common sense. The underlying purpose of the reenactment rule is to make sure legislators are not operating in the blind when they amend legislation, and to make sure the public can become apprised of changes in the law. (*Hellman, supra*, 114 Cal. at p. 152.) An expressly stated amendatory fragment, which indisputably is within the reach of the reenactment rule, certainly offers more in the way of notice of an amendment than does the cryptic language and uncodified context of Assembly Bill No. 816.

It is true the reenactment rule does not apply to the addition of new code sections or the enactment of entirely independent acts that impliedly affect other code sections. (*Hellman, supra*, 114 Cal. at pp. 151–153; *Johnson v. City of Glendale* (1936) 12 Cal.

App. 2d 389, 393 [55 P.2d 580].) These exceptions to the reenactment rule are needed because "[t]o say that every statute which thus affects the operation of another is therefore an amendment of it would introduce into the law an element of uncertainty which no one can estimate. It is impossible for the wisest legislator to know in advance how every statute proposed would affect the operation of existing laws." (*Hellman, supra*, 114 Cal. at p. 152.)

But Assembly Bill No. 816 is an appropriations measure for the Act; Assembly Bill No. 816 mentions by name the Fund and accounts within it. (Stats. 1994, ch. 195, §§ 53, 54.) By its terms, Assembly Bill No. 816 redirects moneys from the Fund's health education and research accounts to programs paying for medical care for indigents. Against this backdrop, a conclusion that Assembly Bill No. 816 violates the reenactment rule does not disrupt orderly legislative processes or inject the judiciary impermissibly into the legislative realm.

Apparently, there are no California decisions involving an alleged substantive amendment like Assembly Bill No. 816. However, the Washington Supreme Court has dealt with a strikingly similar situation. In *Flanders v. Morris* (1977) 88 Wn.2d 183 [558 P.2d 769], an uncodified appropriations bill for a public assistance program added an age restriction to the other statutory restrictions without changing the language of the relevant statute.

The *Flanders* court concluded that the appropriations bill violated Washington's reenactment rule, which stated, like California's: "No act shall ever be revised or amended by mere reference to its title, but the act revised or the section amended shall be set forth at full length." (Wn. Const., art. II, § 37; see *Flanders v. Morris, supra*, 558 P.2d at p. 771.) The court in Flanders noted that previous decisions had set forth the following reason for the reenactment rule: "'The [rule] was undoubtedly framed for the purpose of avoiding confusion, ambiguity, and uncertainty in the statutory law through the existence of separate and disconnected legislative provisions, original and amendatory, scattered through different volumes or different portions of the same volume. Such a provision, among other things, forbids amending a statute simply by striking out or inserting certain words, phrases, or clauses, a proceeding formerly common, through which laws became complicated and their real meaning often difficult of ascertainment. The result desired by such a provision is to have in a section as amended a complete section, so that no further search will be required to determine the provisions of such section as amended.'" (558 P.2d at p. 773.)

To this reason the *Flanders* court added another related one: "Another important purpose of Const. art. 2, § 37, not mentioned above, is the necessity of insuring that legislators are aware of the nature and content of the law which is being amended and the effect of the amendment upon it.... [¶] For 37 years, the statutory law of this state has provided for public assistance on the basis of need with no age restriction. The new restriction is clearly an amendment to [the relevant statute], adding to the restrictions already enumerated there. However, the statute will never reflect this change but will continue to read as it always has, with no age restriction. One seeking the law on the subject would have to know one must look under an 'appropriations' title in the *uncodified* session laws to find the amendment. The fact that the [appropriations] bill is not codified strikes at the very heart and purpose of Const. art. 2, § 37." (558 P. 2d at p. 774, italics in original, citation omitted.

We could not have said it any better. If Assembly Bill No. 816 amends the percentages set forth in section 30124, subdivision (b) or makes any other substantive amendment to the Act, it violates the reenactment rule.

Disposition

The judgment is affirmed.

SCOTLAND, J., concurred.

Notes and Questions

1. An appropriations measure violated the constitutional reenactment rule and did not effectively amend an initiative despite being passed by four-fifths vote of the Legislature where there was no change to the statutory allocation language. The purpose of the constitutional reenactment rule, which prohibits amending a section of a statute unless the section is reenacted as amended, is to avoid enactment of statutes in terms so blind that legislators themselves are deceived in regard to their effect, and the public, from difficulty of making the necessary examination and comparison, fails to become apprised of changes made.

2. The rule clearly applies to acts which are in terms amendatory of some former act. It does not apply to the addition of new code sections or enactment of entirely independent acts that impliedly affect other code sections.

3. The main purpose of the annual budget bill is that of itemizing recommended expenditures for the ensuing fiscal year. Annual budget acts, like all other enactments of the Legislature, are subject to the provisions of Constitution Article IV, Section 9 which sets forth the "single subject" rule.

4. Thus, the budget bill may deal only with the one subject of appropriations to support the annual budget, and may not constitutionally be used to grant authority to a state agency that the agency does not otherwise possess or to substantively amend and change existing statutory law.

5. In this case, the Legislature unsuccessfully argued that it had amended an initiative statute by securing the required 4/5 vote to amend the law. However, the court did not agree. "For purposes of appellate review, the State has conceded that the challenged appropriations from the health education account and the research account were not spent on the health education programs and research subjects mandated by section 30122, subdivision (b). Instead, these appropriations were used to pay for medical services for indigents, primarily children." Was the fact that the appropriated funds were used for an unauthorized purpose a basis for the court's ruling?

6. The first ruling of the court dealt with AB 816 as an appropriations measure. Why did the court rule that this bill was "legally invalid"?

7. The second ruling of the court dealt with AB 816 as an amendment to the underlying Act (Prop. 99). Why did the court rule that this bill "runs afoul" of existing law?

8. The court explained the exceptions to the state Constitution's reenactment rule: "It is true the reenactment rule does not apply to the addition of new code sections or the enactment of entirely independent acts that impliedly affect other code sections."

Planned Parenthood Affiliates v. Swoap

(1985) 173 Cal.App.3d 1187

OPINION

KLINE, P. J.

Petitioners, a coalition of nonprofit corporations which provide comprehensive family planning services, a regional family planning council, and a low-income recipient of state family planning services, filed a writ of mandate seeking to compel respondents State Secretary of Health and Welfare David B. Swoap, Director of the State Department of Health Services Kenneth Kizer, Chief Officer of the State Office of Family Planning Frederick E. Walgenbach, State Controller Kenneth Cory, and State Treasurer Jesse M. Unruh, to refrain from enforcing section 33.35 of the Budget Act of 1985–1986 which contains restrictive language regarding the use of family planning funds for organizations providing abortion-related services.

The 1985–1986 California State Budget was introduced in the Senate as Senate Bill (SB) No. 150 and in the Assembly as Assembly Bill (AB) No. 222. On May 24, 1985, SB 150 was amended to add section 33.35; AB 222 did not include this provision. The Senate and Assembly versions of the budget were sent to a six-member conference committee composed of three members from each house. The conference committee voted to reject section 33.35 and to adopt the Assembly version of that portion of the budget which did not include section 33.35. On June 13, 1985, a two-thirds majority of both houses voted to adopt SB 150 as amended by the conference committee.

After SB 150 was enrolled and sent to the Governor, it was discovered that the bill as adopted included section 33.35. Due to staff error, there was no amendment to SB 150 reflecting the deletion of section 33.35. Members of the conference committee and the Speaker of the Assembly notified the Governor that section 33.35 was contrary to the action of the conference committee and had been left in the budget bill by mistake. The Speaker specifically requested that the Governor "delete the language in order to properly reflect the Budget as voted on by both Houses of the Legislature." On June 28, 1985, the Governor signed SB 150 into law stating that he had not deleted section 33.35, as requested, because he opposed the use of public funds to finance abortions and abortion services. On June 29, 1985, the Department of Health Services notified all agencies receiving state family planning funds that organizations "which perform, promote, or advertise abortions, or receive compensation, advantage, benefit or gain from abortion referrals" may not be eligible for reimbursement.

On July 3, 1985, petitioners filed an original petition in this court seeking mandate to bar enforcement of section 33.35. On July 10, 1985, we issued an order to show cause and stayed enforcement of section 33.35 pending the hearing.

On July 10, 1985, respondents Swoap, Kizer, and Walgenbach sent contracts for fiscal year 1985–1986 to eligible family planning agencies which included the restrictive language of section 33.35. On the same day, respondent State Health Director Kizer issued a statement to such agencies regarding the implementation of section 33.35. Under these guidelines, pregnancy termination procedures would be allowed where the mother's life is at risk, in cases of rape or incest, or where the procedure is incidental to, or a complication of, another treatment. Counties and the University of California would be exempt from the restrictions imposed by section 33.35.

The parties and the amici devote their attention chiefly to the issues of whether section 33.35 unconstitutionally conditions receipt of state funds on the forfeiture of fundamental constitutional rights and denies equal protection of the law. It is unnecessary for us to reach these issues, however, because we find that section 33.35 represents an attempt by the Legislature to amend existing law in violation of the dictates of article IV, section 9, of the California Constitution.

I.

Before addressing the state constitutional issue we deem dispositive; it is necessary to first lay to rest petitioners' unusual contention that section 33.35 should be stricken in order to effectuate the legislative intent. Emphasizing the undisputed fact that section 33.35 remained in the Budget Act solely as a result of clerical error, and relying upon the unopposed affidavits of members of each house of the Legislature who declare that the provision was voted down by a four-to-two vote in a conference committee, petitioners invoke the familiar principle of statutory construction that when the legislative intent may be ascertained it will be given effect by the courts "'even though it may not be consistent with the strict letter of the statute.'" (*Dickey v. Raisin Proration Zone No. 1* (1944) 24 Cal. 2d 796, 802 [151 P.2d 505, 157 A.L.R. 324], quoting *In re Haines* (1925) 195 Cal. 605, 612 [234 P. 883]; *County of Sacramento v. Hickman* (1967) 66 Cal. 2d 841, 849, fn. 6 [59 Cal. Rptr. 609, 428 P.2d 593].) Where necessary in order to effectuate the legislative intent, the "words or phrases [of a statute] may be changed, added or *stricken out.*" (*In re Sekuguchi* (1932) 123 Cal. App. 537, 538 [11 P.2d 655], italics added.)

The difficulty with this argument is that we are not here confronted with an ambiguous statute in need of interpretation. Petitioners are not genuinely asking us to construe the words of section 33.35, but to repeal it. This we cannot do. While certain legislative reports may be indicative of legislative intent (*People v. Superior Court (Douglass)* (1979) 24 Cal. 3d 428, 434 [155 Cal. Rptr. 704, 595 P.2d 139]), "they cannot be used to nullify the language of the statute as it was in fact enacted." (*San Mateo City School Dist. v. Public Employment Relations Bd.* (1983) 33 Cal. 3d 850, 863 [191 Cal. Rptr. 800, 663 P.2d 523].) Nor can the understanding of individual legislators who cast their votes in favor of a measure be used for this purpose. (*Ibid*) The question before us is not the meaning but the validity of section 33.35 as an expression of the legislative will. The salutary principle has long been established in California that the judicial branch may not go behind the record evidence of a statute and inquire whether it genuinely reflects the will of the Legislature. "If an Act is properly enrolled, authenticated, and deposited with the Secretary of State, it is conclusive evidence of the legislative will at the time of its passage." (*People v. Burt* (1872) 43 Cal. 560, 564.)

The seminal case regarding this principle is *Sherman v. Story* (1866) 30 Cal. 253. The defendant in that case, who challenged the validity of a particular Act of 1866, offered legislative journals and oral testimony, all apparently uncontradicted, that certain proposed amendments that were rejected in the Assembly were nonetheless (presumably by mistake) incorporated into the act by the enrolling clerk of the Senate, "and thereby, although in fact not adopted by either House, became a part of the Act, as it now appears." (*Id.*, at p. 255.) "In other words, it is claimed to be competent to show, by the kind of evidence indicated, that the Act now appearing of record in the Office of the Secretary of State, duly authenticated by the certificates of the Secretary of the Senate and Clerk of the Assembly, the signatures of the President of the Senate and Speaker of the Assembly, and the approval of the Governor of the State, never did pass either House, and is, therefore, not a valid law." (*Id.*, at pp. 255–256.) In a lengthy opinion, the Supreme Court declined to look behind the "solemn official record" (*id.*, at p. 278), observing that "[w]hen we once depart from [this] principle — from a sound rule of law — where shall we stop? Do not the circumstances of this case open to our vision a vista of absurdities into which we shall stumble if we attempt to explore forbidden fields for evidence of a vague, shadowy and unsatisfactory character upon which to overthrow the enrolled statutes of the land?" (*Id.*, at p. 279.)

Sherman v. Story was subsequently reaffirmed in *County of Yolo v. Colgan* (1901) 132 Cal. 265 [64 P. 403], which is also pertinent to the case at hand. In *County of Yolo* the journal of the Senate showed that the vote on the statute in question was "ayes, twenty, noes, three"; though the number of aye votes necessary for Senate enactment of the bill was twenty-one. The appellant contended that the measure never became law "because it did not receive, in the senate, the number of votes required by the constitutional provision that 'no bill shall become a law without the concurrence of a majority of the members elected to each house.'" (*Id.*, at p. 267.) After assaying the relevant case law, the court rejected this claim, observing, inter alia, that "[t]he law-making power of the state is vested, by the constitution, in the legislature; and while the constitution has prescribed the formalities to be observed in the passage of bills and the creation of statutes, the power to determine whether these formalities have been complied with is necessarily vested in the legislature itself, since, if it were not, it would be powerless to enact a statute. The constitution has not provided that this essential power thus vested in the legislature shall be subject to review by the courts, while it has expressly provided that no person charged with the exercise of powers properly belonging to one of the three departments — the legislative, executive, and judicial — into which the powers of the government are divided, shall exercise any functions appertaining to either of the others." (*Id.*, at pp. 274–275.)

Since the irregularity relied upon by petitioners is not apparent from a reading of the budget bill as enacted, and can be established only through extrinsic evidence, this case is not within the exception to the rule of *Sherman v. Story* which permits judicial inquiry if the irregularity in legislative proceedings appears on the face of the challenged measure. (*People v. County of Santa Clara* (1951) 37 Cal. 2d 335, 338–340 [231 P.2d 826]; *People v. City of San Buenaventura* (1931) 213 Cal. 637, 642 [3 P.2d 3].)

We note, finally, that if, as appears to have been the case, section 33.35 was enacted by mistake, it is not the first time this has occurred in connection with the annual budget bill, a complex measure invariably enacted in exigent circumstances involving, among other constraints, a constitutionally mandated time restriction. (Cal. Const., art. IV, § 12, subd. (c). ["The Legislature shall pass the budget bill by midnight on June 15 of each year."]) As the Attorney General correctly points out, the mistakes that inevitably occur in the budget bill are ordinarily corrected by the Legislature in the form of a "cleanup" bill. (See, e.g., Stats. 1981, ch. 169, § 45, which was enacted "[i]n order to correct technical errors in the Budget Bill of 1981 … and to more accurately effect the intention of the Conference Committee…." (*Ibid.*) A cleanup bill to repeal section 33.35 (Sen. Bill No. 1469) was introduced in the Senate on June 20, 1985, and presumably will be acted upon in due course. In any event, from all that appears, the Legislature, which has not sought our intervention, possesses the ability to correct its mistakes without judicial assistance.

Accordingly, we hold that section 33.35 of the Budget Act of 1985–1986, which has received the necessary approval of each house of the Legislature and has been duly enrolled and approved by the Governor, cannot be impeached by extrinsic evidence that it does not genuinely reflect the will of the Legislature.

II.

The necessary judicial assumption that section 33.35 is a valid reflection of the will of the Legislature does not, of course, immunize that provision from constitutional scrutiny. Among the applicable state constitutional requirements claimed here to be infringed is the so-called single subject rule of article IV, section 9, which declares that: "A statute shall embrace but one subject, which shall be expressed in its title. If a statute embraces a subject not expressed in its title, only the part not expressed is void. A statute may not be amended by reference to its title. A section of a statute may not be amended unless the section is re-enacted as amended."

This provision, which has ancient roots and exists in one form or another in the constitutions of most of our sister states, has two purposes. One of its functions "is to prevent legislators and the public from being entrapped by misleading titles to bills whereby legislation relating to one subject might be obtained under the title of another." (*Abeel v. Clark* (1890) 84 Cal. 226, 228 [24 P. 383]; *Ex parte Liddell* (1892) 93 Cal. 633, 636 [29 P. 251]; *Matter of Maginnis* (1912) 162 Cal. 200, 203 [121 P. 723]; *Heron v. Riley* (1930) 209 Cal. 507, 510 [289 P. 160]; *People v. Superior Court* (1937) 10 Cal. 2d 288, 293 [73 P.2d 1221].) But prevention of the passage of acts bearing misleading titles is not the principal purpose of the one subject rule. As has been stated, "[t]he primary and universally recognized purpose ... is to prevent log-rolling in the enactment of laws...." (Ruud, "No Law Shall Embrace More Than One Subject" (1958) 42 Minn.L.Rev. 389, 391.) As our Supreme Court has pointed out, "[i]n times past an abuse had grown up, which consisted in attaching to a bill dealing with one matter of legislation a clause entirely foreign to that subject matter, to the end that, hidden under the cloak of the meritorious legislation, the obnoxious measure might 'ride through.' Such 'riders,' as they came to be designated, not infrequently embraced ill-digested and pernicious legislation, relief bills, private appropriation measures, and the like, which would not have carried if the legislative mind had been directed to them. It was to cure this evil that the constitution made it mandatory that a bill should embrace but one subject-matter, and to meet the case of such a 'rider' actually slipping through, declared that any matter foreign to the title of the bill should be held void." (*Ex parte Hallawell* (1909) 155 Cal. 112, 114 [99 P. 490]; see also *Brosnahan v. Brown* (1982) 32 Cal. 3d 236, 251 [186 Cal. Rptr. 30, 651 P.2d 274]; 1A Sutherland, op. cit., *supra*, § 17.01, p. 2 and cases there cited; Luce, Legislative Procedure, *supra*, at pp. 548–552.)

In order to minimize judicial interference in the activities of the legislative branch, the single subject rule is to be construed liberally. "However numerous the provisions of an act may be, if they can be fairly considered as falling within the subject-matter of legislation, or as proper methods for the attainment of the end sought by the act, there is no conflict with the constitutional provision...." (*Ex parte Kohler* (1887) 74 Cal. 38, 41 [15 P. 436]; *Matter of Maginnis, supra*, 162 Cal. 200, 204.) In other words, the rule "was not designed as a loophole of escape from, or a means for the destruction of, legitimate legislation." (*Heron v. Riley, supra*, 209 Cal. 507, 510.) Accordingly, a provision is deemed germane for purposes of the single subject rule if it is "auxiliary to and promotive of the main purpose of the act or has a necessary and natural connection with that purpose...." (*Metropolitan Water Dist. v. Marquardt* (1963) 59 Cal. 2d 159, 172–173 [28 Cal. Rptr. 724, 379 P.2d 28].)

The main purpose of the annual budget bill is that of "itemizing recommended expenditures" for the ensuing fiscal year. (Cal. Const., art. IV, § 12, subd. (c).) As provided in our Constitution, "[n]o bill except the budget bill may contain more than one item of appropriation, and that for one certain, expressed purpose." (Art. IV, § 12, subd. (d).) A legislative "appropriation" has been judicially defined as one "by which a named sum of money has been set apart in the treasury and devoted to the payment of a particular claim or demand." (*Stratton v. Green* (1872) 45 Cal. 149, 151; *Wood v. Riley* (1923) 192 Cal. 293, 303 [219 P. 966].)

The title of the Budget Act of 1985–1986, which pursuant to article IV, section 9, defines the "subject" to which the substance of section 33.35 must be germane, is: "An act making appropriations for the support of the government of the State of California and for several public purposes in accordance with the provisions of Section 12 of Article IV of the Constitution of the State of California, and declaring the urgency thereof, to take effect immediately." (Stats. 1985, ch. 111.)

Respondents contend that section 33.35 does not violate the single subject rule because "the Legislature may control enforcement of budgets through the Budget Act, and item 33.35 is clearly worded to maintain the integrity of the separate budget allocations for planning and abortion." Respondents also maintain that section 33.35 does not amend existing law and is totally consistent with Welfare and Institutions Code section 14500 et seq., the statutory basis for the family planning program. Respondents state that section 33.35 "simply clarifies the separation between funding for abortions and the funding for [family] planning."

While it is true, as we have said, that the single subject rule is to be construed liberally to uphold proper legislation, it is also true, and courts must keep in mind, that the annual budget bill is particularly susceptible to abuse of that rule. "History tells us that the general appropriation bill presents a special temptation for the attachment of riders. It is a necessary and often popular bill which is certain of passage. If a rider can be attached to it, the rider can be adopted on the merits of the general appropriation bill without having to depend on its own merits for adoption." (Ruud, "No Law Shall Embrace More Than One Subject,", supra, 42 Minn.L.Rev. at p. 413.)

In California, legislators and state agencies have repeatedly been reminded by the Attorney General that "[a]nnual budget acts, like all other enactments of the Legislature, are subject to the provisions of section [9], Article IV, of the California Constitution," which sets forth the single subject rule. (29 Ops.Cal.Atty.Gen. 161, 167 (1957); accord 27 Ops.Cal.Atty.Gen. 111, 113 (1956); 27 Ops.Cal.Atty.Gen. 345, 346 (1956); 39 Ops.Cal.Atty.Gen. 200, 204 (1962); 64 Ops.Cal.Atty.Gen. 910, 917 (1981).)

Quoting with approval from one of these opinions, our Supreme Court recently agreed that "'"the budget bill may deal only with the one subject of appropriations to support the annual budget,"' and thus '"may not constitutionally be used to grant authority to a state agency that the agency does not otherwise possess"' or to '"substantively amend and chang[e] [e]xisting statute law."'" (*Association for Retarded Citizens v. Department of Developmental Services* (1985) 38 Cal. 3d 384, 394 [211 Cal. Rptr. 758, 696 P.2d 150], quoting 64 Ops.Cal.Atty.Gen. 910, 917 (1981).)

An amendment has been described as "'a legislative act designed to change some prior or existing law by adding or taking from it some particular provision.'" (*Franchise Tax Bd. v. Cory* (1978) 80 Cal. App. 3d 772, 777 [145 Cal. Rptr. 819], quoting *Assets Reconstruction Corp. v. Munson* (1947) 81 Cal. App. 2d 363, 368 [184 P.2d 11].) "'Whether an act is amendatory of existing law is determined not by title alone, or by declarations in the new act that *it purports to amend* existing law. On the contrary, it is determined by an examination and comparison of its provisions with existing law. If its aim is to clarify or correct uncertainties which arose from the enforcement of the existing law, or to reach situations which were not covered by the original statute, the act is amendatory, *even though in its wording* it does not purport to amend the language of the prior act.'" (Italics in original.) (Id, at p. 777, quoting *Balian Ice Cream v. Arden Farms Co.* (S.D.Cal. 1950) 94 F. Supp. 796, 798–799.)

In *Franchise Tax Bd. v. Cory, supra,* 80 Cal. App. 3d 772, the Legislature sought by "control language" in the budget bill to clarify and restrict the auditing and sampling methods to be used in connection with appropriations for audits by the Franchise Tax Board of political candidates' financial reports. The Governor "item vetoed" this control language but not the appropriation. The Legislature then urged the state Controller not to allow use of the funds appropriated in a manner contrary to the control language. The court held that the control language was an invalid attempt to amend the Political Reform Act (Gov. Code, § 9000 et seq.) without compliance with the initiative amendment procedures required by Government Code section 81012, subdivision (a). In reaching its decision the court noted that, although the audit provisions of the act did not by their terms conflict with the control language, the latter added to the act by clarifying the standards to be used and by significantly restricting the manner of conducting audits. As such the control language undertook to amend the act and was invalid.

Guided in our reasoning by this analysis, we find that section 33.35 amends existing provisions of the family planning act (Welf. & Inst. Code, § 14500 et seq.) and therefore violates the single subject rule.

A major purpose of the family planning act is "[t]o make available to citizens of the state of childbearing age *comprehensive medical knowledge,* assistance and services relating to the planning of families." (Welf. & Inst. Code, § 14501, subd. (a), italics added.) In furtherance of this purpose, the Office of Family Planning is required, among other things, "to establish in each county a viable program for the dispensation of family planning, infertility and *birth control information and techniques*" (*id.,* § 14501, subd. (f), italics added) to pursue "scientific investigation into … existing and new … *birth control techniques*" (*id.,* § 14501, subd. (g), italics added); and to establish education and training programs for health care practitioners "in rendering advice on … *birth control techniques and information.*" (*Id.,* § 14501, subd. (h), italics added.) The Office of Family Planning is also directed to "enter into contracts and agreements with individuals, colleges, universities, associations, corporations, municipalities and other units of government … which may provide for payment by the state within the limit of funds available for material, equipment and services." (*Id.,* § 14501, subd. (i).)

"Birth control," as that term is used in the family planning act, clearly includes abortion. Regulations implementing that act that were recently issued by the Office of Family Planning provide that agencies funded under the act must provide each of their clients' family planning information "that enables her or him to make informed decisions based on full knowledge of *all possible options.*" (Dept. of Health Services, Office of Family Planning, Guidebook for Family Planning Agencies (July 1, 1985) § 4, par. B., p. A.1.8, italics added.) The regulations specifically instruct that in providing "pregnancy counselling and referral" under the family planning act, "[a]ll applicable alternatives (prenatal care, adoption, infertility care, *pregnancy termination,* contraception) must be presented in an unbiased manner" (*id.,* § 5, par. C., subd. 5b(1), p. A.1.16, italics added), so that the client understands "the advantages" as well as "the disadvantages" of her alternatives. (*Id.,* § 5, par. C., subd. 5b(1)(b), p. A.1.17.) Moreover, section 14503 states that "Family planning services shall include, but not be limited to: (a) Medical treatment and procedures defined as family planning services under the published Medi-Cal scope of benefits." (Welf. & Inst. Code, § 14503.) It is undisputed that abortions performed by a physician, whether in a hospital, clinic, or office, are medical services funded under the California Medi-Cal program. (*Committee to Defend Reproductive Rights v. Myers* (1981) 29 Cal. 3d 252, 258 [172 Cal. Rptr. 866, 625 P.2d 779, 20 A.L.R.4th 1118].)

Even if we were to agree with respondents that section 33.35 "simply clarifies" funding arrangements for abortion and other services authorized under the family planning act we would nonetheless be compelled to conclude that it impermissibly amends that act within the meaning of the single subject rule; for, as stated in *Franchise Tax Bd. v. Cory, supra,* 80 Cal. App. 3d 772, an act is amendatory "'[i]f its aim is to *clarify* or correct uncertainties which arose from the enforcement of the existing law, or to reach situations which were not covered by the original statute, ...'" (*Id.,* at p. 777, italics added.) But section 33.35, construed objectively, does not simply clarify the family planning act; quite the contrary, its prohibition on the granting of family planning funds "to any group, clinic, or organization which performs, promotes, or advertises abortions" is a manifest restriction of activities authorized under the family planning act. At the very least, section 33.35 imposes substantive conditions that nowhere appear in existing law.

Because section 33.35 of the Budget Act of 1985–1986 grants authority to a state agency that the agency does not otherwise possess, and in this manner amends the family planning act, said section violates the single subject rule of article IV, section 9, of the California Constitution and is invalid.

The foregoing conclusion makes it unnecessary to discuss the other constitutional objections urged upon us with great force by petitioners.

Petitioners are entitled to recover their costs in these proceedings, including reasonable attorneys' fees pursuant to Code of Civil Procedure section 1021.5. (*Committee to Defend Reproductive Rights v. Myers, supra,* 29 Cal.3d at pp. 285–286.) Because this matter commenced as an original proceeding in this court, we are unable to follow the ordinary practice of remanding the request for fees to the court in which the trial was held for the purpose of taking evidence on, and fixing, the reasonable amount of fees to be awarded. (See, e.g., *Serrano v. Priest* (1977) 20 Cal. 3d 25, 50 [141 Cal. Rptr. 315, 569 P.2d 1303].) Nor is a case closely related to this one still pending before any trial court in this appellate district. (See *Committee to Defend Reproductive Rights v. Cory* (1982) 132 Cal. App. 3d 852, 859 [183 Cal. Rptr. 475]; *Committee to Defend Reproductive Rights v. Rank* (1984) 151 Cal. App. 3d 83, 88 [198 Cal. Rptr. 630].) Therefore, unless the parties are able to agree within 30 days as to the appropriate amount of costs and fees, the matter may be submitted to this court on affidavits. (*Choudhry v. Free* (1976) 17 Cal. 3d 660, 669 [131 Cal. Rptr. 654, 552 P.2d 438].)

A peremptory writ shall issue, directing respondents to refrain from enforcing the unconstitutional provisions of the Budget Act of 1985–1986 challenged herein.

ROUSE, J., and SMITH, J., concurred.

Notes and Questions

1. One of the purposes of Constitution Article IV, Section 9, which provides that a statute may only embrace a "single subject," is to prevent legislators and the public from being entrapped by misleading titles to bills whereby legislation relating to one subject might be obtained under the title of another.

2. However, the primary and universally recognized purpose of such a rule is to prevent log-rolling in the enactment of laws by preventing the use of legislative "riders" from expanding the subject matter of a particular piece of legislation.

3. In this case, the court is called upon to determine whether a section of the annual budget act should be enforced, even though the Legislature mistakenly did not remove the provision before sending the bill to the Governor for final action. The mistake was discovered after the bill had already been sent to the Governor's desk, but the Governor refused to strike the provisions as the Legislature asked.

4. According to the court, "The parties and the amici devote their attention chiefly to the issues of whether section 33.35 unconstitutionally conditions receipt of state funds on the forfeiture of fundamental constitutional rights and denies equal protection of the law." Why did the court rule that it was unnecessary for it to make a determination of these constitutional claims?

5. Why did the court describe the Legislature's argument — "petitioners' unusual contention" — that this section of the annual budget act should be stricken in accord with the intent of the Legislature? How did the court handle the extrinsic aids of legislative intent that clearly supported the Legislature's argument? Is ambiguity always required to allow a court to use extrinsic aids for interpretation?

6. The court noted that the Attorney General correctly pointed out a method for the Legislature to correct any "mistakes that inevitably occur in the budget bill." What is that method?

7. The court noted that the single subject rule is to be construed liberally to uphold proper legislation, but the court also stated that "the annual budget bill is particularly susceptible to abuse of that rule." What is the basis for this statement by the court?

8. The court held that "section 33.35 amends existing provisions of the family planning act (Welf. & Inst. Code, § 14500 et seq.) and therefore violates the single subject rule." Does this mean that the annual budget act cannot amend any existing statutes?

G. Budget Bills and the Single Subject Rule

For purposes of the single subject rule involving legislation, the budget bill is subject to the same requirement. In other words, the budget bill's provisions must be reasonably germane to the same subject. The single subject rule applies to the budget trailer bills as well, which is why the legislature normally adopts about two dozen budget trailer bills that enact statutory changes necessary to implement the budget bill and its appropriations funding.

San Joaquin Helicopters v. Department of Forestry and Fire Protection

(2003) 110 Cal.App.4th 1549

OPINION

Morrison, J.

San Joaquin Helicopters appeals from denial of its petition for a writ of mandate challenging the validity of an interim contract between State of California (the State) Department of Forestry and Fire Protection (CDF) and DynCorp Technical Services for maintenance services on aircraft used in fighting fires. San Joaquin Helicopters contends CDF and the Department of General Services (DGS) had no authority to enter into the interim contract while its bid protest was pending; the State's reliance on section 6.05 of the State Contracting Manual to authorize the interim contract was misplaced as the manual was not adopted as a regulation pursuant to the Administrative Procedure Act; and Government Code section 14615.1, which purports to exempt DGS from the requirements of the Administrative Procedure Act when acting under the State Contracting Manual, is invalid as it was enacted in violation of the single-subject rule of article IV, section 9 of the California Constitution.

We conclude section 6.05 of the State Contracting Manual gave CDF and DGS authority to enter into the interim contract while the bid protest was pending. Government Code section 14615.1 exempted DGS, in actions taken with respect to the State Contracting Manual, from the requirements of the Administrative Procedure Act and its enactment did not violate the single-subject rule. We affirm the judgment.

. . . .

DISCUSSION

I

. . . .

II

Generally, state agencies are required to secure competitive bids for contracts for services. (Pub. Contract Code, § 10340.) A service contract may be awarded without competitive bidding if it meets the conditions prescribed by DGS pursuant to section 10348, subdivision (a) of the Public Contract Code. (*Id.*, § 10340, subd. (a).) Regulations authorized by section 10348 were adopted and then repealed. (Cal. Code Regs., tit. 2, §§ 1896.200–1896.203.)

In entering into a single source contract with DynCorp during the bid protest, the State acted pursuant to section 6.05 of the State Contracting Manual, which permits a sole source contract in that situation "[i]f there is no existing contractor or if the contractor does not wish to continue." San Joaquin Helicopters contends that since section 6.05 of the State Contracting Manual was not adopted pursuant to the Administrative Procedure Act, it is without legal effect. (See *United Systems of Arkansas, Inc. v. Stamison* (1998) 63 Cal.App.4th 1001, 1008 [74 Cal.Rptr.2d 407] [provision of State Administrative Manual is a regulation subject to APA].) The State and DynCorp contend section 6.05 of the State Contracting Manual did not have to comply with the Administrative Procedure Act because it was expressly exempted by Government Code section 14615.1. San Joaquin Helicopters contends Government Code section 14615.1, which was originally enacted as part of Senet Bill 1645 in the 1998 session, is unconstitutional because its enactment violated the single-subject rule.

The single-subject rule is set forth in article IV, section 9 of the California Constitution, which provides in part as follows: "A statute shall embrace but one subject, which shall be expressed in its title. If a statute embraces a subject not expressed in its title, only the part not expressed is void." "The single subject rule essentially requires that a statute have only one subject matter and that the subject be clearly expressed in the statute's title. The rule's primary purpose is to prevent 'log-rolling' in the enactment of laws. This disfavored practice occurs when a provision unrelated to a bill's main subject matter and title is included in it with the hope that the provision will remain unnoticed and unchallenged. By invalidating these unrelated clauses, the single subject rule prevents the passage of laws that otherwise might not have passed had the legislative mind been directed to them. [Citation.]" (*Homan v. Gomez* (1995) 37 Cal.App.4th 597, 600 [43 Cal.Rptr.2d 647].)

The requirements of section 9 relating to the subject of an act and its title are independent provisions. "A statute must comply with both the requirement that it be confined to one subject and with the command that this one subject be expressed in its title. [Citations.]" (*Harbor v. Deukmejian* (1987) 43 Cal.3d 1078, 1096.) The title of Senate Bill 1645 is: "An act to amend Section 14664 of, and to add Section 14615.1 to, the Government Code, to add Article 6.5 (commencing with Section 10389.1) to Chapter 2 of Part 2 of Division 2 of the Public Contract Code, and to amend Section 2 of Chapter 625 of the Statutes of 1991, Section 1 of Chapter 648 of the Statutes of 1992, Section 1 of Chapter 317 of the Statutes of 1993, and Section 1 of Chapter 391 of the Statutes of 1994, relating to state property." (Stats. 1998, ch. 731.) San Joaquin Helicopters does not challenge the title.

The single-subject rule is not to receive a narrow or technical construction, but it is to be liberally construed to uphold proper legislation and not used to invalidate legitimate legislation. (*Evans v. Superior Court* (1932) 215 Cal. 58, 62 [8 P.2d 467].) "Numerous provisions, having one general object, if fairly indicated in the title, may be united in one act. Provisions governing projects so related and interdependent as to constitute a single scheme may be properly included within a single act. [Citation.] The legislature may insert in a single act all legislation germane to the general subject as expressed by its title and within the field of legislation suggested thereby. [Citation.] Provisions which are logically germane to the title of the act and are included within its scope may be united. The general purpose of a statute being declared, the details provided for its accomplishment will be regarded as necessary incidents. [Citations.] ... A provision which conduces to the act, or which is auxiliary to and promotive of its main purpose, or has a necessary and natural connection with such purpose is germane within the rule. [Citation.]" (*Id.* at pp. 62–63.) "[A] measure complies with the rule if its provisions are either functionally related to one another or are reasonably germane to one another or the objects of the enactment." (*Harbor v. Deukmejian, supra,* 43 Cal.3d 1078, 1100.)

There is a similar single-subject rule for initiatives. Article II, section 8, subdivision (d) of the California Constitution provides: "An initiative measure embracing more than one subject may not be submitted to the electors or have any effect." The reasonably germane test for the statutory single-subject rule is also applied to the initiative single-subject rule. (*Perry v. Jordan* (1949) 34 Cal.2d 87, 92–93 [207 P.2d 47].) Therefore, cases applying the rule to initiatives are useful in applying the single-subject rule to legislation.

Not only is a statute limited to a single subject, that subject cannot be one of excessive generality. In *Brosnahan v. Brown* (1982) 32 Cal.3d 236 [186 Cal.Rptr. 30, 651 P.2d 274], the Supreme Court upheld Proposition 8, known as The Victims' Bill of Rights, against a single-subject challenge. The court found each of its several facets was reasonably germane to the general subject of promoting the rights of actual or potential crime victims. (*Id.* at p. 247.) The court cautioned, however, that initiative proponents did not have a blank check to draft measures containing unduly diverse or extensive provisions bearing no reasonable relationship to each other or a general object. "The single-subject rule indeed is a constitutional safeguard adopted to protect against multifaceted measures of undue scope. For example, the rule obviously forbids joining disparate provisions which appear germane only to topics of excessive generality such as 'government' or 'public welfare.'" (*Id.* at p. 253.)

Bills or initiatives of excessive generality have been struck down because they violate the single-subject rule. In *Harbor v. Deukmejian, supra,* 43 Cal.3d 1078, the bill at issue was a trailer bill that amended, repealed or added approximately 150 sections to over 20 codes. The single subject of "fiscal affairs" or "'statutory adjustments'" was too broad to comply with the single-subject rule. (*Id.* at pp. 1100–1101.) A proposed initiative that would restrict legislative salaries and transfer reapportionment from the Legislature to the Supreme Court could not be upheld under the general subject of voter involvement or voter approval of political issues. (*Senate of the State of California v. Jones* (1999) 21 Cal.4th 1142, 1162–1163 [90 Cal.Rptr.2d 810 988 P.2d 1089].)

In *California Trial Lawyers Assn. v. Eu* (1988) 200 Cal.App.3d 351 [245 Cal.Rptr. 916], this court invalidated a proposed initiative for no fault insurance. Inconspicuously placed in the middle of a 120-page document were two provisions addressing campaign contributions and conflicts of interests of elected officials who receive such contributions. We found no connection between the stated purpose of the initiative to reign in increasing insurance premiums and these two provisions. (*Id.* at pp. 358–359.) That the initiative's provisions all had an effect on the business of insurance was insufficient to satisfy the reasonably germane test. "Contemporary society is structured in such a way that the need for and provision of insurance against hazards and losses pervades virtually every aspect of life. Association's approach would permit the joining of enactments so disparate as to render the constitutional single-subject limitation nugatory." (*Id.* at p. 360.)

An initiative designed to reduce toxic pollution, protect seniors from fraud and deceit in the issuance of insurance policies, raise health and safety standards in nursing homes, preserve the integrity of the election process, and fight apartheid violated the single-subject rule. (*Chemical Specialties Manufacturers Assn., Inc. v. Deukmejian* (1991) 227 Cal.App.3d 663.) The proponents' objective of providing the public with accurate information in advertising was too broad a subject, especially where the initiative required unrelated state agencies to take actions. (*Id.* at p. 671.)

While the single subject may not be one of excessive generality, a bill or initiative designed as comprehensive reform is allowable. In *Evans v. Superior Court, supra,* 215 Cal. 58, an act to establish a Probate Code, containing approximately 1700 sections and covering wills, succession, administration of estates, and wards and guardians complied with the single-subject rule as each provision was germane to and had a connection to probate law and procedure. (*Id.* at p. 64.) Various initiatives to accomplish comprehensive reform have also been upheld against a single-subject challenge. (See, e.g., *Amador Valley Joint Union High Sch. Dist. v. State Bd. of Equalization* (1978) 22 Cal.3d 208, 229–232 [upholding the Jarvis-Gann Initiative (Proposition 13)]; *Fair Political Practices Com. v. Superior Court* (1979) 25 Cal.3d 33, 41 [upholding Political Reform Act of 1974 (Proposition 9)]; *Brosnahan v. Brown, supra,* 32 Cal.3d 236, 245–253 [upholding the Victims' Bill of Rights (Proposition 8)]; *Raven v. Deukmejian* (1990) 52 Cal.3d 336, 346–349 [upholding Crime Victims Justice Reform Act of 1999 (Proposition 115)]; *Legislature v. Eu* (1991) 54 Cal.3d 492, 512–514 [upholding The Political Reform Act of 1990 (Proposition 140)].)

Budget bills that substantively change existing law violate the single-subject rule. "'''[T]he budget bill may deal only with one subject of appropriations to support the annual budget,'" and thus "'may not constitutionally be used to grant authority to a state agency that the agency does not otherwise possess'" or to "'substantively amend and change [e]xisting statute law.'"' [Citations.]" (*Planned Parenthood Affiliates v. Swoap* (1985) 173 Cal.App.3d 1187, 1199.) Thus, a section of a budget bill that restricted family planning funds for organizations that provided abortion-related services violated the single-subject rule. (*Id.* at p. 1201.) And a provision of a budget bill that excluded those convicted of certain sex crimes from receiving family visits in prison also violated the constitutional provision. (*Homan v. Gomez, supra,* 37 Cal.App.4th 597, 600–602.)

With the parameters of the single-subject rule in mind, we turn to the provisions of SB 1645. The first section of SB 1645, the one at issue here, adds section 14615.1 to the Government Code. That section exempts DGS from the Administrative Procedure Act in maintaining, developing, or prescribing processes, procedures, or policies in connection with the administration of its duties under certain provisions of the Government Code and the Public Contract Code. It applies to actions taken by DGS with respect to the State Administrative Manual and the State Contracting Manual. (Stats. 1998, ch. 731, § 1.) The other provisions of SB 1645 grant the director of DGS authority to sell, convey or exchange properties not needed by state agencies with the consent of the agency, require DGS to first offer surplus state personal property to school districts, authorize the director of DGS to sell, exchange or lease certain specified surplus state property, exempt certain of these transfers from the California Environmental Quality Act, require the reservation of certain mineral rights, and rescind the director's existing authority to sell, exchange, or lease specified parcels. (Stats. 1998, ch. 731, §§ 1.1–14.)

San Joaquin Helicopters contends the subject of the bill is limited to the disposal of surplus state property. The first section of SB 1645 violates the single-subject rule because it relates to an entirely different subject, exempting DGS from the Administrative Procedure Act in maintaining, developing or prescribing processes, procedures or policies. This exemption is not functionally related or reasonably germane to the disposal of surplus state property. (*Harbor v. Deukmejian, supra*, 43 Cal.3d 1078, 1100.) Further, San Joaquin Helicopters contends there is evidence of improper "logrolling" in the inclusion of Government Code section 14615.1 in SB 1645. First, section 14615.1 was added to SB 1645 only one week before the bill was passed by the Legislature. Second, the bill was referred to solely as the surplus property bill, even after it was passed, by both the bill's author and the Legislative Counsel's Digest.

The State and DynCorp respond first that San Joaquin Helicopters ignores the strong presumption in favor of finding a statute constitutional. (*County of Sonoma v. State Energy Resources Conservation etc. Com.* (1985) 40 Cal.3d 361, 368.) "In considering the constitutionality of a legislative act we presume its validity, resolving all doubts in favor of the Act. Unless conflict with a provision of the state or federal Constitution is clear and unquestionable, we must uphold the Act. [Citations.]" (*California Housing Finance Agency v. Elliott* (1976) 17 Cal.3d 575, 594 [131 Cal.Rptr. 361, 551 P.2d 1193].)

Second, the single-subject rule "is not to receive a narrow or technical construction in all cases, but is to be construed liberally to uphold proper legislation, all parts of which are reasonably germane. [Citation.] The provision was not enacted to provide means for the overthrow of legitimate legislation. [Citation.]" (*Evans v. Superior Court, supra*, 215 Cal. at p. 62.)

Presuming SB 1645 is a constitutional enactment and giving the single-subject rule a liberal construction, the subject of SB 1645 can be viewed as the operation and administration of DGS with respect to state property. Government Code section 14615.1, which exempts DGS processes, procedures and policies from the Administrative Procedure Act, is reasonably germane to this general subject. The operation and administration of DGS with respect to state property is not a subject of excessive generality like government, public welfare, fiscal affairs, the business of insurance, or truth in advertising. It is limited to one state agency and its functions with respect to a certain type of property, state property. While most contracts for supplies, services and construction relate directly to state property (as here, maintenance for state aircraft), it is true that some service contracts may not relate to state property, such as the provision of services for indigents or prisoners. "'[I]t is well established that a [measure] may have "collateral effects" without violating the single-subject rule. [Citations.]' [Citation.]" (*Manduley v. Superior Court* (2002) 27 Cal.4th 537, 578 [117

Cal.Rptr.2d 168, 41 P.3d 3] [upholding the Gang Violence and Juvenile Crime Prevention Act of 1998 (Proposition 21) despite the collateral effect of changes to the lock-in date for determining strike offenses.])

Nor do we find persuasive San Joaquin Helicopters' evidence of "log-rolling." The addition of Government Code section 14615.1 occurred late in the legislative process, only one week before the bill was passed. But as the trial judge, a former legislator, noted: "A week is a century in the Legislature." More importantly, the provision was not hidden, as were the provisions for campaign contributions and conflicts of interest in *California Trial Lawyers Assn. v. Eu, supra*, 200 Cal.App.3d 351. The addition of Government Code section 14615.1 was prominently featured as the first section of the bill. It was clearly described in the Legislative Counsel's Digest: "This bill would provide that the processes, procedures, or policies maintained, developed, or prescribed by the department in connection with the administration of its duties under specified provisions of the Public Contract Code or the State Contract Act shall be exempt from the Administrative Procedure Act, including actions taken by the department with respect to the State Administrative Manual and the State Contracting Manual." (Stats. 1998, ch. 731.)

The enactment of Government Code section 14625.1 as part of SB 1465 did not violate the constitutional single-subject rule.

III

San Joaquin Helicopters contends that even if Government Code section 14615.1, as originally enacted, did not violate the single-subject rule, the State still could not rely on that statute to exempt section 6.05 of the State Contracting Manual from the Administrative Procedure Act. That is so because the original version of Government Code section 14615.1 applied only to the State Contract Act, which governs public works projects, and not contracts for services. In 2000, Government Code section 14615.1 was amended to apply the exemption to all contracts under part 2 division 2 of the Public Contract Code, not just public works contracts under the State Contract Act.

As originally enacted, Government Code section 14615.1 provided: "Where the Legislature directs or authorizes the department to maintain, develop, or prescribe processes, procedures, or policies in connection with the administration of its duties under this chapter, Chapter 2 (commencing with Section 14650), *or the State Contract Act (Part 2 (commencing with Section 10100) of Division 2 of the Public Contract Code)*, the action by the department shall be exempt from the Administrative Procedure Act (Chapter 3.5 (commencing with Section 11340), Chapter 4 (commencing with Section 11370), Chapter 4.5 (commencing with Section 11400), and Chapter 5 (commencing with Section 11500)). This section shall apply to actions taken by the department with respect to the State Administrative Manual and the State Contracting Manual." (Stats. 1998, ch. 731, § 1, italics added.)

San Joaquin's [sic] Helicopters' argument is based on the publishers' titles in the annotated versions (both West's and Deering's) of the Public Contract Code. Part 2 of division 2 of the Public Contract Code is entitled "Contracting by State Agencies." It consists of several chapters. Chapter 1 (Pub. Contract Code, §§ 10100–10265) is entitled "State Contract Act" and deals with public works projects. Chapter 2 (Pub. Contract Code, § 10290 et seq.) provides for state procurement of materials, supplies, equipment, and services. The contract at issue here falls under chapter 2. In 2000, Government Code section 14615.1 was amended. (Stats. 2000, ch. 590, § 4.) The amendment deleted the reference to the State Contract Act and instead referred only to "Part 2 (commencing with Section 10100) of Division 2 of the Public Contract Code." (*Ibid.*)

San Joaquin Helicopters contends that since the original version of Government Code section 14615.1 referred expressly to "the State Contract Act," it referred only to chapter 1 of part 2 of division 2 of the Public Contract Code. Thus, the exemption from the Administrative Procedure Act was not available to actions taken under section 6.05 of the State Contracting Manual with respect to a contract for services.

San Joaquin Helicopters further contends the enactment of the amendment to Government Code section 14615.1 violated the single-subject rule because it was included in a bill, SB 2066, that otherwise dealt exclusively with school facilities.

The trial court found it unnecessary to determine if the amendment to Government Code section 14615.1, SB 2066, violated the single-subject rule. The court concluded the amendment was only a technical correction to clean up the language and not to make a substantive change. Government Code section 14615.1, as originally enacted, applied to all of part 2 of division 2 of the Public Contract Code, not just chapter 1. Finding the legislative history unhelpful on this issue, the court relied primarily on the conclusion there was no rational basis to limit Government Code section 14615.1 to only chapter 1.

"Initially, '[a]s in any case of statutory interpretation, our task is to determine afresh the intent of the Legislature by construing in context the language of the statute.' [Citation.] In determining such intent, we begin with the language of the statute itself. [Citation.] That is, we look first to the words the Legislature used, giving them their usual and ordinary meaning. [Citation.] 'If there is no ambiguity in the language of the statute, "then the Legislature is presumed to have meant what it said, and the plain meaning of the language governs."' [Citation.] 'But when the statutory language is ambiguous, "the court may examine the context in which the language appears, adopting the construction that best harmonizes the statute internally and with related statutes."' [Citation.]" (*People v. Superior Court* (*Zamudio*) (2000) 23 Cal.4th 183, 192–193 [96 Cal.Rptr.2d 463, 999 P.2d 873].)

San Joaquin Helicopters contends there is no ambiguity in the statute; it clearly refers only to the State Contract Act or chapter 1. Since we must seek to give meaning to every word (*Harris v. Capital Growth Investors XIV* (1991) 52 Cal.3d 1142, 1159 [278 Cal.Rptr. 614, 805 P.2d 873]), the original version of Government Code section 14615.1 must be limited to the State Contract Act and the amendment made a substantive change.

We agree that the literal language of Government Code section 14615.1 as originally enacted is not ambiguous. We disagree, however, as to what the reference to "the State Contract Act" means. Based on the publishers' titles in the annotated codes, San Joaquin Helicopters asserts it means only Chapter 1. It is well established, however, that the publishers' titles are unofficial and not part of the act as adopted by the Legislature. (*People v. Avanessian* (1999) 76 Cal.App.4th 635, 641–642 [90 Cal.Rptr.2d 367] and fn. 6.) "Title or chapter headings are unofficial and do not alter the explicit scope, meaning, or intent of a statute. [Citations.]" (*DaFonte v. Up-Right, Inc.* (1992) 2 Cal.4th 593, 602 [7 Cal.Rptr.2d 238, 828 P.2d 140].) In contrast to the publishers' titles, Public Contract Code section 10100 provides: "This *part* may be cited as the State Contract Act." (Italics added.) The Legislature gave the title "State Contract Act" to the part, not the chapter. While part 2 contained only one chapter when originally enacted (Stats. 1981, ch. 306, § 2, pp. 1434–1447), section 10100 literally applies to the entire part 2. Thus, the Legislature's reference to the "State Contract Act" refers to all of part 2 of division 2 and there is no ambiguity or conflict in this reference in Government Code section 14615.1.

This plain meaning interpretation of Government Code section 14615.1 — that it applies to all of part 2 of division 2 of the Public Contract Code — is reinforced by the statutory scheme. Government Code section 14615.1 applies to the duties of DGS under two specified chapters of the Government Code, as well as portions of the Public Contract code. These two chapters in the Government Code are "General Provisions" (Gov. Code, § 14600 et seq.), including the designation of a procurement officer in DGS (Gov. Code, § 14620), and "*Powers and Duties, Generally*" (Gov. Code, § 14650 et seq.; original italics). Since these two chapters cover the broad range of duties of DGS, it is reasonable to conclude the reference to duties under the Public Contract Code was also intended to be broad.

The reference to the State Contracting Manual supports this view. The last sentence of section 14615.1 provides: "This section shall apply to actions taken by the department with respect to the State Administrative Manual and the State Contracting Manual." (Gov. Code, § 14615.1.) The State Contracting Manual states that it "deals primarily with services, consultant services contracts, and interagency agreements." While the manual does apply to certain small public works projects, it is unlikely the Legislature would have made specific reference to exempting actions under the State Contracting Manual if the exemption applied in only a very few cases.

DynCorp has provided selected portions of the State Administrative Manual and the State Contracting Manual and requested that we take judicial notice of them, as well as of certain bills. We grant DynCorp's motion. (Evid. Code, §§ 452, subd. (c); 459, subd. (a).) We also grant the State's motion for judicial notice. (Evid. Code, §§ 452; 459, subd. (a).)

The background of the statute also supports the interpretation offered by the State and DynCorp. Three months before SB 1645 was passed, this court issued its decision in *United Systems of Arkansas, Inc. v. Stamison, supra,* 63 Cal.App.4th 1001. We held the State could not rely on a provision of the State Administrative Manual that changed the protest procedures for bids for electronic data processing goods and services because that provision was a regulation and it had not been adopted in accordance with the Administrative Procedure Act. (*Id.* at pp. 1007–1012.) The enactment of Government Code section 14615.1, exempting DGS from the Administrative Procedure Act in actions taken under the State Administrative Manual and the State Contracting Manual, appears to be a direct legislative response to our decision. Since the contract at issue in United Systems of Arkansas was not a public works contract, the reasonable interpretation is that the Legislature intended the exemption from the Administrative Procedure Act to be broader so as to cover contracts such as the one at issue in United Systems of Arkansas.

Finally, the legislative history of SB 2066 shows that in analyses of the bill the amendment to Government Code section 14615.1 was referred to simply as a technical correction. While the view of a subsequent Legislature is not dispositive of the intent of a previous Legislature, it certainly lends support in determining the reasonable interpretation.

San Joaquin Helicopters contends the 1998 version of Government Code section 14615.1 cannot apply to all of part 2 of division 2 of the Public Contract Code because such an interpretation would require a disfavored implied repeal of Public Contract Code section 10383.8. Section 10383.8 is contained in article 5.5 of chapter 2 of part 2 of division 2 of the Public Contract Code. It provides that DGS may make rules and regulations as necessary to carry out its duties with respect to federal surplus personal property. Those regulations are to be adopted in accordance with the Administrative Procedure Act. (Pub. Contract Code, § 10383.8.) San Joaquin Helicopters contends that if Government Code section 14615.1 applies to chapter 2 and exempts regulations thereunder from the Administrative Procedure Act, it directly conflicts with and thus must repeal by implication the provisions of Public Contract Code section 10383.8.

San Joaquin Helicopters ignores that under its analysis there must be a repeal by implication, either by the 1998 version of Government Code section 14615.1 or the 2000 version, which unquestionably applies to chapter 2. Since a disfavored repeal by implication cannot be avoided, there is no reason to adopt its interpretation of the proper scope of the 1998 version. In any event, it is unnecessary to find a repeal by implication under either version of Government Code section 14615.1. Public Contract Code section 10383.8 and Government Code section 14615.1 can be harmonized under the rules applying to specific and general statutes. Public Contract Code section 10383.8 is a more specific statute and thus its provisions as to regulations for federal surplus personal property are an exception to the more general provisions of Government Code section 14615.1. (*Medical Board v. Superior Court* (2001) 88 Cal.App.4th 1001, 1018 [106 Cal.Rptr.2d 381].)

The plain meaning and the reasonable interpretation of the 1998 version of Government Code section 14615.1 is that the Legislature meant the entire part 2 of division 2 of the Public Contract Code by its reference to "the State Contract Act," and intended the section to apply to the duties of DGS under all of part 2 of division 2 of the Public

Contract Code. Since Government Code section 14615.1 was validly enacted as part of SB 1645, the State could rely on it to exempt section 6.05 of the State Contracting Manual from the requirements of the Administrative Procedure Act.

San Joaquin Helicopters asserts the amendment to Government Code section 14615.1 violated the single-subject rule and complains that the State and DynCorp offer no authority for the proposition that a technical amendment need not comply with the single-subject rule. First, since we have concluded that the 1998 version of Government Code section 14615.1 applied to chapter 2, the State need not rely on the 2000 amendment. Second, the primary purpose of the single-subject rule is to prevent log-rolling, the passage of laws that might otherwise not have passed if considered singly. (*Homan v. Gomez, supra*, 37 Cal.App.4th 597, 600.) An amendment that makes no substantive change in the law is not susceptible to log-rolling since there is no reason to oppose a technical correction. In short, such an amendment has no "subject" to analyze under the single-subject rule. (Cf. *Association for Retarded Citizens v. Department of Developmental Services* (1985) 38 Cal.3d 384, 394 [211 Cal.Rptr. 758, 696 P.2d 150] [budget bill may not substantively amend and change existing law].)

. . . .

DISPOSITION

The judgment is affirmed.

We concur: SCOTLAND, P.J., BLEASE, J.

Notes and Questions

1. The single subject rule is not to receive a narrow or technical construction, but it is to be liberally construed to uphold proper legislation and not used to invalidate legitimate legislation. Budget bills that substantively change existing law violate the single subject rule. The budget bill may deal only with one subject of appropriations to support the annual budget and thus may not constitutionally be used to grant authority to a state agency that the agency does not otherwise possess or to substantively amend and change existing statutory law.

2. The single subject rule essentially requires that a statute have only one subject matter and that the subject be clearly expressed in the statute's title. Provisions governing projects so related and interdependent as to constitute a single scheme may be properly included within a single act. The Legislature may insert in a single act all legislation germane to the general subject as expressed by its title and within the field of legislation suggested thereby without violating the single subject rule.

3. The plaintiff believed the provisions of the State Contracting Manual had to be adopted pursuant to the Administrative Procedure Act, and the failure to do so would make the changes have no legal effect. What was the basis for the court's ruling against this claim?

4. The court noted prior appellate court decisions that ruled, "Budget bills that substantively change existing law violate the single-subject rule." Should that be the rule in all instances? Can you think of an appropriate exception to this stringent rule?

5. Did San Joaquin Helicopters take a narrow view of the single-subject rule? Did the APA exemption constitute "an entirely different subject" from the surplus land provisions of the act?

6. The court noted that. "'[I]t is well established that a [measure] may have "collateral effects" without violating the single-subject rule.'" How well defined are "collateral effects"? Does this term provide sufficient guidance to the Legislature in its efforts to comply with the constitutionally-mandated single subject rule?

7. This case includes a statutory construction analysis regarding the title of the act that was amended by the bill central to the dispute in this case. Was it as clear as the court stated, "Thus, the Legislature's reference to the 'State Contract Act' refers to all of part 2 of division 2 and there is no ambiguity or conflict in this reference in Government Code section 14615.1"?

H. Line-Item Veto

1. California Governor's Line-Item Veto Authority

Article IV of the California Constitution concerns the legislative branch of government. However, it also describes powers of the Governor and the role that he or she plays in the legislative process. Specifically, Section 10 of Article IV deals with legislation and the authority of the state's chief executive.

Of particular interest is Subdivision (e) which grants the Governor line-item veto authority for the budget and appropriations bills. While the Governor of California has this authority, the President of the United States does not have such authority. The following is the language of this constitutional subdivision:

> (e) The Governor may reduce or eliminate one or more items of appropriation while approving other portions of a bill. The Governor shall append to the bill a statement of the items reduced or eliminated with the reasons for the action. The Governor shall transmit to the house originating the bill a copy of the statement and reasons. Items reduced or eliminated shall be separately reconsidered and may be passed over the Governor's veto in the same manner as bills.

As a result of this constitutional grant of authority, the Governor has the authority to (1) reduce a line-item or (2) eliminate the item of spending entirely. In the budget bill, which is the only measure that has multiple appropriations, the Governor can reduce or eliminate line items of the state budget and still approve the budget bill in chief.

Just as with other bills that the Governor may veto, he or she must explain the reason for his or her veto and follow the same process used for other vetoed bills. Subdivision (a) of Section 10 provides for the veto of bills, explaining that the Governor must return the bill to its house of origin with any objections to the bill. If

2/3 majorities of both houses vote to override the veto, then the bill becomes a statute.

So, too, any budget or appropriations bills in which items of spending were reduced or eliminated may be subject to a veto override, and the items reduced or eliminated must be separately considered for purposes of a veto override. If the veto override is successful, then the reduced or eliminated appropriation is restored as approved by the Legislature.

Notes and Questions

1. The governor is not empowered to decide how many subjects are contained in a bill presented to him for signature and to veto parts of a bill which he determines constitute separate subjects. (*Harbor v. Deukmejian* (1987) 43 Cal.3d 1078, rehearing denied.)

I. Appropriations Measures

1. What Is an Appropriations Measure?

What is an "appropriations measure"? Unfortunately, California law does not define this term. However, it is used frequently. California's Legislative Counsel defines an appropriation as "the amount of money made available for expenditure by a specific entity for a specific purpose, from the General Fund or other designated state fund or account."

California's Constitution Article IV, Sections 8 and 10 note "appropriations for the usual current expenses of the State." Section 12 of Article IV mentions "appropriations for the salaries and expenses of the Legislature." Nonetheless, the state Constitution does not define the term. Appropriation is used in numerous other articles of the California Constitution and throughout many of the codes, again without definition.

The common definition of an appropriation bill, sometimes called a spending bill, is essentially any measure that authorizes or makes an expenditure of government funds. It requires adoption by the Legislature and approval by the Governor for purposes of appropriating state dollars.

In California, the main appropriations measure is the annual state budget bill. Article IV, Section 12(d) provides that the budget bill is the only measure that may contain more than one item of appropriation. In addition, appropriations from the General Fund of the State, except appropriations for the public schools and appropriations in the budget and trailer bills that make appropriations related to the budget bill, must be passed by a 2/3 majority vote of both houses of the Legislature.

Notes and Questions

1. Should the California Constitution be amended to provide a definition for "appropriation"? Should the Legislature provide a statutory definition for the term?

St. John's Well Child & Family Center v. Schwarzenegger

(2010) 50 Cal.4th 960

OPINION

GEORGE, C.J. —

We granted review in this original writ proceeding to address the propriety of the Governor's use of the so-called "line-item veto" under the asserted authority of article IV, section 10, subdivision (e) of the California Constitution, to further reduce funding that already had been reduced by the Legislature in its midyear adjustments to the Budget Act of 2009. The Court of Appeal, First Appellate District, Division Two, denied the requested writ of mandate and upheld the Governor's action. Upon review, we agree with that court's disposition of the matter. Because the Court of Appeal's decision (by Kline, P.J., with Lambden & Richman, JJ., concurring) persuasively sets forth and analyzes the issues presented by this case, we adopt substantial parts of it as our own, as modified below to fully reflect our views and to address the arguments that differ from those advanced in the appellate court.

I.

. . . .

In the context of the constitutionally prescribed budget process, the power to *appropriate* public funds belongs exclusively to the Legislature. With respect to a bill containing appropriations, the Governor has three options: (1) to sign the bill, (2) to veto the measure in its entirety (Cal. Const., art. IV, § 10, subd. (a)), or (3) to "*reduce or eliminate one or more items of appropriation*" (*id.*, subd. (e) (hereafter article IV, section 10(e)), italics added). The question posed by this case is whether the Governor exceeded his limited powers under article IV, section 10(e), by using his line-item authority to further reduce funding levels set forth in midyear reductions that the Legislature had made to the Budget Act of 2009 (Stats. 2009, 3d Ex. Sess. 2009–2010, ch. 1, approved by Governor, Feb. 20, 2009) (hereafter 2009 Budget Act), thereby imposing a reduction of appropriated sums greater than the reduction made by the Legislature.

Petitioners and interveners contend that the action taken by the Governor exceeded constitutional limits, because the individual budget cuts he made were not imposed on "items of appropriation" (art. IV, § 10(e)) that could be individually vetoed or reduced. They further contend that, in taking this action, the Governor purported to exercise authority belonging solely to the Legislature, in violation of article III, section 3 of the California Constitution.

Petitioners and interveners sought original relief in the Court of Appeal (pursuant to Cal. Const., art. VI, § 10; Code Civ. Proc., §§ 387, 1085; & Cal. Rules of Court, rule 8.485 et seq.) to enjoin the Controller from enforcing or taking any steps to enforce the Governor's actions concerning certain provisions of Assembly Bill No. 1 (2009–2010 4th Ex. Sess.) (hereafter Assembly Bill 4X 1), as revised by the Governor's line-item reduction of funding with regard to those provisions. (See Assem. Bill 4X 1, as amended by Sen., July 23, 2009, and approved by Governor, July 28, 2009 [with certain deletions, revisions, and reductions (hereafter Governor's July 28 Message)], enacted as Stats. 2009, 4th Ex. Sess. 2009–2010, ch. 1 (hereafter revised 2009 Budget Act).) Because of the importance and urgency of the issues presented, the Court of Appeal exercised its original jurisdiction (*Legislature v. Eu* (1991) 54 Cal.3d 492, 500; *Raven v. Deukmejian* (1990) 52 Cal.3d 336, 340....)

II.

On February 20, 2009, the Governor signed into law the 2009 Budget Act, which set forth various appropriations of state funds for the 2009–2010 fiscal year. Thereafter, California's economy worsened; the revenue assumptions upon which the 2009 Budget Act was based proved to be far too optimistic, and the state's overall cash-flow positions continued to deteriorate. The Governor, pursuant to California Constitution, article IV, section 10, subdivision (f) proclaimed a fiscal crisis, and the Legislature assembled in special session to address the fiscal emergency. Following months of negotiations, the Legislature passed Assembly Bill 4X 1 on July 23, 2009. The final revised budget package enacted as Assembly Bill 4X 1 consisted of 547 pages, set forth in 583 sections, and represented an effort to address more than $24 billion in budget shortfalls, including $15.6 billion in cuts, nearly $4 billion in additional revenues, more than $2 billion in borrowing, approximately $1.5 billion in fund shifts, and more than $1 billion in deferrals and other adjustments.

On July 28, 2009, the Governor exercised his line-item authority to reduce or eliminate several items contained in Assembly Bill 4X 1, and then signed the measure into law. (Rev. 2009 Budget Act.) The Governor eliminated numerous separate line items contained in various sections of Assembly Bill 4X 1. The effect of these reductions was to further decrease the total amount appropriated in the 2009 Budget Act by more than $488 million. Many of the items reduced by the Governor already had been reduced by the Legislature in Assembly Bill 4X 1 from the amounts appropriated in the 2009 Budget Act. The Governor's signing message explained that his cuts to the spending bill were for the most part designed "to increase the reserve and to reduce the state's structural deficit." (Governor's July 28 Message [concerning Assem. Bill 4X 1, §§ 18.00, 18.10, 18.20, 18.40]; see also *id.* [same, concerning §§ 17.50, 18.50].) This original mandamus proceeding by petitioners and interveners followed, challenging the Governor's use of line-item reductions with respect to seven sections of Assembly Bill 4X 1 — specifically, section 568 and sections 570 through 575....

III.

The question presented by this case as a matter of first impression is whether, after the Legislature has made midyear reductions to appropriations that originally appeared in the 2009 Budget Act, the Governor's line-item power encompasses the authority to make further reductions. Although this particular issue is novel, we find guidance in our decision in *Harbor v. Deukmejian* (1987) 43 Cal.3d 1078 (*Harbor*), in which we extensively described the constitutional framework within which a Governor exercises his or her line-item authority.

"The California Constitution declares that the legislative power of the state is vested in the Legislature (art. IV, § 1) and the executive power [is vested] in the Governor (art. [V], § 1). Unless permitted by the Constitution, the Governor may not exercise legislative powers. (Art. III, § 3.) He may veto a bill 'by returning it with any objections to the house of origin' and it will become law only if 'each house then passes the bill by rollcall vote ... two thirds of the membership concurring....' [Art. IV, § 10, subd. (a).] If the Governor fails to act within a certain period of time, the measure becomes law without his signature. (Art. IV, § 10, subd. [(b)].) The Governor's veto power is more extensive with regard to appropriations. *He may 'reduce or eliminate one or more items of appropriation while approving other portions of a bill.'* Such items may be passed over his veto in the same manner as vetoed bills. (Art. IV, § 10, subd. [(e)].)" (*Harbor, supra,* 43 Cal.3d at p. 1084, italics added.)

Our decision in *Harbor,* agreeing with the petitioners in that case, observed: "[I]n vetoing legislation, the Governor acts in a legislative capacity, and ... in order to preserve the system of checks and balances upon which our government is founded, he may exercise legislative power only in the manner expressly authorized by the Constitution." (*Harbor, supra,* 43 Cal.3d at p. 1084.) Because the Constitution authorizes the Governor only "to veto a 'bill' or to reduce or eliminate 'items of appropriation[,]' the Governor may not veto part of a bill which is not an 'item of appropriation.'" (*Ibid.*)

After tracking the historical development of the veto power from its origins in Rome, where the tribune of plebeians had the power to disapprove measures recommended by the senate, we explained in *Harbor* that "[t]he word, 'veto' means 'I forbid' in Latin. Then, as now, the effect of the veto was negative, frustrating an act without substituting anything in its place." (*Harbor, supra,* 43 Cal.3d at p. 1085, citing Zinn, The Veto Power of the President (1951) 12 F.R.D. 209.) After evolving in the United States as "an integral part of the system of checks and balances" (*Harbor,* at p. 1085), the veto power at the federal level has been circumscribed by the limitation that the President may approve or reject a bill in its entirety, but may not select portions of a bill for disapproval. "As a much-quoted early case commented, 'the executive, in every republican form of government, has only a qualified and destructive legislative function, and never creative legislative power.' (*State v. Holder* (1898) 23 So. 643, 645.)" (*Harbor,* at p. 1086.) Significantly, although "the rule prohibiting selective exercise of the veto is unyielding in the federal system, most states have provided an exception for items of appropriation." (*Ibid.*; see *Thirteenth Guam Legislature v. Bordallo* (D. Guam 1977) 430 F.Supp. 405, 410.)

"In California, the Constitution of 1849 included a gubernatorial veto provision similar to that contained in the United States Constitution. (Cal. Const. of 1849, art. IV, § 17....) The Constitution of 1879 added the item veto power, allowing the Governor to 'object to one or more items' of appropriation in a bill which contained several 'items of appropriation.' (Cal. Const. of 1879, art. IV, § 16.) By constitutional initiative in 1922, the Governor was empowered *not only to eliminate 'items of appropriation' but to reduce them,* while approving other portions of a bill. (Art. IV, § 10, subd. ([e]).) The 1922 amendment also directed the Governor to submit a budget to the Legislature containing his recommendation for state expenditures. (Art. IV, § 12, subd. (a).)" (*Harbor, supra,* 43 Cal.3d at p. 1086, italics added.)

The ballot argument in favor of the 1922 constitutional initiative that empowered the Governor to exercise line-item authority to reduce an item of appropriation stated in relevant part: "The budget system will save the taxpayer money, because all state appropriations will be handled in a business way, duplications prevented and extravagance avoided. *The proposed measure will also enable the Governor to reduce an appropriation to meet the financial condition of the treasury,* which under our present system he cannot do. Frequently a worthy measure is vetoed because the legislature passes a bill carrying an appropriation for which sufficient funds are not available. Under present conditions the Governor is compelled to veto the act, no matter how meritorious, because of the excessive appropriation, whereas, if he had the power given by the proposed constitutional amendment, he could approve the bill with a modified appropriation to meet the condition of the treasury." (Ballot Pamp., Gen. Elec. (Nov. 7, 1922) argument in favor of Prop. 12, pp. 78–79, italics added.)

Neither the so-called "item veto," nor the "line-item veto" allowing the Governor to eliminate or reduce items of appropriation, confers the power to selectively veto *general* legislation. (*Harbor, supra,* 43 Cal.3d at p. 1087; *Lukens v. Nye* (1909) 156 Cal. 498, 501–503.) The Governor has no authority to veto part of a bill that is not an "item of appropriation." (*Harbor,* at pp. 1084–1085, 1088–1089.) "[A]rticle III, section 3 provides that one branch of government may not exercise the powers granted to another 'except as permitted by this Constitution.' Case law, commentators, and historians have long recognized that in exercising the veto the Governor acts in a legislative capacity. [Citations.] ... [¶] It follows that in exercising the power of the veto the Governor may act only as permitted by the Constitution. That authority is to veto a 'bill' (art. IV, § 10, subd. (a)) or to 'reduce or eliminate one or more items of appropriation' (*id.,* subd. ([e]).)" (*Harbor, supra,* 43 Cal.3d at pp. 1088–1089.)

The dispositive issue, then, is whether the funding in question — specified in the seven sections of Assembly Bill 4X 1 that the Governor further reduced — encompassed "items of appropriation" (Cal. Const., art. IV, § 10(e)) as to which the Governor could exercise his line-item authority.

IV.

Petitioners and interveners contend that, because the items at issue in Assembly Bill 4X 1 *reduced* the amounts previously appropriated in the 2009 Budget Act, these items were not "appropriations." They maintain that a "reduction" cannot be an "appropriation," and observe that there are no instances in which a California governor previously has exercised line-item authority in this manner.

Subsequent to the passage of the 1922 constitutional amendment empowering the Governor to exercise line-item authority, we addressed in two significant decisions the question of what constitutes an "item of appropriation" subject to the Governor's line-item power. (*Harbor, supra,* 43 Cal.3d 1078; *Wood v. Riley* (1923) 192 Cal. 293.) We review these cases for guidance.

A.

1.

Wood v. Riley, supra, 192 Cal. 293, was decided in 1923, shortly after the Constitution was amended to allow the Governor to use line-item authority to reduce as well as to eliminate "items of appropriation." That case involved the Legislature's action of adding to a budget bill a proviso requiring the Controller to transfer to the state Department of Education, as an additional administrative allotment for the department, 1 percent of the appropriations that had been set aside for salaries and support of several teachers' colleges and special schools. (*Wood v. Riley,* at pp. 294–296.) The Governor vetoed this set-aside proviso. (*Id.,* at p. 296.) The Director of Education sought to enforce the proviso, notwithstanding the Governor's disapproval, arguing that the Governor had attempted to veto part of a sentence in an appropriation bill that did not appropriate money, but that simply provided for a transfer, as a matter of bookkeeping, of a percentage of funds already appropriated. (*Id.,* at p. 297; see *Harbor, supra,* 43 Cal.3d at p. 1091, fn. 13.) We upheld the exercise of the veto, finding that *although the set-aside proviso took no new money from the state treasury,* the proviso nevertheless constituted "*a specific setting aside of an amount, not exceeding a definite fixed sum, for the payment of certain particular claims or demands....* It appears in no other light than as amounting to an item of appropriation in that it adds an additional amount to the funds already provided for the administration of the office of the director of education through the sums appropriated for the use of the state board of education and the superintendent of public instruction. This court has held that 'by a specific appropriation' was understood 'an Act by which a named sum of money has been set apart in the treasury and devoted to the payment of a particular claim or demand[.] ... The proviso, therefore, appears to fill all the requirements of *a distinct item of appropriation of so much of a definite sum of money as may be required for a designated purpose connected with the state government.*" (*Wood v. Riley, supra,* 192 Cal. at pp. 303–304, italics added.)

This court also was persuaded that the Legislature had sought to insulate from the veto an additional appropriation for the "general administrative office" within the department—something the Legislature would have had no authority to do had it directly appropriated funds for that office. (*Wood v. Riley, supra,* 192 Cal. at pp. 304–305.) We explained: "It is very clear that the situation presented is that no appropriation having been recommended by the Governor, or included in the proposed budget bill, for the payment of the 'salaries and support of the general administrative office of the division of normal and special schools,' other than the general provisions for the support of the state board of education and the state superintendent of schools, the legislature attempted, by the inclusion of the proviso in the bill, to make such additional appropriation for such purpose under the guise of an administrative allotment. Therefore, looked at in the light of what it was intended to accomplish, and what it would have accomplished if allowed to stand, one cannot escape the conviction that it worked an appropriation. It added a specific amount to the allowance already made for the use of the state board of education and the state superintendent of schools." (*Ibid.*) We concluded the Legislature could not "by indirection, defeat the purpose of the constitutional amendment giving the Governor power to control the expenditures of the state, when it could not accomplish that purpose directly or by an express provision in appropriation bills." (*Id.,* at p. 305.) In other words, we determined in *Wood v. Riley* that a provision that took no additional funds from the state treasury nevertheless constituted an "appropriation" under the newly adopted constitutional provision — and hence that this provision was subject to the Governor's proper exercise of his line-item authority.

2.

. . . .

On review, we held that the Governor's purported veto of section 45.5 of the trailer bill, relating to timing of the benefits, was unauthorized, because this provision was not an "item of appropriation," and hence the Governor could not selectively veto the item without vetoing the entire bill. (*Harbor, supra,* 43 Cal.3d at pp. 1090–1091.) In making the determination that section 45.5 was not an "item of appropriation," we recognized that "[t]he term has been defined in various ways. *Wood v. Riley, supra,* 192 Cal. 293, 303, defines it as 'a specific setting aside of an amount, not exceeding a definite sum, for the payment of certain particular claims or demands ... not otherwise expressly provided for in the appropriation bill.' It 'adds an additional amount to the funds already provided.' In *Bengzon* [*v. Secretary of Justice* (1937) 299 U.S. 410] the term was described as a bill whose 'primary and specific aim ... is to make appropriations of money from the public treasury.' (299 U.S. 410 at p. 413.) Other cases employ somewhat different definitions (e.g., *Jessen Associates, Inc. v. Bullock* (Tex. 1975) 531 S.W.2d 593, 599 ['setting aside or dedicating of funds for a specified purpose']; *Commonwealth v. Dodson* (1940) 176 Va. 281 [11 S.E.2d 120, 127] ['an indivisible sum of money dedicated to a stated purpose'])." (*Harbor, supra,* 43 Cal.3d at p. 1089.)

We determined that the provision at issue did not qualify "as an item of appropriation under any of these definitions. It does not set aside money for the payment of any claim and makes no appropriation from the public treasury, nor does it add any additional amount to funds already provided for. Its effect is substantive. Like thousands of other statutes, it directs that a department of government act in a particular manner with regard to certain matters. Although as is common with countless other measures, the direction contained therein will require the expenditure of funds from the treasury, this does not transform a substantive measure to an item of appropriation. We agree with petitioners that section 45.5 only expresses the Legislature's intention that the AFDC appropriation, whatever its amount, must be used to provide benefits to recipients from the date of application under certain circumstances." (*Harbor, supra,* 43 Cal.3d at pp. 1089–1090.)

We proceeded to reject the Governor's complaint that the Legislature had attempted to separate the appropriation and its purpose into discrete measures in order to evade a veto of the entire indivisible measure. (*Harbor, supra,* 43 Cal.3d at pp. 1090–1091.) We observed: "Both were specified in the [1984] Budget Act, that is, over $1.5 billion was appropriated for the purpose of funding AFDC. The Governor is bound by this 'purpose' as set forth in the budget. If the Legislature chooses to budget by a lump sum appropriation, [the Governor] may eliminate or reduce the amount available for the purpose as set forth therein. Here, the Governor not only reduced the 'item of appropriation' as set forth in the budget, but he divided it into its supposed component parts, assigned a purpose and amount to the part he disapproved, reduced the total by that amount, and attempted to veto a portion of a substantive bill which he claims contains the 'subject of the appropriation.' We are aware of no authority that even remotely supports the attempted exercise of the veto in this manner." (*Id.,* at pp. 1090–1091.)

Finally, we concluded that even the Legislature's attempt to avoid the Governor's veto did not provide a sufficient basis to conclude that section 45.5 was not an "item of appropriation." We found that no definition of the term "item of appropriation" as used in the Constitution — including the use of that term in *Wood v. Riley, supra,* 192 Cal. 293 — could "reasonably embrace a provision like section 45.5, which does not set aside a sum of money to be paid from the public treasury." (*Harbor, supra,* 43 Cal.3d at p. 1092.) We explained that the circumstance that "in *Wood* the term 'item of appropriation' was construed in such a way as to facilitate the Governor's power to veto a portion of the budget bill which could reasonably be encompassed within the meaning of that term does not provide authority for holding ... that the Governor may veto part of a general bill — a power denied him by the Constitution — in order to foil an alleged legislative attempt to evade the veto." (*Id.,* at p. 1092.)

B.

As in the situation presented in *Wood v. Riley, supra,* 192 Cal. 293, and unlike that before the court in *Harbor, supra,* 43 Cal.3d 1078, the challenged items presented to the Governor in Assembly Bill 4X 1 each "appear[] to fill all the requirements of a distinct item of appropriation of so much of a *definite sum of money* as may be required *for a designated purpose* connected with the state government." (*Wood v. Riley,* at p. 304, italics added.) Assembly Bill 4X 1 "set aside a sum of money to be paid from the public treasury" (*Harbor,* at p. 1092), albeit a sum smaller than that initially appropriated in the 2009 Budget Act.

Petitioners, interveners, and their amici curiae insist that only an *increase* in spending authority can constitute an appropriation. They emphasize that none of the definitions of "item of appropriation" contained in the cases refer to a *decrease* in the spending authorized by a previously enacted budget, and they maintain that such a reduction may not be deemed an item of appropriation. They further argue that because the 2009 Budget Act *already* had set aside sums of money to be paid by the treasury for specific purposes, those items and the sections of Assembly Bill 4X 1 that proposed only reductions to existing, previously enacted appropriations did not satisfy the requirement of money set aside for a particular purpose. The argument, in other words, is that a reduction in a set-aside cannot itself be considered a set-aside or an appropriation. We disagree.

The cases do not require, as petitioners and interveners suggest, that *solely* items that add amounts to funds already provided can constitute "items of appropriation." We concluded that Governor Deukmejian's claim failed in *Harbor* because section 45.5 of the trailer bill did not qualify "as an item of appropriation under *any* of [the] definitions" we reviewed. (*Harbor, supra,* 43 Cal.3d at p. 1089, italics added.) We observed that the provision "does not set aside money for the payment of any claim and makes no appropriation from the public treasury, nor does it add any additional amount to funds already provided for. Its effect is *substantive.*" (*Ibid.,* italics added.) Furthermore, unlike section 45.5 at issue in *Harbor,* which did not refer to any sum of money, much less a definite or ascertainable sum, the Assembly Bill 4X 1 items here at issue specified definite amounts by which the original appropriations would be reduced.

Whether spending authority is increased or decreased, it still fundamentally remains spending authority. Although described as reductions in specified items and sections, each of the provisions at issue in Assembly Bill 4X 1 nevertheless directs the "specific setting aside of an amount, not exceeding a definite fixed sum, for the payment of certain particular claims or demands." (*Wood v. Riley, supra,* 192 Cal. at p. 303; see *Harbor, supra,* 43 Cal.3d at p. 1092.) The items in Assembly Bill 4X 1 that were eliminated or further reduced by the Governor's exercise of line-item authority *capped* the spending authority at an amount less than that set forth in the 2009 Budget Act. The Controller could not thereafter disburse, nor could the recipients of the funds thereafter draw upon, any amount larger than that set aside by the Legislature for the specified purposes. (*Wood v. Riley,* at p. 303 [once enacted, an appropriation "'cannot be thereafter increased except by further legislative appropriation'"], citing, among other authority, *Stratton v. Green* (1872) 45 Cal. 149, 151.)

There is no substantive difference between a Governor's reduction of an item of appropriation in the original 2009 Budget Act, to which interveners and petitioners raise no objection, and a Governor's reduction of that same item in a subsequent amendment to the 2009 Budget Act—that is, Assembly Bill 4X 1. Both actions involve changes in authorized spending.

Interveners insist in their reply brief that the Governor was entitled, in essence, to only one bite at the budget apple. They concede that although he "had the authority to reduce or eliminate each of the items of appropriation at issue here when they were first passed in February, 2009," he nevertheless did not possess that same authority a few months later with regard to "the legislative reductions made in July." We discern no reason why the Governor should have the power to reduce items of appropriation when first enacted, and yet not retain that same power when the Legislature, in response to changed circumstances, sees fit to amend those same appropriations. In both instances, the Governor holds constitutionally granted authority to reduce the allocation of state expenditures.

. . . .

C.

Our determination that the challenged actions concerned authorized reductions of "items of appropriation" is further supported by the structure and content of Assembly Bill 4X 1 itself.

We begin with the observation that this bill constitutes an amendment to the 2009 Budget Act. (See *People v. Kelly* (2010) 47 Cal.4th 1008, 1027 ["an amendment includes a legislative act that changes an existing ... statute by taking away from it"] (*Kelly*); *Planned Parenthood Affiliates v. Swoap* (1985) 173 Cal.App.3d 1187, 1199 [an amendment is a legislative act *changing* prior or existing law by adding or taking from it some particular provision].) As noted above, this extensive and multi-itemed budget bill contains hundreds of sections, some of which *increased* spending over what was appropriated in the 2009 Budget Act. In many other respects, Assembly Bill 4X 1 decreased numerous appropriations made in the 2009 Budget Act.

....

D.

After the Governor exercised his line-item authority, the Legislative Counsel issued an opinion, cited by interveners, concluding that "an item or section of a bill that proposes only to make a reduction in an existing item of appropriation previously enacted in the Budget Act of 2009 is not itself an item of appropriation" and therefore, "in vetoing items of sections of [Assembly Bill 4X 1] that proposed only reductions to existing appropriations enacted by the Budget Act of 2009, the Governor exceeded his 'line-item' veto authority." (Ops. Cal. Legis. Counsel, No. 0920928 (Aug. 5, 2009) Governor's Line-Item Veto Authority: Reductions to Existing Appropriations, pp. 1, 4.)

Although "an opinion of the Legislative Counsel is entitled to respect, its weight depends on the reasons given in its support." (*Santa Clara County Local Transportation Authority v. Guardino* (1995) 11 Cal.4th 220, 238.) Indeed, quite recently, in *Kelly, supra,* 47 Cal.4th 1008, we found unpersuasive the analysis put forth by the Legislative Counsel relating to the legislation at issue in that case. (*Id.,* at p. 1043, fn. 60.) We come to a similar conclusion in the present case.

Opinions of the Legislative Counsel ordinarily are "prepared to assist the Legislature in its consideration of pending legislation" (*California Assn. of Psychology Providers v. Rank* (1990) 51 Cal.3d 1, 17), and therefore such opinions often shed light on legislative intent. Like the Legislative Counsel's opinion at issue in *Kelly*, however, the opinion at issue in the present case was not prepared in order to assist in the consideration of *pending legislation* — it was rendered, instead, *after* the legislation was enacted, and it addressed possible *future litigation* arising from that legislation. Insofar as the opinion expresses a view concerning the constitutionality of the Governor's exercise of authority with regard to Assembly Bill 4X 1, it is entitled to no more weight than the views of the parties. Legislative intent — that is, whether the Legislature *intended* that the items at issue be subject to the Governor's power — is irrelevant to our present inquiry focused upon the *constitutional scope* of that power.

E.

In the Court of Appeal, petitioners argued that the language employed by the Legislature in Assembly Bill 4X 1, to effectuate reductions in prior appropriations, differentiates between those provisions that "amended" sections of the 2009 Budget Act and those provisions (here at issue) that merely "added" sections to that act. Petitioners asserted in the court below that items in the former category are "arguably expose[d] … to the [G]overnor's line-item power" but that "no such authority exists … with respect to" to the latter category of items — those here at issue.

In response, the Court of Appeal observed: "In essence, petitioners argue that the Legislature may do by indirection that which it cannot do directly, that is, it may insulate certain items of appropriation from the Governor's line-item veto power by the language used, whereas other items having the identical effect of reducing the sums appropriated in the 2009 Budget Act would be subject to that power. This, the Legislature may not do. (See *Wood v. Riley, supra,* 192 Cal. at pp. 304–305.) As amici curiae former Governors observe: 'If by simple wordsmithing the legislative branch can create an omnibus spending bill limiting the Governor's oversight only to veto of the entire bill, then the budgetary process is reduced to a game of 'chicken' daring a [G]overnor to bring state government to a halt through a veto.' [¶] Whether identified in Assembly Bill 4X 1 as amendments of, revisions to, or additions to the 2009 Budget Act, it is clear that every provision of Assembly Bill 4X 1 changed a section of the 2009 Budget Act…. Consequently, the sections that were 'added'—like those that expressly 'amended' the 2009 Budget Act—reenacted those provisions and were subject to the line-item veto or reduction by the Governor. (See also *People v. Western Fruit Growers* (1943) 22 Cal.2d 494, 501.)"

In their briefing in this court, petitioners and interveners contend that the Court of Appeal, in reaching its decision, incorrectly relied upon the "reenactment rule" of article IV, section 9 of the California Constitution. The purpose of this rule, they argue, is merely to "prevent the title of a subsequent act from being made a cloak or artifice to distract attention from the substance of the act and to protect legislators and the public from being entrapped by misleading titles…." (*Estate of Henry* (1944) 64 Cal.App.2d 76, 82.)

    ….

V.

Interveners' contention that the amounts designated by the items of Assembly Bill 4X 1 at issue should not be reducible by the Governor is based in part upon a separation-of-powers theory, also advanced by amici curiae SEIU California State Council et al. This claim is premised upon (1) the absence in California's Constitution of explicit gubernatorial authority to increase or decrease the size of spending cuts made by the Legislature in response to a declaration of fiscal emergency, and (2) language in *Harbor, supra,* 43 Cal.3d 1078, emphasizing that, as interveners put it, "the power to veto, reduce or eliminate is not the power to create or increase." Specifically, interveners cite our observations in *Harbor* that "[t]he word 'veto' means 'I forbid' in

Latin" and that "the effect of the veto [is] negative, frustrating an act without substituting anything in its place." (*Id.*, at p. 1085.)

In the view of interveners, when undertaking the challenged line-item reductions, "the Governor sought to use his power to *increase* what the Legislature had done. The Legislature had made a policy determination regarding how much state spending had to be cut in response to the fiscal crisis and where those spending cuts were to be made. The Governor, however, disagreed with the Legislature's policy determinations. He wanted to make *more* cuts in order to keep a larger budget reserve." According to interveners, the Governor's preference for a larger budget reserve is a policy determination belonging to the legislative, not the executive, branch.

The determination whether the items in Assembly Bill 4X 1 at issue constitute appropriations cannot be made by characterizing the Governor's use of line-item authority as "increasing" the Legislature's reductions and then categorizing that act as impermissibly affirmative or "creative." Treating the exercise of line-item authority as an *increase in the reduction*, rather than as a *decrease in the appropriation* is as arbitrary as differentiating between the description of a glass of water as half full and a description of the same vessel as half empty. By increasing the Legislature's reduction, the Governor decreases the size of the appropriation. What matters is not whether the Governor's act is seen as being affirmative or negative, but rather its purpose and practical effect.

The difference of opinion between the Legislature and the Governor underlying these budget cuts was not whether the amount of particular items of appropriation enacted in the 2009 Budget Act needed to be reduced, but the *magnitude* of the necessary reductions. What mattered in the end were the amounts set aside for particular purposes; the Legislature sought greater appropriations than did the Governor. Although the Governor's exercise of line-item authority may be said to have "increased" the reductions made by the Legislature as to the items at issue, the most significant effect of the Governor's actions, and their purpose, was to further reduce the amounts set aside by the Legislature. The Governor's wielding of line-item authority was therefore quintessentially negative; it lowered the cap on the spending authority for specified purposes, providing precisely the type of check on the Legislature intended by the constitutional initiative that adopted the line-item provision, which empowered the Governor "to reduce an appropriation to meet the financial condition of the treasury...." (Ballot Pamp., Gen. Elec. (Nov. 7, 1922) argument in favor of Prop. 12, p. 79.)

Interveners' separation-of-powers argument thus begs the question. True, the Governor's challenged acts were legislative in nature and, "[a]s an executive officer, [the Governor] is forbidden to exercise any legislative power or function *except as ... the Constitution expressly provide[s]*." (*Lukens v. Nye, supra,* 156 Cal. at p. 501, italics added.) Thus, the question before us is not whether the gubernatorial act at issue was legislative in nature, but whether it was constitutionally authorized. As we earlier explained, the act undertaken by the Governor was authorized by the opening sentence of article IV, section 10(e) of our Constitution: "The Governor may reduce or eliminate one or more *items of appropriation* while approving other portions of a bill." (Italics added.)

Similarly, as discussed above, we conclude there is no persuasive reason to hold that the Governor is prevented from exercising line-item authority with respect to *changes* that the Legislature has made to items of appropriation. As emphasized above, the power to "reduce an appropriation to meet the financial condition of the treasury" was bestowed upon the Governor by the people of California in 1922 through constitutional amendment. When, as in the situation presented by the matter now before us, the Legislature finds it necessary to change its appropriations in light of worsened fiscal circumstances, the public's interest in fiscal responsibility is arguably even greater, and there is no indication that those who drafted and enacted article IV, section 10(e) would not have intended the Governor to maintain this same power over state expenditures under these circumstances.

Interveners assert that the foregoing analysis would permit the Governor to "eliminate" a reduction to a previously enacted appropriation, thereby allowing *more* spending than the Legislature authorized — a result that, they maintain, would not constitute use of the "veto" as a "negative" check on the Legislature, but the opposite. We need not address this issue or related issues, because they are not presented by the case before us. We note, however, that the Governor's line-item power does not give him the last word. The Legislature retains the ability to override the Governor's reduction of items of appropriation in the same manner as other bills, by separately reconsidering and passing them by a two-thirds majority of each house. (Cal. Const., art. IV, § 10, subds. (a), (e).)

VI.

Article IV, section 10(e) grants the Governor the limited legislative authority to eliminate or reduce "items of appropriation." For the reasons set forth in this opinion, we conclude that the budget reductions here at issue were "items of appropriation" within the meaning of that constitutional provision, and that therefore the Governor's exercise of line-item authority to reduce those appropriations, while approving other portions of Assembly Bill 4X 1, was consistent with his constitutional powers.

VII.

The judgment rendered by the Court of Appeal, denying the petition for writ of mandate, is affirmed.

KENNARD, J., BAXTER, J., CHIN, J., MORENO, J., CORRIGAN, J., and RYLAARSDAM, concurred.

Notes and Questions

1. In the context of the constitutionally prescribed budget process, the power to appropriate public funds belongs exclusively to the Legislature. Neither the so-called "item veto," nor the "line-item veto" allowing the Governor to eliminate or reduce items of appropriation confers the power to selectively veto general legislation. The governor has no authority to veto part of a bill that is not an "item of appropriation."

2. The court noted that an uncodified section of the law expressing the Legislature's findings and declarations states the law in this case. Would it matter if these statements of legislative intent were codified (rather than uncodified in this statute)?

3. An initial issue raised was whether the statute violated the separation of powers doctrine, as well as a ballot initiative that was approved by the voters. However, "the People do not pursue these arguments on appeal." Would these arguments be persuasive if they had been made on appeal?

4. The court explained that, "An issue that often arises in litigation involving the constitutionality of a legislative enactment under article II, section 10 of the California Constitution is whether the legislative enactment in question in fact amends an initiative statute." How does the Legislature determine whether its bill amends an initiative statute?

5. Why did the court characterize Senate Bill 1437 as presenting a classic example of legislation that addresses a subject related to, but distinct from, an area addressed by an initiative?

6. The court relied upon the ballot materials to "buttress our conclusion that voters intended Proposition 7 to strengthen the punishments for persons convicted of murder, not to reaffirm or amend the substantive offense of murder." They made a similar determination that "the legislative history of Senate Bill 1437 does not assist the People either." What were the bases for these determinations by the court in this case?

7. The court took the position that "the question we must ask ourselves is whether Senate Bill 1437 addresses a matter that the initiative specifically authorizes or prohibits." Why did the court take this approach? What was its ruling in regard to this question?

2. Reduction of Appropriations Amounts

As part of the annual state budget process, the Legislature and Governor review all of the expenditures of the state, whether from the general fund, federal funds, or special funds. As a part of this annual budget review process, the two branches of government can reduce the amounts of their annual appropriations. This can be done by the Legislature in the annual budget bill, or it can be done by the Governor through the use of his or her line-item veto authority.

Notes and Questions

1. Budget bills that substantively change existing law violate the single subject rule, because a substantive bill making a change to existing law can be vetoed in its entirety by the Governor and incorporating such a bill into a budget bill makes it impossible for the Governor to properly exercise his veto. The legislative power is circumscribed by the requirement that the legislative acts be bicamerally enacted and presented to the head of the executive branch for approval or veto.

2. A bill making an appropriation of zero dollars is not a substantive act but is simply an act of non-appropriation which, by operation of the statute, has the auto-

matic legal effect of freeing agencies from the obligation to implement the mandate for that year. When there is a lump sum appropriation intended for multiple purposes, but does not specifically allocate amounts to each of these purposes, the Governor may use the line-item veto to reduce the lump sum amount, but the Governor may not attribute the amount of the reduction to a specific purpose.

3. When the Governor exercises the power of the veto, he is acting in a legislative capacity and he may only act as permitted by the Constitution. The Governor possesses the constitutional authority to reduce or eliminate an item of appropriation in the budget bill passed by the Legislature.

4. Under the statute providing that no local agency shall be required to implement a mandate if the mandate has been "specifically identified by the Legislature in the Budget Act for the fiscal year as being one for which reimbursement is not provided for that fiscal year," making an appropriation of zero dollars is not a substantive act but is simply an act of non-appropriation which, by operation of the statute, has the automatic legal effect of freeing local agencies from the obligation to implement the mandate for that year.

5. When there is a lump-sum appropriation which is intended for multiple purposes, but does not specifically allocate amounts to each of those purposes, the Governor may use the line-item veto to reduce the lump sum appropriations, but the Governor may not attribute the amount of the reduction to a specific purpose and thereby transform his reduction of the lump sum into a veto of the use of the remaining appropriation for the disfavored purpose.

6. If a general appropriation specifically includes small appropriations, the Governor may veto one or more of the smaller appropriations and, in such a situation, the Governor may, but is not required to, reduce the larger appropriation in an equivalent amount. The constitutional provision requiring the Legislature either to fund or suspend local agency mandates does not prohibit the Governor from applying a line-item veto to reduce an appropriation funding a local agency mandate to zero.

7. The Legislature cannot shield an appropriation from the Governor's line-item veto simply by not using the language of an appropriation in the budget bill, particularly when the state Constitution requires that the Legislature choose between a full appropriation of a specific amount or nothing at all.

J. Regular Versus Special Sessions

The California Legislature can meet in regular, special or joint sessions. A "session" is the designated period of time in which the Legislature meets. A "joint" session, which can occur in a regular or special session, is one in which both houses (Assembly and Senate) meet for a specified purpose. Due to its physical size, joint sessions are normally held in the Assembly Chamber.

There is a misconception that the Assembly and Senate always meet separately. However, the Assembly and Senate may meet together in a joint session. The purpose of a joint session is to receive special information, such as the Governor's State of the State address or to hear from a foreign dignitary.

The Constitution provides the dates of convening and adjourning the regular session. Other than that, the Legislature has freedom to set its own calendar of meetings and recesses. Generally, the Legislature begins meeting the first week in January each year and concludes its work for the year either in mid-September (odd-numbered year) or August 31 (even-numbered year).

In terms of the period of time in which the Legislature meets, they may do so in either regular or special session. A "regular" session is the one convened in December of the even-numbered year. Pursuant to Article IV, Section 3(a) of the state constitution, "the Legislature shall convene in regular session at noon on the first Monday in December of each even-numbered year and each house shall immediately organize. Each session of the Legislature shall adjourn sine die by operation of the Constitution at midnight on November 30 of the following even-numbered year."

A "special" session, on the other hand, is one convened pursuant to a proclamation issued by the Governor. Pursuant to Article IV, Section 3(b) of the state Constitution, "on extraordinary occasions the Governor by proclamation may cause the Legislature to assemble in special session. When so assembled it has power to legislate only on subjects specified in the proclamation but may provide for expenses and other matters incidental to the session."

A common misconception is that the Governor can call a special session for any reason. However, under Article IV, Section 3(b), it is "on extraordinary occasions" that the Governor by proclamation can force the Legislature to assemble in special session. This is also the reason why "special sessions" are formally called "extraordinary sessions."

Another common misconception is that the Legislature must enact bills when called into special session. While the Legislature must convene the special session once it has been called by the Governor, there is no legal requirement that any legislation be enacted, nor even be voted upon. But the Constitution does limit what the Legislature can consider during a special session — "it has power to legislate only on subjects specified in the proclamation, but may provide for expenses and other matters incidental to the special session."

Aside from the fact that a special session is limited to the subject matter for which it was called, there are no significant differences in legislative process between a regular and special session. However, the effective dates for bills enacted during a special session are somewhat different than those for a regular session.

Regular session bills, except urgency clause bills that take effect when the Governor signs them, generally take effect on the following January 1. On the other hand, special session bills take effect on the 91st day after adjournment of the special session,

Finally, note that regular sessions of the Legislature, and any special sessions not previously adjourned, are adjourned sine die at midnight on November 30 of each even-numbered year. As such, neither a regular nor a special session will continue indefinitely.

K. Calling Special Sessions

In some instances, the Governor determines that a special, or extraordinary, session of the Legislature is necessary to be held in order to address a specific issue, such as budget situation or a major public disaster. The California Constitution calls for the state's chief executive to call for such a special session.

The Governor must issue a proclamation calling the Legislature into special session and specifying what the reason is for the special session to be convened. While the Legislature must then convene in special session, the Legislature does not have to actually enact any particular legislation in a special session. It is only required to convene the special session. And the Legislature can thereafter adjourn the special session by both houses adopting a resolution by majority vote to terminate the special session.

In *Martin v. Riley* (1942) 20 Cal.2d 28, the Court said,

> The duty of the Legislature in special session to confine itself to the subject matter of the call is of course mandatory. It has no power to legislate on any subject not specified in the proclamation.

> But when the Governor has submitted a subject to the Legislature, the designation of that subject opens for legislative consideration matters relating to, germane to and having a natural connection with the subject proper. Any matter of restriction or limitation becomes advisory or recommendatory only and not binding on the Legislature.

Notes and Questions

1. Legislation providing for the dissolution and winding down of redevelopment agencies did not exceed the scope of the Governor's emergency proclamation finding a fiscal emergency so as to violate the constitutional provision in Article IV, section 10 granting the Governor the power to cause the Legislature to assemble in special session by proclamation to legislate on the subject specified in the proclamation, or the provision governing the issuance of the proclamation declaring the fiscal emergency. (*City of Cerritos v. State of California* (2015) 239 Cal.App.4th 1020, review denied.)

2. Although it was possible for the Legislature to have addressed the declared fiscal crisis in a different manner, the legislation helped alleviate a declared fiscal crisis by boosting state revenues and by helping to balance the budget, which was all the constitutional provision required. (*City of Cerritos v. State of California* (2015) 239 Cal.App.4th 1020, review denied.)

Chapter Twelve

Statutory Interpretation

A. A Note about this Chapter

Entire textbooks, as well as casebooks, have been written on the topic of statutory interpretation, and this casebook does not attempt to supplant any of those. When talking about the California legislative process, we need to discuss statutory interpretation within this context, and that is the purpose of including this section in the casebook.

It is an overview regarding relevant consideration of the key aspects of this topic and its interaction with the California legislative process. It is not an exhaustive treatment, but provides an important introduction to several of the key concepts in order to understand statutory interpretation in the context of the California legislative process.

B. California Law and Its "Maxims of Jurisprudence"

While California statutes do not provide general canons of statutory construction, readers can find in the California Civil Code "Maxims of Jurisprudence." These maxims are set forth in Division 4, General Provisions, Part 4, of the Civil Code, contained in §§ 3509–3548.

So, what are these maxims? A "maxim" is generally defined as "a short, pithy statement expressing a general truth or rule of conduct." As you can read below, these sections of the Civil Code indeed provide short statements that express a rule of jurisprudence, although some may be difficult to decipher.

Part 4 of the Civil Code, which was enacted in 1872, contains 38 code sections, each setting forth a short legal rule. While most were placed in statute in 1872, some of these maxims were added to the Code in 1965. In Civil Code § 3509, we are told that "[t]he maxims of jurisprudence hereinafter set forth are intended not to qualify any of the foregoing provisions of this code, but to aid in their just application." Hopefully, that is clear to all.

The following are the jurisprudential maxims and their associated code section, along with the year they were placed in the Civil Code:

- When the reason of a rule ceases, so should the rule itself. [1872] (Section 3510)

- Where the reason is the same, the rule should be the same. [1872] (Section 3511)

- One must not change his purpose to the injury of another. [1872] (Section 3512)

- Any one may waive the advantage of a law intended solely for his benefit. But a law established for a public reason cannot be contravened by a private agreement. [1872] (Section 3513)

- One must so use his own rights as not to infringe upon the rights of another. [1872] (Section 3514)

- He who consents to an act is not wronged by it. [1872] (Section 3515)

- Acquiescence in error takes away the right of objecting to it. [1872] (Section 3516)

- No one can take advantage of his own wrong. [1872] (Section 3517)

- He who has fraudulently dispossessed himself of a thing may be treated as if he still had possession. [1872] (Section 3518)

- He who can and does not forbid that which is done on his behalf, is deemed to have bidden it. [1872] (Section 3519)

- No one should suffer by the act of another. [1872] (Section 3520)

- He who takes the benefit must bear the burden. [1872] (Section 3521)

- One who grants a thing is presumed to grant also whatever is essential to its use. [1872] (Section 3522)

- For every wrong there is a remedy. [1872] (Section 3523)

- Between those who are equally in the right, or equally in the wrong, the law does not interpose. [1872] (Section 3524)

- Between rights otherwise equal, the earliest is preferred. [1872] (Section 3525)

- No man is responsible for that which no man can control. [1872] (Section 3526)

- The law helps the vigilant, before those who sleep on their rights. [1872] (Section 3527)

- The law respects form less than substance. [1872] (Section 3528)

- That which ought to have been done is to be regarded as done, in favor of him to whom, and against him from whom, performance is due. [1872] (Section 3529)

- That which does not appear to exist is to be regarded as if it did not exist. [1872] (Section 3530)

- The law never requires impossibilities. [1872] (Section 3531)

- The law neither does nor requires idle acts. [1872] (Section 3532)

- The law disregards trifles. [1872] (Section 3533)

- Particular expressions qualify those which are general. [1872] (Section 3534)

- Contemporaneous exposition is in general the best. [1872] (Section 3535)

- The greater contains the less. [1872] (Section 3536)

- Superfluity does not vitiate. [1872] (Section 3537)

- That is certain which can be made certain. [1872] (Section 3538)

- Time does not confirm a void act. [1872] (Section 3539)
- The incident follows the principal, and not the principal the incident. [1872] (Section 3540)
- An interpretation which gives effect is preferred to one which makes void. [1872] (Section 3541)
- Interpretation must be reasonable. [1872] (Section 3542)
- Where one of two innocent persons must suffer by the act of a third, he, by whose negligence it happened, must be the sufferer. [1872] (Section 3543)
- Private transactions are fair and regular. [1965] (Section 3545)
- Things happen according to the ordinary course of nature and the ordinary habits of life. [1965] (Section 3546)
- A thing continues to exist as long as is usual with things of that nature. [1965] (Section 3547)
- The law has been obeyed. [1965] (Section 3548)

Notes and Questions

1. Are these maxims of jurisdiction applicable today? How might you describe one or more of these maxims using today's sayings?

C. Overview of Statutory Construction in California

For those working in and around the state Capitol, it is important to understand the general rules of statutory construction, even as non-lawyers. What is the purpose of statutory construction? The general rules of statutory construction are used in interpreting statutes by the courts. However, by understanding these rules, those drafting statutes can be guided by the rules that the courts will use in interpreting those statutes. That is why even non-lawyers should familiarize themselves with the rules.

While courts are not required to follow these rules of statutory construction in every instance, they are intended to guide the courts in determining what the intent of the Legislature was in enacting the particular statute. The general rule of statutory construction is to effectuate the intent of the Legislature, which basically requires the courts to give the statutory language its usual and ordinary meaning.

The fundamental rule of statutory construction is known as the "plain language" rule. This rule provides that, when the meaning of a statute is clear and unambiguous, there is usually no need for a court to apply any of the rules of statutory construction, because the "plain meaning" of the statute can be ascertained without resorting to the use of extrinsic aids. Under this rule, if the statute is clear, then the courts presume that the Legislature meant what it wrote in the statute, and the courts give effect to the plain meaning of the statute.

In order to resort to the general rules of statutory construction, a court determines that there is ambiguity in the statutory language and, as a result, it is unclear what was intended by the Legislature in enacting the statute. The courts have determined that a party demonstrates statutory ambiguity by providing an alternative meaning to the statutory language. As a result, if the statutory language can be given more than one interpretation, then a court generally must consider extrinsic aids to determine the purpose of the statute and the intent of the Legislature.

Among the extrinsic aids are the legislative history of a statute, the public policy surrounding its enactment, the statutory scheme in which the language exists, and other related items. In this regard, the language of a statute should be construed in light of the rest of the statutory scheme in which the particular statute is found. The goal of the courts is to harmonize the parts of the statute by considering the context of the statutory framework. For example, statutes related to the same subject should be interpreted consistently.

In regards to interpreting general versus specific statutes, if a specific statute is deemed to be inconsistent with a general statute that covers the same subject matter, then the specific statute is usually deemed to be an exception to rule provided by the general statute. In addition, as a general rule of statutory construction, courts must construe an exemption in a statute narrowly.

In a similar vein, a more recently enacted statute generally is given more weight than an earlier enacted statute. In other words, if two statutes cannot be reconciled and appear to be in conflict, the recently-enacted statute will take precedence over the earlier-enacted statute.

Another important rule is that, when interpreting a statute, a court will give significance to each word in a statute in determining the legislative purpose. So, the last antecedent rule provides that any qualifying words are to be applied to the words or phrases immediately preceding the qualifying word(s) and are not interpreted as extending to other words.

One type of rule of statutory construction provides that, where general words follow a list of particular items, the general words will be interpreted to apply only to those items of the same general nature or class as those set forth in the statute.

Another statutory construction rule provides that a statute which lists specific items will prevent the inclusion of other items. Also, courts generally interpret the word "may" as being permissive, while the word "shall" is interpreted to be mandatory.

There is also an important rule that statutes are presumed to operate prospectively, rather than retroactively, unless there is evidence that the Legislature intended the statute to be applied retroactively. So, the presumption is against retroactive application, unless the Legislature has plainly determined by express statement or other indicia that it was their intent to apply the statute retroactively.

Again, the fundamental role of the courts in interpreting a statute is to determine the intent of the Legislature and give effect to the legislative purpose. When the statute is unclear or ambiguous, then the courts are to look to the variety of extrinsic aids to assist them. The California courts have provided explicit guidance regarding which extrinsic aids are permitted to be used. In this regard, the legislative history, as well as the general circumstances surrounding the enactment of the statute, can and should be considered by the courts in order to properly determine the intent of the Legislature.

Finally, the courts generally give deference to the interpretation of a statute given by an administrative agency that has expertise and is charged with interpreting and enforcing a statute. While not necessarily a rule of statutory construction, it is important to take this point into consideration when there is an agency determination regarding the meaning of a statute.

The rules governing statutory construction are well established by numerous court decisions. The basic objective is to ascertain and effectuate the intent of the Legislature. This process begins with the language of the statute itself. If the statutory language is clear, then there is no need for further construction or reviewing the intent of the Legislature. Of course, when the language of a statute is ambiguous, the courts refer to indicia of legislative intent including the bill's legislative history, public policy, or analyses and arguments contained in the official legislative records.

Notes and Questions

1. Are California's general rules of statutory construction consistent with those of other states? While treatises have been written about statutory interpretation, which are some of the key rules that courts in California apply?

2. "Our fundamental task in interpreting a statute is to determine the Legislature's intent so as to effectuate the law's purpose. We first examine the statutory language, giving it a plain and commonsense meaning. We do not examine that language in isolation, but in the context of the statutory framework as a whole in order to determine its scope and purpose and to harmonize the various parts of the enactment. If the language is clear, courts must generally follow its plain meaning unless a literal interpretation would result in absurd consequences the Legislature did not intend. If the statutory language permits more than one reasonable interpretation, courts may consider other aids, such as the statute's purpose, legislative history, and public policy." (*Coalition of Concerned Communities, Inc. v. City of Los Angeles* (2004) 34 Cal.4th 733, 737.)

3. "Fidelity to their aims requires us to approach an interpretive problem not as if it were a purely logical game, like a Rubik's Cube, but as an effort to divine the human intent that underlies the statute." (*Burris v. Superior Court* (2005) 34 Cal.4th 1012, 1017.)

D. Guidance for Interpreting California Codes

California's statutes, of which there are more than half a million, are contained in 29 separate codes. In an effort to provide guidance to those needing to interpret these statutes, each Code begins with a "General Provisions" section. Within these General Provisions are codified directives, which generally include the following:

- The general provisions found in these initial sections of the code govern the construction of the code.

- Titles and section hearings do not determine how provisions of the code are to be interpreted.

- Present tense also means past and future tenses.

- The singular includes the plural.

- The word "shall" is mandatory, while the word "may" is permissive.

Below is additional guidance that is found is almost all of the Codes, but I have included some that are unique to that particular code.

Business & Professions Code

The provisions of this code in so far as they are substantially the same as existing statutory provisions relating to the same subject matter shall be construed as restatements and continuations thereof, and not as new enactments.

No action or proceeding commenced before this code takes effect, and no right accrued, is affected by the provisions of this code, but all procedure thereafter taken therein shall conform to the provisions of this code so far as possible.

Unless the context otherwise requires, the general provisions hereinafter set forth shall govern the construction of this code.

Division, part, chapter, article and section headings contained herein shall not be deemed to govern, limit, modify, or in any manner affect the scope, meaning, or intent of the provisions of this code.

Whenever any reference is made to any portion of this code or of any other law of this state, such reference shall apply to all amendments and additions thereto now or hereafter made.

The present tense includes the past and future tenses; and the future, the present.

Each gender includes the other two genders.

The singular number includes the plural, and the plural the singular.

If any provision of this code, or the application thereof, to any person or circumstance, is held invalid, the remainder of the code, or the application of such provision to other persons or circumstances, shall not be affected thereby.

Civil Code

No part of it is retroactive, unless expressly so declared.

The rule of the common law, that statutes in derogation thereof are to be strictly construed, has no application to this code. The code establishes the law of this state respecting the subjects to which it relates, and its provisions are to be liberally construed with a view to effect its objects and to promote justice.

The provisions of this code, so far as they are substantially the same as existing statutes or the common law, must be construed as continuations thereof, and not as new enactments.

Words and phrases are construed according to the context and the approved usage of the language; but technical words and phrases, and such others as may have acquired a peculiar and appropriate meaning in law, or are defined in the succeeding section, are to be construed according to such peculiar and appropriate meaning or definition.

Words used in this code in the present tense include the future as well as the present; words used in the masculine gender include the feminine and neuter; the singular number includes the plural, and the plural the singular; the word person includes a corporation as well as a natural person; county includes city and county; writing includes printing and typewriting; oath includes affirmation or declaration; and every mode of oral statement, under oath or affirmation, is embraced by the term "testify," and every written one in the term "depose."

Code of Civil Procedure

Whenever any act of a secular nature, other than a work of necessity or mercy, is appointed by law or contract to be performed upon a particular day, which day falls upon a holiday, such act may be performed upon the next business day with the same effect as if it had been performed upon the day appointed.

No statute, law, or rule is continued in force because it is consistent with the provisions of this code on the same subject; but in all cases provided for by this code, all statutes, laws, and rules heretofore in force in this state, whether consistent or not with the provisions of this code, unless expressly continued in force by it, are repealed and abrogated. This repeal or abrogation does not revive any former law heretofore repealed, nor does it affect any right already existing or accrued, or any action or proceeding already taken, except as in this code provided; nor does it affect any private statute not expressly repealed.

Commercial Code

This code shall be liberally construed and applied to promote its underlying purposes and policies

This code being a general act intended as a unified coverage of its subject matter, no part of it shall be deemed to be impliedly repealed by subsequent legislation if such construction can reasonably be avoided.

If any provision or clause of this code or its application to any person or circumstance is held invalid, the invalidity does not affect other provisions or applications of the code which can be given effect without the invalid provision or application, and to this end the provisions of this code are severable.

In this code, unless the statutory context otherwise requires: (1) words in the singular number include the plural, and those in the plural include the singular; and (2) words of any gender also refer to any other gender.

Whether a time for taking an action required by this code is reasonable depends on the nature, purpose, and circumstances of the action.

Whenever this code creates a "presumption" with respect to a fact, or provides that a fact is "presumed," the trier of fact must find the existence of the fact unless and until evidence is introduced that supports a finding of its nonexistence.

Corporations Code

Title, division, part, chapter, article, and section headings contained herein do not in any manner affect the scope, meaning, or intent of the provisions of this code.

The masculine gender includes the feminine and neuter.

"Shall" is mandatory and "may" is permissive.

Education Code

The code establishes the law of this state respecting the subjects to which it relates, and its provisions and all proceedings under it are to be liberally construed, with a view to effect its objects and to promote justice.

The time in which any act provided by this code is to be done is computed by excluding the first day, and including the last, unless the last day is a holiday, and then it is also excluded.

Elections Code

Whenever a power is granted to, or a duty is imposed upon, a public officer, the power may be exercised or the duty may be performed by a deputy of the officer or by a person authorized, pursuant to law, by the officer, unless this code expressly provides otherwise.

Evidence Code

The rule of the common law, that statutes in derogation thereof are to be strictly construed, has no application to this code. This code establishes the law of this state respecting the subject to which it relates, and its provisions are to be liberally construed with a view to effecting its objects and promoting justice.

Family Code

A provision of this code, insofar as it is the same in substance as a provision of a uniform act, shall be construed to effectuate the general purpose to make uniform the law in those states which enact that provision.

"Shall" is mandatory and "may" is permissive. "Shall not" and "may not" are prohibitory.

Financial Code

"Section" means a section of this code unless some other statute is specifically mentioned, and "subdivision" means a subdivision of the section in which the term occurs unless some other section is expressly mentioned.

The existence of corporations formed or existing on the date this code takes effect is not affected by the enactment of this code nor by any change in the requirements for the formation of corporations, nor by the amendment or repeal of the laws under which they were formed or created.

Fish and Game Code

Unless the provisions or the context otherwise requires, the definitions in this chapter govern the construction of this code and all regulations adopted under this code.

This code shall not impair any privilege granted or right acquired under any of the laws of this state prior to the date it takes effect.

Unless otherwise specified by statute, any notice or other written communication required to be sent to any person by this code or regulations adopted pursuant thereto, is sufficient notice if sent by first-class mail to the last address furnished to the department by that person.

Unless the provision or context otherwise requires, a provision of this code that applies to a whole animal also applies to a part of the animal.

Food and Agriculture Code

It is hereby declared, as a matter of legislative determination, that the provisions of this code are enacted in the exercise of the power of this state for the purposes of promoting and protecting the agricultural industry of the state and for the protection of the public health, safety, and welfare. In all civil actions, the provisions of this code shall be liberally construed for the accomplishment of these purposes and for the accomplishment of the purposes of the several divisions of this code, and in criminal actions, the rule of construction set forth in Section 4 of the Penal Code shall be the rule of construction for this code.

Unless a different penalty is expressly provided, a violation of any provision of this code is a misdemeanor.

Whenever any notice, report, statement, or record is required by this code, it shall be in writing unless it is expressly provided that it may be oral.

In all matters which arise under this code, proof of the fact of possession by any person engaged in the sale of a commodity establishes a rebuttable presumption that the commodity is for sale. This presumption is a presumption affecting the burden of producing evidence.

It is hereby declared, as a matter of legislative determination, that the provisions of this section are enacted in the exercise of the power of this state for the purpose of protecting and furthering the public health and welfare.

Government Code

The Legislature hereby declares its intent that the terms "man" or "men" where appropriate shall be deemed "person" or "persons" and any references to the terms "man" or "men" in sections of this code be changed to "person" or "persons" when such code sections are being amended for any purpose. This act is declaratory and not amendatory of existing law.

Harbors and Navigation Code

If any provision of this code, or the application thereof to any person or circumstance, is held invalid, the remainder of the code, or the application of such provision to other persons or circumstances, shall not be affected thereby.

Health and Safety Code

"Person" means any person, firm, association, organization, partnership, business trust, corporation, limited liability company, or company.

Insurance Code

As used in this code, the word "shall" is mandatory, and the word "may" is permissive, unless otherwise apparent from the context.

Provisions of this code relating to a particular class of insurance or a particular type of insurer prevail over provisions relating to insurance in general or insurers in general.

Labor Code

Whenever, by the provisions of this code, an administrative power is granted to a public officer or a duty imposed upon such an officer, the power may be exercised or the duty performed by a deputy of the officer or by a person authorized pursuant to law.

Military and Veterans Code

"Oath" includes affirmation.

Penal Code

No part of this code is retroactive, unless expressly so declared.

The rule of the common law, that penal statutes are to be strictly construed, has no application to this code. All its provisions are to be construed according to the fair import of their terms, with a view to effect its objects and to promote justice.

In the case of any ambiguity or conflict in interpretation, the code section or particular provision of the code section shall take precedence over the descriptive language. The descriptive language shall be deemed as being offered only for ease of reference unless it is otherwise clearly apparent from the context that the descriptive language is intended to narrow the application of the referenced code section or particular provision of the code section.

The several sections of this code which declare certain crimes to be punishable as therein mentioned, devolve a duty upon the court authorized to pass sentence, to determine and impose the punishment prescribed.

In every crime or public offense, there must exist a union, or joint operation of act and intent, or criminal negligence.

Probate Code

A provision of this code, insofar as it is the same in substance as a provision of a uniform act, shall be so construed as to effectuate the general purpose to make uniform the law in those states which enact that provision.

"Division" means a division of this code.

"Part" means a part of the division in which that term occurs.

"Chapter" means a chapter of the division or part, as the case may be, in which that term occurs.

"Article" means an article of the chapter in which that term occurs.

"Section" means a section of this code.

"Subdivision" means a subdivision of the section in which that term occurs.

"Paragraph" means a paragraph of the subdivision in which that term occurs.

"Subparagraph" means a subparagraph of the paragraph in which that term occurs.

Public Contract Code

The Legislature finds and declares that placing all public contract law in one code will make that law clearer and easier to find.

California public contract law should be efficient and the product of the best of modern practice and research.

To encourage competition for public contracts and to aid public officials in the efficient administration of public contracting, to the maximum extent possible, for similar work performed for similar agencies, California's public contract law should be uniform.

Public Resource Code

All persons who, at the time this code goes into effect, hold office under any of the acts repealed by this code, which offices are continued by this code, continue to hold the same according to the former tenure thereof.

Public Utilities Code

The definitions in the Public Utilities Act (Chapter 1 (commencing with Section 201) of Part 1 of Division 1), shall govern the construction of this code.

"City" includes city and county and "incorporated town," but does not include "unincorporated town" or "village."

Revenue and Taxation Code

No act in all the proceedings for raising revenue by taxation is illegal on account of informality or because not completed within the required time.

The courts of this state shall recognize and enforce liabilities for taxes lawfully imposed by any other state, or the political subdivisions thereof, which extends a like comity to this state.

Whenever any notice or other communication is required by this code to be mailed by registered mail, the mailing of such notice or other communication by certified mail shall be deemed to be sufficient compliance with the requirements of law.

Streets and Highways Code

As used in this code, unless the particular provision or the context otherwise requires, "highway" includes bridges, culverts, curbs, drains, and all works incidental to highway construction, improvement, and maintenance.

Unemployment Insurance Code

Whenever any reference is made to any person, officer, board, or agency by any provision of this code, the reference applies to any other person, officer, board, or agency to whom the functions vested in the person, officer, board, or agency referred to are transferred.

The Legislature hereby declares its intent that the term "workmen's compensation" shall hereafter also be known as "workers' compensation." In furtherance of this policy, it is the desire of the Legislature that references to the term "workmen's compensation" in this code be changed to "workers' compensation" when such code sections are being amended for any purpose. This act is declaratory and not amendatory of existing law.

Vehicle Code

If any portion of this code is held unconstitutional, such decision shall not affect the validity of any other portion of this code.

Water Code

The standard miner's inch of water is equivalent to one and one-half cubic feet of water per minute, measured through any aperture or orifice.

Welfare and Institutions Code

It is the purpose of this code, in establishing programs and services which are designed to provide protection, support or care of children, to provide protective services to the fullest extent deemed necessary by the juvenile court, probation department or other public agencies designated by the board of supervisors to perform the duties prescribed by this code to insure that the rights or physical, mental or moral welfare of children are not violated or threatened by their present circumstances or environment.

Notes and Questions

1. When you are dealing with legislative research or understanding particular provisions of law, it is always important to consult the beginning section of the relevant code where these specific provisions appear. These will help you interpret the sections that appear in that particular code.

E. California's Use of Statutory Construction Guidelines in Statutes

The courts in California, as well as across the country, utilize certain canons or rules of statutory construction. Essentially, statutory construction is how the courts interpret and ultimately apply the statutes or laws enacted by the state and federal legislatures. If a statute is not clear, meaning that it is ambiguous, then a court will have to apply these rules to determine how the statute will be applied. The following is a compilation of California statutes that utilize these directives:

Government Code, Title 5, Division 2, Part 1, Chapter 4, Article 4.6, Prop. 218 Omnibus Implementation Act, Section 53751

(f) The court in *Howard Jarvis Taxpayers Ass'n v. City of Salinas* (2002) 98 Cal.App.4th 1351 failed to follow long-standing principles of statutory construction by disregarding the plain meaning of the term "sewer." Courts have long held that statutory construction rules apply to initiative measures, including in cases that apply specifically to Proposition 218 (see *People v. Bustamante* (1997) 57 Cal.App.4th 693; *Keller v. Chowchilla Water Dist.* (2000) 80 Cal.App.4th 1006). When construing statutes, courts look first to the words of the statute, which should be given their usual, ordinary, and commonsense meaning (*People v. Mejia* (2012) 211 Cal.App.4th 586, 611). The purpose of utilizing the plain meaning of statutory language is to spare the courts the necessity of trying to divine the voters' intent by resorting to secondary or subjective indicators.

Public Resource Code Division 13, Chapter 2.6, General, Section 21083.1

It is the intent of the Legislature that courts, consistent with generally accepted rules of statutory construction, shall not interpret this division or the state guidelines adopted pursuant to § 21083 in a manner which imposes procedural or substantive requirements beyond those explicitly stated in this division or in the state guidelines.

Insurance Code Division 1, Part 2, Chapter 1, Article 14.2, California Insurance Guarantee Association, Section 1063.17

(g) Nothing in this section shall be construed to prohibit the board of governors of the association or its investment and audit committees from holding a closed meeting or a closed session of an open and public meeting to discuss any of the following subjects: ...

(7) Statutory construction and other advice received from legal counsel to the association, whether in connection with litigation or otherwise.

Government Code Title 7, Division 1, Chapter 3, Article 10.7, Low- and Moderate-Income Housing within the Coastal Zone, Section 65590

(h) With respect to the requirements of §§ 65583 and 65584, compliance with the requirements of this section is not intended and shall not be construed as any of the following:

(1) A statutory interpretation or determination of the local government actions which may be necessary to comply with the requirements of those sections; except that compliance with this section shall be deemed to satisfy the requirements of paragraph (2) of subdivision (c) of § 65583 for that portion of a local government's jurisdiction which is located within the coastal zone.

Code of Civil Procedure, Part 4, Title 1, Of the General Principles of Evidence, Sections 1858 and 1859

Sec. 1858. In the construction of a statute or instrument, the office of the Judge is simply to ascertain and declare what is in terms or in substance contained therein, not to insert what has been omitted, or to omit what has been inserted; and where there are several provisions or particulars, such a construction is, if possible, to be adopted as will give effect to all.

Sec. 1859. In the construction of a statute the intention of the Legislature, and in the construction of the instrument the intention of the parties, is to be pursued, if possible; and when a general and particular provision are inconsistent, the latter is paramount to the former. So, a particular intent will control a general one that is inconsistent with it.

F. California's "Plain English" Statutes

One of the directives in drafting legislation is the "plain English" rule. The purpose of this rule is for the bill drafter to use straightforward language that can be easily understood and interpreted as the Legislature intended. In that regard, the Legislature has enacted a number of statutes over the years that specifically require the use of "plain English" language. The following is a compilation of those statutes:

Government Code Title 2, Division 3, Part 1, Chapter 3.5, Article 2, Definitions, Section 11342.580

"Plain English" means language that satisfies the standard of clarity provided in Section 11349.

Civil Code Division 3, Part 4, Title 1.6A, Article 2, Section 1786.29

(b) An investigative consumer reporting agency shall provide a consumer seeking to obtain a copy of a report or making a request to review a file, a written notice in simple, plain English and Spanish setting forth the terms and conditions of his or her right to receive all disclosures, as provided.

Food and Agriculture Code Division 5, Part 3, Chapter 1, Article 4, Section 10786

(a)(2) If the department issues an administrative penalty pursuant to paragraph (1), the department shall issue a Notice of Violation to the alleged offender or the offender's agent. The notice shall be written in plain English and shall inform the offender as to how the offender may challenge the administrative penalty.

Health and Safety Code Division 107, Part 5, Chapter 1, Section 128765

(b) The reports published pursuant to Section 128745 shall include an executive summary, written in plain English to the maximum extent practicable, that shall include, but not be limited to, a discussion of findings, conclusions, and trends concerning the overall quality of medical outcomes, including a comparison to reports from prior years, for the procedure or condition studied by the report.

Health and Safety Code Division 107, Part 2, Chapter 2, Article 2, Section 127350

(d)(3) Each hospital's community benefit report shall contain an explanation of the methodology used to determine the hospital's costs, written in plain English.

Civil Code Division 3, Part 2, Title 2, Section 1633

(i)The application that is transmitted electronically pursuant to subdivision (a) shall comply with all applicable federal and state securities laws and regulations relating to disclosures to prospective customers.... Disclosures shall be written in plain English.

Health and Safety Code Division 2, Chapter 3.2, Article 6, Section 1569.69

(a)(6) Residential care facilities for the elderly shall encourage pharmacists and licensed medical professionals to use plain English when preparing labels on medications supplied to residents. As used in this section, "plain English" means that no abbreviations, symbols, or Latin medical terms shall be used in the instructions for the self-administration of medication.

Corporations Code Title 1, Division 1.5, Chapter 11, Section 3502

(e) The special purpose MD&A and any special purpose current report shall be written in plain English and shall be provided in an efficient and understandable manner, avoiding repetition and disclosure of immaterial information.

Government Code Title 2, Division 4, Part 1, Chapter 3.5, Article 5, Section 11346.2

(a)(1) The agency shall draft the regulation in plain, straightforward language, avoiding technical terms as much as possible, and using a coherent and easily readable style. The agency shall draft the regulation in plain English.

Bottom of Form

Family Code Division 17, Chapter 2, Article 1, Section 17406

(c) In all requests for services of the local child support agency or Attorney General pursuant to Section 17400 relating to actions involving paternity or support ... the local child support agency or Attorney General shall give notice.... Notice shall be in bold print and in plain English and shall be translated into the language understandable by the recipient when reasonable.

Government Code Title 2, Division 3, Part 1, Chapter 3.5, Article 5, Section 11346.5

(a)(3) An informative digest drafted in plain English in a format similar to the Legislative Counsel's digest on legislative bills.

G. Researching the Legislative History of an Enacted California Statute

For those who need to research the legislative history of a bill that was enacted into law in the state of California, there are a number of options to use. This article briefly describes some of those avenues for the reader to pursue.

<u>Be sure you are generally familiar with how bills are enacted in California.</u>

Some questions to ask yourself:

- Do you have a general understanding of the legislative process in California?
- Do you know the differences between the Assembly and Senate, policy and fiscal committees, and bill analyses completed for committee and floor deliberations?
- Do you understand which entities create documents that are considered during the legislative process, including non-legislative ones, such as the Department of Finance and state agencies?

It is important for researching the legislative history of an enacted statute in California to possess a basic understanding of what legislative history research consists of and where to look for insights into what the Legislature intended when it enacted a new law or amended an existing statute.

An insistence upon going beyond simply reading the statute allows one to consider valuable extrinsic evidence of what was intended by the Legislature in the adoption of the particular statute of interest.

<u>Decide how much time you have to spend on this research project.</u>

Some questions to ask yourself:

- How quickly do you need the legislative history materials?
- How much time do you have to conduct research into this statute's legislative history?

In general, state legislative history is elusive, and California, like many other states, is no exception to this rule. For example, as opposed to the *Congressional Record* which is basically a verbatim recording of federal legislative proceedings, the California Legislature does not publish transcripts of its floor debates or committee hearings. Unfortunately, there is not as much valuable material available, and the hunt for insights into legislative intent can be time-consuming and may not always be productive.

As a result, it is important to avoid potential frustration and decide before you embark on your research how much time you are willing to devote to this task. Keep in mind that many state courts will look at the "plain meaning" of a statute when determining legislative intent, and so, your legislative intent research may ultimately be ignored by the courts.

<u>Check California legislative history resources.</u>

Some questions to ask yourself:

- Is the material found online (generally since 1993) sufficient or do you need to visit the State Archives for older legislative materials?
- What information is actually available for the particular statute and preceding bill?

The Office of the Legislative Counsel in California (www.leginfo.legislature.ca.gov) has placed relevant legislative materials online since 1993, including all versions of a bill's text, all of the committee and floor analyses, all of the committee and floor votes, and bill histories.

In addition, the California State Archives has a vast collection of original legislative papers that can be accessed by source and session year (e.g., authors' files, committee and study files, Governor's Chaptered Bill Files, party caucus files, Senate Floor analyses files, agency files, Law Revision Commission Study Files).

Interested persons can phone in research requests to the State Archives at (916) 653-2246, but be prepared to wait as they often have backlogs. "Walk-ins" receive priority treatment, and the $.25 per page cost must be paid in advance for any photocopied documents.

Consult an annotated code to identify relevant session laws.

Some questions to ask yourself:

- Which bill affected the statute (now the code section) of interest to you?
- What was the law prior to the adoption of the statute?
- Did the statute add, amend or repeal sections of law?

Following the text of each statute, you will find references to the statute's session laws. You will need the information, primarily the bill number, to guide your legislative history research.

Review the text of the session laws.

Session laws are all the laws from a given legislative session in the order in which they were passed, and they include uncodified acts that never become part of the codified laws. On occasion, a bill's preamble will include a statement of purpose, often referred to as findings and declarations in California. This might assist you in ascertaining the Legislature's intent.

You will also want to compare versions of the statute if it has been amended though the legislative process. You should also review the different versions of a bill, including all of its amendments. What words, phrases or even entire code sections changed due to this bill?

Courts have ruled that contemporaneous, unpassed legislation may be a significant indicator of the intent underlying legislation passed during the same session, for example. Were there any similar bills that did not pass during the same legislative session?

Check Lexis or Westlaw's legislative history databases.

Online research tools can be helpful. For example, Legislative Research & Intent LLC, which is a commercial provider of legislative history research, supplies numerous complimentary research assistance and resources at www.lrihistory.com. Companies such as LRI conduct legislative intent research and certify the documents they find and can provide expert testimony in court.

Commercial databases also provide helpful legislative intent documents in numerous states, including in California.

<u>Review the California Assembly and Senate Journals.</u>

Some questions to ask yourself:

- What happened in the Legislature during the process of adopting this statute?
- What is the statute's legislative history?
- Which committees considered the bill?

The Journals do not always provide valuable legislative history because they have limited information. However, letters of intent by the author, committee reports, and similar information are contained in the Journals.

<u>Compare versions of the bill.</u>

By comparing different versions of a bill, you can identify which text has been added or deleted from a bill. Sometimes, these additions or deletions can help clarify the legislative intent behind the bill.

The dates of all versions of the bill — as introduced, amended, enrolled, and chaptered — along with the Legislative Counsel's Digest are set forth on the first page of all California bills. Always note when your language of interest came into print and any relevant amendments.

Previous legislation that is related, but failed, is relevant to ascertaining legislative intent. In other words, the history of predecessor failed bills can be considered relevant when the legislative effort spans multiple sessions.

<u>Check the California Assembly and Senate websites.</u>

Pursuant to the California Constitution, the Assembly and Senate must make videos and audios of all legislative committee hearings and floor sessions and post them on their respective websites. As a result, there are video files of committee hearings and floor sessions from January 2018 to present.

<u>Look for media coverage.</u>

Some questions to ask yourself:

- Why was the statute adopted?
- What needs prompted its adoption?
- What problem or issue was the Legislature trying to correct or address?

It may be helpful to review news coverage prior to, during, and after the enactment of the statute you are examining. Press reports may provide useful information that could give insights into legislative intent.

<u>Contact the California State Assembly or State Senate committees and author's office.</u>

Some questions to ask yourself:

- What has happened since the statute was created?
- What has been the response of the courts, the agency charged with administering the statute, the legislature, the public, scholars, etc.?

Several state legislative offices have potentially useful materials (i.e., legislator offices, committee offices, partisan offices, floor analysis offices), especially when it comes to more recent legislation, as well as agency analyses and bill files. Access to records held by these offices varies widely depending on the personalities involved and their willingness to make their files available to members of the public. The Legislative Open Records Act, Gov't Code §§ 9070, *et seq.* assures public access as specified.

Other documents to check related to legislative history and intent.

The following is a list of key documents that California courts have generally accepted as evidence concerning legislative history and intent of statutes:

- Interim hearing study and/or transcript and related files. Excerpts from testimony at public legislative hearings which preceded the enactment of a statute may be of some relevance in ascertaining legislative intent.

- Other formal studies and/or recommendations, such as those published by the California Law Revision Commission or a state agency.

- Bill Background Worksheets, which are requested by the committee and filled out by the author's office, sometimes with attachments.

- Policy and fiscal committee analyses (both partisan and nonpartisan versions).

- Department of Finance fiscal reports.

- Floor analyses for third reading (both partisan and nonpartisan versions).

- Statements by the author for committee and floor purposes.

- The legislative author's letter to the Governor. Note that the courts can be more friendly toward such a letter if the letter casts light on the history of a measure and is a reiteration of legislative discussion and events, and not merely an expression of personal opinion.

- Statements by proponents and opponents, such as letters, testimony, position papers, etc.

- Analyses by state agencies.

- Opinions by the Legislative Counsel and the Attorney General.

- Enrolled Bill Reports to the governor from various state entities, such as the Legislative Counsel, agencies and departments, and the governor's staff.

Although not exhaustive, these avenues can point readers in the right direction for purposes of researching statutes enacted in California.

H. What Is Cognizable Legislative History?

Kaufman & Broad Communities, Inc. v. Performance Plastering, Inc.

(2005) 133 Cal. App. 4th 26

OPINION ON REHEARING OF RULING ON MOTION FOR JUDICIAL NOTICE OF LEGISLATIVE HISTORY DOCUMENTS

Sims, J.

Pursuant to rule 22(a) of the California Rules of Court, appellant Performance Plastering, Inc., has moved this court to take judicial notice of various documents that, in the view of appellant, constitute cognizable legislative history of a 1998 amendment to Revenue and Taxation Code section 19719 (Assembly Bill 1950 (AB 1950)). (Stats.1998, ch. 856, § 2.)

I

Legislative History Generally

Before turning to the specifics of appellant's request for judicial notice, we have some general comments about requests for judicial notice of legislative history received by this court.

Many attorneys apparently believe that every scrap of paper that is generated in the legislative process constitutes the proper subject of judicial notice. They are aided in this view by some professional legislative intent services. Consequently, it is not uncommon for this court to receive motions for judicial notice of documents that are tendered to the court in a form resembling a telephone book. The various documents are not segregated and no attempt is made in a memorandum of points and authorities to justify each request for judicial notice. This must stop. And the purpose of this opinion is to help attorneys to better understand the role of legislative history and to encourage them to request judicial notice only of documents that constitute cognizable legislative history.

Preliminarily, we note that resort to legislative history is appropriate only where statutory language is ambiguous. As the California Supreme Court has said, "Our role in construing a statute is to ascertain the Legislature's intent so as to effectuate the purpose of the law. [Citation.] In determining intent, we look first to the words of the statute, giving the language its usual, ordinary meaning. If there is no ambiguity in the language, we presume the Legislature meant what it said, and the plain meaning of the statute governs. [Citation.]" (*Hunt v. Superior Court* (1999) 21 Cal. 4th 984, 1000, 90 Cal. Rptr. 2d 236, 987 P.2d 705, followed in *Curle v. Superior Court* (2001) 24 Cal. 4th 1057, 1063, 103 Cal. Rptr. 2d 751, 16 P.3d 166; accord: *Hoechst Celanese Corp. v. Franchise Tax Bd.* (2001) 25 Cal. 4th 508, 519, 106 Cal. Rptr. 2d 548, 22 P.3d 324.) Thus, "[o]nly when the language of a statute is susceptible to more than one reasonable construction is it appropriate to turn to extrinsic aids, including the legislative history of the measure, to ascertain its meaning." (*Diamond Multimedia Systems,*

Inc. v. Superior Court (1999) 19 Cal. 4th 1036, 1055, 80 Cal. Rptr. 2d 828, 968 P.2d 539, followed in *People v. Farell* (2002) 28 Cal. 4th 381, 394, 121 Cal. Rptr. 2d 603, 48 P.3d 1155; accord: *Esberg v. Union Oil Co.* (2002) 28 Cal. 4th 262, 269, 121 Cal. Rptr. 2d 203, 47 P.3d 1069; *Briggs v. Eden Council for Hope & Opportunity* (1999) 19 Cal. 4th 1106, 1119–1120, 81 Cal. Rptr.2d 471, 969 P.2d 564, and authorities cited therein; *Professional Engineers in Cal. Government v. State Personnel Bd.* (2001) 90 Cal. App. 4th 678, 688–689, 109 Cal. Rptr. 2d 375, but see *Kulshrestha v. First Union Commercial Corp.* (2004) 33 Cal. 4th 601, 613, fn. 7, 15 Cal. Rptr. 3d 793, 93 P.3d 386.)

Nonetheless, we will not require a party moving for judicial notice of legislative history materials to demonstrate the ambiguity of the subject statute at this juncture. This is so for two reasons. First, the ambiguity *vel non* of a statute will often be the central issue in a case, and parties would incur needless expense briefing the issue twice — once in a motion for judicial notice and again in a party's brief on the merits. Second, motions for judicial notice of legislative history materials are decided by writ panels of three justices who may not be the justices later adjudicating the case on the merits. The panel adjudicating the case on the merits should not be stuck with an earlier determination, by a different panel, as to the ambiguity *vel non* of a statute.

Even though we will grant motions for judicial notice of legislative history materials without a showing of statutory ambiguity, we do so with the understanding that the panel ultimately adjudicating the case may determine that the subject statute is unambiguous, so that resort to legislative history is inappropriate.

Even where statutory language is ambiguous, and resort to legislative history is appropriate, as a general rule in order to be cognizable, legislative history must shed light on the collegial view of the Legislature *as a whole.* (See *California Teachers Assn. v. San Diego Community College Dist.* (1981) 28 Cal. 3d 692, 701, 170 Cal. Rptr. 817, 621 P.2d 856.) Thus, to pick but one example, our Supreme Court has said, "We have frequently stated ... that the statements of an individual legislator, including the author of a bill, are generally not considered in construing a statute, as the court's task is to ascertain the intent of the Legislature as a whole in adopting a piece of legislation. [Citations.]" (*Quintano v. Mercury Casualty Co.* (1995) 11 Cal. 4th 1049, 1062, 48 Cal. Rptr. 2d 1, 906 P.2d 1057.)

In order to help this court determine what constitutes properly cognizable legislative history, and what does not, in the future motions for judicial notice of legislative history materials in this court should be in the following form:

1. The motion shall identify each separate document for which judicial notice is sought as a separate exhibit;

2. The moving party shall submit a memorandum of points and authorities citing authority why each such exhibit constitutes cognizable legislative history.

To aid counsel in this respect, we shall now set forth a list of legislative history documents that have been recognized by the California Supreme Court or this court as constituting cognizable legislative history together with a second list of documents that do *not* constitute cognizable legislative history in this court.

DOCUMENTS CONSTITUTING COGNIZABLE LEGISLATIVE
HISTORY IN THE COURT OF APPEAL FOR THE
THIRD APPELLATE DISTRICT

A. Ballot Pamphlets: Summaries and Arguments/Statement of Vote (*Robert L. v. Superior Court* (2003) 30 Cal. 4th 894, 903, 135 Cal. Rptr. 2d 30, 69 P.3d 951; *Jahr v. Casebeer* (1999) 70 Cal. App. 4th 1250, 1255–1256, 1259, 83 Cal. Rptr. 2d 172; *Aguimatang v. California State Lottery* (1991) 234 Cal. App. 3d 769, 790–791, 286 Cal. Rptr. 57.)

B. Conference Committee Reports (*Crowl v. Commission on Professional Competence* (1990) 225 Cal. App. 3d 334, 347, 275 Cal. Rptr. 86.)

C. Different Versions of the Bill (*Quintano v. Mercury Casualty Co., supra,* 11 Cal.4th at p. 1062, fn. 5, 48 Cal. Rptr. 2d 1, 906 P.2d 1057; *People v. Watie* (2002) 100 Cal. App. 4th 866, 884, 124 Cal. Rptr. 2d 258; *San Rafael Elementary School Dist. v. State Bd. of Education* (1999) 73 Cal. App. 4th 1018, 1025, fn. 8, 87 Cal. Rptr. 2d 67; *People v. Patterson* (1999) 72 Cal. App. 4th 438, 442–443, 84 Cal. Rptr. 2d 870.)

D. Floor Statements (*Dowhal v. SmithKline Beecham Consumer Healthcare* (2004) 32 Cal. 4th 910, 926, fn. 6, 12 Cal. Rptr. 3d 262, 88 P.3d 1; *People v. Drennan* (2000) 84 Cal. App. 4th 1349, 1357–1358, 101 Cal. Rptr. 2d 584; *In re Marriage of Siller* (1986) 187 Cal. App. 3d 36, 46, fn. 6, 231 Cal. Rptr. 757.)

E. House Journals and Final Histories (*People v. Patterson, supra,* 72 Cal.App.4th at pp. 442–443, 84 Cal. Rptr. 2d 870 [procedural history of bill from Assembly final history]; *Joyce G. v. Superior Court* (1995) 38 Cal. App. 4th 1501, 1509, 45 Cal. Rptr. 2d 805; *Natural Resources Defense Council v. Fish & Game Com.* (1994) 28 Cal. App. 4th 1104, 1117, 33 Cal. Rptr. 2d 904, fn. 11 [House Conference Report]; *Rosenthal v. Hansen* (1973) 34 Cal. App. 3d 754, 760, 110 Cal. Rptr. 257 [appendix to Journal of the Assembly]; *Rollins v. State of California* (1971) 14 Cal. App. 3d 160, 165, fn. 8, 92 Cal. Rptr. 251 [appendix to Journal of the Senate].)

F. Reports of the Legislative Analyst (*Heavenly Valley v. El Dorado County Bd. of Equalization* (2000) 84 Cal. App. 4th 1323, 1339–1340, 101 Cal. Rptr. 2d 591; *People v. Patterson, supra,* 72 Cal.App.4th at p. 443, 84 Cal. Rptr. 2d 870; *Board of Administration v. Wilson* (1997) 52 Cal. App. 4th 1109, 1133, 61 Cal. Rptr. 2d 207; *Aguimatang v. California State Lottery, supra,* 234 Cal.App.3d at p. 788, 286 Cal. Rptr. 57; *People v. Gulbrandsen* (1989) 209 Cal. App. 3d 1547, 1562, 258 Cal. Rptr. 75.)

G. Legislative Committee Reports and Analyses (*Hutnick v. United States Fidelity & Guaranty Co.* (1988) 47 Cal. 3d 456, 465, fn. 7, 253 Cal. Rptr. 236, 763 P.2d 1326.)

Assembly Committee on Criminal Law and Public Safety (*People v. Baniqued* (2000) 85 Cal. App. 4th 13, 27, fn. 13, 101 Cal. Rptr. 2d 835.)

Assembly Committee on Finance, Insurance and Commerce (*Martin v. Wells Fargo Bank* (2001) 91 Cal. App. 4th 489, 496, 110 Cal. Rptr. 2d 653.)

Assembly Committee on Governmental Organization (*Aguimatang v. California State Lottery, supra,* 234 Cal.App.3d at p. 788, 286 Cal. Rptr. 57.)

Assembly Committee on Health (*Kaiser Foundation Health Plan, Inc. v. Zingale* (2002) 99 Cal. App. 4th 1018, 1025, 121 Cal. Rptr. 2d 741; *Khajavi v. Feather River Anesthesia Medical Group* (2000) 84 Cal. App. 4th 32, 50, 100 Cal. Rptr. 2d 627; *Zabetian v. Medical Board* (2000) 80 Cal. App. 4th 462, 468, 94 Cal. Rptr. 2d 917; *Clemente v. Amundson* (1998) 60 Cal. App. 4th 1094, 1106, 70 Cal. Rptr. 2d 645.)

Assembly Committee on Human Services (*Golden Day Schools, Inc. v. Department of Education* (1999) 69 Cal. App. 4th 681, 692, 81 Cal. Rptr. 2d 758.)

Assembly Committee on Insurance (*Santangelo v. Allstate Ins. Co.* (1998) 65 Cal. App. 4th 804, 814, fn. 8, 76 Cal. Rptr. 2d 735.)

Assembly Committee on Judiciary (*Guillemin v. Stein* (2002) 104 Cal. App. 4th 156, 166, 128 Cal. Rptr. 2d 65; *CalFarm Ins. Co. v. Wolf* (2001) 86 Cal. App. 4th 811, 816, fn. 8, 820, 103 Cal. Rptr. 2d 584, fns. 27–28; *In re Marriage of Perry* (1998) 61 Cal. App. 4th 295, 309, fn. 3, 71 Cal. Rptr. 2d 499; *Peltier v. McCloud River R.R. Co.* (1995) 34 Cal. App. 4th 1809, 1819, fn. 5, 41 Cal. Rptr. 2d 182.)

Assembly Committee on Labor, Employment and Consumer Affairs (*Jensen v. BMW of North America, Inc.* (1995) 35 Cal. App. 4th 112, 138, 41 Cal. Rptr. 2d 295.)

Assembly Committee on Public Employees and Retirement (*Board of Administration v. Wilson, supra,* 52 Cal.App.4th at p. 1133, 61 Cal. Rptr. 2d 207.)

Assembly Committee on Public Safety (*People v. Blue Chevrolet Astro* (2000) 83 Cal. App. 4th 322, 329, 99 Cal. Rptr. 2d 609; *People v. Johnson* (2000) 77 Cal. App. 4th 410, 419, 91 Cal. Rptr. 2d 596; *People v. Sewell* (2000) 80 Cal. App. 4th 690, 695, 95 Cal. Rptr. 2d 600; *People v. Patterson, supra,* 72 Cal.App.4th at pp. 442–443, 84 Cal. Rptr. 2d 870; *Sommerfield v. Helmick* (1997) 57 Cal. App. 4th 315, 319, 67 Cal. Rptr. 2d 51; *Ream v. Superior Court* (1996) 48 Cal. App. 4th 1812, 1819, fn. 5, 1820–1821, 56 Cal. Rptr. 2d 550 [interim hearing report and analysis of assembly bill]; *People v. Frye* (1994) 21 Cal. App. 4th 1483, 1486, 27 Cal. Rptr. 2d 52.)

Assembly Committee on Retirement (*Praiser v. Biggs Unified School Dist.* (2001) 87 Cal. App. 4th 398, 407, fn. 16, 104 Cal. Rptr. 2d 551.)

Assembly Committee on Revenue and Tax (*Sunrise Retirement Villa v. Dear* (1997) 58 Cal. App. 4th 948, 959, 68 Cal. Rptr. 2d 416.)

Assembly Committee on Water, Parks and Wildlife (*Natural Resources Defense Council v. Fish & Game Com., supra,* 28 Cal.App.4th at p. 1118, 33 Cal. Rptr. 2d 904 [bill analysis work sheet].)

Assembly Committee on Ways and Means (*People v. Patterson, supra,* 72 Cal.App.4th at pp. 442–443, 84 Cal. Rptr. 2d 870; *Clemente v. Amundson, supra,* 60 Cal.App.4th at p. 1106, 70 Cal. Rptr. 2d 645.)

Assembly Interim Committee on Municipal and County Government (*Board of Trustees v. Leach* (1968) 258 Cal. App. 2d 281, 286, 65 Cal. Rptr. 588.)

Assembly Office of Research (*Forty-Niner Truck Plaza, Inc. v. Union Oil Co.* (1997) 58 Cal. App. 4th 1261, 1273, 68 Cal. Rptr. 2d 532.

Assembly Staff Analysis (*Clemente v. Amundson, supra,* 60 Cal.App.4th at p. 1107, 70 Cal. Rptr. 2d 645).

Assembly Subcommittee on Health, Education and Welfare Services (*A.H. Robins Co. v. Department of Health* (1976) 59 Cal. App. 3d 903, 908–909, 130 Cal. Rptr. 901.)

Senate Committee on Appropriations Fiscal Summary of Bill (*People v. Patterson, supra,* 72 Cal.App.4th at p. 443, 84 Cal. Rptr. 2d 870.)

Senate Committee on Business and Professions (*Hassan v. Mercy American River Hospital* (2003) 31 Cal. 4th 709, 722, 3 Cal. Rptr. 3d 623, 74 P.3d 726 [Senate committee staff analysis]; *Khajavi v. Feather River Anesthesia Medical Group, supra,* 84 Cal.App.4th at p. 50, 100 Cal. Rptr. 2d 627; *Forty-Niner Truck Plaza, Inc. v. Union Oil Co., supra,* 58 Cal.App.4th at p. 1273, 68 Cal. Rptr. 2d 532 [bill analysis work sheet].)

Senate Committee on Criminal Procedure (*People v. Blue Chevrolet Astro, supra,* 83 Cal.App.4th at p. 329, 99 Cal. Rptr. 2d 609.)

Senate Committee on Education (*Praiser v. Biggs Unified School Dist., supra,* 87 Cal.App.4th at p. 407, fn. 15, 104 Cal. Rptr. 2d 551; *Golden Day Schools, Inc. v. Department of Education, supra,* 69 Cal.App.4th at p. 692, 81 Cal. Rptr. 2d 758.)

Senate Committee on Health and Human Services (*In re Raymond E.* (2002) 97 Cal. App. 4th 613, 617, 118 Cal. Rptr. 2d 376.)

Senate Committee on Health and Welfare (*Zabetian v. Medical Board, supra,* 80 Cal.App.4th at p. 468, 94 Cal. Rptr. 2d 917; *Clemente v. Amundson, supra,* 60 Cal.App.4th at p. 1105, 70 Cal. Rptr. 2d 645 [request for approval of Senate bill].)

Senate Committee on Judiciary (*Martin v. Szeto* (2004) 32 Cal. 4th 445, 450, 9 Cal. Rptr. 3d 687, 84 P.3d 374 [background information]; *Boehm & Associates v. Workers' Comp. Appeals Bd.* (2003) 108 Cal. App. 4th 137, 146, 133 Cal. Rptr. 2d 396; *Westly v. U.S. Bancorp* (2003) 114 Cal. App. 4th 577, 583, 7 Cal. Rptr. 3d 838; *Wood v. County of San Joaquin* (2003) 111 Cal. App. 4th 960, 970, 4 Cal. Rptr. 3d 340; *People v. Robinson* (2002) 104 Cal. App. 4th 902, 905, 128 Cal. Rptr. 2d 619; *Guillemin v. Stein, supra,* 104 Cal.App.4th at p. 167, 128 Cal. Rptr. 2d 65; *In re Michael D.* (2002) 100 Cal. App. 4th 115, 122–123, 121 Cal. Rptr. 2d 909; *In re Raymond E., supra,* 97 Cal.App.4th at p. 617, 118 Cal. Rptr. 2d 376; *People v. Patterson, supra,* 72 Cal.App.4th at p. 443, 84 Cal. Rptr. 2d 870; *In re Marriage of Perry, supra,* 61 Cal.App.4th at p. 309, fn. 3, 71 Cal. Rptr. 2d 499.)

Senate Committee on Revenue and Taxation (*Heavenly Valley v. El Dorado County Bd. of Equalization, supra,* 84 Cal.App.4th at p. 1340, 101 Cal. Rptr. 2d 591; *Sacramento County Fire Protection Dist. v. Sacramento County Assessment Appeals Bd.* (1999) 75 Cal. App. 4th 327, 335, 89 Cal. Rptr. 2d 215; *Sunrise Retirement Villa v. Dear, supra,* 58 Cal.App.4th at p. 959, 68 Cal. Rptr. 2d 416.)

Senate Rules Committee (*Guillemin v. Stein, supra,* 104 Cal.App.4th at p. 166, 128 Cal. Rptr. 2d 65.)

Senate Conference Committee (*Golden Day Schools, Inc. v. Department of Education, supra,* 69 Cal.App.4th at p. 692, 81 Cal. Rptr. 2d 758.)

Senate Interim Committee on Fish and Game (*California Trout, Inc. v. State Water Resources Control Bd.* (1989) 207 Cal. App. 3d 585, 597, 255 Cal. Rptr. 184.)

Senate Subcommittee on Mental Health (*Clemente v. Amundson, supra,* 60 Cal.App.4th at p. 1104, fn. 10, 70 Cal. Rptr. 2d 645.)

H. Legislative Counsel's Digest (*Pacific Gas & Electric Co. v. Department of Water Resources* (2003) 112 Cal. App. 4th 477, 482–483, 5 Cal. Rptr. 3d 283; *People v. Allen* (2001) 88 Cal. App. 4th 986, 995, 106 Cal. Rptr. 2d 253; *Heavenly Valley v. El Dorado County Bd. of Equalization, supra,* 84 Cal.App.4th at p. 1339, 101 Cal. Rptr. 2d 591; *People v. Harper* (2000) 82 Cal. App. 4th 1413, 1418, 98 Cal. Rptr. 2d 894; *Alt v. Superior Court* (1999) 74 Cal. App. 4th 950, 959, fn. 4, 88 Cal. Rptr. 2d 530; *Construction Industry Force Account Council v. Amador Water Agency* (1999) 71 Cal. App. 4th 810, 813, 84 Cal. Rptr. 2d 139; *People v. Prothero* (1997) 57 Cal. App. 4th 126, 133, fn. 7, 66 Cal. Rptr. 2d 779; *Peltier v. McCloud River R.R. Co., supra,* 34 Cal.App.4th at p. 1819, fn. 5, 41 Cal. Rptr. 2d 182.)

I. Legislative Counsel's Opinions/Supplementary Reports (*Trinkle v. California State Lottery* (2003) 105 Cal. App. 4th 1401, 1410, fn. 7, 129 Cal. Rptr. 2d 904; *Trinkle v. Stroh* (1997) 60 Cal. App. 4th 771, 778, fn. 4, 70 Cal. Rptr. 2d 661; *People v. $31,500 United States Currency* (1995) 32 Cal. App. 4th 1442, 1460–1461, 38 Cal. Rptr. 2d 836.)

J. Legislative Party Floor Commentaries

Senate Republican Floor Commentaries (*Pacific Gas & Electric Co. v. Department of Water Resources, supra,* 112 Cal.App.4th at p. 498, 5 Cal. Rptr. 3d 283.)

K. Official Commission Reports and Comments

California Constitution Revision Commission (*Katzberg v. Regents of University of California* (2002) 29 Cal. 4th 300, 319, fn. 18, 127 Cal. Rptr. 2d 482, 58 P.3d 339 [proposed revision].)

California State Government Organization and Economy Commission (*Department of Personnel Administration v. Superior Court* (1992) 5 Cal. App. 4th 155, 183, 6 Cal. Rptr. 2d 714.)

Law Revision Commission (*Estate of Dye* (2001) 92 Cal. App. 4th 966, 985, 112 Cal. Rptr. 2d 362; *Estate of Della Sala* (1999) 73 Cal. App. 4th 463, 469, 86 Cal. Rptr. 2d 569; *Estate of Reeves* (1991) 233 Cal. App. 3d 651, 656, 284 Cal. Rptr. 650; *In re Marriage of Schenck* (1991) 228 Cal. App. 3d 1474, 1480, fn. 2, 279 Cal. Rptr. 651.

L. Predecessor Bills (*City of Richmond v. Commission on State Mandates* (1998) 64 Cal. App. 4th 1190, 1199, 75 Cal. Rptr. 2d 754.)

M. Statements by Sponsors, Proponents and Opponents Communicated to the Legislature as a Whole

Assembly Bill Digest by Assembly Speaker (*People v. Drennan, supra,* 84 Cal.App.4th at p. 1357, 101 Cal. Rptr. 2d 584.)

Floor Statement by Sponsoring Legislator (*In re Marriage of Siller, supra,* 187 Cal.App.3d at p. 46, fn. 6, 231 Cal. Rptr. 757.)

N. Transcripts of Committee Hearings *Lantzy v. Centex Homes* (2003) 31 Cal. 4th 363, 376, 2 Cal. Rptr. 3d 655, 73 P.3d 517; *Hoechst Celanese Corp. v. Franchise Tax Bd.* (2001) 25 Cal. 4th 508, 519, fn. 5, 106 Cal. Rptr. 2d 548, 22 P.3d 324.)

O. Analyses by Legislative Party Caucuses (e.g. Senate Democratic and Republican) (*People v. Allen, supra,* 88 Cal.App.4th at p. 995, fn. 16, 106 Cal. Rptr. 2d 253; *Golden Day Schools, Inc. v. Department of Education, supra,* 69 Cal.App.4th at p. 691–692, 81 Cal. Rptr. 2d 758; *Forty-Niner Truck Plaza, Inc. v. Union Oil Co., supra,* 58 Cal.App.4th at p. 1273, 68 Cal. Rptr. 2d 532.)

Assembly Office of Research Report (*Crowl v. Commission on Professional Competence, supra,* 225 Cal.App.3d at pp. 346–347, 275 Cal. Rptr. 86 [staff report].)

Assembly Committee on Judiciary (*Wood v. County of San Joaquin, supra,* 111 Cal.App.4th at p. 969, 4 Cal. Rptr. 3d 340; *Rieger v. Arnold* (2002) 104 Cal. App. 4th 451, 463, 128 Cal. Rptr. 2d 295; *Guillemin v. Stein, supra,* 104 Cal.App.4th at p. 167, 128 Cal. Rptr. 2d 65.)

Office of Assembly Floor Analyses (*People v. Patterson, supra,* 72 Cal.App.4th at p. 443, 84 Cal. Rptr. 2d 870.)

Office of Senate Floor Analyses (*Pacific Gas & Electric Co. v. Department of Water Resources, supra,* 112 Cal.App.4th at p. 497, 5 Cal. Rptr. 3d 283; *People v. Robinson, supra,* 104 Cal.App.4th at p. 905, 128 Cal. Rptr. 2d 619; *In re Raymond E., supra,* 97 Cal.App.4th at pp. 616–617, 118 Cal. Rptr. 2d 376; *Khajavi v. Feather River Anesthesia Medical Group, supra,* 84 Cal.App.4th at p. 50, 100 Cal. Rptr. 2d 627; *People v. Chavez* (1996) 44 Cal. App. 4th 1144, 1155–1156, 52 Cal. Rptr. 2d 347.)

P. Enrolled Bill Reports (*Elsner v. Uveges* (2004) 34 Cal. 4th 915, 934, fn. 19, 22 Cal. Rptr. 3d 530, 102 P.3d 915.)

DOCUMENTS *NOT* CONSTITUTING LEGISLATIVE HISTORY IN THE COURT OF APPEAL FOR THE THIRD APPELLATE DISTRICT

A. Authoring Legislator's Files, Letters, Press Releases and Statements Not Communicated to the Legislature as a Whole

Files (*People v. Patterson, supra,* 72 Cal.App.4th at p. 444, 84 Cal. Rptr. 2d 870.)

General (*People v. Garcia* (2002) 28 Cal. 4th 1166, 1176, fn. 5, 124 Cal. Rptr. 2d 464, 52 P.3d 648.)

Letters from Bill's Author to Governor Without an Indication the Author's Views Were Made Known to the Legislature as a Whole (*Heavenly Valley v. El Dorado County Bd. of Equalization, supra,* 84 Cal.App.4th at p. 1340–1341, 101 Cal. Rptr. 2d 591; *People v. Patterson, supra,* 72 Cal.App.4th at pp. 443–444, 84 Cal. Rptr. 2d 870.)

Statements by Bill's Author About Bill's Intended Purpose (*People v. Patterson, supra,* 72 Cal.App.4th at p. 443, 84 Cal. Rptr. 2d 870.)

B. <u>Documents with Unknown Author and Purpose</u> (*State Compensation Ins. Fund v. Workers' Comp. Appeals Bd.* (1985) 40 Cal. 3d 5, 10, fn. 3, 219 Cal. Rptr. 13, 706 P.2d 1146.)

C. <u>Handwritten Document Copies, without Author, Contained in Assemblymember's Files</u> (*Amwest Surety Ins. Co. v. Wilson* (1995) 11 Cal. 4th 1243, 1263, fn. 13, 48 Cal. Rptr. 2d 12, 906 P.2d 1112.)

D. <u>Letter from Consultant to the State Bar Taxation Section to Governor</u> (*Heavenly Valley v. El Dorado County Bd. of Equalization, supra,* 84 Cal.App.4th at pp. 1340–1341, 101 Cal. Rptr. 2d 591.)

E. <u>Letter from the Family Law Section of the State Bar of California to Assembly-member or Senator</u> (*In re Marriage of Pendleton & Fireman* (2000) 24 Cal. 4th 39, 47, 99 Cal. Rptr. 2d 278, 5 P.3d 839.)

F. <u>Letters to Governor Urging Signing of Bill</u> (*California Teachers Assn. v. San Diego Community College Dist., supra,* 28 Cal.3d at p. 701, 170 Cal. Rptr. 817, 621 P.2d 856; *Heavenly Valley v. El Dorado County Bd. of Equalization, supra,* 84 Cal.App.4th at p. 1327, fn. 2, 101 Cal. Rptr. 2d 591.)

G. <u>Letters to Particular Legislators, Including Bill's Author</u> (*Quintano v. Mercury Casualty Co., supra,* 11 Cal.4th at p. 1062, fn. 5, 48 Cal. Rptr. 2d 1, 906 P.2d 1057; *Heavenly Valley v. El Dorado County Bd. of Equalization, supra,* 84 Cal.App.4th at p. 1327, fn. 2, 101 Cal. Rptr. 2d 591.)

H. <u>Magazine Articles</u> (*Cortez v. Purolator Air Filtration Products Co.* (2000) 23 Cal. 4th 163, 168, 96 Cal. Rptr. 2d 518, 999 P.2d 706.)

I. <u>Memorandum from a Deputy District Attorney to Proponents of Assembly Bill</u> (*People v. Garcia, supra,* 28 Cal.4th at p. 1176, fn. 5, 124 Cal. Rptr. 2d 464, 52 P.3d 648.)

J. <u>Proposed Assembly Bill Which Was Withdrawn by Author</u> (*Heavenly Valley v. El Dorado County Bd. of Equalization, supra,* 84 Cal.App.4th at p. 1342, 101 Cal. Rptr. 2d 591.)

K. <u>State Bar's View of the Meaning of Proposed Legislation</u> (*Peltier v. McCloud River R.R. Co., supra,* 34 Cal.App.4th at p. 1820, 41 Cal. Rptr. 2d 182.)

L. <u>Subjective Intent Reflected by Statements of Interested Parties and Individual Legislators, Including Bill's Author, Not Communicated to Legislature as a Whole</u> (*Quintano v. Mercury Casualty Co., supra,* 11 Cal.4th at p. 1062, 48 Cal. Rptr. 2d 1, 906 P.2d 1057; *Collins v. Department of Transportation* (2003) 114 Cal. App. 4th 859, 870, fn. 11, 8 Cal. Rptr. 3d 132.)

M. <u>Views of Individual Legislators, Staffers, and Other Interested Persons</u>

Document Related to Bill from File of Assembly Committee on Ways and Means

Material on Bill from File of Assembly Committee on Public Safety

Material on Bill from File of Assembly Republican Caucus

Material on Bill from File of Author

Material on Bill from File of Office of Senate Floor Analyses

Material on Bill from File of Senate Committee on Appropriations

Material on Bill from File of Senate Committee on the Judiciary

Postenrollment Documents Regarding Bill (*People v. Patterson, supra,* 72 Cal.App.4th at pp. 442–443, 84 Cal. Rptr. 2d 870.)

II

Appellant's Specific Requests

We now turn to the documents for which judicial notice is sought.

A.

The first document is entitled "AB 1950 (Torlakson) Construction Defect Litigation Reform [¶] Fact Sheet." Nothing in appellant's motion suggests this document was made available to the Legislature as a whole. Rather, it appears to reflect the personal view of Assemblymember Tom Torlakson. Appellant argues that judicial notice is appropriate because the document was located in the file of a legislative committee. We acknowledge that in *James v. St. Elizabeth Community Hospital* (1994) 30 Cal. App. 4th 73 at page 81, 35 Cal. Rptr. 2d 372, this court considered the contents of a document simply because it was found in the files of a committee. But, upon reflection, we now conclude that this practice should not be further condoned. Many pieces of paper that are never seen by members of the committee, let alone by the Legislature as a whole, find their way into committee files. Unlike committee reports, which are routinely available to the Legislature as a whole, these random documents are not reliable indicia of legislative intent. Because there is no showing that Assemblymember Torlakson's "Fact Sheet" was communicated to the Legislature as a whole, it does not constitute cognizable legislative history, and the request for judicial notice of this document is denied. (See *Quintano v. Mercury Casualty Co., supra,* 11 Cal.4th at p. 1062, 48 Cal. Rptr. 2d 1, 906 P.2d 1057; *People v. Patterson, supra,* 72 Cal.App.4th at p. 444, 84 Cal. Rptr. 2d 870.)

B.

Next is the Assembly Judiciary Committee Report dated April 21, 1998, pertaining to AB 1950. The request for judicial notice is granted with respect to this document. (*Guillemin v. Stein, supra,* 104 Cal.App.4th at p. 166, 128 Cal. Rptr. 2d 65, and authorities cited at p. 525 of this opinion, *ante.*)

C.

Next is the Senate Judiciary Committee Report pertaining to AB 1950. The request for judicial notice is granted with respect to this document. (*Martin v. Szeto, supra,* 32 Cal.4th at p. 450, 9 Cal. Rptr. 3d 687, 84 P.3d 374, and authorities cited at p. 526 of this opinion, *ante.*)

D.

Next, and finally, are three enrolled bill reports on AB 1950, prepared respectively by the Office of Insurance Advisor, the Department of Real Estate, and the Franchise Tax Board.

Generally, "enrolled bill" refers to a bill that has passed both houses of the Legislature and that has been signed by the presiding officers of the two houses. (1 Sutherland, Statutes and Statutory Construction (6th ed.2002) § 15:1, p. 814.) In some states, enrollment also includes signature by the Governor (*ibid.*), but not in California.

California law provides that bills ordered enrolled by the Senate or Assembly are delivered to the clerk of the house ordering the enrollment. (Gov.Code, § 9502.) The clerk delivers the bills to the State Printer. (§ 9503.) The State Printer shall "engross or enroll (print) them" and return them to the clerk. (§§ 9504–9505.) "If the enrolled copy of a bill or other document is found to be correct, [it shall be presented] to the proper officers for their signatures. When the officers sign their names thereon, as required by law, *it is enrolled.*" (§ 9507, italics added.) Enrolled bills are then transmitted to the Governor for his approval. (§ 9508.) If the Governor approves it and deposits it with the Secretary of State, it becomes the official record and is given a chapter number. (§ 9510.)

Thus, an enrolled bill is one that has been passed by the Senate and Assembly but has not yet been signed by the Governor.

An "enrolled bill report" is prepared by a department or agency in the executive branch that would be affected by the legislation. Enrolled bill reports are typically forwarded to the Governor's office before the Governor decides whether to sign the enrolled bill.

In *McDowell v. Watson* (1997) 59 Cal. App. 4th 1155 at pages 1161 through 1162, footnote 3 [69 Cal. Rptr. 2d 692] (*McDowell*), the Fourth Appellate District opined that enrolled bill reports should not be considered for legislative intent:

> "[I]t is not reasonable to infer that enrolled bill reports prepared by the executive branch for the Governor were ever read by the Legislature.
>
> "We recognize that courts have sometimes cited the latter materials as indicia of legislative intent. [Numerous citations.] However, none of those opinions address[es] the propriety of doing so. Accordingly, we decline to follow their example. 'Such a departure from past rules of statutory construction, we believe, should be effected only after full discussion and exposure of the issue.' (*California Teachers Assn. v. San Diego Community College Dist.* [(1981)] 28 Cal.3d [692] 701 [170 Cal. Rptr. 817, 621 P.2d 856].)
>
> "We also note that *Commodore Home Systems, Inc. v. Superior Court* (1982) 32 Cal. 3d 211 at pages 218 through 219 [185 Cal. Rptr. 270, 649 P.2d 912], has been relied upon as authority for considering enrolled bill reports to determine legislative intent. [Citations.] However, that reliance is misplaced, because the Supreme Court in *Commodore* specifically noted that it had been requested to take notice of those reports and that the opposing party had not objected. [Citation.] Moreover, while *Commodore* cites authority for taking judicial notice of such executive acts, it does not address the relevance of that evidence to determining legislative intent." (*McDowell, supra,* 59 Cal.App.4th at p. 1162, fn. 3, 69 Cal. Rptr. 2d 692; see also *Whaley*

v. Sony Computer Entertainment America, Inc. (2004) 121 Cal. App. 4th 479, 487, fn. 4, 17 Cal. Rptr. 3d 88 [following *McDowell*].)

This court has twice followed *McDowell, supra,* 59 Cal. App. 4th 1155, 69 Cal. Rptr. 2d 692, in declining judicial notice of enrolled bill reports. (See *Lewis v. County of Sacramento* (2001) 93 Cal. App. 4th 107, 121, fn. 4, 113 Cal. Rptr. 2d 90; *People v. Patterson, supra,* 72 Cal.App.4th at p. 444, 84 Cal. Rptr. 2d 870.)

On the other hand, in *People v. Allen* (2001) 88 Cal. App. 4th 986, 106 Cal. Rptr. 2d 253, this court said, "While enrolled bill reports prepared by the executive branch for the Governor do not necessarily demonstrate the Legislature's intent [citation], they can *corroborate* the Legislature's intent, as reflected in legislative reports, by reflecting a contemporaneous common understanding shared by participants in the legislative process from both the executive and legislative branches." (*Id.* at p. 995, fn. 19, 106 Cal. Rptr. 2d 253.)

And in *People v. Carmony* (2005) 127 Cal. App. 4th 1066, 26 Cal. Rptr. 3d 365, this court recently took judicial notice of an enrolled bill report without discussion. (*Id.* at p. 1078, 26 Cal. Rptr. 3d 365.)

For practical purposes, these inconsistencies have been resolved by a 2004 decision of our Supreme Court in *Elsner v. Uveges, supra,* 34 Cal. 4th 915, 22 Cal. Rptr. 3d 530, 102 P.3d 915. There, the court took judicial notice of an enrolled bill report prepared by the Department of Industrial Relations. (*Id.* at p. 934, 22 Cal. Rptr. 3d 530, 102 P.3d 915.) The court said, "Uveges challenges Elsner's reliance on the enrolled bill report, arguing that it is irrelevant because it was prepared after passage. However, we have routinely found enrolled bill reports, prepared by a responsible agency contemporaneous with passage and before signing, instructive on matters of legislative intent. [Citations.]" (*Id.* at p. 934, fn. 19, 22 Cal. Rptr. 3d 530, 102 P.3d 915.)

We are obligated to follow *Elsner.* (*Auto Equity Sales, Inc. v. Superior Court* (1962) 57 Cal. 2d 450, 455, 20 Cal. Rptr. 321, 369 P.2d 937.) We hereby grant appellant's motion for judicial notice of the enrolled bill reports, and we leave it to the panel deciding this case to determine the extent to which these reports may be "instructive."

Nonetheless, we respectfully add that we continue to find the logic of *McDowell, supra,* 59 Cal. App. 4th 1155, 69 Cal. Rptr. 2d 692, unassailable. In fact, enrolled bill reports cannot reflect the intent of the Legislature because they are prepared by the executive branch, and then not until after the bill has passed the Legislature and has become "enrolled." Moreover, to permit consideration of enrolled bill reports as cognizable legislative history gives the executive branch an unwarranted opportunity to determine the meaning of statutes. That is the proper and exclusive duty of the judicial branch of government. "'[T]he determination of the meaning of statutes is a judicial function....' [Citation.]" (*People v. Franklin* (1999) 20 Cal. 4th 249, 256, 84 Cal. Rptr. 2d 241, 975 P.2d 30.)

But we do not write on a clean slate.

We concur: SCOTLAND, P.J., and DAVIS, J.

Notes and Questions

1. Does this appellate court decision demonstrate that state court judges understand the legislative process in this state? Do the items of extrinsic evidence demonstrate that the judicial branch has a thorough understanding of the legislative process and how to find appropriate evidence of legislative intent?

2. "Many attorneys apparently believe that every scrap of paper that is generated in the legislative process constitutes the proper subject of judicial notice. They are aided in this view by some professional legislative intent services." Why do you think the court views legislative intent services that assist attorneys in researching and analyzing legislative materials in a negative manner?

3. "And the purpose of this opinion is to help attorneys to better understand the role of legislative history and to encourage them to request judicial notice only of documents that constitute cognizable legislative history." Did the court's opinion achieve this goal?

4. What are the two reasons the court gave for not requiring a party moving for judicial notice of legislative history materials to demonstrate the ambiguity of the subject statute at this juncture?

5. According to the court, the fundamental rule is: "Even where statutory language is ambiguous, and resort to legislative history is appropriate, as a general rule in order to be cognizable, legislative history must shed light on the collegial view of the Legislature *as a whole*. (See *California Teachers Assn. v. San Diego Community College* (1981) 28 Cal.3d 692, 701.)

6. The bulk of this court opinion sets forth a list of legislative history documents that have been recognized by the California Supreme Court or the Third District Court of Appeal as constituting cognizable legislative history, together with a second list of documents that do *not* constitute cognizable legislative history in the Third District Court of Appeal. Do you believe these lists are exhaustive of all possible legislative history materials?

7. Regarding the first item of legislative history, Assemblymember Torlakson's "Fact Sheet," why did the court rule that it did not constitute cognizable legislative history, and the request for judicial notice of this document was denied?

8. On the issue of "enrolled bill reports (EBRs)," the Supreme Court allows EBRs as cognizable legislative history. However, these are prepared only for the Governor's review and after a bill has passed both houses of the Legislature. What is the justification for allowing EBRs if they were not available to the legislature "as a whole"?

I. Legislative Intent and California Courts

In determining the intent of the Legislature in enacting state laws, California courts have historically taken a limited view of legislative materials that can be used to determine intent. The courts generally rely upon certain types of legislative history documents to gain an understanding of the meaning of a statute and, ultimately, to apply the Legislature's intent when interpreting a statute.

The determination of legislative intent is important, because there are instances in which there are legitimate legal disputes between parties as to what statutory language may mean or what was intended by the language. In these cases, both parties will attempt to argue that their interpretation is the correct one that should be adopted by the court. Obviously, it is up to the judiciary to determine whose view is the correct one.

The concern from this author's perspective is that the courts utilize an unrealistic viewpoint in determining which legislative intent materials can be properly used by a court to make a determination. For example, the courts have determined that documents available to all legislators are the proper ones to use. Of course, this is based upon the assumption, which is not likely correct, that all legislators read all of the materials before casting their votes. That assumption is probably not a realistic view of what actually happens in the legislative process.

Readers should understand that this statement is not meant as a criticism of the Legislature or any individual legislators. Instead, it is simply an acknowledgement that legislators cannot be expected to read every bill and all of the background materials and analyses and thoroughly understand the intent behind each and every measure and the particular wording used in the legislation when they are voting on thousands of bills each year.

The other point from this author's perspective is that California's legislative history is lacking, particularly in comparison to the materials produced by the federal government. In a similar manner to the prior concern expressed, this is not a criticism of the California legislative process; rather, it is an acknowledgement that there is limited, insightful material produced in conjunction with the consideration of legislation.

For example, Congress uses a committee mark-up session to delve deeply into the legislative language being used in a bill. They review in detail the language and discuss and debate it, and there are transcripts of those hearings. In the California Legislature, on the other hand, committees rarely get into the details of bill language. There may be debate generally over the policy of a particular bill, but rarely any discussion about the bill's actual language.

Also, at the federal level, there is the benefit of the *Congressional Record*, basically a verbatim transcript of debate and discussion regarding pending legislation, which is obviously very helpful for reviewing legislative intent. However, the *Assembly Daily Journal* and the *Senate Daily Journal* do not have anything in detail regarding legislative debate. As such, the main source of legislative intent in the California Legislature is a committee analysis.

Unfortunately, committee and floor bill analyses rarely provide details or insights into why specific bill language was or was not used in a bill. Generally, the bill analyses explain existing law, changes to the law being made by the proposed bill, arguments for and against the bill, and a few staff comments. However, rarely is specific language discussed and reasons why that particular language was used. As a result, there are definite limitations in gleaning insight into the language used by the Legislature when it comes to bills.

Because of these factors, California courts' reliance on certain legislative materials is important, but the courts may be taking an unnecessarily narrow view of which items can be appropriately used to determine the intent of the Legislature. One possible reason is that the judicial branch does not have a fundamental understanding of the legislative process.

In making determinations regarding which documents are properly considered by a court of law in determining legislative intent, the courts have shown a limited understanding of the legislative process, and they need to have greater familiarity with the legislative process in order to properly determine what true and accurate statements of legislative intent are and how they are made by members of the legislative branch of government.

As we live and operate in a legal world dominated by statutes, it is of increasing importance for our courts to properly interpret those statutes and determine what particular legislative language means. Our state statutes sometimes have ambiguities, and courts must look to the legislative history to determine what those statutory words were intended to mean. Sometimes a statute's plain reading can be followed, but at other times, that may not be so easy, and courts will have to rely upon the limited evidence of legislative intent that is available.

Notes and Questions

1. Does the judicial branch's basis for determining legislative intent reflect the realities of the legislative process? Should the judiciary adopt a different view of legislative intent?

J. Judicial Policymaking

The judiciary may not undertake to evaluate the wisdom of the policies embodied in legislation, according to state courts. In other words, the judicial branch does not review whether the law is good or bad public policy. Instead, judges review whether the law comports with the Constitution and was adopted properly.

Kollander Construction, Inc. v. Superior Court

(2002) 98 Cal.App.4th 304

OPINION

HASTINGS, J.—

We issued an Order to Show Cause in this original proceeding and requested briefing on whether Code of Civil Procedure section 1008 is unconstitutional to the extent that it purports to deprive trial courts of their inherent power to reconsider interim rulings. We agree with Division Seven of this District which held in *Darling, Hall & Rae v. Kritt* (1999) 75 Cal. App. 4th 1148, 1156 that trial courts retain their inherent power notwithstanding the language of section 1008 which provides that compliance with its provisions is jurisdictional. But we conclude we need not reach the constitutional issue in this case because the facts support the trial court's finding that new circumstances arose to support reconsideration of the trial court's denial of a section 473 motion to set aside a dismissal.

BACKGROUND

The underlying action is one for personal injury brought by real party in interest Dionicia Alvarez. The action was filed on behalf of Ms. Alvarez by attorney Mayra Fornos and alleged that Ms. Alvarez was injured when she fell into an excavation made by defendants Century Communications Corporation and Multi-Cable, Inc. when they were repairing or installing cable service at a specified location.

. . . .

DISCUSSION

Code of Civil Procedure section 1008, subdivision (a), provides in relevant part: "When an application for an order has been made to a judge, or to a court, and refused in whole or in part, or granted, or granted conditionally, or on terms, any party affected by the order may, within 10 days after service upon the party of written notice of entry of the order and based upon new or different facts, circumstances, or law, make application to the same judge or court that made the order, to reconsider the matter and modify, amend, or revoke the prior order."

Prior to 1992, section 1008 allowed a motion for reconsideration solely upon "an alleged different state of facts." (Stats. 1978, ch. 631, § 2; see also, *Imperial Beverage Co. v. Superior Court* (1944) 24 Cal. 2d 627, 634.) Section 1008 purported to be neither jurisdictional nor exclusive. (*Id.* at pp. 633–634; *Salowitz Organization, Inc. v. Traditional Industries, Inc.* (1990) 219 Cal. App. 3d 797, 807–808). The trial court retained its inherent power to reconsider interim rulings. (*Greenberg v. Superior Court* (1982) 131 Cal. App. 3d 441, 445.)

Section 1008 was amended in 1992 and added the language "new or different facts, circumstances, or law" as grounds for reconsideration. (Code Civ. Proc., § 1008, subd. (a); Stats. 1992, ch. 460, § 4.) The purpose of the amendment was to reduce the number of motions for reconsideration by making the diligence requirements of the statute stricter, and by making the statutory procedure exclusive and jurisdictional. (*Baldwin v. Home Savings of America* (1997) 59 Cal. App. 4th 1192, 1199.) To effect this purpose, subdivision (e) was added: "This section specifies the court's *jurisdiction* with regard to applications for reconsideration of its orders and renewals of previous motions, and applies to all applications to reconsider any order of a judge or court, or for the renewal of a previous motion, whether the order deciding the previous matter or motion is interim or final. *No application to reconsider any order or for the renewal of a previous motion may be considered by any judge or court unless made according to this section.*" (Italics added.)

Without reaching the question of whether these new restrictions constitutionally impinged upon the inherent power of a trial court to reconsider its interim rulings, several appellate courts have enforced the expressed intent of the Legislature to impose jurisdictional and exclusive procedures on motions for reconsideration. (See *Pazderka v. Caballeros Dimas Alang, Inc.* (1998) 62 Cal. App. 4th 658, 669–670; *Baldwin v. Home Savings of America, supra,* 59 Cal.App.4th at p. 1200; *Garcia v. Hejmadi* (1997) 58 Cal. App. 4th 674, 686; *Wilson v. Science Applications Internat. Corp.* (1997) 52 Cal. App. 4th 1025, 1031; *Lucas v. Santa Maria Public Airport Dist.* (1995) 39 Cal. App. 4th 1017, 1027; *Gilberd v. AC Transit* (1995) 32 Cal. App. 4th 1494, 1499; and *Morite of California v. Superior Court* (1993) 19 Cal. App. 4th 485, 490–491.)

A court's inherent powers are neither confined by nor dependent on statute. (*Walker v. Superior Court* (1991) 53 Cal. 3d 257, 267.) The inherent power to reconsider interim rulings is derived from the Constitution. (*Id.* at pp. 266–267.) Under article VI, section 1, of the California Constitution, "[t]he judicial power of this State is vested in the Supreme Court, courts of appeal, superior courts, and municipal courts, all of which are courts of record."

The California Constitution also provides for two other branches of government, the legislative branch and the executive branch. (See Cal. Const., art. IV, § 1 [legislative]; Cal. Const., art. V, § 1 [executive].)

Separate powers are divided coequally among the three, with each branch vested with certain "core" functions that may not be usurped by another branch. (*People v. Bunn* (2002) 27 Cal. 4th 1, 14; Cal. Const., art. III, § 3.) The core power of the judiciary is "to resolve 'specific controversies' between parties." (*People v. Bunn, supra,* 27 Cal.4th at p. 15.) The legislative branch is granted the "far-reaching power to weigh competing interests and determine social policy." (*Id.* at p. 15.)

"Notwithstanding these principles, it is well understood that the branches share common boundaries.... [Citations.] [¶] Indeed, the 'sensitive balance' underlying the tripartite system of government assumes a certain degree of mutual oversight and influence. [Citations.]" (*People v. Bunn, supra,* 27 Cal.4th at p. 14.) Thus, the Legislature does not necessarily violate the separation of powers doctrine when it legislates with regard to an inherent judicial power or function. (*Superior Court v. County of Mendocino* (1996) 13 Cal. 4th 45, 57.) "The ... Legislature may put reasonable restrictions upon constitutional functions of the courts provided they do not defeat or materially impair the exercise of those functions." (*Brydonjack v. State Bar* (1929) 208 Cal. 439, 444.)

It is a core function of the courts to ensure the orderly and effective administration of justice. (*Walker v. Superior Court, supra,* 53 Cal.3d at pp. 266–267.) "'One of the powers which has always been recognized as inherent in courts, which are protected in their existence, their powers, and jurisdiction by constitutional provisions, has been the right to control [their] order or business, and to so conduct the same that the rights of all suitors before them may be safeguarded. This power has been recognized as judicial in its nature, and as being a necessary appendage to a court organized to enforce rights and redress wrongs.'" (*Lorraine v. McComb* (1934) 220 Cal.

753, 756.) The inability to correct an error prior to trial and appeal is "'a serious impediment to a fair and speedy disposition of causes.'" (*De La Beckwith v. Superior Court* (1905) 146 Cal. 496, 500.) "A court could not operate successfully under the requirement of infallibility in its interim rulings. Miscarriage of justice results where a court is unable to correct its own perceived legal errors, ..." (*People v. Castello* (1998) 65 Cal. App. 4th 1242, 1249.)

More recently, Division Seven of this District considered the separation of powers doctrine, and found no constitutional invalidity after construing section 1008 as not affecting the court's ability to reevaluate its own interim rulings on its own motion. (*Darling, Hall & Rae v. Kritt, supra,* 75 Cal.App.4th at p. 1156.) The court found the line of cases holding section 1008 jurisdictional to be inapplicable, reasoning that section 1008, subdivision (a) applies only to applications made to the court by parties, not only by its very terms, but also because the intent of the Legislature was "to conserve the court's resources by constraining litigants who would attempt to bring the same motion over and over." (*Darling, Hall & Rae v. Kritt, supra,* 75 Cal.App.4th at p. 1157.) The court also explained that the statute does not restrict reconsiderations sua sponte, because "these same judicial resources would be wasted if the court could not, on its own motion, review and change its interim rulings"; and such a restriction, therefore, would be an impairment of the court's powers prohibited by the separation of powers doctrine of the California Constitution. (*Ibid.*)

While we agree with Division Seven that judicial resources would be wasted if the court could not review and change its interim rulings, we do not see how the manner of bringing erroneous rulings to the court's attention would in any way mitigate that waste. If section 1008 can be said to create an unreasonable impediment to the orderly and effective administration of justice, it can make no difference whether the error is brought to the attention of the court by the parties or by the insight of the judge alone. "Whether the trial judge has an unprovoked flash of understanding in the middle of the night or is prompted to rethink an issue by the stimulus of a motion is constitutionally immaterial to the limitation on the power of the Legislature to regulate the judiciary. [Citation.]" (*Remsen v. Lavacot* (2001) 87 Cal. App. 4th 421, 427, quoting Miller & Horton, About Face (Mar. 2000) 23 L.A. Law. 43, 49.)

Division One of the Fourth District Court of Appeal has suggested in dictum that the language of section 1008 should be read as directory only, to the extent that it could be interpreted as unconstitutionally restricting more than applications made by the parties. (See *People v. Castello, supra,* 65 Cal.App.4th at pp. 1247–1250.)

We agree with that court that when a statute is found to violate the separation of powers doctrine, it should not be construed as mandatory. (See *Lorraine v. McComb, supra,* 220 Cal. at p. 757.) Statutes should be interpreted to preserve their constitutionality, if possible. (*Dyna-Med, Inc. v. Fair Employment & Housing Com.* (1987) 43 Cal. 3d 1379, 1387.)

On the other hand, language of a statute may not be disregarded in defiance of the clear intent of the Legislature. (See *Razeto v. City of Oakland* (1979) 88 Cal. App.

3d 349, 351.) Thus, if we read language into the statute, we must "steer clear of 'judicial policymaking' in the guise of statutory reformation, and ... avoid encroaching on the legislative function in violation of the separation of powers doctrine." (*Kopp v. Fair Pol. Practices Com.* (1995) 11 Cal. 4th 607, 661.) We may reform (or "rewrite") a statute to render it constitutional only "when we can say with confidence that (i) it is possible to reform the statute in a manner that closely effectuates policy judgments clearly articulated by the enacting body, and (ii) the enacting body would have preferred the reformed construction to invalidation of the statute." (*Kopp v. Fair Pol. Practices Com., supra*, 11 Cal.4th at p. 661.)

Thus, the question with regard to section 1008 becomes whether the Legislature clearly articulated its policy judgment when it amended the statute by adding the jurisdictional language of subdivision (e). If so, did the Legislature clearly re-articulate its policy judgment when it amended section 1008 in 1998 to specify that it applies to all applications for interim orders? (See Code Civ. Proc., § 1008, subd. (g); Stats. 1998, ch. 200, § 2.)

If we were to answer those questions in the affirmative, yet construe section 1008 as directory only with regard to applications made by the parties to reconsider an interim ruling, we would be rewriting the statute in defiance of express policy judgments clearly articulated by the Legislature. The result would be a violation on our part of the separation of powers doctrine. (See *Kopp v. Fair Pol. Practices Com., supra*, 11 Cal.4th at p. 661.) Since the Constitution would not allow such a result, our only recourse would be to invalidate the statute. (See *id.* at p. 661; Cal. Const., art. III, § 3.)

At the same time, however, long-established policy obliges us not to "reach out and unnecessarily pronounce upon the constitutionality of any duly enacted statute." (*Palermo v. Stockton Theatres, Inc.* (1948) 32 Cal. 2d 53, 65.) We are constrained to avoid constitutional questions where other grounds are available and dispositive of the issues of the case. (E.g., *Santa Clara County Local Transportation Authority v. Guardino* (1995) 11 Cal. 4th 220, 230.) [1d] Here, invalidation of section 1008 is unnecessary because the trial court concluded new circumstances were presented which supported the grant of the motion for reconsideration. We agree.

Litigants have the right to a full and fair hearing on "critical pretrial matters." (*Titmas v. Superior Court* (2001) 87 Cal. App. 4th 738, 742.) At the hearing on the 473 motion, the trial court granted petitioners an opportunity to respond to the Elias declaration. Instead, petitioners filed a complete new set of points and authorities and a new declaration which addressed not only the Elias declaration but also facts originally addressed by Fornos in her declaration filed with the original motion. Petitioners also raised new issues. Instead of relying on their original argument that the dismissal was not a mistake, petitioners urged that a mistake was made, but it was inexcusable, and that real party's showing was insufficient to establish excusable neglect. McKenzie's supplemental declaration was supported with twelve new exhibits, including excerpts from depositions taken prior to the dismissal, showing that Kollander Construction was the successor to All American Cable Vision, and a letter showing that it was Kollander who was on the job on that date. The court's order denying the 473 motion contained numerous references to petitioners' newly submitted authorities and to their counsel's supplemental declaration.

While it was within the court's discretion to permit petitioners to file a response to Elias's declaration (*Alvak Enterprises v. Phillips* (1959) 167 Cal. App. 2d 69, 74), the length and breadth of the response far exceeded the scope of the anticipated filing. Parties should be given opportunity to brief the new issues that arise after submission, "so that the ensuing order does not issue like a 'bolt from the blue out of the trial judge's chambers.' [Citations.]" (*Monarch Healthcare v. Superior Court* (2000) 78 Cal. App. 4th 1282, 1286.) Indeed, a motion for reconsideration is the appropriate response to the denial of that opportunity. (*Id.* at pp. 1286–1287.)

Petitioners do not contend that the trial court abused its discretion in granting the 473 motion, but contend that we should grant the petition, because they realized while preparing it that the signature on Fornos' declarations does not appear to be the same as that on the complaint and the dismissal with prejudice.

A party may not object to the genuineness of a signature for the first time in the reviewing court. (See *Burnett v. Lyford* (1892) 93 Cal. 114, 117.)

Petitioners assert that because their failure to object was inadvertent, they may raise the issue for the first time here. They rely on *Clark v. Bradley* (1951) 106 Cal. App. 2d 537, but Clark merely held that a new trial was properly granted when all counsel and the court did not realize that the evidence had been inadvertently offered and admitted. (See 106 Cal.App.2d at pp. 544–545.) Since it does not appear that petitioners' inadvertence was shared by real party or the trial court, Clark is inapplicable, and any objection to Fornos' signature has been waived.

DISPOSITION

The petition for writ of mandate or other extraordinary relief is denied. The alternative writ, having served its purpose, is discharged, and the temporary stay order is lifted upon finality of this decision. Real party in interest shall have her costs.

VOGEL (C.S.), P.J., and CURRY, J., concurred.

Notes and Questions

1. If a court reads language into the statute, it must steer clear of judicial policymaking in the guise of statutory reformation and avoid encroaching on the legislative function in violation of the separation of powers doctrine.

2. A court may reform or rewrite a statute to render it constitutional only when it can say with confidence that (1) it is possible to reform the statute in a manner that closely effectuates policy judgments clearly articulated by the enacting body and (2) the enacting body would have preferred the reformed construction to invalidation of the statute.

3. The court in this case noted that, "without reaching the question of whether these new restrictions constitutionally impinged upon the inherent power of a trial court to reconsider its interim rulings, several appellate courts have enforced the ex-

pressed intent of the Legislature to impose jurisdictional and exclusive procedures on motions for reconsideration." Does this approach strike the right balance between inherent powers in the judicial branch and the separation of powers doctrine?

4. As a general rule, the appellate court agreed that, when a statute is found to violate the separation of powers doctrine, it should not be construed as mandatory. In this case, why did the court find it unnecessary to invalidate the statute at issue?

K. Conflict between Two or More Statutes

When two or more statutes that were enacted during the same legislative session actually conflict with each other, then the later enacted statute prevails. This is the general rule in California, which is also found in the state's Government Code.

In re Thierry S.
(1977) 19 Cal.3d 727
OPINION

WRIGHT, J.

Thierry S. was declared a ward of the juvenile court after a finding was made that he was a person described in Welfare and Institutions Code section 602. He appeals from the ensuing judgment (a dispositional order granting probation) and asserts on both statutory interpretation and constitutional grounds that his arrest without a warrant for an alleged misdemeanor was illegal because the offense was not committed in the presence of the arresting officer. He argues that evidence obtained as a result of such arrest and custody which followed was tainted and should have been suppressed by the juvenile court.

In light of applicable rules of statutory interpretation, we agree with the minor's statutory contentions and conclude that a warrant is required before a minor may be arrested or taken into temporary custody based on the alleged commission of a misdemeanor outside the presence of the arresting officer. Lack of compliance with the warrant requirement in the present case tainted evidence essential to the wardship finding and, accordingly, we reverse the judgment.

An extended recitation of the facts in this case is not essential to our resolution of the central issue before us. Although there is considerable disagreement over the necessity of obtaining a warrant before taking a juvenile into custody under circumstances such as those in the present case, the People have never disputed the minor's assertion that if he was taken into custody illegally the evidence relied upon by the juvenile court was tainted by that initial illegality. Consequently, we summarize only the most basic facts.

Deputy Sheriff Bolts was dispatched to a local schoolyard in response to a citizen's telephone call. When he arrived, he saw the minor and another juvenile seated on the ground, their legs bound by a rope. An adult approached Deputy Bolts and indicated that he had detained the two boys after he had observed them standing near the broken window of a schoolroom which had apparently been vandalized only a short time before his arrival. Based on the representation of the citizen-informant and an inspection of the damaged schoolroom, Bolts concluded that there was probable cause to believe that the juveniles were responsible for the damage and that they therefore fell within section 602 as minors who had violated the law defining misdemeanor vandalism (Pen. Code, § 594, subd. (c)). He informed the boys that they were under arrest and transported them to a local detention facility from which they were ultimately released to the custody of their parents. At about the time of their release, Bolts observed certain physical evidence which later connected the boys with vandalism of a number of railroad signal boxes and produced other evidence relied upon by the juvenile court in reaching its section 602 finding. The finding is based solely on evidence of the railroad vandalism and no further action was taken in regard to the schoolroom incident.

The minor relies on section 625.1 as imposing by negative implication a requirement that a warrant must be obtained before a peace officer can take a juvenile into temporary custody based on the alleged commission of a misdemeanor outside of the arresting officer's presence. The People, on the other hand, argue that section 625, subdivision (a) rather than section 625.1 controls in such situations and further contend that section 625 expressly authorizes peace officers to take juveniles into "temporary custody" without a warrant for violation of a criminal law as long as any such arrest is based upon reasonable cause. The minor, in response, does not dispute that section controlled the taking of minors into custody pursuant to section 602 prior to the enactment of section 625.1. He argues, however, that when section 625.1 was enacted in 1971 it took precedence over section 625 insofar as arrests pursuant to section 602 were concerned. Resolution of these conflicting claims necessitates a review of the statutory history of both section 625 and section 625.1 and also involves the application of certain rules of statutory interpretation including those set forth in Government Code section 9605.

At common law it was the general rule that a warrant was required for a misdemeanor arrest unless the offense amounted to a breach of the peace and was committed in the presence of the arresting officer. (5 Am. Jur.2d, Arrest, § 28, p. 718; 1 Torcia, Wharton's Criminal Procedure (12th ed. 1974) Arrest, § 63, p. 168; Comment, Arrest With and Without a Warrant (1927) 75 U.Pa.L.Rev. 485–486.) The warrant requirement was designed as a protection against the abuses of arbitrary arrests and continues to serve that purpose today. As society became increasingly complex and personal mobility increased, however, the need for public security resulted in the development of statutes expanding the authority of peace officers to undertake misdemeanor arrests. In California the breach of the peace requirement was eliminated and officers are now authorized to make misdemeanor arrests without a warrant as long as the arresting officer has reasonable cause to believe that such an offense has been committed in his presence. (Pen. Code, § 836.)

Prior to 1960, Penal Code section 836 provided the only statutory standard for misdemeanor arrests in either adult or juvenile contexts. In that year the Governor's Special Study Commission on Juvenile Justice issued a report on the juvenile court law, culminating a three-year comprehensive review of that subject. The commission's report contained findings and proposed a large number of statutory changes designed to make the juvenile court law, which had gone without basic revision since its enactment in 1915, more responsive to the needs of a modern and more complex society. One recommendation was the enactment of a provision in the Welfare and Institutions Code specifically authorizing warrantless juvenile misdemeanor arrests if based on reasonable cause to believe that a minor had broken any state or federal law or local ordinance. (Rep. of the Governor's Special Study Com. on Juvenile Justice (1960) pt. I, pp. 42–43, 65 (hereinafter, Report).)

In support of its recommendation the commission noted that under the then existing state of the law there was little uniformity in the arrest procedures used by various law enforcement agencies throughout the state. Its research revealed that only a few agencies generally complied with the warrant requirement of Penal Code section 836 when arresting minors, while most police and sheriff's departments simply took juveniles into custody ignoring the fact that the misdemeanor had not been committed in the presence of the arresting officer. Other departments commonly utilized the premise that the minor was not receiving proper parental control or was in danger of leading "an idle, dissolute, lewd, or immoral life" (former § 700, subds. (b), (k), enacted Stats. 1937, ch. 369, repealed Stats. 1961, ch. 1616, § 1) as grounds for an arrest. Some agencies even charged such minors with felonies because of concern over the possibility of false arrest suits. (Report, pt. I, p. 43, pt. II, p. 96.) In view of the foregoing practices the commission concluded that warrantless misdemeanor juvenile arrests based solely on probable cause, i.e., without the "in the presence of the arresting officer" requirement of Penal Code section 836, should be expressly authorized by statute. In addition, because a minor falls within the jurisdiction of the juvenile court whenever he violates any law or ordinance defining crime (§ 602), the commission further concluded that introduction of a warrant requirement by inclusion of an "in the presence" requirement in the new provision would serve no useful purpose.

The result of the commission's recommendation was the enactment of section 625, subdivision (a) which in relevant part then provided as it does now that a peace officer may, without a warrant, take a minor into temporary custody when the officer "has reasonable cause for believing that such minor is a person described in Sections 600, 601, or 602, ..." (Stats. 1961, ch. 1616, § 2, italics added; see fn. 4, *ante*.) Our concern is with the statute's reference to section 602, for it is that provision which confers authority to arrest a juvenile based on the alleged violation of a criminal law. (See fn. 1, *ante*.) No relevant changes were made in section 625 until 1971. In that year a sequence of events occurred involving the amendment of section 625 and the enactment of section 625.1 which gives rise to the dispute over the validity of the arrest in the present case.

Three bills affecting the right of peace officers to undertake misdemeanor juvenile arrests pursuant to section 625 were enacted into statutes during the 1971 session of the Legislature. Two of these bills, Assembly Bill No. 910 (A.B. 910) and Assembly Bill No. 911 (A.B. 911), were concerned solely with the question of juvenile arrests, while the third, Assembly Bill No. 2887 (A.B. 2887), was an omnibus measure which, with a few exceptions, lowered the age of majority from 21 to 18 years by amending a broad range of statutes. One of the many statutes amended by A.B. 2887 to lower an age reference was section 625. A.B. 911 was also designed to amend section 625 but, as we discuss hereinafter, despite the fact that it was enacted and chaptered in the Statutes of 1971, the relationship between A.B. 911 and A.B. 2887 was such that A.B. 911 never acquired the force of law and thus section 625 was never amended thereby. A.B. 910 enacted section 625.1 which, as we have seen, established a stricter standard for misdemeanor juvenile arrests by imposing the "in the presence of the arresting officer" requirement for all warrantless arrests with exceptions not here pertinent. The chaptering sequence of these three bills, and in particular that of A.B. 911 and A.B. 2887 constitutes the central factor in the statutory interpretation analysis involved in this case.

When they were first introduced into the Assembly, only one of the three bills in question, A.B. 910, affected section 625. Among other things, A.B. 910 proposed to amend section 625 by adding language which would have had the effect of prohibiting peace officers from making warrantless arrests of juveniles for alleged misdemeanor violations unless the offenses were committed in the presence of the arresting officers. A.B. 910 and A.B. 911 were later completely redrafted in the Senate to propose a two-pronged statutory scheme for temporary juvenile detentions. First, as redrafted A.B. 910 proposed enactment of a new section 625.1 which would be exclusively concerned with standards for juvenile arrests based on alleged violations of any laws defining crime. (See § 602.) Second, A.B. 911 as redrafted proposed to amend section 625, subdivision (a), contingent on the previous enactment of section 625.1, by deletion of the reference to section 602. The effect of the redrafted versions of A.B. 910 and A.B. 911 would have been that section 625 would thereafter have controlled only juvenile detentions pursuant to sections 600 or 601, while new section 625.1 would have been the sole authorization in the Welfare and Institutions Code for arrests pursuant to section 602 — criminal law violations. As we have already noted, the significant feature of new section 625.1 was that it imposed an "in the presence of the arresting officer" standard in misdemeanor cases and thus, unlike section 625, established a warrant requirement when that standard is not met.

At the time that A.B. 910 and A.B. 911 were undergoing major revision in the Senate, A.B. 2887 contained no provision affecting section 625. Because subdivision (c) of section 625 contained a reference to the age of 21 years, it was necessary to provide for the reduction of that reference to 18 years. As a result, A.B. 2887 was amended by adding a new provision proposing the necessary change in section 625. In order to accommodate the two different amendments to section 625 proposed by A.B. 911 and A.B. 2887, when A.B. 910 and A.B. 911 were redrafted by the Senate a procedure referred to as "double-jointing" took place in regard to A.B. 911. Explication of this term requires a brief summary of the process whereby a bill becomes an operative statute.

After a single version of a bill has been passed by both houses of the Legislature, it can be enacted into a statute in one of three ways. First, the Governor may sign it within certain time limits set forth in the Constitution. Second, the Governor may veto the bill and return it to the Legislature which may in turn enact the bill into a statute by a two-thirds vote in both houses. Finally, if the Governor fails to take any action on the bill within the constitutional time limits, it automatically becomes a statute. (Cal. Const., art. IV, § 10, subd. (a).)

At any one session of the Legislature more than one bill affecting a particular code section or uncodified law may be enacted into a statute. When a conflict is presented by two or more of such recently enacted statutes it is necessary to provide a procedure to determine which of the conflicting statutes will take precedence. The Constitution itself provides no such mechanism and, therefore, the Legislature consistent with pre-existing judicial authority has provided for rules controlling such situations by enacting Government Code section 9605.

The second paragraph of Government Code section 9605 establishes the rule that when two or more bills enacted at the same session of the Legislature conflict, the statute which is enacted last prevails. When as in the present case two conflicting bills are signed by the Governor during the same session of the Legislature, the bill signed last is the one which takes precedence, for a bill is not enacted into a statute until it has been signed by the Governor and transmitted by him to the Secretary of State. (*Davis v. Whidden* (1897) 117 Cal. 618, 622 [49 P. 766]; see Note, Statutory Construction: Conflicting Acts Passed at the Same Session: Higher Chapter Number Prevails (1956) 3 UCLA L.Rev. 417, fn. 4.) In recognition of this long established rule, the Legislature has provided in Government Code section 9510 a means whereby the order in which bills have been signed can be routinely ascertained: After the Governor has signed and dated a bill it is deposited in the office of the Secretary of State where it is assigned a consecutive chapter number corresponding to the order in which it was received. The order of receipt is presumed to be the order in which the bill was approved by the Governor and thereafter when two or more statutes enacted at the same session conflict, the highest chaptered statute is presumed to prevail. The "highest chapter number test" has long been the rule in this state and the Governor, the Assembly, the Senate, and the judiciary have consistently relied upon it when acting upon and when interpreting legislation. (*In re McManus* (1954) 123 Cal.App.2d 395, 399–400 [266 P.2d 929].)

As a consequence of the highest chapter number rule, the Legislature has developed the procedure known as "double-jointing." In the simplest case of two pending bills affecting the same code section in a conflicting manner, double-jointing consists of drafting an alternative version of the code section in question incorporating the changes proposed by both bills which is then included in at least one of the two bills. In addition to the alternative version of the code section a statement of legislative intent is also added to the bill and it provides that if both bills are enacted and affect the same code section, then the amendments proposed by both bills shall be given effect in the form set forth in the alternative version of the code section.

Because the double-jointing provision now before us (see fn. 13 *post*) does not purport to make exception to the highest chapter number rule, however, the double-jointing procedure followed in the instant case would achieve the desired result (incorporation of the changes proposed by both bills) only if the statute which is enacted last contains the alternative version of the code section being amended with a relevant declaration of legislative intent. Although the double-jointing procedure took place in the present case it was ineffective because, as we next describe, A.B. 911 and A.B. 2887 were not signed by the Governor in the order contemplated by the Legislature and thus the last-enacted of the two statutes failed to contain the necessary alternative version of section 625.

When A.B. 2887 was amended by the Senate to include a provision affecting section 625, that provision of the bill proposed amendment of only subdivision (c) by providing that the age reference therein would be reduced from 21 to 18 years. It is highly significant that the bill retained the reference to section 602 in subdivision (a) of section 625.

As stated earlier, when the Senate redrafted A.B. 911 it used a double-jointing procedure by providing for alternative amendments to section 625. Section 1 of A.B. 911 would have made only one change in section 625, deletion of the reference to section 602 in subdivision (a). Due to the fact that A.B. 2887 proposed an amendment of only subdivision (c) of section 625, an alternative version of the amendment to section 625 was proposed. Section 2 of A.B. 911 incorporated both the change proposed by A.B. 2887 and that proposed by section 1 of A.B. 911. Thus section 2 of A.B. 911 proposed not only that section 625 would be amended to delete the reference to section 602 in subdivision (a), but it also proposed that the age reference in subdivision (c) would be reduced from 21 to 18 years.

In order to specify which of the two versions of the amendment to section 625 contained in A.B. 911 and the one version contained in A.B. 2887 would take precedence in the event that both A.B. 911 and A.B. 2887 were enacted into statutes, a statement of legislative intent was incorporated as section 3 of A.B. 911. In sum that statement provided that if A.B. 911 and A.B. 2887 were both enacted into statutes in a form which would affect section 625, and A.B. 2887 was chaptered before A.B. 911 (in other words, if A.B. 911 was approved by the Governor after A.B. 2887), then the amendments proposed by both bills would be given effect in the alternative version of section 625 contained in section 2 of A.B. 911.

Despite the fact that both bills were enacted into statutes the chaptering sequence specified by section 3 of A.B. 911 never occurred because the Governor signed the bills in the reverse order from that in which they were received from the Legislature. A.B. 2887 was enrolled and sent to the Governor by the Legislature on November 23 while A.B. 911 was not sent to him until seven days later on November 30. Had the bills been approved in that same order section 3 of A.B. 911 would have taken complete effect and section 625 would have been amended to reflect the changes proposed by both bills. Although both bills were eventually approved by the Governor on December 14, A.B. 911 was signed before A.B. 2887.

The effect of this reversed order of enactment was that A.B. 911 was chaptered lower (ch. 1730) than A.B. 2887 (ch. 1748) and therefore pursuant to the highest chapter number rule as set forth in Government Code section 9605 and the failure of the terms of the double-jointing provision to make any exception thereto, the version of section 625 contained in A.B. 2887 prevailed over both versions of section 625 contained in A.B. 911. Thus, on the effective date of the statutes enacted in the 1971 legislative session, March 4, 1972, the only amendment of section 625 which occurred was reduction of the age reference in subdivision (c). The reference to section 602 in subdivision (a) of section 625 was unaffected and it remained as it had since that section was first enacted in 1961.

By itself, the reference to section 602 in subdivision (a) of section 625 creates no ambiguity in the statutory scheme for misdemeanor juvenile arrests. An ambiguity appears, however, because section 625.1 (Stats. 1971, ch. 1415; A.B. 910) also became an operative statute for the first time on March 4, 1972, the effective date of the amendment to section 625. Because both section 625 and section 625.1 now purport to provide for section 602 arrest situations, an obvious conflict exists.

It has been suggested that there is in fact no conflict between section 625 and section 625.1 because the enactment of A.B. 911 resulted in an amendment of section 625 by the removal of the section 602 reference contained in subdivision (a) of section 625. Therefore, it is argued, section 625.1 is the sole authority in the Welfare and Institutions Code controlling section 602 arrests. Such an argument ignores the highest chapter number rule by which A.B. 2887 is deemed to have negated the purported intent to remove the section 602 reference contained in subdivision (a) of section 625. It is claimed, however, that the rule, as adopted by the Legislature in Government Code section 9605, is in violation of article IV, section 10 of the Constitution. That section specifies the manner in which the Governor may act on a bill which has been sent to him after passage by both houses of the Legislature. Because that constitutional provision fails to grant to the Governor the authority to control legislation by the order in which he approves such bills, it is urged that the highest chapter number rule is an abridgment of the division of powers set forth in the Constitution.

The foregoing contention is nothing more than a request that we overrule our decision in *Davis v. Whidden, supra,* 117 Cal. 618, 622, wherein we held that a bill does not become a statute until it is approved by the Governor, and thus conflicts between statutes enacted at the same legislative session must be resolved by examination of their order of approval by the Governor. We are urged to hold in place of this long-established rule that conflicts between such statutes are to be resolved by examination of the order of their passage by the Legislature. (Compare *People v. Mattes* (1947) 396 Ill. 348 [71 N.E.2d 690].)

No persuasive grounds are urged which convince us that the highest chapter number rule violates the division of powers doctrine set forth in the Constitution. It does not necessarily follow that because article IV, section 10 does not expressly grant to the Governor the power to control the order in which legislation may take effect, that such a procedure infringes legislative prerogatives. The separation of powers doctrine is necessarily conditioned by the constitutional provision which manifestly involves the Governor in the legislative process to the extent provided therein. It provides not only how, through the Governor's action or inaction a legislative bill becomes a statute but also, inferentially at least, when enactment occurs. As it provides the Governor with the right to control, within limits, when an enactment occurs, it cannot be denied that he may elect, again within limits, the relative order in which enactments may occur. It appears, moreover, that the Legislature has not sacrificed any control to the Governor, as it retains the power to condition the operation of a statute or a series of statutes on the action the Governor may take in respect thereto. It could have, had it chosen to do so, provided "double jointing" provisions in both A.B. 911 and A.B. 2887 which would have insured the particular result it desired regardless of the order of approval by the Governor because in either case the last enacted statute would have contained an alternative version of section 625. We reaffirm our holding in *Davis v. Whidden, supra,* 117 Cal. 618, 622, and continue to follow the highest chapter number rule as set forth in Government Code section 9605.

As we have previously noted, the significant difference between the two statutes in question is that section 625.1 imposes an "in the presence of the arresting officer" requirement for warrantless juvenile misdemeanor arrests, while section 625 contains no similar limitation. In order to resolve the conflict between these differing arrest provisions we turn to the doctrine of implied repeal.

When two or more statutes concern the same subject matter and are in irreconcilable conflict the doctrine of implied repeal provides that the most recently enacted statute expresses the will of the Legislature, and thus to the extent of the conflict impliedly repeals the earlier enactment. Repeals by implication, however, are not favored and there is a presumption against operation of the doctrine. (*Cal. Drive-in Restaurant Assn. v. Clark* (1943) 22 Cal.2d 287, 292 [140 P.2d 657, 147 A.L.R. 1028].) "They are recognized only when there is no rational basis for harmonizing the two potentially conflicting statutes [citation], and the statutes are 'irreconcilable, clearly repugnant, and so inconsistent that the two cannot have concurrent operation. The courts are bound, if possible, to maintain the integrity of both statutes if the two may stand together.'" (*In re White* (1969) 1 Cal.3d 207, 212 [81 Cal.Rptr. 780, 460 P.2d 980].)

Insofar as section 625.1 imposes an "in the presence of the arresting officer" requirement for warrantless juvenile misdemeanor arrests and section 625 contains no such limitation, there is no rational way in which the two statutes may be reconciled. We must, accordingly, ascertain which statute constitutes the later enactment. Section 625.1 was enacted in the 1971 legislative session and became effective on March 4, 1972. Although section 625 as amended also became effective on that date, it was amended only as to an unrelated matter. Government Code section 9605 provides for the instant precedence issue: "Where a section or part of a statute is amended, it is not considered as having been repealed and reenacted in the amended form. *The portions which are not altered are to be considered as having been the law from the time when they were enacted.*" (Italics added.) In the present case, the amendment of subdivision (c) in section 625 by the age of majority bill (Stats. 1971, ch. 1748; A.B. 2887) did not, as we have already indicated, alter the reference to section 602 contained in subdivision (a) of the statute. It therefore follows that subdivision (a) of section 625 dates from 1961 when it was first enacted. (Stats. 1961, ch. 1616, § 2.) Accordingly, insofar as section 625, subdivision (a) conflicts with section 625.1 on the subject of misdemeanor juvenile arrests, the former section was impliedly repealed by enactment of section 625.1 in 1971.

In view of the foregoing, the arrest of Thierry in 1975 was governed by section 625.1. Because he was arrested without a warrant for the alleged commission of a misdemeanor which had not been committed in the presence of the arresting officer, the arrest was invalid. As a consequence of that illegal arrest the evidence relied upon by the juvenile court was tainted and should have been suppressed. Because there is no other material evidence that the minor came within the provisions of section 602, the finding cannot be supported.

The judgment is reversed.

TOBRINER, Acting C.J., MOSK, J., RICHARDSON, J., SULLIVAN, J., and KAUS, J., concurred.

Notes and Questions

1. The presumption established by Gov't Code § 9605 providing that when two or more statutes enacted at the same session conflict, the highest chapter statute is presumed to prevail is rebuttable and can be overcome by evidence that the Governor actually approved bills in a different order than indicated by the chapter numbers. The highest chapter number rule does not violate the division of powers doctrine.

2. When two conflicting bills are signed by the Governor during the same session of the Legislature, the bill signed last is the one which takes precedence. Does this rule make sense in the legislative process? Is there another statutory presumption that could be utilized to deal with two measures that conflict? Is it the responsibility of the legislative branch, or even the judicial branch, to address these conflicts between two bills?

3. There was a total of three bills that impacted the defendant in this case. There was a conflict between two of these bills, A.B. 910 and A.B. 911. The chaptering sequence of these three bills, and in particular that of A.B. 911 and A.B. 2887, "constitutes the central factor in the statutory interpretation analysis involved in this case."

4. The court discussed the legislative process of "double-jointing" language and its impact on which bill becomes the operative statute. How did the court explain that the double-jointing language was ineffective?

5. As the court explained, the state Constitution itself does not provide a procedure or mechanism for resolving conflicting statutes. As a result, the Legislature enacted

Government Code § 9605. "When as in the present case two conflicting bills are signed by the Governor during the same session of the Legislature, the bill signed last is the one which takes precedence, for a bill is not enacted into a statute until it has been signed by the Governor and transmitted by him to the Secretary of State." The court noted that "the 'highest chapter number test' has long been the rule in this state and the Governor, the Assembly, the Senate, and the judiciary have consistently relied upon it when acting upon and when interpreting legislation. (*In re McManus* (1954) 123 Cal.App.2d 395, 399–400.)"

6. What was the basis for the argument that the highest chapter number rule violates Article IV, Section 10 of the state Constitution?

L. Statutory Inconsistencies

Sacramento Newspaper Guild, Local 92 of the American Newspaper Guild, AFL-CIO v. Sacramento County Board of Supervisors

(1968) 263 Cal.App.2d 41

OPINION

FRIEDMAN, J.

At the behest of plaintiff Newspaper Guild, the trial court issued a preliminary injunction restraining the Sacramento County board of supervisors and its committees from holding any closed meeting at which three or more members were present except under the statutory exceptions for personnel and national security matters. The lawsuit was premised upon asserted violations of California's public meeting law, known as the Brown Act. (Gov. Code, §§ 54950–54960.) The board of supervisors and its members appeal from the order granting the preliminary injunction.

Immediate occasion for the lawsuit was a luncheon gathering at the Elks Club in Sacramento on February 8, 1967.participants were the five county supervisors, the county counsel, county executive, county director of welfare and several members of the Central Labor Council, AFL-CIO. The subject of discussion was a strike of the Social Workers Union against the county and the county's effort to enforce an injunction secured in connection with the strike. Newspaper reporters sought but were denied admission to the gathering. In their amended complaint the plaintiffs described not only the February 8 occurrence but alleged threatened future meetings of the supervisors, the county counsel and county executive with third persons selected by them.

Pending the appeal this court issued a limited writ of supersedeas permitting the supervisors to confer with the county counsel under conditions in which the lawyer-client privilege would obtain, but otherwise maintaining enforceability of the trial court decree (*Sacramento Newspaper Guild v. Sacramento County Board of Supervisors,* 255 Cal. App. 2d 51 [62 Cal. Rptr. 819].)

The Brown Act opens with section 54950, which states the law's intent that the "actions [of local legislative bodies] be taken openly and that their deliberations be conducted openly." At its core is section 54953, which declares: "All meetings of the legislative body of a local agency shall be open and public. ..." Both these declarations were in the original version of the Brown Act adopted in 1953. As the legislative body of a local agency, a county board of supervisors is subject to the act. (§§ 54951, 54952.) One feature of the act is section 54957, which permits executive sessions to consider (a) matters affecting the national security and (b) employment and dismissal of personnel. The 1961 Legislature made several additions to the Brown Act (Stats. 1961, ch. 1671), among them a definition of the phrase "action taken" in section 54952.6 and a new misdemeanor penalty provision in section 54959.

A provision of the Brown Act, section 54960, authorizes any "interested person" to seek legal restraint against violations or threatened violations. Defendants do not question the Newspaper Guild's standing to sue. The complaint alleges that the Newspaper Guild is a labor organization composed of professional working newspaper men and women. Whether that allegation makes out adequate standing to sue is at least questionable. (See *United States ex rel. Stowell v. Deming* (1927) 19 F.2d 697, 698, cert. den. 275 U.S. 531 [72 L. Ed. 410, 48 S. Ct. 28]; *Adler v. City Council of Culver City* (1960) 184 Cal. App. 2d 763, 775 [7 Cal. Rptr. 805]; *Associated Boat Industries v. Marshall* (1951) 104 Cal. App. 2d 21, 22 [230 P.2d 379].) The right to disclosure is an attribute of citizenship, not possessed in any increased degree by persons or groups whose interest in access to news is economic. (See *Oxnard Publishing Co. v. Superior Court* (1968) fn. * (Cal.App.) [68 Cal. Rptr. 83].) Section 54950's broad declaration of the public's right to disclosure should logically extend standing to any county elector. Had the county raised the issue in the trial court, amendment of the complaint to add appropriate parties and allegations would have been little more than a matter of mechanics. Under the circumstances, there is substantial compliance with section 54960.

Although all five of the county supervisors were present at the Elks Club luncheon of February 8, 1967, and although the subject or [sic] discussion was a matter of county governmental interest, defendants contend that the trial court erred in viewing it as a meeting within the scope of the Brown Act. They rely upon *Adler v. City Council of Culver City, supra,* 184 Cal.App.2d at pp. 770–774, which held the statute applicable only to formal meetings for the transaction of official business, inapplicable to informal sessions. The Newspaper Guild, on the other hand, argues that the 1961 amendments of the Brown Act were designed to nullify the Adler decision. (See 42 Ops. Cal. Atty. Gen. 61 (1963); Comment, Access to Governmental Information in California, 54 Cal.L.Rev. 1650, 1653–1655 (1966); cf. Herlick, California's Secret Meeting Law, 37 State Bar J. 540 (1962).)

Section 54953 is unequivocal in its central thrust upon official sessions for the transaction of official business, but somewhat ambiguous as it encounters peripheral gatherings or conversations among board members where public business is a topic.

Interpretation to accomplish legislative intent is a truism of the law. Instead of appraising the accuracy of Adler as an interpretation of the pre-1961 law and analyzing the 1961 amendments so far as they bear upon Adler, we prefer to interpret the public meeting provision by examining the current enactment of which it forms a part. Attempts to define "meeting" by synonyms or by coupling it with modifying adjectives involve a degree of question-begging. Interpretation requires inquiry into the Brown Act's objective and into the functional character of the gatherings or sessions to which the legislature intended it to apply.

There is nothing in the Brown Act to demarcate a narrower application than the range of governmental functions performed by the agency. Although the Brown Act artificially classifies it as a legislative body, a board of supervisors actually performs legislative, executive and even quasi-judicial functions. (*Chinn v. Superior Court* (1909) 156 Cal. 478, 481 [105 P. 580]; *Fraser v. Alexander* (1888) 75 Cal. 147, 152 [16 P. 757].) Section 54950 is a deliberate and palpable expression of the act's intended impact. It declares the law's intent that deliberation as well as action occur openly and publicly. Recognition of deliberation and action as dual components of the collective decision-making process brings awareness that the meeting concept cannot be split off and confined to one component only, but rather comprehends both and either.

To "deliberate" is to examine, weigh and reflect upon the reasons for or against the choice. (See Webster's New International Dictionary (3d ed.)) public choices are shaped by reasons of fact, reasons of policy or both. Any of the agency's functions may include or depend upon the ascertainment of facts. (*Walker v. County of Los Angeles* (1961) 55 Cal. 2d 626, 635 [12 Cal. Rptr. 671, 361 P.2d 247].) Deliberation thus connotes not only collective discussion, but the collective acquisition and exchange of facts preliminary to the ultimate decision.

The act supplies additional internal evidence that deliberative gatherings are "meetings," however confined to investigation and discussion. Section 54952.6 defines the phrase "action taken." (Fn. 3, *supra*.) This definition leads to two other provisions where this phrase, or an approximation of it, appears: the declaration of legislative intent in section 54950 and the misdemeanor declaration in section 54959 (fns. 2 and 3, *supra*). In section 54950 the notion of action-taking is juxtaposed to that of deliberation, indicating that deliberation and action, however they may coalesce, are functionally discernible steps, both of which must be taken in public view. The misdemeanor penalty in section 54959, in contrast, is limited to a meeting "where action is taken." Critics of open meeting laws have been troubled by the prospect of criminal prosecutions against public officials who make the wrong guess when confronted with an ambiguous situation. (See Comment, Open Meeting Legislation, 75 Harv.L.Rev. 1199, 1211 (1962); Comment, 54 Cal.L.Rev. supra, at p. 1662.) Apparently sharing this concern, the Legislature has made the criminal sanction narrower than the law's declaration of intended coverage. Not every violation of the Brown Act is a violation of section 54959. The misdemeanor penalty is focused on the meeting where action is taken, not on the meeting confined to deliberation. The narrow, carefully designed criminal penalty evidences the act's broader scope when no crime is involved, that is, when deliberation is unaccompanied by "action taken."

Section 54952 defines the "legislative body" of a local agency to include its committees. Boards of supervisors have investigatory powers which they may delegate to committees, which in turn may "send for persons and papers." (Gov. Code, §§ 25170–25171.) Without troubling the lexicographers, one recognizes a committee as a subordinate body charged with investigating, considering and reporting to the parent body upon a particular subject. Normally, committees investigate, consider and report, leaving the parent body to act. By the specific inclusion of committees and their meetings, the Brown Act demonstrates its general application to collective investigatory and consideration activity stopping short of official action.

Extrinsic as well as intrinsic evidence of legislative intent impels rejection of a narrow interpretation. Tendencies toward secrecy in public affairs have been the subject of extensive criticism and comment. Such governmental phenomena as "managed" news, secret meetings and closed records are disparaged as inimical to the goals and needs of a self-governing nation. The suppression of public information at the local government level in California was the subject of investigation by an Assembly Interim Committee on Judiciary, which submitted its report at the 1953 legislative session. (Progress Report to the Legislature, Assembly Interim Com. on Judiciary (1953) Reg. Sess.) pp. 13–62.) The committee's recommendations included the proposed measure which later became the Brown Act. The report noted widespread evasion of existing open meeting statutes through unannounced "sneak" meetings and through indulgence in euphemisms such as executive session, conference, caucus, study or work session, and meeting of the committee of the whole. (*Ibid.*, pp. 21–23.) The report declared: "It is now apparent to this committee that there is a real need for legislative action. Legislative and administrative groups and officials through devious ways are depriving us, the public, of our inalienable right to be present and to be heard at all deliberations of governmental bodies wherein decisions affecting the public are being made." (*Ibid.*, p. 21.) In presenting and recommending the measure later known as the Brown Act, the committee stated: "The committee is of the opinion that there is a genuine and compelling need for legislative action of a nature designed to curb this misuse of democratic process by public bodies who would legislate in secret. Unless for proper security reasons, the public has the right to be present and to be heard during all phases of legislative enactment by any governmental agency. This right is a source of strength to our Country and must be protected at all costs." (*Ibid.*, p. 61.)

In this area of regulation, as well as others, a statute may push beyond debatable limits in order to block evasive techniques. An informal conference or caucus permits crystallization of secret decisions to a point just short of ceremonial acceptance. There is rarely any purpose to a nonpublic pre-meeting conference except to conduct some part of the decisional process behind closed doors. Only by embracing the collective inquiry and discussion stages, as well as the ultimate step of official action, can an open meeting regulation frustrate these evasive devices. As operative criteria, formality and informality are alien to the law's design, exposing it to the very evasions it was designed to prevent. Construed in the light of the Brown Act's objectives, the term "meeting" extends to informal sessions or conferences of the board members designed for the discussion of public business.

The Elks Club luncheon, attended by the Sacramento County Board of Supervisors, was such a meeting.

Defendants, nevertheless, contend that the occasion was a lawful exercise of the lawyer-client privilege existing between the supervisors and the county counsel, as their attorney; that the pending lawsuit to restrain striking and picketing by county-employed social workers furnished the occasion for exercise of the privilege. Defendants point out that the former law denied the privilege where persons other than the attorney and client were present; that section 952 of the new Evidence Code now extends the privilege to limited situations involving the presence of third persons.

Evidence Code section 952 confers the privilege upon information communicated "in confidence" to the lawyer and upon advice given by the lawyer. The privilege cannot be invoked where the client's communication was not intended to be confidential. (*City & County of San Francisco v. Superior Court* (1951) 37 Cal. 2d 227, 234–235 [231 P.2d 26].)

Participants in the Elks Club luncheon testified at the preliminary injunction hearing. In substance they said that the luncheon took place because the labor representatives wanted to discuss the social workers' strike and to ascertain whether a strike sanction by the central labor council would involve that body in the lawsuit. One supervisor testified that he had attended as a guest of the central labor council, but had no knowledge of the discussion topic until he arrived. Another supervisor testified that he had attended to ascertain the attitude of the central labor council regarding the strike litigation. A third supervisor filed an affidavit. None of these supervisors stated that he or any other supervisor had said anything to the county counsel in confidence. None claimed attendance for the purpose of getting the county counsel's legal advice and none claimed receiving any. If any communication passed between the supervisors and their attorney at the Elks Club luncheon, the record fails to reveal it.

Where the privilege against disclosure is claimed, its opponent has the burden of proving nonconfidentiality. (Evid. Code, § 917.) Here, although a courtroom occasion occurred, the privilege against testifying was not claimed. The assertion appears belatedly, in the form of argument urging a legal characterization. There is no evidentiary basis at all for the characterization. The luncheon meeting of February 8, 1967, finds no shelter under the lawyer-client privilege. The trial court correctly concluded that it violated section 54953.

Aside from the statutory exceptions for national security and personnel matters, the preliminary injunction prohibits nonpublic meetings of three or more supervisors "for whatever purpose." Defendants object to the breadth of the injunction, asserting that the Brown Act should not be construed to prevent conferences between the supervisors and the county counsel for the purpose of seeking and receiving confidential legal advice. Defendants rely upon an opinion of the Attorney General, 36 Ops. Cal. Atty. Gen. 175 (1960), holding that in narrowly limited situations, where a public discussion of legal problems would benefit the agency's adversary and injure the public interest, the board members may meet privately with their attorney. Defendants' position is supported by a brief filed by the County Counsel of Los Angeles County as amicus curiae.

The Brown Act, specifically section 54953, broadly encompasses "all meetings." Viewed as a statutory microcosm, its demand is forthright, offering no internal interstice for private lawyer-client consultations. It is not a microcosm, however, but one element in a structure of constitutional and statutory policies covering the powers, duties and procedures of local agencies of government. Another part of this legal structure is the privilege attaching to confidential lawyer-client communications. This privilege was for almost a century expressed in Code of Civil Procedure section 1881, subdivision 2, and has now been recodified in the Evidence Code. [7a] California decisional law assumes without discussion that the privilege is just as available to public agency clients and their lawyers as to their private counterparts. (*Holm v. Superior Court* (1954) 42 Cal. 2d 500, 506–508 [267 P.2d 1025, 268 P.2d 722]; *Jessup v. Superior Court* (1957) 151 Cal. App. 2d 102, 108–111 [311 P.2d 177].) Codifying this notion, the Evidence Code distinctly includes public agencies and entities among the clients who may assert the privilege.

Traditionally the district attorney has served both as public prosecutor and as civil attorney for California counties and their officials. He fulfills this dual role in those counties which have not established separate civil law offices. (§§ 26520–26528.) When the office of county counsel is established by charter or by act of the supervisors under state law, that officer usually assumes the civil law functions as attorney for the county and its board of supervisors. (§§ 26529, 27640–27645.) Subject to charter restrictions, supervisors may also employ special counsel to furnish representation and advice in civil legal matters. (§§ 25203, 31001.)

Plaintiffs do not dispute the availability of the lawyer-client privilege to public officials and their attorneys. They view it as a barrier to testimonial compulsion, not a procedural rule for the conduct of public affairs. The view is too narrow.

The privilege against disclosure is essentially a means for achieving a policy objective of the law. The objective is to enhance the value which society places upon legal representation by assuring the client full disclosure to the attorney unfettered by fear that others will be informed. (*Greyhound Corp. v. Superior Court* (1961) 56 Cal. 2d 355, 396 [15 Cal. Rptr. 90, 364 P.2d 266]; *Holm v. Superior Court, supra*, 42 Cal.2d at pp. 506–507; 8 Wigmore on Evidence (McNaughton rev. 1961) § 2291; Comment, Attorney-Client Privilege in California, 10 Stan.L.Rev. 297–300 (1958); Louisell, Confidentiality, Conformity and Confusion: Privileges in Federal Court Today, 31 Tulane L. Rev. 101 (1956).) The privilege serves a policy assuring private consultation. If client and counsel must confer in public view and hearing, both privilege and policy are stripped of value. Considered in isolation from the Brown Act, this assurance is available to governmental as well as private clients and their attorneys.

Thus, the structure of laws governing local public boards includes two separate substructures, one in the Government Code demanding open meetings, the other in the Evidence Code assuring confidential lawyer-client conferences. Each expresses a separate policy objective, but neither refers expressly to the other in terms of dominance or reconciliation. At this point we assume without deciding that the Evidence Code, enacted in 1965, merely recodified and continued the existing statutory, lawyer-client privilege of public agencies; that the Brown Act, adopted in 1953, is really the later of the two statutes.

When a later statute supersedes or substantially modifies an earlier law but without expressly referring to it, the earlier law is repealed or partially repealed by implication.

The courts assume that in enacting a statute the Legislature was aware of existing, related laws and intended to maintain a consistent body of statutes. (*Stafford v. Realty Bond Service Corp.* (1952) 39 Cal. 2d 797, 805 [249 P.2d 241]; *Lambert v. Conrad* (1960) 185 Cal. App. 2d 85, 93 [8 Cal. Rptr. 56]; 1 Sutherland, Statutory Construction (3d ed.) §2012, pp. 461–466.) Thus, there is a presumption against repeals by implication; they will occur only where the two acts are so inconsistent that there is no possibility of concurrent operation, or where the later provision gives undebatable evidence of an intent to supersede the earlier; the courts are bound to maintain the integrity of both statutes if they may stand together. (*Warne v. Harkness* (1963) 60 Cal. 2d 579, 588 [35 Cal. Rptr. 601, 387 P.2d 377]; *Penziner v. West American Finance Co.* (1937) 10 Cal. 2d 160, 176 [74 P.2d 252]; *Smith v. Mathews* (1909) 155 Cal. 752, 758 [103 P. 199]; see *Williams v. Los Angeles Metropolitan Transit Authority* (1968) 68 Cal. 2d 599, 603 [68 Cal. Rptr. 297, 440 P.2d 497].) Also, relevant when the seeming inconsistencies appear in separate codes is the rule declaring that the codes blend into each other and constitute a single statute for the purposes of statutory construction. (*Pesce v. Department of Alcoholic Beverage Control* (1958) 51 Cal. 2d 310, 312 [333 P.2d 15]; *People v. Vassar* (1962) 207 Cal. App. 2d 318, 322 [24 Cal. Rptr. 481].)

One of the provisions of the Brown Act, section 54958, declares its application to local legislative bodies "notwithstanding the conflicting provisions of any other state law." Failing to designate what if any laws are superseded, such a clause has no greater force than a repeal by implication; it subordinates or repeals existing law only to the extent that the two laws are irreconcilable. (*Penziner v. West American Finance Co., supra*, 10 Cal.2d at pp. 174–175; 45 Cal.Jur. 2d, Statutes, §69, p. 590; 1 Sutherland, op. cit., §2013, pp. 466–468.)

The question, then, is whether the public meeting requirement of section 54953 abrogates by implication the statutory policy assuring opportunity for private legal consultation by public agency clients; or, in equivalent terms, whether the Brown Act supplies unmistakable evidence of a legislative intent to abolish that statutory policy. That policy is just as meaningful, as financially important, to public as to private clients. Public agencies are constantly embroiled in contract and eminent domain litigation and, with the expansion of public tort liability, in personal injury and property damage suits. Large-scale public services and projects expose public entities to potential tort liabilities dwarfing those of most private clients. Money actions by and against the public are as contentious as those involving private litigants. The most casual and naive observer can sense the financial stakes wrapped up in the conventionalities of a condemnation trial. Government should have no advantage in legal strife; neither should it be a second-class citizen. We reiterate what we stated in the supersedeas aspect of this suit, *Sacramento Newspaper Guild v. Sacramento County Board of Supervisors, supra*, 255 Cal.App.2d at page 54: "Public agencies face the same hard realities as other civil litigants. An attorney who cannot confer with his client outside his opponent's presence may be under insurmountable handicaps. A panoply of constitutional, statutory, administrative and fiscal arrangements covering state and local government expresses a policy that litigating public agencies strive with their legal adversaries on fairly even terms. We need not pause for citations to demonstrate the obvious. There is a public entitlement to the effective aid of legal counsel in civil litigation. Effective aid is impossible if opportunity for confidential legal advice is banned."

. . . .

At various legislative sessions after 1953 bills were introduced, but not passed, expressly amending the Brown Act to permit board members and their attorneys to confer on property acquisition or pending litigation. A recommendation to the same general effect was made by an interim committee in 1965. (The Right to Know, 12 Assembly Interim Com. Report No. 10, Governmental Organization (1965), California Legislature, pp. 41–44.) The record and briefs point to the failure of these proposals as alleged evidence of the 1953 Legislature's design to abrogate the public lawyer-client privilege. The unpassed bills of later legislative sessions evoke conflicting inferences. Some legislators might propose them to replace an existing prohibition; others to clarify an existing permission. A third group of legislators might oppose them to preserve an existing prohibition, and a fourth because there was no need to clarify an existing permission. The light shed by such unadopted proposals is too dim to pierce statutory obscurities. As evidences of legislative intent, they have little value. (See *Ambrose v. Cranston* (1968) 261 Cal. App. 2d 137, 143–144 [68 Cal. Rptr. 22]; Willard and MacDonald, The Effect of An Unsuccessful Attempt to Amend a Statute, 44 Cornell L. Q. 336 (1958).)

The two enactments are capable of concurrent operation if the lawyer-client privilege is not overblown beyond its true dimensions. As a barrier to testimonial disclosure, the privilege tends to suppress relevant facts, hence is strictly construed. (*Greyhound Corp. v. Superior Court, supra*, 56 Cal.2d at p. 396.) As a barrier against public access to public affairs, it has precisely the same suppressing effect, hence here too must be strictly construed. As noted earlier, the assurance of private legal consultation is restricted to communications "in confidence," private clients, relatively free of regulation, may set relatively wide limits on confidentiality. Public board members, sworn to uphold the law, may not arbitrarily or unnecessarily inflate confidentiality for the purpose of deflating the spread of the public meeting law. Neither the attorney's presence nor the happenstance of some kind of lawsuit may serve as the pretext for secret consultations whose revelation will not injure the public interest.

To attempt a generalization embracing the occasions for genuine confidentiality would be rash. The Evidence Code lawyer-client provisions may operate concurrently with the Brown Act, neither superseding the other by implication.

Because the Brown Act did not abolish the statutory opportunity of boards of supervisors to confer privately with their attorney on occasions properly requiring confidentiality, the preliminary injunction is too broad. The preliminary injunction is modified by adding at its end a new paragraph 6, to read as follows:

> "6. This preliminary injunction shall not prevent the Sacramento County Board of Supervisors from consulting privately with the county counsel or other attorney representing the board under circumstances in which the lawyer-client privilege conferred by sections 950 through 962 of the California Evidence Code may lawfully be claimed."

As so modified, the preliminary injunction order is affirmed. Each party is to bear its own costs on appeal.

PIERCE, P.J., and REGAN, J., concurred.

Notes and Questions

1. When seeming inconsistencies appear in separate codes, the codes must be considered as blending into each other and constituting a single statute for purposes of statutory construction. Two laws on the same subject will be so construed as to maintain the integrity of both, if reasonably possible to do so, as courts are bound to uphold the prior act if both may well subsist together, but if they cannot be reconciled, the last act governs and repeals the former acts so far as they are repugnant.

2. This case demonstrates the tension between official sessions of a local government body wherein official business is transacted and what the court deemed "peripheral gatherings or conversations among board members where public business is a topic." The court also explored the differences between deliberation and action.

3. The court found that, because the statute includes committees and their meetings, "the Brown Act demonstrates its general application to collective investigatory and consideration activity stopping short of official action."

4. In the meeting between the labor union and the supervisors, none of the supervisors claimed attendance for the purpose of getting the county counsel's legal advice and none claimed receiving any such advice. The record did not show that there was any communication between the supervisors and their attorney. What was the impact of this?

5. The court described the presumption against repeals by implication as occurring "only where the two acts are so inconsistent that there is no possibility of concurrent operation, or where the later provision gives undebatable evidence of an intent to supersede the earlier; the courts are bound to maintain the integrity of both statutes if they may stand together."

Wong Him v. City & County of San Francisco

(1948) 87 Cal.App.2d 80

OPINION

Bray, J.

Appeal from a judgment of the Superior Court of San Francisco after order sustaining demurrers of respondents city and county of San Francisco and State of California without leave to amend.

The main question here is whether the adoption in 1945 of section 175 of the Revenue and Taxation Code repealed by implication section 3637 of that code.

Appellant, Henry Wong Him, was the owner of two lots in the city and county of San Francisco. In the year 1927–28, the city levied its taxes on the realty, and, in addition, on the personal property located thereon. The complaint alleges that this assessment was illegal and invalid because the personal property belonged to persons other than the appellant and other than the legal and assessed owner of the property. The taxes were unpaid, and on June 25, 1928, the property was marked sold to the state by the city and county for nonpayment of the taxes levied for that fiscal year. On September 6, 1933, the city tax collector made and executed a deed to the State of California for failure to pay taxes. This action was brought on October 22, 1946, under chapter 5.7, part 6, division 1, of the Revenue and Taxation Code and against the city and state, to contest the validity of the tax deed. The deed was alleged to be invalid because the levy upon which the tax was originally based was illegal and void, and because no legal notice of the sale under which the property was deeded to the state was made or given by the city. The demurrers of the respondents on the ground that the action was barred by section 175 were sustained without leave to amend.

Appellant concedes that if section 175 is applicable to this action, then it was not brought in time, as under that section the latest date to bring it would have been September 15, 1946. He, however, contends that section 3637, rather than 175, applies, and under that section the action could be brought any time up until January 1, 1948.

Chapter 5.7 of the Revenue and Taxation Code, entitled "Taxpayer's Action to Contest the Validity of Tax Sale or Tax Deed," was originally added to the code in 1941. Section 3620 thereof sets forth the purpose of the chapter, and section 3637 provides the limitation of the remedy. The same Legislature which had passed section 175 had, just a few weeks before, extended the operation of section 3637. Section 175 was approved by the governor June 25, 1945, and became effective September 15, 1945. (Stats. 1945, ch. 1017, p. 1963.) Sections 3620 and 3637 were amended and became effective immediately as urgency measures on May 31, 1945. (Stats. 1945, ch. 637, p. 1172.) Respondents' sole contention is that sections 3637 and 175 are inconsistent and irreconcilable, and therefore there was a repeal by implication when the latter was added to the code. Appellant, however, contends that there is no inconsistency; that section 175 presents a new remedy, making the procedure for that remedy the procedure under chapter 5.7 and placing its own statutes of limitation thereon, and, therefore, there is no repeal by implication.

In order to apply this doctrine, there must, of course, be an irreconcilable conflict between the two. 23 California Jurisprudence, page 694, section 84, quoted with approval in *Burger v. Hirni*, 50 Cal. App. 2d 709, 711 [123 P.2d 891], states: "Presumption Against Repeal by Implication. It is elementary that the repeal of statutes by implication is not favored, especially where the prior enactment has been judicially construed and is generally understood and acted upon. Likewise, in the absence of express terms it will be presumed that the legislature did not intend by a later act to repeal a former one, if by a fair and reasonable construction effect can be given to both. To overcome this presumption, the two acts must be irreconcilable — i.e., clearly repugnant — as to the vital matters to which they relate, and so inconsistent that the two cannot have concurrent operation, or it must be apparent that the later statute is a revision of the entire subject matter and designed as a substitute for the earlier act, or the intent to effect a repeal must be otherwise expressed in unmistakable language. Accordingly, where there are two laws upon the same subject, they will, if reasonably possible, be so construed as to maintain the integrity of both, the courts being bound to uphold the prior act if the two may well subsist together, though if the two cannot be reconciled, the last act will, of course, govern, and repeals the former in so far as the two are repugnant. The theory of repeal by inadvertence will not be considered if another result may be reached by the application of any rule of construction; ..."

Section 175 was added as chapter 3 to part 1 ("General Provisions"), division 1 ("Property Taxation"), of the Revenue and Taxation Code, and reads: "Chapter 3. Limitation of Actions. § 175. Tax deeds: Presumption where action not commenced in year: Manner of prosecution. All deeds heretofore and hereafter issued to the State of California or to any taxing agency, including taxing agencies which have their own system for the levying and collection of taxes, by reason of delinquency of property taxes or assessments levied by any taxing agency or revenue district, shall be conclusively presumed to be valid unless held to be invalid in an appropriate proceeding in a court of competent jurisdiction to determine the validity of said deed commenced within one year after the execution of said deed, or within one year after the effective date of this section, whichever be later. Such proceedings may be prosecuted within the time limits above specified in the manner and subject to the provisions of Sections 3618 to 3636 of this code."

Section 3637, as originally enacted on May 19, 1941, provided that an action brought under chapter 5.7 must be commenced within one year after the date of execution of the tax deed, or one year after the effective date of said chapter. (Stats. 1941, ch. 293, p. 1439.) The amendment of May 22, 1943, limited the time to one year after the date of execution of the tax deed or one year after January 2, 1945. (Stats. 1943, ch. 709, p. 2465.) As amended on May 31, 1945, and as it now reads, the section provides: "Any proceedings brought in accordance with the provisions of this chapter can only be commenced within one year after the date of execution of the tax deed, or within one year after January 2, 1947, whichever is later." (Stats. 1945, ch. 637, p. 1172.)

Whether section 175 provides a new remedy, and whether it is wholly inconsistent with section 3637, depends upon the legislative meaning and intent in enacting section 3620, determining who may bring an action under chapter 5.7. The latter section has always been passed as an urgency measure, and, as last amended, effective May 31, 1945, reads: "The owner of any real property deeded to the State for taxes, or sold to the State by operation of law prior to July 1, 1939, or any other person who may redeem such property, may bring an action in the superior court of the county wherein the real property is located, to contest the validity of the tax sale or the tax deed to the State."

Appellant contends that this section limits the remedy of chapter 5.7 to the owner of any real property deeded or sold to the state prior to July 1, 1939, and that the addition of section 175 provides a new remedy for all tax deeds, and, specifically, for tax deeds made after 1939. He contends that before the passage of section 175 there was no provision for any such proceedings as to deeds made after July 1, 1939. Respondents, on the other hand, contend that the proper interpretation of this section is that it permits the bringing of an action on property deeded to the state, no matter when the deed was made, but limits the bringing of an action for property sold, but not deeded, prior to July 1, 1939. Thus, the question here is — does section 3620 limit the relief under chapter 5.7 to property deeded or sold prior to July 1, 1939, or does the limitation apply only to property sold but not deeded? If the date refers to both deeds and sales, then the remedy is strictly limited; whereas section 175 applies to all tax deeds without restriction as to date.

As originally enacted in 1941, chapter 5.7 was entitled "Taxpayer's Action to Contest the Validity of Tax Deed" and section 3620 read as follows: "The owner of any real property deeded to the State for taxes, or any other person who may redeem such property, may bring an action in the superior court of the county wherein the real property is located to contest the validity of the tax deed to the State."

In 1937, in the case of *Otis v. Los Angeles County*, 9 Cal. 2d 366 [70 P.2d 633], the court held the tax levy of Los Angeles County for the fiscal year 1933–34 invalid and excessive, thereby invalidating all tax deeds resulting from such levy. The statement of the facts constituting the urgency of the measure indicates that the Legislature had in mind the effect of the decision in the Otis case, for, after declaring that numerous levies by taxing agencies had been, directly or indirectly, declared invalid by court decision, it stated: "Many taxpayers are willing to pay these delinquent taxes and to redeem properties from tax sale if a quick and immediate remedy can be afforded for so doing. No such remedy now exists which has met with the approval of title companies and attorneys for public bodies. It is estimated that large amounts of delinquent taxes, necessary to the continued welfare of the fiscal systems of local governments, will be immediately paid upon the adoption of a quick and simple remedy by which such tax liabilities can be determined in an action brought by the taxpayer." (Stats. 1941, ch. 293, p. 1440.)

On May 22, 1943, chapter 5.7 was again amended in several particulars. The title of the chapter was amended to read: "Taxpayer's Action to Contest the Validity of Tax Sale or *Tax Deed*." (Emphasis added.) An amendment to section 3620 authorized an action to contest the validity of a tax sale as well as a tax deed. It read in part as follows: "The owner of any real property *deeded to the State for taxes*, or sold to the State by operation of law, prior to July 1, 1935, or any other person ..." (Emphasis added.)

Thus, it appears that section 3620 as originally enacted in 1941 limited actions to owners of real property deeded to the state, and no limitation was made in that section as to the time when the deed was made. The same year that section 3620 was enacted, section 3637 was also passed. It provided: "Any proceeding brought in accordance with the provisions of this chapter can only be commenced within one year after the date of execution of the tax deed, or within one year after the effective date of this chapter, whichever is later." (Stats. 1941, p. 1439.) Reading the two sections together, it is clear that the Legislature was referring not only to deeds executed prior to the enactment of the chapter, but also to deeds thereafter to be executed, and that as to deeds already executed, actions thereon must be brought within one year after the effective date of the chapter (1941), and as to deeds thereafter executed, the actions must be brought within one year from their execution.

In 1943, when section 3620 was amended (Stats. 1943, p. 2463) by adding the words "or sold to the State by operation of law, prior to July 1, 1935" (thus for the first time covering property sold but not deeded), section 3637 was also amended, changing the date for the commencement of proceedings to one year after the date of the execution of the deed, "or within one year after January 2, 1945, whichever is later." (Stats. 1943, p. 2465.) From the fact that a comma precedes the words "prior to July 1, 1935" in section 3620, it would appear at first blush that the right of action was limited to property either sold or deeded prior to that date. However, as the Legislature in amending section 3637 that year provided that actions could be brought within one year after the execution of the deed or within one year after January 2, 1945, it is obvious that the limitation in section 3620 "prior to July 1, 1935" was intended to apply only to property tax sold but not deeded. If the property had to be deeded prior to July 1, 1935, how could a suit commenced in 1943 and after, be brought "within one year after the execution of the deed"?

The same reasoning applies to the amendments of 1945. Section 3620 was amended by changing the date, and leaving out the above-mentioned comma, so that the section now reads: "The owner of any real property deeded to the State for taxes, or sold to the State by operation of law prior to July 1, 1939 ..." (Stats. 1945, p. 1172.) Section 3637 was amended to provide that the proceedings must be commenced "within one year after the date of execution of the tax deed, or within one year after January 2, 1947, whichever is later." (Stats. 1945, p. 1172.) By leaving out the comma in section 3620, any ambiguity between that section and section 3637 was eliminated. To give any meaning to the latter section, it necessarily follows that section 3620 means that actions may be brought on property deeded to the state at any time (other than as limited by section 3637), but on property sold, but not deeded, the sale must have been prior to July 1, 1939.

Were it not that the Legislature in its repeated reenactment of these sections intended to place no limitation in section 3620 on tax deeded property, there would be no reason for inserting in section 3637 the language "within one year after the date of execution of the tax deed." Actions on property tax sold prior to 1939, but not deeded, must be brought within one year of January 2, 1947. To give any meaning to the language providing that actions on tax deeded property may be brought within one year of the execution of the deed, it obviously follows that there must be no limitation on the date of the deed. A suit brought in 1945 on a deed executed prior to July 1, 1939, could not possibly be brought within one year of the deed's execution.

In the amicus curiae brief of the county of Los Angeles there appears a photostatic copy of Assembly Bill No. 2003, as it was first introduced in the 1945 Legislature. This bill later became the law which amended sections 3620 and 3637. It appears from such photostat that the elimination of the comma above referred to which was contained in the 1943 amendment was deliberate, and not through inadvertence, as it is shown in the bill with a line drawn through it. While this circumstance is by no means controlling, it is significant in view of the apparent ambiguity between sections 3620 and 3637 as they appeared in the 1943 amendments.

Tax proceedings are in invitum, and tax laws must be strictly construed in favor of the taxpayers. (*Whitmore v. Brown*, 207 Cal. 473 [279 P. 447]; 24 Cal.Jur. pp. 27, 28; *County of Los Angeles v. Jones*, 13 Cal. 2d 554 [90 P.2d 802]; *Anglo Cal. Nat. Bank v. Leland*, 9 Cal. 2d 347 [70 P.2d 937].) The construction given here broadens rather than restricts the remedy provided in chapter 5.7. To hold otherwise would eliminate all property tax deeded subsequent to July 1, 1939, from the benefits of the chapter.

While the language in the emergency clauses of both the 1943 and 1945 acts may be ambiguous and subject to the interpretation that the Legislature is referring only to property either tax deeded or sold prior to a specific date, the action of the Legislature in each time changing both section 3620 and 3637, conclusively shows that such interpretation is not the correct one.

The construction we are giving these sections is the same as the construction which the attorney general contends in his brief has been given since 1943 by his office and the County Counsel of Los Angeles, in actual practice in actions, many in number, which have been filed pursuant to the provisions of chapter 5.7.

Contemporaneous administrative construction, "Although not necessarily controlling ... is entitled to great weight." (*Coca-Cola Co. v. State Bd. of Equalization*, 25 Cal. 2d 918 [156 P.2d 1].) However, in view of our holding, it becomes unnecessary to consider such alleged administrative construction.

The Legislature in passing section 175 evidently had chapter 5.7 in mind, as they referred to all but two sections thereof. The last line of the section states: "Such proceedings may be prosecuted within the time limits above specified in the manner and subject to the provisions of sections 3618 to 3636 of this code." While the failure to mention section 3637 can be interpreted two ways, the better interpretation, in view of the history of that section, together with that of section 3620, is that the Legislature intended by section 175 to repeal by implication that portion of section 3637 which refers to actions on tax deeds.

Section 3620 supplies the basis for the remedial proceedings provided for in chapter 5.7, and applies to all tax deeds whenever executed. Up to 1945, the only limitation of time in which to bring such proceedings was that provided in section 3637. When, in that year, the Legislature enacted section 175 of the same chapter, providing a different limitation upon the time in which proceedings as to all tax deeds could be brought, it is manifest that the legislative intent was to repeal by implication section 3637 insofar as it applied to actions on tax deeded property. *Boyd v. Huntington*, 215 Cal. 473, 482 [11 P.2d 383], quoted with approval in *Division of Labor Law Enforcement v. Moroney*, 28 Cal. 2d 344, 346 [170 P.2d 3], stated: "'a general statute will not repeal by implication a former one which is special or which is limited in its application unless there is something in the general law that makes it manifest that the legislature contemplated and intended a repeal.'" The two acts are clearly inconsistent and repugnant to each other, as applied to tax deeded property, and therefore meet the test set forth in the quotation from *Burger v. Hirni* heretofore given. As section 175 applies to the subject matter of this litigation, and as this action was not brought in time thereunder, the judgment of the court is correct, and is affirmed.

PETERS, P.J., and WARD, J., concurred.

Notes and Questions

1. As the court described the presumption against repeal by implication, it is elementary that the repeal of statutes by implication is not favored, especially where the prior enactment has been judicially construed and is generally understood and acted upon. Likewise, in the absence of express terms, it will be presumed that the Legislature did not intend by a later act to repeal a former one, if by a fair and reasonable construction, effect can be given to both. To overcome this presumption, the two acts must be irreconcilable. Is requiring express terms too high a threshold for the courts to utilize?

2. The main question in this case was whether the adoption of a different Revenue and Taxation Code section repealed by implication another existing CRTC code section. As the court explained, "The same Legislature which had passed section 175 had, just a few weeks before, extended the operation of section 3637. Section 175 was approved by the governor June 25, 1945, and became effective September 15, 1945. Sections 3620 and 3637 were amended and became effective immediately as urgency measures on May 31, 1945."

3. The court case centers on the "sole contention that sections 3637 and 175 are inconsistent and irreconcilable, and therefore there was a repeal by implication when the latter was added to the code." Without an inconsistency between the two sections, there is no argument for implicating the repeal by implication doctrine. "In order to apply this doctrine, there must, of course, be an irreconcilable conflict between the two. 23 California Jurisprudence, page 694, section 84...."

4. The court provided a helpful explanation of the doctrine, including that "it is elementary that the repeal of statutes by implication is not favored." The courts, in applying this doctrine, also look to see if there are express terms that show the Legislature intended repeal of the former statute. Fundamentally, the two statutes must be "irreconcilable — i.e., clearly repugnant — as to the vital matters to which they relate." Moreover, the courts view the inconsistency as creating a situation where "the two [statutes] cannot have concurrent operation."

5. When the court reviewed the two statutes, and "read the two sections together," the court found that the Legislature was referring to the same type of land deeds.

6. What is the impact of this statement by the court: "From the fact that a comma precedes the words 'prior to July 1, 1935' in section 3620 ..."? What is the impact of this determination by the court: "Section 3620 was amended by changing the date, and leaving out the above-mentioned comma, so ..."?

7. What is the impact on this case of the following general rule: "Tax proceedings are in invitum, and tax laws must be strictly construed in favor of the taxpayers" (*Whitmore v. Brown*, 207 Cal. 473....)"?

M. Multiple Bills on the Same Topic

No abridgment of the separation of powers doctrine can validly be predicated on the fact that Constitution Article IV, Section 10 (specifying the manner in which the Governor may act on bills sent to him after passage by both houses of the Legislature) does not expressly grant him the authority to control legislation by the order in which he approves bills.

Government Code §§ 9510 and 9605 may effectively allow him to do so in the case of multiple bills intended to amend the same code section or statute either by virtue of the order in which he signs them, or by virtue of the order in which, having signed them, he transmits them to the Secretary of State who must give them consecutive chapter numbers in the order of their receipt, thereby raising the presumption that the latest enactment to be received was the latest to be approved and thus the one to be given precedence.

The separation of powers doctrine is maintained because, regardless of the actual or presumed order of approval by the Governor, the Legislature may ensure the particular result it desires by inserting "double jointing" provisions in the bills. (*In re S.* (1977) 19 Cal.3d 139.)

N. Reformation of Statutes

Kopp v. Fair Political Practices Commission

(1995) 11 Cal.4th 607

OPINION

LUCAS, C.J. —

I. INTRODUCTION AND SUMMARY

In 1988 the voters enacted Proposition 73, which was designed to reform financing of statewide and local political campaigns. (See Gov. Code, §§ 82041.5, 85100–85400, 89001.) Five provisions of that measure are at issue in this litigation: Section 85301, subdivision (a) (hereafter section 85301(a)) limits to $1,000 per *fiscal year,* contributions by a "person" to a candidate or to committees controlled by the candidate. Section 85302 limits to $2,500 per *fiscal year,* contributions by a "person" to a "political committee, broad based political committee, or political party." Section 85303, subdivision (a) (hereafter section 85303(a)) limits to $2,500 per *fiscal year,* contributions by a "political committee" to a "candidate or any committee controlled by that candidate." Subdivision (b) (hereafter section 85303(b)) of the same section limits to $5,000 per *fiscal year,* contributions by a "broad based political committee or political party" to a "candidate or any committee controlled by that candidate." Finally, section 85304 bans transfer of contributions between a candidate's own committees and between candidates.

In 1990, in a suit in which petitioners in the present litigation were allowed to intervene on behalf of the defendant (respondent herein Fair Political Practices Commission), the federal district court held the "fiscal year" measure of sections 85301–85303 unconstitutional, and enjoined enforcement of those sections and section 85304. (*Service Employees v. Fair Political Practices* (E.D.Cal. 1990) 747 F. Supp. 580 (*Service Employees I*).) The United States Court of Appeals for the Ninth Circuit affirmed the judgment of the district court (Service *Emp. Intern. v. Fair Political Prac. Com'n* (9th Cir. 1992) 955 F.2d 1312 (*Service Employees II*)), and the high court denied certiorari review. (505 U.S. 1230 [120 L.Ed.2d 922, 112 S.Ct. 3056, 3057].)

In this original proceeding (see Cal. Const., art. VI, § 10; Cal. Rules of Court, rule 56(a)) brought by petitioners State Senator Quentin Kopp and Assemblyman Ross Johnson, cosponsors of Proposition 73, we issued an alternative writ of mandate to respondent Fair Political Practices Commission directing it to show cause why a peremptory writ of mandate should not issue ordering respondent to enforce sections 85301–85304. Respondent filed an answer taking a neutral position on the issue. We granted the motions of Common Cause to intervene on behalf of petitioners, and of the California Legislature and four legislators to intervene on behalf of respondent. In addition, we accepted amicus curiae briefs from other interested entities and legislators.

The issue is one of state law: assuming enforcement of the challenged sections as enacted would violate the federal Constitution, *may,* and if so, *should,* the statutes be *judicially reformed* in a manner that avoids the fiscal year measure?

As explained below, we reject claims by interveners on behalf of respondent that the doctrine of res judicata or considerations of comity bar consideration of the issue raised. Nor does the federal appeals court's judgment affirming the federal district court's injunction against enforcement of sections 85301–85304 render those sections incapable of reformation by this court in this litigation.

We also reject the view that a court lacks authority to rewrite a statute in order to preserve its constitutionality or that the separation of powers doctrine, which vests legislative power in the Legislature and judicial power in the courts (Cal. Const., art. IV, § 1; *id.*, art. VI, § 1), invariably precludes such judicial rewriting. Under established decisions of this court and the United States Supreme Court, a reviewing court may, in appropriate circumstances, and consistently with the separation of powers doctrine, reform a statute to conform it to constitutional requirements in lieu of simply declaring it unconstitutional and unenforceable. (1a) The guiding principle is consistency with the Legislature's (or, as here, the electorate's) intent: a court may reform a statute to satisfy constitutional requirements if it can conclude with confidence that (i) it is possible to reform the statute in a manner that closely effectuates policy judgments clearly articulated by the enacting body, and (ii) the enacting body would have preferred such a reformed version of the statute to invalidation of the statute. We conclude, however, that we should not reform section 85304 and, under this test, we may not reform sections 85301(a), 85302, or 85303(a) and (b).

We will not reform the "inter-candidate" aspect of section 85304's transfer ban because the federal appeals court found that section unconstitutional on First Amendment and overbreadth grounds unrelated to reformation of the fiscal year measures of sections 85301(a) and 85303(a) and (b), and hence its order in this regard will not be implicated by our judgment herein, whether or not we reform the latter two sections.

Nor will we reform section 85301(a) or section 85303(a) and (b) — each of which regulates contributions to individual candidates — because, as illustrated by the starkly divergent positions of petitioners and intervener on their behalf, on one hand, and the justices joining Justice Baxter's concurring and dissenting opinion, on the other hand, the statutes cannot be reformed in a fashion that closely effectuates policy judgments clearly articulated by the electorate. Specifically, because the "per election" approach advocated by petitioners and Common Cause would allow candidates less funding than the electorate contemplated, and because the so-called "modified election cycle" reformation advocated by Justice Baxter's concurring and dissenting opinion would allow candidates more funds than the electorate planned (and would remove any regulation of the pace of contributions for nonpartisan offices), neither reformation would closely effectuate policy judgments clearly expressed by the electorate, and hence neither reformation is permissible.

Finally, for related reasons, we will not reform section 85302, which regulates contributions to political committees or parties.

. . . .

B. *Reformation of "constitutionally invalid" statutory provisions*

In a related argument, interveners for respondent assert that when the federal courts declared sections 85301–85304 unconstitutional, those statutes ceased to exist, and hence cannot be judicially reformed because there is nothing left to reform. They cite authority for the proposition that an *invalidated* statute "is not a law; it confers no rights; it imposes no duties; it affords no protection; it creates no office; it is, in legal contemplation, as inoperative as though it had never been passed." (*Norton v. Shelby County* (1886) 118 U.S. 425, 442 [30 L.Ed. 178, 186, 6 S.Ct. 1121] (*Norton*); accord, *Reclamation District v. Superior Court* (1916) 171 Cal. 672, 676 [154 P. 845] (*Reclamation District*).) They concede "numerous exceptions to that principle" — including the rule that "the text of an unconstitutional statute can be rendered legally operative by amending it to repair the constitutional defect" (1 Sutherland, Statutory Construction (5th ed. 1994) Limitations on Legislative Power, § 2.07, p. 38, fn. omitted; see *County of Los Angeles v. Jones* (1936) 6 Cal.2d 695, 708 [59 P.2d 489]), but assert the latter rule is inapplicable here, because petitioners propose repair by judicial *reformation*, rather than legislative *amendment*.

As petitioners observe, more recent decisions have approached the problem differently from *Norton, supra,* 118 U.S. 425, and *Reclamation District, supra,* 171 Cal. 672. "They proceed on the principle that a statute declared unconstitutional is void in the sense that it is inoperative or unenforceable, but not void in the sense that it is repealed or abolished...." (*Jawish v. Morlet* (App.D.C. 1952) 86 A.2d 96, 97, and cases cited [when decision declaring statute unconstitutional is subsequently overruled, statute is restored by overruling decision without necessity of reenactment]; *Ballew v. State* (1974) 292 Ala. 460 [296 So.2d 206] [construing state statute in manner rendering it enforceable despite federal court's earlier decision holding same statute unconstitutional, void, and subject to injunction].) In this regard, we find *Dombrowski v. Pfister, supra,* 380 U.S. 479, persuasive. In that case the high court enjoined enforcement of an unconstitutionally overbroad state statute, but specifically acknowledged the state's authority thereafter to seek and obtain, in state court, a judicial "narrowing" reformation of the invalidated statute. (*Id.* at pp. 491 492 [14 L.Ed.2d at pp. 31 32.)

In any event, we note that neither decision of the federal courts in the *Service Employees* litigation purported to "invalidate" the statutes at issue here, as interveners on behalf of respondent use that term. The federal district court concluded that "because [sections 85301–85303] are measured by a fiscal year, they violate the Constitution of the United States and are *unenforceable*." (*Service Employees I, supra,* 747 F. Supp. at p. 590, italics added.) In turn, the federal appeals court simply agreed with "the district court's decision that all of Proposition 73's contribution limits that are measured on a fiscal year basis are constitutionally infirm" (*Service Employees II, supra,* 955 F.2d at p. 1321), and affirmed the district court's judgment. (*Id.* at p. 1323.) We therefore reject interveners' premise; the federal appeals court did not "invalidate" sections 85301–85304; instead, it *enjoined enforcement* of those sections *as written*.

To the extent interveners on behalf of respondent suggest a statute that has been labeled "constitutionally invalid" is to be treated "as though it had never been passed," and hence as not susceptible to judicial reformation, *Dombrowski v. Pfister, supra,* 380 U.S. 479, and our own cases reject that view. Indeed, the leading authority on the general subject of unconstitutional enactments, cited by both petitioners and interveners for respondent, describes with approval one of our cases (*Quong Ham Wah Co. v. Industrial Acc. Com.* (1920) 184 Cal. 26 [192 P. 1021, 12 A.L.R. 1190]), in which, it notes, we judicially reformed a workers' compensation statute by extending benefits to the class expressly excluded by statute (*id.* at p. 39 et seq.), *after* first finding the statute violated the federal Constitution (184 Cal. at pp. 36–38). (Field, The Effect of an Unconstitutional Statute (1935, reprint ed. 1971), p. 274.) We have recently reaffirmed that same judicial authority to reform constitutionally "invalid" statutes. In *Del Monte v. Wilson* (1992) 1 Cal.4th 1009 [4 Cal.Rptr.2d 826, 824 P.2d 632], we held two veterans' benefits statutes "*invalid* as violative of the equal protection clause of the Fourteenth Amendment of the United States Constitution." (*Id.* at p. 1026, italics added.) Nevertheless, we went on to judicially reform both statutes by extending the statutory benefits to those expressly excluded by the statutes. (*Ibid.*; see *post,* at p. 650.)

Numerous other decisions have long recognized the propriety of such judicial action. (See, e.g., *In re Edgar M.* (1975) 14 Cal.3d 727, 736, 737 [122 Cal.Rptr. 574, 537 P.2d 406] [holding statute as enacted unconstitutional, and then reforming to preserve constitutionality]; see also *Davis v. Michigan Dept. of Treasury* (1989) 489 U.S. 803, 817–818 [103 L.Ed.2d 891, 906–907, 109 S.Ct. 1500] [holding state benefits statute unconstitutional as enacted, and remanding to state court to elect between reformation and invalidation]; *Wengler v. Druggists Mutual Ins. Co.* (1980) 446 U.S. 142, 152–153 [64 L.Ed.2d 107, 116–117, 100 S.Ct. 1540] [same]; *Orr v. Orr* (1979) 440 U.S. 268, 283–284 [59 L.Ed.2d 306, 321–322, 99 S.Ct. 1102] [same]; *Stanton v. Stanton* (1975) 421 U.S. 7, 17–18 [43 L.Ed.2d 688, 696–697, 95 S.Ct. 1373] [same].) In view of this authority, we reject the position of interveners for respondent, that sections 85301 through 85304 were rendered legally nonexistent (and hence not susceptible to judicial reformation) by the federal appeals court's judgment affirming the district court's order enjoining enforcement of those sections.

C. *Summary*

We summarize our disposition of interveners' objections to consideration of the state law reformation issue in this writ proceeding as follows: when faced with a question of whether to reform a state statute, the function of a federal court is to divine, to the best of its ability, how the state's highest court would resolve that state law issue. (*Eubanks v. Wilkinson, supra,* 937 F.2d 1118, 1122.) As noted above, neither federal court in the *Service Employees* litigation did so, and instead both relied solely on federal law in concluding the statutes should not be reformed.

Contrary to suggestions of interveners on behalf of respondent, we conclude that a state supreme court is not constrained by principles of res judicata, collateral estoppel, or comity, to keep silent on a state law statutory reformation issue, when the question is presented to it in litigation such as this. Nor does the federal appeals court's judgment affirming the injunction against enforcement of sections 85301 through 85304 render those sections legally nonexistent and hence not susceptible to judicial reformation. Our sovereign duty as a state court of last resort (see *Scott v. Bank One Trust Co., N.A., supra,* 577 N.E.2d 1077, 1080), consistent with principles of federalism and comity, requires that we not automatically accept the federal court's ruling on this important state law issue, but consider the reformation question afresh ourselves and reach a different conclusion if state law leads us to that result.

For these reasons we issued an order to show cause in this matter, and now proceed to address the issue presented therein, namely, whether we may, and if so, should reform and order respondent to enforce sections 85301(a), 85302, 85303(a) and (b), and the inter-candidate transfer ban of section 85304.

IV. THE AUTHORITY OF A COURT TO REFORM A STATUTE TO PRESERVE ITS CONSTITUTIONALITY

Interveners and amicus curiae on behalf of respondent assert this court lacks authority to reform statutes, and that if we were to claim such authority, we would step out of legitimate judicial bounds and improperly invade the Legislature's domain. They rely on numerous cases such as *Metromedia, Inc. v. City of San Diego* (1982) 32 Cal.3d 180, 187 [185 Cal.Rptr. 260, 649 P.2d 902] and *Blair v. Pitchess* (1971) 5 Cal.3d 258, 282 [96 Cal.Rptr. 42, 486 P.2d 1242, 45 A.L.R.3d 1206] — decisions in which we broadly stated we may not rewrite a statute even to preserve its constitutionality. As we shall explain, those cases, with one antique and unpersuasive exception, are *all* distinguishable. Moreover, as we shall explain directly below, numerous decisions of the United States Supreme Court and lower federal courts and sister states, and numerous decisions of this court, amply support the propriety of judicial reformation — including "rewriting" — of statutes to preserve constitutionality when (i) doing so closely effectuates policy judgments clearly articulated by the enacting body, and (ii) the enacting body would have preferred such a reformed version of the statute over the invalid and unenforceable statute.

Because much of the jurisprudence of our own cases rests on and flows from decisions of the United States Supreme Court addressing judicial authority to reform statutes to preserve them against constitutional infirmity, we will first survey in some detail decisions of the high court, and to a lesser extent, lower federal and state courts. (*Post,* pt. IV. A.) Thereafter, we will review California cases on that question (*post,* pt. IV. B.), and finally, as noted, we will consider cases in which we have disclaimed such authority (*post,* pt. IV. C.).

....

4. *Judicial reformation of otherwise vague or overbroad criminal statutes*

Finally, the high court has endorsed the propriety of judicial reformation of statutes in the context of otherwise vague or overbroad criminal statutes — namely, criminal obscenity statutes — and has encouraged state courts to do so as well.

In *Miller v. California* (1973) 413 U.S. 15 [37 L.Ed.2d 419, 93 S.Ct. 2607] (*Miller*), the high court confirmed that "obscene" materials are not protected by the First Amendment, but limited the scope of nonprotected materials to those that, inter alia, "portray sexual conduct in a patently offensive way." (*Id.* at p. 24 [37 L.Ed.2d at pp. 430–431].) The court required that, in order to be regulated, such conduct be "specifically defined by the applicable state law, as written or authoritatively construed." (*Ibid.,* fn. omitted.) Thereafter the court gave "a few plain examples of what a state statute could define for regulation" under its standard: "(a) Patently offensive representations or descriptions of ultimate sex acts, normal or perverted, actual or simulated [, and] [¶] (b) Patently offensive representation or descriptions of masturbation, excretory functions, and lewd exhibition of the genitals." (*Id.* at p. 25 [37 L.Ed.2d at p. 431].)

Justice Brennan, dissenting in a companion case (*Paris Adult Theater I v. Slaton* (1973) 413 U.S. 49 [37 L.Ed.2d 446, 93 S.Ct. 2628]), asserted the court's *Miller* standard would "invalidate virtually every state law relating to the suppression of obscenity" (*id.* at p. 95, fn. 13 [37 L.Ed.2d at p. 480] (dis. opn. of Brennan, J.).) In response, the *Miller* court stated: "We do not hold … that all States … must now enact new obscenity statutes. Other existing state statutes, as construed heretofore or hereafter, may well be adequate. See *United States v. 12 200-Ft. Reels of Film* [(1973) 413 U.S. 123,] at [p.] 130 n. 7 [37 L.Ed.2d 500, 507]." (*Miller, supra,* 413 U.S. at p. 24, fn. 6 [37 L.Ed.2d at p. 430].)

In the cited footnote 7 of *United States v. 12 200-Ft. Reels of Film* (1973) 413 U.S. 123, 130 [37 L.Ed.2d 500, 507, 93 S.Ct. 2665] (*12 200-Ft. Reels of Film*), the high court stated: "[W]hile we must leave to state courts the construction of state legislation, we do have a duty to authoritatively construe federal statutes where "'a serious doubt of constitutionality is raised"' and "'a construction of the statute is fairly possible by which the question may be avoided.'" *United States v. Thirty-Seven Photographs,* 402 U.S. 363, 369 (1971) [28 L.Ed.2d 822, 829–830, 91 S.Ct. 1400], (opinion of White, J.).… If and when such a 'serious doubt' is raised as to the vagueness of the words 'obscene,' 'lewd,' 'lascivious,' 'filthy,' 'indecent,' or 'immoral' as used to describe regulated material in 19 U.S.C. § 1305(a) and 18 U.S.C. § 1462, … we are prepared to construe such terms as limiting regulated material to patently offensive representations or descriptions of that specific 'hard core' sexual conduct given as examples in *Miller v. California,* [*supra,* 413 U.S.] at [page] 25 [37 L.Ed.2d at page 431]. See *United States v. Thirty-Seven Photographs, supra,* [402 U.S.] at [pages] 369–374 [28 L.Ed.2d at pages 829–835 (opinion of White, J.).…"

Subsequently, citing footnote 7 of *12 200-Ft. Reels of Film, supra,* 413 U.S. 123, 130 [37 L.Ed.2d 500, 507], and *Thirty-Seven Photographs, supra,* 402 U.S. 363, 369 [28 L.Ed.2d 822, 829–830], the high court imposed its elaborate saving gloss — i.e., the specific "hard core" sexual conduct given as examples in *Miller, supra,* 413 U.S. at page 25 [37 L.Ed.2d at page 431] — to preserve against a vagueness challenge a federal statute prohibiting mailing of obscene materials. (*Hamling v. United States* (1974) 418 U.S. 87, 113–116 [41 L.Ed.2d 590, 618–620, 94 S.Ct. 2887].) Thereafter, most state courts (see, e.g., *State v. A Motion Picture Entitled "The Bet"* (1976) 219

Kan. 64 [547 P.2d 760, 767], and cases cited), including our own (see *Bloom v. Municipal Court* (1976) 16 Cal.3d 71, 81 [127 Cal.Rptr. 317, 545 P.2d 229]) did the same, thereby grafting onto the various states' statutes the detailed gloss articulated by the high court in *Miller*. In doing so the state courts determined — most often only by implication — that reformation was an appropriate exercise of judicial power, and that reformation of the statutes, rather than invalidating them, was most consistent with legislative intent.

More recently, in *Brockett v. Spokane Arcades, Inc.* (1985) 472 U.S. 491 [86 L.Ed.2d 394, 105 S.Ct. 2794] (*Spokane Arcades*), the high court approved a similar reformation of a state statute that employed the term "lust" in its definition of regulated obscene matter. The United States Court of Appeals for the Ninth Circuit had invalidated the entire statute on the ground the term was unconstitutionally overbroad because it reached material that merely stimulated "normal sexual responses" in addition to material that was properly subject to regulation — i.e., that evincing a "morbid and shameful interest in sex." (*Id.* at p. 495 [86 L.Ed.2d at p. 400], citing *J-R Distributors, Inc. v. Eikenberry* (9th Cir. 1984) 725 F.2d 482, 490–491.) The high court reversed.

The court first declined to *construe* the term "lust" as referring only to conduct that could properly be regulated. (*Spokane Arcades, supra,* 472 U.S. at pp. 500–501 [86 L.Ed.2d at pp. 403–404].) The court then noted that a "'statute may be in part constitutional and in part unconstitutional, and … if the parts are wholly independent of each other, that which is constitutional may stand while that which is unconstitutional will be rejected.'" (472 U.S. at p. 502 [86 L.Ed.2d at p. 405].) Cautioning that "a federal court should not extend its invalidation of a statute further than necessary to dispose of the case before it," (*ibid.*) the court concluded the statute could be saved through a combination of severance and tacit insertion of limiting language. "Unless there are countervailing considerations, the [state] law should have been invalidated *only insofar as the word 'lust' is to be understood as reaching protected materials.*" (*Id.* at p. 504 [86 L.Ed.2d at p. 406], italics added.) The court observed that state law disfavored invalidating the entire statute and favored severance (*id.* at p. 506 [86 L.Ed.2d at pp. 407–408]), and surmised that the state legislature would prefer a statute that was so severed and limited by a definition of "lust" that excludes material that merely stimulates "normal sexual responses." Accordingly, it reversed the judgment invalidating the statute. (*Id.* at p. 507 [86 L.Ed.2d at p. 408].)

Although all decisions in which courts preserve enactments by severance are to some extent examples of judicial reformation, the significance of *Spokane Arcades, supra,* 472 U.S. 491, lies in the *type* of severance it employed. The court *severed* from the statute any *meaning* of "lust" that would include material that merely stimulates "normal sexual responses." In other words, the court implicitly introduced into the statute words of limitation — confining the reach of the otherwise overbroad term "lust" to cover only material "whose predominant appeal is to a 'shameful or morbid interest'" in sex (*id.* at p. 498 [86 L.Ed.2d at p. 402]) — in order to uphold the statute's validity. (See also *United States v. Treasury Employees* (1995) 513 U.S. ___, ___ [130 L.Ed.2d 964, 986–988, 115 S.Ct. 1003] (maj. opn. of Stevens, J.); *id.* at p. ___ [130

L.Ed.2d at pp. 992–994] (conc. dis. opn. of O'Connor, J.); *id.* at p. ___ [130 L.Ed.2d at pp. 1002–1003] (dis. opn. of Rehnquist, C.J.) [all recognizing authority of court to "rewrite" statute to preserve constitutionality].)

B. *Reformation of statutes by California courts*

Our own cases reveal that, consistently with *Welsh* [*v. United States*, (1970) 398 U.S. 333, 344–367 [26 L. Ed. 2d 308, 321–334, 90 S. Ct. 1792], *supra*, and its numerous high court predecessors and progeny, it is appropriate in some situations for courts to reform — i.e., "rewrite" — enactments in order to avoid constitutional infirmity, when doing so "is more consistent with legislative intent than the result that would attend outright invalidation." (*Arp v. Workers' Comp. Appeals Bd.* (1977) 19 Cal.3d 395, 407–408 [138 Cal.Rptr. 293, 563 P.2d 849] (*Arp*).) As explained below, like the high court, we have reformed statutes to preserve their constitutionality in cases concerning classifications otherwise invalid under the equal protection clause, and in cases involving criminal statutes otherwise unconstitutionally vague or overbroad. In addition, our decisions have reformed statutes to confer necessary procedural due process protections, to avoid classifications impermissible under the First Amendment, and to avoid nullification under the judicial powers provision of our own Constitution.

1. *Guiding principles: The Arp case*

Although *Arp, supra*, 19 Cal.3d 395, was a case in which we ultimately determined *not* to reform a constitutionally infirm statute, that decision both confirms the propriety of such a judicial role in appropriate cases, and provides guidance on the reformation question posed here.

In *Arp, supra*, a unanimous opinion by Justice Richardson, we considered a widower's challenge to a section of the Labor Code governing workers' compensation benefits. Former Labor Code section 3501, subdivision (a), provided that a widow was conclusively presumed to be totally dependent on her deceased husband, but created no such presumption for a widower. Instead, under the statutory scheme, a widower was forced to establish the fact and extent of dependency on his deceased wife. Following high court decisions cited above (e.g., *Frontiero v. Richardson, supra*, 411 U.S. 677; *Weinberger v. Wiesenfeld, supra*, 420 U.S. 636; *Califano v. Goldfarb, supra*, 430 U.S. 199), we held the statute infirm under the equal protection clauses of the state and federal Constitutions. (*Arp, supra*, 19 Cal. 3d at p. 407.)

We then addressed "the question of remedy. Petitioner urges upon us the course adopted in *Goldfarb, Wiesenfeld* and *Frontiero*: extension of statutory benefits to males and females alike, without regard to actual dependency. [Citation.] [¶] Although *courts do not lack the power to remedy a constitutional defect by literally rewriting statutory language*, it is a comparatively drastic alternative, to be invoked sparingly, and *only when the result achieved by such a course is more consistent with legislative intent than the result that would attend outright invalidation.* [Citations.]" (*Arp, supra*, 19 Cal. 3d at pp. 407–408, italics added.)

We noted that in *Weinberger v. Wiesenfeld, supra*, 420 U.S. 636, the high court "in effect held that substitution of the word 'parent' for the word 'mother' was consistent with Congressional intent to subsidize parental care for minor children" (*Arp, supra,* 19 Cal.3d at p. 408), and that the similar reformation in *Califano v. Goldfarb, supra,* 430 U.S. 199, was also consistent with Congress's intent. (19 Cal. 3d at p. 408.)

We concluded, however, that "[o]ur own case is somewhat different," in that there was "clear, if antique" evidence that the Legislature *"did not want* widowers to receive compensation in excess of their actual, demonstrable financial loss: it *repealed* the original limited presumption affording surviving husbands total dependency benefits on a showing of only partial dependency. [Citations.]" (19 Cal.3d at pp. 408–409, italics in original.) In addition, we observed that extension in such "benefits" cases posed a special problem that militated in favor of legislative reformation. We observed that "[s]uch action would undoubtedly have some impact on workers' compensation insurance rates, since the present rate structure presumably has been carefully calculated without reference to the additional risk of maximum payout for all cases of female fatalities …" (*id.* at p. 409) and that under those circumstances "legislative preference is uncertain" and hence "judicial caution is appropriate." (*Id.* at p. 410.) In closing, we also noted that invalidation rather than extension would not substantially disrupt the overall workers' compensation scheme, or impose "any unfair hardship to an employee's survivors" (*ibid.*), because other valid parts of the scheme remained to protect those interests. (*Ibid.*)

Arp, supra, 19 Cal.3d 395, thus stands for the proposition that courts possess the authority, in appropriate cases, "to remedy a constitutional defect by literally rewriting statutory language" when doing so is "more consistent with legislative intent than the result that would attend outright invalidation," but that such judicial action is improper when the suggested reformation is *inconsistent* with the Legislature's intent, or when that intent *cannot be ascertained.* As explained below, both before and since *Arp, supra,* 19 Cal.3d 395, we have reformed statutes to remedy constitutional defects consistently with the principles that governed our resolution of *Arp.*

2. Reformation of statutes to avoid vagueness, overbreadth, or procedural due process problems

In a substantial number of cases we have imposed saving constructions on otherwise unconstitutionally vague terms, thus preserving statutes while at the same time adding a crucial judicial gloss that, in practical effect, operates as a judicial reformation of the statute. As noted above, one such case was *Bloom v. Municipal Court, supra,* 16 Cal.3d 71, 81, in which we — like most other state courts — added a substantial textual gloss to our "obscenity" statute (Pen. Code, § 311.2) in order to save it against a claim that it was void for vagueness. After reviewing the high court decisions described above, including *12 200-Ft. Reels of Film, supra,* 413 U.S. 123, and *Thirty-Seven Photographs, supra,* 402 U.S. 363, we held our Penal Code section "is … limited to patently offensive representations or descriptions of the specific 'hard core' sexual conduct given as examples in *Miller I*[, *supra,* 415 U.S. at page 25 (37 L.Ed.2d at p. 431)], i.e., 'ultimate sexual acts, normal or perverted, actual or simulated,' and masturbation, excretory functions, and lewd exhibitions of the genitals.'" (*Bloom, supra,* 16 Cal.3d at p. 81.)

Thereafter, in *Pryor v. Municipal Court* (1979) 25 Cal.3d 238, 256–257 [158 Cal.Rptr. 330, 599 P.2d 636], we concluded that Penal Code section 647, subdivision (a) (disorderly conduct), was unconstitutionally vague. The statute made criminal one "'[w]ho solicits anyone to engage in or who engages in lewd or dissolute conduct in any public place or in any place open to the public or exposed to public view.'" (25 Cal.3d at pp. 243–244, italics omitted.) In order to preserve the statute, we revised its scope, "arriv[ing] at the following construction of section 647, subdivision (a): The terms 'lewd' and 'dissolute' in this section are synonymous, and refer to conduct which involves the touching of the genitals, buttocks or female breast for the purpose of sexual arousal, gratification, annoyance or offense, if the actor knows or should know of the presence of persons who may be offended by his conduct. The statute prohibits such conduct only if it occurs in any public place or in any place open to the public or exposed to public view; it further prohibits the solicitation of such conduct to be performed in any public place or in any place open to the public or exposed to public view...." (25 Cal.3d at pp. 256–257.)

In numerous other cases we have similarly reformed partly overbroad or vague statutes — and in doing so imposed what amounts to a judicial reformation of the statutory terms. (See, e.g., *City of Los Angeles v. Belridge Oil Co.* (1954) 42 Cal.2d 823, 832–833 [271 P.2d 5]; *In re Kay* (1970) 1 Cal.3d 930, 943 [83 Cal.Rptr. 686, 464 P.2d 142]; *In re Bushman* (1970) 1 Cal.3d 767, 773 [83 Cal.Rptr. 375, 463 P.2d 727]; *Morrison v. State Board of Education* (1969) 1 Cal.3d 214, 225, 232–233 [82 Cal.Rptr. 175, 461 P.2d 375], and cases cited; *Barrows v. Municipal Court* (1970) 1 Cal.3d 821,

Apparently because neither petitioners nor intervener on their behalf discusses these cases, interveners and amicus curiae on behalf of respondent do not discuss them or challenge their applicability to the present litigation. We assume that if pressed, they might attempt to distinguish them on the ground we were not forced in those cases to *disregard* language and to *substitute* reformed language; instead, we simply placed a saving "construction" on the statutory language, thereby constricting the reach of the statute. The distinction, in our view, suggests a difference of degree, not kind. In each of the cited vagueness and overbreadth cases we declined to give effect to the "plain words" meaning of the statutes, and instead reformed the statutes to in order to save and make them enforceable. In practical effect, in all of these cases, we "rewrote" each statute in order to preserve its constitutionality.

3. *Reformation of statutes to avoid violation of state constitutional prohibition*

In re Edgar M., supra, 14 Cal.3d 727 (*Edgar M.*), a unanimous opinion by Chief Justice Wright, illustrates the permissible limits of judicial reformation of a statute in order to conform it to constitutional principles. In *Edgar M.,* we considered a constitutional challenge to Welfare and Institutions Code section 558, which governed a juvenile's application for rehearing after a referee's decision declaring the minor a ward of the court and removing him from his home. The statute provided: "'If all of the proceedings before the referee have been taken down by an official reporter, the judge of the juvenile court may, after reading the transcript of such proceedings, grant or deny such application. If proceedings before the referee have not been taken down by an official reporter, such application shall be *granted* as of right. If an application for rehearing is not granted within 20 days following the date of its receipt, it shall be *deemed denied.* However, the court, for good cause, may extend such period beyond 20 days, but not in any event beyond 45 days, following the date of receipt of the application, at which time the application for rehearing shall be *deemed denied unless it is granted within such period.'"* (14 Cal.3d at pp. 736–737, italics added.)

Because the latter two sentences purported to give binding effect to a juvenile referee's decision without requiring any action by a trial court, we concluded they violated constitutional restrictions on a referee's powers. Instead of invalidating the statute, however, we sought a "construction of the [statute] that will eliminate this invalid application and yet preserve the parts and applications of the [statute] which do not violate the constitutional provisions and which the Legislature would have intended to put into effect if it had foreseen the constitutional restriction." (*Edgar M., supra,* 14 Cal. 3d at p. 736.) We determined that we could best effectuate the Legislature's intent "by altering the operative effect" of the statute's language rather than striking the two offending sentences altogether: "To strike the last two sentences from the section would remove the limits on the time during which an application for rehearing could be pending and awaiting action.... The section would then read as it did in ... 1961.... However, the Legislature showed its dissatisfaction with this omission by introducing the sentences into the section by amendments in 1963 [citations]. The salutary purpose of the amendments was to prevent indefinite prolongation of uncertainty concerning the status of a referee's order as the order of a court." (*Edgar M., supra,* 14 Cal.3d at p. 737.)

Our opinion explained: "We believe that the legislative intent will be more fully effectuated within the constitutional restraint by altering the operative effect of these sentences rather than striking them altogether. The quoted portion of section 558 provides that if the proceedings before the referee have *not* been taken down by an official reporter, an application for rehearing must be granted as a matter of right. If the proceedings *have* been taken down by a reporter but the judge does not ... act on the application within the required period, the proceedings should be treated as a practical matter as if they had been unreported. Thus, we conclude that we can best harmonize the statutory purpose with the constitutional command by requiring that applications which would be 'deemed denied' under the section's literal wording be instead granted as of right, thereby applying to unacted-upon applications based on reported proceedings the rule which the Legislature has laid down for applications based on unreported proceedings." (*Edgar M., supra,* 14 Cal.3d at p. 737.) Clearly, in *Edgar M.,* we substantially reformed — indeed, "rewrote" — two sentences of the statute in order to conform it to constitutional principles, and to effectuate, as closely as possible, the Legislature's intent, which we gleaned from the statute and its history.

Amicus curiae on behalf of respondent attempts to dismiss *Edgar M.* as an aberration — "to say the least, an unusual case ... [embodying a] 'forced, strained, and unsatisfactory principle of statutory construction.'" (Quoting *People v. Belton* (1979) 23 Cal.3d 516, 531 [153 Cal.Rptr. 195, 591 P.2d 485] (dis. opn. of Jefferson, J.).) Interveners on behalf of respondent, on the other hand, accept the analysis and result in *Edgar M., supra,* 14 Cal.3d 727, as being consistent with the Legislature's intent, but attempt to distinguish the present case on the ground that "the electorate's intent with regard to Proposition 73 is much harder to discern." We agree with interveners' implicit concession that *Edgar M., supra,* cannot be dismissed, as amicus curiae would suggest, as some kind of mutant decision, and that the dispositive inquiry in the present case centers on the electorate's intent.

4. *Reformation of underinclusive enactments to avoid First Amendment problems*

In *City and County of San Francisco v. Eller Outdoor Advertising* (1987) 192 Cal.App.3d 643 [237 Cal.Rptr. 815] (*Eller*), the Court of Appeal considered the constitutionality of San Francisco's ordinance regulating both commercial and noncommercial signs. The court found the ordinance constitutional in most part, but held one aspect of the measure, which set out exemptions from regulation, conflicted with the First Amendment.

The suspect categories of exempted signs were contained in four subdivisions of section 603 of the ordinance. Subdivision (c) exempted "'Temporary display posters, without independent structural support, in connection with political campaigns and with civic non-commercial health, safety, and welfare campaigns'"; subdivision (d) exempted "'[t]emporary displays of a patriotic, religious, charitable or civic character'"; subdivision (f) exempted "'Commemorative plaques'"; and subdivision (h) exempted "'Religious symbols attached to buildings....'" (*Eller, supra,* 192 Cal.App.3d at pp. 649–650, fn. 3.)

Following decisions of the high court, the Court of Appeal concluded that by these exemptions the city had impermissibly attempted "'in the area of noncommercial speech[,] to evaluate the strength of, or distinguish between, various communicative interests. [Citations.] With respect to noncommercial speech, the City may not choose the appropriate subjects for public discourse....'" (*Eller, supra,* 192 Cal.App.3d at pp. 661–662, quoting *Metromedia, Inc. v. San Diego* (1981) 453 U.S. 490, 514–515 [69 L.Ed.2d 800, 819–820, 101 S.Ct. 2882].) The *Eller* court concluded these exemption provisions were "incompatible with the First Amendment" under *Metromedia, supra,* 453 U.S. 490, and proceeded to determine "whether the defect we have noted requires invalidation of the entire ordinance or whether the offending provisions can be construed in such a way as to save its constitutionality." (*Eller, supra,* 192 Cal.App.3d at pp. 662, 663.)

The *Eller* court noted that in *Metromedia, Inc. v. City of San Diego, supra,* 32 Cal.3d 180, 187–191, we declined to reform a similar local ordinance principally because the enactors' intent to impose a comprehensive ban on practically all noncommercial signs was incompatible with reformation of the ordinance to exempt noncommercial signs. (*Eller, supra,* 192 Cal.App.3d at p. 663.) As the Court of Appeal observed, however, the San Francisco ordinance revealed the opposite intent, i.e., to exempt "the vast majority of noncommercial expression." (*Id.* at p. 664.)

The court concluded: "In light of the ordinance's apparent purpose to allow most forms of noncommercial speech, little violence is done to the legislative purpose to interpret the exceptions created in subdivisions (c) and (d) of section 603 to embrace *all* categories of noncommercial messages, thereby preserving the ordinance's neutrality and saving it from the constitutional problem raised by the United States Supreme Court in *Metromedia*[, *Inc. v. San Diego, supra,* 453 U.S. 490]. Given the high degree of tolerance for noncommercial communication exhibited by San Francisco's sign legislation, we believe that, had the [board of supervisors] foreseen the First Amendment difficulties created by section 603, they would have chosen an interpretation which broadened, rather than narrowed permissible areas of ideological expression. [¶] Finally, in order to avoid vagueness problems with the term 'temporary' [in section 603, subdivision (d)], we construe that phrase in accord with the modifying description set forth in section 603, subdivision (c) itself., i.e., signs 'without independent structural support.'" (*Eller, supra,* 192 Cal.App.3d at pp. 664–665.)

In other words, the *Eller* court reformed section 603 of San Francisco's ordinance by, inter alia, extending the exemption for *most* noncommercial signs to *all* noncommercial signs. In practical effect, the court *rewrote* the section to apply to "*All noncommercial signs, including*" those listed in the various subdivisions, in order to effectuate the local legislature's intent.

5. *Reformation of underinclusive statutes to avoid equal protection violation*

Even before *Arp, supra,* 19 Cal.3d 395, we recognized a court's authority to extend underinclusive statutory classifications and thereby reform statutes in order to avoid an equal protection violation. For example, in *Hayes v. Superior Court* (1971) 6 Cal.3d 216, 224 [98 Cal.Rptr. 449, 490 P.2d 1137], we unanimously reformed a statute that unreasonably discriminated against defendants convicted in California but imprisoned out of state, by extending to those persons the benefits enjoyed by those convicted and imprisoned in California. (*Id.* at p. 225.) In so reforming the statute, we stressed that doing so was most consistent with the apparent legislative intent, and explained: "A statutory classification which arbitrarily excludes some but not all of those similarly situated in relation to the legitimate purposes of the statute does not necessarily invalidate the entire statute. (*Skinner v. Oklahoma*[, *supra,*] 316 U.S. 535, 543 [86 L.Ed. 1655, 1661]; *In re King* (1970) ... 3 Cal.3d 226, 237 [90 Cal.Rptr. 15, 474 P.2d 983].) In light of the purposes and history of a particular statute or an overall statutory scheme *a reviewing court may correct a discriminatory classification by invalidating the invidious exemption and thus extending statutory benefits to those whom the Legislature unconstitutionally excluded.*" (*Hayes v. Superior Court, supra,* 6 Cal.3d at p. 224, italics added.)

Two years later, in *Sykes v. Superior Court* (1973) 9 Cal.3d 83 [106 Cal.Rptr. 786, 507 P.2d 90], we quoted and followed *Hayes v. Superior Court, supra,* 6 Cal.3d 216, and unanimously extended to those who establish a right to retrial by way of a writ the same statutory protections afforded those who establish a right to retrial by other legal processes. (*Sykes v. Superior Court, supra,* 9 Cal.3d at pp. 92–93.) Then, in *In re Kapperman* (1974) 11 Cal.3d 542 [114 Cal.Rptr. 97, 522 P.2d 657], we extended a statutory right to "presentence credit" to those imprisoned before the effective date of the legislation, despite the Legislature's expressed intent to confine the benefit to those imprisoned after that date. In so reforming the statute we again quoted and followed *Hayes v. Superior Court, supra,* 6 Cal.3d 216, and expressed our conviction that such a "correction" was "consistent with probable legislative intent." (*In re Kapperman, supra,* 11 Cal.3d at p. 550.)

As noted above, we reaffirmed the authority of a court to "rewrite" a statute in order to avoid invalidity for under inclusion in *Arp, supra,* 19 Cal.3d 395, 407 et seq. (See *ante,* pp. 641–643.) Shortly after we decided *Arp, supra,* the Court of Appeal relied on that decision in *Fenske v. Board of Administration* (1980) 103 Cal.App.3d 590 [163 Cal.Rptr. 182] to extend a disability retirement benefits statute otherwise unconstitutional under the equal protection clause. The court reasoned that extension rather than invalidation was most consistent with the Legislature's intent. (*Id.* at pp. 597–598.)

Most recently, in a unanimous opinion by Justice Mosk, we followed these cases and the high court cases discussed *ante,* at pages 632–636, and reformed two benefits statutes that we found "invalid" under the equal protection clause. (*Del Monte v. Wilson, supra,* 1 Cal.4th 1009, 1026.) Military and Veterans Code sections 890 and 980 granted state veterans' benefits, but limited those benefits to veterans who were natives or residents of California at the time of their entry into active service. In selecting reformation over invalidation, we judicially *extended* the benefits of the statutes to those who had been *excluded* by the Legislature, i.e., those who were *not* natives or residents of California at the time of their entry into active service. (1 Cal. 4th at p. 1026.) In so doing we were "guided by the intent of the Legislature to aid veterans." (*Ibid.,* citing [*Califano v.*] *Westcott, supra,* 443 U.S. 76, 89 [61 L.Ed.2d 382, 393], and *Welsh, supra,* 398 U.S. 333, 361 [26 L.Ed. 308, 330–331] (conc. opn. of Harlan, J.).)

. . . .

C. *Cases broadly asserting courts lack authority to "rewrite" statutes in order to preserve them against invalidity under the Constitution*

As noted previously, amicus curiae and interveners on behalf of respondent assert we lack authority to reform a statute in order to make the law consistent with the Constitution. The high court, sister-state, and California cases discussed immediately above (pt. IV. A. B.) amply refute that assertion. As we explain below, those decisions also serve to distinguish the numerous cases relied on by amicus curiae and interveners on behalf of respondent, in which we (and the high court) have broadly stated that a court lacks authority to "rewrite" a statute even to preserve its constitutionality.

As interveners and amicus curiae on behalf of respondent note, one of our most recent assertions in this regard was in *Metromedia, Inc. v. City of San Diego, supra,* 32 Cal.3d 180, in which we said: "There are limits, however, to the ability of a court to save a statute through judicial construction. As we explained in *Blair v. Pitchess* (1971) 5 Cal.3d 258 [96 Cal.Rptr. 42, 486 P.2d 1242, 45 A.L.R.3d 1206], '"[t]his court cannot…, in the exercise of its power to interpret, rewrite the statute. If this court were to insert in the statute all or any of the … qualifying provisions [required to make it constitutional], it would in no sense be interpreting the statute as written, but would be rewriting the statute in accord with the presumed legislative intent. That is a legislative and not a judicial function.'" (P. 282, quoting *Seaboard Acceptance Corp. v. Shay* (1931) 214 Cal. 361, 369 [5 P.2d 882]; see *Flood v. Riggs* (1978) 80 Cal.App.3d 138, 156–157 [145 Cal.Rptr. 573]." (*Metromedia, Inc. v. City of San Diego, supra,* 32 Cal.3d at p. 187.) Interveners and amicus curiae on behalf of respondents assert we should be guided by this and similar statements in numerous other cases and conclude we have no authority to reform a statute in order to preserve and conform it to constitutional requirements.

Close examination of the numerous cases cited by interveners and amicus curiae on behalf of respondent reveals, however, that with one antique exception, the decisions are all distinguishable from the federal and state cases cited *ante,* part IV. A. and B. Most involved situations in which reformation was inappropriate under the standard articulated today, because it was *not* possible to reform the statutes in a manner that closely effectuated policy judgments clearly articulated by the Legislature or enacting body. The remaining cases are distinguishable on a variety of grounds: some involved no constitutional infirmity; others did not involve reformation at all; and some of the decisions and authority affirmatively support the power of courts to reform in order to preserve constitutionality.

Metromedia, Inc. v. City of San Diego, supra, 32 Cal.3d 180, falls into the first category. The City of San Diego enacted an ordinance that banned erection of off-site billboards. After the superior court held the ordinance unconstitutional under the First Amendment, we reversed. (*Metromedia, Inc. v. City of San Diego* (1980) 26 Cal.3d 848 [164 Cal.Rptr. 510, 610 P.2d 407] (*Metromedia I*).) The United States Supreme Court in turn reversed our decision, holding that to the extent the ordinance banned noncommercial billboards, it violated the First Amendment. (*Metromedia, Inc. v. San Diego, supra,* 453 U.S. 490. Significantly, the high court did not declare the ordinance unenforceable, but instead remanded to our court to consider an issue of state law, i.e., whether the ordinance should be "sustain[ed] ... by limiting its reach to commercial speech." (*Id.* at p. 521, fn. 26 [69 L.Ed.2d at p. 824].) We construed the high court's order as requiring us to determine "whether the constitutionality of the ordinance could be saved by a limiting judicial construction of its terms or by severance of unconstitutional provisions from the balance of the enactment" (*Metromedia, Inc. v. City of San Diego, supra,* 32 Cal.3d at p. 182 (*Metromedia III*)), and proceeded to address those issues.

We began our discussion with the statement quoted above (and by interveners and amicus curiae on behalf of respondent), to the effect that we may not, in the exercise of our power to interpret or construe a statute consistently with the constitution, "rewrite" it. (*Metromedia III, supra,* 32 Cal.3d at p. 187.) Thereafter, we stressed that the intent of the ordinance drafters was to ban *both* commercial and noncommercial off-site billboards. We stated: "It does not appear, however, that the city intended to limit its ban to billboards which carried commercial messages. To the contrary, *the city's concern was not with the message but with the structure.*" (*Ibid.,* italics added.)

We found it "clear that the San Diego City Council, in enacting the ordinance in question, intended to include noncommercial billboards" (*id.* at p. 189), but noted that purpose could not be given effect under high court authority. (*Ibid.*)

Any judicial reformation of the San Diego ordinance by limiting its coverage to commercial billboards would have required rewriting in a manner that *ignored* the city's principal concern — the physical existence of *all* off-site billboards — and it would have substituted for that expressed concern an intention patently inconsistent with the rest of the ordinance, i.e., to ban only off-site *commercial* billboards. As we explained, such a reformed ordinance would *not* have closely effectuated the legislative purpose of the ordinance, because "the effect of such [a reformed] ordinance would depend on the extent to which persons are willing to purchase billboard space for noncommercial advertising" (*Metromedia III, supra,* 32 Cal.3d at p. 190), and "it would offer no assurance that a substantial number of billboards, or any particular billboard, would be removed, or that the erection of new billboards would be inhibited." (*Ibid.*) We concluded that the city's "legislative purpose may be better served by an ordinance which bans most off-site billboards than [a judicially reformed] one which draws a distinction based on the content of the billboard's message." (*Id.* at p. 191.)

Metromedia III, supra, was thus a case in which judicial reformation was inappropriate: It was impossible to reform the ordinance in a manner that closely effectuated policy judgments clearly articulated by the local legislature.

All but one of the remaining cases cited by amicus curiae and interveners on behalf of respondent are also distinguishable. In many of the cases, reformation designed to closely effectuate the enacting body's policy judgments was impossible because the enacting body's intent was plainly *inconsistent* with a saving or reformed construction of the enactment. In some of the cases, reformation designed to closely effectuate the enacting body's policy judgments was impossible because the enacting body's intent was *unascertainable.*

Other cases cited by interveners and amicus curiae on behalf of respondent illustrate another important limitation on a court's authority to reform statutes: they concern situations in which crucial policy judgments were *not* clearly articulated by the enacting body, and in which it was thus impossible to reform unconstitutional enactments because doing so would have required the court to substitute or render policy judgments. In *Blair v. Pitchess, supra,* 5 Cal.3d 258, for example, the plaintiffs sued to enjoin enforcement of the state's "claim and delivery" law, a detailed statutory scheme (former Code Civ. Proc., §§ 509–521, enacted 1872) under which the plaintiff in an action to recover possession of property could post a bond, pay a fee, and require a law enforcement officer to seize property from the defendant, all *before* adjudication of the underlying property claim. We found the scheme so wholly infected with both Fourth Amendment (unreasonable search and seizure) and Fifth Amendment (seizure of property without due process of law) infirmities that, we concluded, the statutes could not be salvaged: "[I]n order to create a constitutional prejudgment replevin remedy, there must be provision for a determination of probable cause by a magistrate and for a hearing prior to any seizure, except in those few instances where important state or creditor interests justify summary process. No such safeguards can by any reasonable construction be found in sections 509 through 521; *nor do those sections provide any clue as to which state or creditor interests are sufficiently important to warrant summary procedures.* Consequently, we are compelled to invalidate the statute in its entirety and await a legislative redrafting." (*Blair v. Pitchess, supra,* 5 Cal.3d at p. 283, italics added.) Thereafter the Legislature overhauled the scheme, making scores of changes in response to our decision. (See Code Civ. Proc., §§ 511.101–514.040.)

Still other cases cited by interveners on behalf of respondent are distinguishable on yet another ground: they involved no constitutional infirmity, and hence did not pose the issue addressed herein, i.e., the conditions under which a court may reform an enactment in order to preserve its constitutionality. Indeed, as we implied in *People v. One 1940 Ford V-8 Coupe, supra,* 36 Cal.2d 471 (*One 1940 Ford V-8 Coupe*), the prospect that an enactment might be declared unconstitutional and unenforceable is a crucial factor that militates in favor of, and in appropriate situations mandates, judicial reformation of an enactment. In *One 1940 Ford V-8 Coupe, supra,* we specifically distinguished the simple statutory construction issue before us from the statutory reformation question posed in another case, in which an "exception" was "read into the statute" to avoid constitutional due process problems. (36 Cal.2d at pp. 475–476.) We declined to engage in the same reformation in *One 1940 Ford V-8 Coupe, supra,* precisely because "no constitutional obstacles" were presented on the facts of that case. (*Id.* at p. 476.)

Finally, two cases cited by interveners on behalf of respondent actually hold reformation to be appropriate, and hence do not support their view. In the same vein, we question interveners' reliance on 2A Sutherland, Statutory Construction (5th ed. 1992) Intrinsic Aids, section 47.38, page 291. The cited authority strongly supports rather than defeats the propriety of judicial reformation. It asserts that, in appropriate situations, courts may insert or add words "to prevent unconstitutionality" (*ibid.,* fn. omitted) and that "[a] majority of cases permit the elimination or disregarding of words in a statute" or "the substitution of one word for another if necessary to carry out the legislative intent or express clearly manifested meaning." (*Id.,* §§ 47.37, p. 283, 47.36, p. 277, fn. omitted.) Indeed, the cited page on which interveners rely contains the following: "*Although some courts have been hesitant to supply or insert words, the better practice requires that a court enforce the legislative intent or statutory meaning where it is clearly manifested. The inclusion of words necessary to clear expression of the intent or meaning is in aid of legislative authority. The denial of the power to insert words when the intent or meaning is clear is more of a usurpation of the legislative power because the result can be the destruction of the legislative purpose.*" (*Id.,* § 47.38, p. 291, italics added, fn. omitted.)

As we acknowledged above, one antique case cited by interveners and amicus curiae on behalf of respondent supports their view. But, as explained below, it also serves to illustrate why courts have, in the intervening century, cautiously recognized the propriety of judicial reformation in order to preserve the constitutionality of statutes.

People v. Perry (1889) 79 Cal. 105 [21 P. 423] (*Perry*) was an action by one Davidson, who was appointed in November 1887 by Governor Waterman to be a member of the Board of Health of the City and County of San Francisco. Davidson sued Perry, who had been appointed seven months earlier to the same office by the former Governor, Bartlett. The question posed was whether the appointed office carried a fixed term, or whether the holder served at the pleasure of the Governor. The state Constitution had, since 1863, granted the Legislature authority to set the term, not exceeding four years, for such offices. (*Perry, supra,* 79 Cal. at pp. 113–114.) Nevertheless, in 1870, the Legislature set the office term at five years. (*Id.* at pp. 112–113.)

The court, with only four justices participating in the case, held the clause of the statute fixing the term at five years unconstitutional. It rejected Perry's suggestion that the statute be reformed to set out a four-year term, and concluded that because "no term has been declared by law, … [Perry] held [his office] at the pleasure of the governor, and [Davidson's] title is valid." (*Perry, supra,* 79 Cal. at p. 114.) In reaching this conclusion, the court explained: "[W]e know of no precedent for holding that a clause of a statute, which as enacted is unconstitutional, may be changed in meaning in order to give it some operation, when admittedly it cannot operate as the legislature intended. This would, it seems to us, be making a law, and not merely correcting an excess of authority." (*Perry, supra,* 79 Cal. at p. 115.)

Although the *Perry* court's reluctance to reform the statute in order to preserve its constitutionality was consistent with the jurisprudence of the day (in which, for example, common and nonprejudicial errors in criminal litigation regularly gave rise to reversals of judgments), we conclude *Perry*'s 19th century view of the permissible judicial role regarding reformation of otherwise unconstitutional statutes is dubious authority today. Indeed, in hindsight, it is apparent that the court's professed reluctance to invade the legislative domain actually did far more violence to the legislative scheme than would the proposed reformation. (See 2A Sutherland, Statutory Construction, *supra,* § 47.38, p. 291, quoted *ante,* at p. 658.) The Legislature plainly intended to establish an office of fixed term lasting for as many years as the Constitution allowed. The *Perry* court's refusal to reform the statute to provide for a four-year fixed term wholly frustrated the Legislature's clear and principal intent. Moreover, as explained, *ante,* at pages 641–653, the result in *Perry* is inconsistent with the case law of this court over the past two decades. For these reasons, although we agree with interveners that *Perry, supra,* supports their position, we decline to afford that case any weight.

Although we do not otherwise question the analysis or holdings of the cases relied on by amicus curiae and interveners on behalf of respondent, for the reasons set out above we conclude the various cited statements from *Metromedia III, supra,* 32 Cal.3d 180, and its predecessors and successors (to the effect that a court may never "rewrite" a statute even to preserve its constitutionality), are distinguishable and overbroad dicta. Moreover, as explained above (pt. IV. A. B.), we — and the high court — have expressly and implicitly contradicted and repudiated those overbroad statements in a substantial number of decisions in which we and the high court have reformed — i.e., rewritten — enactments to avoid various types of constitutional infirmities.

        . . . .

D. *Summary: the propriety of, and standards for, judicial reformation of statutes*

In all of the high court and California cases discussed *ante,* part IV. A. and B., the underlying principle is the same. Contrary to dictum in cases like *Metromedia III, supra,* 32 Cal. 3d at page 187, and consistent with our statement in *Arp, supra,* 19 Cal.3d at page 407, a court may reform — i.e., "rewrite" — a statute in order to preserve it against invalidation under the Constitution, when we can say with confidence that (i) it is possible to reform the statute in a manner that closely effectuates policy judgments clearly articulated by the enacting body, and (ii) the enacting body would have preferred the reformed construction to invalidation of the statute. By applying these factors, courts may steer clear of "judicial policymaking" in the guise of statutory reformation, and thereby avoid encroaching on the legislative function in violation of the separation of powers doctrine. (See Cal. Const., art. IV, § 1; *id.,* art. VI, § 1.)

In articulating a reformation designed to effectuate the Legislature's or electorate's intent, courts search for phrasing that would disturb as little as possible the language of the statutes as enacted. At the same time, however, we focus not only on the *number of words* involved in a proposed reformation, but more important, on the *quality* of the proposed change. As a general matter, it is impermissible for a court to reform by supplying terms that disserve the Legislature's or electorate's *policy* choices. By contrast, when legislative (or the electorate's) intent regarding policy choice is clear, a revision that effectuates that choice is not impermissible merely because it requires insertion of more words than it removes.

In summary, and to paraphrase Justice Ginsburg, *supra,* [Some Thoughts on Judicial Authority to Repair Unconstitutional Legislation (1979)] 23 Clev. St. L.Rev. at page 324, we conclude courts may legitimately employ the power to reform in order to effectuate policy judgments clearly articulated by the Legislature or electorate, when invalidating a statute would be far more destructive of the electorate's will. And, "of course ... ultimate authority to recast or scrap the law in question remains with the political branches [and, as in this case, the electorate]." (*Ibid.*)

Before deciding the specific reformation question posed in this proceeding, we briefly address generally the reformation of initiative statutes.

V. REFORMATION OF INITIATIVE STATUTES

Interveners on behalf of respondent assert courts are precluded from reforming initiative statutes, because such judicial action would operate free from the procedural protections that apply to legislative amendment of initiative statutes. Petitioners and intervener on their behalf, joined by the dissenting justices today, advance the opposite view, asserting a court should be especially willing to reform initiative statutes, especially those that concern legislative elections. We accept neither view.

Interveners on behalf of respondents observe that initiative statutes, "[f]or better or worse ... are meant to be set in stone. The Legislature is prohibited from amending them without going back to the people" unless the initiative provides otherwise. (See Cal. Const., art. II, § 10, subd. (c) [The Legislature "may amend or repeal an initiative statute by another statute that becomes effective only when approved by the electors

unless the initiative statute permits amendment or repeal without their approval."].)
Proposition 73 permits legislative amendment "to further its purposes," but allows
such amendment only by a two-thirds vote. (§§ 81012, subd. (a), 85103.) Interveners
on behalf of respondent conclude that judicial reformation of the statutes at issue
here is tantamount to an amendment of them, and that such action is barred by
article II, section 10, subdivision (c) of the state Constitution.

We reject the view that courts are barred from reforming initiative statutes. As
described above, we have recognized and applied substantial safeguards to ensure
both that any proposed reformation closely effectuates policy judgments clearly articulated by the electorate, and that the electorate would have preferred the reformed
version of the statute over the constitutionally invalid and unenforceable version.
More important, nothing we might do by way of reformation would impair the Legislature's authority under article II, section 10, subdivision (c) of the California Constitution, to amend or repeal initiative statutes such as section 85301(a) or section
85303(a) and (b).

Although the concerns raised by interveners on behalf of respondent do not justify
a conclusion that courts are precluded from reforming initiative statutes, those same
points militate against the opposite view of petitioners and their supporters, i.e., that
courts should be especially willing to reform such statutes. Granted, we have said the
people's initiative power is to be jealously guarded and liberally construed. (*Raven
v. Deukmejian* (1990) 52 Cal.3d 336, 341 [276 Cal.Rptr. 326, 801 P.2d 1077].) But we
perceive no principled basis for a general presumption favoring judicial reformation
in such cases. Nor do we find persuasive Justice Baxter's suggested "special" presumption favoring reformation of initiative statutes that the Legislature may be expected to dislike. (See conc. dis. opn. of Baxter, J., *post,* at pp. 686–687.) We conclude
that in all cases, reformation should be tested objectively against the standard set out
herein.

VI. REFORMATION OF SECTIONS 85301–85304

A. *Preliminary observations regarding sections 85302 and 85304*

As an initial matter, we narrow substantially the scope of our inquiry. [W]e view
the federal courts' decisions as reflecting an implied determination that unless the
limitations on contributions to candidates set out in sections 85301(a), 85303(a) and
(b) are enforceable, section 85302, which regulates contributions to political committees
and parties, would itself remain unenforceable. We agree with that determination,
and accordingly defer our consideration of whether section 85302 may be reformed.

We further confine the scope of our inquiry by determining, at the threshold, that
there is no basis for reforming section 85304, which establishes both intra- and inter-
candidate transfer bans. As explained above, the intra-candidate aspect of section
85304, which the courts found to constitute an unconstitutional *spending* limitation,
is not at issue in this proceeding. (See *ante,* pp. 617 619; see generally, *Buckley v.
Valeo, supra,* 424 U.S. 1, 54–59 [46 L.Ed.2d 659, 707–710].) As also explained above,
the inter-candidate transfer ban aspect of section 85304, which appears to operate

as a *contribution* limitation, was invalidated by the federal court of appeals on *dual* grounds, one of which was that the section is overbroad because it prohibits both large *and small* transferred contributions, and is thus "not 'closely drawn to avoid unnecessary abridgment of associational freedoms'" as required by *Buckley v. Valeo, supra,* 424 U.S. 1, 25 [46 L.Ed.2d 659, 691]. (*Service Employees II, supra,* 955 F.2d at p. 1323.) Contrary to the view of petitioners and intervener on their behalf, the federal appeals court's analysis and conclusion in this latter regard would not be undermined by reformation of the "fiscal year" measure of sections 85301 and 85303, and hence section 85304 will remain as enacted and enjoined.

We thus focus on whether sections 85301(a) and 85303(a) and (b) (regulating contributions to *candidates*) may be reformed in a manner that renders them constitutional.

B. *Whether it is possible to reform sections 85301 and 85303 in a manner that closely effectuates policy judgments clearly articulated by the electorate*

The enjoined sections reflect three key policy judgments: First, the sections establish a maximum dollar amount for particular contributions. Second, the sections regulate the pace at which those contributions may be made. Finally, the sections implicitly establish the rights to contribute and to accept a theoretical maximum aggregate amount of funds. A proper reformation must closely effectuate each of these policy judgments.

As noted above, the federal appeals court broached the question whether the sections might be reformed or saved by merely striking the word "fiscal" from the term "fiscal year," but declined to do so because that would create an annual measure and hence lead to the same discriminatory effect perceived as unconstitutional. We agree.

The federal appeals court also considered striking the term "fiscal year" and replacing it with the term "election cycle," but declined do so because, it reasoned, "we would be at a loss to know what the dollar amounts of the limitations should be." (*Service Employees II, supra,* 955 F.2d at p. 1321.)

Petitioners and intervener on their behalf eschew the "election cycle" approach suggested by the federal appeals court, and propose instead that the statutes be reformed by inserting a "per election" measure similar to that employed in an analogous federal statute. (See 2 U.S.C. § 431(1)(A) ["The term 'election' means [¶] . . . a general [or] . . . primary . . . election. . . ."].)

We conclude, however, that such a reformation would not closely effectuate policy judgments clearly articulated by the electorate. Granted, it would retain the maximum amounts for particular contributions established by the sections, and it would effectuate the pacing requirement, at least in the closing months of a campaign, when contributions are arguably most important. But it would promote those policy judgments at the expense of reducing the theoretical maximum aggregate amount of funds that could be contributed to and accepted by most candidates. Specifically, although the "per election" approach would generally maintain the theoretical maximum aggregate amount of funds that could be contributed to and accepted by most candidates for offices with two-year terms (i.e., Assembly races), it would reduce by 50 percent . . .

the theoretical maximum aggregate amount of funds that could be contributed or accepted for all partisan offices with four-year terms (i.e., Senate races and most statewide offices), and it would reduce by 75 percent … the theoretical maximum aggregate amount of funds that could be contributed or accepted for many if not most nonpartisan offices with four-year terms (i.e., most local government offices).

Intervener on behalf of petitioners acknowledges these consequences of the proposed "per election" reformation, but insists this approach is nevertheless consistent with the electorate's intent. First, focusing on section 85301(a), intervener on behalf of petitioners asserts the section was not intended to "*ensure* that contributors would be allowed to donate up to the $4,000 … maximum amounts theoretically allowed for four-year offices under the initiative's fiscal year limits. Rather, … the voters were primarily motivated by a desire to restrict the size of particular contributions to *no more than* $1,000.…*" Second, intervener on behalf of petitioners cites the corresponding provisions of Proposition 68—a rival campaign reform measure that received a lesser number of affirmative votes at the same election at which Proposition 73 was enacted, and which, accordingly, remains "inoperative." (See *Taxpayers to Limit Campaign Spending v. Fair Pol. Practices Com., supra,* 51 Cal.3d 744, 771; *Gerken, supra,* 6 Cal.4th 707, 720.) Intervener observes that under the proposed "per election" reformation of sections 85301(a) and 85303(a) and (b), the maximum contribution to any given statewide or legislative candidate would be the same as the amount set out in the corresponding provisions of Proposition 68. Intervener on behalf of petitioners concludes from this that the voters intended to enact the reduced theoretical maximum aggregate contribution amounts that would result under a "per election" reformation of sections 85301(a) and 85303(a) and (b).

As interveners and amicus curiae for respondent suggest, and as Justice Baxter's concurring and dissenting opinion shows, the argument of intervener for petitioners does not withstand scrutiny. First, assuming for purposes of analysis that the electorate's "primary" motivation was to restrict the size of *particular* contributions, this affords no ground to presume that the statute was not also purposefully designed to accomplish precisely what it would have done in practice, i.e., afford each individual or institutional contributor the opportunity to give, and each candidate the opportunity to accept, a theoretical maximum aggregate amount of contributions—in other words, up to $4,000, $10,000, and $20,000, for a Senate candidate under sections 85301(a) and 85303(a) and (b), respectively.

Second, Proposition 68 is *inoperative* because the voters stated a preference for its rival, Proposition 73. (*Gerken, supra,* 6 Cal.4th 707, 720.) The fact that a majority of the electorate voted for Proposition 68 and the lesser maximum aggregate contribution amounts contained therein cannot, and does not, negate the fact that a *greater majority* voted for Proposition 73 and its *more generous* maximum aggregate contribution amounts. Moreover, because the lower aggregate contribution limitations set out in Proposition 68 were part of a package that also would have established spending limitations and partial public matching funds for campaigns (see inoperative §§ 85400–85405, 85500–85506, proposed by Prop. 68 and approved by electors June 7, 1988), the contribution amounts are to that extent deflated, and hence not "transferable" to Proposition 73, which specifically bans public financing of campaigns. (See § 85300.)

We conclude a "per election" reformation of sections 85301(a) and 85303(a) and (b) would not closely effectuate the right of contributors to give, and candidates to accept, the theoretical maximum aggregate amount of contributions contemplated by the statutes as enacted. Accordingly, we decline to reform the statutes in the fashion advocated by petitioners and interveners on their behalf.

We also decline to revise the statutes in the manner suggested by Justice Baxter. He and the justices joining his concurring and dissenting opinion would reform the three statutes "to limit campaign contributions and loans to candidates to no more than $1,000 (for § 85301, subd. (a)), $2,500 (for § 85303, subd. (a)) and $5,000 (for § 85303, subd. (b)) multiplied by the number of years of the term of office sought by the candidate, and in partisan races, to further incorporate a 'per election' pacing mechanism so that no more than one-half the total allowable amount may be contributed prior to the primary election and no more than one-half of the total allowable amount may be contributed between the primary election and the general election." (Conc. dis. opn. of Baxter, J., *post,* at p. 689.)

Because no party advocated or anticipated a reformation similar to that suggested by Justice Baxter, we sought briefing on the issues raised by such a reformation. Our letter asked, inter alia, whether "(i) it would be necessary or possible to reform the statutes in a manner that closely replicates the total theoretical maximum contribution amounts that would have been allowed under the statutes as enacted, and (ii) would it be necessary or possible for such a judicial reformation to retain a mechanism regulating the pace of contributions, similar to that existing in the statutes as enacted?"

The opponents of reformation — interveners and amicus curiae on behalf of respondent — answered that both objectives are necessary, but neither is possible without this court engaging in extensive rewriting of the statutes or without imposing its own policy judgments in place of those reflected in the statutes as enacted.

Petitioners, although not clearly addressing the questions posed, significantly declined to embrace any suggestion that reformation must allow candidates to receive the theoretical maximum aggregate contributions that would have been allowed under Proposition 73 as enacted.

Intervener on behalf of petitioners argued it would be improper to reform the statutes in a manner that permits candidates to receive the theoretical maximum aggregate amounts allowable under the statutes as enacted. It acknowledged that its own "per election" approach would diminish substantially the theoretical maximum, but asserted that problem is more theoretical than real, because most fundraising occurs toward the close of a campaign — i.e., near the primary and general election stages. Moreover, intervener claimed, a reformation that attempts to replicate the total theoretical maximum aggregate contribution amounts that would have been allowed under the statutes as enacted, would require improper "wholesale rewriting" of the statutes, and would be unnecessary in any event because it would conflict with the voters' primary intent, which was to "restrict the size of particular contributions...."

The supplemental brief of respondent is perhaps most significant. Respondent reaffirmed its neutrality on the ultimate question of whether the statutes *should* be reformed. At the same time, it strongly suggested that if we do reform, we should do so in the manner suggested by petitioners, and *not* in a manner that attempts to replicate the theoretical maximum aggregate contributions that would have been allowed under the statutes as written (i.e., Justice Baxter's approach) because that would "in effect .. . raise the contribution dollar amount above the level which voters were attempting to impose" and allow last-minute lump-sum payments well over the $1,000, $2,500, and $5,000 per fiscal year limitations, thus benefiting candidates who do not face competitive primaries. In this vein, respondent's supplemental brief repeatedly asserted that petitioners' proposed reformation, compared with a scheme (such as proposed by Justice Baxter) that attempts to preserve total campaign contributions in the amounts allowed under Proposition 73, "*best* adheres to the original statutory scheme and preserves the original intent of the electorate." (Italics added.) Respondent also repeatedly asserted that petitioners' approach, compared with a scheme that attempts to preserve total campaign contributions in the amounts allowed under Proposition 73, is "*closest* to [that] contemplated by Proposition 73." (Italics added.) Finally, respondent asserted that although it would be possible to administer a scheme that permits candidates to receive the theoretical aggregate maximums that they would have been allowed under the statutes as enacted, such a scheme would be undesirable because it would be neither simple nor uniform and it would be difficult to administer because, inter alia, there would be at least nine different contribution formulas for candidates for various offices.

In other words, no party or amicus curiae endorses Justice Baxter's approach.

We conclude the reasoning underlying the supplemental briefing forecloses the extensive and novel reformation proposed by Justice Baxter. Indeed, that proposed reformation is impermissible because it is the mirror image of the "per election" approach: Although it would closely effectuate the policy of protecting rights to contribute and to accept a theoretical maximum aggregate amount of funds, as explained below, it would advance that policy at the expense of *doubling,* and in some cases, *quadrupling* the maximum amount of particular contributions. Moreover, in a significant category of elections, it would impose *no* pacing regulation, thus allowing lump-sum contributions barred by the statutes as enacted.

Under Justice Baxter's approach, in the 12 months before a general election, Senate candidates in partisan races would be allowed to receive $4,000 from individuals — $2,000 for the primary, and $2,000 for the general election. By contrast, under the statutes as enacted, during the same period the same candidates would have been limited to $2,000, i.e., $1,000 during the fiscal year in which the primary is held and $1,000 during the fiscal year in which the general election is held. Similarly, under Justice Baxter's approach, in the 12 months before an election, candidates in nonpartisan local contests for 4-year terms — i.e., candidates in most mayoral, council, and supervisorial races — would be allowed to receive $4,000 from individuals at any time. Again, by contrast, under the statutes as enacted, during the same period the same candidates would have been limited to $1,000 (with the possibility of another $1,000 in the event of a runoff election held in a subsequent fiscal year).

The $1,000, $2,500, and $5,000 caps on contribution amounts set out in sections 85301(a) and 85303(a) and (b), together with the pacing mechanism limiting contributions by fiscal year, were obviously intended to limit the opportunity for lump-sum contributions at any time during a campaign. By doubling and in some cases quadrupling those contribution amounts, and by allowing a substantial category of candidates to solicit and accept those contributions in a lump sum at any time, Justice Baxter's proposed reformation would substantially disserve the electorate's policy choices.

Having concluded that neither proposed reformation is permissible, we need not decide whether the electorate would have preferred either of them to invalidation. We observe, however, that an affirmative response is not so self-evident as petitioners and Justice Baxter suggest. As noted above, petitioners' "per election" reformation would impose regulations *stricter* than those set out in the statutes as enacted, and we might assume, at least for purposes of analysis, that the electorate would have preferred *that* reformation over invalidation. But, as also noted above, Justice Baxter's "modified election cycle" reformation would produce a scheme considerably more *lenient* than the statutes as enacted. We would be extremely reluctant to presume that the electorate might have preferred such a "half loaf" compromise over invalidation. Indeed, we find it at least as likely that the electorate would prefer to start anew in order to create a comprehensive and coherent scheme, rather than settle for a makeshift and ill-fitting law that might actually hamper future campaign financing reform by creating an illusion that full and complete reform had been achieved. Accordingly, we conclude that it would be impossible to determine *with confidence* that the electorate would have preferred the reformation proposed by Justice Baxter over invalidation.

VII. CONCLUSION

Contrary to interveners and amicus curiae on behalf of respondent, the separation of powers doctrine guides, but does not invariably preclude, judicial rewriting of statutes to preserve constitutionality. Consistent with the doctrine, a court has authority to reform statutes by rewriting them to preserve constitutionality when it can conclude with confidence that (i) it is possible to reform the statute in a manner that closely effectuates policy judgments clearly articulated by the enacting body, and (ii) the enacting body would have preferred such a reformed version of the statute to invalidation of the statute. Indeed, in an appropriate case it would be our duty to rewrite in order "to prevent unconstitutionality." (2A Sutherland, Statutory Construction, *supra,* Intrinsic Aids, § 47.38, p. 291.) As observed above, the "better practice requires that a court enforce the legislative intent or statutory meaning where it is clearly manifested. The inclusion of words necessary to clear expression of the intent or meaning is in aid of legislative authority. *The denial of the power to insert words when the intent or meaning is clear is more of a usurpation of the legislative power because the result can be the destruction of the legislative purpose.*" (*Ibid.,* italics added; see also *id.,* § 47.37, p. 283; *id.,* § 47.36, p. 277.) And, as also noted above, when legislative (or the electorate's) intent regarding policy choice is clear, a revision that effectuates that choice is not impermissible merely because it requires insertion of more words than it removes.

We also conclude, however, that reformation is inappropriate here, and cannot be accomplished consistently with the limitations placed on courts by the separation of powers doctrine. We decline to reform section 85304 because the federal appeals court's analysis of, and conclusion regarding, that section would not be undermined by reformation of the "fiscal year" measure of sections 85301(a) and 85303(a) and (b). In turn, we may not reform sections 85301(a) and 85303(a) and (b) (and, accordingly, we may not reform section 85302) because it is impossible to do so in a manner that closely effectuates policy judgments clearly articulated by the electorate. The "per election" approach would allow persons to give, and candidates to accept, less funding than the electorate contemplated. By contrast, Justice Baxter's novel and unsupported "modified election cycle" approach would allow candidates more funds than the electorate planned, and it would remove any regulation of the pace of contributions for the numerous nonpartisan municipal and county elections throughout the state. Because neither reformation would closely effectuate policy judgments clearly expressed by the electorate, it follows that either would impermissibly intrude on the policy-making functions reserved to the Legislature and the people (Cal. Const., art. IV, § 1), and hence neither reformation is permissible.

Accordingly, we deny the relief requested by petitioners.

WERDEGAR, J., concurred.

Notes and Questions

1. As a general matter, it is impermissible for a court to reform a statute to save it from invalidation under the Constitution by supplying terms that disserve the Legislature's or electorate's policy choices. By contrast, when legislative intent regarding a policy choice is clear, revision that effectuates that choice is not impermissible merely because it requires insertion of more words than it removes.

2. The Court made clear at the outset that its decision was based upon interpreting and applying state law, saying that the issue presented was "may, and if so, should, the statutes be judicially reformed in a manner that avoids the fiscal year measure"? The Court then spent many pages of its opinion reviewing federal and state court decisions, including those from other jurisdictions, to ultimately "reject the view that a court lacks authority to rewrite a statute in order to preserve its constitutionality or that the separation of powers doctrine, which vests legislative power in the Legislature and judicial powers in the courts (citations) invariably precludes such judicial rewriting."

3. On what basis did the Court in this case reject the application of the res judicata and collateral estoppel doctrines? In other words, how could the state court entertain the same cause of action that had already been resolved by a federal court decision?

4. How is the "public interest" exception generally applied by the federal and state courts? How was it used in this case?

5. How did this Court handle the argument that, when the federal court declared provisions of the initiative to be unconstitutional, "those statutes ceased to exist, and hence cannot be judicially reformed because there is nothing left to reform"?

6. What is the legal significance between "invalidating" a statute and "enjoining enforcement" of a statute?

7. The Court in this case clearly articulated that Courts can reform or "rewrite" a statute to preserve the statute's constitutionality. The court set forth two requirements to be met before a court could undertake reformation. What are those?

8. Is there a distinction between ascertaining the intent of the Legislature and determining the electorate's intent with a ballot measure? Is the intent of the voters "much harder to discern"?

9. Did the Court articulate a clear test for determining "whether the enacting body would prefer a reformed version of a statute over invalidation of the statute"? Are there "other factors" for a court to use to determine whether the Legislature or electorate would have intended reformation over invalidation?

10. The Court did note that, "There are limits, however, to the ability of a court to save a statute through judicial construction." (Citing *Blair v. Pitchess* (1971) 5 Cal.3d 258.) What is an example of those limits? How does a court determine if such a limit exists in a particular dispute?

11. At what point does reformation constitute "judicial policymaking"? In other words, when does reforming a statute by the judicial branch impermissibly encroach on the lawmaking function granted to the legislative branch, thereby violating the separation of powers doctrine?

12. The Court provided several important guideposts on reforming a statute. For example, the Court said it would "focus not only on the *number of words* involved in a proposed reformation, but more important, on the *quality* of the proposed change." In addition, the Court also made clear that, "as a general matter, it is impermissible for a court to reform by supplying terms that disserve the Legislature's or electorate's *policy* choices."

O. Certainty of Statutory Language

Lockheed Aircraft Corporation v. Superior Court of Los Angeles County

(1946) 28 Cal.2d 481

OPINION

GIBSON, C.J.

The Lockheed Aircraft Corporation, hereinafter called defendant, was sued by eighteen of its former employees, hereinafter referred to as plaintiffs, claiming they had been wrongfully discharged pursuant to rules adopted and enforced by defendant regulating and controlling their political activities in violation of section 1101 of the Labor Code.

Defendant's demurrer to the complaint having been overruled, it answered denying the existence of the rules and regulations above referred to and alleged by way of affirmative defense that it was engaged in the manufacture of airplanes for the federal government under contracts which required it to protect its plants from entry by persons of unknown loyalty or suspected disloyalty to the United States, and that it did not have sufficient information and belief as to the respective plaintiffs to satisfy itself of their unquestioned patriotism and loyalty.

Defendant here seeks to prevent further proceedings in connection with the taking of the deposition of its president, contending that section 1101 of the Labor Code, which underlies plaintiffs' action, is unconstitutional and that therefore respondent court is without jurisdiction of the subject matter.

In *Rescue Army v. Municipal Court, ante,* p. 460 [171 P.2d 8], we held that if the statute under which a defendant is charged with crime is unconstitutional a court purporting to act thereunder will be restrained by prohibition in a proper case. In so far as the jurisdictional question is concerned, there is no difference between the case of a criminal prosecution for a purported offense which does not exist because of the invalidity of the statute creating it and the case of a civil suit in which the cause of action was created by a void statute.

Plaintiffs have not disputed defendant's contention that the cause of action is based entirely upon the statute, nor have they objected to the propriety of this application for prohibition on the ground that some other adequate remedy is available. And the District Court of Appeal, in its opinion, prior to our granting of a hearing, passed on the merits of the several challenges to the constitutionality of section 1101. Thus, the court below has assumed that prohibition was a proper remedy to raise the constitutional issues, and the parties now join in urging us to pass upon those issues. The proceedings in the respondent court were interrupted many months ago and to avoid further delay we make the same assumption, solely for the purpose of this opinion, for we are satisfied that under all the circumstances a present disposition of the constitutional questions will serve to expedite, rather than disturb, the orderly processes of justice. (See *Rescue Army v. Municipal Court, ante,* p. 460 [171 P.2d 8].) We therefore proceed to a consideration of the arguments advanced against the constitutionality of section 1101 of the Labor Code.

The section reads as follows: "No employer shall make, adopt, or enforce any rule, regulation, or policy: (a) Forbidding or preventing employees from engaging or participating in politics or from becoming candidates for public office. (b) Controlling or directing or tending to control or direct the political activities or affiliations of employees."

The first contention made by defendant is that section 1101 is so uncertain and ambiguous that it is unconstitutional.

All presumptions and intendments favor the validity of a statute and mere doubt does not afford sufficient reason for a judicial declaration of invalidity.

Statutes must be upheld unless their unconstitutionality clearly, positively and unmistakably appears. (*Collins v. Riley*, 24 Cal.2d 912, 915 [152 P.2d 169]; *People v. Superior Court*, 10 Cal.2d 288, 298 [73 P.2d 1221]; See, also, *Jersey Maid Milk Products Co. v. Brock*, 13 Cal.2d 620, 636 [91 P.2d 577], and cases cited.)

A statute should be sufficiently certain so that a person may know what is prohibited thereby and what may be done without violating its provisions, but it cannot be held void for uncertainty if any reasonable and practical construction can be given to its language. As stated in *Pacific Coast Dairy v. Police Court*, 214 Cal. 668, at page 676 [8 P.2d 140, 80 A.L.R. 1217], "Mere difficulty in ascertaining its meaning, or the fact that it is susceptible of different interpretations will not render it nugatory. Doubts as to its construction will not justify us in disregarding it."

Defendant asserts that it cannot determine whether subdivision (b) of the section, which prevents an employer from controlling or directing the political activities or affiliations of employees, prohibits an employer from discharging persons who advocate the overthrow of the government by force or violence, or whose loyalty to the United States has not been established to the satisfaction of the employer.

The Merriam Webster Dictionary, second edition, defines "political" as "Of or pertaining to the exercise of the rights and privileges or the influence by which the individuals of a state seek to determine or control its public policy; having to do with the organization or action of individuals, parties, or interests that seek to control the appointment or action of those who manage the affairs of state." The same authority defines "politics" as "The science and art of government; the science dealing with the organization, regulation, and administration of a state, in both its internal and external affairs; political science.... The theory or practice of managing or directing the affairs of public policy or of political parties; hence, political affairs, principles, convictions, opinions, sympathies, or the like...."

Whether the statute is read alone, or in conjunction with the quoted definitions, there is no intimation or implication of any intent to protect any individual or group advocating the overthrow of the government by force or violence. On the contrary, the words "politics" and "political" imply orderly conduct of government, not revolution. Likewise, there is no intent to protect the members of any organization as such, regardless of the varying shades of political beliefs which may be asserted or alleged to be espoused by the group. In each case, the interference proscribed by the statute is interference with "political activities or affiliations," and the test is not membership in or activities connected with any particular group or organization, but whether those activities are related to or connected with the orderly conduct of government and the peaceful organization, regulation and administration of the government. We find nothing in the section which is intended to prevent an employer engaged in producing vital war materials from discharging an employee who advocates the overthrow of our government by force or whose loyalty to the United States has not been established to the satisfaction of the employer.

The statute is also said to be uncertain because it "does not designate whether the prohibited rule, regulation or policy be a published rule, regulation or policy or an unpublished one." The matter of publication is a false issue. The statute provides that "No employer shall make, adopt, or enforce any rule, regulation or policy," hence evidence of publication or lack of publication is material only in so far as it may tend to prove or disprove the existence of any such rule or policy. The word "policy" is defined as "A settled or definite course or method adopted and followed by a government, institution, body, or individual." (Merriam Webster Dictionary (2d. ed.).)

Defendant next contends that section 1101 constitutes an unjustifiable and arbitrary limitation on the liberty of contract in violation of both the state and federal Constitutions.

The right to contract is not absolute and unqualified, and reasonable restrictions are not prohibited by the constitutional provisions.

Unless it is shown that the restraint here involved is unreasonable or unjustifiable, it must be presumed that the Legislature determined that the measure was necessary for the general welfare of the people and for the protection of rights connected with the use of the ballot. The wisdom of the policy underlying the statute is a matter solely for the Legislature, and where it is determined that a restriction or regulation is necessary to protect a fundamental right and the statute is reasonably designed to achieve that purpose, the courts will not interfere. The right to ballot would be endangered if citizens were deprived of any incidents of that right or if they were hampered in their advocacy of or opposition to measures which may be placed upon the ballot. We cannot say that section 1101 is not properly designed to achieve the result intended by the Legislature or that there is an arbitrary or unreasonable limitation of the right to contract.

A violation of section 1101 is made a misdemeanor by section 1103, and defendant contends the statute is therefore penal in character and does not create any civil right of action. This argument ignores section 1105 which provides that "Nothing in this chapter shall prevent the injured employee from recovering damages from his employer for injury suffered through a violation of this chapter." The contract of employment must be held to have been made in the light of, and to have incorporated, the provisions of existing law. (*Stockton Sav. & Loan Bank v. Massanet*, 18 Cal.2d 200, 206 [114 P.2d 593]; *Guardianship of Ounjuian*, 4 Cal.2d 659, 661 [52 P.2d 220]; *Mott v. Cline*, 200 Cal. 434, 446 [253 P. 718].) Hence, upon violation of the section, an employee has a right of action for damages for breach of his employment contract.

Defendant also contends that section 1101 is unconstitutional because its enforcement assertedly deprives an employer of the right of free speech and prevents him from publishing his political beliefs or views among his employees. There is nothing in the section which, expressly or by implication, has any such effect.

The facts and issues have not been sufficiently established or clarified to justify a present consideration of such matters as the possible effect of sections 2920–2928 of the Labor Code, or of various federal statutes governing the performance of contracts with the federal government relating to war materials. We do not deem it proper to consider those matters in this proceeding when the cause of discharge has not yet been established.

Defendant also seeks to restrain respondent court from enforcing compliance with a subpoena duces tecum issued on the taking of the deposition, asserting that the affidavit in support thereof is defective in that it does not sufficiently describe and identify the desired records. It is well established that prohibition cannot be used to prevent the enforcement of a subpoena duces tecum on the ground the affidavit is defective. (*C.S. Smith Met. M. Co. v. Superior Court*, 16 Cal.2d 226 [105 P.2d 587].) If the questions relating to the sufficiency of the affidavit are not properly disposed of by objections in the trial court, and contempt proceedings ensue, the remedies of certiorari and habeas corpus are considered adequate. (*State Bd. of Equalization v. Superior Court*, 20 Cal.2d 467, 471 [127 P.2d 4]; *Wessels v. Superior Court*, 200 Cal. 403 [253 P. 135]; *Commercial Bk. v. Superior Court*, 192 Cal. 395, 397 [220 P. 422].)

The alternative writ is discharged, and the application for a peremptory writ is denied.

SHENK, J., EDMONDS, J., CARTER, J., TRAYNOR, J., SCHAUER, J., and SPENCE, J., concurred.

Notes and Questions

1. As the Court noted, "A statute should be sufficiently certain so that a person may know what is prohibited thereby and what may be done without violating the provisions thereof, but cannot be held void for uncertainty if any reasonable and practical construction can be given to the language." It did not find the statute at issue in this case uncertain.

2. The Court also explained that courts are constrained in their review of a statute to the language, not the policy. "The wisdom of the policy underlying the statute is a matter solely for the Legislature, and where it is determined that a restriction or regulation is necessary to protect a fundamental right and the statute is reasonably designed to achieve that purpose, the courts will not interfere."

P. Effect of a Declaratory Statute

While a declaratory statute cannot bind courts with respect to the application of the original statute to transactions which occurred or rights of action which occurred prior to the passage of the declaratory statute, the statute declaratory of the former statute has the same effect as if it were embodied in the original statute at the time of its passage in the absence of any intervening rights. *Clayton v. Schultz* (1935) 4 Cal.2d 425, held:

> [4] Respondents contend that so much of the 1929 amendment as is declara-
> tory of the meaning of the said statutes, with intent to give them a retro-

spective operation, is unconstitutional. In view of the nature and purpose of the amendment, so far as here applicable, we see no reason to declare it unconstitutional. [5] While a declaratory statute cannot bind the courts with respect to application of the original statute to transactions which occurred or rights of action which accrued prior to passage of the declaratory act, yet, in the absence of intervening rights, an act declaratory of a former one has the same effect as if embodied in the original act at the time of its passage. (12 C.J., p. 811, sec. 247.)

Chapter Thirteen

Comparing California with Other Jurisdictions

A. Comparing Congress and the Legislature in the Lawmaking Process

Of interest to those involved in the legislative process, insights into the California Legislature and the United States Congress allow us to examine the strengths and weaknesses of these branches of government and whether there are possible improvements that could made in the federal or state lawmaking processes.

Both the U.S. Congress and the California Legislature draw their authority from the federal and state Constitutions and are provided extensive powers and duties in statute. While they obviously deal with different levels of government, Congress and the California Legislature share similar roles in the lawmaking process. Each legislative body proposes and adopts legislation to be implemented by the executive branch of government.

The legislative branches of the state and federal governments are similar in many regards, but they are also different in several aspects. Obviously, the California Legislature is based upon the Congress, and they both are featured in the state and federal Constitutions. Both bodies generally make laws and have investigatory powers, adopt budgets, and confirm certain executive branch appointments. But the differences in the legislative process can be profound.

For example, several elected officials who have worked in both the federal and state legislative bodies have noted that, while a legislator can introduce any bill desired in Congress or the Legislature, the state Legislature actually ensures that each bill is debated and voted upon. In Congress, while thousands of bills are introduced each year, many of those bills do not even get a hearing, let alone a vote. And congressional leaders limit debate and amendments on measures that do get heard and debated.

The Constitution of the United States (Article I, Sections 1–10) spells out the authority of Congress to make laws. The U.S. Supreme Court has broadly interpreted this authority for the legislative branch. However, the Court has also negated this authority when finding it conflicts with the Tenth Amendment to the Constitution.

The Tenth Amendment to the U.S. Constitution provides: "The powers not delegated to the United States, nor prohibited by it to the states, are reserved to the states respectively, or to the people." Thus, the scope of policymaking by the California Legislature is very broad just based on the Tenth Amendment to the federal Constitution. State statutes can be adopted on nearly any matter if they do not conflict with federal law or violate the provisions of the California or federal Constitutions.

The California Constitution (Article IV) and the state Government Code (§§ 9000– 10606) establish some of the procedures by which legislation is proposed, considered, and acted upon at the state level. In general, these state constitutional provisions and state statutes direct the Legislature to adopt specific rules for the development and consideration of legislation. In turn, the Senate and Assembly have adopted the Senate Rules, Assembly Rules and Joint Rules.

In both Congress and the Legislature, the political parties and the party leaders dictate most of the legislative process, as well as the ultimate outcome of legislation. This is due to the fact that the majority party enjoys a majority of members on the committees (thus generally ensuring they control the fate of legislation) and on the Floors, because the vast majority of bills require a simple majority vote for passage.

Both the U.S. Senate and the U.S. House of Representatives use an elaborate system of committees and subcommittees to consider legislation and the federal budget. Currently, the Senate has 16 standing committees and nearly 100 subcommittees, while the House has 22 standing committees and nearly 150 subcommittees. These committees and subcommittees are where legislation is heard, amended, passed to the floor, or held in committee.

Given the size of Congress (with 100 Senators and 435 Representatives), there is a heavy reliance on seniority and the expertise of members in determining committee membership. The selection of committee and subcommittee chairs is determined by party leaders. The California Legislature relies less on seniority, but certainly takes into account the expertise and political needs of its members to determine committee composition.

Neither the California Senate nor the Assembly has formal rules regarding how seniority and years of experience dictate the selection of committee chairs, committee memberships, leadership positions, office space, number of staff, etc. Instead, party politics play a primary role in affecting these decisions. Traditionally, the leadership of each house recognizes the experience, expertise, and preferences of its members in making committee assignments and leadership assignments.

Like the Legislature, a majority vote is required for most actions of the U.S. House and Senate, as well as its committees and subcommittees. While one party does largely control the houses of Congress, House and Senate rules regarding debate and bringing matters to a vote often require supermajority votes (usually three-fifths or two-thirds). The most prominent example occurs within the U.S. Senate where rules provide that debate is virtually unlimited.

These rules allow a minority of U.S. Senators not only to forestall action on legislation (by use of a filibuster), but also to bring the entire operation of the Senate to a virtual standstill. Debate can be terminated through a motion for "cloture" —

but this motion requires 60 votes to pass. Thus, while a majority party may have votes to pass a piece of legislation, the minority party can procedurally prevent the legislation from ever coming to a vote on the Floor of the U.S. Senate. Neither the U.S. House, nor the California Legislature have such a rule.

At both levels of government, through the annual federal and state budgets, Congress and the Legislature can provide or remove funding and direct executive branch agency activities through budget control language. Congress can direct one of its many control agencies (GAO, CBO, or legislative committees), and the Legislature can do the same (through the LAO, State Auditor, or legislative committees), to investigate the agency's actions to regulate or implement laws. Executive branch agencies can be pressured via numerous informal and behind-the-scenes techniques applied by legislative committees, party leaders, or individual legislators.

Like Congress, both the California Senate and Assembly use a committee system. The various committees (currently 22 standing committees in the Senate and 31 standing committees in the Assembly), the number of members on each committee, and other details are addressed in the respective Rules of the Assembly and Senate. Some committees have subcommittees, especially in the Budget Committee. Most bills go through two committees in each house of the Legislature, a policy committee and a fiscal committee. However, some bills have two policy committee hearings due to their subject matter.

In these state Legislature committees, the authors present their bills, and the committees hear public testimony, discuss the legislation, and then vote. Authors of bills retain significant authority to negotiate and compromise on the language of their individual pieces of legislation. These legislators can propose author's amendments, they can accept or reject amendments proposed by the committee, or they can drop their proposals entirely. The formative review of legislation occurs in these committees, but the committees do not tend to take over authorship of legislation, as is the practice in Congress.

Another important distinction between federal and state legislative committees is how bills are processed. In the committees of the Legislature, the general practice is to work out language changes prior to the hearing so that hearings are only a brief debate on the merits of the bill between proponents and opponents, nominal discussion by committees, and a vote to either pass or defeat the bill. This is often due to the time limits of committee hearings and the sheer volume of bills that are considered and acted upon in the California Legislature.

On the other hand, in Congressional committees, their hearings are called "markup" sessions because the committee members debate and amend legislation in their committees rather than just debate the measures. Congressional committees engage in lengthy committee hearings to debate specific language changes to federal legislation. Their process of amending bills is open and part of the public hearing process.

In addition, the annual state budget is treated differently in the committee process in the Legislature. Each house (Senate and Assembly) refers the budget to its respective and fairly large Budget Committee, which in turn is divided into subcommittees (five in the Senate and six in the Assembly) where that committee will accept, reject or amend the Governor's budget proposals. These subcommittee decisions are usually ratified by the house's full budget Committee, before a two-house conference committee is convened to resolve any remaining issues between the Assembly and Senate before final action on the state budget.

In looking at the productivity of these two legislative bodies of our federal and state governments, there were 12,298 bills and resolutions introduced in the 112th Congress (the 2011–12 Session), but only 238 measures (1.9%) became law. At the federal level, rarely do more than 5% of bills introduced in a session become law. On the other hand, in California, there are usually about 4,500 bills introduced during the two-year legislative session and usually between 1,500 and 2,000 bills are signed into law, more than one-third of them.

As we would expect, the roles of Congress and the Legislature are similar in the lawmaking process, with some limited exceptions. Their interactions with the President and the Governor, respectively, are similar as well. Because the chief executives determine the ultimate fate of legislation due to their power to sign or veto bills, the President and the Governor are able to greatly influence the legislative process in a similar manner. The role of the chief executive is examined in detail in another chapter.

Notes and Questions

1. What is a federal legislative procedure that the California Legislature should consider adopting? Explain how this procedure would enhance the state lawmaking process.

2. What is a California legislative procedure that the U.S. Congress should consider adopting? Explain how this procedure would enhance the federal lawmaking process.

B. Comparing California's Legislative Branch to Other States

California state government is not unique among the other states. All 50 states provide for a republican form of government in their individual constitutions. All the states are based upon the federal government with three branches: legislative, executive, and judicial.

California's Legislature is comprised of two houses — State Assembly and State Senate. The Assembly has 80 members elected every two years, and the Senate has 40 members elected every four years. The maximum number of years that can be served is 12 years — either in a single house or combined. A majority vote is required for most legislation, although a 2/3 majority vote is required for certain measures, such as urgency clause bills and tax increases.

With one exception, all states are bicameral, as they all have upper and lower houses of differing sizes. For the lower house, half a dozen states provide four-year terms, while the remaining states provide two-year terms. The sizes of the houses range from 42 to 400 members. For the upper house, a dozen states provide two-year terms, while the remaining states provide four-year terms.

The sizes of the upper houses range from 21 to 67 members. About 35 states do not have term limits for maximum service. About 22 states have a simple majority vote requirement for all measures. The remaining states have a hybrid system requiring both simple and super majority votes for measures that are considered.

Notes and Questions

1. What is a difference that exists between California's Legislature and other states' legislatures that should be adopted in California? Why should that change be made?

C. Differences between Legislative Processes: Congress v. California Legislature

Having worked in both Washington, DC and Sacramento, I am often asked about the differences in the two legislative processes. California's Legislature is obviously based upon the federal legislative branch and, as you would expect, they share many things in common. Nonetheless, their specific rules for the legislative are different.

We can answer the "differences" question in broader terms to appreciate some of the major distinctions between the federal legislative process and the state legislative process. This brief section is my take on some of those major distinctions.

<u>Bills</u>

In both the Congress and the California Legislature, legislators can introduce any bill they would like. However, in Congress, bills are rarely given a hearing. In the Legislature, basically everything gets heard. A bill may die at its first hearing, but at least there was a public hearing on the measure. It would be extraordinary if a California legislator were denied a hearing on his or her bill. A committee chair may do so, but that is not a custom and practice of either house.

To appreciate this point, take a look at the numbers: During an average two-year session of Congress, about 10,000 bills are introduced. Roughly 80% of those are referred to committee without any further action. About 4–5% get signed into law. As such, while thousands of bills are introduced each year in Congress, most do not get a hearing, let alone a vote.

In contrast, during an average two-year session of the California Legislature, about 4,500 bills are introduced. Roughly 45% of these bills reach the Governor's desk and about 85% of those get signed into law (meaning more than a third get signed into law after introduction). Clearly, in California, opportunities for hearings and votes are a predominant aspect of the process.

Sponsored Bills

All bills in Congress are "sponsored," because that is the term they use for the author of the bill (i.e., the Member of Congress). On the other hand, in the California Legislature, "sponsor" means the individual or group that brought the bill idea to the legislator. The legislator who authors the bill is called the "author." This use of terminology is critical in either Capitol city.

Committee Hearings

In Congress, federal legislators conduct committee "mark-up sessions" on bills and can spend a good amount of time going line-by-line reviewing bill language. In the Legislature, almost no amending occurs in a committee hearing, and debate is usually limited to the policy arguments for and again a measure. That is probably because they have to hear so many bills.

In the California Legislature, the general practice is to attempt to work out bill amendments before the hearing. When disputes arise in committee, they may be worked out in the context of the public committee hearing. Members of the committee (or the committee's analysis of the bill) may suggest amendments, which the author can usually accept or reject. The author can also ask that the vote be postponed and the bill be brought back to the committee for a future hearing and vote.

In contrast, Congress uses the public hearing to gather information — including support and opposition — regarding a bill, but amendments and revisions are not immediately decided upon in the context of that hearing. Instead, bills that are expected to receive majority support go through a process called "mark up."

Here, in a subsequent meeting, members of the committee and their staff go through the proposal in detail and decide on appropriate changes. Each amendment or revision is voted up or down, and the committee also votes on whether to send the bill forward with amendments, or whether to table or postpone action.

Importantly, while the mark-up session is generally open to the public, the sessions are conducted without testimony or participation from outside parties, including the author (if not a member of the committee) or interest groups for and against the bill.

Record of Proceedings

California does not have anything like the *Congressional Record*, which is essentially a verbatim transcript of congressional proceedings. While committee hearings and floor sessions in the Legislature are videotaped, and available to order, the *Senate Daily Journal* and the *Assembly Daily Journal* do not include transcripts of debates or statements made by legislators. Instead, they merely document the major actions taken on legislation. As such, there are definite limits on documentation in the Legislature related to determining legislative intent.

Calendar

The California Legislature is bound by its calendar and the deadlines for bills to be introduced, heard in committee, considered by the respective houses, and sent to the Governor. This is like most legislatures, whether they are part-time or full-time sessions. Congress, on the other hand, convenes through the calendar year, every year, and with large chunks of time out of Washington.

The practical implication of this is that, absent rule waivers, bills in the Legislature must move through the process according to those calendar deadlines whereas, in Congress, bills can be introduced and considered throughout the year without concern for any deadlines in general.

Omnibus Bills

California pretty well follows its germaneness rule, meaning that bill amendments have to relate to the main subject of the bill as introduced. On the other hand, Congress enacts most policy changes through omnibus spending measures often with entirely unrelated subject matter scattered through the bill. Although more policy is getting done in the state budget process, those policy changes are still contained in single, related subject matter bills.

Vote Requirements

In both Congress and the Legislature, vote requirements matter, but really only in one house of Congress — the Senate. In Congress, most legislation (except for an override of the President's veto and a few other limited measures) only needs a simple majority to pass. One might conclude that Congress has an easier job of passing legislation, but this is not the case because of rules regarding debate.

The rules of the U.S. Senate and the House of Representatives enable legislative leaders to structure and limit debate more than in the California Legislature. The major exception occurs with the rules of the Senate, where floor debate is virtually unlimited. Historically, this has led to use of the "filibuster," where members bring the operations of the Senate to a standstill through endless debate of a proposal.

The only way to limit debate when faced with a filibuster is through a "Motion for Cloture." which requires a three-fifths (3/5th) vote. Thus, unless 60 Senators vote to limit debate, the use of the filibuster can prevent a measure from ever coming to a vote. Effectively, this means on many occasions that a bill cannot really pass the Senate unless it has 60 votes. As such, a block of just 41 Senators can prevent a bill from passing the Senate.

On the other hand, the California Constitution specifies many kinds of legislation that require a supermajority (two-thirds) vote, including: tax increases, most appropriations bills, proposals to amend the California Constitution, urgency bills, and a vote to override a Governor's veto, plus many other related to specific laws (e.g., amendments to the Political Reform Act require a super majority vote).

Direct Democracy

The U.S. Constitution does not provide for the initiative or referendum processes. However, the California Constitution allows for both forms of direct democracy. As such, the people can propose statutes and constitutional amendments for consideration on the statewide ballot through use of an initiative, and they can repeal most laws (with a few exceptions) adopted by the Legislature and Governor through use of a referendum.

Notes and Questions

1. What is a key distinction between the federal and state legislative processes? Which is better?

2. Should California's Legislature adopt a particular Congressional process? If so, why?

Appendix A

California Constitution, Article IV

ARTICLE IV LEGISLATIVE [SEC. 1–SEC. 28]

(Heading of Article 4 amended Nov. 8, 1966, by Prop. 1-a. Res.Ch. 139, 1966 1st Ex. Sess.)

SEC. 1.

The legislative power of this State is vested in the California Legislature which consists of the Senate and Assembly, but the people reserve to themselves the powers of initiative and referendum.

(Sec. 1 added Nov. 8, 1966, by Prop. 1-a. Res.Ch. 139, 1966 1st Ex. Sess.)

SEC. 1.5.

The people find and declare that the Founding Fathers established a system of representative government based upon free, fair, and competitive elections. The increased concentration of political power in the hands of incumbent representatives has made our electoral system less free, less competitive, and less representative.

The ability of legislators to serve unlimited number of terms, to establish their own retirement system, and to pay for staff and support services at state expense contribute heavily to the extremely high number of incumbents who are reelected. These unfair incumbent advantages discourage qualified candidates from seeking public office and create a class of career politicians, instead of the citizen representatives envisioned by the Founding Fathers. These career politicians become representatives of the bureaucracy, rather than of the people whom they are elected to represent.

To restore a free and democratic system of fair elections, and to encourage qualified candidates to seek public office, the people find and declare that the powers of incumbency must be limited. Retirement benefits must be restricted, state-financed incumbent staff and support services limited, and limitations placed upon the number of terms which may be served.

(Sec. 1.5 added Nov. 6, 1990, by Prop. 140. Initiative measure.)

SEC. 2.

(a) (1) The Senate has a membership of 40 Senators elected for 4-year terms, 20 to begin every 2 years.

  (2) The Assembly has a membership of 80 members elected for 2-year terms.

(3) The terms of a Senator or a Member of the Assembly shall commence on the first Monday in December next following her or his election.

(4) During her or his lifetime a person may serve no more than 12 years in the Senate, the Assembly, or both, in any combination of terms. This subdivision shall apply only to those Members of the Senate or the Assembly who are first elected to the Legislature after the effective date of this subdivision and who have not previously served in the Senate or Assembly. Members of the Senate or Assembly who were elected before the effective date of this subdivision may serve only the number of terms allowed at the time of the last election before the effective date of this subdivision.

(b) Election of members of the Assembly shall be on the first Tuesday after the first Monday in November of even-numbered years unless otherwise prescribed by the Legislature. Senators shall be elected at the same time and places as members of the Assembly.

(c) A person is ineligible to be a member of the Legislature unless the person is an elector and has been a resident of the legislative district for one year, and a citizen of the United States and a resident of California for 3 years, immediately preceding the election, and service of the full term of office to which the person is seeking to be elected would not exceed the maximum years of service permitted by subdivision (a) of this section.

(d) When a vacancy occurs in the Legislature the Governor immediately shall call an election to fill the vacancy.

(Sec. 2 amended June 5, 2012, by Prop. 28. Initiative measure.)

SEC. 3.

(a) The Legislature shall convene in regular session at noon on the first Monday in December of each even-numbered year and each house shall immediately organize. Each session of the Legislature shall adjourn sine die by operation of the Constitution at midnight on November 30 of the following even-numbered year.

(b) On extraordinary occasions the Governor by proclamation may cause the Legislature to assemble in special session. When so assembled it has power to legislate only on subjects specified in the proclamation but may provide for expenses and other matters incidental to the session.

(Sec. 3 amended June 8, 1976, by Prop. 14. Res.Ch. 5, 1976.)

SEC. 4.

(a) To eliminate any appearance of a conflict with the proper discharge of his or her duties and responsibilities, no Member of the Legislature may knowingly receive any salary, wages, commissions, or other similar earned income from a lobbyist or lobbying firm, as defined by the Political Reform Act of 1974, or from a person who, during the previous 12 months, has been under a contract with the Legislature. The Legislature shall enact laws that define earned income. However, earned income does not include any community property interest in the income of a spouse. Any Member who knowingly receives any salary, wages, commissions, or other similar earned income from a lobbyist employer, as defined by the Political Reform Act of 1974, may not, for a period of one year following its receipt, vote upon or make, participate in making, or in any way attempt to use his or her official position to influence an action or decision before the Legislature, other than an action or decision involving a bill described in subdivision (c) of Section 12 of this article, which he or she knows, or has reason to know, would have a direct and significant financial impact on the lobbyist employer and would not impact the public generally or a significant segment of the public in a similar manner. As used in this subdivision, "public generally" includes an industry, trade, or profession.

(b) Travel and living expenses for Members of the Legislature in connection with their official duties shall be prescribed by statute passed by rollcall vote entered in the journal, two-thirds of the membership of each house concurring. A Member may not receive travel and living expenses during the times that the Legislature is in recess for more than three calendar days, unless the Member is traveling to or from, or is in attendance at, any meeting of a committee of which he or she is a member, or a meeting, conference, or other legislative function or responsibility as authorized by the rules of the house of which he or she is a member, which is held at a location at least 20 miles from his or her place of residence.

(c) The Legislature may not provide retirement benefits based on any portion of a monthly salary in excess of five hundred dollars ($500) paid to any Member of the Legislature unless the Member receives the greater amount while serving as a Member in the Legislature. The Legislature may, prior to their retirement, limit the retirement benefits payable to Members of the Legislature who serve during or after the term commencing in 1967.

When computing the retirement allowance of a Member who serves in the Legislature during the term commencing in 1967 or later, allowance may be made for increases in cost of living if so provided by statute, but only with respect to increases in the cost of living occurring after retirement of the Member. However, the Legislature may provide that no Member shall be deprived of a cost of living adjustment based on a monthly salary of five hundred dollars ($500) which has accrued prior to the commencement of the 1967 Regular Session of the Legislature.

(Sec. 4 amended June 5, 1990, by Prop. 112. Res.Ch. 167, 1989.)

SEC. 4.5.

Notwithstanding any other provision of this Constitution or existing law, a person elected to or serving in the Legislature on or after November 1, 1990, shall participate in the Federal Social Security (Retirement, Disability, Health Insurance) Program and the State shall pay only the employer's share of the contribution necessary to such participation. No other pension or retirement benefit shall accrue as a result of service in the Legislature, such service not being intended as a career occupation. This Section shall not be construed to abrogate or diminish any vested pension or retirement benefit which may have accrued under an existing law to a person holding or having held office in the Legislature, but upon adoption of this Act no further entitlement to nor vesting in any existing program shall accrue to any such person, other than Social Security to the extent herein provided.

(Sec. 4.5 added Nov. 6, 1990, by Prop. 140. Initiative measure.)

SEC. 5.

(a) (1) Each house of the Legislature shall judge the qualifications and elections of its Members and, by rollcall vote entered in the journal, two-thirds of the membership concurring, may expel a Member.

(2) (A) Each house may suspend a Member by motion or resolution adopted by rollcall vote entered in the journal, two-thirds of the membership concurring. The motion or resolution shall contain findings and declarations setting forth the basis for the suspension. Notwithstanding any other provision of this Constitution, the house may deem the salary and benefits of the Member to be forfeited for all or part of the period of the suspension by express provision of the motion or resolution.

(B) A Member suspended pursuant to this paragraph shall not exercise any of the rights, privileges, duties, or powers of his or her office, or utilize any resources of the Legislature, during the period the suspension is in effect.

(C) The suspension of a Member pursuant to this paragraph shall remain in effect until the date specified in the motion or resolution or, if no date is specified, the date a subsequent motion or resolution terminating the suspension is adopted by rollcall vote entered in the journal, two-thirds of the membership of the house concurring.

(b) No Member of the Legislature may accept any honorarium. The Legislature shall enact laws that implement this subdivision.

(c) The Legislature shall enact laws that ban or strictly limit the acceptance of a gift by a Member of the Legislature from any source if the acceptance of the gift might create a conflict of interest.

(d) No Member of the Legislature may knowingly accept any compensation for appearing, agreeing to appear, or taking any other action on behalf of another person before any state government board or agency. If a Member knowingly accepts any compensation for appearing, agreeing to appear, or taking any other action on behalf of another person before any local government board or agency, the Member may not, for a period of one year following the acceptance of the compensation, vote upon or make, participate in making, or in any way attempt to use his or her official position to influence an action or decision before the Legislature, other than an action or decision involving a bill described in subdivision (c) of Section 12, which he or she knows, or has reason to know, would have a direct and significant financial impact on that person and would not impact the public generally or a significant segment of the public in a similar manner. As used in this subdivision, "public generally" includes an industry, trade, or profession. However, a Member may engage in activities involving a board or agency which are strictly on his or her own behalf, appear in the capacity of an attorney before any court or the Workers' Compensation Appeals

Board, or act as an advocate without compensation or make an inquiry for information on behalf of a person before a board or agency. This subdivision does not prohibit any action of a partnership or firm of which the Member is a member if the Member does not share directly or indirectly in the fee, less any expenses attributable to that fee, resulting from that action.

(e) The Legislature shall enact laws that prohibit a Member of the Legislature whose term of office commences on or after December 3, 1990, from lobbying, for compensation, as governed by the Political Reform Act of 1974, before the Legislature for 12 months after leaving office.

(f) The Legislature shall enact new laws, and strengthen the enforcement of existing laws, prohibiting Members of the Legislature from engaging in activities or having interests which conflict with the proper discharge of their duties and responsibilities. However, the people reserve to themselves the power to implement this requirement pursuant to Article II.

(Sec. 5 amended June 7, 2016, by Prop. 50. Res.Ch. 127, 2014.)

SEC. 6.

For the purpose of choosing members of the Legislature, the State shall be divided into 40 Senatorial and 80 Assembly districts to be called Senatorial and Assembly Districts. Each Senatorial district shall choose one Senator and each Assembly district shall choose one member of the Assembly.

(Sec. 6 added June 3, 1980, by Prop. 6. Res.Ch. 78, 1978.)

SEC. 7.

(a) Each house shall choose its officers and adopt rules for its proceedings. A majority of the membership constitutes a quorum, but a smaller number may recess from day to day and compel the attendance of absent members.

(b) Each house shall keep and publish a journal of its proceedings. The rollcall vote of the members on a question shall be taken and entered in the journal at the request of 3 members present.

(c) (1) Except as provided in paragraph (3), the proceedings of each house and the committees thereof shall be open and public. The right to attend open and public proceedings includes the right of any person to record by audio or video means any and all parts of the proceedings and to broadcast or otherwise transmit them; provided that the Legislature may adopt reasonable rules pursuant to paragraph (5) regulating the placement and use of the equipment for recording or broadcasting the proceedings for the sole purpose of minimizing disruption of the proceedings. Any aggrieved party shall have standing to challenge said rules in an action for declaratory and injunctive relief, and the Legislature shall have the burden of demonstrating that the rule is reasonable.

(2) Commencing on January 1 of the second calendar year following the adoption of this paragraph, the Legislature shall also cause audiovisual recordings to be made of all proceedings subject to paragraph (1) in their entirety, shall make such recordings

public through the Internet within 24 hours after the proceedings have been recessed or adjourned for the day, and shall maintain an archive of said recordings, which shall be accessible to the public through the Internet and downloadable for a period of no less than 20 years as specified by statute.

(3) Notwithstanding paragraphs (1) and (2), closed sessions may be held solely for any of the following purposes:

(A) To consider the appointment, employment, evaluation of performance, or dismissal of a public officer or employee, to consider or hear complaints or charges brought against a Member of the Legislature or other public officer or employee, or to establish the classification or compensation of an employee of the Legislature.

(B) To consider matters affecting the safety and security of Members of the Legislature or its employees or the safety and security of any buildings and grounds used by the Legislature.

(C) To confer with, or receive advice from, its legal counsel regarding pending or reasonably anticipated, or whether to initiate, litigation when discussion in open session would not protect the interests of the house or committee regarding the litigation.

(4) A caucus of the Members of the Senate, the Members of the Assembly, or the Members of both houses, which is composed of the members of the same political party, may meet in closed session.

(5) The Legislature shall implement this subdivision by concurrent resolution adopted by rollcall vote entered in the journal, two-thirds of the membership of each house concurring, or by statute, and in the case of a closed session held pursuant to paragraph (3), shall prescribe that reasonable notice of the closed session and the purpose of the closed session shall be provided to the public. If there is a conflict between a concurrent resolution and statute, the last adopted or enacted shall prevail.

(d) Neither house without the consent of the other may recess for more than 10 days or to any other place.

(Sec. 7 amended Nov. 8, 2016, by Prop. 54. Initiative measure.)

SEC. 7.5.

In the fiscal year immediately following the adoption of this Act, the total aggregate expenditures of the Legislature for the compensation of members and employees of, and the operating expenses and equipment for, the Legislature may not exceed an amount equal to nine hundred fifty thousand dollars ($950,000) per member for that fiscal year or 80 percent of the amount of money expended for those purposes in the preceding fiscal year, whichever is less. For each fiscal year thereafter, the total aggregate expenditures may not exceed an amount equal to that expended for those purposes in the preceding fiscal year, adjusted and compounded by an amount equal to the percentage increase in the appropriations limit for the State established pursuant to Article XIII B.

(Sec. 7.5 added Nov. 6, 1990, by Prop. 140. Initiative measure.)

SEC. 8.

(a) At regular sessions no bill other than the budget bill may be heard or acted on by committee or either house until the 31st day after the bill is introduced unless the house dispenses with this requirement by rollcall vote entered in the journal, three fourths of the membership concurring.

(b) (1) The Legislature may make no law except by statute and may enact no statute except by bill. No bill may be passed unless it is read by title on 3 days in each house except that the house may dispense with this requirement by rollcall vote entered in the journal, two thirds of the membership concurring.

(2) No bill may be passed or ultimately become a statute unless the bill with any amendments has been printed, distributed to the members, and published on the Internet, in its final form, for at least 72 hours before the vote, except that this notice period may be waived if the Governor has submitted to the Legislature a written statement that dispensing with this notice period for that bill is necessary to address a state of emergency, as defined in paragraph (2) of subdivision (c) of Section 3 of Article XIII B, that has been declared by the Governor, and the house considering the bill thereafter dispenses with the notice period for that bill by a separate rollcall vote entered in the journal, two thirds of the membership concurring, prior to the vote on the bill.

(3) No bill may be passed unless, by rollcall vote entered in the journal, a majority of the membership of each house concurs.

(c) (1) Except as provided in paragraphs (2) and (3) of this subdivision, a statute enacted at a regular session shall go into effect on January 1 next following a 90-day period from the date of enactment of the statute and a statute enacted at a special session shall go into effect on the 91st day after adjournment of the special session at which the bill was passed.

(2) A statute, other than a statute establishing or changing boundaries of any legislative, congressional, or other election district, enacted by a bill passed by the Legislature on or before the date the Legislature adjourns for a joint recess to reconvene in the second calendar year of the biennium of the legislative session, and in the possession of the Governor after that date, shall go into effect on January 1 next following the enactment date of the statute unless, before January 1, a copy of a referendum petition affecting the statute is submitted to the Attorney General pursuant to subdivision (d) of Section 10 of Article II, in which event the statute shall go into effect on the 91st day after the enactment date unless the petition has been presented to the Secretary of State pursuant to subdivision (b) of Section 9 of Article II.

(3) Statutes calling elections, statutes providing for tax levies or appropriations for the usual current expenses of the State, and urgency statutes shall go into effect immediately upon their enactment.

(d) Urgency statutes are those necessary for immediate preservation of the public peace, health, or safety. A statement of facts constituting the necessity shall be set forth in one section of the bill. In each house the section and the bill shall be passed separately, each by rollcall vote entered in the journal, two thirds of the membership concurring. An urgency statute may not create or abolish any office or change the salary, term, or duties of any office, or grant any franchise or special privilege, or create any vested right or interest.

(Sec. 8 amended Nov. 8, 2016, by Prop. 54. Initiative measure.)

SEC. 8.5.

An act amending an initiative statute, an act providing for the issuance of bonds, or a constitutional amendment proposed by the Legislature and submitted to the voters for approval may not do either of the following:

(a) Include or exclude any political subdivision of the State from the application or effect of its provisions based upon approval or disapproval of the measure, or based upon the casting of a specified percentage of votes in favor of the measure, by the electors of that political subdivision.

(b) Contain alternative or cumulative provisions wherein one or more of those provisions would become law depending upon the casting of a specified percentage of votes for or against the measure.

(Sec. 8.5 added June 2, 1998, by Prop. 219. Res.Ch. 34, 1996.)

SEC. 9.

A statute shall embrace but one subject, which shall be expressed in its title. If a statute embraces a subject not expressed in its title, only the part not expressed is void. A statute may not be amended by reference to its title. A section of a statute may not be amended unless the section is re-enacted as amended.

(Sec. 9 added Nov. 8, 1966, by Prop. 1-a. Res.Ch. 139, 1966 1st Ex. Sess.)

SEC. 10.

(a) Each bill passed by the Legislature shall be presented to the Governor. It becomes a statute if it is signed by the Governor. The Governor may veto it by returning it with any objections to the house of origin, which shall enter the objections in the journal and proceed to reconsider it. If each house then passes the bill by rollcall vote entered in the journal, two-thirds of the membership concurring, it becomes a statute.

(b) (1) Any bill, other than a bill which would establish or change boundaries of any legislative, congressional, or other election district, passed by the Legislature on or before the date the Legislature adjourns for a joint recess to reconvene in the second calendar year of the biennium of the legislative session, and in the possession of the Governor after that date, that is not returned within 30 days after that date becomes a statute.

(2) Any bill passed by the Legislature before September 1 of the second calendar year of the biennium of the legislative session and in the possession of the Governor on or after September 1 that is not returned on or before September 30 of that year becomes a statute.

(3) Any other bill presented to the Governor that is not returned within 12 days becomes a statute.

(4) If the Legislature by adjournment of a special session prevents the return of a bill with the veto message, the bill becomes a statute unless the Governor vetoes the bill within 12 days after it is presented by depositing it and the veto message in the office of the Secretary of State.

(5) If the 12th day of the period within which the Governor is required to perform an act pursuant to paragraph (3) or (4) of this subdivision is a Saturday, Sunday, or holiday, the period is extended to the next day that is not a Saturday, Sunday, or holiday.

(c) Any bill introduced during the first year of the biennium of the legislative session that has not been passed by the house of origin by January 31 of the second calendar year of the biennium may no longer be acted on by the house. No bill may be passed by either house on or after September 1 of an even-numbered year except statutes calling elections, statutes providing for tax levies or appropriations for the usual current expenses of the State, and urgency statutes, and bills passed after being vetoed by the Governor.

(d) The Legislature may not present any bill to the Governor after November 15 of the second calendar year of the biennium of the legislative session.

(e) The Governor may reduce or eliminate one or more items of appropriation while approving other portions of a bill. The Governor shall append to the bill a statement of the items reduced or eliminated with the reasons for the action. The Governor shall transmit to the house originating the bill a copy of the statement and reasons. Items reduced or eliminated shall be separately reconsidered and may be passed over the Governor's veto in the same manner as bills.

(f) (1) If, following the enactment of the budget bill for the 2004–05 fiscal year or any subsequent fiscal year, the Governor determines that, for that fiscal year, General Fund revenues will decline substantially below the estimate of General Fund revenues upon which the budget bill for that fiscal year, as enacted, was based, or General Fund expenditures will increase substantially above that estimate of General Fund revenues, or both, the Governor may issue a proclamation declaring a fiscal emergency and shall thereupon cause the Legislature to assemble in special session for this purpose. The proclamation shall identify the nature of the fiscal emergency and shall be submitted by the Governor to the Legislature, accompanied by proposed legislation to address the fiscal emergency.

(2) If the Legislature fails to pass and send to the Governor a bill or bills to address the fiscal emergency by the 45th day following the issuance of the proclamation, the Legislature may not act on any other bill, nor may the Legislature adjourn for a joint recess, until that bill or those bills have been passed and sent to the Governor.

(3) A bill addressing the fiscal emergency declared pursuant to this section shall contain a statement to that effect.

(Sec. 10 amended March 2, 2004, by Prop. 58. Res.Ch. 1, 2003–04 5th Ex. Sess.)

SEC. 11.

The Legislature or either house may by resolution provide for the selection of committees necessary for the conduct of its business, including committees to ascertain facts and make recommendations to the Legislature on a subject within the scope of legislative control.

(Sec. 11 amended Nov. 7, 1972, by Prop. 4. Res.Ch. 81, 1972.)

SEC. 12.

(a) Within the first 10 days of each calendar year, the Governor shall submit to the Legislature, with an explanatory message, a budget for the ensuing fiscal year containing itemized statements for recommended state expenditures and estimated state revenues. If recommended expenditures exceed estimated revenues, the Governor shall recommend the sources from which the additional revenues should be provided.

(b) The Governor and the Governor-elect may require a state agency, officer or employee to furnish whatever information is deemed necessary to prepare the budget.

(c) (1) The budget shall be accompanied by a budget bill itemizing recommended expenditures.

(2) The budget bill shall be introduced immediately in each house by the persons chairing the committees that consider the budget.

(3) The Legislature shall pass the budget bill by midnight on June 15 of each year.

(4) Until the budget bill has been enacted, the Legislature shall not send to the Governor for consideration any bill appropriating funds for expenditure during the fiscal year for which the budget bill is to be enacted, except emergency bills recommended by the Governor or appropriations for the salaries and expenses of the Legislature.

(d) No bill except the budget bill may contain more than one item of appropriation, and that for one certain, expressed purpose. Appropriations from the General Fund of the State, except appropriations for the public schools and appropriations in the budget bill and in other bills providing for appropriations related to the budget bill, are void unless passed in each house by rollcall vote entered in the journal, two-thirds of the membership concurring.

(e) (1) Notwithstanding any other provision of law or of this Constitution, the budget bill and other bills providing for appropriations related to the budget bill may be passed in each house by rollcall vote entered in the journal, a majority of the membership concurring, to take effect immediately upon being signed by the Governor or upon a date specified in the legislation. Nothing in this subdivision shall affect the vote requirement for appropriations for the public schools contained in subdivision (d) of this section and in subdivision (b) of Section 8 of this article.

(2) For purposes of this section, "other bills providing for appropriations related to the budget bill" shall consist only of bills identified as related to the budget in the budget bill passed by the Legislature.

(f) The Legislature may control the submission, approval, and enforcement of budgets and the filing of claims for all state agencies.

(g) For the 2004–05 fiscal year, or any subsequent fiscal year, the Legislature may not send to the Governor for consideration, nor may the Governor sign into law, a budget bill that would appropriate from the General Fund, for that fiscal year, a total amount that, when combined with all appropriations from the General Fund for that fiscal year made as of the date of the budget bill's passage, and the amount of any General Fund moneys transferred to the Budget Stabilization Account for that fiscal year pursuant to Section 20 of Article XVI, exceeds General Fund revenues for that fiscal year estimated as of the date of the budget bill's passage. That estimate of General Fund revenues shall be set forth in the budget bill passed by the Legislature.

(h) Notwithstanding any other provision of law or of this Constitution, including subdivision (c) of this section, Section 4 of this article, and Sections 4 and 8 of Article III, in any year in which the budget bill is not passed by the Legislature by midnight on June 15, there shall be no appropriation from the current budget or future budget to pay any salary or reimbursement for travel or living expenses for Members of the Legislature during any regular or special session for the period from midnight on June 15 until the day that the budget bill is presented to the Governor. No salary or reimbursement for travel or living expenses forfeited pursuant to this subdivision shall be paid retroactively.

(Sec. 12 amended Nov. 2, 2010, by Prop. 25. Initiative measure.)

SEC. 12.5.

Within 10 days following the submission of a budget pursuant to subdivision (a) of Section 12, following the proposed adjustments to the Governor's Budget required by subdivision (e) of Section 13308 of the Government Code or a successor statute, and following the enactment of the budget bill, or as soon as feasible thereafter, the Director of Finance shall submit to the Legislature both of the following:

(a) Estimates of General Fund revenues for the ensuing fiscal year and for the three fiscal years thereafter.

(b) Estimates of General Fund expenditures for the ensuing fiscal year and for the three fiscal years thereafter.

(Sec. 12.5 added Nov. 4, 2014, by Prop. 2. Res.Ch. 1, 2013–14 2nd Ex. Sess.)

SEC. 13.

A member of the Legislature may not, during the term for which the member is elected, hold any office or employment under the State other than an elective office.

(Sec. 13 amended Nov. 5, 1974, by Prop. 11. Res.Ch. 96, 1974.)

SEC. 14.

A member of the Legislature is not subject to civil process during a session of the Legislature or for 5 days before and after a session.

(Sec. 14 added Nov. 8, 1966, by Prop. 1-a. Res.Ch. 139, 1966 1st Ex. Sess.)

SEC. 15.

A person who seeks to influence the vote or action of a member of the Legislature in the member's legislative capacity by bribery, promise of reward, intimidation, or other dishonest means, or a member of the Legislature so influenced, is guilty of a felony.

(Sec. 15 amended Nov. 5, 1974, by Prop. 11. Res.Ch. 96, 1974.)

SEC. 16.

(a) All laws of a general nature have uniform operation.

(b) A local or special statute is invalid in any case if a general statute can be made applicable.

(Sec. 16 amended Nov. 5, 1974, by Prop. 7. Res.Ch. 90, 1974.)

SEC. 17.

The Legislature has no power to grant, or to authorize a city, county, or other public body to grant, extra compensation or extra allowance to a public officer, public employee, or contractor after service has been rendered or a contract has been entered into and performed in whole or in part, or to authorize the payment of a claim against the State or a city, county, or other public body under an agreement made without authority of law.

(Sec. 17 added Nov. 8, 1966, by Prop. 1-a. Res.Ch. 139, 1966 1st Ex. Sess.)

SEC. 18.

(a) The Assembly has the sole power of impeachment. Impeachments shall be tried by the Senate. A person may not be convicted unless, by rollcall vote entered in the journal, two thirds of the membership of the Senate concurs.

(b) State officers elected on a statewide basis, members of the State Board of Equalization, and judges of state courts are subject to impeachment for misconduct in office. Judgment may extend only to removal from office and disqualification to hold any office under the State, but the person convicted or acquitted remains subject to criminal punishment according to law.

(Sec. 18 added Nov. 8, 1966, by Prop. 1-a. Res.Ch. 139, 1966 1st Ex. Sess.)

SEC. 19.

(a) The Legislature has no power to authorize lotteries, and shall prohibit the sale of lottery tickets in the State.

(b) The Legislature may provide for the regulation of horse races and horse race meetings and wagering on the results.

(c) Notwithstanding subdivision (a), the Legislature by statute may authorize cities and counties to provide for bingo games, but only for charitable purposes.

(d) Notwithstanding subdivision (a), there is authorized the establishment of a California State Lottery.

(e) The Legislature has no power to authorize, and shall prohibit, casinos of the type currently operating in Nevada and New Jersey.

(f) Notwithstanding subdivisions (a) and (e), and any other provision of state law, the Governor is authorized to negotiate and conclude compacts, subject to ratification by the Legislature, for the operation of slot machines and for the conduct of lottery games and banking and percentage card games by federally recognized Indian tribes on Indian lands in California in accordance with federal law. Accordingly, slot machines, lottery games, and banking and percentage card games are hereby permitted to be conducted and operated on tribal lands subject to those compacts.

(f) Notwithstanding subdivision (a), the Legislature may authorize private, nonprofit, eligible organizations, as defined by the Legislature, to conduct raffles as a funding mechanism to provide support for their own or another private, nonprofit, eligible organization's beneficial and charitable works, provided that (1) at least 90 percent of the gross receipts from the raffle go directly to beneficial or charitable purposes in California, and (2) any person who receives compensation in connection with the operation of a raffle is an employee of the private nonprofit organization that is conducting the raffle. The Legislature, two-thirds of the membership of each house concurring, may amend the percentage of gross receipts required by this subdivision to be dedicated to beneficial or charitable purposes by means of a statute that is signed by the Governor.

(Sec. 19 amended March 7, 2000, by Prop. 1A (Res.Ch. 142, 1999) and Prop. 17 (Res.Ch. 123, 1999).)

SEC. 20.

(a) The Legislature may provide for division of the State into fish and game districts and may protect fish and game in districts or parts of districts.

(b) There is a Fish and Game Commission of 5 members appointed by the Governor and approved by the Senate, a majority of the membership concurring, for 6-year terms and until their successors are appointed and qualified. Appointment to fill a vacancy is for the unexpired portion of the term. The Legislature may delegate to the commission such powers relating to the protection and propagation of fish and game as the Legislature sees fit. A member of the commission may be removed by concurrent resolution adopted by each house, a majority of the membership concurring.

(Sec. 20 added Nov. 8, 1966, by Prop. 1-a. Res.Ch. 139, 1966 1st Ex. Sess.)

SEC. 21.

To meet the needs resulting from war-caused or enemy-caused disaster in California, the Legislature may provide for:

(a) Filling the offices of members of the Legislature should at least one fifth of the membership of either house be killed, missing, or disabled, until they are able to perform their duties or successors are elected.

(b) Filling the office of Governor should the Governor be killed, missing, or disabled, until the Governor or the successor designated in this Constitution is able to perform the duties of the office of Governor or a successor is elected.

(c) Convening the Legislature.

(d) Holding elections to fill offices that are elective under this Constitution and that are either vacant or occupied by persons not elected thereto.

(e) Selecting a temporary seat of state or county government.

(Sec. 21 amended Nov. 5, 1974, by Prop. 11. Res.Ch. 96, 1974.)

SEC. 22.

It is the right of the people to hold their legislators accountable. To assist the people in exercising this right, at the convening of each regular session of the Legislature, the President pro Tempore of the Senate, the Speaker of the Assembly, and the minority leader of each house shall report to their house the goals and objectives of that house during that session and, at the close of each regular session, the progress made toward meeting those goals and objectives.

(Sec. 22 added June 5, 1990, by Prop. 112. Res.Ch. 167, 1989.)

SEC. 28.

(a) Notwithstanding any other provision of this Constitution, no bill shall take effect as an urgency statute if it authorizes or contains an appropriation for either (1) the alteration or modification of the color, detail, design, structure or fixtures of the historically restored areas of the first, second, and third floors and the exterior of the west wing of the State Capitol from that existing upon the completion of the project of restoration or rehabilitation of the building conducted pursuant to Section 9124 of the Government Code as such section read upon the effective date of this section, or (2) the purchase of furniture of different design to replace that restored, replicated, or designed to conform to the historic period of the historically restored areas specified above, including the legislators' chairs and desks in the Senate and Assembly Chambers.

(b) No expenditures shall be made in payment for any of the purposes described in subdivision (a) of this section unless funds are appropriated expressly for such purposes.

(c) This section shall not apply to appropriations or expenditures for ordinary repair and maintenance of the State Capitol building, fixtures and furniture.

(Sec. 28 added June 3, 1980, by Prop. 3. Res.Ch. 56, 1978.)

Appendix B

Finding California Laws

Like the federal government, California laws are found in three places: The State Constitution, statutes (the Codes), and regulations. The hierarchy of laws is the same as federal laws, with the constitution at the top, followed by statutes, and ending with regulations. The following is an overview of the three sources of laws in California:

The California Constitution is one of the longest constitutions in the nation at about 110 pages in length. The following are the articles of the constitution:

Article I Declaration of Rights

Article II Voting, Initiative and Referendum, and Recall

Article III State of California

Article IV Legislative

Article V Executive

Article VI Judicial

Article VII Public Officers and Employees

Article IX Education

Article X Water

Article X A Water Resources Development

Article X B Marine Resources Protection Act of 1990

Article XI Local Government

Article XII Public Utilities

Article XIII Taxation

Article XIII A [Tax Limitation]

Article XIII B Government Spending Limitation

Article XIII C [Voter Approval for Local Tax Levies]

Article XIII D [Assessment and Property-Related Fee Reform]

Article XIV Labor Relations

Article XV Usury

Article XVI Public Finance

Article XVIII Amending and Revising the Constitution

Article XIX Motor Vehicles Revenues

Article XIX A Loans from the Public Transportation Account or Local Transportation Fund

Article XIX B Motor Vehicle Fuel Sales Tax Revenues and Transportation Improvement Funding

Article XIX C [Enforcement of Certain Provisions]

Article XX Miscellaneous Subjects

Article XXI Redistricting of Senate, Assembly, Congressional and Board of Equalization Districts

Article XXII [Architectural and Engineering Services]

Article XXXIV Public Housing Project Law

Article XXXV Medical Research

Next comes the statutes. A sense of the scope of state statutes can be gained by noting the titles of California's 29 codes which contain about 150,000 statutes. The following are the codes:

Business and Professions Code

Civil Code

Code of Civil Procedure

Commercial Code

Corporations Code

Education Code

Elections Code

Evidence Code

Family Code

Financial Code

Fish and Game Code

Food and Agricultural Code

Government Code

Harbors and Navigation Code

Health and Safety Code

Insurance Code

Labor Code

Military and Veterans Code

Penal Code

Probate Code

Public Contract Code

Public Resources Code

Public Utilities Code

Revenue and Taxation Code

Streets and Highways Code

Unemployment Insurance Code

Vehicle Code

Water Code

Welfare and Institutions Code

California has over 200 state agencies that make public policy via their authority to adopt regulations. They adopt between 500–600 new regulations each year. The website of the Office of Administrative Law (OAL) provides direct access to the *California Code of Regulations* (CCR), which is organized under the following 27 titles:

Title 1. General Provisions

Title 2. Administration

Title 3. Food and Agriculture

Title 4. Business Regulations

Title 5. Education

Title 7. Harbors and Navigation

Title 8. Industrial Relations

Title 9. Rehabilitative and Developmental Services

Title 10. Investment

Title 11. Law

Title 12. Military and Veterans Affairs

Title 13. Motor Vehicles

Title 14. Natural Resources

Title 15. Crime Prevention and Corrections

Title 16. Professional and Vocational Regulations

Title 17. Public Health

Title 18. Public Revenues

Title 19. Public Safety

Title 20. Public Utilities and Energy

Title 21. Public Works

Title 22. Social Security

Title 23. Waters

Title 24. Building Standards Code

Title 25. Housing and Community Development

Title 26. Toxics

Title 27. Environmental Protection

Title 28. Managed Health Care

The laws of the State of California are found in these three locations. Of course, there are also court decisions that interpret the State Constitution, statutes and regulations. So, capital lawyers need to monitor state and federal court decisions interpreting these California laws.

Index of Topics